PROFESSIONAL

# Java® for Web Applications

Nicholas S. Williams

Professional Java® for Web Applications

Published by
John Wiley & Sons, Inc.
10475 Crosspoint Boulevard
Indianapolis, IN 46256
www.wiley.com



Published simultaneously in Canada

ISBN: 978-1-118-65646-4
ISBN: 978-1-118-65651-8 (ebk)
ISBN: 978-1-118-90931-7 (ebk)

Manufactured in the United States of America

10 9 8 7 6 5 4 3 2 1



**Library of Congress Control Number:** 2013958292

# ABOUT THE AUTHOR

**NICK WILLIAMS** is a Software Engineer for UL Workplace Health and Safety in Franklin, Tennessee. A computer science graduate from Belmont University, he has been active in commercial and open source software projects for more than 9 years. He is the founder of `DNSCrawler.com`, a site for free DNS and IP troubleshooting tools, and NWTS Java Code, an open source community that specializes in obscure Java libraries that meet niche needs. In 2010, the Nashville Technology Council named him the Software Engineer of the Year for Middle Tennessee. Nick is a committer for Apache Logging (including Log4j) and Jackson Data Processor JSR 310 Data Types. He has also contributed new features to Apache Tomcat 8.0, Spring Framework 4.0, Spring Security 3.2, Spring Data Commons 1.6, Spring Data JPA 1.4, and JBoss Logging 3.2; serves as a contributor on several other projects, including OpenJDK; and is a member of the Java Community Process (JCP).

Nick currently lives in Tennessee with his wife Allison. You can find him on Twitter @Java_Nick (`https://twitter.com/Java_Nick`).

# ABOUT THE TECHNICAL EDITORS

**JAKE RADAKOVICH** joined UL Workplace Health and Safety in 2009, and currently serves as Software Developer on the Occupational Health Manager product. Prior to that, he was a research assistant at Middle Tennessee State University working on AlgoTutor, a web-based algorithm development tutoring system. He holds a BS in Computer Science and Mathematics from Middle Tennessee State University. You can follow Jake on Twitter @JakeRadakovich (`https://twitter.com/JakeRadakovich`).

**MANUEL JORDAN ELERA** is an autodidactic developer and researcher who enjoys learning new technologies for his own experiments and creating new integrations. He won the 2010 Springy Award and was a Community Champion and Spring Champion in 2013. In his little free time, he reads the Bible and composes music on his guitar. Manuel is a Senior Member in the Spring Community Forums known as dr_pompeii. You can read about him and contact him through his blog at `http://manueljordan.wordpress.com/` and you can follow him on his Twitter account, @dr_pompeii (`https://twitter.com/dr_pompeii`).

# CREDITS

**ACQUISITIONS EDITOR**
Mary James

**PROJECT EDITOR**
Maureen Spears Tullis

**TECHNICAL EDITORS**
Michael Jordan Elera
Jake Radakovich

**TECHNICAL PROOFREADER**
Jonathan Giles

**SENIOR PRODUCTION EDITOR**
Kathleen Wisor

**COPY EDITOR**
Apostrophe Editing Services

**EDITORIAL MANAGER**
Mary Beth Wakefield

**FREELANCER EDITORIAL MANAGER**
Rosemarie Graham

**ASSOCIATE DIRECTOR OF MARKETING**
David Mayhew

**MARKETING MANAGER**
Ashley Zurcher

**BUSINESS MANAGER**
Amy Knies

**VICE PRESIDENT AND EXECUTIVE GROUP PUBLISHER**
Richard Swadley

**ASSOCIATE PUBLISHER**
Jim Minatel

**PROJECT COORDINATOR, COVER**
Todd Klemme

**PROOFREADERS**
Nancy Carrasco
Josh Chase, Word One

**INDEXER**
Robert Swanson

**COVER DESIGNER**
Wiley

**COVER IMAGE**
iStockphoto.com/ElementalImaging

# ACKNOWLEDGMENTS


#### THANKS TO...

My wife Allison, whose unwavering support and persistent reminders about deadlines during this stressful year made this book possible.

My parents and siblings, who told me that I could do anything I put my mind to.

Drs. Joyce Blair Crowell and William Hooper, whose dedicated instruction and mentoring made my career possible.

Dr. Sarah Ann Stewart, who believed in me when I thought surely calculus and proofs spelled doom for my education.

Mrs. Lockhart, who inspired me to write.

Jay, for introducing me to Mary, and to Mary and Maureen for making this book a reality.

Jake, for being absurd. Oh, and for agreeing to be my technical editor.

# CONTENTS

# INTRODUCTION

**THOUGH MANY DON'T REALIZE IT, MOST PEOPLE USE JAVA EVERY DAY.** It's all around you — it's in your TV, in your Blu-ray player, and on your computer; some popular smart phones run a Java-based operating system; and it powers many of the websites you use every day. When you think of Java, you may naturally picture browser applets or desktop applications with user interfaces that don't match other applications on the operating system. You may even think of that annoying system tray notification that tells you to update Java (seemingly) constantly.

But Java is much more than just these daily, visible reminders you may be exposed to. Java is a powerful language, but much of its capability lies in the power of the platform. Although the Java SE platform provides indispensable tools for creating console, desktop, and browser applications, the Java EE platform extends this platform significantly to help you create rich, powerful web applications. This book covers these tools and shows you how to create modern and useful enterprise Java web applications.

## WHO THIS BOOK IS FOR

This book is for software developers and engineers who already have a proficient knowledge in the Java language and the Java Platform, Standard Edition (Java SE). It is a self-guided, self-study book that existing Java developers can use to expand their Java knowledge and grow their skillset from applets or console or desktop applications to enterprise web applications. You can read this book from start to finish to cover all the topics in order, or you can pick and choose topics that interest you and use this book more as a reference. Although some chapters occasionally refer to examples from previous chapters, an effort was made to make each chapter as self-sustaining as possible. The examples are all available for download from `wrox.com`, which should help you when an example relies on another example from a previous chapter.

This book can also be useful for developers with existing Java Platform, Enterprise Edition (Java EE) experience who want to refresh their skills or learn about new features in the latest Java EE version. Software architects might also find this book useful because it covers several web software development concepts and patterns in addition to specific tools and platform components. This book could help architects apply new ideas to their teams' projects and processes.

If you're a manager of a software development team, you may also find this book helpful. Undoubtedly you strive every day to communicate effectively with the developers and engineers that you oversee. By reading this book, you can expand your knowledgebase, understand the tools your developers use to more successfully communicate, and make recommendations to your team to solve certain problems. After reading this book, you may also decide to purchase several copies for your team to improve their skillsets and apply the concepts within your projects.

Finally, teachers and students can apply this book to a classroom environment. Used as a textbook, it can be invaluable for 300 and 400 level courses to instruct students in real-world skills that can help them succeed in the workplace beyond graduation.

## WHO THIS BOOK IS NOT FOR

This book is not for readers who have no experience with Java and have never written or compiled Java-based applications. If you have no prior Java experience, you will likely find it difficult to understand the text and examples in this book. This is because this book does not cover the Java language syntax or the specifics of the Java SE platform. It is assumed the reader is comfortable writing, compiling, and debugging Java code and is familiar with the standard platform. Very few explanations are given about standard Java features and tools, except where those features were added in Java SE 8.

In addition, the reader is expected to have a basic understanding of the following technologies and concepts. Although some of them may seem obvious, it's important to note that if you are unfamiliar with one or more of these concepts you may have difficulty with some chapters in the book.

- The Internet and the TCP and HTTP protocols
- HyperText Markup Language (HTML), including HTML 5
- Extensible Markup Language (XML)
- JavaScript or ECMAScript, including jQuery and browser debugging tools
- Cascading Style Sheets (CSS)
- Structured Query Language (SQL) and relational databases, specifically MySQL (If you are familiar with other relational databases, you can adapt to MySQL easily.)
- Transactions and transactional concepts, such as Atomicity, Consistency, Isolation, Durability (ACID)
- Use of an Integrated Development Environment (IDE)
- Execution of simple command-line tasks (You do not need to be a command-line guru.)

## WHAT YOU WILL LEARN IN THIS BOOK

In this book, you learn about the Java EE platform version 7 and many of the technologies within it. You'll start with an introduction to what exactly the Java EE platform is and how it evolved, followed by an introduction to application servers and Servlet containers and how they work. You'll then proceed to explore Spring Framework, publish-subscribe, Advanced Message Queuing Protocol (AMQP), object-relational mappers (O/RMs), Hibernate ORM, Spring Data, full-text searching, Apache Lucene, Hibernate Search, Spring Security, and OAuth. Throughout this book you will also explore the following components of Java EE 7:

- Servlets 3.1 – JSR 340
- JavaServer Pages (JSP) 2.3 – JSR 245
- Java Unified Expression Language (JUEL or just EL) 3.0 – JSR 341
- Java API for WebSockets – JSR 356

- Bean Validation (BV) 1.1 – JSR 349
- Java Message Service (JMS) 2.0 – JSR 343
- Java Persistence API (JPA) 2.1 – JSR 338
- Java Transaction API (JTA) 1.2 — JSR 907

You'll also make extensive use of lambda expressions and the new JSR 310 Java 8 Date and Time API, both additions to Java SE 8.

## Part I: Creating Enterprise Applications

Here you explore Servlets, filters, listeners, and JavaServer Pages (JSP). You'll learn about how Servlets respond to HTTP requests and how filters assist them. You'll easily create powerful user interfaces based on JSP. Combining the power of JSP tags and the brand-new Expression Language 3.0, you'll then create Java-free views easily maintained by UI developers who have little or no Java knowledge. You'll learn about HTTP sessions and how they can help you create rich user experiences that span multiple pages in your application. You'll explore the brand-new technology called WebSockets, which helps you create richer, more interactive user interfaces by providing full-duplex, bidirectional communications between your application and the client (such as a browser). As a final note, you'll learn about application logging best practices and technologies, something that will become critical as you create complex applications with lots of code.

## Part II: Adding Spring Framework Into the Mix

In this part of the book you start working with Spring Framework and Spring MVC. You'll explore topics such as dependency injection (DI), inversion of control (IoC), and aspect-oriented programming (AOP). You'll configure advanced Spring Framework projects using both XML and annotation-based configuration, and you'll use Spring tools to support your bean validation and internationalization needs. You'll create both RESTful and SOAP web services using Spring MVC controllers and Spring Web Services, and you'll learn how to use the flexible messaging systems built in to Spring Framework. You'll also learn about the Advanced Message Queuing Protocol (AMQP) and configure and use a RabbitMQ installation.

## Part III: Persisting Data with JPA and Hibernate ORM

This part focuses on data persistence and different approaches to storing your objects in your databases. After understanding some of the basic issues with using raw JDBC for persisting your entities, you'll learn about object-relational mappers (O/RMs) and explore Hibernate ORM and its API. You'll then take a look at the Java Persistence API, an abstraction that allows you to program to a common API regardless of the O/RM implementation. Next you'll explore Spring Data and how it can help you create persistence applications without writing any persistence code. You'll also learn several methods for searching your persisted data and explore Hibernate Search with Apache Lucene as a potential full-text searching tool.

## Part IV: Securing Your Application with Spring Security

The final part of the book introduces you to the concepts of authentication and authorization and shows you several techniques that can be used for both. It then helps you integrate Spring Security into your Spring Framework applications. You'll also learn how to secure your web services using OAuth 1.0a and OAuth 2.0 and create a custom access token type to make your OAuth 2.0 implementation stronger.

# WHAT YOU WILL NOT LEARN IN THIS BOOK

This book does not teach you about basic Java syntax or the Java SE platform, though it will briefly explain some new features added in Java SE 7 and 8. It will also not teach you how to write Java-based console or desktop applications or applets. If you are looking for a book on these topics, Wrox has a variety of titles to choose from.

More important, this book **does not teach you how to administer a Java EE application server environment.** There are dozens of different application servers and web containers, and no two are managed identically. Which application server you use strongly depends on the nature of your application, your business requirements, your business practices, and your server environment. It would be impractical to teach you how to administer even a few of the most common application servers. The best way to learn how to deploy and administer your Java EE application server or web container of choice is to consult its documentation and, in some cases, experiment. (Because the use of a web container is necessary to complete the examples in this book, Chapter 2 covers the basic tasks of installing, starting, stopping, and deploying applications to Apache Tomcat.)

Refer back to the introductory section titled "Who This Book Is Not For" — this book does not cover the basics of the technologies and concepts listed in that section. It also does not cover the following Java EE 7 components, which are unsupported by most simple web containers and unnecessary when using Spring Framework and its related projects.

- Java API for RESTful Web Services (JAX-RS) 2.0 – JSR 339
- JavaServer Faces (JSF) 2.2 – JSR 344
- Enterprise JavaBeans (EJB) 3.2 – JSR 345
- Contexts and Dependency Injection (CDI) 1.1 – JSR 346
- JCache – JSR 107
- State Management – JSR 350
- Batch Applications for the Java Platform – JSR 352
- Concurrency Utilities for Java EE – JSR 236
- Java API for JSON Processing – JSR 353

# WHAT TOOLS YOU WILL NEED

You'll need several different tools to complete and run the examples in this book. To start, be sure you have the following installed or enabled on your computer:

- Apache Maven version 3.1.1 or newer
- A command line for certain tasks, and an operating system that provides access to the command line (In other words, you cannot compile and run the examples on a smartphone or tablet.)
- A quality text editor useful for tasks such as editing configuration files. You should never use Windows Notepad or Apple TextEdit as a text editor. If you are looking for a quality text editor, consider:
  - **Windows** — Notepad++ or Sublime Text 2.
  - **Mac OS X** — TextWrangler, Sublime Text 2, or Vim.
  - **Linux** — Sublime Text 2 or Vim.

## Java Development Kit for Java SE 8

You must have the Java Development Kit (JDK) for Java SE 8 installed on your machine. Java SE 8 is scheduled to release on March 18, 2014. You should be able to download the JDK from Oracle's standard Java SE Downloads site (`http://www.oracle.com/technetwork/java/javase/downloads/index.html`). However, if you purchased this book prior to the release of Java SE 8, you may need to download the Early Access JDK from its Java.net project site (`https://jdk8.java.net/download.html`). (Don't worry, you won't have to compile it.) Always get the latest version of the JDK, and download the version and architecture appropriate for your machine. If your machine contains a 64-bit processor and 64-bit operating system, you should download the 64-bit Java installer.

## Integrated Development Environment

You need an integrated development environment, or IDE, for compiling and executing the code samples and general experimentation. An IDE, sometimes also called an interactive development environment, is a software application with coding, building, deploying, and debugging facilities for software developers to use when creating software. There are many different Java IDEs available, and some are better than others. A lot of what makes one IDE better than another is simply perspective and personal practices — an IDE that is perfect for one developer may not be so easy for another developer to use. Generally, however, IDEs that include intelligent code suggestions, code completion, code generation, syntax checking, spell checking, and framework integration (Spring Framework, JPA, Hibernate ORM, and so on) are going to be much more useful and provide you with a much more productive work environment than IDEs without these features.

You may already have an IDE that you use regularly, or you may simply use your favorite text editor and a command line. If you have an IDE, it may or may not be up to the task of running the examples in this book. When choosing an IDE (or evaluating whether you current IDE is sufficient), you should get one with intelligent code completion and suggestions, syntax checking, and integration with Java EE, Spring Framework, Spring Security, Spring Data, JPA, and Hibernate ORM. This means it should have the ability to evaluate your Java EE, Spring, JPA, and Hibernate configurations and tell you whether there are any errors or problems with those configurations. This introduction briefly tells you about three polyglot IDEs and makes a recommendation for this book.

## NetBeans IDE 8.0

NetBeans — a free IDE — is the standard, Oracle-sponsored Java IDE, similar to how Microsoft Visual Studio is the standard IDE for .NET development. It is not, however, the most popular Java IDE. Only NetBeans IDE 8.0 has support for Java SE 8 and Java EE 7 — previous versions do not. NetBeans provides a strong feature set and built-in support for all Java EE features. It also supports C, C++, and PHP development. You can also extend NetBeans's functionality using plug-ins, and plug-ins are available for Spring Framework and Hibernate ORM. However, the NetBeans feature set is not as rich as other IDEs, so it is not recommended for this book. The code examples in this book are not available as NetBeans downloads, but you should be able to import the samples as Maven projects if you prefer to use NetBeans. You can download NetBeans at `https://netbeans.org/`.

## Eclipse Luna IDE 4.4 for Java EE Developers

Eclipse is another free IDE and the most popular Java IDE worldwide. One of its strengths is its extensibility, which goes beyond its support for plug-ins. Using the Eclipse platform, you can completely customize the IDE for specific tasks and workflows. It already has plug-ins and extensions for Spring Framework, Spring Data, Spring Security, Hibernate ORM, and more. The Spring community offers a customized version of Eclipse — called Spring Tool Suite — that is very well suited for working with Spring-based projects. However, in this author's opinion, Eclipse is a very difficult IDE to use effectively and efficiently. Very simple tasks often require a great amount of effort. Historically, compatible Eclipse releases have trailed Java SE and EE releases considerably. At the time this book was written, the Eclipse community had not yet released an Eclipse IDE version compatible with Java SE 8 and Java EE 7. Therefore, it is not recommended that you choose Eclipse IDE for running the examples in this book. If you do choose to use — or continue to use — Eclipse, you should make sure you get Eclipse Luna IDE 4.4 for Java EE Developers, which is scheduled for release in June 2014. This may require downloading a pre-release edition, and that edition may not support all the topics covered in this book. You can download Eclipse IDE at `http://www.eclipse.org/downloads/`.

Due to the popularity of Eclipse IDE, the code examples for this book will be available to download as Eclipse projects as soon as Eclipse Luna 4.4 is capable of running them.

### IntelliJ IDEA 13 Ultimate Edition

JetBrains's IntelliJ IDEA is a feature-rich Java IDE with both Community (free) and Ultimate (paid) editions. It is, again in this author's opinion, the easiest to use and most powerful Java IDE available. Its code suggestions and completion and framework support are unmatched in any other IDE. In addition, it has historically provided better early support for experimental versions of Java SE and Java EE before they release. IntelliJ IDEA 12, for example, provided Java SE 8 support as early as December 2012 — a full 15 months before Java SE 8 was released and 18 months before Eclipse IDE supported it. If you like to test new versions of Java SE and Java EE before they come out, and use them immediately after their release, IntelliJ IDEA is essentially your only option.

This power does come at a cost, however. The Community Edition is useful for many different types of Java SE projects, but not Java EE projects. You need to purchase the Ultimate Edition to realize the full support for Java EE, Spring projects, and Hibernate ORM. The Ultimate Edition is priced reasonably and competitively for companies, individuals, and students, at a fraction of the cost that you would pay for equivalent editions of Microsoft Visual Studio. Educational institutions can get free licenses for official classroom use, and established open source organizations can get free licenses for their projects. You can download a 30-day free trial of IntelliJ IDEA 13 Ultimate Edition at `http://www.jetbrains.com/idea/download/`, and you can purchase a license (or obtain a free license if you qualify) for your download at any time. ***In addition, the back of this book contains a coupon for a free 90-day personal license of IntelliJ IDEA 13 Ultimate!*** We recommend you use IntelliJ IDEA Ultimate Edition for all the code examples in this book. Until Eclipse Luna 4.4 is capable of running the examples, the code downloads will initially be available only as IntelliJ IDEA projects.

Be sure to download the latest version of IntelliJ IDEA. Although version 13.0.x is the most current version as of the date this book was published, 13.1.x is scheduled for release sometime in April 2014 with several Spring Framework and Java EE 7 support improvements, and 14.0.x will likely be released in December 2014.

## Java EE 7 Web Container

The final tool you'll need while reading this book is a Java EE web container that implements the Servlet, JSP, JUEL, and WebSocket specifications in Java EE 7. This topic is covered more thoroughly in Chapter 2, where you review the most popular web containers and application servers and learn how to download, install, and use Apache Tomcat 8.0.

# CONVENTIONS USED IN THIS BOOK

Several conventions are used throughout this book to help draw your attention to certain items or demonstrate something in code. This section covers those conventions by example.

> **NOTE** *Notes indicate notes, tips, hints, tricks, reminders, and other interesting information loosely related to the current discussion. You'll want to pay attention to these boxes.*

> **WARNING** *Warnings hold important information that is directly relevant to the surrounding text and should not be forgotten. Warnings can indicate pitfalls, dangers, and potential for loss or corrupted data. Pay close attention to these boxes.*

You may see several styles in the text:

- New terms and important words are *highlighted* when introduced. This may not be the first time these words appear in the text, but it will be the first time they are explained.
- Keyboard strokes appear as Ctrl+S, Ctrl+Alt+F8, and so on.
- Filenames, URIs that aren't URLs, class and method names, primitive types, and code within the text `appear like this`.
- Code variables, method and constructor parameter names, and request parameters look like *`this`*.
- Values the user must enter in dialog boxes, prompts, or form fields are **`bold and monospace`**.

Finally, when reading sample code within the text, it may be presented in two different ways:

```
We use a monofont type with no highlighting for most lines of code.
```

```
We use bold to emphasize code that's especially important, to show changes from
previous examples, or to draw attention to it when mentioning it in the text.
```

In most cases, code examples are simply written inline, between paragraphs. However, when they are particularly long they will be referenced by number in the text and appear as code listings, as in the sample Listing I-1.

**LISTING I-1: A Sample Code Listing**

```
This is what a code listing will look like.
```

Finally, you will occasionally see an icon in the margin next to a paragraph. This icon will always be referenced in the paragraph it is next to and indicates a toolbar button that you will need to use to perform a task discussed in that paragraph.

# CODE EXAMPLES

As with any software development book, this book makes extensive use of code examples to demonstrate the topics explained. For the most part, these examples are full IDE projects that you can just open in your IDE, compile, and execute. All the examples are available for download from the `wrox.com` code download site. Just go to `http://www.wrox.com/go/projavaforwebapps` and click the Download Code tab. You can download all the code samples as a single ZIP file or a ZIP file for each chapter. Within the download for each chapter you'll find two versions of each sample: an IntelliJ IDEA project and an Eclipse project. You should use the version applicable to the IDE you chose. If you are not using one of these two IDEs, your IDE should be able to import the IntelliJ IDEA project as a simple Maven project.

> **NOTE** *Remember, the Eclipse version of the code samples will not be available until Eclipse Luna 4.4 is capable of running them. If you are reading this book before that milestone, you can download the IntelliJ IDEA example projects.*

Near the beginning of the book, you can create the examples from scratch in your IDE without downloading them from the code site (if that's what you want). However, as the examples get more complex this will not be possible. The most critical code is printed in the book, but printing every line of code is not practical — it would make this book considerably longer, and thus make it more expensive for you. In addition, much of the omitted code is repetitive. For example, the Spring Framework configuration is nearly identical for most of the example projects in Parts II through IV. In these cases, it makes much more sense to simply show you how the configuration has changed from previous chapters rather than re-printing the entire configuration. For this reason, you need to download most of the code examples from the `wrox.com` code download site if you want to execute and test the examples.

On the first page of each chapter, you'll see an area titled "Wrox.com Code Downloads for This Chapter." This section lists the names of all the code examples used in the chapter and reminds you of the link for downloading the code samples. A handful of chapters do not contain code example downloads, but most do.

## MAVEN DEPENDENCIES

The code examples in this book make extensive use of third-party dependencies, such as Spring Framework, Hibernate ORM, and Spring Security. Including these dependency JARs in the code downloads on the download site would make these downloads unnecessarily large and cause you to download many hundreds of megabytes over the course of the book. To eliminate this problem, the code samples use Apache Maven and its dependency management capabilities. All the sample projects are Maven projects. When opening each project in your IDE, the IDE should automatically resolve the dependencies in your local Maven repository or, if necessary, download them to your local Maven repository.

On the first page of each chapter you'll see an area titled "New Maven Dependencies for This Chapter." This section lists the Maven dependencies that, in addition to all previous dependencies, you'll use in that chapter. You can also consult the `pom.xml` file in each example project to view its dependencies. Some chapters do not introduce new Maven dependencies, but most do.

Each Maven dependency has a *scope* that defines which classpath that dependency is available on. The most common scope — "compile" scope — indicates that the dependency is available to your project on the compile classpath, the unit test compile and execution classpaths, and the eventual runtime classpath when you execute your application. In a Java EE web application, this means the dependency is copied into your deployed application. "Runtime" scope indicates that the dependency is available to your project on the unit test execution and runtime execution classpaths, but unlike compile scope it is not available when you compile your application or its unit tests. A runtime dependency is copied into your deployed application. Finally, "provided" scope indicates that the container in which your application executes provides the dependency on your behalf. In a Java EE application, this means the dependency is already on the Servlet container's or application server's classpath and is not copied into your deployed application. Maven and your IDE ensures provided dependencies are available when you compile your application and its unit tests. There are other Maven scopes as well, but these are the only scopes you use in this book.

Some of the Maven dependencies you see in the text and the sample projects have exclusions that ignore certain dependencies of those dependencies — these are called *transient dependencies*. To a large extent, these exclusions are usually redundant and are shown only for clarity. When a dependency relies on an older version of a dependency than a version you are already using, the exclusion makes it clear that there is a discrepancy there, and also avoids problems caused by Maven's nearness algorithm. However, some of the exclusions exist because newer versions of Java SE or Java EE provide the dependency already, or because the dependency ID changed. When this is the reason an exclusion exists, it is noted in the text.

## WHY SECURITY IS AT THE END OF THE BOOK

Quite frankly, application security gets in the way. The technologies and techniques you must use to add authentication and authorization to your products can clutter your code and make the process of learning more difficult. It's natural to think about security first, and it's never wrong to keep security in mind at all times. However, with the right tools, it's fairly easy to add authentication and authorization to an existing project after it is complete (or nearly so). This book focuses first on creating quality web applications with rich feature sets using industry standard tools. Once you have all the skills you need to create powerful applications, Part IV of this book shows you how to add authentication and authorization to an existing application to secure it from unauthorized and malicious access.

## ERRATA

We strove to make this text as thorough and accurate as possible, but nobody is perfect and mistakes do happen. Occasionally this book may contain errors that require correction. If you find factual errors, spelling mistakes, or faulty pieces of code, we want to hear about it! By providing your feedback, you could save other readers' time and effort trying to troubleshoot something that isn't working, and at the same time improve future editions of this book.

To read the discovered errata for this book, go to `http://www.wrox.com/` and use the search box to find this title. Searching for its ISBN is the fastest way to locate it. On this book's page, click the Errata link. Here you can view all the errata that has been submitted by readers and verified by Wrox editors. If you don't spot the errata you found, go to `http://www.wrox.com/contact/techsupport.shtml` and complete the form there to report the problem. After we verify the error and come up with a correction, we will post it to this book's errata page and fix the problem for future editions.

# PART I
# Creating Enterprise Applications

# Introducing Java Platform, Enterprise Edition

**IN THIS CHAPTER**

- Java SE and Java EE version timeline
- Introducing Servlets, filters, listeners, and JSPs
- Understanding WAR, and EAR files, and the class loader hierarchy

**WROX.COM CODE DOWNLOADS FOR THIS CHAPTER**

There are no code downloads for this chapter.

**NEW MAVEN DEPENDENCIES FOR THIS CHAPTER**

There are no Maven dependencies for this chapter.

## A TIMELINE OF JAVA PLATFORMS

The Java language and its platforms have had a long and storied history. From its invention in the mid-'90s to an evolution drought from 2007 to nearly 2012, Java has gone through many changes and encountered its share of controversy. In the earliest days, Java, known as the Java Development Kit or JDK, was a language tightly coupled to a platform composed of a small set of essential *application programming interfaces* (*APIs*). Sun Microsystems unveiled the earliest alpha and beta versions in 1995, and although Java was extremely slow and primitive by today's standards, it began a revolution in software development.

## In the Beginning

Java's history is summarized in Figure 1-1, a timeline of Java platforms. As of the publication of this book, the Java language and the Java SE platform have always evolved together — new versions of each always release at the same time and are tightly coupled to one another. The platform was called the JDK through version 1.1 in 1997, but by version 1.2 it was clear that the JDK and the platform were not synonymous. Starting with version 1.2 in late 1998, the Java technology stack was divided into the following key components:

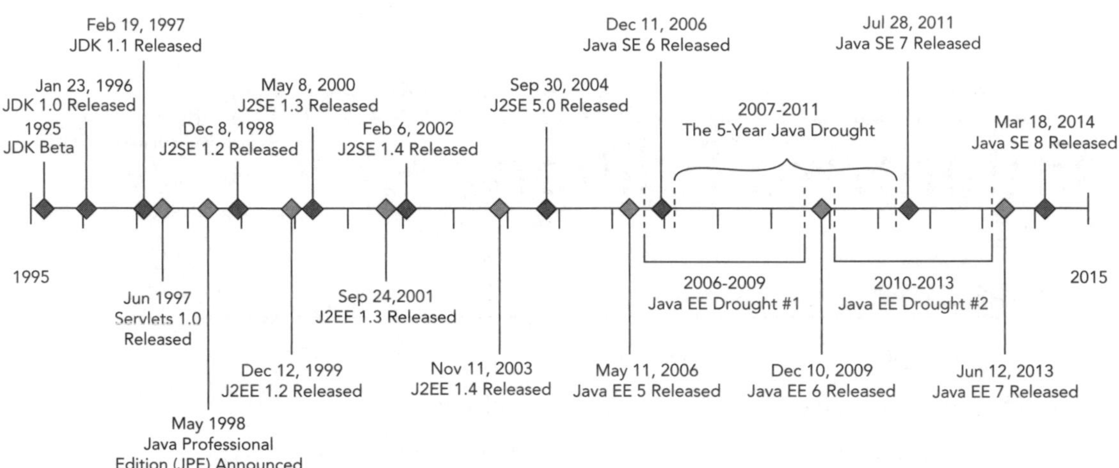


**FIGURE 1-1:** A timeline showing the correlation of the evolution of Java Platform, Standard Edition and Java Platform, Enterprise Edition. The events on top of the timeline represent Java SE milestones while the events on the bottom represent Java EE milestones.

- *Java* is the language and includes a strict and strongly typed syntax with which you should be very familiar by now.
- *Java 2 Platform, Standard Edition*, also known as *J2SE*, referred to the platform and included the classes in the `java.lang` and `java.io` packages, among others. It was the building block that Java applications were built upon.
- A *Java Virtual Machine*, or *JVM*, is a software virtual machine that runs compiled Java code. Because compiled Java code is merely bytecode, the JVM is responsible for compiling that bytecode to machine code before running it. (This is often called the *Just In Time Compiler* or *JIT Compiler.*) The JVM also takes care of memory management so that application code doesn't have to.
- The *Java Development Kit*, or *JDK*, was and remains the piece of software Java developers use to create Java applications. It contains a Java language compiler, a documentation generator, tools for working with native code, and (typically) the Java source code for the platform to enable debugging platform classes.
- The *Java Runtime Environment*, or *JRE*, was and remains the piece of software end users download to run compiled Java applications. It includes a JVM but does not contain any of the development tools bundled in the JDK. The JDK, however, does contain a JRE.

All five of these components have historically been specifications, not implementations. Any company may create its own implementation of this Java technology stack, and many companies have. Though Sun offered a standard implementation of Java, J2SE, the JVM, the JDK, and the JRE, IBM, Oracle, and Apple also created competing implementations that offered different features.

The IBM implementation was born out of need — Sun didn't offer binaries capable of running on IBM operating systems, so IBM created its own. The situation was similar for the Apple Mac OS operating system, so Apple rolled its own implementation as well. Although the implementations offered by these companies were all free as in beer, they were not free as in freedom, so they were not considered open source software. As such, the open source community quickly formed the OpenJDK project, which provided an open source implementation of the Java stack.

Still more companies created less popular implementations, some of which compiled your application to machine code for a target architecture to improve performance by avoiding JIT compilation. For the vast majority of users and developers, the Sun Java implementation was both sufficient and preferred. After Oracle's purchase of Sun, the Sun and Oracle implementations became one and the same.

Not shown in Figure 1-1 is the development of other languages capable of using the J2SE and running on the JVM. Over the years, dozens of languages appeared that can compile to Java bytecode (or machine code, in some cases) and run on the JVM. The most high-profile of these are Clojure (a Lisp dialect), Groovy, JRuby (a Java-based Ruby implementation), Jython (a Java-based Python implementation), Rhino, and Scala.

## The Birth of Enterprise Java

This brief history lesson might seem unnecessary — as an existing Java developer, you have likely heard most of this before. However, it's important to include the context of the history of the Java Platform, Standard Edition, because it is tightly woven into the birth and evolution of the Java Platform, Enterprise Edition. Sun was already aware of the need for more advanced tools for application development, particularly in the arena of the growing Internet and the popularity of web applications. In 1998, shortly before the release of J2SE 1.2, Sun announced it was working on a product called the Java Professional Edition, or JPE. Work had already begun on a technology known as *Servlets*, which are miniature applications capable of responding to HTTP requests. In 1997, Java Servlets 1.0 released alongside the Java Web Server with little fanfare because it lacked many features that the Java community wanted.

After several internal iterations of Servlets and the JPE, Sun released *Java 2 Platform, Enterprise Edition* (or *J2EE*) version 1.2 on December 12, 1999. The version number corresponded with the current Java and J2SE version at the time, and the specification included:

- Servlets 2.2
- JDBC Extension API 2.0
- Java Naming and Directory Interface (JNDI) 1.0
- JavaServer Pages (JSP) 1.2
- Enterprise JavaBeans (EJB) 1.1

- Java Message Service (JMS) 1.0
- Java Transaction API (JTA) 1.0
- JavaMail API 1.1
- JavaBeans Activation Framework (JAF) 1.0.

Like J2SE, J2EE was a mere specification. Sun provided a *reference implementation* of the specification's components, but companies were free to create their own as well. Many implementations evolved, and you learn about some of them in the next chapter. These implementations included and still include open source and commercial solutions. The J2EE quickly became a successful complement to the J2SE, and over the years some components were deemed so indispensable that they have migrated from J2EE to J2SE.

## Java SE and Java EE Evolving Together

J2EE 1.3 released in September 2001, a little more than a year after Java and J2SE 1.3 and before Java/J2SE 1.4. Most of its components received minor upgrades, and new features were added into the fold. The following joined the J2EE specification, and the array of implementations expanded and upgraded:

- Java API for XML Processing (JAXP) 1.1
- JavaServer Pages Standard Tag Library (JSTL) 1.0
- J2EE Connector Architecture 1.0
- Java Authentication and Authorization Service (JAAS) 1.0

At this point the technology was maturing considerably, but it still had plenty of room for improvement.

J2EE 1.4 represented a major leap in the evolution of the Java Platform, Enterprise Edition. Released in November 2003 (approximately a year before Java/J2SE 5.0 and 2 years after Java/J2SE 1.4), it included Servlet 2.4 and JSP 2.0. It was in this version that the JDBC Extension API, JNDI, and JAAS specifications were removed because they had been deemed essential to Java and moved to Java/J2SE 1.4. This version also represented the point at which J2EE components were broken up into several higher-level categories:

- **Web Services Technologies:** Included JAXP 1.2 and the new Web Services for J2EE 1.1, Java API for XML-based RPC (JAX-RPC) 1.1, and Java API for XML Registries (JAXR) 1.0
- **Web Application Technologies:** Included the Servlet, JSP, and JSTL 1.1 components, as well as the new Java Server Faces (JSF) 1.1
- **Enterprise Application Technologies:** Included EJB 2.1, Connector Architecture 1.5, JMS 1.1, JTA, JavaMail 1.3, and JAF
- **Management and Security Technologies:** Included Java Authorization Service Provider Contract for Containers (JACC) 1.0, Java Management Extensions (JMX) 1.2, Enterprise Edition Management API 1.0, and Enterprise Edition Deployment API 1.1

## The Era of the Name Changes

Enter the era of the name changes, which are often a source of confusion for Java developers. They are highlighted here so that you fully understand the naming conventions used in this book and how they relate to the previous naming conventions you may already be familiar with. Java and J2SE 5.0 were released in September 2004, and included generics, annotations, and enums, three of the most radical language syntax changes in Java history. This version number was a departure from previous patterns, made more confusing by the fact that the J2SE APIs and the `java` command-line tool reported the version number as being 1.5. Sun had made the decision to drop the 1 from the publicized version number and go by the minor version, instead. It quickly recognized that the "dot-oh" on the end of the version number was a source of confusion and quickly began referring to it as simply version 5.

About the same time, the decision was made to retire the name Java 2 Platform, Standard Edition in favor of Java Platform, Standard Edition and to abbreviate this new name Java SE. The changes were made formal with Java SE 6, released in December 2006, and to this day the name and version convention has remain unchanged. Java SE 6 is internally 1.6, Java SE 7 is internally 1.7, and Java SE 8 is internally 1.8.

The same name and number change decisions were applied to J2EE, but because J2EE 1.5 was set to release between J2SE 5.0 and Java SE 6, the changes were applied a version early. Java Platform, Enterprise Edition 5, or Java EE 5, was released in May 2006, approximately 18 months after J2SE 5.0 and 7 months before Java SE 6. Internally Java EE 5 is 1.5, Java EE 6 is 1.6, and Java EE 7 is 1.7. Whenever you see the terms J2SE or Java SE, they are interchangeable, and the preferred and accepted name today is Java EE. Likewise, J2EE and Java EE are interchangeable, but Java EE is preferred today. The rest of this book refers to them exclusively as Java SE and Java EE.

Java EE 5 grew and included numerous changes and improvements again, and today it is still one of the most widely deployed Java EE versions. It included the following changes and additions:

- JAXP and JMX moved to J2SE 5.0 and were not included in Java EE 5.
- Java API for XML-based Web Services (JAX-WS) 2.0, Java Architecture for XML Binding (JAXB) 2.0, Web Service Metadata for the Java Platform 2.0, SOAP with Attachments API for Java (SAAJ) 1.2, and Streaming API for XML (StAX) 1.0 were added to Web Services Technology.
- Java Persistence API (JPA) 1.0 and Common Annotations API 1.0 were added to Enterprise Applications Technology.

## The Java SE and EE Droughts

The release of Java SE 6 in December 2006, marked the beginning of a drought for Java SE releases that lasted approximately 5 years. This time was a period of frustration and even anger for many in the Java community. Sun continued to promise new language features and APIs for Java SE 7, but the schedule continued to slip year after year with no end in sight. Meanwhile other technologies, such as the C# language and .NET platform, caught up to and surpassed Java in language features and platform APIs, causing some to speculate whether Java had reached the end of its useful life. To make matters worse, Java EE entered its own drought period and by 2009, more than 3 years had passed since Java EE 5 was released. All was not lost, however. Java EE 6 development picked up in early 2009, and it released in December 2009, 3 years and 7 months after Java EE 5, and 3 years almost to the day after Java SE 6.

By this time, Java Enterprise Edition became enormous:

- SAAJ, StAX, and JAF moved to Java SE 6.
- The Java API for RESTful Web Services (JAX-RS) 1.1 and Java APIs for XML Messaging (JAXM) 1.3 specifications were added to Web Services Technologies.
- The Java Unified Expression Language (JUEL or just EL) 2.0 was added to Web Application Technologies.
- Management and Security Technologies saw the addition of Java Authentication Service Provider Interface for Containers (JASPIC) 1.0.
- Enterprise Application Technologies realized the most dramatic increase in features, including Contexts and Dependency Injection for Java (CDI) 1.0, Dependency Injection for Java 1.0, Bean Validation 1.0, Managed Beans 1.0, and Interceptors 1.1, in addition to updates to all its other components.

Java EE 6 also represented a major turning point in the architecture of Java EE on two fronts:

- This version introduced annotation-based and programmatic application configuration to complement the traditional XML configuration used for more than a decade.
- This version marked the introduction of the Java EE Web Profile.

To account for the fact that Java EE had become so large (and maintaining and updating certified implementations was becoming increasingly difficult), the Web Profile certification program offered the opportunity to certify Java EE implementations that included only a subset of the entire Java EE platform. This subset included the features deemed to be most critical to a large number of applications and excluded specifications that are used only by a small minority of applications. As of Java EE 6:

- None of the Web Services or Management and Security components are part of the Java EE Web Profile.
- The Web Profile includes everything from Web Application Technologies and everything from Enterprise Application Technologies except Java EE Connector Architecture, JMS, and JavaMail.

It was during the 5-year Java drought that Oracle Corporation bought Sun Microsystems in January 2010. Coupled with the Java SE drought, this brought a whole new set of concerns for the Java community. Oracle was never known for its agility or willingness to cooperate with open source projects, and many people feared Oracle had bought Sun to shut Java down. However, this turned out not to be the case.

Early on, Oracle began reorganizing the Java team, creating communication pipelines with the open source community, and releasing roadmaps for future Java SE and Java EE versions that were more realistic than anything Sun had promised. Work began anew on Java SE 7, which released on

(Oracle's) schedule in June 2011, almost 5 years after Java SE 6. A second Java EE drought ended with the release of Java EE 7 in June 2013, 3 years and 7 months after Java EE 6. Oracle now says it is on track to begin releasing new versions of both platforms every 2 years, on alternate years. It remains to be seen whether that will come to pass.

# Understanding the Most Recent Platform Features

Java SE 7 and 8 and Java EE 7 have brought major changes to the language and supporting APIs and resulted in a rejuvenation of Java technologies. You use these new features throughout this book, so this section provides an overview of them.

## Java SE 7

Originally, Java SE 7 had a very ambitious feature list, but after acquiring Sun, Oracle quickly admitted that achieving the goals for Java SE 7 would take many, many years. Every feature was the most important feature to some group of users, so the decision was made to defer some of them to future versions. The alternative was to delay the release of Java SE 7 until 2015 or later — an option that was not acceptable.

Java SE 7 included support for dynamic languages as well as compressed 64-bit pointers (for improved performance on 64-bit JVMs). It also added several language features that made developing Java applications more productive. Perhaps one of the most useful changes was *diamonds*, a shortcut for generic instantiation. Prior to Java 7, both the variable declaration and the variable assignment for generic types had to include the generic type arguments. For example, here is a declaration and assignment for a very complex `java.util.Map` variable:

```
Map<String, Map<String, Map<Integer, List<MyBean>>>> map =
        new Hashtable<String, Map<String, Map<Integer, List<MyBean>>>>();
```

Of course, this declaration contains a lot of redundant information. Assigning anything other than a `Map<String, Map<String, Map<Integer, List<MyBean>>>>` to this variable would be illegal, so why should you have to specify all those type arguments again? Using Java 7 diamonds, this declaration and assignment becomes much simpler. The compiler infers the type arguments for the instantiated `java.util.Hashtable`.

```
Map<String, Map<String, Map<Integer, List<MyBean>>>> map = new Hashtable<>();
```

Another common complaint about Java prior to Java 7 is the management of closable resources as it relates to `try-catch-finally` blocks. In particular, consider this nasty bit of JDBC code:

```
Connection connection = null;
PreparedStatement statement = null;
ResultSet resultSet = null;
try
{
    connection = dataSource.getConnection();
    statement = connection.prepareStatement(...);
    // set up statement
    resultSet = statement.executeQuery();
    // do something with result set
}
```

```
catch(SQLException e)
{
    // do something with exception
}
finally
{
    if(resultSet != null) {
        try {
            resultSet.close();
        } catch(SQLException ignore) { }
    }

    if(statement != null) {
        try {
            statement.close();
        } catch(SQLException ignore) { }
    }

    if(connection != null && !connection.isClosed()) {
        try {
            connection.close();
        } catch(SQLException ignore) { }
    }
}
```

Java 7's *try-with-resources* has drastically simplified this task. Any class implementing `java.lang.AutoCloseable` is eligible for use in a try-with-resources construct. The JDBC `Connection`, `PreparedStatement`, and `ResultSet` interfaces extend this interface. When you use try-with-resources as shown in the following example, the resources you declare within the `try` keyword's parentheses are automatically closed in an implicit `finally` block. Any exceptions thrown during this cleanup are added to an existing exception's suppressed exceptions or, if there is no existing exception, are thrown after the resources have all been closed.

```
try(Connection connection = dataSource.getConnection();
    PreparedStatement statement = connection.prepareStatement(...))
{
    // set up statement
    try(ResultSet resultSet = statement.executeQuery())
    {
        // do something with result set
    }
}
catch(SQLException e)
{
    // do something with exception
}
```

Another improvement made to try-catch-finally is the addition of *multi-catch*. As of Java 7 you can now catch multiple exceptions within a single `catch` block, separating the exception types with a single pipe. For example:

```
try
{
    // do something
```

```
}
catch(MyException | YourException e)
{
    // handle these exceptions the same way
}
```

One caveat to keep in mind is that you can't multi-catch two or more exceptions such that one inherits from another. For example, the following is prohibited because `FileNotFoundException` extends `IOException`:

```
try {
    // do something
} catch(IOException | FileNotFoundException e) {
    // handle these exceptions the same way
}
```

Of course, this can easily be considered a matter of common sense. In this case, you would simply catch `IOException`, which would catch both types of exceptions.

A few other miscellaneous language features in Java 7 include *binary literals* for bytes and integers (you can write the literal `1928` as `0b11110001000`) and *underscores in numeric literals* (you can write the same literals as `1_928` and `0b111_1000_1000`, if desired). In addition, you can finally use `String`s as `switch` arguments.

## Java EE 7

Java EE 7, released on June 12, 2013, contains a number of changes and new features. You'll cover many of these new features throughout this book, so they are not detailed here. In summary, the changes to Java EE 7 are as follows:

- JAXB was added to Java SE 7 and is no longer included in Java EE.
- Batch Applications for the Java Platform 1.0 and Concurrency Utilities for Java EE 1.0 were added to Enterprise Application Technologies.
- Web Application Technologies picked up Java API for WebSockets 1.0 (which you learn about in Chapter 10) and Java API for JSON Processing 1.0.
- The Java Unified Expression Language has been significantly expanded to include lambda expressions and an analog of the Java SE 8 Collections Stream API. (You learn more about this in Chapter 6.)
- The Web Profile was expanded slightly to include specifications more likely to be required in common web applications: JAX-RS, Java API for WebSockets, and Java API for JSON Processing.

## Java SE 8

The new features in Java SE 8 can come in very handy as you work the examples in this book. Perhaps most visible is the addition of *lambda expressions* (unofficially known as *closures*). Lambda expressions are anonymous functions that are defined, and possibly called, without being assigned a type name or bound to an identifier. Lambda expressions are particularly useful for anonymously implementing those one-method interfaces that are so common in Java applications. For example, a `Thread` that was previously instantiated with an anonymous `Runnable` like this:

```
public String doSomethingInThread(String someArgument)
{
    ...
    Thread thread = new Thread(new Runnable() {
        @Override
        public void run()
        {
            // do something
        }
    });
    ...
}
```

can now be simplified with a lambda expression:

```
public String doSomethingInThread(String someArgument)
{
    ...
    Thread thread = new Thread(() -> {
        // do something
    });
    ...
}
```

Lambda expressions can have arguments, return types, and generics. And where desired, you can use a *method reference* instead of a lambda expression to pass a reference to an interface-matching method. The following code is also equivalent to the previous two instantiations of `Thread`. You can also assign method references and lambda expressions to variables.

```
public String doSomethingInThread(String someArgument)
{
    ...
    Thread thread = new Thread(this::doSomething);
    ...
}

public void doSomething()
{
    // do something
}
```

One of the biggest complaints among Java users since its earliest days is the lack of a decent date and time API. `java.util.Date` has always been rife with problems, and the addition of `java.util.Calendar` just made many problems worse. Java SE 8 finally addresses that with JSR 310, a new date and time API. This API is based largely on Joda Time, but with improvements to the underlying architecture to fix problems in it that the Joda Time inventor pointed out. This API is a revolutionary addition to the Java SE platform APIs and finally brings a powerful and well-designed date and time API to Java.

## A Continuing Evolution

As you can tell, the Java SE and EE platforms were born together and have evolved hand-in-hand for nearly two decades. It's probable that they will continue to evolve together for many years or decades to come. You should be fairly familiar with Java SE, but it's possible you know absolutely nothing about using Java EE. It's also possible you're familiar with older Java EE versions but want to learn more about the new features in Java EE.

Part I of this book teaches you about the most important features in Java EE, including:

- Application servers and web containers (Chapter 2)
- Servlets (Chapter 3)
- JSPs (Chapters 4, 6, 7, and 8)
- HTTP sessions (Chapter 5)
- Filters (Chapter 9)
- WebSockets (Chapter 10).

# UNDERSTANDING THE BASIC WEB APPLICATION STRUCTURE

A lot of components go into making a Java EE web application. First, you have your code and the third-party libraries it depends on. Then you have the deployment descriptor, which includes instructions for deploying and starting your application. You also have the `ClassLoaders` responsible for isolating your application from other web applications on the same server. Finally, you must package your application somehow, and for that you have WAR and EAR files.

## Servlets, Filters, Listeners, and JSPs

Servlets are a key component of any Java EE web application. Servlets, which you learn about in Chapter 3, are Java classes responsible for accepting and responding to HTTP requests. Nearly every request to your application goes through a Servlet of some type, except those requests that are erroneous or intercepted by some other component. A filter is one such component that can intercept requests to your Servlets. You can use filters to meet a variety of needs, from data formatting, to response compression, to authentication and authorization. You explore the various uses of filters in Chapter 9.

As with many other different types of applications, web applications have a life cycle. There are both startup and shutdown processes, and many different things happen during these stages. Java EE web applications support various types of listeners, which you learn about throughout Parts I and II. These listeners can notify your code of multiple events, such as application startup, application shutdown, HTTP session creation, and session destruction.

Perhaps one of the most powerful Java EE tools at your disposal is the JavaServer Pages technology, or JSP. JSPs provide you with the means to easily create dynamic, HTML-based graphical user interfaces for your web applications without having to manually write `Strings` of HTML to an `OutputStream` or `PrintWriter`. The topic of JSPs encompasses many different facets, including the

JavaServer Pages Standard Tag Library, the Java Unified Expression Language, custom tags, and internationalization and localization. You will spend significant time on these features in Chapter 4 and Chapters 6 through 9.

Of course, there are many more features in Java EE than just Servlets, filters, listeners, and JSPs. You will cover many of these in this book, but not all of them.

## Directory Structure and WAR Files

Standard Java EE web applications are deployed as WAR files or "exploded" (unarchived) web application directories. You should already be familiar with *JAR*, or *Java Archive*, files. Recall that a JAR file is simply a ZIP-formatted archive with a standard directory structure recognized by JVMs. There is nothing proprietary about the JAR file format, and any ZIP archive application can create and read JAR files. A *Web Application Archive*, or *WAR*, file is the equivalent archive file for Java EE web applications.

All Java EE web application servers support WAR file application archives. Most also support exploded application directories. Whether archived or exploded, the directory structure convention, as shown in Figure 1-2, is the same. Like a JAR file, this structure contains classes and other application resources, but those classes are not stored relative to the application root as in a JAR file. Instead, the class files live in `/WEB-INF/classes`. The `WEB-INF` directory stores informational and instructional files that Java EE web application servers use to determine how to deploy and run the application. Its `classes` directory acts as the package root. All your compiled application class files and other resources live within this directory.

Unlike standard JAR files, WAR files can contain bundled JAR files, which live in `/WEB-INF/lib`. All the classes in the JAR files in this directory are also available to the application on the application's classpath. The `/WEB-INF/tags` and `/WEB-INF/tld` directories are reserved for holding JSP tag files and tag library descriptors, respectively. You'll explore the topic of tag files and tag libraries thoroughly in Chapter 8. The `i18n` directory is not actually part of the Java EE specifications, but it is a convention that most application developers follow for storing internationalization (i18n) and localization (L10n) files.

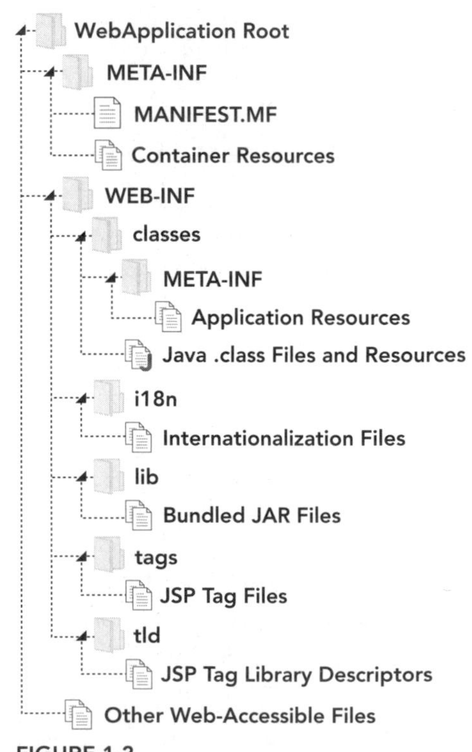

FIGURE 1-2

You probably also noticed the presence of two different `META-INF` directories. This can be a source of confusion for some developers, but if you remember the simple classpath rules, you can easily differentiate the two. Like JAR file `META-INF` directories, the root-level `/META-INF` directory contains the application manifest file. It can also contain resources for specific web containers or application servers. For example, Apache Tomcat (which you'll learn about in Chapter 2) looks for and uses a `context.xml` file in this directory to help customize how the application is deployed in Tomcat. None of these files are part of the Java EE specification, and the supported files can vary from one application server or web container to the next.

Unlike JAR files, the root-level /META-INF directory is *not* on the application classpath. You cannot use the ClassLoader to obtain resources in this directory. /WEB-INF/classes/META-INF, however, is on the classpath. You can place any application resources you desire in this directory, and they become accessible through the ClassLoader. Some Java EE components specify files that belong in this directory. For example, the Java Persistence API (which you'll learn about in Part III of this book) specifies two files — one named persistence.xml and another orm.xml — that live in /WEB-INF/classes/META-INF.

Most files contained within a WAR file or exploded web application directory are resources directly accessible through a URL. For example, the file /bar.html relative to the root of an application deployed to http://example.org/foo is accessible from http://example.org/foo/bar.html. In the absence of any filter or security rules to the contrary, this holds true for *all* resources in your application except those resources under the /WEB-INF and /META-INF directories. The files in these directories are protected resources that are not accessible via URL.

## The Deployment Descriptor

The deployment descriptor is the metadata that describes the web application and provides instructions to the Java EE web application server for deploying and running the web application. Traditionally, all this metadata came from the deployment descriptor file, /WEB-INF/web.xml. This file contains definitions for Servlets, listeners, and filters, and configuration options for HTTP sessions, JSPs, and the application in general. Servlet 3.0 in Java EE 6 added the ability to configure web applications using annotations and a Java configuration API. It also added the notion of web fragments — JAR files within your application can contain Servlets, filters, and listeners configured in /META-INF/web-fragment.xml deployment descriptors within the necessary JAR files. Web fragments can also use annotations and the Java configuration API.

This change to the deployment of web applications in Java EE 6 added significant complexity to the task of organizing this process. To ease this complexity, you can configure the order of your web fragments so that they are scanned and activated in a specific sequence. This happens one of two ways:

- Each web fragment's web-fragment.xml file can contain an <ordering> element that uses nested <before> and <after> tags to control whether the web fragment activates before or after other web fragments. These tags contain nested <name> elements to specify the name of another fragment relative to which the current fragment should be ordered. <before> and <after> can alternatively contain nested <others> elements to indicate that the fragment should activate before or after any other fragments not specifically named.
- If you didn't create a particular web fragment and don't have control over its contents, you can still control the order of your web fragments within your application's deployment descriptor. The <absolute-ordering> element in /WEB-INF/web.xml, together with its nested <name> and <others> elements, configures an absolute order for bundled web fragments that overrides any order instructions that come with the web fragments.

By default, Servlet 3.0 and newer environments scan web applications and web fragments for Java EE web application annotations for configuring Servlets, listeners, filters, and more. You can disable this scanning and disable annotation configuration by adding the attribute `metadata-complete="true"` to the root `<web-app>` or `<web-fragment>` elements as needed. You can also disable all web fragments in your application by adding `<absolute-ordering />` (without any nested elements) to your deployment descriptor.

You learn more about the web application deployment descriptor and annotation configuration throughout Part I of the book. In Part II, you explore the container initializer and programmatic configuration with the Java API, and see how it can make bootstrapping Spring Framework easier and testable.

## Class Loader Architecture

When working with Java EE web applications, it's essential to understand the `ClassLoader` architecture because it differs from the architecture to which you are accustomed in standard Java SE applications. In a typical application, the `java.*` classes that come with the Java SE platform are loaded in a special root `ClassLoader` that cannot be overridden. This is a security measure that prevents malicious code from, for example, replacing the `String` class or redefining `Boolean.TRUE` and `Boolean.FALSE`.

After this `ClassLoader` comes the extension `ClassLoader`, which loads classes from the extensions JARs in the JRE installation directory. Finally, the application `ClassLoader` loads all other classes in the application. This forms a hierarchy of `ClassLoaders`, with the root serving as the earliest ancestor for all `ClassLoaders`. When a lower-level `ClassLoader` is asked to load a class, it always delegates to its parent `ClassLoader` first. This continues up until the root `ClassLoader` is checked. With the exception of the root `ClassLoader`, a `ClassLoader` loads a class from its collection of JARs and directories *only* if its parent `ClassLoader` first fails to find the class.

This method of class loading is called the *parent-first class loader delegation model*, and although it works great for many types of applications, it is not ideal for most Java EE web applications. A server that runs Java EE web applications is typically extraordinarily complex and a number of vendors could provide its implementation. The server could use some of the same third-party libraries that your application uses, but they may be of conflicting versions. In addition, different web applications could also provide conflicting versions of the same third-party libraries, leading to even more problems. To solve these problems, you need a *parent-last class loader delegation model*.

In Java EE web application servers, each web application is assigned its own isolated `ClassLoader` that inherits from the common server `ClassLoader`. By isolating the applications from each other, they cannot access each other's classes. This not only eliminates the risk of conflicting classes, but it also serves as a security measure preventing web applications from interfering with or harming other web applications. In addition, a web application `ClassLoader` (typically) asks its parent to load a class only if it can't load the class itself first. In this way, the class loading is delegated to the parent last instead of the parent first, and web application classes and libraries are preferred over those that the server supplies. To maintain the protected status of bundled Java SE classes, web application `ClassLoaders` still check the root `ClassLoader` before attempting to load any classes. Although this delegation model is more preferable for web applications in nearly all cases, there are still rare circumstances in which it is not appropriate. For this reason, Java EE-compliant servers provide the capability of changing the delegation model from parent-last back to parent-first.

## Enterprise Archives

You've learned about WAR files, but there's another type of Java EE archive that you should know about: *EAR* files. An *Enterprise Archive* is a collection of JAR files, WAR files, and configuration files compressed into a single, deployable archive (in ZIP format, just like JARs and WARs).

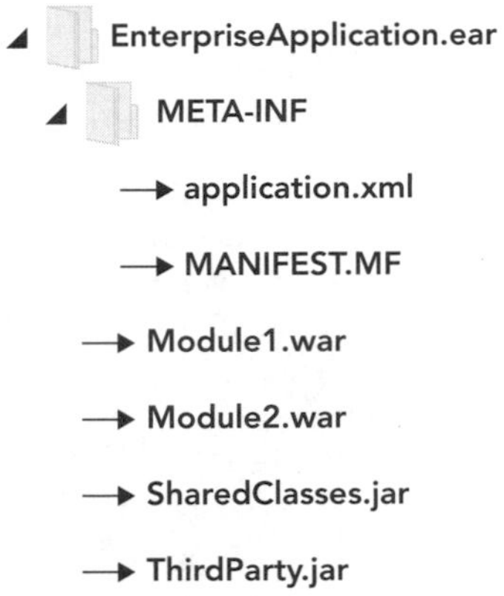

EnterpriseApplication.ear
META-INF
→ application.xml
→ MANIFEST.MF
→ Module1.war
→ Module2.war
→ SharedClasses.jar
→ ThirdParty.jar

**FIGURE 1-3**

Figure 1-3 shows a sample EAR file. As with a WAR file, the root `/META-INF` directory contains the archive manifest and is not available to the application classpath. The `/META-INF/application.xml` file is a special deployment descriptor that describes how to deploy the various components included within the EAR file. At the root level of an EAR file are all the web application modules included within it — one WAR file for each module. There is nothing special about these WAR files; they can have all the same contents and features as a normal, standalone WAR file. The EAR file can also contain JAR libraries, which can serve many purposes. The JAR files can contain Enterprise JavaBeans declared in the `/META-INF/application.xml` deployment descriptor, or they can be simple third-party libraries that two or more WAR modules share within the enterprise archive.

As you might have figured, enterprise archives also come with their own `ClassLoader` architecture. Typically, an additional `ClassLoader` is inserted into the hierarchy between the server `ClassLoader` and the web application `ClassLoaders` assigned to each module. This `ClassLoader` isolates the enterprise application from other enterprise applications but enables multiple modules in a single EAR to share common libraries contained within the EAR. This new `ClassLoader` can use either the parent-last (default) or parent-first delegation models. The web application `ClassLoaders` can then either delegate parent-first (enabling EAR library classes to take precedence) or parent-last (enabling WAR classes to take precedence).

Although it is useful to understand enterprise archives, they are a feature of the full Java EE specification, and most web container-only servers (such as Apache Tomcat) do not support them. As such, they are not discussed further in this book.

> **WARNING** *The* `ClassLoader` *examples described in this section are just that — examples. Though the Java EE specifications do describe parent-first and parent-last class loading, different implementations achieve these models in different ways, and each server could have certain nuances that might cause problems depending on your needs. You should always read the documentation of the server you choose so that you can determine whether the* `ClassLoader` *architecture of that particular server is appropriate for you.*

## SUMMARY

In this chapter you explored the histories of the Java Platform, Standard Edition and Java Platform, Enterprise Edition and learned how the two platforms evolved together over the last 19 years. You were briefly introduced to some of the topics covered in this book — Servlets, filters, listeners, JSPs, and more — and saw how Java EE applications are structured, both internally and on the filesystem. You then learned about web application archives and enterprise archives and how they serve as vessels for transporting and deploying Java EE applications.

The rest of the book explores these topics in much greater detail, answering the many questions that you likely have after reading the last several pages. In Chapter 2 you take a closer look at application servers and web containers, what they are, and how to choose one for your purposes. You also learn how to install and use Tomcat for the examples in this book.

# Using Web Containers

## IN THIS CHAPTER

- Choosing a web container
- Installing Tomcat on your machine
- Deploying and undeploying applications in Tomcat
- Debugging Tomcat from IntelliJ IDEA
- Debugging Tomcat from Eclipse

### WROX.COM CODE DOWNLOADS FOR THIS CHAPTER

You can find the `wrox.com` code downloads for this chapter `http://www.wrox.com/go/projavaforwebapps` on the Download Code tab. The code for this chapter is divided into the following major examples:

- sample-deployment WAR Application File
- Sample-Debug-IntelliJ Project
- Sample-Debug-Eclipse Project

### NEW MAVEN DEPENDENCIES FOR THIS CHAPTER

There are no Maven dependencies for this chapter.

## CHOOSING A WEB CONTAINER

In the previous chapter you were introduced to the Java Platform, Enterprise Edition, and the concepts of Servlets, filters, and other Java EE components. You also learned about some of the new features in Java 7 and 8. Java EE web applications run within Java EE *application servers* and *web containers* (also known as *Servlet containers*, and this book uses the terms interchangeably).

Although the Java EE specification is full of many smaller sub-specifications, most web containers implement only the Servlet, JSP, and JSTL specifications. This is different from full-blown Java EE application servers, which implement the entire Java EE specification. Every application server contains a web container, which is responsible for managing the life cycle of Servlets, mapping request URLs to Servlet code, accepting and responding to HTTP requests, and managing the filter chain, where applicable. However, standalone web containers are often lighter-weight and easier to use when you don't require the entire feature set of Java EE.

Choosing a web container (or an application server, for that matter) is a task that requires careful research and consideration for the requirements of your project. You have many options for choosing a web container, and each has its advantages and challenges. You may use a variety of web containers. For example, you may decide to use Apache Tomcat for local testing on your developers' machines while using GlassFish for your production environment. Or you may write an application that your customers deploy on their own servers, in which case you probably want to test on many different application servers and web containers.

In this section you learn about some common web containers and application servers, and in the remaining sections you take a closer look at the one you use for the rest of this book.

## Apache Tomcat

Apache Tomcat is the most common and popular web container available today. Sun Microsystems software engineers originally created this web container as the Sun Java Web Server, and it was the original reference implementation of the Java EE Servlet specification. Sun later donated it to the Apache Software Foundation in 1999, and at that point it became Jakarta Tomcat and eventually Apache Tomcat. It is also interesting to note that Apache's evolution of Tomcat led to the development of the Apache Ant build tool, which thousands of commercial and open source projects use today.

Tomcat's primary advantages are its small footprint, simple configuration, and long history of community involvement. Typically, developers can be up-and-running with a functional Tomcat installation in 5 to 10 minutes, including download time. Tomcat requires very little configuration out-of-the-box to run well on a development machine, but it can also be tuned significantly to perform well in high-load, high-availability production environments. You can create large Tomcat clusters to handle huge volumes of traffic reliably. Tomcat is often used in commercial production environments due to its simplicity and lightweight profile. However, Tomcat lacks the sophisticated web management interface than many of its competitors offer for configuring the server. Instead, Tomcat provides only a simple interface for basic tasks, such as deploying and undeploying applications. For further configuration, administrators must manipulate a collection of XML and Java properties files. In addition, because it is not a full application server, it lacks many Java EE components, such as the Java Persistence API, the Bean Validation API, and the Java Message Service.

As you can imagine, this makes Tomcat great for many tasks but does make deploying more complex enterprise applications challenging and, sometimes, impossible. If you like Tomcat but need a full Java EE application server, you can turn to Apache TomEE, which is built on Tomcat but offers a full implementation of all the Java EE components. Being built on Tomcat, it has the full force of the Tomcat community and more than a decade of testing behind it. Apache also offers Geronimo, another open source full Java EE application server.

> **NOTE** *TomEE and Geronimo are both Oracle-certified Java EE application servers, meaning they have been verified to be in compliance with all aspects of the Java EE specification. Because Tomcat is only a web container, it has no such certification. However, its huge user base and active community ensure that it accurately implements the Java EE components it provides.*

Tomcat provides implementations of the Servlet, Java Server Pages (JSP), Java Unified Expression Language (EL), and WebSocket specifications. Table 2-1 lists several Tomcat versions and the specifications they implement. Only Tomcat 6, 7, and 8 are still supported. Versions 3.3, 4.1, and 5.5 reached end of life years ago. You can read more about Apache Tomcat on the Tomcat website (`http://tomcat.apache.org/`).

**TABLE 2-1:** Tomcat Versions and Their Specifications

| TOMCAT VERSION | JAVA EE* | SERVLET | JSP | EL | WEBSOCKET | MIN. JAVA SE VERSION |
|---|---|---|---|---|---|---|
| 3.3.x | 1.2 | 2.2 | 1.1 | – | – | 1.1 |
| 4.1.x | 1.3 | 2.3 | 1.2 | – | – | 1.3 |
| 5.5.x | 1.4 | 2.4 | 2.0 | – | – | 1.4 |
| 6.0.x | 5 | 2.5 | 2.1 | 2.1 | – | 5.0 |
| 7.0.x | 6 | 3.0 | 2.2 | 2.2 | – | 6 |
| 8.0.x | 7 | 3.1 | 2.3 | 3.0 | 1.0 | 7 |

* The Java EE column indicates only the equivalent Java EE version; Tomcat is not an application server and does not implement Java EE. A hyphen in a column indicates that the Tomcat version did not implement that particular specification.

## GlassFish

GlassFish Server is an open source and commercial full Java EE application server implementation. It provides all the features in the Java EE specification, including a web container, and is currently the reference implementation for the Java EE specification. Its web container is actually a derivative of Apache Tomcat; however, it has evolved considerably since the Tomcat core was forked to create GlassFish, and the code is hardly recognizable today. The open source edition of GlassFish offers community support, whereas the commercial Oracle GlassFish Server provides paid, commercial support through Oracle Corporation. Oracle is only offering commercial support through Java EE 7. Starting with Java EE 8, GlassFish will not include a commercial support option.

One of GlassFish's strengths is its management interface, which provides a graphical web user interface, a command-line interface, and configuration files to configure anything within the server. Server administrators can even use the management interface to deploy new GlassFish instances within a GlassFish cluster. As the reference implementation, it is also always the first server to roll out a new version whenever the specification is updated. The first version of GlassFish was released in May 2006, and implemented the Java EE 5 specification. In September 2007, version 2.0 added support for full clustering capabilities. Version 3.0 — the reference implementation for Java EE 6, released in December 2009 — included several enterprise improvements. This version represented a turning point in GlassFish's popularity, and it became extremely simple to manage an enterprise clustered GlassFish environment. In July 2011, version 3.1.1 improved several enterprise features and added support for Java SE 7, though Java SE 6 was still the minimum required version. GlassFish 4.0 released in June 2013 as the reference implementation of Java EE 7 and requires a minimum Java SE 7.

You can read more about GlassFish, and download it if you want, at `https://glassfish.java.net/`.

## JBoss and WildFly

Red Hat's JavaBeans Open Source Software Application Server (JBoss AS) was the second-most popular Java EE server, next to Tomcat, as of early 2013. Historically, JBoss AS has been a web container with Enterprise JavaBeans support and some other Java EE features. Eventually it became Web Profile-certified and, in 2012, became certified as a full Java EE application server. Over time, the name JBoss also became synonymous with a development community (like Apache) that provided several products, as well as the commercial JBoss Enterprise Application Platform. The application server retained the name JBoss AS through version 7.1.x, but in 2012, the community decided that the name was the source of too much confusion due to other JBoss projects. The application server was renamed to WildFly as of version 8.0, released in early 2014.

Similar to GlassFish, WildFly is open source with free support provided by the JBoss Community and paid, commercial support provided by Red Hat. It has a comprehensive set of management tools and provides clustering and high-availability capabilities like Tomcat and GlassFish. JBoss AS versions 4.0.x through 4.2.x were built atop Tomcat 5.5 and supported Java EE 1.4 features. Version 5.0 introduced Java EE 5 support and a brand new web container, and 5.1 contained early implementations of some Java EE 6 features (although it was still a Java EE 5 application server). JBoss AS 6.0 implemented the Java EE 6 Web Profile, but it did not seek or obtain a Java EE 6 application server certification. JBoss AS 7.0 represented a complete rewrite of the product to dramatically decrease its footprint and increase its performance, and also supported only the Java EE 6 web profile. It was not until JBoss AS 7.1 that it again became a full application server, achieving Java EE 6 certification more than 2 years after Java EE 6 was released. WildFly 8.0 is a full Java EE 7 application server and requires a minimum of Java SE 7. (Actually, all Java EE 7 application servers and web containers require a minimum of Java SE 7.)

You can learn more about and download JBoss AS 7.1 and earlier at `http://www.jboss.org/jbossas`, whereas you can find WildFly 8.0 at `http://www.wildfly.org/`.

## Other Containers and Application Servers

There are many other web containers, such as Jetty and Tiny, and open source full Java EE application servers, such as JOnAS, Resin, Caucho, and Enhydra. There are also a number of commercial full application servers, of which Oracle WebLogic and IBM WebSphere are the most popular. Table 2-2 shows some of these servers and the versions that supported various Java EE specifications.

**TABLE 2-2:** Container and Application Server Versions

| SERVER | J2EE 1.2 | J2EE 1.3 | J2EE 1.4 | JAVA EE 5 | JAVA EE 6 | JAVA EE 7 |
|---|---|---|---|---|---|---|
| Jetty* | 3.x | 4.x | 5.x | 6.x: J2SE 1.4<br>7.x: Java SE 5.0 | 8.x: Java SE 6<br>9.0.x: Java SE 7 | 9.1.x |
| WebLogic | 6.x | 7.x-8.x | 9.x | 10.x: Java SE 6<br>11g PS5: Java SE 7 | 12c | 12.1.4** |
| WebSphere | 4.x | 5.x | 6.x | 7.x | 8.x: Java SE 6<br>8.5.x: Java SE 7 | 9.x** |

* Web container only; not a full application server

** These are speculated versions — Oracle and IBM have not officially announced Java EE 7 support yet.

Each web container or application server has its own advantages and disadvantages. The task of picking an application server cannot be covered in a single chapter and is beyond the scope of this book. The needs of your organization's project must be understood, and the right web container or application server that meets those needs should be chosen. Operational budgets must be considered because commercial application servers tend to have an extremely high cost of licensing. All these factors will impact your decision, and you may pick a server that isn't even listed in this book.

### Why You'll Use Tomcat in This Book

Many of the advantages of Apache Tomcat (which is referred to simply as Tomcat for the rest of this book) have already been outlined. Perhaps most important for this book is the ease with which developers can start using Tomcat. By far, Tomcat is easier to get running quickly than any other web container, and it provides all the features that you need to complete the examples in this book. In addition, all the major Java IDEs provide tools to run, deploy on, and debug Tomcat, making it easier for you to develop your application.

Although some developers prefer using other web containers — and with the right knowledge nearly any web container can serve you well on a development machine — it's hard to make a case against using Tomcat. By using Tomcat for this book, you can focus on the code and development practices, paying little-to-no attention to the management of your container. The rest of this chapter helps you get Tomcat installed and set up on your machine. It also introduces you to deploying and undeploying applications with the Tomcat manager and debugging Tomcat in your Java IDE.

## INSTALLING TOMCAT ON YOUR MACHINE

Before you can install Tomcat on your machine, you need to download it from the Tomcat project site. Go to `http://tomcat.apache.org/download-80.cgi` to find the Tomcat 8.0 downloads page, and scroll down to the "Binary Distributions" section. There are many downloads on this page, and the only ones you need for this book are under the "Core" heading. As a Windows user, the two downloads you are concerned with are the "32-bit/64-bit Windows Service Installer" (works for any system architecture) and the "32-bit Windows zip" *or* "64-bit Windows zip" (depending on your machine architecture). If you run on Linux, Mac OS X, or some other operating system, you need the non-Windows zip, which is just called "zip."

## Installing as a Windows Service

Many developers want to install Tomcat as a Windows service. This has several advantages, especially in a quality assurance or production environment. It makes management of JVM memory and other resources easier, and it greatly simplifies starting Tomcat automatically when Windows boots. However, in a development environment, installing Tomcat as a service can have some drawbacks. This technique installs only the service and does not install the command-line scripts that run Tomcat from the command line. Most IDEs use these command-line scripts to run and debug Tomcat from within the IDE. You may install Tomcat as a service by downloading the "32-bit/64-bit Windows Service Installer," but you also need to download the "Windows zip" to run Tomcat from your IDE.

This book does not cover installing Tomcat as a windows service because you would usually do this only for production or QA environments. The documentation on the Tomcat website is very helpful if you want to explore this further. Of course, if you are not using Windows, the Windows installer will be of no use to you. There are ways to start Tomcat automatically in other operating systems, but they are also outside the scope of this book.

## Installing as a Command-Line Application

Most application developers need to run Tomcat only as a command-line application and usually only from their IDE. To do this, follow these steps:

1. Download the architecture-appropriate Windows zip (if you use Windows) or the non-Windows zip (if you use anything else) from the Tomcat 8.0 download page and unzip the directory.
2. Place the contents of the Tomcat directory in this zip file into the folder `C:\Program Files\Apache Software Foundation\Tomcat 8.0` on your local machine (or into the appropriate directory for a server in your operating system). For example, the `webapps` directory should now be located at `C:\Program Files\Apache Software Foundation\Tomcat 8.0\webapps`.
3. If you use Windows 7 or newer, you need to change some permissions to make Tomcat accessible from your IDE. Right-click the `Apache Software Foundation` directory in `C:\Program Files` and click Properties. On the Security tab, click the Edit button. Add your user or the Users group, and give that entry full control over the directory.
4. To configure Tomcat for its first use, start by opening the file `conf/tomcat-users.xml` in your favorite text editor. Place the following tag between the `<tomcat-users>` `</tomcat-users>` XML tags:

```
<user username="admin" password="admin" roles="manager-gui,admin-gui" />
```

> **WARNING** *This configures an admin user that you can use to log in to Tomcat's web management interface. Of course, this username and password combination is very insecure and should never be used for production or publicly facing servers. However, for testing on your local machine it is sufficient.*

5. Open the `conf/web.xml` file. Search the file for the text `org.apache.jasper.servlet.JspServlet`. Below the tag that contains this text are two `<init-param>` tags. You learn about Servlet init parameters in the next chapter, but for now add the following init parameters below the existing init parameters:

```
<init-param>
    <param-name>compilerSourceVM</param-name>
    <param-value>1.8</param-value>
</init-param>
<init-param>
    <param-name>compilerTargetVM</param-name>
    <param-value>1.8</param-value>
</init-param>
```

   By default, Tomcat 8.0 compiles JavaServer Pages files with Java SE 6 language support even if it runs on Java SE 8. These new Servlet init parameters instruct Tomcat to compile JSP files with Java SE 8 language features, instead.

6. After you make these changes and save these files, you should now be ready to start up Tomcat and make sure that it runs properly. Open up a command prompt and change your directory to the Tomcat home directory (`C:\Program Files\Apache Software Foundation\Tomcat 8.0`).

7. Type the command **`echo %JAVA_HOME%`** (or **`echo $JAVA_HOME`** on a non-Windows operating system) and press Enter to check whether the `JAVA_HOME` environmental variable is properly set to your Java Development Kit (JDK) home directory. If it is not, configure the environmental variable, and then log out and back in before proceeding (see the Note that follows). Tomcat cannot run without this variable properly set.

8. Type the command **`bin\startup.bat`** (or **`bin/startup.sh`** if you do not use Windows) and press Enter. A Java console window should open showing the output of the running Tomcat process. After a few seconds, you should see the message "INFO [main] org.apache.catalina.startup.Catalina.start Server startup in 1827 ms" or something similar in the console window. This means Tomcat has started properly.

> **NOTE** *When starting, Tomcat initially looks for the* `JRE_HOME` *environmental variable and uses that if it is set. If it isn't, it next looks for the* `JAVA_HOME` *variable. If neither is set, Tomcat fails to start. However, to debug Tomcat you* must *have* `JAVA_HOME` *set, so it's best to simply go ahead and configure that.*

9. Open your favorite Web browser and navigate to `http://localhost:8080/`. You should see a page that looks like Figure 2-1. This means that Tomcat is running and JSPs are compiling properly with Java SE 8. If this screen does not come up or you observe an error

in the Java console, you need to check the preceding steps and possibly consult the Tomcat documentation.

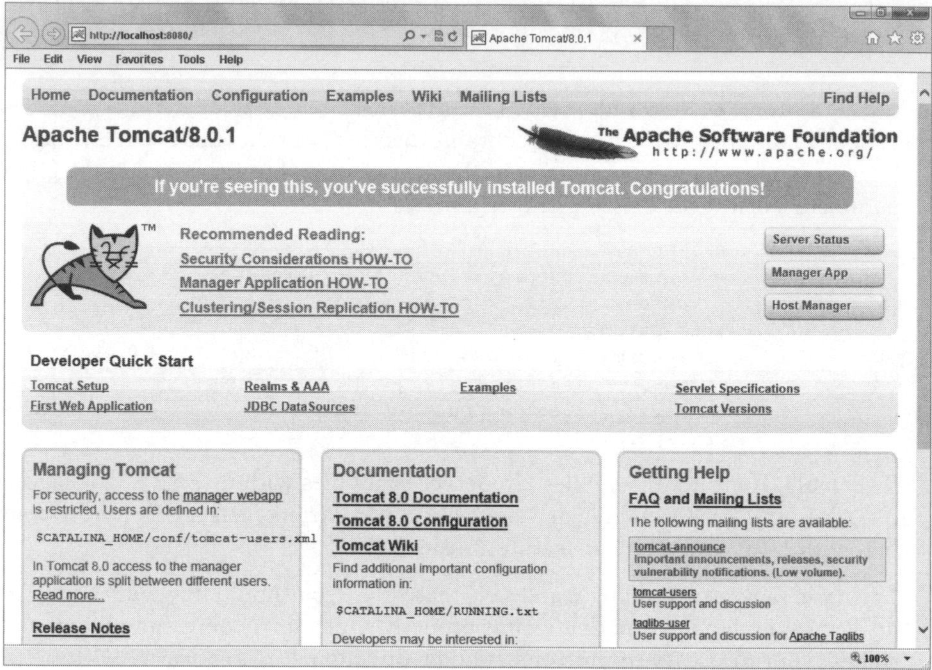


FIGURE 2-1

When you finish using Tomcat, you can stop it by running the command **`bin\shutdown.bat`** (or **`bin/shutdown.sh`**) in the command prompt in the Tomcat 8.0 home directory. The Java console window should close, and Tomcat will stop. However, do not do this yet; in the next section, you explore deploying and undeploying applications in Tomcat. (If you have already shut down Tomcat, don't worry about it. It's easy to start it back up again.)

> **WARNING** *The earliest releases of Tomcat 8.0 do not support compiling JSPs for Java 8. You'll know that this is the case for your release if you see "WARNING: Unknown source VM 1.8 ignored" or similar in the Java console. If so, you need to complete the following steps for "Configuring a Custom JSP Compiler."*

## Configuring a Custom JSP Compiler

Tomcat ships with and uses the Eclipse JDT compiler for compiling JavaServer Pages files in web applications. (You learn more about JSP files and how they compile in Chapter 4.) This enables Tomcat to run properly without requiring a JDK installation. Using the Eclipse compiler, all you need is a simple Java Runtime Edition (JRE) installation. Because JSPs are usually very simple, the Eclipse compiler is typically quite adequate for any Tomcat environment. However, there are circumstances for which you don't want to use the Eclipse compiler. Perhaps you find a bug in the Eclipse compiler that prevents one of your JSPs from compiling. Or if a new version of Java comes out with language features you want to use in your JSPs, it could be some time before Eclipse has a compatible compiler. Whatever reason you may have, you can easily configure Tomcat to use the JDK compiler instead of Eclipse.

1. Open Tomcat's `conf/web.xml` file back up and find the `JspServlet` again.
2. Add the following init parameter, which tells the Servlet to use Apache Ant with the JDK compiler to compile JSPs instead of the Eclipse compiler.

```
<init-param>
    <param-name>compiler</param-name>
    <param-value>modern</param-value>
</init-param>
```

3. Tomcat doesn't have a way to use the JDK compiler directly, so you must have the latest version of Ant installed on your system. You also need to add the JDK's `tools.jar` file and Ant's `ant.jar` and `ant-launcher.jar` files to your classpath. The easiest way to do this is to create a `bin\setenv.bat` file and add the following line of code to it (ignore new lines here), replacing the file paths as necessary for your system.

```
set "CLASSPATH=C:\path\to\jdk8\lib\tools.jar;C:\path\to\ant\lib\ant.jar;
C:\path\to\ant\lib\ant-launcher.jar"
```

Of course, this applies only to Windows machines. For non-Windows environments, you should instead create a `bin/setenv.sh` file with the following contents, replacing the file paths as necessary for your system:

```
export CLASSPATH=/path/to/jdk8/lib/tools.jar:/path/to/ant/lib/ant.jar:
/path/to/ant/lib/ant-launcher.jar
```

When running Tomcat with such a custom JSP compilation configuration, be sure to carefully observe the output in the Tomcat logs. If Tomcat cannot find Ant or Ant cannot find the JDK compiler, Tomcat automatically falls back to the Eclipse compiler and outputs only a warning to the logs.

## DEPLOYING AND UNDEPLOYING APPLICATIONS IN TOMCAT

In this section you learn how to deploy and undeploy Java EE web applications in Tomcat. You have two options for accomplishing this:

- Manually by placing the application in the `webapps` directory
- Using the Tomcat manager application

If you have not already done so, you should download the `sample-deployment.war` sample application from the Chapter 2 section on the `wrox.com` download site. This is what you should use to practice deployment and undeployment.

## Performing a Manual Deploy and Undeploy

Deploying an application manually on Tomcat is simple — just place the `sample-deployment.war` file in Tomcat's `webapps` directory. If Tomcat is running, within a few moments Tomcat should automatically unpack the application file into a directory with the same name minus the `.war` extension. If Tomcat is not running, you can start it, and the application file will unpack as Tomcat starts. When the application has unpacked, open your browser and navigate to `http://localhost:8080/sample-deployment/`. You should see a page that looks like Figure 2-2. This means that the sample application has successfully deployed.

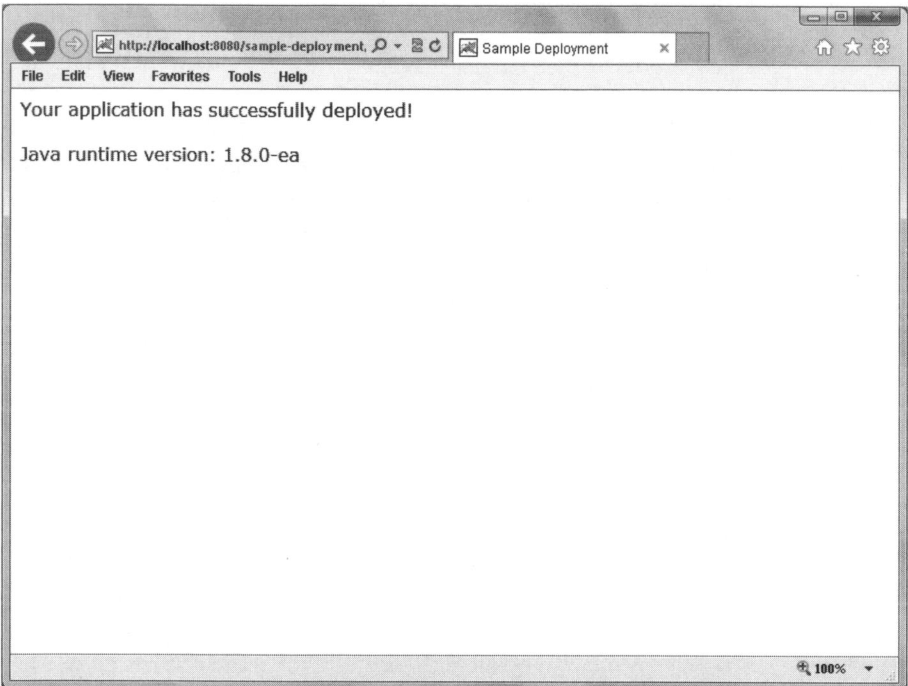


FIGURE 2-2

Undeploying the application is as simple as reversing the process. Delete the `sample-deployment.war` file and wait a few moments. When Tomcat detects that the file was deleted, it undeploys the application and deletes the unpacked directory, and the application will no longer be accessible from your browser. You do not need to shut down Tomcat to perform this task.

## Using the Tomcat Manager

You can also deploy a Java EE application using the Tomcat manager web interface. To do so, follow these steps:

1. Open your browser and navigate to `http://localhost:8080/manager/html`.
2. When you are prompted for a username and password, enter **admin** for the username and **admin** for the password (or whatever you configured in `conf/tomcat-users.xml`). The page you are presented with should look like Figure 2-3.

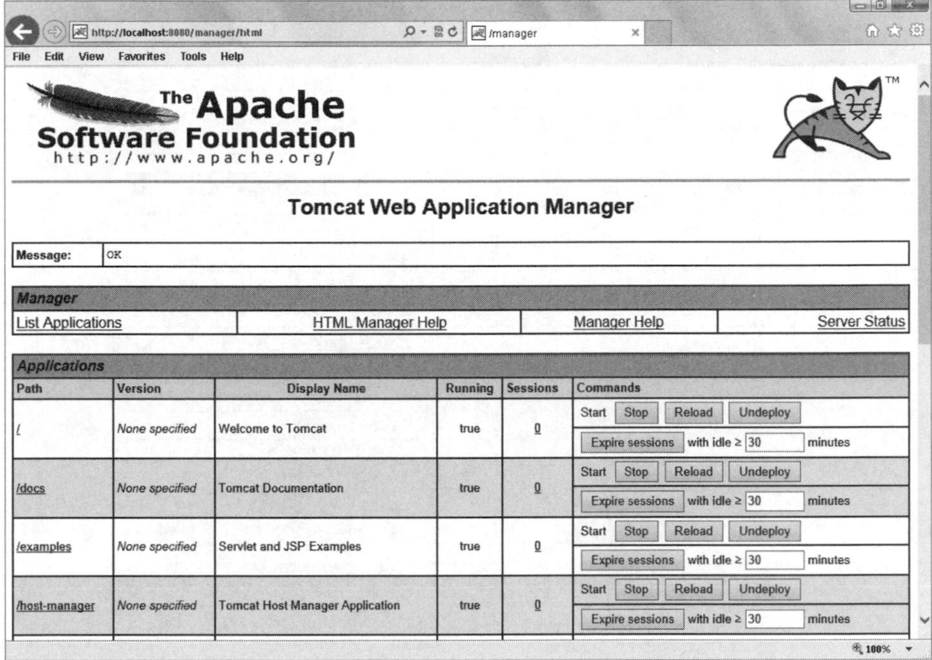


FIGURE 2-3

3. Scroll down to the Deploy section and find the form “WAR file to deploy.” In the “Select WAR file to upload” field, choose the `sample-deployment.war` file from your filesystem, as shown in Figure 2-4, and then click the Deploy button. The WAR file uploads to Tomcat, which deploys the application. The `sample-deployment` directory is again created in Tomcat’s `webapps` directory. When complete, Tomcat returns you to the list of applications where you can see that the sample application has been deployed, as shown in Figure 2-5.
4. Like before, you can go to `http://localhost:8080/sample-deployment/` and view the sample page in the sample application.

You have now deployed the application using the Tomcat manager.

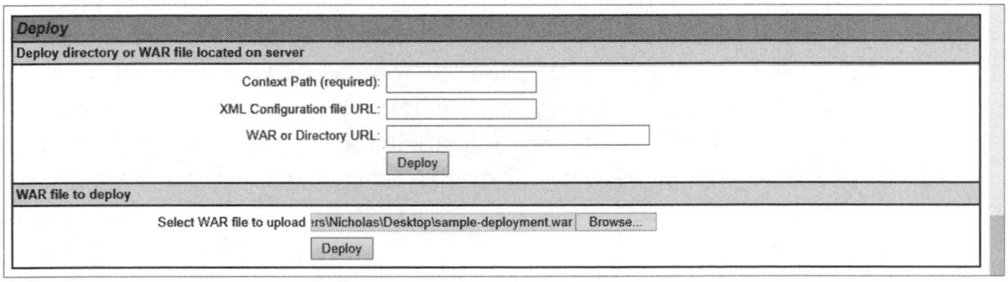

FIGURE 2-4

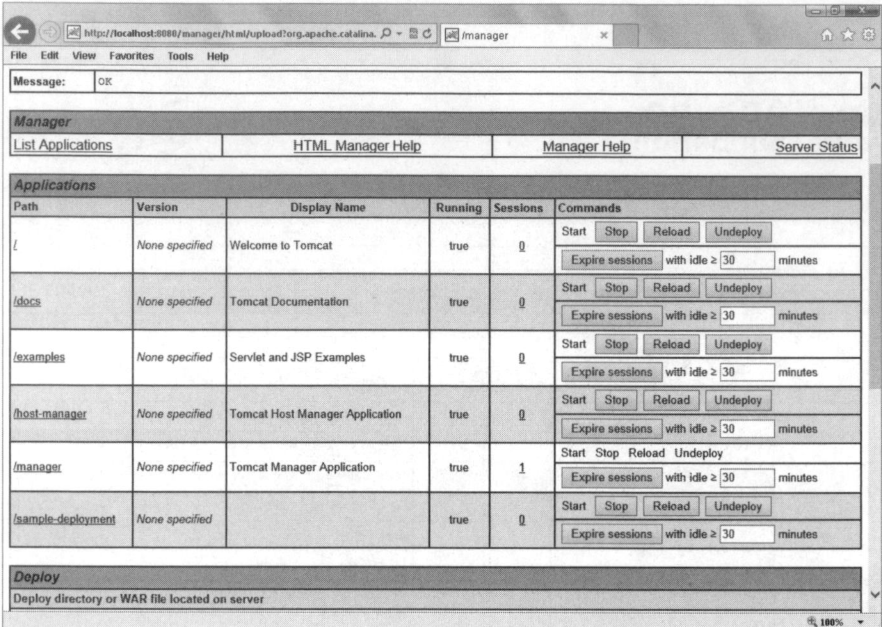


FIGURE 2-5

Undeploying is just as easy to accomplish. On the Tomcat manager page you saw earlier, you should notice an Undeploy button next to the sample application (refer to Figure 2-5). Click this button and the sample application will be undeployed and removed from the `webapps` directory. When complete, you can no longer access the application at `http://localhost:8080/sample-deployment/`.

## DEBUGGING TOMCAT FROM YOUR IDE

As a Java EE developer, one of the most important skills you can hold is the ability to deploy and debug applications in Tomcat from your Java IDE. This provides you with immeasurable troubleshooting skills for determining why an application won't run or figuring out why the bug your customer reported occurs. This section covers setting up, running, and debugging web applications in Tomcat using both IntelliJ IDEA and Eclipse. You can read both sets of instructions or just the set that pertains to the IDE you have chosen — that choice is up to you.

Throughout the rest of this book is very little instruction for doing this. This keeps the text decoupled from any particular IDE. You also do not see any IDE-specific screenshots after this chapter. Be sure you are familiar and comfortable with deploying and debugging applications in Tomcat using your IDE before moving on, even if that means going over this section several times.

### Using IntelliJ IDEA

If you use IntelliJ IDEA 13 or newer, you have just a few simple steps to take to get up and running with your web applications. The first thing you need to do is set up IntelliJ to recognize your local Tomcat or other container installation. This is a one-time-only step — you set it up once in your global IDE settings, then you can use the application server for any web application project. Next, set up each web application project to use your configured container. Finally, you just need to start your application from IntelliJ and place breakpoints where you'd like to debug your application.

## Setting Up Tomcat 8.0 in IntelliJ

To start, you need to configure Tomcat in IntelliJ's list of application servers.

1. Open up IntelliJ's IDE settings dialog. With a project open you can go to File ➪ Settings, or click the Settings icon in the toolbar (shown here in the margin), or press Ctrl + Alt + S. If you don't have a project open, you can click the Configure button and then the Settings button.
2. In the left pane of the Settings dialog, click Application Servers under IDE Settings. Initially, you have no application servers configured.
3. Click the green plus icon to add a new application server. Click the browse button next to the Tomcat Home field to browse for and select the Tomcat home directory (for example, `C:\Program Files\Apache Software Foundation\Tomcat 8.0`). Then click OK. IntelliJ should automatically detect your Tomcat version, and the dialog should look like Figure 2-6.

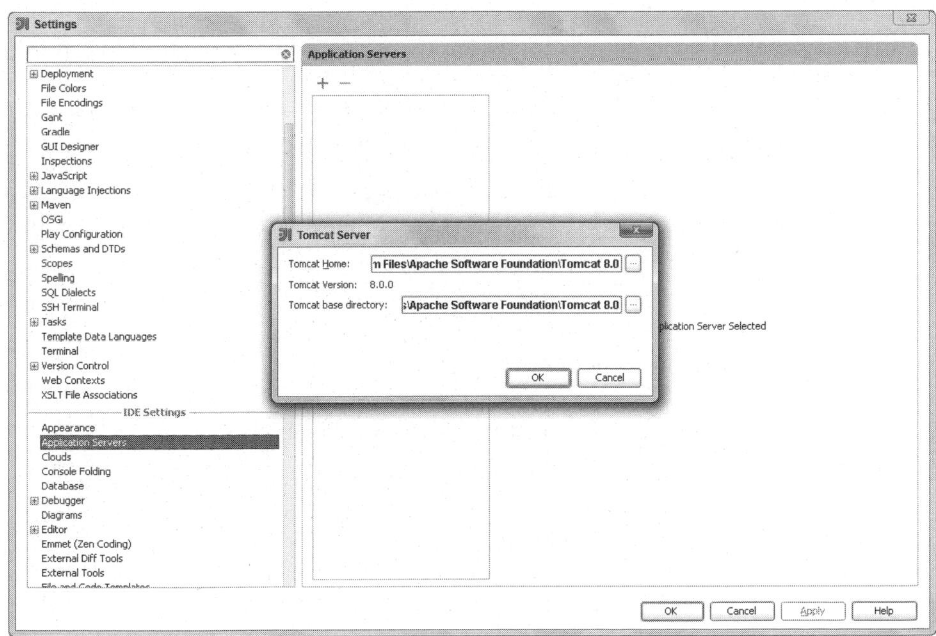


FIGURE 2-6

4. Click OK again to complete adding Tomcat to your list of application servers, and change the name if you want. All the IntelliJ code samples you can download for this book assume an application server name of **Tomcat 8.0**, so for maximum ease you should rename it to Tomcat 8.0 if it is named something else.
5. Click Apply to save the changes and OK to close the Settings dialog.

## Adding a Tomcat Configuration to a Project

After you create a project and are ready to deploy it to Tomcat from IntelliJ, you need to add a Tomcat run/debug configuration to your project.

1. Click the run/debug configurations icon (a down arrow) on the toolbar, then click Edit Configurations.

2. In the dialog that appears, click the green plus icon, scroll to the bottom of the Add New Configuration menu, hover over Tomcat Server, and click Local. This creates a run/debug configuration for running your project against a local Tomcat, as shown in Figure 2-7.
3. If Tomcat 8.0 is the only application server you have added to IntelliJ, it is automatically selected as the application server this run/debug configuration will use. If you have other application servers configured, one of those might be selected, in which case you need to click the "Application server" drop-down and select Tomcat 8.0 instead.
4. Name the run configuration something meaningful. In Figure 2-7 and in all the sample IntelliJ projects you download for this book, the run configuration is named Tomcat 8.0 like the application server it uses.
5. You'll probably see a warning that no artifacts are marked for deployment. Correcting this is simple. Click the Deployment tab and then the green plus icon under the "Deploy at the server startup" heading. Click Artifact, and then click the exploded war file artifact. Click OK. Change the "Application context" name for the artifact deployment to the server-relative URL you want it deployed to, as shown in Figure 2-8.
6. Click Apply and then OK to save the run/debug configuration and dismiss the dialog.

You can download the Sample-Debug-IntelliJ project from the `wrox.com` code download site to view a sample web application already configured to run on your local Tomcat 8.0 application server. (However, you still need to set up your Tomcat 8.0 installation in IntelliJ's IDE settings.)

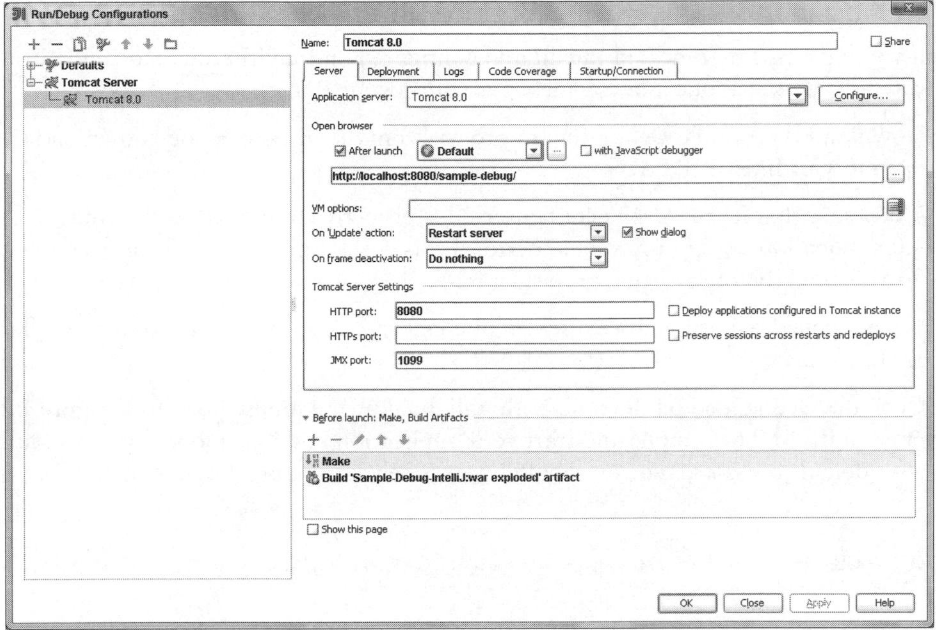


FIGURE 2-7

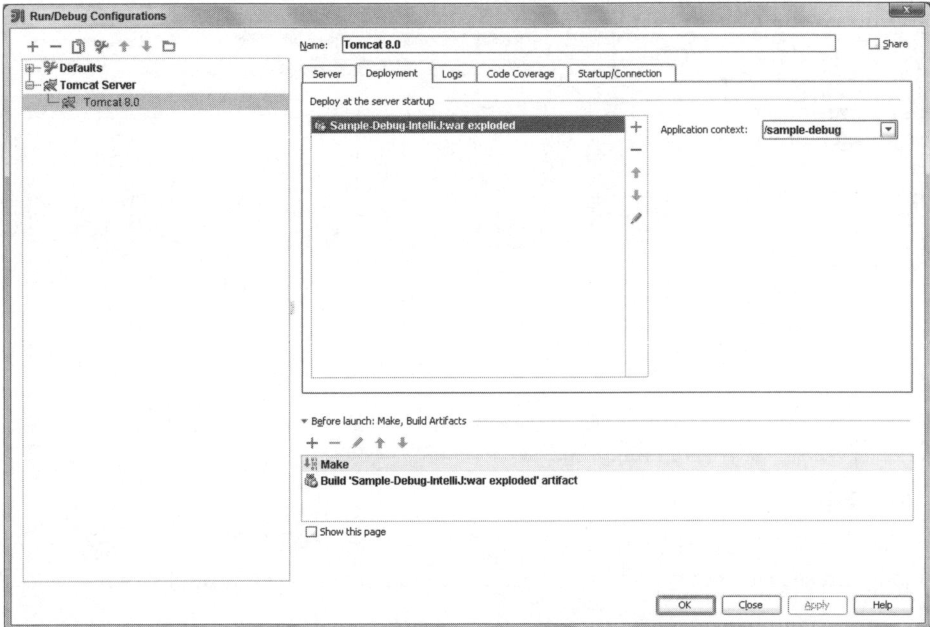


FIGURE 2-8

## Starting an Application and Hitting Breakpoints

Now that you have set up Tomcat in IntelliJ and configured an IntelliJ project to run in Tomcat, you're ready to start the application and debug it within your IDE.

1. Download the Sample-Debug-IntelliJ project from the `wrox.com` code download site, and open it with IntelliJ IDEA.
2. Make sure that its run/debug configuration is properly configured to use your local Tomcat 8.0 application server. You should perform this check for each sample project you download for this book before attempting to start it.
3. When opened, you should see a screen like Figure 2-9, with two breakpoints in place for `index.jsp`.
4. Click the Debug icon on the toolbar (highlighted by the mouse pointer in Figure 2-9) or press Shift + F9 to compile and start your application in debug mode. IntelliJ should launch your default browser, and you should immediately hit the breakpoints in `index.jsp`.

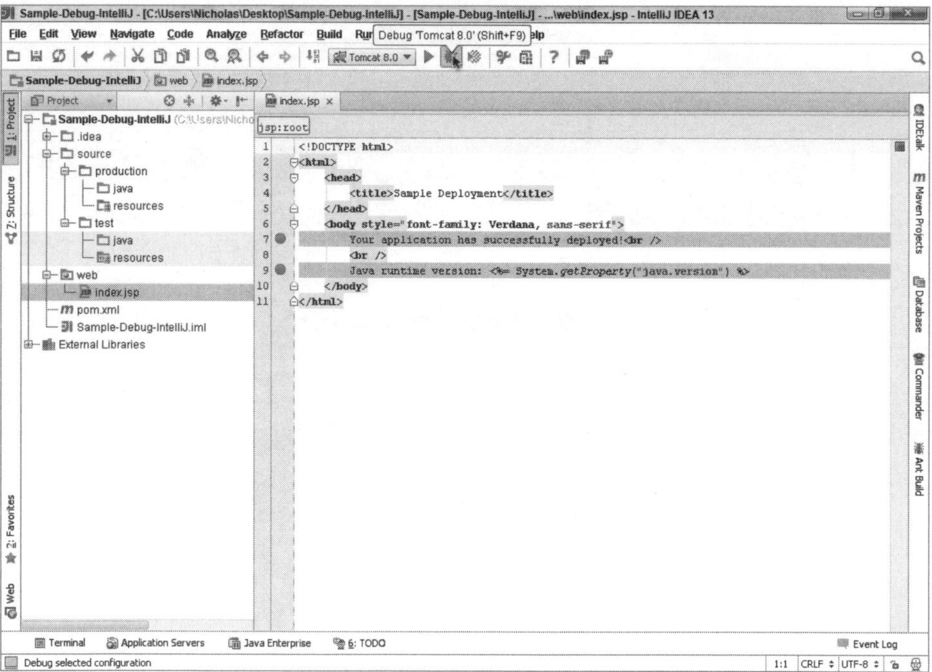


FIGURE 2-9

You should again see the webpage from Figure 2-2 to indicate that your application successfully deployed.

> **NOTE** *IntelliJ may actually access* `http://localhost:8080/sample-debug/` *before launching your browser. It does this to ensure that your application has been properly deployed. If this is the case, you will hit the breakpoints twice — once when IntelliJ accesses the application and once when your browser opens and accesses the application.*

## Using Eclipse

Using Tomcat in Eclipse has some similarities to using Tomcat in IntelliJ IDEA, but it also has many differences, and the screens look very different. The same basic process still applies — you need to set up Tomcat in Eclipse's global settings, configure it for a project, and start and debug the project. In this last part of this section. you learn how to use Tomcat from Eclipse in case you have chosen that as your IDE for this book.

> **WARNING** *As discussed in the introduction, as of the date this book was published, Eclipse does not yet support Java SE 8, Java EE 7, or Tomcat 8.0. You must wait until Eclipse 4.4 Luna is released in June 2014 to realize support for these technologies. As such, the Eclipse instructions and figures in this section may not be completely accurate, and you should respond as needed to changes made to the release version of Eclipse Luna.*

### Setting Up Tomcat 8.0 in Eclipse

To begin, you must configure Tomcat 8.0 as a runtime environment in Eclipse's global preferences. To do so, follow these steps:

1. Open your Eclipse IDE for Java EE Developers and go to Windows ➪ Preferences.
2. In the Preferences dialog that appears, expand Server, and then click Runtime Environments. A Server Runtime Environments panel appears where you can manage the application servers and web containers available to all your Eclipse projects.
3. Click the Add button to open the New Server Runtime Environment dialog.
4. Expand the Apache folder and select Apache Tomcat v8.0, making sure you select the "Create a new local server" check box. Then click the Next button.
5. On the next screen, click the Browse button and browse to your Tomcat 8.0 home directory (for example, `C:\Program Files\Apache Software Foundation\Tomcat 8.0`). Then click OK.
6. In the JRE drop-down, select your local Java SE 8 JRE installation. Name the server whatever you want. The Eclipse sample projects you download throughout this book assume that the server is named Apache Tomcat v8.0, which is the Eclipse default. At this point you should see a screen like Figure 2-10.

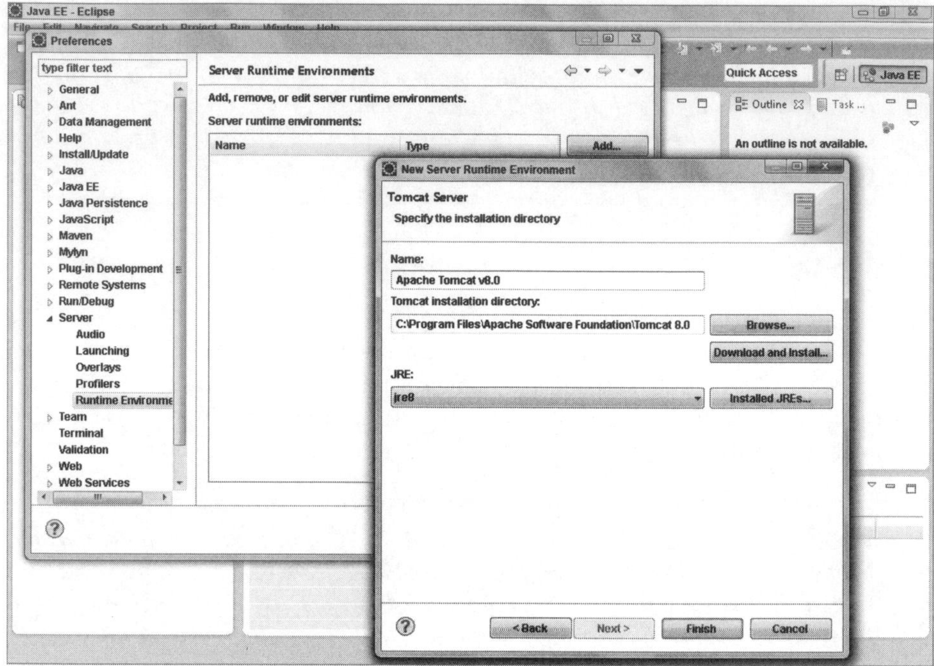


FIGURE 2-10

7. Click the Finish button to complete adding your local Tomcat server to Eclipse, and then click OK to close the preferences dialog.

You are now ready to use Tomcat 8.0 in your Eclipse projects.

One other thing to note is that, by default, Eclipse uses a built-in browser to open your web applications. You should disable this feature and use a mainstream browser, instead, such as Google Chrome, Mozilla Firefox, or Microsoft Internet Explorer. To change this setting, go to the Window ➪ Web Browser menu, and select something other than “0 Internal Web Browser.” The option “1 Default System Web Browser” should be sufficient in most cases, but it’s easy to change this setting frequently to meet your needs at any given time.

## Using the Tomcat Server in a Project

When creating a new project in Eclipse, you have to select the configured runtime server you are going to use for that project on the first dialog, as shown in Figure 2-11. However, this configures only the libraries for your application. It does not select the Tomcat 8.0 server you created. For that, follow these steps:

1. After you create or open the project, go to Project ➪ Properties and click the Server menu item on the left side of the project Properties dialog that appears.
2. By default, the selected server is “<None>,” so you should change it to “Tomcat v8.0 Server at localhost” instead, as shown Figure 2-12.

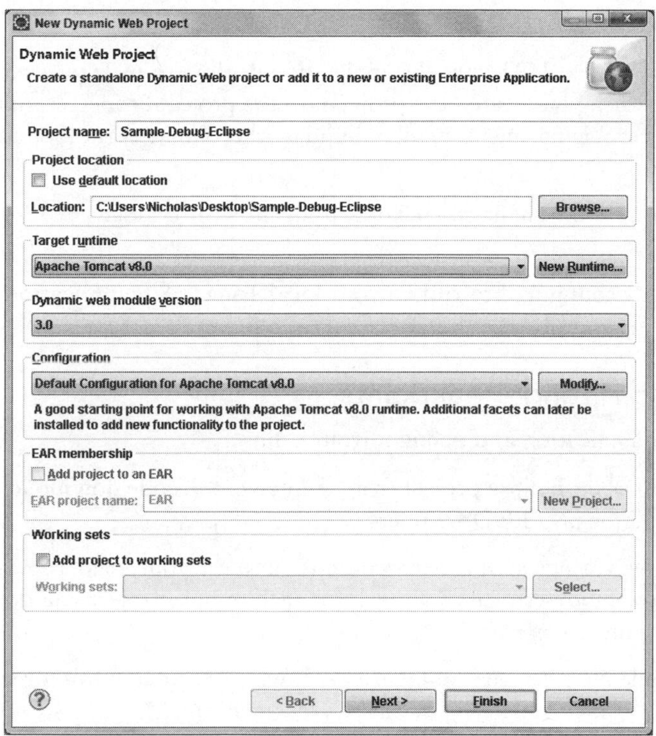


FIGURE 2-11

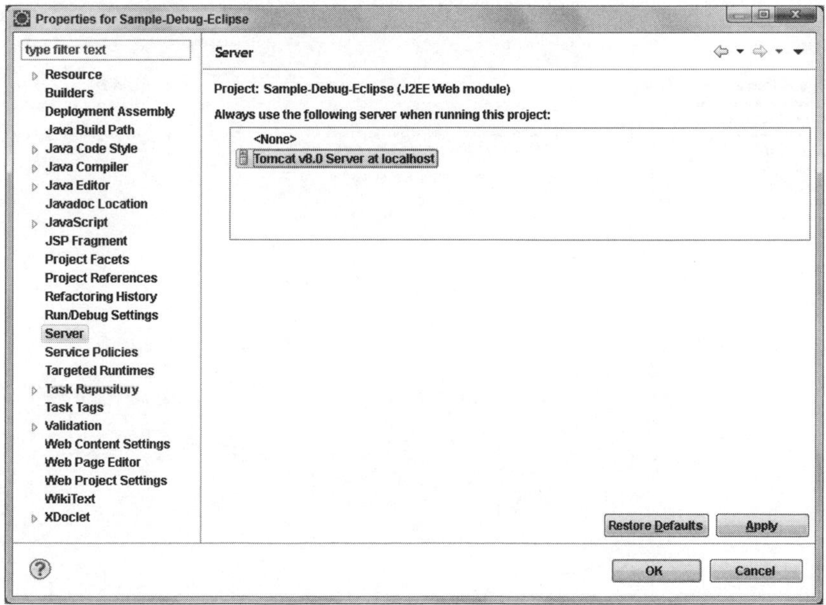


FIGURE 2-12

3. Click Apply to save the changes.
4. Change the application context URL that the application deploys to in Tomcat (assuming you didn't configure it when you created the project). In the project Properties dialog, you can click the Web Project Settings menu item and update the "Context root" field to change this setting.
5. After clicking Apply to save the changes, click OK to dismiss the dialog.

You can download the Sample-Debug-Eclipse project from the `wrox.com` code download site to view a sample web application already configured to run on your local Tomcat 8.0 application server. (However, you still need to set up your Tomcat 8.0 installation in Eclipse's IDE preferences.)

## Starting an Application and Hitting Breakpoints

You're now ready to start your application and debug it from Eclipse.

1. Download the Sample-Debug-Eclipse project from the `wrox.com` code download site, and open it with Eclipse IDE for Java EE Developers.
2. Make sure that its server settings are properly configured to use your local Tomcat 8.0 application server. You should perform this check for each sample project you download for this book before attempting to start it.
3. When opened you should see a screen like Figure 2-13, with one breakpoint already in place for `index.jsp`.

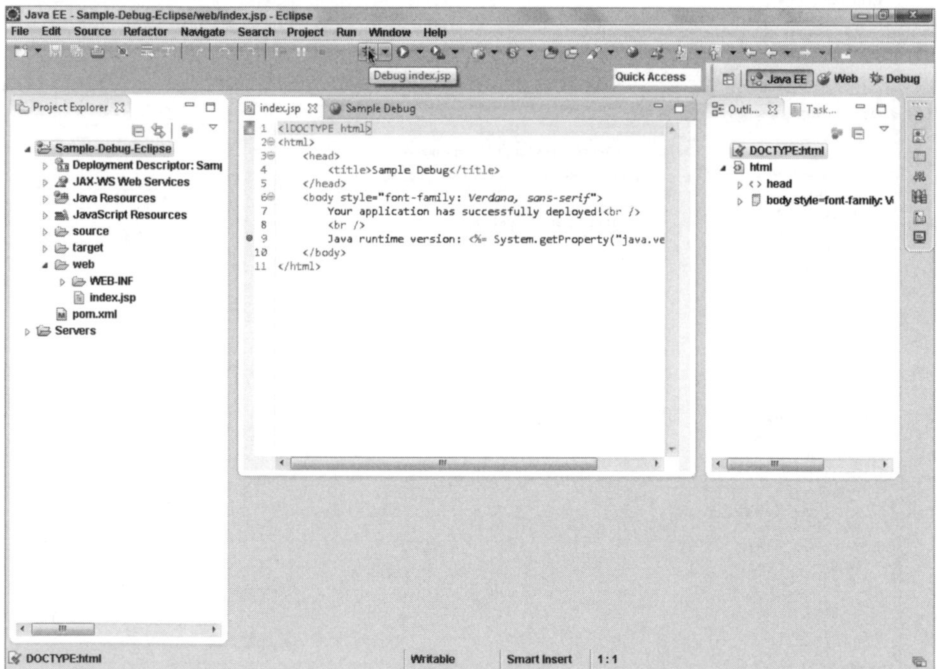


FIGURE 2-13

4. Click the Debug icon in the toolbar (highlighted by the mouse pointer in Figure 2-13) to compile and start your application in debug mode. Eclipse should launch the configured browser, and you should immediately hit the breakpoint in `index.jsp`. You can again see the webpage from Figure 2-2 to indicate that your application successfully deployed.

5. To continue from the breakpoint, click the continue icon (shown here in the margin) on the Eclipse toolbar.

> **WARNING** *When you run Tomcat from Eclipse, Eclipse overrides any custom* `conf\setenv.bat` *or* `conf/setenv.sh` *file that you create to configure advanced JSP compilation. If you do not want to use the Eclipse JDT compiler to compile your JSPs, you need to add the* `CLASSPATH` *configuration in this file to some other Tomcat configuration file. Consult the Tomcat documentation to determine the appropriate file to place this in.*

> **NOTE** *You likely noticed that the JSP in Eclipse only has one breakpoint, whereas the JSP in IntelliJ IDEA has two breakpoints. The Eclipse JSP debugger is much more limited than the IDEA JSP debugger, so placing a breakpoint on Line 7 in this JSP is not possible in Eclipse.*

## SUMMARY

In this chapter, you learned about Java EE application servers and web containers and explored several popular implementations of both. You installed Tomcat 8.0 on your local machine, configured JSP compilation, started it from the command line, and experimented with deploying and undeploying applications in Tomcat. Finally, you learned how to configure and run Tomcat 8.0 and debug your applications using both IntelliJ IDEA and Eclipse IDE for Java EE Developers.

In the next chapter you create Servlets and learn how Java EE web applications work.

# 3

# Writing Your First Servlet

## IN THIS CHAPTER

- Creating a Servlet class
- Configuring a Servlet for deployment
- Understanding `doGet()`, `doPost()` and other methods
- Using parameters and accepting form submissions
- Configuring your application using init parameters
- Uploading files from a form
- Making your application safe for multithreading

## WROX.COM CODE DOWNLOADS FOR THIS CHAPTER

You can find the `wrox.com` code downloads for this chapter at `www.wrox.com/go/projavaforwebapps` on the Download Code tab. The code for this chapter is divided into the following major examples:

- Hello-World Project
- Hello-User Project
- Customer-Support-v1 Project

## NEW MAVEN DEPENDENCIES FOR THIS CHAPTER

In this chapter, you'll need your first Maven dependency, shown in the following code. You'll use this dependency for every chapter throughout the rest of the book.

```
<dependency>
    <groupId>javax.servlet</groupId>
    <artifactId>javax.servlet-api</artifactId>
    <version>3.1.0</version>
    <scope>provided</scope>
</dependency>
```

In the last chapter, you became familiar with application servers and web containers and learned how to run, deploy to, and debug Apache Tomcat 8.0 from your Java IDE. In this chapter, you begin building web applications by first exploring the world of Servlets. Throughout this chapter and the rest of the book, you'll continually change and improve these applications, deploying them to Tomcat for testing and debugging.

# CREATING A SERVLET CLASS

In the Java Platform, Enterprise Edition, a *Servlet* is what receives and responds to requests from the end user. The Java EE API specification defines a Servlet as follows:

> *A Servlet is a small Java program that runs within a Web server. Servlets receive and respond to requests from Web clients, usually across HTTP, the HyperText Transfer Protocol.*
>
> `http://docs.oracle.com/javaee/7/api/javax/servlet/Servlet.html`

Servlets are the core classes in any web application, the only classes that either perform the work of responding to requests or delegate that work to some other part of the application. Unless some filter prematurely terminates a request (discussed in Chapter 9), every request to your application goes through some Servlet. The web container in which you run your application will have one or more built-in Servlets. These Servlets handle serving JavaServer Pages, displaying directory listings (if you have them enabled) and accessing static resources, such as HTML pages and graphics. You won't need to worry about these Servlets yet (in some cases, ever). In this chapter, you learn how to write and configure the custom Servlets that make up your application.

Every Servlet implements the `javax.servlet.Servlet` interface, but usually not directly. `Servlet` is a simple interface, containing methods for initializing and destroying the Servlet and servicing requests. However, the `service` method will be called for any request of any type, even if it is not an HTTP request (theoretically, assuming your web container supports such a request). As an example, in the future it's possible that new Servlets could be added to Java EE to support File Transfer Protocol (FTP). For that reason, there are various Servlet classes that you can extend instead. As of Java EE 7, the only Servlet protocol currently supported is HTTP.

## What to Extend

In almost all cases, Servlets inherit from `javax.servlet.GenericServlet`. `GenericServlet` is still a protocol-independent Servlet with the lone, abstract `service` method, but it contains several helper methods for logging and getting information about the application and Servlet configuration (more on that later in the section "Configuring a Servlet for Deployment").

For responding to HTTP-specific requests, `javax.servlet.http.HttpServlet` extends `GenericServlet` and implements the service method to accept only HTTP requests. Then, it provides empty implementations for methods corresponding to each HTTP method type, as illustrated in Table 3-1.

**TABLE 3-1:** Empty Implementations for HTTP Method Types

| METHOD | SERVLET METHOD | PURPOSE |
|---|---|---|
| `GET` | `doGet()` | Retrieves the resource at the specified URL |
| `HEAD` | `doHead()` | Identical to GET, except only the headers are returned |
| `POST` | `doPost()` | Typically used for web form submission |
| `PUT` | `doPut()` | Stores the supplied entity at the URL |
| `DELETE` | `doDelete()` | Deletes the resource identified by the URL |
| `OPTIONS` | `doOptions()` | Returns which HTTP methods are allowed |
| `TRACE` | `doTrace()` | Used for diagnostic purposes |

> **NOTE** *Most web programmers are familiar with the* `GET` *and* `POST` *methods and use them the majority of the time. If you are not familiar with the various HTTP methods or would like to learn more, now is the time to click* `http://www.w3.org/Protocols/rfc2616/rfc2616-sec9.html` *to see the RFC-2616 specification section on method definitions* at `http://www.w3.org/Protocols/rfc2616/rfc2616-sec9.html`.

With no exceptions in this book, your Servlets will always extend `HttpServlet`. It provides all the tools you need to selectively accept and respond to different types of HTTP requests, and its methods accept `javax.servlet.http.HttpServletRequest` and `javax.servlet.http.HttpServletResponse` arguments instead of `javax.servlet.ServletRequest` and `javax.servlet.ServletResponse` so that you have easy access to HTTP-specific attributes of the requests your Servlet services. You should begin by creating a new, empty Servlet that extends `HttpServlet`:

```
package com.wrox;

import javax.servlet.http.HttpServlet;

public class HelloServlet extends HttpServlet
{

}
```

> **NOTE** *In order for this code to compile, you need to have the Java EE Servlet API library on your compile classpath. This is where the Maven artifact listed on the first page of this chapter comes into play. In each chapter you will need the listed Maven artifacts in order to compile any examples in that chapter.*

In this form, your Servlet is already prepared to accept any HTTP request and respond to it with a 405 Method Not Allowed error. This is how you control which HTTP methods your Servlet responds to: Any HTTP Servlet methods you do not override will be responded to with an HTTP status 405. A Servlet that does not handle any requests is, of course, not very useful, so override the `doGet` method to add support for the HTTP method `GET`:

```
package com.wrox;

import javax.servlet.ServletException;
import javax.servlet.http.HttpServlet;
import javax.servlet.http.HttpServletRequest;
import javax.servlet.http.HttpServletResponse;
import java.io.IOException;

public class HelloServlet extends HttpServlet
{
    @Override
    protected void doGet(HttpServletRequest request, HttpServletResponse response)
            throws ServletException, IOException
    {
        response.getWriter().println("Hello, World!");
    }
}
```

Now your Servlet is equipped to respond to `GET` requests and return the plain text response "Hello, World!" in the response body. The code in this example is fairly straightforward. Calling `getWriter` on the *`response`* parameter returns a `java.io.PrintWriter`, a common Java class used for writing text to an output stream. Next, the code calls the `println` method on the `PrintWriter` to write the text "Hello, World!" to the output stream. Notice that you don't have to worry about any of the details of the raw HTTP request or response. The web container takes care of interpreting the request and reading the headers and parameters from the socket. After your method returns, it takes care of formatting the response headers and body and writing them back to the socket.

> **NOTE** *Notice that you did not call the* `close` *method on the* `PrintWriter` *that you obtained from the* `response`*. Generally speaking, in Java you only need to close resources that you create. The web container created this resource, so it is responsible for closing it. Even if you had assigned the instance to a local variable and called several methods on it, this would still be the case.*

You obviously could do a lot more in this `doGet` method, such as using request parameters, and you haven't taken a look at the other methods yet. Rest assured, you'll get to both soon.

## Using the Initializer and Destroyer

While you get your first Servlet up and running, you should probably know about the `init` and `destroy` methods. When a web container first starts a Servlet, it calls that Servlet's `init` method. This is sometimes, though not always, when the application is deployed. (You learn how to control this in the next section.) Later when the web container shuts down the Servlet, it calls the Servlet's `destroy` method. These methods are not the same as the Java constructor and finalizer, and they are not called at the same time as the constructor and finalizer. Normally, these methods do nothing, but you can override them to perform some action:

```
@Override
public void init() throws ServletException
{
    System.out.println("Servlet " + this.getServletName() + " has started.");
}

@Override
public void destroy()
{
    System.out.println("Servlet " + this.getServletName() + " has stopped.");
}
```

> **NOTE** *You should know that another* `init` *method accepts a single argument of type* `javax.servlet.ServletConfig`*. This method is specified in the* `Servlet` *interface, but* `GenericServlet` *takes care of implementing this method for you and then calls the no-argument overload of* `init` *overridden in the previous code example. In this way, you do not have to call* `super.init(servletConig)` *from your own* `init` *method implementation.*
>
> *Although you* can *override the original method, you shouldn't do so because if you forgot to call the super method, the Servlet might not initialize correctly. If you need to access the* `ServletConfig`*, it's much easier to just call the* `getServletConfig` *method. You learn more about the* `ServletConfig` *class throughout Parts I and II of this book.*

You can do many things with these two methods. More important, `init` is called after the Servlet is constructed but before it can respond to the first request. Unlike when the constructor is called, when `init` is called all the properties have been set on the Servlet, giving you access to the `ServletConfig` and `javax.servlet.ServletContext` objects. (You learn what to do with these in the "Configuring your Application Using Init Parameters" section.) So, you may use this method to read a properties file or connect to a database using JDBC, for example. The `init` method is called when the Servlet starts. If the Servlet is configured to start automatically when the web application is deployed and started, that is when it is called. Otherwise, it is not called until the first request for that Servlet is received.

Likewise, `destroy` is called immediately after the Servlet can no longer accept any requests. This typically happens either when the web application is stopped or undeployed or when the web container shuts down. Because it is called immediately upon undeployment or shutdown, you do not have to wait for garage collection to trigger the finalizer before cleaning up resources such as temporary files or disconnecting from databases no longer in use. This is particularly important because if your application is undeployed but the server continues running, it may be several minutes or even hours before garbage collection runs. If you clean up your resources in the finalizer instead of the `destroy` method, this could result in your application undeploying partially or failing to undeploy. Thus, you should always use the `destroy` method to clean up resources held by your Servlet between requests.

The previous code example uses the `init` and `destroy` methods to log when the Servlet starts and stops, respectively. When you run your application in the next section, these log messages appear in the output window of your IDE's debugger. Later in this chapter you put these methods to better use.

# CONFIGURING A SERVLET FOR DEPLOYMENT

Now that you have created your Servlet, it's time to put it in action. Although you have a working class that can respond to HTTP `GET` requests with a clever greeting, you have not written instructions for the web container to deploy the Servlet with the application. Chapter 1 introduced you to the deployment descriptor (`web.xml`) and the structure of a web application, and in Chapter 2 you learned how to deploy and debug an application using your IDE. In this section, you create the `web.xml` file in your `WEB-INF` directory and configure your Servlet for deployment. You then deploy the application using your IDE and see that greeting in your browser. Finally, you put some breakpoints in your code and examine when certain methods are called.

## Adding the Servlet to the Descriptor

As you've learned, the deployment descriptor instructs the web container how the application should be deployed. Specifically, it defines all the listeners, Servlets, and filters that should deploy with the application and the settings the application should use to do this. First, take a look at a (mostly) empty `web.xml` file:

```
<?xml version="1.0" encoding="UTF-8"?>
<web-app xmlns="http://xmlns.jcp.org/xml/ns/javaee"
         xmlns:xsi="http://www.w3.org/2001/XMLSchema-instance"
         xsi:schemaLocation="http://xmlns.jcp.org/xml/ns/javaee
                             http://xmlns.jcp.org/xml/ns/javaee/web-app_3_1.xsd"
         version="3.1">

    <display-name>Hello World Application</display-name>

</web-app>
```

> **WARNING** *If you have worked with deployment descriptors in previous Java EE versions, this might look slightly unfamiliar to you. This is because the XML schema URIs for* `web.xml` *and other configuration files have changed since Java EE 6. You must use the new URIs for your application to be Java EE 7 compliant.*

In the previous example, the code in bold indicates to the application server what the name of the application is. On the Tomcat manager screen that lists all the installed applications, the name between the <display-name> tags appears beside your application. The version attribute in the opening <web-app> tag indicates which Servlet API version the application is written for — in this case, version 3.1.

Now you need to tell the web container to create an instance of the Servlet you wrote earlier, so you must add a Servlet tag to the descriptor file between the beginning and ending <web-app> tags:

```
<servlet>
    <servlet-name>helloServlet</servlet-name>
    <servlet-class>com.wrox.HelloServlet</servlet-class>
</servlet>
```

Earlier in the chapter, you learned about the Servlet init method and when it would normally be called. In this example, the init method is called when the first request arrives for the Servlet after the web application starts. Normally, this is sufficient for most uses. However, if the init method does many things, Servlet startup might become a time-intensive process, and this could make the first request to that Servlet take several seconds or even several minutes! Obviously, this is not desirable. A simple tweak to the servlet configuration can make the servlet start up immediately when the web application starts:

```
<servlet>
    <servlet-name>helloServlet</servlet-name>
    <servlet-class>com.wrox.HelloServlet</servlet-class>
    <load-on-startup>1</load-on-startup>
</servlet>
```

The emboldened code instructs the web container to start the Servlet as soon as the web application starts. If multiple Servlet configurations contain this tag, they start up in the order of the values within the tags, with the previously used value "1" coming first and higher numbers later. If two or more Servlets have the same value in the <load-on-startup> tag, those conflicting Servlets start in the order they appear in the descriptor file, still after other Servlets with lower numbers and before other Servlets with higher numbers.

## Mapping the Servlet to a URL

You have instructed the application server to start the Servlet but have not yet told it what URL requests the Servlet should respond to. This is a simple matter:

```
<servlet-mapping>
    <servlet-name>helloServlet</servlet-name>
    <url-pattern>/greeting</url-pattern>
</servlet-mapping>
```

With this configuration, all requests to the application-relative URL /greeting are handled by the helloServlet. (Notice that the <servlet-name> tags within the <servlet> and <servlet-mapping> tags match each other. This is how the web container associates the two.) If the application is deployed at http://www.example.net, the Servlet responds to requests directed to the URL http://www.example.net/greeting. Of course, you are not limited to this one mapping. You could map several URLs to the same Servlet:

```
<servlet-mapping>
    <servlet-name>helloServlet</servlet-name>
    <url-pattern>/greeting</url-pattern>
    <url-pattern>/salutation</url-pattern>
    <url-pattern>/wazzup</url-pattern>
</servlet-mapping>
```

In this case, all three URLs act as aliases for the same logical endpoint: the `helloServlet`. Why, you might ask, do you need to give a Servlet instance a name and then map a request to the name of that instance? Why can't you just map the URL directly to the Servlet class? Well, what if you have two different store Servlets in an online shopping application, for example? Those stores might have identical logic but connect to different databases. This can be achieved simply:

```
<servlet>
    <servlet-name>oddsStore</servlet-name>
    <servlet-class>com.wrox.StoreServlet</servlet-class>
</servlet>
<servlet>
    <servlet-name>endsStore</servlet-name>
    <servlet-class>com.wrox.StoreServlet</servlet-class>
</servlet>

<servlet-mapping>
    <servlet-name>oddsStore</servlet-name>
    <url-pattern>/odds</url-pattern>
</servlet-mapping>
<servlet-mapping>
    <servlet-name>endsStore</servlet-name>
    <url-pattern>/ends</url-pattern>
</servlet-mapping>
```

Now you have two instances of the same Servlet class, but they have different names and are mapped to different URLs. Two examples ago, you had three URLs all pointing to the *same Servlet instance*. However, in this example you have *two different Servlet instances*. You might wonder how the two different instances know which stores they are. A quick call to `this.getServletName()` from anywhere in the servlet code returns either "oddsStore" or "endsStore" depending on which instance it is. Recall that you used this method earlier when you were logging calls to the initializer and the destroyer.

Rewinding a bit, you now have the simple, completed `web.xml` descriptor file:

```
<?xml version="1.0" encoding="UTF-8"?>
<web-app xmlns="http://xmlns.jcp.org/xml/ns/javaee"
         xmlns:xsi="http://www.w3.org/2001/XMLSchema-instance"
         xsi:schemaLocation="http://xmlns.jcp.org/xml/ns/javaee
                             http://xmlns.jcp.org/xml/ns/javaee/web-app_3_1.xsd"
         version="3.1">

    <display-name>Hello World Application</display-name>

    <servlet>
        <servlet-name>helloServlet</servlet-name>
        <servlet-class>com.wrox.HelloServlet</servlet-class>
    </servlet>
```

```
    <servlet-mapping>
        <servlet-name>helloServlet</servlet-name>
        <url-pattern>/greeting</url-pattern>
    </servlet-mapping>

</web-app>
```

## Running and Debugging Your Servlet

After it's saved, compile your application and check to make sure you have an IDE run configuration set up to run your project in your local Tomcat 8.0 instance. (If you don't remember how to do this, refer back to Chapter 2). The application should deploy to `/hello-world`. You can also just download the Hello-World IDE project from the `wrox.com` code download site — it is already configured to deploy properly. When this is done, follow these steps:

1. Click the debug icon in your IDE to start the web container in debug mode. Your IDE deploys your application to the web container after it starts.
2. Open your favorite web browser and navigate to `http://localhost:8080/hello-world/greeting`. You should now see the screen in Figure 3-1.

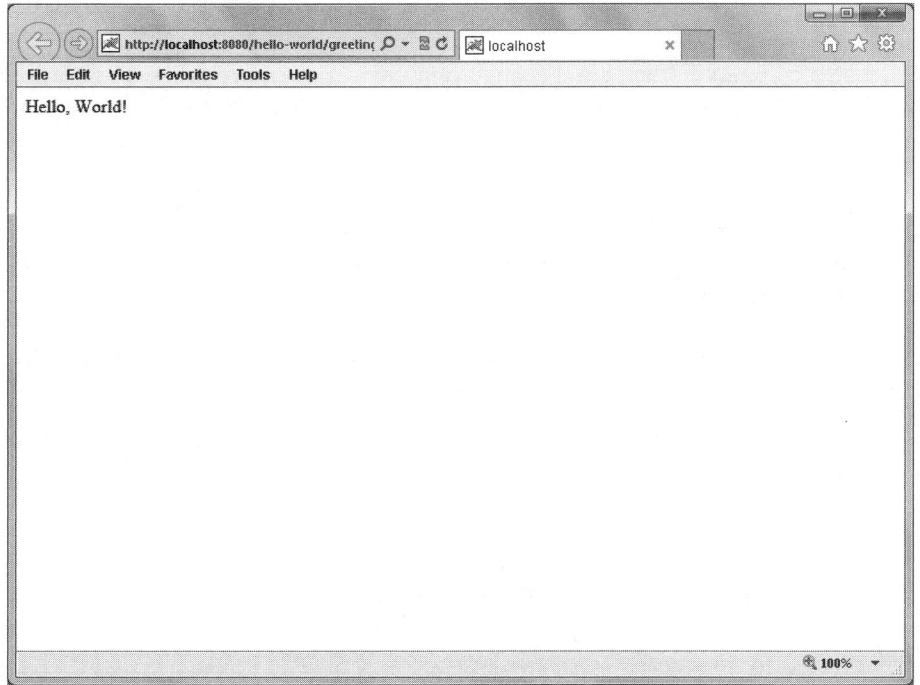


FIGURE 3-1

3. A good way to understand what happened is to place some breakpoints in the `HelloServlet` and run this experiment again. You should stop your debugger (which shuts down Tomcat) so that you can hit a breakpoint in the initializer as well. Place breakpoints

in the single lines of code in the `doGet`, `init`, and `destroy` methods of your Servlet; then restart your debugger. After Tomcat starts and your application deploys, you will notice that you did not hit any breakpoints yet (because `<load-on-startup>` is not present in the deployment descriptor).

4. Refresh the greeting page in your browser and you should hit the breakpoint in the `init` method of your IDE. This means that Tomcat has activated the just-in-time initialization of your Servlet: It was not initialized until the first request came in.
5. Just like it would if the `init` method were taking a long time to complete, the request from your browser remains on hold until you continue your debugger, so do that now. You should immediately hit the breakpoint in the `doGet` method. Now the Servlet services the request, but your browser still waits on a response.
6. Continue your debugger a second time, and now the response is sent to your browser.

At this point, you can press the Refresh button on your browser as many times as you like, and you will hit the breakpoint only in the `doGet` method. The `init` method is not called again until some action destroys the Servlet (for example, Tomcat shutting down) and then it starts again. Up until this point, you have not yet hit the breakpoint in the `destroy` method. You want to do that now, but unfortunately, if you stop Tomcat from your IDE, it detaches the debugger before the breakpoint is hit, so you need to stop Tomcat from the command line. To do this, follow these steps:

1. Open up a command prompt and change your current directory to the Tomcat home directory (`C:\Program Files\Apache Software Foundation\Tomcat 8.0` on a Windows machine, remember).
2. Type the command **bin\shutdown.bat** (or **bin/shutdown.sh** if you are not running Windows) and press Enter.
3. In your IDE window, you should immediately hit the breakpoint in the `destroy` method. Tomcat does not completely shut down until you continue your debugger.

As mentioned earlier, you can change the configuration of your Servlet so that it is initialized when the application starts. Try that now.

1. Update your Servlet declaration in the deployment descriptor to add the code in bold in the following example:

```
<servlet>
    <servlet-name>helloServlet</servlet-name>
    <servlet-class>com.wrox.HelloServlet</servlet-class>
    <load-on-startup>1</load-on-startup>
</servlet>
```

2. With the breakpoints still in place in your Servlet, start your debugger again. You should immediately hit the breakpoint in the `init` method before you make the first request to the Servlet.
3. Continue the debugger and then refresh your browser. Now you should hit the breakpoint only in the `doGet` method; the Servlet was initialized on application startup and does not need to be initialized again.

Now that you have created your first Servlet and are familiar with the life cycle of a Servlet, you are encouraged to experiment with different method calls on the Servlet and on the *`request`* and *`response`* parameters in the `doGet` method. In the next section, you explore `doGet`, `doPost`, and other methods further to better understand `HttpServletRequest` and `HttpServletResponse`.

> **NOTE** *You should consult (and bookmark) the API documentation for Java EE 7 located at* `http://docs.oracle.com/javaee/7/api/` *for information on the available methods and their purposes.*

# UNDERSTANDING DOGET(), DOPOST(), AND OTHER METHODS

In the previous section you learned about the `doGet` method and other methods that map to the various HTTP request methods. But what exactly can you do in these methods? More important, what *should* you do in these methods? The short answers to these questions are "just about anything" and "not very much," respectively. This section explores some of the things you can do and how to do them.

## What Should Happen during the service Method Execution?

The `Servlet` class's `service` method, as you learned earlier, services all incoming requests. Ultimately, it must parse and handle the data on the incoming request based on the protocol in use and then return a protocol-acceptable response to the client. If the `service` method returns without sending response data back to the socket, the client will likely observe a network error, such as "connection reset." In the HTTP protocol specifically, the `service` method should understand the headers and parameters that the client sends and then return a proper HTTP response that at least includes the minimum HTTP headers (even if the response body itself is empty). In reality, the implementation of this is complex (and involves many steps) and may differ from web container to web container.

The beauty of extending `HttpServlet` is that you don't have to worry about any of these details. Although the reality is that the `service` method must do many things before responding to the user, the developer using `HttpServlet` must do little. Actually, in the Hello-World project you used in the last two sections, if you remove the single line of code from the `doGet` method and run the application, everything still works fine! A properly structured HTTP response with zero-length content returns to the client. The only requirement is that you override the `doGet` method (or `doPost` or `doPut` or whatever you want to support); you don't need to put anything in it. But how useful is this, really?

The answer to that is "not at all." Just because you *can* return an empty response doesn't mean you *should*. This is where `HttpServletRequest` and `HttpServletResponse` come in. These parameters in the various methods defined by `HttpServlet` enable you to read parameters passed from the client, accept files uploaded from a posted form, read the raw data contained in the request body (for doing things such as handling PUT requests or accepting JSON request bodies), read request headers and manipulate response headers, and write response content back to the client. These are some of the many things that you *can* do when servicing a request, and in reality you usually *should* do one or more of these things.

# Using HttpServletRequest

The `HttpServletRequest` interface is an extension of `ServletRequest` that provides additional HTTP protocol-specific information about a received request. It specifies dozens of methods that you can use to obtain details about an HTTP request. It also permits you to set request attributes (different from request parameters).

> **NOTE** *You'll learn about request attributes and the inspection of authentication details in the next chapter. This book does not cover the details of every method (for that, you can consult the API documentation) but covers the most important features.*

## Getting Request Parameters

Perhaps the most important capability of `HttpServletRequest`, and one you explore through examples in the next section, is to retrieve request parameters passed by the client. Request parameters come in two different forms: via *query parameters* (also called *URI parameters*), or in an `application/x-www-form-urlencoded` or `multipart/form-data` encoded request body (typically called *post variables* or *form variables*). Query parameters are supported with all request methods and are contained in the first line of data in an HTTP request, as in the following example:

```
GET /index.jsp?productId=9781118656464&category=Books HTTP/1.1
```

> **NOTE** *Technically speaking, the RFC specification for the HTTP protocol does not disallow query parameters in any of the HTTP methods. However, many web servers ignore query parameters passed to* `DELETE`, `TRACE`, *and* `OPTIONS`, *and the usefulness of query parameters in such requests is questionable. So, it is best to not rely on query parameters for these types of requests. This book does not cover all the rules and intricacies of the HTTP protocol. That exercise is left up to you.*

In this example, there are two query parameters contained in the request: *`productId`*, which has this book's ISBN as its value, and *`category`*, which has the value Books. These same parameters could also be passed in the request body as post variables. Post variables can, as the name implies, be included only in `POST` requests. Consider the following example:

```
POST /index.jsp?returnTo=productPage HTTP/1.1
Host: www.example.com
Content-Length: 48
Content-Type: application/x-www-form-urlencoded

addToCart&productId=9781118656464&category=Books
```

This POST request has post variables (instructing the website to add this book to the cart) *and* query parameters (instructing the website to return to the product page when the task is complete). Although there is a difference in the delivery of these two types of parameters, they are essentially the same, and they convey essentially the same information. The Servlet API does not differentiate between the two types of parameters. A call to any of the parameter-related methods on a request object returns parameters whether they were delivered as query parameters or post variables.

The getParameter method returns a single value for a parameter. If the parameter has multiple values, getParameter returns the first value, whereas getParameterValues returns an array of values for a parameter. If the parameter has only one value, this method returns an array with one element in it. The getParameterMap method returns a java.util.Map<String, String[]> containing all the parameter names mapped to their values, whereas the getParameterNames method returns an enumeration of the names of all the available parameters; both are useful for iterating over all the request parameters.

> **WARNING** *The first time you call* getParameter, getParameterMap, getParameterNames, *or* getParameterValues *on a request object, the web container determines whether the request contains post variables, and if it does it reads and parses those post variables by obtaining the request's* InputStream. *The* InputStream *of a request can be read only once. If you call* getInputStream *or* getReader *on a request containing post variables and then later attempt to retrieve parameters in that request, the attempt to retrieve the parameters results in an* IllegalStateException. *Likewise, if you retrieve parameters on a request containing post variables and then later call* getInputStream *or* getReader, *the call to* getInputStream *or* getReader *fails with an* IllegalStateException.
>
> Simply *put, any time you anticipate that a request may contain post variables, it's best to use only the parameter methods and leave* getInputStream *and* getReader *alone.*

## Determining Information about the Request Content

Several methods are available to help determine the type, length, and encoding of the content of the HTTP request. The getContentType method returns the *MIME content type* of the request, such as application/x-www-form-urlencoded, application/json, text/plain, or application/zip, to name a few. A MIME content type describes that the data it marks contains some type. For example, ZIP archives files have a MIME content type of application/zip to indicate that they contain ZIP archive data.

The getContentLength and getContentLengthLong methods both return the number of bytes in the request body (the *content length*), with the latter method being useful for requests whose content might exceed 2 gigabytes (unusual, but not impossible). The getCharacterEncoding method returns the *character encoding* (such as UTF-8 or ISO-8859-1) of the request contents whenever the request contains character-type content. (text/plain, application/json, and application/x-www-form-urlencoded are some examples of character-type MIME content types.) Although these methods can come in handy in many situations, none of them are necessary if you get post variables from the request body using the parameter methods.

> **NOTE** *The Servlet 3.1 specification in Java EE 7 is the first version that supports the* `getContentLengthLong` *method. Before this version, you had to call* `getHeader("Content-Length")` *and convert the returned* `String` *to a* `long` *for requests that could be larger than 2,147,483,647 bytes.*

## Reading the Contents of a Request

The methods `getInputStream`, which returns a `javax.servlet.ServletInputStream`, and `getReader`, which returns a `java.io.BufferedReader`, can both be used to read the contents of the request. Which one is best completely depends on the context in which the request contents are being read. If the contents are expected to be character-encoded data, such as UTF-8 or ISO-8859-1 text, using the `BufferedReader` is typically the easiest route to take because it lets you easily read `char` data. If, however, the request data is binary in nature, you must use the `ServletInputStream` so that you can access the request content in `byte` format. You should never use them both on the same request. After a call to either method, a call to the other will fail with an `IllegalStateException`. Remember the preceding warning, and do not use these methods on a request with post variables.

## Getting Request Characteristics Such as URL, URI, and Headers

There are many request characteristics that you may need to know about, such as the URL or URI the request was made with. These are easy to obtain from the request object:

- `getRequestURL`: Returns the entire URL that the client used to make the request, including protocol (`http` or `https`), server name, port number, and server path but not including the query string. So, in a request to `http://www.example.org/application/index.jsp?category=Books`, `getRequestURL` returns `http://www.example.org/application/index.jsp`.
- `getRequestURI`: This is slightly different from `getRequestURL` in that it returns only the server path part of the URL; using the previous example, that would be `/application/index.jsp`.
- `getServletPath`: Similar to `getRequestURI`, this returns even less of the URL. If the request is `/hello-world/greeting?foo=world`, the application is deployed as `/hello-world` on Tomcat, and the servlet-mappings are `/greeting`, `/salutation`, and `/wazzup`, `getServletPath` returns only the part of the URL used to match the servlet mapping: `/greeting`.
- `getHeader`: Returns the value of a header with the given name. The case of the header does not have to match the case of the string passed into the method, so `getHeader("content-type")` can match the `Content-Type` header. If there are multiple headers with the same name, this returns only the first value. In such cases, you would want to use the `getHeaders` method to return an enumeration of all the values.
- `getHeaderNames`: Returns an enumeration of the names of all the headers in the request — a great way to iterate over the available headers.

- `getIntHeader`: If you have a particular header that you know is always a number, you can call this to return the value already converted to a number. It throws a `NumberFormatException` if the header cannot be converted to an integer.
- `getDateHeader`: You can call this to return the (millisecond) Unix timestamp-equivalent of a header value that represents a valid timestamp. It throws an `IllegalArgumentException` if the header value is not recognized as a date.

### Sessions and Cookies

The `getSession` and `getCookies` methods are mentioned only long enough to tell you that this chapter doesn't cover them, but they are both important citizens in the `HttpServletRequest` realm. You can learn more about these is Chapter 5.

## Using HttpServletResponse

As the `HttpServletRequest` interface extends `ServletRequest` and provides access to the HTTP protocol-specific properties of a request, the `HttpServletResponse` interface extends `ServletResponse` and provides access to the HTTP protocol-specific properties of a response. You use the response object to do things such as set response headers, write to the response body, redirect the request, set the HTTP status code, and send cookies back to the client. Again, the most common features of this object are covered here.

### Writing to the Response Body

The most common thing you'll do with a response object, and something you have already done with a response object, is write content to the response body. This might be HTML to display in a browser, an image that the browser is retrieving, or the contents of a file that the client is downloading. It could be plain text or binary data. It might be just a few bytes long or it could be gigabytes long.

The `getOutputStream` method, which returns a `javax.servlet.ServletOutputStream`, and the `getWriter` method, which returns a `java.io.PrintWriter`, both enable you to write data to the response. Like their counterparts in `HttpServletRequest`, you would probably want to use the `PrintWriter` for returning HTML or some other character-encoded text to the client because this makes it easy to write encoded `Strings` and `chars` to the response. However, for sending binary data back, you must use the `ServletOutputStream` to send the response `bytes`. Also, you should never use both `getOutputStream` and `getWriter` in the same response. After a call to one, a call to the other will fail with an `IllegalStateException`.

While you're writing to the response body, it might be necessary to set the content type or encoding. You can do this with `setContentType` and `setCharacterEncoding`. You may call these methods as many times as you like; the last call to the method is the one that matters. However, if you plan to call `setContentType` and `setCharacterEncoding` along with `getWriter`, you must call `setContentType` and `setCharacterEncoding` *before* `getWriter` so that the returned writer is configured for the correct character encoding. Calls made after `getWriter` are ignored. If you do not call `setContentType` and `setCharacterEncoding` before calling `getWriter`, the returned writer uses the container's default encoding.

At your disposal, you also have the `setContentLength` and `setContentLengthLong` methods. In almost all cases, these do not need to be called. The web container sets the `Content-Length` header as it finalizes your response, and it is safest to let it do so.

> **NOTE** *The Servlet 3.1 specification in Java EE 7 is the first version that supports the* `setContentLengthLong` *method. Before this version, you had to call* `setHeader("Content-Length", Long.toString(length))` *for responses that could be larger than 2,147,483,647 bytes.*

### Setting Headers and Other Response Properties

Serving as counterparts to methods in `HttpServletRequest`, you can call `setHeader`, `setIntHeader`, and `setDateHeader` to set nearly any header value you desire. If the existing response headers already include a header with the name you are setting, the value of that header will be overridden. To avoid this, you can instead use `addHeader`, `addIntHeader`, or `addDateHeader`. These versions do not override existing header values, but instead add additional values for the given headers. You can also call `getHeader`, `getHeaders` `getHeaderNames`, and `containsHeader` to investigate which headers have already been set on the response.

In addition, you can use:

- `setStatus`: To set the HTTP response status code
- `getStatus`: To determine what the current status of the response is
- `sendError`: To set the status code, indicate an optional error message to write to the response data, direct the web container to provide an error page to the client, and clear the buffer
- `sendRedirect`: To redirect the client to a different URL

This section covered most of the things you can do while servicing an HTTP request in your Servlet and noted important details and cautions where necessary. In the past several sections you have used the Hello-World project to demonstrate working with Servlets. In the next section, you move on to a slightly more complex example.

## USING PARAMETERS AND ACCEPTING FORM SUBMISSIONS

In this section, you make your Hello-World project a little more dynamic by accepting parameters and form submissions. You also explore annotation configuration and temporarily forego the deployment descriptor. For the examples in this section, you can follow along in the completed Hello-User project, or you can simply incorporate the changes into your existing project as they are covered.

Several changes have been made to the project. The first thing you should notice is that the `doGet` method is much more complex now:

```
private static final String DEFAULT_USER = "Guest";

@Override
protected void doGet(HttpServletRequest request, HttpServletResponse response)
        throws ServletException, IOException
{
    String user = request.getParameter("user");
    if(user == null)
        user = HelloServlet.DEFAULT_USER;

    response.setContentType("text/html");
    response.setCharacterEncoding("UTF-8");

    PrintWriter writer = response.getWriter();
    writer.append("<!DOCTYPE html>\r\n")
            .append("<html>\r\n")
            .append("    <head>\r\n")
            .append("        <title>Hello User Application</title>\r\n")
            .append("    </head>\r\n")
            .append("    <body>\r\n")
            .append("        Hello, ").append(user).append("!<br/><br/>\r\n")
            .append("        <form action=\"greeting\" method=\"POST\">\r\n")
            .append("            Enter your name:<br/>\r\n")
            .append("            <input type=\"text\" name=\"user\"/><br/>\r\n")
            .append("            <input type=\"submit\" value=\"Submit\"/>\r\n")
            .append("        </form>\r\n")
            .append("    </body>\r\n")
            .append("</html>\r\n");
}
```

The code in bold is new. It is doing a little logic now:

- It tests if the `user` parameter is included in the request and, if it is not, it uses the *`DEFAULT_USER`* constant instead.
- It sets the content type of the response to `text/html` and the character encoding to UTF-8.
- It gets a `PrintWriter` from the response and writes out a compliant HTML5 document (note the HTML5 DOCTYPE), including the greeting (now directed at a particular user) and a form for supplying your username.

You might wonder how the `doGet` method can receive the form submission when the method type for the form is set to `POST`. This is handled with the simple `doPost` implementation, which is also new:

```
@Override
protected void doPost(HttpServletRequest request, HttpServletResponse response)
```

```
            throws ServletException, IOException
    {
        this.doGet(request, response);
    }
```

This implementation simply delegates to the doGet method. Either a query parameter or a post variable named *user* can trigger the greeting to change.

The last thing you should notice is the annotation just above the Servlet declaration:

```
@WebServlet(
        name = "helloServlet",
        urlPatterns = {"/greeting", "/salutation", "/wazzup"},
        loadOnStartup = 1
)
public class HelloServlet extends HttpServlet
{
...
}
```

> **NOTE** *You'll notice that the class imports have been left off of the newest* HelloServlet *code example. As your code gets more complex, the imports can begin to take up many dozens of lines of code. This is too much to print in this book efficiently. A good IDE, like the one you use for this book, can recognize the class names and suggest the imports for you, taking the hard work out of your hands. With few exceptions,* import *and* package *statements are omitted from the rest of the examples in this book. New classes will be in the* com.wrox *package unless otherwise stated.*

If you also take a look at the deployment descriptor, you'll notice that the Servlet declaration and mapping were removed from the web.xml file. (Or if you made these changes to the existing project, you should remove everything in the deployment descriptor except for the <display-name> tag.) The annotation in the previous example replaces the XML that you wrote in your previous project and adds a little bit more.

You still get an instance of HelloServlet named *helloServlet*; it still starts when the application starts; and it is still mapped to the /greeting URL. It is also now mapped to the /salutation and /wazzup URLs. As you can tell, this is a much more direct and concise approach to instantiating and mapping servlets. However, it has some drawbacks, which are pointed out throughout the rest of the chapter. For now, compile your project and start Tomcat in your debugger; then go to http://localhost:8080/hello-world/greeting in your browser. You should see a screen as shown in Figure 3-2.

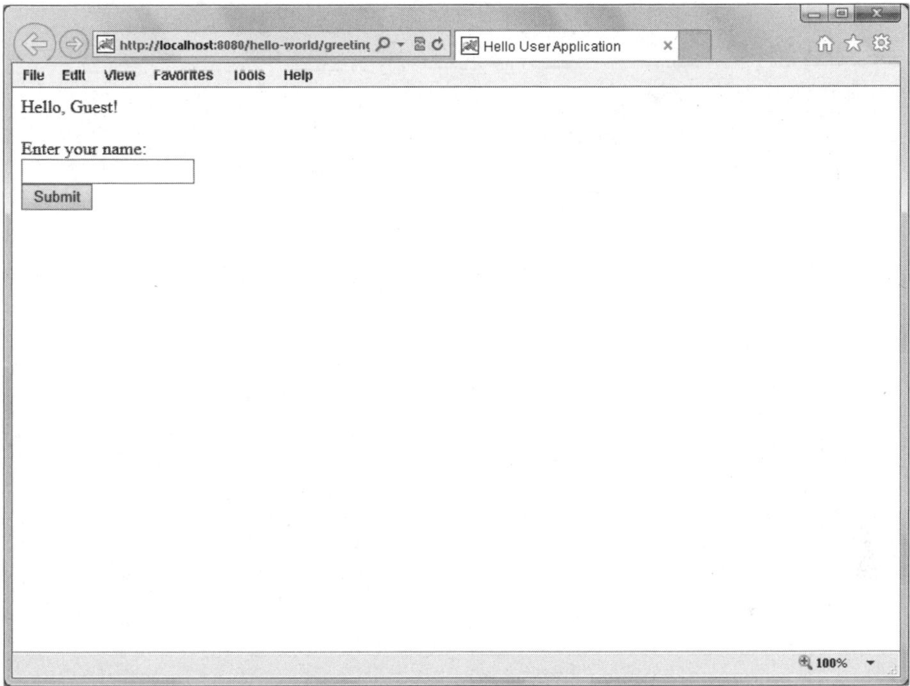


FIGURE 3-2

To understand what this Servlet can do, first add the query string `user=Allison` to the URL so that it is `http://localhost:8080/hello-world/greeting?user=Allison`. The screen should now change and, instead of saying "Hello, Guest!" it should say "Hello, Allison!" In this case the request was serviced by the `doGet` method, which found the *`user`* query parameter and output it to the screen.

You can confirm this by placing breakpoints in `doGet` and `doPost` and refreshing the page. Now, type your name in the form field on the screen and click the Submit button. If you examine the URL in the address bar, it does not have any query parameters. Instead, your name was included in the request as a post variable, and when the `doPost` method serviced the request and delegated to the `doGet` method, the call to `getParameter` retrieved the post variable, resulting in your name displaying on the screen. Hitting the breakpoints will confirm that this has happened.

Remember from the previous section that single parameter values are not the only thing your Servlets can accept. You can also accept multiple parameter values. The most common example of this is a set of related check boxes, where the user is permitted to check one or more values. Refer to the code Listing 3-1, the `MultiValueParameterServlet`, mapped to `/checkboxes`. Compile and run this code in Tomcat using your debugger and navigate your browser to `http://localhost:8080/hello-world/checkboxes`. The `doGet` method in this Servlet prints out a simple form with five check boxes. The user can select any number of these check boxes and click Submit, which is serviced by the `doPost` method. This method retrieves all the fruit values and lists them on the screen using an unordered list. Try this out by selecting various combinations of check boxes and clicking Submit.

**LISTING 3-1: MultiValueParameterServlet.java**

```
@WebServlet(
        name = "multiValueParameterServlet",
        urlPatterns = {"/checkboxes"}
)
public class MultiValueParameterServlet extends HttpServlet
{
    @Override
    protected void doGet(HttpServletRequest request, HttpServletResponse response)
            throws ServletException, IOException
    {
        response.setContentType("text/html");
        response.setCharacterEncoding("UTF-8");

        PrintWriter writer = response.getWriter();
        writer.append("<!DOCTYPE html>\r\n")
              .append("<html>\r\n")
              .append("    <head>\r\n")
              .append("        <title>Hello User Application</title>\r\n")
              .append("    </head>\r\n")
              .append("    <body>\r\n")
              .append("        <form action=\"checkboxes\" method=\"POST\">\r\n")
              .append("Select the fruits you like to eat:<br/>\r\n")
              .append("<input type=\"checkbox\" name=\"fruit\" value=\"Banana\"/>")
              .append(" Banana<br/>\r\n")
              .append("<input type=\"checkbox\" name=\"fruit\" value=\"Apple\"/>")
              .append(" Apple<br/>\r\n")
              .append("<input type=\"checkbox\" name=\"fruit\" value=\"Orange\"/>")
              .append(" Orange<br/>\r\n")
              .append("<input type=\"checkbox\" name=\"fruit\" value=\"Guava\"/>")
              .append(" Guava<br/>\r\n")
              .append("<input type=\"checkbox\" name=\"fruit\" value=\"Kiwi\"/>")
              .append(" Kiwi<br/>\r\n")
              .append("<input type=\"submit\" value=\"Submit\"/>\r\n")
              .append("        </form>")
              .append("    </body>\r\n")
              .append("</html>\r\n");
    }

    @Override
    protected void doPost(HttpServletRequest request, HttpServletResponse response)
            throws ServletException, IOException
    {
        String[] fruits = request.getParameterValues("fruit");

        response.setContentType("text/html");
        response.setCharacterEncoding("UTF-8");

        PrintWriter writer = response.getWriter();
        writer.append("<!DOCTYPE html>\r\n")
              .append("<html>\r\n")
              .append("    <head>\r\n")
              .append("        <title>Hello User Application</title>\r\n")
```

```
                .append("    </head>\r\n")
                .append("    <body>\r\n")
                .append("        <h2>Your Selections</h2>\r\n");

        if(fruits == null)
            writer.append("        You did not select any fruits.\r\n");
        else
        {
            writer.append("        <ul>\r\n");
            for(String fruit : fruits)
            {
                writer.append("        <li>").append(fruit).append("</li>\r\n");
            }
            writer.append("        </ul>\r\n");
        }

        writer.append("    </body>\r\n")
                .append("</html>\r\n");
    }
}
```

This section has shown you the various ways that you can use request parameters within your Servlet methods. You have explored query parameters and post variables, along with single-value and multivalve parameters. In the next section you learn about various ways to configure your application using init parameters.

## CONFIGURING YOUR APPLICATION USING INIT PARAMETERS

When writing a Java web application, the need will inevitably arise to provide ways of configuring your application and the Servlets within it. There are many ways to do that using numerous technologies, and you explore a few of those in this book. The simplest means of configuring your application, through context *initialization parameters* (usually shortened to *init parameters*) and Servlet init parameters, is covered in this section. These parameters can be put to any number of uses, from defining connection information for communicating with a relational database, to providing an e-mail address to send store order alerts to. They are defined at application startup and cannot change without restarting the application.

### Using Context Init Parameters

Earlier you emptied the deployment descriptor file and replaced your Servlet declaration and mappings with annotations on the actual classes. Although this is one thing (added in the Servlet 3.0 specification in Java EE 6) that you can do without the deployment descriptor, several things still require the deployment descriptor. Context init parameters are one such feature. You declare context init parameters using the `<context-param>` tag within the `web.xml` file. The following code example shows two context init parameters added to the deployment descriptor:

```
<context-param>
    <param-name>settingOne</param-name>
    <param-value>foo</param-value>
```

```
    </context-param>
    <context-param>
        <param-name>settingTwo</param-name>
        <param-value>bar</param-value>
    </context-param>
```

This creates two context init parameters: *`settingOne`* having a value of `foo` and *`settingTwo`* having a value of `bar`. You can easily obtain and use these parameter values from anywhere in your Servlet code. The `ContextParameterServlet` demonstrates this ability:

```
@WebServlet(
        name = "contextParameterServlet",
        urlPatterns = {"/contextParameters"}
)
public class ContextParameterServlet extends HttpServlet
{
    @Override
    protected void doGet(HttpServletRequest request, HttpServletResponse response)
            throws ServletException, IOException
    {
        ServletContext c = this.getServletContext();
        PrintWriter writer = response.getWriter();

        writer.append("settingOne: ").append(c.getInitParameter("settingOne"))
              .append(", settingTwo: ").append(c.getInitParameter("settingTwo"));
    }
}
```

If you compile, debug, and navigate to `http://localhost:8080/hello-world/contextParameters`, you can see these parameters listed on the screen. Every Servlet in your application shares these init parameters, and their values are the same across all servlets. There may be cases, however, in which you need a setting that applies to only a single Servlet. For this purpose you would use Servlet init parameters.

> **NOTE** *It should be noted that as of Servlet 3.0 you can call the* `setInitParameter` *method on the* `ServletContext` *as an alternative to defining context init parameters using* `<context-param>`. *However, this method can only be called within the* `contextInitialized` *method of a* `javax.servlet.ServletContextListener` *(which you learn about in Chapter 9) or the* `onStartup` *method of a* `javax.servlet.ServletContainerInitializer` *(which you learn about in Chapter 12). Even so, changing the values would require recompiling your application, so XML is usually the best option for context init parameters.*

## Using Servlet Init Parameters

Consider the code for the `ServletParameterServlet` class. You may immediately notice that it is not annotated with `@WebServlet`. Don't worry; you learn why in a minute. The code is otherwise nearly identical to the `ContextParameterServlet`. Instead of getting your init parameters from the `ServletContext` object, you obtain them from the `ServletConfig` object:

```
public class ServletParameterServlet extends HttpServlet
{
    @Override
    protected void doGet(HttpServletRequest request, HttpServletResponse response)
            throws ServletException, IOException
    {
        ServletConfig c = this.getServletConfig();
        PrintWriter writer = response.getWriter();

        writer.append("database: ").append(c.getInitParameter("database"))
              .append(", server: ").append(c.getInitParameter("server"));
    }
}
```

Of course, just having the Servlet code isn't enough. The following XML added to the deployment descriptor declares and maps the servlet and also does a little bit more:

```
<servlet>
    <servlet-name>servletParameterServlet</servlet-name>
    <servlet-class>com.wrox.ServletParameterServlet</servlet-class>
    <init-param>
        <param-name>database</param-name>
        <param-value>CustomerSupport</param-value>
    </init-param>
    <init-param>
        <param-name>server</param-name>
        <param-value>10.0.12.5</param-value>
    </init-param>
</servlet>
<servlet-mapping>
    <servlet-name>servletParameterServlet</servlet-name>
    <url-pattern>/servletParameters</url-pattern>
</servlet-mapping>
```

The `<init-param>` tag, like the `<context-param>` tag for the Servlet context, creates an init parameter specific to this Servlet. If you compile, debug, and navigate to `http://localhost:8080/hello-world/servletParameters`, you can see the *`database`* and *`server`* parameters specified in the deployment descriptor. So why, you might ask, can't you use annotations for this like you can for the rest of the Servlet mapping? Well, technically you can. You can achieve the same result as in the previous code by removing the initialization and mapping from the deployment descriptor and adding this annotation to the Servlet declaration:

```
@WebServlet(
        name = "servletParameterServlet",
        urlPatterns = {"/servletParameters"},
        initParams = {
                @WebInitParam(name = "database", value = "CustomerSupport"),
                @WebInitParam(name = "server", value = "10.0.12.5")
        }
)
public class ServletParameterServlet extends HttpServlet
{
...
}
```

The drawback to doing this, however, is that the values of the Servlet init parameters can no longer be changed without recompiling the application. Sure, there may be settings that you wouldn't want to change without recompiling the application, but at that point why not just make them class constants? The advantage of putting Servlet init parameters in the deployment descriptor is that a server administrator needs to change only a few lines of XML and restart the deployed application to effect the change. If such settings contain connection information for a relational database, the last thing you want to do is to recompile the application to change the IP address of the database server!

The next section introduces a new feature of `HttpServletRequests` added in the Servlet 3.0 specification and a new example application that you improve upon throughout the rest of the book.

### THE DRAWBACKS OF @CONFIG

As mentioned earlier there are advantages and disadvantages to using annotation-based configuration (often simply called @Config) in your web application. The primary advantage is the lack of XML and the direct, concise annotation language used to configure your application. However, there are numerous drawbacks to this approach as well.

One example of this is the inability to create multiple instances of a single Servlet class. You saw earlier in the chapter how such a pattern might be used. This is impossible using annotations and can be accomplished only using XML configuration or programmatic Java configuration.

In Chapter 9, you learn about filters and why it's important to carefully construct the order the filters execute in. You can make filters execute in a specific order when declaring them using XML configuration or programmatic Java configuration. If you declare your filters using `@javax.servlet.annotation.WebFilter`, however, it is impossible to make them execute in a specific order (something many feel is a glaring oversight in the Servlet 3.0 and 3.1 specifications). Unless your application has only one filter, `@WebFilter` is virtually useless.

There are many smaller things that still require the XML deployment descriptor to accomplish, such as defining error-handling pages, configuring JSP settings, and providing a list of welcome pages. Thankfully, you can mix-and-match XML, annotation, and programmatic Java, and configuration, so you can use each when it's most convenient. Throughout this book, you use all three techniques.

## UPLOADING FILES FROM A FORM

Uploading files to Java EE Servlets has nearly always been possible, but it used to require considerable effort. The task was so complex that Apache Commons made an entire project, called Commons FileUpload, to handle all the work. Thus, what seemed to be the simple requirement of accepting file upload submissions required introducing a third-party dependency in your application. Servlet 3.0 in Java EE 6 changed all that when it introduced the multipart configuration options for Servlets and the `getPart` and `getParts` methods in `HttpServletRequest`.

You can use this feature as a launching point for your interchapter example application: the Customer Support project. Although each chapter has smaller examples to demonstrate specific points, each chapter also includes a new version of the Customer Support project that incorporates the new topics learned in that chapter.

## Introducing the Customer Support Project

The setup is a global website serving customers around the world for Multinational Widget Corporation. Your product managers have been tasked with adding an interactive customer support application to the company's website. It should enable users to post questions or support tickets and enable employees to respond to those inquiries. Support tickets and comments alike should contain file attachments. For urgent matters, customers should enter a chat window with a dedicated support representative. And, to top it all off, because this is Multinational Widget Corporation, the entire application should be localizable in as many languages as the company decides to translate. That's not asking much, right?

Oh, yea. It needs to be really secure, too.

Obviously you can't tackle this all at once, especially with how little you've learned so far, so for each chapter you either tackle a small feature or improve upon code written in the chapter before. For the rest of this chapter, refer to the Customer-Support-v1 project. The project is relatively simple right now. It consists of three pages, handled by `doGet`: a list of tickets, a page to create tickets, and a page to view a ticket. It also has the capability of downloading a file attached to a ticket and of accepting a `POST` request to create a new ticket. Although the code is not complex and consists largely of concepts you have already covered in this chapter, there is too much to print it all here. You need to follow along in the code downloaded from the website.

## Configuring the Servlet for File Uploads

In the project you can find a `Ticket` class, an `Attachment` class, and the `TicketServlet` class. The `Ticket` and `Attachment` classes are simple *POJOs — plain old Java objects*. The `TicketServlet` does all the hard work at this time, so start by looking at its declaration and fields:

```
@WebServlet(
        name = "ticketServlet",
        urlPatterns = {"/tickets"},
        loadOnStartup = 1
)
@MultipartConfig(
        fileSizeThreshold = 5_242_880, //5MB
        maxFileSize = 20_971_520L, //20MB
        maxRequestSize = 41_943_040L //40MB
)
public class TicketServlet extends HttpServlet
{
    private volatile int TICKET_ID_SEQUENCE = 1;

    private Map<Integer, Ticket> ticketDatabase = new LinkedHashMap<>();
...
}
```

Already you should see some things you recognize and some things you don't. The `@MultipartConfig` annotation instructs the web container to provide file upload support for this servlet. It has several important attributes you should look at. The first, which is not shown here, is `location`. This instructs the web container in which directory to store temporary files if it needs to. In most cases, however, it is sufficient to omit this field and let the application server use its default temporary directory. The `fileSizeThreshold` tells the web container how big the file has to be before it is written to the temporary directory.

In this example, uploaded files smaller than 5 megabytes are kept in memory until the request completes and then they become eligible for garbage. After a file exceeds 5 megabytes, the container instead stores it in `location` (or default) until the request completes, after which it deletes the file from disk. The last two parameters, `maxFileSize` and `maxRequestSize`, place limits on uploaded files: `maxFileSize` in this example prohibits an uploaded file from exceeding 20 megabytes, whereas `maxRequestSize` prohibits the total size of a request from exceeding 40 megabytes, regardless of the number of file uploads it contains. That's really all there is to it. The Servlet is now configured to accept file uploads.

> **NOTE** *As with configuring Servlet init parameters using annotations, the multipart configuration parameters in the previous example cannot be changed without recompiling the application. If you anticipate server administrators' needing to customize these settings without recompiling the application, you need to use the deployment descriptor instead of* `@WebServlet` *and* `@MultipartConfig`. *Within the* `<servlet>` *tag you can place a* `<multipart-config>` *tag, and within that you can use the* `<location>`, `<file-size-threshold>`, `<max-file-size>`, *and* `<max-request-size>` *tags.*

You may also notice that the "ticket database" isn't a database at all (Or is it? It's a medium for storing data, no?), but rather a simple hash map. Eventually in Part III of this book you back your application with a relational database. For now, however, you want to get the user interface right and understand the business requirements so that product management at Multinational Widget Corporation is happy. After that, you can worry about persisting your data.

Now that you understand what you've seen so far, take a look at the `doGet` implementation:

```
@Override
protected void doGet(HttpServletRequest request, HttpServletResponse response)
        throws ServletException, IOException
{
    String action = request.getParameter("action");
    if(action == null)
        action = "list";
    switch(action)
    {
        case "create":
            this.showTicketForm(response);
            break;
        case "view":
            this.viewTicket(request, response);
            break;
```

```
            case "download":
                this.downloadAttachment(request, response);
                break;
            case "download":
            default:
                this.listTickets(response);
                break;
        }
    }
```

There's too much to do to put everything in the doGet method; before long, you could have a method that spans hundreds of lines. In this example, the doGet method uses a primitive action/executor pattern: The action is passed in through a request parameter, and the doGet method sends the request to an executor (method) based on that action. The doPost method is similar:

```
    @Override
    protected void doPost(HttpServletRequest request, HttpServletResponse response)
            throws ServletException, IOException
    {
        String action = request.getParameter("action");
        if(action == null)
            action = "list";
        switch(action)
        {
            case "create":
                this.createTicket(request, response);
                break;
            case "download":
            default:
                response.sendRedirect("tickets");
                break;
        }
    }
```

One new thing you can notice in doPost is the use of the redirect method. You learned about this method a few sections ago. In this case, if the client performs a POST with a missing or invalid *action* parameter, his browser is redirected to the page that lists tickets. Most of the methods in this class are nothing new: use of parameters, use of the PrintWriter to output content to the client's browser, and so on. Not all the code can fit in this book, but there are some new features used here that you should look at. The following example is a snippet of the downloadAttachment method, only the part that contains something new you haven't seen yet:

```
        response.setHeader("Content-Disposition",
                "attachment; filename=" + attachment.getName());
        response.setContentType("application/octet-stream");

        ServletOutputStream stream = response.getOutputStream();
        stream.write(attachment.getContents());
```

This simple bit of code is responsible for handing off the file download to the client's browser. The Content-Disposition header, as set, forces the browser to ask the client to save or download the file instead of just opening the file inline in the browser. The content type is a generic, binary content type that keeps the data from having some kind of character encoding applied to it. (A more correct implementation would know the attachment's actual MIME content type and use that value, but that task is outside the scope of this book.) Finally, the ServletOutputStream is used to write the file contents to the response. This may not be the most efficient way to write the file contents to the response because it may suffer memory issues for large files. If you anticipate permitting large file downloads, you shouldn't store files in-memory, and you should copy the bytes from a file's `InputStream` to the `ResponseOutputStream`. You should then `flush` the `ResponseOutputStream` frequently so that bytes are continuously streaming back to the user's browser instead of buffering in memory. The exercise of improving this code is left up to you.

## Accepting a File Upload

Lastly, take a look at the `createTicket` method and the method that it uses, `processAttachment`, in Listing 3-2. These methods are particularly important because they deal with handling a file upload — something you have not done yet. The `processAttachment` method gets the `InputStream` from the multipart request and copies it to the `Attachment` object. It uses the `getSubmittedFileName` method added in Servlet 3.1 to identify the original file name before it was uploaded. The `createTicket` method uses this method and other request parameters to populate the `Ticket` object and add it to the database.

**LISTING 3-2: Part of TicketServlet.java**

```
private void createTicket(HttpServletRequest request,
                          HttpServletResponse response)
        throws ServletException, IOException
{
    Ticket ticket = new Ticket();
    ticket.setCustomerName(request.getParameter("customerName"));
    ticket.setSubject(request.getParameter("subject"));
    ticket.setBody(request.getParameter("body"));

    Part filePart = request.getPart("file1");
    if(filePart != null)
    {
        Attachment attachment = this.processAttachment(filePart);
        if(attachment != null)
            ticket.addAttachment(attachment);
    }

    int id;
    synchronized(this)
    {
        id = this.TICKET_ID_SEQUENCE++;
        this.ticketDatabase.put(id, ticket);
    }

    response.sendRedirect("tickets?action=view&ticketId=" + id);
}

private Attachment processAttachment(Part filePart)
        throws IOException
{
    InputStream inputStream = filePart.getInputStream();
    ByteArrayOutputStream outputStream = new ByteArrayOutputStream();
```

```
        int read;
        final byte[] bytes = new byte[1024];

        while((read = inputStream.read(bytes)) != -1)
        {
            outputStream.write(bytes, 0, read);
        }

        Attachment attachment = new Attachment();

        attachment.setName(filePart.getSubmittedFileName());
        attachment.setContents(outputStream.toByteArray());

        return attachment;
    }
```

One thing you may notice in the `createTicket` method is the use of a `synchronized` block to lock access to the ticket database. You explore this a little more in the next and final section of the chapter.

# MAKING YOUR APPLICATION SAFE FOR MULTITHREADING

Web applications are, by nature, multithreaded applications. At any given time, zero, one, or a thousand people may be using your web application simultaneously, and your code must anticipate and account for this. There are dozens of different facets to this topic, and entire books have been written about multithreading and managing concurrency in applications. Obviously, this book cannot possibly cover all the important multithreading discussions. However, you should know two things above all else when considering concurrency in your web applications.

## Understanding Requests, Threads, and Method Execution

Every web container is, of course, slightly different. But in the Java EE world, generally speaking, a web container contains some type of thread pool, possibly called the *connector pool* or *executor pool*.

When the container receives a request, it looks for an available thread in the pool. If it does not find an available thread and the thread pool has already reached its maximum size, the request enters a queue — first in first out — and waits for an available thread. (Typically, there is also a higher limit, called the `acceptCount` setting in Tomcat, which defines the maximum number of connections that can be queued before the container starts rejecting connections.) Once a thread is available, the container borrows the thread from the pool and hands the request off to be handled by the thread. At this point, the thread is no longer available for any other incoming requests. In a normal request, the thread and request will be linked throughout the life of the request. As long as the request is processed by your code, that thread will be dedicated to the request. Only when the request has completed and the content of your response has been written back to the client will the thread be free from the request and return to the pool to service another request.

Creating and destroying threads includes a lot of overhead that can slow an application down, so employing a pool of reusable threads in this manner eliminates this overhead and improves performance.

The thread pool has a configurable size that determines how many connections can be serviced at once. Although this is not a discussion of the techniques and practices of managing application servers, hardware limitations place a practical limit on the size of this pool, after which increasing the pool size achieves no performance gains (and often can hurt performance). The default maximum pool size in Tomcat is 200 threads, and this number can be increased or decreased. You must understand this because it means that, in a worst-case scenario, 200 different threads (or more, if you increase the number) could be executing the same method in your code on the same instance of that code simultaneously. Therefore, you should consider the way that code functions so that simultaneous executions of the code in multiple threads do not result in exceptional behavior.

> **NOTE** *On the subject of requests and threads, there are circumstances during which a thread may not be devoted to a request for the entire life of the request. Servlet 3.0 in Java EE 6 added the concept of asynchronous request contexts. Essentially, when your Servlet services a request, it can call* `ServletRequest`*'s* `startAsync` *method. This returns a* `javax.servlet.AsyncContext` *object in which that request resides. Your Servlet can then return from the Servlet's* `service` *method without responding to the request, and the thread will be returned to the pool. The request does not close, but instead stays open, unanswered. Later, when some event occurs, your application can retrieve the response object from the* `AsyncContext` *and use it to send a response to the client. You learn more about using asynchronous request contexts in Chapter 9. This approach is often employed for a technique called long polling, something that Chapter 10 discusses.*

## Protecting Shared Resources

The most typical complication when coding for a multithreaded application is the access of shared resources. Objects and variables created during the execution of a method are safe as long as that method is executing — other threads do not have access to them. However, static and instance variables in a Servlet, for example, could be accessed by multiple threads simultaneously (remember: in the worst case, even 200 threads simultaneously). It's important to synchronize access to these shared resources to keep their contents from becoming corrupt and possibly causing errors in your application.

You can employ a few techniques to protect shared resources from these problems. Consider the first line of code in the `TicketServlet`:

```
private volatile int TICKET_ID_SEQUENCE = 1;
```

In Java, it is sometimes possible for one thread to read the previous value of a variable even after the value has been changed in another thread. This can cause consistency issues in some circumstances. The `volatile` keyword in this case establishes a happens-before relationship for all future reads of the variable and guarantees that other threads will always see the latest value of the variable.

Next, recall the synchronized block of code in the `createTicket` method from Listing 3-2:

```
synchronized(this)
{
    id = this.TICKET_ID_SEQUENCE++;
    this.ticketDatabase.put(id, ticket);
}
```

Two things are happening in this block of code: the `TICKED_ID_SEQUENCE` is incremented and its value retrieved, and the `Ticket` is inserted into the hash map of tickets. Both of these variables are instance variables of the Servlet, meaning multiple threads may have access to them simultaneously. Putting these actions within the synchronized block guarantees that no other thread can execute these two lines of code at the same time. The thread currently executing this block of code has exclusive access to execute the block until it completes. Of course, care should always be taken when using synchronized code blocks or methods because incorrect application of synchronization can result in a deadlock, a problem beyond the scope of this book.

> **WARNING** *One final thing to keep in mind when writing your Servlet methods: **Never** store request or response objects in static or instance variables. Just don't do it. There is no maybe — it **will** cause problems for you. Any objects and resources that belong to a request should exist only as local variables and method arguments.*

## SUMMARY

In this chapter, you were introduced to the `Servlet` interface and `GenericServlet` and `HttpServlet` abstract classes, along with the `HttpServletRequest` and `HttpServletResponse` interfaces. You learned how to service incoming requests and respond to them appropriately using the request and response objects. You experimented with the deployment descriptor and explored how to configure Servlets using `web.xml` and annotations. You also discovered one of the most important tasks when dealing with HTTP requests: handling request parameters, including query parameters and post variables, and accepting file uploads through form submissions. You were introduced to context and Servlet init parameters and how to use them to configure your application. Finally, you learned about request threads and thread pools and why multithreading considerations are so important in web application programming.

At this point, you should have a firm grasp on the basics of creating and using Servlets in your web application. One of the major inconveniences you may have noticed during this chapter is the complexity and cumbersomeness of writing simple HTML to the response. In the next chapter you explore the answer to this problem and how it makes life much easier in the Java EE world: JavaServer Pages.

# Using JSPs to Display Content

## IN THIS CHAPTER

- Using `<br />` is easier than `output.println("<br />")`
- Creating your first JSP
- Using Java within a JSP (and why you shouldn't)
- Combining Servlets and JSPs
- A note about JSP Documents (JSPX)

## WROX.COM CODE DOWNLOADS FOR THIS CHAPTER

You can find the `wrox.com` code downloads for this chapter at `www.wrox.com/go/projavaforwebapps` on the Download Code tab. The code for this chapter is divided into the following major examples:

- Hello-World-JSP Project
- Hello-User-JSP Project
- Customer-Support-v2 Project

## NEW MAVEN DEPENDENCIES FOR THIS CHAPTER

In addition to the Maven dependency introduced in the previous chapter, you will also need the following Maven dependencies. The exclusions are necessary because the JSTL implementation defines transient dependencies on older versions of the JSP and Servlet specifications that have different Maven artifact IDs than the current versions.

```
<dependency>
    <groupId>javax.servlet.jsp</groupId>
    <artifactId>javax.servlet.jsp-api</artifactId>
    <version>2.3.1</version>
    <scope>provided</scope>
```

```
        </dependency>

        <dependency>
            <groupId>javax.servlet.jsp.jstl</groupId>
            <artifactId>javax.servlet.jsp.jstl-api</artifactId>
            <version>1.2.1</version>
            <scope>compile</scope>
        </dependency>

        <dependency>
            <groupId>org.glassfish.web</groupId>
            <artifactId>javax.servlet.jsp.jstl</artifactId>
            <version>1.2.2</version>
            <scope>compile</scope>
            <exclusions>
                <exclusion>
                    <groupId>javax.servlet</groupId>
                    <artifactId>servlet-api</artifactId>
                </exclusion>
                <exclusion>
                    <groupId>javax.servlet.jsp</groupId>
                    <artifactId>jsp-api</artifactId>
                </exclusion>
                <exclusion>
                    <groupId>javax.servlet.jsp.jstl</groupId>
                    <artifactId>jstl-api</artifactId>
                </exclusion>
            </exclusions>
        </dependency>
```

In the last chapter you learned about Servlets and handling requests, responses, request parameters, file uploads, Servlet configuration, and more. However, you may have noticed a serious inconvenience when writing the Servlet code to output HTML content to the response: Repeatedly calling methods on the `ServletOutputStream` or `PrintWriter` classes to output the content and having to put HTML content within Java `String`s, requiring escaping of quotation marks, is a real pain. In this chapter, you explore JavaServer Pages and how they can make your life a whole lot easier.

## <BR /> IS EASIER THAN OUTPUT.PRINTLN("<BR />")

Java is a powerful language. It has many capabilities and features that make it useful, flexible, and easy to use. Chances are, you are reading this book because you like Java and want to learn how to do more with it. So what's up with this?

```
PrintWriter writer = response.getWriter();
writer.append("<!DOCTYPE html>\r\n")
      .append("<html>\r\n")
      .append("    <head>\r\n")
      .append("        <title>Hello World Application</title>\r\n")
      .append("    </head>\r\n")
      .append("    <body>\r\n")
      .append("        Nick says, \"Hello, World!\"\r\n")
      .append("    </body>\r\n");
      .append("</html>\r\n");
```

The number of ways this is inconvenient and cumbersome is rather long. Significantly more code must be written to achieve this. More file space is needed to store the code. Time is wasted writing and testing the code. Verbosity with line endings (`\r\n`) is necessary to make HTML source that is readable in the browser's View Source feature. Any quotation marks that appear in the HTML must be escaped so that they do not prematurely terminate the `String` literal. And — perhaps one of the worst problems — code editors cannot easily (in most cases, at all) recognize and validate HTML code within `Strings` to tell you if you're doing something wrong. Surely there is a better way. After all, it's just text. If you wrote the previous example in a plain HTML file, it would be simple:

```
<!DOCTYPE html>
<html>
    <head>
        <title>Hello World Application</title>
    </head>
    <body>
        Hello, World!
    </body>
</html>
```

Fortunately, the creators of the Java EE specification realized that this system would quickly become unwieldy and designed *JavaServer Pages*, also known as *JSPs*, to answer the need.

## Why JSPs Are Better

The problem with the most-recent code example is that it's a static HTML document. It may have been easier to write and it will likely be infinitely easier to maintain than the example written in Java, but there's nothing dynamic about it. JSPs are essentially a hybrid solution, combining Java code and HTML tags. JSPs can contain any HTML tag in addition to Java code, built-in JSP tags (Chapter 7), custom JSP tags (Chapter 8), and something called the Expression Language (Chapter 5). Many of these features you learn about in later chapters.

In this chapter, you explore the basic rules of JSPs and learn about the syntax, directives, declarations, scriptlets, and expressions of the JSP technology. You also learn about the life cycle of a JSP and how it is ultimately used to send a response back to the user.

There are alternatives to JSPs. Perhaps the most common alternative is Facelets, part of the broader JavaServer Faces technology (or JSF for short, making it easy to confuse with JSP). There are also templating frameworks, such as Velocity, Freemarker, SiteMesh, and Tiles, that all, in some fashion, supplement or replace the features provided by JSPs. This book cannot possibly cover all the options and variations of presentation technologies that work with the Servlet 3.1 specification. It will, therefore, focus on the most popular and widely used technology.

The following example, which you can find in the `index.jsp` file of the Hello-World-JSP project on the `wrox.com` downloads page, re-creates the Hello-World project from Chapter 2, but uses a JSP instead of a Servlet to display the greeting to the user.

```
<%@ page contentType="text/html;charset=UTF-8" language="java" %>
<!DOCTYPE html>
<html>
    <head>
        <title>Hello World Application</title>
```

```
    </head>
    <body>
        Hello, World!
    </body>
</html>
```

This example is nearly identical to the original HTML-only example earlier in the section. The only new code is the first line, highlighted in bold. This is one of several JSP *directives* that you will examine in more detail in the section "Creating Your First JSP." This particular directive sets the content type and character encoding of the page, something you previously did with the `setContentType` and `setCharacterEncoding` method calls on the `HttpServletResponse`. Everything else in this JSP is plain HTML, transmitted back to the client as-is in the response. The interesting question is, "What's actually happening behind the scenes?"

## What Happens to a JSP at Run Time

A JSP is really just a fancy Servlet. Perhaps you have heard the phrase "syntactic sugar." Ultimately, in one way or another, all popular languages programmers use today on a regular basis are syntactic sugar. Take Java, for example, as a code you write with. When you compile Java code, it is turned into *bytecode*. The bytecode is what matters — not the Java code. In fact, many different statements in Java can turn into identical bytecode. But to take it a step further, bytecode is not the final rendering of a Java program. This bytecode is still platform-independent, but that is not sufficient to run on varying operating systems.

When Java runs in the JRE, the Just In Time compiler compiles it into *machine code*, which is specific to the platform it runs on. Ultimately, it's this machine code that is executed. Even lower-level languages, such as C, are simply syntactic sugar for the machine code they actually get compiled to. JSPs are another form of syntactic sugar. At run time, the JSP code is interpreted by the JSP compiler, which parses out all the special features in the JSP code and translates them to Java code. The Java class created from each JSP implements `Servlet`. Then, the Java code goes through the same cycle it normally does. Still at run time, it is compiled into bytecode and then into machine code. Finally, the JSP-turned-Servlet responds to requests like any other Servlet.

To investigate this, for these steps:

1. Compile the Hello-World-JSP project in your IDE, start your debugger, and open your browser to `http://localhost:8080/hello-world/`. You should see the all-too-familiar greeting on your screen.
2. Browse your file system to the Tomcat 8.0 home directory (`C:\Program Files\Apache Software Foundation\Tomcat 8.0` on Windows) and go into the directory `work\Catalina\localhost\hello-world`. Tomcat puts all compiled JSPs for the application in this directory, but it also leaves behind the intermediate Java files it generates so that you can inspect and troubleshoot with them.
3. Continue going down further directories until you come across the `index_jsp.java` file. Open it (not the `index_jsp.class` file) in your favorite text editor.

What you should find is a class that extends `org.apache.jasper.runtime.HttpJspBase`. This abstract class extends — you may have guessed — `HttpServlet`. `HttpJspBase` provides some base functionality that will be used by all JSPs that Tomcat compiles, and when your JSP is executed, ultimately the `service` method on that Servlet is executed, which eventually executes the `_jspService` method.

If you inspect the `_jspService` method, you'll find a series of method calls writing your HTML to the output stream. This code should look very familiar to you because it's not that different from the Java code that you replaced with this JSP. Of course, the JSP Servlet class does not look the same on every web container. The `org.apache.jasper` classes, for example, are Tomcat-specific classes. Your JSP compiles differently on each different web container you run it on. The important point is that there is a standard specification for the behavior and syntax of JSPs, and as long as the web containers you use are compliant with the specification, your JSPs should run the same on all of them, even if the Java code they get translated into looks completely different.

JSPs, just like your normal Servlets, can also be debugged at run time. To demonstrate this, place a breakpoint on the line of your JSP that contains "Hello, World," and then refresh your browser. At this point you should hit the breakpoint in the JSP, and you should notice a few things. First, you can hit breakpoints directly within the JSP code! You don't have to place breakpoints in the translated JSP Servlet class; Java, Tomcat, and your IDE can match the breakpoint in the JSP to code executing in the run time. You should also notice that, although the breakpoint might be in the JSP code, the debugger clearly is not. The stack will show that your run time has paused within the `_jspService` method, and the variables window shows you all the instance and local variables defined within that scope in the `index_jsp` class.

> **WARNING** *IntelliJ IDEA has much better JSP debugging facilities than does Eclipse IDE. If you are using Eclipse, it's possible that you may not be able to place a breakpoint in this JSP at all. As of now, Eclipse only lets you place breakpoints in the Java code embedded in your JSPs, while IntelliJ allows breakpoints in any JSP code.*

Like all other Servlets running in your web container, JSPs have a life cycle. In some web containers, such as Tomcat, the JSP is translated and compiled just in time when the first request to that JSP arrives. For future requests, the JSP is already compiled and ready to use. This, as you can imagine, introduces some performance impacts. Although the performance hit generally comes only on the first request, leaving all subsequent requests to run at a decent speed, this is still unwanted in some production environments. Because of this, many web containers give you the option of precompiling all of an application's JSPs as it deploys. This, of course, significantly slows down deployment for large applications. If you have many thousands of JSPs, your application could conceivably take 10 minutes to deploy instead of just 1. It's up to the organization to decide which configuration meets its needs best. Regardless of the time of compilation, after the first request arrives, the JSP Servlet will be instantiated and initialized, and then the first request can be serviced.

By this point you should realize that the code you write in your JSP ultimately is translated into some version of the code you would have had to write anyway if you didn't have JSPs. So why, you might ask, should one even bother with JSPs? The fact remains that the JSP is a much easier file format for producing markup for display in a web browser than writing straight Java code. If this can improve the speed, efficiency, and accuracy of your development process, the question actually is, "Why *wouldn't* you use JSPs?"

# CREATING YOUR FIRST JSP

You've explored a JSP that was already written for you, so now work on creating your own JSP. You need to know some things about how JSPs are structured and what you can put in JSPs. You go over some of the basic need-to-knows in this section and then delve a little further in the next.

## Understanding the File Structure

In the previous chapter you explored Servlets and answered the question, "What must you do in the `service` method?" The answer was that you *must* appropriately respond to the HTTP request with a valid HTTP response, but because `HttpServlet` takes care of all of that for you, your `doGet` and `doPost` methods could literally be empty methods (as useless as that was). As it turns out, the question in this case is still the same. There are many things that must happen when a JSP is executed, but all those "musts" are handled for you.

To demonstrate this, create a file named `blank.jsp` in the web root of an empty project; delete all its contents (your IDE might put some code in there for you — delete it all); and redeploy your project. Alternatively, just use the Hello-World-JSP you downloaded from `wrox.com`, which already contains a `blank.jsp`. When you go to `http://localhost:8080/hello-world/blank.jsp`, you don't get any errors. Everything works fine; you just get a useless blank page back. Now put the following code in it, redeploy, and reload:

```
<!DOCTYPE html>
<html>
    <head>
        <title>Hello World Application</title>
    </head>
    <body>
        Hello, World!
    </body>
</html>
```

There's just a slight difference between `blank.jsp` and `index.jsp` now, that being the missing special tag that's on the first line of `index.jsp`. And yet, the content still displays the same. This is because JSPs by default have a content type of `text/html` and a character encoding of ISO-8859-1. However, this default character encoding is incompatible with many special characters like those in non-English languages, which can interfere with efforts to localize your application. So, at a minimum, your JSP needs to contain HTML to display to the user. However, to ensure that HTML displays correctly in all browsers on all systems in many languages, you'll want to include certain JSP tags to control the data sent to the client, such as setting the character encoding to the localization-friendly UTF-8.

Several different types of tags can be used in JSPs, and you explore more of them in the next section. Of the directive tag type, there is one that you have already seen:

```
<%@ page ... %>
```

This directive tag provides you with some controls over how the JSP is translated, rendered, and transmitted back to the client. In the `index.jsp` example, the `page` directive looks like this:

```
<%@ page contentType="text/html;charset=UTF-8" language="java" %>
```

The `language` attribute tells the container which *JSP scripting language* this JSP uses. A JSP scripting language (not to be confused with interpreted scripting languages) is a language that can be embedded in a JSP for scripting certain actions. Currently, Java is the only supported scripting language for JSPs, but this attribute leaves that open for extension someday.

Technically, you can omit this attribute. Because Java is the only supported JSP scripting language, and in addition Java is the default in the specification, Java is implied when this attribute is missing. The `contentType` attribute tells the container the value of the `Content-Type` header that should be sent back along with the response. The `Content-Type` header contains both the content type and the character encoding, separated with a semicolon. If you recall reading the `index_jsp.java` file, it contained the Java that this attribute was translated to:

```
response.setContentType("text/html;charset=UTF-8");
```

It should be noted that the previous code snippet is the equivalent of the following two lines of code, which you saw in your Hello-User project from Chapter 3:

```
response.setContentType("text/html");
response.setCharacterEncoding("UTF-8");
```

And furthermore, these are both equivalent to the following line of code:

```
response.setHeader("Content-Type", "text/html;charset=UTF-8");
```

As you can see, there are several ways to accomplish the same task. The `setContentType` and `setCharacterEncoding` methods are convenience methods. Which method you use is up to you; although, you should generally pick one and stick to it to avoid confusion. However, as most of your content code from here on will be JSP-based, you'll mostly just be concerned with the `contentType` attribute of the page directive.

## Directives, Declarations, Scriptlets, and Expressions

In addition to the various HTML and JSP tags you can use within a JSP, there are several unique structures that define a sort of JSP language. They are *directives*, *declarations*, *scriptlets*, and *expressions*. In the simplest terms, they look like this:

```
<%@ this is a directive %>
<%! This is a declaration %>
<% this is a scriptlet %>
<%= this is an expression %>
```

### Using Directives

Directives are used to direct the JSP interpreter to perform an action (such as setting the content type) or make an assumption about the file (such as which scripting language it uses), to import a class, to include some other JSP at translation time, or to include a JSP tag library.

### Using Declarations

You use declarations to declare something within the scope of your JSP Servlet class. For example, you could define instance variables, methods, or classes within a declaration tag. You need to remember that these declarations all are made within the generated JSP Servlet class, so any classes you define are actually inner classes of the JSP Servlet class.

## Using Scriptlets

Like a declaration, a scriptlet also contains Java code. However, scriptlets have a different scope. Although code within a declaration is copied to the JSP Servlet class body at translation time and must therefore be used to *declare* some field, type, or method, scriptlets are copied to the body of the `_jspService` method you looked at earlier. Any local variables that are in scope within this method execution will be in scope within your scriptlets, and any code that is legal within a method body is legal within a scriptlet. So, you can define local variables, but not instance fields. You can use conditional statements, manipulate objects, and perform arithmetic, all things you cannot do within a declaration. You can even define classes (as odd as that may sound, but it is legal in Java to have class definitions within a method), but the classes do not have scope outside the `_jspService` method. A class, method, or variable defined within a declaration can be used within a scriptlet, but a class or variable defined within a scriptlet cannot be used within a declaration.

## Using Expressions

Expressions contain simple Java code that returns something that can be written to the client output, and expressions output the return variable of that code to the client. So, you could have an arithmetic calculation within an expression because that results in a numeric value that can be displayed. You could call some method that returns a `String` or number or other primitive because that results in a displayable returned value. Essentially, any code that can legally be the entire right side of an assignment statement can be placed within an expression. Expressions execute within the same method scope as scriptlets; that is, expressions get copied into the `_jspService` method just like scriptlets do.

Take a look at the following example code. It doesn't actually do anything useful, but it demonstrates the variety of things you can do within directives, declarations, scriptlets, and expressions.

```
<%@ page contentType="text/html;charset=UTF-8" language="java" %>
<%!
    private final int five = 0;

    protected String cowboy = "rodeo";

    //The assignment below is not declarative and is a syntax error if uncommented
    //cowboy = "test";

    public long addFive(long number)
    {
        return number + 5L;
    }

    public class MyInnerClass
    {

    }
    MyInnerClass instanceVariable = new MyInnerClass();

    //WeirdClassWithinMethod is in method scope, so the declaration below is
    // a syntax error if uncommented
```

```
        //WeirdClassWithinMethod bad = new WeirdClassWithinMethod();
    %>
    <%
        class WeirdClassWithinMethod
        {

        }
        WeirdClassWithinMethod weirdClass = new WeirdClassWithinMethod();
        MyInnerClass innerClass = new MyInnerClass();
        int seven;
        seven = 7;
    %>
    <%= "Hello, World" %><br />
    <%= addFive(12L) %>
```

## Putting It All Together

Create a JSP file named `gibberish.jsp` in the web root of an empty project, and put the preceding gibberish code in there (or just use the JSP in the Hello-World-JSP project). Compile and run your application and go to `http://localhost:8080/hello-world/gibberish.jsp`. Obviously, this page isn't useful in the browser; the point that you should understand is in the source file. Go back into the Tomcat work directory and find the `gibberish_jsp.java` file. Examine how the code in your JSP got translated into Java code in the JSP Servlet class to gain a better understanding of the differing purposes of directives, declarations, scriptlets, and expressions.

# Commenting Your Code

Like nearly every other language or markup in existence, JSP also has a method for commenting code. There are four different ways that you can comment code within a JSP:

- XML comments
- Traditional Java line comments
- Traditional Java block comments
- JSP comments.

The XML comment (also known as the HTML comment) is syntax you are most likely already familiar with:

```
<!-- This is an HTML/XML comment -->
```

This type of comment is passed through to the client because it is standard XML and HTML markup. The browser ignores it, but it appears in the source of the response. *More important, any JSP tags within this comment will still be evaluated.* This is essential to remember because commenting out code with this style of comment does not prevent Java code within from executing. To demonstrate this, consider the following example:

```
<!-- This is an HTML/XML comment: <%= someObject.dumpInfo() %> -->
```

If `someObject.dumpInfo()` returns "connections=5, errors=12, successes=3847," the response sent back to the client's browser will contain the following HTML comment in it:

```
<!-- This is an HTML/XML comment: connections=5, errors=12, successes=3847 -->
```

You can use any legal Java comment within declarations and scriptlets in JSPs. This includes, as mentioned previously, line comments and block comments. In the following example, all the code in bold is commented out and will not be evaluated:

```
<%
    String hello = "Hello, World!"; // this is a comment
    //long test = 12L;
    /*int i = 0;
    int j = 12;*/
    String goodbye = "Goodbye, World!";
%>
```

The new type of comment that you have not used yet is the JSP comment. The syntax of the JSP comment closely resembles an XML/HTML comment, with the only difference being the percent sign instead of the exclamation point at the beginning, and the percent sign at the end:

```
<%-- This is a JSP comment --%>
```

Just as with the XML/HTML comment, everything between the `<%--` and the `--%>` is considered commented. Not only is it not sent to the browser, it isn't even interpreted/translated by the JSP compiler. Whereas all three of the previously covered comment types appear in the JSP Servlet java file, this last comment type does not. To the translator, it does not even exist. This is especially useful for commenting out some range of code that includes JSP scriptlets, expressions, declarations, directives, and markup that you do not want to be evaluated or sent to the browser.

## Adding Imports to Your JSP

In Java when you use a class directly, you must either reference it using its fully qualified class name, or you must include an import statement at the top of the Java code file. The rules are the same in JSPs. Any time a JSP contains Java code that uses a class directly, it must either use the fully qualified class name or include an import directive in the JSP file. And just as every class in the `java.lang` package is imported implicitly in Java files, similarly every class in the `java.lang` package is implicitly imported in JSP files.

Importing Java classes in JSPs is different but just as easy as importing Java classes in a Java code file. Importing one or more classes is as simple as adding an import attribute to the page directive you learned about earlier:

```
<%@ page import="java.util.*,java.io.IOException" %>
```

In this example, you use a comma to separate multiple imports, and the result is that the `java.io.IOException` class and all the members of the `java.util` package are imported. Of course, you do not have to use a separate directive to import classes. You could combine this with the example seen earlier:

```
<%@ page contentType="text/html;charset=UTF-8" language="java"
         import="java.util.*,java.io.IOException" %>
```

You also don't have to combine multiple imports into a single directive using a comma separator. You could use multiple directives to accomplish this task:

```
<%@ page import="java.util.Map" %>
<%@ page import="java.util.List" %>
<%@ page import="java.io.IOException" %>
```

Something to consider when doing this is that every JSP tag that results in no output, and also every directive, declaration, and scriptlet, results in an empty line being output to the client. So, if you have many page directives for imports followed by various declarations and scriptlets, you could end up with dozens of blank lines in your output. To compensate for this, JSP developers often chain the end of one tag to the beginning of the next:

```
<%@ page import="java.util.Map"
%><%@ page import="java.util.List"
%><%@ page import="java.io.IOException" %>
```

This code example has the exact same logical outcome as the previous example, but it results in only one blank line at the top of the output instead of three. In the section "Combining Servlets and JSPs," you will learn about a deployment descriptor setting that trims this white space entirely.

# Using Directives

Earlier you were introduced to the directive, a JSP feature denoted with a beginning `<%@` and an ending `%>`. There are three different types of directives, which are discussed at this time.

## Changing Page Properties

You have already explored some features of the `page` directive, such as the `contentType`, `language`, and `import` attributes. There are also many more features of the `page` directive. As explained earlier, the `page` directive provides you with some controls over how the JSP is translated, rendered, and transmitted back to the client. Here are some of the other attributes that may be included in this directive:

### pageEncoding

Specifies the character encoding used by your JSP and is equivalent to `setCharacterEncoding` on `HttpServletResponse`. Instead of `contentType="text/html;charset=UTF-8"`, you could write `contentType="text/html" pageEncoding="UTF-8"`.

### session

This must either be `true` or `false`, and indicates whether the JSP participates in HTTP sessions. By default it is `true`, giving you access to the implicit *`session`* variable in the JSP (covered in the section "Using Java within a JSP (and Why You Shouldn't)"). If you set it to `false`, you cannot use the implicit *`session`* variable. If your application does not use sessions and you want to improve performance, setting this to `false` might be a good idea. You learn more about HTTP sessions in Chapter 5.

### isELIgnored

This attribute specifies whether expression language (EL) is parsed and translated for this JSP. You learn more about EL in Chapter 6. Prior to the JSP 2.0 specification, the default value was `true`, meaning you had to set it to `false` for every JSP in which you wanted to use EL. As of JSP 2.0 (you use JSP 2.3 in this book) the default value is `false`, so you should never need to worry about this setting.

### buffer and autoFlush

These attributes are closely related, and their defaults are "8kb" and `true`, respectively. They control whether the output of the JSP is sent immediately to the browser as it is generated or buffered and sent in batches. The `buffer` attribute specifies the size of the JSP buffer or "none" (the output will not be buffered), whereas `autoFlush` indicates whether the buffer will be flushed automatically after it reaches its size limit. If `buffer` is set to "none" and `autoFlush` is set to `false`, an exception occurs when the JSP is translated to Java. If `autoFlush` is set to `false` and the buffer becomes full, an exception occurs. This is a handy way to ensure that the content a JSP generates does not exceed a certain length.

With `autoFlush` set to `true` (the default), the smaller your buffer, the more often data will be flushed to the client, and the larger the buffer, the less often data will be flushed to the client. Disabling the buffer entirely with `buffer="none"` can improve the performance of your JSPs because it decreases memory consumption and CPU overhead. However, this is not without its setbacks. Using no buffer can result in sending more packets to the browser, which can increase bandwidth consumption marginally. Also, when the first character of the response begins flowing to the client, the HTTP response headers must be committed and sent before the response. Because of this, you cannot set response headers (`response.setHeader(...)`) or forward the JSP (`<jsp:forward />`) after the buffer has flushed, and you cannot set response headers or forward the JSP *at all* in a JSP where the buffer has been disabled. This may be an acceptable sacrifice to improve server-side performance in certain circumstances.

### errorPage

If an error occurs during the execution of the JSP, this attribute instructs the container what JSP to forward the request to.

### isErrorPage

This attribute indicates that this JSP is serving as an error page (by default, it is `false`). If set to `true`, this enables the implicit *`exception`* variable on the page. You would do this on JSPs that you forward to when errors occur, or that you have defined in the container as error-handling JSPs.

### isThreadSafe

`true` by default, this tells the container that the JSP can safely serve multiple requests simultaneously. If changed to `false`, the container only serves requests to this JSP one-by-one. A good rule of thumb is to *never* change this. Remember, "If your JSP isn't thread safe, you're doing it wrong."

### extends

This attribute specifies which class your JSP Servlet should inherit from. Using this is not portable from one web container to another, and it should never be necessary. Just don't do it.

### Other Attributes

In most of your JSPs, `contentType` (and optionally `pageEncoding`) are the only attributes of the `page` directive that you will ever change from the default values. The `session` and `isErrorPage` attributes are probably the two most common of the other attributes. Occasionally, you may need to disable buffering. With each JSP, you should evaluate your options and decide which attributes should be changed to suit your application's needs.

## Including Other JSPs

Including other JSPs in a JSP is easy, but there are some interesting rules and options to keep in mind. The first tool that you can use to include another JSP in your JSP is the `include` directive. It is straightforward:

```
<%@ include file="/path/to/some/file.jsp" %>
```

The `file` attribute provides the container with the path to the JSP file that should be included. If it is absolute, the path resolves from the web root of the application, so a file named `included.jsp` in the `WEB-INF` directory could be included with path `/WEB-INF/included.jsp`. If the path is relative, it resolves from the same directory the including JSP exists in. The `include` directive is evaluated at translation time. Before the JSP is translated to Java, the `include` directive is replaced (virtually) with the contents of the included JSP file. After this happens, the combined contents are then translated to Java and compiled. Thus, as you can see, this process is static and only occurs once.

To demonstrate this, follow these steps:

1. Create a JSP called `includer.jsp` in the web root of your Hello-World-JSP project and place the following line of code in it (deleting any code your IDE generated). Alternatively, just use the Hello-World-JSP project.

   ```
   <%@ include file="index.jsp" %>
   ```

2. Compile and debug your application and navigate to `http://localhost:8080/hello-world/includer.jsp` in your favorite browser. You should see the familiar page, which means your include has worked.
3. Now go into the Tomcat work directory and open the `includer_jsp.java` file that Tomcat created. You should immediately notice that, other than the class name, it is identical to `index_jsp.java`. This is because the JSP was included statically at translation time.

There is a different way to include other JSPs that results in a dynamic (run time) inclusion instead of a static (translation time) inclusion. You use the `<jsp:include>` tag to achieve this:

```
<jsp:include page="/path/to/some/page.jsp" />
```

The `<jsp:include>` tag doesn't have a `file` attribute; it has a `page` attribute. The path is still relative to the current file or absolute from the web root, just like with the `include` directive. But it is not included at translation time. Instead, the included file is compiled separately. At run time, the request is temporarily forwarded to the included JSP, the resulting output of that JSP is written to the response, and then the control returns back to the including JSP. This can easily be seen by creating a file named `dynamicIncluder.jsp` in your project's web root with the following line of code (or use the Hello-World-JSP project):

```
<jsp:include page="index.jsp" />
```

Compile and debug again and navigate to `http://localhost:8080/hello-world/dynamicIncluder.jsp`, then open the `dynamicIncluder_jsp.java` file that Tomcat created. You can see now that the content of this Java file is quite different. The most interesting line in the file is:

```
org.apache.jasper.runtime.JspRuntimeLibrary.include(request, response, "index.jsp",
                                                    out, false);
```

This sends the request and response down into another method, which runs the included JSP, writes its contents to the response, and returns.

Both of these methods of inclusion have their strengths and weaknesses. The `include` directive is fast because it is evaluated only once, and all variables defined in the including JSP are in scope and can be referenced by the included JSP. But this method makes your JSP (and the `_jspService` method, as a result) longer, which is important to keep in mind because the bytecode of compiled Java methods can't be longer than 65,534 bytes. The `<jsp:include>` tag does not cause this problem, but it also does not perform as well because it must be evaluated every page load, and variables defined in the including JSP are out of scope and cannot be used in the included JSP. Ultimately, you must decide which is appropriate each time you need to include a file, but in most cases, the `include` directive is a good choice.

> **NOTE** *By default, web containers translate and compile files ending in* `.jsp` *and* `.jspx` *(which you learn about later) as JSPs. You may have also seen the extension* `.jspf`*. JSPF files are generally called JSP Fragments and are not compiled by the web container. Although there are no hard-and-fast rules governing JSPF files (you can technically configure most web containers to compile them if you want), there are some agreed-upon best practices. JSPF files represent fragments of JSPs that cannot stand alone and should always be included, not accessed directly. This is why web containers do not normally compile them. Actually, in many cases a JSPF file references variables that can exist only if it is included in another JSP file. For this reason, JSPF files should be included only using the* `include` *directive because variables defined in the including JSP must be in scope in the included JSP.*

### Including Tag Libraries

Chapters 7 and 8 talk more about tag libraries, but they are mentioned now because of how they are included. You use the `taglib` directive to reference a tag library so that you can use the tags defined by that tag library in your JSP. Like the `include` directive, the `taglib` directive is quite simple:

```
<%@ taglib uri="http://java.sun.com/jsp/jstl/core" prefix="c" %>
```

The `uri` attribute specifies the URI namespace that the tag library is defined under, and the `prefix` attribute defines the alias with which you reference the tags in that library. You learn more about what this means in Chapter 7.

## Using the <jsp> Tag

All JSPs support a special kind of tag with an XMLNS prefix of `jsp`. This tag has many uses and features. Most of the features are used in JSP Documents (XML versions of JSPs that you learn about in the last section of this chapter) or relics from older versions of JSP in which some things were much harder to do than they are now (and so are not covered here). However, you should learn about a few useful features of this tag.

You have already learned about `<jsp:include>` and how it differs from the `include` directive. A similar tag is the `<jsp:forward>` tag. This enables you to forward a request from the JSP it is currently executing in to some other JSP. Unlike a `<jsp:include>`, the request does not return to the original JSP. This is not a redirect; the client's browser does not see the change. Also, anything the JSP writes to the response stays in the response when the forward occurs; it is not erased, like it would be with a redirect. Using the `<jsp:forward>` tag is simple:

```
<jsp:forward page="/some/other/page.jsp" />
```

In this example the request is internally forwarded to `/some/other/page.jsp`. Any response content generated before the tag still goes to the client's browser. Any code that comes after the tag is ignored and not evaluated. This is how this tag differs from the `<jsp:include>` tag. If the code after the `<jsp:forward>` tag were not ignored, this tag would behave just like the `<jsp:include>` tag.

Three other related tags are `<jsp:useBean>`, `<jsp:getProperty>`, and `<jsp:setProperty>`. The `<jsp:useBean>` tag declares the presence of a JavaBean on the page, whereas `<jsp:getProperty>` retrieves properties (using getter methods) from beans declared with `<jsp:useBean>`. Similarly, `<jsp:setProperty>` sets properties (using setter methods). A Java bean in this case is any instantiated object. `<jsp:useBean>` instantiates a class to create a bean, and this bean can then be accessed using the other two bean tags, custom tags, and JSP scriptlets and expressions. The advantage to declaring a bean in this way is that it makes the bean available to other JSP tags; if you simply declared the bean in a scriptlet, it would only be available to scriptlets and expressions.

Finally, there is the `<jsp:plugin>` tag, which is a handy tool for embedding Java Applets in the rendered HTML. This tag removes the risk of messing up the careful structure of `<object>` and `<embed>` tags necessary to get Java Applets to work in all browsers. It handles creating these HTML tags for you so that the Applet should work in all mainstream browsers that support the Java plug-in. Here is an example of using the `<jsp:plugin>` tag:

```
<jsp:plugin type="applet" code="MyApplet.class" jreversion="1.8">
    <jsp:params>
        <jsp:param name="appletParam1" value="paramValue1"/>
    </jsp:params>
    <jsp:fallback>
        The browser you are using does not support Java Applets. You might
        consider switching browsers.
    </jsp:fallback>
</jsp:plugin>
```

Note that `<jsp:plugin>` can also contain standard object/embed HTML attributes such as `name`, `align`, `height`, `width`, `hspace`, and `vspace`. These attributes are copied to the HTML markup.

> **NOTE** *Java Applets are a completely different subject from web applications and are outside the scope of this book. If you want to learn more about Java Applets, most beginner Java books cover the topic.*

# USING JAVA WITHIN A JSP (AND WHY YOU SHOULDN'T!)

In this section you explore using Java within a JSP a little more by replacing the Servlet in the Hello-User project (from the previous chapter) with just a JSP. Then you briefly consider why using Java in a JSP is discouraged (and why there's actually a deployment descriptor setting to disable it). For the rest of this section you use the Hello-User-JSP project on the `wrox.com` download site.

## Using the Implicit Variables in a JSP

JSP files have several *implicit variables* (objects) available for use within scriptlets and expressions in the JSP. They are considered implicit because you do not have to define or declare them anywhere in your code. The JSP specification requires that the translator and compiler of the JSP provide these variables, with the exact names specified. The variables have *method scope*. They are defined at the beginning of the Servlet method that the JSP executes in (in Tomcat 8.0, the `_jspService` method). This means you cannot use them within any code you place inside JSP declarations. Declarations have *class scope*. Because the implicit variables are in scope only within the method that the JSP executes in, code inside declarations cannot use them. You can see an example of how the implicit variables are defined by looking at the `_jspService` method of any of the previously compiled JSPs you examined in the last section:

```
public void _jspService(final javax.servlet.http.HttpServletRequest request,
                        final javax.servlet.http.HttpServletResponse response)
        throws java.io.IOException, javax.servlet.ServletException
{
    final javax.servlet.jsp.PageContext pageContext;
    javax.servlet.http.HttpSession session = null;
    final javax.servlet.ServletContext application;
    final javax.servlet.ServletConfig config;
    javax.servlet.jsp.JspWriter out = null;
    final java.lang.Object page = this;
    javax.servlet.jsp.JspWriter _jspx_out = null;
    javax.servlet.jsp.PageContext _jspx_page_context = null;

    try {
        response.setContentType("text/html;charset=UTF-8");
        pageContext = _jspxFactory.getPageContext(this, request, response,
                null, true, 8192, true);
        _jspx_page_context = pageContext;
        application = pageContext.getServletContext();
        config = pageContext.getServletConfig();
        session = pageContext.getSession();
        out = pageContext.getOut();
        _jspx_out = out;
        ...
    }
    ...
}
```

The code isn't exactly the picture of clean code, but the important parts of the code are bold so that you can understand what's going on. The bold code emphasizes the declaration or assignment (or both) of implicit variables required by the JSP specification. Variables that are not bold (such as *`_jspx_out`* or *`_jspx_page_context`*) are Tomcat-specific variables that are not guaranteed to exist and should never be used in your JSP. Eight implicit variables are in this code, but the JSP specification defines nine implicit variables. Now take a look at each of these implicit variables, and then you'll understand why one is missing.

## request and response

The *`request`* variable is an instance of `HttpServletRequest` and the *`response`* variable is an instance of `HttpServletResponse`, both of which you learned about in detail in Chapter 3. Anything you can do with a request in a Servlet you can also do in a JSP, including getting request parameters, getting and setting attributes, and even reading from the response body. The same rules you learned about in the last chapter apply here. However, there are some restrictions on what you can do with the response object in a JSP. These restrictions are not contract restrictions, so they are not enforced at compile time. Instead, they are enforced at run time because violating them could cause unexpected behavior or even errors. For example, you should not call `getWriter` or `getOutputStream` because the JSP is already writing to the response output. You also should not set the content type or character encoding, flush or reset the buffer, or change the buffer size. These are all things that the JSP does, and if your code does them, too, it can cause problems.

## session

This variable is an instance of `HttpSession`. You learn more about sessions in the next chapter. Remember from the previous section that the `page` directive has a `session` attribute that defaults to `true`. This is why the *`session`* variable is available in the previous code example and will be available by default in all of your JSPs. If you set the `page` directive's `session` attribute to `false`, the *`session`* variable in the JSP is not defined and cannot be used.

## out

The `JspWriter` instance *`out`* is available for you to use in all your JSPs. It is a `Writer`, just like what you get from calling the `getWriter` method on `HttpServletResponse`. If for some reason you need to write directly to the response, you should use the *`out`* variable. However, in most cases you can simply use an expression or write text or HTML content in the JSP.

## application

This is an instance of the `ServletContext` interface. Recall from Chapter 3 that this interface gives you access to the configuration of the web application as a whole, including all the context init parameters. Why this variable was named *`application`* instead of *`context`* or *`servletContext`* is a mystery.

## config

The *`config`* variable is an instance of the `ServletConfig` interface. Unlike the *`application`* variable, its name actually reflects what it is. As you learned in Chapter 3, you can use this object to access the configuration of the JSP Servlet, such as the Servlet init parameters.

## pageContext

This object, an instance of the `PageContext` class, provides several convenience methods for getting request attributes and session attributes, accessing the request and response, including other files, and forwarding the request. You will probably never need to use this class within a JSP. It will, however, come in handy when you write custom JSP tags in Chapter 8.

### page

The *page* variable is an interesting object to examine. It is an instance of `java.lang.Object`, which initially makes it seem unuseful. However, it essentially is the *this* variable from the JSP Servlet object. So, you could cast it to `Servlet` and use methods defined on the `Servlet` interface. It is also a `javax.servlet.jsp.JspPage` (which extends `Servlet`) and a `javax.servlet.jsp.HttpJspPage` (which extends `JspPage`), so you could cast it to either of those and use methods defined on those interfaces. In reality, you will probably never have a reason to use this variable. It may be useful if other JSP scripting languages are ever supported. However, the JSP 2.3 specification, section 1.8.3 note "a," says that *page* is always a synonym for *this* when the scripting language is Java. Thus, anything you can do with *page* (such as get the Servlet name or access methods or instance variables you defined in a JSP declaration) you can also do with *this*.

### exception

This is the variable that was missing from the previous code example. Recall from the previous section that you can specify as `true` the `isErrorPage` attribute on the `page` directive to indicate that the JSP's purpose is to handle errors. Doing so makes the *exception* variable available for use within the JSP. Because the default value for `isErrorPage` is `false` and you have not used it anywhere, the *exception* variable has not been defined in any JSPs you created. If you create a JSP with `isErrorPage` set to `true`, the implicit *exception* variable, a `Throwable`, is defined automatically.

> **NOTE** *You can read the JavaServer Pages 2.3 specification document on the JSP specification page at* `http://download.oracle.com/otndocs/jcp/jsp-2_3-mrel2-spec/`.

## Trying Out the Implicit Variables

Now that you understand the available implicit variables and their purposes, you should explore this more by writing some JSP code that uses the implicit variables. In your project, create a `greeting.jsp` file in the web root, and place the following code in it (or just use the Hello-User-JSP project):

```
<%@ page contentType="text/html;charset=UTF-8" language="java" %>
<%!
    private static final String DEFAULT_USER = "Guest";
%>
<%
    String user = request.getParameter("user");
    if(user == null)
        user = DEFAULT_USER;
%>
<!DOCTYPE html>
<html>
    <head>
```

```
            <title>Hello User Application</title>
        </head>
        <body>
            Hello, <%= user %>!<br /><br />
            <form action="greeting.jsp" method="POST">
                Enter your name:<br />
                <input type="text" name="user" /><br />
                <input type="submit" value="Submit" />
            </form>
        </body>
    </html>
```

Compare this to the code you wrote in `HelloServlet.java` for the Hello-User project in the previous chapter. There's much less to it, but it accomplishes the same thing. Notice the use of a declaration to define the *`DEFAULT_USER`* variable, a scriptlet to look for the *`user`* request parameter and default it if it is not set, and an *`expression`* to output the value of the user variable. Now compile and debug this code and go to `http://localhost:8080/hello-world/greeting.jsp` in your browser. Try entering a name in the input field and clicking the Submit button — the post variable is detected and used. Now try going to `http://localhost:8080/hello-world/greeting.jsp?user=Allison`, and you should see that the query parameter is also detected and used. You are encouraged to explore the Java code that Tomcat translated your JSP into.

Another thing you did in the Hello-User project was create a Servlet to demonstrate using multiple-value parameters. This, too, can be replicated using JSPs. Create a file in your project web root named `checkboxes.jsp` (or use the Hello-User-JSP project):

```
<%@ page contentType="text/html;charset=UTF-8" language="java" %>
<!DOCTYPE html>
<html>
    <head>
        <title>Hello User Application</title>
    </head>
    <body>
        <form action="checkboxesSubmit.jsp" method="POST">
            Select the fruits you like to eat:<br />
            <input type="checkbox" name="fruit" value="Banana" /> Banana<br />
            <input type="checkbox" name="fruit" value="Apple" /> Apple<br />
            <input type="checkbox" name="fruit" value="Orange" /> Orange<br />
            <input type="checkbox" name="fruit" value="Guava" /> Guava<br />
            <input type="checkbox" name="fruit" value="Kiwi" /> Kiwi<br />
            <input type="submit" value="Submit" />
        </form>
    </body>
</html>
```

This file replicates the output of the `doGet` method in the `MultiValueParameterServlet.java` file from the Hello-User project. Next, create `checkboxesSubmit.jsp` (also in the Hello-User-JSP project):

```
<%@ page contentType="text/html;charset=UTF-8" language="java" %>
<%
    String[] fruits = request.getParameterValues("fruit");
%>
<!DOCTYPE html>
<html>
```

```
    <head>
        <title>Hello User Application</title>
    </head>
    <body>
        <h2>Your Selections</h2>
        <%
            if(fruits == null)
            {
        %>You did not select any fruits.<%
            }
            else
            {
        %><ul><%
                for(String fruit : fruits)
                {
                    out.println("<li>" + fruit + "</li>");
                }
        %></ul><%
            }
        %>
    </body>
</html>
```

This file replicates the logic and output of the `doPost` method from the `MultiValueParameterServlet` class. Notice how the bold code jumps in and out of scriptlets, using Java only where the logic requirements demand and leaving the scriptlets to use straight output instead of writing with the implicit *out* variable. The exception is inside the `for` loop, which demonstrates one use case for the *out* variable. This could have just as easily been replaced with `%><li><%= fruit %></li><%` to accomplish the same thing. Now compile and debug the project and go to `http://localhost:8080/hello-world/checkboxes.jsp` in your browser. You should see a page like that in Figure 4-1. Experiment with different combinations of the check boxes, and verify that it behaves identically to the Hello-User project in Chapter 3. Try replacing the use of *out* in the `for` loop with `%><li><%= fruit %></li><%`. When you recompile and run the project again, the output should not change.

Finally, create a file named `contextParameters.jsp` to explore the use of the *application* implicit variable and the retrieval of context init parameters. Alternatively, use the file already in the Hello-User-JSP project.

```
<%@ page contentType="text/html;charset=UTF-8" language="java" %>
<!DOCTYPE html>
<html>
    <head>
        <title>Hello User Application</title>
    </head>
    <body>
        settingOne: <%= application.getInitParameter("settingOne") %>,
        settingTwo: <%= application.getInitParameter("settingTwo") %>
    </body>
</html>
```

Also, you need to have some context init parameters defined in your deployment descriptor, just like in Chapter 3:

```
<context-param>
    <param-name>settingOne</param-name>
    <param-value>foo</param-value>
</context-param>
<context-param>
    <param-name>settingTwo</param-name>
    <param-value>bar</param-value>
</context-param>
```

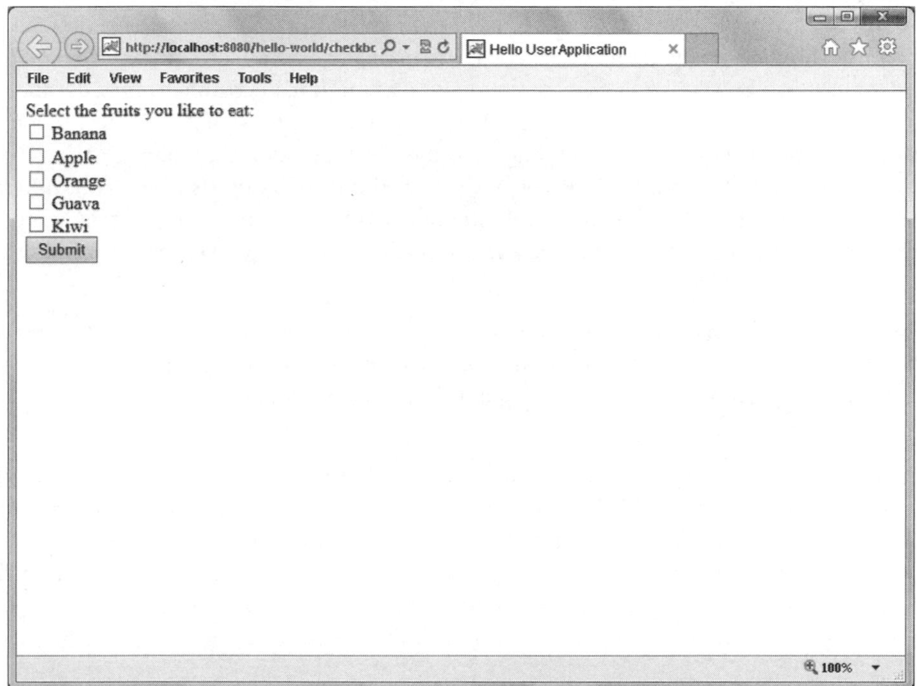


FIGURE 4-1

Now compile, debug, and navigate to `http://localhost:8080/hello-world/contextParameters.jsp`. As with the Servlet-based Hello-User project, you should see the values of the context init parameters.

## Why You Shouldn't Use Java in a JSP

There are plenty of advantages to using Java within a JSP, and in addition to the uses previously pointed out so far in this chapter, you are likely thinking of other uses as you read this paragraph. The coolest thing about using Java in a JSP is that almost anything you can do in a normal Java class you can do in a JSP. However, one of the biggest dangers of using Java in a JSP is that almost anything you can do in a normal Java class you can do in a JSP. These sentences might sound crazy, but it's true. Think about all the things you can do in Java code. Here are a few to help you out.

You could connect to, query, and manipulate a relational database (or NoSQL database, as the case may be). You could also access and write to files on the server file system. You could connect to remote servers, perform REST web service transactions, and interact with system peripherals. You could even do some number crunching, sort a binary tree with one billion nodes, traverse a large data set looking for suspicious data, or search a Document Object Model for a particular set of nodes. Now raise your hand if you think any of these things are good ideas in a JSP.

Java is a powerful language, and the problem with having all that power at your fingertips is that it's so hard not to use it. Depending on the application, any one of those tasks might be tasks you need to perform within a web application. But consider this: In a cleanly structured application, would it be appropriate to put all the database access, file manipulation, and number crunching code in a single class? Probably not. Most likely, you would have several classes that performed specialized functions and then use those classes wherever needed. JavaServer Pages is a technology that was designed for the *presentation layer*, also known as the *view*. Although it's possible to mix database access with the presentation layer, or to mix number crunching with the presentation layer, it is not a good idea. Functional languages, scripting languages, and other languages that execute from the top of a file to the bottom of a file, such as PHP, certainly have their uses. But it's likely you didn't pick Java as your platform of choice so that you could make pages written in this manner. Chances are you picked Java for its elegance, strong typing, and strict object-oriented structure, among other reasons.

Additionally, in most organizations, user interface developers are responsible for creating the presentation layer. These developers rarely have experience writing Java code, and providing them with that ability can be dangerous. Instead, it often makes sense to provide them with a less-powerful set of tools to work with.

In a well-structured, cleanly coded application, the presentation layer is separated from the business logic, which is likewise separated from the data persistence layer. It's actually possible to create JSPs that display dynamic content without a single line of Java inside the JSP. This enables application developers to concentrate on the business and data logic while user interface developers work on the JSPs. You may wonder how this is possible, but you will not be disappointed. You learn the first step in the next section, and explore even more powerful JSP technologies in Chapters 6, 7, and 8.

# COMBINING SERVLETS AND JSPS

For the rest of this chapter you improve the customer support application you began working on in Chapter 3. You can follow along with the examples and find the entire source code in the Customer-Support-v2 project on the `wrox.com` download site. When dealing with complex logic, data validation, data persistence, and a detailed presentation layer, it makes the most sense to use a combination of Servlets and JSPs instead of using exclusively one or the other. In this section, you separate the business logic of customer support from the presentation layer.

## Configuring JSP Properties in the Deployment Descriptor

Earlier in the chapter you learned about the `page` directive and the many attributes it provides to enable you to customize how your JSP is translated, compiled, and processed. If you have many JSPs with similar properties, however, it can be cumbersome to place this `page` directive at the top of every JSP file. Fortunately, there is a way to configure common JSP properties within the deployment descriptor. In the `web.xml` file, which should be empty except for the `<display-name>`, add the following contents:

```
<jsp-config>
    <jsp-property-group>
        <url-pattern>*.jsp</url-pattern>
        <url-pattern>*.jspf</url-pattern>
        <page-encoding>UTF-8</page-encoding>
        <scripting-invalid>false</scripting-invalid>
        <include-prelude>/WEB-INF/jsp/base.jspf</include-prelude>
        <trim-directive-whitespaces>true</trim-directive-whitespaces>
        <default-content-type>text/html</default-content-type>
    </jsp-property-group>
</jsp-config>
```

## Understanding JSP Property Groups

The `<jsp-config>` tag contains any number of `<jsp-property-group>` tags. These property groups are used to differentiate properties for different groups of JSPs. For example, you may want to define one set of common properties for all JSPs in the `/WEB-INF/jsp/admin` folder and a different set of common properties for all the JSPs in the `/WEB-INF/jsp/help` folder. You differentiate these property groups by defining distinct `<url-pattern>` tags for each `<jsp-property-group>`. In the previous code example, the `<url-pattern>` tags indicate that this property group applies to all files ending in `.jsp` and `.jspf`, anywhere in the web application. If you want to treat JSPs in one folder differently from JSPs in another in the fashion mentioned just earlier, you could have two (or more) `<jsp-property-group>` tags, with one having `<url-pattern>/WEB-INF/jsp/admin/*.jsp</url-pattern>` and the other having `<url-pattern>/WEB-INF/jsp/help/*.jsp</url-pattern>`.

Consider some important rules when dealing with the `<url-pattern>` tag:

- If some file in your applications matches a `<url-pattern>` in both a `<servlet-mapping>` and a JSP property group, whichever match is more specific wins. For example, if one matching `<url-pattern>` were `*.jsp` and the other were `/WEB-INF/jsp/admin/*.jsp`, the one with `/WEB-INF/jsp/admin/*.jsp` would win. If the `<url-pattern>` tags are identical, the JSP property group wins over the Servlet mapping.
- If some file matches a `<url-pattern>` in more than one JSP property group, the more specific match wins. If two or more most-specific matches are identical, the first matching JSP property group in the order it appears in the deployment descriptor wins.
- If some file matches a `<url-pattern>` in more than one JSP property group and more than one of those property groups contains `<include-prelude>` or `<include-coda>` rules, the include rules from *all* the JSP property groups are applied for that file, even though only one of the property groups is used for the other properties.

To understand that last bullet point, consider the following hypothetical property groups:

```
<jsp-property-group>
    <url-pattern>*.jsp</url-pattern>
    <url-pattern>*.jspf</url-pattern>
    <page-encoding>UTF-8</page-encoding>
    <include-prelude>/WEB-INF/jsp/base.jspf</include-prelude>
</jsp-property-group>
<jsp-property-group>
    <url-pattern>/WEB-INF/jsp/admin/*.jsp</url-pattern>
    <url-pattern>/WEB-INF/jsp/admin/*.jspf</url-pattern>
```

```
        <page-encoding>ISO-8859-1</page-encoding>
        <include-prelude>/WEB-INF/jsp/admin/include.jspf</include-prelude>
    </jsp-property-group>
```

A file named /WEB-INF/jsp/user.jsp would match only the first property group. It would have a character encoding of UTF-8 and the /WEB-INF/jsp/base.jspf file would be included at the beginning. On the other hand, /WEB-INF/jsp/admin/user.jsp would match both property groups. Because the second property group is a more specific match, this file would have a character encoding of ISO-8859-1. However, both /WEB-INF/jsp/base.jspf *and* /WEB-INF/jsp/admin/include.jspf would be included at the beginning of this file. This can get very confusing, so you are urged to keep your JSP property groups as simple as possible.

## Using JSP Properties

The <include-prelude> tag in the Customer Support project's deployment descriptor tells the container to include the /WEB-INF/jsp/base.jspf file *at the beginning* of every JSP that belongs in this property group. This is useful for defining common variables, tag library declarations, or other resources that should be made available to all JSPs in the group. Similarly, an <include-coda> tag defines a file to be included *at the end* of every JSP in the group. You can use both of these tags more than once in a single JSP group. You might, for example, create header.jspf and footer.jspf files to include at the beginning and end, respectively, of every JSP. These files could contain header and footer HTML content to work as a sort of template for your application. Of course, you must take care when doing this, because you could easily include these files in places you don't intend.

The <page-encoding> tag is identical to the pageEncoding attribute of the page directive. Because JSPs already have a content type of text/html by default, you could simply specify a <page-encoding> of UTF-8 to change the content type character encoding of your JSPs from text/html;ISO-8859-1 to text/html;UTF-8. You could also use the <default-content-type> tag to override text/html with some other default content type.

A particularly useful property is <trim-directive-whitespaces>. This property instructs the JSP translator to remove from the response output any white space only text created by directives, declarations, scriptlets, and other JSP tags. Earlier in this chapter you learned how to chain the end of one directive to the beginning of the next to prevent extra new lines from appearing in the response. This tag takes care of that for you so that you can write cleaner code.

Also mentioned earlier was the possibility to use the deployment descriptor to completely disable Java within JSPs. The <scripting-invalid> tag serves that purpose. The default value and value in your code, false, permits Java in all JSPs in the group. Later in the book you change this value to true. Once true, using Java within a matching JSP results in a translation error. The <el-ignored> tag is similar and corresponds to the isELIgnored attribute of the page directive. If true, expression language is prohibited in the group's JSPs (resulting in a translation error if EL is used). This defaults to false (allow expression language), and you can leave it that.

There are a handful of other JSP property group tags that you will probably never use. <is-xml> indicates that matching JSPs are JSP documents (which you learn about in the next section). The <deferred-syntax-allowed-as-literal> tag is an expression language feature you learn about in Chapter 6. <buffer> corresponds to the buffer attribute of the page directive that you learned about earlier in the chapter. Finally, <error-on-undeclared-namespace> indicates whether an error is raised if a tag with unknown namespace is used within a matching JSP, and defaults to false.

Except for <url-pattern>, all of the tags within <jsp-property-group> are optional, but they must appear in the following order, with unused tags omitted: <url-pattern>, <el-ignored>, <page-encoding>, <scripting-invalid>, <is-xml>, <include-prelude>, <include-coda>, <deferred-syntax-allowed-as-literal>, <trim-directive-whitespace>, <default-content-type>, <buffer>, <error-on-undeclared-namespace>.

In the Customer Support project you have included /WEB-INF/jsp/base.jspf in all JSPs in the application. (The web container is smart enough not to apply this include rule to base.jspf itself.) Its contents are simple:

```
<%@ page import="com.wrox.TicketServlet, com.wrox.Attachment" %>
<%@ taglib prefix="c" uri="http://java.sun.com/jsp/jstl/core" %>
```

This accomplishes two things: It imports these classes for all JSPs and declares the JSTL core tag library with an XMLNS prefix of c. You learn more about the JSTL in Chapter 7. You may wonder why this file is placed in the /WEB-INF/jsp directory instead of in the web root. Remember that files within the WEB-INF directory are protected from web access. Placing the JSP file in this directory prevents users from accessing the JSP from their browser. You would want to do this for any JSP that you do not want browsers to access directly, such as JSPs that rely on session and request attributes provided by a forwarding Servlet and JSPs that are only included.

The last thing you should look at before moving on is the index.jsp file in the web root of the Customer Support project. This is a web application *directory index file*, and its existence in the web root means it can respond to requests for the deployed application root (/) without being directly identified in the URL. It has two simple lines of code in it:

```
<%@ page session="false" %>
<c:redirect url="/tickets" />
```

The second line of code redirects the user to the /tickets Servlet URL relative to the deployed application. The first line of code disables sessions in the index.jsp file to prevent the unnecessary *JSESSIONID* parameter from being automatically appended to the redirect URL (which happens when a session is created and the client is redirected in the same request).

# Forwarding a Request from a Servlet to a JSP

A typical pattern when combining Servlets and JSPs is to have the Servlet accept the request, do any business logic processing and data storage or retrieval necessary, prepare a model that can easily be used in a JSP, and then forward the request to the JSP. The methods in the Customer Support application's TicketServlet need a few changes to make this happen. You can apply these changes yourself or just view them in the project you downloaded.

## Using the Request Dispatcher

You should first address the showTicketForm method because it is the simplest to change. You need to change its signature to also accept an HttpServletRequest and then replace the entire contents with a simple forward to the JSP:

```
private void showTicketForm(HttpServletRequest request,
                            HttpServletResponse response)
        throws ServletException, IOException
{
```

```
        request.getRequestDispatcher("/WEB-INF/jsp/view/ticketForm.jsp")
               .forward(request, response);
    }
```

The new code for this method introduces you to a new feature of the `HttpServletRequest`. The `getRequestDispatcher` method obtains a `javax.servlet.RequestDispatcher`, which handles internal forwards and includes for a specific path (in this case `/WEB-INF/jsp/view/ticketForm.jsp`). With this object, you can forward the current request to that JSP by calling the `forward` method. Note that this is not a redirect: The user's browser does not receive a redirect status code, and the browser URL bar does not change. Instead, the internal request handling is forwarded to a different part of the application. After you call `forward`, your Servlet code should never manipulate the response again. Doing so could result in errors or erratic behavior. Now create the JSP file that this method forwards to (or view it in the project you downloaded):

```
<%@ page session="false" %>
<!DOCTYPE html>
<html>
    <head>
        <title>Customer Support</title>
    </head>
    <body>
        <h2>Create a Ticket</h2>
        <form method="POST" action="tickets" enctype="multipart/form-data">
            <input type="hidden" name="action" value="create"/>
            Your Name<br/>
            <input type="text" name="customerName"><br/><br/>
            Subject<br/>
            <input type="text" name="subject"><br/><br/>
            Body<br/>
            <textarea name="body" rows="5" cols="30"></textarea><br/><br/>
            <b>Attachments</b><br/>
            <input type="file" name="file1"/><br/><br/>
            <input type="submit" value="Submit"/>
        </form>
    </body>
</html>
```

## Designing for the Presentation Layer

This isn't an impressive example because all you've done is copy some code from Java to JSP — not a new thing at this point. You are not using sessions yet, so that has been disabled in the JSP. You should next change the `TicketServlet`'s `viewTicket` method, which is more complicated. A good approach to take is to think of your presentation, first — what data elements does it need to work? — and then code your Servlet method to provide that information. With this in mind, start with the `/WEB-INF/jsp/view/viewTicket.jsp` file:

```
<%@ page session="false" %>
<%
    String ticketId = (String)request.getAttribute("ticketId");
    Ticket ticket = (Ticket)request.getAttribute("ticket");
%>
<!DOCTYPE html>
<html>
    <head>
```

```
        <title>Customer Support</title>
    </head>
    <body>
        <h2>Ticket #<%= ticketId %>: <%= ticket.getSubject() %></h2>
        <i>Customer Name - <%= ticket.getCustomerName() %></i><br /><br />
        <%= ticket.getBody() %><br /><br />
        <%
            if(ticket.getNumberOfAttachments() > 0)
            {
                %>Attachments: <%
                int i = 0;
                for(Attachment a : ticket.getAttachments())
                {
                    if(i++ > 0)
                        out.print(", ");
                    %><a href="<c:url value="/tickets">
                        <c:param name="action" value="download" />
                        <c:param name="ticketId" value="<%= ticketId %>" />
                        <c:param name="attachment" value="<%= a.getName() %>" />
                    </c:url>"><%= a.getName() %></a><%
                }
            }
        %>
        <a href="<c:url value="/tickets" />">Return to list tickets</a>
    </body>
</html>
```

Creating this JSP should show you that the presentation layer needs a *`ticketId`* and a *`ticket`* to display correctly (the code in bold). The `viewTicket` method can be changed to provide these variables and forward the request to the JSP:

```
private void viewTicket(HttpServletRequest request,
                        HttpServletResponse response)
        throws ServletException, IOException
{
    String idString = request.getParameter("ticketId");
    Ticket ticket = this.getTicket(idString, response);
    if(ticket == null)
        return;

    request.setAttribute("ticketId", idString);
    request.setAttribute("ticket", ticket);

    request.getRequestDispatcher("/WEB-INF/jsp/view/viewTicket.jsp")
           .forward(request, response);
}
```

The first few lines of the method perform the business logic of parsing the request parameter and getting the ticket from the database. Then the code in bold adds two attributes to the request. This is the primary purpose of *request attributes*. They can be used to pass data between different elements of the application that are handling the same request, such as between a Servlet and a JSP. Request attributes are different from request parameters: Request attributes are `Objects` while request parameters are `Strings`, and clients cannot pass in attributes like they can parameters. Request attributes exist solely for internal use within your application. If the Servlet places a `Ticket` into a request attribute, the JSP retrieves it as a `Ticket`. During the life of the request, any component of the application that has access to the `HttpServletRequest` instance has access to the request attributes. When the request has completed, the request attributes are discarded.

The last method you need to change is the `listTickets` method. Again, begin by creating the `/WEB-INF/jsp/view/listTickets.jsp` presentation file in the Customer Support application. Because request attributes are `Objects`, you must cast them when you retrieve them. In this case, the cast to a `Map<Integer, Ticket>` is an unchecked operation, so you need to suppress the warning.

```
<%@ page session="false" import="java.util.Map" %>
<%
    @SuppressWarnings("unchecked")
    Map<Integer, Ticket> ticketDatabase =
            (Map<Integer, Ticket>)request.getAttribute("ticketDatabase");
%>
<!DOCTYPE html>
<html>
    <head>
        <title>Customer Support</title>
    </head>
    <body>
        <h2>Tickets</h2>
        <a href="<c:url value="/tickets">
            <c:param name="action" value="create" />
        </c:url>">Create Ticket</a><br /><br />
        <%
            if(ticketDatabase.size() == 0)
            {
                %><i>There are no tickets in the system.</i><%
            }
            else
            {
                for(int id : ticketDatabase.keySet())
                {
                    String idString = Integer.toString(id);
                    Ticket ticket = ticketDatabase.get(id);
                    %>Ticket #<%= idString %>: <a href="<c:url value="/tickets">
                        <c:param name="action" value="view" />
                        <c:param name="ticketId" value="<%= idString %>" />
                    </c:url>"><%= ticket.getSubject() %></a> (customer:
        <%= ticket.getCustomerName() %>)<br /><%
                }
            }
        %>
    </body>
</html>
```

As you can see, this JSP needs the *`ticketDatabase`*, so you should change the `listTickets` method to provide this variable and forward the request:

```
    private void listTickets(HttpServletRequest request,
                             HttpServletResponse response)
            throws ServletException, IOException
    {
```

```
        request.setAttribute("ticketDatabase", this.ticketDatabase);

        request.getRequestDispatcher("/WEB-INF/jsp/view/listTickets.jsp")
               .forward(request, response);
    }
```

## Testing the Updated Customer Support Application

At this point your Servlet code should look much less cluttered. You have moved the presentation code into JSPs and focused on business logic in the Servlet. There are two methods from the previous version of the `TicketServlet`, `writeHeader` and `writeFooter`, that are now unused and can be removed. These made writing presentation code in the Servlet slightly easier, but now you don't need that. Finally, `doGet` and `doPost` had to be updated to reflect the changed signature of the methods they call.

Compile the customer support application and run Tomcat in your IDE debugger. Navigate in your favorite browser to `http://localhost:8080/support/`. You should be redirected to `http://localhost:8080/support/tickets` because of the redirect code in the `index.jsp` file. You should see the page in Figure 4-2. Create a few tickets, uploading attachments with some and not with others; view tickets; and download attachments. Overall, the application should function identically to version 1 created in Chapter 3. However, now that you are no longer writing presentation layer code in Java, it is much easier to improve and expand the application.

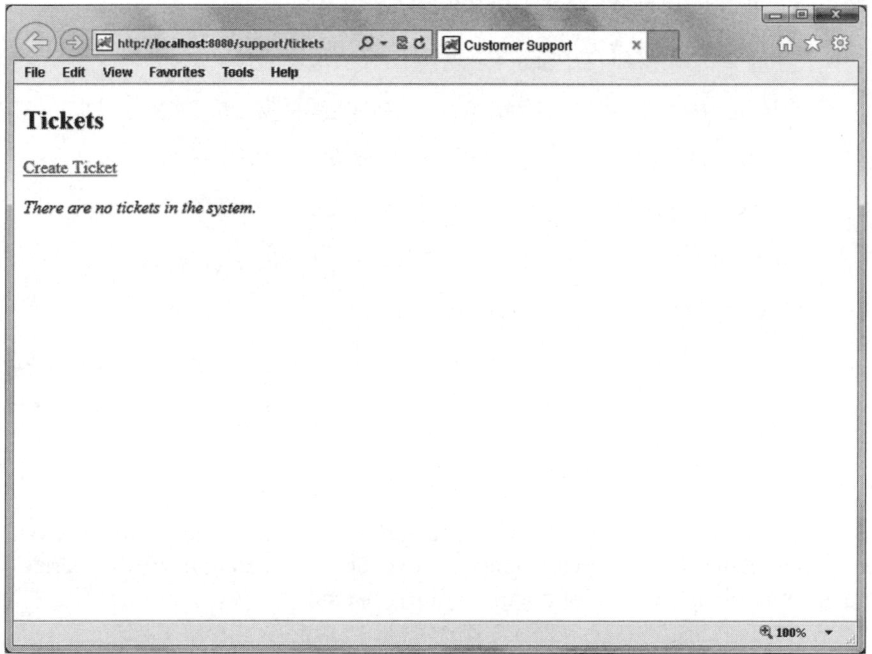


FIGURE 4-2

In the next chapter you continue improving the customer support application by introducing session support and the ability to add comments to support tickets.

# A NOTE ABOUT JSP DOCUMENTS (JSPX)

Earlier in the chapter you saw a passing reference to a technology known as JSP Documents, which end in the `.jspx` extension. They are not as widely used as standard JSPs, and although they support the same features, they do so in different ways. Overall, the increased difficulty and code that comes with using JSP Documents instead of JSPs can be nontrivial, as demonstrated in this section. Also, due to the lesser popularity of JSP Documents, you can find fewer examples and code samples online that use JSP Documents, and it may be harder to find forum and mailing list users with experience in JSP Documents to help you with any questions you might have. For this reason, JSP Documents are not used in this book. Only in this chapter do you see an example of JSP Documents for the purpose of understanding the difference between the two related technologies. Nevertheless, the technology exists in case you prefer working with pure XML.

JSP Documents are XML Documents (hence their name), and therefore many of the features you have seen, such as directives, cannot work the same way. XML Documents must adhere to a strict schema or they will fail to parse correctly. The main advantage to using JSP Documents over standard JSPs is that it's slightly easier to detect problems with the JSPs at compile time instead of run time. However, in many cases this benefit is not worth the added cost of dealing with JSP Documents. Table 4-1 lists several JSP features and compares their JSP syntax to their JSP Document syntax.

**TABLE 4-1:** Comparison of JSP Features and JSP Document Features

| FEATURE | JSP SYNTAX | JSP DOCUMENT SYNTAX |
|---|---|---|
| Page Directive | `<%@ page %>` | `<jsp:directive.page />` |
| Include Directive | `<%@ include %>` | `<jsp:directive.include />` |
| Tag Library Directive | `<%@ taglib %>` | `xmlns:prefix="Library URI"` |
| Declaration | `<%! ... %>` | `<jsp:declaration> ... </jsp:declaration>` |
| Scriptlet | `<% ... %>` | `<jsp:scriptlet> ... </jsp:scriptlet>` |
| Expression | `<%= ... %>` | `<jsp:expression> ... </jsp:expression>` |
| Comment | `<%-- ... --%>` | `<!-- ... -->` |

You should notice two patterns in this table:

- Everything is a `jsp` tag. Directives, declarations, scriptlets, and expressions are all XML tags now, with the `jsp` namespace prefix. The only exception is the tag library directive, which becomes an attribute of the root document tag, instead.
- You no longer differentiate between JSP comments and XML comments. All comments are XML comments. (Of course, inside declarations and scriptlets, you can still use Java comments.)

To demonstrate how this can change a document, consider Listing 4-1. This is a simple JSP file with all the features covered in this chapter. Then, compare that code to Listing 4-2, the JSP

Document-equivalent of Listing 4-1. Notice how the directives, declarations, scriptlets, expressions, and comments all change. Pay particular attention to the XML doctype, the `<jsp:root>` element, and the XMLNS attributes. As you can see, JSPs are noticeably easier to work with than JSP Documents.

**LISTING 4-1: A standard JSP file**

```
<%@ page contentType="text/html;charset=UTF-8" language="java" %>
<%@ include file="/WEB-INF/jsp/base.jspf" %>
<%@ taglib prefix="c" uri="http://java.sun.com/jsp/jstl/core" %>
<%!
    private static final String DEFAULT_USER = "Guest";
%>
<%
    String user = request.getParameter("user");
    if(user == null)
        user = DEFAULT_USER;
%>
<%--<%= "This code is commented" %>--%>
<!DOCTYPE html>
<html>
    <head>
        <title>Hello User Application</title>
    </head>
    <body>
        Hello, <%= user %>!<br /><br />
        <form action="greeting.jsp" method="POST">
            Enter your name:<br />
            <input type="text" name="user" /><br />
            <input type="submit" value="Submit" />
        </form>
    </body>
</html>
```

**LISTING 4-2: The JSP Document-equivalent of Listing 4-1**

```
<?xml version="1.0" encoding="UTF-8"?>
<jsp:root xmlns="http://www.w3.org/1999/xhtml" version="2.0"
          xmlns:jsp="http://java.sun.com/JSP/Page"
          xmlns:c="http://java.sun.com/jsp/jstl/core">
    <jsp:directive.page contentType="text/html;charset=UTF-8" language="java" />
    <jsp:directive.include file="/WEB-INF/jsp/base.jspx" />
    <jsp:declaration>
        private static final String DEFAULT_USER = "Guest";
    </jsp:declaration>
    <jsp:scriptlet>
        String user = request.getParameter("user");
        if(user == null)
            user = DEFAULT_USER;
```

*continues*

**LISTING 4-2** *(continued)*

```
        </jsp:scriptlet>
        <!--<jsp:expression>"This code is commented"</jsp:expression> -->
        <!DOCTYPE html>
        <html>
            <head>
                <title>Hello User Application</title>
            </head>
            <body>
                Hello, <jsp:expression>user</jsp:expression>!<br /><br />
                <form action="greeting.jsp" method="post">
                    Enter your name:<br />
                    <input type="text" name="user" /><br />
                    <input type="submit" value="Submit" />
                </form>
            </body>
        </html>
    </jsp:root>
```

## SUMMARY

In this chapter you explored the world of JSPs and learned how they can make your life easier by simplifying the task of writing HTML markup to the response output. You were introduced to directives, declarations, scriptlets, and expressions. You learned about the various ways you can comment out code in JSPs and about the many ways you can include Java code in a JSP file. You also discovered the nine implicit Java variables available in your JSP and read about why using Java scriptlets and declarations is discouraged. Finally, you applied these principles and improved the Customer Support application by adding JSP properties to the deployment descriptor and separating the business logic in the Servlet from the presentation code in the JSP.

In the next chapter you learn about HTTP sessions, their purpose, and how to use them in Java EE web applications.

# 5

# Maintaining State Using Sessions

## IN THIS CHAPTER

- Why sessions are necessary
- Working with cookies and URL parameters
- How to store data in a session
- Making sessions useful
- How to cluster an application that uses sessions

## WROX.COM CODE DOWNLOADS FOR THIS CHAPTER

You can find the `wrox.com` code downloads for this chapter at `www.wrox.com/go/projavaforwebapps` on the Download Code tab. The code for this chapter is divided into the following major examples:

- Shopping-Cart Project
- Session-Activity Project
- Customer-Support-v3 Project

## NEW MAVEN DEPENDENCIES FOR THIS CHAPTER

There are no new Maven dependencies for this chapter. Continue to use the Maven dependencies introduced in all previous chapters.

# UNDERSTANDING WHY SESSIONS ARE NECESSARY

So far you've learned about web applications, web containers, Servlets, JSPs, and how Servlets and JSPs work together. You have also learned about the life cycle of a request, and it should be clear at this point that the tools you have been introduced to so far do not enable you to associate multiple requests coming from the same client and share data between those requests. You might think that you can use the IP address as a unique identifier and all requests from an IP address within some timeframe must belong to the same client. Unfortunately, due to Network Address Translation (NAT) this is not reliable. Thousands of students at a college campus can literally all use the same IP address, hidden behind a NAT router. For this reason the concept of *HTTP sessions* has achieved nearly universal adoption by all HTTP server-side technologies, and Java EE has session support written into its specification.

Not every application needs sessions. The Hello World examples you've seen in this book certainly don't need sessions. So far the Customer Support application hasn't needed sessions. It has been more like an anonymous message board. But if you think about the requirements Multinational Widget Corporation has for its customer support site, you may quickly realize that at some point you must create user accounts, and those users need to log in to the application. Customer support requests may contain private information, such as server configuration files that other customers shouldn't see. Certainly you need a way to restrict access to certain support tickets so that only the posting customer and members of MWC's support team can access any given ticket. You could have users provide a username and password on every page they access, but it's a fair bet customers aren't going to be happy with that solution.

## Maintaining State

Sessions are used to maintain state between one request and the next. HTTP requests are completely stateless on their own. From the server's perspective, the request begins when the user's web browser opens a socket to the server, and it ends when the server sends the last packet back to the client and closes the connection. At that point there is no longer a link between the user's browser and the server, and when the next connection comes in, there is no way to tie the new request to the previous request.

Applications often cannot function correctly in such a stateless manner. A classic example is the online shopping website. Nearly every online shopping site these days requires you to create a username and password before purchasing, but consider even the few that don't. When browsing the store, you find a product you like, so you add that product to your shopping cart. You continue browsing the store and find another product you like. You add it to your shopping cart as well. When you view your shopping cart, you see that both products you added remain in your shopping cart. Somehow, between every request you made, the website knew those requests were coming from the same browser on the same computer and associated that with your shopping cart. Nobody else can see your shopping cart or the items in it — it is exclusively tied to your computer and browser. This scenario is an analogy to a real-life shopping experience. You enter your favorite grocery store, and as you walk in the door, you grab a shopping cart or basket. (You get a session from the server.) You walk through the store and pick up items as you go, placing them in your cart (adding them to the session). When you get to the cash register, you remove the items from the cart and give them to the cashier, who scans them and takes your money. (You check out using your session.) As you walk out the door, you return your shopping cart or basket. (You close your browser or log out, ending your session.)

In this example, the cart or basket maintains your state as you walk through the store. Without the cart, neither you nor the store could keep up with everything you needed to purchase. If no state were maintained between requests, you would have to "walk in," grab one item, pay for it, "walk out" (end the request), and repeat the entire process again for each item you wanted to purchase. Sessions are the engine behind maintaining state between requests, and without them the web would be a very different place.

### Remembering Users

Another scenario to consider is the user forum website. Almost universally in online forums, users are known by their usernames or "handles." As a user enters the forums, he logs in, providing a username and password to prove his identity. (The merit of username/password authentication as proof of identity is an argument reserved for Chapter 25.) From that point he can add forum threads, respond to threads, participate in private messages with other users, report threads or responses to moderators, and possibly mark threads as favorites. Notice that the user logged in only a single time during that entire timeline. The system needed a way to remember who he was between each request, and sessions provided that.

### Enabling Application Workflow

Often users need some form of workflow to complete a task using an advanced web application. In the case of creating a news article for publication on a news site, for example, the journalist might first go to a screen where she can enter a title, tagline, and body and format the elements appropriately. On the next page she might then select one or more photos associated with the article and indicate how they should be displayed. She might also upload or record some video to be placed in the article. Finally, she would probably be presented with a list of similar articles or a search field to find similar articles so that she could indicate which ones should be placed in a Related Articles box.

After all these steps had been completed, the article would be published. This entire scenario represents the idea of a workflow. The workflow contains many steps in it, each step part of the completion of a single task. To tie all these steps together to complete the workflow, the requests must have state maintained between them. The shopping cart example is actually a subset of the broader idea of workflows.

## USING SESSION COOKIES AND URL REWRITING

Now that you understand the importance of sessions, you are probably wondering how they work. There are two different components to this: first, the generic theory behind web sessions and how they are implemented; and second, the specifics behind the session implementation in Java EE web applications. Both are covered in this section.

In the general theory of web sessions, a session is some file, memory segment, object, or container managed by the server or web application that contains various data elements assigned to it.

These data elements could be a username, a shopping cart, workflow details, and more. The user's browser does not hold or maintain any of this data. It is managed solely by the server or web application code. The only missing piece is a link between this container and the user's browser. For this purpose, sessions are assigned a randomly generated string called a session ID. The first time a session is created (as a result of a request being received), the session ID for that session is conveyed back to the user's browser as part of the response. Every subsequent request from that user's browser includes the session ID in some fashion. When the application receives the request with the session ID, it can then link the existing session to that request. This is demonstrated in Figure 5-1.

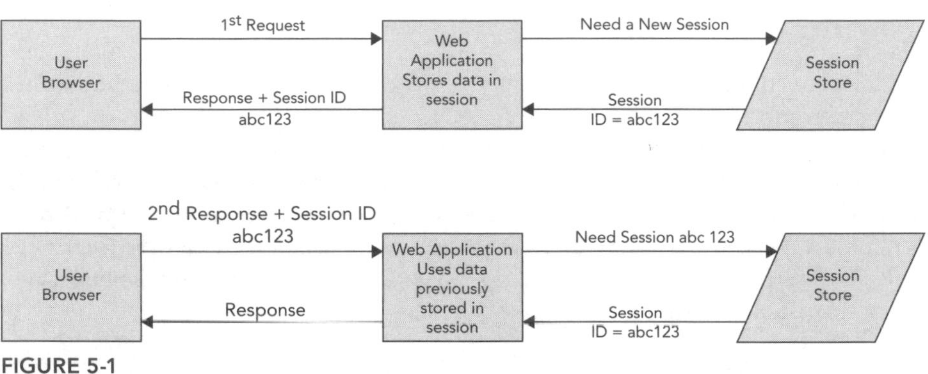


FIGURE 5-1

> **NOTE** *You may wonder why the session ID is random instead of a simple sequential ID. The reason for this is compelling: A sequential ID would be predictable, and a predictable ID would make hijacking other users' sessions trivial.*

The remaining problem to be solved is how the session ID is passed from server to browser and back. There are two techniques used to accomplish this: *session cookies* and *URL rewriting.*

## Understanding the Session Cookie

Fortunately, a solution already exists in HTTP 1.1 that enables servers to send session IDs back to browsers so that the browsers include the session IDs in future requests. This is the technology called HTTP cookies. If you are unfamiliar with cookies, they are essentially a mechanism whereby arbitrary data can be passed from the server to the browser via the `Set-Cookie` response header, stored locally on the user's computer, and then transmitted back from the browser to the server via the `Cookie` request header. Cookies can have various attributes, such as a domain name, a path, an expiration date or maximum age, a secure flag, and an HTTP-only flag.

The `Domain` attribute instructs the browser for which domain names it should send the cookie back, whereas the `Path` attribute enables the cookie to further be restricted to a certain URL relative to the domain. Every time a browser makes a request of any type, it finds all cookies that match the domain and path for the site and sends those cookies along with the request. `Expires` defines an absolute expiration date for the cookie, whereas the mutually exclusive `Max-Age` attribute defines the number of seconds before the cookie expires. If a cookie's expiration date is in the past, the browser deletes it immediately. (This is how you delete a cookie — set its expiration date to the past.) If a cookie does not have an `Expires` or `Max-Age` attribute, it is deleted when the browser is closed. If the `Secure` attribute is present (it does not need to have a value) the browser will send the cookie back only over HTTPS. This protects the cookie from being transmitted unencrypted. Finally, the `HttpOnly` attribute restricts the cookie to direct browser requests. Other technologies, such as JavaScript and Flash, will not have access to the cookie.

Web servers and application servers use cookies to store session IDs on the client side so that they can be transmitted back to the server with each request. With Java EE application servers, the name of this session cookie is `JSESSIONID` by default. Examine the following headers from a series of requests and responses between a client browser and a Java EE web application deployed at `http://www.example.com/support`. This is what you would expect to see if tracing the HTTP requests and responses with a network-stiffing tool like Fiddler or Wireshark.

***REQUEST 1***

```
GET /support HTTP/1.1
Host: www.example.com
```

***RESPONSE 1***

```
HTTP/1.1 302 Moved Temporarily
Location: https://www.example.com/support/login
Set-Cookie: JSESSIONID=NRxclGg2vG7kI4MdlLn; Domain=.example.com; Path=/; HttpOnly
```

***REQUEST 2***

```
GET /support/login HTTP/1.1
Host: www.example.com
Cookie: JSESSIONID=NRxclGg2vG7kI4MdlLn
```

***RESPONSE 2***

```
HTTP/1.1 200 OK
Content-Type: text/html;charset=UTF-8
Content-Length: 21765
```

***REQUEST 3***

```
POST /support/login HTTP/1.1
Host: www.example.com
Cookie: JSESSIONID=NRxclGg2vG7kI4MdlLn
```

***RESPONSE 3***

```
HTTP/1.1 302 Moved Temporarily
Location: http://www.example.com/support/home
Set-Cookie: remusername=Nick; Expires=Wed, 02-Jun-2021 12:15:47 GMT;
    Domain=.example.com; Path=/; HttpOnly
```

***REQUEST 4***

```
GET /support/home HTTP/1.1
Host: www.example.com
Cookie: JSESSIONID=NRxclGg2vG7kI4MdlLn; remusername=Nick
```

***RESPONSE 4***

```
HTTP/1.1 200 OK
Content-Type: text/html;charset=UTF-8
Content-Length: 56823
```

The `Set-Cookie` headers in the responses are used to send cookies to the user's browser for storage. Likewise, the `Cookie` headers in the requests are used to send cookies back to the web server. In this imaginary scenario, the user navigates to some support site and gets redirected to the login page. While redirected, the user's browser also gets a session ID cookie from the server. When the user's browser goes to the login page, it includes the session ID cookie in its request. From then on, each time the browser sends a new request, it includes the `JSESSIONID` cookie. The server does not send it again because it knows the browser already has it.

After a successful login, the server also sends back a *`remusername`* cookie. This is unrelated to the session and in this case represents a technique the site uses to auto-populate the user's username whenever he goes to the login page. Future requests will always contain this cookie; although, future responses do not reset it. Notice that the `JSESSIONID` cookie has no expiration date, whereas the *`remusername`* cookie does. The *`remusername`* cookie will expire in the year 2021 (a long time from now, after which the user will probably have a different computer), whereas the `JSESSIONID` cookie will expire as soon as the user closes his browser.

> **NOTE** *The* `remusername` *cookie is used here simply to demonstrate another use for cookies and how multiple cookies are transmitted in the* `Cookie` *request header. The actual feature — remembering usernames — is not related to this discussion.*

One of the obstacles to using cookies to transmit session IDs is that users can disable cookie support in their browsers, thereby completely eliminating this method of transmitting session IDs. However, over the past decade this has become less and less of a concern, with one major search and e-mail provider and one major social network requiring cookies to be enabled for users of their websites.

## Session IDs in the URL

Another popular method for transmitting session IDs is through URLs. The web or application server knows to look for a particular pattern containing the session ID in the URL and, if found, retrieves the session from the URL. Different technologies use different strategies for embedding and locating session IDs in the URL. For example, PHP uses a query parameter named *`PHPSESSID`*:

```
http://www.example.com/support?PHPSESSID=NRxclGg2vG7kI4MdlLn&foo=bar&high=five
```

Java EE applications use a different approach. The session ID is placed in a matrix parameter in the last path segment (or directory) in the URL. This frees up the query string so that the session ID does not conflict with other parameters in the query string.

```
http://www.example.com/support;JSESSIONID=NRxclGg2vG7kI4MdlLn?foo=bar&high=five
```

The specific technique that a given technology uses is immaterial to the end result: Embed the session ID in the URL and you avoid needing to use cookies. You might wonder, however, how the session ID in a request URL gets to the browser in the first place. A request URL is only effective for conveying the session ID from the browser to the server. So where does the session ID come from? The answer is that the session ID must be embedded in every URL that the application sends back in every response, including links on the page, form actions, and 302 redirects. Consider the previous example of the login scenario using cookies. The following headers demonstrate the same set of transactions using URL embedding instead of cookies:

***REQUEST 1***

```
GET /support HTTP/1.1
Host: www.example.com
```

***RESPONSE 1***

```
HTTP/1.1 302 Moved Temporarily
Location: https://www.example.com/support/login;JSESSIONID=NRxclGg2vG7kI4MdlLn
```

***REQUEST 2***

```
GET /support/login;JSESSIONID=NRxclGg2vG7kI4MdlLn HTTP/1.1
Host: www.example.com
```

***RESPONSE 2***

```
HTTP/1.1 200 OK
Content-Type: text/html;charset=UTF-8
Content-Length: 21796
...
<form action="http://www.example.com/support/login;JSESSIONID=NRxclGg2vG7kI4MdlLn"
      method="post">
...
```

***REQUEST 3***

```
POST /support/login;JSESSIONID=NRxclGg2vG7kI4MdlLn HTTP/1.1
Host: www.example.com
```

***RESPONSE 3***

```
HTTP/1.1 302 Moved Temporarily
Location: http://www.example.com/support/home;JSESSIONID=NRxclGg2vG7kI4MdlLn
```

***REQUEST 4***

```
GET /support/home;JSESSIONID=NRxclGg2vG7kI4MdlLn HTTP/1.1
Host: www.example.com
```

***RESPONSE 4***

```
HTTP/1.1 200 OK
Content-Type: text/html;charset=UTF-8
Content-Length: 56854
...
<a href="http://www.example.com/support/somewhere;JSESSIONID=NRxclGg2vG7kI4MdlLn">
...
```

In this case, notice that the session ID is being returned to the browser via the `Location` header, form action, and link tag. As you can see, the browser is never actually "aware" of the session ID like it is with a session cookie. Instead, the server rewrites the `Location` header URL and the URLs in any response content (links, form actions, and other URLs) so that any URLs the browser uses to access the server already have the session ID embedded in them. The important point about this is that the session ID *must be embedded in the* `Location` *header URL and in every single URL in the markup*. This is no trivial task and can often be downright inconvenient. For this purpose, the Java EE Servlet API comes with a few conveniences that make this simple.

For starters, the `HttpServletResponse` interface defines two methods that rewrite URLs to include embedded session IDs if necessary: `encodeURL` and `encodeRedirectURL`. Any URL that will be placed in a link, form action, or other markup can first be passed to the `encodeURL` method, which returns an appropriately "encoded" version of the URL. Any URL passed to the `sendRedirect` response method can be passed to the `encodeRedirectURL` method, which returns an appropriately "encoded" version of that URL. The word "encoded" here means that the *`JSESSIONID`* matrix parameter will be embedded in the last path segment of the URL only if all four of the following conditions are met:

- A session is active for the current request. (Either it requested a session by passing in a session ID, or the application code created a new session.)
- The `JSESSIONID` cookie was not present in the request.
- The URL is not an absolute URL and is a URL within the same web application.
- Session URL rewriting is enabled in the deployment descriptor (more on this in the section "Storing Data in a Session").

The second condition is the troublesome condition. The only way to detect if a user's browser allows cookies is to set a cookie and then look for that cookie to be returned on the next request. However, you need a session to associate one request with another; otherwise, how would you know whether the request was simply the first request from a different user or a second request from the same user without a cookie? Therefore, the second condition always assumes that the lack of a *`JSESSIONID`* cookie means the user's browser doesn't support cookies, with the understanding that this means URLs will *always* get encoded on the *first* request to a session-enabled application even if the user's browser supports cookies. The unfortunate side effect is that sometimes URLs contain the *`JSESSIONID`* matrix parameter even if the user's browser accepted the `JSESSIONID` cookie.

Of course, the `HttpServletRequest` methods are just part of the toolset available to help you embed session IDs in URLs. The `<c:url>` tag, which is discussed more in Chapter 7, also embeds session IDs in URLs.

## Session Vulnerabilities

As you can imagine, sessions are not without their vulnerabilities, and I would be remiss if I did not warn you about them. The bad news is that these vulnerabilities can cause serious problems for your users, and if you transact sensitive or personal information (such as credit card numbers or healthcare data) it can mean huge penalties for your business. The good news is that there are easy ways to address these vulnerabilities, which you will learn about as well. Of course, I cannot possibly cover all potential vulnerabilities in your applications as there are thousands of ways to compromise web applications. The developer should always be diligent and well informed on matters of security. In mission-critical, sensitive applications, it would be wise to use a commercial scanner of some type that scans your application for weaknesses.

For more information about web application and session vulnerabilities and how to detect and address them, visit the Open Web Application Security Project (OWASP) website (`https://www.owasp.org/`).

## The Copy and Paste Mistake

Perhaps one of the easiest ways a session can be compromised is for an unsuspecting user to copy and paste the URL from his browser into an e-mail, forum posting, chat room, or other public area. Embedding session IDs in URLs, which you read about earlier in this section, is the source of this problem. Remember the URLs passed back and forth between the client and server? Those URLs, session ID and all, appear in the address bar in the client's browser. If the user decides to share a page in your application with his friends and copies and pastes the URL from the address bar, the session ID is included in the URL his friends see. If they go to that URL before the session expires, *they then assume the identity of the user who shared the URL*. The obvious problem with this is that the user's friends might see personal information accidentally.

The more dangerous scenario is that a nefarious character finds the link and uses it to hijack the user's session. He can then change the account e-mail address, obtain a password reset link, and finally change the password — giving the attacker complete control over the user's account and everything in it.

As innocent as the origin of this problem is — a user copying and pasting a URL from his address bar — the only infallible method of addressing this vulnerability is to completely disable embedding session IDs in URLs. Although this may sound like a drastic measure with potentially catastrophic consequences for the usability of your application, remember what was said earlier about how commonplace it has become for major Internet companies to require cookies when using their sites. Cookies have become a fact of life for web users today, and the vulnerabilities inherent in cookies are far less common and dangerous than this one.

## Session Fixation

The *session fixation attack* is similar to the copy-and-paste mistake, except that the "unsuspecting user" in this case is the attacker, and the victims are the users who use a link containing a session ID. An attacker might go to some website known to accept session IDs embedded in the URL. The attacker will obtain a session ID in this manner (either through a URL or by examining the browser's cookies) and then send a URL containing that session ID to a victim, through a forum or (most often) an e-mail. At this point, when the user clicks the link to go to the website, his session ID is fixed to what was in the URL — a session ID the attacker knows about. If the user then logs in to the website during this session, the attacker will also be logged in because he shares the session ID, giving him access to the user's account.

There are two ways to address the issue:

- As with the copy-and-paste mistake, you can simply disable the embedding of session IDs in URLs *and also* disallow your application from accepting session IDs via URLs (something you explore in the section "Storing Data in a Session").
- Employ *session migration* after login. When the user logs in, change the session ID, or copy the session details to a new session and invalidate the original session. (Either method achieves the same thing: assigning a different session ID to the newly "logged in" session.) The attacker still has the original session ID, which is no longer valid and not connected to the user's session.

**WARNING** *There is another type of session fixation attack in which a malicious website writes a session ID cookie using another website's domain name, effectively setting the session ID for the other website in the victim's browser. This attack has the same effect as the URL session fixation attack. However, there is no way for web applications to protect against this vulnerability without disabling sessions altogether. This vulnerability is actually a* browser vulnerability, *not a vulnerability of web applications.*

All *modern browsers have fixed this vulnerability for cross-domain attacks (site* `example.net` *sets a cookie for site* `example.com`*). However, site* `malicious.example.net` *could still set a session cookie for domain* `.example.net`*, which would then be picked up by site* `vulnerable.example.net`*. This problem can be avoided altogether by following a simple rule:* Don't share a domain name with untrusted applications.

## Cross-Site Scripting and Session Hijacking

You have already read about the copy-and-paste mistake which, when exploited by a malicious party, becomes a session fixation attack. There is another form of *session hijacking* that utilizes JavaScript to read the contents of a session cookie. An attacker, who exploits a site's vulnerability to *cross-site scripting attacks*, injects JavaScript into a page to read the contents of a session ID cookie using the JavaScript DOM property `document.cookie`. After the attacker retrieves a session ID from an unsuspecting user, he can then assume that session ID by creating a cookie on his own machine or using URL embedding, thereby assuming the identity of the victim.

The most obvious defense against this attack is to secure your site against cross-site scripting, which is a topic outside the scope of this book (see the previously mentioned OWASP website). However, doing this can be tricky and difficult, and attackers are constantly finding new ways to effect cross-site scripting attacks. An alternative defense, which you should *always* use in conjunction with this, is flagging all your cookies with the `HttpOnly` attribute. This attribute allows the cookie to be used only when the browser makes an HTTP (or HTTPS) request, whether that request happens via link, manual entry of a URL in the address bar, form submission, or AJAX request. More important, `HttpOnly` completely disables the ability of JavaScript, Flash, or some other browser scripting or plugin to obtain the contents of the cookie (or even know of its existence). This stops the cross-site scripting session hijacking attack in its tracks. Session ID cookies should always include the `HttpOnly` attribute.

**NOTE** *Although the* `HttpOnly` *attribute prevents JavaScript from accessing the cookie using the* `document.cookie` *DOM property, AJAX requests originating from JavaScript code* will *still include the session ID cookie because the browser, not the JavaScript code, is responsible for forming the AJAX request headers. This means the server will still be able to associate the AJAX requests with the user's session.*

## Insecure Cookies

The final vulnerability you should consider is the *man-in-the-middle attack* (*MitM attack*), the classic data interception attack whereby an attacker observes a request or response as it travels between the client and server and obtains information from the request or response. This attack gave rise to Secure Sockets Layer and Transport Layer Security (SSL/TLS), the foundation of the HTTPS protocol. Securing your web traffic using HTTPS effectively foils the MitM attack and prevents session ID cookies from being stolen. The problem, however, is that a user might first try to go to your site using HTTP. Even if you redirect them to HTTPS, the damage is already done: Their browser has transmitted the session ID cookie to your server unencrypted, and an observing attacker can steal the session ID.

The `Secure` cookie flag was created to address this very issue. When your server sends the session ID cookie to the client in the response, it sets the `Secure` flag. This tells the browser that the cookie should be transmitted only over HTTPS. From then on, the cookie will only be transmitted encrypted, and attackers cannot intercept it. The drawback is that your site must *always* be behind HTTPS for this to work. Otherwise, as soon as you redirect the user to HTTP, the browser can no longer transmit the cookie and the session will be lost. For this reason, you must weigh the security needs of your application and determine if the data you are protecting is sensitive enough to warrant the performance overhead and hassle of securing every request with HTTPS.

## The Strongest Possible Defense

One final option you should understand when dealing with the security of your sessions is the SSL/TLS Session ID. To improve the efficiency of the SSL protocol by eliminating the need to perform an SSL handshake on every request, the SSL protocol defines its own type of session ID. The *SSL Session ID* is established during the SSL handshake and then used in subsequent requests to tie requests together for determining which keys should be used for encryption and decryption. This very concept duplicates the notion of the HTTP session ID. However, the SSL Session ID is not transmitted or stored using cookies or URLs and is extremely secure. (You can learn more about how the SSL Session ID works by reviewing RFC 2246 "The TLS Protocol.") It is inordinately difficult to obtain an SSL Session ID for which you are not authorized. Some extremely high-security websites, such as those of financial institutions, reuse the SSL Session ID as the HTTP session ID, thereby eliminating cookies *and* URL encoding and still maintaining state between requests.

This is an extremely secure method of establishing a session ID across requests and is nearly invulnerable. Plus, when SSL vulnerabilities are found, they are usually dealt with in a matter of weeks and eliminated by browser updates. However, there are understandably some drawbacks to using this technique; otherwise, everyone would use it. In older versions of the Java EE specification, there was no standard way to specify this, so developers had to use container-specific classes to achieve using SSL Session IDs, and this configuration was sometimes hit-or-miss. In the Java EE 6.0 specification, an option was added (which you learn about in the next section) to easily instruct the web container to use SSL session IDs, so configuration is no longer a major concern (though not many sites are using this yet). In addition, as with the `Secure` cookie flag, it requires that your site *always* be behind HTTPS. If you are concerned enough about security to enable this feature, however, you probably intend for your entire site to always be behind HTTPS, so this will likely not be an issue for you.

Another problem with reusing the SSL Session ID is that the web container must be responsible for the SSL communications. If you use a web server or load balancer to manage your SSL communications — something common in clustered server environments — the web container will not know what the SSL Session ID is. In such a clustered environment, the user's request must also always be routed to the same server. Finally, depending on server and browser, the life of the SSL Session ID can be very long or very short, so it's hard to rely on this as an HTTP session ID replacement.

Now that you have been introduced to sessions, learned about the `JSESSIONID` cookie and URL rewriting, and explored some of the vulnerabilities inherent in sessions and how to address them, it's time to start using sessions in your Java EE applications.

# STORING DATA IN A SESSION

As you learn about using sessions in Java EE, you will be using the Shopping-Cart example project found on the `wrox.com` code download site. You will not create an entire shopping site with payment systems and related features. You will simply explore the concept of using sessions to aggregate data collected across multiple pages (in this case, products added to a shopping cart). You can create the project yourself or follow along in the Shopping-Cart project. Your project should start with the deployment descriptor `<jsp-config>` from Chapter 4 and the following `/WEB-INF/jsp/base.jspf` file:

```
<%@ taglib prefix="c" uri="http://java.sun.com/jsp/jstl/core" %>
```

Also, you should have a simple `index.jsp` file in your web root for redirecting to your store Servlet:

```
<c:redirect url="/shop" />
```

## Configuring Sessions in the Deployment Descriptor

In many cases, HTTP sessions are ready to go in Java EE and require no explicit configuration. However, configure them you can, and for security purposes you should. You configure sessions in the deployment descriptor using the `<session-config>` tag. Within this tag, you can configure the method by which sessions are tracked, the age after which sessions timeout, and the details of the session ID cookie, if you use that. Many of these have default values that you never need to change. The following code demonstrates all the possible deployment descriptor settings for sessions.

```
    <session-config>
        <session-timeout>30</session-timeout>
        <cookie-config>
            <name>JSESSIONID</name>
            <domain>example.org</domain>
            <path>/shop</path>
            <comment><![CDATA[Keeps you logged in. See our privacy policy for
                more information.]]></comment>
            <http-only>true</http-only>
            <secure>false</secure>
            <max-age>1800</max-age>
        </cookie-config>
        <tracking-mode>COOKIE</tracking-mode>
```

```
        <tracking-mode>URL</tracking-mode>
        <tracking-mode>SSL</tracking-mode>
    </session-config>
```

All of the tags within `<session-config>` and `<cookie-config>` are optional, but they must appear in the order shown in this example (excluding omitted tags). The `<session-timeout>` tag specifies how long sessions should remain inactive, in minutes, before being invalidated. If the value is 0 or less, the session never expires. If this tag is omitted, the container default applies. Tomcat's default container is 30, which can be changed in the Tomcat configuration. If you want consistency, you should explicitly set the timeout using this tag. In this example the timeout is 30 minutes. Each time a user with a certain session ID makes a request to your application, the timer resets on his session's inactivity. If he goes more than 30 minutes without making a request, his session is considered invalid and he is given a new session. The `<tracking-mode>` tag, which was added in Servlet 3.0/ Java EE 6, indicates which technique the container should use for tracking session IDs. The legal values are:

- `URL` — The container only embeds session IDs in URLs. It does not use cookies or SSL session IDs. This approach is not very secure.
- `COOKIE` — The container uses session cookies for tracking session IDs. This technique is very secure.
- `SSL` — The container uses SSL Session IDs as HTTP session IDs. This method is the most secure approach available but requires all requests to be HTTPS for it to work properly.

You may use `<tracking-mode>` more than once to tell the container it can use multiple strategies. For example, if you specify both `COOKIE` and `URL`, the container prefers cookies but uses URLs when cookies are not available (as described in the previous section). Specifying `COOKIE` as the only tracking mode tells the container to *never* embed sessions in URLs and always assume the user has cookies enabled. Likewise, specifying `URL` as the only tracking mode tells the container to *never* use cookies. If you enable the `SSL` tracking mode, you cannot also enable the `COOKIE` or `URL` modes. SSL Session IDs must be used on their own; the container cannot fall back to cookies or URLs in the absence of HTTPS.

The `<cookie-config>` tag applies only when `COOKIE` is specified as one of the (or the only) tracking modes. Tags within it customize the session cookies that the container returns to the browser:

- The `<name>` tag enables you to customize the name of the session cookie. The default is *`JSESSIONID`*, and you will probably never need to change that.
- The `<domain>` and `<path>` tags correspond to the `Domain` and `Path` attributes of the cookie. The web container appropriately defaults these for you so that you should usually not need to customize them. The `Domain` defaults to the domain name used to make the request during which the session was created. The `Path` defaults to the deployed application context name.
- The `<comment>` tag adds a `Comment` attribute to the session ID cookie, providing the opportunity to add arbitrary text. This is often used to explain the purpose of the cookie and point users to the site's privacy policy. Whether you use this is entirely up to you. If you omit this tag, the `Comment` attribute is not added to the cookie.

- The `<http-only>` and `<secure>` tags correspond to the `HttpOnly` and `Secure` cookie attributes, and both default to `false`. For increased security you should always customize `<http-only>` to `true`. `<secure>` should be changed to `true` only if you have HTTPS enabled.
- The final tag, `<max-age>`, specifies the `Max-Age` cookie attribute that controls when the cookie expires. By default, the cookie has no expiration date, which means it expires when the browser closes. Setting this to -1 has the same effect. Expiring the cookie when the browser closes is almost always what you want. You customize this value in seconds (unlike `<session-timeout>`, which is in minutes), but doing so could cause the cookie to expire and session tracking to fail while the user is in the middle of actively using your application. It's best to leave this one alone and not use this tag.

> **NOTE** *As of Servlet 3.0/Java EE 6, you can skip the deployment descriptor and configure most of these options programmatically using the* `ServletContext`. *Use the* `setSessionTrackingModes` *method to specify a* `Set` *of one or more* `javax.servlet.SessionTrackingMode` *enum constants.* `getSessionCookieConfig` *returns a* `javax.servlet.SessionCookieConfig` *— use this object to configure any of the* `<cookie-config>` *settings. You can configure the tracking modes or cookie configuration only within a* `ServletContextListener`*'s* `contextInitialized` *method or a* `ServletContainerInitializer`*'s* `onStartup` *method. You learn about listeners in the "Applying Sessions Usefully" section, and* `ServletContainerInitializers` *in Chapter 12. Currently you cannot configure the session timeout programmatically — this oversight should be corrected in Java EE 8.*

Now that you understand the available options, the session configuration for the Shopping-Cart project is as follows:

```
<session-config>
    <session-timeout>30</session-timeout>
    <cookie-config>
        <http-only>true</http-only>
    </cookie-config>
    <tracking-mode>COOKIE</tracking-mode>
</session-config>
```

This causes sessions to last 30 minutes, instructs the container to only use cookies for session tracking and makes session cookies contain the `HttpOnly` attribute for security. It accepts all the other default values and does not specify a comment for the cookie. URL session tracking is disabled because it is not secure. For the rest of the book, you will always use this session configuration.

> **NOTE** *As noted earlier, the most secure approach would be to use SSL Session IDs. A secure compromise uses cookies but sets the cookie* `Secure` *attribute to require HTTPS. This book does not demonstrate either of these techniques because doing so would require generating a self-signed SSL certificate and learning the complexities of configuring SSL in Tomcat. Both of these topics are beyond the scope of this book and can be explored more in the Tomcat documentation.*

## Storing and Retrieving Data

In your project create a Servlet called `com.wrox.StoreServlet` and annotate it as a Servlet with the URL pattern `/shop`. In addition, create a simple map in your Servlet representing a product database. (Or, just use the Shopping-Cart project.)

```
@WebServlet(
        name = "storeServlet",
        urlPatterns = "/shop"
)
public class StoreServlet extends HttpServlet
{
    private final Map<Integer, String> products = new Hashtable<>();

    public StoreServlet()
    {
        this.products.put(1, "Sandpaper");
        this.products.put(2, "Nails");
        this.products.put(3, "Glue");
        this.products.put(4, "Paint");
        this.products.put(5, "Tape");
    }
}
```

You can use this product database to "browse" products and link cart items back to product names.

### Using Sessions in Your Servlets

Create a simple implementation of the `doGet` method supporting three actions: `browse`, `addToCart`, and `viewCart`:

```
    @Override
    protected void doGet(HttpServletRequest request, HttpServletResponse response)
            throws ServletException, IOException
    {
        String action = request.getParameter("action");
        if(action == null)
            action = "browse";

        switch(action)
        {
            case "addToCart":
                this.addToCart(request, response);
                break;

            case "viewCart":
                this.viewCart(request, response);
                break;

            case "browser":
            default:
                this.browse(request, response);
                break;
        }
    }
```

The `browse` and `viewCart` methods of your Servlet should be quite simple, adding a request attribute and forwarding on to a JSP:

```
private void viewCart(HttpServletRequest request, HttpServletResponse response)
        throws ServletException, IOException
{
    request.setAttribute("products", this.products);
    request.getRequestDispatcher("/WEB-INF/jsp/view/viewCart.jsp")
            .forward(request, response);
}

private void browse(HttpServletRequest request, HttpServletResponse response)
        throws ServletException, IOException
{
    request.setAttribute("products", this.products);
    request.getRequestDispatcher("/WEB-INF/jsp/view/browse.jsp")
           .forward(request, response);
}
```

These methods are similar in that they both add the products database to a request attribute, but they forward to different JSPs. Now take a look at the `addToCart` method:

```
private void addToCart(HttpServletRequest request,
                       HttpServletResponse response)
        throws ServletException, IOException
{
    int productId;
    try
    {
        productId = Integer.parseInt(request.getParameter("productId"));
    }
    catch(Exception e)
    {
        response.sendRedirect("shop");
        return;
    }

    HttpSession session = request.getSession();
    if(session.getAttribute("cart") == null)
        session.setAttribute("cart", new Hashtable<Integer, Integer>());

    @SuppressWarnings("unchecked")
    Map<Integer, Integer> cart =
            (Map<Integer, Integer>)session.getAttribute("cart");
    if(!cart.containsKey(productId))
        cart.put(productId, 0);
    cart.put(productId, cart.get(productId) + 1);

    response.sendRedirect("shop?action=viewCart");
}
```

This method is definitely more complicated. First, it gets and parses the product ID for the product being added to the cart. After that the code in bold calls some new session-related methods that you haven't looked at yet. The `getSession` method on `HttpServletRequest` comes in two forms: `getSession()` and `getSession(boolean)`.

A call to `getSession()` calls `getSession(true)`, which returns the existing session if one exists and creates a new session if a session does not already exist. (It never returns `null`.) A call to `getSession(false)`, on the other hand, returns the existing session if one exists and `null` if no session exists. There are reasons for calling `getSession` with an argument of `false` — for example, you may want to test whether a session has already been created — but in most cases you simply call `getSession()`. The `getAttribute` method returns an object stored in the session. It has a counterpart, `getAttributeNames`, which returns an enumeration of the names of all the attributes in the session. The `setAttribute` method binds an object to the session. In this example, the code looks for the *`cart`* attribute, adds it if it does not exist, and then retrieves the simple *`cart`* map from the session. It then looks for the product ID in the cart and adds it with a quantity of zero if it does not exist. Finally, it increments the quantity of that product in the cart.

## Using Sessions in Your JSPs

The Servlet code can handle the logic in your application, but you need some JSPs to display the product list and shopping cart. Start by creating `/WEB-INF/jsp/view/browse.jsp`:

```
<%@ page import="java.util.Map" %>
<!DOCTYPE html>
<html>
    <head>
        <title>Product List</title>
    </head>
    <body>
        <h2>Product List</h2>
        <a href="<c:url value="/shop?action=viewCart" />">View Cart</a><br /><br />
        <%
            @SuppressWarnings("unchecked")
            Map<Integer, String> products =
                    (Map<Integer, String>)request.getAttribute("products");

            for(int id : products.keySet())
            {
                %><a href="<c:url value="/shop">
                    <c:param name="action" value="addToCart" />
                    <c:param name="productId" value="<%= Integer.toString(id) %>"/>
                </c:url>"><%= products.get(id) %></a><br /><%
            }
        %>
    </body>
</html>
```

This JSP has little new in it, and simply lists out all the products. You will explore the `<c:url>` and `<c:param>` tags further in Chapter 7. Clicking a product name adds it to the cart. Next create `/WEB-INF/jsp/view/viewCart.jsp`:

```
<%@ page import="java.util.Map" %>
<!DOCTYPE html>
<html>
    <head>
        <title>View Cart</title>
    </head>
    <body>
```

```
        <h2>View Cart</h2>
        <a href="<c:url value="/shop" />">Product List</a><br /><br />
        <%
            @SuppressWarnings("unchecked")
            Map<Integer, String> products =
                    (Map<Integer, String>)request.getAttribute("products");
            @SuppressWarnings("unchecked")
            Map<Integer, Integer> cart =
                    (Map<Integer, Integer>)session.getAttribute("cart");

            if(cart == null || cart.size() == 0)
                out.println("Your cart is empty.");
            else
            {
                for(int id : cart.keySet())
                {
                    out.println(products.get(id) + " (qty: " + cart.get(id) +
                            ")<br />");
                }
            }
        %>
    </body>
</html>
```

This JSP uses the implicit *session* variable you learned about in Chapter 4 to access the shopping cart `Map` stored in the session. It then lists out all the items in the cart and their quantities. Notice that the `session` attribute of the `page` directive is no longer set to `false` (it defaults to `true`), which enables you to use the *session* variable in the JSP.

## Compiling and Testing

Now that everything is in place, compile your project, and run Tomcat in your IDE debugger.

1. Navigate in your browser to `http://localhost:8080/shopping-cart/` and you see the list of products.
2. Click View Cart to view your cart, which will be empty because you haven't added anything yet.
3. Click Product List to return to the product list and then click a product name to add it to your cart. You should now see the cart, which has the item in it.
4. Return to the product list and add a different product to the cart. Now you should see both items in your cart. The session is successfully storing data between requests.
5. Add another product and also add some of the same products. More products should appear in your cart, and the quantities should increase for products you've added again.

After a while, your cart should look like Figure 5-2.

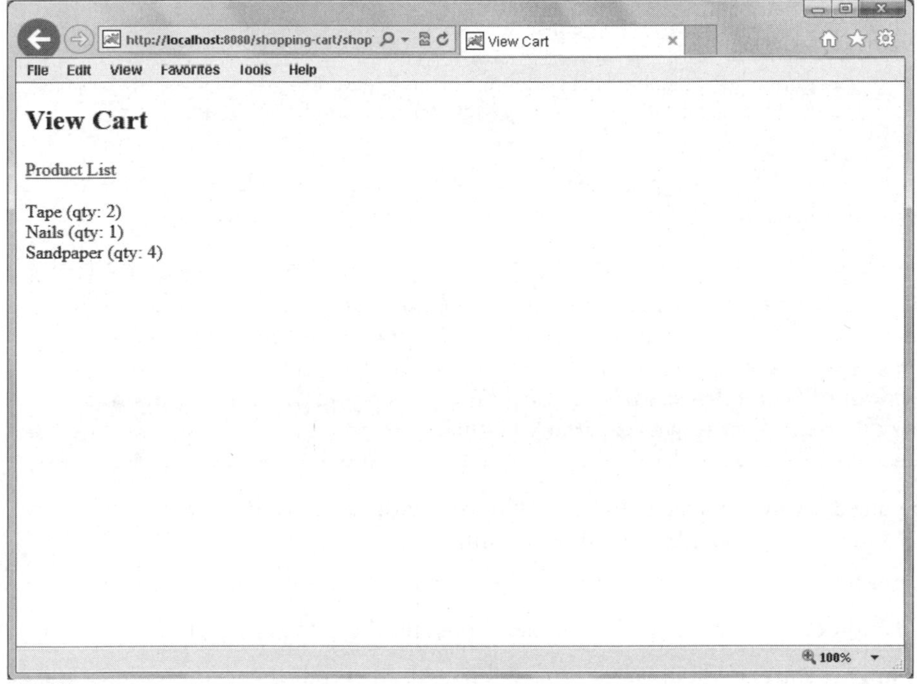


FIGURE 5-2

To further test that the session is working properly, open your application in a different browser, and click View Cart. The cart in the new browser should be empty, whereas the cart in your original browser should still have items in it. This demonstrates that not only is your cart persisting between requests, but also that it belongs *only* to your individual session in that browser. No other users can see it.

The final test is to close and re-open the original browser window that had cart items in it. Now the cart should be empty. This is because your session cookie expired when you closed the browser, and when you went back to your application, you got a new session. The old session, however, sticks around for a while until you undeploy the application or shut down Tomcat, or the session times out due to inactivity. There is no (easy) way to get that session back in your browser.

## Removing Data

So far the session is useful, but you shouldn't have to close and re-open your browser to empty your cart. That's where the `removeAttribute` method of the session comes in.

1. Add a new case to your `doGet` method:

```
case "emptyCart":
    this.emptyCart(request, response);
    break;
```

2. Add the `emptyCart` method implementation:

```
private void emptyCart(HttpServletRequest request,
```

```
                              HttpServletResponse response)
            throws ServletException, IOException
    {
        request.getSession().removeAttribute("cart");
        response.sendRedirect("shop?action=viewCart");
    }
```

As you can see, this is the simplest method in your Servlet. The code removes the *cart* attribute from your session and then redirects you to view your empty cart.

> **NOTE** *It should be pointed out that you could have instead called* `getAttribute` *to retrieve the* `Map` *and then called the* `clear` *method on the* `Map`*. This would also empty the cart and would be slightly more efficient because over time it would lead to fewer garbage collections. However, this example demonstrates the use of the* `removeAttribute` *method.*

3. You now need a way to navigate to the link to empty the cart. Modify `/WEB-INF/jsp/view/viewCart.jsp` and add the following link to it:

   ```
   <a href="<c:url value="/shop?action=emptyCart" />">Empty Cart</a><br /><br />
   ```

4. Compile and debug your application and add some products to your cart.
5. After your cart starts to fill up, click Empty Cart. All the products in your cart should go away, leaving you with an empty cart.

You can do some other things with sessions that you won't experiment with here but that you need to know about. The most obvious thing you might want to do is retrieve the session ID to use for some purpose. Calling the `getId` method on the `HttpSession` object easily accomplishes this. Also there are the `getCreationTime` and `getLastAccessedTime` methods. Although `getCreationTime` obviously returns the time (Unix timestamp in milliseconds) that the session object was created, the `getLastAccessedTime` method can be a bit counterintuitive.

This is not the last time that your code used the session object in some way. Instead, it is the timestamp of the last request that included the session ID for that session in it (URL, cookie, or SSL session) — in other words, the last time the *user* accessed the session. The `isNew` method can be handy: It returns `true` if the session was created during the current request, which means the user's browser has not yet received the session ID.

`getMaxInactiveInterval` returns the maximum time (in seconds) that this session can be inactive (no requests containing the session ID) before it expires. Its counterpart is `setMaxInactiveInterval`, which enables you to change the inactivity window. By default, `getMaxInactiveInterval` returns the value you set in `<session-timeout>`. The `setMaxInactiveInterval` method overrides this configured setting to make it shorter or longer for this specific session.

To understand why you might need to do this, consider an application where certain users (administrators) have a lot of power and can see sensitive information. You might want their

```
            catch(UnknownHostException e)
            {
                e.printStackTrace();
            }
            visits.add(now);
        }

        private void viewSessionActivity(HttpServletRequest request,
                                         HttpServletResponse response)
                throws ServletException, IOException
        {
            request.getRequestDispatcher("/WEB-INF/jsp/view/viewSessionActivity.jsp")
                   .forward(request, response);
        }
    }
```

The final thing to look at in this project is the `/WEB-INF/jsp/view/viewSessionActivity.jsp` file in Listing 5-2. It's less complicated than it looks. All it's doing is displaying all the page visit data accrued in the session in a readable manner. Now to test this, follow these steps:

1. Compile and debug your application and navigate to `http://localhost:8080/session-activity/do/home/` in your browser. You should see some information about your session, an indication that the session is new, and information about the request you just made.
2. Start adding paths and query parameters to the end of the URL. Try different URLs and wait different amounts of time between each request. You can even replace `home/` with something else — just make sure you leave `/do/` in the URL.

After a while, you should start to see something like Figure 5-3 emerge. Your application is tracking request activity and persisting it between requests to display to the user.

**LISTING 5-2: viewSessionActivity.jsp**

```
<%@ page import="java.util.Vector, com.wrox.PageVisit, java.util.Date" %>
<%@ page import="java.text.SimpleDateFormat" %>
<%!
    private static String toString(long timeInterval)
    {
        if(timeInterval < 1_000)
            return "less than one second";
        if(timeInterval < 60_000)
            return (timeInterval / 1_000) + " seconds";
        return "about " + (timeInterval / 60_000) + " minutes";
    }
%>
<%
    SimpleDateFormat f = new SimpleDateFormat("EEE, d MMM yyyy HH:mm:ss Z");
%>
<!DOCTYPE html>
<html>
    <head>
        <title>Session Activity Tracker</title>
    </head>
    <body>
```

*continues*

**LISTING 5-2** *(continued)*

```
        <h2>Session Properties</h2>
        Session ID: <%= session.getId() %><br />
        Session is new: <%= session.isNew() %><br />
        Session created: <%= f.format(new Date(session.getCreationTime()))%><br />

        <h2>Page Activity This Session</h2>
        <%
            @SuppressWarnings("unchecked")
            Vector<PageVisit> visits =
                    (Vector<PageVisit>)session.getAttribute("activity");

            for(PageVisit visit : visits)
            {
                out.print(visit.getRequest());
                if(visit.getIpAddress() != null)
                    out.print(" from IP " + visit.getIpAddress().getHostAddress());
                out.print(" (" + f.format(new Date(visit.getEnteredTimestamp())));
                if(visit.getLeftTimestamp() != null)
                {
                    out.print(", stayed for " + toString(
                            visit.getLeftTimestamp() - visit.getEnteredTimestamp()
                    ));
                }
                out.println(")<br />");
            }
        %>
    </body>
</html>
```

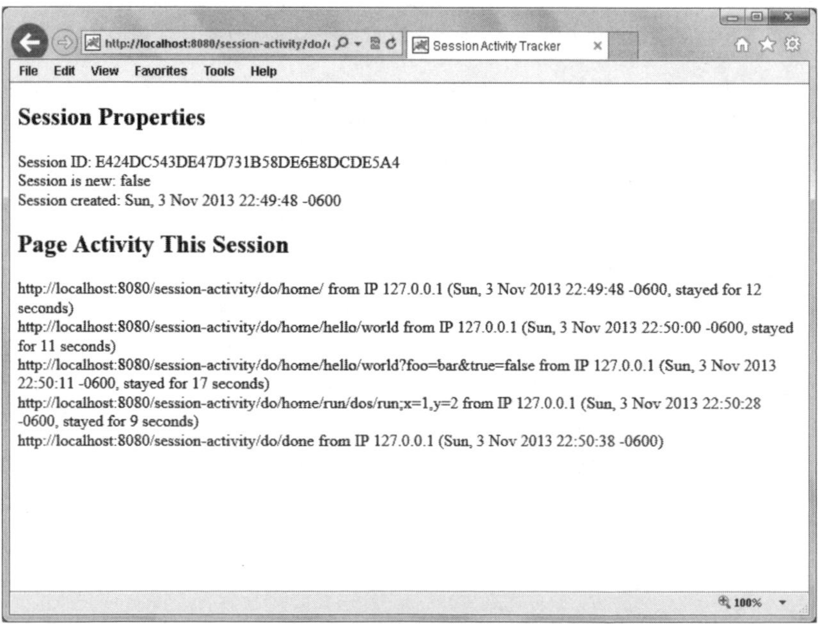


**FIGURE 5-3**

# APPLYING SESSIONS USEFULLY

At this point you should be well acquainted with how sessions work and how to use sessions in Java EE web applications. There are many things you can do with sessions. In addition, some extra tools are available to help you track when sessions are created, destroyed, and updated. You explore those further in this section. For the rest of the chapter, you'll work with the Customer-Support-v3 project found on the `wrox.com` code download site and integrate sessions into the Customer Support application.

## Adding Login to the Customer Support Application

In the last chapter you disabled sessions in the customer support application by adding `session="false"` to the page attributes in all the JSPs. You want to use sessions now, and this can prevent you from doing that, so remove the `session="false"` attribute from all the JSPs in version 3 of the Customer Support application. Remember that this attribute value defaults to `true`, so removing the attribute altogether enables sessions.

You should also add the `<session-config>` XML from the Shopping-Cart application to the deployment descriptor so that sessions are configured for better security and session IDs don't end up in URLs. It should be obvious at this point that the Customer Support application needs some form of user database with logins. In this section, you'll add a very rudimentary, unsecure login capability to your application. In the last part of the book several chapters cover securing your application with a more comprehensive authentication and authorization system, so you can keep it simple for now.

### Setting Up the User Database

Add a `LoginServlet` class to your application and create a static, in-memory user database in it:

```
@WebServlet(
        name = "loginServlet",
        urlPatterns = "/login"
)
public class LoginServlet extends HttpServlet
{
    private static final Map<String, String> userDatabase = new Hashtable<>();

    static {
        userDatabase.put("Nicholas", "password");
        userDatabase.put("Sarah", "drowssap");
        userDatabase.put("Mike", "wordpass");
        userDatabase.put("John", "green");
    }
}
```

As you can see, the user database is a simple map of usernames to passwords without respect to any sort of varying permissions level. Users can either access the system or they can't, and passwords are not stored in a secure manner. The `doGet` method is responsible for displaying the login screen, so create that now.

```
@Override
protected void doGet(HttpServletRequest request, HttpServletResponse response)
        throws ServletException, IOException
{
    HttpSession session = request.getSession();
    if(session.getAttribute("username") != null)
    {
        response.sendRedirect("tickets");
        return;
    }

    request.setAttribute("loginFailed", false);
    request.getRequestDispatcher("/WEB-INF/jsp/view/login.jsp")
           .forward(request, response);
}
```

The first thing the method in the previous example does is check to see if a user is already logged in (a *`username`* attribute exists) and redirect them to the ticket screen if they are. If the user is not logged in, it sets a *`loginFailed`* request attribute to `false` and forwards the request to the login JSP. When the login form on the JSP is submitted, it posts to the `doPost` method:

```
@Override
protected void doPost(HttpServletRequest request, HttpServletResponse response)
        throws ServletException, IOException
{
    HttpSession session = request.getSession();
    if(session.getAttribute("username") != null)
    {
        response.sendRedirect("tickets");
        return;
    }

    String username = request.getParameter("username");
    String password = request.getParameter("password");
    if(username == null || password == null ||
            !LoginServlet.userDatabase.containsKey(username) ||
            !password.equals(LoginServlet.userDatabase.get(username)))
    {
        request.setAttribute("loginFailed", true);
        request.getRequestDispatcher("/WEB-INF/jsp/view/login.jsp")
               .forward(request, response);
    }
    else
    {
        session.setAttribute("username", username);
        request.changeSessionId();
        response.sendRedirect("tickets");
    }
}
```

There's not a lot new in the `doPost` method. It again makes sure that the user isn't already logged in, and then checks the username and password against the "database." If the login failed it sets the *`loginFailed`* request attribute to `true` and sends the user back to the login JSP. If the credentials match, it sets the *`username`* attribute on the session, changes the session ID, and then redirects the user to the ticket screen. The `changeSessionId` method (code in bold) is a new feature in Servlet 3.1 from Java EE 7 that protects against the session fixation attacks you read about earlier in the chapter by migrating the session (changing the session ID).

## Creating the Login Form

Next create `/WEB-INF/jsp/view/login.jsp` and put a login form in it:

```
<!DOCTYPE html>
<html>
    <head>
        <title>Customer Support</title>
    </head>
    <body>
        <h2>Login</h2>
        You must log in to access the customer support site.<br /><br />
        <%
            if(((Boolean)request.getAttribute("loginFailed")))
            {
                %>
        <b>The username or password you entered are not correct. Please try
            again.</b><br /><br />
                <%
            }
        %>
        <form method="POST" action="<c:url value="/login" />">
            Username<br />
            <input type="text" name="username" /><br /><br />
            Password<br />
            <input type="password" name="password" /><br /><br />
            <input type="submit" value="Log In" />
        </form>
    </body>
</html>
```

This simple page writes out a login form to the screen and, using the *`loginFailed`* attribute, notifies users when their login credentials were rejected. Together with the `LoginServlet`, it completes the simple login feature. However, this doesn't stop users from accessing the ticket screens. You need to add a check in the `TicketServlet` to make sure users are logged in before displaying ticket information or letting them post tickets. This is easily accomplished by adding the following code to the top of the `doGet` and `doPost` methods in the `TicketServlet`:

```
        if(request.getSession().getAttribute("username") == null)
        {
            response.sendRedirect("login");
            return;
        }
```

Now that users log in before creating tickets, your code already has access to their names when they create new tickets. This means you don't need the name field on the ticket form anymore. In the `TicketServlet`'s `createTicket` method, change the current code, which sets the ticket's customer name using the request parameter, so that it now uses the username from the session as shown in the following code. You can also remove the "Your Name" (`customerName`) input field from `/WEB-INF/jsp/view/ticketForm.jsp`.

```
ticket.setCustomerName(
        (String)request.getSession().getAttribute("username")
);
```

## Testing the Log In

Now that your application requires logins, follow these steps to test it:

1. Compile the project and debug it using your IDE.
2. Navigate to the application in your browser (`http://localhost:8080/support/`) and you should immediately be taken to the login page.
3. Try logging in with incorrect usernames and passwords (both of which are case-sensitive) and you should be denied entry.
4. Try a valid username and password, and you should land on the list of tickets.
5. Create a few tickets like you did in previous chapters, and your username should be attached to them.
6. Close your browser, re-open it, and log back in using a different username and password.
7. Create another ticket and you can see that the new ticket has the name of the user you're currently logged in as, while the old tickets have the other user's name.

## Adding a Logout Link

When testing, you had to close your browser to log out of the Customer Support application. This may not be desirable and is not the hallmark of an enterprise application. Adding a logout link is trivial enough. First, tweak the code at the top of the `LoginServlet`'s `doGet` method to add support for logging the user out:

```
HttpSession session = request.getSession();
if(request.getParameter("logout") != null)
{
    session.invalidate();
    response.sendRedirect("login");
    return;
}
else if(session.getAttribute("username") != null)
{
    response.sendRedirect("tickets");
    return;
}
```

The only other thing you need to do is add a logout link to the top of the `listTickets.jsp`, `ticketForm.jsp`, and `viewTicket.jsp` files in `/WEB-INF/jsp/view`, just above the `<h2>` headers:

```
<a href="<c:url value="/login?logout" />">Logout</a>
```

Now rebuild and run again, and log in to your application. You should see a logout link on top of every page. Click the logout link and you will return to the login page, indicating that you have successfully been logged out.

## Detecting Changes to Sessions Using Listeners

One of the more useful features of sessions in Java EE is the idea of session events. When changes are made to sessions (for example, session attributes are added or removed), the web container can notify your application of these changes. This is achieved through a form of the publish-and-subscribe model, enabling you to decouple the code in your application that needs to be aware of session changes from the code that makes changes to sessions. This is especially useful if some third-party code — such as Spring Framework or Spring Security — makes changes to sessions in your application because it enables you to detect these changes without changing the third-party code. The tools that you use to detect these changes are called listeners.

Several listeners are defined in the Servlet API and most, though not all of them, listen for some form of session activity. You subscribe to an event by implementing the listener interface corresponding to that event and then (in most cases) either adding a `<listener>` configuration to your deployment descriptor or (as of Servlet 3.0/Java EE 6) annotating the class with `@javax.servlet.annotation.WebListener` (but not both).

You may implement as few or as many listener interfaces as you need in a single class; although of course, you wouldn't want to put code that didn't logically belong together in the same class. When something happens that triggers the publication of an event to which your code is subscribed, the container invokes the method on your class corresponding to that event.

> **NOTE** *Starting in Servlet 3.0/Java EE 6, instead of annotating a listener class with* `@WebListener` *or declaring it in your deployment descriptor you can programmatically register it using* `ServletContext`*'s* `addListener` *method. You can only call this method within a* `ServletContextListener`*'s* `contextInitialized` *method or a* `ServletContainerInitializer`*'s* `onStartup` *method. Of course, any* `ServletContextListener` *you use to do this has to be registered as well (using one of these three approaches). You learn more about* `ServletContainerInitializers` *in Chapter 12.*

One of the listener interfaces you can implement is the `javax.servlet.http.HttpSessionAttributeListener` interface. It has three methods that are notified when session attributes are added, updated (replaced) or removed.

A particularly interesting listener is `javax.servlet.http.HttpSessionBindingListener`. Unlike most other listeners, you do not add deployment descriptor configurations for or annotate `HttpSessionBindingListeners`. If a class implements this interface, it becomes aware of its status as a session attribute. For example, if class `Foo` implements `HttpSessionBindingListener` and you add an instance of `Foo` to an `HttpSession` using `setAttribute`, the container calls that instance's `valueBound` method. Likewise, the container call's the instance's `valueUnbound` method when you remove it from the session using `removeAttribute`.

The two listeners you look at more closely in this section are `HttpSessionListener` and `HttpSessionIdListener` in the `javax.servlet.http` package. Create a `SessionListener` class in your project that implements both of these interfaces and annotate it with `@WebListener` (or follow along in the Customer-Support-v3 project):

```
@WebListener
public class SessionListener implements HttpSessionListener, HttpSessionIdListener
{
...
}
```

`@WebServlet` is not the only way to notify the container that your code is subscribing to these events. You could instead register it programmatically or declare the listener in the deployment descriptor as follows (though the example will stick to the annotation because it is the easiest technique).

```
<listener>
    <listener-class>com.wrox.SessionListener</listener-class>
</listener>
```

The `HttpSessionListener` interface defines the `sessionCreated` and `sessionDestroyed` methods. `sessionCreated`, intuitively, is called whenever a new session is created. `sessionDestroyed` is called whenever something causes the session to no longer be valid. This could be an explicit call to the session's `invalidate` method in code, or it could be an implicit invalidation due to an inactivity timeout. The following code implements these methods:

```
@Override
public void sessionCreated(HttpSessionEvent e)
{
    System.out.println(this.date() + ": Session " + e.getSession().getId() +
            " created.");
}

@Override
public void sessionDestroyed(HttpSessionEvent e)
{
    System.out.println(this.date() + ": Session " + e.getSession().getId() +
            " destroyed.");
}
```

As you can see, you use these events to log when a session is created or destroyed. This is a common use case for this particular listener because often administrators want to log this information in some way for record-keeping purposes. `HttpSessionIdListener` defines only one method, `sessionIdChanged`. This method, called whenever the session ID is changed using the request's `changeSessionId` method, is implemented in the following code:

```
@Override
public void sessionIdChanged(HttpSessionEvent e, String oldSessionId)
{
    System.out.println(this.date() + ": Session ID " + oldSessionId +
            " changed to " + e.getSession().getId());
}
```

All three of these methods use a simple helper method to add a timestamp to the session activity log entries.

```
    private SimpleDateFormat formatter =
            new SimpleDateFormat("EEE, d MMM yyyy HH:mm:ss");
...
```

```
    private String date()
    {
        return this.formatter.format(new Date());
    }
```

Now compile, debug, and navigate to your application. Immediately a logging message should appear in your debug window indicating that a session was created. Log in to the application, and you should observe another logging message that the session ID changed. This is the session fixation protection that you added to the project a few pages ago. Finally, when you log out of the application, two more log entries appear — one indicating that your session was destroyed and another indicating that a new session was created (because you returned to the login page). You now have a mechanism to log session activity in your application.

> **NOTE** *When you first start the debugger but before you open your browser, you may already see a logging message indicating that one or more sessions were destroyed. This is completely normal. Tomcat persists sessions to the filesystem when it is shut down so that the data in them is not lost and then attempts to restore the serialized sessions to memory when Tomcat starts back up. If the persisted sessions expired before Tomcat restored them, Tomcat notifies* `HttpSessionListeners` *that the sessions expired just as if Tomcat was never stopped. This is fairly standard behavior among web containers and can be disabled in most cases, but that is outside the scope of this book. Consult your container's documentation.*

## Maintaining a List of Active Sessions

In addition to logging session activity, you can use the `HttpSessionListener` and `HttpSessionIdListener` to maintain a list of active sessions in the application, something the Servlet API specification does not provide for directly.

To accomplish this, start by creating the `SessionRegistry` class in Listing 5-3. This class is fairly simple. It maintains a static `Map` with session IDs as keys and corresponding session objects as values. This may seem inefficient at first, but remember that these session objects already exist in memory for another purpose. The session objects are not being duplicated; this class simply stores another set of references to them, which is a relatively lightweight thing to do compared to the potential memory footprint of the session objects themselves. Because the class contains only static methods, its constructor is private to prevent instantiation.

**LISTING 5-3: SessionRegistry.java**

```
public final class SessionRegistry
{
    private static final Map<String, HttpSession> SESSIONS = new Hashtable<>();
```

*continues*

**LISTING 5-3** *(continued)*

```
        public static void addSession(HttpSession session)
        {
            SESSIONS.put(session.getId(), session);
        }

        public static void updateSessionId(HttpSession session, String oldSessionId)
        {
            synchronized(SESSIONS)
            {
                SESSIONS.remove(oldSessionId);
                addSession(session);
            }
        }

        public static void removeSession(HttpSession session)
        {
            SESSIONS.remove(session.getId());
        }

        public static List<HttpSession> getAllSessions()
        {
            return new ArrayList<>(SESSIONS.values());
        }

        public static int getNumberOfSessions()
        {
            return SESSIONS.size();
        }

        private SessionRegistry() { }
    }
```

This registry stores references to all the active sessions, but you must add and remove sessions somehow. For that, follow these steps:

1. Expand the `SessionListener` you created earlier. Add the following code to the `sessionCreated` method:

   ```
   SessionRegistry.addSession(e.getSession());
   ```

2. Add the following code to the `sessionDestroyed` method:

   ```
   SessionRegistry.removeSession(e.getSession());
   ```

3. Add the following code to the `sessionIdChanged` method:

   ```
   SessionRegistry.updateSessionId(e.getSession(), oldSessionId);
   ```

Now sessions will be added to and removed from your registry at the appropriate times, but you still need a way to display these sessions. A simple `SessionListServlet` handles the request:

```
@WebServlet(
        name = "sessionListServlet",
        urlPatterns = "/sessions"
)
```

```
public class SessionListServlet extends HttpServlet
{
    @Override
    protected void doGet(HttpServletRequest request, HttpServletResponse response)
            throws ServletException, IOException
    {
        if(request.getSession().getAttribute("username") == null)
        {
            response.sendRedirect("login");
            return;
        }

        request.setAttribute("numberOfSessions",
                SessionRegistry.getNumberOfSessions());
        request.setAttribute("sessionList", SessionRegistry.getAllSessions());
        request.getRequestDispatcher("/WEB-INF/jsp/view/sessions.jsp")
               .forward(request, response);
    }
}
```

The code for `/WEB-INF/jsp/view/sessions.jsp`, which takes care of displaying the sessions, is contained in Listing 5-4.

To test this you need two different Internet browsers (not just two windows of the same browser):

1. Rebuild and debug your application, and open the first browser to the support application URL.
2. After logging in, navigate to `http://localhost:8080/support/sessions`. You should see your current session listed in the list of sessions.
3. Open the second browser, log in to the support application, and navigate to `http://localhost:8080/support/sessions` in that browser as well. You should see a screen similar to the one in Figure 5-4.
4. Reload the first browser you opened, and the new session should appear there too. This means you are successfully maintaining a list of sessions.

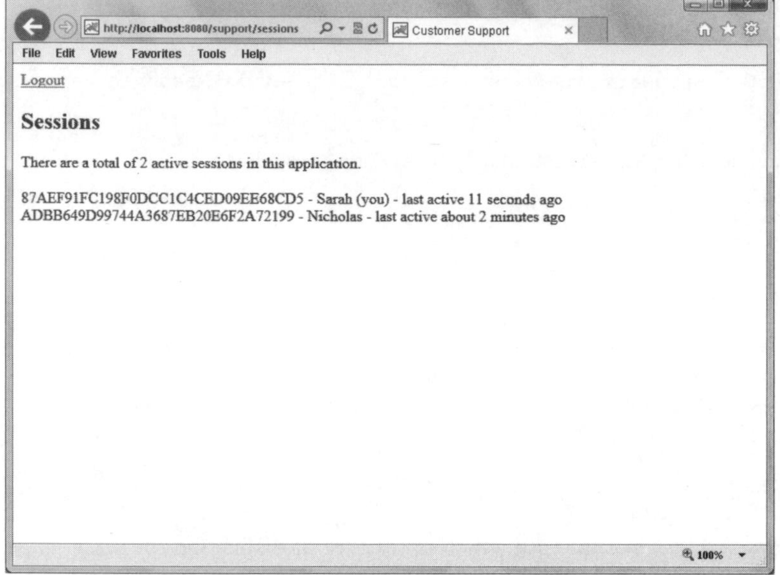


FIGURE 5-4

**LISTING 5-4: sessions.jsp**

```
<%@ page import="java.util.List" %>
<%!
    private static String toString(long timeInterval)
    {
        if(timeInterval < 1_000)
            return "less than one second";
        if(timeInterval < 60_000)
            return (timeInterval / 1_000) + " seconds";
        return "about " + (timeInterval / 60_000) + " minutes";
    }
%>
<%
    int numberOfSessions = (Integer)request.getAttribute("numberOfSessions");
    @SuppressWarnings("unchecked")
    List<HttpSession> sessions =
            (List<HttpSession>)request.getAttribute("sessionList");
%>
<!DOCTYPE html>
<html>
    <head>
        <title>Customer Support</title>
    </head>
    <body>
        <a href="<c:url value="/login?logout" />">Logout</a>
        <h2>Sessions</h2>
        There are a total of <%= numberOfSessions %> active sessions in this
        application.<br /><br />
        <%
            long timestamp = System.currentTimeMillis();
            for(HttpSession aSession : sessions)
```

```
            {
                out.print(aSession.getId() + " - " +
                        aSession.getAttribute("username"));
                if(aSession.getId().equals(session.getId()))
                    out.print(" (you)");
                out.print(" - last active " +
                        toString(timestamp - aSession.getLastAccessedTime()));
                out.println(" ago<br />");
            }
        %>
    </body>
</html>
```

> **NOTE** *The sessions listed in this example are only the ones in the currently running instance of Tomcat. If your application was deployed to multiple Tomcat instances, you would see different sessions listed, depending on which Tomcat instance your request to the application landed on, because the page would still list only sessions on that particular Tomcat instance. The solution to this problem involves properly configuring your application for clustering and setting up session replication in your container. These topics are explored in the next section.*

# CLUSTERING AN APPLICATION THAT USES SESSIONS

In the time you spend working with enterprise applications, you will undoubtedly come across the need to cluster an application. Clustering provides several advantages, notably adding redundancy and scalability to your application. Properly clustered applications can suffer failures or even endure routine maintenance without end users ever experiencing downtime. In a very well-managed environment, administrators can even roll out upgrades to applications without causing downtime. As you can tell, clustering is an invaluable member of the web application toolset.

Clustering does not come without its downsides, however, and there are challenges that must be overcome. One of the biggest of these challenges is the passing of messages between instances of an application running on separate machines, sometimes even on disparate or disconnected networks or in different regions of the world. For decades engineers have been re-imagining and redesigning cluster messaging systems, constantly searching for that "perfect" messaging framework that is stable, reliable, and fast. Advanced Message Queuing Protocol (AMQP), Java Message Service (JMS), and Microsoft Message Queuing (MSMQ) are three competing technologies that have emerged as a result. Of course, there are other challenges with application clustering than just messaging, and the one you look at in this section is managing sessions in a cluster.

Understanding this section requires you to have some basic knowledge of what load balancing is, how it works, and what some of the common load balancing strategies are. These are topics that would require considerable time to discuss and are outside the scope of this book.

## Using Session IDs in a Cluster

The immediate problem you might see with session clustering is that sessions exist as objects in memory and as such only reside on a single instance of a web container. In a purely round-robin or load-smart load balancing scenario, two consecutive requests from the same client may go to different web containers. The first web container instance would assign a session ID to the first request it received, and then when the next request came in to a different instance of the web container, the second instance would not recognize the session ID and would create and assign a new session ID. At this point, sessions would be useless.

One solution to this problem is to employee sticky sessions. The idea of sticky sessions is that the load balancing mechanism is session-aware and always sends a request from the same session to the same server. This can be accomplished in a number of ways and depends largely on the load balancing technology. For example, the load balancer may be made aware of the web container's session cookie and know that it is a session cookie, therefore using it as a mechanism for determining when requests should go to the same server. Or some load balancers can add their own session cookies to responses and recognize those cookies in subsequent requests. (Yes, a single request can belong to many different sessions, as long as the session cookie names or session ID transmission techniques are all different.)

A potential downside to both of these techniques is that the web container cannot use SSL/HTTPS because that would prevent the load balancer from inspecting or modifying requests or responses. However, many load balancers support handling the encryption and decryption of HTTPS traffic, so you haven't really made your application less secure; you've just moved the encryption mechanism from the server to the load balancer. (Some organizations even prefer this setup, but remember that it prevents you from using SSL Session IDs as your HTTP session IDs.) Finally, some load balancers use a combination of source and destination IP addresses to determine when to send multiple requests to the same server, but this can be troublesome for the same reason that using IP addresses to establish HTTP sessions is a bad idea.

The most common load balancing approach administrators of a Tomcat environment take is to use an Apache HTTPD or Microsoft IIS web server to load balance requests between Apache Tomcat instances. The Apache Tomcat Connector (`http://tomcat.apache.org/connectors-doc/`) provides a mechanism for interfacing these web servers with Tomcat. The connector's mod_jk component is an Apache HTTPD module that forwards requests to Tomcat and provides sticky sessions capability using Tomcat's session IDs. Likewise, isapi_redirect is the IIS connector that provides the same capability when using IIS. As load increases even more, you can set up a dumb round-robin load balancer to balance requests between multiple HTTPD or IIS web servers.

This multi-layer approach, demonstrated in Figure 5-5, can achieve extremely high performance and availability while maintaining session affinity. The connector (mod_jk or isapi_redirect) uses a Tomcat concept known as the session ID *jvmroute* to determine which Tomcat instance to send each request to. Consider the following session ID:

```
AA64E92624FFEA976C4148DF5BC6BA03
```

In a load-balanced environment with multiple Tomcat instances, each Tomcat instance would have a jvmroute configured in the `<Connector>` element in Tomcat's `conf/server.xml` configuration file. That jvmroute is appended to the end of all session IDs. In a cluster with three Tomcat instances having jvmroutes `tcin01`, `tcin02` and `tcin03`, that same session ID would instead look like this if the session originated on instance `tcin02`:

```
AA64E92624FFEA976C4148DF5BC6BA03.tcin02
```

From then on the web server connector (mod_jk or isapi_redirect) would recognize that this session belonged to Tomcat instance `tcin02` and would always send requests in that session to that instance. If your application were secured with HTTPS, the web server would have to be in charge of certificates and encryption/decryption for this to work. The advantage of using mod_jk or isapi_redirect for this is that they have access to the SSL Session ID and re-transmit that ID to Tomcat, allowing SSL session tracking to work properly. This exact sticky-session load balancing approach also works with GlassFish behind Apache HTTPD/mod_jk and IIS/isapi_redirect.

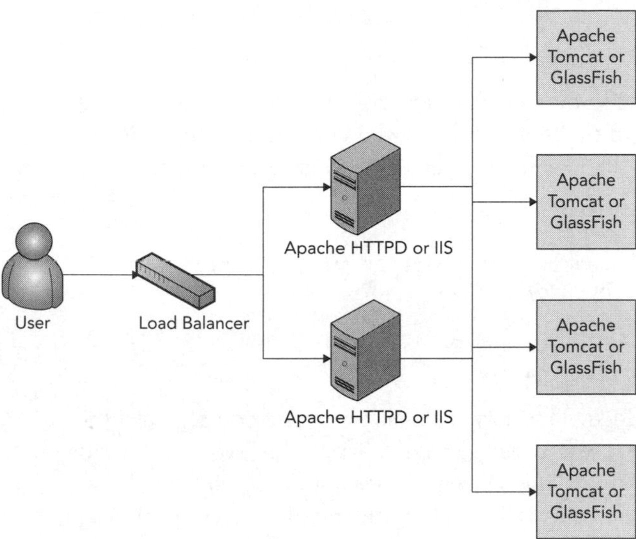


**FIGURE 5-5**

The exact details of configuring mod_jk, isapi_redirect, and Tomcat's and GlassFish's jvmroute are outside the scope of this book and vary from one version to the next. Consult the Tomcat and GlassFish documentation for instructions. WebLogic, WebSphere, and other containers offer similar but ultimately different approaches that are covered in detail in their documentation as well.

## Understand Session Replication and Failover

The major problem with using sticky sessions is that it may support scalability, but it does not support high availability. If the Tomcat instance that created a particular session goes down, the session is lost and the user must log in again. Even worse, the user could potentially lose unsaved work. For this purpose sessions can be replicated throughout the cluster so that all sessions are available to all web container instances regardless of the instances from which they originated. Enabling session replication in your application is easy to accomplish. You just need to add the `<distributable>` tag to the deployment descriptor:

```
<distributable />
```

That's all there is to it. There are no attributes, nested tags, or content for this tag. The presence of this in the deployment descriptor tells the web container to replicate sessions across the cluster, if one exists. When a session is created in one instance, it is replicated to the other instances. If a session attribute is changed, that session is re-replicated to the other instances so that they have the latest version of the session.

Of course, it isn't *actually* this simple. For instance, this only *marks* your application as supporting distributable sessions. It does not configure your web container's session replication mechanism (which is a complex topic not discussed in this book). It also does not automatically mean your application follows best practices. You must be careful which session attributes you set (if they are not `Serializable`, an `IllegalArgumentException` is thrown when you call `setAttribute`) and how you update those session attributes. Consider this code snippet from the Shopping-Cart project:

```
@SuppressWarnings("unchecked")
Map<Integer, Integer> cart =
        (Map<Integer, Integer>)session.getAttribute("cart");
if(!cart.containsKey(productId))
    cart.put(productId, 0);
cart.put(productId, cart.get(productId) + 1);
```

The web container does not (and cannot) know that the Map containing the cart items has changed in this way. Because of this, the change to the session will not be replicated, which means that other container instances cannot know about the new item in the cart. This can be addressed simply:

```
@SuppressWarnings("unchecked")
Map<Integer, Integer> cart =
        (Map<Integer, Integer>)session.getAttribute("cart");
if(!cart.containsKey(productId))
    cart.put(productId, 0);
cart.put(productId, cart.get(productId) + 1);
session.setAttribute("cart", cart);
```

Notice the code in bold that has been added. This may seem silly because you replaced the `cart` session attribute with the same object that was already assigned to it. However, calling this method tells the container that the session has changed and causes the session to be replicated again. Any time you change an object assigned to a session attribute, you must call `setAttribute` again to ensure the change is replicated.

There is also a listener associated with the concept of session replication. Any objects added to sessions as attributes can implement the `javax.servlet.http.HttpSessionActivationListener` interface. When a session is about to be serialized to replicate to other servers, the `sessionWillPassivate` method is called, giving the object bound to the session an opportunity to perform some action first. When the session is deserialized in another container, the `sessionDidActivate` method is called to notify the attribute that it has been deserialized.

One final note: Sticky sessions and session replication are not mutually exclusive concepts. Often the two are combined to achieve session failover — sessions are still replicated, but requests in the same session are sent to the same instance until that instance fails, at which point the requests are sent to a different instance that already knows about the session. You can use several techniques to increase the efficiency of your application using sticky session failover, but they are outside the scope of this book. The documentation for your web container should describe the replication features it supports and how to use them.

## SUMMARY

In this chapter you have been introduced to the concept of sessions and how sessions are established between the client and server. You learned about some of the many potential security vulnerabilities associated with sessions and how each of them can be addressed, and you also learned about the most secure session ID transmission method of all: using the SSL session ID. You explored employing sessions in Java EE using a shopping cart application and added login support to the Customer Support application. You also discovered how to detect changes to sessions and used that to establish a registry of sessions within your application. Finally, you were introduced to the concepts behind clustering sessions and learned about some of the challenges and approaches to session clustering. In the next three chapters, you explore some technologies that make working with JSPs easier than ever before and help you get rid of Java within JSPs for good.

# Using the Expression Language in JSPs

## IN THIS CHAPTER

- All about Expression Language
- How to write with the EL syntax
- How to use scoped variables in EL expressions
- How to access collections with Java 8 streams in EL expressions
- Switching out Java code with Expression Language

## WROX.COM CODE DOWNLOADS FOR THIS CHAPTER

You can find the `wrox.com` code downloads for this chapter at `www.wrox.com/go/projavaforwebapps` on the Download Code tab. The code for this chapter is divided into the following major examples:

- User-Profile Project
- Customer-Support-v4 Project

## NEW MAVEN DEPENDENCIES FOR THIS CHAPTER

In addition to Maven dependencies introduced in previous chapters, you also need the following Maven dependency:

```
<dependency>
    <groupId>javax.el</groupId>
    <artifactId>javax.el-api</artifactId>
    <version>3.0.0</version>
    <scope>provided</scope>
</dependency>
```

# UNDERSTANDING EXPRESSION LANGUAGE

Up to this point, you have used Java to output dynamic content from your JSPs. However, recall that Chapter 4 covers how the use of declarations, scriptlets, and expressions is discouraged. Not only does this provide a great deal of power (sometimes too much) to your JSPs, but it also makes writing JSPs difficult for UI developers with little or no Java background. There must be an easier way to display data and perform simple operations than using Java code. You might think that the `<jsp>` tags could provide a solution, and indeed these tags can be used to replace certain Java operations. However, these tags are clunky and awkward to use. What's needed is something easily read, familiar to both Java developers and UI developers, and with a simple set of rules and operators to make data access and manipulation easier.

## What It's For

Expression Language (EL) was originally developed as part of the JSP Java Standard Tag Library (JSTL), something you learn about in the next chapter, to support the rendering of data on JSP pages without the use of scriptlets, declarations, or expressions. It was inspired by and largely based on the ECMAScript (the foundation of JavaScript) and XPath languages. At the time it was referred to as the Simplest Possible Expression Language (SPEL) but later shortened to Expression Language. EL was part of the JSTL 1.0 specification that came out with JSP 1.2 and could be used only in attributes of JSTL tags. In JSP 2.0 and JSTL 1.1 the EL specification (due to its popularity) was moved from the JSTL specification to the JSP specification and became available for use anywhere in a JSP, not just within JSTL tag attributes.

While this was happening, work had commenced on JavaServer Faces, built on JSP 1.2 as an alternative to plain JSP. JSF also needed its own expression language. However, there were several drawbacks to reusing the EL as it existed for JSPs. For one, JSF needed to control the evaluation of expressions to certain points of the JSF life cycle. An expression might need to be evaluated during page rendering but also during a postback to the JSF page. In addition, JSF needed better support for method expressions than the EL offered. As a result, two separate but extremely similar expression languages formed — one for JSP 2.0 and one for JSF 1.0.

Obviously having two separate Java expression languages was not ideal, so when work began on the JSP 2.1 specification, an effort was underway to merge the JSP 2.0 Expression Language with the JSF 1.1 Expression Language. The result was the Java Unified Expression Language (JUEL) for JSP 2.1 and JSF 1.2.

Despite being shared by JSP and JSF, EL did not get its own JSR but continued to be a part of the JSP specification, although it did have its own specification document and JAR artifact. This remained the case for EL in JSP 2.2. EL continues to expand and improve, and as of Java EE 7 it was moved into its own JSR (JSR 341) and updated to support lambda expressions and an equivalent of the Java 8 Collections Stream API, marking Java Unified Expression Language 3.0 (or EL 3.0 for short). EL 3.0 was released with Java EE 7, Servlet 3.1, JSP 2.3, and JSF 2.2 in 2013. In this chapter you explore EL 3.0 as it pertains to JSPs, learning about JSF-related features only where pertinent comparisons can be made. Most of the chapter centers on syntax, and where features that are new to EL 3.0 are demonstrated, this is indicated.

## Understanding the Base Syntax

The base syntax for EL delineates expressions that require evaluation from the rest of the JSP page syntax. The JSP interpreter must detect when an EL expression begins and ends so that it can parse and evaluate the expression separately from the rest of the page. There are two different types of the base EL syntax: *immediate evaluation* and *deferred evaluation*.

### Immediate Evaluation

Immediate evaluation EL expressions are those that the JSP engine should parse and evaluate at the time of page rendering. This means that as the JSP code is being executed from top to bottom, the EL expression is evaluated as soon as the JSP engine comes across it and before the execution of the rest of the page continues. EL expressions that should be immediately evaluated look like the following example, where `expr` is a valid EL expression.

```
${expr}
```

The dollar sign and opening and closing brackets define the boundaries of the EL expression. Everything inside the brackets gets evaluated as an EL expression. More important, this means that you can't use this syntax for any other purpose in your JSPs; otherwise, it will get evaluated as an EL expression and could result in an EL syntax error. If you ever needed to write something with this syntax out to the response, you would need to escape the dollar sign:

```
\${not an EL expression}
```

The backslash before the dollar sign indicates to the JSP engine that this is not, in fact, an EL expression and should not be evaluated. The previous example would have literally been written to the response as `${not an EL expression}`. You could also have used the dollar sign XML entity `$` instead of `\$` and it would have resulted in the same outcome.

```
&#36;{not an EL expression}
```

Although the JSP engine would also ignore this, many find using the backslash easier. It's simply a matter of personal preference. Of course, you might legitimately need to put a backslash before an expression that you do, actually, want evaluated. This *requires* the use of the backslash XML entity:

```
&#92;${EL expression to evaluate}
```

In this case, the EL expression will be evaluated and rendered after the backslash.

### Deferred Evaluation

Deferred evaluation EL expressions are a part of the Unified Expression Language that primarily supports the needs of JavaServer Faces. Although the deferred syntax is legal in JSPs, it is not normally seen in JSPs. Deferred syntax looks nearly identical to immediate syntax, again where `expr` is a valid EL expression:

```
#{expr}
```

In JSF, deferred expressions can be evaluated either when the page is rendered or during a postback to the page, or possibly even both. The specifics of this are not pertinent to this book, but you must understand that this is different from JSP, which does not have a sense of life cycles that JSF has. In JSP, the `#{}` deferred syntax, which is only valid in JSP tag attributes, can be used to defer the evaluation of the EL expression until later in the rendering process *of the tag*. Instead of the EL expression being evaluated before the attribute value is bound to the tag (like it would be with `${}`), the tag attribute gets a reference to the unevaluated EL expression. The tag can then later invoke a method to evaluate the EL expression when it's appropriate. This can be useful and is explored more in Chapter 8, but it is rarely used.

One potential problem with deferred syntax is that some templating languages and JavaScript frameworks use the `#{}` syntax for substitutions. Because of this, if you use these substitutions, you would normally have to escape them so that they aren't confused with deferred evaluation EL expressions:

```
\#{not an EL expression}
&#35;{also not an EL expression}
```

However, this may not work for some frameworks that utilize this syntax, and it can be a real pain if you need to use this often or if you have a lot of existing JSPs that need to work with EL 2.1 or higher. (Also, the XML entity isn't compatible with JavaScript.) Because of this, there is another option for preventing a `#{}` literal from being evaluated as a deferred expression. Within the `<jsp-config>` section of the deployment descriptor, you can add the following tag to any `<jsp-property-group>`:

```
<deferred-syntax-allowed-as-literal>true</deferred-syntax-allowed-as-literal>
```

This permits the `#{}` syntax to be used in a literal manner and prevents you from having to escape the hash tag in this case. If you need to control this for individual JSPs, you can use the `deferredSyntaxAllowedAsLiteral="true"` attribute of the `page` directive in any JSP, instead.

For the remainder of this book, you will only see immediate evaluation EL syntax in example code and you will not use deferred evaluation EL syntax, with one exception. In the Chapter 8 discussion on custom tag and function libraries, you'll explore the `<deferred-value>` and `<deferred-method>` options when defining custom tags. This also necessitates demonstrating the deferred syntax.

## Placing EL Expressions

Simply put, EL expressions can be used just about anywhere in a JSP, with a few minor exceptions. To start, EL expressions cannot be used within any directives, so don't even try it. Directives (`<%@ page %>`, `<%@ include %>`, and `<%@ taglib %>`) are evaluated when the JSP is compiled, but EL expressions are evaluated later when the JSP is rendered, so it cannot work. Also, EL expressions are not valid within JSP declarations (`<%! %>`), scriptlets (`<% %>`), or expressions (`<%= %>`). If used within any of these, an EL expression will simply be ignored or, worse, could result in a syntax error.

Other than that, EL expressions can be placed just about anywhere. One place you might see EL expressions is within simple literal text written to the screen:

```
The user will see ${expr} text and will know that ${expr} is good.
```

This example includes two EL expressions that, when evaluated, are placed inline with the text that displays. If the first expression evaluated to "red" and the second expression evaluated to "it," the user would see the following:

```
The user will see red text and will know that it is good.
```

In addition, expressions can be used within standard HTML tag attributes as in the following example.

```
<input type="text" name="something" value="${expr}" />
```

HTML tag attributes are not the only place that EL expressions are allowed. You can also use them in JSP tag attributes, as demonstrated with the following code.

```
<c:url value="/something/${expr}/${expr}" />
<c:redirect url="${expr}" />
```

As you can see, EL expressions do not have to make up the entire attribute value. Instead, any one or more parts of the attribute value can include EL expressions. You might wonder about other HTML features, such as JavaScript or Cascading Style Sheets. The JSP engine does not parse things of this nature and writes them out to the response as if they were literal text, so these, also, may contain EL expressions in either quoted or literal form:

```
<script type="text/javascript" lang="javascript">
    var employeeName = '${expr}';
    var booleanValue = ${expr};
    var numericValue = ${expr};
</script>
<style type="text/css">
    span.error {
        color: ${expr};
        background-image: url('/some/place/${expr}.png');
    }
</style>
```

So far you have learned about the different types of EL expressions and where EL expressions can be placed, but you may wonder what exactly `expr` looks like. In the next section you learn about what you can put within an EL expression.

## WRITING WITH THE EL SYNTAX

EL expressions, like any other language, have a specific syntax. Like Java, JavaScript, and most other languages, that syntax is strict, and violating it will result in syntax errors when your JSP is rendered. Unlike Java, however, EL syntax is loosely typed and has many implicit type conversions built in, similar to languages like PHP or JavaScript. The primary rule for an expression is that it should evaluate to some value. You cannot declare variables within an expression or perform some kind of assignment or operation that does not result in a value. (For example, `${object.method()}` is only valid if `method` has a non-`void` return type.) EL is not designed to replace Java; instead, it is designed to provide you with the tools you need to create JSPs without Java.

> **NOTE** *Although you cannot* declare *variables within an EL expression, you can* assign *variables as of the EL 3.0 specification. Using the standard assignment operator* `=`*, you can assign* `A = B` *within an expression as long as* `B` *is some value that can be written out to the page. So, the expression* `${x = 5}` *will result in assigning* `5` *to* `x` *and also in rendering* `5` *in place of the EL expression.*

## Reserved Keywords

As with any other language, one of the first things you should know about EL is its list of reserved keywords. These are words that should be used only for their prescribed purpose. Variables, properties, and methods should have names equal to these reserved words.

- `true`
- `false`
- `null`
- `instanceof`
- `empty`
- `div`
- `mod`
- `and`
- `or`
- `not`
- `eq`
- `ne`
- `lt`
- `gt`
- `le`
- `ge`

You'll recognize the first four words as also being Java reserved keywords. You can use these in the same manner you would use their counterparts in Java. The `empty` keyword is used to validate whether some `Collection`, `Map`, or array contains any values, or whether some `String` has a length of one or more characters. If any of these are `null` or "empty," the expression evaluates to `true`; otherwise, it evaluates to `false`.

```
${empty x}
```

The `div` and `mod` keywords map to the Java mathematical operations divide (`/`) and modulus (`%`), respectively, and are merely alternatives to the mathematical symbols. You can still use `/` and `%` if you prefer. The `and`, `or`, and `not` keywords map to the Java logical operators `&&`, `||`, and `!`, respectively. As with the mathematical operators, you can still use traditional logical operators if you prefer. Finally, the `eq`, `ne`, `lt`, `gt`, `le`, and `ge` operators are alternatives to the Java relational operators `==`, `!=`, `<`, `>`, `<=`, and `>=`, respectively, which can also still be used if you prefer.

## Operator Precedence

Just like with other languages, all the previous operators, together with other operators in the EL, have an order of precedence that is important to understand. This order is mostly intuitive and not dissimilar from operator precedence in Java. More important, as with Java and arithmetic equations, operators of equal precedence are considered in the order they appear in an expression, from left to right.

The first operators evaluated in an EL expression are the bracket `[]` and dot (`.`) resolution operators. Consider the following expression:

```
${myCollection["key"].memberName["anotherKey"]}
```

The engine first resolves the value mapped to *key* in the `myCollection` object. It then resolves the `memberName` method, field, or property within the *key* value found in `myCollection`. Finally, it locates the *anotherKey* value within the value that `memberName` evaluates to. After these operators are considered, the grouping parentheses operators `()` are considered. These operators are used to change the precedence of other operators, just as they are in Java or arithmetic equations.

The third set of operators considered includes the unary negative sign (-), `not`, `!`, and `empty`. Next, the EL engine evaluates the arithmetic operators multiply (`*`), divide (`/`), and `div`, and modulus (`%`) and `mod`, which are followed by the addition (`+`) and binary subtraction (-) operators, just like they are ordered in mathematical equations. After this the EL string concatenation operator `+=` (new to EL 3.0) is evaluated. Next, it evaluates the comparison relational operators `<` (or `lt`), `>` (or `gt`), `<=` (or `le`), and `>=` (or `ge`), followed by the equality relational operators `==` (or `eq`) and `!=` (or `ne`). After this, it evaluates all the `&&` and `and` operators from left to right, then all the `||` and `or` operators from left to right, and then all the `?` and `:` conditional operators from left to right.

The next thing that the EL engine evaluates is the lambda expression operator (`->`), new in the EL 3.0 specification. This has the same syntactic and semantic purpose as the Java 8 lambda expression operator. However, you do not need to be running on Java 8 for EL lambda expressions to be valid. After this, the EL engine evaluates the assignment `=` operator, which was also added in the EL 3.0 specification. This operator assigns the value of some expression on the right side of the operator to the variable on the left side of the operator. The resulting value of the expression is then the value of the variable on the left side of the operator. Consider the following expression.

```
${x = y + 3}
```

Now assume that, at execution time, the value of *y* is 4. The result of the expression `y + 3` is 7, thus 7 is assigned to *x*. Because the resulting value of the expression is *x*, the value of `${x = y + 3}` is 7.

The final operator that the EL engine evaluates is the semicolon (`;`) operator, also a new feature in EL 3.0. This operator mimics the comma (`,`) operator in C, allowing the specification of several expressions with the values of all but the last expression being discarded. To understand this, refer to the following expression.

```
${x = y + 3; object.callMethod(x); 'Hello, World!'}
```

This combination EL expression has four expressions within it.

- The expression `y + 3` is evaluated, resulting in 7 assuming *y* is 4.
- That value is assigned to *x*.

- The `callMethod` method is invoked on the `object` variable and passed `x` (7) as its argument.
- The string literal "Hello, World!" is evaluated. The result of this expression is the result of the expression after the last semicolon only: "Hello, World!"

The results of the `x = y + 3` expression and the `object.callMethod(x)` expression are discarded. This is especially useful to assign some value to an EL variable and then include that value in some other part of the expression instead of just outputting the value.

To help you keep all this straight, the following list summarizes the order of precedence from top (highest) to bottom (lowest) with only the symbols and none of the clutter. Remember that operators with the same precedence are evaluated in the order they appear in an expression, from left to right.

```
[], .
()
unary -, !, not, empty
*, /, div, %, mod
+ math, binary -
+= string
<, lt, >, gt, <=, le, >=, ge
==, eq, !=, ne
&&, and
||, or
?, :
->
=
;
```

> **NOTE** *In Java, you test for equality between objects using the* `equals` *method. For example, to test if two Strings were equal, you would use* `"Hello".equals("Hello")`, *not* `"Hello" == "Hello"`. *The latter tests that the two references are the same instance, not that the two objects are equal. However, in EL expressions you use the* `==` *or* `eq` *operators to test for object equality instead of calling the* `equals` *method. (There is no equivalent for testing if two references are the same in EL.) Likewise, you use* `!=` *or* `ne` *instead of* `!"Hello".equals("Hello")`.
>
> *The use of the relational comparison operators* `<`, `lt`, `>`, `gt`, `<=`, `le`, `>=`, *and* `ge` *is similar to the equality operators. Any two objects that implement the* `java.lang.Comparable` *interface can be compared with comparison operators as long as the types are the same or one can be coerced to the other. So,* `${o1 >= o2}` *and* `${o1 ge o2}` *in EL are equivalent to* `o1.compareTo(o2) >= 0` *in Java, and* `${o1 < o2}` *and* `${o1 lt o2}` *are equivalent to* `o1.compareTo(o2) < 0`.

## Literal Values

The Unified Expression Language has a support for specifying literal values with a specific syntax. You have already seen the `true`, `false`, and `null` keywords, which are all literal values.

In addition, EL can have string literal values. Unlike Java, where string literals are always surrounded by double quotes, string literals in EL can be surrounded by *either* double *or* single quotes, similar to PHP and JavaScript. So, both of the expressions in the following example are valid.

```
${"This string will be rendered on the user's screen."}
${'This string will also be "rendered" on the screen.'}
```

As you can see, there are advantages and disadvantages to using either type of string literal, and in many cases you will simply use the one that's easiest for the particular case. If some string has a single quote within it, it's probably easiest to use double quotes for the literal. Similarly, if the string has a double quote in it, it's probably easiest to use a single quote literal.

One thing you must be careful about, however, is using EL expression string literals within JSP tag attributes. Because these are both evaluated by the JSP engine, the quotes surrounding an attribute value and the quotes surrounding a string literal conflict. Thus, both of the EL expression attribute values in the following example are invalid and result in syntax errors:

```
<c:url value="${"value"}" />
<c:url value='${'value'}' />
```

There are two valid ways to address this conflict. You can either use opposite quote types for the attribute and literal, or you can escape the literal quotes. All four lines of code in the following example are valid.

```
<c:url value="${'value'}" />
<c:url value='${"value"}' />
<c:url value="${\"value\"}" />
<c:url value='${\'value\'}' />
```

Generally, you will find it is easier to simply use opposite quotes instead of escaping. But what if your string literal itself contains a single or double quote and you need to put the expression in an attribute value? There's no way around it at this point. You must escape *something*. The six lines of code in the following example are all valid ways of dealing with this.

```
<c:url value="${'some \"value\"'}" />
<c:url value='${"some \"value\""}' />
<c:url value="${'some \'value\''}" />
<c:url value='${"some \'value\'"}' />
<c:url value="${\"some 'value'\"}" />
<c:url value='${\'some "value"\'}' />
```

Need to mix and match single and double quotes within a string literal that exists within an attribute value? This is where things start to get hairy:

```
<c:url value="${'some attribute\'s \"value\"'}" />
<c:url value='${"some \"attribute\" \'value\'"}' />
```

As you can tell, this can quickly spiral out of control. Where possible, it's best to keep your string literals simple. The last thing to note about string literals is that, as of Expression Language 3.0 in Java EE 7, you can concatenate string literals within EL expressions somewhat like you do within Java. All three lines in the following example are equivalent and result in the same output.

```
The user will see ${expr} text and will ${expr}.
${'The user will see ' += expr += " text and will " += expr += '.'}
${"The user will see " += expr += ' text and will ' += expr += "."}
```

If *expr* results in some object that is not a `String`, it will be coerced to a `String` by calling the `toString` method on that object.

Numeric literals in EL are simplified over those in Java, and you can even perform arithmetic between certain objects that you could not in Java. Consider the following three integer-type numeric literals:

```
${105}
${-132147483648}
${139223372036854775807}
```

- The first literal is an implicit `int` and is treated like one when the expression is evaluated.
- The second literal is too large to be an `int`. In Java, this would be a syntax error unless you appended an `L` to the end of the number to indicate it was a `long`, but in EL it simply becomes a `long` implicitly.
- The third literal is too large to even be a `long`, so it is treated as a `BigInteger` implicitly.

All these conversions happen under the hood without your involvement. Then there are the decimal types:

```
${105.509}
${34000000000000000000000000000000000000001.0}
${1.79769313486231570e+309}
```

Similar to the integer types, these literals are an implicit `float`, `double`, and `BigDecimal`, respectively. It should be noted that although the default literal decimal type in Java is `double`, the default decimal type in EL is `float` unless a larger precision is required. Keep this in mind when you work with EL expressions. You cannot explicitly specify the literal type — it is always handled implicitly.

EL expressions make mathematical operations much easier because all type conversions and precision upgrades are implicit and because the arithmetic operators can be used on `BigInteger` and `BigDecimal` types. Consider the following expression, which adds two numbers and returns the resulting value:

```
${12 + 1.79769313486231570e+309}
```

The number on the left side of the addition operator is an `int`, whereas the number on the right side is an implicit `BigDecimal`. To do this in Java would normally require the following code:

```
new BigDecimal(12).add(new BigDecimal("1.79769313486231570e+309"));
```

However, the EL engine takes care of everything for you. First, it coerces `12` from an `int` to a `BigDecimal`; then it turns the addition operator into a call to the `add` method.

> **NOTE** *In Java, numbers can be expressed as standard (base-10, `83`) literals, octal (base-8, `0123`) literals, hexadecimal (base-16, `0x53`) literals, or binary (base-2, `0b01010011`) literals. In EL expressions, only base-10 literals are permitted. There is no equivalent for literals in the other bases. Also, while underscores are permitted within numeric literals (`1_491_188`, `0b0101_0011`) in Java to make it easier to distinguish groups of numbers in a literal (as a replacement for commas, for example), this is not permitted in EL expressions. Number literals must be contiguous.*

Three other primitive literals to consider are `char`s, `byte`s, and `short`s. You do not normally need to use these data types in EL expressions, but it is possible that some method you might call in an EL expression could expect a `char`, `byte`, or `short` as an argument. EL does not contain specific literals for these types but will coerce other literals into `char`s, `byte`s, and `short`s when necessary.

For `char`s, a `null`, `''` string literal, or `""` string literal will be coerced into the null byte character (`0x00`). A single-character string literal (single or double quote) will be coerced into its equivalent `char`. An integer-type number will also be coerced into a `char` as long as its value is between 0 and 65,535. Any other type, any multicharacter string, or any number outside the range of 0 and 65,535 will result in an error.

Any integer-type number will also be coerced into a `byte` or `short` when necessary, as long as the number does not extend beyond the range of the `byte` or `short` it is being coerced to. Otherwise, the attempted coercion will result in an error.

The final literal type is not a primitive but rather a literal for creating various collections. Collection literals construction is a feature proposed as an improvement to the Java Collections API in Java 8 that did not make the final feature cut and instead was deferred to Java 9 (for now). It did make it into Expression Language 3.0, however. You can create a collection within an EL expression whenever needed. The syntax is rather intuitive, is quite similar to syntaxes in JavaScript and other languages, and is in line with the proposed syntax for Java 9. You can construct `Set`s, `List`s, and `Map`s with EL collection literals, and they will all be constructed as instances of the default implementations. A literal `Set` will become a `HashSet<Object>`, a literal `List` will become an `ArrayList<Object>`, and a literal `Map` will become a `HashMap<Object, Object>`. Consider first the `Set` literal:

```
{1, 2, 'three', 4.00, x}
```

This constructs a `HashSet<Object>` with five elements of varying types. The fifth object, `x`, could be anything. Commas separate elements in the literal `Set`. You might need to create a `Set`, for example, to pass in as an argument to a method call:

```
${someObject.someMethod({1, 2, 'three', 4.00, x})}
```

Constructing a `List` is nearly identical to constructing a `Set` except that it uses brackets instead of braces, and it works exactly the same as arrays in JavaScript/JSON:

```
[1, 2, 'three', [x, y], {'foo', 'bar'}]
```

Notice that the fourth element of this `ArrayList<Object>` is another `List`, and the fifth element is a `Set`. You can nest collection literals in this manner to insert collection objects into other collection objects. As with `Set`s, elements in `List`s are separated with commas.

The final collection literal, which creates a `HashMap<Object, Object>`, is identical to the object literal syntax in JavaScript and JSON:

```
{'one': 1, 2: 'two', 'key': x, 'list': [1, 2, 3]}
```

Elements here, too, are separated with commas. However, `Map`s are more complicated because they require keys mapped to values instead of just values. So each element in this literal is a pair of objects separated by a colon, with the object on the left of the colon being the key and the object on the right of the colon being the value. The *`list`* key in this literal is mapped to a `List` object with values 1, 2, and 3.

## Object Properties and Methods

EL provides a simplified syntax for accessing properties in JavaBeans in addition to the standard syntax you are used to for accessing public accessor methods. You cannot access public fields from EL expressions. Consider a class named `Shirt` with a public field named *`size`*. Assuming a variable name of *`shirt`*, you might think that you could access *`size`* with the following EL expression:

```
${shirt.size}
```

However, this is not allowed. When the EL engine sees this syntax, it is looking for a property on *`shirt`*, not a field. But what is a property? Consider an altered `Shirt` where *`size`* is a properly encapsulated private field with standard JavaBean accessor and mutator methods `getSize` and `setSize`. Now the expression `shirt.size` becomes a shortcut for calling `shirt.getSize()`. This can work for any field of any type. As long as it has a standard JavaBean accessor method, it can be accessed in this way. If `Shirt` had a field named *`styleCategory`* with an accessor `getStyleCategory`, it could be accessed with `shirt.styleCategory`. For `boolean` fields (and only `boolean` fields) the accessor can start with either `get` or `is`. So for a field named *`expired`* with either a `getExpired` or `isExpired` accessor, you could access the field with `shirt.expired`.

This is not the only technique that you can use to access properties within a JavaBean. In the spirit of the ECMAScript and XPath languages, you can also access properties using the `[]` operator. The following expressions also access the *`size`*, *`styleCategory`*, and *`expired`* properties using the `getSize`, `getStyleCategory`, and `getExpired` or `isExpired` methods, respectively.

```
${shirt["size"]}
${shirt["styleCategory"]}
${shirt["expired"]}
```

In earlier versions of EL, you could access only JavaBeans properties. You could not call methods on objects. However, EL 2.1 added the ability to call object methods in JSPs. So, you could get the size of a `Shirt` with `${shirt.getSize()}` instead of `${shirt.size}`, but why would you? The latter is certainly easier. Method invocation mostly comes in handy when a value-returning method also requires some input.

Suppose you had an immutable class ComplexNumber that represents mathematical complex numbers (combination of a real number and an imaginary number in the form a + b*i*). That class would undoubtedly have a plus method that enables you to add some other number to it. (Possibly that method is overloaded so that you could add an integer, a double, or another ComplexNumber.) You can call the plus method and pass in an argument, and the resulting ComplexNumber would be the value of the expression:

```
${complex.plus(12)}
```

In this example, the toString method is implicitly called on the resulting ComplexNumber so that the string representation of the ComplexNumber is rendered. However, suppose you wanted the *i* in the string representation to be properly italicized so that it looks like a proper mathematical representation of a complex number. You might have a toHtmlString method on the ComplexNumber class to achieve this. You can thus render it like so:

```
${complex.plus(12).toHtmlString()}
```

These are chained method calls identical to the way you would perform this operation in standard Java code.

## EL Functions

In EL, a function is a special tool mapped to a static method on a class. Like schema-compliant XML tags, functions are mapped to a namespace. The overall syntax of a function call is as follows, where [ns] is the namespace, [fn] is the function name, and [a1] through [a*n*] are arguments:

```
${[ns]:[fn]([a1[, a2[, a3[, ...]]]])}
```

Functions are defined within Tag Library Descriptors (TLDs), which may sound strange because functions are not tags. This is a carryover from the earliest days of EL when it was part of the Java Standard Tag Library (JSTL) specification and EL could be used only within JSP tag attributes. Because the TLD concept already supported the idea of namespaces, it made sense for EL function definitions to remain within TLDs.

You learn more about TLDs and defining tags and functions in Chapter 8. However, there is already a set of functions defined in the JSTL that meet many of the needs developers have within JSPs today. All the functions deal with strings in some way — trimming, searching, joining, splitting, escaping, and more. By convention, the JSTL function library has a namespace of fn; however, you may make it whatever you like in the taglib directive. You experiment with using EL functions in the next section, but here are some of the more common JSTL EL functions and what they do.

- ${fn:contains(String, String)} — This function tests whether the first string contains one or more instances of the second string and returns true if it does.
- ${fn:escapeXml(String)} — If a string you are outputting could contain special characters, you can use this function to escape those special characters. < becomes <, > becomes >, & becomes &, and " becomes ". This is an especially important tool in the prevention of cross-site scripting (XSS) attacks.

- `${fn:join(String[], String)}` — This function joins an array of strings together using the specified string as a delimiter. For example, this could be useful for comma-separating an array of e-mail addresses together into one string for display on the page.
- `${fn:length(Object)}` — If the argument is a string, this function invokes and returns the result of calling the `length` method on the specified string. If it is a `Collection`, `Map`, or array, it returns the size of that `Collection`, `Map`, or array. No other types are supported. This is perhaps the most useful function in the JSTL.
- `${fn:toLowerCase(String)}` and `${fn:toUpperCase(String)}` — You can use these functions to change the case of a string to all lowercase or all uppercase.
- `${fn:trim(String)}` — This function trims all white space from both ends of the specified string.

There are still more functions available in the JSTL, and you can read about the rest of them by clicking at `http://docs.oracle.com/javaee/5/jstl/1.1/docs/tlddocs/fn/tld-summary.html`. This is the documentation for JSTL 1.1 in Java EE 5. Unfortunately, there is no readily available HTML documentation for JSTL 1.2 in Java EE 6 and 7.

## Static Field and Method Access

New in Expression Language 3.0, you can now access the public static fields and public static methods within any class on your JSP's class path. You could argue (and some have) that this puts too much power in the hands of JSP authors and enables them to do practically anything they could normally do with a scriptlet. It's up to you to decide whether that is a good thing or a bad thing, but the feature exists and cannot be disabled in EL 3.0.

You access static fields and methods the same way you would in Java — using the fully-qualified class name and field or method name separated with the dot operator. For example, you can access the `MAX_VALUE` constant on the `Integer` class with the following expression:

```
${java.lang.Integer.MAX_VALUE}
```

The class name must be fully qualified unless the class is imported using the JSP `page` directive. Remember that in JSPs, like Java, all classes in `java.lang` are implicitly imported for you. Because of this, the previous expression could be written like this instead:

```
${Integer.MAX_VALUE}
```

With this you can access static fields or methods on any class your JSP has access to. It's important to note that you can only *read* the value of these fields. You cannot write to them. (Of course, if a field is also final, you couldn't normally write to it anyway.) Calling a static method on a class is just as easy. Suppose you wanted to reverse the order of the bits in a number and see how the value of the number changed:

```
${java.lang.Integer.reverse(42)}
${Integer.reverse(24)}
```

This expression calls the static `reverse` method on the `Integer` class and passes the number 42 as its argument. In addition to calling named static methods, you can also invoke a constructor on a class, which returns an instance of that class that you can further access properties of, invoke methods on, or simply coerce to a string for output.

```
${com.wrox.User()}
${com.wrox.User('First', 'Last').firstName}
```

Although the static method access can entirely replace the behavior of EL functions and function libraries, that doesn't mean that function libraries are unnecessary. The previous static method call to `Integer.reverse` might be convenient, but with a theoretical `int` function library mapped to the static methods of `Integer`, the following expression is still more convenient:

```
${int:reverse(42)}
```

That may not seem much shorter, but imagine a much longer class name, and you should quickly see why function libraries are still of great use. One of the areas in which static field access could be most handy is with enums, which you learn about next.

## Enums

Chances are you've been exposed to Java enums at some point, and if you've been using Java for a while, you are probably familiar with how useful and powerful they can be. Traditionally, enums in EL have been coerced to and from strings when necessary. For example, say your JSP had an in-scope variable named *`dayOfWeek`* and it represented one of the values from the `java.time.DayOfWeek` enum in the new Java 8 Date and Time API. You could test whether *`dayOfWeek`* is Saturday with the following boolean expression:

```
${dayOfWeek == 'SATURDAY'}
```

The *`dayOfWeek`* variable here is converted to a `String` and compared to "SATURDAY." This is unlike Java, where this conversion would never happen automatically. Although this is handy, it is certainly not type-safe. If you misspell Saturday (or if Saturday ever ceases being a day of the week) your IDE would probably not catch it, and if you compile JSPs during a continuous integration build to check for JSP compile-time errors, that would not catch it either. However, as of EL 3.0 you can use the static field access syntax to achieve type-safe enum constant reference. After all, enum constants are just public static final fields of their enum types:

```
${dayOfWeek == java.time.DayOfWeek.SATURDAY}
```

And, if you import `DayOfWeek` into your JSP, the expression is nearly as simple as the string-as-enum expression (and more like what you'd see in Java code):

```
${dayOfWeek == DayOfWeek.SATURDAY}
```

These last two techniques are type-safe and will be validated by your IDE and at compile time. Whichever you use is up to you, but we recommend a type-safe way.

## Lambda Expressions

Expression Language 3.0 counts lambda expressions among its many new features. A *lambda expression* is an anonymous function that, typically, is passed as an argument to a higher-order function (such as a Java method). In the most general sense, lambda expressions are a list of parameter names (or some placeholder if the function has no parameters), followed by some type of operator, and finally the function body. In some languages supporting lambda expressions, this order is reversed or otherwise different. Lambda expression syntax in EL is nearly identical to that of Java 8 lambda expressions. The primary difference between the two is that in Java the body of a lambda expression can contain anything that's legal in a Java method, whereas in EL the body of a lambda expression is another EL expression.

Just like with Java lambda expressions, EL lambda expressions use the arrow operator `->` to separate the expression parameters on the left side from the expression in the right side. Also, again as with Java lambda expressions, the parentheses around the expression parameter are optional if there is exactly one parameter. The following expressions are valid EL lambda expressions:

```
a -> a + 5
(a, b) -> a + b
```

Of course, by themselves these lambda expressions are not complete EL expressions. Something must be done with the lambda expressions. They could be evaluated immediately:

```
${(a -> a + 5)(4)}
${((a, b) -> a + b)(4, 7)}
```

In the preceding EL expressions, the lambda expressions are declared and evaluated immediately. The resulting outputs of the two EL expressions are 9 and 11, respectively. Note that the lambda expression itself is surrounded by parentheses. This disambiguates the lambda expression from everything around it and enables you to execute it immediately. You could also define an EL lambda expression for use at a later time:

```
${v = (a, b) -> a + b; v(3, 15)}
```

The output of the second expression in this case is 18 because it executes the lambda expression defined before the semicolon. The lambda expression *v* can now be used in any other EL expression that follows this expression on the page. This is especially useful if the lambda is very complex.

Finally, you could also pass an EL lambda expression as an argument to a method called within an EL expression.

```
${users.stream().filter(u -> u.lastName == 'Williams' ||
    u.lastName == 'Sanders ').toArray()}
```

## Collections

Collections can be easily accessed in EL using the dot `.` and bracket `[]` operators. How you use the operators depends on what type of collection it is. Remember that in the Java Collections API, all collections are either `Collections` or `Maps`. Within the hierarchy of `Maps`, you simply have many different types of maps, all of which share a common foundation: Some key is associated with some value. The `Collection` hierarchy is a little more complicated. Within it you have `Sets`, `Lists`, and `Queues`. Because each type of collection has a different way in which you access its values, EL supports each one slightly differently.

Accessing values in a `Map` is quite simple and mimics the accessing of properties on JavaBeans. Suppose you have a `Map` named *map* with a key *`username`* mapped to the value "Jonathon" and a key *`userId`* mapped to the value "27." You could access these two properties of the map using the bracket operators, as in the following example:

```
${map["username"]}
${map["userId"]}
```

However, this is not the only technique you can use to access the `Map` values. You could also treat the keys like bean properties and access their values using the dot operator:

```
${map.username}
${map.userId}
```

Although the second technique certainly involves fewer characters (always three fewer, to be exact), some people find the first technique more natural and more like how you would access `Map` values in languages that support operator overloading. You should use whichever you are more comfortable with. However, you should also note some restrictions on using the dot operator for accessing `Map` values. Simply put, if a key couldn't be an identifier in Java, you must use brackets instead of the dot operator to access the value mapped to that key. This means that your key can't contain spaces, periods, or hyphens, can't start with a number, and can't contain most special characters. (Although, there are a few surprising special characters that Java supports in identifiers, such as the dollar sign ($) and accented characters such as å, é, è, î, ö, ü, ñ, and so on.) If it contains any characters that aren't valid in Java identifiers, you must use brackets. If you're not sure, err on the side of caution and use brackets.

Accessing `List`s is equally simple; however, it may surprise you just how forgiving it is. Consider a `List` (cleverly named *`list`*) with values "blue," "red," and "green," in order from 0 to 2. You would access the values using the bracket operator just as if the `List` were actually an array. The following code demonstrates this.

```
${list[0]}
${list[1]}
${list[2]}
```

You cannot treat the `List` indexes as properties and access them with the dot operator. This results in syntax errors:

```
${list.0} <%-- The EL interpreter will complain about a syntax error --%>
```

However, EL does permit you to use string literals instead of numbers to index the `List`, just as if it were a `Map` with the `List` indexes serving as the keys:

```
${list["0"]}
${list['1']}
${list[2]}
```

The only rule when using string literals is that the strings must be convertible to integers; otherwise, your code results in runtime errors. Although this is certainly flexible, there is no reason to use string literals as `List` indexes, and doing so can result in other developers' confusing your `List` (probably not named *`list`*) for a `Map`. We recommend using numeric literals instead.

The values of the other two types of collections, `Set`s and `Queue`s, cannot be accessed using EL. These collections do not provide a means of directly accessing a value, such as an index with a `List` or a key with a `Map`. There are no "get" methods on `Set`s and `Queue`s. You can access the values in these types of collections only by using iteration — something you explore in the next chapter. However, as with all types of collections, you can test whether `Set`s and `Queue`s are empty using the `empty` operator:

```
${empty set}
${empty queue}
```

You can do more things with collections using EL collection streams, and you explore that more in the collection streams section later in this chapter.

## USING SCOPED VARIABLES IN EL EXPRESSIONS

Expression Language's sense of scoped variables and how variables are resolved makes it especially useful and powerful. Recall from Chapter 4 that JSPs have a set of implicit variables (`request`, `response`, `session`, `out`, `application`, `config`, `pageContext`, `page`, and `exception`) that you can use to obtain information from the request, session, and execution environment and affect the response. EL has a similar set of implicit variables; however, it also has an idea of implicit scope in which unknown variables are resolved. This enables you to obtain information from a variety of sources with minimal code. You explore these topics in this section.

For this section you use the User-Profile project available for download on the `wrox.com` code site. If you create it from scratch, be sure to create your `web.xml` file using the `<jsp-config>` from Chapter 4 and the `<session-config>` from Chapter 5, and create an `index.jsp` with the lone tag `<c:redirect url="/profile" />`.

The `/WEB-INF/jsp/base.jspf` file, which you have used in previous chapters, has changed slightly. Instead of just declaring the `c` tag library, it now also declares the `fn` function library, which you use in this section:

```
<%@ taglib prefix="c" uri="http://java.sun.com/jsp/jstl/core" %>
<%@ taglib prefix="fn" uri="http://java.sun.com/jsp/jstl/functions" %>
```

### A NOTE ABOUT SCOPES

There are four different attribute scopes mentioned in this section (page, request, session, and application), but you may not understand the difference between them or what exactly they are. Each of these scopes has a progressively larger and longer scope than the previous one. You should already be familiar with the request scope: It begins when the server receives the request and ends when the server completes sending the response back to the client. The request scope exists anywhere that has access to the request object, and the attributes bound to the request are no longer bound after the request completes.

In Chapter 5 you learned about sessions and session attributes, so by now you may have figured out that the session scope persists between requests, and that any code with access to the `HttpSession` object can access the session scope. When the session has been invalidated, its attributes are unbound and the scope ends.

The page and application scopes are somewhat different. The page scope encapsulates attributes for a particular page (JSP) and request. When a variable is bound to the page scope, it is available only to that JSP page and only during the life of the request. Other JSPs and Servlets cannot access the page scope-bound variable, and when the request completes, the variable is unbound. With access to the `JspContext` or `PageContext` object, you can store and retrieve attributes that exist within the page scope using the `setAttribute` and `getAttribute` methods. The application scope is the broadest scope, existing across all requests, sessions, JSP pages, and Servlets. The `ServletContext` object you learned about in Chapter 3 represents the application scope, and attributes that are stored in it live in the application scope.

## Using the Implicit EL Scope

The EL defines 11 implicit variables in the scope of EL expressions, and you will learn about them all later in this section. However, the implicit scope is more useful and more commonly used because of its capability to resolve an attribute in the request, session, page, or application scope. When an EL expression references a variable, the EL evaluator resolves the variable using the following procedure:

1. It checks if the variable is one of the 11 implicit variables.
2. If the variable is not one of the 11 implicit variables, the EL evaluator next looks for an attribute in the page scope (`PageContext.getAttribute("variable")`) that has the same name (case-sensitive) as the variable. If it finds a matching page scope attribute, it uses the attribute value as the variable's value.
3. Finding no matching page attribute, the evaluator next looks for a request attribute (`HttpServletRequest.getAttribute("variable")`) with the same name as the variable and uses the attribute if it is found.
4. The evaluator looks for a session attribute (`HttpSession.getAttribute("variable")`) and uses it if found.
5. The evaluator looks for an application attribute (`ServletContext .getAttribute("variable")`) and uses it if found.
6. After the evaluator looks in all these places, if it finds no implicit variable or attribute matching the variable name, it raises an error.

The beauty of this feature is you do not need to retrieve an instance of the `HttpServletRequest` or `HttpSession` to use attributes on either of those objects. This is demonstrated in the `ProfileServlet` and `profile.jsp` file in the User-Profile project. Start by looking at the `com.wrox.User` class, which has several private fields with matching accessor and mutator methods:

```
public class User
{
    private long userId;
    private String username;
    private String firstName;
    private String lastName;
    private Map<String, Boolean> permissions = new Hashtable<>();
```

```
    ...
        // mutators and accessors
    ...
    }
```

This is a simple POJO that you can use to hold information about your "user." You need to view this information somehow, so next create a very simple `ProfileServlet`:

```
@WebServlet(
        name = "profileServlet",
        urlPatterns = "/profile"
)
public class ProfileServlet extends HttpServlet
{
    @Override
    protected void doGet(HttpServletRequest request, HttpServletResponse response)
            throws ServletException, IOException
    {
        User user = new User();
        user.setUserId(19384L);
        user.setUsername("Coder314");
        user.setFirstName("John");
        user.setLastName("Smith");

        Hashtable<String, Boolean> permissions = new Hashtable<>();
        permissions.put("user", true);
        permissions.put("moderator", true);
        permissions.put("admin", false);
        user.setPermissions(permissions);

        request.setAttribute("user", user);
        request.getRequestDispatcher("/WEB-INF/jsp/view/profile.jsp")
               .forward(request, response);
    }
}
```

So far, you haven't seen anything new. The Servlet creates a new `User` instance, sets some values on it, adds some permissions to it, creates a request attribute to hold the *`user`* object, and then forwards the request on to the view. The important code is contained in the `/WEB-INF/jsp/view/profile.jsp` file, which displays the user profile information in the browser:

```
<%--@elvariable id="user" type="com.wrox.User"--%>
<!DOCTYPE html>
<html>
    <head>
        <title>User Profile</title>
    </head>
    <body>
        User ID: ${user.userId}<br />
        Username: ${user.username} (${user.username.length()} characters)<br />
        Full Name: ${fn:escapeXml(user.lastName) += ', '
            += fn:escapeXml(user.firstName)}
        <br /><br />
        <b>Permissions (${fn:length(user.permissions)})</b><br />
```

```
            User: ${user.permissions["user"]}<br />
            Moderator: ${user.permissions["moderator"]}<br />
            Administrator: ${user.permissions["admin"]}<br />
        </body>
    </html>
```

There is a lot of interesting stuff in this JSP, and you will dissect it in a minute. For now, compile and fire up your debugger; then navigate to `http://localhost:8080/user-profile/profile` in your browser. You should see the page from the screen shot in Figure 6-1.

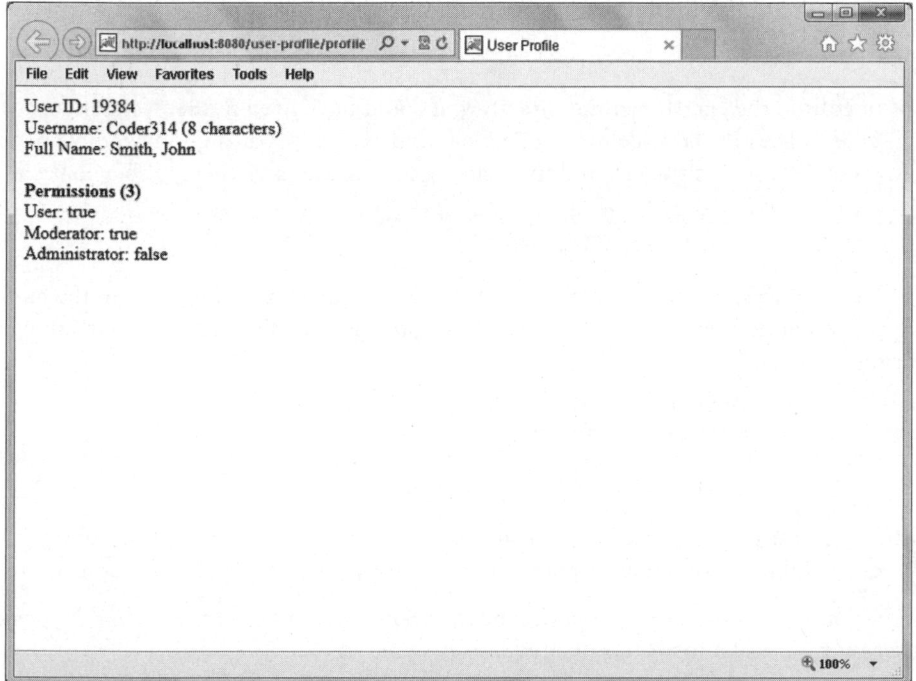


FIGURE 6-1

Now take a look at this JSP line by line to get a better understanding of how it works. First there's the new, weird JSP comment at the top of the file:

```
<%--@elvariable id="user" type="com.wrox.User"--%>
```

This comment tag is not really needed, and in fact if you remove it, recompile, and rerun your application, it still works. (Go ahead; try it!) So what does it do? The special `@elvariable` comment is a convention that developers use to type-hint for their IDE. This comment tells the IDE "Yes, a *`user`* variable exists in the implicit scope on this page, and its type is `com.wrox.User`." The advantage this gains you is that because the IDE knows the variable exists and what its type is, it can now provide auto-completion and intelligent suggestions that it could not otherwise provide. It can also validate that your EL expression is correct.

Even if you do not use an IDE or use one that does not support this convention, other developers maintaining your JSPs at a later date can quickly know what the EL variable type is. Your JSP-writing time will be much easier spent if you get in the habit of using `@elvariable` comments.

Next, you should notice the User ID line:

```
User ID: ${user.userId}<br />
```

Here, the *user* attribute that you added to the request in the Servlet code has been accessed as an EL variable using the implicit scope in the JSP page, and you have used the bean property *userId* instead of calling the accessor method directly. The line directly below it does the same with the username but also calls the length method on the username `String`.

```
Username: ${user.username} (${user.username.length()} characters)<br />
```

Note that instead of calling the length method directly you could have used the `fn:length` function, but that is used later in the code for a collection, and this serves as a good example of the alternative. Next, your JSP escapes the last and first name and concatenates them with a comma:

```
Full Name: ${fn:escapeXml(user.lastName) += ', '
    += fn:escapeXml(user.firstName)}
```

Note the use of the `fn:escapeXml` function to escape HTML characters that might be in the name and the `+=` string concatenation operator to combine all the strings. The final part of your JSP prints out the user's permissions:

```
<b>Permissions (${fn:length(user.permissions)})</b><br />
User: ${user.permissions["user"]}<br />
Moderator: ${user.permissions["moderator"]}<br />
Administrator: ${user.permissions["admin"]}<br />
```

The `fn:length` function outputs the number of elements in the user's *permissions* collection, and the other three lines are all using the bracket operators to access values in the *permissions* `Map`.

As an exercise, edit your `ProfileServlet` and change the `request.setAttribute("user", user)` line to put the user on the session instead of the request:

```
request.getSession().setAttribute("user", user);
```

Now compile and rerun your application. You don't need to make any changes to the JSP. The *user* attribute may be in a different scope (session instead of request) but is still in the implicit scope so that you can access it from EL expressions as an EL variable. When it was bound to the request, the *user* attribute existed until the request was complete, and then it was made eligible for garbage collection. Now that it is bound to the session, it is available to other requests from the same client, even if they go to different pages. However, this is not the only scope you could bind the *user* attribute to. Replace `request.getSession()` with `this.getServletContext()` and bind it to the application context:

```
this.getServletContext().setAttribute("user", user);
```

Now compile and rerun again without making any changes to the JSP. Again the user attribute was still in the implicit scope and accessible from your EL expression. You can access anything in the four supported scopes in this manner, which greatly simplifies your task of writing JSPs.

## Using the Implicit EL Variables

As mentioned earlier in this section, there are 11 implicit EL variables available for use within EL expressions. With one exception, they are all `Map` objects. Most are used to access attributes from some scope, request parameters, or headers.

- *`pageContext`* is an instance of the `PageContext` class and is the only implicit EL variable that is not a `Map`. You should be familiar with `PageContext` from Chapter 4 and earlier in this section. Using this variable you can access the page error data and exception object (if applicable), the expression evaluator, the output writer, the JSP Servlet instance, the request and response, the `ServletContext`, the `ServletConfig`, and the session.
- *`pageScope`* is a `Map<String, Object>` containing all the attributes bound to the `PageContext` (page scope).
- *`requestScope`* is a `Map<String, Object>` of all the attributes bound to the `ServletRequest`. Using this, you can access these attributes without calling a method on the request object.
- *`sessionScope`* is also a `Map<String, Object>`, and it contains all the session attributes from the current session.
- *`applicationScope`* is the last of the scopes, a `Map<String, Object>` containing all the attributes bound to the `ServletContext` instance.
- *`param`* and *`paramValues`* are similar in that they both provided access to the request parameters. The *`param`* variable is a `Map<String, String>` and contains only the first value from any parameter with multiple values (similar to `getParameter` from `ServletRequest`), whereas the `Map<String, String[]>` *`paramValues`* contains all the values of every parameter (`getParameterValues` from `ServletRequest`). *`param`* is easier to use if you know a request parameter has only one value.
- *`header`* and *`headerValues`* provide access to the request headers, with `Map<String, String>` *`header`* containing only the first value of any multivalue headers and `Map<String, String[]>` *`headerValues`* containing all values for every header. Like *`param`*, *`header`* is easier to use if you know a header has only one value.
- *`initParam`* is a `Map<String, String>` containing all the context init parameters from the `ServletContext` instance for this application.
- *`cookie`* is a `Map<String, javax.servlet.http.Cookie>` containing all the cookies that the user's browser sent along with the request. The keys in this map are the cookie names. It should be noted that it is possible to have two cookies with the same name (but different paths), and in that case this `Map` will contain only the first cookie with a given name in the order it existed in the request. This order might vary from one request to the next. There is no way in EL to access any of the other duplicate cookies with the same name without iterating over all the cookies. (Iteration with EL is something you learn how to do in the next chapter.)

To demonstrate the various EL implicit variables and how they can be used, create a file named `info.jsp` in the web root of your project and put the following code in it:

```
<%
    application.setAttribute("appAttribute", "foo");
    pageContext.setAttribute("pageAttribute", "bar");
    session.setAttribute("sessionAttribute", "sand");
    request.setAttribute("requestAttribute", "castle");
%>
<!DOCTYPE html>
<html>
    <head>
        <title>Information</title>
    </head>
    <body>
        Remote Address: ${pageContext.request.remoteAddr}<br />
        Request URL: ${pageContext.request.requestURL}<br />
        Session ID: ${pageContext.request.session.id}<br />
        Application Scope: ${applicationScope["appAttribute"]}<br />
        Page Scope: ${pageScope["pageAttribute"]}<br />
        Session Scope: ${sessionScope["sessionAttribute"]}<br />
        Request Scope: ${requestScope["requestAttribute"]}<br />
        User Parameter: ${param["user"]}<br />
        Color Multi-Param: ${fn:join(paramValues["colors"], ', ')}<br />
        Accept Header: ${header["Accept"]}<br />
        Session ID Cookie Value: ${cookie["JSESSIONID"].value}<br />
    </body>
</html>
```

The first four lines of the JSP set attributes within the various scopes, for the purposes of demonstration. The lines within the HTML body print out varying information about the request, attributes on the different scopes, parameters in the URL, headers, and cookies. Compile and debug your application; then go to `http://localhost:8080/user-profile/info.jsp?user=jack&colors=green&colors=red` in your browser. You should see a good deal of information printed out to the screen. If the Session ID Cookie Value line is empty, this means that your session was just created and the browser did not send a cookie yet; refresh the page and a value should appear here.

One last JSP demonstrates the priority of the various scopes when resolving variables in the implicit EL scope. Create a file named `scope.jsp` in the web root, and put the following code in it.

```
<%
    pageContext.setAttribute("a", "page");
    request.setAttribute("a", "request");
    session.setAttribute("a", "session");
    application.setAttribute("a", "application");

    request.setAttribute("b", "request");
    session.setAttribute("b", "session");
    application.setAttribute("b", "application");

    session.setAttribute("c", "session");
```

```
    application.setAttribute("c", "application");

    application.setAttribute("d", "application");
%>
<!DOCTYPE html>
<html>
    <head>
        <title>Scope Demonstration</title>
    </head>
    <body>
        a = ${a}<br />
        b = ${b}<br />
        c = ${c}<br />
        d = ${d}<br />
    </body>
</html>
```

The majority of this JSP is setup code, with only four EL expressions making up the demonstration. The a attribute has conflicting values in all four scopes, b in three, and c in two. The d attribute is present only in the application scope. The value displayed next to each name on the page will be the name of the scope with the highest precedence among the scopes with conflicting values. Compile and run your application and navigate to `http://localhost:8080/user-profile/scope.jsp`. The output should look identical to what follows, indicating that the EL engine looks for implicitly scoped variables first in the page scope and then in the request, session, and application scopes, in that order.

```
a = page
b = request
c = session
d = application
```

## ACCESSING COLLECTIONS WITH THE STREAM API

One of the biggest additions to Expression Language 3.0 in Java EE 7 is support for the Collections Stream API introduced in Java SE 8. Because the API is supported natively in EL 3.0, you do not need to run your application in Java 8 to take advantage of this new EL feature. In this section, you learn the basics of the Stream API and how to use it in your JSPs.

> **NOTE** *In an early, prerelease version of Expression Language 3.0, the specification included an implementation of Microsoft LINQ (Language Integrated Query). This added collection-querying capabilities using the LINQ standard query operators. The final specification was rewritten to remove the LINQ features and replace them with an equivalent to the Stream API. This provides consistency across the Java language and Expression Language specifications.*

The basis of the Stream API is the no-argument `stream` method present on every `Collection`. This method returns a `java.util.stream.Stream` that can filter and otherwise manipulate a copy of the collection. The `java.util.Arrays` class also provides many static methods for retrieving `Streams` from various arrays. Using this `Stream`, you can perform many different operations. Some of these operations return other `Streams`, allowing you to create a *chained pipeline* of operations. This pipeline consists of a *pipeline source* (the `Stream`), the *intermediate operations* (such as filtering and sorting), and finally a *terminal operation* (such as converting the results to a `List` that can be iterated and displayed).

In EL 3.0, you can call the `stream` method on any EL variable that is a Java array or a `Collection`. The returned `Stream` isn't actually a `java.util.stream.Stream` because EL 3.0 must work in Java 7, where `Stream`s do not exist yet. Instead, the returned `Stream` is an EL-specific implementation of the Stream API. For example, the following EL expression filters a `Collection` of books by title, reduces the properties available for each book to just the title and author, and returns a `List` of the results:

```
books.stream().filter(b->b.title == 'Professional Java for Web Applications')
      .map(b->{ 'title':b.title, 'author':b.author })
      .toList()
```

## Understanding Intermediate Operations

As mentioned earlier, intermediate operations filter, sort, reduce, transform, or otherwise alter a collection of values so that the collection ends up in the desired state. It's important to understand that when performing intermediate operations on a `Stream`, the original `Collection` or array is never altered. The operations affect only the contents of the stream. You'll find many different intermediate operations, and you learn about the most common and useful ones in this section. You can learn about the rest of them by downloading and reading the JSR 341 specification PDF from the specification download page (`http://download.oracle.com/otndocs/jcp/el-3_0-fr-eval-spec/index.html`).

### Filtering the Stream

The `filter` operation is probably the operation you will use most often. It filters the contents of the `Stream`, typically reducing the number of objects contained therein. The `filter` operation accepts a *predicate argument* — a lambda expression that returns a `boolean` and accepts a single argument whose type is the element type of the `Stream`. Given a List<E> where `E` is the element type, `stream` returns a Stream<E>. Calling `filter` on this Stream<E>, you supply a Predicate<E> with the signature `E -> boolean`. You then use properties of `E` to determine whether to include that particular `E` in the resulting Stream<E>. To better understand this, consider the following expression:

```
${books.stream().filter(b -> b.author == "John F. Smith")}
```

The predicate in this case is the lambda expression that accepts a book as an argument and tests whether the book's author is John F. Smith. When passed to the `filter` operation, the predicate applies to every book in the `Stream`, and the resulting `Stream` contains only those books for which the predicate returns `true`.

You can also use the special `distinct` operation to filter out duplicate values. The following expression removes the duplicate 3s and 5s from the `List`:

```
${[1, 2, 3, 3, 4, 5, 5, 5, 5, 6].stream().distinct()}
```

## Manipulating Values

You can manipulate the values in a Stream using the forEach operation. Like filter, forEach accepts a lambda expression that is evaluated for every element in the Stream. However, this lambda expression is a *consumer*, meaning it has no return value. You can use this to manipulate the values in the Stream, likely to transform them in some way. Here is one potential use case:

```
${books.stream().forEach(b -> b.setLastViewed(Instant.now()))}
```

## Sorting the Stream

You sort the stream using the sorted operation. For a Stream<E>, the sorted operation accepts a java.util.Comparator<E>. As a Java developer, you are probably familiar with this interface, which can be represented with the lambda expression (E, E) -> int. This lambda expression or Comparator compares two elements in the Stream using an efficient sorting algorithm that is unspecified and implementation-specific. The following expression sorts books by their title:

```
${books.stream().sorted((b1, b2) -> b1.title.compareTo(b2.title))}
```

A variation of the sorted operation exists that does not accept any arguments. Instead, it assumes that the elements in the Stream implement the java.lang.Comparable interface, meaning you can naturally sort them. The following naturally orders the list of numbers from least to greatest. The resulting list is -2, 0, 3, 5, 7, 8, 19.

```
${[8, 3, 19, 5, 7, -2, 0].stream().sorted()}.
```

## Limiting the Stream Size

You can limit the number of elements in the Stream using the limit and substream operations. Use limit to simply truncate the Stream after the specified number of elements. substream is more useful for pagination because you can specify a start index (inclusive) and end index (exclusive).

```
${books.stream().limit(10)}
${books.stream().substream(10, 20)}
```

## Transforming the Stream

Using the map operation, you can transform the elements in the Stream to some other type of element. The map operation accepts a *mapper* that expects one type of element and returns a number. Given a Stream<S>, map expects a lambda expression whose sole argument is of type S. If the lambda expression then returns a different type R, the resulting Stream is a Stream<R>. The following takes a List<Book>, retrieves a Stream<Book>, and transforms it into a Stream<String> containing only the book titles:

```
${books.stream().map(b -> b.title)}
```

Of course, you can return more complex types. You might have a different type, DisplayableBook, with a limited set of properties. Or you could create an implicit List or Map, returning a Stream<List<Object>> or Stream<Map<Object, Object>>:

```
${books.stream().map(b -> [b.title, b.author])}
${books.stream().map(b -> {"title":b.title, "author":b.author})}
```

# Using Terminal Operations

After you filter, sort, or otherwise transform your `Stream`, you need to perform some final operation that converts the `Stream` back into a useful value, `Collection`, or array. This type of operation is a terminal operation. It is terminal because unlike intermediate operations, which all return `Streams` that can be further acted on, this operation does not return a `Stream`. It evaluates any intermediate operations deferred for performance reasons and then converts the final result as desired. Ultimately, you must always perform a terminal operation. A `Stream` is not very useful by itself; you need a final value to act on.

## Returning a Collection

You can use the `toArray` and `toList` operations to return a Java array or `List` of the final result element type. For example, the following expressions return a `String[]` and `List<String>` of book titles, respectively:

```
${books.stream().map(b -> b.title).toArray()}
${books.stream().map(b -> b.title).toList()}
```

If you performed any `sorted` intermediate operations on the `Stream`, the resulting array or `List` will be in the order indicated with those operations. You can also use the `iterator` operation to return a suitable `java.util.Iterator`.

## Using Aggregate Functions

You can aggregate the values in the `Stream` using the `min`, `max`, `average`, `sum`, and `count` operations. The `count` operation can operate on any type of `Stream`, whereas the `average` and `sum` operations require the final `Stream` element types to be coercible to `Numbers`. `count` returns the number of elements in the `Stream` as a `long`; `average` returns the average of all the `Stream` elements as an `Optional<? extends Number>`; and `sum` returns the sum of all the `Stream` elements as a `Number`. An `Optional` is a placeholder that can report whether the returned value was `null` and provide the returned value when requested.

The `min` and `max` operations are both interesting. They both return `Optional<E>` where `E` is the element type of the resulting `Stream`. Without any arguments, these operations require that the `Stream` elements implement `Comparable`. However, you can provide a `Comparator` argument to these operations when wanted.

The following expressions represent some common use cases for these aggregating terminal operations:

```
${books.stream().map(b -> b.price()).min()}
${books.stream().map(b -> b.price()).max()}
${books.stream().filter(b -> b.author == "John F. Smith")
        .map(b -> b.price()).average()}
${books.stream().filter(b -> b.author == "John F. Smith").count()}
${cartItems.stream().map(i -> i.price() * i.quantity()).sum()}
```

## Returning the First Value

You can use the `findFirst` operation to return the first element in the resulting `Stream`. For a `Stream<E>` it returns an `Optional<E>` because the `Stream` might be empty, meaning there is no first element to return.

```
${books.stream().filter(b -> b.author == "John F. Smith").findFirst()}
```

# Putting the Stream API to Use

For a simple exercise in the use of the Stream API, you add a JSP to the User-Profile project and filter, map, and sort a `List` of `Users`. Start by adding a constructor to the `User` object (and also adding a default constructor so that previous code won't break).

```
public User() { }

public User(long userId, String username, String firstName, String lastName)
{
    this.userId = userId;
    this.username = username;
    this.firstName = firstName;
    this.lastName = lastName;
}
```

Now create a `collections.jsp` file in the web root of the project and put the following code in it:

```
<%@ page import="com.wrox.User" %>
<%@ page import="java.util.ArrayList" %>
<%
    ArrayList<User> users = new ArrayList<>();
    users.add(new User(19384L, "Coder314", "John", "Smith"));
    users.add(new User(19383L, "geek12", "Joe", "Smith"));
    users.add(new User(19382L, "jack123", "Jack", "Johnson"));
    users.add(new User(19385L, "farmer-dude", "Adam", "Fisher"));
    request.setAttribute("users", users);
%>
<!DOCTYPE html>
<html>
    <head>
        <title>Collections and Streams</title>
    </head>
    <body>
        ${users.stream()
                .filter(u -> fn:contains(u.username, '1'))
                .sorted((u1, u2) -> (x = u1.lastName.compareTo(u2.lastName);
                     x == 0 ? u1.firstName.compareTo(u2.firstName) : x))
                .map(u -> {'username':u.username, 'first':u.firstName,
                     'last':u.lastName})
                .toList()}
    </body>
</html>
```

The setup code at the top of the file creates some users and adds them to the list. Then the EL expression filters the list to users whose usernames contain the number 1; orders by the last name and then first name; selects the username, first name, and last name from each matching user; and then evaluates immediately to a `List`. Finally, the `List` is automatically coerced to a `String` for display on the screen (using the `List`'s `toString` method). Notice the use of the semicolon and assignment (`=`) operators in the `sorted` lambda expression — this allows you to compare the last names only once, assign the comparison to a variable (`x`), and then test the value of `x`, returning it if the last names are different and comparing the first names if the last names are the same. The body of the `sorted` lambda expression is surrounded by parentheses (in bold) because the lambda operator (`->`) has a higher precedence than the assignment and semicolon operators.

You can test this out by compiling and running your application and going to `http://localhost:8080/user-profile/collections.jsp` in your browser.

> **NOTE** *In Chapter 4 you explored using Java code in JSPs and learned about some of the many reasons using Java within JSPs is discouraged. The introduction of the Stream API to the Expression Language provides a lot of additional power for the JSP author to manipulate collections significantly. If you get in the habit of using the Stream API in JSPs routinely, you may find that you have started putting business logic in the presentation layer instead of the Java code. Only you can decide whether this is appropriate for your needs, but it is something to keep in mind. You will not see use of the Stream API in JSPs anywhere else in the book — these types of operations are performed only in the Java code from now on.*

## REPLACING JAVA CODE WITH EXPRESSION LANGUAGE

In this section you begin replacing some of the Java code in your JSPs in the ongoing customer support application with EL expressions. The Customer-Support-v4 project on the `wrox.com` code download site contains these changes. You cannot replace all the Java code yet. For that, we will need the next chapter. Start by updating your `/WEB-INF/jsp/base.jspf` file to contain a tag library declaration for the JSTL function library:

```
<%@ page import="com.wrox.Ticket, com.wrox.Attachment" %>
<%@ taglib prefix="c" uri="http://java.sun.com/jsp/jstl/core" %>
<%@ taglib prefix="fn" uri="http://java.sun.com/jsp/jstl/functions" %>
```

You do not need to make any changes to Java code in this section. Everything you change will be within JSPs. The `ticketForm.jsp` view in `/WEB-INF/jsp/view` is already devoid of any Java code, so there is nothing you can do to improve that. `viewTicket.jsp`, on the other hand, has several things that can be replaced. The new code for this file is in Listing 6-1.

Notice that the new code has `@elvariable` type hints at the top for *`ticketId`* and *`ticket`*, and that the *`ticketId`* Java variable has been removed. The *`ticket`* Java variable has not been removed, however, because EL expressions cannot replace everything the *`ticket`* variable is being used for — such as iterating over the attachments. The new EL expressions have been highlighted in bold.

**LISTING 6-1: viewTicket.jsp**

```
<%--@elvariable id="ticketId" type="java.lang.String"--%>
<%--@elvariable id="ticket" type="com.wrox.Ticket"--%>
<%
    Ticket ticket = (Ticket)request.getAttribute("ticket");
%>
<!DOCTYPE html>
<html>
    <head>
        <title>Customer Support</title>
    </head>
    <body>
        <a href="<c:url value="/login?logout" />">Logout</a>
        <h2>Ticket #${ticketId}: ${ticket.subject}</h2>
        <i>Customer Name - ${ticket.customerName}</i><br /><br />
        ${ticket.body}<br /><br />
        <%
            if(ticket.getNumberOfAttachments() > 0)
            {
                %>Attachments: <%
                int i = 0;
                for(Attachment a : ticket.getAttachments())
                {
                    if(i++ > 0)
                        out.print(", ");
                    %><a href="<c:url value="/tickets">
                        <c:param name="action" value="download" />
                        <c:param name="ticketId" value="${ticketId}" />
                        <c:param name="attachment" value="<%= a.getName() %>" />
                    </c:url>"><%= a.getName() %></a><%
                }
                %><br /><br /><%
            }
        %>
        <a href="<c:url value="/tickets" />">Return to list tickets</a>
    </body>
</html>
```

The `/WEB-INF/jsp/view/sessions.jsp` file is another JSP that could use EL expressions. You can find the new code for this file in Listing 6-2. The only changes to this JSP are the `@elvariable` type hint and the lone EL expression in bold. None of the rest of the Java code can be replaced at this time because of the need for recursion and formatting the time interval.

**LISTING 6-2: sessions.jsp**

```
<%--@elvariable id="numberOfSessions" type="java.lang.Integer"--%>
<%@ page import="java.util.List" %>
<%!
    private static String toString(long timeInterval)
    {
        if(timeInterval < 1_000)
            return "less than one second";
        if(timeInterval < 60_000)
            return (timeInterval / 1_000) + " seconds";
        return "about " + (timeInterval / 60_000) + " minutes";
    }
%>
<%
    @SuppressWarnings("unchecked")
    List<HttpSession> sessions =
            (List<HttpSession>)request.getAttribute("sessionList");
%>
<!DOCTYPE html>
<html>
    <head>
        <title>Customer Support</title>
    </head>
    <body>
        <a href="<c:url value="/login?logout" />">Logout</a>
        <h2>Sessions</h2>
        There are a total of ${numberOfSessions} active sessions in this
        application.<br /><br />
        <%
            long timestamp = System.currentTimeMillis();
            for(HttpSession aSession : sessions)
            {
                out.print(aSession.getId() + " - " +
                        aSession.getAttribute("username"));
                if(aSession.getId().equals(session.getId()))
                    out.print(" (you)");
                out.print(" - last active " +
                        toString(timestamp - aSession.getLastAccessedTime()));
                out.println(" ago<br />");
            }
        %>
    </body>
</html>
```

Now compile and run the customer support application and go to `http://localhost:8080/support/` in your browser. Log in, create a few tickets, and view the tickets. Go to `http://localhost:8080/support/sessions` and view the list of sessions. Everything should work the same way it did in Chapter 5, but now EL takes care of some of your output.

## SUMMARY

In this chapter you learned about the history of the Java Unified Expression Language, the basic EL syntax, and what EL expressions are used for. You explored reserved words, operators, literal values, accessing object properties and methods, EL functions and the JSTL function library, static field and method access, enums, lambda expressions, and collections operators. You were introduced to the four different scopes and the implicit EL scope, and learned about the eleven implicit EL variables. You also learned about the Stream API and its addition to EL 3.0. Finally, you replaced some Java code with EL expressions in the customer support application that you started in Chapter 3.

It should be clear by now that although EL expressions can replace a lot of Java code, they do not do everything you need to replace *all* the Java code in your JSPs. For example, you cannot loop within EL expressions or have blocks of code evaluated based on whether some expression is true. For this you need the Java Standard Tag Library, which you explore in the next chapter.

# Using the Java Standard Tag Library

## IN THIS CHAPTER

- Understanding JSP tags and the JSTL
- How to implement the Core tag library (C namespace)
- How to use the Formatting tag library (FMT namespace)
- How to use the Database Access tag library (SQL namespace)
- How to use the XML Processing tag library (XML namespace)
- Swapping Java code with JSP tags

## WROX.COM CODE DOWNLOADS FOR THIS CHAPTER

You can find the `wrox.com` code downloads for this chapter at `http://www.wrox.com/go/projavaforwebapps` on the Download Code tab. The code for this chapter is divided into the following major examples:

- Address-Book Project
- Address-Book-i18n Project
- Customer-Support-v5 Project

## NEW MAVEN DEPENDENCIES FOR THIS CHAPTER

There are no new Maven dependencies for this chapter. Continue to use the Maven dependencies introduced in all previous chapters.

# INTRODUCING JSP TAGS AND THE JSTL

Up to this point it has been absolutely necessary to use Java to do certain things in JSPs. The ability to add Java to your JSPs is convenient to be sure, but remember that your UI developers, accustomed to HTML, JavaScript, and CSS, will likely not write Java code. Your goal is to have Java-free JSPs, but so far you do not have the tools to do that yet. The Expression Language was helpful in replacing some Java code, but you experienced in the last chapter how much you still have to rely on Java code even using EL. In fact, you really haven't even tapped in to the power of EL yet because you are still too limited by having to use Java code.

You have already seen a small sampling of JSP tags and the JSTL in previous chapters with the `<c:url>` and `<c:redirect>` tags. This was simply unavoidable because the alternatives were too unfriendly to even show you. However, these tags were mentioned only in passing, and the details of them and the JSTL were left to this chapter. You also saw part of the JSTL when you explored the JSTL function library (with the `fn` namespace) in the previous chapter, but this was necessary because it is really a function library, not a tag library, and it is meant exclusively for use in EL expressions. You can't use the JSTL function library outside of EL expressions. In this chapter you learn about the concept of JSP tags and the JSTL in detail, and you finally replace the unsightly Java code in your JSPs with a combination of JSP tags and EL expressions.

## Working with Tags

JSP tags are a special syntax of the JavaServer Pages technology that looks like any normal HTML or XML tag. JSP tags are also called *actions* because that's what they do. A JSP tag performs some action, such as creating or restricting output. The JSP and JSTL specifications refer almost exclusively to actions, but this book calls them *tags*. Because they are outside of the scope of any standard HTML-specified tag, JSP tags require an XML namespace to be referenced correctly. However, writing XML can be a very tedious and unforgiving task, as you saw with the brief introduction to JSP Documents (`.jspx`) in Chapter 4. In particular, the need to adhere to a strict XML document syntax is sometimes difficult even for seasoned programmers. Thus the idea of the JSP tag syntax includes some shortcuts to make writing JSPs easier. The first of these shortcuts is the `taglib` directive, which you explored in Chapter 4 and have used since then.

```
<%@ taglib prefix="c" uri="http://java.sun.com/jsp/jstl/core" %>
<%@ taglib prefix="fn" uri="http://java.sun.com/jsp/jstl/functions" %>
```

This directive is an alternative to the XMLNS technique for referencing XML namespaces in XML documents:

```
<jsp:root xmlns="http://www.w3.org/1999/xhtml" version="2.0"
          xmlns:jsp="http://java.sun.com/JSP/Page"
          xmlns:c="http://java.sun.com/jsp/jstl/core"
          xmlns:fn="http://java.sun.com/jsp/jstl/functions">
```

The use of this directive prevents XML document parsers from parsing your JSP, but it also prevents you from having to worry about XML standards compliance (the other important shortcut). Instead, the JSP engine in your web container understands the special JSP syntax and knows how to parse it, and (these days) all major Java IDEs also understand the JSP syntax and can alert you to syntax errors and other issues in your JSP.

The `prefix` attribute in a `taglib` directive (or the XML namespace) represents the namespace with which the tag library is referenced throughout the JSP page. The tag prefix is suggested in the Tag Library Descriptor file (TLD) for that tag library but is declared in the `taglib` directive using the `prefix` attribute. Thus the prefix can be whatever you set it to in the `prefix` attribute, but generally developers stick to using the prefix suggested in the TLD to prevent confusion among other developers.

The `uri` attribute indicates the URI defined in the TLD for that tag library. This is how the JSP parser locates the appropriate TLD for the referenced tag library: It finds the TLD containing the same URI.

> **NOTE** *The URI is a naming convention, not actually the location of the TLD (and not a real URL). In fact, in most cases navigating to the URI in your browser can result in a 404 Not Found or similar error. The TLDs you use are included with your application in some fashion, whether in the container, in your application's JAR files, or in your application's* `WEB-INF` *directory. The URI is merely a technique for uniquely identifying a TLD so that the tags you use can be correctly associated with the appropriate TLD.*

When the JSP parser encounters a `taglib` directive, it locates the TLD file for that tag library, using the URI, by looking for it in a variety of locations. These locations are indicated in the JSP specification as follows, in order from highest to lowest precedence:

1. If the container is a Java EE-compliant container, the parser looks for any matching TLD files that are part of the Java EE specification, including the JSP tag library, the Java Standard Tag Library, and any JavaServer Faces libraries.
2. It then checks explicit `<taglib>` declarations within the `<jsp-config>` section of the deployment descriptor.
3. If the parser still hasn't located a matching TLD file, it checks any TLD files contained within the `META-INF` directory of any JAR files placed in your application's `/WEB-INF/lib` directory, or any TLD files placed in your application's `/WEB-INF` directory or in any subdirectories of `/WEB-INF`, recursively.
4. Finally, the parser checks any other TLD files that ship as part of the web container or application server. (These are usually custom to the web container, and as such using them ties your application specifically to that web container and makes it non-portable.)

An explicit `<taglib>` declaration is normally not needed unless the TLD you are referencing does not contain a URI (legal, but unusual), it is not located within one of the other locations previously listed (something you can avoid by putting it in the right place), or you need to override a TLD with a conflicting URI supplied in some third-party JAR file that you don't have control over (a more likely but still unusual scenario). Explicit `<taglib>` declarations look like this:

```
<jsp-config>
    ...
    <taglib>
        <taglib-uri>http://www.example.org/xmlns/jsp/custom</taglib-uri>
        <taglib-location>/tld/custom.tld</taglib-location>
    </taglib>
    ...
</jsp-config>
```

In this example the `<taglib-uri>` value `http://www.example.org/xmlns/jsp/custom` would be compared against the `taglib` directive `uri` attribute. If they matched, it would use the TLD specified (`/tld/custom.tld`), relative to the root of the web application. Notice this configuration does not specify a prefix. This is because it is not a tag library declaration, like the `taglib` directive. It's simply a map telling the container where the TLD file for the specified tag library URI lives. The use of explicit `<taglib>` declarations is almost universally avoidable, so you will not use them in any examples in this book.

After a `taglib` directive is correctly configured to resolve to the appropriate TLD, you can use the tags within that library in your JSP. All JSP tags follow the same basic syntax:

```
<prefix:tagname[ attribute=value[ attribute=value[ ...]]] />

<prefix:tagname[ attribute=value[ attribute=value[ ...]]]>
    content
</prefix:tagname>
```

In this syntactic notation, `prefix` denotes the JSP tag library prefix, also known as the *namespace* (which is the standard XML nomenclature). `tagname` is the name of the tag as defined in the TLD. Attribute values are quoted with either single quotes (`'`) or double quotes (`"`) but are never unquoted. Two attributes in the same tag can use different quoting styles, but if an attribute value starts with a single quote, it must end with a single quote, and if it starts with a double quote, it must end with a double quote. There must be white space between attributes, but in a self-closing tag, the white space before the `/>` is optional. All JSP tags must either be valid XML self-closing tags (`<prefix:tagname />`) or they must have matching closing tags (`<prefix:tagname></prefix:tagname>`). Non-XML self-closing tags without matching closing tags (`<prefix:tagname>`) are syntax errors.

When you write a JSP, note that one tag library is already implicitly included for use in all your JSPs. This is the JSP tag library (prefix `jsp`), and you do not need to place a `taglib` directive in a JSP to use it. (In a JSP document, however, you do need to add an XMLNS declaration for the `jsp` tag library.) You have already seen uses of tags in the JSP tag library in previous chapters, such as `<jsp:include>`, `<jsp:forward>`, `<jsp:plugin>`, `<jsp:useBean>`, and so on. You have also seen how the JSP tag library can be used in JSP Documents with `<jsp:root>`, `<jsp:directive>`, `<jsp:declaration>`, `<jsp:scriptlet>`, and `<jsp:expression>`. All these tags are already available to you in any JSP you write.

Remember from Chapter 2 that there are full, Java EE-compliant application servers, and then there are more limited Java EE web containers. Application servers implement the entire Java EE specification, whereas web containers implement the Servlet and JSP specifications — and maybe a handful of other specifications that the creators of the web container thought important. Most web containers also implement the EL specification because it used to be part of the JSP specification and today remains inextricably linked to the JSP specification. All web containers support using tag libraries with JSPs because this support is part of the JSP specification. However, some web containers do not implement the Java Standard Tag Library (JSTL) specification, because the specific tag libraries in the JSTL are easily decoupled from the generic concept of tag libraries. Tomcat has historically been one of these web containers, and to this day, it does not implement the JSTL. However, this does not mean that you cannot use JSTL in applications you plan on deploying in Tomcat!

> **NOTE** *Tomcat implements the Servlet API, JSP, Expression Language, and WebSocket API implementations. Other web containers may implement more or fewer specifications, and this may vary from one version to the next. Be sure to consult the documentation for your particular web container to determine which specifications it supports.*

Recall from Chapter 4 that you added three new Maven dependencies to your example code. One of these was the JSP API, which simply enables you to compile against the JSP features in your IDE. Another dependency is for the Servlet API. These Maven dependencies have "provided" scope because Tomcat already includes the JSP API library, and as such you do not need to include it in your deployed application. The other two dependencies you added were the JSTL API (the interfaces, abstract classes, and tag descriptions for the JSTL) and the JSTL implementation provided by GlassFish (the JSTL TLD, concrete classes, and implementations of the interfaces). If Tomcat provided a JSTL implementation, you still would need JSTL Maven dependencies, but they would have "provided" scope. Because Tomcat does not provide a JSTL implementation, these libraries are in "compile" scope so that they deploy with your application. This enables you to use JSTL in your application despite Tomcat's lack of a JSTL implementation.

There are five tag libraries in the Java Standard Tag Library specification:

- Core (`c`)
- Formatting (`fmt`)
- Functions (`fn`)
- SQL (`sql`)
- XML (`x`)

You already learned about the Functions library in Chapter 6 while you were exploring the Expression Language. The rest of this chapter is devoted to using the other four libraries and also touches on why using the XML and SQL libraries is generally discouraged. For reference, you can view the TLD documentation for Java EE 5's JSTL 1.1 at `http://docs.oracle.com/javaee/5/jstl/1.1/docs/tlddocs/`. Unfortunately, there is no public documentation for Java EE 6's JSTL 1.2, but the changes between these versions were very minor. No new tags were added — just clarifications in the specification. There was no new JSTL version in Java EE 7.

## USING THE CORE TAG LIBRARY (C NAMESPACE)

The Core tag library, as the name implies, contains nearly all the core functionality you need to replace the Java code in your JSPs. This includes tools for conditional programming, looping and iterating, and outputting content. When you work on the Customer Support application at the end of this chapter, you will find that almost every line of Java code is replaced with some tag from the Core library. You have already seen a couple of tags from the Core library, so you should be familiar with its `taglib` directive:

```
<%@ taglib prefix="c" uri="http://java.sun.com/jsp/jstl/core" %>
```

There are many tags in the Core library, none of them unimportant. However, some of them are more commonly used than others, and you learn about them first.

### <c:out>

The `<c:out>` tag is probably the most commonly used (and sometimes the most misunderstood) tag in the Core tag library. Its purpose is to assist in the outputting of content to your JSPs. You might immediately wonder how this is different from simply using an EL expression to output content. Perhaps more confusing is that `<c:out>` is almost always used with one or more EL expressions!

```
<c:out value="${someVariable}" />
```

Although in this case `<c:out>` may very well be equivalent to simply writing `${someVariable}`, there are some differences. First, in this case, the use of `<c:out>` is actually equivalent to `${fn:escapeXml(someVariable)}`. This is because, by default, `<c:out>` escapes reserved XML characters (`<`, `>`, `'`, `"`, and `&`) just like `fn:escapeXml` does. You can disable this behavior by setting the `escapeXml` attribute to false:

```
<c:out value="${someVariable}" escapeXml="false" />
```

However, in most cases you would never want to do this. The default escaping of reserved XML characters helps protect your site from cross-site scripting and various injection attacks, and also helps prevent unexpected special characters from breaking the functionality of your site. There is also the `default` attribute, which specifies a default value if the one provided in the `value` attribute is `null`.

```
<c:out value="${someVariable}" default="Value not specified." />
```

The `default` attribute can also contain an EL expression. (Any attribute in almost any tag can, for that matter.)

```
<c:out value="${someVariable}" default="${someOtherValue}" />
```

Instead of the `default` attribute, you could use nested contents and achieve the same thing. This enables you to use HTML tags, JavaScript, and other JSP tags to generate the default value.

```
<c:out value="${someVariable}">default value</c:out>
```

Finally, note how the `value` attribute works. Normally, the value specified by the EL expression in the `value` attribute is coerced to a `String` and that `String` is written to the output. However, if the EL expression returns a `java.io.Reader`, the contents of that reader are read and then written to the output.

## <c:url>

The `<c:url>` tag properly encodes URLs, and rewrites them if necessary to add the session ID, and can also output URLs in your JSP. (In the examples in this book, session IDs in URLs are disabled to prevent session fixation attacks, so you will not see URL rewriting with this tag in action.) The tag accomplishes this behavior together with the `<c:param>` tag, which specifies query parameters to include in the URL. If the URL is a relative URL, the tag prepends the URL with the context path for your application so that the browser receives the correct absolute URL. Consider the following use of the `<c:url>` tag:

```
<c:url value="http://www.example.net/content/news/today.html" />
```

Because this URL is an absolute URL and contains no spaces or other special characters to encode, it is not changed in any way. Using the `<c:url>` tag for such a purpose is really pointless. However, if you had query parameters that you need to include in the URL, that would be a different story.

```
<c:url value="http://www.example.net/content/news/today.jsp">
    <c:param name="story" value="${storyId}" />
    <c:param name="seo" value="${seoString}" />
</c:url>
```

In this case the `<c:url>` tag will properly form and encode the query string. The *`story`* parameter might not be a problem, but the *`seo`* parameter (likely a search engine optimization string) could contain spaces, question marks, ampersands, and other special characters, all of which are encoded to ensure that they do not corrupt the URL. Where the `<c:url>` tag is probably most helpful, however, is in the encoding of relative URLs.

Consider that your application is deployed to `http://www.example.org/forums/` and you place the following link tag in your HTML:

```
<a href="/view.jsp?forumId=12">Product Forum</a>
```

When a user clicked that link, they would be taken to `http://www.example.org/view.jsp?forumId=12`. You probably meant for that URL to be relative to the forum application, not the entire website. You could easily change your link to point to `/forums/view.jsp?forumId=12`, but what if you write a forums application that anyone can download and use on their website. You don't know whether they're going to deploy the application to `/forums`, `/discussion`, `/boards`, or even just `/`. This is where the `<c:url>` tag shines.

```
<a href="<c:url value="/view.jsp">
    <c:param name="forumId" value="12" />
</c:url>">Product Forum</a>
```

Notice that the `<c:url>` tag here is actually embedded within the attribute of an HTML tag. This is completely legal and quite common. The `<c:url>` tag gets parsed and replaced when the JSP engine renders your JSP, and it treats everything that isn't special JSP syntax as plain text. If your application is deployed to `/forums`, the resulting link points to `/forums/view.jsp?forumId=12`. If it's deployed to `/boards`, it'll be `/boards/view.jsp?forumId=12`. This saves you the trouble of worrying about what context path your application is deployed to. Of course, it's possible that you really wanted the URL to go back to the root of the site. Or maybe you needed it to go to some other deployed application. This is easily accomplished, too, by adding the `context` attribute to the tag.

```
<c:url value="/index.html" context="/"/>
<c:url value="/item.jsp?itemId=15" context="/store" />
```

The first tag produces a URL going to the root context, `/index.html`. The second tag produces a URL going to the `/store` context, `/store/item.jsp?itemId=15`.

By default, the `<c:url>` tag outputs the resulting URL to the response. If you have a URL you are going to use multiple times on the page, you can save the resulting URL to a scoped variable instead:

```
<c:url value="/index.jsp" var="homepageUrl" />
<c:url value="/index.jsp" var="homepageUrl" scope="request" />
```

The `var` attribute specifies the name of the EL variable to create and save the resulting URL to. By default it is saved to the page scope (remember the four EL variable scopes: page, request, session, and application), which is normally sufficient. If for some reason you need to save it to a different scope, you can use the `scope` attribute to explicitly specify the scope. Notice that the value of `var` is a plain string, not an EL expression. Although an EL expression can work here, it is useless that way. You are telling the JSP the name of the attribute you want created in the scope, so it should always be a plain string value.

The first tag in the previous example creates a *`homepageUrl`* attribute in the page scope. The second tag creates the same attribute, but in the request scope instead. Regardless of which scope you save the URL to, you can then reference the URL later in the page with (in this example) `${homepageUrl}`.

```
<a href="${homepageUrl}">Home</a>
```

For maximum safety, flexibility, and portability, it is recommended that *all* URLs in JSPs get encoded with `<c:url>` unless the URL is an external URL with no query parameters. Even in that case, using `<c:url>` is still legal and even encouraged in case the URL contains special characters that need encoding.

## <c:if>

It is likely obvious to you that the `<c:if>` tag is a conditional tag for controlling when certain content in rendered. Using the `<c:if>` tag is quite straightforward:

```
<c:if test="${something == somethingElse}">
    execute only if test is true
</c:if>
```

The `test` attribute specifies a condition that must evaluate to `true` for the nested content within the `<c:if>` tag to be evaluated. If `test` evaluates to `false`, everything within the tag is ignored. If you have some complex condition that you want to test only once but use multiple times on the page, you can save it to a variable using the `var` attribute (and optionally specify a different `scope`):

```
<c:if test="${someComplexExpressionIsTrue}" var="itWasTrue" />
...
<c:if test="${itWasTrue}">
    do something
</c:if>
...
<c:if test="${itWasTrue}">
    do something else
</c:if>
```

You might immediately wonder if there is a <c:else> to accompany <c:if>. There is not. <c:if> is meant for simple, all-or-nothing conditional blocks. For more complex if/else-if/else logic, you need something more powerful than <c:if>.

## <c:choose>, <c:when>, and <c:otherwise>

The <c:choose>, <c:when>, and <c:otherwise> tags are the more powerful counterpart to the <c:if> tag and provide more complex if/else-if/else logic. The <c:choose> tag acts as a frame to indicate the beginnings and end of the complex conditional block. It has no attributes and may contain only white space, <c:when>, and <c:otherwise> nested within. There must be at least one and may be unlimited <c:when> tags within a <c:choose>, and all the <c:when> tags must come before the <c:otherwise> tag. <c:when> has one attribute, test, which indicates the condition that must evaluate to true for the content within that <c:when> to execute. Any content or other JSP tags may be nested within <c:when>. Only one <c:when> tag will have its contents evaluated: The first one whose test is true. The <c:choose> short-circuits to the end after a <c:when> tag has evaluated to true.

There may be at most one (optional) <c:otherwise> tag, and it must be the last tag within <c:choose>. It has no attributes, may contain any nested content, and always has its contents executed if and only if none of the <c:when> tags within the same <c:choose> evaluate to true.

```
<c:choose>
    <c:when test="${something}">
        "if"
    </c:when>
    <c:when test="${somethingElse}">
        "else if"
    </c:when>
    ...
    <c:otherwise>
        "else"
    </c:otherwise>
</c:choose>
```

From the previous code, you can see that the first <c:when> is like the initial if in Java. It is evaluated first, and if it's true everything within it is executed and everything else is ignored. The second <c:when> and all other <c:when>s are analogous to else if. They are tested only if every <c:when> before them evaluate to false. The <c:otherwise> tag is like the final else: the backup case that is always evaluated when everything else fails. Of course, your <c:choose> could have just one <c:when> and nothing else:

```
<c:choose>
    <c:when test="${something}">
        "if"
    </c:when>
</c:choose>
```

However, in this case it's much easier to just write <c:if test="${something}">...</c:if>. When complexity is required, <c:choose> can manage it. When your if needs no elses, <c:if> is probably the way to go.

## <c:forEach>

The `<c:forEach>` tag is used for iteration and repeats its nested body content some fixed number of times or while iterating over some collection or array of objects. It can act like a standard Java `for` loop or a Java `for-each` loop depending on which attributes you use. For example, say you want to replace the following Java loop with a `<c:forEach>`:

```
for(int i = 0; i < 100; i++)
{
    out.println("Line " + i + "<br />");
}
```

The equivalent `<c:forEach>` tag is as follows:

```
<c:forEach var="i" begin="0" end="100">
    Line ${i}<br />
</c:forEach>
```

In this case, every number between 0 and 100 prints to the screen. The `begin` attribute must be at least 0. If `end` is less than `begin`, the loop never executes. You can also increment *i* by more than 1, if you want to, using the `step` attribute (which must be greater than or equal to 1):

```
<c:forEach var="i" begin="0" end="100" step="3">
    Line ${i}<br />
</c:forEach>
```

In this case, every third number between 0 and 100 prints to the screen.

Using `<c:forEach>` to iterate over some collection of objects is a matter of utilizing different attributes.

```
<c:forEach items="${users}" var="user">
    ${user.lastName}, ${user.firstName}<br />
</c:forEach>
```

The expression within `items` must evaluate to some `Collection`, `Map`, `Iterator`, `Enumeration`, object array, or primitive array. If `items` is a `Map`, the `Map.Entry`s are iterated by calling the `entrySet` method. If `items` is an `Iterator` or `Enumeration`, remember that you cannot rewind these types to the beginning after iteration begins, so you can only iterate over them once. If `items` is `null`, no iteration is performed, just as if the collection were empty. This does not cause a `NullPointerException`. If you have some other class that implements `Iterable` but is not one of these types, you can use it by calling the `iterator` method on the object (`items="${object.iterator()}"`). The `var` attribute specifies the name of the variable to which each element should be assigned for each loop iteration. The previous example is equivalent to the following Java `for-each` loop:

```
for(User user : users)
{
    out.println(user.getLastName() + ", " + user.getFirstName() + "<br />");
}
```

You can skip collections elements in `<c:forEach>` using the `step` attribute, just like you would for iterating over numbers. You can also use the `begin` attribute to begin iteration at the specified index (inclusive) and the `end` attribute to end iteration at the specified index (inclusive). This is useful to implement paging of a collection of objects, for example.

Finally, whether you use `<c:forEach>` as a `for` loop of numbers or a `for-each` loop over a collection of objects, you can use the `varStatus` attribute to make a variable available within the loop containing the current status of the iteration.

```
<c:forEach items="${users}" var="user" varStatus="status">
    ${status.begin}
    ${status.end}
    ${status.step}
    ${status.count}
    ${status.current}
    ${status.index}
    ${status.first}
    ${status.last}
</c:forEach>
```

In this example the *`status`* variable encapsulates the status of the current iteration. The properties of this status object (an instance of `javax.servlet.jsp.jstl.core.LoopTagStatus`) follow:

- *`begin`* — Contains the value of the `begin` attribute from the loop tag.
- *`end`* — Contains the value of the `end` attribute from the loop tag.
- *`step`* — Contains the value of the `step` attribute from the loop tag.
- *`index`* — Returns the current index from the iteration. This value increases by *`step`* for each iteration.
- *`count`* — Returns the count of the number of iterations performed so far (including the current iteration). This value increases by 1 for each iteration, even if *`step`* is greater than 1. The value starts at 1 with the first iteration and is never equal to `status.index`.
- *`current`* — This contains the current item from the iteration. If you also use the `var` attribute to export the item as a variable, this is the same as that. In the previous example, `status.current` equals *`user`*.
- *`first`* — This is `true` if the current iteration is the very first iteration (if `status.count` is equal to 1). Otherwise it is `false`.
- *`last`* — This is `true` if the current iteration is the very last iteration. Otherwise it is `false`.

One final thing to consider when using `<c:forEach>` is the impact of EL deferred syntax (`#{}`). If you intend to use some tag within the loop that requires deferred syntax in an attribute, and you want to use the variable created as specified in `var` within that deferred syntax, you must also use deferred syntax for the EL expression in `<c:forEach>`'s `items` attribute. Otherwise, the deferred syntax referencing the element variable will not work.

## <c:forTokens>

The `<c:forTokens>` tag is nearly identical to the `<c:forEach>` tag. It contains many of the same attributes (`var`, `varStatus`, `begin`, `end`, and `step`) that behave in the same way as their `<c:forEach>` counterparts when operating in a `for-each` loop over a collection of objects. The major difference with `<c:forTokens>` is that the `items` attribute accepts a `String`, not a collection, and the additional `delims` attribute specifies one or more characters with which to split the `String` into tokens. The tag, then, loops over those tokens.

```
<c:forTokens items="This,is,a,cool,tag." delims="," var="word">
    ${word}<br />
</c:forTokens>
```

## <c:redirect>

You have already seen the `<c:redirect>` tag in use in the `index.jsp` files of many of the sample projects. This tag redirects the user to another URL, just as the name implies. After adding the HTTP `Location` header to the response and changing the HTTP response status code, it aborts execution of the JSP. Because it changes response headers, `<c:redirect>` must be called before the response has started streaming back to the client. Otherwise, it is not successful in redirecting the client, and the client instead receives a truncated response (with everything after the `<c:redirect>` tag in the JSP missing). `<c:redirect>` follows the same rules as `<c:url>` regarding URL encoding, rewriting for session IDs, and adding query parameters using nested `<c:param>` tags. The following examples are all possible uses of the `<c:redirect>` tag; however, this is certainly not an exhaustive example.

```
<c:redirect url="http://www.example.com/" />

<c:redirect url="/tickets">
    <c:param name="action" value="view" />
    <c:param name="ticketId" value="${ticketId}" />
</c:redirect>

<c:redirect url="/browse" context="/store" />
```

## <c:import>

The `<c:import>` tag is a particularly interesting action that enables the retrieval of the contents of the resource at a particular URL. Those contents can then be inlined to the response, saved to a `String` variable, or saved to a `Reader` variable. As with `<c:url>` and `<c:redirect>`, the URL can be for the local context, for another context, or for an external site and is properly encoded and rewritten when necessary. Nested `<c:param>` tags can also specify query parameters to encode into the URL. The `var` attribute specifies the name of the `String` variable to which the content should be saved, and the `scope` attribute can specify the scope of the `String` variable. The `varReader` attribute specifies the name of the `Reader` variable that should be made available for reading the content.

If you use `varReader` to export a `Reader` variable, you cannot use `<c:param>`, and you must use the `Reader` within the nested content of the `<c:import>` tag. The `Reader` variable will not be available after the closing `</c:import>` tag. (This ensures that the JSP engine has the opportunity to close the `Reader`.)

You should never use `var` and `varReader` together; doing so will result in an exception. With neither the `var` nor the `varReader` attributes specified, the content of the resource at the URL is inlined in the JSP. The following examples demonstrate some of the ways that you can use `<c:import>`.

```
<c:import url="/copyright.jsp" />

<c:import url="/ad.jsp" context="/store" var="advertisement" scope="request">
    <c:param name="category" value="${forumCategory}" />
</c:import>

<c:import url="http://www.example.com/embeddedPlayer.do?video=f8ETe9238MNTte"
```

```
            varReader="player" charEncoding="UTF-8">
        <wrox:writeVideoPlugin reader="${player}" />
    </c:import>
```

The first example inlines the contents from the application's local `copyright.jsp` in the page. The second saves the contents of `ad.jsp?category=${forumCategory}` to a `String` named *`advertisement`* in the request scope, properly encoding the *`category`* query parameter. The third fetches some external resource and exports it as a `Reader` object named *`player`*. The imaginary `<wrox:writeVideoPlugin>` tag then uses *`player`* in some way that is unimportant here.

Notice also the use of the `charEncoding` attribute. Chances are you will never use this attribute. However, if the target resource does not return a `Content-Type` header (very unusual) and the content type is something other than ISO-8859-1, you need to specify what the character encoding is by specifying the `charEncoding` attribute.

## <c:set> and <c:remove>

You can use the `<c:set>` tag to set the value of a new or existing scope variable and use its counterpart, `<c:remove>`, to remove a variable from scope.

```
<c:set var="myVariable" value="Hello, World!" />
...
${myVariable}
...
<c:remove var="myVariable" scope="page" />

<c:set var="complexVariable" scope="request">
    nested content including other JSP tags
</c:set>
...
${complexVariable}
...
<c:remove var="complexVariable" scope="request" />
```

As with most other tags that expose scope variables, you can use the `scope` attribute to specify what scope the variable is defined in. (The default is page scope.) Be careful with `<c:remove>` because its `scope` attribute does not work the same: If you do not specify `scope`, all attributes with matching names in all scopes are removed. This is probably not what you want to happen, so you should always use the `scope` attribute.

In addition to the uses previously shown, you can also use `<c:set>` to change the value of a property on a bean.

```
<c:set target="${someObject}" property="propertyName" value="Hello, World!" />

<c:set target="${someObject}" property="propertyName">
    nested content including other JSP tags
</c:set>
```

When used in this manner, the `target` attribute should always be an EL expression that evaluates to either a `Map` or some other bean with mutator methods ("setters") that are used to set property values. The previous examples are both equivalent to calling `someObject.setPropertyName(...)` for a bean or `someObject.put("propertyName", ...)` for a `Map` in Java code.

## Putting Core Library Tags to Use

To get a feel for how the Core tag library works, this section creates an application that lists out contacts in an address book. You can create the address book from scratch or follow along with the Address-Book project available on the wrox.com code download site. Create the standard application with a deployment descriptor containing the standard JSP and session configurations you used in Chapter 6. The index.jsp welcome file should redirect to the /list servlet using the <c:redirect> tag:

```
<c:redirect url="/list" />
```

The base JSP page /WEB-INF/jsp/base.jsp should contain taglib directives for the Core and Function libraries from the JSTL:

```
<%@ taglib prefix="c" uri="http://java.sun.com/jsp/jstl/core" %>
<%@ taglib prefix="fn" uri="http://java.sun.com/jsp/jstl/functions" %>
```

You need something to list, so start by creating a simple Contact POJO with basic information you would find in an address book. Notice in the following code sample that Contact uses the new Java 8 Date and Time API and implements Comparable so that it can be sorted appropriately. The mutator and accessor methods and contents of the constructor have been omitted for brevity.

```
public class Contact implements Comparable<Contact>
{
    private String firstName;
    private String lastName;
    private String phoneNumber;
    private String address;
    private MonthDay birthday;
    private Instant dateCreated;

    public Contact() { }

    public Contact(String firstName, String lastName, String phoneNumber,
                   String address, MonthDay birthday,
                   Instant dateCreated) { ... }

    ...

    @Override
    public int compareTo(Contact other)
    {
        int last = lastName.compareTo(other.lastName);
        if(last == 0)
            return firstName.compareTo(other.firstName);
        return last;
    }
}
```

The ListServlet in Listing 7-1 responds to requests; it contains a static Set of contacts that serves as a database of sorts and is prepopulated with a handful of contacts. The doGet method adds an empty contacts Set to a request attribute if the *empty* parameter is present, or the static Set if the parameter is not present, and then redirects to the /WEB-INF/jsp/view/list.jsp file found in Listing 7-2.

Notice in `list.jsp` the use of `<c:choose>`, `<c:when>`, and `<c:otherwise>` to display a message if the address book is empty and otherwise execute the code to loop over the list. `<c:forEach>` performs this task, and `<c:out>` ensures that the `String` values are properly escaped so that they do not contain XML characters. Finally, the `<c:if>` tag makes sure that the birthday displays only if it is not null.

**LISTING 7-1: ListServlet.java**

```
@WebServlet(
        name = "listServlet",
        urlPatterns = "/list"
)
public class ListServlet extends HttpServlet
{
    private static final SortedSet<Contact> contacts = new TreeSet<>();

    static {
        contacts.add(new Contact("Jane", "Sanders", "555-1593", "394 E 22nd Ave",
                MonthDay.of(Month.JANUARY, 5),
                Instant.parse("2013-02-01T15:22:23-06:00")
        ));
        contacts.add(new Contact( "John", "Smith", "555-0712", "315 Maple St",
                null, Instant.parse("2012-10-15T09:31:17-06:00")
        ));
        contacts.add(new Contact("Scott", "Johnson", "555-9834", "424 Oak Dr",
                MonthDay.of(Month.NOVEMBER, 17),
                Instant.parse("2013-04-04T19:45:01-06:00")
        ));
    }

    @Override
    protected void doGet(HttpServletRequest request, HttpServletResponse response)
            throws ServletException, IOException
    {
        if(request.getParameter("empty") != null)
            request.setAttribute("contacts", Collections.<Contact>emptySet());
        else
            request.setAttribute("contacts", contacts);
        request.getRequestDispatcher("/WEB-INF/jsp/view/list.jsp")
               .forward(request, response);
    }
}
```

**LISTING 7-2: list.jsp**

```
<%--@elvariable id="contacts" type="java.util.Set<com.wrox.Contact>"--%>
<!DOCTYPE html>
<html>
    <head>
        <title>Address Book</title>
    </head>
    <body>
        <h2>Address Book Contacts</h2>
```

*continues*

**LISTING 7-2** *(continued)*

```
            <c:choose>
                <c:when test="${fn:length(contacts) == 0}">
                    <i>There are no contacts in the address book.</i>
                </c:when>
                <c:otherwise>
                    <c:forEach items="${contacts}" var="contact">
                        <b>
                            <c:out value="${contact.lastName}, ${contact.firstName}" />
                        </b><br />
                        <c:out value="${contact.address}" /><br />
                        <c:out value="${contact.phoneNumber}" /><br />
                        <c:if test="${contact.birthday != null}">
                            Birthday: ${contact.birthday}<br />
                        </c:if>
                        Created: ${contact.dateCreated}<br /><br />
                    </c:forEach>
                </c:otherwise>
            </c:choose>
        </body>
    </html>
```

Compile and debug your project and navigate to `http://localhost:8080/address-book/list?empty` in your browser. You should see the message that there are no contacts in the address book, meaning that the `<c:when>` test evaluated to `true`. Now take the *`empty`* parameter off the URL, and you should see a screen like that in Figure 7-1. For the most part this looks okay, but the dates are not formatted in a friendly manner, and there is no support for alternative languages. In the next section you learn more about implementing these.

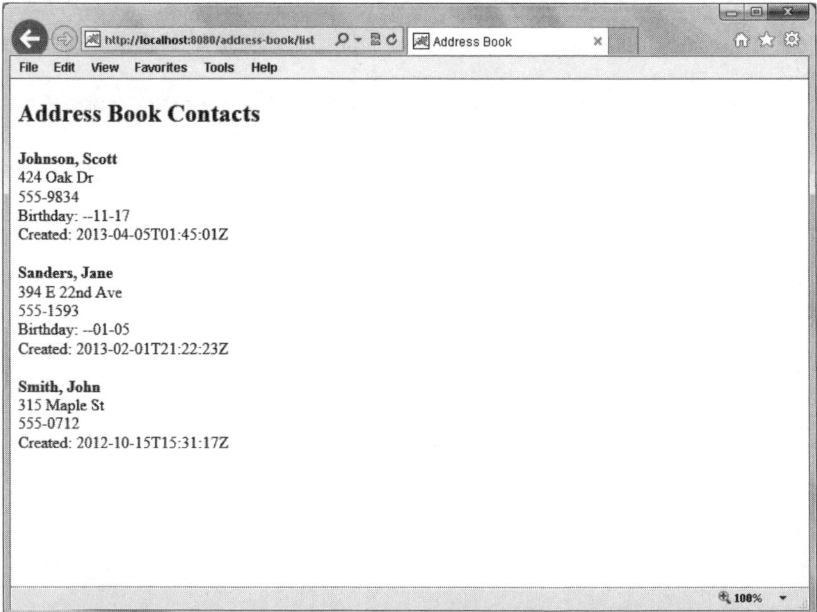


FIGURE 7-1

# USING THE INTERNATIONALIZATION AND FORMATTING TAG LIBRARY (FMT NAMESPACE)

If you intend to create enterprise Java applications for deployment on the web and target large, international audiences, you will ultimately need to *localize* your application to particular regions of the world. This is achieved through *internationalization* (often abbreviated i18n), which is the process of designing an application so that it can adapt to different regions, languages, and cultures without redesigning or rewriting the application for new regions.

After an application is internationalized, you can utilize the internationalization framework to *localize* the application by adding support for the target regions, languages, and cultures. Often the terms localization (often abbreviated L10n) and internationalization are confused, which is understandable considering that they are so interrelated. One handy way to remember the difference is, "First you internationalize through architecture, and then you localize through translation."

## Internationalization and Localization Components

There are three components to internationalization and localization:

- Text must be translatable and translated so that users who speak and understand other languages can use your application.
- Dates, times, and numbers (including currencies and percentages) must be formatted correctly for different locales. For example, 12,934.52 in the United States is actually 12 934,52 in France and 12.934,52 in Germany.
- Prices must be convertible so that they can display in a local currency to match the client's region of the world.

Often, the conversion of currencies is omitted — and for good reason. Displaying prices in different currencies to users can be extremely challenging, inaccurate, and out of date, and today most business financial institutions provide mechanisms for converting your currency to the user's currency during checkout. In many cases it is perfectly sufficient to simply display prices in U.S. dollars. Due to the complexities of this topic, this book does not cover currency conversion.

The JSTL provides a tag library that supports both internationalization and localization efforts in your applications: the Internationalization and Formatting library, whose prefix is `fmt`. In this section you learn about how to use and configure the Formatting library to internationalize your application so that you can later localize it. You often see the term *locale*, which is an identifier representing a specific region, culture, and/or political area. Locales always contain a *two-letter lowercase language code* as specified by ISO 639-1. You can view a list of all these codes at `http://www.loc.gov/standards/iso639-2/php/code_list.php`. This page displays 2-letter ISO 639-1 and 3-letter ISO 639-2 codes. You will only use the 2-letter codes for this book.

For languages where the language code is too ambiguous (Mexican Spanish is slightly different from Spanish in Spain, for example) the locale can optionally contain a *two-letter uppercase country code* as specified by ISO 3166-1, which you can view at `http://www.iso.org/iso/home/standards/country_codes/iso-3166-1_decoding_table.htm`.

In a locale code, the language code always comes first. If a country code is specified, it comes next, with an underscore separating the language and country codes. Occasionally, a locale is also associated with a variant, which is not included as part of the locale code. You do not usually need to worry about variants, but for more information on them, you should see the API documentation for the `java.util.Locale` class. `Locale` is used to represent locales in Java and the JSTL.

The Internationalization and Formatting tag library is divided into two main categories:

- Tags that support internationalization (i18n tags)
- Tags that support date, time, and number formatting (formatting tags)

I18n tags have a sense of resource bundles, which define locale-specific objects. Resource bundles consist of keys that correspond to entries in the bundle and are defined using an arbitrary basename of the developer's choosing with the locale code appended to the basename to form the full resource bundle name. A given key typically has entries in every resource bundle, one for each language and country supported. In this section you learn first about all the i18n tags and then the formatting tags.

The `taglib` directive for the Internationalization and Formatting library follows:

```
<%@ taglib prefix="fmt" uri="http://java.sun.com/jsp/jstl/fmt" %>
```

> **NOTE** *One of the traditional complaints about the JSTL Internationalization and Formatting tag library is that it is more difficult to use than it should be. However, this is sometimes also seen as a matter of personal preference, with other developers thinking the JSTL support for i18n and localization is quite adequate. A lot of this depends on your particular needs, and in Chapter 15 you will use Spring Framework i18n tools to explore internationalization more thoroughly and understand your other options.*

## <fmt:message>

Perhaps the i18n tag that you will use the most (maybe the only i18n tag you will ever use), `<fmt:message>` resolves a localized message in a resource bundle and then either inlines that message on the page or saves it to an EL variable. The required `key` attribute specifies the key of the localization message to resolve in the resource bundle. You use the optional `bundle` attribute to indicate which localization context, created with `<fmt:setBundle>`, should be used for locating the key. This overrides the default bundle. The optional `var` attribute specifies an EL variable to save the localized message to, and the corresponding `scope` attribute can control which scope the variable goes in. Localization messages can also be parameterized using the `<fmt:param>` tag nested within the `<fmt:message>` tag. Say your application had one resource bundle translated for two languages — U.S. English (`en_US`) and Mexican Spanish (`es_MX`) — and each translation contained an entry for the localization message `store.greeting`. The English value for `store.greeting` might look like this:

```
store.greeting=There are {0} products in the store.
```

The Spanish value is similar, except that it is translated:

```
store.greeting=Hay {0} productos en la tienda.
```

The `{0}` token in each message indicates a placeholder that some parameter should replace. Placeholders are zero-based but they do not have to appear in numerical order within the message. Some languages use very different word orders, meaning a parameter may need to be replaced at different places in different languages. Placeholders can also be duplicated when desirable — you may want to insert the same parameter into a message multiple times. Within your JSP, you reference the localization message using the following code.

```
<fmt:message key="store.greeting">
    <fmt:param value="${numberOfProducts}" />
</fmt:message>
```

If `numberOfProducts` were 63, users would see the following output depending on their selected locale:

```
English: There are 63 products in the store.
Spanish: Hay 63 productos en la tienda.
```

The nested `<fmt:param>` tags correspond to the placeholders in order starting from 0. So the first `<fmt:param>` tag specifies a value for `{0}`, the second for `{1}`, and so on, regardless of what order the placeholders actually appear in the localized message. (Messages do not need to have placeholders in them, and you can use `<fmt:message>` without `<fmt:param>`. If a message does contain a placeholder and no `<fmt:param>` is specified for it, the placeholder is left as-is in the message.) Instead of the `value` attribute, you can specify the parameter value by placing it within the `<fmt:param>` opening and closing tags.

```
<fmt:message key="store.greeting">
    <fmt:param>${numberOfProducts}</fmt:param>
</fmt:message>
```

You should also note that the `key` attribute isn't strictly required; rather, the message key is. There is an alternative way of specifying the message key without using the `key` attribute:

```
<fmt:message>some.message.key</fmt:message>

<fmt:message>
    store.greeting
    <fmt:param value="${numberOfProducts}" />
</fmt:message>
```

Although this method is supported, it is rarely used, and many IDEs do not validate message keys unless they are placed within the `key` attribute. In this book, message keys are always specified in the `key` attribute.

> **NOTE** *If you ever see a* `<fmt:message>` *replaced with* `??????`*, this means you failed to validly specify a message key (either with the* `key` *attribute or in the tag body). If some message (such as* `store.greeting`*) is ever replaced with* `???<key>???` *(such as* `???store.greeting???`*), this means that the message key could not be found in the configured resource bundle.*

## <fmt:setLocale>

The `<fmt:setLocale>` tag sets the locale used to resolve resource bundle messages for i18n and formatting. The `value` attribute specifies the locale and can be either a `String` locale code (such as `en_US`) or an EL expression evaluating to an instance of `Locale`. If `value` is a locale code, the `variant` attribute can also be specified to indicate a variant of the locale. The locale is saved to an EL variable with the name *`javax.servlet.jsp.jstl.fmt.locale`* and becomes the default locale in the specified `scope` (which defaults to page scope). If you use this tag, it should come before any other i18n or formatting tags to ensure that the correct locale is used. However, you should not normally need the `<fmt:setLocale>` tag. Internationalized applications typically have a mechanism (such as loading saved locale settings from a user account) by which the locale is automatically set before the request ever gets forwarded to a JSP. You explore this further in Chapter 15.

```
<fmt:setLocale value="en_US" />

<fmt:setLocale value="${locale}" />
```

## <fmt:bundle> and <fmt:setBundle>

I18n tags in JSTL rely on a localization context to inform them of the current resource bundle and locale. You can use `<fmt:setLocale>` and other techniques to specify the locale in the current localization context. `<fmt:bundle>` and `<fmt:setBundle>` are two ways to indicate the resource bundle that should be used. When an i18n tag needs to know its localization context, it looks in several places, using the first specified localization context it finds in this order of precedence:

- If the `bundle` attribute of the `<fmt:message>` tag is specified, it uses that value with preference over all other bundles that might apply to the tag.
- If the i18n tag is nested with a `<fmt:bundle>` tag, it uses this bundle (unless overridden by the `bundle` attribute on `<fmt:message>`).
- If the default localization context is specified using the context init parameter or EL variable named *`javax.servlet.jsp.jstl.fmt.localizationContext`*, it uses that bundle. You learn how to specify this later in this section.

Although the `<fmt:bundle>` tag creates an ad-hoc localization context that affects only the nested tags within, `<fmt:setBundle>` exports a localization context to an EL variable that i18n tags can later use by referencing the bundle variable in the `bundle` attribute. The name of the exported variable is specified in the `var` attribute and has the scope specified in `scope` (which defaults to page scope). If you do not specify `var`, the localization context is saved to the EL variable named *`javax.servlet.jsp.jstl.fmt.localizationContext`* and becomes the default localization context for that scope. The following example demonstrates the precedence of bundle definitions.

```
<fmt:setBundle basename="Errors" var="errorsBundle" />

<fmt:bundle basename="Titles">
    <fmt:message key="titles.homepage" />

    <fmt:message key="errors.notFound" bundle="${errorsBundle}" />
</fmt:bundle>

<fmt:message key="others.greeting" />
```

The basename attribute indicates the base name of the resource bundle — that is, the beginning of the resource bundle file, before the locale code is appended to it. The <fmt:message> tag outputting the titles.homepage message will use the Titles bundle defined by the <fmt:bundle> tag within which it is nested, whereas the errors.notFound message will resolve using the Errors bundle defined in the <fmt:setBundle> tag. Finally, the others.greeting message will resolve using the default localization context.

As with <fmt:setLocale>, you will rarely (if ever) use the <fmt:bundle> and <fmt:setBundle> tags. There are tools that make managing this easier, and they are discussed later in this section and more in depth in Chapter 15.

## <fmt:requestEncoding>

The <fmt:requestEncoding> tag sets the character encoding for the current request using the var attribute so that request parameters are correctly decoded with the character encoding appropriate to the given locale. You do not need to use this tag and do not see it used in this book for two reasons:

- Your Java servlets process request parameters before any <fmt:requestEncoding> tag has a chance to change the request character encoding.
- All modern browsers include a Content-Type request header with a character encoding for any requests whose encoding differs from ISO-8859-1. They all also use the character encoding returned by the last response from the site the request is sent to. This eliminates the need to manually set the request character encoding.

This tag is a legacy tag that originates from an era where the encoding of request attributes was rarely known and had to be guessed. The developer could make an educated guess about the encoding based on the selected language. Today, because of the behavior of modern browsers, the need to do this has gone away.

## <fmt:timeZone> and <fmt:setTimeZone>

The formatting tags that handle dates and times need a locale and a time zone to function properly. The locale comes from the localization context, which you read about earlier in the discussion about <fmt:bundle> and <fmt:setBundle>, and is determined using the same rules defined in that section. However, the idea of a time zone, while sometimes correlated to the region or language specified in the locale, is not strictly tied to the locale. Someone from the United States may visit Tokyo, for example, and want to use your application in English with standard U.S. date and time formatting while seeing the dates and times in Tokyo time. For this reason and many others, time zones and locales are separate in Java and in the JSTL. Formatting tags that require time zones resolve the time zone to use with the given strategy, in order of precedence:

- If a date and time formatting tag has a value specified for its timeZone attribute, use that value with preference over all other time zones.
- If the tag is nested within a <fmt:timeZone> tag, use the time zone specified by <fmt:timeZone>.

- If the context init parameter or EL variable named *javax.servlet.jsp.jstl.fmt.timeZone* is specified, use that time zone.
- Otherwise, use the time zone provided by the container (typically the JVM time zone, the time zone of the underlying operating system).

The `<fmt:timeZone>` tag is the time zone analog to the `<fmt:bundle>` action. It creates an ad-hoc time zone scope within which any nested tags use the given time zone. Its only attribute is `value`, which can be an EL expression evaluating to a `java.util.TimeZone`, or to a `String` matching any legal time zone ID as specified in the IANA Time Zone Database. You can learn about these IDs on the IANA website (`http://www.iana.org/time-zones`) or in the API documentation for `TimeZone`. If `value` is `null` or empty, the GMT time zone is assumed.

The `<fmt:setTimeZone>` tag, on the other hand, acts like the `<fmt:setBundle>` tag and exports the `value` specified time zone to a scope variable. The `var` attribute specifies the name of the EL variable to export the time zone to in the scope specified by `scope` (which defaults to page scope, as usual). If `var` is omitted, the time zone is saved to the EL variable named *javax.servlet.jsp.jstl.fmt.timeZone* and becomes the default time zone for that scope.

```
<fmt:setTimeZone value="America/Chicago" var="timeZoneCst" />

<fmt:timeZone value="${someTimeZone}">
    tags nested here use someTimeZone
</fmt:timeZone>

<fmt:timeZone value="${timeZoneCst}">
    tags nested here use America/Chicago
</fmt:timeZone>
```

## <fmt:formatDate> and <fmt:parseDate>

The `<fmt:formatDate>` tag, as the name implies, formats the specified date (and/or time) using the default or specified locale and the default or specified time zone. The formatted date is then either inlined or saved to the variable specified in the attribute `var` with the indicated `scope`. The `timeZone` attribute specifies a different `TimeZone` or `String` time zone ID to format the date. The date value is specified using the value attribute. Currently, `value` must be an EL expression evaluating to an instance of `java.util.Date`; neither `java.util.Calendar` nor the Java 8 Date & Time API classes are supported. In the next chapter, you create a custom tag library with an improved date formatting tag that supports these newer classes. A future version of the JSTL will likely support these types.

How a date is formatted is determined using the locale combined with the `type`, `dateStyle`, `timeStyle`, and `pattern` attributes. `type` should be one of "date," "time," or "both" to indicate whether to output just the date, just the time, or the date followed by the time, respectively. The `dateStyle` and `timeStyle` attributes both follow the semantics defined in the API documentation for `java.text.DateFormat` and must be one of "default" (conveniently, the default), "short," "medium," "long," or "full." These attributes specify how the date and time, respectively, are formatted in relation to their locales. If you need to you can also specify a custom formatting pattern according to the `java.text.SimpleDateFormat` rules using the `pattern` attribute. In this case the `type`, `dateStyle`, and `timeStyle` attributes are ignored. Doing this also ignores the styles that come with the locale (though the months are still localized to the language), so it's best to avoid using `pattern` if at all possible.

```
<fmt:formatDate value="${someDate}" type="both" dateStyle="long"
                timeStyle="long" />

<fmt:formatDate value="${someDate}" type="date" dateStyle="short"
                var="formattedDate" timeZone="${differentTimeZone}" />
```

Given a date of the 3rd day of October in the year 2013 at the time 15:22:37 in the default time zone of America/Chicago, the first example outputs "October 3, 2013 3:22:37 PM CDT" for the U.S. English locale and "3 October 2013 15:22:37 CDT" for the France French locale. The second example formats the date only and in a shorter format in the time zone specified by `${differentTimeZone}` and saves it to the *`formattedDate`* variable. The value of *`formattedDate`* is "10/3/13" for the U.S. English locale and "03/10/13" for the France French locale.

If `<fmt:parseDate>` sounds to you like the opposite of `<fmt:formatDate>`, you're exactly right. `<fmt:parseDate>` has all the same attributes and rules as `<fmt:formatDate>`, but it reverses the process. It takes formatted `Strings` like what `<fmt:formatDate>` would output and parses them into `Date` objects. Typically, you would always assign this to a variable using the `var` attribute; otherwise, it's not very useful. Also, instead of specifying the date to parse using the `value` attribute, you can specify it as the body content within the tag.

## <fmt:formatNumber> and <fmt:parseNumber>

The `<fmt:formatNumber>` tag is an extremely powerful action that enables the formatting of numbers (integer-style and decimals), currencies, and percentages. It has many attributes and not all of them apply to all situations. First, know that this tag, like so many others you have seen, has `var` and `scope` attributes that behave as you are accustomed. If `var` is omitted, the formatted number is inlined in the JSP. Now consider the need to format a currency and assume *`number`* is a scope variable with the value 12349.15823.

```
<fmt:formatNumber type="currency" value="${number}" />
```

This outputs "$12,349.16" for the U.S. English locale and "12.349,16 €" for the Spain Spanish locale. You should immediately see the problem: The number was represented with two different currency symbols without a currency conversion taking place. This would be inaccurate and confusing for any users of your application. Because of this, you should always specify the `currencyCode` attribute, which can be any valid ISO 4217 currency code. (You can view this list at `http://en.wikipedia.org/wiki/ISO_4217`).

```
<fmt:formatNumber type="currency" value="${number}" currencyCode="USD" />
```

The output of this is still "$12,349.16" for the U.S. English locale but is now "12.349,16 USD" for the Spain Spanish locale, which is correct. The `currencySymbol` attribute can also be used to override the currency symbol used, but it is best to leave this alone. The tag can correctly determine the currency symbol based on the currency code you specify. Both of these attributes are ignored if `type` is not "currency."

Another valid `type` value (and the default) is "number." This formats a number as a generic number. By default it rounds numbers to three digits and groups digits of numbers according to the locale.

```
<fmt:formatNumber type="number" value="${number}" />
```

This outputs "12,349.158" for the U.S. English locale and "12.349,158" for the Spain Spanish locale. You use the `maxFractionDigits` attribute to increase and decrease the rounding accuracy by specifying the number of digits after the decimal separator and the `maxIntegerDigits` to specify the maximum number of digits before the decimal separator. (Don't ever use `maxIntegerDigits` because it can truncate your numbers. For example, if set to 3, the number 12345 becomes 345.) The `minFractionDigits` is used to pad zeroes onto the end of the decimal portion of the number out to the specified number of digits, and likewise `minIntegerDigits` is used to pad zeroes onto the beginning of the integer portion of the number. The `groupingUsed` attribute (default `true`) specifies whether digits should be grouped in the formatted number. If `false`, the output from the previous example would have been "12349.158" and "12349,158." These five attributes are all accepted for all three number `types`.

The third and final valid `type` value is "percent" and is used to format the number as a percentage.

```
<fmt:formatNumber type="percent" value="0.8572" />
```

The output of this is "86%" for both the U.S. English locale and the Spain Spanish locale because the default strategy is to round percentages to whole numbers. If the `maxFractionDigits` attribute were set to 2, the values would be "85.72%" and "85,72%". Notice that the number is automatically multiplied by 100 for you so that it is converted to a percentage. The default value for `maxFractionDigits` is locale-specific for currencies, 3 for numbers and 0 for percentages. There is also a `pattern` attribute with which you can specify a custom pattern to format the number according to the `java.text.DecimalFormat` rules. You generally want to avoid using this attribute.

Like `<fmt:parseDate>`, `<fmt:parseNumber>` reverses the process of `<fmt:formatNumber>`. It does not have the `maxFractionDigits`, `maxIntegerDigits`, `minFractionDigits`, `minIntegerDigits`, or `groupingUsed` attributes because that information is not needed to parse numbers. It does contain the additional attributes `integerOnly` (which specifies whether to ignore the fraction part of the number and defaults to `false`) and `parseLocale` (which specifies the locale to use when parsing the number, if other than the default locale). Also like `<fmt:parseDate>`, you can specify the number to parse in the `value` attribute or in the tag body content.

## Putting i18n and Formatting Library Tags to Use

To explore the i18n and Formatting library further, you can expand upon the Address-Book project you created earlier in the book and internationalize it. You can continue to add to the previous project, or you can follow along in the Address-Book-i18n project from the `wrox.com` code download site. The first thing you should do is add a new context init parameter in the deployment descriptor.

```
<context-param>
    <param-name>javax.servlet.jsp.jstl.fmt.localizationContext</param-name>
    <param-value>AddressBook-messages</param-value>
</context-param>
```

This establishes a resource bundle from which localized messages can be loaded. But where does the container locate this bundle? It looks for a file anywhere on your class path named `AddressBook-messages_[language]_[region].properties`. If it does not find that file, it looks for `AddressBook-messages_[language].properties`. If it doesn't find that either, it switches to the fallback locale (English) and looks for its bundle. To satisfy this need, create a file named `AddressBook-messages_en_US.properties` in the `source/production/resources` directory of your IDE project. All the files in this `resources` directory will get copied to the `/WEB-INF/classes` directory at build time.

```
title.browser=Address Book
title.page=Address Book Contacts
message.noContacts=There are no contacts in the address book.
label.birthday=Birthday
label.creationDate=Created
```

You also want a translated version of this file so that you can test switching languages, so create a file named `AddressBook-messages_fr_FR.properties` in the same directory.

```
title.browser=Carnet d'Adresses
title.page=Contacts du Carnet d'Adresses
message.noContacts=Il n'y a pas des contacts dans le carnet d'adresses.
label.birthday=Anniversaire
label.creationDate=Établi
```

You need a way to easily change the language the page displays in, so add the following code to the top of the `doGet` method in the `ListServlet`. The `Config` class here is imported from `javax.servlet.jsp.jstl.core.Config`.

```
        String language = request.getParameter("language");
        if("french".equalsIgnoreCase(language))
            Config.set(request, Config.FMT_LOCALE, Locale.FRANCE);
```

Because the `<fmt:formatDate>` tag doesn't support the Java 8 Date and Time API, you need a way to access the old-style `Date` object, so add the following method to the `Contact` POJO. (If this seems like a hack to you, that's because it is. It's the easiest way right now to get the `Date` object for formatting. In the next chapter you create a way to format the new API without this hack.)

```
    public Date getOldDateCreated()
    {
        return new Date(this.dateCreated.toEpochMilli());
    }
```

Finally, add the `taglib` directive you learned about earlier in the chapter to the `/WEB-INF/jsp/base.jspf` file. Now that all the groundwork has been laid, take a look at the new (substantially changed) `list.jsp` in Listing 7-3. All literal text is replaced with `<fmt:message>` tags referencing the keys from your properties files. The process of placing the `<fmt:message>` tags in the JSP is the internationalization of your application. The process of creating the properties files that contain the translations is the localization of your application.

Also note the use of `<fmt:formatDate>` to format the creation date for display on the page and how the code that displays the birthday has changed. Now test it all out by compiling and debugging your project and going to `http://localhost:8080/address-book/list` in your browser. You can see that it looks the same for the most part, except that the birthday and creation date are both displaying in a friendly manner. Add `?language=french` to the URL, and the page should now display in French instead of English, as shown in Figure 7-2. Add `&empty` to the URL and you see in French the message that there are no contacts. You have successfully internationalized and localized your application.

**LISTING 7-3: list.jsp**

```
<%--@elvariable id="contacts" type="java.util.Set<com.wrox.Contact>"--%>
<!DOCTYPE html>
<html>
    <head>
        <title><fmt:message key="title.browser" /></title>
    </head>
    <body>
        <h2><fmt:message key="title.page" /></h2>
        <c:choose>
            <c:when test="${fn:length(contacts) == 0}">
                <i><fmt:message key="message.noContacts" /></i>
            </c:when>
            <c:otherwise>
                <c:forEach items="${contacts}" var="contact">
                    <b>
                        <c:out value="${contact.lastName}, ${contact.firstName}" />
                    </b><br />
                    <c:out value="${contact.address}" /><br />
                    <c:out value="${contact.phoneNumber}" /><br />
                    <c:if test="${contact.birthday != null}">
                        <fmt:message key="label.birthday" />:
                        ${contact.birthday.month.getDisplayName(
                            'FULL', pageContext.response.locale
                        )} ${contact.birthday.dayOfMonth}<br />
                    </c:if>
                    <fmt:message key="label.creationDate" />:
                    <fmt:formatDate value="${contact.oldDateCreated}" type="both"
                                    dateStyle="long" timeStyle="long" />
                    <br /><br />
                </c:forEach>
            </c:otherwise>
        </c:choose>
    </body>
</html>
```

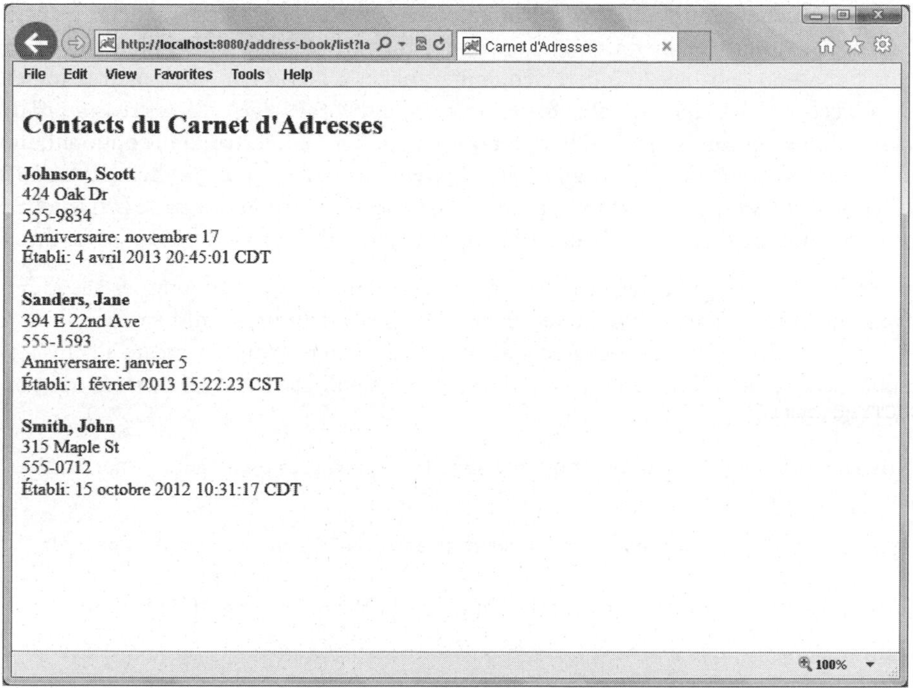


FIGURE 7-2

## USING THE DATABASE ACCESS TAG LIBRARY (SQL NAMESPACE)

The JSTL contains a library of tags that provides transactional access to relational databases. The standard prefix for this library is `sql`, and its `taglib` directive is similar to previous directives you have seen.

```
<%@ taglib prefix="sql" uri="http://java.sun.com/jsp/jstl/sql" %>
```

Generally speaking, performing database actions within the presentation layer (JSPs) is frowned upon and should be avoided if at all possible. Instead, such code should go in the business logic of the application, typically a Servlet or, more appropriately, a repository that the Servlet uses. For this reason, this book does not dive deeply into the details of the SQL tag library and strongly discourages you from using this library. However, this tag library is sometimes useful, especially for prototyping new applications or quickly testing theories or concepts, so an overview of its use is warranted.

The actions in the SQL library provide you with the capability of querying data with `SELECT` statements; accessing and iterating the results of those queries; updating data with `INSERT`, `UPDATE`, and `DELETE` statements; and performing any number of these actions within a transaction. Typically, the tags in this library operate using a `javax.sql.DataSource`. The `<sql:query>`, `<sql:update>`, `<sql:transaction>`, and `<sql:setDataSource>` tags all have `dataSource` attributes for specifying the data source that should be used to perform that action.

The `dataSource` attribute must either be a `DataSource` or a `String`. If it's a `DataSource`, it is used as-is. If it's a `String`, the container attempts to resolve the `String` as a JNDI name for a `DataSource`. If a matching `DataSource` is not found, the container makes a last-ditch effort by treating the `String` as a JDBC connection URL and attempts to connect using the `java.sql.DriverManager`. If none of these works, an exception is thrown. For all tags the `dataSource` attribute is optional, in which case the container looks for the EL variable named *`javax.servlet.jsp.jstl.sql.dataSource`* in the default scope (set using a context init parameter or `<sql:setDataSource>`). If it is a `String` or a `DataSource`, the same logic previously described is applied. Otherwise, an exception is thrown.

Queries are performed using the `<sql:query>` tag and update actions using the `<sql:update>` tag. For either tag, the SQL statement can be specified in the `sql` attribute or in the nested body content. Nested tags can be used to specify prepared statement parameters. You can create a transaction with `<sql:transaction>`, and all nested query and update tags will use that transaction, but you must keep in mind two rules:

- Only the `<sql:transaction>` tag may specify a `dataSource` attribute (nested tags within it may not).
- If you query data, you must iterate over that data within the transaction as well.

The following code demonstrates some of the things possible with the SQL tag library:

```
<sql:transaction dataSource="${someDataSource}" isolation="read_committed">
    <sql:update sql="UPDATE dbo.Account
                     SET Balance = Balance - ?, LastTransaction = ?
                     WHERE AccountId = ?">
        <sql:param value="${transferAmount}" />
        <fmt:parseDate var="transactionDate" value="${effectiveDate}" />
        <sql:dateParam value="${transactionDate}" />
        <sql:param value="${sourceAccount}" />
    </sql:update>
    <sql:update>
        UPDATE dbo.Account SET Balance = Balance + ?, LastTransaction = ?
        WHERE AccountId = ?
        <sql:param value="${transferAmount}" />
        <sql:dateParam value="${someLaterDate}" />
        <sql:param value="${destinationAccount}" />
    </sql:update>
</sql:transaction>

<sql:query var="results" sql="SELECT * FROM dbo.User WHERE Status = ?">
    <sql:param value="${statusParameter}" />
</sql:query>

<c:forEach items="${results.rows}" var="user">
    ...
</c:forEach>
```

## USING THE XML PROCESSING TAG LIBRARY (X NAMESPACE)

Like the SQL tag library, the XML Processing tag library is not recommended for use and is not covered in-depth in this book. When it was invented, XML was the only widespread standard with which applications shared data, and having the ability to parse and traverse XML was crucial. Today, more and more applications support the JSON standard as an alternative to XML, and several highly efficient libraries can map objects to JSON or XML and back to objects. These tools are easier to use than the XML tag library and can take care of data transformation where it belongs — in the business logic.

The XML tag library, whose prefix is `x`, is based on the XPath standard and consists of nodes or node sets, variable bindings, functions, and namespace prefixes. It contains many actions similar to the tags in the Core tag library but designed specifically to work with XPath expressions against an XML document. The `taglib` directive and a small sampling of what can be done with the XML library are demonstrated in the following code.

```
<%@ taglib prefix="x" uri="http://java.sun.com/jsp/jstl/xml" %>

<c:import url="http://www.example.news/feed.xml" var="feed" />
<x:parse doc="${feed}" var="parsedDoc" />

<x:out select="$parsedDoc/feed/title" />

<x:forEach select="$parsedDoc/feed/stories//story">
    <x:out select="@title" /><br />
    <x:out select="@url" /><br /><br />
</x:forEach>
```

## REPLACING JAVA CODE WITH JSP TAGS

In Chapter 6, you replaced a few lines of Java code with Expression Language (EL) in the JSPs for the Customer Support application. However, you simply could not change much because you did not have the tools yet. In this section you see nearly all of the JSP Java code replaced with JSTL tags. You can follow along in the Customer-Support-v5 project from the `wrox.com` code download site. Start by looking at the `/WEB-INF/jsp/view/login.jsp` page. As shown in the following code sample, not much has changed (because there wasn't much Java code to begin with). The `@elvariable` type hint has been added to the first line of the page above the doctype, and the only scriptlet on the page was replaced with the `<c:if>` tag.

```
<%--@elvariable id="loginFailed" type="java.lang.Boolean"--%>
...
        You must log in to access the customer support site.<br /><br />
        <c:if test="${loginFailed}">
            <b>The username and password you entered are not correct. Please try
                again.</b><br /><br />
        </c:if>
        <form method="POST" action="<c:url value="/login" />">
...
```

/WEB-INF/jsp/view/viewTicket.jsp has been changed more, and again all the Java code in the file is now gone. You can see this change in Listing 7-4. The series of scriptlets and expressions that listed links to the attachments has been replaced with a <c:if> test of the number of attachments, a <c:forEach> loop over the list of attachments, and another <c:if> tag using the loop tag status variable to determine whether to print a comma before the current attachment. Also, most EL expressions have been placed within the value attribute of <c:out> tags. This protects the application from injection of HTML and JavaScript. The <c:out> tags escape any XML reserved characters as long as the escapeXml attribute is left with its default true value. It's good to get into the habit of always using <c:out> to output String variables. However, variables that you know with certainty are non-char primitives (integers, decimals, and so on) do not need escaping.

**LISTING 7-4: viewTicket.jsp**

```
<%--@elvariable id="ticketId" type="java.lang.String"--%>
<%--@elvariable id="ticket" type="com.wrox.Ticket"--%>
<!DOCTYPE html>
<html>
    <head>
        <title>Customer Support</title>
    </head>
    <body>
        <a href="<c:url value="/login?logout" />">Logout</a>
        <h2>Ticket #${ticketId}: <c:out value="${ticket.subject}" /></h2>
        <i>Customer Name - <c:out value="${ticket.customerName}" /></i><br /><br />
        <c:out value="${ticket.body}" /><br /><br />
        <c:if test="${ticket.numberOfAttachments > 0}">
            Attachments:
            <c:forEach items="${ticket.attachments}" var="attachment"
                       varStatus="status">
                <c:if test="${!status.first}">, </c:if>
                <a href="<c:url value="/tickets">
                    <c:param name="action" value="download" />
                    <c:param name="ticketId" value="${ticketId}" />
                    <c:param name="attachment" value="${attachment.name}" />
                </c:url>"><c:out value="${attachment.name}" /></a>
            </c:forEach><br /><br />
        </c:if>
        <a href="<c:url value="/tickets" />">Return to list tickets</a>
    </body>
</html>
```

The /WEB-INF/jsp/view/listTickets.jsp file in Listing 7-5 uses many of the same features to replace Java code as Listing 7-4 but also utilizes the more complex <c:choose>, <c:when>, and <c:otherwise> to replace the old if-else code. The <c:when> tests whether the ticket database is empty and prints, "There Are No Tickets in the System" if it is. Otherwise (hence the name of the tag) the <c:forEach> loop iterates over the database. Notice here that the items attribute of <c:forEach> resolves to a Map, so each iteration exposes a Map.Entry<Integer, Ticket> variable. It's easy to access the int key with entry.key and the corresponding Ticket value with entry .value. The <c:out> tag outputs user input in a safe way.

One final note about Listing 7-5: The `@elvariable` type hint is wrapped for the purposes of printing in this book; however, it must be all on one line for your IDE to recognize it.

**LISTING 7-5: listTickets.jsp**

```
<%--@elvariable id="ticketDatabase"
                type="java.util.Map<Integer, com.wrox.Ticket>"--%>
<!DOCTYPE html>
<html>
    <head>
        <title>Customer Support</title>
    </head>
    <body>
        <a href="<c:url value="/login?logout" />">Logout</a>
        <h2>Tickets</h2>
        <a href="<c:url value="/tickets">
            <c:param name="action" value="create" />
        </c:url>">Create Ticket</a><br /><br />
        <c:choose>
            <c:when test="${fn:length(ticketDatabase) == 0}">
                <i>There are no tickets in the system.</i>
            </c:when>
            <c:otherwise>
                <c:forEach items="${ticketDatabase}" var="entry">
                    Ticket ${entry.key}: <a href="<c:url value="/tickets">
                        <c:param name="action" value="view" />
                        <c:param name="ticketId" value="${entry.key}" />
                    </c:url>"><c:out value="${entry.value.subject}" /></a>
                    (customer: <c:out value="${entry.value.customerName}" />)<br />
                </c:forEach>
            </c:otherwise>
        </c:choose>
    </body>
</html>
```

The only JSP remaining that still contains Java code at this point is `/WEB-INF/jsp/view/sessions.jsp`. This JSP contains a definition for a special method that converts a time interval into friendly text, such as "less than a second" or "about *x* minutes." Unfortunately, nothing you have learned in this chapter can easily replace that method or how it's used. If you really need to, you could calculate this value in some Servlet code and forward to the JSP with a list of POJOs instead of a list of `HttpSessions`. However, that would be more work than necessary, so you can leave replacing this Java code as an exercise to complete in the next chapter.

Now compile and fire up your application and go to `http://localhost:8080/support/` to log in. Create some tickets, view the list of tickets, and view the tickets you created. Include some HTML tags, quotes, and apostrophes in your ticket titles and bodies. In the previous version of the project these would have been printed literally and interpreted as HTML in your browser. You can view the page source to see how they are now escaped properly and don't pose a danger to your application anymore.

## SUMMARY

In this chapter you have learned about all the features that the Java Standard Tag Library (JSTL) brings to the table, and also a little bit more about JSP tags in general and how they are created. You've explored the various facets of the Core tag library and the Internationalization and Formatting tag library, and also took a brief look at accessing databases and parsing XML in JSPs. You saw how to replace Java code with JSP tags and how the JSTL covers almost everything you could need to do in a JSP, and you replaced nearly all the presentation layer Java code in the Customer Support application that you are working on for Multinational Widget Corporation.

You may have noticed that some things could be done better or more easily (such as formatting dates using the Java 8 Date and Time API) if you could create your own tags, and that the clever time interval formatter in the session list still uses Java code. In the next chapter you learn about creating custom tags, functions, and tag and function libraries, and you apply that to get rid of any remaining Java in your JSPs. Finally, recall that you did not internationalize and localize the Customer Support application. In Chapter 15 you study internationalization more in-depth using tools provided by Spring Framework that make the task substantially easier.

# Writing Custom Tag and Function Libraries

## IN THIS CHAPTER

- All about TLDs, tag files, and tag handlers
- Creating an HTML template using a tag file
- How to create a more useful date formatting tag handler
- Abbreviating strings using an EL function
- How to replace Java code with custom JSP tags

### WROX.COM CODE DOWNLOADS FOR THIS CHAPTER

You can find the `wrox.com` code downloads for this chapter at `www.wrox.com/go/projavaforwebapps` on the Download Code tab. The code for this chapter is divided into the following major examples:

- c.tld
- fn.tld
- Template-Tags Project
- Customer-Support-v6 Project

### NEW MAVEN DEPENDENCIES FOR THIS CHAPTER

In addition to the Maven dependencies introduced in previous chapters, you also need the following Maven dependency:

```
<dependency>
    <groupId>org.apache.commons</groupId>
    <artifactId>commons-lang3</artifactId>
```

```
        <version>3.1</version>
        <scope>compile</scope>
    </dependency>
```

## UNDERSTANDING TLDS, TAG FILES, AND TAG HANDLERS

In Chapter 7 you explored the Java Standard Tag Library (JSTL) and also got a brief introduction to the Tag Library Descriptor (TLD), a special file that describes the tags and/or functions in a library. In this chapter you learn more about the TLD and how tags and functions are declared within them. You also learn how to create tag handlers and tag files.

All JSP tags result in execution of some tag handler. The tag handler is an implementation of `javax.servlet.jsp.tagext.Tag` or `javax.servlet.jsp.tagext.SimpleTag` and contains the Java code necessary to achieve the tag's wanted behavior. A tag handler is specified within a tag definition in a TLD, and the container uses this information to map a tag in a JSP to the Java code that should execute in place of that tag.

However, tags do not always have to be written as Java classes explicitly. Just like the container can translate and compile JSPs into `HttpServlets`, it can also translate and compile tag files into `SimpleTags`. Tag files are not as powerful as straight Java code, and you cannot do things like parse nested tags within a tag file like you can with an explicit tag handler, but tag files do have the advantages of using simple markup like JSPs and allowing the use of other JSP tags within them. A tag definition in a TLD can point to either a tag handler class or to a tag file. However, you do not have to create a TLD to use a tag defined in a tag file. The `taglib` directive enables you to do this using the `tagdir` attribute:

```
<%@ taglib prefix="myTags" tagdir="/WEB-INF/tags" %>
```

Notice how this `taglib` directive is different from others you have seen. Instead of specifying a URI for a TLD file containing the tag library's definitions, it specifies a directory in which tag files can be found. Any `.tag` or `.tagx` files within the `tagdir` directory are bound to the `myTags` namespace in this case. Tag files in an application *must* be within the `/WEB-INF/tags` directory, but they may also be within a subdirectory of this directory. You could use this to have multiple name spaces of tag files in your application, as in the following example.

```
<%@ taglib prefix="t" tagdir="/WEB-INF/tags/template" %>
<%@ taglib prefix="f" tagdir="/WEB-INF/tags/formats" %>
```

> **NOTE** *The difference between* `.tag` *and* `.tagx` *is the same as the difference between* `.jsp` *and* `.jspx`*. The* `.tag` *files contain JSP syntax while* `.tagx` *files contain JSP Document (XML) syntax. For more information on the difference between JSP and JSP Document syntax, refer to "A Note About JSP Documents" in Chapter 4.*

JSP tag files can also be defined in JAR files within your application's `/WEB-INF/lib` directory, but the rules are slightly different. Whereas tag files in your application must be in `/WEB-INF/tags` and can be declared either in a TLD *or* with a `taglib` directive pointing to the directory, tag files in a JAR file are placed in the `/META-INF/tags` directory and *must* be declared within a TLD in the `/META-INF` directory (or subdirectory) of the same JAR file.

## Reading the Java Standard Tag Library TLD

To write custom tag and function libraries, you must understand the JSP tag library XSD and how to write tags with it. The best way to demonstrate this is by example, and using something you are already familiar with should be helpful, so take a look at the TLD for the Core tag library from the JSTL. You can find this within the `org.glassfish.web:javax.servlet.jsp.jstl` Maven artifact JAR file (look for the `/META-INF/c.tld` file), or you can download it from the `wrox.com` code download site. Start by looking at the initial declaration within the file:

```
<?xml version="1.0" encoding="UTF-8" ?>
<!--...Copyright (c) 2010 Oracle and/or its affiliates. All rights reserved...-->
<taglib xmlns="http://java.sun.com/xml/ns/javaee"
    xmlns:xsi="http://www.w3.org/2001/XMLSchema-instance"
    xsi:schemaLocation="http://java.sun.com/xml/ns/javaee
                    http://java.sun.com/xml/ns/javaee/web-jsptaglibrary_2_1.xsd"
    version="2.1">
    ...
</taglib>
```

If you are at all familiar with XML, you know that this just sets up the document root element and declares that the document is using the XML schema definition `web-jsptaglibrary_2_1.xsd`. This XML schema defines how a TLD is structured, just like `web-app_3_1.xsd` in `web.xml` defines how the deployment descriptor is structured. The only thing of importance about the JSP tag library XSD that is not obvious from reading through a TLD file is that the schema uses a strict element sequence, meaning that any elements you use must come in a certain order, or your TLD file will not validate. The first five elements within the document root declare general information about the tag library.

```
<description>JSTL 1.2 core library</description>
<display-name>JSTL core</display-name>
<tlib-version>1.2</tlib-version>
<short-name>c</short-name>
<uri>http://java.sun.com/jsp/jstl/core</uri>
```

For this code:

- The `<description>` and `<display-name>` elements provide useful names that XML tools (such as your IDE) can display, but are irrelevant to the actual content of the TLD and are completely optional. You can actually have as many `<description>`s and `<display-name>`s as you want (as long as order is maintained), allowing you to specify different display names and descriptions for different languages. Another optional element not shown here is `<icon>`, which must always come after `<display-name>` and before `<tlib-version>`. Don't worry about `<icon>`; you will never need to use it.
- `<tlib-version>` is a required element. Any TLDs you create must have exactly one of these. It defines the version of your tag library and must contain only numbers and periods (groups of numbers that can be separated only with a single period).
- `<short-name>` indicates the preferred and default prefix (or namespace) for this tag library and is also required. It cannot contain white space or start with a number or underscore.
- The fifth element shown here, `<uri>`, defines the URI for this tag library. This element is not required, and (as explained in Chapter 7) the lack of a URI means that the `<jsp-config>`

in the deployment descriptor must contain a `<taglib>` declaration for this tag library to be useable. It's best to always use `<uri>` despite the fact that it's optional, and remember that it doesn't have to be (and really shouldn't be) a URL to an actual resource. Your TLD can have only one `<uri>`.

## Defining Validators and Listeners

The next element in the Core TLD defines a validator.

```
<validator>
  <description>
      Provides core validation features for JSTL tags.
  </description>
  <validator-class>
      org.apache.taglibs.standard.tlv.JstlCoreTLV
  </validator-class>
</validator>
```

Validators extend the `javax.servlet.jsp.tagext.TagLibraryValidator` class to validate a JSP at compile time to ensure it uses the library correctly. The validator in this case performs checks that, for example, make sure the `<c:param>` tag is nested only within tags that support it (such as `<c:url>` and `<c:import>`). Validator elements have nested, in order, zero or more `<description>` elements, exactly one required `<validator-class>` element, and zero or more `<init-param>` elements (which work like you're accustomed to in the deployment descriptor). A tag library can have zero or more validators. Validators are difficult to implement because doing so requires you to actually parse the JSP syntax. Because validators are almost never needed and extremely complicated, they are not covered in this book.

Validators are mentioned here only because they must be declared after the `<uri>` element and before any `<listener>` elements. Listener declarations are identical to their counterparts in the deployment descriptor, and any valid Java EE listener class (`ServletContextListener`, `HttpSessionListener`, and others) can be declared here. However, it is extremely unusual for listeners to be declared within a TLD, and you do not see examples of that in this book. You may declare zero or more listeners in a TLD, and immediately following that you may declare zero or more tags, which are the next things you see in the Core TLD.

## Defining Tags

The `<tag>` element is the workhorse of the TLD and is responsible for defining tags in your tag library.

```
<tag>
  <description>
      Catches any Throwable that occurs in its body and optionally
      exposes it.
  </description>
  <name>catch</name>
  <tag-class>org.apache.taglibs.standard.tag.common.core.CatchTag</tag-class>
  <body-content>JSP</body-content>
  <attribute>
      <description>
Name of the exported scoped variable for the
```

```
exception thrown from a nested action. The type of the
scoped variable is the type of the exception thrown.
        </description>
        <name>var</name>
        <required>false</required>
        <rtexprvalue>false</rtexprvalue>
    </attribute>
  </tag>
```

It may have zero or more nested `<description>`, `<display-name>`, and `<icon>` elements, just like `<taglib>`. Generally, only `<description>` is used here. After these comes the required `<name>` element, which specifies the name of the JSP tag. In this case, the full tag name is `<c:catch>`, where `c` is the `<short-name>` (prefix) for the tag library and `catch` is the `<name>` of the tag. A tag can obviously have only one name. The `<tag-class>` element comes next and indicates the tag handler class (`Tag` or `SimpleTag`) responsible for executing the tag. Not shown in this example is the optional `<tei-class>` element, which comes next and specifies an extension of `javax.servlet.jsp.tagext.TagExtraInfo` for this tag. `TagExtraInfo` classes can validate the attributes used in a tag at translation time to ensure that their uses are proper. You may see these occasionally, but not often. In the Core tag library only the `<c:import>` and `<c:forEach>` tags provide extra info classes.

Next, `<body-content>` specifies what type of content is allowed nested within the tag. Its valid values are:

- `empty` — This indicates that the tag may not contain any nested content and must be an empty tag.
- `scriptless` — Tags with this body content type may have template text, EL expressions, and JSP tags within them, but no scriptlets or expressions. (Declarations are never allowed within the nested body content of a tag.)
- `JSP` — his indicates that the tag's nested content may be any content that is otherwise valid in the JSP (including scripting, if that is enabled in the JSP, but no declarations).
- `tagdependent` — This tells the container not to evaluate the nested content of the tag, but instead to let the tag evaluate the content itself. Usually this means the content is a different language, such as SQL, XML, or encoded data.

After `<body-content>` come zero or more `<variable>` elements, which is not shown in the previous example and, indeed, cannot be found in any of the JSTL TLDs. These elements provide information about variables defined as a result of using this tag. The `<variable>` element has the following subelements that provide additional information about defined variables:

- `<description>` — This is an optional description for the variable.
- `<name-given>` — The (required) name of the variable created by this tag. This should be a valid Java identifier.
- `<name-from-attribute>` — The (required) name of an attribute whose value determines what the name of the variable will be. Note that this element conflicts with `<name-given>`. You must specify both of these elements, but only one of them should ever have a value. The other should always be empty. The `<name-from-attribute>` element must always refer to the name of a tag attribute whose type is `String`, which does not allow runtime expressions in its value, and which is used to specify the name of the variable.

- `<variable-class>` — This optional element indicates the fully qualified Java class name of the defined variable's type. If not provided, it is assumed to be `String`.
- `<declare>` — This Boolean element, which defaults to `true`, indicates whether the variable defined is a new variable that will require a declaration. If `false`, it means the variable is already defined elsewhere and is merely changing.
- `<scope>` — Indicates the scope in which this variable will be defined. The default value is `NESTED`, which means that the variable is only available to code and actions *nested within the tag*. The other valid values are `AT_BEGIN`, which indicates that the variable is in scope for code nested within the tag *and* code coming after the tag, and `AT_END`, which means that the variable is only in scope for code that comes after the tag and *not* for code nested within the tag.

> **NOTE** *What exactly is a variable in this case? Why doesn't the JSTL use this element in its TLDs? Unfortunately, there's a lot of incomplete or inaccurate information online about* `<variable>`*s in the TLD (even the XML schema document doesn't make it clear), and as always the whole story can be found in the official JSP specification document. A variable, in this case, kind of refers to both an EL variable* and *a Java (scripting) variable. In your tag handler or tag file, you create or assign a value to an EL variable by calling* `pageContext.setAttribute`, `jspContext.setAttribute`, *or* `getJspContext().setAttribute` *(depending on what type of handler or file it is). The* `<variable>` *attribute in your TLD tells the container to expect this EL variable* and to copy its value to a scripting variable. *(Some IDEs also use variable definitions to assist the developer in using the tag.) Without a* `<variable>`*, users of your tag* can *still access the variables you define, using EL. With a* `<variable>`*, on the other hand, users of your tag can access the variables you define using EL* or *Java code. Because the use of scripting in JSPs is discouraged (see Chapter 4), developers rarely use* `<variable>`*, and you will not see examples of it in this book.*

> **WARNING** *The* `TagExtraInfo` *class also provides a way to specify variables defined by a tag. However, that is an old method of achieving this and should not be used anymore. You should only use* `<variable>` *elements in your TLD for this purpose.*

After the `<variable>`s for your tag, you can define zero or more `<attribute>`s, something demonstrated in the `<c:catch>` tag defined previously. Attributes, as the name implies, define the attributes that can be specified for this tag. There are several subelements of an `<attribute>` that specify the details of the attribute it defines.

- `<description>` — This optionally specifies a description for this attribute.
- `<name>` — This required element indicates the name of this attribute. The value must be a valid Java identifier.

- <required> — This is an optional Boolean value that indicates whether this attribute is required when using this tag. The default value is false.
- <rtexprvalue> — This optional Boolean element, which defaults to false, indicates whether the attribute allows runtime expressions (EL or scripting expressions) to specify the attribute value. If true, runtime expressions are permitted. If false, attribute values are considered static and runtime expressions result in a translation-time error.
- <type> — This optional element specifies the fully qualified Java class name of the attribute type. If not specified, the type is assumed to be an Object.
- <deferred-value> — The presence of this optional element indicates that the attribute value is a deferred EL value expression, and as a result the tag handler will be passed the attribute value as a javax.el.ValueExpression. Normally, the container evaluates an expression before binding its return value to the attribute value. With deferred value, the unevaluated ValueExpression is bound to the attribute, instead. The tag handler can then later evaluate that expression zero or more times as needed. By default, it is assumed that the value of this expression will be coerced into an Object, but a nested <type> element can specify a more precise type, which is especially helpful when using this attribute in an IDE.
- <deferred-method> — The presence of this optional element indicates that the attribute value is a deferred EL method expression, and as a result the tag handler will be passed the attribute value as a javax.el.MethodExpression. This is similar to <deferred-value> except for the expression type. By default it is assumed that the signature of the method in the expression is void method(), but you can use the nested <method-signature> element to specify a more precise signature (such as void execute(java.lang.String) or boolean test(java.lang.Object)) so that the expected return type and the number and type of parameters are correctly documented. The method name here isn't actually important and the container ignores it.
- <fragment> — If this optional Boolean element is set to true, it makes the attribute type javax.servlet.jsp.tagext.JspFragment and tells the container not to evaluate the JSP content contained in the attribute value. The tag handler can then manually evaluate the fragment zero or more times. If omitted, the default is false. Using <fragment>, code that uses the tag can specify the value of the attribute using a nested <jsp:attribute> tag instead of an actual XML attribute, as in the following example. This is the case even if the body content is set to empty.

```
<myTags:doSomething>
    <jsp:attribute name="someAttribute">
        Any <b>content</b> <fmt:message key="including.jsp.tags" />.
    </jsp:attribute>
</myTags:doSomething>
```

A related element not often seen, <dynamic-attributes>, follows any <attribute> tags. You can specify this Boolean element exactly once or you can omit it. The default value is false, and it indicates whether attributes not otherwise specified by <attribute> elements are still permitted. Where this is most often seen is in a JSP tag that ultimately outputs an HTML tag. The code for that tag could obtain the dynamic attributes and then copy them from the JSP tag to the HTML tag at run time. Spring Framework's form tag library, which you explore in Part II of this book, uses dynamic attributes for this exact reason. Dynamic attributes always permit EL and scriptlet expressions as values. To use dynamic attributes your tag handler class must implement `javax.servlet.jsp.tagext.DynamicAttributes`.

Following `<dynamic-attributes>` is the optional `<example>` element (of which there can only be one). This is related to `<description>` and contains simple text providing examples of using the tag. Finally, your tag can have zero or more `<tag-extension>`s. This tag provides additional information about a tag useful for consumption by some tool, such as an IDE or validator. Tag extensions never affect the behavior of the tag or the container. They are abstract and do not contain any subelements; instead, the developer is responsible for defining a schema for the tag extensions he wants to implement. Tag extensions are unusual and complicated and are not covered in this book.

## Defining Tag Files

You have already seen how you can use the `taglib` directive to collect a directory of tag files into a namespace of custom tags, and you now know that tag files are essentially JSPs with slightly different semantics. You learn the details of these semantics later in this section. However, you should also know how to define tag files within a Tag Library Descriptor. Remember that tag files shipped inside of JAR libraries must be defined inside a TLD. Also, if you have one or more tag files that you would like to group with one or more tag handlers or JSP functions into the same namespace, you need to define those tag files within the TLD even if they are not shipped inside of JAR libraries.

After all the `<tag>` elements in your TLD, you can place zero or more `<tag-file>` elements to define tag files that belong to your library. Within the `<tag-file>` element are the optional `<description>`, `<display-name>`, and `<icon>` elements that you should be accustomed to by now. Typically, only the `<description>` is specified. The `<name>` element is analogous to `<tag>`'s `<name>` element and specifies what the name of the tag following the prefix is. The next element is `<path>`, which specifies the path to the `.tag` file implementing this custom tag. The value of `<path>` must start with `/WEB-INF/tags` in web applications and `/META-INF/tags` in JAR files. The final two elements are `<example>` and `<tag-extension>`, which serve the same purpose as their counterparts within the `<tag>` element. You will not find an example of `<tag-file>` within the JSTL TLDs, but the following XML demonstrates its basic use.

```
<tag-file>
  <description>This tag outputs bar.</description>
  <name>foo</name>
  <path>/WEB-INF/tags/foo.tag</path>
</tag-file>
```

## Defining Functions

After defining tag files in your TLD, you may define zero or more JSP functions using the `<function>` element. This is not demonstrated in `c.tld`, but you can view the JSTL functions defined within `fn.tld`, which you can also find in `/META-INF/` in the Maven artifact or download from the `wrox.com` download site. If you open this file, you can see the familiar header with the tag library description, display name, version, short name, and URI. The next thing you see is the first function:

```
<function>
  <description>
    Tests if an input string contains the specified substring.
  </description>
  <name>contains</name>
  <function-class>
    org.apache.taglibs.standard.functions.Functions
  </function-class>
  <function-signature>
    boolean contains(java.lang.String, java.lang.String)
  </function-signature>
  <example>
    &lt;c:if test="${fn:contains(name, searchString)}">
  </example>
</function>
```

As you can see, defining a function in a TLD is extraordinarily simple. Bypassing the `<description>`, `<display-name>`, `<icon>`, and `<name>` elements you are already familiar with for `<tag>` and `<tag-file>`, the important elements in this example are `<function-class>` and `<function-signature>`. The function class is just the fully qualified name of a standard Java class, and the function signature is literally the signature of a static method on that class. Any public static method on any public class can become a JSP function in this manner. The last two elements that you may use within `<function>` are `<example>` and `<function-extension>`, which are analogous to the `<example>` and `<tag-extension>` elements within tag and tag file definitions.

> **WARNING** *The* `<example>` *for the* `fn:contains` *function contains characters reserved in the XML language. This is bad practice, and very strict XML validators may flag this as an issue. You should always place content like this within a CDATA block (*`<![CDATA[ special content goes here ]]>`*).*

## Defining Tag Library Extensions

After all `<tag>`s, `<tag-file>`s, and `<function>`s in your TLD, you may define zero or more tag library extensions using the `<taglib-extension>` element. Tag library extensions, like tag extensions and function extensions, do not affect tag or container behavior and simply exist to support tooling. Their concept is abstract and there are no predefined subelements within `<taglib-extension>`; instead, the developer is expected to know what he wants to use the extension for and define the schema himself. This author has never seen a tag extension, function extension, or tag library extension in practice, and so they are not covered in this book.

# Comparing JSP Directives and Tag File Directives

As discussed earlier in this chapter, tag files work essentially like JSP files do. They contain the same syntax and must follow the same basic rules, and at run time they get translated and compiled into Java just like JSPs do. Tag files can use any normal template text (including HTML), any other JSP tag, declarations, scriptlets, expressions, and expression language. It should not be surprising, however, that there are some minor differences between the two file formats, mainly concerning the directives available for tag files. In Chapter 4 you learned about the `page`, `include`, and `taglib` directives and how to use them in JSPs. Tag files can also use the `include` and `taglib` directives to include files and other tag libraries in the JSP, but there is no `page` directive in tag files. The `include` directive can be used to include `.jsp`, `.jspf`, and other `.tag` files in a `.tag` file, or `.jspx` and other `.tagx` files in a `.tagx` file. Using a `taglib` directive in a tag file is identical to using one in a JSP file.

Instead of the `page` directive, tag files have a `tag` directive. This directive replaces the necessary functionality from JSP's `page` directive and also replaces many of the configuration elements from a `<tag>` element in a TLD file. The `tag` directive has the following attributes, none of which are required:

- `pageEncoding` — This is equivalent to the `page` directive `pageEncoding` attribute and sets the character encoding of the tag's output.
- `isELIgnored` — Equivalent to its counterpart in the `page` directive, this instructs the container not to evaluate EL expressions in the tag file and defaults to `false`.
- `language` — This specifies the scripting language used in the tag file (currently only Java is supported), just like the `language` attribute in the `page` directive.
- `deferredSyntaxAllowedAsLiteral` — Just like the `page` directive attribute, this tells the container to ignore and not parse deferred EL syntax within the tag file.
- `trimDirectiveWhitespaces` — This tells the container to trim white space around directives, equivalent to the same attribute on the `page` directive.
- `import` — This attribute works just like the `page` directive's `import` attribute. You can specify one or more comma-separated Java classes to import in this attribute, and you can use the attribute multiple times in the same `tag` directive or across multiple `tag` directives.
- `description` — This is the equivalent of the `<description>` element in a TLD file, and specifying it can be helpful for developers to understand your tag better.
- `display-name` — Equivalent to the `<display-name>` element in a TLD, there is usually no need to specify this.
- `small-icon` and `large-icon` — These attributes essentially replace the `<icon>` element in a TLD, and you should never need to specify them.
- `body-content` — This is the replacement for `<body-content>` in a TLD, with one minor change: Its valid values are `empty`, `scriptless`, and `tagdependent`. The `JSP` value available in a TLD is not valid for the body content of a tag specified in a tag file. Due to the limitations of how tag files work, you cannot use scriptlets or expressions within the nested body content when using a tag that was defined in a tag file. `scriptless` is the default value for this attribute.
- `dynamic-attributes` — This string attribute is the counterpart of the `<dynamic-attributes>` element in a TLD and indicates whether dynamic attributes are enabled. By default the value is blank, which means that dynamic attributes are not supported. To enable dynamic attributes, set its value to the name of the EL variable you want created to hold all of the dynamic attributes. The EL variable will have a type of `Map<String, String>`. The map keys will be dynamic attribute names, and the values attribute values.

- `example` — You can use this attribute to indicate example tag usage just like with the `<example>` element in a TLD, but it is very difficult to effectively do this in a directive attribute.

Notice that equivalent directive attributes are missing for the `<name>`, `<tag-class>`, `<tei-class>`, `<variable>`, `<attribute>`, and `<tag-extension>` elements. The tag name is inferred from and always equal to the tag filename (minus the `.tag` extension), and `<tag-class>` is not needed because the tag file *is* the tag handler (or will be, after the container compiles it). There is no way to specify a `TagExtraInfo` class or a tag extension for tag files because there is simply no equivalent. This leaves `<variable>` and `<attribute>`, which are replaced with the `variable` and `attribute` directives, respectively.

The `variable` directive provides `description`, `name-given`, `name-from-attribute`, `variable-class`, `declare`, and `scope` attributes that are equivalent to their identically named elements in a TLD. It also provides an additional attribute, `alias`, which enables you to specify a local variable name that you can use to reference the variable within your tag file. The `attribute` directive has `description`, `name`, `required`, `rtexprvalue`, `type`, `fragment`, `deferredValue`, `deferredValueType`, `deferredMethod`, and `deferredMethodSignature` attributes that correspond to elements in a TLD.

## CREATING YOUR FIRST TAG FILE TO SERVE AS AN HTML TEMPLATE

Now that you are familiar with the details of Tag Library Descriptors and tag files, it's time to create your first custom JSP tag. The simplest way to create a custom tag is by writing a tag file and using a `taglib` directive with the `tagdir` attribute. You need to follow along in the Template-Tags project on the `wrox.com` code download site because some of the code in the next several sections is too long to print in this book. Note the standard deployment descriptor has changed slightly since Chapter 7: `<scripting-invalid>false</scripting-invalid>` has changed to `<scripting-invalid>true</scripting-invalid>` to disable Java in JSPs. The project also has an `index.jsp` file in the web root that redirects to `/index` with `<c:url>`, and a `/WEB-INF/jsp/base.jspf` file with the following tag library declarations:

```
<%@ taglib prefix="c" uri="http://java.sun.com/jsp/jstl/core" %>
<%@ taglib prefix="fmt" uri="http://java.sun.com/jsp/jstl/fmt" %>
<%@ taglib prefix="fn" uri="http://java.sun.com/jsp/jstl/functions" %>
<%@ taglib prefix="template" tagdir="/WEB-INF/tags/template" %>
```

Next, create a simple Servlet that can respond to requests to `/index`. Right now it may look like overkill for such a simple action, but in later sections you will add some more logic to this.

```
@WebServlet(
        name = "indexServlet",
        urlPatterns = "/index"
)
public class IndexServlet extends HttpServlet
{
    @Override
```

```
    protected void doGet(HttpServletRequest request, HttpServletResponse response)
            throws ServletException, IOException
    {
        String view = "hello";

        request.getRequestDispatcher("/WEB-INF/jsp/view/" + view + ".jsp")
               .forward(request, response);
    }
}
```

One of the most powerful things you can do with tag files is establish a system of HTML templates for your application to use. This templating system can take care of many of the repetitive tasks needed on pages across your application, cutting down on duplicated code and making it easier to change the design of your site. To demonstrate this, create a `/WEB-INF/tags/template/main.tag` file containing the basic JSP layout that most pages in your application use.

```
<%@ tag body-content="scriptless" dynamic-attributes="dynamicAttributes"
        trimDirectiveWhitespaces="true" %>
<%@ attribute name="htmlTitle" type="java.lang.String" rtexprvalue="true"
              required="true" %>
<%@ include file="/WEB-INF/jsp/base.jspf" %>
<!DOCTYPE html>
<html<c:forEach items="${dynamicAttributes}" var="a">
    <c:out value=' ${a.key}="${fn:escapeXml(a.value)}"' escapeXml="false" />
</c:forEach>>
    <head>
        <title><c:out value="${fn:trim(htmlTitle)}" /></title>
    </head>
    <body>
        <jsp:doBody />
    </body>
</html>
```

Now examine the previous code example:

- The first directive in this file establishes that uses of the tag can contain body content, that it supports dynamic attributes, that dynamic attributes are accessible with the `dynamicAttributes` EL variable, and that directive white space should be trimmed. Note the use of the `trimDirectiveWhitespace` attribute to accomplish this; the `<jsp-config>` in the deployment descriptor *does not affect tag files*, so you need to do this manually in each tag file.
- The second directive establishes the explicit `htmlTitle` attribute.
- The third attribute includes the `base.jspf` file, again because `<jsp-config>` does not affect tag files.
- The `<c:forEach>` loop copies all the dynamic attributes into the `<html>` tag. This isn't something you would normally need to do, but it does demonstrate how useful dynamic attributes can be.
- The `<c:out>` tag in the loop may seem unnecessary, but it is done this way for a reason: This ensures that the space between each attribute is not ignored, that the attribute values are escaped properly, and that the quotes around the attribute values are not escaped.

- The `htmlTitle` attribute is output as the document `<title>` using `<c:out>` and the EL expression trimming its value.
- The special `<jsp:doBody>` tag is used within the HTML `<body>`. This tag, which can be used only within tag files, tells the container to evaluate the content of the JSP tag call and place it inline. You could also specify the `var` or `varReader` attributes and the scope attribute to output the evaluated body content to a variable instead of `inlining` it.

Now to put all this to use, create the `/WEB-INF/jsp/view/hello.jsp` file that calls the `<template:main>` tag you have created.

```
<template:main htmlTitle="Template Homepage">
    Hello, Template!
</template:main>
```

That's all there is to it! Compile the application and start your debugger; then navigate to `http://localhost:8080/template-tags/index`. If you view the response source for the resulting page, you see that the document title is "Template Homepage" and that the text "Hello, Template!" was placed within the document body. You have successfully created your first custom JSP tag! In the next section you demonstrate the power of this HTML template more fully when you create another page to show off your next custom tag.

## CREATING A MORE USEFUL DATE FORMATTING TAG HANDLER

In the previous chapter, you explored the JSTL and learned about internationalization, localization, and the standard `fmt` tag library. You may recall that you were promised you would create a replacement for the `<fmt:formatDate>` tag, which was so limited in its capabilities. Some of the major drawbacks you may have noticed with this tag were its inability to format anything other than a `java.util.Date`, place the time before the date when needed, or place a token string between the date and time. The first drawback required you to always convert all date and time instances to a `Date`, and the second and third required you to either use two `<fmt:formatDate>` tags or use the `pattern` attribute, neither of which is ideal.

To create a better formatting tag, start by thinking about the date types you would like to support. Obviously, you would want to support `Date` and probably also `Calendar`. Then there's the Java 8 Date and Time API, which has many different types representing dates and times. Thankfully, the API has a common interface, `java.time.temporal.TemporalAccessor`, that all the major types representing dates and times implement. Add some code to the `doGet` method of `IndexServlet` to put dates of each type on the page model.

```
        if(request.getParameter("dates") != null)
        {
            request.setAttribute("date", new Date());
            request.setAttribute("calendar", Calendar.getInstance());
            request.setAttribute("instant", Instant.now());
            view = "dates";
        }
```

Now that you know what you need your tag to do, think about how you want to use it. Create a TLD file that specifies the behavior and attributes for the new date formatting tag. Doing this before actually writing the tag handler is an way of writing an interface based on use cases and then coding to the interface. The tag definition in your TLD is the interface in this case. Listing 8-1 declares a `wrox` tag library with the URI `http://www.wrox.com/jsp/tld/wrox` and specifies a single tag conveniently named `formatDate`.

The entire tag declaration is more than 100 lines long—too long to print in this book. You need to download the Template-Tags project from the `wrox.com` code download site to see the whole thing. The tag has many of the same attributes as `<fmt:formatDate>`, and as you read the TLD, you can understand the purpose for each attribute through its description.

**LISTING 8-1: wrox.tld**

```
<?xml version="1.0" encoding="ISO-8859-1"?>
<taglib xmlns="http://java.sun.com/xml/ns/javaee"
        xmlns:xsi="http://www.w3.org/2001/XMLSchema-instance"
        xsi:schemaLocation="http://java.sun.com/xml/ns/javaee
        http://java.sun.com/xml/ns/javaee/web-jsptaglibrary_2_1.xsd"
        version="2.1">

    <tlib-version>1.0</tlib-version>
    <short-name>wrox</short-name>
    <uri>http://www.wrox.com/jsp/tld/wrox</uri>

    <tag>
        <description><![CDATA[...]]></description>
        <name>formatDate</name>
        <tag-class>com.wrox.tag.FormatDateTag</tag-class>
        <body-content>empty</body-content>
        <attribute>
            <description>...</description>
            <name>value</name>
            <required>true</required>
            <rtexprvalue>true</rtexprvalue>
        </attribute>
        <attribute>
            ...
        </attribute>
        ...
        <dynamic-attributes>false</dynamic-attributes>
    </tag>

</taglib>
```

Implementing this tag is not a simple task. The `FormatDateTag` class, which extends `TagSupport` and utilizes Java 8 lambda expressions and method references to take care of some of the harder work, contains several hundred lines of code, and is too long to print in this book. You can find the implementation of this class in the Template-Tags project on the `wrox.com` code download site. There are many important things to note about this class.

First, the static fields are used to make the reflective access to the Apache/GlassFish JSTL implementation more efficient. The Apache classes have already implemented the hard work of resolving the locale and time zone information according to the JSTL specification, which consists of several hundred lines of code that it would not be ideal to duplicate. Of course, using these classes requires you to stick to that specific JSTL implementation, which isn't always ideal either. In a true enterprise application, you would probably want to copy the relevant Open Source code into your application so that it was more portable. For demonstration purposes, using the Apache classes is adequate. The private `getLocale` and `getTimeZone` methods use these static fields to invoke the protected methods in the Apache classes.

The `init` method, which is called from the constructor and the `release` method, resets all the tag attributes to their default values. This is important because containers pool and reuse tag handlers to improve efficiency, and between each use of the tag they call the `release` method to reset it before setting all the attributes again. A series of mutator methods ("setters") set all of the values for the tag attributes. The `org.apache.commons.lang3.StringUtils` class from Apache Commons Lang makes testing the string attributes for `null` or blank easier in these methods. The `setTimeZone` method enables a `String`, `java.util.TimeZone`, `java.time.ZoneId`, or `null` value and throws an exception if some other type is passed in.

The `doEndTag` method is the method that the container invokes when it is ready to close the tag. For tags that permit body content, `doStartTag` and `doAfterBody` could also be overridden to execute code at different times, but because this tag doesn't allow body content, only `doEndTag` needs be overridden. The `doEndTag` outputs nothing and removes the scope variable (if applicable) if the date value is `null`. It then invokes one of two `formatDate` methods based on the value type and either outputs the formatted date or sets it to the specified scope variable. The two `formatDate` methods set up the appropriate formatters for the differing date types and then pass those formatters to the third `formatDate` method, which executes them in the proper order depending on the `timeFirst` and `separateDateTimeWith` attribute values. Before Java 8, this would require `DateFormat` and `DateTimeFormatter` to inherit from a common interface, but they do not. Using Java 8 lambdas, references to the format methods of each formatter are passed instead and invoked when necessary.

To use the newly created tag, add a `taglib` directive to `/WEB-INF/jsp/base.jspf`:

```
<%@ taglib prefix="wrox" uri="http://www.wrox.com/jsp/tld/wrox" %>
```

Now create the `/WEB-INF/jsp/view/dates.jsp` view to format the dates previously created in the Servlet.

```
<%--@elvariable id="date" type="java.util.Date"--%>
<%--@elvariable id="calendar" type="java.util.Calendar"--%>
<%--@elvariable id="instant" type="java.time.Instant"--%>
<template:main htmlTitle="Displaying Dates Properly">
    <b>Date:</b>
    <wrox:formatDate value="${date}" type="both" dateStyle="full"
                     timeStyle="full" /><br />
    <b>Date, time first with separator:</b>
    <wrox:formatDate value="${date}" type="both" dateStyle="full"
                     timeStyle="full" timeFirst="true"
                     separateDateTimeWith=" on " /><br />
    <b>Calendar:</b>
    <wrox:formatDate value="${calendar}" type="both" dateStyle="full"
                     timeStyle="full" /><br />
    <b>Instant:</b>
    <wrox:formatDate value="${instant}" type="both" dateStyle="full"
                     timeStyle="full" /><br />
```

```
        <b>Instant, time first with separator:</b>
        <wrox:formatDate value="${instant}" type="both" dateStyle="full"
                         timeStyle="full" timeFirst="true"
                         separateDateTimeWith=" on " /><br />
    </template:main>
```

Compile and debug your application and go to `http://localhost:8080/template-tags/index?dates` in your browser. You should see all three dates formatted, two of them twice each with different formats, just as specified. This new tag you have created is much more flexible and powerful than the stock `<fmt:formatDate>` tag that comes with the JSTL.

## UNDERSTANDING THE DIFFERENT TYPES OF TAG HANDLERS

You can write tag handlers in different ways to achieve many different tasks, and this book simply cannot cover all the possibilities. But it's important to understand the general differences between these different tag types. All tags must implement either the `Tag` interface or `SimpleTag` interface, both of which extend the `JspTag` marker interface. `Tag` is the classic tag handler that has been around since the earliest days of JSP tags, whereas `SimpleTag` was added in JSP 2.0 to make tags — well — simpler to write.

`SimpleTag` may be simpler to use for many tasks, but among these advantages come a key disadvantage: `SimpleTag` classes are instantiated, used exactly once, and then thrown away. `Tag` instances can be pooled and reused, which can net significant performance gains on heavily used tags or tags that carry around many resources. However, you can't ignore how much easier it is to implement a loop, for example, in a `SimpleTag`. (The `invoke` method in this case is writing the invoked body to the JSP output, but passing in a `Writer` instead of `null` causes the body to be written to that `Writer`.)

```
public void doTag() throws JspException, IOException
{
    while(condition-is-true)
    {
        this.getJspContext().setAttribute("someElVariable", value);
        this.getJspBody().invoke(null);
    }
}
```

Compare this to how complex it is to implement the same loop in a `Tag` (implementing `IterationTag`, which extends `Tag`):

```
public int doStartTag() throws JspException
{ // this is invoked exactly once
    if(condition-is-true)
    {
        this.pageContext.setAttribute("someElVariable", value);
        return Tag.EVAL_BODY_INCLUDE;
    }
```

```
        return Tag.SKIP_BODY;
    }

    public int doAfterBody() throws JspException
    { // this is invoked as many times as needed
        if(condition-is-true)
        {
            this.pageContext.setAttribute("someElVariable", value);
            return Tag.EVAL_BODY_AGAIN;
        }
        return Tag.SKIP_BODY;
    }

    public int doEndTag() throws JspException
    { // this is invoked exactly once
        return Tag.EVAL_PAGE;
    }
```

You must evaluate each tag you need to create to determine whether it necessitates prioritizing performance over convenience. Keep in mind that `doStartTag` may return only `Tag.SKIP_BODY` or `Tag.EVAL_BODY_INCLUDE`; `doAfterBody` may return only `Tag.SKIP_BODY` or `IterationTag.EVAL_BODY_AGAIN`; and `doEndTag` may return only `Tag.SKIP_PAGE` or `Tag.EVAL_PAGE`.

The following list indicates the various tag interfaces you can implement (and the helper classes you should actually extend) and when you would implement each.

- `SimpleTag extends JspTag` — Use this for all tags that do not require the performance gains achieved through pooling. You should normally extend `SimpleTagSupport`.
- `Tag extends JspTag` — Use this poolable tag handler for most simple tags that do not do things like loop or access their body content. (The body content can still be evaluated with this tag, just not accessed.) You should normally extend `TagSupport`.
- `LoopTag extends Tag` — This tag is not often used, as it is only useful for looping over collections (or arrays) of objects. You should normally extend `LoopTagSupport`.
- `IterationTag extends Tag` — This is a more useful iteration tag that can iterate based on any condition, including looping over collections of objects. You should normally extend `IterationTagSupport`.
- `BodyTag extends IterationTag` — This iteration tag enables the output of the evaluated body to be buffered into a `BodyContent` object that can later be used for some other purpose (like saving the output to a variable). This is achieved by returning `BodyTag.EVAL_BODY_BUFFERED` from `doStartTag` instead of `Tag.EVAL_BODY_INCLUDE` and then accessing the body content in `doEndTag`. You should normally extend `BodyTagSupport`.

## CREATING AN EL FUNCTION TO ABBREVIATE STRINGS

Recall from earlier in the chapter that you can use a TLD to define EL functions as well as tags. Remember that EL function definitions are simple; all you need is a public static method of some class and you can define an EL function that maps to that. You don't even have to write the static method yourself. It can be something from the Java SE library, the Java EE library, or a completely different third-party library. Consider `StringUtils` from the Apache Commons Lang library. It has a very handy method, `abbreviate`, that ensures a string does not exceed a certain length. If the string is too long, it gets shortened and an ellipsis (...) is added to the end of the string. This can be a very useful action in the world of web applications, in which user input can often be long and sometimes needs to be shortened for summary display or to keep the page layout from being thrown off.

To turn this useful method into an EL function that can easily be called from your JSPs, follow these steps:

1. Open the `wrox.tld` file and add the following `<function>` below the date formatting `<tag>`:

```
<function>
    <description>...</description>
    <name>abbreviateString</name>
    <function-class>org.apache.commons.lang3.StringUtils</function-class>
    <function-signature>
        java.lang.String abbreviate(java.lang.String,int)
    </function-signature>
</function>
```

   It should be obvious how much easier it is to define an EL function than a JSP tag. The `<function-class>` element specifies the fully qualified class name that the method belongs to and the `<function-signature>` element specifies which method on the class makes up the function.

2. Now add a little bit more logic to the `doGet` method of your `IndexServlet`:

```
        else if(request.getParameter("text") != null)
        {
            request.setAttribute("shortText", "This is short text.");
            request.setAttribute(
                    "longText",
                    "This is really long text that should get cut
off at 32 chars."
            );
            view = "text";
        }
```

3. Create a `/WEB-INF/jsp/view/text.jsp` view to demonstrate using the EL function.

```
<%--@elvariable id="shortText" type="java.lang.String"--%>
<%--@elvariable id="longText" type="java.lang.String"--%>
<template:main htmlTitle="Abbreviating Text">
    <b>Short text:</b> ${wrox:abbreviateString(shortText, 32)}<br />
    <b>Long text:</b> ${wrox:abbreviateString(longText, 32)}<br />
</template:main>
```

**4.** Compile and start up the Template-Tags project one more time and navigate to `http://localhost:8080/template-tags/index?text` in your browser.

You should see that your new EL function has abbreviated only the second string and has added an ellipsis to the end of that string.

## REPLACING JAVA CODE WITH CUSTOM JSP TAGS

Previously you were promised that you would finally get to replace all Java code in the Customer Support application JSPs with JSP tags you created in this chapter. Indeed, you can do this with everything you have learned in this chapter. You can follow along in the Customer-Support-v6 project available on the `wrox.com` code download site, or you can make the changes noted here. You should start by changing `<scripting-invalid>false</scripting-invalid>` in your deployment descriptor to `<scripting-invalid>true</scripting-invalid>`. This change proves that you have replaced all Java code in your JSPs because any JSPs with Java code cannot compile with this setting enabled.

Now copy the `com.wrox.tag.FormatDateTag` class and `/WEB-INF/tld/wrox.tld` file from the Template-Tags project to the support project; you can use the date formatting tag and string abbreviating function in the support application. You can also add another function to the TLD. Create a `TimeUtils` class like the following:

```
public final class TimeUtils
{
    public static String intervalToString(long timeInterval)
    {
        if(timeInterval < 1_000)
            return "less than one second";
        if(timeInterval < 60_000)
            return (timeInterval / 1_000) + " seconds";
        return "about " + (timeInterval / 60_000) + " minutes";
    }
}
```

You can then add a function to the bottom of the TLD that calls the method in the `TimeUtils` class.

```
    <function>
        <description>
            Formats a time interval in an attractive way, such as "less than one
            second" or "ten seconds" or "about 12 minutes".
        </description>
        <name>timeIntervalToString</name>
        <function-class>com.wrox.TimeUtils</function-class>
        <function-signature>
            java.lang.String intervalToString(long)
        </function-signature>
    </function>
```

Make sure the `/WEB-INF/jsp/base.jspf` file has the appropriate `taglib` declarations in it.

```
<%@ taglib prefix="c" uri="http://java.sun.com/jsp/jstl/core" %>
<%@ taglib prefix="fmt" uri="http://java.sun.com/jsp/jstl/fmt" %>
<%@ taglib prefix="fn" uri="http://java.sun.com/jsp/jstl/functions" %>
<%@ taglib prefix="wrox" uri="http://www.wrox.com/jsp/tld/wrox" %>
<%@ taglib prefix="template" tagdir="/WEB-INF/tags/template" %>
```

You're almost ready to begin changing your JSPs. You'll also create a few tag files to help you template the support application and avoid duplicating presentation code. Start with `/WEB-INF/tags/template/main.tag` in Listing 8-2, which is much more complex than the template tag from the Template-Tags project.

Notice that two of the attributes for this tag are simple strings, but the `headContent` and `navigationContent` attributes are JSP fragments. This allows those attributes to contain JSP content that you can later evaluate. In the proper place, the tag evaluates these fragments using the `<jsp:invoke>` tag. This is similar to `<jsp:body>` except that it acts on fragment attributes instead of the tag body content.

**LISTING 8-2: main.tag**

```
<%@ tag body-content="scriptless" trimDirectiveWhitespaces="true" %>
<%@ attribute name="htmlTitle" type="java.lang.String" rtexprvalue="true"
              required="true" %>
<%@ attribute name="bodyTitle" type="java.lang.String" rtexprvalue="true"
              required="true" %>
<%@ attribute name="headContent" fragment="true" required="false" %>
<%@ attribute name="navigationContent" fragment="true" required="true" %>
<%@ include file="/WEB-INF/jsp/base.jspf" %>
<!DOCTYPE html>
<html>
    <head>
        <title>Customer Support :: <c:out value="${fn:trim(htmlTitle)}" /></title>
        <link rel="stylesheet"
              href="<c:url value="/resource/stylesheet/main.css" />" />
        <jsp:invoke fragment="headContent" />
    </head>
    <body>
        <h1>Multinational Widget Corporation</h1>
        <table border="0" id="bodyTable">
            <tbody>
                <tr>
                    <td class="sidebarCell">
                        <jsp:invoke fragment="navigationContent" />
                    </td>
                    <td class="contentCell">
                        <h2><c:out value="${fn:trim(bodyTitle)}" /></h2>
                        <jsp:doBody />
                    </td>
                </tr>
            </tbody>
        </table>
    </body>
</html>
```

You might wonder how you're supposed to specify an attribute that contains JSP content; after all, such a value might be many lines long and contain other JSP tags. `/WEB-INF/tags/template/loggedOut.tag` in Listing 8-3 demonstrates this. When you use a JSP tag, you typically specify all the attributes as normal XML attributes and then the contents within the tag make up the entire tag body. However, when an attribute value is too long or contains JSP content, you can use the `<jsp:attribute>` tag within the tag body to specify the attribute value.

At this point the attribute is specified within the tag body content, so to specify the *real* tag body content you need to use the `<jsp:body>` tag. Everything in this tag becomes the tag body for the enclosing tag (`<template:main>` in this case). Listing 8-4, `/WEB-INF/tags/template/basic.tag`, demonstrates this again but with a lot more content in the fragment attributes. This tag specifies several links that go within the sidebar of the page on every page that uses this template tag. It also provides `extraHeadContent` and `extraNavigationContent` attributes to allow consuming pages to add extra content to the head tag or sidebar.

Although tag files cannot technically extend one another, this is essentially what you are doing. The `main` tag sets up a foundation for the template and the `loggedOut` and `basic` tags build upon that foundation. Now you can see the full power of tag files.

**LISTING 8-3: loggedOut.tag**

```
<%@ tag body-content="scriptless" trimDirectiveWhitespaces="true" %>
<%@ attribute name="htmlTitle" type="java.lang.String" rtexprvalue="true"
              required="true" %>
<%@ attribute name="bodyTitle" type="java.lang.String" rtexprvalue="true"
              required="true" %>
<%@ include file="/WEB-INF/jsp/base.jspf" %>
<template:main htmlTitle="${htmlTitle}" bodyTitle="${bodyTitle}">
    <jsp:attribute name="headContent">
        <link rel="stylesheet"
              href="<c:url value="/resource/stylesheet/login.css" />" />
    </jsp:attribute>
    <jsp:attribute name="navigationContent" />
    <jsp:body>
        <jsp:doBody />
    </jsp:body>
</template:main>
```

**LISTING 8-4: basic.tag**

```
<%@ tag body-content="scriptless" trimDirectiveWhitespaces="true" %>
<%@ attribute name="htmlTitle" type="java.lang.String" rtexprvalue="true"
              required="true" %>
<%@ attribute name="bodyTitle" type="java.lang.String" rtexprvalue="true"
              required="true" %>
<%@ attribute name="extraHeadContent" fragment="true" required="false" %>
<%@ attribute name="extraNavigationContent" fragment="true" required="false" %>
<%@ include file="/WEB-INF/jsp/base.jspf" %>
<template:main htmlTitle="${htmlTitle}" bodyTitle="${bodyTitle}">
    <jsp:attribute name="headContent">
        <jsp:invoke fragment="extraHeadContent" />
```

*continues*

**LISTING 8-4** *(continued)*

```
        </jsp:attribute>
        <jsp:attribute name="navigationContent">
            <a href="<c:url value="/tickets" />">List Tickets</a><br />
            <a href="<c:url value="/tickets">
                <c:param name="action" value="create" />
            </c:url>">Create a Ticket</a><br />
            <a href="<c:url value="/sessions" />">List Sessions</a><br />
            <a href="<c:url value="/login?logout" />">Log Out</a><br />
            <jsp:invoke fragment="extraNavigationContent" />
        </jsp:attribute>
        <jsp:body>
            <jsp:doBody />
        </jsp:body>
    </template:main>
```

> **NOTE** *You may have noticed two CSS files used in these tags,* `/resource/stylesheet/main.css` *and* `/resource/stylesheet/login.css`. *These style sheets make the application more attractive but are not required for the application to function properly, so they are not printed in this book. You can find them in the Customer-Support-v6 project on the* `wrox.com` *code download site.*

Now you need just a few simple changes to the Java classes in the application. First, add a creation date field and appropriate mutator and accessor to the Ticket class:

```
    private OffsetDateTime dateCreated;
```

In the `TicketServlet` class, add the following line to the `createTicket` method to assign a value to the creation date field:

```
        ticket.setDateCreated(OffsetDateTime.now());
```

In the `doGet` method of `SessionListServlet`, add the following request attribute before the request dispatcher forwards the request:

```
        request.setAttribute("timestamp", System.currentTimeMillis());
```

You are now ready to change the JSPs in `/WEB-INF/jsp/view` to use the new `template` and `wrox` tag libraries. `login.jsp` is simple and uses the `<template:loggedOut>` tag:

```
<%--@elvariable id="loginFailed" type="java.lang.Boolean"--%>
<template:loggedOut htmlTitle="Log In" bodyTitle="Log In">
    You must log in to access the customer support site.<br /><br />
    <c:if test="${loginFailed}">
        <b>The username and password you entered are not correct. Please try
            again.</b><br /><br />
    </c:if>
    <form method="POST" action="<c:url value="/login" />">
        Username<br />
        <input type="text" name="username" /><br /><br />
        Password<br />
        <input type="password" name="password" /><br /><br />
        <input type="submit" value="Log In" />
    </form>
</template:loggedOut>
```

All the other tickets use the `<template:basic>` tag. `ticketForm.jsp` hasn't changed at all except for using the template:

```
<template:basic htmlTitle="Create a Ticket" bodyTitle="Create a Ticket">
    <form method="POST" action="tickets" enctype="multipart/form-data">
        <input type="hidden" name="action" value="create"/>
        Subject<br />
        <input type="text" name="subject"><br /><br />
        Body<br />
        <textarea name="body" rows="5" cols="30"></textarea><br /><br />
        <b>Attachments</b><br />
        <input type="file" name="file1"/><br /><br />
        <input type="submit" value="Submit"/>
    </form>
</template:basic>
```

In addition to using the template, `viewTicket.jsp` now uses the `<wrox:formatDate>` tag to display the date the ticket was created:

```
<%--@elvariable id="ticketId" type="java.lang.String"--%>
<%--@elvariable id="ticket" type="com.wrox.Ticket"--%>
<template:basic htmlTitle="${ticket.subject}"
                bodyTitle="Ticket #${ticketId}: ${ticket.subject}">
    <i>Customer Name - <c:out value="${ticket.customerName}" /><br />
    Created <wrox:formatDate value="${ticket.dateCreated}" type="both"
                             timeStyle="long" dateStyle="full" /></i><br /><br />
    <c:out value="${ticket.body}" /><br /><br />
    <c:if test="${ticket.numberOfAttachments > 0}">
        Attachments:
        <c:forEach items="${ticket.attachments}" var="attachment"
                   varStatus="status">
            <c:if test="${!status.first}">, </c:if>
            <a href="<c:url value="/tickets">
                    <c:param name="action" value="download" />
                    <c:param name="ticketId" value="${ticketId}" />
                    <c:param name="attachment" value="${attachment.name}" />
                </c:url>"><c:out value="${attachment.name}" /></a>
        </c:forEach><br /><br />
    </c:if>
</template:basic>
```

`listTickets.jsp` uses not only the date formatter, but also the `wrox:abbreviateString` EL function to truncate ticket subjects to 60 characters:

```
<%--@elvariable id="ticketDatabase"
                type="java.util.Map<Integer, com.wrox.Ticket>"--%>
<template:basic htmlTitle="Tickets" bodyTitle="Tickets">
    <c:choose>
        <c:when test="${fn:length(ticketDatabase) == 0}">
            <i>There are no tickets in the system.</i>
        </c:when>
        <c:otherwise>
            <c:forEach items="${ticketDatabase}" var="entry">
                Ticket ${entry.key}: <a href="<c:url value="/tickets">
                    <c:param name="action" value="view" />
                    <c:param name="ticketId" value="${entry.key}" />
                </c:url>">
```

```
                <c:out value="${wrox:abbreviateString(entry.value.subject, 60)}" />
                </a><br />
                <c:out value="${entry.value.customerName}" /> created ticket
                <wrox:formatDate value="${entry.value.dateCreated}" type="both"
                                timeStyle="short" dateStyle="medium" /><br />
                <br />
            </c:forEach>
        </c:otherwise>
    </c:choose>
</template:basic>
```

Notice that `sessions.jsp` experienced the largest change. All the Java code for declaring the method, looping over the sessions, and outputting data is gone, replaced by 100 percent JSP code using `<c:forEach>`, `<c:out>`, `<c:if>`, and `wrox:timeIntervalToString`.

```
<%--@elvariable id="timestamp" type="long"--%>
<%--@elvariable id="numberOfSessions" type="int"--%>
<%--@elvariable id="sessionList"
                type="java.util.List<javax.servlet.http.HttpSession>"--%>
<template:basic htmlTitle="Active Sessions" bodyTitle="Active Sessions">
    There are a total of ${numberOfSessions} active sessions in this
    application.<br /><br />
    <c:forEach items="${sessionList}" var="s">
        <c:out value="${s.id} - ${s.getAttribute('username')}" />
        <c:if test="${s.id == pageContext.session.id}"> (you)</c:if>
         - last active
        ${wrox:timeIntervalToString(timestamp - s.lastAccessedTime)} ago<br />
    </c:forEach>
</template:basic>
```

You can now compile and run your application and go to `http://localhost:8080/support/login` in your browser. Log in to the support application to create, view, and list tickets. Notice the formatted dates on the view and list pages, and the convenient sidebar on the left side of the page. Create a ticket with a long subject and see how it gets chopped off before wrapping on the list page. You now have all the tools you need to create useful, dynamic JSPs without any Java code embedded in them.

# SUMMARY

In this chapter you learned about creating custom JSP tags and EL functions. You explored the Tag Library Descriptor (TLD) by taking a look at TLDs from the Java Standard Tag Library (JSTL) and by creating your own TLD. You examined the concept of tag files and used this technology to create powerful HTML templates to serve as a base for your application's pages. You created a better date and time formatting tag that provides more flexible formatting options and supports `Date`, `Calendar`, and the Java 8 Date and Time API, while maintaining the locale and time zone contract established in the JSTL. At this point you know everything you could need to know to create Java-free JSPs.

From here on you switch gears and look at more advanced technologies. In the next chapter you explore filters and how you can usefully apply them to your applications.

# Improving Your Application Using Filters

## IN THIS CHAPTER

- The purpose of filters
- How to create, declare, and map filters
- How to properly order your filters
- Using filters with asynchronous request handling
- Exploring practical uses for filters
- Using filters to simplify authentication

## WROX.COM CODE DOWNLOADS FOR THIS CHAPTER

You can find the `wrox.com` code downloads for this chapter at `http://www.wrox.com/go/projavaforwebapps` on the Download Code tab. The code for this chapter is divided into the following major examples:

- Filter-Order Project
- Filter-Async Project
- Compression-Filter Project
- Customer-Support-v7 Project

## NEW MAVEN DEPENDENCIES FOR THIS CHAPTER

There are no new Maven dependencies for this chapter. Continue to use the Maven dependencies introduced in all previous chapters.

# UNDERSTANDING THE PURPOSE OF FILTERS

Filters are application components that can intercept requests to resources, responses from resources, or both, and act on those requests or responses in some manner. Filters can inspect and modify requests and responses, and they can even reject, redirect, or forward requests.

A relatively new addition to the Servlet specification, filters were added in Servlet 2.3, improved in Servlet 2.4, and haven't really changed much since then. The `javax.servlet.Filter` interface is very simple and involves the `HttpServletRequest` and `HttpServletResponse` that you are already familiar with. Like Servlets, filters can be declared in the deployment descriptor, programmatically, or with annotations, and they can have init parameters and access the `ServletContext`. The number of uses for filters is really limited only by your imagination; in this section you explore some of the most common applications.

## Logging Filters

Filters can be especially useful for logging activity in your application. You'll learn about the concepts of and tools involved with logging in Chapter 11, but one scenario applications developers sometimes face is the need to log every request to the application and what the result of each request is (status code, length, and possibly other information). Usually the web container provides facilities for request logging, but if you need proprietary information displayed in your request log, you can use a filter to log requests instead. You can also use filters to add tracking information that will be used for all logging operations for the request. This is called fish tagging, and you'll learn more about it in Chapter 11.

## Authentication Filters

When you need to ensure that only authorized people access your application, this typically involves performing a check on each request to ensure the user is "logged in." The meaning of that term may vary from application to application, but the tedium of performing this check in every Servlet is universal. Filters can make the job easier by centralizing authentication and authorization checks into one location that intercepts all secured requests.

At the end of this chapter, you add a filter to the ongoing Customer Support project that does just this and removes duplicate code throughout the application. In Part IV, you explore Spring Security and use it to add authentication and authorization to your applications. Filters are the foundation for Spring Security and make up a large part of its functionality.

## Compression and Encryption Filters

Though it is not always the case (and is becoming less and less common every day), there are still times in which Internet bandwidth is extremely limited and CPU resources are more abundant. In these cases, it's often desirable to spend the necessary CPU cycles compressing data before transmitting it over the wire. You can use a filter to accomplish this: When the request comes in, it remains unaltered, but as the response goes back out to the user, the filter compresses it. This, of course, requires that the user can decompress the response. In the section "Investigating Practical Uses for Filters," you see what's involved in writing a response compression filter.

Filters can also be useful for handling decryption of requests and encryption of responses. Typically, you rely on HTTPS for this; something the web container or web server can natively handle. However, if the consumers of your resources are not a browser or other web client but instead some other application, they could employ a proprietary encryption system understood only by those two applications. In this case, a filter is a prime candidate for decrypting requests as they come in and encrypting responses as they go out. Understand that this is an unusual scenario, and you really should rely on industry-standard tools such as HTTPS for securing your application's communications.

### Error Handling Filters

Let's face it: As hard as software developers try to handle errors that arise during the execution of their software, sometimes errors slip through the cracks. When the software is an operating system, the nasty symptom is often a system halt, affectionately referred to in the technology world as "the blue screen of death." With desktop applications, the user might receive a notice that "the application has quit unexpectedly."

With web applications, the result is typically an HTTP response code of 500, often accompanied by a plain HTML page with the words "Internal Server Error" and some diagnostic information. For applications run locally (such as on an intranet), this diagnostic information is usually not harmful and it might actually be useful for the developer to figure out what went wrong. But for web applications run remotely, this diagnostic information can potentially reveal sensitive system information that hackers can use to compromise a system.

For these reasons, you should display a more friendly, generic error page to users (often styled like the rest of your web application) and log the error or notify a system administrator as necessary. A filter is the perfect tool for this task. You can wrap request handling in a `try-catch` block, thus catching and logging any errors. This results in the request being forwarded to a generic error page that does not contain any diagnostic or sensitive information.

## CREATING, DECLARING, AND MAPPING FILTERS

Creating a filter is as simple as implementing the `Filter` interface. Its `init` method is called when the filter is initialized and provides access to the filter's configuration, its init parameters, and the `ServletContext`, just like the `init` method in a `Servlet`. Similarly, the `destroy` method is called when the web application is shut down. The `doFilter` method is called when a request comes in that is mapped to the filter. It provides access to the `ServletRequest`, `ServletResponse`, and `FilterChain` objects. Although you can use filters to filter more than just HTTP requests and responses, in reality, for your uses, the request is always an `HttpServletRequest` and the response is always an `HttpServletResponse`. In fact, at the moment the Servlet API specification does not support any protocols besides HTTP. Within `doFilter` you can either reject the request or continue it by calling the `doFilter` method of the `FilterChain` object; you can alter the request and the response; and you can wrap the request and response objects.

### Understanding the Filter Chain

Although only one Servlet can handle a request, any number of filters may intercept a request. Figure 9-1 demonstrates how the filter chain accepts an incoming request and passes it from filter to filter until all matching filters have been processed, finally passing it on to the Servlet. Calling `FilterChain.doFilter()` triggers the continuation of the filter chain. If the current filter is the last filter in the chain, calling `FilterChain.doFilter()` returns control to the Servlet container, which passes the request to the Servlet. If the current filter does not call `FilterChain.doFilter()`, the chain is interrupted, and the Servlet and any remaining filters never handle the request.

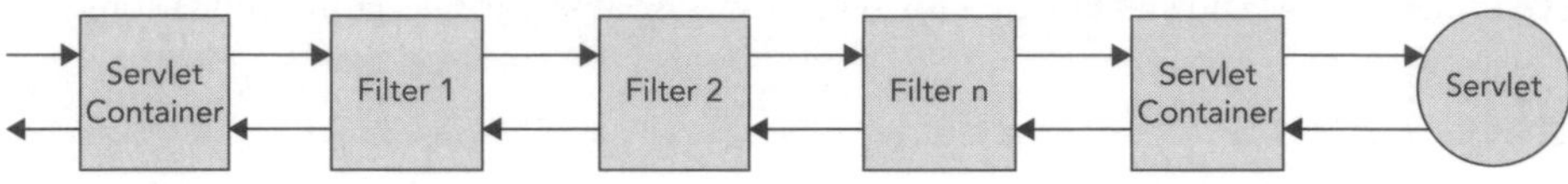


**FIGURE 9-1**

In this way, the filter chain is very much like a stack (and, indeed, the series of method executions do go on the Java stack). When a request comes in, it goes to the first filter, which is added to the stack. When that filter continues the chain, the next filter is added to the stack. This continues until the request goes to the Servlet, which is the last item added to the stack. As the request completes and the Servlet's `service` method returns, the Servlet is removed from the stack and control passes back to the last filter. When its `doFilter` method returns, that filter is removed from the stack and control returns to the previous filter. This continues until control has returned to the first filter. When its `doFilter` method returns, the stack is empty and request processing completes. Because of this, a filter can take action on a request both before and after the destination Servlet services it.

## Mapping to URL Patterns and Servlet Names

Just like Servlets, filters can be mapped to URL patterns. This determines which filter or filters will intercept a request. Any request matching a URL pattern to which a filter is mapped first goes to that filter before going to any matching Servlets. Using URL patterns, you can intercept not only requests to your Servlets, but also to other resources, such as images, CSS files, JavaScript files, and more.

Sometimes, mapping to a particular URL is inconvenient. Possibly you have several URLs — even dozens — that are already mapped to a Servlet, and you want to also map a filter to those URLs. Instead of mapping your filter to a URL or URLs, you can map it to one or more Servlet names. If a request is matched to a Servlet, the container looks for any filters mapped to that Servlet's name and applies them to the request. Later in this section, you learn about how to map filters to URLs and Servlet names. Whether you map your filters using URL patterns, Servlets names, or both, a filter can intercept multiple URL patterns and Servlet names, and multiple filters can intercept the same URL pattern or Servlet name.

## Mapping to Different Request Dispatcher Types

In a Servlet container, you can dispatch requests in any number of ways. There are:

- **Normal requests** — These originate from the client and include a URL targeted for a particular web application in the container.

- **Forwarded requests** — These trigger when your code calls the `forward` method on a `RequestDispatcher` or uses the `<jsp:forward>` tag. Though they are related to the original request, they are handled internally as a separate request.
- **Included requests** — Similarly, using `<jsp:include>` and calling `include` on a `RequestDispatcher` result in separate, internal include requests related to the original requests. (Remember that this is contrary to `<%@ include %>`.)
- **Error resource requests** — These are requests to error pages for handling HTTP errors such as `404 Not Found`, `500 Internal Server Error`, and so on.
- **Asynchronous requests** — These are requests that are dispatched from the `AsyncContext` during the handling of any other request.

Prior to Servlet 2.4, filters applied only to resources for typical requests. Servlet 2.4 added the ability to map filters to forwarded requests, include requests, and error resources, greatly expanding their capabilities. In Servlet 3.0 (Java EE 6), the new asynchronous request handling presented a challenge for filter writers: Because the Servlet's `service` method returns before the request's response has been sent, the capability of the filter chain is compromised. To compensate for this, Servlet 3.0 added the new asynchronous dispatcher type for filters intercepting requests dispatched from the `AsyncContext`. Asynchronous filters should be implemented with caution because they can be invoked multiple times (potentially in different threads) for a single asynchronous request. This is covered in more detail in the next section.

You indicate which dispatcher type or types a filter should apply to when you declare and map a filter, which you learn about in the remainder of this section.

## Using the Deployment Descriptor

Before any filters you write can intercept requests, you must declare and map them just like you do your Servlets. As with Servlets, you can accomplish this in multiple ways. The traditional way is in the deployment descriptor using the `<filter>` and `<filter-mapping>` elements (analogous to the `<servlet>` and `<servlet-mapping>` elements). `<filter>` elements must contain at least a name and a class but may also include a description, display name, icon, and one or more init parameters.

```
<filter>
    <filter-name>myFilter</filter-name>
    <filter-class>com.wrox.MyFilter</filter-class>
</filter>
```

The previous code snippet demonstrates a simple filter declaration within the deployment descriptor. Unlike Servlets, filters cannot be loaded on the first request. A filter's `init` method is always called on application startup: After `ServletContextListeners` initialize, before Servlets initialize, and in the order the filter appears in the deployment descriptor.

After a filter has been declared, you can map it to any number of URLs or Servlet names. Filter URL mappings can also include wildcards, just like Servlet URL mappings.

```
<filter-mapping>
    <filter-name>myFilter</filter-name>
    <url-pattern>/foo</url-pattern>
    <url-pattern>/bar/*</url-pattern>
```

```
        <servlet-name>myServlet</servlet-name>
        <dispatcher>REQUEST</dispatcher>
        <dispatcher>ASYNC</dispatcher>
    </filter-mapping>
```

In this case, the filter responds to any request to the application-relative URLs `/foo` and `/bar/*`, as well as any requests that end up being serviced by the Servlet named *`myServlet`*. The two `<dispatcher>` elements mean that it can respond to normal requests and requests dispatched from the `AsyncContext`. The valid `<dispatcher>` types are `REQUEST`, `FORWARD`, `INCLUDE`, `ERROR`, and `ASYNC`. A filter mapping may have zero or more `<dispatcher>` elements. If none are specified, a single, default `REQUEST` dispatcher is assumed.

## Using Annotations

As with Servlets, you can declare and map filters using annotations. The `@javax.servlet.annotation.WebFilter` annotation contains attributes that substitute for all the options in the deployment descriptor. The following code has the equivalent effect of the previous filter declaration and mapping in the deployment descriptor:

```
@WebFilter(
        filterName = "myFilter",
        urlPatterns = { "/foo", "/bar/*" },
        servletNames = { "myServlet" },
        dispatcherTypes = { DispatcherType.REQUEST, DispatcherType.ASYNC }
)
public class MyFilter implements Filter
```

The primary disadvantage of using annotations to declare and map filters is the inability to order those filters on the filter chain. Filters have a particular order (which you learn about in the next section) that is very important to their proper interaction. If you want to control the order in which your filters execute without using the deployment descriptor, you need to use programmatic configuration. Hopefully, the future Java EE 8 will include the capability of ordering annotated filters.

## Using Programmatic Configuration

You can configure filters programmatically with the `ServletContext`, just like Servlets, listeners, and other components. Instead of using the deployment descriptor or annotations, you can call methods on the `ServletContext` to register and map filters. Because this must be done before the `ServletContext` finishes starting, it is typically accomplished within a `ServletContextListener`'s `contextInitialized` method. (You can also add filters within a `ServletContainerInitializer`'s `onStartup` method, which you learn more about in Part II.)

```
@WebListener
public class Configurator implements ServletContextListener
{
    @Override
    public void contextInitialized(ServletContextEvent event)
    {
```

```
        ServletContext context = event.getServletContext();

        FilterRegistration.Dynamic registration =
                context.addFilter("myFilter", new MyFilter());
        registration.addMappingForUrlPatterns(
                EnumSet.of(DispatcherType.REQUEST, DispatcherType.ASYNC),
                false, "/foo", "/bar/*"
        );
        registration.addMappingForServletNames(
                EnumSet.of(DispatcherType.REQUEST, DispatcherType.ASYNC),
                false, "myServlet"
        );
    }
}
```

In this example, the filter is added to the `ServletContext` using the `addFilter` method. This returns a `javax.servlet.FilterRegistration.Dynamic`, which you can use to add filter mappings for URL patterns and Servlet names. The `addMappingForUrlPatterns` and `addMappingForServletNames` methods both accept a `Set` of `javax.servlet.DispatcherTypes` as the first argument. As with the deployment descriptor, if the dispatcher types argument is `null`, the default `REQUEST` dispatcher is assumed:

```
        registration.addMappingForUrlPatterns(null, false, "/foo", "bar/*");
```

The second method parameter indicates the filter's order relative to filters in the deployment descriptor. If `false` (as in this case), the programmatic filter mapping is ordered before any filter mappings in the deployment descriptor. If `true`, mappings in the deployment descriptor come first. You'll learn more about filter order in the next section. The final parameter is a vararg parameter for specifying the URL patterns (for `addMappingForUrlPatterns`) or Servlet names (for `addMappingForServletNames`) to map the filter to.

## ORDERING YOUR FILTERS PROPERLY

So far throughout this chapter, you have seen several references to the filter order, but you are undoubtedly wondering what exactly that is. Filter order determines where in the filter chain a filter appears, which in turn determines when one filter processes a request in relation to other filters. In some cases it does not matter what order your filters process requests; in other cases, however, it can be critical — it completely depends on how you are using filters. For example, a filter that sets up logging information for a request (or enters the request in a log) should probably come before any other filters because other filters might alter the fate of the request. As discussed earlier, you cannot order filters declared using annotations, making them virtually useless for most enterprise applications. You will use the deployment descriptor or programmatic configuration extensively, but you will probably never use annotations for configuring filters.

### URL Pattern Mapping versus Servlet Name Mapping

Defining the filter order is simple: Filters that match a request are added to the filter chain in the order their mappings appear in the deployment descriptor or programmatic configuration. (And remember, if you configure some filters in the deployment descriptor and others programmatically, you can determine whether a programmatic mapping comes before the XML mappings using the second argument to the `addMapping*` methods.) Filter order is demonstrated in Figure 9-2, where different requests match different filters but always in the same order. However, the order is not quite as simple as that: URL mappings are given preference over Servlet name mappings. If two filters match a request, one by a URL pattern and the other by a Servlet name, the filter that matches by URL pattern always is present on the chain *before* the filter that matches by Servlet name, as shown in Figure 9-3, even if its mapping appears afterward. To demonstrate this, consider the following mappings:

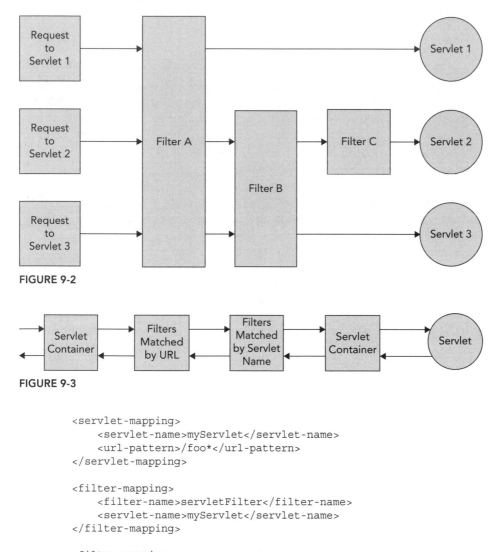

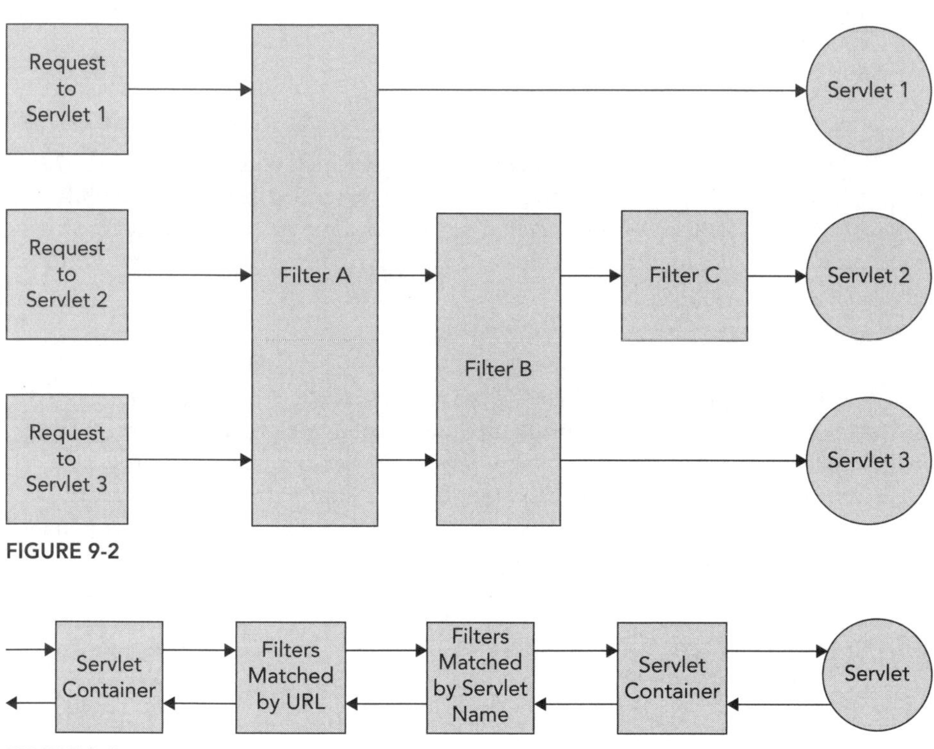


FIGURE 9-2

FIGURE 9-3

```
<servlet-mapping>
    <servlet-name>myServlet</servlet-name>
    <url-pattern>/foo*</url-pattern>
</servlet-mapping>

<filter-mapping>
    <filter-name>servletFilter</filter-name>
    <servlet-name>myServlet</servlet-name>
</filter-mapping>

<filter-mapping>
    <filter-name>myFilter</filter-name>
    <url-pattern>/foo*</url-pattern>
```

```
    </filter-mapping>

    <filter-mapping>
        <filter-name>anotherFilter</filter-name>
        <url-pattern>/foo/bar</url-pattern>
    </filter-mapping>
```

If a normal request comes in to the URL `/foo/bar`, it will match all three filters. The filter chain will consist, in order, of *myFilter*, *anotherFilter*, and then *servletFilter*. `myFilter` executes before `anotherFilter` because that's the order they appear in the deployment descriptor. They both execute before `servletFilter` because URL mappings always come before Servlet-name mappings. If the request is a forward, include, error dispatch, or asynchronous dispatch, it will not match any of these filters, because the mappings do not specify any `<dispatcher>`s explicitly.

## Exploring Filter Order with a Simple Example

To better understand how filter order works, take a look at the Filter-Order project on the `wrox.com` code download site. It contains three Servlets and three filters. The following code snippet, `ServletOne`, is identical to its counterparts `ServletTwo` and `ServletThree`, except that all occurrences of "One" have been replaced with "Two" and "Three," respectively:

```
@WebServlet(name = "servletOne", urlPatterns = "/servletOne")
public class ServletOne extends HttpServlet
{
    @Override
    protected void doGet(HttpServletRequest request, HttpServletResponse response)
            throws ServletException, IOException {
        System.out.println("Entering ServletOne.doGet()");
        response.getWriter().write("Servlet One");
        System.out.println("Leaving ServletOne.doGet()");
    }
}
```

Similarly, the following `FilterA` is identical to `FilterB` and `FilterC`:

```
public class FilterA implements Filter
{
    @Override
    public void doFilter(ServletRequest request, ServletResponse response,
                         FilterChain chain) throws IOException, ServletException {
        System.out.println("Entering FilterA.doFilter()");
        chain.doFilter(request, response);
        System.out.println("Leaving FilterA.doFilter()");
    }

    @Override
    public void init(FilterConfig config) throws ServletException { }

    @Override
    public void destroy() { }
}
```

The filters are mapped to requests in the deployment descriptor as follows so that they match the mappings shown in Figure 9-2.

```
<filter>
    <filter-name>filterA</filter-name>
    <filter-class>com.wrox.FilterA</filter-class>
</filter>

<filter-mapping>
    <filter-name>filterA</filter-name>
    <url-pattern>/*</url-pattern>
</filter-mapping>

<filter>
    <filter-name>filterB</filter-name>
    <filter-class>com.wrox.FilterB</filter-class>
</filter>

<filter-mapping>
    <filter-name>filterB</filter-name>
    <url-pattern>/servletTwo</url-pattern>
    <url-pattern>/servletThree</url-pattern>
</filter-mapping>

<filter>
    <filter-name>filterC</filter-name>
    <filter-class>com.wrox.FilterC</filter-class>
</filter>

<filter-mapping>
    <filter-name>filterC</filter-name>
    <url-pattern>/servletTwo</url-pattern>
</filter-mapping>
```

To try this out:

1. Compile the application and start Tomcat from your IDE.
2. Go to `http://localhost:8080/filters/servletOne` in your browser. You can see several messages printed to the standard output from Tomcat in your IDE:

    ```
    Entering FilterA.doFilter().
    Entering ServletOne.doGet().
    Leaving ServletOne.doGet().
    Leaving FilterA.doFilter().
    ```

3. Change the address in your browser to `/servletTwo` and observe the new output:

    ```
    Entering FilterA.doFilter().
    Entering FilterB.doFilter().
    Entering FilterC.doFilter().
    Entering ServletTwo.doGet().
    Leaving ServletTwo.doGet().
    Leaving FilterC.doFilter().
    Leaving FilterB.doFilter().
    Leaving FilterA.doFilter().
    ```

    Notice how the Filter chain progresses from A to C and then the Servlet. Then after the Servlet completes processing the request, the chain exits in reverse order from C to A.

4 Change the address in your browser to `/servletThree`. Its output should look like the following code.

```
Entering FilterA.doFilter().
Entering FilterB.doFilter().
Entering ServletThree.doGet().
Leaving ServletThree.doGet().
Leaving FilterB.doFilter().
Leaving FilterA.doFilter().
```

5. Make any changes to the mappings that you can think of to explore how it affects the execution of the filter chain. Try changing one or more of the URL mappings to Servlet name mappings and notice how the filter chain changes again.

## Using Filters with Asynchronous Request Handling

As mentioned in the previous section, filters that apply to asynchronous request handling can be tricky to correctly implement and configure. The key problem with asynchronous request handling is that the Servlet's `service` method can return before a response is sent to the client. Request handling can then be delegated to another thread or completed based on some event.

For example, the service method (or, by extension, the `doGet`, `doPost`, or other method) could start the `AsyncContext`, register a listener for some type of hypothetical message (such as a chat request received), and then return. Then, when the hypothetical message listener receives a message, it could send the response back to the user. Using this technique, a request thread is not blocked waiting while the request handling is paused. A filter that intercepts such a request would complete before the response is actually sent because when service returns, FilterChain's doChain method returns.

Filters mapped to the `ASYNC` dispatcher intercept internal requests made as a result of calling one of `AsyncContext`'s `dispatch` methods. To demonstrate this more complex filtering, look at the Filter-Async on the `wrox.com` code download site. Its `AnyRequestFilter` wraps the request and response (something you explore more in the next section) and can filter any type of request. If it detects that the Servlet started an `AsyncContext`, it prints that information and indicates whether the `AsyncContext` is using the original request and response or the unwrapped request and response.

```
public class AnyRequestFilter implements Filter
{
    private String name;

    @Override
    public void init(FilterConfig config)
    {
        this.name = config.getFilterName();
    }

    @Override
    public void doFilter(ServletRequest request, ServletResponse response,
                         FilterChain chain) throws IOException, ServletException
    {
```

```
            System.out.println("Entering " + this.name + ".doFilter().");
            chain.doFilter(
                    new HttpServletRequestWrapper((HttpServletRequest)request),
                    new HttpServletResponseWrapper((HttpServletResponse)response)
            );
            if(request.isAsyncSupported() && request.isAsyncStarted())
            {
                AsyncContext context = request.getAsyncContext();
                System.out.println("Leaving " + this.name + ".doFilter(), async " +
                        "context holds wrapped request/response = " +
                        !context.hasOriginalRequestAndResponse());
            }
            else
                System.out.println("Leaving " + this.name + ".doFilter().");
        }

        @Override
        public void destroy() { }
    }
```

This filter is instantiated and mapped three times in `web.xml`. All three mappings can intercept any URL, but the *`normalFilter`* instance intercepts only normal requests; the *`forwardFilter`* intercepts only forwarded requests; and the *`asyncFilter`* intercepts only requests dispatched from the `AsyncContext`. Notice the addition of `<async-supported>true</async-supported>` to each `<filter>` element. This tells the container that the filter is prepared for asynchronous requests. If a filter without `<async-supported>` enabled filters a request, attempting to start an `AsyncContext` in that request will result in an `IllegalStateException`.

The `NonAsyncServlet` is very straightforward: It responds to requests to `/regular` and forwards to the `nonAsync.jsp` view.

```
@WebServlet(name = "nonAsyncServlet", urlPatterns = "/regular")
public class NonAsyncServlet extends HttpServlet
{
    @Override
    protected void doGet(HttpServletRequest request, HttpServletResponse response)
            throws ServletException, IOException
    {
        System.out.println("Entering NonAsyncServlet.doGet().");
        request.getRequestDispatcher("/WEB-INF/jsp/view/nonAsync.jsp")
                .forward(request, response);
        System.out.println("Leaving NonAsyncServlet.doGet().");
    }
}
```

`AsyncServlet` in Listing 9-1 is much more complex. To make logging very clear, it generates a unique ID for the current request. If the *unwrap* parameter is not present, it starts the `AsyncContext` with `startAsync(ServletRequest, ServletResponse)`. This ensures the `AsyncContext` gets the request and response as passed into `doGet`. If a filter wrapped the request or response, the wrapper is what the `AsyncContext` uses. However, if the *unwrap* is present, the `doGet` starts the `AsyncContext` using the no-argument `startAsync` method. In this case, the `AsyncContext` gets the original request and response, not the wrapped request and response. Notice the call to `AsyncContext`'s `start(Runnable)` method (using Java 8 method references). Using this tells the container to run the `Runnable` with its internal thread pool. You could also simply start your own thread, but using the container's thread pool is safer and avoids resource exhaustion.

**LISTING 9-1: AsyncServlet.java**

```
@WebServlet(name = "asyncServlet", urlPatterns = "/async", asyncSupported = true)
public class AsyncServlet extends HttpServlet
{
    private static volatile int ID = 1;

    @Override
    protected void doGet(HttpServletRequest request, HttpServletResponse response)
            throws ServletException, IOException
    {
        final int id;
        synchronized(AsyncServlet.class)
        {
            id = ID++;
        }
        long timeout = request.getParameter("timeout") == null ?
                10_000L : Long.parseLong(request.getParameter("timeout"));

        System.out.println("Entering AsyncServlet.doGet(). Request ID = " + id +
                ", isAsyncStarted = " + request.isAsyncStarted());

        final AsyncContext context = request.getParameter("unwrap") != null ?
                request.startAsync() : request.startAsync(request, response);
        context.setTimeout(timeout);

        System.out.println("Starting asynchronous thread. Request ID = " + id +
                ".");

        AsyncThread thread = new AsyncThread(id, context);
        context.start(thread::doWork);

        System.out.println("Leaving AsyncServlet.doGet(). Request ID = " + id +
                ", isAsyncStarted = " + request.isAsyncStarted());
    }

    private static class AsyncThread
    {
        private final int id;
        private final AsyncContext context;

        public AsyncThread(int id, AsyncContext context) { ... }

        public void doWork()
        {
            System.out.println("Asynchronous thread started. Request ID = " +
                    this.id + ".");

            try {
```

*continues*

**LISTING 9-1** *(continued)*

```
                Thread.sleep(5_000L);
            } catch (Exception e) {
                e.printStackTrace();
            }

            HttpServletRequest request =
                    (HttpServletRequest)this.context.getRequest();
            System.out.println("Done sleeping. Request ID = " + this.id +
                    ", URL = " + request.getRequestURL() + ".");

            this.context.dispatch("/WEB-INF/jsp/view/async.jsp");

            System.out.println("Asynchronous thread completed. Request ID = " +
                    this.id + ".");
        }
    }
}
```

Now experiment with these Servlets and filters:

1. Compile the application and start Tomcat from your IDE; then go to `http://localhost:8080/filters/regular` in your browser. You should see the following in the output window of the debugger. Notice that *`normalFilter`* intercepted the request to the Servlet, and *`forwardFilter`* intercepted the forwarded request to the JSP.

```
Entering normalFilter.doFilter().
Entering NonAsyncServlet.doGet().
Entering forwardFilter.doFilter().
In nonAsync.jsp.
Leaving forwardFilter.doFilter().
Leaving NonAsyncServlet.doGet().
Leaving normalFilter.doFilter().
```

2. Go to `http://localhost:8080/filters/async`. The following debugger output appears immediately. Notice that *`normalFilter`* intercepts the request but completes before the response is actually sent.

```
Entering normalFilter.doFilter().
Entering AsyncServlet.doGet(). Request ID = 1, isAsyncStarted = false
Starting asynchronous thread. Request ID = 1.
Leaving AsyncServlet.doGet(). Request ID = 1, isAsyncStarted = true
Leaving normalFilter.doFilter(), async context holds wrapped request/response=true
Asynchronous thread started. Request ID = 1.
```

After a 5-second wait, the `AsyncThread` inner class sends the response to the user, and the following debugger output appears. When the request is dispatched to the JSP using the `AsyncContext`'s dispatch method, *`asyncFilter`* intercepts the internal request to that JSP.

```
Done sleeping. Request ID = 1, URL = http://localhost:8080/filters/async.
Asynchronous thread completed. Request ID = 1.
```

```
Entering asyncFilter.doFilter().
In async.jsp.
Leaving asyncFilter.doFilter().
```

3. Go to `http://localhost:8080/filters/async?unwrap` and wait for the response to complete. The following debugger output appears (some of it after 5 seconds). It's identical except that, in this case, the `AsyncContext` holds the original request and response instead of the wrapped request and response (the bold output changed).

```
Entering normalFilter.doFilter().
Entering AsyncServlet.doGet(). Request ID = 2, isAsyncStarted = false
Starting asynchronous thread. Request ID = 2.
Leaving AsyncServlet.doGet(). Request ID = 2, isAsyncStarted = true
Leaving normalFilter.doFilter(), async context holds wrapped request/response=false
Asynchronous thread started. Request ID = 2.
Done sleeping. Request ID = 2, URL = http://localhost:8080/filters/async.
Asynchronous thread completed. Request ID = 2.
Entering asyncFilter.doFilter().
In async.jsp.
Leaving asyncFilter.doFilter().
```

4. Go to `http://localhost:8080/filters/async?timeout=3000`. The following debugger output appears, and then 5 seconds later the sleep completes, and retrieving the request from the `AsyncContext` results in an `IllegalStateException`. This is because the `AsyncContext` timeout expired and the response was closed before the `AsyncThread` inner class could complete its work.

```
Entering normalFilter.doFilter().
Entering AsyncServlet.doGet(). Request ID = 3, isAsyncStarted = false
Starting asynchronous thread. Request ID = 3.
Leaving AsyncServlet.doGet(). Request ID = 3, isAsyncStarted = true
Leaving normalFilter.doFilter(), async context holds wrapped request/response=true
Asynchronous thread started. Request ID = 3.
```

It should be clear by now how complex and powerful asynchronous request handling is. The important point is that if you handle the response using the `AsyncContext` directly, the code executes outside the scope of any filters. However, if you use `AsyncContext`'s `dispatch` method to internally forward the request to a URL, a filter mapped for `ASYNC` requests can intercept the internal forward and apply whatever additional logic is required. You must decide when each approach is appropriate, but in most cases you will have no need for asynchronous request handling. No other parts of this book use asynchronous request handling.

## INVESTIGATING PRACTICAL USES FOR FILTERS

The beginning of the chapter discussed many practical uses for filters. The Compression-Filter project on the `wrox.com` code download site demonstrates two of these uses: a logging filter and a response compression filter. The project contains a simple Servlet mapped to `/servlet` that responds with "This Servlet response may be compressed." It also contains a simple `/index.jsp` file that responds with "This content may be compressed." This project uses the following `ServletContextListener` to programmatically configure the filters for the application.

```
@WebListener
public class Configurator implements ServletContextListener
{
    @Override
    public void contextInitialized(ServletContextEvent event) {
        ServletContext context = event.getServletContext();

        FilterRegistration.Dynamic registration =
                context.addFilter("requestLogFilter", new RequestLogFilter());
        registration.addMappingForUrlPatterns(null, false, "/*");

        registration = context.addFilter("compressionFilter",
                new CompressionFilter());
        registration.setAsyncSupported(true);
        registration.addMappingForUrlPatterns(null, false, "/*");
    }

    @Override
    public void contextDestroyed(ServletContextEvent event) { }
}
```

## Adding a Simple Logging Filter

The `RequestLogFilter` class in Listing 9-2 is the first filter in the filter chain for all requests to the application. It times how long a request takes to process and logs information about every request that comes in to the application — the IP address, timestamp, request method, protocol, response status and length, and time to process the request — similar to the Apache HTTP log format. The logging happens in the `finally` block so that any exceptions thrown further down the filter chain do not prevent the logging statement from being written.

**LISTING 9-2: RequestLogFilter.java**

```
public class RequestLogFilter implements Filter
{
    @Override
    public void doFilter(ServletRequest request, ServletResponse response,
                         FilterChain chain) throws IOException, ServletException {
        Instant time = Instant.now();
        StopWatch timer = new StopWatch();
        try {
            timer.start();
            chain.doFilter(request, response);
        } finally {
            timer.stop();
            HttpServletRequest in = (HttpServletRequest)request;
            HttpServletResponse out = (HttpServletResponse)response;
            String length = out.getHeader("Content-Length");
            if(length == null || length.length() == 0)
                length = "-";
```

```
            System.out.println(in.getRemoteAddr() + " - - [" + time + "]" +
                    " \"" + in.getMethod() + " " + in.getRequestURI() + " " +
                    in.getProtocol() + "\" " + out.getStatus() + " " + length +
                    " " + timer);
        }
    }

    @Override
    public void init(FilterConfig filterConfig) throws ServletException { }

    @Override
    public void destroy() { }
}
```

> **NOTE** *The* `RequestLogFilter` *will not work properly with asynchronous request handling. If a Servlet starts an* `AsyncContext`, `doFilter` *will return before the response has been sent, meaning the filter will log incomplete or incorrect information. Making this filter work correctly for asynchronous requests is a significant and complex task that is left as an exercise for the reader to consider.*

## Compressing Response Content Using a Filter

The `CompressionFilter` in Listing 9-3 is significantly more complex than the `RequestLogFilter`. When thinking about compressing the response, you might think that you should execute the filter chain and then perform the compression logic on the way back out. Remember, however, that response data can begin flowing back to the client before the Servlet has completed servicing the request. It can also begin flowing back to the client *after* the Servlet has completed servicing the request, in the case of asynchronous request handling. Because of this, if you want to alter the response content, you must wrap the response object passed further down the chain. The `CompressionFilter` does just this.

Take a minute to read over the code and examine what `CompressionFilter` is doing. First, it checks to see if the client has included an `Accept-Encoding` request header containing the "gzip" encoding. This is a very important check because if it hasn't, this means the client may not understand gzip-compressed responses. If it has, it sets the `Content-Encoding` header to "gzip" and then wraps the response object with an instance of the private inner class `ResponseWrapper`. This class, in turn, wraps the `PrintWriter` or `ServletOutputStream` that sends data back to the client with the private inner class `GZIPServletOutputStream`. This wrapper contains an internal `java.util.zip.GZIPOutputStream`. Response data is first written to the `GZIPOutputStream`, and when the request completes, it finishes compression and writes the compressed response to the wrapped `ServletOutputStream`. The `ResponseWrapper` also prevents any Servlet code from setting the content length header for the response because the content length cannot be known until after the response is compressed.

**LISTING 9-3: CompressionFilter.java**

```
public class CompressionFilter implements Filter
{
    @Override
    public void doFilter(ServletRequest request, ServletResponse response,
                         FilterChain chain) throws IOException, ServletException {
        if(((HttpServletRequest)request).getHeader("Accept-Encoding")
                .contains("gzip")) {
            System.out.println("Encoding requested.");
            ((HttpServletResponse)response).setHeader("Content-Encoding", "gzip");
            ResponseWrapper wrapper =
                    new ResponseWrapper((HttpServletResponse)response);
            try {
                chain.doFilter(request, wrapper);
            } finally {
                try {
                    wrapper.finish();
                } catch(Exception e) {
                    e.printStackTrace();
                }
            }
        } else {
            System.out.println("Encoding not requested.");
            chain.doFilter(request, response);
        }
    }

    @Override
    public void init(FilterConfig filterConfig) throws ServletException { }

    @Override
    public void destroy() { }

    private static class ResponseWrapper extends HttpServletResponseWrapper
    {
        private GZIPServletOutputStream outputStream;
        private PrintWriter writer;

        public ResponseWrapper(HttpServletResponse request) {
            super(request);
        }

        @Override
        public synchronized ServletOutputStream getOutputStream()
                throws IOException {
            if(this.writer != null)
                throw new IllegalStateException("getWriter() already called.");
            if(this.outputStream == null)
                this.outputStream =
                        new GZIPServletOutputStream(super.getOutputStream());
            return this.outputStream;
        }

        @Override
```

```
    public synchronized PrintWriter getWriter() throws IOException {
        if(this.writer == null && this.outputStream != null)
            throw new IllegalStateException(
                    "getOutputStream() already called.");
        if(this.writer == null) {
            this.outputStream =
                    new GZIPServletOutputStream(super.getOutputStream());
            this.writer = new PrintWriter(new OutputStreamWriter(
                    this.outputStream, this.getCharacterEncoding()
            ));
        }
        return this.writer;
    }

    @Override
    public void flushBuffer() throws IOException {
        if(this.writer != null)
            this.writer.flush();
        else if(this.outputStream != null)
            this.outputStream.flush();
        super.flushBuffer();
    }

    @Override
    public void setContentLength(int length) { }

    @Override
    public void setContentLengthLong(long length) { }

    @Override
    public void setHeader(String name, String value) {
        if(!"content-length".equalsIgnoreCase(name))
            super.setHeader(name, value);
    }

    @Override
    public void addHeader(String name, String value) {
        if(!"content-length".equalsIgnoreCase(name))
            super.setHeader(name, value);
    }

    @Override
    public void setIntHeader(String name, int value) {
        if(!"content-length".equalsIgnoreCase(name))
            super.setIntHeader(name, value);
    }

    @Override
    public void addIntHeader(String name, int value) {
        if(!"content-length".equalsIgnoreCase(name))
            super.setIntHeader(name, value);
    }

    public void finish() throws IOException {
```

*continues*

**LISTING 9-3** *(continued)*

```
                if(this.writer != null)
                    this.writer.close();
                else if(this.outputStream != null)
                    this.outputStream.finish();
            }
        }

        private static class GZIPServletOutputStream extends ServletOutputStream
        {
            private final ServletOutputStream servletOutputStream;
            private final GZIPOutputStream gzipStream;

            public GZIPServletOutputStream(ServletOutputStream servletOutputStream)
                    throws IOException {
                this.servletOutputStream = servletOutputStream;
                this.gzipStream = new GZIPOutputStream(servletOutputStream);
            }

            @Override
            public boolean isReady() {
                return this.servletOutputStream.isReady();
            }

            @Override
            public void setWriteListener(WriteListener writeListener) {
                this.servletOutputStream.setWriteListener(writeListener);
            }

            @Override
            public void write(int b) throws IOException {
                this.gzipStream.write(b);
            }

            @Override
            public void close() throws IOException {
                this.gzipStream.close();
            }

            @Override
            public void flush() throws IOException {
                this.gzipStream.flush();
            }

            public void finish() throws IOException {
                this.gzipStream.finish();
            }
        }
    }
```

The wrapper pattern is a very common pattern that you will likely see applied in many filters. Both the request and response objects can be wrapped; however, wrapping the response is usually more common. Wrapping the response allows you to intercept any method calls on the wrapped response, facilitating the ability to modify the response data. You can also use a very similar filter to that in Listing 9-3 to encrypt response data rather than compress it. The request object could be wrapped to decrypt its contents.

To try out the logging and compression filters:

1. Compile your application and start Tomcat from your IDE.
2. Go to `http://localhost:8080/compression/` and `http://localhost:8080/compression/servlet` in your browser.
3. Using the developer tools built for you browser, start monitoring the headers of requests to and responses from the application. (Microsoft Internet Explorer and Google Chrome have built-in developer tools that can do this, and the Firebug plug-in for Mozilla Firefox has this capability.) You should see a screen like that in Figure 9-4.

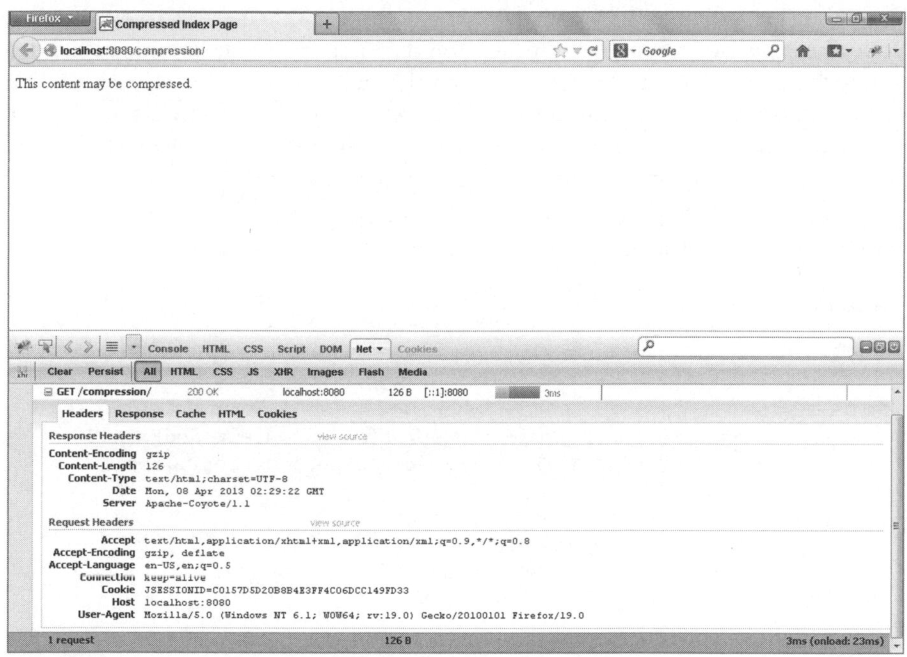


FIGURE 9-4

Notice that the `Accept-Encoding` request header contains the "gzip" encoding, and the `Content-Encoding` response header has the value "gzip." This means that your browser is announcing it can accept gzip-encoded responses, and the compression filter is obliging the request and compressing the response data before sending it to the browser.

## SIMPLIFYING AUTHENTICATION WITH A FILTER

One critical use for filters in web applications is for securing applications against unwanted access. The Customer Support application you are making for Multinational Widget Corporation uses a very primitive authentication mechanism for securing its pages. You have probably already noticed that many places in the application contain the same, duplicated code to check for authentication:

```
if(request.getSession().getAttribute("username") == null)
{
    response.sendRedirect("login");
    return;
}
```

At some point you might have thought a better solution is to create a public static method on some class to perform this check and call it everywhere. For sure, this reduces duplicated code, but it still results in performing that method call in multiple places. As the number of servlets in your application increased, so would have the number of calls to that static method.

After what you have learned in this chapter, it should be clear that a filter is a better place to put this code. The Customer-Support-v7 project on the `wrox.com` code download site demonstrates this by adding the `Configurator` listener class and the `AuthenticationFilter` class. The previous code snippet has been removed from the `doGet` and `doPost` methods in `TicketServlet` and the `doGet` method in `SessionListServlet`. The configurator is simple: It declares the `AuthenticationFilter` and maps it to `/tickets` and `/sessions`:

```
@WebListener
public class Configurator implements ServletContextListener
{
    @Override
    public void contextInitialized(ServletContextEvent event)
    {
        ServletContext context = event.getServletContext();

        FilterRegistration.Dynamic registration = context.addFilter(
                "authenticationFilter", new AuthenticationFilter()
        );
        registration.setAsyncSupported(true);
        registration.addMappingForUrlPatterns(
                null, false, "/sessions", "/tickets"
        );
    }

    @Override
    public void contextDestroyed(ServletContextEvent event) { }
}
```

As you add more Servlets or other protected resources (such as JSPs) to your application, you only need to add their URL patterns to the filter registration to ensure that users log in before accessing those resources. Of course, this filter does not protect the login Servlet because you do not want to protect the login screen. You also do not need to protect any of the CSS, JavaScript, or image resources because they do not contain sensitive data. The `AuthenticationFilter` performs the authentication check on every request of any HTTP method and redirects users to the login screen if they are not logged in:

```
public class AuthenticationFilter implements Filter
{
    @Override
    public void doFilter(ServletRequest request, ServletResponse response,
                         FilterChain chain) throws IOException, ServletException
    {
        HttpSession session = ((HttpServletRequest)request).getSession(false);
        if(session != null && session.getAttribute("username") == null)
            ((HttpServletResponse)response).sendRedirect("login");
        else
            chain.doFilter(request, response);
    }

    @Override
    public void init(FilterConfig config) throws ServletException { }

    @Override
    public void destroy() { }
}
```

One beautiful thing about this change is that if you alter the authentication algorithm, you only need to change the filter to continue protecting the resources in your application. Previously, you would have had to make changes to every Servlet. Test out these changes by compiling, starting up Tomcat in your IDE, and navigating to `http://localhost:8080/support` in your browser. Even though the authentication check has been removed from all the Servlets, you are still asked to log in before viewing or creating tickets, or viewing the list of sessions.

## SUMMARY

In this chapter you explored the purpose of filters and the many reasons you might use them. You learned about the `Filter` interface and how to create, declare, and map filters in your applications. You experimented with the all-important filter chain, and learned how the order in which filters are executed can be unimportant in some scenarios and quite critical in others. You were introduced to the concept of asynchronous request handling and used filters to explore that topic further and gain an understanding of how tricky asynchronous request handling can be. Finally, after exploring the three different ways of declaring and mapping filters — in the deployment descriptor, using annotations, and programmatically — you experimented with a logging filter, a response compression filter, and an authentication filter.

In the next chapter you explore the technology of WebSockets, how they dramatically improve interactive web applications, and how to use them in Java and JavaScript. An interesting point is that the code in Tomcat that makes WebSockets possible actually uses a filter to intercept all WebSocket-bound requests in your application and send them to your WebSocket endpoints (which you learn about more in the next chapter). So, without even doing anything, your application already has filters inspecting and, if necessary, modifying requests.

# 10

# Making Your Application Interactive with WebSockets

## IN THIS CHAPTER

- How Ajax evolved to WebSockets
- A discussion on the WebSocket APIs
- Using WebSockets to create multiplayer games
- Communicating in a cluster with WebSockets
- How to add chatting to a web application

## WROX.COM CODE DOWNLOADS FOR THIS CHAPTER

You can find the `wrox.com` code downloads for this chapter at `http://www.wrox.com/remtitle.cgi?isbn=1118656464` on the Download Code tab. The code for this chapter is divided into the following major examples:

- Game-Site Project
- Simulated-Cluster Project
- Customer-Support-v8 Project

## NEW MAVEN DEPENDENCIES FOR THIS CHAPTER

In addition to the Maven dependencies introduced in previous chapters, you also need the following Maven dependencies:

```
<dependency>
    <groupId>javax.websocket</groupId>
    <artifactId>javax.websocket-api</artifactId>
```

```
        <version>1.0</version>
        <scope>provided</scope>
    </dependency>

    <dependency>
        <groupId>org.apache.commons</groupId>
        <artifactId>commons-lang3</artifactId>
        <version>3.1</version>
        <scope>compile</scope>
    </dependency>

    <dependency>
        <groupId>com.fasterxml.jackson.core</groupId>
        <artifactId>jackson-core</artifactId>
        <version>2.3.2</version>
        <scope>compile</scope>
    </dependency>

    <dependency>
        <groupId>com.fasterxml.jackson.core</groupId>
        <artifactId>jackson-annotations</artifactId>
        <version>2.3.2</version>
        <scope>compile</scope>
    </dependency>

    <dependency>
        <groupId>com.fasterxml.jackson.core</groupId>
        <artifactId>jackson-databind</artifactId>
        <version>2.3.2</version>
        <scope>compile</scope>
    </dependency>

    <dependency>
        <groupId>com.fasterxml.jackson.datatype</groupId>
        <artifactId>jackson-datatype-jsr310</artifactId>
        <version>2.3.2</version>
        <scope>compile</scope>
    </dependency>
```

## EVOLUTION: FROM AJAX TO WEBSOCKETS

In the beginning, man created HTML and saw that it was not enough. Users wanted web pages that interacted with them. The answer to this was JavaScript. In the early days of JavaScript, there was almost no standardization between browsers (in the earliest days, only one browser supported it) and JavaScript was extremely slow and insecure. Over the years it has improved significantly in speed, security, and capability. With many JavaScript frameworks available on the web, you can now create extremely rich, single-page web applications with very little JavaScript. The biggest driver of this innovation was the adoption of a technology known as Ajax.

## Problem: Getting New Data from the Server to the Browser

*Ajax*, an acronym for *Asynchronous JavaScript and XML*, has become synonymous with the idea of asynchronously communicating (or synchronously, for that matter) with a remote server using JavaScript. It does not necessitate the use of XML, as the name implies. (JSON is often used instead of XML, and in such cases it can still be called Ajax or may also be called *AJAJ*.) With Ajax, web applications in the browser could now communicate with server-side components without the browser page changing or refreshing. This communication could happen completely transparently, without the user knowing, and it could be used to send new data to the server or fetch new data from the server. This, however, was the crux of the problem: The browser could only fetch new data from the server. But the browser doesn't necessarily know when new data is available to fetch. The server knows that. Just like only the browser knows when it has new data to send to the server, only the server knows when it has new data to send to the browser. For example, when two users are chatting in a web application, only the server knows when user A has sent a message to user B. User B's browser won't know until it contacts the server. Even with something as powerful as Ajax, this was a difficult problem to solve.

Over the past 14 years, dozens of solutions have emerged, some of them widely supported, whereas others were extremely browser-specific. This book doesn't cover all of them, nor would that be useful. However, four major approaches have served as the basis for the varying solutions to this problem, and understanding them and their weaknesses is key to understanding the need for something better.

> **NOTE** *The actual details of making Ajax requests and receiving responses using JavaScript is not important to the discussion in this chapter and outside the scope of this book. If you are unfamiliar with this topic, there are thousands of Ajax tutorials available online.*

## Solution 1: Frequent Polling

Perhaps one of the most prevalent approaches to this problem is *frequently polling* the server for new data. The concept is fairly simple: At a regular interval, often once per second, the browser sends an Ajax request to the server polling for new data. If the browser has new data to send to the server, that data hitches a ride on the request. If the server has new data for the browser, it replies with the new data. If it does not, it replies with no content. (This may mean an empty JSON object or XML document, or a `Content-Length` header of 0.) This protocol looks something like the four requests represented in Figure 10-1, except there are usually many more requests and responses.

The downside to this protocol is huge and obvious: An enormous number of wasted requests could be made and replied to needlessly. Notice that the second and third requests in the figure achieved nothing! Add to this the overhead of establishing a connection, sending and receiving headers, and tearing down a connection, and a lot of processing and network resources are wasted to find out that the server has no new data for the browser. Though this technique is still in widespread use due to the sheer simplicity of implementing it, it was clear early on that it was not a good solution to this problem.

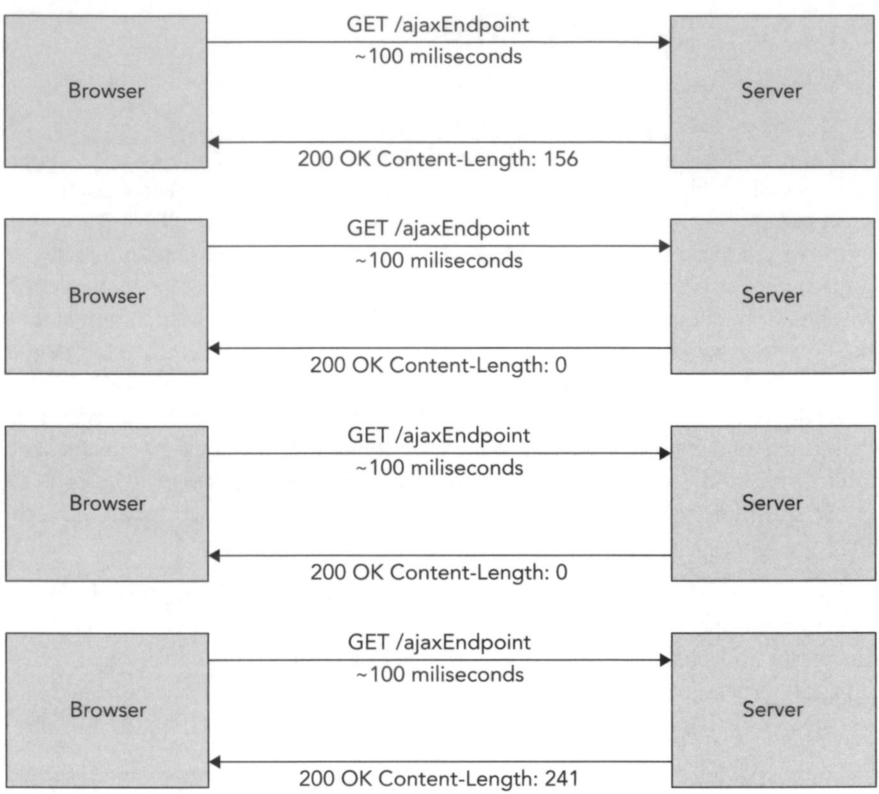


**FIGURE 10-1**

## Solution 2: Long Polling

*Long polling*, represented in Figure 10-2, is similar to frequent polling, except that the server doesn't respond until it has data to send back to the browser. This is more efficient because fewer compute and network resources are wasted, but it brings some problems of its own to the table:

- **What if the browser has new data to send to the server before the server responds?** The browser must either make a separate, parallel request, or it must terminate the current request (from which the server must recover gracefully) and begin another one.
- **Connection timeouts are built into the TCP and HTTP specifications.** Because of this, the server and client must periodically close and re-establish a connection. Sometimes the connection closes as often as every 60 seconds, although some implementations have been successful at holding a connection for several minutes.
- **A connection limit mandate exists in the HTTP/1.1 specification.** Browsers must permit no more than two simultaneous connections to any given hostname. If one connection is constantly tied up waiting for data to be pushed from the server, it cuts in half the number of connections that can be used to fetch web pages, graphics, and other resources from the server.

Regardless of these issues, this is a popular approach that has gained widespread use over the past several years and is often generically referred to as *Comet* (an ironic play on words with Ajax, as both names can refer to cleaning products).

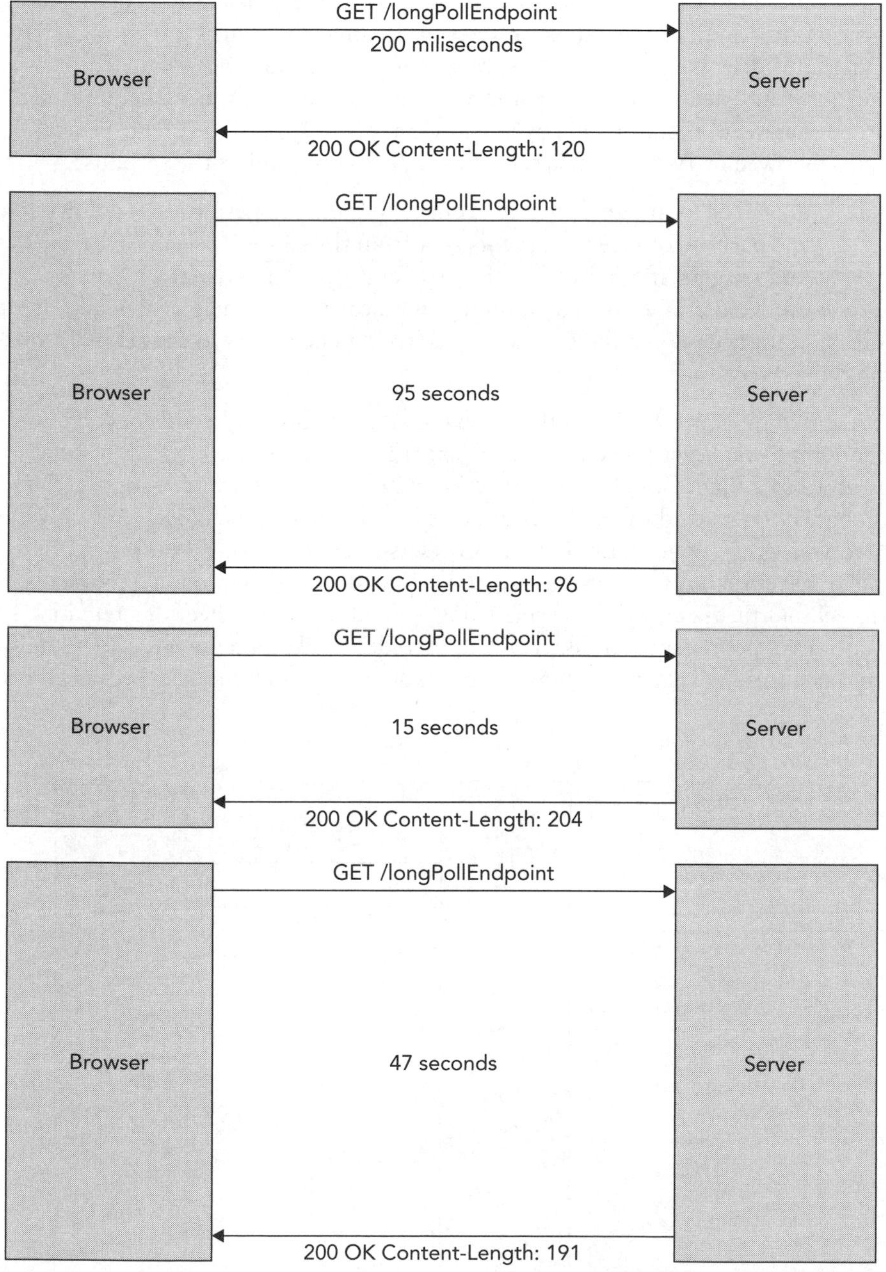


**FIGURE 10-2**

## Solution 3: Chunked Encoding

Very similar to the long polling solution, *chunked encoding* takes advantage of an HTTP/1.1 feature that enables servers to respond to requests without advertising a content length. In place of the `Content-Length: n` header, a response can contain a `Transfer-Encoding: chunked` header. This tells the browser that the response is coming in "chunks." In the response, each chunk starts with a number indicating the length of the chunk, a series of optional characters indicating chunk extensions (irrelevant to this discussion), and a `CRLF` (carriage return + line feed) sequence. This is then followed by the data contained in that chunk and another `CRLF`. Any number of chunks can follow, and they can be separated, theoretically, by any amount of time, small or great. When a zero-length chunk (a `0` followed by two `CRLF`s) is sent, this indicates the end of the response.

How you typically use chunked encoding to solve the problem at hand is to establish a connection at the beginning for the sole purpose of receiving events sent from the server. Each chunk from the server is a new event and triggers another call to the JavaScript `XMLHttpRequest` object's `onreadystatechange` event handler. Occasionally, though not nearly as often as with long polling, the connection has to be refreshed. When the browser needs to send new data to the server, it does so with a second short-lived request.

This protocol is represented in Figure 10-3. On the left-hand side, the browser *sends* new data to the "upstream endpoint," whenever it needs to, using short-lived requests. On the right-hand side, the browser establishes a single, long-lived connection with the "downstream endpoint," and the server uses that connection to send the browser updates in chunks. Chunked encoding solves the major timeout problem present with long polling (browsers tolerate responses taking a long time to *complete* much better than responses taking a long time to *start* — large file downloads are the perfect example), but the issue with browsers being limited to two connections remains. Additionally, with both long polling and chunked encoding, older browsers tended to indefinitely display a message in the status bar that the page was still loading — though modern browsers have eliminated this behavior.

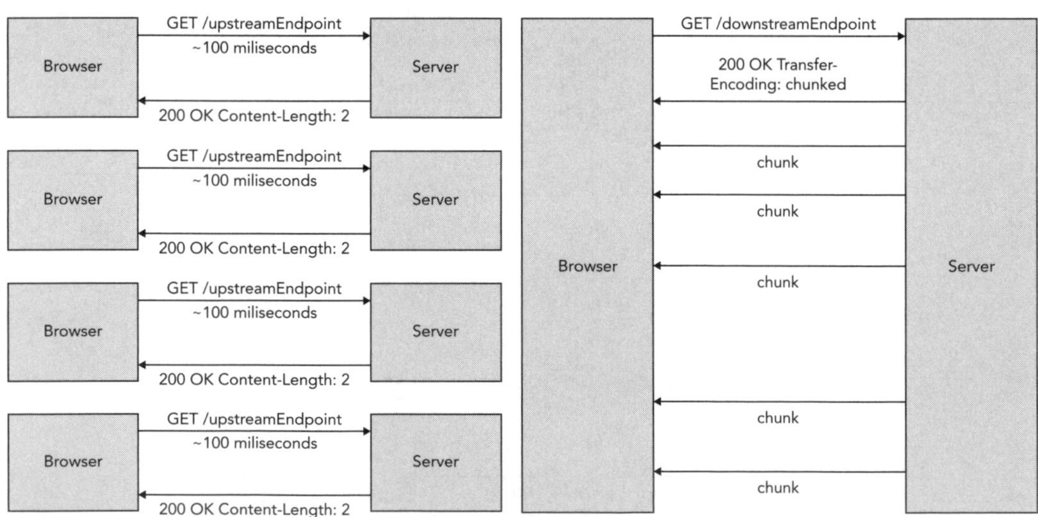


**FIGURE 10-3**

## Solution 4: Applets and Adobe Flash

Early in this evolutionary process, many realized that what all of these solutions were emulating was true full-duplex communications between a browser and server over a single connection. Simply put, this was not going to happen using Ajax and `XMLHttpRequest`. A popular, though short-lived, approach to this problem was to use Java Applets or Adobe Flash movies, demonstrated in Figure 10-4. Essentially, the developer would create a 1-pixel-square transparent Applet or Flash movie and embed it in the page. This plug-in would then establish an ordinary TCP socket connection (instead of an HTTP connection) to the server. This eliminated all of the restrictions and limitations present in the HTTP protocol. When the server sent messages to the browser, the Applet or Flash movie would call a JavaScript function with the message data. When the browser had new data for the server, it would call a Java or Flash method using a JavaScript DOM function exposed by the browser plug-in, and that method would forward the data on to the server.

This protocol achieved true full-duplex communications over a single connection and eliminated issues such as timeouts and concurrent connection limitations (and even avoided the security constraint placed on Ajax connections that they must originate from a page on the same fully qualified domain name). But it came at a high cost: It required third-party (Java or Flash) plug-ins, which were inherently insecure, slow, and memory-intensive. Because there were no security protocols built in to this solution and each developer was left to his own devices, it also revealed some interesting vulnerabilities.

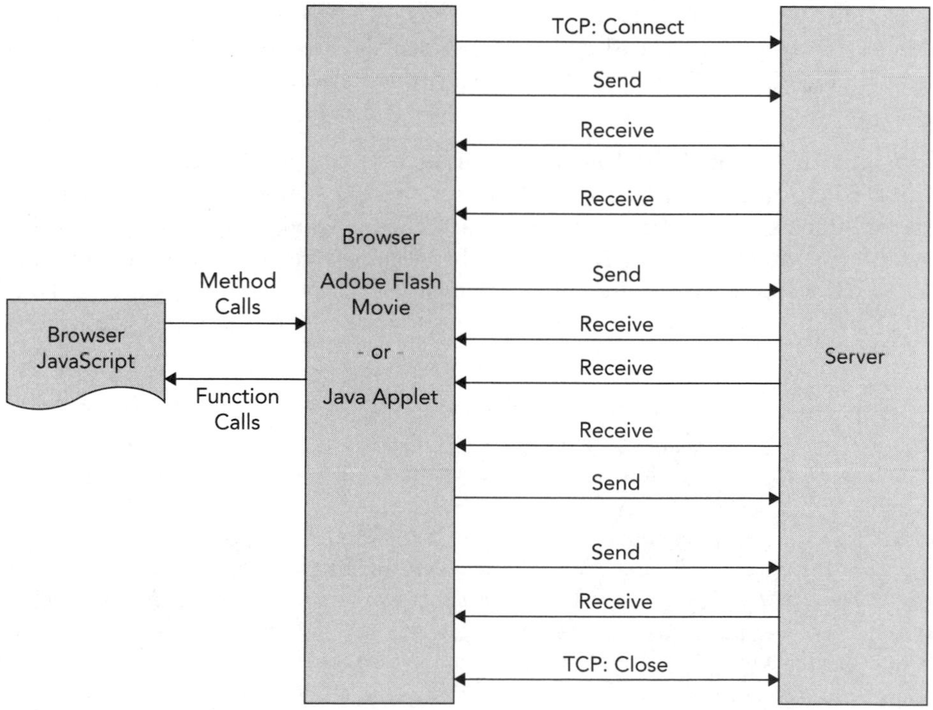


**FIGURE 10-4**

This technology took off for a while, but not long after that, the mobile web took the technology world by storm. Browsers in most popular mobile device operating systems would not (and to this day still do not) run Java or Flash plug-ins. With an increasing percentage of Internet traffic coming from mobile devices (one-quarter of all traffic as of late 2012), web developers quickly abandoned this approach to getting data from the server. They needed something better. They needed a solution that used raw TCP connections, was secure, was fast, could be easily supported on mobile platforms, and didn't require browser plug-ins to accomplish.

## WebSockets: The Solution Nobody Knew Kind of Already Existed

The HTTP/1.1 specification in RFC 2616 was formalized in 1999. It provided the framework for all HTTP communications used for more than a decade to the present day. Section 14.42 included a rarely used, often overlooked featured called *HTTP Upgrade.*

### The HTTP/1.1 Upgrade Feature

The premise is simple: Any HTTP client (not just browsers) can include the header name and value `Connection: Upgrade` in a request. To indicate what the client wants to upgrade to, the additional `Upgrade` header must specify a list of one or more protocols. These protocols should be something incompatible with HTTP/1.1, such as IRC or RTA. The server, if it accepts the upgrade request, returns the response code `101 Switching Protocols` along with a response `Upgrade` header with a single value: the first protocol that the server supports from the list of the requested protocols. Originally, this feature was most often used to upgrade from HTTP to HTTPS, but was subject to man-in-the-middle attacks because the entire connection wasn't secured. Thus, the technique was quickly replaced with the `https` URI scheme. Since then, `Connection: Upgrade` has largely fallen out of use.

The most important feature of an HTTP Upgrade is that the resulting protocol can be anything. It ceases to be an HTTP connection after the Upgrade handshake is complete and can even turn into a persistent, full-duplex TCP socket connection. Theoretically speaking, you could use HTTP Upgrade to establish any kind of TCP communications between any two endpoints with a protocol of your own design. However, browsers aren't about to turn JavaScript developers loose on the TCP stack (nor should they), so some protocol needed to be agreed upon. Thus, the WebSockets protocol was born.

> **NOTE** *If a particular resource on a server accepts only HTTP Upgrade requests and a client connects to this resource without requesting an upgrade, the server can respond with* `426 Upgrade Required` *to indicate that an upgrade is mandatory. In this case the response could also include the* `Connection: Upgrade` *header and the* `Upgrade` *header containing a list of the upgrade protocols the server supports. If a client requests an upgrade to a protocol the server doesn't support, the server responds with* `400 Bad Request` *and can include the* `Upgrade` *header containing a list of the upgrade protocols the server supports. Finally, if the server does not accept upgrade requests, it responds with* `400 Bad Request`.

## WebSocket Protocol Sits on Top of HTTP/1.1 Upgrade

A *WebSocket* connection, represented in Figure 10-5, begins with a not-so-unordinary HTTP request to a URL with a special scheme. The URI schemes `ws` and `wss` correspond to their HTTP counterparts `http` and `https`, respectively. The `Connection: Upgrade` header is present along with the `Upgrade: websocket` header, instructing the server to upgrade the connection to the WebSocket protocol, a persistent, full-duplex communications protocol formalized as RFC 6455 in 2011. After the handshake is completed, text and binary messages are sent in either direction at the same time without closing and re-establishing the connection. At this point, there is essentially no difference between client and server — they have equal capabilities and power over the connection, and are simply *peers*.

> **NOTE** *The* `ws` *and* `wss` *schemes aren't strictly part of the HTTP protocol, since HTTP requests and request headers don't actually include URI schemes. Instead, HTTP requests include only the server-relative URL in the first line of the request and the domain name in the* `Host` *header. The specialized WebSocket schemes are mainly used to inform browsers and APIs as to whether you intend to connect using SSL/TLS (*`wss`*) or no encryption (*`ws`*).*

There are many advantages to the way the WebSocket protocol is implemented:

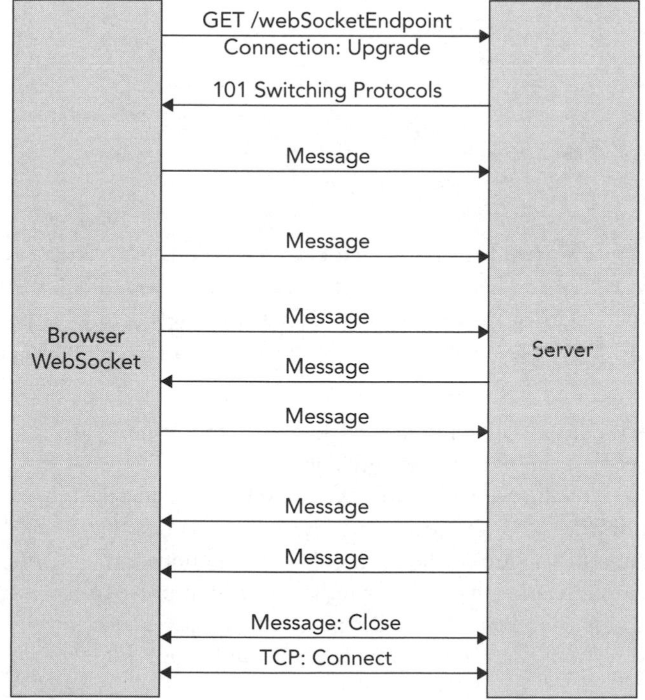


**FIGURE 10-5**

- Because the connection is established on port 80 (`ws`) or 443 (`wss`), the same ports used for HTTP, almost no firewalls block WebSocket connections.
- The protocol integrates naturally into Internet browsers and HTTP servers because the handshake takes place over HTTP.
- Heartbeat messages called *pings* and *pongs* are sent back and forth to keep WebSocket connection alive nearly indefinitely. Essentially, one peer periodically sends a tiny packet to the other (the ping), and the other peer responds with a packet containing the same data (the pong). This establishes that both peers are still connected.
- Messages are framed on your behalf without any extra code so that the server and client both know when a message starts and when all its content arrives.
- The closing of the WebSocket connection involves a special close message that can contain reason codes and text explaining why the connection was closed.
- The WebSocket protocol can *securely* allow cross-domain connections, eliminating restrictions placed on Ajax and `XMLHttpRequest`.
- The HTTP specification requiring browsers to limit simultaneous connections to two per hostname does not apply after the handshake is complete because the connection ceases to be an HTTP connection.

The handshake request headers in a WebSocket connection are simple. A typical WebSocket upgrade request may appear as follows if studied in a traffic analyzer like Wireshark or Fiddler:

```
GET /webSocketEndpoint HTTP/1.1
Host: www.example.org
Connection: Upgrade
Upgrade: websocket
Origin: http://example.com
Sec-WebSocket-Key: x3JJHMbDL1EzLkh9GBhXDw==
Sec-WebSocket-Version: 13
Sec-WebSocket-Protocol: game
```

You should already be familiar with the HTTP prelude (`GET /webSocketEndpoint HTTP/1.1`) and the `Host` header. Also the `Connection` and `Upgrade` headers were previously explained. The `Origin` header is a security mechanism that protects against unwanted cross-domain requests. The browser sets this header to the domain from which the web page was served, and the server checks that value against a list of "approved" domains.

The `Sec-WebSocket-Key` header is a specification conformance check: The browser generates a random key, base64 encodes it, and places it in the request header. The server appends `258EAFA5-E914-47DA-95CA-C5AB0DC85B11` to the request header value, SHA-1 hashes it, and returns the hashed value base64 encoded in the `Sec-WebSocket-Accept` response header. `Sec-WebSocket-Version` indicates the current version of the protocol that the client implements, and `Sec-WebSocket-Protocol` is an optional header that further indicates which protocol is used on top of the WebSocket protocol. (This is a protocol you define, such as `chat`, `game`, or `stockticker`.) The following is what the response to the previous request might look like:

```
HTTP/1.1 101 Switching Protocols
Server: Apache 2.4
Connection: Upgrade
Upgrade: websocket
Sec-WebSocket-Accept: HSmrc0sMlYUkAGmm5OPpG2HaGWk=
Sec-WebSocket-Protocol: game
```

At this point, the HTTP connection goes away and is replaced by a WebSocket connection using the same, underlying TCP connection. The biggest hurdle to the success of this connection is HTTP proxies, which historically don't handle HTTP Upgrade requests well (nor, for that matter, HTTP traffic in general). Browsers typically try to detect if the connection is going over a proxy and issue an HTTP CONNECT before the handshake, but this does not always work. Truly the most reliable way to use WebSockets is to *always* use SSL/TLS (`wss`). Proxies typically leave SSL/TLS connections alone and let them do their own thing, and with this strategy, your WebSocket connections can work in nearly all circumstances. It's also secure: The traffic is encrypted, in both directions, using the same industry-tested security as HTTPS.

Although all these details — upgrades, headers, protocols, framing, and binary and text messages — may sound daunting, the good news is that you don't have to worry about any of it. There are several APIs that cover all the protocol's difficult tasks and leave you only the task of creating your application on top of it.

> **WARNING** *The WebSocket protocol is a very new technology relative to the timeframe that browsers typically adopt technologies. As such, you need to have very modern browsers installed on your client machine to use WebSockets. The examples throughout this chapter require you to have two* different *browsers (not just two windows — two actual different browsers). These browsers need to be from the following list or newer:*
>
> - *Microsoft Internet Explorer 10.0 (must have Windows 7 SP1 or newer)*
> - *Mozilla Firefox 18.0*
> - *Google Chrome 24.0*
> - *Apple Safari 6.0*
> - *Opera 12.1*
> - *Apple Safari iOS 6.0*
> - *Google Android Browser 4.4*
> - *Microsoft Internet Explorer Mobile 10.0*
> - *Opera Mobile 12.1*
> - *Google Chrome for Android 30.0*
> - *Mozilla Firefox for Android 25.0*
> - *Blackberry Browser 7.0*

### The Many Uses of WebSockets

The WebSocket protocol has virtually unlimited uses, much of which includes browser applications, but some of which exists outside of Internet browsers. You see examples from both categories in this chapter. Though this book cannot list them all, the following is a taste of the many uses for WebSockets:

- JavaScript Chat
- Multiplayer online games (Mozilla hosts a fun, involved MMORPG called BrowserQuest written entirely in HTML5 and JavaScript using WebSockets.)
- Live Stock Ticker
- Live Breaking News Ticker
- HD Video Streaming (Yes, believe it or not, it really is that fast and powerful.)
- Communications between nodes in an application cluster
- Bulk, transactional data transfer between applications across the network
- Real-time monitoring of remote system or software status and performance

## UNDERSTANDING THE WEBSOCKET APIS

One key thing you should understand about WebSockets is that they are not just for communication between browsers and servers. Two applications written in any framework supporting WebSockets can, theoretically, establish communications over WebSockets. Therefore, many of the WebSocket implementations available contain both client and server endpoint tools. This is true, for example, in Java and .NET. JavaScript, however, is meant to serve only as a client endpoint of a WebSocket connection. In this section, you learn about using the JavaScript WebSocket client endpoint first, and then move on to the Java client endpoint and finally the Java server endpoint.

> **NOTE** *When this book refers to the JavaScript capabilities, it's referring solely to JavaScript as implemented by Internet browsers. Some JavaScript frameworks, such as Node.js, can run outside of the context of a browser and provide additional capabilities (including a WebSocket server) that are not discussed in this book. Learning about these frameworks is an exercise outside the scope of this book.*

### HTML5 (JavaScript) Client API

As noted previously, all modern browsers offer WebSocket support, and that support is standardized across supporting browsers. The World Wide Web Consortium (W3C) formalized the requirements and interface for WebSocket communications within a browser as an extension of HTML5. Although you use JavaScript to perform WebSocket communications, the `WebSocket` interface is actually part of HTML5. All browsers provide WebSocket communications through an implementation of the `WebSocket` interface. (If you remember the early days of Ajax, when different browsers had different classes and functions for performing Ajax requests, this will be a pleasant surprise for you.)

## Creating a WebSocket Object

Creating a `WebSocket` object is straightforward:

```
var connection = new WebSocket('ws://www.example.net/stocks/stream');
var connection = new WebSocket('wss://secure.example.org/games/chess');
var connection = new WebSocket('ws://www.example.com/chat', 'chat');
var connection = new WebSocket('ws://www.example.com/chat', {'chat.v1','chat.v2'});
```

The first parameter to the `WebSocket` constructor is the required URL of the WebSocket server to which you want to connect. The optional second argument can be a string or array of strings defining one or more client-defined protocols that you want to accept. Remember that these protocols are of your own implementation and are not managed by the WebSocket technology. This argument simply provides a mechanism for passing the information along if you need to do so.

## Using the WebSocket Object

There are several properties in the WebSocket interface. The first, `readyState`, indicates the current state of the WebSocket connection. Its value is always either `CONNECTING` (the number 0), `OPEN` (1), `CLOSING` (2) or `CLOSED` (3).

```
if(connection.readyState == WebSocket.OPEN) { /* do something */ }
```

It is primarily used internally; however, it is useful to ensure you do not attempt to send messages when the connection is not open. Unlike `XMLHttpRequest`, `WebSocket` does not have an `onreadystatechange` event that gets called whenever any type of event happens, forcing you to check `readyState` to determine a course of action. Instead, `WebSocket` has four separate events representing the four distinct things that can happen to a WebSocket:

```
connection.onopen = function(event) { }
connection.onclose = function(event) { }
connection.onerror = function(event) { }
connection.onmessage = function(event) { }
```

The event names clearly indicate when these events are triggered. Importantly, the `onclose` event is triggered when `readyState` changes from `CLOSING` to `CLOSED`. When the handshake completes and onopen is called (`readyState` changes from `CONNECTING` to `OPEN`), the read-only `url`, `extensions` (server-provided extensions) and `protocol` (server-selected protocol) object properties are set and fixed. The event object passed in to onopen is a standard JavaScript `Event` with nothing particularly interesting in it. The Event passed in to `onclose`, however, does have three useful properties: `wasClean`, `code`, and `reason`. You can use these to report improper closures to the user:

```
connection.onclose = function(event) {
    if(!event.wasClean)
        alert(event.code + ': ' + event.reason);
}
```

The legal closure codes are defined in RFC 6455 Section 7.4 (`http://tools.ietf.org/html/rfc6455#section-7.4`). Code 1000 is normal and all other codes are abnormal. The `onerror` event contains a data property containing the error object, which could be any number of things (typically it is a string message). This event is triggered only for client-side errors; protocol errors result in closure of the connection. onmessage is the event handler you must deal with most carefully. Its event also contains a data property. This property is a string if the message is text message, a Blob if the message is a binary message and the WebSocket's binaryType property is set to "blob" (default), or an ArrayBuffer if the message is a binary message and binaryType is set to "arraybuffer." You should typically set binaryType immediately after instantiating the WebSocket object and leave it at that value for the rest of the connection; however, it is legal to change the value whenever needed.

```
var connection = new WebSocket('ws://www.example.net/chat');
connection.binaryType = 'arraybuffer';
...
```

The WebSocket object has two methods: send and close. The close method accepts an optional close code as its first argument (default 1000) and an optional string reason as its second argument (default blank). The send method, which accepts a string, Blob, ArrayBuffer, or ArrayBufferView as its sole argument, is the only place you are likely to use the WebSocket interface's bufferedAmount property. bufferedAmount indicates how much data from previous send calls is still waiting to be sent to the server. Although you may continue to send data even if data is still waiting to be sent, sometimes you may want to push new data to the server only if no data is still waiting:

```
connection.onopen = function() {
    var intervalId = window.setInterval(function() {
        if(connection.readyState != WebSocket.OPEN) {
            window.clearInterval(intervalId);
            return;
        }
        if(connection.bufferedAmount == 0)
            connection.send(updatedModelData);
    }, 50);
}
```

The previous example sends fresh data at most every 50 milliseconds but, if the buffer has outgoing data in it still, it waits another 50 milliseconds and tries again. If the connection is not open, it stops sending data and clears the interval.

## Java WebSocket APIs

The Java API for WebSocket was formalized in the JCP as JSR 356 and included in Java EE 7. It contains both a client and a server API. The client API is the foundational API: It specifies a set of classes and interfaces in the javax.websocket package that include all the necessary common functionality for a WebSocket peer. The server API contains javax.websocket.server classes and interfaces that use and/or extend client classes to provide additional functionality. As such, there are two artifacts for this API: the client-only artifact and the full artifact (which includes client and server classes and interfaces). Both APIs contain many classes and interfaces, and not all of them are covered here. That's what the API documentation is for (which you can find at http://docs.oracle.com/javaee/7/api/ with the rest of the Java EE documentation). The rest of this section highlights the important details of the two APIs. The example code throughout the chapter can give you a better idea of exactly how to use the APIs.

## The Client API

The client API is built on the `ContainerProvider` class and the `WebSocketContainer`, `RemoteEndpoint`, and `Session` interfaces. `WebSocketContainer` provides access to all the WebSocket client features, and the `ContainerProvider` class provides a static `getWebSocketContainer` method for obtaining the underlying WebSocket client implementation. `WebSocketContainer` provides four overloaded `connectToServer` methods that all accept a `URI` to connect to a remote endpoint and initiate a handshake. These methods accept either a POJO instance of any type annotated with `@ClientEndpoint`, a `Class<?>` for a POJO of any type annotated with `@ClientEndpoint`, an instance of the `Endpoint` class, or a `Class<? extends Endpoint>`. If you use either of the `Class`-variety methods, the class you supply must have a zero-argument constructor and will be instantiated on your behalf.

If you use the `Endpoint` or `Class<? extends Endpoint>` methods, you must also supply a `ClientEndpointConfig`. When the handshake is complete, the `connectToServer` method returns a `Session`. You can do many things with the `Session` object, most notably close the `Session` (which closes the WebSocket connection) or send messages to the remote endpoint.

> **NOTE** *The Java API for WebSocket specifies an API, not an implementation. You can program against this API, but at run time you need an implementation to back it. If your application runs in a Java EE application server or a web container supporting WebSockets, client and server implementations are provided for you already. If it runs standalone, you need to find a standalone client or server implementation (depending on your needs) to deploy with your application.*

The WebSocket `Endpoint` has `onOpen`, `onClose`, and `onError` methods that are called on those events, whereas `@ClientEndpoint` classes can have (optional) methods annotated `@OnOpen`, `@OnClose`, and `@OnError`. `@ClientEndpoint` classes and classes extending `Endpoint` can specify one or more methods annotated with `@OnMessage` to handle receiving messages from the remote endpoint. Using annotated classes and methods, you have a lot of flexibility in what method parameters you can require.

`@OnOpen` methods can have:

- One optional `Session` parameter
- One optional `EndpointConfig` parameter

`@OnClose` methods can have:

- One optional `Session` parameter
- One optional `CloseReason` parameter

`@OnError` methods can have:

- One optional `Session` parameter
- One required `Throwable` parameter

`@OnMessage` methods are more complex. In addition to the standard optional `Session` parameter, they must have exactly one of the following combinations of parameters:

- One `String` to receive an entire text message
- One `String` plus one `boolean` to receive a text message in chunks, with the `boolean` set to `true` on the last chunk
- One Java primitive or primitive wrapper to receive an entire text message converted to that type
- One `java.io.Reader` to receive a text message as a blocking stream
- One `byte[]` or one `java.nio.ByteBuffer` to receive an entire binary message
- One `byte[]` or one `ByteBuffer`, plus one `boolean` to receive a binary message in chunks
- One `java.io.InputStream` to receive a binary message as a blocking stream
- One `PongMessage` for custom handling of heartbeat responses
- Any Java object if the endpoint has a `Decoder.Text`, `Decoder.Binary`, `Decoder.TextStream`, or `Decoder.BinaryStream` registered to convert that type. The message type of text or binary must match the registered decoder.

An endpoint can have only one method each to handle open, close, and error events; however, it may have up to three message-handling methods: no more than one for text messages, no more than one for binary messages, and no more than one for pong messages. One final note about the client API: The WebSocket Maven dependency used in this chapter is for the server API, which includes a dependency on the client API. If you ever need to write a Java application that is *only* a WebSocket client, you need only the client API Maven dependency:

```
<dependency>
    <groupId>javax.websocket</groupId>
    <artifactId>javax.websocket-client-api</artifactId>
    <version>1.0</version>
    <scope>provided</scope>
</dependency>
```

## The Server API

The server API depends on the entire client API and adds only a handful of classes and interfaces. `ServerContainer` extends `WebSocketContainer` and adds methods to programmatically register `ServerEndpointConfig` instances or classes annotated with `@ServerEndpoint`. In a Servlet environment, you obtain a `ServerContainer` instance by calling `ServletContext.getAttribute("javax.websocket.server.ServerContainer")`. In a standalone application, you need to follow the instructions of the particular WebSocket implementation you are using to get a `ServerContainer` instance.

However, in nearly all use cases (including all uses within Java EE web containers) you never actually need to obtain a `ServerContainer`. Instead, simply annotate your server endpoint class or classes with `@ServerEndpoint`; the WebSocket implementation can scan your classes for this annotation and automatically pick up and register your server endpoints for you. The container creates a new instance of your endpoint class each time it receives a new WebSocket connection for that endpoint and disposes of each instance after its connection closes.

When using `@ServerEndpoint`, you specify at least the required `value` attribute, which indicates the application-relative URL that this endpoint responds to. The URL path, which must start with a leading slash, can contain template parameters. So, for example, consider the following annotation:

```
@ServerEndpoint("/game/{gameType}")
```

If your application were deployed at `http[s]://www.example.org/app`, this server endpoint would respond to `ws[s]://www.example.org/app/game/chess`, `ws[s]://www.example.org/app/game/checkers`, and so on. Then, any `@OnOpen`, `@OnClose`, `@OnError`, or `@OnMessage` method in the server endpoint could have an optional additional parameter annotated with `@PathParam("gameType")`, and the container would provide "chess" and "checkers," respectively, as the values to that parameter. The event handling methods in your server endpoints work just like the event handling methods in your client endpoints. The difference between server and client only matters at the time of handshake. After the handshake is complete and the connection is established, the server and client become peers and are completely equal endpoints with the same capabilities and responsibilities.

> **NOTE** *Because the primary purpose of the WebSocket protocol is communications between the server and browser, this chapter contains a lot of JavaScript code. Some of this code includes extensive use of the jQuery JavaScript library. This book would have to be hundreds of pages longer to teach you about JavaScript programming for the web, so it is assumed that you have a basic working knowledge of both JavaScript and jQuery (used to make easier, shorter examples). If you are not familiar with JavaScript, you are encouraged to take a break now and go find a JavaScript and jQuery book or tutorial. Otherwise, some of the code could be hard to follow.*

## CREATING MULTIPLAYER GAMES WITH WEBSOCKETS

You saw earlier that one of the many things WebSockets can do is facilitate communication for multiplayer online games, even Massively Multiplayer Online Role Playing Games (MMORPGs). In this section, you create a simple multiplayer game to demonstrate the power of WebSockets. The key for multiplayer games is responsiveness: When a player takes some action, his opponents must see that action as soon as possible. This is especially critical for battle and action sequences, where opponents must compete in real time.

It would take many thousands of lines of code to create an action-packed game where responsiveness was critical. Instead, you can implement a simple, two-player Tic-tac-toe game. Tic-tac-toe (also known as Xs and Os or Noughts and Crosses) is a simplistic strategy game where the player's goal is to place three Xs or Os (whichever is his piece) in a row vertically, horizontally, or diagonally. Although Tic-tac-toe certainly does not require responsiveness, this example still demonstrates just how responsive WebSockets can be. You should follow along in the Game-Site project available on the `wrox.com` code download site. Only some of the code is printed in this book, and there are graphics and style sheets that are necessary for the game.

## Implementing the Basic Tic-Tac-Toe Algorithm

Online Tic-tac-toe can be played against either a human opponent or a computer. The algorithm gets very complex when you include computer play because you must implement some artificial intelligence algorithms that are beyond the scope of this book. Besides, that wouldn't be as good a demonstration of WebSockets. Instead, your Tic-tac-toe game requires two human opponents. The core algorithm is contained within the `TicTacToeGame` class. This class is important to the project but doesn't perform any WebSocket operations. This is an example of separation of concerns — the game is abstracted into its own class so that any user interface, including a WebSocket interface, can use the game logic.

Because the class contains nothing new, it is not printed in this book. Open the Game-Site project and review `TicTacToeGame`. It contains some simple methods for retrieving a player's name — whose ever turn it is — including whether the game is a tie or over, and who the winner is (if anyone). The `move` method checks whether the intended move is legal, executes the move, and then calls other methods to calculate if the game is over and who the winner is. `calculateWinner` implements the algorithm for determining the winner of the game. Finally, several static methods serve as a mechanism for starting, joining, and coordinating games.

## Creating the Server Endpoint

Enough with game logic, what you really came here to see is the Java WebSocket code. This is found in the `TicTacToeServer` class in Listing 10-1. The `TicTacToeGame` could be used by any user interface code to play Tic-tac-toe, but `TicTacToeServer` acts as a gateway for two WebSocket Sessions to interact with a `TicTacToeGame`. This requires some careful machinations. (Imagine if this were an unlimited-player game!)

The `onOpen` method gets the game ID and username from the path parameters (this game site is obviously not worried about security) and then, depending on whether the user is starting a new game or joining an existing game, creates or completes a `Game` object. The inner `Game` class associates the `Session` objects for the two players with their `TicTacToeGame` instance. When both users have joined, the `GameStartedMessage` is sent to both endpoints using the internal `sendJsonMessage` helper method.

**LISTING 10-1: TicTacToeServer.java**

```
@ServerEndpoint("/ticTacToe/{gameId}/{username}")
public class TicTacToeServer
{
    private static Map<Long, Game> games = new Hashtable<>();
    private static ObjectMapper mapper = new ObjectMapper();

    @OnOpen
    public void onOpen(Session session, @PathParam("gameId") long gameId,
                       @PathParam("username") String username) {
        try {
            TicTacToeGame ticTacToeGame = TicTacToeGame.getActiveGame(gameId);
            if(ticTacToeGame != null) {
                session.close(new CloseReason(
                        CloseReason.CloseCodes.UNEXPECTED_CONDITION,
```

```
                    "This game has already started."
            ));
        }
        List<String> actions = session.getRequestParameterMap().get("action");
        if(actions != null && actions.size() == 1) {
            String action = actions.get(0);
            if("start".equalsIgnoreCase(action)) {
                Game game = new Game();
                game.gameId = gameId;
                game.player1 = session;
                TicTacToeServer.games.put(gameId, game);
            } else if("join".equalsIgnoreCase(action)) {
                Game game = TicTacToeServer.games.get(gameId);
                game.player2 = session;
                game.ticTacToeGame = TicTacToeGame.startGame(gameId, username);
                this.sendJsonMessage(game.player1, game,
                        new GameStartedMessage(game.ticTacToeGame));
                this.sendJsonMessage(game.player2, game,
                        new GameStartedMessage(game.ticTacToeGame));
            }
        }
    } catch(IOException e) {
        e.printStackTrace();
        try {
            session.close(new CloseReason(
                    CloseReason.CloseCodes.UNEXPECTED_CONDITION, e.toString()
            ));
        } catch(IOException ignore) { }
    }
}

@OnMessage
public void onMessage(Session session, String message,
                      @PathParam("gameId") long gameId) {
    Game game = TicTacToeServer.games.get(gameId);
    boolean isPlayer1 = session == game.player1;
    try {
        Move move = TicTacToeServer.mapper.readValue(message, Move.class);
        game.ticTacToeGame.move(
                isPlayer1 ? TicTacToeGame.Player.PLAYER1 :
                        TicTacToeGame.Player.PLAYER2,
                move.getRow(), move.getColumn()
        );
        this.sendJsonMessage((isPlayer1 ? game.player2 : game.player1), game,
                new OpponentMadeMoveMessage(move));
        if(game.ticTacToeGame.isOver()) {
            if(game.ticTacToeGame.isDraw()) {
                this.sendJsonMessage(game.player1, game,
                        new GameIsDrawMessage());
                this.sendJsonMessage(game.player2, game,
                        new GameIsDrawMessage());
            } else {
                boolean wasPlayer1 = game.ticTacToeGame.getWinner() ==
                        TicTacToeGame.Player.PLAYER1;
                this.sendJsonMessage(game.player1, game,
```

*continues*

**LISTING 10-1** *(continued)*

```
                            new GameOverMessage(wasPlayer1));
                    this.sendJsonMessage(game.player2, game,
                            new GameOverMessage(!wasPlayer1));
                }
                game.player1.close();
                game.player2.close();
            }
        } catch(IOException e) {
            this.handleException(e, game);
        }
    }

    @OnClose
    public void onClose(Session session, @PathParam("gameId") long gameId) {
        Game game = TicTacToeServer.games.get(gameId);
        if(game == null)
            return;
        boolean isPlayer1 = session == game.player1;
        if(game.ticTacToeGame == null) {
            TicTacToeGame.removeQueuedGame(game.gameId);
        } else if(!game.ticTacToeGame.isOver()) {
            game.ticTacToeGame.forfeit(isPlayer1 ? TicTacToeGame.Player.PLAYER1 :
                    TicTacToeGame.Player.PLAYER2);
            Session opponent = (isPlayer1 ? game.player2 : game.player1);
            this.sendJsonMessage(opponent, game, new GameForfeitedMessage());
            try {
                opponent.close();
            } catch(IOException e) {
                e.printStackTrace();
            }
        }
    }

    private void sendJsonMessage(Session session, Game game, Message message) {
        try {
            session.getBasicRemote()
                    .sendText(TicTacToeServer.mapper.writeValueAsString(message));
        } catch(IOException e) {
            this.handleException(e, game);
        }
    }

    private void handleException(Throwable t, Game game) {
        t.printStackTrace();
        String message = t.toString();
        try {
            game.player1.close(new CloseReason(
                    CloseReason.CloseCodes.UNEXPECTED_CONDITION, message
            ));
        } catch(IOException ignore) { }
        try {
            game.player2.close(new CloseReason(
```

```
                    CloseReason.CloseCodes.UNEXPECTED_CONDITION, message
            ));
        } catch(IOException ignore) { }
    }

    private static class Game {
        public long gameId;
        public Session player1;
        public Session player2;
        public TicTacToeGame ticTacToeGame;
    }

    public static class Move {
        private int row;
        private int column;
        // accessor and mutator methods
    }

    public static abstract class Message {
        private final String action;
        public Message(String action) {
            this.action = action;
        }
        public String getAction() { ... }
    }
    public static class GameStartedMessage extends Message {
        private final TicTacToeGame game;
        public GameStartedMessage(TicTacToeGame game) {
            super("gameStarted");
            this.game = game;
        }
        public TicTacToeGame getGame() { ... }
    }
    public static class OpponentMadeMoveMessage extends Message {
        private final Move move;
        public OpponentMadeMoveMessage(Move move) {
            super("opponentMadeMove");
            this.move = move;
        }
        public Move getMove() { ... }
    }
    public static class GameOverMessage extends Message {
        private final boolean winner;
        public GameOverMessage(boolean winner) {
            super("gameOver");
            this.winner = winner;
        }
        public boolean isWinner() { ... }
    }
    public static class GameIsDrawMessage extends Message {
        public GameIsDrawMessage() {
            super("gameIsDraw");
        }
    }
    public static class GameForfeitedMessage extends Message {
```

*continues*

**LISTING 10-1** *(continued)*

```
            public GameForfeitedMessage() {
                super("gameForfeited");
            }
        }
    }
```

In this system, messages sent from the browser to the server are always `Moves` (an inner class), whereas messages sent from the server to the browser are always `Messages` (another inner class). WebSocket messages here are exchanged in text format, and the Jackson Data Processor library serializes `Messages` into outgoing messages and deserializes incoming messages into `Moves`. When `onMessage` is called, that means a player has made a move and sent that move to the endpoint. The server endpoint registers the move with the `TicTacToeGame` and then notifies the opponent of the move by sending a WebSocket message over the opposing `Session`. If the game is over, it sends both players the `GameOverMessage` or `GameIsDrawMessage` as appropriate and then closes both `Sessions`. If a connection is closed, `onClose` makes sure that the game was over or never started. If the game is in progress, the user who closed their `Session` forfeited the game. (Likely they closed their browser or navigated away from the page.)

Of course, all this is useless without a user interface, and you might wonder how that `TicTacToeGame` got created in the first place. This is all coming up next.

## Writing the JavaScript Game Console

To create the user interface, the first thing you need is a Servlet for starting or joining games, getting usernames for players, and forwarding requests to the appropriate JSPs. `TicTacToeServlet` accomplishes exactly that. First, a user starts a game by simply entering a username for that game session. Next, the game is added to a list of pending games. When another user comes to the site, he sees the list of pending games and choses one to join. When he joins that game by providing his username, the game will move from pending to in-progress. The `list.jsp` page is where pending games are listed and contains the UI code for starting a new game as well. There shouldn't be much new or exciting in either the Servlet or this JSP, so they aren't printed here.

The `game.jsp` page in Listing 10-2 is where all the fun JavaScript code is happening. You'll notice at the top the inclusion of the `ticTacToe.css` style sheet, the jQuery JavaScript library, and the Bootstrap JavaScript library and CSS file. Without these doing some of the boring non-WebSockets work, you would have to write many more lines of code. The game surface is a basic `div` layout with three rows and three columns. To simplify the code, the local player is always Os and the opponent is always Xs. (Although typically the first player to move is Xs.) When it's your turn, you can hover over each game square and, if it's a legal move, the square displays a faded O in it. Clicking a square commits to that move and cannot be undone.

When the document has loaded, the code checks that the browser supports WebSockets and displays an error if it does not. It then connects to the server and, when the connection is established, it displays a message about waiting for the opponent to join. An `onbeforeunload` event is added to the `window` object to ensure that the user forfeits if he closes the browser or leaves the page. The `onclose` event ensures that the closure of the connection was clean and the `onerror` event handles errors. `onmessage` handles the five different types of messages the server could send (`GameStartedMessage`, `OpponentMadeMoveMessage`, `GameOverMessage`, `GameIsDrawMessage`, and

GameForfeitedMessage), clears squares that the opponent claims, and notifies the user when the game is over. Finally, the move function, which is called when you click a game square, sends your moves to the server.

**LISTING 10-2: game.jsp**

```
<%--@elvariable id="action" type="java.lang.String"--%>
<%--@elvariable id="gameId" type="long"--%>
<%--@elvariable id="username" type="java.lang.String"--%>
<!DOCTYPE html>
<html>
    <head>
        <title>Game Site :: Tic Tac Toe</title>
        <link rel="stylesheet" href="http://cdnjs.cloudflare.com/ajax/libs/twitter-
bootstrap/2.3.1/css/bootstrap.min.css" />
        <link rel="stylesheet"
              href="<c:url value="/resource/stylesheet/ticTacToe.css" />" />
        <script src="http://code.jquery.com/jquery-1.9.1.js"></script>
        <script src="http://cdnjs.cloudflare.com/ajax/libs/twitter-bootstrap/2.3.1/
js/bootstrap.min.js"></script>
    </head>
    <body>
        <h2>Tic Tac Toe</h2>
        <span class="player-label">You:</span> ${username}<br />
        <span class="player-label">Opponent:</span>
        <span id="opponent"><i>Waiting</i></span>
        <div id="status"> </div>
        <div id="gameContainer">
            <div class="row">
                <div id="r0c0" class="game-cell" onclick="move(0, 0);"> </div>
                <div id="r0c1" class="game-cell" onclick="move(0, 1);"> </div>
                <div id="r0c2" class="game-cell" onclick="move(0, 2);"> </div>
            </div>
            <div class="row">
                <div id="r1c0" class="game-cell" onclick="move(1, 0);"> </div>
                <div id="r1c1" class="game-cell" onclick="move(1, 1);"> </div>
                <div id="r1c2" class="game-cell" onclick="move(1, 2);"> </div>
            </div>
            <div class="row">
                <div id="r2c0" class="game-cell" onclick="move(2, 0);"> </div>
                <div id="r2c1" class="game-cell" onclick="move(2, 1);"> </div>
                <div id="r2c2" class="game-cell" onclick="move(2, 2);"> </div>
            </div>
        </div>
        <div id="modalWaiting" class="modal hide fade">
            <div class="modal-header"><h3>Please Wait...</h3></div>
            <div class="modal-body" id="modalWaitingBody"> </div>
        </div>
        <div id="modalError" class="modal hide fade">
            <div class="modal-header">
                <button type="button" class="close" data-dismiss="modal">&times;
                </button>
                <h3>Error</h3>
```

*continues*

**LISTING 10-2** *(continued)*

```
        </div>
        <div class="modal-body" id="modalErrorBody">A blah error occurred.
        </div>
        <div class="modal-footer">
            <button class="btn btn-primary" data-dismiss="modal">OK</button>
        </div>
    </div>
    <div id="modalGameOver" class="modal hide fade">
        <div class="modal-header">
            <button type="button" class="close" data-dismiss="modal">&times;
            </button>
            <h3>Game Over</h3>
        </div>
        <div class="modal-body" id="modalGameOverBody"> </div>
        <div class="modal-footer">
            <button class="btn btn-primary" data-dismiss="modal">OK</button>
        </div>
    </div>
    <script type="text/javascript" language="javascript">
        var move;
        $(document).ready(function() {
            var modalError = $("#modalError");
            var modalErrorBody = $("#modalErrorBody");
            var modalWaiting = $("#modalWaiting");
            var modalWaitingBody = $("#modalWaitingBody");
            var modalGameOver = $("#modalGameOver");
            var modalGameOverBody = $("#modalGameOverBody");
            var opponent = $("#opponent");
            var status = $("#status");
            var opponentUsername;
            var username = '<c:out value="${username}" />';
            var myTurn = false;

            $('.game-cell').addClass('span1');

            if(!("WebSocket" in window))
            {
                modalErrorBody.text('WebSockets are not supported in this ' +
                        'browser. Try Internet Explorer 10 or the latest ' +
                        'versions of Mozilla Firefox or Google Chrome.');
                modalError.modal('show');
                return;
            }

            modalWaitingBody.text('Connecting to the server.');
            modalWaiting.modal({ keyboard: false, show: true });

            var server;
            try {
                server = new WebSocket('ws://' + window.location.host +
                        '<c:url value="/ticTacToe/${gameId}/${username}">
                            <c:param name="action" value="${action}" />
```

```
            </c:url>');
} catch(error) {
    modalWaiting.modal('hide');
    modalErrorBody.text(error);
    modalError.modal('show');
    return;
}

server.onopen = function(event) {
    modalWaitingBody
            .text('Waiting on your opponent to join the game.');
    modalWaiting.modal({ keyboard: false, show: true });
};

window.onbeforeunload = function() {
    server.close();
};

server.onclose = function(event) {
    if(!event.wasClean || event.code != 1000) {
        toggleTurn(false, 'Game over due to error!');
        modalWaiting.modal('hide');
        modalErrorBody.text('Code ' + event.code + ': ' +
                event.reason);
        modalError.modal('show');
    }
};

server.onerror = function(event) {
    modalWaiting.modal('hide');
    modalErrorBody.text(event.data);
    modalError.modal('show');
};

server.onmessage = function(event) {
    var message = JSON.parse(event.data);
    if(message.action == 'gameStarted') {
        if(message.game.player1 == username)
            opponentUsername = message.game.player2;
        else
            opponentUsername = message.game.player1;
        opponent.text(opponentUsername);
        toggleTurn(message.game.nextMoveBy == username);
        modalWaiting.modal('hide');
    } else if(message.action == 'opponentMadeMove') {
        $('#r' + message.move.row + 'c' + message.move.column)
                .unbind('click')
                .removeClass('game-cell-selectable')
                .addClass('game-cell-opponent game-cell-taken');
        toggleTurn(true);
    } else if(message.action == 'gameOver') {
        toggleTurn(false, 'Game Over!');
        if(message.winner) {
            modalGameOverBody.text('Congratulations, you won!');
        } else {
```

*continues*

**LISTING 10-2** *(continued)*

```
                            modalGameOverBody.text('User "' + opponentUsername +
                                    '" won the game.');
                        }
                        modalGameOver.modal('show');
                    } else if(message.action == 'gameIsDraw') {
                        toggleTurn(false, 'The game is a draw. ' +
                                'There is no winner.');
                        modalGameOverBody.text('The game ended in a draw. ' +
                                'Nobody wins!');
                        modalGameOver.modal('show');
                    } else if(message.action == 'gameForfeited') {
                        toggleTurn(false, 'Your opponent forfeited!');
                        modalGameOverBody.text('User "' + opponentUsername +
                                '" forfeited the game. You win!');
                        modalGameOver.modal('show');
                    }
                };

                var toggleTurn = function(isMyTurn, message) {
                    myTurn = isMyTurn;
                    if(myTurn) {
                        status.text(message || 'It\'s your move!');
                        $('.game-cell:not(.game-cell-taken)')
                                .addClass('game-cell-selectable');
                    } else {
                        status.text(message ||'Waiting on your opponent to move.');
                        $('.game-cell-selectable')
                                .removeClass('game-cell-selectable');
                    }
                };

                move = function(row, column) {
                    if(!myTurn) {
                        modalErrorBody.text('It is not your turn yet!');
                        modalError.modal('show');
                        return;
                    }
                    if(server != null) {
                        server.send(JSON.stringify({ row: row, column: column }));
                        $('#r' + row + 'c' + column).unbind('click')
                                .removeClass('game-cell-selectable')
                                .addClass('game-cell-player game-cell-taken');
                        toggleTurn(false);
                    } else {
                        modalErrorBody.text('Not connected to came server.');
                        modalError.modal('show');
                    }
                };
            });
        </script>
    </body>
</html>
```

## Playing WebSocket Tic-Tac-Toe

Now that you have reviewed the code and see how all the pieces fit together, you can do the following:

1. Compile the Game-Site project.
2. Start up Tomcat in your debugger, and open up two different browsers (such as Firefox and Safari, or Internet Explorer 10 and Chrome). Make them small enough so that you can place them side-by-side or one on top of the other in your screen.
3. Go to `http://localhost:8080/games/ticTacToe` in both browsers. There should be no games listed yet.
4. Click Start a Game in one browser and enter your name or favorite username in the prompt, and then click OK. You will be taken to the game page and presented with the message about waiting for your opponent.
5. In the other browser, reload the listing page and you should see the pending game listed. Click that game and enter in a *different* name or username in the prompt. As soon as you land on the game page, the waiting message should disappear in the first browser. You'll notice that it is nearly instantaneous. One of the browsers should have a message that says, It's Your Move!, whereas the message in the other says, Waiting on Your Opponent to Move.
6. Go back and forth between browsers making moves. Before long your screen should look something like Figure 10-6 (where John is about to beat Scott with a move in the lower-left corner). Notice how quickly the move from one player shows up in the other player's browser. The delay is imperceptible. The speed and scalability of WebSockets make it an extraordinarily powerful technology.

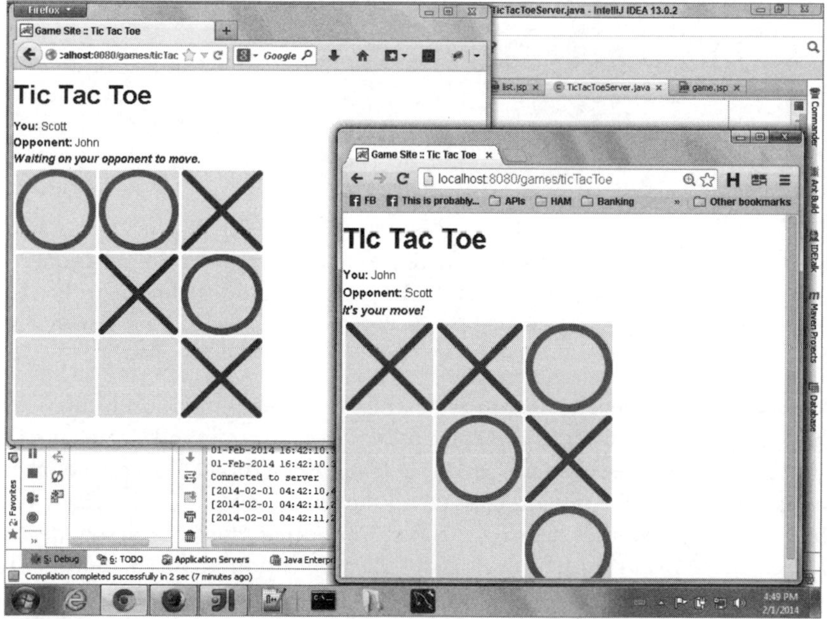


FIGURE 10-6

# USING WEBSOCKETS TO COMMUNICATE IN A CLUSTER

Now that you've seen how Java server endpoints work, and how to communicate with server endpoints using JavaScript, it's time to explore the Java client endpoint. Because the client endpoint can't be used to connect to a browser, you need to connect to some other application. There are many possible uses for this, from data transfers to coordination of distributed activities across multiple servers. There are endless possibilities. As a software developer, chances are you will have to deal with a cluster of servers at some point to scale a web application to handle large numbers of users, and WebSockets might be a way to help application nodes communicate with each other.

## Simulating a Simple Cluster Using Two Servlet Instances

In a standard cluster scenario, nodes would notify each other of their existence through some means, often by sending a packet to an agreed-upon multicast IP address and port. They would then establish communications through some other channel, such as a TCP socket. This is a complicated scenario to replicate in a small example, but you can easily simulate it by using multiple servlets in a single application. On the `wrox.com` code download site, this example is the Simulated-Cluster project. Take a look at `web.xml` first, and you'll notice two Servlet mappings. The first Servlet mapping is in the following code. The second Servlet mapping is identical except that the name, init parameter value, and URL pattern have a 2 in them instead of a 1. If you're wondering why you need this in the deployment descriptor, remember that you can't map the same Servlet twice using annotations. You must use either the deployment descriptor or programmatic configuration to accomplish this.

```
<servlet>
    <servlet-name>clusterNode1</servlet-name>
    <servlet-class>com.wrox.ClusterNodeServlet</servlet-class>
    <init-param>
        <param-name>nodeId</param-name>
        <param-value>1</param-value>
    </init-param>
</servlet>
<servlet-mapping>
    <servlet-name>clusterNode1</servlet-name>
    <url-pattern>/clusterNode1</url-pattern>
</servlet-mapping>
```

The `ClusterNodeServlet` class in Listing 10-3, which extends `HttpServlet`, is annotated with `@ClientEndpoint`. Unlike `@ServletEndpoint`, `@ClientEndpoint` does not mean the class will be instantiated automatically. `@ClientEndpoint` is a marker to tell the container that this is a valid endpoint.

Alternatively, you could implement the `Endpoint` abstract class. *Any* class can be an endpoint. A Servlet is used here only because it's easy and convenient. The `init` method, which is called on the first request, connects to the server endpoint, and the `destroy` method closes the connection. Every time a request comes in, the Servlet sends a message to the cluster about it. The `onMessage` method (annotated with `@OnMessage`) accepts messages echoed from other cluster nodes, and `onClose` (annotated with `@OnClose`) prints an error message if the connection is closed abnormally.

**LISTING 10-3: ClusterNodeServlet.java**

```
@ClientEndpoint
public class ClusterNodeServlet extends HttpServlet
{
    private Session session;
    private String nodeId;

    @Override
    public void init() throws ServletException {
        this.nodeId = this.getInitParameter("nodeId");
        String path = this.getServletContext().getContextPath() +
                "/clusterNodeSocket/" + this.nodeId;
        try {
            URI uri = new URI("ws", "localhost:8080", path, null, null);
            this.session = ContainerProvider.getWebSocketContainer()
                    .connectToServer(this, uri);
        } catch(URISyntaxException | IOException | DeploymentException e) {
            throw new ServletException("Cannot connect to " + path + ".", e);
        }
    }

    @Override
    public void destroy() {
        try {
            this.session.close();
        } catch(IOException e) {
            e.printStackTrace();
        }
    }

    @Override
    protected void doGet(HttpServletRequest request, HttpServletResponse response)
            throws ServletException, IOException {
        ClusterMessage message = new ClusterMessage(this.nodeId,
                "request:{ip:\"" + request.getRemoteAddr() +
                "\",queryString:\"" + request.getQueryString() + "\"}");
        try(OutputStream output = this.session.getBasicRemote().getSendStream();
            ObjectOutputStream stream = new ObjectOutputStream(output)) {
            stream.writeObject(message);
        }
        response.getWriter().append("OK");
    }

    @OnMessage
    public void onMessage(InputStream input) {
        try(ObjectInputStream stream = new ObjectInputStream(input)) {
            ClusterMessage message = (ClusterMessage)stream.readObject();
            System.out.println("INFO (Node " + this.nodeId +
                    "): Message received from cluster; node = " +
                    message.getNodeId() + ", message = " + message.getMessage());
        } catch(IOException | ClassNotFoundException e) {
            e.printStackTrace();
        }
```

*continues*

**LISTING 10-3** *(continued)*

```
    }

    @OnClose
    public void onClose(CloseReason reason) {
        CloseReason.CloseCode code = reason.getCloseCode();
        if(code != CloseReason.CloseCodes.NORMAL_CLOSURE) {
            System.err.println("ERROR: WebSocket connection closed unexpectedly;" +
                    " code = " + code + ", reason = " + reason.getReasonPhrase());
        }
    }
}
```

## Transmitting and Receiving Binary Messages

You probably noticed that the `ClusterNodeServlet` used Java serialization to send and receive the `ClusterMessage implements Serializable` messages over the WebSocket connection. To do this, the WebSocket messages have to be binary. This is different from the Tic-tac-toe server endpoint, which translates messages to and from JSON and sends and receives them as text messages. Java serialization is faster than JSON, so when possible it's better to use Java serialization. However, you can only do so when both peers are Java. If only one peer is Java, you have to use a different serialization technology, such as JSON. Although `ClusterNodeServlet` sends and receives binary messages using `OutputStreams` and `InputStreams`, `ClusterNodeEndpoint` in Listing 10-4 uses `byte` arrays. In this case, this takes slightly more code because `ObjectOutputStreams` and `ObjectInputStreams` are already needed to perform the serialization and deserialization. In some cases using `byte` arrays will be easier, and in others using `ByteBuffers` or streams will be easier, so it's valuable to learn both approaches. It all depends on where your data comes from or what you want to do with it. If you need to send data that already exists as a `byte` array, it's easier to just use that `byte` array. On the other hand, if you're already dealing with streams, it's usually easier to just stick to streams.

The endpoint's only responsibilities are echoing messages sent from one node to all the other nodes and notifying connected nodes when other nodes join or leave the cluster. In another cluster scenario, you might not have a central endpoint that collects and echoes all messages. Instead, each node might connect directly to all other nodes. It all depends on your use case and the needs of your application.

**LISTING 10-4:** ClusterNodeEndpoint.java

```
@ServerEndpoint("/clusterNodeSocket/{nodeId}")
public class ClusterNodeEndpoint
{
    private static final List<Session> nodes = new ArrayList<>(2);

    @OnOpen
    public void onOpen(Session session, @PathParam("nodeId") String nodeId) {
        System.out.println("INFO: Node [" + nodeId + "] connected to cluster.");
        ClusterMessage message = new ClusterMessage(nodeId, "Joined the cluster.");
        try {
            byte[] bytes = ClusterNodeEndpoint.toByteArray(message);
            for(Session node : ClusterNodeEndpoint.nodes)
```

```
                node.getBasicRemote().sendBinary(ByteBuffer.wrap(bytes));
        } catch(IOException e) {
            System.err.println("ERROR: Exception when notifying of new node");
            e.printStackTrace();
        }
        ClusterNodeEndpoint.nodes.add(session);
    }

    @OnMessage
    public void onMessage(Session session, byte[] message) {
        try {
            for(Session node : ClusterNodeEndpoint.nodes) {
                if(node != session)
                    node.getBasicRemote().sendBinary(ByteBuffer.wrap(message));
            }
        } catch(IOException e) {
            System.err.println("ERROR: Exception when handling message on server");
            e.printStackTrace();
        }
    }

    @OnClose
    public void onClose(Session session, @PathParam("nodeId") String nodeId) {
        System.out.println("INFO: Node [" + nodeId + "] disconnected.");
        ClusterNodeEndpoint.nodes.remove(session);
        ClusterMessage message = new ClusterMessage(nodeId, "Left the cluster.");
        try {
            byte[] bytes = ClusterNodeEndpoint.toByteArray(message);
            for(Session node : ClusterNodeEndpoint.nodes)
                node.getBasicRemote().sendBinary(ByteBuffer.wrap(bytes));
        } catch(IOException e) {
            System.err.println("ERROR: Exception when notifying of left node");
            e.printStackTrace();
        }
    }

    private static byte[] toByteArray(ClusterMessage message) throws IOException {
        try(ByteArrayOutputStream output = new ByteArrayOutputStream();
            ObjectOutputStream stream = new ObjectOutputStream(output)) {
            stream.writeObject(message);
            return output.toByteArray();
        }
    }
}
```

## Testing the Simulated Cluster Application

Testing the simulated cluster application is fairly straightforward. Just take the following steps:

1. Compile the application and start Tomcat from your IDE.
2. Go to `http://localhost:8080/cluster/clusterNode1` in your favorite browser, and you should see the following message in the debugger output. This is the result of the first Servlet instance's `init` method being called and connecting to the WebSocket server endpoint.

```
INFO: Node [1] connected to cluster.
```

3. Now go to `http://localhost:8080/cluster/clusterNode2`. You should see a couple of messages this time. In this case the second Servlet instance connected to the endpoint, and when it sent a message, the endpoint echoed that message back to the first Servlet.

```
INFO: Node [2] connected to cluster.
INFO (Node 1): Message received from cluster; node = 2, message =
Joined the cluster.
INFO (Node 1): Message received from cluster; node = 2, message =
request:{ip:"127.0.0.1",queryString:""}
```

4. Try the first URL again, but this time add a query string to it: `http://localhost:8080/cluster/clusterNode1?hello=world&foo=bar`. Notice this time there is no connection message because both Servlets are started now.

```
INFO (Node 2): Message received from cluster; node = 1, message =
request:{ip:"127.0.0.1",queryString:"hello=world&foo=bar"}
```

5. One last time, try the second URL again, also with a query string: `http://localhost:8080/cluster/clusterNode2?baz=qux&animal=dog`.

```
INFO (Node 1): Message received from cluster; node = 2, message =
request:{ip:"127.0.0.1",queryString:"baz=qux&animal=dog"}
```

6. If you want to experiment further, create another instance of the Servlet and map it to `/clusterNode3`; then compile and start the application again. Try going to all three URLs, and you'll see that whenever a Servlet responds to a `GET` request, the other two Servlets receive a WebSocket message about it.

This may seem like a juvenile example, but it's a simple way to demonstrate how the Java WebSocket client and server APIs can work together. It is also a good opportunity for you to learn about using `byte` arrays, `ByteBuffers`, and streams for binary messages. This approach might be very useful for you in some clustered applications, and you may need a different set of technologies in other clustered applications. You explore more options in Chapter 18.

> **NOTE** *You may have noticed that the Servlet instances in this project were set to initialize on the first request instead of on application start-up. There is a very important reason for this: The* `ClusterNodeServlet` *connects to the WebSocket endpoint in the* `init` *method. If the application is in the process of starting when the Servlets initialize, they won't connect to the endpoint. Thus, the Servlets must initialize after application start-up.*

## ADDING "CHAT WITH SUPPORT" TO THE CUSTOMER SUPPORT APPLICATION

Perhaps the most ubiquitous example of the usefulness of WebSockets is Internet chatting. Many applications provide chatting capabilities from your desktop and most use some kind of service provider through which chat messages are routed. Chat is also common on websites, with many social networks, forums, and online communities offering chat capabilities. Typically, chat works one of two ways:

- **Chat room** — This has more than two, and usually unlimited, participants. Chat rooms are also usually public, requiring only membership on the site to join.
- **Private chat** — This usually has only two participants. Nobody else can see the contents of the chat.

Whether a chat is private or in a chat room, the server-side implementation is essentially the same: The server accepts connections, associates all the related connections, and echoes incoming messages to all associated connections. It also publishes interesting events, such as when somebody connects to or disconnects from the chat. The only big difference is how many connections are associated with each other.

Multinational Widget Corporation needs support chat in its Customer Support application. Support chat is a basic concept: In an urgent situation, a customer might need live help. The customer could log on to the support site and enter a private chat with a customer support representative. Typically, this would be offered only during certain hours. Also, usually customers have the ability to download or have the chat log e-mailed to them at the end of the chat session. In this section, you use WebSockets to add "Chat with Support" to the Customer Support application. You should follow along in the Customer-Support-v8 project available on the `wrox.com` code download site because there is not enough room in this book to print it all.

There are some changes to the `main.css` style sheet and a new `chat.css` style sheet to correctly style the chat pages. The `/WEB-INF/tags/template/main.tag` file now includes some third-party CSS and JavaScript libraries and defines a couple of JavaScript functions for use on any pages. Also, `basic.tag` now has links for creating a new chat with support or viewing pending chat requests.

Normally, only customer support representatives could view and respond to pending chat requests, but the customer support application doesn't have full security with user permissions yet. You'll add that in Part IV of this book. The `ChatServlet` has a fairly simple task: It manages the listing, creating, and joining of chat sessions. The `doPost` method sets the `Expires` and `Cache-Control` headers to ensure the browser doesn't cache the chat page. `/WEB-INF/jsp/view/chat/list.jsp` is responsible for listing pending chats for customer support personnel to respond to. Finally, the `Configurator` class now also maps the `AuthenticationFilter` to the `/chat` URL so that the `ChatServlet` is protected.

## Using Encoders and Decoders to Translate Messages

Earlier in the chapter you learned about all the possible parameters you could specify for `@OnMessage` methods. Remember:

- You can specify any Java object as a parameter as long as you provide a decoder capable of translating incoming text or binary messages into that object.
- You can send any object using the `sendObject` methods of `RemoteEndpoint.Basic` or `RemoteEndpoint.Async` as long as you provide an encoder capable of translating that object into a text or binary message.
- You provide encoders by implementing `Encoder.Binary`, `Encoder.BinaryStream`, `Encoder.Text`, or `Encoder.TextStream` and specifying their classes in the `encoders` attribute of `@ClientEndpoint` or `@ServerEndpoint`.

➤ You can implement Decoder.Binary, Decoder.BinaryStream, Decoder.Text, or Decoder.TextStream and use the decoders attribute of the endpoint annotations to provide decoders for your messages.

```
public class ChatMessage
{
    private OffsetDateTime timestamp;
    private Type type;
    private String user;
    private String content;

    // accessor and mutator methods

    public static enum Type
    {
        STARTED, JOINED, ERROR, LEFT, TEXT
    }
}
```

The previous code for the ChatMessage shows that it is a simple POJO. The WebSocket API needs both an encoder and a decoder so that your chat application can send and receive messages. Listing 10-5 contains a simple class that encodes and decodes ChatMessages. It uses the Jackson Data Processor to encode and decode the messages. The encode method takes a ChatMessage and an OutputStream, encodes the message by converting it to JSON, and writes it to the OutputStream. The decode method does the opposite: Given an InputStream, it reads and deserializes the JSON ChatMessage. The init and destroy methods are specified in both the Encoder and Decoder interfaces. They are not used here, but could come in handy if you ever need to initialize or release resources that your encoders and decoders use.

**LISTING 10-5: ChatMessageCodec.java**

```
public class ChatMessageCodec
        implements Encoder.BinaryStream<ChatMessage>,
                    Decoder.BinaryStream<ChatMessage>
{
    private static final ObjectMapper MAPPER = new ObjectMapper();
    static {
        MAPPER.findAndRegisterModules();
        MAPPER.configure(JsonGenerator.Feature.AUTO_CLOSE_TARGET, false);
    }

    @Override
    public void encode(ChatMessage chatMessage, OutputStream outputStream)
            throws EncodeException, IOException {
        try {
            ChatMessageCodec.MAPPER.writeValue(outputStream, chatMessage);
        } catch(JsonGenerationException | JsonMappingException e) {
            throw new EncodeException(chatMessage, e.getMessage(), e);
        }
    }

    @Override
```

```
    public ChatMessage decode(InputStream inputStream)
            throws DecodeException, IOException {
        try {
            return ChatMessageCodec.MAPPER.readValue(
                    inputStream, ChatMessage.class
            );
        } catch(JsonParseException | JsonMappingException e) {
            throw new DecodeException((ByteBuffer)null, e.getMessage(), e);
        }
    }

    @Override
    public void init(EndpointConfig endpointConfig) { }

    @Override
    public void destroy() { }
}
```

## Creating the Chat Server Endpoint

The server endpoint uses the following `ChatSession` class to associate a user requesting a chat with the support representative who responds. It includes the opening message and a log of all messages sent during the chat.

```
public class ChatSession
{
    private long sessionId;
    private String customerUsername;
    private Session customer;
    private String representativeUsername;
    private Session representative;
    private ChatMessage creationMessage;
    private final List<ChatMessage> chatLog = new ArrayList<>();

    // accessor and mutator methods

    @JsonIgnore
    public void log(ChatMessage message) { ... }

    @JsonIgnore
    public void writeChatLog(File file) throws IOException {
        ObjectMapper mapper = new ObjectMapper();
        mapper.findAndRegisterModules();
        mapper.configure(JsonGenerator.Feature.AUTO_CLOSE_TARGET, false);
        mapper.configure(SerializationFeature.WRITE_DATES_AS_TIMESTAMPS, false);

        try(FileOutputStream stream = new FileOutputStream(file))
        {
            mapper.writeValue(stream, this.chatLog);
        }
    }
}
```

The `ChatEndpoint` class in Listing 10-6 receives chat connections and coordinates them appropriately. Some of the code has been omitted due to its length, but concepts that are new to you have been included. Nested within the class is the `EndpointConfigurator` class, which overrides the `modifyHandshake` method. At handshake time, this method is called and exposes the underlying HTTP request.

You can get the `HttpSession` object from this request, and in this case you want the HTTP session to make sure the user is logged in and also close the WebSocket session if the user logs out. This is also why the endpoint is an `HttpSessionListener`. When a session gets invalidated, the `sessionDestroyed` method is called, and the endpoint ends the chat session. One thing to keep in mind is that a new instance of this class is created at startup as a web listener, and a new instance is created each time a client endpoint connects to the server endpoint. That's why all the fields are static: so that the information about the `Sessions`, `HttpSessions`, and `ChatSessions` can be coordinated between instances.

The `onOpen` method, called when a new handshake has completed, first checks to make sure an `HttpSession` was associated with the `Session` (in the `modifyHandshake` method) and that the user is logged in. If the chat session ID is 0 (a new session has been requested), a new chat session is created and added to the list of pending sessions. If it is greater than 0, a representative is joining a requested session and messages are sent to both clients. When `onMessage` receives a message from either client, it echoes that message back to both clients. When a `Session` is closed, an error occurs, or an `HttpSession` is destroyed, a message is sent to the other user notifying her that the chat is over, and both connections are closed.

**LISTING 10-6: ChatEndpoint.java**

```
@ServerEndpoint(value = "/chat/{sessionId}",
        encoders = ChatMessageCodec.class,
        decoders = ChatMessageCodec.class,
        configurator = ChatEndpoint.EndpointConfigurator.class)
@WebListener
public class ChatEndpoint implements HttpSessionListener
{
    ...
    private static final Map<Long, ChatSession> chatSessions = new Hashtable<>();
    private static final Map<Session, ChatSession> sessions = new Hashtable<>();
    private static final Map<Session, HttpSession> httpSessions =
            new Hashtable<>();
    public static final List<ChatSession> pendingSessions = new ArrayList<>();

    @OnOpen
    public void onOpen(Session session, @PathParam("sessionId") long sessionId) {
        HttpSession httpSession = (HttpSession)session.getUserProperties()
                .get(ChatEndpoint.HTTP_SESSION_PROPERTY);
        try {
            if(httpSession==null || httpSession.getAttribute("username")==null) {
                session.close(new CloseReason(
                        CloseReason.CloseCodes.VIOLATED_POLICY,
                        "You are not logged in!"
                ));
```

```
                return;
            }
            String username = (String)httpSession.getAttribute("username");
            session.getUserProperties().put("username", username);
            ChatMessage message = new ChatMessage();
            message.setTimestamp(OffsetDateTime.now());
            message.setUser(username);
            ChatSession chatSession;
            if(sessionId < 1) {
                message.setType(ChatMessage.Type.STARTED);
                message.setContent(username + " started the chat session.");
                chatSession = new ChatSession();
                synchronized(ChatEndpoint.sessionIdSequenceLock) {
                    chatSession.setSessionId(ChatEndpoint.sessionIdSequence++);
                }
                chatSession.setCustomer(session);
                chatSession.setCustomerUsername(username);
                chatSession.setCreationMessage(message);
                ChatEndpoint.pendingSessions.add(chatSession);
                ChatEndpoint.chatSessions.put(chatSession.getSessionId(),
                        chatSession);
            } else {
                message.setType(ChatMessage.Type.JOINED);
                message.setContent(username + " joined the chat session.");
                chatSession = ChatEndpoint.chatSessions.get(sessionId);
                chatSession.setRepresentative(session);
                chatSession.setRepresentativeUsername(username);
                ChatEndpoint.pendingSessions.remove(chatSession);
                session.getBasicRemote()
                        .sendObject(chatSession.getCreationMessage());
                session.getBasicRemote().sendObject(message);
            }
            ChatEndpoint.sessions.put(session, chatSession);
            ChatEndpoint.httpSessions.put(session, httpSession);
            this.getSessionsFor(httpSession).add(session);
            chatSession.log(message);
            chatSession.getCustomer().getBasicRemote().sendObject(message);
        } catch(IOException | EncodeException e) {
            this.onError(session, e);
        }
    }

    @OnMessage
    public void onMessage(Session session, ChatMessage message) {
        ChatSession c = ChatEndpoint.sessions.get(session);
        Session other = this.getOtherSession(c, session);
        if(c != null && other != null) {
            c.log(message);
            try {
                session.getBasicRemote().sendObject(message);
                other.getBasicRemote().sendObject(message);
            } catch(IOException | EncodeException e) {
                this.onError(session, e);
            }
        }
```

*continues*

**LISTING 10-6** *(continued)*

```
        }

        @OnClose
        public void onClose(Session session, CloseReason reason) { ... }

        @OnError
        public void onError(Session session, Throwable e) { ... }

        @Override
        public void sessionDestroyed(HttpSessionEvent event) { ... }

        @Override
        public void sessionCreated(HttpSessionEvent event) { /* do nothing */ }

        @SuppressWarnings("unchecked")
        private synchronized ArrayList<Session> getSessionsFor(HttpSession session) {
            try {
                if(session.getAttribute(WS_SESSION_PROPERTY) == null)
                    session.setAttribute(WS_SESSION_PROPERTY, new ArrayList<>());
                return (ArrayList<Session>)session.getAttribute(WS_SESSION_PROPERTY);
            } catch(IllegalStateException e) {
                return new ArrayList<>();
            }
        }

        private Session close(Session s, ChatMessage message) { ... }

        private Session getOtherSession(ChatSession c, Session s) { ... }

        public static class EndpointConfigurator
                extends ServerEndpointConfig.Configurator {
            @Override
            public void modifyHandshake(ServerEndpointConfig config,
                                        HandshakeRequest request,
                                        HandshakeResponse response) {
                super.modifyHandshake(config, request, response);
                config.getUserProperties().put(
                        ChatEndpoint.HTTP_SESSION_PROPERTY, request.getHttpSession()
                );
            }
        }
    }
```

## Writing the JavaScript Chat Application

The `/WEB-INF/jsp/view/chat/chat.jsp` file contains the user interface for the support chat. Much of the code is presentation, connection, and error handling, which you have seen before with the Tic-tac-toe game. Of particular importance are the `onmessage` event and the `send` function, which deal with receiving and sending binary messages, respectively. Because this application uses JSON to send messages between the browser and the server, it would have been easier to use text messages instead of binary messages. However, you have not yet seen how to handle binary WebSocket messages in JavaScript, so this example demonstrates that.

```
server.onmessage = function(event) {
    if(event.data instanceof ArrayBuffer) {
        var message = JSON.parse(String.fromCharCode.apply(
                null, new Uint8Array(event.data)
        ));
        objectMessage(message);
        if(message.type == 'JOINED') {
            otherJoined = true;
            if(username != message.user)
                infoMessage('You are now chatting with ' +
                        message.user + '.');
        }
    } else {
        modalErrorBody.text('Unexpected data type [' +
                typeof(event.data) + '].');
        modalError.modal('show');
    }
};

send = function() {
    if(server == null) {
        modalErrorBody.text('You are not connected!');
        modalError.modal('show');
    } else if(!otherJoined) {
        modalErrorBody.text(
                'The other user has not joined the chat yet.');
        modalError.modal('show');
    } else if(messageArea.get(0).value.trim().length > 0) {
        var message = {
            timestamp: new Date(), type: 'TEXT', user: username,
            content: messageArea.get(0).value
        };
        try {
            var json = JSON.stringify(message);
            var length = json.length;
            var buffer = new ArrayBuffer(length);
            var array = new Uint8Array(buffer);
            for(var i = 0; i < length; i++) {
                array[i] = json.charCodeAt(i);
            }
            server.send(buffer);
            messageArea.get(0).value = '';
        } catch(error) {
            modalErrorBody.text(error);
            modalError.modal('show');
        }
    }
};
```

Now compile and start the Customer-Support-v8 application, and open two different Internet browsers to `http://localhost:8080/support`. Log in to the support application in both browsers as *different users*. (Remember, you can view the available usernames and passwords in the `LoginServlet` code.) In one browser, click Chat with Support to request a chat session. In the other browser click View Chat Requests and then click the chat session you previously opened. Type messages in each browser and click Send. You should soon see something like Figure 10-7. You are now chatting with yourself through both browsers.

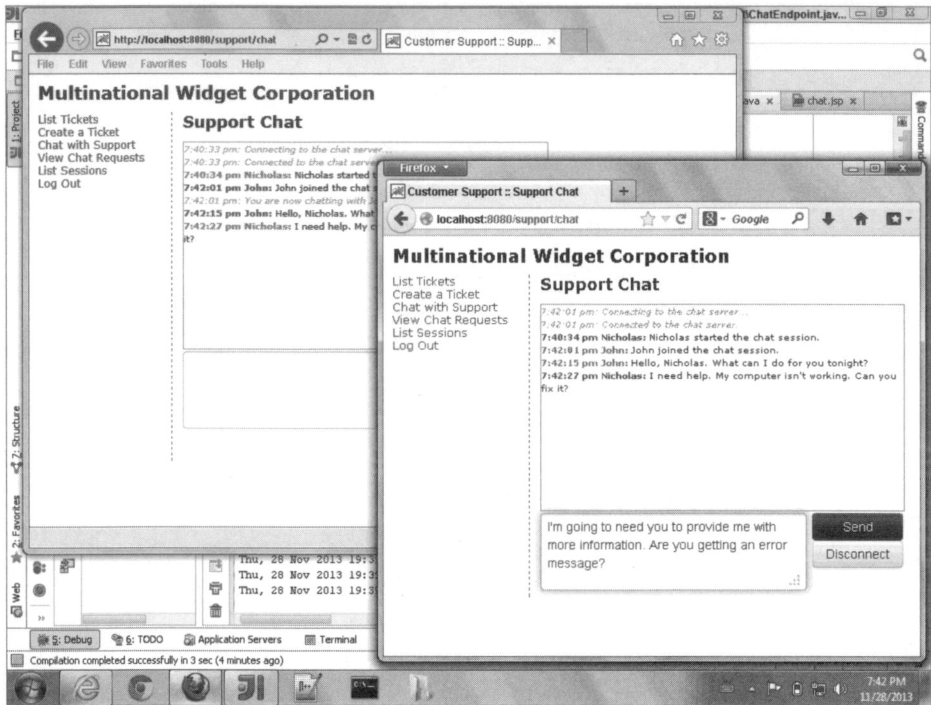


FIGURE 10-7

# SUMMARY

WebSockets are an extremely useful, powerful new technology in the Internet world. Like the HTTP protocol, which underwent many changes in its early days, the WebSockets protocol is likely to undergo many changes in the coming years as well. Currently, it has a framework for extensions, but no existing extensions. That is likely to change as more and more developers begin using the technology. There are endless uses for WebSockets, and you explored several of those uses in this chapter. You created a multiplayer game of Tic-tac-toe, used WebSockets to communicate within nodes in an application cluster, and added support chat to the Customer Support application. You learned about the technologies that led to WebSockets and how WebSockets solved many of the problems those technologies couldn't. By now you should be familiar with the protocol and the Java and JavaScript APIs necessary to use it.

In the next chapter you learn about application logging principles and the technologies you can use to facilitate debugging and tracing your application and identifying errors that occur.

# 11

# Using Logging to Monitor Your Application

## IN THIS CHAPTER

- All about logging
- What are the different logging levels?
- What logging facility is right for you?
- How to integrate logging into your application
- Include logging in the Customer Support application

## WROX.COM CODE DOWNLOADS FOR THIS CHAPTER

You can find the `wrox.com` code downloads for this chapter at `http://www.wrox.com/go/projavaforwebapps` on the Download Code tab. The code for this chapter is divided into the following major examples:

- Logging-Integration Project
- Customer-Support-v9 Project

## NEW MAVEN DEPENDENCIES FOR THIS CHAPTER

In addition to the Maven dependencies introduced in previous chapters, you also need the following Maven dependencies:

```
<dependency>
    <groupId>org.apache.logging.log4j</groupId>
    <artifactId>log4j-api</artifactId>
    <version>2.0</version>
    <scope>compile</scope>
```

```
</dependency>

<dependency>
    <groupId>org.apache.logging.log4j</groupId>
    <artifactId>log4j-core</artifactId>
    <version>2.0</version>
    <scope>runtime</scope>
</dependency>

<dependency>
    <groupId>org.apache.logging.log4j</groupId>
    <artifactId>log4j-jcl</artifactId>
    <version>2.0</version>
    <scope>runtime</scope>
</dependency>

<dependency>
    <groupId>org.apache.logging.log4j</groupId>
    <artifactId>log4j-slf4j-impl</artifactId>
    <version>2.0</version>
    <scope>runtime</scope>
</dependency>

<dependency>
    <groupId>org.apache.logging.log4j</groupId>
    <artifactId>log4j-taglib</artifactId>
    <version>2.0</version>
    <scope>runtime</scope>
</dependency>
```

# UNDERSTANDING THE CONCEPTS OF LOGGING

Imagine a scenario: You have a report of a bug in your application. Given precise replication steps from customer support, you can duplicate the bug every time. The problem is, as soon as you hit a breakpoint in the debugger, the problem goes away. Vanishes without an explanation. This likely (though not certainly) means the problem is related to multithreading, and hitting a breakpoint slows the execution down enough to mask the problem. So how are you supposed to figure out what the problem is? Application logging is critical to successful debugging, troubleshooting, monitoring, and error reporting in your application. In this chapter you explore the concepts of logging; learn about logging façades, APIs, and implementations; and integrate logging into an application.

## Why You Should Log

*As a personal choice, we tend not to use debuggers beyond getting a stack trace or the value of a variable or two. One reason is that it is easy to get lost in details of complicated data structures and control flow; we find stepping through a program less productive than thinking harder and adding output statements and self-checking code at critical places. Clicking over statements takes longer than scanning the output of judiciously-placed displays. It takes less time to decide where to put print statements than to single-step to the critical section of code, even assuming we know where that is. More important, debugging statements stay with the program; debugger sessions are transient.*

KERNIGHAN, BRIAN W. AND ROB PIKE. *THE PRACTICE OF PROGRAMMING*. READING: ADDISON WESLEY LONGMAN, INC., 1999. 119.

There are many reasons you should log. The preceding quote highlights some important points about logging — and about the drawbacks of debuggers. It should be noted that much time has passed since that book was published, and debuggers have come a long way. The ease of firing up a debugger in an IDE and stepping through an application's execution cannot be understated in today's world. In many ways the Java debugger is the best around, and debugger integration in today's Java IDEs makes inspection and even modification of static, instance, and stack variables a simple matter. In most Java IDEs, you can evaluate an arbitrary expression at run time when stopped at a breakpoint, and you can change, recompile, and reload code without restarting the Java virtual machine.

But even with all that, debugging is not enough. The hypothetical presented earlier is one of many examples in which a debugger gets in the way. In addition, sometimes a debugger is simply not available. Consider a situation in which a customer issue cannot be replicated in a development environment, or even a quality assurance environment. In most cases, attaching a debugger to your customer's running production application is simply not an option.

Let's face it: Bugs are not planned. You write your application to be perfect, but bugs surface anyway. They always will. There are many techniques you can employ and tools you can use to detect and minimize bugs in your code, but you will never avoid them completely. So, it makes sense that you should plan to troubleshoot a bug without a debugger.

Debugging your application is not the only reason you should log, though. Often you need to be notified of important events such as errors, changes in application configuration, unexpected behavior, component startup or shutdown, user logins, data changes, and more. You may also want to simply monitor your application to make sure it is working and undergoing activity of some sort. All of these needs — and more — demonstrate why you should log.

In the earliest days of Java (`java.util.logging` wasn't part of the framework until Java 1.4), many developers used `System.err.println()` and `System.out.println()` to "log" errors and interesting information. Even today, many applications and even libraries are still filled with statements such as these. These streams can be redirected to separate files, which does have some usefulness, but their lack of granularity and "always on" disposition causes logs to fill up quickly and hinders the performance of the application. Ideally, you want something that is easily customizable, can be configured to display a little or a lot of information, can display different information depending on the package or class, and (most important) does not hinder performance.

## What Content You Might Want to See in Logs

Given the ideal logging system described previously — customizable, configurable, variable by package or class, and performs well — think about all the information you would want to put in a log file. You can probably think of a number of things, and really the possibilities are technically endless, but here are some basic ideas to get you started:

- **When an application crashes or exits unexpectedly, it is essential to log in as much detail as possible, everything that led up to the crash.** This may include messages, stack traces, thread dumps, and even heap dumps. JVM crashes are not easy events to log. Most of the time the very nature of the crash prevents logging facilities from working. Because of this, most JVMs have tools built in to note when these events occur. For example, the Oracle and OpenJDK JVMs have the command line option-`XX:+HeapDumpOnOutOfMemoryError` that makes Java generate a heap dump when the JVM runs out of memory. Consult your JVM manufacturer's documentation for more information.
- **When errors occur, you should log any information you have about that error (type, message, stack trace, and what the application was doing when the error occurred).** Then, with all that important data stored in a log somewhere, you can display to users only a minimal error message telling them that something went wrong without divulging details that could compromise your system (such as file paths or SQL queries).
- **Sometimes issues arise that aren't quite errors and don't stop an action from continuing but should probably be brought to somebody's attention at a later time.** These issues indicate a potential, but not definite, problem with your application. You should log these types of situations, including a detailed message and what the application was doing. Sometimes, a stack trace is also applicable to these situations. You might consider these "warnings."
- **There are certain important events that you might want to see in your logs.** Logging things such as the creation of entities, the starting of components, a successful user login, or the execution of tasks help you know that your system is working properly.
- **When you want to track down a problem, you want to see detailed information about the execution of methods and routines, often including the value of applicable variables.** However, you probably don't want to see this data all the time, and creating that much data could hinder performance.
- **In the toughest debugging scenarios, you may need to see when any method is entered or exited, as well as the parameter values and return value for each method.** In any loops that are executing, you might require data from each iteration. This, of course, is a ton of information in a high-load scenario, so you definitely don't want it on all the time, and probably not for all methods, even when you do turn it on. In fact, sometimes you may even want to limit this type of logging detail to a specific user or other criteria.
- **Often you need to audit activities in your application.** If your field is security, healthcare, or legal, the law sometimes mandates keeping a record of who did what and when! At some point, you will likely need a mechanism for keeping track of these things. Make no mistake: This is just another form of logging. There may be unique features to this type of logging, and it may have to be separate from any other logging, but it is still just logging.

This is by no means an exhaustive list. The needs of every developer and project are different, and it's likely you have already thought of something not on this list. However, these key concepts are common to almost all applications, and you should keep them in mind both when writing your application and when designing your logging system.

## How Logs Are Written

An important thing to keep in mind is that a "log" is not necessarily a file in and of itself. Often when you think of logging, you naturally think of a file. After all, at some point your log contents will probably end up in a file somewhere. But this does not mean that your log contents are written directly to a flat file to later be read manually in eye-bleeding sessions. (Although you could certainly do that if you prefer.) Logs can be written any number of ways to any number of media. Sometimes, logs are written to multiple locations simultaneously, or written to a primary media falling over to a backup media if the primary media fails. Sometimes logs are written asynchronously so that your application can continue processing while the logged information is queued waiting to be written. In some circumstances, logging must even be transaction-safe so that the action stops if logging fails. All these things, and your application's business needs, affect how logs are written.

Generally speaking, there are some common mechanisms that people use for storing application logs. You may want to use one or more of these, or come up with something on your own.

### The Console

A time-tested mechanism, console logging is effectively equivalent to using `System.out.println()`. Although you can gain many advantages using a logging system, the output of the log is the same place: stdout. The thing about console logging is that, unless the process's standard output redirects using operating system facilities (which often happens), the contents of the console are gone after the application exits or the data falls off the end of the console buffer. However, console logging can be extraordinarily useful during development cycles and when other mechanisms fail. It is nearly always configured as at least a failover logging mechanism for most applications.

### Flat Files

Another traditional logging method, flat files are perhaps the easiest media to write logs to and the most difficult media to read logs from. The primary advantage flat files have over console logging is that they are persistent by nature (until you delete them), but that's about where the advantages end.

Typically, flat-file logging consists of a single line in the file per log entry, but because log messages sometimes take up multiple lines (like stack traces), it can be difficult to apply this pattern programmatically. Standard flat-file logs are decently easy to read with the human eye, but nearly impossible to filter or sift through. There are some variations of flat-file logging that, in some cases, improve on this problem slightly:

- **XML logging persists each log event using a standardized XML syntax.** The primary advantage of this is that it's both human readable AND machine readable, meaning programs can be written to read log contents and display them programmatically with filtering capabilities. However, XML is an extremely bloated format and can often triple or quadruple the size of your logs (or worse!).
- **JSON logging is similar to XML except that it stores log contents in the JavaScript Object Notation format.** This means much less bloat than XML, but on the other hand makes it slightly harder for humans to read.

- **On Linux operating systems, syslog is a facility that all processes can write to.** The specifics of this are outside the scope of this book, but essentially log events are written to flat files managed by the operating system logging tool and stored in a central location in a standardized format. Windows offers a similar functionality through the Windows Event Log, and that data is stored in XML and comes with a log viewer built in to the operating system.

The concept of rolling files can be applied to all these patterns (and, in the case of syslog and Event Log, is applied automatically). When a logging system is set up to use rolling files, it periodically changes the file it is logging to. Sometimes this rolling is time-based — Tomcat, for example, gets a fresh set of log files every day — whereas other times, when a log file reaches a certain size, log files get backed up to an indexed filename and a new log file starts.

## Sockets

A less common method for logging, sockets are nonetheless quite useful in some situations. Log events are translated into some network-communicable form and then sent over the network to some other location. Sometimes the receiving application is on the same machine; sometimes it is on a different machine on the same network; and sometimes it is on a different network (even the other side of the world). In nearly all cases, the other end of the socket connection is a dedicated logging server whose sole purpose is receiving and persisting logs in some way.

## SMTP and SMS

Although sending an e-mail for logging events may sound strange, think about how badly you want to know when an error occurs in your application. E-mail and SMS log notifications are rarely sent for typical run-of-the-mill logging events. In every case that this author has seen, e-mail and SMS were reserved for severe application errors only, such as exceptions that caused the abortion of a system action or caused a component to fail to start. This notifies the system administrator that a problem needs to be looked at right away.

## Databases

It is very common today for applications to log to a database of some type and for obvious reasons. Databases are efficient, transaction safe means of storage that are extremely easy to query and filter data from. If you are logging audit data, chances are you will have to use a database to store those logs. The disadvantages to logging to a database may also be obvious. The first is speed: Writing data to an indexed table with the overhead of the network stack and a database is much slower (on a small scale) than writing to a flat file. But then there's the issue of database size: Many databases have limits on how much data they can hold and, even when those limits are lifted, performance suffers drastically. Inserts can take large fractions of seconds or more. For many, this is an unreasonable price to pay for logging that can be easily filtered.

Enter NoSQL databases, which lack many of the problems that relational databases present to logging systems. These databases store data in a nonrelational manner, which removes much of the overhead and enables well-performing storage of many hundreds of gigabytes or even terabytes of data. One of the most popular databases to use for such a task is MongoDB, a NoSQL document database. This database stores data in the Binary JSON (BSON) format, which is an extremely compressed and efficient means of storage.

MongoDB sacrifices read performance — it can be quite slow when filtering large datasets — and exchanges it for write performance. Inserting data into MongoDB can be orders of magnitude faster than popular relational database systems when database size exceeds several gigabytes. This is a huge plus for logging systems, which you want to impact application performance as little as possible. MongoDB, like most other document databases, is not fully ACID-compliant, but if you structure your documents correctly, you can reduce the chances of losing data to about the same as with an ACID RDBMS.

# USING LOGGING LEVELS AND CATEGORIES

In the previous section, you explored some of the concepts of logging, including an overview of the various types of information you might want to see in your application logs. As you explored this topic, it probably became clear to you very quickly that there are different types or severity of logging events, and that not all types are logged all the time. This is commonly known as the concept of logging *levels*. Sometimes, levels are not enough. Often you need the finest logging details from only specific parts of your application, not from the entire thing. If you could just *categorize* your logging events, your logging data would become even more useful. In this section, you investigate logging levels and categories. You also look at the concept of log sifting and how it relates to and differs from log categorization.

## Why Are There Different Logging Levels?

Chances are you have already answered this question. So far in this chapter, you've identified a lot of information that should be included in logs; some of it indicative of serious errors, and other types represent extremely fine and numerous debugging detail. If you had all this detail turned on all the time, your logs could grow by megabytes per second. (Trust me, I've seen it happen.) Not only would this seriously hinder the performance of the application, but also your logs would become essentially useless. When you have multiple megabytes of log data to sort through for a single second of application execution, you might as well not have any logs.

Levels indicate the severity or relative importance of a logged event. The word "relative" is used here because that's exactly what it is: One logging level is either more or less important than another logging level. The name of a logging level itself does not define the actual importance of the message it conveys; it just defines the importance of the message as compared to some other message. In some systems, logging levels are merely integers and nothing more. In other systems, logging levels are assigned a name to provide some semblance of semantic usefulness. There is no agreed-upon standard for the number, order, or name of logging levels. Nearly every system you use can define these differently, and it's up to you to determine what works best for you.

## Logging Levels Defined

Although there is not an agreed-upon standard, some common patterns appear in most logging systems written for Java applications. Logging levels are typically named to give them some high-level meaning, and in most systems anywhere from six to ten distinct levels exist. Table 11-1 lists the most common types in order from most severe to most trivial and the equivalent constant as defined in `java.util.logging.Level`.

TABLE 11-1: Common Logging Levels

| GENERIC NAME | Level CONSTANT | SEMANTIC MEANING |
|---|---|---|
| Fatal Error / Crash | No equivalent | Indicates an error of the severest form. Usually these errors result in a crash or at least premature termination of the application. |
| Error | `SEVERE` | Indicates that a serious problem has occurred |
| Warning | `WARNING` | Indicates that some event has occurred that may or may not be a problem and probably needs to be looked at |
| Information | `INFO` | As the name implies, this indicates informational items that could be useful for application monitoring and debugging. |
| Configuration Details | `CONFIG` | Events with this level typically contain details about configuration information. You often see this at application or component startup. |
| Debug | `FINE` | Indicates debugging information and often includes the values of variables |
| Trace Level 1<br>Trace Level 2 | `FINER`<br>`FINEST` | These levels represent different levels of application tracing. Many logging frameworks define only a single trace level. One possible way to use these levels separately would be to utilize `FINER` for logging executed SQL statements and `FINEST` for logging entry into and exiting from method calls. |

It's important to note that these examples are based off of one specific logging system: `java.util.logging` built in to the Java SE APIs. But there are many different logging systems both inside and outside of Java programming, and each defines its own slightly different set of levels. Some systems (such as `java.util.logging`) enable you to extend and define more levels. Other systems do not.

As an example of a different set of levels, consider the logging levels available in the Apache HTTPD 2.2 server logs: `emerg`, `alert`, `crit`, `error`, `warn`, `notice`, `info`, and `debug`. (Version 2.4 adds 8 more levels: `trace1` through `trace8`). The disproportionate number of levels for unusual activity as opposed to debugging highlights a fundamental difference in this system: It was considered more important here to differentiate many different types of errors than many different types of debug information. (Though, that has changed in later versions.) Likewise, your needs may vary based on the use case for your application.

## How Logging Categories Work

The concept of a logging category is slightly more abstract than logging level. In nearly all cases in Java (including all of the examples you see in this chapter), logging categories are represented by named logger instances, and each logger can have a different level assigned to it. Through this pattern, two different classes could have two different loggers, and you could set one to log trace data and the other to log warnings only. In fact, that's exactly how categories are used in most cases: At development time, each class gets its own logger, usually named after the fully qualified class name. Depending on the logging system, a logger hierarchy is usually established so that loggers with undefined level assignments inherit the level from some parent logger.

### How Log Sifting Works

Log sifting is conceptually similar to log categorization but serves a slightly different purpose. Using log sifting, different types or originations of events get logged to different locations (different files, different database tables or documents, and so on). In some ways this is the same idea as categories, except that categories typically define a different logging level as opposed to a different logging destination. Many logging frameworks enable you to sift logs by actually using the category, thus knocking out two problems with one feature. Others provide you with the ability to sift using categories *and* other attributes of a log event (usually determined in a filter of some type). In Java, all major logging frameworks permit sifting based on at least the logging category, if not more attributes of each log event. You explore the topic of sifting more in both of the next two sections.

## CHOOSING A LOGGING FRAMEWORK

After you understand the logging needs of your application, your next task is to choose a logging framework. This might not mean using a third-party framework — it might mean creating your own. However, in almost all cases you can find existing, industry-tested logging frameworks that you can configure to meet your needs, which means creating your own is simply an unnecessary task. In this section you examine two important guidelines to keep in mind and then take a look at some existing logging frameworks.

### API versus Implementation

Consider this scenario: You've written a large, enterprise application with many thousands of classes. Most of these classes (the ones that aren't POJOs) use logging. After careful research, you chose and integrate an industry-standard logging system into your application. A week after going live, your system's engineering team informs you that the syslog output you've chosen is not adequate, and that it needs database logging. Unfortunately, the logging system you've chosen doesn't support database logging. What can you do? You could extend the logging system, but there's a perfectly good logging system out there that already supports database logging, and you'd rather use that. However, if you did that you'd need to change thousands of classes to use a different logging system. The effort could take weeks and cost your company tens of thousands of dollars.

The underlying problem in this scenario is that the logging API you are using is tightly coupled with an underlying implementation. You can't swap out the implementation without changing everywhere in your code where logging is used. You could have avoided this problem if you had simply written a simple logging API to hide the underlying framework from your uses of logging in the code. Then, all you'd have had to do to swap out the framework is change a handful of classes in your API; the rest of your application could continue using your API for logging as it always had. Thankfully, this is not a new concept in the world of logging frameworks, and chances are you won't even have to write the API yourself.

The standard `java.util.logging` framework built in to the Java platform is one example of the separation of logging API from implementation. The `java.util.logging.LogManager` class is responsible for creating and returning `Logger` instances when requested and delegates to a default implementation. Developers can extend `LogManager` and specify a system property to provide an alternative implementation of the standard logging API.

The standard implementation has handlers that can write to the files, streams, sockets, console, and even memory. You might wonder, then, why you can't just use the standard logging facility. The simple answer is, "You can." In many cases and for many applications, the built-in logging system is completely adequate. However, it has a key drawback that makes it downright difficult if not impossible to use in web applications: It loads its configuration from a system property instead of the classpath. Because of this, two web applications deployed in the same container instance cannot have different logging configurations unless the container has extended the base logging implementation. Tomcat does do this, but not all containers do, so relying on this isn't portable. Instead, it's better to find some other solution that combines separate APIs and implementations.

## Performance

Obviously, performance is a huge consideration no matter what part of an application you work on, and logging is no different. Think for just a second, however, about the process of writing to files, sockets, or databases, or sending e-mails. These tasks spend considerable time blocking while input/output operations complete, and blocking is a time-intensive situation. There is simply no way around it: Logging messages takes time, and the vast majority of that time is out of your hands and in that of the operating system — meaning you can't speed it up through software alone.

But, really, if you have a message that you feel is important enough to log, chances are you won't care that it adds a few milliseconds to an activity. So why does performance matter? The key is it doesn't matter (much) when you *are* logging; it matters (drastically) when you *are not* logging. You are likely to fill up your code with trace, debug, and informational statements that you won't want to see most of the time. You essentially want these operations to do absolutely nothing unless you have that level of detail enabled.

The following are the critical situations in which performance can make or break a logging framework:

- Calling a debug method when debug logging is disabled shouldn't add *milliseconds* to an action — it should add *nanoseconds or less*.
- With a well-performing logging system, you should fill your code to the brim with logging statements, turn all logging off, and notice no perceivable difference in application response time. This is the key performance indicator that you should look for when choosing a logging system.

Sure, good performance when you turn on logging is admirable and desirable, but it is meaningless if performance is bad when logging is turned off.

## A Quick Look at Apache Commons Logging and SLF4J

Apache Commons Logging (`http://commons.apache.org/proper/commons-logging/`) and Simple Logging Façade for Java (`http://www.slf4j.org/`) are both Open Source, ultra-thin logging APIs. Neither API contains any implementation code. Instead, developers are expected to pick a logging framework to sit under the API. In a Maven project, the Commons Logging or SLF4J APIs are often given `compile` scope, whereas the implementation is given `runtime` scope, thereby completely preventing the application from using the underlying implementation directly.

Though both APIs have several classes, there are only two classes in each API that you will ever use directly. In Commons Logging, the `LogFactory` class has two static `getLog` methods that return named `Logs`. The `Log` class has methods for logging debug, info, warning, error, and other messages. SLF4J is very similar. The static `getLogger` methods on its `LoggerFactory` class return `Loggers`, which have methods for logging various message levels. The SLF4J API is a bit more flexible because its `Logger` class supports markers, format-syntax `Strings`, and arguments for each logging method. You learn more about this later in this section.

Both of these APIs are heavily used in libraries and are the two most popular for this purpose. Application code is not the only code that needs logging. Often libraries that applications use, especially complex libraries such as Spring Framework or Hibernate, need to log messages as well. This logging helps you, the consumer of the library, understand what is happening and track down problems when things go wrong. However, because libraries do not run but instead are coded against, they have no way of knowing (nor do they care) how logging actually takes place.

Enter the Commons Logging and SLF4J APIs. Both logging APIs ship with absolutely no implementation; instead, they come with adapters to multiple logging frameworks. At run time, they discover the logging framework in use (by convention or configuration) and activate the appropriate adapter to translate logging events from the API to the implementation. Commons Logging provides adapters for Avalon, `java.util.logging`, Log4j 1.2, and LogKit logging. SLF4J provides adapters for (ironically) Commons Logging, `java.util.logging`, and Log4j 1.2 logging. When the APIs do not provide adapters to support a particular logging framework, often the logging frameworks provide adapters. Logback, for example, is a popular implementation to use with SLF4J and provides the SLF4J adapter binding. In the worst-case scenario, both APIs make writing custom adapters easy.

For years, Log4j was the most popular logging framework to use either standalone or underneath Commons Logging or SLF4J. (It was most commonly used with Commons Logging.) However, Log4j had some drawbacks, and in particular suffered from a very narrow interface (no markers, no message formatting, no message arguments) and performance issues. Dissatisfaction with various APIs and frameworks led to the creation of SLF4J (an improvement on Commons Logging), and later Logback (an improvement on Log4j). Logback boasted an extremely useful interface, a strongly performing implementation, and a battery of tests to demonstrate its stability and performance. It didn't take long for work to begin on Log4j 2, the successor to Log4j whose goal was to improve the interface and performance of the original Log4j framework.

## Introducing Log4j 2

Log4j 2 (`http://logging.apache.org/log4j/2.x/`), which was released in February 2014, is a vast improvement over Log4j. It includes significant performance improvements, a greatly expanded interface, and plenty of tests to back it all up. In addition, the API and implementation have been completely separated. The API specifies an interface for developers to log to and also provides hooks for creating an underlying implementation.

Of course, there's also the default implementation, but developers of applications and other logging frameworks are free to use the API hooks to adapt the API to sit on top of other logging implementations. Because there are so many logging frameworks out there and Log4j 2 is still very new, you should still use Commons Logging or SLF4J as your logging API when writing a new *library*. This is because you have no way of knowing what logging frameworks consumers of your library will use, and there is a better chance those logging frameworks will have adapters for Commons Logging or SLF4J than for Log4j 2. However, when writing an application you call the shots. Writing directly against the Log4j 2 API provides more flexibility and could also help performance somewhat, depending on your use of it, and you won't lose the ability to swap out the underlying implementation if you ever need to.

> **NOTE** *Log4j 2 includes several performance metrics on its website. The most important metric — performance when logging is turned off — is impressive: on midline hardware, 3 nanoseconds for calls to* `isDebugEnabled`*, and 4 nanoseconds for calls to* `debug` *when debug is turned off. That's 4 billionths of a second sacrificed to put helpful message logging in your application. To put this in perspective, with all debug logging disabled, your application would have to execute 250,000 debug methods to add 1 millisecond in execution time, or 250,000,000 debug methods per second to double execution time.*
>
> *All this performance is actually roughly the same as Logback performance. Where Log4j 2 really excels is with log filters. In a multithreaded application, tests show Log4j 2 beats Logback by an order of magnitude or more when filter processing is active.*

For the rest of this book, you will log against the Log4j 2 API with the Log4j 2 core implementation underneath it. (In a real-world scenario, you should evaluate the needs of your project and determine which API and implementation work best for you.) You have undoubtedly noticed that this chapter has added five Log4j 2 Maven dependencies. Here is an explanation of each:

- `log4j-api` provides the API for logging. This is the only Log4j dependency that is in `compile` scope in your application because it contains the only classes you should code against.
- `log4j-core` contains the standard Log4j 2 implementation. As you explore Log4j 2 configuration throughout the rest of this chapter, it is the implementation you are configuring, not the API. The API requires no configuration.
- `log4j-jcl` is an adapter to support the Commons Logging API. Several libraries you use in the rest of this book log against the Commons Logging API, and this adapter causes Commons Logging to use Log4j 2 as its implementation.
- `log4j-slf4j-impl` is an SLF4J implementation adapter. Several libraries used throughout the rest of this book log against the SLF4J API, and this adapter causes SLF4J to use Log4j 2 as its implementation.

- `log4j-taglib` is an adapter that includes a JSP Tag Library for logging within your JSPs. Like the previous three dependencies, this dependency is in `runtime` scope for the purposes of writing your application code because you do not need to compile against it. However, if you were to configure a build to compile your JSPs, you would need this dependency to have compile scope for the JSP compilation process.

The Log4j 2 implementation has several key concepts that you should understand. Although the API exposes some of these concepts in a generic sense (this is noted where applicable), it is the integration with the implementation that makes the features possible.

> **WHY NOT USE COMMONS LOGGING OR SLF4J?**
>
> At this point, you may be thinking back to the scenario presented earlier where you need to quickly swap out your logging implementation. While the Log4j 2 API certainly makes this *possible*, it does not make it *easy*. The API is, undoubtedly, written with the implementation in mind. So why don't you use Commons Logging or SLF4J in front of Log4j 2?
>
> Neither the Commons Logging API nor the SLF4J API is as complete and feature-rich as the Log4j 2 API. Choosing Commons Logging or SLF4J means giving up some features, such as fatal logging, any-level logging, custom level logging, easy method entry and exit logging, and message formatting with arguments. Using a logging façade is a much more important thing to do in an independent library than in an application. If you are willing to sacrifice some Log4j 2 features, you can certainly choose SLF4J or Commons Logging over the Log4j 2 API. On the other hand, if you want to utilize all Log4j 2 features and also use a logging façade, you could create your own façade to match the Log4j 2 API. That choice is left up to you. For this book, you will use the Log4j 2 API directly.

## Configuration

The Log4j 2 implementation is completely self-configuring. At the most, the only thing you must do to use Log4j 2 is place logging statements in your code. By default, Log4j 2 can configure itself to log errors and higher and to write log messages to the console. It does this only if all the following steps have failed to locate an explicit configuration:

1. Inspect the `log4j.configurationFile` system property, and load the configuration from that file if it exists.
2. Look for a file named either `log4j2-test.json` or `log4j2-test.jsn` on the classpath, and load the configuration from that file if it exists.
3. Look for a file named `log4j2-test.xml` on the classpath and load the configuration from that file if it exists.
4. Look for a file named either `log4j2.json` or `log4j2.jsn` on the classpath, and load the configuration from that file if it exists.
5. Look for a file named `log4j2.xml` on the classpath, and load the configuration from that file if it exists.

The purpose of the separate `-test` files having higher priority is simple: This covers the cases in which unit (or other) tests are executing, and both files are on the classpath. In the next section you explore Log4j 2 configuration by integrating it into a web application.

## Levels

In the `org.apache.logging.log4j.Level` class, Log4j 2 defines six logging levels and two special-meaning levels, listed in order of their priority (most severe to least severe): `OFF`, `FATAL`, `ERROR`, `WARN`, `INFO`, `DEBUG`, `TRACE`, `ALL`. Note that `OFF` and `ALL` are not levels you would actually log against; instead, you would assign these levels to a particular `org.apache.logging.log4j.Logger` or `org.apache.logging.log4j.core.Appender`, `OFF` meaning "do not log anything" and `ALL` meaning "log everything." `Level` is, by necessity, exposed through the API, but how it is used to control the logging of messages is configured through the implementation.

Originally, `Level` was an enum, meaning it could not be extended. Shortly before Log4j 2 was released, `Level` was changed from an enum to a final class with a private constructor and a factory method `forName(String name, int intLevel)`. This method returns the existing `Level` if it exists and creates a new `Level` if it does not. The enum `org.apache.logging.log4j.spi.StandardLevel` helps map custom `Levels` you create to standard levels when logging to bridge APIs like SLF4J. There is always exactly one instance of a `Level` of any given name. This means you can easily create your own custom `Levels` using the following technique and you can compare a value to a `Level` using the == operator instead of `equals`.

```
public final class CustomLevels
{
    public static final Level CONFIG = Level.forName("CONFIG", 350);
    public static final Level NOTICE = Level.forName("NOTICE", 450);
    public static final Level DIAG   = Level.forName("DIAG", 550);
}
```

## Loggers

Loggers and categories are synonymous in Log4j 2, and you must deal with the `Logger` class in every class you log in. You obtain a `Logger` by calling one of the `getLogger` methods of `org.apache.logging.log4j.LogManager`. When you have a `Logger` instance you can log errors, warnings, and other messages. `Loggers` have names in Log4j 2, just like they do in most APIs and implementations. The `Logger` name defines the logging category, and by convention that name is the fully qualified class name of the class using the `Logger` (each class has its own `Logger` instance).

Multiple calls to `getLogger` with the same name or class result in the exact same instance of `Logger`, not in multiple instances with the same name (in other words, `Loggers` are cached). Any two `Loggers` can have different `Level` settings and be assigned to zero or more `Appenders`. `Logger` names in Log4j 2 follow a dot-separated hierarchy, with more specific `Loggers` inheriting the `Level` and `Appenders` of ancestor `Loggers`. This is demonstrated in Table 11-2. This table deals only with `Levels`, but the inheritance rules are essentially the same for `Appenders`. The Assigned Level column represents `Levels` that you might assign in your Log4j configuration.

**TABLE 11-2:** Inheritance Hierarchy for Log4j 2 Loggers

| LOGGER | ASSIGNED LEVEL | EFFECTIVE LEVEL | LEVEL INHERITED FROM |
|---|---|---|---|
| `root` (special) | `WARN` | `WARN` | n/a |
| `com` | – | `WARN` | `root` |
| `com.wrox` | `INFO` | `INFO` | – |
| `com.wrox.chat` | `DEBUG` | `DEBUG` | – |
| `com.wrox.shop` | – | `INFO` | `com.wrox` |
| `com.example.test` | – | `WARN` | `root` |

## Appenders

`Appenders` are responsible for actually writing log contents to their destination. `Appenders` have essentially the same inheritance rules as `Levels` when assigned to `Loggers`, with the exception that the inheritance also has an `additivity` property that determines whether an `Appender` adds to or overrides other inherited `Appenders`.

For example, if the `root` logger is assigned to a console `Appender` and `com.wrox` is assigned to a file `Appender`, log messages written to `com.wrox`, `com.wrox.chat`, and others go to *both* the console *and* the file, whereas log messages written to `root` or `com.example.test` go only to the console. However, if you set the `additivity` property to `false` for `com.wrox`, messages written to `com.wrox`, `com.wrox.chat`, and others go only to the file. (They stop at that `Appender`.) If `com.wrox`'s `additivity` property is still `false` and `com.wrox.shop` has a syslog `Appender` with `additivity` set to `true` (default), messages written to `com.wrox.shop` go to syslog and the file, but not to the console.

## Layouts

`Appenders` often use `Layouts` to determine how to format their output. The most common type of `Layout` is a pattern-based `Layout` that defines a series of tokens replaced at write-time with data from a logging message. There are also HTML, XML, syslog, and serialized layouts, to name a few examples. You explore the `PatternLayout` more in the next section.

## Filters

Log4j 2 `Filters`, not to be confused with Servlet filters, provide a mechanism whereby log messages can be examined to determine if or how they should be written. The result of a `Filter` evaluation is either `ACCEPT`, `DENY`, or `NEUTRAL`, just like with network firewalls. `ACCEPT` indicates that the message should be written and all other `Filters` should be ignored. If a `Filter` evaluation results in `ACCEPT`, even the message `Level` is ignored, and the message is logged even if its `Level` is not high enough. `DENY` is the opposite: This means that the message is immediately rejected, and the following filters do not get the opportunity to evaluate the message. `NEUTRAL` indicates that the `Filter` neither accepts nor denies the message, and other `Filters` may evaluate it further.

In a Log4j 2 configuration, `Filters` can be attached to four different stages of the architecture: the context configuration, the `Logger` configuration, the `Appender` reference, or the `Appender` configuration. When a message is logged, its first stop is any context-wide `Filters` in the order they were declared. This happens before the `Level` is evaluated. Assuming the context `Filters` say `NEUTRAL`, the message then goes to have its `Level` evaluated. If it passes the `Level` test, its next stop is the `Logger` configuration `Filters`. After this come the `Appender` reference Filters, which determine whether the `Logger` should route the message to a particular `Appender`. (This can be used to sift messages into different files or database tables, for example.) Finally, `Filters` on individual `Appenders` determine whether the `Appender` should write the message.

`Filters` can act on all sorts of information. A common pattern is to include `Marker` objects with logging messages and have `Filters` examine those `Marker` objects. (This is especially useful for sifting.) `Filters` can also look at the contents of a message, the message type, exceptions attached to a message, and data stored in the currently running `Thread`, just to name a few things. For that matter, `Filters` can use something as unrelated to the current message as the system time to determine how to act on a message. You'll see an example for configuring a `Filter` in the next section.

## INTEGRATING LOGGING INTO YOUR APPLICATION

Using and configuring Log4j is a fairly simple task. As described in the last section, you can get away with as little as simply putting logging statements in your application:

```
private static final Logger log = LogManager.getLogger();

@Override
protected void doGet(HttpServletRequest request, HttpServletResponse response)
        throws ServletException, IOException
{
    if(request.getParameter("action") == null)
        log.error("No action specified.");
}
```

Log4j 2 can configure itself with the default configuration and start writing logging messages to the console. Of course, this default configuration is likely not sufficient for you. Chances are you're going to need more than just errors logged (you'll probably want warnings and possibly informational messages), and you'll likely want the logs to go somewhere other than the console. You can easily achieve both with a configuration file.

> **NOTE** *If you are used to configuring previous versions of Log4j, you should keep two important things in mind. First, Log4j 2 does not support configuration through Java properties files anymore. You must use either XML or JSON. Second, Log4j 2's XML schema is not the same as Log4j's XML schema. If you have existing* `log4j.xml` *files in any of your applications, you cannot simply rename those files to* `log4j2.xml`*. You must adopt the new configuration schema.*

## Creating the Log4j 2 Configuration Files

Remember that Log4j 2 looks for two different configuration files (`log4j2` and `log4j2-test`), and that it supports three different extensions for those files (`.xml`, `.json`, and `.jsn`). The `.json` and `.jsn` extensions are both for JSON-format configurations. JSON configurations are much more easily read and written with code than XML configurations, so if you want to programmatically create Log4j 2 configurations, JSON is probably the way to go. If you're creating your configuration by hand, XML is an easier choice, so that's what you use here. You can follow along in the Logging-Integration project available for download on the `wrox.com` code download site.

The project is simple, containing a single servlet with some methods that execute correctly and others that do not. The first thing you must do is create the appropriate configuration files. When you create the standard configuration file, this also affects how logging behaves when unit tests run. Because the standard configuration file instructs Log4j 2 to log to a file and you probably don't want that when running unit tests, you should first create a `log4j2-test.xml` file in the `resources` directory of your project's `test` folder:

```
<?xml version="1.0" encoding="UTF-8"?>
<configuration status="WARN">
    <appenders>
        <Console name="Console" target="SYSTEM_OUT">
            <PatternLayout
                    pattern="%d{HH:mm:ss.SSS} [%t] %-5level %logger{36} - %msg%n"/>
        </Console>
    </appenders>
    <loggers>
        <root level="debug">
            <appender-ref ref="Console"/>
        </root>
    </loggers>
</configuration>
```

> **NOTE** *There is no official XML schema for the Log4j configuration files. The XML that you can use is flexible and also varies depending on which extensions and plugins are on the classpath, thus the configuration file cannot be strictly validated against a schema. You can learn more about which XML elements and attributes are valid in the Log4j Configuration Documentation at* `http://logging.apache.org/log4j/2.x/manual/configuration.html`.

This configuration file is nearly identical to the implicit default configuration. The only differences here are that the configuration status `Logger` `Level` changed from `OFF` to `WARN` and the root `Logger` `Level` changed from `ERROR` to `DEBUG`, both of which are more appropriate for testing situations.

You are already familiar with the `root` `Logger` (the ancestor of all `Logger`s in Log4j 2), but you may wonder what the configuration status `Logger` is. Log4j, too, needs to log messages when things aren't quite working right. It does this through a special `Logger` called the `StatusLogger`. This `Logger`'s sole purpose is to log events occurring within the logging system itself. As an example, say you create a socket Appender that cannot connect to its destination server. In this case it would log this failure using the StatusLogger. The default setting for the StatusLogger, OFF, suppresses all these messages from the logging system. Here, that Level has been changed to WARN (by changing the <configuration> element's status attribute).

Now that you have an adequate test configuration, create a log4j2.xml file in the resources directory of your project's production source folder:

```
<?xml version="1.0" encoding="UTF-8"?>
<configuration status="WARN">
    <appenders>
        <Console name="Console" target="SYSTEM_OUT">
            <PatternLayout
                    pattern="%d{HH:mm:ss.SSS} [%t] %-5level %logger{36} - %msg%n"/>
        </Console>
        <RollingFile name="WroxFileAppender" fileName="../logs/application.log"
                     filePattern="../logs/application-%d{MM-dd-yyyy}-%i.log">
            <PatternLayout>
                <pattern>%d{HH:mm:ss.SSS} [%t] %X{id} %X{username} %-5level
%c{36} %l: %msg%n</pattern>
            </PatternLayout>
            <Policies>
                <SizeBasedTriggeringPolicy size="10 MB" />
            </Policies>
            <DefaultRolloverStrategy min="1" max="4" />
        </RollingFile>
    </appenders>
    <loggers>
        <root level="warn">
            <appender-ref ref="Console" />
        </root>
        <logger name="com.wrox" level="info" additivity="false">
            <appender-ref ref="WroxFileAppender" />
            <appender-ref ref="Console">
                <MarkerFilter marker="WROX_CONSOLE" onMatch="NEUTRAL"
                              onMismatch="DENY" />
            </appender-ref>
        </logger>
        <logger name="org.apache" level="info">
            <appender-ref ref="WroxFileAppender" />
        </logger>
    </loggers>
</configuration>
```

There's some new and interesting stuff here. First, the rolling file Appender is configured to write to application.log in the Tomcat logs directory. (This assumes that your IDE starts Tomcat from the bin directory, which is typical; in a real-world scenario, you want to make these paths configurable.) Although Log4j 2 has a simpler file Appender that writes to a file, this Appender can roll the log in one or more scenarios, such as the log reaching a certain size, the date changing, the application starting, or any combination of those three. In this case, the Appender is configured to roll the log file every time it reaches 10 megabytes and to keep no more than four backed up logs.

> **NOTE** *If, when running the application, you can't find the* `application.log` *file in Tomcat's* `logs` *directory, try changing the relative path to an absolute path of a directory on your system and then restart the application.*

The `PatternLayout` has many patterns that can log event information, and you can learn about them all (and other layouts) in the Log4j Layout Documentation at `http://logging.apache.org/log4j/2.x/manual/layouts.html`. In this case, the file `Appender` pattern has substituted `%c` for `%logger` (the former is shorthand for the latter) and added `%l`, which prints the class, method, file, and line number where the logging message occurred. It has also added `%X{id}` (a fish tag) and `%X{username}`, which are properties on the `ThreadContext` — you learn about these next. You'll also notice that the pattern for the file `Appender`, in addition to actually being a different pattern, is configured using a different XML format than the console `Appender`. You can specify properties of `Appenders`, `Filters`, `Loggers`, and so on as tag attributes *or* as nested tags. The two approaches are interchangeable.

Finally, the new `Logger` configurations in this file say that all `Loggers` in the `com.wrox` and `org.apache` hierarchies have the level of `INFO` and that the `Loggers` in `com.wrox` are not additive — they do not inherit the console `Appender` and only log to the file `Appender`. However, notice the `com.wrox` `<appender-ref>` element for the console `Appender` has a nested `<MarkerFilter>` element with it. This filter says that `Loggers` in the `com.wrox` hierarchy *can* log to the console `Appender`, but only for events containing a `Marker` named `WROX_CONSOLE`. You can learn about the various `Filters` available in the Log4j Filter Documentation at `http://logging.apache.org/log4j/2.x/manual/filters.html`. The following incomplete configuration shows all of the valid locations for `Filter` configuration elements (shown in bold):

```
<?xml version="1.0" encoding="UTF-8"?>
<configuration>
    ...
    <FilterName ... /><!-- This is a context-wide filter -->
    <appenders>
        <AppenderName name="someAppender">
            <FilterName ... /><!-- This is an appender filter -->
            ...
        </AppenderName>
        ...
    </appenders>
    <loggers>
        <logger name="someLogger" level="info">
            <FilterName ... /><!-- This is a logger filter -->
            ...
            <appender-ref ref="someAppender">
                <FilterName ... /><!-- This is an appender reference filter -->
                ...
            </appender-ref>
            ...
        </logger>
        ...
    </loggers>
</configuration>
```

This book cannot show you all the possible ways to configure Log4j, as there are many. If you want more information, a good place to start is the Log4j Manual at `http://logging.apache.org/log4j/2.x/manual/index.html`.

## Utilizing Fish Tagging with a Web Filter

When using any logging framework, you should *fish tag* requests so that you can group together logging messages belonging to the same request and analyze them. The `org.apache.logging.log4j.ThreadContext` stores properties in the current thread until the `ThreadContext` is cleared. Any events logged in the same thread between when a property is added to the `ThreadContext` and when it is removed can be associated with that property. If there are many concurrent web requests executing, unique fish tags for each request enable you to identify all the messages logged during that particular request.

A fish tag is typically something strongly unique, such as a UUID. The `ThreadContext` can store anything else useful for distinguishing logging events, such as the username of the user who is logged in. The following `LoggingFilter` adds the fish tag (*`id`*) and session username (*`username`*) to the `ThreadContext` at the beginning of the request and clears the `ThreadContext` as the request completes. The pattern discussed previously then prints these properties with `%X{id}` and `%X{username}`. Because the filter supports multiple dispatcher types and may execute multiple times in a single request, it only sets the fish tag and username properties if they have not already been set, and it only clears the `ThreadContext` for the same invocation that set the fish tag and username properties:

```
@WebFilter(urlPatterns = "/*", dispatcherTypes = {
        DispatcherType.REQUEST, DispatcherType.ERROR, DispatcherType.FORWARD,
        DispatcherType.INCLUDE, DispatcherType.ASYNC
})
public class LoggingFilter implements Filter
{
    @Override
    public void doFilter(ServletRequest request, ServletResponse response,
                         FilterChain chain) throws IOException, ServletException {
        boolean clear = false;
        if(!ThreadContext.containsKey("id")) {
            clear = true;
            ThreadContext.put("id", UUID.randomUUID().toString());
            HttpSession session = ((HttpServletRequest)request).getSession(false);
            if(session != null)
                ThreadContext.put("username",
                        (String)session.getAttribute("username"));
        }

        try {
            chain.doFilter(request, response);
        } finally {
            if(clear)
                ThreadContext.clear();
        }
    }

    ...
}
```

> **WARNING** *Recall the lessons you learned in Chapter 9 about asynchronous request handling. If you set values on the* `ThreadContext` *at the beginning of an asynchronous request, those values will be cleared before the request completes. For this reason, you must be very careful whenever you use the* `ThreadContext` *with asynchronous requests. The Web Applications and JSPs section of the Log4j 2 manual online includes helpful information about using all aspects of Log4j with asynchronous contexts.*

## Writing Logging Statements in Java Code

Using Log4j 2 `Logger` instances is extremely straightforward. Overloaded methods exist for each of the logging `Levels`, and these enable you to specify `Strings`, `Objects`, or `Messages` as messages, provide one or more parameters to substitute in a `String` message, provide `Throwables` whose stack traces should be logged, and provide `Markers` to flag an event. Take a look at Listing 11-1, which uses a `Logger` to log activity in the `ActionServlet`. A singleton `Logger` is created for all instances of the Servlet. Then methods like `info`, `warn`, and `error` write log messages. The special methods `entry` and `exit` log at the `TRACE` level and are shorthand for tracing program execution through method calls and returns. Many more methods are available on this `Logger` interface, and you should read its API documentation available at `http://logging.apache.org/log4j/2.x/javadoc.html` to learn more.

> **NOTE** `LogManager`*'s no-argument* `getLogger` *method returns a* `Logger` *whose name is equal to the fully-qualified class name of the class calling* `getLogger`*. In the case of Listing 11-1, that name is* `com.wrox.ActionServlet`*. You could also use the* `getLogger` *method that accepts a* `Class` *argument, which would return a* `Logger` *named after that* `Class`*. If you want to use something other than class names as* `Logger` *names, you could use the* `getLogger` *method that accepts a* `String` *argument — the name of the* `Logger`*.*

**LISTING 11-1: ActionServlet.java**

```
@WebServlet(name = "actionServlet", urlPatterns = "/files")
public class ActionServlet extends HttpServlet
{
    private static final Logger log = LogManager.getLogger();

    @Override
    protected void doGet(HttpServletRequest request, HttpServletResponse response)
            throws ServletException, IOException {
        String action = request.getParameter("action");
        if(action != null) {
            log.info("Received request with action {}.", action);
            String contents = null;
            switch(action) {
```

*continues*

**LISTING 11-1** *(continued)*

```
                case "readFoo":
                    contents = this.readFile("../foo.bar", true);
                    break;
                case "readLicense":
                    contents = this.readFile("../LICENSE", false);
                    break;
                default:
                    contents = "Bad action " + action + " specified.";
                    log.warn("Action {} not supported.", action);
            }
            if(contents != null)
                response.getWriter().write(contents);
        } else {
            log.error("No action specified.");
            response.getWriter().write("No action specified.");
        }
    }

    protected String readFile(String fileName, boolean deleteWhenDone) {
        log.entry(fileName, deleteWhenDone);

        try {
            byte[] data = Files.readAllBytes(new File(fileName).toPath());
            log.info("Successfully read file {}.", fileName);
            return log.exit(new String(data));
        } catch(IOException e) {
            log.error(MarkerManager.getMarker("WROX_CONSOLE"),
                    "Failed to read file {}.", fileName, e);
            return null;
        }
    }
}
```

Now compile and start up the application and go to `http://localhost:8080/logging-integration/files` in your browser. The `application.log` file should appear in the Tomcat logs directory and have an error in it. Adding `?action=badAction` to the URL and reloading the log file reveals a new informational message and warning in the file. Changing the action to `readLicense` reads the Tomcat license file back to the browser. Only informational messages appear in the log this time. Finally, change the action to `readFoo` and an error, complete with exception stack trace, appears in the log file. This time the error also appeared in the console (debugger) output because it included the `Marker` named `WROX_CONSOLE`. Notice the fish tag for each message logged and how it is the same for multiple messages logged in the same request. You should experiment with the Log4j configuration file and change the `level` and `additivity` attributes to see how the data logged changes.

> **NOTE** *The relative file name used to access the Tomcat license file only works if your IDE starts Tomcat from Tomcat's* `bin` *directory, which is typical. If your IDE starts Tomcat from some other directory, you may need to change the path to this file to get it to work.*

## Using the Log Tag Library in JSPs

As mentioned earlier, Log4j 2 comes with a tag library that enables you to log messages in JSPs without using scripting. This book won't go into a lot of detail on this subject because, generally speaking, there is much less need for logging in the presentation layer. In fact, as long as your JSPs don't have any business logic in them, you'll never need to log in them. With that said, you can include the tag library with the following `taglib` directive:

```
<%@ taglib prefix="log" uri="http://logging.apache.org/log4j/tld/log" %>
```

The Logging-Integration project has a `logging.jsp` file in the web root that demonstrates how to use these logging tags:

```
<log:entry />
<!DOCTYPE html>
<html>
    <head>
        <title>Test Logging</title>
    </head>
    <body>
        <log:info message="JSP body displaying." />
        Messages have been logged.
        <log:info>JSP body complete.</log:info>
    </body>
</html>
<log:exit />
```

Each JSP in your application that uses one or more `log` tags automatically has a unique `Logger` created for it. You can override this `Logger` using the `<log:setLogger>` tag or the logger attribute on most of the other tags. Try out the JSP logging by starting the application and going to `http://localhost:8080/logging-integration/logging.jsp` in your browser. Depending on the logging level you have configured, you see different messages appear in the log.

## Logging in the Customer Support Application

The Customer-Support-v9 project on the `wrox.com` code download site has had all uses of `System.out`, `System.err`, and `Throwable.printStackTrace()` removed from its code and replaced with Log4j 2 logging. In addition, more logging statements were added throughout the application. Finally, the `LoggingFilter` was copied from the previous example and added to the beginning of the filter chain in the `Configurator` so that all requests are fish tagged.

You should download and review these changes, but they are not detailed here because it's redundant to what you've already learned. The default logging level for all `Loggers` in the `com.wrox` hierarchy is set to `INFO` and the only `INFO` event so far is when a user logs in. Most other logging events are `DEBUG`, `TRACE`, `WARN`, or `ERROR`. Because of this, you won't see much in the `support.log` file when you run the Customer Support application. Rest assured, this will change in Part II when you start using Spring Framework.

## SUMMARY

In this chapter you learned the fundamentals of application logging and why logging in your applications is so important. You investigated several common logging patterns and explored the concepts of categories and logging levels. You also learned about the importance of separating a logging API from its underlying implementation, saving you headaches down the road. You were introduced to several popular logging APIs and implementations, such as Apache Commons Logging, SLF4J, Logback, Log4j 1.x, and Log4j 2. Finally, you learned details for using and configuring Log4j 2 and experimented with integrating it into a web application. Throughout the rest of the book, logging is quietly present in every chapter. Each project you work on contains a Log4j 2 configuration and logging statements. This way, you can get into the habit of consistently logging whenever you program.

This wraps up Part I, where you learned about various aspects of web application development using Java SE, Java EE, Servlets, JSPs, filters, WebSockets, application servers, web containers, and more. By now, you should have a firm grasp on the basics, and you should be able to write fairly complex applications. In Part II you start growing your enterprise development skillset as you learn about Spring Framework and how it supplements, enhances, and — in some cases — supplants parts of the Java Platform, Enterprise Edition.

# PART II
# Adding Spring Framework Into the Mix

# 12

# Introducing Spring Framework

## IN THIS CHAPTER

- Understanding Spring Framework
- The benefits of Spring Framework
- What are application contexts?
- How to bootstrap Spring Framework
- How to configure Spring Framework
- How to use Bean Definition Profiles

## WROX.COM CODE DOWNLOADS FOR THIS CHAPTER

You can find the `wrox.com` code downloads for this chapter at `http://www.wrox.com/go/projavaforwebapps` on the Download Code tab. The code for this chapter is divided into the following major examples:

- Spring-One-Context-XML-Config Project
- Spring-XML-Config Project
- Spring-Hybrid-Config Project
- Spring-Java-Config Project

## NEW MAVEN DEPENDENCIES FOR THIS CHAPTER

In addition to the Maven dependencies introduced in previous chapters, you also need the following Maven dependencies:

```
<dependency>
    <groupId>javax.inject</groupId>
    <artifactId>javax.inject</artifactId>
```

```
        <version>1</version>
        <scope>compile</scope>
    </dependency>

    <dependency>
        <groupId>javax.annotation</groupId>
        <artifactId>javax.annotation-api</artifactId>
        <version>1.2</version>
        <scope>runtime</scope>
    </dependency>

    <dependency>
        <groupId>org.springframework</groupId>
        <artifactId>spring-webmvc</artifactId>
        <version>4.0.0.RELEASE</version>
        <scope>compile</scope>
    </dependency>
```

## WHAT IS SPRING FRAMEWORK?

Spring Framework is an application container for Java that supplies many useful features, such as Inversion of Control, Dependency Injection, abstract data access, transaction management, and more. It was conceived in 2002 in response to industry complaints that the Java EE specification was sorely lacking and very difficult to use. Its first major release in 2004 was a game changer for Java EE applications and was followed by 2.0 in 2006, 2.5 in 2007, 3.0 in 2009, 3.1 in 2011, and 3.2 in 2012. Released in December 2013, the latest major version, Spring Framework 4.0, contains many enhancements, including support for Java SE 8, Java EE 7, WebSockets, and Groovy 2.

Though Spring Framework rose from the Enterprise Edition world, it is by no means strictly restricted to an EE environment. Often considered an alternative to or supplement for Enterprise JavaBeans (EJB, a Java EE server-side component for building enterprise applications in a modular fashion using encapsulated Beans), the Spring Framework container can run in any Java EE Application Server, Java EE Web Container, or Java SE standalone application (including server daemons and desktop applications).

EJB, on the other hand, is an Application Server-specific framework not found in desktop applications or even Web Containers such as Apache Tomcat and Jetty. Spring Framework is more than just a replacement for EJB, however; it provides many features that to this day Java EE still does not have replacements for. Over the years, Spring has evolved from a framework to a community, spawning many related projects such as Spring Security (which you learn about in Part IV of this book), Spring Data (which you learn about in Part III), Spring Integration, Spring Batch, Spring Mobile, Spring for Android, Spring Social, Spring Boot, and Spring.NET (the C# .NET port of Spring Framework), just to name a few.

To be sure, Spring Framework is not a requirement to develop rich Java web applications. You can create full-featured web applications with everything you have learned in this book up to this point. Spring Framework is a productivity framework: It makes developing applications of all types in a rapid way with modular concepts and testable code *easier*. It abstracts away the concepts of "requests" and "responses" and enables you to write application code that can be utilized from many different interfaces. *When used properly, Spring Framework is the most powerful tool in your Java development toolbox.*

## Inversion of Control and Dependency Injection

One of Spring Framework's core features is support for the closely related concepts of *Inversion of Control* (*IoC*) and *Dependency Injection* (*DI*). IoC is a software design pattern whereby an *assembler*, in this case Spring Framework, binds object coupling at run time instead of compile time. When some component of program logic, Service A for example, depends on another component of program logic, Service B, that dependency is fulfilled when the application runs instead of Service A instantiating Service B directly (which would be bound at compile time). This enables application developers to program against a set of interfaces, which can be swapped out in different environments without recompiling the code. One place this is handy is in a testing environment: "Mock" or "test" services can be provided while running unit tests; then the same code can be deployed to a production environment with more "real" services.

Though this can theoretically be achieved in any number of ways, DI is the most common technique. Using DI, a piece of program code (in Spring Framework, a class) declares that it depends on another piece of program code (an interface), and at run time the assembler injects an instance (usually but not always a singleton) of that dependency.

## Aspect-Oriented Programming

Because Spring Framework handles the instantiation and injection of dependencies, it can wrap instances of the dependencies it injects to decorate method calls with other behavior. For example, using Spring Security you can annotate methods to indicate security restrictions placed on those methods, and Spring Framework wraps those method calls with the security checks necessary to fulfill those security restrictions. You can also define your own *cross-cutting concerns* using *aspects*, and Spring Framework decorates all the appropriate methods with these concerns. Cross-cutting concerns are concerns (such as security concerns) that affect multiple components of a program, often without regard to what those components are. *Aspect-oriented programming* is a complement to object-oriented programming that enables application of these concerns through the definition of aspects, which specify how and when to apply the concerns. Spring Framework provides extensive tools for aspect-oriented programming, which you will learn about throughout the rest of the book.

## Data Access and Transaction Management

Spring Framework provides a set of data access tools that simplify the extraction and persistence of Java objects in relational databases. Though these features make unit testing data access drastically easier, some vendor-specify SQL is still required. Spring Framework also provides extensive support for the Java Persistence API (JPA) and object-relational mappers such as Hibernate ORM, which you explore in Part III of this book. Through the Spring Data project, persisting objects in relational databases, and NoSQL databases such as MongoDB and Redis, becomes a simple task. Finally, Spring Framework supports a declarative transactional model whereby execution of an annotated method is wrapped within a transaction and rolled back if the method throws an exception. This is achieved using Spring Framework's AOP support.

## Application Messaging

In any application, messaging is an important concern that needs addressing. For example, certain parts of a program may need to know when another part of the program performs a specified action. The part of the program performing this action could simply depend on the parts interested in the action and call methods on all of them to notify them, but that type of tight coupling is hard to maintain and can get very messy quickly.

Spring Framework provides a loosely coupled messaging system that uses the *publish-subscribe* pattern: Components in a system announce that they are interested in certain messages by subscribing to them, and the producers of these messages publish the messages without caring who is subscribed. This is essentially how Twitter works: People who have interesting (or perhaps noninteresting) things to say tweet those things, and other people who are interested in those types of tweets follow them. Using Spring Framework, a Spring-managed bean subscribes to a particular message type by implementing a generic interface, and other Spring-managed objects publish those messages to Spring Framework, which delivers them to the subscribed parties. This system can be extended and configured to deliver messages across a cluster of applications as well.

## Model-View-Controller Pattern for Web Applications

Spring Framework features a *model-view-controller* (*MVC*) pattern framework that simplifies the process of creating interactive web applications. Instead of manually dealing with the complexities of Servlets, `HttpServletRequests`, `HttpServletResponses`, and forwarding to JSPs, Spring handles these tasks for you. Each method in a controller class is mapped to a different request URL, method, or other property of a request. The model is passed from the controller to the view in the form of a `Map<String, Object>`. The `View` or view name (`String`) returned from the controller method causes Spring to forward to the appropriate JSP view. Request and URL path parameters are automatically converted to primitive or complex controller method arguments.

In addition to typical HTML views, Spring can automatically generate plain text views and file download views and XML or JSON entity views. Through all these features, Spring Framework greatly simplifies working in a Servlet container.

# WHY SPRING FRAMEWORK?

In previous sections, you have learned about many of the features Spring Framework offers, so you may already understand some of the compelling reasons for using Spring Framework in your applications. Its feature set and simplification of the Servlet API are not the only advantages of Spring Framework. The patterns it encourages, which you learn more about throughout this part of the book, provide several benefits that you can undoubtedly appreciate as you strive to create powerful web applications.

## Logical Code Groupings

Consider some of the more complex Servlets you have created in previous chapters of this book. Each had a single `doGet` or `doPost` method, or perhaps both, containing many `if` statements or `switch` blocks responsible for routing the request to any number of methods within the Servlet. In a significantly more complicated enterprise application, you would quickly find this pattern becoming unmanageable and extremely difficult to test. A Servlet handling user profiles, for example, could have dozens of methods, each with a different route logic established in the `doGet` or `doPost` method.

A possible solution might be to create dozens of Servlets instead. Although this would result in a more testable and maintainable code base, the number of Servlets could quickly become as unmanageable as the number of logic branches were previously. If your application contains hundreds of features, each with dozens of pages, you would quickly realize a code base ballooning to thousands of tiny Servlets, which, to many developers, is equally unwanted. If your Servlets could be mapped down to the individual method level instead of only at the class, many problems would be solved.

Using Spring's Web MVC framework, a controller class acts very much like a Servlet with method-level mappings. Each method can have a distinct mapping to a particular URL, request method, parameter existence, header value, content type, and/or expected response type. While your unit tests focus on testing the small units of code that are your controller methods, controller classes can contain many mapped methods that are logically grouped together. Returning to the user profile example, the controller could have dozens of mapped methods representing the different actions that can be taken on user profiles, but no `doGet` or `doPost` method is necessary to route requests to the proper methods. Spring Framework handles all of this analysis and routing for you.

### Multiple User Interfaces Utilizing One Code Base

In a real-world scenario, you may be asked to create an advanced application with thousands of features that should be accessible from desktop applications, web browsers, mobile web browsers, RESTful web services, and SOAP web services. Using only Servlets, this task would quickly become daunting. You would eventually end up duplicating a lot of code or creating your own system in which business logic was abstracted into a set of other classes used from many user interfaces.

Fortunately, Spring Framework provides just such a system, tested and ready for you to use with very little effort. Using Spring, business logic becomes encapsulated in a set of business objects called services. These services perform operations common to all user interfaces, such as ensuring that certain entity properties are properly specified. Your application contains a different set of controllers and views for each user interface, and these use the common business objects to perform critical operations. Controllers, then, are necessary to perform only user interface-specific operations, such as translating form submissions or JSON request bodies into entities and displaying the appropriate view to the user. Unit testing becomes easier, code is reused, and very little effort is necessary to achieve both.

## UNDERSTANDING APPLICATION CONTEXTS

The Spring Framework container comes in the form of one or more *application contexts*, represented by the `org.springframework.context.ApplicationContext` interface. An application context manages a set of *beans*, Java objects that perform business logic, execute tasks, persist and retrieve persisted data, respond to HTTP requests, and more. Spring-managed beans are automatically eligible for dependency injection, message notification, scheduled method execution, bean validation, and other crucial Spring services.

A Spring application always has at least one application context, and sometimes that's all it needs. However, it can also have a hierarchy of multiple application contexts. In such a hierarchy, any Spring-managed beans have access to beans in the same application context, in the parent application context, in the parent's parent application context, and so forth. They do not have access to beans in sibling or child application contexts. This is useful for defining a set of shared application components while isolating other application components from each other. For example, you may want the user and administrative sections of a web application to have no access to each other, but undoubtedly you'll have some shared resources that both sections need.

> **NOTE** *You work with Spring Framework extensively throughout the rest of the book, and you should keep the API documentation handy at all times. Be sure to bookmark the documentation at* `http://docs.spring.io/spring/docs/4.0.x/javadoc-api/` *so that you can reference it whenever you want to know more about a Spring interface, class, annotation, enum, or exception.*

There are a number of interfaces that extend and classes that implement `ApplicationContext`:

- The `ConfigurableApplicationContext` interface is, as the name implies, configurable, whereas the base `ApplicationContext` is only readable.
- The `org.springframework.web.context.WebApplicationContext` and `ConfigurableWebApplicationContext` interfaces are intended for Java EE web applications running in Servlet containers and provide access to the underlying `ServletContext` and, if applicable, `ServletConfig`.
- The concrete classes `ClassPathXmlApplicationContext` and `FileSystemXmlApplicationContext` are designed to load the Spring configuration from XML files in a standalone application, whereas the `XmlWebApplicationContext` achieves the same within Java EE web applications.
- For programmatically configuring Spring using Java instead of XML, the `AnnotationConfigApplicationContext` and `AnnotationConfigWebApplicationContext` classes work in standalone and Java EE web applications, respectively.

In Java EE web applications, Spring handles web requests using a *dispatcher Servlet*, which delegates incoming requests to the appropriate controllers and translates request and response entities as needed. Your web application can have as many instances of the `org.springframework.web.servlet.DispatcherServlet` class as makes sense for your use case.

Each `DispatcherServlet` instance gets its own application context, which has references to the web application's `ServletContext` and its own `ServletConfig`. You might create multiple `DispatcherServlets`, for example, to separate your web user interface from your web services. Because none of these `DispatcherServlets` can access the application context for any other `DispatcherServlets`, it is often desirable to share certain beans (such as business objects or data access objects) in a common root application context. This application context, global to the entire web application, is the parent of all the `DispatcherServlets`' application contexts and is created using the `org.springframework.web.context.ContextLoaderListener`. It, too, has a reference to the web application's `ServletContext`, but because it does not belong to any particular Servlet, it does not have a `ServletConfig` reference.

Although the idea of having multiple `DispatcherServlets` is commonplace in web applications and is used throughout this book, it is only one configuration of infinite possibilities. In any standalone or web application, you can create whatever application context hierarchy your needs justify. As a general rule, you should always have one root application context from which all other application contexts inherit in one way or another, as shown in Figure 12-1.

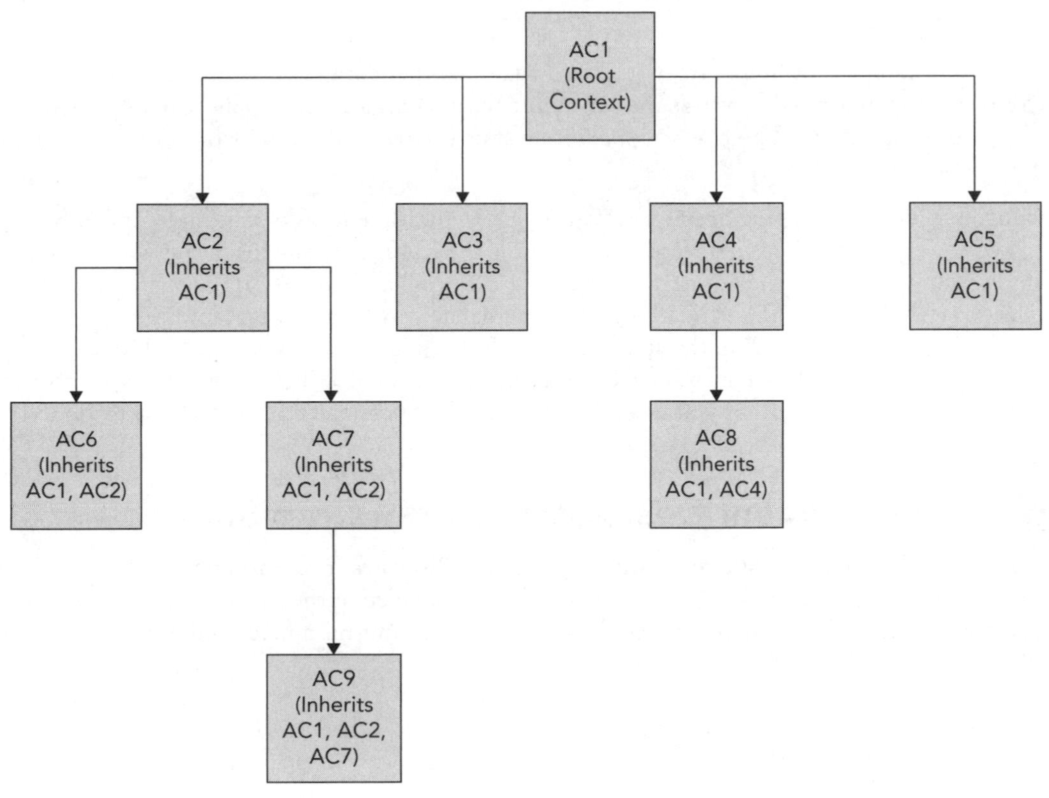


**FIGURE 12-1**

# BOOTSTRAPPING SPRING FRAMEWORK

In the world of computer software, everything must get bootstrapped at some point or another. Consider your desktop, notebook, or mobile computing device: When it turns on, a bootstrap device of some type (typically a BIOS or similar) initializes all the hardware, loads startup instructions from some location (such as the boot sector on a hard drive), and starts the operating system. In this sense, the hardware is a container for the operating system. The operating system is another container — for the software that runs within it.

C programs have a standardized bootstrap mechanism: the `main()` method. All runnable C programs must contain this method to be bootstrapped. A Java Virtual Machine executable, which typically is written in C or C++, contains this `main()` method (or the equivalent for the language it is written in). Language virtual machines, such as the JVM or the .NET Runtime, are containers for other software. For Java applications, instructions in the application manifest file (or provided at the command line) bootstrap the Java application by providing the name of a class with a `public static void main(String...)` method. Tomcat, like any other Java application, has a `public static void main(String...)` method, but Tomcat is yet again another container — a Servlet container for running Java EE web applications. These web applications contain a form of bootstrap instructions: deployment descriptors or meta-information in the form of annotations that instruct Tomcat how to run them.

Like all these examples, Spring Framework is yet again another container. It can run within any Java SE or EE container and serves as the run-time environment for your application. Also like all these examples, Spring must be bootstrapped: It must be started and given instructions for how to run the application it contains.

Configuring and bootstrapping Spring Framework are two different tasks that, independently of each other, can be handled in different ways. While the configuration tells Spring how to run the application it contains, the bootstrap process starts Spring and passes off the configuration instructions to it. In a Java SE application, there is only one way to bootstrap Spring: programmatically, usually within the application's `public static void main(String...)` method. In a Java EE application, you have two choices: You can use the deployment descriptor to bootstrap Spring using XML, or you can programmatically bootstrap Spring within a `javax.servlet.ServletContainerInitializer`.

## Using the Deployment Descriptor to Bootstrap Spring

In traditional Spring Framework applications, you always bootstrapped Spring in the Java EE deployment descriptor. At the very least, this requires an instance of the `DispatcherServlet` given a configuration file in the form of a `contextConfigLocation` init parameter and instructed to load on startup.

```
<servlet>
    <servlet-name>springDispatcher</servlet-name>
    <servlet-class>org.springframework.web.servlet.DispatcherServlet
</servlet-class>
    <init-param>
        <param-name>contextConfigLocation</param-name>
        <param-value>/WEB-INF/servletContext.xml</param-value>
    </init-param>
    <load-on-startup>1</load-on-startup>
</servlet>
<servlet-mapping>
    <servlet-name>springDispatcher</servlet-name>
    <url-pattern>/</url-pattern>
</servlet-mapping>
```

This creates a single Spring application context within the setting of the `DispatcherServlet` and instructs the Servlet container to initialize the `DispatcherServlet` at startup. When initialized, the `DispatcherServlet` loads the context configuration from the `/WEB-INF/servletContext.xml` file and starts the application context. Of course, this creates only one application context for your application, which, as previously explained, is not very flexible. A more complete descriptor bootstrap would look more like this:

```
        <context-param>
            <param-name>contextConfigLocation</param-name>
            <param-value>/WEB-INF/rootContext.xml</param-value>
        </context-param>
        <listener>
            <listener-class>org.springframework.web.context.ContextLoaderListener
    </listener-class>
        </listener>

        <servlet>
            <servlet-name>springDispatcher</servlet-name>
            <servlet-class>org.springframework.web.servlet.DispatcherServlet
    </servlet-class>
            <init-param>
                <param-name>contextConfigLocation</param-name>
                <param-value>/WEB-INF/servletContext.xml</param-value>
            </init-param>
            <load-on-startup>1</load-on-startup>
        </servlet>
        <servlet-mapping>
            <servlet-name>springDispatcher</servlet-name>
            <url-pattern>/</url-pattern>
        </servlet-mapping>
```

The `ContextLoaderListener` is initialized when the web application first starts (because it implements `ServletContextListener`, it initializes before any Servlets), loads the root application context configuration from the `/WEB-INF/rootContext.xml` file specified in the `contextConfigLocation` context init parameter, and starts the root application context.

Note that the `contextConfigLocation` context init parameter is different from the `contextConfigLocation` Servlet init parameter for the `DispatcherServlet`. They do not conflict; the former applies to the entire Servlet context and the latter applies only to the particular Servlet for which it is specified. The root application context created by the listener is automatically set as the parent context for any application contexts created by `DispatcherServlets`.

Although there can be only one root application context of this nature in a web application, there can be as many Servlet application contexts as you can find uses for. In Chapter 17, you can see an example of this when you create a second `DispatcherServlet` for RESTful web services. You can also arbitrarily create other application contexts if needed, though that is typically not applicable in a web application.

Of course, these bootstrap examples have assumed that you are configuring Spring using XML files, which you explore in the "Configuring Spring Framework" section of this chapter. You can also configure Spring with Java instead of XML (also covered in the later section), and bootstrapping a Java configuration from the deployment descriptor is very much the same:

```
        <context-param>
            <param-name>contextClass</param-name>
            <param-value>org.springframework.web.context.support.
```

```
AnnotationConfigWebApplicationContext</param-value>
    </context-param>
    <context-param>
        <param-name>contextConfigLocation</param-name>
        <param-value>com.wrox.config.RootContextConfiguration</param-value>
    </context-param>
    <listener>
        <listener-class>org.springframework.web.context.ContextLoaderListener
</listener-class>
    </listener>

    <servlet>
        <servlet-name>springDispatcher</servlet-name>
        <servlet-class>org.springframework.web.servlet.DispatcherServlet
</servlet-class>
        <init-param>
            <param-name>contextClass</param-name>
            <param-value>org.springframework.web.context.support.
AnnotationConfigWebApplicationContext</param-value>
        </init-param>
        <init-param>
            <param-name>contextConfigLocation</param-name>
            <param-value>com.wrox.config.ServletContextConfiguration
</param-value>
        </init-param>
        <load-on-startup>1</load-on-startup>
    </servlet>
    <servlet-mapping>
        <servlet-name>springDispatcher</servlet-name>
        <url-pattern>/</url-pattern>
    </servlet-mapping>
```

Normally the `ContextLoaderListener` and `DispatcherServlet` create instances of `org.springframework.web.context.support.XmlWebApplicationContext`, which expect Spring's configuration to come in the form of an XML file. The previous example overrides this behavior and uses the `AnnotationConfigWebApplicationContext` instead. This context type expects programmatic context configurations, specified as class names (instead of file names) in the `contextConfigLocation` parameters.

## Programmatically Bootstrapping Spring in an Initializer

Recall that in previous chapters you used a `ServletContextListener` to programmatically configure the Servlets and filters in your application. The downside of using this interface is that the listener's `contextInitialized` method may be called after other listeners. Java EE 6 added a new interface called `ServletContainerInitializer`. Classes implementing `ServletContainerInitializer` have their `onStartup` method called when the application first starts, before any listeners are notified. This is the earliest possible point in the life cycle of the application. You do not configure `ServletContainerInitializers` in the deployment descriptor; instead, you use Java's service provider system to declare a class or classes that implement `ServletContainerInitializer` by listing them, one on each line, in a file named `/META-INF/services/javax.servlet.ServletContainerInitializer`. For example, the following file contents list two classes that implement `ServletContainerInitializer`:

```
com.wrox.config.ContainerInitializerOne
com.wrox.config.ContainerInitializerTwo
```

The downside is that this file cannot exist directly within your application's WAR file or exploded directory — you cannot place the file in your web application's `/META-INF/services` directory. It must be within the `/META-INF/services` directory *of a JAR file included in your application's* `/WEB-INF/lib` *directory.*

Spring Framework provides a bridge interface that makes this much simpler to achieve. The `org.springframework.web.SpringServletContainerInitializer` class implements `ServletContainerInitializer`, and because the JAR containing this class includes a service provider file listing the class's name, its `onStartup` method is called when your application starts up. This class then scans your application for implementations of the `org.springframework.web.WebApplicationInitializer` interface and calls the `onStartup` method of any matching classes it finds. Within a `WebApplicationInitializer` implementation class, you can programmatically configure listeners, Servlets, filters, and more, all without writing a single line of XML. More important, you can bootstrap Spring from within this class.

```
public class Bootstrap implements WebApplicationInitializer
{
    @Override
    public void onStartup(ServletContext container)
    {
        XmlWebApplicationContext rootContext = new XmlWebApplicationContext();
        rootContext.setConfigLocation("/WEB-INF/rootContext.xml");
        container.addListener(new ContextLoaderListener(rootContext));

        XmlWebApplicationContext servletContext = new XmlWebApplicationContext();
        servletContext.setConfigLocation("/WEB-INF/servletContext.xml");
        ServletRegistration.Dynamic dispatcher = container.addServlet(
            "springDispatcher", new DispatcherServlet(servletContext)
        );
        dispatcher.setLoadOnStartup(1);
        dispatcher.addMapping("/");
    }
}
```

This bootstrap is the functional equivalent of the previous deployment descriptor bootstrap that used the Spring XML configuration. The following bootstrap instead uses the Spring Java configuration for a pure Java bootstrap and configuration process.

```
public class Bootstrap implements WebApplicationInitializer
{
    @Override
    public void onStartup(ServletContext container)
    {
        AnnotationConfigWebApplicationContext rootContext =
            new AnnotationConfigWebApplicationContext();
        rootContext.register(com.wrox.config.RootContextConfiguration.class);
        container.addListener(new ContextLoaderListener(rootContext));

        AnnotationConfigWebApplicationContext servletContext =
            new AnnotationConfigWebApplicationContext();
```

```
        servletContext.register(com.wrox.config.ServletContextConfiguration
.class);
        ServletRegistration.Dynamic dispatcher = container.addServlet(
            "springDispatcher", new DispatcherServlet(servletContext)
        );
        dispatcher.setLoadOnStartup(1);
        dispatcher.addMapping("/");
    }
}
```

Of course, you do not have to configure all your application contexts the same way. You can mix and match configuration methods used during the bootstrap process. The following example demonstrates this and also demonstrates how to bootstrap Spring in a standalone application, such as a desktop application or server daemon.

```
public class Bootstrap
{
    public static void main(String... arguments)
    {
        ClassPathXmlApplicationContext rootContext =
            new ClassPathXmlApplicationContext("com/wrox/config/rootContext.xml");

        FileSystemXmlApplicationContext daemonContext =
            new FileSystemXmlApplicationContext(
                new String[] {"file:/path/to/daemonContext.xml"}, rootContext
            );

        AnnotationConfigApplicationContext forkedProcessContext =
            new AnnotationConfigApplicationContext(
                com.wrox.config.ProcessContextConfiguration.class
            );
        forkedProcessContext.setParent(rootContext);

        rootContext.start();
        rootContext.registerShutdownHook();
        daemonContext.start();
        daemonContext.registerShutdownHook();
        forkedProcessContext.start();
        forkedProcessContext.registerShutdownHook();
    }
}
```

Notice the extra effort required to assign the `rootContext` as the parent context for the `daemonContext` and `forkedProcessContext`, and to call the `start` and `registerShutdownHook` methods. In a web application, the `ContextLoaderListener` and `DispatcherServlet` automatically configure the parent application contexts and call their `start` methods on application startup and their `stop` methods on application shutdown. In a standalone application, you must call the `start` method yourself, and then you must call `stop` when your application is shutting down. As an alternative to manually calling `stop`, you can call `registerShutdownHook` to register a shutdown callback with the JVM that will stop the application context automatically when the JVM begins to exit.

## THE DISPATCHER SERVLET MAPPING

The examples you have seen so far, and will continue to see throughout this book, show the `DispatcherServlet` mapped to the URL pattern `/`. Over the years, there has been much confusion about mapping the `DispatcherServlet` to the root of the application URL, and it's easy to find incorrect or incomplete information about it on forums, blogs, and other technical sites.

You can map the `DispatcherServlet` to just about any URL pattern you want. Some common approaches are to map it to the URL patterns `/do/*`, `*.do`, or `*.action`, and some sites use a `*.html` mapping to make pages appear more static than they are. There are some important things to note, however. Most important, don't map a `DispatcherServlet` to the URL pattern `/*`. In most cases the URL pattern must either start with or end with an asterisk, but when mapping to the application root, the lone forward slash *without an asterisk* is sufficient to get the Servlet to respond to all URLs in your application and while still enabling the Servlet container's JSP mechanism to handle JSP requests. A trailing asterisk causes the Servlet container to send even internal JSP requests to that Servlet, which is not desirable. (This is because the container maps its JSP handler Servlet after your Servlets have been mapped, giving it lower precedence.)

If you plan to map the `DispatcherServlet` to the application root, make sure you account for static resources such as HTML pages, CSS and JavaScript files, and images. Some online tutorials demonstrate how to set up Spring Framework to serve static resources, but doing so is not necessary and does not perform well. When any Servlet is mapped to the application root (without an asterisk), more-specific URL patterns always override it. So permitting your Servlet container to serve static resources is as simple as adding mappings for those resources to the Servlet named `default` (which all containers provide automatically). This can be accomplished in the deployment descriptor like so:

```
<servlet-mapping>
    <servlet-name>default</servlet-name>
    <url-pattern>/resources/*</url-pattern>
    <url-pattern>*.css</url-pattern>
    <url-pattern>*.js</url-pattern>
    <url-pattern>*.png</url-pattern>
    <url-pattern>*.gif</url-pattern>
    <url-pattern>*.jpg</url-pattern>
</servlet-mapping>
```

Or programmatically in a `ServletContainerInitializer` (`WebApplicationInitializer`) or `ServletContextListener` like so:

```
servletContext.getServletRegistration("default").addMapping(
    "/resources/*", "*.css", "*.js", "*.png", "*.gif", "*.jpg"
);
```

*continues*

*continued*

The default Servlet does not have to be declared. The Servlet container implicitly declares it on your behalf. The URL patterns shown here are examples—only you can decide where you want to put your static resources and, thus, which URL patterns are appropriate.

## CONFIGURING SPRING FRAMEWORK

Now that you know how to bootstrap Spring Framework, you are ready to learn about configuring it. The remainder of this chapter continues to use both XML and programmatic bootstrapping for its examples, but all future chapters in this book use only programmatic bootstrapping. As you have already seen, you can configure a Spring application context using either XML or Java. Not only can you configure different application contexts in a single application differently, you also can configure a single application context with a mixture of Java and XML. This is an uncommon scenario in modern applications, but it is required in some cases. For example, the Java configuration added in Spring Security 3.2 does not cover every configuration scenario, so for some examples in Part IV of this book you must use Spring Security's XML configuration instead. Also, the Spring Web Services tools you learn about in Chapter 17 have no support for Java configuration at all. When configuring an application context that uses these tools, you can configure the application context using Java but import an XML configuration for Spring Security or Spring Web Services. In this chapter, you learn about all these things.

This section utilizes the Spring-One-Context-XML-Config, Spring-XML-Config, Spring-Hybrid-Config, and Spring-Java-Config projects on the `wrox.com` code download site. You can refer to these projects throughout this section or create the code on your own. For starters, all four projects have the same basic deployment descriptor code you're used to seeing from Part I. You'll continue to use this template deployment descriptor throughout the rest of the book:

```
<display-name>Spring Application</display-name>

<jsp-config>
    <jsp-property-group>
        <url-pattern>*.jsp</url-pattern>
        <url-pattern>*.jspf</url-pattern>
        <page-encoding>UTF-8</page-encoding>
        <scripting-invalid>true</scripting-invalid>
        <include-prelude>/WEB-INF/jsp/base.jspf</include-prelude>
        <trim-directive-whitespaces>true</trim-directive-whitespaces>
        <default-content-type>text/html</default-content-type>
    </jsp-property-group>
</jsp-config>

<session-config>
    <session-timeout>30</session-timeout>
    <cookie-config>
        <http-only>true</http-only>
```

```
        </cookie-config>
        <tracking-mode>COOKIE</tracking-mode>
    </session-config>

    <distributable />
```

You should also update `log4j2.xml` to make sure that all appropriate messages end up in your logs. In the following example all messages get written to the console and to the log file, and although most messages are limited to warnings, classes in the `com.wrox`, `org.apache`, and `org.springframework` packages log at the `INFO` level.

```
        <root level="warn">
            <appender-ref ref="Console" />
            <appender-ref ref="WroxFileAppender" />
        </root>
        <logger name="com.wrox" level="info" />
        <logger name="org.apache" level="info" />
        <logger name="org.springframework" level="info" />
```

All four projects also include the very basic `GreetingService` interface and its `GreetingServiceImpl` implementation.

```
public class GreetingServiceImpl implements GreetingService
{
    @Override
    public String getGreeting(String name)
    {
        return "Hello, " + name + "!";
    }
}
```

The `HelloController` that follows responds to web requests in all four projects. You do not need to be concerned with the semantics of these classes, the annotations in the controller, or the controller-service pattern at this time. You'll learn about these things soon, but right now you should remember that with four identical base projects, you can configure Spring Framework many different ways and achieve the same ends.

```
@Controller
public class HelloController
{
    private GreetingService greetingService;

    @ResponseBody
    @RequestMapping("/")
    public String helloWorld()
    {
        return "Hello, World!";
    }

    @ResponseBody
    @RequestMapping("/custom")
    public String helloName(@RequestParam("name") String name)
    {
        return this.greetingService.getGreeting(name);
```

```
    }

    public void setGreetingService(GreetingService greetingService)
    {
        this.greetingService = greetingService;
    }
}
```

## Creating an XML Configuration

You'll recall that Spring Framework manages beans, and that is the primary thing you'll configure whenever you configure Spring Framework. You'll write some of these beans yourself, like `GreetingServiceImpl` and `HelloController`. Others beans are default *framework beans* that come with Spring Framework, such as implementations of Spring's `ApplicationContext`, `ResourceLoader`, `BeanFactory`, `MessageSource`, and `ApplicationEventPublisher` classes, just for starters.

To tell Spring how to configure all these beans, you use the `<beans>` XML namespace, demonstrated in the Spring-One-Context-XML-Config project. Take a look at its `/WEB-INF/servletContext.xml` file:

```
<?xml version="1.0" encoding="UTF-8"?>
<beans xmlns="http://www.springframework.org/schema/beans"
       xmlns:xsi="http://www.w3.org/2001/XMLSchema-instance"
       xmlns:mvc="http://www.springframework.org/schema/mvc"
       xsi:schemaLocation="http://www.springframework.org/schema/beans
            http://www.springframework.org/schema/beans/spring-beans-4.0.xsd
            http://www.springframework.org/schema/mvc
            http://www.springframework.org/schema/mvc/spring-mvc-4.0.xsd">

    <mvc:annotation-driven />

    <bean name="greetingServiceImpl" class="com.wrox.GreetingServiceImpl" />

    <bean name="helloController" class="com.wrox.HelloController">
        <property name="greetingService" ref="greetingServiceImpl" />
    </bean>

</beans>
```

This simple XML file tells Spring to instantiate `GreetingServiceImpl` and `HelloController` and to inject the `greetingServiceImpl` bean into the `helloController` bean's `greetingService` property. The `<beans>` element is a parent element for containing the Spring configuration. Within it you can use nearly any other Spring configuration element — generally speaking, however, the elements you use within a `<beans>` element almost always result in the creation of beans. You use a `<bean>` element to explicitly construct a bean of a given class, and you can specify constructor arguments and properties for that bean within the `<bean>` element's sub-elements. The `<mvc:annotation-driven>` element instructs Spring to use annotations like `@RequestMapping`, `@RequestBody`, `@RequestParam`, `@PathParam`, and `@ResponseBody` to map requests to controller methods. Using the `<mvc:annotation-driven>` element actually causes certain beans to be created behind the scenes, but you don't have to worry about them just yet. They exist to facilitate mapping requests to controller methods. You learn more about these framework beans throughout the next several chapters.

You can do many things with the `@RequestMapping` annotation and its partners, and you will explore these more in Chapter 13. For now, understand that the URL pattern `/` gets mapped to the `HelloController`'s `helloWorld` method and the URL pattern `/custom` to the `helloName` method. These URL patterns are relative to the `DispatcherServlet`'s URL pattern, not to the web application root URL. However, because the `DispatcherServlet` maps to the application root in this case, it results in the URL patterns also being relative to the application root. If you had mapped the `DispatcherServlet` to `/do/*`, the URL patterns in the `@RequestMapping` annotations wouldn't have changed, but in the browser address bar they would have `/do` in front of them.

You have created the Spring configuration, but you still need to bootstrap it. For that use the deployment descriptor, but you could just as easily use Java bootstrapping if desired. Notice the mapping to the default Servlet for ensuring that Tomcat handles static resources.

```
    <servlet-mapping>
        <servlet-name>default</servlet-name>
        <url-pattern>/resource/*</url-pattern>
    </servlet-mapping>

    <servlet>
        <servlet-name>springDispatcher</servlet-name>
        <servlet-class>org.springframework.web.servlet.DispatcherServlet
</servlet-class>
        <load-on-startup>1</load-on-startup>
        <init-param>
            <param-name>contextConfigLocation</param-name>
            <param-value>/WEB-INF/servletContext.xml</param-value>
        </init-param>
    </servlet>
    <servlet-mapping>
        <servlet-name>springDispatcher</servlet-name>
        <url-pattern>/</url-pattern>
    </servlet-mapping>
```

Now compile the project, start Tomcat, and go to `http://localhost:8080/xml/` in your favorite browser. You should see the text "Hello, World!" on the screen. Next, try the URL `http://localhost:8080/xml/custom?name=Nick`. You should now see "Hello, Nick!" in the browser window. Alter the *name* parameter, and the output should change to match. Your first Spring Framework application is working!

As discussed in an earlier section, often it's desirable to have two different application contexts in a web application. You have created only one here. A typical pattern places all the business logic-related classes in the root application context and the controllers in the Servlet application context. To demonstrate this, switch to the Spring-XML-Config project or make the simple changes yourself.

Remove the `greetingServiceImpl` bean declaration from the `servletContext.xml` file (if you don't remove it, it will be instantiated twice) and create a new `/WEB-INF/rootContext.xml` file containing only that bean:

```
<?xml version="1.0" encoding="UTF-8"?>
<beans xmlns="http://www.springframework.org/schema/beans"
       xmlns:xsi="http://www.w3.org/2001/XMLSchema-instance"
```

```
        xsi:schemaLocation="http://www.springframework.org/schema/beans
            http://www.springframework.org/schema/beans/spring-beans-4.0.xsd">

    <bean name="greetingServiceImpl" class="com.wrox.GreetingServiceImpl" />

</beans>
```

You then just need to add the ContextLoaderListener to the deployment descriptor.

```
    <context-param>
        <param-name>contextConfigLocation</param-name>
        <param-value>/WEB-INF/rootContext.xml</param-value>
    </context-param>
    <listener>
        <listener-class>org.springframework.web.context.ContextLoaderListener
</listener-class>
    </listener>
```

You now have two application contexts: The root application context contains the greetingServiceImpl bean; and the DispatcherServlet's application context inherits all the root context's beans, contains the helloController bean, and initializes annotation-driven controller mapping. To make things a little more interesting, tweak the request mapping on the helloName method of the controller.

```
    @RequestMapping(value = "/", params = {"name"})
    public String helloName(@RequestParam("name") String name)
```

This method is now mapped to the same URL as the helloWorld method, but it requires the *name* parameter to be present in the request. The mere presence or absence of the *name* parameter determines which method Spring sends the request to. To prove that point, compile and start your application again and try the http://localhost:8080/xml/ and http://localhost:8080/xml/?name=Nick URLs.

> **NOTE** *You probably noticed that Spring Framework wrote log messages to the debug console and to your* application.log *file. Is Spring using Log4j? Not directly. Spring uses Apache Commons Logging as its logging API. Because your project has the* org.apache.logging.log4j:log4j-jcl *Commons Logging Bridge artifact on its class path, events that Spring Framework logs to Commons Logging get passed to Log4j and written to your log configuration. Messages* INFO *or higher appear because you set the logging level for* org.springframework *to* INFO *in your Log4j configuration file.*

## Creating a Hybrid Configuration

As you can imagine, configuring Spring Framework with XML can get tedious, and the previous example didn't even demonstrate the MultiActionController and SimpleUrlHandlerMapping classes — a legacy mechanism (removed in Spring Framework 4.0) for mapping requests to controllers that involved extremely verbose XML and strict method signatures accepting HttpServletRequests and HttpServletResponses. In a large enterprise application, you could define hundreds of beans, each requiring three or more lines of XML. This configuration method quickly looks no better than configuring Servlets using XML in the deployment descriptor.

If you're a fan of the explicitness of XML but don't want configuration files that long — configuration files that can become extremely hard to maintain — you can create a hybrid configuration that combines some of the best of both worlds.

At the core of this hybrid configuration are the concepts of *component scanning* and *annotation configuration*. Using component scanning, Spring scans the package or packages you specify for classes with specific annotations. Any classes (in these packages) annotated with `@org.springframework.stereotype.Component` become Spring-managed beans, meaning Spring instantiates them and injects their dependencies.

Other annotations qualify for this component scanning: Any annotation that is annotated with `@Component` becomes a component annotation, and any annotation that is annotated with another component annotation becomes a component annotation. Therefore, classes annotated with `@Controller`, `@Repository`, and `@Service` (all in the same package as `@Component`) also become Spring-managed beans. You can create your own component annotations, too. In Chapter 17 you'll create `@WebController` and `@RestController` annotations marked with `@Controller` to distinguish normal controllers from RESTful web service controllers.

Another key annotation that works in conjunction with annotation configuration is `@org.springframework.beans.factory.annotation.Autowired`. You can annotate any private, protected, or public field, or a public mutator method that accepts one or more arguments, with `@Autowired`. `@Autowired` declares a dependency or dependencies that Spring should inject after instantiation, and it can also mark a constructor. Usually, Spring-managed beans must have zero-argument constructors, but in the presence of a single `@Autowired` constructor on a class, Spring uses that constructor and injects all the constructor arguments.

In any of these cases, if Spring cannot find a matching bean for a dependency, it throws and logs an exception and fails to start. Likewise, if it finds *more than* one matching bean for a dependency, it also throws and logs an exception and fails to start. You can avoid this second problem using either the `@org.springframework.beans.factory.annotation.Qualifier` or the `@org.springframework.context.annotation.Primary` annotations. When used on an `@Autowired` field, method, method parameter, or constructor parameter, `@Qualifier` enables you to specify the name of the bean that should be used. Conversely, you can mark a component-annotated bean with `@Primary` to indicate it should be preferred when it is one of multiple candidate beans that fulfill a dependency.

So, should you use fields, mutators, or constructors with `@Autowired`? That debate has raged for years. Some teams prefer having `@Autowired` fields because it involves the least amount of code. Other teams prefer using `@Autowired` constructors because it makes it impossible to construct an object without satisfying all its dependencies. Still others prefer using `@Autowired` mutators because, though it involves the most code, it avoids having non-private fields while also making unit testing easier because you don't always have to mock every dependency just to construct an instance. Which approach you use in the real world is completely up to you, but in this book you will annotate fields in most cases so that the code examples take up fewer pages.

> **NOTE** *Spring Framework also supports certain Java EE annotations in place of its proprietary annotations.* `@javax.inject.Inject` *is completely synonymous with* `@Autowired`*, and nothing special is required to make it work. You can annotate any field, constructor, or method using* `@Inject` *just like you would with* `@Autowired`*.* `@javax.annotation.Resource` *is also treated synonymously with* `@Autowired`*. Likewise,* `@javax.inject.Named` *is the equivalent of* `@Qualifier` *and has the same effect on* `@Autowired` *or* `@Inject` *properties as* `@Qualifier` *does. (Spring also has support for custom qualifiers using the* `@javax.inject.Qualifier` *meta-annotation.) Which annotations you use is largely up to you; however, the argument can be made that using* `javax.*` *annotations somewhat unties your application from Spring and makes it easier to switch to another framework at a later date.*

As mentioned earlier in the section, Spring provides many default framework beans automatically, and sometimes your beans need instances of those beans. Generally, using framework beans is discouraged because doing so further ties your application to Spring Framework and makes it more difficult to switch to something else. However, you must use these beans when you want to use certain powerful Spring features, such as publish-subscribe messaging. You can ask for any of these beans to be `@Autowired` or `@Inject`ed and Spring will oblige, but many people prefer to obtain these beans differently to make the connection to Spring more apparent. For this, you have the `org.springframework.beans.factory.Aware` interfaces. `Aware` is simply a marker interface for other interfaces to extend indicating awareness of certain framework beans. For example, the `org.springframework.context.ApplicationContextAware` interface specifies a `setApplicationContext` method for providing the `ApplicationContext` instance of the current (not parent) context to your beans. (If you need to, you can then obtain the parent context by calling `ApplicationContext`'s `getParent` method.)

There are many other interfaces that extend `Aware`, but some of the most popular follow:

- `ApplicationEventPublisherAware` for obtaining the bean used to publish application events
- `BeanFactoryAware` for obtaining the `BeanFactory` with which you can manually retrieve or create beans
- `EnvironmentAware` for obtaining an `Environment` object that you can use to get properties from property sources
- `MessageSourceAware` for obtaining the internationalization message source
- `ServletContextAware` for obtaining the `ServletContext` in Java EE web application environments
- `ServletConfigAware` for obtaining the `ServletConfig` in `DispatcherServlet` web application context-managed beans

It's also often desirable to perform some sort of initialization on a class after all its dependencies have been injected but before it is injected as a dependency in any other beans. This is easily achieved merely by implementing the `org.springframework.beans.factory`

.InitializingBean interface. After all configuration of your bean is complete (dependencies are injected and Aware methods have been called), Spring calls its afterPropertiesSet method. If you do not want to tie your application to this proprietary Spring interface, you can instead create exactly one public, void, zero-argument method annotated with @javax.annotation.PostContstruct. It will be called at the same time as afterPropertiesSet normally would.

Whichever you use, it will be called even if your bean declared no dependencies that needed injection. On the flip side, if your bean needs to shut down after references to it have gone away and before Spring shuts down, you can implement org.springframework.beans.factory.DisposableBean's destroy method or create your own public, void, zero-argument method annotated with @javax.annotation.PreDestroy.

> **NOTE** *If you want more advanced control over the life cycle of your beans than* InitializingBean, @PostConstruct, DisposableBean, *or* @PreDestroy *have to offer, take a look at the API documentation for the* org.springframework.context.Lifecycle *and* SmartLifecycle *interfaces.*

Initiating component scanning and annotation configuration is a simple task using the existing deployment descriptor configuration and the rootContext.xml and servletContext.xml files. You can see this change in the Spring-Hybrid-Config project. In the rootContext.xml configuration, simply remove all bean definitions and replace them with the <context:annotation-config> and <context:component-scan> elements:

```
<?xml version="1.0" encoding="UTF-8"?>
<beans xmlns="http://www.springframework.org/schema/beans"
       xmlns:xsi="http://www.w3.org/2001/XMLSchema-instance"
       xmlns:context="http://www.springframework.org/schema/context"
       xsi:schemaLocation="http://www.springframework.org/schema/beans
            http://www.springframework.org/schema/beans/spring-beans-4.0.xsd
            http://www.springframework.org/schema/context
            http://www.springframework.org/schema/context/spring-context-4.0.xsd">

    <context:annotation-config />
    <context:component-scan base-package="com.wrox" />

</beans>
```

The base-package attribute instructs Spring Framework to scan all classes on the class path in the package com.wrox or in any subpackages for @Component, @Controller, @Repository, and @Service. The similar servletContext.xml configuration file still contains the <mvc:annotation-driven> element:

```
<?xml version="1.0" encoding="UTF-8"?>
<beans xmlns="http://www.springframework.org/schema/beans"
       xmlns:xsi="http://www.w3.org/2001/XMLSchema-instance"
       xmlns:context="http://www.springframework.org/schema/context"
       xmlns:mvc="http://www.springframework.org/schema/mvc"
       xsi:schemaLocation="http://www.springframework.org/schema/beans
            http://www.springframework.org/schema/beans/spring-beans-4.0.xsd
```

```
            http://www.springframework.org/schema/context
            http://www.springframework.org/schema/context/spring-context-4.0.xsd
            http://www.springframework.org/schema/mvc
            http://www.springframework.org/schema/mvc/spring-mvc-4.0.xsd">

    <mvc:annotation-driven />

    <context:annotation-config />
    <context:component-scan base-package="com.wrox" />

</beans>
```

You still have two remaining minor things to change:

- You must tell Spring to instantiate the `GreetingServiceImpl`, so annotate the class with `@Service`.

```
@Service
public class GreetingServiceImpl implements GreetingService
```

- You need to tell Spring to inject the `GreetingService` into the `HelloController`, so annotate the mutator method with `@Autowired`.

```
    @Autowired
    public void setGreetingService(GreetingService greetingService)
```

You may already have noticed a problem with this configuration, which you can observe by placing a breakpoint in the `setGreetingService` mutator before starting Tomcat. This break point is hit twice for two different instances of the `HelloController` and `GreetingServiceImpl`. Indeed, you can also see this in the application log file. Spring instantiates the `GreetingServiceImpl` and `HelloController` twice: once in the root application context and once in the `DispatcherServlet`'s application context. Why is this happening?

Remember that component scanning, by default, scans for *all* `@Components`, and you have component scanning enabled in both application contexts. What you really want is to separate your beans. The root application context should hold services, repositories, and other pieces of business logic, whereas the `DispatcherServlet`'s application context should contain web controllers. Fortunately, you have a simple way to alter the default component-scanning algorithm. In the Spring-Hybrid-Config project this has already been done for you. First, the `rootContext.xml` configuration adds an exclusion to the scanning:

```
<context:annotation-config />
<context:component-scan base-package="com.wrox">
    <context:exclude-filter type="annotation"
            expression="org.springframework.stereotype.Controller" />
</context:component-scan>
```

This `exclude-filter` tells Spring to scan for all `@Components` *except* `@Controllers`. Other than this exclusion, the default scan pattern still applies. The `servletContext.xml` configuration takes a slightly different approach and uses a whitelist instead of a blacklist to tell Spring which components to scan for:

```
<mvc:annotation-driven />

<context:annotation-config />
<context:component-scan base-package="com.wrox" use-default-filters="false">
```

```
        <context:include-filter type="annotation"
                expression="org.springframework.stereotype.Controller" />
    </context:component-scan>
```

In this case, the `use-default-filters` attribute set to `false` tells Spring to ignore its standard scanning pattern. Instead of the `exclude-filter` specified in the root context, an `include-filter` tells Spring to scan *only* for `@Controllers`. Even if `use-default-filters` is true, you can still use `include-filters` to add to the default scanning filters.

Although you've removed all the `<bean>` definitions from the configuration files, you can still use `<bean>` and component scanning together. You may have cases in which you cannot use component scanning to register a bean. One example of this is registering a class provided by a third party as a bean: Because you'll have only a compiled version of the class, you can't add Spring annotations to it. Another example is registering framework beans that aren't registered by default, such as Java Persistence API tools. Any time you need to, you can still specify `<bean>` elements in your configuration to supplement what Spring finds through component scanning.

Compile the application and start up Tomcat from your IDE. Go to `http://localhost:8080/hybrid/` and `http://localhost:8080/hybrid/?name=John`, and you'll notice that the application works exactly as it did using an XML-only configuration.

## Configuring Spring with Java Using @Configuration

How you configure Spring is largely a matter of personal preference. Some development teams prefer the verbosity and plain text descriptiveness of XML files. However, there are some distinct disadvantages to configuring Spring using XML:

- **It's hard to debug an XML configuration.** You must download and attach the Spring Framework sources to your project as well as know where to place breakpoints and how to step through it. The source code for Spring is massive, and debugging it is no trivial task.
- **It's impossible to unit test an XML configuration.** Sure, you can programmatically bootstrap your Spring configuration within a unit test, but this isn't a unit test. Because doing this starts your entire application context and wires all your beans, it's actually an integration test. You can't test isolated units of your Spring configuration if it's XML-based.

Spring Framework's pure Java configuration enables you to programmatically configure your Spring container so that you can easily debug and unit test pieces of your configuration. This is also useful for development teams that simply don't like XML.

Earlier in the chapter, you explored bootstrapping programmatic Spring configuration using the `AnnotationConfigWebApplicationContext`. When using this class, you register configuration classes with it via the `register` method. These configuration classes (which must be annotated `@org.springframework.context.annotation.Configuration` and which must have a default constructor) register beans through no-argument methods annotated `@Bean`. You can do many powerful things with `@Configuration` classes, and more important, you can unit test and debug each method, as necessary.

The `@Configuration` annotation is meta-annotated with `@Component`, meaning your `@Configuration` classes are eligible for dependency injection using `@Autowired` or `@Inject`; may implement any of the `Aware` interfaces, `InitializingBean`, or `DisposableBean`; and may have

@PostConstruct and @PreDestroy methods. This is useful if a @Configuration class needs to directly access a framework bean or a bean created in another @Configuration class. It's also useful if it needs to initialize two or more dependent beans after its own dependencies are injected but before Spring calls its @Bean methods.

The fact that @Configuration classes are @Components also means that your @Configuration classes are picked up automatically if you have component scanning enabled on the package that contains them. This can have both intended and unintended consequences. If your @Configuration class enables component scanning on the same package it resides in, your beans could be instantiated twice, which isn't good.

On the other hand, if you divide your application into many modules, each module can have its own @Configuration, and you can create a core @Configuration that component scans for all the modules' @Configurations. The key point to take from this is that you should always be careful when combining @Configuration and component scanning.

Often it is desirable to have externalized values that drive your configuration. For example, your application may require the use of a JNDI data source, but you wouldn't want to hard code the name of that data source. Instead, it is preferable to store the name of the data source in some settings file loaded at configuration time. Using the @org.springframework.context.annotation.PropertySource annotation, you can do just that.

```
@Configuration
@PropertySource({
    "classpath:com/wrox/config/settings.properties",
    "file:config.properties"
})
public class ExampleConfiguration
...
```

To access the properties in the property source, you can use an injected org.springframework.core.env.Environment instance to obtain the values manually, or you can use the @org.springframework.beans.factory.annotation.Value annotation to have the property values injected automatically.

```
...
public class ExampleConfiguration
{
    @Inject Environment environment;

    @Value("my.property.key") String myPropertyValue;
...
```

You might not be able to or want to contain your entire configuration in a single class. For that matter, you might not be able to configure everything with Java. As discussed earlier, some tools may still require XML configuration. The @org.springframework.context.annotation.Import and @ImportResource annotations provide support for these needs.

```
@Configuration
@Import({ DatabaseConfiguration.class, ClusterConfiguration.class })
@ImportResource("classpath:com/wrox/config/spring-security.xml")
public class ExampleConfiguration
...
```

In the previous code snippet, Spring Framework will load the configuration contained in ExampleConfiguration as well as the configuration contained in DatabaseConfiguration, ClusterConfiguration, and spring-security.xml. It does not initialize and execute these configurations in a specific order; instead, it determines if any of the configurations depend on beans provided by any of the other configurations, and initializes the configurations in the proper order to fulfill these dependencies.

Spring Framework has many XML configuration features you've already used that do not involve <bean> definitions. These result in very specific framework bean definitions behind the scenes but enable you to specify the configuration with minimal effort and include things such as <mvc:annotation-driven> and <context:component-scan>. There are replacements for all these XML namespace features using a set of configuration-related annotations. You can mark any @Configuration-annotated class with the following annotations to enable those features. You will learn more about these annotations gradually throughout the rest of the book.

- @ComponentScan replaces <context:component-scan> and enables component scanning on the specified package or packages. Just like its counterpart, you can enable or disable default filters and specify include and exclude filters to fine-tune the component scanning algorithm.
- @EnableAspectJAutoProxy is the replacement for <aop:aspectj-autoproxy> and enables support for handling classes marked with AspectJ's @Aspect annotation and advising methods as appropriate using aspect-oriented programming.
- @EnableAsync replaces parts of Spring's <task:*> namespace and enables Spring's asynchronous @Async method execution. When used with the AsyncConfigurer interface, your @Configuration can fine-tune the configuration of asynchronous behavior.
- @EnableCaching enables Spring's annotation-driven cache-management features and replaces the <cache:*> namespace.
- @EnableLoadTimeWeaving replaces <context:load-time-weaver>. It changes how several features such as @Transactional, @Configurable, @Aspect, and more, work. In most cases you won't often need this feature, but it is covered in Part III when you work with the Java Persistence API. Importantly, it is mutually exclusive with @EnableAspectJAutoProxy.
- @EnableMBeanExport is the replacement for <context:mbean-export> and instructs Spring to expose certain framework beans and any @ManagedResource-annotated beans as JMX MBeans.
- @EnableScheduling replaces the rest of Spring's <task:*> namespace and activates scheduled method execution with @Scheduled, similar to the @Async method execution enabled by @EnableAsync.
- @EnableSpringConfigured activates dependency injection in objects that are not Spring-managed beans and replaces <context:spring-configured>. It requires load time weaving to support this feature, as it must intercept object construction.
- @EnableTransactionManagement replaces <tx:annotation-driven> and enables database transaction management for methods advised with the @Transactional annotation.

- `@EnableWebMvc` activates annotation-driven controller request mapping and replaces `<mvc:annotation-driven>`. This activates a very complex configuration, which you often must customize. You can customize the entire Web MVC configuration by making your `@Configuration` class implement `WebMvcConfigurer` or, more easily, customize only the pieces that you need to by extending `WebMvcConfigurerAdapter`.

The Spring-Java-Config project demonstrates use of a pure Java configuration from `WebApplicationInitializer` bootstrapping to `@Configuration` classes for the root and `DispatcherServlet` application contexts. The `GreetingService`, `GreetingServiceImpl`, and `HelloController` classes have been moved to the `com.wrox.site` package to be separate from the configuration classes in the `com.wrox.config` package. This way, component scanning won't inadvertently detect the `@Configuration` classes.

The first new class in this project, `RootContextConfiguration`, is very simple:

```
@Configuration
@ComponentScan(
        basePackages = "com.wrox.site",
        excludeFilters = @ComponentScan.Filter(Controller.class)
)
public class RootContextConfiguration
{
}
```

The `@ComponentScan` annotation tells Spring to scan classes in the `com.wrox.site` package and all subpackages and exclude `@Controller` classes, just like the hybrid configuration earlier in this section. The new `ServletContextConfiguration` class is very similar, turning off default filters to scan only for `@Controllers`, and enabling the annotation-driven Web MVC features.

```
@Configuration
@EnableWebMvc
@ComponentScan(
        basePackages = "com.wrox.site",
        useDefaultFilters = false,
        includeFilters = @ComponentScan.Filter(Controller.class)
)
public class ServletContextConfiguration
{
}
```

You probably noticed that neither of these classes have any `@Bean` methods. All the beans you need right now are configured automatically using component scanning and `@EnableWebMvc`, so you don't have a need for any `@Bean` methods.

> **NOTE** *In the next section you see an example of manual bean configuration with `@Bean`, and throughout the rest of this book, you see more and more examples of creating custom beans with `@Bean` methods.*

Of course, these configuration classes can't bootstrap themselves, so the `Bootstrap` class implements `WebApplicationInitializer`.

```
public class Bootstrap implements WebApplicationInitializer
{
    @Override
    public void onStartup(ServletContext container) throws ServletException
    {
        container.getServletRegistration("default").addMapping("/resource/*");

        AnnotationConfigWebApplicationContext rootContext =
                new AnnotationConfigWebApplicationContext();
        rootContext.register(RootContextConfiguration.class);
        container.addListener(new ContextLoaderListener(rootContext));

        AnnotationConfigWebApplicationContext servletContext =
                new AnnotationConfigWebApplicationContext();
        servletContext.register(ServletContextConfiguration.class);
        ServletRegistration.Dynamic dispatcher = container.addServlet(
                "springDispatcher", new DispatcherServlet(servletContext)
        );
        dispatcher.setLoadOnStartup(1);
        dispatcher.addMapping("/");
    }
}
```

The init parameters, listener, and `DispatcherServlet` configured in the deployment descriptor earlier in this section have been removed, and `web.xml` now contains just basic JSP and session configuration. The only other change made was for demonstration purposes and not out of necessity: The `HelloController` now uses `@Inject` instead of `@Autowired` to declare its dependencies.

```
@Inject
public void setGreetingService(GreetingService greetingService)
```

Now compile the application, start Tomcat from your IDE, and go to `http://localhost:8080/java/` and `http://localhost:8080/java/?name=Mars`. The application functions identically to the Spring-XML-Config and Spring-Hybrid-Config applications.

## UTILIZING BEAN DEFINITION PROFILES

Java is a flexible language that can run in many environments, so there's no reason your Spring Framework application must be rigid. Spring's *bean definition profiles* enable easily turning entire sections of the configuration on or off with a simple switch at the command line, in the deployment descriptor, or programmatically. This functionality is very handy in many use cases, and undoubtedly you'll have your own ideas by the end of this section. Some examples follow:

- **In an application environment with many tiers, you need some beans to run on one tier while other beans run on another.** Using bean definition profiles, you can deploy a single application to every tier while the activated profile controls which beans are registered.
- **You may write an application for resale to work against many different types of data stores.** When your end users purchase and install the application they indicate which type of data store they want to use. Your application could have a Java Persistence API profile containing JPA repositories for persisting to relational databases and a Spring Data NoSQL profile

containing NoSQL repositories for writing to schema-less data stores. Your users can install the same executable file while a simple configuration switch enables the correct profile.

- **You might want to create different Development, Quality Assurance, and Production profiles.** In the Development profile, you can probably hard-code certain settings, such as a connection to a local database that all developers must create. The Quality Assurance profile, likewise, might also have hard-coded settings that differ from development machines. Undoubtedly, your production environment team needs to change the application's settings without waiting on you to change and recompile it, so the Production profile would load those settings from a properties file that your technicians can change.

## Understanding How Profiles Work

Similar to other technologies that provide configuration profiles (such as Maven), using Spring bean definition profiles has two components: declaration and activation. You can declare profiles using `<beans>` elements in XML configuration files, the `@org.springframework.context.annotation.Profile` annotation on `@Configuration` classes or `@Components`, or both. Any `<beans>` element can contain a profile attribute to indicate that its beans belong to a particular profile. Fortunately, you do not have to create a new configuration file for every profile you want to create because you can nest `<beans>` elements. The following code snippet demonstrates this.

```
<?xml version="1.0" encoding="UTF-8"?>
<beans xmlns="http://www.springframework.org/schema/beans"
       xmlns:xsi="http://www.w3.org/2001/XMLSchema-instance"
       xsi:schemaLocation="http://www.springframework.org/schema/beans
           http://www.springframework.org/schema/beans/spring-beans-4.0.xsd">

    ...
    <beans profile="development,qa">
        <jdbc:embedded-database id="dataSource" type="HSQL">
            <jdbc:script location="classpath:com/wrox/config/sql/schema.sql"/>
            <jdbc:script location="classpath:com/wrox/config/sql/test-data.sql"/>
        </jdbc:embedded-database>
    </beans>

    <beans profile="production">
        <context:property-placeholder location="file:/settings.properties" />
        <jee:jndi-lookup id="dataSource"
                         jndi-name="java:/comp/env/${production.dsn}" />
    </beans>
    ...

</beans>
```

In this example, the two differently configured `DataSource` beans are registered in different profiles. The in-memory embedded HyperSQL database is created if the `development` or `qa` profiles are active, whereas a data source with the configured name is looked up in the JNDI context only if the `production` profile is active. Because both beans implement `DataSource` and have the same bean ID, any `<bean>` can use the reference to the `dataSource` bean, and any `@Component` can have the appropriate `DataSource` injected automatically. You can also achieve this using Java `@Configuration`, as shown in the following code.

```
interface DataConfiguration
{
    DataSource dataSource();
}

@Configuration
@Import({DevQaDataConfiguration.class, ProductionDataConfiguration.class})
@ComponentScan(
        basePackages = "com.wrox.site",
        excludeFilters = @ComponentScan.Filter(Controller.class)
)
public class RootContextConfiguration
{
}

@Configuration
@Profile({"development", "qa"})
public class DevQaDataConfiguration implements DataConfiguration
{
    @Override
    @Bean
    public DataSource dataSource()
    {
        return new EmbeddedDatabaseBuilder()
                .setType(EmbeddedDatabaseType.HSQL)
                .addScript("classpath:com/wrox/config/sql/schema.sql")
                .addScript("classpath:com/wrox/config/sql/test-data.sql")
                .build();
    }
}

@Configuration
@Profile("production")
@PropertySource("file:settings.properties")
public class ProductionDataConfiguration implements DataConfiguration
{
    @Value("production.dsr")
    String dataSourceName;

    @Override
    @Bean
    public DataSource dataSource()
    {
        return new JndiDataSourceLookup()
                .getDataSource("java:/comp/env/" + this.dataSourceName);
    }
}
```

After you have declared your profiles, you can activate them in one or more of several different ways. First, you can use the `spring.profiles.active` context init parameter:

```
<context-param>
    <param-name>spring.profiles.active</param-name>
    <param-value>development</param-value>
</context-param>
```

Or the Servlet init parameter:

```
<servlet>
...
    <init-param>
       <param-name>spring.profiles.active</param-name>
       <param-value>development</param-value>
    </init-param>
...
</servlet>
```

The context parameter affects all Spring application contexts running within the web application, whereas the Servlet init parameter affects only the `DispatcherServlet` application context for which it is set.

You can also use the `-Dspring.profiles.active=development` command-line parameter to activate a profile for all application contexts running throughout the Java Virtual Machine. Using any of these techniques, you can specify multiple profiles to activate, separated with commas (`<param-value>profile1,profile2</param-value>`, `-Dspring.profiles.active=profile1,profile2`). This, of course, means that profile names cannot contain commas.

You can also activate one or more profiles programmatically by calling the `setActiveProfiles` method on a `ConfigurableEnvironment` instance:

```
configurableEnvironment.setActiveProfiles("development");
configurableEnvironment.setActiveProfiles("profile1", "profile2");
```

Using this method affects the application context containing the environment and any children application contexts. Using context or servlet init parameters or command-line properties is typically more common. After all, if you know enough to programmatically set the active profiles, why do you need profiles at all? Programmatically setting profiles is useful for integration testing, however.

One more thing to understand is that the `@Profile` annotation, like `@Component`, can serve as a meta-annotation. This means you can create your own custom annotations that serve as `@Profile` annotations. As an example, consider the following annotation.

```
@Documented
@Retention(value=RetentionPolicy.RUNTIME)
@Target(value={ElementType.TYPE, ElementType.METHOD})
@Profile("development")
public @interface Development
{
}
```

The custom `@Development` annotation has the same force as the `@Profile` annotation with the profile name "development." Now, using `@Development` is equivalent to using `@Profile("development")`. This is especially useful to avoid littering your code with string-literal profile names subject to typos and hard to replace if you decide to change the profile name.

## Considering Antipatterns and Security Concerns

You should keep some important considerations in mind whenever you decide to use bean definition profiles to solve a problem or need:

- **Is there a simpler way to achieve the same result?** If the same beans are created in multiple profiles but with different settings, chances are you can achieve this goal using a property source and one or more properties files. Using profiles for this would typically be an antipattern, adding more complexity than its worth.
- **What are the types of beans present in your profiles?** In most cases, two different profiles should largely have the same beans, albeit possibly different implementations or with more debugging, profiling, or reporting turned on. As a general rule, QA and production profiles should be nearly identical, with the major difference present between the development and QA profiles. Otherwise, you might not be testing everything you should be.
- **What are the security implications of using bean definition profiles?** Generally speaking, you should never use profiles to control security aspects of your application. Because end users can activate or deactivate profiles simply by enabling or disabling a JVM command-line property, they can easily circumvent security restrictions defined in such a way. One obvious antipattern in this case is to disable all product-licensing checks in a development profile but enable them in QA and production profiles. A clever user can then avoid purchasing your application merely by switching from the production to the development profile. There are ways to avoid this, such as stripping out classes during production builds or utilizing a Java `SecurityManager`, but it's best just to avoid this situation altogether.

## SUMMARY

In this chapter you were introduced to the Spring Framework, and you learned about beans, application contexts, and dispatcher Servlets. You then experimented with the many ways to bootstrap and configure Spring Framework. You explored the concepts of Dependency Injection (DI) and Inversion of Control (IoC), aspect-oriented programming, transaction management, publish-subscribe application messaging, and Spring's MVC framework. You also saw the advantages of using Spring Framework over other technologies, and how Spring can make software development easier and more rapid for web applications, desktop applications, and even server daemons.

In the next chapter you take a deeper dive into controllers and the MVC framework to understand the true usefulness of the `@RequestMapping` annotation. Throughout the rest of the book, you'll see many Spring applications. Keep in mind that only you can decide whether to use XML or Java bootstrapping and XML, hybrid, or Java configuration in your real-life Spring applications. However, for the sake of consistency, Java bootstrapping and configuration are used exclusively from here on out.

# 13

# Replacing Your Servlets with Controllers

## IN THIS CHAPTER

- What is @RequestMapping?
- How to utilize Spring Framework's model and view pattern
- Easing your life with form objects
- Keeping the Customer Support application up-to-date

## WROX.COM CODE DOWNLOADS FOR THIS CHAPTER

You can find the wrox.com code downloads for this chapter at http://www.wrox.com/go/projavaforwebapps on the Download Code tab. The code for this chapter is divided into the following major examples:

- Model-View-Controller Project
- Spring-Forms Project
- Customer-Support-v10 Project

## NEW MAVEN DEPENDENCY FOR THIS CHAPTER

In addition to the Maven dependencies introduced in previous chapters, you also need the following Maven dependency:

```
<dependency>
    <groupId>org.springframework</groupId>
    <artifactId>spring-oxm</artifactId>
    <version>4.0.2.RELEASE</version>
    <scope>compile</scope>
</dependency>
```

# UNDERSTANDING @REQUESTMAPPING

In Chapter 12, you were introduced to Spring Framework controllers and how to use the `@RequestMapping` annotation to map requests to methods within your controllers. `@RequestMapping` is an extraordinarily powerful tool in the Spring toolset, enabling you to map a request with the URL, the `Content-Type` or `Accept` header of the request, the HTTP request method, the presence or value of specified request parameters or headers, or any combination of these.

With `@RequestMapping`, you no longer need complex switches or logic branches within Servlet `doGet` or similar methods to select the proper method to execute. Instead, requests are automatically routed to the proper controller and method on your behalf. How a request maps to the proper controller and method is established through the various `@RequestMapping` annotation attributes. A mapped method may have any name, any number of different arguments, and one of numerous supported return types. In this section, you learn about all these capabilities.

## Using @RequestMapping Attributes to Narrow Request Matching

The `@RequestMapping` annotation narrows which requests are mapped to a particular method. You can place `@RequestMapping` on just a controller method or on both a controller class and its methods. Placing the annotation on both a controller class and its methods establishes certain inheritance and precedence rules regarding the mappings. Some `@RequestMapping` attributes established for the controller class are inherited by and additive to those established for the method, whereas others established for the method override those established for the class. Thus, it is important to understand each attribute, its purpose, and whether values on the method add to or override values on the class.

> **NOTE** *Only* `@RequestMappings` *specified on a controller class are considered, not those specified on its superclasses. Thus, you cannot annotate an abstract class and have derived classes inherit the abstract class's mappings.*

### URL Restrictions

You have already used @`RequestMapping` to narrow which requests a method can respond to based on their URLs. Using the `value` attribute (implicitly or explicitly if using other attributes), you can specify any Ant-style URL pattern. This is significantly more flexible than Servlet URL mappings (which may only begin with or end with a wildcard and cannot have multiple wildcards or wildcards in the middle of the URL). Controller method URL mappings are constructed using the Servlet URL mapping for the `DispatcherServlet`, the controller mapping (if applicable), and the method mapping, all separated by forward slashes if not specified. To demonstrate, consider the following methods mapped to different URLs:

```
@RequestMapping("viewProduct")
public String viewProduct(...) { ... }

@RequestMapping("addToCart")
```

```
    public String addProductToCart(...) { ... }

    @RequestMapping("writeReview")
    public String writeProductReview(...) { ... }
```

In this case, if you map the `DispatcherServlet` to the context root (/), the application-relative URLs for these methods become `/viewProduct`, `/addToCart`, and `/writeReview`, respectively. Assuming that you instead map the `DispatcherServlet` to `/store/*`, the URLs for these methods become `/store/viewProduct`, `/store/addToCart`, and `/store/writeReview`, respectively.

> **NOTE** *If you are not familiar with Ant-style patterns, taken a minute to review the Apache Ant pattern documentation at* `http://ant.apache.org/manual/dirtasks.html#patterns`.

If you find that many URLs in a controller share a common element, you can use mapping inheritance to reduce redundancy in your mappings:

```
@RequestMapping("product")
public class ProductController
{
    @RequestMapping("view")
    public String viewProduct(...) { ... }

    @RequestMapping("addToCart")
    public String addProductToCart(...) { ... }

    @RequestMapping("writeReview")
    public String writeProductReview(...) { ... }
}
```

In this case, the method URLs become `/product/view`, `/product/addToCart`, and `/product/writeReview` if the `DispatcherServlet` maps to the context root. Likewise, the URLs become `/store/product/view`, `/store/product/addToCart`, and `/store/product/writeReview` if the `DispatcherServlet` maps to `/store/*`.

Another important aspect of URL mappings is that if a request matches multiple different URL mappings, the most-specific mapping wins. Thus, consider the following mappings:

```
    @RequestMapping("view/*")
    public String viewAll(...) { ... }

    @RequestMapping("view/*.json")
    public String viewJson(...) { ... }

    @RequestMapping("view/id/*")
    public String view(...) { ... }

    @RequestMapping("view/other*")
    public String viewOther(...) { ... }
```

Many different URLs could potentially match more than one of these methods:

- The URL /view/other.json could match the viewAll, viewJson, or viewOther methods, but viewOther is more specific, so it's routed there.
- /view/id/anything.json would likewise match viewAll, viewJson, or view, but it is mapped to view.
- Because viewAll has the least-specific mapping of any of these methods, only requests that match none of the other methods are routed to viewAll.

Using this technique, you can create a catchall method that catches any requests not otherwise mapped to a controller method:

```
public class HomeController
{
    @RequestMapping(value="/*")
    public String catchAll(...) { ... }
}
```

However, this is generally not recommended. When users navigate to an invalid URL on your site, seeing the site homepage instead of a 404-error page can lead to confusion. If Spring Framework finds no methods matching a request, it automatically responds with a 404 error. If you want to customize this error page, you can do so using the <error-page> deployment descriptor element.

One final thing to understand about the @RequestMapping value attribute: It can also accept an array of URL mappings. Because of this, you can map more than one URL to a given method. In this example, the home method responds to the URLs /, /home, and /dashboard:

```
    @RequestMapping({"/", "home", "dashboard"})
    public String home(...) { ... }
```

Though not strictly required, you typically always use the value attribute, even if you use other attributes, too. It rarely makes sense, for example, to map a controller method to POST requests without specifying a URL as well.

## HTTP Request Method Restrictions

You can also narrow the matching of requests to controller methods using HTTP methods. The @RequestMapping method attribute accepts one or more org.springframework.web.bind.annotation.RequestMethod enum constants. If a controller method mapping includes one or more values for the method attribute, a request only maps to this controller method if the request's HTTP method matches one of the specified constants. You might find this particularly useful to map the same URL to different controller methods depending on the HTTP method, as in the following example:

```
@RequestMapping("account")
public class AccountManagementController
{
    @RequestMapping(value="add", method=RequestMethod.GET)
    public String addForm(...) { ... }

    @RequestMapping(value="add", method=RequestMethod.POST)
    public View addSubmit(...) { ... }
}
```

The /account/add URL matches both the addForm and addSubmit methods. GET requests to this URL route to the addForm method, whereas POST requests route to the addSubmit method. A request to the same URL using any other HTTP method is rejected. In fact, it's best practice to always specify the supported HTTP method or methods for every mapping. This makes it more difficult to compromise your application, and also makes it obvious when a form that should be submitted as a POST request (such as a login) accidentally gets submitted with a GET request. RequestMethod supports OPTIONS, HEAD, GET, POST, PUT, DELETE, PATCH, and TRACE.

It's important to understand that, when inherited from the class, the method attribute is a restriction at both levels. A request's HTTP method is checked against the class-level restrictions first. If it makes it past these restrictions, it is then checked against the method-level restrictions. Thus, the following AccountManagementController is semantically the same as the previous version.

```
@RequestMapping(value="account", method={RequestMethod.GET, RequestMethod.POST})
public class AccountManagementController
{
    @RequestMapping(value="add", method=RequestMethod.GET)
    public String addForm(...) { ... }

    @RequestMapping(value="add", method=RequestMethod.POST)
    public View addSubmit(...) { ... }
}
```

## Request Parameter Restrictions

The params attribute of the @RequestMapping annotation is another feature you briefly explored in Chapter 12. Using this attribute you can specify one or more parameter expressions that must hold true. The expression "myParam=myValue" indicates that the *myParam* request parameter must be present and its value must equal "myValue," whereas "myParam!=myValue" indicates that the *myParam* request parameter must not equal "myValue." You can also use the expression "myParam", meaning the *myParam* request parameter must be present with any value (including blank), and "!myParam", meaning the *myParam* request parameter must not be present (blank values are not allowed). If a request does not match all the expressions specified in the params attribute, it does not map to the controller method.

The following request mapping narrows the matching so that the method is invoked only if the employee parameter is present with any value and the confirm parameter is present and equals true:

```
@RequestMapping(value="can", params={"employee", "confirm=true"})
public String can(...) { ... }
```

Like HTTP request method restrictions, parameter restrictions are inherited. Spring Framework first checks the parameter restrictions on the controller class and then checks the parameter restrictions on the method. It only maps the request if it passes both sets of restrictions.

## Request Header Restrictions

Header restrictions using @RequestMapping's headers attribute work nearly identically to parameter restrictions, including the way they are inherited. You can specify value or presence expressions for any header and negate those expressions with an exclamation point, just like with parameter restrictions.

Header restrictions have the additional feature that you can specify value wildcards for media-type headers. So the following request mapping matches only requests that contain the `X-Client` header and whose `Content-Type` header is any text type. Note that header name matching is case-insensitive.

```
@RequestMapping(value="user", headers={"X-Client", "content-type=text/*"})
public User user(...) { ... }
```

### Content Type Restrictions

You can further narrow request mapping using the request content type or the request's expected response content type (or both). Although either of these restrictions are possible using the `headers` attribute, the `consumes` and `produces` attributes are conveniences to make this task easier.

The `consumes` attribute takes one or more media types (or media type wildcards) that must match the request's `Content-Type` header. Thus, it defines what content type the method can consume. Likewise, the `produces` attribute takes one or more media types (or wildcards) that must match the request's `Accept` header. As such, it specifies which content types the method can produce so that Spring can determine whether those match the content types the client expects the response to contain. The following request mapping matches only requests with a `Content-Type` of `application/json` or `text/json` and an `Accept` header containing `application/json` or `text/json`.

```
@RequestMapping(value="song", consumes={"text/json", "application/json"},
                produces={"text/json", "application/json"})
public Song song(...) { ... }
```

If specified in both the class `@RequestMapping` and the method `@RequestMapping`, the `consumes` and `produces` attributes on the method *override* those specified on the class. (In other words, the values for the class are ignored if values are also specified for the method.)

> **NOTE** *Content type restrictions are useful but are not always the best way to achieve* content negotiation. *The "Configuring Content Negotiation" section of this chapter goes into more detail about this topic.*

## Specifying Controller Method Parameters

Controller methods can have any number of parameters of many different types. Spring Framework is extremely flexible as to the number and types of parameters. The simplest methods may have zero parameters, whereas complex methods may have a dozen or more. Spring can understand the purpose of these parameters and provide the proper value at call time. Additionally, some simple configuration can expand the parameter types that Spring understands.

### Standard Servlet Types

When needed, Spring can provide arguments to your methods for numerous parameter types related to the Servlet API. The values passed to these parameters are never `null` because Spring guarantees values for them. Your methods can specify none, any, or all of these parameter types:

- `HttpServletRequest`, for using request properties
- `HttpServletResponse`, for manipulating the response
- `HttpSession`, for manipulating the HTTP session object
- `InputStream` *or* `Reader`, but not both, for reading the request body. You should not close this object when finished with it.
- `OutputStream` *or* `Writer`, but not both, for writing to the response body. You should not close this object when finished with it.
- The `java.util.Locale` that the client has identified should be used for localization purposes (or the default locale, if none is specified).
- An `org.springframework.web.context.request.WebRequest`, which is for using request properties and manipulating the HTTP session object without using the Servlet API directly. You should not use this parameter type if you also have parameters of types `HttpServletRequest`, `HttpServletResponse`, or `HttpSession` in the same method.

## Annotated Request Properties

You can use several parameter annotations (which are all in the package `org.springframework.web.bind.annotation`) to indicate that a method parameter's value should be taken from some property of the request. In most cases, a parameter marked with one of these annotations can be any primitive or primitive wrapper type, `String`, `Class`, `File`, `Locale`, `Pattern`, `java.util.Properties`, or `java.net.URL`, or an array or any `Collection` of any of these types. Spring automatically converts the value to that type, if possible. You can also register your own custom `java.beans.PropertyEditors` or `org.springframework.core.convert.converter.Converters` with Spring Framework to handle other types.

The `@RequestParam` annotation indicates that the annotated method parameter should be derived from the named request parameter. You specify the request parameter name using the `value` attribute (implicitly or explicitly). By default, this annotation indicates that the request parameter is required, and the request will not map without it. You can set the `required` attribute to `false` to disable this behavior (making the request parameter optional), in which case the method argument value is `null` if the request does not contain that request parameter. You can also use the `defaultValue` attribute to specify a value other than `null` to pass in if the request lacks the parameter. The following method accepts a required *`id`* request parameter, an optional *`name`* request parameter with a default value of `null`, and an optional *`key`* request parameter with a blank string as the default value. Request parameter names *are* case sensitive.

```
@RequestMapping("user")
public String user(@RequestParam("id") long userId,
                   @RequestParam(value="name", required=false) String name,
                   @RequestParam(value="key", defaultValue="") String key)
{ ... }
```

> **NOTE** *When using* `@RequestParam`*, you are not strictly required to specify the request parameter name using the* `value` *attribute. Spring Framework will infer that the request parameter name is equal to the method parameter name. However, this works only if your code compiles with local symbol debug information; otherwise, Spring cannot detect the parameter name. As an alternative to enabling local debug symbols, Spring also supports the new parameter name reflection tools added in Java 8, which require your code to be compiled with the* `-parameters` *command-line argument enabled. If you cannot rely on either of these, you should stick to explicitly specifying the request parameter name.*
>
> *If you expect a request parameter to have multiple values, make the corresponding method parameter an array or* `Collection` *of the appropriate type.*

You can also obtain all request parameter values in a `Map` by annotating a single parameter of type `Map<String, String>` or `org.springframework.util.MultiValueMap<String, String>` with `@RequestParam`.

`@RequestHeader` works identically to `@RequestParam` in providing access to request header values. It specifies a required (default) or optional request header to use as the value of the corresponding method parameter. Because HTTP headers can also have multiple values, you should use array or `Collection` parameter types if you expect this to be the case. You can annotate a single parameter of type `Map<String, String>`, `MultiValueMap<String, String>`, or `org.springframework.http.HttpHeaders` with `@RequestHeader` to obtain the values of all request headers. Of the following three methods, `foo` obtains two headers by name, while `bar` and `baz` obtain all headers. Header names *are not* case sensitive.

```
@RequestMapping("foo")
public String foo(@RequestHeader("Content-Type") String contentType,
                  @RequestHeader(value="X-Custom-Header", required=false)
                      Date customHeader)
{ ... }

@RequestMapping("bar")
public String bar(@RequestHeader MultiValueMap<String, String> headers)
{ ... }

@RequestMapping("baz")
public String baz(@RequestHeader HttpHeaders headers)
{ ... }
```

URL mappings in Spring Framework do not have to be static values. Instead, the URL can contain a template indicating that part of the URL is variable and its value is required at run time. *URI template variables* are often much friendlier to search engines and are part of the RESTful web services standard. The following code snippet demonstrates specifying a URI template variable in a URL mapping and using that template variable value as a value for a method parameter by way of `@PathVariable`.

```
@RequestMapping(value="user/{userId}", method=RequestMethod.GET)
public String user(@PathVariable("userId") long userId) { ... }
```

By default, Spring allows template variable values to contain any character other than a period (regular expression `[^\.]*`). You can customize this behavior by specifying a regular expression in the URL mapping to decrease the allowed characters or increase it to include periods. The following mapping is essentially the same as the previous one but restricts the *userId* template variable to numeric characters only. A request URL that does not contain this template variable or that contains invalid characters will not map to the controller method.

```
@RequestMapping(value="user/{userId:\\d+}", method=RequestMethod.GET)
public String user(@PathVariable("userId") long userId) { ... }
```

A URL mapping may contain multiple template variables, and each can have an associated method parameter. In addition, you can annotate a single method parameter of type `Map<String, String>` as `@PathVariable` and it will contain all URI template variable values from the URL.

```
@RequestMapping(value="foo/{var1}/bar/{var2}")
public String fooBar(@PathVariable("foo") String foo,
                     @PathVariable("bar") long bar)
{ ... }

@RequestMapping(value="bar/{var1}/foo/{var2}")
public String barFoo(@PathVariable Map<String, String> variables)
{ ... }
```

RFC 3986 defines the concept of *URI path parameters*. Unlike query parameters, which go in the query string and belong to the URI as a whole, path parameters belong to specific segments of a path.

For example, in the URL `http://www.example.com/hotel/43;floor=8;room=15/guest`, the path parameters *floor* and *room* belong to the path segment *43* (likely the hotel ID in this example). The Servlet API specification requires that path parameters be removed from the URL prior to matching it to a Servlet mapping. For the hotel URL, this means that the URL used to match the request to a Servlet is actually `/hotel/43/guest`. Spring Framework does the same thing when it matches requests to controller method mappings. In addition, Spring provides the `@MatrixVariable` annotation for extracting path parameters as method parameters. Similar to `@RequestParameter`, `@MatrixVariable` has `value`, `required`, and `defaultValue` attributes.

```
@RequestMapping("hotel/{hotelId:\\d+}/guest")
public String guestForRoom(@PathVariable("hotelId") long hotelId,
                           @MatrixVariable("floor") short floorNumber,
                           @MatrixVariable("room") short roomNumber)
{ ... }
```

This mapping matches the previous hotel URL. Because path parameters are ignored when matching requests to URL mappings, the mapping doesn't actually declare the parameters.

`@MatrixVariable` also has a `pathVar` attribute for specifying to which URI template variable (`@PathVariable`) the URI path parameter belongs. The `pathVar` attribute is optional, however. If only one path segment in your URL can contain a path parameter with the given name, you have no reason to specify the `pathVar`. If more than one path segment in your URL can contain a path parameter with the given name, you must specify `pathVar` to disambiguate which parameter you are referencing. The following example is semantically the same as the previous example, but completely unambiguous:

```
    @RequestMapping("hotel/{hotelId:\\d+}/guest")
    public String guestForRoom(@PathVariable("hotelId") long hotelId,
                               @MatrixVariable(pathVar="hotelId", value="floor")
                                   short floorNumber,
                               @MatrixVariable(pathVar="hotelId", value="room")
                                   short roomNumber)
    { ... }
```

## Input-Bound Form Objects

When working with HTML forms, a client submission can often contain a dozen or more fields. Consider a user sign-up form, which could have the username, password, confirmed password, e-mail address, first and last name, phone numbers, addresses, and more.

Although `@RequestParam` is certainly a valuable tool, having dozens of parameters for your method is tedious at best and makes unit testing fragile. Instead of this, Spring Framework enables you to specify a *form object*, also called a *command object*, as one of a controller method's parameters. Form objects are simple POJOs with accessor and mutator methods. They don't have to implement any special interface, and you don't have to mark the controller method parameter with any special annotation for Spring to recognize it as a form object.

```
public class UserRegistrationForm
{
    private String username;
    private String password;
    private String emailAddress;

    // other fields, and mutators and accessors
}

@RequestMapping("user")
public class UserController
{
    @RequestMapping(value="join", method=RequestMethod.POST)
    public String join(UserRegistrationForm form) { ... }
}
```

In this example, Spring looks through the `UserRegistrationForm` class for methods starting with `set`. It then maps request parameters to the form object properties using the parameter names. For example, the `setUsername` method is called with the value of the request parameter *`username`*, and the `setEmailAddress` method is called with the value of the *`emailAddress`* request parameter. If a request parameter doesn't match any form object properties, it is simply ignored. Likewise, if you have form object properties that aren't satisfied with request parameters, they are also ignored. The string-based request parameter values are converted to their destination property types using the registered `PropertyEditors` and `Converters` (the same ones that convert controller method arguments).

Spring can also validate the details of your form object automatically, which means you can avoid embedding that validation logic in your controller method. If you have bean validation enabled and if you mark your form object parameter with `@javax.validation.Valid`, the parameter that immediately follows the form object parameter may be of type `org.springframework.validation.Errors` or `org.springframework.validation.BindingResult`. When Spring calls the method, the value for that parameter is the result of the validation process. If the parameter immediately following the form object parameter is not an `Errors` or `BindingResult` object and validation of the form object fails, Spring simply throws an `org.springframework.web.bind.MethodArgumentNotValidException`.

```
@RequestMapping(value="join", method=RequestMethod.POST)
public String join(@Valid UserRegistrationForm form,
                   BindingResult validation) { ... }
```

The details of how form object validation works, and how you enable it, are covered in Chapter 16.

## Request Body Conversion and Entities

So far, the tools you have seen that coordinate with `@RequestMapping` have dealt with traditional features of `GET` and `POST` web requests: headers, URL query parameters, and `x-www-form-urlencoded` request bodies (form submissions). However, `POST` and `PUT` requests can contain data in formats other than `x-www-form-urlencoded`. For example, in a RESTful web service, a `POST` or `PUT` request may contain a request body in JSON or XML format to represent more complex data than possible with `x-www-form-urlencoded`. Request bodies can also contain binary, base64-encoded data or, for that matter, pretty much any format that the client and server can understand. When this data represents some kind of object, it is often referred to as the *request entity* or *HTTP entity*. Using the `@RequestBody` annotation, Spring automatically converts a request entity to a controller method parameter.

```
public class Account
{
    public long accountId;
    public String accountName;
    public String emailAddress;

    // other fields, and mutators and accessors
}

@RequestMapping("account")
public class AccountController
{
    @RequestMapping(value="update", method=RequestMethod.POST)
    public String update(@RequestBody Account account) { ... }
}
```

By default, `@RequestBody` parameters are required, but you can make them optional using the `required` attribute. Request entities are automatically converted using Spring's HTTP message converters. Although other parameter types, such as `@RequestParam` and `@RequestHeader` parameters, are simple types converted automatically from their string representation to the target type using `PropertyEditors` and `Converters`, request entities must have specialized message converters that can understand both the source format (JSON, XML, binary, and so on) and the destination format (a POJO or other complex object). You learn more about using HTTP message converters in Chapter 17.

Like form objects, you can also mark `@RequestBody` method parameters as `@Valid` to trigger content validation and can optionally follow the parameters with `Error` or `BindingResult` parameters. Again, validation throws a `MethodArgumentNotValidException` if validation fails and there is no `Error` or `BindingResult` parameter following the request entity parameter.

```
@RequestMapping(value="update", method=RequestMethod.POST)
public String update(@Valid @RequestBody Account account,
                     BindingResult validation) { ... }
```

Instead of using `@RequestBody`, your method could take an argument of type `org.springframework.http.HttpEntity<?>`. This type provides access to the request headers (`HttpHeaders`) and to the request body as the type argument specified. So, you could replace the previous method with this:

```
@RequestMapping(value="update", method=RequestMethod.POST)
public String update(HttpEntity<Account> request) { ... }
```

However, validation of the request body object does not happen automatically using the `HttpEntity` parameter, so there is really no compelling benefit to using it.

## Multipart Request Data

In Chapter 3, you learned how to accept file uploads in your Servlets using Servlet 3.0's multipart request support. In a browser environment, you almost always use a multipart request for uploading files along with regular form data. In these cases, the request has a `Content-Type` of `multipart/form-data`, and it contains a part for each form field submitted. Each part of the request, separated by a specified boundary, has a `Content-Disposition` of `form-data` and a name matching the form input name. If the form field is a standard form field, its part simply contains the data from the form field. If the form field is a file-type field for a single file, its part has a `Content-Type` matching the file MIME type and the file contents, binary encoded if necessary.

The following is a sample `POST` of a form with a single field *`username`* with the value "John" and a single-file upload of a text file, similar to what you would see using a network monitoring tool like Wireshark or Fiddler:

```
POST /form/upload HTTP/1.1
Hostname: www.example.org
Content-Type: multipart/form-data; boundary=X3oABba8
Content-Length: 236

--X3oABba8
Content-Disposition: form-data; name="username"

John
--X3oABba8
Content-Disposition: form-data; name="upload"; filename="sample.txt"
Content-Type: text/plain; charset=UTF-8

This is the contents of sample.txt
--X3oABba8--
```

If the form field is a file-type field for multiple files, its part has a `Content-Type` of `multipart/mixed` and contains its own parts, one for each file, as in the following example:

```
POST /form/upload HTTP/1.1
Hostname: www.example.org
Content-Type: multipart/form-data; boundary=X3oABba8
Content-Length: 512

--X3oABba8
Content-Disposition: form-data; name="username"

John
--X3oABba8
Content-Disposition: form-data; name="uploads"
Content-Type: multipart/mixed; boundary=Bc883CXNc

--Bc883CXNc
Content-Disposition: file; filename="sample.txt"
Content-Type: text/plain; charset=UTF-8

This is the contents of sample.txt
--Bc883CXNc
Content-Disposition: file; filename="blank-pixel.gif"
Content-Type: image/gif
Content-Transfer-Encoding: base64

R0lGODlhAQABAHAAACH5BAUAAAAALAAAAAABAAEAAAICRAEAOw==
--Bc883CXNc--
--X3oABba8--
```

Marking a controller method parameter with `@RequestParam` results in Spring pulling that value from the URL query parameter with that name, the `x-www-form-urlencoded` `POST` request body parameter with that name, or from the multipart request part with that name. However, the available `PropertyEditors` and `Converters` convert these parameters only from string values to simple types. File uploads are neither string values nor simple types.

The `@RequestPart` annotation can mark any controller method parameter that should come from a part in a multipart request and should be converted with an HTTP message converter instead of a `PropertyEditor` or `Converter`. Like so many of the other annotations, it also has a `required` attribute that defaults to `true`.

```
@RequestMapping(value="form/upload", method=RequestMethod.POST)
public String upload(@RequestParam("username") String username,
                     @RequestPart("upload") Part upload) { ... }
```

This method can respond to the previously demonstrated multipart request containing a single file. This works because Spring has a built-in HTTP message converter that recognizes file parts. In addition to the `javax.servlet.http.Part` type, you can also convert file uploads to `org.springframework.web.multipart.MultipartFile`. If the file field permits multiple file uploads, as demonstrated in the second multipart request, simply use an array or `Collection` of `Parts` or `MultipartFiles`.

```
@RequestMapping(value="form/upload", method=RequestMethod.POST)
public String upload(@RequestParam("username") String username,
                     @RequestPart("uploads") List<MultipartFile> uploads)
{ ... }
```

You are not limited to using multipart file uploads directly as controller method parameters. Your form objects can contain `Part` or `MultipartFile` fields, and Spring knows automatically that it must obtain the values from file parts and converts the values appropriately.

```
public class UploadForm
{
    private String username;
    private List<Part> uploads;

    // mutators and accessors
}

    @RequestMapping(value="form/upload", method=RequestMethod.POST)
    public String upload(UploadForm form) { ... }
```

So far, you have seen multipart processing used exclusively for file uploads, but for Spring request processing, file uploads are not the only multipart contents supported. Instead of `multipart/form-data`, a request might be `multipart/mixed`. Its parts could then contain any content, including request entities in JSON, XML, or binary form. Spring can then convert these parts to any type for which it has an appropriate HTTP message converter. You can even use validation with non-file parts, just like you can with `@RequestBody` parameters and form objects.

```
    @RequestMapping(value="update", method=RequestMethod.POST)
    public String update(@Valid @RequestPart("account") Account account,
                         BindingResult validation) { ... }
```

It should be noted that using multipart requests in this manner is extremely unusual. Typically, entity requests have a one-part body; multipart requests come from browsers uploading files.

### Model Types

In the next section you explore using models and views in the Spring MVC architecture. It should be noted here, however, that your controller methods may have a single non-annotated parameter of type `Map<String, Object>`, `org.springframework.ui.ModelMap`, or `org.springframework.ui.Model`. A method parameter of one of these types represents the model that Spring passes to your views for rendering, and you may add any attributes to it, as needed, while your method executes.

## Selecting Valid Return Types for Controller Methods

As you have undoubtedly concluded, Spring Framework is extraordinarily flexible as to what method parameters your `@RequestMapping` methods may specify. Likewise, Spring is quite flexible on which types your controller methods may return. Generally speaking, while the method parameters are usually related to the request contents, the return type is typically related to the response. A `void` return type, for example, tells Spring that your method handles writing to the response manually, and so Spring does no further request handling after your method returns. More typically, however, a controller method returns some type (sometimes with an annotation) indicating how Spring should respond to the request.

## Model Types

Controller methods may return a Map<String, Object>, a ModelMap, or a Model. This is an alternative to specifying one of these types as a method parameter. Spring can recognize this return type as the model and determine the view automatically using the configured org.springframework.web.servlet.RequestToViewNameTranslator (defaults to org.springframework.web.servlet.view.DefaultRequestToViewNameTranslator).

## View Types

To instruct Spring to use a specific view to render a response, your controller methods may return a number of view types. The org.springframework.web.servlet.View interface (or any class implementing View) indicates that your method returns an explicit view object. After your method returns, request handling is passed off to that view. Spring Framework provides dozens of View implementations (such as RedirectView, for example), or you may create your own. Your controller methods may also return a String indicating the *name* of a view to resolve. You learn more about view resolution in the next section. Finally, your methods may return an org.springframework.web.servlet.ModelAndView. This class provides the ability to return both a View and a model type, or a String view name and a model type, at the same time.

## Response Body Entities

Just like request bodies can contain HTTP entities (request entities), response bodies can contain HTTP entities (*response entities*). Controller methods can return HttpEntity<?> or org.springframework.http.ResponseEntity<?>, and Spring converts the body object in the entity to the correct response content using the appropriate HTTP message converter based on the negotiated content type. HttpEntity permits setting of the response body and various headers. ResponseEntity, which extends HttpEntity, adds the ability to set the response status code in the form of an org.springframework.http.HttpStatus.

```
@RequestMapping(value="user/{userId}", method=RequestMethod.GET)
public ResponseEntity<User> getUser(@PathVariable("userId") long userId)
{
    User user = this.userService.getUser(id);
    return new ResponseEntity<User>(user, HttpStatus.OK);
}
```

If you don't want to use the HttpEntity or ResponseEntity, you can return the body object itself and annotate the method with @ResponseBody, which has the same effect. You can then also annotate the method with @ResponseStatus to specify the response status code (which defaults to 200 OK if you don't use @ResponseStatus).

```
@RequestMapping(value="user/{userId}", method=RequestMethod.GET)
@ResponseBody
@ResponseStatus(HttpStatus.OK)
public User getUser(@PathVariable("userId") long userId)
{
    return this.userService.getUser(id);
}
```

In Chapter 12, you used a return type of `String` with the `@ResponseBody` annotation for one of the examples. When `@ResponseBody` is specified, other handlers for the returned type (such as view resolution) are ignored. Because of this, Spring returned the `String` as the actual response body for that example instead of resolving a view by name. `@ResponseBody` always takes precedence over all other controller method return value handlers.

### Any Return Type

Your methods may return any other object, and Spring assumes this object should be an attribute in the model. It uses the camelCase version of the return type class name as the model attribute name unless the method is annotated with `@ModelAttribute`, in which case Spring uses the name specified in the annotation as the attribute name. In either scenario, Spring determines the view automatically using the configured `RequestToViewNameTranslator`. In the following example, the first method's return value becomes a model attribute named *userAccount*, and the second method's return value becomes a model attribute named *user*.

```
@RequestMapping("user/{userId}")
public UserAccount viewUser(@PathVariable("userId") long userId)
{ ... }

@RequestMapping("user/{userId}")
@ModelAttribute("user")
public UserAccount viewUser(@PathVariable("userId") long userId)
{ ... }
```

### Asynchronous Types

In addition to all the return type options previously listed, controller methods may return `java.util.concurrent.Callable<?>` or `org.springframework.web.context.request.async.DeferredResult<?>`. These types cause Spring to execute the `Callable` or `DeferredResult` in a separate thread using asynchronous request handling, freeing up the request thread to answer another request. You would typically do this for requests that may take a long time to respond to, especially if they spend much of that time blocking for network or disk I/O. The type parameter (return type) for the `Callable` or `DeferredResult` should be the type you would normally return from the controller method if you did not want to invoke asynchronous request handling (`View`, `String`, `ModelMap`, `ModelAndView`, `ResponseEntity`, and so on). You can still annotate the controller method with `@ResponseBody`, `@ResponseStatus`, or `@ModelAttribute` to trigger the appropriate handling after the `Callable` or `DeferredResult` returns. The same cautions expressed in Chapters 9 and 11 regarding asynchronous request handling with filters and logging apply here as well.

## USING SPRING FRAMEWORK'S MODEL AND VIEW PATTERN

As you have probably concluded by this point, Spring Framework's MVC architecture gets its name due to its reliance on the *Model-View-Controller* (*MVC*) design pattern. If you are not familiar with the MVC pattern, it may be helpful at this point to pick up a copy of *Head First Design Patterns* (O'Reilly, ISBN 978-0596007126) and read about it.

To sum it up in one sentence, controllers manipulate data in a model that represents information the user is interested in and pass that model on to the view, which renders the model in a way useful to the user. The user only ever knowingly interacts with the view, but he unknowingly interacts with the controller when he performs actions of some kind. The MVC pattern works great in a Java Enterprise Edition environment, and indeed you have already been using it since Chapter 4! A Servlet can be thought of as a controller, performing actions on behalf of the user when requested. The Servlet manipulates the model in the form of `HttpServletRequest` attributes and then forwards that model on to the view, the JSP, for rendering.

Spring takes this two steps further by separating the model from the request entirely (remember: `Map<String, Object>`, `ModelMap`, or `Model`) and providing the high-level `View` interface that can be implemented in infinite ways. The `InternalResourceView` and `JstlView` implement traditional JSP and JSTL-enhanced-JSP views, respectively. They take care of translating model attributes to request attributes and forwarding the request on to the proper JSP. If you aren't a fan of JSP, you can choose `FreeMarkerView` (which supports the FreeMarker template engine), `VelocityView` (which supports the Apache Velocity template engine), and `TilesView` (which supports the Apache Tiles template engine). You can also implement support for some other template engine.

If you need to transform the model into a JSON or an XML response — typical for RESTful web services and Ajax-backing request endpoints — Spring provides the `MappingJackson2JsonView` and `MarshallingView`. These support JSON and XML, respectively. You can also use the `RedirectView`, which sends a `Location`-header redirect response with status code `302 Found` (for HTTP 1.0 compatibility) or `303 See Other` (the correct status code for HTTP 1.1 clients) depending on how you construct it. Later, in the section "Updating the Customer Support Application," you write your own custom view called `DownloadView` to send the content of a server-side file to the user's browser.

When a controller method returns an implementation of `View`, or `ModelAndView` with an implementation of `View` passed into the `ModelAndView` constructor, Spring uses that `View` directly and requires no further logic to determine how to present your model to the client. If the controller method returns a `String` view name, or a `ModelAndView` constructed with a `String` view name, Spring must resolve that view name into an actual `View` using the configured `org.springframework.web.servlet.ViewResolver`. If the method returns a model or model attribute, Spring must first implicitly translate the request into a view name using the configured `RequestToViewNameTranslator` (as previously described) and *then* resolve that named view using the `ViewResolver`. Finally, when a controller method returns a response entity, `ResponseEntity`, or `HttpEntity`, Spring uses content negotiation to determine which view to present the entity with.

This section covers each of these techniques. Your application may use one of them exclusively or some or all of them throughout your controllers. You can follow along in the Model-View-Controller project available for download on the `wrox.com` code download site.

## Using Explicit Views and View Names

The Model-View-Controller project is bootstrapped and configured programmatically just like you learned in Chapter 12: A `WebApplicationInitializer` starts Spring Framework, which is configured with two `@Configuration` classes, `RootContextConfiguration` and `ServletContextConfiguration`. For this project, all requests are mapped to the `HomeController` class.

## Using the Redirect View

Generally, the most common view you would explicitly return is the `org.springframework.web.servlet.view.RedirectView` for sending the client to a different URL. If the URL begins with a protocol (`http://`, `https://`, and so on) or network prefix (`//`), it is assumed to be an absolute URL. If the URL is relative (no protocol, prefix, or leading forward slash) it is assumed to be relative to the current URL (typical web and file system behavior). Perhaps counter-intuitively, `RedirectView` normally considers URLs starting with a forward slash to be relative to the *server* URL as opposed to the application *context* URL (which, in almost all cases, is not the intended behavior). So, when you construct a `RedirectView`, it is important to enable context-relative absolute URLs, as demonstrated in the first method in the `HomeController`.

```
@RequestMapping("/")
public View home(Map<String, Object> model)
{
    model.put("dashboardUrl", "dashboard");
    return new RedirectView("/{dashboardUrl}", true);
}
```

The second, `true` argument to the `RedirectView` constructor tells `RedirectView` that the URL is context-relative, not server-relative. Notice the replacement template `{dashboardUrl}` in the URL for the `RedirectView`. `RedirectView` replaces such templates with attributes from the model. Of course, in this case it would have been easier to construct the view with the static URL string (`new RedirectView("/dashboard", true)`), but using this template demonstrates the power of the `RedirectView`.

The eventual URL to which the view is redirecting the client is rather useless without a handler method, and the second method in the `HomeController` takes care of this.

```
@RequestMapping(value = "/dashboard", method = RequestMethod.GET)
public String dashboard(Map<String, Object> model)
{
    model.put("text", "This is a model attribute.");
    model.put("date", Instant.now());

    return "home/dashboard";
}
```

This method responds to the `/dashboard` URL, adding text and date attributes and returning the `String` name of a view. But what does this name mean? How does Spring take this name and figure out the view from it?

## Configuring View Resolution

To match this view name to an actual view, Spring needs a `ViewResolver` instance that can understand it. Creating a view resolver is a simple task of instantiating a framework bean within the dispatcher servlet application context. For this, you should use the `InternalResourceViewResolver`, which can turn view names into JSP filenames. This is accomplished with the `viewResolver` method of the `ServletContextConfiguration`.

```
@Bean
public ViewResolver viewResolver()
{
```

```
        InternalResourceViewResolver resolver =
                new InternalResourceViewResolver();
        resolver.setViewClass(JstlView.class);
        resolver.setPrefix("/WEB-INF/jsp/view/");
        resolver.setSuffix(".jsp");
        return resolver;
    }
```

As configured, the view resolver constructs JSP file names using the prefix `/WEB-INF/jsp/view` followed by the view name followed by `.jsp`. There's nothing else you need to do to get view resolution working. You should note that it's important to name the bean `viewResolver`, and thus you must also name the `@Bean` method `viewResolver`.

## Creating a JSP View

Naturally, given the configured view resolver and the view name returned by the `dashboard` handler method, the application needs a `/WEB-INF/jsp/view/home/dashboard.jsp` file. There is nothing special about this JSP file. You can use all the same features within it — scriptlets, expressions, expression language, JSP tags, and more — as you can within any other JSP. Notice the `@elvariable` type hints, which you learned in Part I, help your IDE provide validation and code suggestion services for your JSPs.

```
<%--@elvariable id="text" type="java.lang.String"--%>
<%--@elvariable id="date" type="java.time.Instant"--%>
<!DOCTYPE html>
<html>
    <head>
        <title>Dashboard</title>
    </head>
    <body>
        Text: ${text}<br />
        Date: ${date}
    </body>
</html>
```

The view in this case is simple: It just prints out the two attributes on the model. Notice that you access the model attributes just as you used to access `HttpServletRequest` attributes. You don't have to do anything special because the `JstlView` ensures all your model attributes are exposed as EL variables for the JSP. To test this, compile your application and start Tomcat from your IDE. Go to `http://localhost:8080/mvc` and you should immediately be redirected to `http://localhost:8080/mvc/dashboard`. This is the `RedirectView` doing its job in the `HomeController`'s `home` method. Your browser should now display the text from the model and the current time in ISO 8601 format. This means view resolution is working properly and your JSP view displayed your model through the `JstlView`.

# Using Implicit Views with Model Attributes

If a controller method returns a model or model attribute, Spring must determine which view to use automatically. To do this, it needs a `RequestToViewNameTranslator` bean coupled with a `ViewResolver`.

## Configuring View Name Translation

Although you can create your own `RequestToViewNameTranslator` if needed, the `DefaultRequestToViewNameTranslator` is usually sufficient. It strips off the web application context URL and any file extension at the end of the URL. What remains of the URL becomes the view name. For example, the URL `http://localhost:8080/mvc/foo` turns into the view name `foo`, whereas the URL `http://localhost:8080/mvc/foo/bar.html` turns into the view name `foo/bar`. As with the `ViewResolver`, all you have to do is add a bean to the `ServletContextConfiguration` in order to configure the `RequestToViewNameTranslator`.

```
@Bean
public RequestToViewNameTranslator viewNameTranslator()
{
    return new DefaultRequestToViewNameTranslator();
}
```

You can customize how the `DefaultRequestToViewNameTranslator` translates the name with various configuration methods, but here the default configuration is sufficient. You must name the bean `viewNameTranslator`, so you must also name the `@Bean` method `viewNameTranslator`.

## Using @ModelAttribute

After you configure view name translation, taking advantage of it is simple. The `userHome` method of the `HomeController`, mapped to the `/user/home` URL, creates a `User` object, sets some values on it, and returns the `User`. The `User` class, in this case, is a simple POJO with fields `userId`, `username`, and `name`, accompanied by standard mutators and accessors.

```
@RequestMapping(value = "/user/home", method = RequestMethod.GET)
@ModelAttribute("currentUser")
public User userHome()
{
    User user = new User();
    user.setUserId(1234987234L);
    user.setUsername("adam");
    user.setName("Adam Johnson");
    return user;
}
```

The `@ModelAttribute` annotation tells Spring that the `User` returned should be added to the model with the attribute key *`currentUser`*. Without the annotation, Spring uses the default attribute key *`user`* (based on the class name of the type returned). You need a view to display this user, and based on the configured view name translation, the view name becomes `user/home`, so you can create the JSP `/WEB-INF/jsp/view/user/home.jsp`.

```
<%--@elvariable id="currentUser" type="com.wrox.site.User"--%>
<!DOCTYPE html>
<html>
    <head>
        <title>User Home</title>
    </head>
    <body>
        ID: ${currentUser.userId}<br />
        Username: ${currentUser.username}<br />
```

```
        Name: ${currentUser.name}<br />
    </body>
</html>
```

Now compile the project, start Tomcat from your IDE, and go to `http://localhost:8080/mvc/user/home` in your browser. You should see the ID, username, and name for the user as created in the `userHome` controller method. View name translation and view resolution worked together to detect and display the proper view for the request.

# Returning Response Entities

Getting request entities and returning response entities is a task typically reserved for RESTful web services or other automated tasks. In the majority of cases, browsers are involved in these situations only when a JavaScript application makes an Ajax `GET` from or `POST` to the server. For this reason, HTTP entities and content negotiation are covered in greater detail in Chapter 17. This section covers the basics of handling response entities and configuring message converters and content negotiation.

## Configuring Message Converters

When a server receives a `POST` or `PUT` with a request body, this body is typically called an HTTP entity or request entity, but may also be called a *message*. That message, in whatever format it might be, must be converted to a Java object of some type for your controller methods to consume. This happens based on the `Content-Type` header of the request.

You have already learned about one message converter and may not have even realized it: The `org.springframework.http.converter.FormHttpMessageConverter` is responsible for converting `x-www-form-urlencoded` messages into form objects for your controller methods. Message converters work both ways: They can convert incoming messages to Java objects as well as convert Java objects to outgoing messages. They operate on the simple principle of recognized MIME content types and target Java types. Each converter has one or more supported MIME and Java types, and it can convert messages with those MIME types to Java objects of those types and back. This is the tail end of the content-negotiation process. When Spring establishes a negotiated content type, it picks a converter that supports the source and target type and uses it for the incoming or outgoing entities, or both if applicable. (In a single request, it's possible for the request to include a message of one content type while the server responds with a message of a different content type.)

Spring Framework automatically creates certain message converters on your behalf if you don't configure any manually. In many cases, this automatic configuration is sufficient. For the purposes of demonstration and extra configuration, the Model-View-Controller project configures the message converters manually. To do this, the `ServletContextConfiguration` class must extend `WebMvcConfigurerAdapter` and override the `configureMessageConverters` method.

```
...
public class ServletContextConfiguration extends WebMvcConfigurerAdapter
{
    @Inject ObjectMapper objectMapper;
    @Inject Marshaller marshaller;
```

```
        @Inject Unmarshaller unmarshaller;

        @Override
        public void configureMessageConverters(
                List<HttpMessageConverter<?>> converters
        ) {
            converters.add(new ByteArrayHttpMessageConverter());
            converters.add(new StringHttpMessageConverter());
            converters.add(new FormHttpMessageConverter());
            converters.add(new SourceHttpMessageConverter<>());

            MarshallingHttpMessageConverter xmlConverter =
                    new MarshallingHttpMessageConverter();
            xmlConverter.setSupportedMediaTypes(Arrays.asList(
                    new MediaType("application", "xml"),
                    new MediaType("text", "xml")
            ));
            xmlConverter.setMarshaller(this.marshaller);
            xmlConverter.setUnmarshaller(this.unmarshaller);
            converters.add(xmlConverter);

            MappingJackson2HttpMessageConverter jsonConverter =
                    new MappingJackson2HttpMessageConverter();
            jsonConverter.setSupportedMediaTypes(Arrays.asList(
                    new MediaType("application", "json"),
                    new MediaType("text", "json")
            ));
            jsonConverter.setObjectMapper(this.objectMapper);
            converters.add(jsonConverter);
        }
    ...
    }
```

The `ByteArrayHttpMessageConverter`, `StringHttpMessageConverter`, `FormHttpMessageConverter`, and `SourceHttpMessageConverter` are all converters that Spring would configure automatically. They are configured here, in the same order they would be normally. Order is important because some converters have broader MIME type and Java type nets that might mask other converters you prefer to use.

The `MarshallingHttpMessageConverter` is not typically added to the list of message converters, but it is in this case to support translation to and from XML entities. The `MappingJackson2HttpMessageConverter` *is* normally created automatically as long as the Jackson Data Processor 2 is on the classpath. However, it is created with a default, non-configured `com.fasterxml.jackson.databind.ObjectMapper` and supports only the `application/json` MIME content type. The configuration here adds support for `text/json` and uses a preconfigured `ObjectMapper`.

You undoubtedly noticed that the `org.springframework.oxm.Marshaller`, `org.springframework.oxm.Unmarshaller`, and `ObjectMapper` are injected in the configuration class, and you are probably wondering where they come from. To enable these beans to be configured and shared throughout the application, they are created in the `RootContextConfiguration`. Because the `org.springframework.oxm.jaxb.Jaxb2Marshaller` is both a `Marshaller` and an `Unmarshaller`, it fulfills both dependencies.

```
@Bean
public ObjectMapper objectMapper()
{
    ObjectMapper mapper = new ObjectMapper();
    mapper.findAndRegisterModules();
    mapper.configure(SerializationFeature.WRITE_DATES_AS_TIMESTAMPS, false);
    mapper.configure(DeserializationFeature.ADJUST_DATES_TO_CONTEXT_TIME_ZONE,
            false);
    return mapper;
}

@Bean
public Jaxb2Marshaller jaxb2Marshaller()
{
    Jaxb2Marshaller marshaller = new Jaxb2Marshaller();
    marshaller.setPackagesToScan(new String[] { "com.wrox.site" });
    return marshaller;
}
```

The Jackson `ObjectMapper` configuration does some important things. First, it tells Jackson to find and register all extension modules, such as the JSR 310 (Java 8 Date and Time) support module. It then disables serializing dates as timestamp integers (meaning they will be written as ISO 8601 strings) and adjustment of deserialized dates to the current time zone (so that date strings without time zones are assumed to be UTC). The Jaxb2Marshaller has a fairly simple configuration — it is simply told which package to scan for XML-annotated entities.

## Configuring Content Negotiation

*Content negotiation* is the process whereby the client conveys to the server a list of preferred response content types, in order of preference, and the server chooses a suitable content type from those (or a default if none of them are suitable). The largest and most challenging part of content negotiation is figuring out what format the client wants its data in. If the request contains a request entity, it will also have a `Content-Type` header for that entity, but that is not necessarily the format the client wants the response to be in. (Although it usually is.) Then there's the `Accept` header, meant to indicate which response formats the client is willing to accept. The key here is that the word "formats" is plural; the client may indicate many acceptable formats and a preference or precedence for each one. Older browsers sent long, confusing `Accept` headers that were difficult to comply by and often listed `text/html` last or not at all. Internet Explorer 8 on a Windows 7 machine with Microsoft Office installed sends an `Accept` header of more than 200 bytes with 14 MIME types in it, and *none* of them are `text/html`!

Thankfully, the latest versions of all the major browsers today send sensible `Accept` headers containing at least `text/html`. Also, when using JavaScript applications or RESTful web service clients, the client application has complete control over the `Accept` header, making its contents a much more reliable factor in negotiating content type. To be realistic, the browser is rarely involved in content negotiation anyway. In almost all cases, a request to your web application will fall into one of three categories:

- If it's a request due to someone clicking a link or otherwise entering an address in their browser's address bar, the target is some resource with a fixed content type that isn't subject to negotiation — an HTML page (`text/html` or `application/xhtml+xml`), a file to download, and so on.

- If it's an Ajax request from a client-side JavaScript browser application, the client application has complete control over the `Accept` header for performing content negotiation.
- If it's a client application accessing your web services, it has complete control over the `Accept` header for performing content negotiation.

Content negotiation in Spring uses a multistep approach for determining the content type the client wants to receive back. Sometimes the same message converter is used for the request and the response and sometimes it is not. When the request contains a request entity, the incoming message converter is always chosen based on the request's `Content-Type` header. When the response contains a response entity, the outgoing message converter is chosen in a multistep process:

1. **Spring first looks for a file extension on the request URL.** If it contains a file extension (such as `.html`, `.xml`, `.json`, and so on), it determines the requested format based on that. If it does not contain a file extension, or if the file extension is not recognized, it moves on.
2. **Spring next looks for a request parameter named *`format`*. (You can configure this to change the parameter name.)** If this exists, it uses the requested format (`html`, `xml`, `json`, and so on). If the *`format`* parameter does not exist or is not recognized, it moves on.
3. **Finally, Spring uses the `Accept` header to determine the wanted response format.**

You can customize this entire process to meet your needs. You can completely eliminate one or more steps and change how each step works based on how you want your application to perform content negotiation. (However, you cannot reorder the steps.) The `ServletContextConfiguration` class in the Model-View-Controller project overrides the `configureContentNegotiation` method of `WebMvcConfigurerAdapter` to accomplish this.

```
@Override
public void configureContentNegotiation(
        ContentNegotiationConfigurer configurer)
{
    configurer.favorPathExtension(true).favorParameter(false)
            .parameterName("mediaType").ignoreAcceptHeader(false)
            .useJaf(false).defaultContentType(MediaType.APPLICATION_XML)
            .mediaType("xml", MediaType.APPLICATION_XML)
            .mediaType("json", MediaType.APPLICATION_JSON);
}
```

This configuration enables file extension checking, disables request parameter checking, sets the request parameter name to *`mediaType`* (unnecessary because this is disabled, but shown here for demonstration purposes), and ensures the `Accept` header is not ignored. It also disables using Java Activation Framework (JAF) — a tool that can map file extensions to media types, among other things — in favor of manually specifying the supported media types. Finally, it sets the default content type to `application/xml`, and adds support for `application/xml` and `application/json`.

## Using @ResponseBody

Now that content negotiation is properly configured, you can use it with a controller method. The `getUser` method of the `HomeController` does just that.

```
@RequestMapping(value = "/user/{userId}", method = RequestMethod.GET)
@ResponseBody
public User getUser(@PathVariable("userId") long userId)
{
    User user = new User();
    user.setUserId(userId);
    user.setUsername("john");
    user.setName("John Smith");
    return user;
}
```

Notice the use of `@ResponseBody`, which is what triggers the content negotiation strategy you configured. Also, this method uses URI template variables and the `@PathVariable` annotation to get the user ID from the URL instead of a request parameter. Now compile the application, start Tomcat for your IDE, and go to `http://localhost:8080/mvc/user/12` in your favorite browser. You should see the user represented as XML (shown in Figure 13-1), either because the `Accept` header your browser sends includes `application/xml` or because XML was set as the default in your content negotiation configuration.

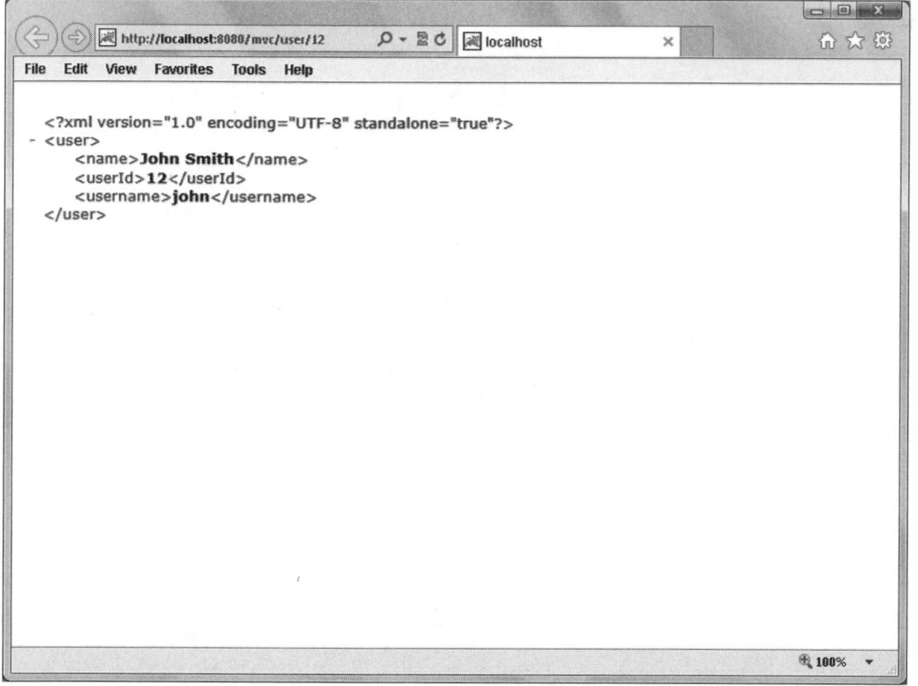


FIGURE 13-1

If you change the ID at the end of the URL, the XML changes to reflect the new ID. Now go to `http://localhost:8080/mvc/user/13.json` and the presentation changes from XML to JSON. (I recommend you use Chrome or Firefox for this because Internet Explorer will prompt you to download a JSON file.) You don't have to change the URL mapping for your controller method because Spring recognizes the extension, ignores it for request mapping, and uses it for content negotiation. Now if you change the extension from JSON to XML, the presentation changes back to XML.

> **NOTE** *The* `Jaxb2Marshaller` *can marshal the* `User` *object to its XML representation because the* `User` *class is annotated with* `@javax.xml.bind.annotation.XmlRootElement`.

## MAKING YOUR LIFE EASIER WITH FORM OBJECTS

Form objects in Spring Framework are one of the biggest conveniences when you write browser-based web applications. The work of locating, casting, and translating request parameters to business objects can be tedious, and that tedium just gets greater with each additional property a business object has. Using form objects is simple, and the Spring-Forms project available on the `wrox.com` code download site demonstrates just how it's done with a simple controller and a few JSP views.

The `UserManagementController` has two private fields and a synchronized private method for generating user IDs atomically. To start, it also has a request handler method `displayUsers` for displaying a list of the existing users.

```
@Controller
public class UserManagementController
{
    private final Map<Long, User> userDatabase = new Hashtable<>();
    private volatile long userIdSequence = 1L;

    @RequestMapping(value = "user/list", method = RequestMethod.GET)
    public String displayUsers(Map<String, Object> model)
    {
        model.put("userList", this.userDatabase.values());
        return "user/list";
    }
...
    private synchronized long getNextUserId()
    {
        return this.userIdSequence++;
    }
}
```

The `User` class is a simple POJO class with fields `userId`, `username`, and `name`, and appropriate mutators and accessors. The `/WEB-INF/jsp/view/user/list.jsp` view provides a link to add a new user and uses the `<c:forEach>` tag to loop over and display the existing users.

```
<%--@elvariable id="userList" type="java.util.Collection<com.wrox.site.User>"--%>
<!DOCTYPE html>
<html>
    <head>
        <title>User List</title>
    </head>
    <body>
        <h2>Users</h2>
        [<a href="<c:url value="/user/add" />">new user</a>]<br />
```

```
        <br />
        <c:forEach items="${userList}" var="user">
            ${user.name} (${user.username})
            [<a href="<c:url value="/user/edit/${user.userId}"/>">edit</a>]<br/>
        </c:forEach>
    </body>
</html>
```

## Adding the Form Object to Your Model

For you to use a form object, it first needs to be accessible in the view displaying the form. The `createUser(Map)` method adds a new `UserForm` object to the model and returns the `user/add` view name. You'd be right to wonder why the code uses both `User` and `UserForm` objects. Admittedly, this is overkill in this case. But it highlights that your business objects won't always look exactly like your form objects.

As an example, you might simply have many fields you don't need or want to display or have users edit on a web form. Also, you may have some fields in a different format or of a different type in your form objects than in your business objects. You might even use more than one form (and, thus, form object) to edit a single business object. Actually, many times you must have separate form objects and business objects, and this example demonstrates how to do that.

```
    @RequestMapping(value = "user/add", method = RequestMethod.GET)
    public String createUser(Map<String, Object> model)
    {
        model.put("userForm", new UserForm());
        return "user/add";
    }
...
    @RequestMapping(value = "user/edit/{userId}", method = RequestMethod.GET)
    public String editUser(Map<String, Object> model,
                           @PathVariable("userId") long userId)
    {
        User user = this.userDatabase.get(userId);
        UserForm form = new UserForm();
        form.setUsername(user.getUsername());
        form.setName(user.getName());
        model.put("userForm", form);

        return "user/edit";
    }
```

Notice that the `editUser(Map, long)` method also adds a `UserForm` to the model, but it does so differently. It first retrieves the `User` being edited, copies that user's information to the form, and then puts the form on the model before returning the `user/edit` view name.

## Using the Spring Framework <form> Tags

The `/WEB-INF/jsp/view/user/add.jsp` and `/WEB-INF/jsp/view/user/edit.jsp` views are quite simple. All they do is set the *`title`* EL variable and include the `/WEB-INF/jsp/view/user/form.jspf` file.

```
<c:set var="title" value="Add User" />
<%@ include file="form.jspf" %>
```

The previous two lines of code make up the entire `add.jsp` file, and `edit.jsp` is nearly identical except that *`title`* is set to "Edit User." The `form.jspf` file outputs the form using the *`userForm`* model attribute.

```
<%--@elvariable id="userForm" type="com.wrox.site.UserForm"--%>
<!DOCTYPE html>
<html>
    <head>
        <title>${title}</title>
    </head>
    <body>
        <h1>${title}</h1>
        <form:form method="post" modelAttribute="userForm">
            <form:label path="username">Username</form:label><br />
            <form:input path="username" /><br />
            <br />
            <form:label path="name">Name:</form:label><br />
            <form:input path="name" /><br />
            <br />
            <input type="submit" value="Save" />
        </form:form>
    </body>
</html>
```

The first thing you probably noticed is the use of tags in the `form` namespace. This tag library, provided by Spring Framework, is a wrapper around standard `<form>`, `<input>`, and `<textarea>` fields and provides automatic field binding to form object contents. When creating a new user, this doesn't mean much. However, when editing an existing user, the values from the model attribute are automatically placed in the form fields that belong to them. This simplifies your code and eliminates the worry over properly escaping values for use in the form. Of course, to use a tag library, you must first declare it. The `form` tag library is declared with all the other tag libraries in the `base.jspf` file, which is automatically included in all your JSPs.

```
<%@ taglib prefix="form" uri="http://www.springframework.org/tags/form" %>
```

The `form` namespace includes 14 tags that encapsulate a wide range of web form features. In addition to its own attributes, each tag supports all the standard HTML attributes for the HTML tag to which it is equivalent. The `<form:form>` tag is the parent tag of all the others, indicating which model attribute form object the form fields will bind to. You don't have to specify the `action` attribute (although you can) because by default `<form:form>` always submits to the URL of the current page. The remaining 13 tags bind to various bean properties of the form object, indicated by the `path` attributes on the tags.

- `<form:errors>` is equivalent to a `<span>` and is related to automatic form object validation. You learn more about this tag in Chapter 16.
- `<form:label>`, which indicates label text for a field, is the equivalent of `<label>`.
- `<form:hidden>` is the equivalent of `<input type="hidden">`.
- `<form:input>`, as you have already seen, is the equivalent of `<input type="text">`.

- `<form:password>` is normally the equivalent of `<input type="password">` and has a `showPassword` attribute (defaulting to `false`) that specifies whether the password should display. When `showPassword` is `true`, this tag is actually equivalent to `<input type="text">`.
- `<form:textarea>` is equivalent to `<textarea>`.
- `<form:checkbox>` is the equivalent of `<input type="checkbox">` and can support multiple types of properties, such as `booleans`, `Booleans`, and numeric types.
- `<form:checkboxes>` is a variation of `<form:checkbox>` that automatically creates multiple check box fields on your behalf. You use the `items` attribute to specify a `Collection`, `Map`, or array of objects with which to generate the tags . The `itemValue` and `itemLabel` attributes specify the names of the field value and field label properties, respectively, for the objects in the collection.
- `<form:radiobutton>` is the equivalent of `<input type="radio">`. Typically, you bind two or more of these to the same `path` (form object property), and Spring automatically selects the proper one based on the property value.
- `<form:radiobuttons>` is to `<form:radiobutton>` as `<form:checkboxes>` is to `<form:checkbox>`. It has the same `items`, `itemValue`, and `itemLabel` attributes to help generate the radio buttons. Both `<form:radiobuttons>` and `<form:checkboxes>` are great for deriving fields from enums.
- `<form:select>` is the equivalent of a `<select>` drop-down or multiselect box. It works with `<form:option>` and `<form:options>`. It automatically selects the correct option based on the value of the `path` the select is bound to.
- `<form:option>` belongs nested within a `<form:select>` and is the equivalent of `<option>`.
- `<form:options>`, like `<form:checkboxes>` and `<form:radiobuttons>`, has `items`, `itemValue`, and `itemLabel` attributes that help generate multiple `<option>` elements.

## Obtaining Submitted Form Data

When a user submits a form to your controller, obtaining the data from that submission is simple. The `createUser(UserForm)` and `editUser(UserForm, long)` methods both receive submitted `UserForm` objects translated automatically from request parameters because of the `FormHttpMessageConverter`.

```
@RequestMapping(value = "user/add", method = RequestMethod.POST)
public View createUser(UserForm form)
{
    User user = new User();
    user.setUserId(this.getNextUserId());
    user.setUsername(form.getUsername());
    user.setName(form.getName());
    this.userDatabase.put(user.getUserId(), user);

    return new RedirectView("/user/list", true, false);
}
```

```
...
    @RequestMapping(value = "user/edit/{userId}", method = RequestMethod.POST)
    public View editUser(UserForm form, @PathVariable("userId") long userId)
    {
        User user = this.userDatabase.get(userId);
        user.setUsername(form.getUsername());
        user.setName(form.getName());

        return new RedirectView("/user/list", true, false);
    }
```

Now compile the application, launch Tomcat from the IDE, and go to `http://localhost:8080/forms/user/list` in your favorite browser. Click the new user link and enter a username and name to create a new user. Add one or two more users, and then try to edit one. You'll notice that Spring automatically bound your `UserForm` object on the model to the form fields in the view. On submission it automatically converted the request parameters to the form object. This is a Spring MVC feature that you can use over and over again, both throughout this book and throughout your time developing Spring Framework applications.

# UPDATING THE CUSTOMER SUPPORT APPLICATION

You should now take a look at the Customer-Support-v10 project available for download from the `wrox.com` code download site. The application has changed significantly from Part I of the book in that it bootstraps Spring Framework, moves existing classes into the `com.wrox.site` package, and replaces Servlets with Spring MVC controllers. In the interest of space this book cannot reprint the entire project. You should, however, understand some key differences.

## Enabling Multipart Support

First, the `Configurator` class has gone away. This class was a `ServletContextListener` that programmatically configured the `LoggingFilter` and `AuthenticationFilter` so that they executed in the proper order. Whenever you configure Servlet API features programmatically, it's best to do so within a single class. The `Bootstrap` class you have come to know in this and the previous chapter is the perfect place for the programmatic configuration of filters that used to be in `Configurator`. Also, because the ticket system enables files to be uploaded as attachments, the `DispatcherServlet` configured in the `Bootstrap` class now has multipart support configured. The `Bootstrap` class for the Customer Support application is in Listing 13-1.

**LISTING 13-1: Bootstrap.java**

```
public class Bootstrap implements WebApplicationInitializer {
    @Override
    public void onStartup(ServletContext container) throws ServletException {
        container.getServletRegistration("default").addMapping("/resource/*");

        AnnotationConfigWebApplicationContext rootContext =
                new AnnotationConfigWebApplicationContext();
        rootContext.register(RootContextConfiguration.class);
```

```
        container.addListener(new ContextLoaderListener(rootContext));

        AnnotationConfigWebApplicationContext servletContext =
                new AnnotationConfigWebApplicationContext();
        servletContext.register(ServletContextConfiguration.class);
        ServletRegistration.Dynamic dispatcher = container.addServlet(
                "springDispatcher", new DispatcherServlet(servletContext)
        );
        dispatcher.setLoadOnStartup(1);
        dispatcher.setMultipartConfig(new MultipartConfigElement(
                null, 20_971_520L, 41_943_040L, 512_000
        ));
        dispatcher.addMapping("/");

        FilterRegistration.Dynamic registration = container.addFilter(
                "loggingFilter", new LoggingFilter()
        );
        registration.addMappingForUrlPatterns(null, false, "/*");

        registration = container.addFilter(
                "authenticationFilter", new AuthenticationFilter()
        );
        registration.addMappingForUrlPatterns(
                null, false, "/ticket", "/ticket/*", "/chat", "/chat/*",
                "/session", "/session/*"
        );
    }
}
```

Enabling multipart support on the `DispatcherServlet` is not quite enough to get file uploads working with Spring MVC. Spring Framework also supports older versions of the Servlet API. Recall that before Servlet 3.0, the Servlet API did not have built-in multipart support and third-party tools were necessary to accomplish file uploads. Spring MVC needs a `MultipartResolver` instance to tell it whether to use Servlet 3.0+ multipart support or some third-party tool. The `ServletContextConfiguration` class has an additional `@Bean` method to create that bean, which must be called `multipartResolver`.

```
    @Bean
    public MultipartResolver multipartResolver()
    {
        return new StandardServletMultipartResolver();
    }
```

## Converting Servlets to Spring MVC Controllers

The `index.jsp` file has been removed and replaced with the `IndexController`. The `SessionListServlet` of old is now the `SessionListController`. The code isn't really that different except that Spring MVC patterns are used instead of `HttpServletRequest` and `HttpServletResponse` tools.

`LoginServlet` has become the `AuthenticationController`. This code has changed somewhat. Instead of `doGet` and `doPost` methods checking for the presence of various request parameters, each action has been replaced with a simple controller method. `ChatServlet` has become the `ChatController`, and `TicketServlet` has become the `TicketController`. These Servlets both used the action pattern, where the *action* request parameter controlled execution of the `doGet` or `doPost` methods. This resulted in lengthy `doGet` and `doPost` methods just to determine which method to execute. Now Spring takes care of that using `@RequestMapping`, eliminating much of the code in these controllers.

The `TicketController` uses a form object for ticket submissions, and this form object uses Spring's `MultipartFile` to gain easy access to uploaded files.

```
public static class Form
{
    private String subject;
    private String body;
    private List<MultipartFile> attachments;

    // mutators and accessors
}
```

This makes the code for the `create` handler method vastly more concise than the code in the Servlet previously was.

```
    @RequestMapping(value = "create", method = RequestMethod.POST)
    public View create(HttpSession session, Form form) throws IOException
    {
        Ticket ticket = new Ticket();
        ticket.setId(this.getNextTicketId());
        ticket.setCustomerName((String)session.getAttribute("username"));
        ticket.setSubject(form.getSubject());
        ticket.setBody(form.getBody());
        ticket.setDateCreated(Instant.now());

        for(MultipartFile filePart : form.getAttachments())
        {
            log.debug("Processing attachment for new ticket.");
            Attachment attachment = new Attachment();
            attachment.setName(filePart.getOriginalFilename());
            attachment.setMimeContentType(filePart.getContentType());
            attachment.setContents(filePart.getBytes());
            if((attachment.getName() != null &&
                    attachment.getName().length() > 0) ||
                    (attachment.getContents() != null &&
                        attachment.getContents().length > 0))
                ticket.addAttachment(attachment);
        }

        this.ticketDatabase.put(ticket.getId(), ticket);

        return new RedirectView("/ticket/view/" + ticket.getId(), true, false);
    }
```

## Creating a Custom Downloading View

The final thing you should note about the new Spring-enabled Customer Support application is the use of the custom `com.wrox.site.DownloadView` class in Listing 13-2 for downloading files from your Spring controllers. You can utilize this reusable view anywhere in the application to send a file attached to the response back to the client for downloading.

**LISTING 13-2: DownloadView.java**

```
public class DownloadingView implements View
{
    private final String filename;
    private final String contentType;
    private final byte[] contents;

    public DownloadingView(String filename, String contentType, byte[] contents)
    {
        this.filename = filename;
        this.contentType = contentType;
        this.contents = contents;
    }

    @Override
    public String getContentType()
    {
        return this.contentType;
    }

    @Override
    public void render(Map<String, ?> model, HttpServletRequest request,
                       HttpServletResponse response) throws Exception
    {
        response.setHeader("Content-Disposition",
                "attachment; filename=" + this.filename);
        response.setContentType("application/octet-stream");

        ServletOutputStream stream = response.getOutputStream();
        stream.write(this.contents);
    }
}
```

This downloading view is greatly simplified and has some hard-coded behavior in it. In the real world, it would likely have several settings for customization. It does the job, though, and one line of code in the `TicketController` sends the attachment to be downloaded in the client's browser.

```
        return new DownloadingView(attachment.getName(),
                attachment.getMimeContentType(), attachment.getContents());
```

As usual, you can test the refactored Customer Support application by compiling the project, starting Tomcat from your IDE, and going to `http://localhost:8080/support/` in your favorite browser. Test the usual features—listing tickets, creating tickets, chatting, and so on. To the user it should seem largely the same, but it is on its way to being a better-designed application.

## SUMMARY

This chapter covered a host of information regarding Spring MVC controllers and request mapping methods. You learned about the infinite ways you can use `@RequestMapping` as well as many other annotations and types to create powerful controller methods that can handle and respond to any type of request. You experimented with Spring's support for the Model-View-Controller pattern and designed form objects that Spring can automatically create from request parameters. Finally, you saw the refactored Customer Support application for the Multinational Widget Corporation, which now uses Spring Framework and controllers instead of Servlets with the action pattern. You then learned how to create your own Spring `View` for pushing file downloads to the client browser.

In the next chapter you explore how services and repositories can enrich your applications further; they help separate the different types of program logic into independent layers that can be abstracted away and mocked for independent testing.

# Using Services and Repositories to Support Your Controllers

## IN THIS CHAPTER

- What is Model-View-Controller plus Controller-Service-Repository?
- Using the root application context instead of a web application context
- Enhancing services with asynchronous and scheduled execution
- Using logic layer separation with WebSockets

## WROX.COM CODE DOWNLOADS FOR THIS CHAPTER

You can find the `wrox.com` code downloads for this chapter at `http://www.wrox.com/go/projavaforwebapps` on the Download Code tab. The code for this chapter is divided into the following major examples:

- Discussion-Board Project
- Customer-Support-v11 Project

## NEW MAVEN DEPENDENCIES FOR THIS CHAPTER

In addition to the Maven dependencies introduced in previous chapters, you also need the following Maven dependencies:

```
<dependency>
    <groupId>org.springframework</groupId>
    <artifactId>spring-websocket</artifactId>
```

```
        <version>4.0.2.RELEASE</version>
        <scope>compile</scope>
    </dependency>
```

## UNDERSTANDING MODEL-VIEW-CONTROLLER PLUS CONTROLLER-SERVICE-REPOSITORY

In Chapter 13, you learned about the powerful tools available to you for replacing Servlets with Spring MVC controllers. You explored the Model-View-Controller (MVC) pattern as implemented in Spring Framework. By now, you're probably quite familiar with the pattern in general, even if you had never seen it before. You may have already noticed a problem with this pattern, however. Despite its simplicities and the fact that controllers are cleaner than Servlets, your controller methods can still get out of hand. Up to this point your business logic has been fairly simple: Save submitted data somewhere in memory. But think about all the other things that need to happen when you create or edit data in your application:

- **Validation** — The data needs to be validated in some way to ensure that the proper rules were followed when creating it. For example, some fields may not be optional, and other fields may have restricted values.
- **Alerts** — These may need to be sent out via e-mail, text message, or mobile notification regarding the change.
- **Other, existing data in the application** — This may need to change. Consider an online forum system, for example, where you typically see the number of posts and the user and date of the last post in each forum. Then, within the forum, each post usually shows you the number of replies and the user and date of the last reply in each post. To improve performance, the statistical data for replies is usually rolled up to the post, while statistical data for posts is usually rolled up to the forum. Thus, when adding a reply to a forum post, you must also update the post and forum data.
- **Data persistence** — Application data is rarely just persisted in memory. Usually it resides in a data store of some type, such as a relational database, a NoSQL database, or a set of flat files. Persisting this data involves a whole set of logic in and of itself, and that logic can sometimes be quite complex and consume a lot of code.

So, with all that in mind, is it really best to put all this logic in a controller? Consider Figure 14-1, which demonstrates the basic operation of the three components in an MVC system. What if after creating a fantastic web application that does exactly what your boss wants, he asks you to add RESTful and SOAP web services to the application? Can you reuse the controllers you created for your web application? Probably not. Instead, you'll find yourself performing a significant refactoring of your codebase to separate out *user interface logic* from *business logic*.

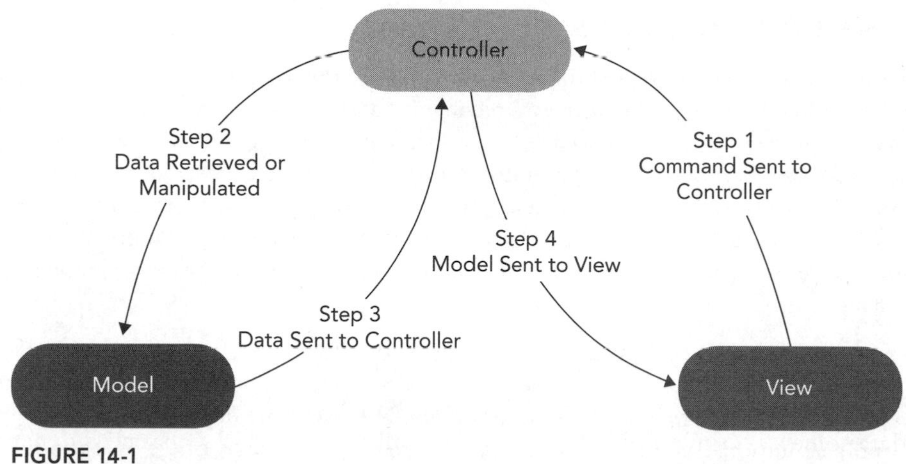


FIGURE 14-1

## Recognizing Different Types of Program Logic

User interface logic is any logic that exists solely to support a particular user interface. If a piece of code logic is needed no matter how the user is interacting with the application, that logic is business logic. However, if that piece of code logic is needed only for a particular user interface, it is user interface logic. In an ideal application, you would want these types of logic separated into different layers. By doing this, you make it possible to easily swap out the user interface or, even better, utilize multiple user interfaces simultaneously, without having to change any business logic. You could also write a library that handles your business logic and then use that library in web applications and desktop applications.

When persisting application data to a data store of some type, often there is a lot of logic dedicated to the persistence of that data and unrelated to other business logic. This *persistence logic* is recognizable by its uselessness when the underlying data store changes dramatically. For example, a piece of code may still be necessary when you change from using MySQL to PostreSQL, but if it becomes unnecessary when you switch to an in-memory data store or a NoSQL database, that probably means it is persistence logic. As with separating user interface logic from business logic, you should also keep persistence logic separate from business logic. Doing so creates two distinct advantages:

- If you decide at a later date to switch the data store to which you persist your data, you can do so without changing your business logic.
- Testing your business logic becomes vastly simpler because you can mock your persistence logic and isolate only the business logic for testing.

Depending on the nature of your applications, you might be able to think of other forms of program logic that can and should be separated into distinct layers. Using `@Component` (or custom annotations meta-annotated with `@Component`) you can create any beans dependent on any other beans, and Spring instantiates and injects as necessary to create your program structure. However, Spring also provides a Controller-Service-Repository pattern that naturally satisfies the need to separate these three common types of program logic. This pattern is not structurally enforced in Spring like the MVC pattern is. Instead, Spring simply provides a set of markers that guide and support the optional implementation of this pattern in your application.

## Repositories Provide Persistence Logic

In the Controller-Service-Repository pattern, repositories are the lowest layer, responsible for all logic related to saving data to a data store and retrieving saved data from a data store. You mark a repository with the `@Repository` annotation to indicate its semantic purpose. With component scanning enabled, `@Repository` classes are automatically instantiated, injected, and managed within the Spring application context they belong to. Typically, each repository is responsible for a single persistence object, or entity. This breaks the repository layer into small units of easily testable code that you can replace one entity at a time if you decide that a particular entity belongs in a different data store.

Repositories are created from interfaces, and dependents of a repository program against its interface instead of against the implementation itself. This way the repository can be faked using a mocking framework like EasyMock or Mockito to facilitate testing its dependents without relying on the real implementation. Typically, repositories that perform similar storage operations inherit from a mutual base class that provides common operations to all similar repositories. Repositories may also consume other repositories but should not consume resources in higher application layers such as services or controllers. (However, this is not something that Spring actively enforces.)

## Services Provide Business Logic

Services are the next layer above repositories. Services encapsulate the business logic of the application and consume other services and repositories but do not consume resources in higher application layers like controllers (again, something that Spring does not actively enforce). Services are marked with the `@Service` annotation, making them eligible for automatic instantiation and dependency injection, among other benefits. Like repositories, services are created from interfaces so that dependent resources may program against an interface. This pattern of basing each layer on a set of interfaces allows each layer to be tested in isolation from all the other layers. From a transactional point of view, the execution of a service method from a higher layer (such as a controller) can be thought of as a transactional *unit of work*. It may perform several operations on multiple repositories and other services in the context that all operations must either succeed or fail as a single unit. When a service method is executed from another service method, it is generally thought of as belonging to the same unit of work that the calling method belongs to.

It should be noted that this concept of unit of work does not imply that it can always be handled with traditional relational database transactions. The operations performed during a unit of work may have multiple consequences across different data stores or file media. These operations may include transmission of intra- or inter-application messages, e-mails, text messages, or mobile notifications that in most cases cannot be rolled back. How this logical unit of work maintains atomicity is outside the scope of this book and must be dealt with on a case-by-case basis. Suffice it to say that, in a simple application dealing with a single ACID-compliant data store, units of work are roughly equivalent to database transactions. Spring does provide support for these transactional needs, and you explore that further in Part III of this book.

Some developers do not like to use the term "service" to describe this layer of the application, as that can sometimes be confused with web services. What you call your business logic layer doesn't matter. You don't even have to use the `@Service` annotation. You could instead use the `@Component` annotation or a custom annotation meta-annotated with `@Component`. What you call it and how you mark it does not change its purpose. The rest of this book, however, refers to them as services.

## Controllers Provide User Interface Logic

You are already quite familiar with the concept of controllers, `@Controller`, `@RequestMapping`, and how that all works together in Spring MVC. Controllers are the top layer of the food chain in the Controller-Service-Repository pattern. In fact, this three-layer system can easily be compared to a natural food chain. In this system, repositories are the plant life and absorb only nutrients from nature (the database). Services are omnivores that consume repositories (plant life) or other services (omnivores). Continuing this analogy to its logical conclusion, controllers are carnivores. They consume services (the omnivores), but they never consume repositories (plant life) directly, and they never consume other controllers. Controllers, in some form or another, control the user interface and, using services for assistance, prepare the model for presentation in the view.

In the MVC paradigm, services and repositories are considered part of the controller (not the `@Controller`). This is shown in Figure 14-2. A `@Controller`, the `@Services` it depends on, the `@Repositorys` those `@Services` depend on, and any caching layers that lie between these components all act together to form the controller in the Model-View-Controller pattern. All these components use the model in some form or another. Ultimately, the `@Controller` — which could be for a web GUI or a web service API — passes the necessary parts of the model to the view for rendering. This view could be a JSP (for a web GUI), or it could be a JSON or XML rendering engine (for a web GUI or a web service API).

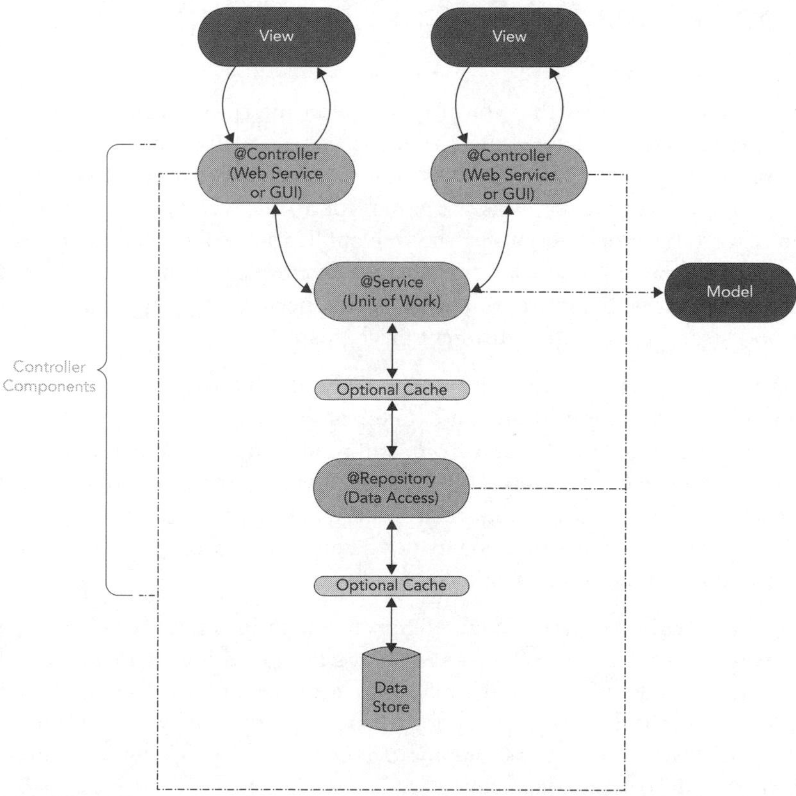


**FIGURE 14-2**

# USING THE ROOT APPLICATION CONTEXT INSTEAD OF A WEB APPLICATION CONTEXT

Think about the `ServletContextConfiguration` class you have become familiar with over the past two chapters. Of course, you can name this class whatever you want to name it, but its purpose remains the same. As the configuration for the Spring application context for the `DispatcherServlet`, this class is responsible for establishing how Spring operates when receiving HTTP requests in a Servlet container. That description immediately limits the scope for this configuration.

Outside of a Servlet container, the `ServletContextConfiguration` has no purpose. The contents of the configuration reflect this. Every bean configured in this class is somehow related to accepting, handling, and responding to HTTP requests. If you were to create a RESTful or SOAP web service for your application, you would likely create a separate `DispatcherServlet` with its own application context and `@Configuration`, and the configuration would be different to reflect the different way the controllers in this context handle requests. You would probably disable unnecessary beans like the `ByteArrayHttpMessageConverter`, `StringHttpMessageConverter`, and `FormHttpMessageConverter`, as these wouldn't be applicable to RESTful or SOAP web services. You also wouldn't need things like the `ViewResolver` and `RequestToViewNameTranslator`.

## Reusing the Root Application Context for Multiple User Interfaces

Given the previous discussion, remember that your different user interfaces typically share the same services. This way, your business logic remains consistent across all user interfaces. To accomplish this, you should not manage your services and repositories in a web application context, but in the root application context that serves as the parent for all the web application contexts. All these services and repositories are inherited by the web application contexts that control the various user interfaces. If at some point you want to create a desktop application using the services and repositories written for your web application, you can use the same root application context configuration, albeit bootstrapped through a different mechanism.

You already spent considerable time in Chapter 12 learning about application context hierarchy and inheritance, configuring a root application context (`RootContextConfiguration`) with a web application context (`ServletContextConfiguration`), and modifying component scanning to scan for only the proper components in each context. Component scanning is the key to this separation. If you use component scanning, you must configure it properly. Otherwise, you may get duplicate bean definitions, or worse some bean definitions may not be picked up. Component scanning works on two principals: package scanning and class filtering.

When using the `@ComponentScan` annotation, you tell Spring which Java package or packages to scan for candidate classes using the `String[] basePackages` attribute. Spring locates all classes belonging to these packages or subpackages and applies the resource filters against each class. The downside of `basePackages` is that it is not type-safe, and so a typo can easily go unnoticed. As an alternative, you can use the `Class<?>[] basePackageClasses` attribute. Spring determines the package names to scan from the classes specified.

For each class that Spring finds in the base packages, it applies the filter or filters configured. Filters are segregated as include filters and exclude filters. If the class triggers any one of the include filters *and* doesn't trigger any of the exclude filters, it becomes a Spring bean, meaning it is constructed, injected, initialized, and anything else that applies to Spring-managed beans. When the `@ComponentScan`'s `useDefaultFilters` attribute is `true` (it is unless explicitly set to `false`), there are no exclude filters and only one include filter by default. The one default include filter flags a class if it is marked with `@Component` or if it is marked with an annotation meta-annotated with `@Component`. Thus, the following two component scan configurations are equivalent:

```
@ComponentScan(basePackages = "com.wrox.site")
@ComponentScan(
        basePackages = "com.wrox.site",
        useDefaultFilters = false,
        includeFilters = @ComponentScan.Filter(value = Component.class,
                                               type = FilterType.ANNOTATION)
)
```

If you specify include or exclude filters, they are in addition to the default filter if `useDefaultFilters` is `true`. If you set `useDefaultFilters` to `false`, the filters you specify replace the default filter. You can customize component scan filters quite extensively.

You could, for example, create your own set of annotations and tell Spring to scan for those. You could also use assignable type filters, which trigger when a class extends or implements the class or one of the classes specified. Another possibility is to use `org.springframework.context.annotation.FilterType.CUSTOM`, in which case the class or classes specified should be implementations of `org.springframework.core.type.filter.TypeFilter`. Or you could apply a combination of some or all of these techniques with or without the default filters in place.

Take a look at the following component scan configuration, which comes from the `RootContextConfiguration` you have seen previously.

```
@ComponentScan(
        basePackages = "com.wrox.site",
        excludeFilters = @ComponentScan.Filter(Controller.class)
)
```

This configuration scans the `com.wrox.site` package for any classes that pass the default filters but *aren't* marked with `@Controller`. So classes marked with `@Component`, `@Service`, `@Repository`, or any annotations marked with those annotations become beans, but `@Controllers` don't. This is the complement of the component scan configuration for `ServletContextConfiguration`, which finds *only* beans annotated with `@Controller`.

```
@ComponentScan(
        basePackages = "com.wrox.site",
        useDefaultFilters = false,
        includeFilters = @ComponentScan.Filter(Controller.class)
)
```

Using these component scans for the separate application contexts accomplishes the objective: Business logic and repository logic are centralized in the root application context, whereas user interface logic lives in the Servlet application context. Recall from Chapter 13 that if you don't specify these component-scanning filters in the root and Servlet application contexts, your beans are instantiated multiple times — once in each context.

## Moving Your Business Logic from Controllers to Services

In a perfect world every engineer gets to write every program from the ground up using the best tools and the best practices available. In the real world you are usually required to work with legacy applications that don't always use the good tools or good practices. Not only must you maintain these applications and address issues reported by your users, often you also must add new features to them, and often adding these new features requires refactoring the code to support new business needs.

Think about a simple discussion board and what type of business logic it might require. Assuming you have no categories or other ways to classify or group discussions, your users need the ability to create discussions and reply to discussions. When creating a discussion, you should make sure that its title and body are not blank. When replying to a discussion, you should not only check that the reply isn't blank, but also that the reply is written for a discussion that actually exists. Both discussions and replies need to be timestamped, but this timestamp is automatic, not user-supplied, so it is business logic. In this hypothetical scenario you have an existing application with two controllers. The `BoardController` provides the ability to list and create discussions, whereas the `DiscussionController` permits viewing a discussion and replying to it. These controllers encompass the entire codebase for your application, minus configuration and views. They manage user interface logic, perform business logic, and persist discussions and replies to the database.

Now your boss assigns you three new tasks:

- Users have requested to receive e-mails when discussions they post or reply to are replied to.
- Users have also requested the ability to view the board and discussions as RSS feeds.
- The server administrators want to automatically delete topics that were posted or last replied to more than a year ago to save on storage and improve performance.

Think about some of the changes you need to make to support these new features. Each discussion requires a list of all unique users who have replied to the discussion to make sending notifications easier. As is usually the case, users will eventually ask to unsubscribe from a discussion, so keeping this list on the discussion instead of aggregating it from all replies every time is much simpler and less expensive. Also, each discussion needs to have a date field that represents the last time it was replied to or when it was posted if there are no replies. Both of these changes pose a problem because these updates to a discussion when replies are posted are triggered from the `DiscussionController`, but the `BoardController` contains the logic for saving discussion records. Also, you already have methods that retrieve discussions and replies from the database and return JSP views. Now you need new methods that do the same things but return RSS views. This smells of code duplication.

It shouldn't take you long to realize you need to separate your business logic from your user interface logic before you can approach any of these tasks. You'll do exactly that in the rest of this section using the Discussion-Board project available for download on the `wrox.com` code download site. To get a good idea of what kind of interface your services need, take a look at the request handler methods of the `BoardController` and `DiscussionController`. Don't worry about the code right now. Just think about the interface. The `BoardController` contains methods for listing and creating discussions.

```
@Controller
@RequestMapping("discussion")
public class BoardController
{
    @RequestMapping(value = {"", "list"}, method = RequestMethod.GET)
    public String listDiscussions(Map<String, Object> model) { ... }

    @RequestMapping(value = "create", method = RequestMethod.GET)
    public String createDiscussion(Map<String, Object> model) { ... }

    @RequestMapping(value = "create", method = RequestMethod.POST)
    public View createDiscussion(DiscussionForm form) { ... }
}
```

The `DiscussionController`, meanwhile, contains methods for viewing a discussion and replying to it.

```
@Controller
@RequestMapping("discussion/{discussionId:\\d+}")
public class DiscussionController
{
    @RequestMapping(value = {"", "*"}, method = RequestMethod.GET)
    public String viewDiscussion(Map<String, Object> model,
                                 @PathVariable("discussionId") long id) { ... }

    @RequestMapping(value = "reply", method = RequestMethod.POST)
    public ModelAndView reply(ReplyForm form,
                              @PathVariable("discussionId") long id) { ... }
}
```

Think about the POJOs you need to support this. For simplicity, assume users are just e-mail addresses that you can represent with `String`s instead of some user object. You need a `Discussion` object and a `Reply` object for persisting data with and passing to the view.

```
public class Discussion
{
    private long id;
    private String user;
    private String subject;
    private String uriSafeSubject;
    private String message;
    private Instant created;
    private Instant lastUpdated;
    private Set<String> subscribedUsers = new HashSet<>();

    // mutators and accessors
}

public class Reply
{
    private long id;
    private long discussionId;
```

```
    private String user;
    private String message;
    private Instant created;

    // mutators and accessors
}
```

It seems logical to have a service for each entity. Based on what you know about the controllers, the `DiscussionService` and `ReplyService` interfaces should be simple. Notice that the `ReplyService` has no method for getting an individual `Reply` by its ID. There's no business need for it right now. If you ever need to add the ability to edit a reply, then you would need to add this method.

```
public interface DiscussionService
{
    List<Discussion> getAllDiscussions();
    Discussion getDiscussion(long id);
    void saveDiscussion(Discussion discussion);
}

public interface ReplyService
{
    List<Reply> getRepliesForDiscussion(long discussionId);
    void saveReply(Reply reply);
}
```

Now at this moment how your service implementations work doesn't matter. You can already refactor your controllers to use the interfaces of the services. If you take a look at the code for the `BoardController`, you can see how simple it is. Its methods contain only the code necessary to support interacting with the user. `createDiscussion`, in particular, doesn't even set all of the properties on the `Discussion`. It sets only user-provided properties, leaving it up to the service to set the generated properties, such as the ID and URI-safe subject. It doesn't need to know how this happens, nor does it care.

```
    @Inject DiscussionService discussionService;

    @RequestMapping(value = {"", "list"}, method = RequestMethod.GET)
    public String listDiscussions(Map<String, Object> model)
    {
        model.put("discussions", this.discussionService.getAllDiscussions());
        return "discussion/list";
    }

    @RequestMapping(value = "create", method = RequestMethod.GET)
    public String createDiscussion(Map<String, Object> model)
    {
        model.put("discussionForm", new DiscussionForm());
        return "discussion/create";
    }

    @RequestMapping(value = "create", method = RequestMethod.POST)
    public View createDiscussion(DiscussionForm form)
    {
        Discussion discussion = new Discussion();
        discussion.setUser(form.getUser());
        discussion.setSubject(form.getSubject());
```

```
        discussion.setMessage(form.getMessage());
        this.discussionService.saveDiscussion(discussion);

        return new RedirectView("/discussion/" + discussion.getId() + "/" +
                discussion.getUriSafeSubject(), true, false);
    }
```

The code for the `DiscussionController` is equally simple. Most of the work is delegated to the `DiscussionService` and the `ReplyService`, leaving the controller to concern itself with only the user interface.

```
    @Inject DiscussionService discussionService;
    @Inject ReplyService replyService;

    @RequestMapping(value = {"", "*"}, method = RequestMethod.GET)
    public String viewDiscussion(Map<String, Object> model,
                                 @PathVariable("discussionId") long id)
    {
        Discussion discussion = this.discussionService.getDiscussion(id);
        if(discussion != null)
        {
            model.put("discussion", discussion);
            model.put("replies", this.replyService.getRepliesForDiscussion(id));
            model.put("replyForm", new ReplyForm());
            return "discussion/view";
        }

        return "discussion/errorNoDiscussion";
    }

    @RequestMapping(value = "reply", method = RequestMethod.POST)
    public ModelAndView reply(ReplyForm form,
                              @PathVariable("discussionId") long id)
    {
        Discussion discussion = this.discussionService.getDiscussion(id);
        if(discussion != null)
        {
            Reply reply = new Reply();
            reply.setDiscussionId(id);
            reply.setUser(form.getUser());
            reply.setMessage(form.getMessage());
            this.replyService.saveReply(reply);

            return new ModelAndView(new RedirectView("/discussion/" + id + "/" +
                    discussion.getUriSafeSubject(), true, false));
        }

        return new ModelAndView("discussion/errorNoDiscussion");
    }
```

## Using Repositories for Data Storage

When you start to write the implementations of `DiscussionService` and `ReplyService`, you quickly realize much of the necessary code is dedicated to saving data to and retrieving data from the database. To keep the service code purely business-related, it's best to create a repository layer to deal with data persistence. This makes your service methods more concise and easily testable. The interfaces for the `DiscussionRepository` and the `ReplyRepository` are simple and, unsurprisingly, mirror the service interfaces significantly.

```
public interface DiscussionRepository
{
    List<Discussion> getAll();
    Discussion get(long id);
    void add(Discussion discussion);
    void update(Discussion discussion);
}

public interface ReplyRepository
{
    List<Reply> getForDiscussion(long id);
    void add(Reply reply);
    void update(Reply reply);
}
```

Now that you have an interface for persisting data to program against, you can implement the services. The `DefaultDiscussionService`'s `getDiscussion` method doesn't have any additional business logic (although someday you may need to have it), but `getAllDiscussions` sorts the list before returning it and `saveDiscussion` performs some interesting tasks. First, it sterilizes the subject to make it safe for a URI and sets the sterilized value to the `uriSafeSubject` property. This is used when creating URLs for discussions to make them search engine-friendly. It also updates the `lastUpdated` timestamp. Finally, if the discussion is new, it updates the creation timestamp and subscribes the user who created it before adding the discussion; otherwise, it updates the discussion.

```
@Service
public class DefaultDiscussionService implements DiscussionService
{
    @Inject DiscussionRepository discussionRepository;

    @Override
    public List<Discussion> getAllDiscussions()
    {
        List<Discussion> list = this.discussionRepository.getAll();
        list.sort((d1, d2) -> d1.getLastUpdated().compareTo(d2.getLastUpdated()));
        return list;
    }

    @Override
    public Discussion getDiscussion(long id)
    {
        return this.discussionRepository.get(id);
    }

    @Override
    public void saveDiscussion(Discussion discussion)
    {
        String subject = discussion.getSubject();
        subject = Normalizer.normalize(subject.toLowerCase(), Normalizer.Form.NFD)
                .replaceAll("\\p{InCombiningDiacriticalMarks}+", "")
                .replaceAll("[^\\p{Alnum}]+", "-")
```

```
                .replace("--", "-").replace("--", "-")
                .replaceAll("[^a-z0-9]+$", "")
                .replaceAll("^[^a-z0-9]+", "");
        discussion.setUriSafeSubject(subject);

        Instant now = Instant.now();
        discussion.setLastUpdated(now);

        if(discussion.getId() < 1)
        {
            discussion.setCreated(now);
            discussion.getSubscribedUsers().add(discussion.getUser());
            this.discussionRepository.add(discussion);
        }
        else
            this.discussionRepository.update(discussion);
    }
}
```

> **NOTE** *The* `getAllDiscussions` *method shows off the power of Java 8 lambda expressions, and in some cases, it might be appropriate to do sorting of this nature in Java code. However, in most cases sorting is much more efficient in the database itself, and usually you pass sorting instructions on to the repository somehow.*

`DefaultReplyService`'s `getRepliesForDiscussion` method also sorts the list returned by the repository before returning it. `saveReply` uses both the repository and the `DiscussionService` (notice, again, the use of the interface instead of the implementation) to perform some business tasks. If the reply is new, it subscribes the replier to the discussion, sets the reply creation timestamp, and adds the reply. If it's not new it just updates the reply. Either way, it then saves the discussion using the `DiscussionService`. This ensures that all business rules are still followed.

```
@Service
public class DefaultReplyService implements ReplyService
{
    @Inject ReplyRepository replyRepository;
    @Inject DiscussionService discussionService;

    @Override
    public List<Reply> getRepliesForDiscussion(long discussionId)
    {
        List<Reply> list = this.replyRepository.getForDiscussion(discussionId);
        list.sort((r1, r2) -> r1.getId() < r2.getId() ? -1 : 1);
        return list;
    }

    @Override
    public void saveReply(Reply reply)
    {
        Discussion discussion =
                this.discussionService.getDiscussion(reply.getDiscussionId());
```

```
            if(reply.getId() < 1)
            {
                discussion.getSubscribedUsers().add(reply.getUser());
                reply.setCreated(Instant.now());
                this.replyRepository.add(reply);
            }
            else
            {
                this.replyRepository.update(reply);
            }
            this.discussionService.saveDiscussion(discussion);
        }
    }
```

> **NOTE** *The* `getRepliesForDiscussion` *method is a key example of where sorting may actually be appropriate in the Java code instead of the database because this data set size is always extremely limited. However, do you think this logic is appropriate in the service, or is it more appropriate in the controller, instead?*

Now the only thing left is to implement the repositories. For this example, just use an in-memory map like you have for all the other projects in the book so far. The `InMemoryDiscussionRepository` is fairly predictable, but it should be noted that the code becomes more complex if you actually persist to a database of some type.

```
@Repository
public class InMemoryDiscussionRepository implements DiscussionRepository
{
    private final Map<Long, Discussion> database = new Hashtable<>();
    private volatile long discussionIdSequence = 1L;

    @Override
    public List<Discussion> getAll()
    {
        return new ArrayList<>(this.database.values());
    }

    @Override
    public Discussion get(long id)
    {
        return this.database.get(id);
    }

    @Override
    public void add(Discussion discussion)
    {
        discussion.setId(this.getNextDiscussionId());
        this.database.put(discussion.getId(), discussion);
    }

    @Override
    public void update(Discussion discussion)
    {
```

```
            this.database.put(discussion.getId(), discussion);
        }

        private synchronized long getNextDiscussionId()
        {
            return this.discussionIdSequence++;
        }
    }
```

InMemoryReplyRepository is interesting because of its getForDiscussion method, which uses a lambda expression like a WHERE clause in a SQL statement to exclude the replies that don't belong to the selected discussion. Notice the use of the volatile keyword, which ensures different threads never see stale values of ID sequence fields.

```
    @Repository
    public class InMemoryReplyRepository implements ReplyRepository
    {
        private final Map<Long, Reply> database = new Hashtable<>();
        private volatile long replyIdSequence = 1L;

        @Override
        public List<Reply> getForDiscussion(long id)
        {
            ArrayList<Reply> list = new ArrayList<>(this.database.values());
            list.removeIf(r -> r.getDiscussionId() != id);
            return list;
        }

        @Override
        public synchronized void add(Reply reply)
        {
            reply.setId(this.getNextReplyId());
            this.database.put(reply.getId(), reply);
        }

        @Override
        public synchronized void update(Reply reply)
        {
            this.database.put(reply.getId(), reply);
        }

        private synchronized long getNextReplyId()
        {
            return this.replyIdSequence++;
        }
    }
```

Now it's time to test it all. There's not enough space to print all the JSP views in the book, but they're all there in the Discussion-Board project to take a look at if you want. When you're ready, compile the application and start Tomcat from your IDE; then go to http://localhost:8080/board/. Try creating and replying to various discussions. When you're satisfied that the code works, take a look back over it all and imagine how much uglier the code would have been — and how much harder to test and extend it would have been — if you had put all this code in the controllers.

The task of creating the RSS views that users are asking for is suddenly much easier now that you can reuse the service calls. This book doesn't cover that particular task, but feel fry to do it yourself!

# IMPROVING SERVICES WITH ASYNCHRONOUS AND SCHEDULED EXECUTION

With refactoring to separate business logic from UI logic out of the way, you still have two tasks to tackle: deleting old discussions automatically and notifying users of replies. Think about both of these tasks for a minute. You probably realize that automatically deleting old discussions means no user interaction, indicating that no controller calls a service method to perform this task. So what does call this method?

Also, what you may not have thought of is how long it can take to send e-mails to multiple people about a reply. E-mails sent to users should not reveal the e-mail addresses of other users — that's a privacy breach. At the same time, using the blind carbon copy (BCC) feature tends to land e-mails in the spam filter — or worse, land your e-mail server on a blacklist. So, if you need to notify 20 people about a reply, you must send 20 e-mails, and this can take more than a few seconds. So how do you do this without hurting performance for the user? You must do this in a background thread, asynchronously.

Spring Framework has tools to tackle both these responsibilities. When you schedule tasks to run on some schedule, or execute code asynchronously, one of the biggest obstacles is thread management. Your web application cannot simply spin up as many threads as it wants to whenever it wants. Thread growth must be controlled to prevent thread usage from over-taxing the hardware your application runs on. In a Servlet container, creating threads and leaving them running can result in memory leaks — and those almost always end badly.

The problem that most developers forget — or don't know about — is that creating and destroying threads often involves a lot of overhead, and that can cause performance issues, also. What you really need is a central thread pool that reuses threads instead of creating and destroying, and that queues tasks to execute when the pool is exhausted running other tasks. Not only does Spring provide such a system, it also provides the annotations `@org.springframework.scheduling.annotation.Async` and `@org.springframework.scheduling.annotation.Scheduled` to indicate that a method should run asynchronously and automatically (without manual execution), respectively.

You cannot just go slap some annotations on methods that need them without some configuration, however. First, you need to enable these features. Next, `@Async` methods and `@Scheduled` methods do not use the same thread pool by default, but you want them to. Using the same thread pool ensures that you can always use resources in the most efficient manner possible. As such, it's important to take a minute and understand the plumbing that supports this.

## Understanding Executors and Schedulers

Spring Framework defines the distinct but closely related concepts of *executors* and *schedulers*. An executor is exactly what it sounds like: It executes tasks. The contract does not mandate that this happen asynchronously; instead, that is handled differently in different implementations. Schedulers are responsible for remembering when a task is supposed to execute, and then executing it on time (using an executor).

- The `java.util.concurrent.Executor` interface defines an executor that can execute a simple `Runnable`.
- Spring extends this interface with `org.springframework.core.task.TaskExecutor`.
- Spring also provides the `org.springframework.scheduling.TaskScheduler` interface that specifies several methods for scheduling tasks to run one or more times at some point in the future.

There are many implementations of both these Spring interfaces, and most of them implement both interfaces. The most common of these is the `org.springframework.scheduling.concurrent.ThreadPoolTaskScheduler`, which provides both an executor and a scheduler (backed by the executor) and a thread pool for executing tasks in an orderly and efficient manner. When your application shuts down, this class makes sure that all the threads it created are shut down properly to prevent memory leaks and other issues.

This class also implements the `java.util.concurrent.ThreadFactory` interface. Because of this, you can define a `ThreadPoolTaskScheduler` bean, and it fulfills any dependencies you have on an `Executor`, `TaskExecutor`, `TaskScheduler`, or `ThreadFactory`. This is about to come in handy because you need it to configure asynchronous and scheduled method execution.

## Configuring a Scheduler and Asynchronous Support

To enable asynchronous method execution on `@Async` methods, annotate your `@Configuration` class with `@EnableAsync`. Likewise, to enable scheduled method execution on `@Scheduled` methods, use the `@EnableScheduling` annotation. You want to place these annotations on the `RootContextConfiguration` to share this configuration across all beans in your application. However, `@EnableAsync` and `@EnableScheduling` by themselves simply establish default asynchronous and scheduling configurations. To customize this behavior, you need to implement the `AsyncConfigurer` interface to return the proper asynchronous executor and implement the `SchedulingConfigurer` class to assign the proper executor to the scheduler.

```
@Configuration
@EnableAsync(proxyTargetClass = true)
@EnableScheduling
...
public class RootContextConfiguration
        implements AsyncConfigurer, SchedulingConfigurer
{
    private static final Logger log = LogManager.getLogger();
    private static final Logger schedulingLogger =
            LogManager.getLogger(log.getName() + ".[scheduling]");

    ...

    @Bean
    public ThreadPoolTaskScheduler taskScheduler()
    {
        log.info("Setting up thread pool task scheduler with 20 threads.");
```

```
        ThreadPoolTaskScheduler scheduler = new ThreadPoolTaskScheduler();
        scheduler.setPoolSize(20);
        scheduler.setThreadNamePrefix("task-");
        scheduler.setAwaitTerminationSeconds(60);
        scheduler.setWaitForTasksToCompleteOnShutdown(true);
        scheduler.setErrorHandler(t -> schedulingLogger.error(
                "Unknown error occurred while executing task.", t
        ));
        scheduler.setRejectedExecutionHandler(
                (r, e) -> schedulingLogger.error(
                        "Execution of task {} was rejected for unknown reasons.",r
                )
        );
        return scheduler;
    }

    @Override
    public Executor getAsyncExecutor()
    {
        Executor executor = this.taskScheduler();
        log.info("Configuring asynchronous method executor {}.", executor);
        return executor;
    }

    @Override
    public void configureTasks(ScheduledTaskRegistrar registrar)
    {
        TaskScheduler scheduler = this.taskScheduler();
        log.info("Configuring scheduled method executor {}.", scheduler);
        registrar.setTaskScheduler(scheduler);
    }
}
```

Only new parts of this class are shown; existing parts are hidden. The `proxyTargetClass` attribute in the `@EnableAsync` annotation tells Spring to use the CGLIB library to proxy classes with asynchronous or scheduled methods instead of using Java interface proxies. This allows you to have asynchronous and scheduled methods on your beans that aren't specified in an interface. If you set this attribute to `false`, only interface-specified methods could be executed on a schedule or asynchronously. The new `@Bean` method exposes the scheduler as a bean that any of your beans may use. The `getAsyncExecutor` method (specified in `AsyncConfigurer`) tells Spring to use the same scheduler for asynchronous method execution, and the `configureTasks` method (specified in `SchedulingConfigurer`) tells Spring to use the same scheduler for scheduled method execution.

You may immediately wonder how this can possibly work. `getAsyncExecutor` and `configureTasks` each call `taskScheduler`, so aren't two `TaskSchedulers` instantiated? And isn't a third `TaskScheduler` instantiated when Spring calls the `@Bean` method? Actually, only one `TaskScheduler` is instantiated. Spring proxies calls to all `@Bean` methods so that they are never called more than once. The result of the first invocation of a `@Bean` method is cached and used for all future invocations. This allows multiple methods in your configuration to use other `@Bean` methods. Because of this, only one `TaskScheduler` is instantiated in this configuration, and that instance is used for the bean definition, in the `getAsyncExecutor` method, and in the `configureTasks` method. When you execute the example later, the log statements in these methods will prove this.

## Creating and Using @Async Methods

Spring Framework provides support for `@Async` methods by wrapping affected beans in a proxy. When Spring injects a bean with `@Async` methods in other beans that depend on it, it actually injects the proxy, not the bean itself. Those beans then call methods on the proxy. For normal methods, the proxy just delegates directly to the underlying method. For methods annotated with `@Async` or `@javax.ejb.Asynchronous`, the proxy instructs the executor to execute the method and then returns immediately. How this works has one important consequence: If a bean calls one of its own `@Async` methods, that method will *not* execute asynchronously because `this` cannot be proxied. Because of this, if you want to call a method asynchronously, it must be on another object. (And that object must be a Spring-managed bean, of course.)

> **NOTE** *This isn't entirely true. With Java interface-based proxies, you cannot proxy* `this`*. With CGLIB proxies, you can proxy* `this` *by overriding every method in the original class. This is how configuration* `@Bean` *method caching works — Spring always proxies* `@Configuration` *classes using CGLIB. Because you have enabled CGLIB proxies here, you can call* `@Async` *methods on the same class, and they will execute asynchronously. However, you should not rely on this — a configuration change could break it.*

The `NotificationService` and `FakeNotificationService` in the Discussion-Board project demonstrate how this works. Notice that the method is marked `@Async` on both the interface and the implementation. This is not strictly required. However, when the intention is for all implementations to execute asynchronously, it's considered polite to annotate the interface so that consumers are aware of this.

```
public interface NotificationService
{
    @Async
    void sendNotification(String subject, String message,
                          Collection<String> recipients);
}

@Service
public class FakeNotificationService implements NotificationService
{
    private static final Logger log = LogManager.getLogger();

    @Override
    @Async
    public void sendNotification(String subject, String message,
                                 Collection<String> recipients)
    {
        log.info("Started notifying recipients {}.", recipients);
        try {
            Thread.sleep(5_000L);
        } catch (InterruptedException ignore) { }
        log.info("Finished notifying recipients.");
    }
}
```

The DefaultReplyService obtains an @Injected NotificationService and, with a few simple lines of code, calls the asynchronous method in saveReply if the reply is new.

```
Set<String> recipients = new HashSet<>(discussion.getSubscribedUsers());
recipients.remove(reply.getUser()); // no need to email replier
this.notificationService.sendNotification(
        "Reply posted", "Someone replied to \"" + discussion.getSubject()
        + ".\"", recipients
);
```

# Creating and Using @Scheduled Methods

Creating @Scheduled methods isn't all that different from creating @Async methods. All you have to do is write a method that does what you want and annotate it. The only important thing to note about @Scheduled methods is that they can't have any parameters. (How would Spring know what to use as arguments?) Just because a method is @Scheduled doesn't mean you can't call in manually. You can, any time you want to; though you certainly don't have to. In fact, you can also annotate a @Scheduled method with @Async so that it executes asynchronously if executed manually.

The scheduled execution you need in the Discussion-Board project deletes discussions that were posted longer than a year ago or replied to longer than a year ago, whichever was more recent. This first requires some tweaks to the repositories to support deletions. In ReplyRepository and its implementation, you now need a deleteForDiscussion method.

```
@Override
public synchronized void deleteForDiscussion(long id)
{
    this.database.entrySet()
            .removeIf(e -> e.getValue().getDiscussionId() == id);
}
```

DiscussionRepository and its implementation also need a delete method. However, deletions need to cascade to replies, so this class needs an @Injected ReplyRepository.

```
@Override
public void delete(long id)
{
    this.database.remove(id);
    this.replyRepository.deleteForDiscussion(id);
}
```

Now that the repositories support deleting, you just need to add a @Scheduled method to the DefaultDiscussionService:

```
@Scheduled(fixedDelay = 15_000L, initialDelay = 15_000L)
public void deleteStaleDiscussions()
{
    Instant oneYearAgo = Instant.now().minus(365L, ChronoUnit.DAYS);
    log.info("Deleting discussions stale since {}.", oneYearAgo);

    List<Discussion> list = this.discussionRepository.getAll();
    list.removeIf(d -> d.getLastUpdated().isAfter(oneYearAgo));

    for(Discussion old : list)
        this.discussionRepository.delete(old.getId());
}
```

This method starts executing 15 seconds after Spring starts and executes again and again with 15 seconds between the end of one invocation and the start of the next. You can use `@Scheduled` in many different ways to control when a method executes. Notice that `deleteStaleDiscussions` isn't part of the `DiscussionService` interface, but the method still executes on a schedule because `@EnableAsync`'s `proxyTargetClass` attribute is set to `true`. (Of course, in the real world this method would execute much less often, such as once per day.)

Now that you have asynchronous and scheduled methods created and configured, compile the application, start up Tomcat from your IDE, and go to `http://localhost:8080/board/`. Watch the log and you can see that the `TaskScheduler` is instantiated only once and the scheduled method executes every 15 seconds. Create discussions and replies and you can see the asynchronous notification method writing to the log. The 5-second sleep during the method proves that it is executing asynchronously because, as you see, the server responds in much less than 5 seconds when you post a reply.

# APPLYING LOGIC LAYER SEPARATION TO WEBSOCKETS

If you take a look at the Customer-Support-v11 project on the `wrox.com` code download site, you can see that its business logic has also been moved into services, leaving the controllers to worry only about user interface logic.

- `InMemoryUserRepository`, which implements `UserRepository`, stores all the users in memory.
- `TemporaryAuthenticationService`, which implements `AuthenticationService`, uses the `UserRepository` interface.
- The `AuthenticationController` now uses the `AuthenticationService` interface to conduct business logic.
- Likewise, you should see the `InMemoryTicketRepository`, the `DefaultTicketService` that uses the `TicketRepository` interface, and the `TicketController` that now uses the `TicketService` interface.
- The authentication code uses the `java.security.Principal` interface now, and the `AuthenticationFilter` wraps the underlying connection to expose the `Principal` as a shortcut alternative to querying the session attributes. To see where this can come in handy, take a look at the `POST`-handling `create` method on the `TicketController`. It now takes a `Principal` instead of the `HttpSession` as its first parameter, and Spring knows how to supply that value.

## Adding Container-Managed Objects to the Spring Application Context

Another thing that has changed is that the former class `SessionRegistry` is now an interface of instance methods, and the `DefaultSessionRegistry` implements it. This works fine for the `SessionListController`, but by now you should realize that the `SessionListener` causes problems. `SessionListener` is instantiated and managed by the Servlet container, not by Spring

Framework. That's why `SessionRegistry` used to be a class of static methods. So how does the `SessionListener` get a hold of the `SessionRegistry` bean instance?

You actually have a few options here. One, which uses `bytecode` instrumentation and Aspect-Oriented Programming, is very automatic at run time. The only thing you have to do is annotate classes that aren't Spring-managed beans with `@org.springframework.beans.factory.annotation.Configurable` if you want them converted to Spring beans automatically upon instantiation. However, the configuration necessary to accomplish this is quite tricky, and it wouldn't be fair to hide all the magic from you without explaining how it works.

Alternatively, you can programmatically add an existing object to the Spring application context at run time. The first thing you must do is remove the `@WebListener` annotation from `SessionListener` because the order in which the listener is invoked can be unpredictable with this annotation. Instead, programmatically configure the listener in the `Bootstrap` class to make sure that it is invoked *after* Spring's `ContextLoaderListener`.

```
        ...
        container.addListener(new ContextLoaderListener(rootContext));
        container.addListener(SessionListener.class);
        ...
```

Now, you need to change `SessionListener` so that it also implements `ServletContextListener`. This way the `SessionListener` can initialize itself within Spring when the container starts up, right after Spring starts up.

```
public class SessionListener
        implements HttpSessionListener, HttpSessionIdListener,
        ServletContextListener
{
    ...
}
```

You can use the `contextInitialized` method in the listener to get the root application context from the `ServletContext`, retrieve the bean factory from the application context, and configure the `SessionListener` instance as a bean in the root application context.

```
    @Override
    public void contextInitialized(ServletContextEvent event)
    {
        WebApplicationContext context =
                WebApplicationContextUtils.getRequiredWebApplicationContext(
                        event.getServletContext());
        AutowireCapableBeanFactory factory =
                context.getAutowireCapableBeanFactory();
        factory.autowireBeanProperties(this,
                AutowireCapableBeanFactory.AUTOWIRE_BY_TYPE, true);
        factory.initializeBean(this, "sessionListener");
        log.info("Session listener initialized in Spring application context.");
    }
```

When the `contextInitialized` method completes execution, the `SessionRegistry` implementation is injected, and the `SessionListener` can begin using it immediately.

> **WARNING** *The listener may now be eligible for wiring and other amenities, but it is not a fully-fledged Spring bean. Other beans cannot have the listener* `@Autowired` *or* `@Injected` *into them, and calling the* `getBean` *method of* `ApplicationContext` *does not return the listener. This is because the listener is never placed into the bean registry for the application context. You can partially resolve this by calling the bean factory's* `registerSingleton` *method, but some services will still not work, such as scheduled method execution and post-construction/pre-destruction callback methods.*

## Using the Spring WebSocket Configurator

As you likely already realize, WebSocket server endpoints are also container-managed objects. You can, therefore, use the same technique to wire up your WebSocket server endpoints that you used for your `SessionListener`. You might wonder why Spring doesn't have a controller-equivalent replacement for WebSocket endpoints. The answer to this question is simple: Controllers were meant to be a flexible replacement for Servlets that abstracted away the details of the underlying connection. The Java WebSockets API already does a good job of this, and it is unnecessary for Spring to replace it. However, to avoid having to programmatically register a server endpoint with Spring every time it is instantiated (remember, you get a new endpoint instance for each connection), Spring provides first-class support for server endpoints by way of the `org.springframework.web.socket.server.endpoint.SpringConfigurator`.

The `SpringConfigurator` class extends `javax.websocket.server.ServerEndpointConfig.Configurator` to ensure that instances of your server endpoint are properly injected and initialized before any of the event- or message-handling methods are called. Normally, you declare your endpoint using the `SpringConfigurator`, as in the following example:

```
@ServerEndpoint(value="/chat/{sessionId}", configurator=SpringConfigurator.class)
```

However, the `ChatEndpoint.EndpointConfigurator` class already extends `ServerEndpointConfig.Configurator` to expose the `HttpSession` as a user property, and `ChatEndpoint` uses this custom configurator. So, you just need to change the custom configurator to extend `SpringConfigurator` instead of `ServerEndpointConfig.Configurator`.

```
public static class EndpointConfigurator extends SpringConfigurator
{
    @Override
    public void modifyHandshake(ServerEndpointConfig config,
                                HandshakeRequest request,
                                HandshakeResponse response) { ... }
}
```

That's really all there is to it. With this simple change, your `EndpointConfigurator` can have `@Autowired` or `@Injected` properties and implement any of the magic Spring interfaces (such as the `Aware` interfaces), just like a first-class bean. However, as with the listener, the endpoint is never placed in the singleton bean registry, meaning other beans cannot access it and it is not eligible for pre-destroy life-cycle notification or scheduled method execution (although post-construct methods will work). If you want the endpoint to exist in the bean registry and be eligible for these services, you can declare a singleton instance of the endpoint in the root application context configuration, instead:

```
@Bean
public ChatEndpoint chatEndpoint()
{
    return new ChatEndpoint();
}
```

When you do this, the `SpringConfigurator` (or extending class) specified in the `@ServerEndpoint` annotation no longer returns a new instance for every WebSocket connection. Instead, it returns that singleton instance to handle every connection. Thus, one instance of the endpoint handles multiple connections, just like a Servlet or controller. This requires careful coordination, because if you do this the endpoint can no longer hold the `Session`, `HttpSession`, `ChatSession`, `Principal`, and other objects as instance variables — they have to be looked up on the invocation of every method. So then what are the benefits of using a singleton `ChatEndpoint` bean? First, it consumes less memory, especially if you have many thousands of WebSocket connections. Also, it takes less time to establish a connection, because Spring only injects dependencies once instead of on each connection. In the Customer-Support-v11 application, the endpoint is not configured this way, but instead adheres to the traditional model of one endpoint instance per WebSocket connection. Refactoring it to be a singleton bean is an exercise left up to the reader.

## Remember: A WebSocket Is Just Another Interface for Business Logic

At first it might seem very difficult to separate business logic from user interface logic in a WebSocket endpoint. In some ways it's very much like a controller and can react to each incoming message like a controller might react to an incoming HTTP request. Admittedly, the fact that server endpoints can send messages to clients without first receiving messages (something that controllers cannot do) definitely complicates matters. The lines are blurred here. Nobody can tell you where to draw the line; only you and your organization can make that determination. However, it's important to keep in mind that, whatever way you spin it, a WebSocket connection is just another interface for some unit of business logic. A service *can* be extracted from the tangle of business and user interface logic.

Recall that previous `ChatEndpoint` versions also implemented `HttpSessionListener` to receive notifications of logouts or session timeouts mid-chat. The use case was that if a user logged out of his web session in a separate window from the chat, the chat needed to end for security reasons.

However, implementing `HttpSessionListener` was a messy solution because it meant that the container created a singleton instance of `ChatEndpoint` that didn't actually handle connections, and a host of static fields were needed to maintain information about the `Session`-to-`HttpSession` link across instances of the `ChatEndpoint`. Fortunately, there's a cleaner way to do that now. The `SessionRegistry` has two new methods that enable beans to register callbacks to execute when a session is destroyed.

```
void registerOnRemoveCallback(Consumer<HttpSession> callback);
void deregisterOnRemoveCallback(Consumer<HttpSession> callback);
```

`ChatEndpoint` has an `@Injected` `SessionRegistry`, and in its `@PostContsruct` method, it registers a callback. Notice that the callback is registered and deregistered using Java 8 method references (bold), which makes the code significantly cleaner.

```
private final Consumer<HttpSession> callback = this::httpSessionRemoved;

...

@PostConstruct
public void initialize()
{
    this.sessionRegistry.registerOnRemoveCallback(this.callback);
}

private void httpSessionRemoved(HttpSession httpSession)
{
    if(httpSession == this.httpSession)
    {
        synchronized(this)
        {
            if(this.closed)
                return;
            log.info("Chat session ended abruptly by {} logging out.",
                    this.principal.getName());
            this.close(ChatService.ReasonForLeaving.LOGGED_OUT, null);
        }
    }
}

private void close(ChatService.ReasonForLeaving reason, String unexpected)
{
    ...
    this.sessionRegistry.deregisterOnRemoveCallback(this.callback);
    ...
}
```

This code is much cleaner and completely eliminates the need for a complex map of `Sessions` to `HttpSessions` and `HttpSessions` to `Sessions`.

> **NOTE** *You might wonder why the* `ChatEndpoint` *has the* `callback` *instance variable instead of simply passing* `this::httpSessionRemoved` *to the* `registerOnRemoveCallback` *and* `deregisterOnRemoveCallback` *methods. Method references (*`this::something`*) in Java have no object identity. Because of this, the references passed to* `registerOnRemoveCallback` *and* `deregisterOn-RemoveCallback` *would appear to be different instances, making it impossible to deregister the callback. Using the* `callback` *instance variable solves this problem.*

`ChatEndpoint` also uses a scheduled method — `sendPing` — to send ping messages every 25 seconds. Browsers respond to pings with pongs, and this keeps a connection alive if no other activity occurs for a period of time. The WebSocket container does not send pings automatically on your behalf, so it's up to your code to accomplish this. This would be a perfect application of Spring Framework's scheduled method execution, eliminating the need to manage a thread for sending ping messages. However, you can't just mark `sendPing` with `@Scheduled` because `ChatEndpoint` is not a singleton bean. Spring Framework only supports `@Scheduled` on singleton beans, and would ignore it on the `ChatEndpoint`.

To solve this problem, you need to use Spring's `TaskScheduler` bean directly. The following code sends pings and accepts pongs. After the `ChatEndpoint` is constructed, it schedules `sendPing` to run after 25 seconds and every 25 seconds thereafter. When the connection closes, it cancels all future execution of `sendPing`.

```
private static final byte[] pongData =
        "This is PONG country.".getBytes(StandardCharsets.UTF_8);
...
private ScheduledFuture<?> pingFuture;
...
@Inject TaskScheduler taskScheduler;
...

private void sendPing()
{
    if(!this.wsSession.isOpen())
        return;
    log.debug("Sending ping to WebSocket client.");
    try
    {
        this.wsSession.getBasicRemote()
                .sendPing(ByteBuffer.wrap(ChatEndpoint.pongData));
    }
    catch(IOException e)
    {
        log.warn("Failed to send ping message to WebSocket client.", e);
    }
}

@OnMessage
public void onPong(PongMessage message)
{
    ByteBuffer data = message.getApplicationData();
    if(!Arrays.equals(ChatEndpoint.pongData, data.array()))
        log.warn("Received pong message with incorrect payload.");
    else
        log.debug("Received good pong message.");
}

@PostConstruct
public void initialize()
{
    ...
    this.pingFuture = this.taskScheduler.scheduleWithFixedDelay(
            this::sendPing,
            new Date(System.currentTimeMillis() + 25_000L),
            25_000L
    );
}

...

private void close(ChatService.ReasonForLeaving reason, String unexpected)
{
    ...
```

```
            if(!this.pingFuture.isCancelled())
                this.pingFuture.cancel(true);
            ...
        }
```

The ChatService (implemented in DefaultChatService) handles business logic, such as creating ChatSession objects (and assigning them IDs), maintaining the list of pending chat sessions, and writing messages to a chat log. This leaves the ChatEndpoint class to concern itself only with handling WebSocket Session objects and sending and receiving messages, using the @Injected ChatService for business logic application.

One of the ways the ChatEndpoint is less complicated now is when you replace the system of maps between different session types with instance variables for the user's WebSocket Session (wsSession) and the opposite party's WebSocket Session (otherWsSession). One challenge in achieving this is notifying the user requesting a chat session when the customer service representative connects to and responds to that chat session. Java 8 lambdas make this a trivial task by simply declaring an event handler on the ChatSession object.

```
public class ChatSession
{
    ...
    private Consumer<Session> onRepresentativeJoin;
    ...
    public void setRepresentative(Session representative)
    {
        this.representative = representative;
        if(this.onRepresentativeJoin != null)
            this.onRepresentativeJoin.accept(representative);
    }

    public void setOnRepresentativeJoin(Consumer<Session> onRepresentativeJoin)
    {
        this.onRepresentativeJoin = onRepresentativeJoin;
    }
    ...
}
```

Now when a new chat session is created, the customer session uses a simple lambda expression to respond to the act of the support representative joining the session. When the support representative joins and the setRepresentative method is called, this triggers the callback that ensures both sides know about the presence of each other.

```
public void onOpen(Session session, @PathParam(sessionId) long sessionId)
{
    ...
            if(sessionId < 1)
            {
                CreateResult result =
                        this.chatService.createSession(this.principal.getName());
                this.chatSession = result.getChatSession();
                this.chatSession.setCustomer(session);
                this.chatSession.setOnRepresentativeJoin(
                        s -> this.otherWsSession = s
                );
```

```
                session.getBasicRemote().sendObject(result.getCreateMessage());
            }
            else
            {
                JoinResult result = this.chatService.joinSession(sessionId,
                        this.principal.getName());
                if(result == null)
                {
                    log.warn("Attempted to join non-existent chat session {}.",
                            sessionId);
                    session.close(new CloseReason(
                            CloseReason.CloseCodes.UNEXPECTED_CONDITION,
                            "The chat session does not exist!"
                    ));
                    return;
                }
                this.chatSession = result.getChatSession();
                this.chatSession.setRepresentative(session);
                this.otherWsSession = this.chatSession.getCustomer();
                session.getBasicRemote()
                        .sendObject(this.chatSession.getCreationMessage());
                session.getBasicRemote().sendObject(result.getJoinMessage());
                this.otherWsSession.getBasicRemote()
                        .sendObject(result.getJoinMessage());
            }
    ...
}
```

Now that you've reviewed the updates to the Customer Support application and have a grasp for the improvements made, compile the project, start Tomcat, and go to `http://localhost:8080/support` to give it a try. Create tickets and look at the session list, which all work as they did before, but on a simpler code base. Be sure to open a second browser and try out the Support Chat feature to see how it works, as well.

# SUMMARY

In this chapter you explored complementing the Model-View-Controller pattern with Controller-Service-Repository. You learned why it's important to separate user interface logic, business logic, and data persistence logic into separate layers, and saw how much simpler this made your code. Simpler code is easier to test and generally more stable, which should always be a goal in software development. You also learned how to separate these different layers, and you discovered the support Spring Framework offers you through the `@Controller`, `@Service`, and `@Repository` annotations.

Later in the chapter you discovered the powerful asynchronous and scheduled method execution tools that Spring offers, and used them to do things, such as send e-mail notifications in the background and clear old data out of the data store periodically. Finally, you learned about wiring and initializing non-Spring beans and about Spring Framework's support for managing WebSocket endpoints.

In the next chapter you revisit an old topic, internationalization and localization, and learn how much simpler Spring Framework makes the task of readying your application for global distribution.

# 15

# Internationalizing Your Application with Spring Framework i18n

## IN THIS CHAPTER

- The importance of Spring Framework i18n
- Using Spring's internationalization and localization APIs
- Configuring Spring's internationalization support
- How to internationalize your code
- Internationalizing the Customer Support application

## WROX.COM CODE DOWNLOADS FOR THIS CHAPTER

You can find the `wrox.com` code downloads for this chapter at `http://www.wrox.com/go/projavaforwebapps` on the Download Code tab. The code for this chapter is divided into the following major examples:

- Localized-Application Project
- Customer-Support-v12 Project

## NEW MAVEN DEPENDENCIES FOR THIS CHAPTER

There are no new Maven dependencies for this chapter. Continue to use the Maven dependencies introduced in all previous chapters.

# WHY DO YOU NEED SPRING FRAMEWORK I18N?

In Chapter 7 you learned about internationalization (i18n) and localization (L10n) using the JSTL Internationalization and Formatting tag library (`fmt`). If you have not read Chapter 7, you do not need to go back and read it now; however, if you don't understand internationalization, localization, or the formatting tag library, you *should* go back and read the "Using the Internationalization and Formatting tag library" section of Chapter 7. That section gives you a basic overview of the principals of internationalization and localization and introduces you to using the formatting tag library to achieve these objectives. More important, it covers language codes, region and country codes, variants, `Locale`, and `TimeZone`, which you must understand to effectively use Spring Framework's internationalization support. This chapter uses many of these concepts and technologies but does not re-cover these topics.

In this chapter you explore Spring Framework's internationalization and localization facilities and learn how using them is much simpler than using the container's facilities directly. You will come to understand message sources and more Spring JSP tags, and you will finally internationalize and localize the Customer Support application.

## Making Internationalization Easier

One of the things you probably decided about the Internationalization and Formatting tag library is that it isn't exactly the easiest to use. First, you must configure your resource bundles in your deployment descriptor, or in a `ServletContainerInitializer` or `ServletContextListener`, using the `javax.servlet.jsp.jstl.fmt.localizationContext` context parameter. The bundles must be classes or files present on the classpath (in `/WEB-INF/classes`), despite your possibly wanting to obtain them from somewhere else (such as a database, or even just a different file).

Also, you have to implement a way to detect the locale the user wants to use. `HttpServletRequest` does include `getLocale` and `getLocales` methods, which derive the wanted locales from the `Accept-Language` HTTP request header and return the system default `Locale` in the absence of that header, but this mechanism works only in limited circumstances. The user must use a computer configured with his preferred language (not always the case, especially on public computers) and the browser must support the `Accept-Language` header (typical these days, but not guaranteed). After you determine the wanted locale, you must then configure the tag library to use that locale using the `javax.servlet.jsp.jstl.core.Config` class and the `Config.FMT_LOCALE` constant. Oh, and don't forget about remembering to manually change locale settings from request to request, which also isn't supported automatically.

Spring provides simplifications for all these tasks, enabling you to do less work to support your international users. In addition to this, you can use Spring's i18n support throughout your code rather than just inside JSPs. Spring's i18n support leverages, and in some cases wraps, the i18n support built into the Java SE and Java EE platforms and the JSTL. In this chapter, you learn about all these features and more. You also learn about the internationalization and localization concepts they empower.

## Localizing Error Messages Directly

One of the drawbacks of Java SE and EE internationalization is the strict reliance on strings as localization keys. To be sure, you ultimately have to look up error codes, and the easiest way to do this is with strings. However, it's easier if things such as `Throwables` and validation error objects can pass directly to localization APIs without always making a call to determine the error code before looking up the localized message. Using Spring Framework's `MessageSourceResolvable` you can do just that. You can pass any object that implements this interface to any Spring i18n API and resolve it automatically. In the section "Internationalizing Your Code," you use this to adopt a reliable pattern for handling, logging, and propagating exceptions. In Chapter 16, you use this feature even more for bean validation errors.

## USING THE BASIC INTERNATIONALIZATION AND LOCALIZATION APIS

Before you dive into internationalizing your applications, you should be familiar with some basic classes and APIs. Some of these are platform classes and APIs, so they may be familiar to you already. The rest are Spring Framework classes and APIs, and you must understand how these work together.

### Understanding Resource Bundles and Message Formats

Just like the standard tag library, Spring Framework i18n uses *resource bundles* and *message formats*. It also uses an abstraction above resource bundles called *message sources* to support an easier API for obtaining localized messages. In practice, a resource bundle is an implementation of `java.util.ResourceBundle`. A `ResourceBundle` is a collection (not a `Collection`) of message keys that are mapped to localized *message formats*. The important point to notice here is that the keys are message formats, not messages themselves.

Of course, message formats (`java.text.MessageFormat`) look a lot like localized string messages when stored in a database or properties file. But these message formats can actually contain a variety of placeholder templates that are replaced at run time with supplied argument values. If the types of the values are specified as number, date, or time types, they are automatically formatted properly for the given locale. For example, the following are all U.S. English-localized message formats:

```
The road is long and windy.
There are {0} cats on the farm.
There are {0,number,integer} cats on the farm.
With a {0,number,percentage} discount, the final price is {1,number,currency}.
The value of Pi to seven significant digits is {0,number,#.######}.
My birthdate: {0,date,short}. Today is {1,date,long} at {1,time,long}.
My birth day: {0,date,MMMMMM-d}. Today is {1,date,MMM d, YYYY} at {1,time,hh:mma).
There {0,choice,0#are no cats|1#is one cat|1<are {0,number,integer} cats}.
```

Importantly, placeholders are numbered, and when using the message codes, you specify the arguments in the same order as the placeholder numbers, not in the order the placeholders appear in the message. This is because the placeholders might appear in a different order in other languages.

Placeholders always follow one of the following syntaxes, where # is the placeholder number and italic text represents user-supplied values:

```
{#}
{#,number}
{#,number,integer}
{#,number,percent}
{#,number,currency}
{#,number,custom format as specified in java.text.DecimalFormat}
{#,date}
{#,date,short}
{#,date,medium}
{#,date,long}
{#,date,full}
{#,date,custom format as specified in java.text.SimpleDateFormat}
{#,time}
{#,time,short}
{#,time,medium}
{#,time,long}
{#,time,full}
{#,time,custom format as specified in java.text.SimpleDateFormat}
{#,choice,choice format as specified in java.text.ChoiceFormat}
```

The `number`, `date`, and `time` placeholders follow the same formatting rules as established in the `<fmt:formatNumber>` and `<fmt:dateFormat>` tags. This means the date and time placeholders do not currently support the Java 8 Date and Time API. Unfortunately, support for these types is not scheduled until the Java 9 SE release.

When you specify resource bundles using the context parameter `javax.servlet.jsp.jstl.fmt.localizationContext`, its value is one or more (comma-separated) strings representing the basenames for resource bundles. The JSTL then knows to use these basenames to locate resource bundles when internationalization tags are used. When the JSTL needs to localize a message, it calls one of the `getBundle` methods on the `ResourceBundle` class and specifies the basename and `Locale`. `ResourceBundle` then constructs a list of possible matching resource bundle names of the following formats:

```
[baseName]_[language]_[script]_[region]_[variant]
[baseName]_[language]_[script]_[region]
[baseName]_[language]_[script]
[baseName]_[language]_[region]_[variant]
[baseName]_[language]_[region]
[baseName]_[language]
```

If the `Locale` does not contain a variant, the first and fourth names are omitted from the list. If it does not contain a region, the second and fifth names are omitted, and the first and fourth names simply contain the script and variant or language and variant, respectively, separated by two underscores (for example, `baseName_en__JAVA`). If the `Locale` does not contain a script, the first three names are all omitted. The resulting list is then checked for existing resource bundles with those names.

For each bundle name in the list, ordered with the precedence of the previous list of bundle name formats, `ResourceBundle` first attempts to load and instantiate a class extending `ResourceBundle` with the specified bundle name and then returns that class. If no class is found,

`ResourceBundle` then replaces any periods (`.`) in the name with forward slashes (`/`), appends `.properties` to the name, and then looks for a file on the classpath with that name, returning a `PropertyResourceBundle` for that file if it exists. If, after searching all bundle names, `ResourceBundle` does not find a matching bundle, it uses the fallback `Locale` to generate a new list of possible bundle names and searches again. If it still does not find a matching bundle, it looks for a class and then a file matching just the basename with no other qualifiers, and then throws an exception if no bundle is found.

When a `ResourceBundle` is found and returned, it can then be used to resolve message codes to message format strings. The bundle file consists of standard Java properties-style messages, with keys using message codes and values using `MessageFormat` strings. You can construct `MessageFormat` instances from these value strings.

If the basenames you specify in the `javax.servlet.jsp.jstl.fmt.localizationContext` context parameter are files, you can see how easy this might be to manage. For example, you might have basenames labels and errors with the following files on your classpath:

```
labels_en.properties
labels_en_US.properties
labels_en_GB.properties
labels_fr_FR.properties
errors_en.properties
errors_en_US.properties
errors_en_GB.properties
errors_fr_FR.properties
```

Each of these results in its own `ResourceBundle` over time. However, what if you want to store your messages in a database? You either need a different class for each locale supported, with most classes performing essentially the same logic (selecting values from the database), or you have to implement your own system for resolving `ResourceBundle` instances. (And even then you still need a separate *instance* for each supported locale.) This is because a given `ResourceBundle` instance supports only one locale at a time. Checking the API documentation for `ResourceBundle` confirms that, indeed, the methods for resolving messages contain no `Locale` parameters. You should quickly realize that this pattern is unsustainable.

## Message Sources to the Rescue

Spring message sources provide an abstraction of and wrapper around resource bundles. Message sources, which implement the `org.springframework.context.MessageSource` interface, provide three simple methods for resolving a `String` message using a `MessageSourceResolvable` object and `Locale`, or a `String` message code, object array arguments list, default message, and `Locale`. The fact that these methods accept `Locale`s means you need only a single `MessageSource` instance to obtain a localized message for any locale. Furthermore, because they return messages that have already been formatted instead of message formats, `MessageSource`s eliminate one more step (formatting the message) from the task of localizing messages.

Out-of-the-box, Spring Framework provides two implementations of `MessageSource`:

- `org.springframework.context.support.ResourceBundleMessageSource`
- `org.springframework.context.support.ReloadableResourceBundleMessageSource`

ResourceBundleMessageSource actually has a collection of ResourceBundles backing it. It uses the getBundle method of ResourceBundle to locate its bundles, so it essentially uses the exact same strategy (meaning bundle properties files must be on the classpath in /WEB-INF/classes).

One downside of ResourceBundles detected with getBundle is that they are cached forever (until the JVM shuts down, that is), and sometimes that isn't desirable. The ReloadableResourceBundleMessageSource is, as the name implies, reloadable. It is not backed with a ResourceBundle (despite its name), but it follows similar bundle detection rules. Using basenames, it locates bundle files (only files, not classes) using the same algorithm as ResourceBundle. However, these files can be either on the classpath (if the basename starts with classpath:) or on the file system relative to the context root. Because files loaded on the classpath are typically cached forever, using classpath resources makes the ReloadableResourceBundleMessageSource unreloadable, so this is usually avoided. A typical place to put bundle files for this message source is in /WEB-INF/i18n. Using the MessageSource API is simple:

```
@Inject MessageSource messageSource;

...

    this.messageSource.getMessage("foo.message.key", new Object[] {
            argument1, argument2, argument3
    }, user.getLocale());

    this.messageSource.getMessage("foo.message.key", new Object[] {
            argument1, argument2, argument3
    }, "This is the default message. Args: {0}, {1}, {2}.", user.getLocale());
```

Undoubtedly, you should see how much easier MessageSource implementations are to use within Java code. Your Java code no longer requires knowing the right basename, locating a ResourceBundle for the basename and Locale, resolving a message format from the bundle, and then formatting the message. Instead, it just needs to call a single method on an injected MessageSource implementation. This would be infinitely useful in a desktop application. But, in a well-designed web application, how often do you really localize within the Java code?

There are certainly uses cases for using the MessageSource API directly in a web application. For example, when you send e-mails or other notifications you need to localize the contents of those notifications. Also, some web services localize returned error messages if the Accept-Language request header is specified. However, most of your localization takes place in your JSPs, and what good does a MessageSource do you there? The JSTL clearly expects ResourceBundles, not MessageSources.

## Using Message Sources to Internationalize JSPs

Spring supports this need by providing the org.springframework.context.support.MessageSourceResourceBundle. (Notice the similarity to ResourceBundleMessageSource; be sure not to confuse these.) MessageSourceResourceBundle extends ResourceBundle and exposes an underlying MessageSource for a particular Locale, delegating calls on the ResourceBundle methods to the underlying MessageSource. Whenever you access a JSP using JstlView, Spring MVC automatically sets up the MessageSourceResourceBundle for the user-specified or default

`Locale` using the `javax.servlet.jsp.jstl.fmt.LocalizationContext` so that `<fmt:message>` works properly.

Of course, this works only for JSPs you access when using `JstlView` (either directly or with a view resolver) from a Spring MVC controller. There are other JSPs that you might access without Spring, such as error pages or simple pages that don't require a controller. Because Spring is not involved in the request life cycle for these types of JSPs, it cannot set up the `MessageSourceResourceBundle` automatically.

There are two different tactics you can use to get a `MessageSourceResourceBundle` for internationalizing these JSPs that aren't controlled by Spring Framework:

- The easiest approach is to simply use the `<spring:message>` tag from the Spring tag library instead of the `<fmt:message>` tag. The `<spring:message>` tag, which you learn more about later in this chapter, has several advantages over the `<fmt:message>` tag. One of those advantages is the ability to use a `MessageSource` directly.
- If you do not want to or cannot use the `<spring:message>` tag for some reason, the other approach is to create a `Filter` that applies to all the JSP requests not handled by Spring Framework. This filter, which you need to wire with Spring, would then use the `org.springframework.web.servlet.support.JstlUtils` class to mimic the behavior of the `JstlView` and set up the `LocalizationContext`. Of course, if you use a technique other than `Accept-Language` to set the user locale, you need to make sure the user locale is discovered and set before this filter executes on the filter chain.

The following hypothetical filter accomplishes this second approach.

```
public class JstlLocalizationContextFilter implements Filter
{
    private ServletContext servletContext;
    @Inject MessageSource messageSource;

    @Override
    public void doFilter(ServletRequest request, ServletResponse response,
                         FilterChain chain) throws IOException, ServletException
    {
        JstlUtils.exposeLocalizationContext(
                (HttpServletRequest)request, this.messageSource
        );
        chain.doFilter(request, response);
    }

    @Override
    public void init(FilterConfig config) throws ServletException
    {
        this.servletContext = config.getServletContext();
        WebApplicationContext context =
                WebApplicationContextUtils.getRequiredWebApplicationContext(
                        this.servletContext);
        AutowireCapableBeanFactory factory =
                context.getAutowireCapableBeanFactory();
        factory.autowireBeanProperties(this,
                AutowireCapableBeanFactory.AUTOWIRE_BY_TYPE, true);
        factory.initializeBean(this, "jstlLocalizationContextFilter");
```

```
            this.messageSource = JstlUtils.getJstlAwareMessageSource(
                    this.servletContext, this.messageSource
            );
        }

        @Override
        public void destroy() { }
    }
```

# CONFIGURING INTERNATIONALIZATION IN SPRING FRAMEWORK

Now that you understand how message sources and resource bundles work, you are probably eager to learn how to configure them. Configuring a message source in Spring is easy and requires only a few lines of code. However, that's not all that it takes to get internationalization working properly in Spring.

Most sites provide some way for users to change their locale, and it's likely that you also want to provide this capability. In addition to temporarily changing their locale, many users will want to permanently set their locale using some sort of user profile setting. These are all things that you must consider. This section discusses the different options, and shows you how to configure internationalization in Spring Framework. You use the Localized-Application project, available on the `wrox.com` code download site, during this section and the next. It contains the `Bootstrap`, `RootContextConfiguration`, and `ServletContextConfiguration` classes that pick up from the previous chapter.

## Creating a Message Source

Creating a message source in Spring Framework is a simple task. All you have to do is create a `@Bean` method in the `RootContextConfiguration` class and return the `MessageSource` implementation of your choice. The bean must be named `messageSource`.

```
...
private static final Logger schedulingLogger =
        LogManager.getLogger(log.getName() + ".[scheduling]");

@Bean
public MessageSource messageSource()
{
    ReloadableResourceBundleMessageSource messageSource =
            new ReloadableResourceBundleMessageSource();
    messageSource.setCacheSeconds(-1);
    messageSource.setDefaultEncoding(StandardCharsets.UTF_8.name());
    messageSource.setBasenames(
            "/WEB-INF/i18n/messages", "/WEB-INF/i18n/errors"
    );
    return messageSource;
}

@Bean
public ObjectMapper objectMapper()
...
```

In this case you use the `ReloadableResourceBundleMessageSource`. You probably immediately noticed that the cache time in seconds was set to -1. This disables reloading and makes the message source cache messages forever (until the JVM restarts).

Why, you may ask, don't you just use the `ResourceBundleMessageSource` instead? The `ReloadableResourceBundleMessageSource` isn't backed with actual `ResourceBundles` like the `ResourceBundleMessageSource`, so it performs better than `ResourceBundleMessageSource` — but only if you disable reloading. With reloading enabled (`cacheSeconds > 0`), it takes about twice as long to resolve messages as does `ResourceBundleMessageSource`. Setting the cache time to -1 is the best-performing configuration you can use in a production environment. In a development environment, you might want to set the cache time to a positive number so that you can change localized messages without restarting Tomcat. This is a perfect candidate for Spring's Bean Definition Profiles, which you learned about in Chapter 12.

Another thing you probably noticed about the message source configuration is that the default encoding has been set to UTF-8. Spring must know what encoding your properties files are in so that it can read them properly. There's actually another property, `fileEncodings`, which you can use to set the encodings of individual files. The `defaultEncoding` property sets the encoding for only those files not found in the `fileEncodings` property. Because UTF-8 can encode any character from any known language with as little space as possible, in most cases you just want to set the default encoding to UTF-8 and ensure that all your properties files are encoded in UTF-8. This is vastly simpler than trying to manage different encodings for each file depending on the language it contains.

Finally, the message source is configured with the basenames `/WEB-INF/i18n/messages` and `/WEB-INF/i18n/errors`. This means that the message source will look for filenames like `/WEB-INF/i18n/messages_en_US.properties`, `/WEB-INF/i18n/errors_fr_FR.properties`, and so on.

Of course, this is just one option of infinite possibilities. Spring comes with only two message sources, both of which use files to load messages, but you may implement `MessageSource` in any way you need and return that implementation instead. For example, some types of applications host multiple customers, each with many employees or members, and those customers may want to customize the localization for their accounts. This is much easier to manage in a database of some sort, rather than a collection of properties files. Perhaps the perfect solution is a key-value NoSQL database, such as Redis, RavenDB, or MongoDB (which is actually a document database but works great for key-value storage as well). Using a NoSQL repository (perhaps with Spring Data Redis or Spring Data MongoDB), you can easily create a `MessageSource` that retrieves messages from the database.

## Understanding Locale Resolvers

In concept, *locale resolvers* are similar to view resolvers. Spring uses a locale resolver as a strategy for determining the locale for the current request so that it can determine how to localize messages (and so that it can tell the JSTL how to localize messages). Locale resolvers provide a way to obtain the user's locale without relying solely on the `Accept-Language` header. (Though the default implementation, `org.springframework.web.servlet.i18n.AcceptHeaderLocaleResolver`, does just that.) Because you don't want to rely solely on the `Accept-Language` header, and you want to provide a way for users to change their locale to something other than their browser's locale, you don't want to use the default `LocaleResolver` implementation. A common alternative to the default is `org.springframework.web.servlet.i18n.SessionLocaleResolver`. This resolver uses the following strategy:

- `SessionLocaleResolver` looks on the current session for the session attribute whose name is equal to the `SessionLocaleResolver.LOCALE_SESSION_ATTRIBUTE_NAME` constant. If the attribute exists its value is returned.
- `SessionLocaleResolver` next checks whether its `defaultLocale` property is set and returns it if it is.
- Finally, `SessionLocaleResolver` returns the value of `getLocale` on the `HttpServletRequest` (which comes from the `Accept-Language` header).

Setting up the locale resolver is as simple as creating a new `@Bean` in your configuration. The `DispatcherServlet` detects the resolver and automatically uses it for all locale-fetching actions. For example, your request handler methods may have a parameter of type `Locale`, and Spring automatically uses the value provided by the `LocaleResolver` to supply that argument.

`JstlUtils` also uses this resolver to determine the user's locale. Because `HttpServletRequest` automatically returns the server default encoding if no `Accept-Language` header exists, that is sufficient for a fallback, and you do not need to set a default locale on the `SessionLocaleResolver` in most cases. (In fact, setting the default locale prevents the resolver from using the `Accept-Language` header.) When configuring the `LocaleResolver` `@Bean`, you should place it in the `ServletContextConfiguration`. Using the `RootContextConfiguration` would cause all `DispatcherServlet`s to use the same `LocaleResolver`, which is not desirable. The bean must be named `localeResolver`.

```
...
}

@Bean
public LocaleResolver localeResolver()
{
    return new SessionLocaleResolver();
}

@Bean
public ViewResolver viewResolver()
...
```

The `DispatcherServlet` is responsible for setting a `LocaleResolver` request attribute on each incoming request using the resolver that you configure. This makes the `LocaleResolver` available to any code executed by the `DispatcherServlet` or any code that has access to the request object after the `DispatcherServlet` has set the attribute. It should be clear, then, that error pages and other non-view JSPs do not have access to the `LocaleResolver`. In the previous section you used a custom `JstlLocalizationContextFilter` to configure the message source for these pages. You can tweak it slightly to also set the `LocaleResolver` on the request.

```
...
private ServletContext servletContext;
private LocaleResolver = new SessionLocaleResolver();
```

```
    @Inject MessageSource messageSource;

    @Override
    public void doFilter(ServletRequest request, ServletResponse response,
                         FilterChain chain) throws IOException, ServletException
    {
        request.setAttribute(
                DispatcherServlet.LOCALE_RESOLVER_ATTRIBUTE, this.localeResolver
        );
        JstlUtils.exposeLocalizationContext(
                (HttpServletRequest)request, this.messageSource
        );
    ...
```

This code does not use an `@Injected` `LocaleResolver` because the filter is wired using the root application context, but the `localeResolver` bean exists on the child `DispatcherServlet` application context. The `LocaleResolver` implementations are all very lightweight objects, so it's okay to have a duplicate resolver here.

## Using a Handler Interceptor to Change Locales

Now your application can determine the user's desired locale, but how do you set that session attribute if the user wants a different locale? For this you need a handler interceptor. The `org.springframework.web.servlet.HandlerInterceptor` interface determines how to intercept requests handled in the `DispatcherServlet`, similar to a `Filter`. Its `preHandle` method is executed after the `DispatcherServlet` receives the request but before it executes the handler method on the controller. The `postHandle` method is executed after the handler method returns but before the view is rendered. The `afterCompletion` method executes after the view renders and right before `DispatcherServlet` returns control to the container.

If you have filter-like behavior you need to implement, you want to do it with a Spring-managed bean, and the behavior needs to apply only to requests served by the `DispatcherServlet`, using a `HandlerInterceptor` is a great way to do it.

The `org.springframework.web.servlet.i18n.LocaleChangeInterceptor` is a `HandlerInterceptor` for changing the locale when requested. On each request to the `DispatcherServlet`, it looks for a request parameter, which defaults to *`locale`* but can be customized. If this request parameter exists, the interceptor converts the `String` parameter to a `Locale` and then uses the `LocaleResolver`'s `setLocale` method to set the locale. This way, the `LocaleResolver` is responsible for determining both how to retrieve the locale *and* how to set the locale.

To set up the `LocaleChangeInterceptor` or any other interceptors, you override the `addInterceptors` method of `WebMvcConfigurerAdapter` in your `ServletContextConfiguration` class. If you want to customize the request parameter that the interceptor checks for, you could instantiate the interceptor, call the `setParamName` method, and then add it to the registry.

```
    ...
    }

    @Override
```

```
    public void addInterceptors(InterceptorRegistry registry)
    {
        super.addInterceptors(registry);

        registry.addInterceptor(new LocaleChangeInterceptor());
    }

    @Bean
    public LocaleResolver localeResolver()
    ...
```

Now, on any page you can add a link to change locales and simply submit it to the current page. This not only changes the locale for the current page, it also changes the locale for all subsequent pages the user visits until his session times out or he closes his browser.

## Providing a User Profile Locale Setting

If your application is one that users can sign up for and log in to, chances are they're going to want to set their locale once and have that locale used automatically every time they come back to the site. Speaking in the abstract, you can provide a profile settings page somewhere for users to change various settings like their name, e-mail address, password, time zone, and locale, among others. But how do you use this setting, and how do you make changes to it immediately visible?

You have a couple of options at your disposal to utilize user profile locale settings. First, you can simply use an `@Injected` `LocaleResolver` on your login controller and your profile controller. When users authenticate or update their profile, you simply call `setLocale` on the resolver to update their current locale.

One disadvantage of this technique — a problem that also exists with the `SessionLocaleResolver` in general — is that the application forgets a user's locale after he logs out and closes his browser, or his session times out. When he returns, the application may display in a different language. In these cases, you may want to create a custom `LocaleResolver` that prefers the logged-in user's locale and uses a cookie value as a backup. Because the `org.springframework.web.servlet.i18n.CookieLocaleResolver` already takes care of much of that for you, you could just extend that resolver.

```
public class UserCookieHeaderLocaleResolver extends CookieLocaleResolver
{
    @Override
    public Locale resolveLocale(HttpServletRequest request)
    {
        Locale locale = null;
        Principal user = request.getUserPrincipal();
        if(user != null && user instanceof FooPrincipal)
            locale = ((FooPrincipal)user).getLocale();

        if(locale == null)
            locale = super.resolveLocale(request);
        return locale;
    }
}
```

Because you have several options on how to achieve this task and those options largely depend on your authentication mechanism and user API, this example is not demonstrated in the Localized-Application project.

## Including Time Zone Support

When internationalizing your application, locale is not the only topic that you should consider. In addition to language and region, time zones are a major issue for web application users. The majority of users want to see times displayed on a page in their time zone, not the server time zone, especially if that server is on the other side of the world. Often it can be difficult to even know what day it is in different parts of the world! Spring Framework 4.0 now includes first-class support for time zones, including the `java.util.TimeZone` and `java.time.ZoneId` classes. Spring includes `PropertyEditors` for these types, so you can specify `TimeZone` and `ZoneId` method parameters in your controller methods and Spring can convert request parameters, path variables, and header values for these method parameters.

Spring can also resolve the user's time zone and provide it to your controller methods, similar to how it resolves and provides the user's locale to your controller methods. However, this mechanism functions differently than locale resolution. There are no `TimeZone` or `ZoneId` resolvers, and there are no change interceptors. Time zones are handled differently than locales, and they are not normally changed on the fly like locales are. Since the earliest days of Spring, you have been able to manually set the current `Locale` using the `org.springframework.context.i18n.LocaleContextHolder`. This tool serves as both a replacement for and supplement to the various `LocaleResolvers`, ensuring that you can always manipulate the `Locale` whenever needed. The `Locale` is stored in a `ThreadLocal` variable, following the request throughout the rest of its entire lifecycle.

As of Spring 4.0, `LocaleContextHolder` also supports setting and retrieving the current `TimeZone`. You can use the static methods in this class for setting the user's `TimeZone`, and Spring automatically sets the JSTL `TimeZone` property and provides access to `TimeZone` and `ZoneId` controller method parameters. This makes the task of managing user `TimeZones` in your applications much simpler. All you have to do is determine which `TimeZone` a user wants to use and set that `TimeZone` on the `LocaleContextHolder`.

## Understanding How Themes Can Improve Internationalization

Spring Framework has a concept of *themes* that is very similar to internationalization support. Themes are collections of Cascading Style Sheets, JavaScript files, images, and other resources necessary to style your site. The `Theme` interface represents a theme, and the available `ThemeResolvers` (including a `SessionThemeResolver` and a `CookieThemeResolver`) can resolve the appropriate theme for a user. Not surprisingly, the `ThemeChangeInterceptor` uses a configurable request parameter that defaults to *`theme`* to update the user's selected theme. The themes feature even provides a `ResourceBundleThemeSource`, nearly identical to the `ResourceBundleMessageSource`, which loads key-to-resource-path instructions from properties files. Finally, when creating your views you use the `<spring:theme>` tag, again nearly identical to the `<spring:message>` tag, to output the appropriate resource URLs for a particular theme.

At this point you're probably wondering what this has to do with internationalization and localization, other than the API being so similar. Remember that, when internationalizing an application, language *content* isn't the only thing you must account for. Different languages around the world also print in *different directions*.

- English and other western languages read left-to-right and then top-to-bottom.
- Middle Eastern languages such as Arabic and Hebrew typically read right-to-left then top-to-bottom.
- Even more difficult, Japanese, Chinese, and Korean read top-to-bottom and then right-to-left.
- Mongolian reads top-to-bottom and then left-to-right.

If you thought simply translating your application was hard, wait until you try to account for all four language directions!

Spring Framework themes can actually be a big help here. Instead of using a standard `ThemeResolver` you can create a custom `ThemeResolver` that sets the theme based on the current locale. Using `java.awt.ComponentOrientation`'s `getOrientation(Locale)` method, you can detect the appropriate text direction based on the `Locale` and then return the correct theme for that text direction. You also want a custom `LocaleResolver` and `LocaleChangeInterceptor` that prevent the user from selecting a locale that you don't support (such as Mongolian). Because the `Theme` is always based on the `Locale`, you don't need a `ThemeChangeInterceptor`. After this is configured, you can change the text direction of your views using nothing but CSS, greatly reducing the amount of work you have to do over other solutions (such as having custom views for each text direction).

> **NOTE** *This topic is obviously advanced, and the complexities of, and issues that arise from, supporting multiple text directions are numerous and outside the scope of this book. For this reason, this is the only mention you will see about text direction in this book. Hopefully, it gives you ideas for how to better support your international users.*

## INTERNATIONALIZING YOUR CODE

In Chapter 7, you experimented with internationalizing your JSPs using `<fmt:message>`, `<fmt:formatDate>`, and `<fmt:formatNumber>`. This section does not rehash the details of the Formatting and Internationalization Tag Library, but you can use it to internationalize your JSPs. The Localize-Application project contains a `HomeController` with one mapping in it. The simple handler method adds just a few items to the model and returns a view name.

```
@Controller
public class HomeController
{
    @RequestMapping(value = "/", method = RequestMethod.GET)
```

```
        public String index(Map<String, Object> model)
        {
            model.put("date", Instant.now());
            model.put("alerts", 12);
            model.put("numCritical", 0);
            model.put("numImportant", 11);
            model.put("numTrivial", 1);

            return "home/index";
        }
    }
```

The `/WEB-INF/i18n/messages_en_US.properties` file contains messages localized for U.S. English.

```
title.alerts=Server Alerts Page
alerts.current.date=Current Date and Time:
number.alerts=There {0,choice,0#are no alerts|1#is one alert|1<are \
  {0,number,integer} alerts} in the log.
alert.details={0,choice,0#No alerts are|1#One alert is|1<{0,number,integer} \
  alerts are} critical. {1,choice,0#No alerts are|1#One alert is|1<{1,number,\
  integer} alerts are} important. {2,choice,0#No alerts are|1#One alert \
  is|1<{2,number,integer} alerts are} trivial.
```

Finally, the `/WEB-INF/i18n/messages_es_MX.properties` file contains messages localized for Mexican Spanish.

```
title.alerts=Server Alertas Página
alerts.current.date=Fecha y hora actual:
number.alerts={0,choice,0#No hay alertas|1#Hay una alerta|1<Hay \
  {0,number,integer} alertas} en el registro.
alert.details={0,choice,0#No hay alertas son críticos|1#Una alerta es \
  crítica|1<{0,number,integer} alertas son críticos}. \
  {1,choice,0#No hay alertas son importantes|1#Una alerta es importante\
  |1<{1,number,integer} alertas son importantes}. \
  {2,choice,0#No hay alertas son triviales|1#Una alerta es trivial\
  |1<{2,number,integer} alertas son triviales}.
```

## Using the <spring:message> Tag

If you are familiar with the `<fmt:message>` tag, the `<spring:message>` tag should come naturally because it is very similar but ultimately better. The `code` attribute is the equivalent of the `key` attribute for `<fmt:message>` and specifies the message code. Both tags have `var` and `scope` attributes responsible for exporting the localized value to an EL variable instead of printing it on the page inline. `<spring:message>` does not have an equivalent for the `bundle` attribute because `<spring:message>` uses a `MessageSource` instead of a `ResourceBundle`.

The `javaScriptEscape` attribute is especially useful because, if set to `true`, it causes the characters `"` and `'` in the final, formatted message to be replaced with `\"` and `\'`, respectively, so that it is safe for use in JavaScript strings. By default, this attribute is `false`, and it has no equivalent in `<fmt:message>`. The `htmlEscape` attribute, also unique to `<spring:message>`, escapes special characters `<`, `>`, `&`, `"`, and `'` in the final, formatted message with their equivalent entity escape sequences if its value is `true`. By default, its value is `false`.

If most or all the `<spring:message>` tags on a page should be HTML escaped, you can use the tag `<spring:htmlEscape defaultHtmlEscape="true" />` in your JSP to affect all `<spring:message>` tags that follow it. If most or all the `<spring:message>` tags in your entire application should be HTML escaped, you can set the context init parameter `defaultHtmlEscape` to `true` in the deployment descriptor or programmatically, and this will affect all `<spring:message>` tags in your application. For purposes of precedence, the `htmlEscape` attribute of `<spring:message>`, if explicitly set, always overrides the `<spring:htmlEscape>` tag and the context init parameter, and the `<spring:htmlEscape>` tag, if explicitly used, always overrides the context init parameter.

```
<context-param>
    <param-name>defaultHtmlEscape</param-name>
    <param-value>true</param-value>
</context-param>
```

The final difference between `<fmt:message>` and `<spring:message>` comes in how you specify the message to localize. When you use `<fmt:message>`, you can specify the message using only the `key` attribute or tag body as the message code and, if necessary, nested `<fmt:param>` tags for format parameter arguments. `<spring:message>` is much more flexible, enabling you to use any of the following three strategies. These are all mutually exclusive; you cannot use more than one of these per use of the `<spring:message>` tag. You can specify the message:

- **Traditionally using the `code` attribute or tag body as the message code and, if necessary, nested `<spring:argument>` tags for format parameter arguments.** The `<spring:argument>` tag, added in Spring 4.0, works just like the `<fmt:param>` tag. You can also optionally specify a default message format using the `text` attribute, and that value is used if the message code does not resolve. You should not use this strategy with the `arguments`, `argumentSeparator`, or `message` attributes.
- **Using the `code` attribute or tag body as the message code and, if necessary, provide a delimited list of arguments in the `arguments` attribute.** By default, the delimiter is a single comma, but you can customize the delimiter using the `argumentSeparator` attribute. You can also optionally specify a default message format using the `text` attribute, and that value is used if the message code does not resolve. You should not use this strategy with the `message` attribute or `<spring:argument>` nested tag.
- **Using an instance of `MessageSourceResolvable` for the `message` attribute using an EL expression.** Because a `MessageSourceResolvable` provides its own codes, arguments, and default messages, you should not use this with the `code`, `arguments`, `argumentSeparator`, or `text` attributes, a tag body, or nested `<spring:argument>` tags.

Use of the `<spring:message>` and `<fmt:message>` tags together is demonstrated in the `/WEB-INF/jsp/view/home/index.jsp` file of the Localized-Application project. You'll notice that this file contains absolutely no string literals, but instead uses message internationalization for all text output. This is how it should be done.

```
<%--@elvariable id="date" type="java.util.Date"--%>
<%--@elvariable id="alerts" type="int"--%>
<%--@elvariable id="numCritical" type="int"--%>
<%--@elvariable id="numImportant" type="int"--%>
<%--@elvariable id="numTrivial" type="int"--%>
```

```
<!DOCTYPE html>
<html>
    <head>
        <title><spring:message code="title.alerts" /></title>
    </head>
    <body>
        <h2><spring:message code="title.alerts" /></h2>
        <i><fmt:message key="alerts.current.date">
            <fmt:param value="${date}" />
        </fmt:message></i><br /><br />
        <fmt:message key="number.alerts">
            <fmt:param value="${alerts}" />
        </fmt:message><c:if test="${alerts > 0}">
             <spring:message code="alert.details">
                <spring:argument value="${numCritical}" />
                <spring:argument value="${numImportant}" />
                <spring:argument value="${numTrivial}" />
            </spring:message>
        </c:if>
    </body>
</html>
```

## Handling Application Errors Cleanly

As you well know by now, application errors happen. You can't prevent them completely. Eventually, something goes wrong and your application does not function properly. Usually, this causes a thrown exception. In Chapter 11, you learned about how logging can help you handle these errors cleanly. However, hiding all errors from users is not an acceptable alternative to displaying all error stack traces to users. When something goes wrong, users need to know. You should log technical details, but you should display a useful error message for users to help them understand what went wrong in the least technical terms possible. This error message must also be localized. You do not want this internationalization to affect the messages written to your logs, just what displays to the user.

You have many different ways to approach this, and it is outside the scope of this book to cover all the possibilities. Instead, this book presents a pattern for your consideration and demonstrates how it can greatly simplify your application development.

When an exception of some expected (but not wanted) type occurs, such as a `SQLException` when executing SQL statements using JDBC, the natural tendency is to catch the exception and log it. This is okay, but you still need to report that error message to the user somehow. You could rethrow the exception, but then how does a higher layer in the application know that it has already been logged? Also if you simply rethrow the exception, how does a useful error message get presented to the user? A view catching an exception thrown three layers down, after all, has no idea in what context the exception was thrown, and therefore has no ability to create a useful error message for it.

To tackle the first problem, you can create your own custom exception and throw it instead of rethrowing the original exception. You might name it `LoggedException` and then institute a policy that `LoggedExceptions` should never be logged and should be rethrown if caught. All the `LoggedException` constructors require that you include the underlying exception as the cause. This certainly solves the first problem, but it doesn't solve the second.

A good way to tackle the second problem is to make `LoggedException` implement `MessageSourceResolvable`. Then, it contains its own error code, default message, and arguments that you can use to internationalize display of the exception. However, if you think about this for a minute, you will quickly realize that some circumstances require you to throw internationalized exceptions without first catching an underlying exception. So, what you really need is an `InternationalizedException` that just implements `MessageSourceResolvable`, and a `LoggedException` that extends it. Listing 15-1 shows the `InternationalizedException` from the Localized-Application project.

**LISTING 15-1: InternationalizedException.java**

```
public class InternationalizedException extends RuntimeException
        implements MessageSourceResolvable {
    private static final long serialVersionUID = 1L;
    private static final Locale DEFAULT_LOCALE = Locale.US;

    private final String errorCode;
    private final String[] codes;
    private final Object[] arguments;

    public InternationalizedException(String errorCode, Object... arguments) {
        this(null, errorCode, null, arguments);
    }

    public InternationalizedException(Throwable cause, String errorCode,
                                      Object... arguments) {
        this(cause, errorCode, null, arguments);
    }

    public InternationalizedException(String errorCode, String defaultMessage,
                                      Object... arguments) {
        this(null, errorCode, defaultMessage, arguments);
    }

    public InternationalizedException(Throwable cause, String errorCode,
                                      String defaultMessage,Object... arguments) {
        super(defaultMessage == null ? errorCode : defaultMessage, cause);
        this.errorCode = errorCode;
        this.codes = new String[] { errorCode };
        this.arguments = arguments;
    }

    @Override
    public String getLocalizedMessage() {
        return this.errorCode;
    }

    public String getLocalizedMessage(MessageSource messageSource) {
        return this.getLocalizedMessage(messageSource, this.getLocale());
    }

    public String getLocalizedMessage(MessageSource messageSource,Locale locale) {
        return messageSource.getMessage(this, locale);
```

```
        }

        @Override
        public String[] getCodes() {
            return this.codes;
        }

        @Override
        public Object[] getArguments() {
            return this.arguments;
        }

        @Override
        public String getDefaultMessage() {
            return this.getMessage();
        }

        protected final Locale getLocale() {
            Locale locale = LocaleContextHolder.getLocale();
            return locale == null ? InternationalizedException.DEFAULT_LOCALE:locale;
        }
    }
```

The `getLocale` method and `getLocalizedMessage` methods aren't strictly required but do make it easier to use the exception from within Java code. This exception can be thrown anywhere in your code with or without a causing exception. Extending it is the `LoggedException`, as shown in Listing 15-2. This exception doesn't even have any methods or fields; it just restricts the possible constructors to require the user to supply a causing exception.

**LISTING 15-2: LoggedException.java**

```
    public class LoggedException extends InternationalizedException {
        private static final long serialVersionUID = 1L;

        public LoggedException(Throwable cause, String errorCode,
                               Object... arguments) {
            this(cause, errorCode, null, arguments);
        }

        public LoggedException(Throwable cause, String errorCode,
                               String defaultMessage, Object... arguments) {
            super(cause, errorCode, defaultMessage, arguments);
        }
    }
```

You already realize the advantage of logging an exception and throwing the `LoggedException` in its place, which keeps higher layers from catching the exception and relogging it. To demonstrate how easy it is to localize the exception, follow these steps:

1. Add the following to the handler method of your `HomeController`.

   ```
   model.put("exception", new InternationalizedException(
           "bad.food.exception", "You ate bad food."
   ));
   ```

2. Add a translation for the message in /WEB-INF/i18n/errors_en_US.properties:

```
bad.food.exception=You ate bad food.
```

3. In /WEB-INF/i18n/errors_es_MX.properties, use:

```
bad.food.exception=Comiste comida en mal estado.
```

4. Update /WEB-INF/jsp/view/home/index.jsp to display the exception using <spring:message>.

```
            ...
            </c:if>
            <c:if test="${exception != null}"><br /><br />
                <spring:message message="${exception}" />
            </c:if>
        </body>
    </html>
```

To test out the Localized-Application project, compile it, start Tomcat from your IDE, and go to http://localhost:8080/i18n/ in your favorite browser. You should see the page, nicely displayed in English. Go to http://localhost:8080/i18n/?locale=es_MX and the page should change to Spanish. More important, you can now go back to http://localhost:8080/i18n/ without the *locale* parameter as many times as you like, and the page still displays in Spanish. Only when you go to http://localhost:8080/i18n/?locale=en_US does the page revert to English and stay that way even without the *locale* parameter.

> **NOTE** *If you visit the application on a computer whose locale is set to Spanish, the page should actually display in Spanish first, not English, assuming your browser sends the* Accept-Language *header. If that's the case, reverse the instructions and try* en_US *as the first locale value, instead.*

## Updating the Customer Support Application

The Customer-Support-v12 project, which you can get from the wrox.com code download site, is now internationalized using virtually the same configuration as the Localized-Application project. The only difference is that the Customer Support application has an additional resource bundle basename in the message source configuration.

```
        messageSource.setBasenames(
                "/WEB-INF/i18n/titles", "/WEB-INF/i18n/messages",
                "/WEB-INF/i18n/errors"
        );
```

The i18n files /WEB-INF/i18n/errors_en_US.properties, messages_en_US.properties, and titles_en_US.properties contain dozens of messages between them. There is no localization for any other language. Most of the internationalization is routine use of <spring:message>, but the /WEB-INF/jsp/view/chat/chat.jsp file is an interesting example. This file is full of JavaScript string literals that need to be localized. <spring:message> with javaScriptEscape set to true is handy for this, but that's not the only dilemma. For example, take a look at this message in messages_en_US.properties, which ultimately will be placed in a JavaScript string:

```
message.chat.joined=You are now chatting with {0}.
```

This message is parameterized and requires you to complete arguments. So how does this work when the parameter is not available at time of view rendering, but instead must be populated by JavaScript? Well, quite simply, the formatter just ignores extra replacement templates when arguments don't exist for them, so this message is written to the JavaScript code as `'You are now chatting with {0}.'` at render time. Using that value, then, just requires calling the `replace` method on the JavaScript string to replace the parameter with the appropriate argument.

```
infoMessage('<spring:message code="message.chat.joined" javaScriptEscape="true"/>'
        .replace('{0}', message.user));
```

The final challenge when internationalizing the Customer Support application is dealing with chat messages. Unlike all other localized messages, which resolve when the view renders, the `ChatService` and `ChatController` output messages over the WebSocket connection must also be localized. The `<spring:message>` and `<fmt:message>` tags do you no good here.

## Using the Message Source Directly

To solve this problem, the `ChatMessage` needs to consist of a message code and arguments and be localized programmatically. The `ChatController` uses the `MessageSource` directly to accomplish this. The first step to take is to refactor the `ChatMessage` class.

```
public class ChatMessage implements Cloneable
{
    private Instant timestamp;
    private Type type;
    private String user;
    private String contentCode;
    private Object[] contentArguments;
    private String localizedContent;
    private String userContent;

    // mutators and accessors
    // enum
    // clone

    static abstract class MixInForLogWrite
    {
        @JsonIgnore public abstract String getLocalizedContent();
        @JsonIgnore public abstract void setLocalizedContent(String l);
    }

    static abstract class MixInForWebSocket
    {
        @JsonIgnore public abstract String getContentCode();
        @JsonIgnore public abstract void setContentCode(String c);
        @JsonIgnore public abstract Object[] getContentArguments();
        @JsonIgnore public abstract void setContentArguments(Object[] c);
    }
}
```

The new `MixInForLogWrite` and `MixInForWebSocket` inner classes are special classes to support the Mix-In Annotations feature of Jackson Data Processor. The `localizedContent` should not be written to the chat log file because it is localized for a particular user. Likewise, the `contentCode` and `contentArguments` don't need to be transmitted over the WebSocket connection because the message is localized already. On the other hand, the user supplies the `userContent` property, and thus you cannot localize it. You must transmit and write this property to the log as-is. To use these Mix-In Annotations, first add a `@PostConstruct` method to the `DefaultChatService`.

```
@PostConstruct
public void initialize()
{
    this.objectMapper.addMixInAnnotations(ChatMessage.class,
            ChatMessage.MixInForLogWrite.class);
}
```

You can now add a different Mix-In class to the `ObjectMapper` in the `ChatMessageDecoderCodec` using the static initializer. Because this is a different `ObjectMapper` instance, it won't interfere with the Mix-In you just added in the `DefaultChatService`.

```
    MAPPER.addMixInAnnotations(ChatMessage.class,
            ChatMessage.MixInForWebSocket.class);
```

Next, you need to refactor the `DefaultChatService` to use message codes and arguments instead of static messages.

```
public CreateResult createSession(String user)
{
    ...
    message.setContentCode("message.chat.started.session");
    message.setContentArguments(user);
    ...
}

public JoinResult joinSession(long id, String user)
{
    ...
    message.setContentCode("message.chat.joined.session");
    message.setContentArguments(user);
    ...
}

public ChatMessage leaveSession(ChatSession session, String user,
                                ReasonForLeaving reason)
{
    ...
    if(reason == ReasonForLeaving.ERROR)
        message.setType(ChatMessage.Type.ERROR);
    message.setType(ChatMessage.Type.LEFT);
    if(reason == ReasonForLeaving.ERROR)
        message.setContentCode("message.chat.left.chat.error");
    else if(reason == ReasonForLeaving.LOGGED_OUT)
        message.setContentCode("message.chat.logged.out");
    else
        message.setContentCode("message.chat.left.chat.normal");
    message.setContentArguments(user);
    ...
}
```

At this point everything compiles, but the endpoint is not yet localizing messages. It first needs a `MessageSource` and a `Locale`:

```
    private Locale locale;
    private Locale otherLocale;
    ...
    @Inject MessageSource messageSource;
```

The locales can't be injected, so the `modifyHandshake` method of the `ChatEndpoint.EndpointConfigurator` class gets the `Locale` from Spring and adds it to the WebSocket `Session`.

```
            config.getUserProperties().put(LOCALE_KEY,
                    LocaleContextHolder.getLocale());
```

The `onOpen` method of the `ChatEndpoint` assigns the locale.

```
        this.locale = EndpointConfigurator.getExposedLocale(session);
        ...
                this.otherWsSession = this.chatSession.getCustomer();
                this.otherLocale = EndpointConfigurator
                        .getExposedLocale(this.otherWsSession);
```

The `ChatEndpoint` also needs an internal helper method to make localization easier. Calling this method, you can clone and localize a `ChatMessage` in one line of code.

```
    private ChatMessage cloneAndLocalize(ChatMessage message, Locale locale)
    {
        message = message.clone();
        message.setLocalizedContent(this.messageSource.getMessage(
                message.getContentCode(), message.getContentArguments(), locale
        ));
        return message;
    }
```

You can localize all the places where internally generated `ChatMessages` are sent. Remember that you cannot localize user-generated `ChatMessages` because they contain user content, not message codes.

```
...
                session.getBasicRemote().sendObject(this.cloneAndLocalize(
                        result.getCreateMessage(), this.locale
                ));
...
                session.getBasicRemote().sendObject(this.cloneAndLocalize(
                        this.chatSession.getCreationMessage(), this.locale
                ));
                session.getBasicRemote().sendObject(this.cloneAndLocalize(
                        result.getJoinMessage(), this.locale
                ));
                this.otherWsSession.getBasicRemote()
                        .sendObject(this.cloneAndLocalize(
                                result.getJoinMessage(), this.otherLocale
                        ));
...
                        this.wsSession.getBasicRemote()
                                .sendObject(this.cloneAndLocalize(
```

```
                                message, this.locale
                        ));
                this.wsSession.close(closeReason);
    ...
                    this.otherWsSession.getBasicRemote()
                            .sendObject(this.cloneAndLocalize(
                                    message, this.otherLocale
                            ));
                    this.otherWsSession.close(closeReason);
```

Now that the internationalization of the Customer Support application is complete, compile it, start Tomcat from your IDE, and go to `http://localhost:8080/support/`. Log in and browse around. Create, list, and view tickets, and view the list of sessions. Log in from another browser and engage in a chat session. Internationalization and localization clearly take a great deal of effort, but the tools provided by Spring Framework make the task much easier.

# SUMMARY

In this chapter, you have learned a great deal about internationalization (i18n) and localization (L10n) in both concept and practice. You have witnessed how difficult these tasks are and experimented with all the Spring Framework tools provided to make it easier. You internationalized JSP views, using `<spring:message>` and `<fmt:message>`, and Java strings, using Spring's `MessageSource`. You also learned about all your options when configuring Spring's internationalization and localization support and were introduced to a Logged and Internationalized Exception pattern. Finally, you got a look at support for user time zones and a brief introduction on the complexities of text direction in non-western locales.

In the next chapter, you learn about JSR 303/JSR 349 automatic bean validation and Hibernate Validator. The chapter relates closely to this one, and you will find that the skills and tools you discovered in this chapter are indispensable as you familiarize yourself with bean validation.

# 16

# Using JSR 349, Spring Framework, and Hibernate Validator for Bean Validation

## IN THIS CHAPTER

- An Introduction to Bean Validation
- Configuring validation in the Spring Framework container
- Adding constraint validation annotations to your beans
- Configuring Spring beans for method validation
- Writing your own validation constraints
- Integrating validation in the Customer Support application

## WROX.COM CODE DOWNLOADS FOR THIS CHAPTER

You can find the `wrox.com` code downloads for this chapter at `http://www.wrox.com/go/projavaforwebapps` on the Download Code tab. The code for this chapter is divided into the following major examples:

- HR-Portal Project
- Custom-Constraints Project
- Customer-Support-v13 Project

## NEW MAVEN DEPENDENCIES FOR THIS CHAPTER

In addition to the Maven dependencies introduced in previous chapters, you also need the following Maven dependencies:

```
<dependency>
    <groupId>javax.validation</groupId>
    <artifactId>validation-api</artifactId>
    <version>1.1.0.Final</version>
    <scope>compile</scope>
</dependency>

<dependency>
    <groupId>org.hibernate</groupId>
    <artifactId>hibernate-validator</artifactId>
    <version>5.1.0.Final</version>
    <scope>runtime</scope>
    <exclusions>
        <exclusion>
            <groupId>org.jboss.logging</groupId>
            <artifactId>jboss-logging</artifactId>
        </exclusion>
    </exclusions>
</dependency>

<dependency>
    <groupId>org.jboss.logging</groupId>
    <artifactId>jboss-logging</artifactId>
    <version>3.2.0.GA</version>
    <scope>runtime</scope>
</dependency>
```

# WHAT IS BEAN VALIDATION?

In a large application, chances are that you'll have many different types of objects that get "saved" in some fashion. The meaning of the word saved here doesn't matter; the objects might get stored in a collection in memory, transmitted over a network connection to some other system, or persisted to a database.

Whatever the goal, you undoubtedly have rules that these objects must follow. An object representing a user, for example, is probably required to have a non-null, non-blank value in the username field. An item added to a shopping cart requires a product identifier and a quantity, and the quantity must be greater than zero. An e-mail sent might require the recipient address, subject, and body fields to have values. An employee added to a human resources system must have a first and last name, and a date of birth that is before some date.

Sometimes these *business rules* can get quite complex. For example, a property representing an e-mail address must match the following regular expression to be a valid RFC 2822 address. (And even this expression isn't complete because it omits non-English characters, as well as quoted and bracketed characters in the domain part.)

```
^[a-z0-9`!#$%^&*'{}?/+=|_~-]+(\.[a-z0-9`!#$%^&*'{}?/+=|_~-]+)*@
    ([a-z0-9]([a-z0-9-]*[a-z0-9])?)+(\.[a-z0-9]([a-z0-9-]*[a-z0-9])?)*$
```

It should not take a lot to convince you that evaluating these business rules throughout your application can become cumbersome and downright inefficient when code like evaluating that e-mail address regular expression is duplicated many times over. At the very least, evaluating all these rules consumes many lines of code. Consider this sample evaluation of an employee entity.

```
    if(employee.getFirstName() == null ||
            employee.getFirstName().trim().length() == 0)
        throw new ValidationException("validate.employee.firstName");
    if(employee.getLastName() == null || employee.getLastName().trim().length() == 0)
        throw new ValidationException("validate.employee.lastName");
    if(employee.getGovernmentId() == null ||
            employee.getGovernmentId().trim().length() == 0)
        throw new ValidationException("validate.employee.governmentId");
    if(employee.getBirthDate() == null ||
            employee.getBirthDate().isAfter(yearsAgo(18)))
        throw new ValidationException("validate.employee.birthDate");
    if(employee.getGender() == null)
        threw new ValidationException("validate.employee.gender");
    if(employee.getBadgeNumber() == null ||
            employee.getBadgeNumber().trim().length() == 0)
        throw new ValidationException("validate.employee.badgeNumber");
    if(employee.getAddress() == null || employee.getAddress().trim().length() == 0)
        throw new ValidationException("validate.employee.address");
    if(employee.getCity() == null || employee.getCity().trim().length() == 0)
        throw new ValidationException("validate.employee.city");
    if(employee.getState() == null || employee.getState().trim().length() == 0)
        throw new ValidationException("validate.employee.state");
    if(employee.getPhoneNumber() == null ||
            employee.getPhoneNumber().trim().length() == 0)
        throw new ValidationException("validate.employee.phoneNumber");
    if(employee.getEmail() == null || employee.getEmail().trim().length() == 0 ||
            !EMAIL_REGEX.matcher(employee.getEmail()).matches())
        throw new ValidationException("validate.employee.email");
    if(employee.getDepartment() == null ||
            lookupService.getDepartment(employee.getDepartment()) == null)
        throw new ValidationException("validate.employee.department");
    if(employee.getLocation() == null ||
            lookupService.getLocation(employee.getLocation()) == null)
        throw new ValidationException("validate.employee.location");
    if(employee.getPosition() == null ||
            lookupService.getPosition(employee.getPosition()) == null)
        throw new ValidationException("validate.employee.position");
    if(employee.getManager() == null && !"President".equals(employee.getPosition()))
        throw new ValidationException("validate.employee.manager");
```

Are you tired yet? You haven't even written the code to save the employee! This code just tests whether you're *allowed* to save the employee. Worse, you'll find out about only one violation at a time, meaning you may have to submit the employee multiple times to get it right. You could, instead, add to a collection of error codes and throw the exception if the collection is not empty after validation, but that's yet again more code.

Thankfully, there's an easier way. Bean Validation is a Java EE API for automatically validating declared business rules on Java beans. It consists of a metadata model — a set of annotations with which you declare the business rules for a given class — and an API for using the validation tools.

JSR 303 is the original specification for JavaBean Validation 1.0, and it was added as part of the Java EE 6 platform. JavaBean Validation 1.1, specified in JSR 349, is the successor to JSR 303 in Java EE 7. It includes a couple of major improvements, such as supporting validation of method arguments and return values, and enabling Unified Expression Language expressions within validation error messages. You use Hibernate Validator 5.1 to power Bean Validation in this book.

## Why Hibernate Validator?

JSR 349 is just the specification of the metadata model and the validation API. You still require an implementation of this API to make Bean Validation in your applications work. Hibernate Validator 5.0 is the reference implementation for JSR 349, meaning it is compliant with the specification. In addition, you can generally count on it to be ahead of other implementations as far as identifying and fixing issues because it is the most used of any Bean Validation implementation. (Hibernate Validator 5.1 includes several important enhancements, bug fixes, and performance improvements to better support JSR 349.)

In fact, Hibernate Validator was the inspiration for the Bean Validation standard, which is evident from the fact that Hibernate Validator's version number is far ahead of the specification's version number. Hibernate Validator has been around for many years. Originally it was part of the Hibernate ORM project (which you learn about in Part III of this book) and provided declarative validation of entities before they were persisted to the database. It eventually became its own project and, after more years still, evolved into the Bean Validation standard.

## Understanding the Annotation Metadata Model

Bean Validation works by way of annotating fields, methods, and more, to indicate that a particular constraint applies to the annotated target. Any annotation whose retention policy is run time (meaning the annotation survives compilation and is available in class metadata at run time) and which is annotated with `@javax.validation.Constraint` represents a constraint annotation. The API comes with several predefined constraint annotations, but you can create your own and provide corresponding `javax.validation.ConstraintValidator` implementations that correspond to your custom annotations. A `ConstraintValidator` is responsible for evaluating a particular constraint type. The API does not define `ConstraintValidators` for the built-in constraints because it is up to the implementation how to handle these built-in annotations.

Constraint annotations may be placed on fields, methods, or method parameters. When placed on a field, this indicates that the validator should check that field for constraint compliance whenever the validation method is called on an instance of the class. When placed on a JavaBean accessor method, this simply serves as an alternative to annotating the underlying field. Annotating an interface method indicates that the constraint should be applied against the return value of the method after method execution. Annotating one or more method parameters of an interface method means that the constraints should be applied against the method parameters before method execution.

These last two patterns facilitate a programming style known as *programming by contract* or *PbC*. The creator of the interface specifies a contract that the interface follows, such as certain return values never being `null`, or certain method parameters having to follow certain rules. Consumers of the interface can then rely on that contract, and implementers and consumers of the interface alike know that the contract is enforced if they violate it.

When using Bean Validation annotations as PbC constraints, you must create a proxy to validate the target implementation classes. This requires some form of dependency injection for consumers of an interface to actually call the proxy of its implementation. Full Java EE application servers implementing Java EE 7 provide the capability to DI proxied implementations that are appropriately validated. When using simple Servlet containers such as Tomcat, however, you must provide some other DI solution.

### Using Bean Validation with Spring Framework

Obviously, Spring Framework's dependency injection is the solution to this problem. Spring Framework automatically proxies Spring-managed beans that use Java Bean Validation. Calls to annotated methods are intercepted and validated appropriately, whether to check that the consumer provides valid arguments or that the implementation returns legal values. As such, it is quite common to use Bean Validation on `@Services` because these are the conceptual Spring-managed beans that handle business logic. Spring Framework also validates any form objects or other constraint-annotated arguments passed to controller handler methods if the parameters are marked with `@javax.validation.Valid`.

In this chapter, you explore how to configure Bean Validation in Spring Framework and how to use all the provided constraint annotations to apply business rules to your beans. You also learn how to create your own, custom constraint annotations for rules that aren't satisfied by the built-in constraints.

## CONFIGURING VALIDATION IN THE SPRING FRAMEWORK CONTAINER

Before you can easily use any of the validation tools, you must first set up Bean Validation in the Spring Framework configuration. This is not to say that configuring Bean Validation in Spring is *required* to use the validator, as the following standard validation code still works, even without the Spring container:

```
ValidatorFactory factory = Validation.buildDefaultValidatorFactory();
Validator validator = factory.getValidator();
Set<ConstraintViolation<Employee>> violations = validator.validate(employee);
if(violations.size() > 0)
    throw new ConstraintViolationException(violations);
```

But you don't want to have to use it like that. You want this to be automatic, which means Spring Framework's dependency injection and proxy support have to get involved. To accomplish this you must configure four things:

- A validator
- Message localization for the validator
- A method validation processor
- Spring MVC form validation

For this, use the HR-Portal project, available for download from the `wrox.com` code download site.

> **NOTE** *You've likely noticed that the Maven dependency for Hibernate Validator excludes the transient JBoss Logging API dependency (Hibernate projects use this instead of Commons Logging as their logging API), and that a runtime JBoss Logging dependency is separately declared. The* `hibernate-validator` *artifact declares a dependency on a* `jboss-logging` *version that doesn't support Log4j 2, so it is necessary to declare a newer dependency that does. The exclusion isn't strictly necessary, but is shown for clarity.*

> **WARNING** *Prior to Spring Framework 4.0, Spring's support for Bean Validation 1.0 was specifically targeted to Hibernate Validator 4.2 or 4.3. This is because Hibernate Validator provided some nonstandard features that were necessary to solve certain problems, such as integration with Spring i18n. As of Spring 4.0, any Bean Validation 1.1 implementation works because these features are standardized in 1.1. However, if you, for some reason, are restricted to Bean Validation 1.0, you must still use Hibernate Validator.*

## Configuring the Spring Validator Bean

Spring Framework had support for automatic validation of objects long before the Bean Validation standard was formalized. The `org.springframework.validation.Validator` interface specifies a tool for validating objects based on annotation constraints. Those constraints and their application were originally defined in a separate project know as Spring Modules Validation, which was killed before it left beta status in favor of the emerging JSR 303 standard. Now this Spring `Validator` interface serves as a façade for the Bean Validation API.

It's important to understand this because Spring's validation reports errors using the `org.springframework.validation.Errors` interface, as opposed to returning a `Set<javax.validation.ConstraintViolation<?>>`. This `Errors` interface provides access to one or more `org.springframework.validation.ObjectErrors` and one or more `org.springframework.validation.FieldErrors`. To this day, you may use either the Spring `Validator` or the `javax.validation.Validator` to suit your preferences in most cases, but in one particular case, you must use the Spring `Validator` and its `Errors`.

> **NOTE** *To avoid confusion, when you see the code word "*`Validator`*" throughout the rest of this book, it refers to the* `javax.validation.Validator` *unless specified otherwise. However, if it is preceded with the word "Spring" as in "Spring* `Validator`*" it refers to the* `org.springframework.validation.Validator`.

When configuring Spring Framework's validation support, you define a special type of bean (a class that extends `org.springframework.validation.beanvalidation.SpringValidatorAdapter`) that implements both `Validator` and Spring `Validator`. Internally, this bean uses a `Validator` to support the operations of both interfaces. You have the choice of using either of the following:

- `javax.validation.beanvalidation.CustomValidatorBean`
- `javax.validation.beanvalidation.LocalValidatorFactoryBean.`

In most cases, you want to use the `LocalValidatorFactoryBean` because it supports retrieval of the underlying `Validator` and enables you to use the same `MessageSource` and bundle files that you use for internationalizing the rest of your application. At its simplest, configuring Spring Framework's `LocalValidatorFactoryBean` is as simple as instantiating it and returning it in a `@Bean` method in the `RootContextConfiguration` class:

```
@Bean
public LocalValidatorFactoryBean localValidatorFactoryBean()
{
    return new LocalValidatorFactoryBean();
}
```

The `LocalValidatorFactoryBean` automatically detects the Bean Validation implementation on the classpath, whether that's Hibernate Validator or some other implementation, and uses its default `javax.validation.ValidatorFactory` as the backing factory. There's no need to set up the `META-INF/validation.xml` file usually required to take advantage of Bean Validation in your application. However, sometimes there is more than one Bean Validation Provider on the classpath (for example, when running within a full Java EE application server such as GlassFish or WebSphere). In these cases, which provider Spring selects is unpredictable (it might even change each time!), so you should set the provider class manually if you prefer the provider to be predictable.

```
@Bean
public LocalValidatorFactoryBean localValidatorFactoryBean()
{
    LocalValidatorFactoryBean validator = new LocalValidatorFactoryBean();
    validator.setProviderClass(HibernateValidator.class);
    return validator;
}
```

The only downside to doing this is that it requires Hibernate Validator to be a compile-time dependency instead of a runtime dependency. This pollutes your compile time classpath, meaning your IDE will sometimes make code suggestions that you don't want. You can avoid this by loading the class dynamically, which of course has its own downside in that any mistakes in the name will not be caught at compile time.

```
@Bean
public LocalValidatorFactoryBean localValidatorFactoryBean()
        throws ClassNotFoundException
{
    LocalValidatorFactoryBean validator = new LocalValidatorFactoryBean();
    validator.setProviderClass(Class.forName(
            "org.hibernate.validator.HibernateValidator"
    ));
    return validator;
}
```

Because setting the provider class manually is not necessary when using Tomcat, the examples in this book do not do this.

## Setting Up Error Code Localization

In the next section, you explore adding constraint annotations to your classes and entities. When you do this, you can specify an error message to accompany each constraint. Alternatively, you can specify an error code.

Error codes enable you to internationalize the constraints you use so that they are localized before you display them to the user. The default internationalization in Bean Validation uses resource bundle files `ValidationMessages.properties`, `ValidationMessages_[language].properties`, `ValidationMessages_[language]_[region].properties`, and so on. These files must be on the classpath (in `/WEB-INF/classes`). However, using any Bean Validation 1.1 implementation, you can provide your own internationalization using a `javax.validation.MessageInterpolator`. (Hibernate Validator 4.2 and 4.3 also supplied nonstandard support for interpolators before Bean Validation 1.1 was released.) Either way, you also need to specify the `Locale` for the validator to use each time it's activated.

Again, Spring comes to the rescue, making it easy to provide a custom `MessageInterpolator` and eliminate the worry over the `Locale`. You need only to set the validation `MessageSource` on the `LocalValidatorFactoryBean` defined in `RootContextConfiguration` and it automatically provides an interpolator backed by that `MessageSource`:

```
...

@Bean
public MessageSource messageSource()
{
    ReloadableResourceBundleMessageSource messageSource =
            new ReloadableResourceBundleMessageSource();
    messageSource.setCacheSeconds(-1);
    messageSource.setDefaultEncoding(StandardCharsets.UTF_8.name());
    messageSource.setBasenames(
            "/WEB-INF/i18n/titles", "/WEB-INF/i18n/messages",
            "/WEB-INF/i18n/errors", "/WEB-INF/i18n/validation"
    );
    return messageSource;
}

@Bean
public LocalValidatorFactoryBean localValidatorFactoryBean()
{
    LocalValidatorFactoryBean validator = new LocalValidatorFactoryBean();
    validator.setValidationMessageSource(this.messageSource());
    return validator;
}

...
```

Now that you have configured the `LocalValidatorFactoryBean` to use your `MessageSource`, you can create your localized validation messages alongside all the other localized messages in your application and also take advantage of Spring's support for tracking the `Locale` of the current user so that messages are properly localized at run time.

## Using a Method Validation Bean Post-Processor

Spring Framework uses the concept of *bean post-processors* to configure, customize, and, if necessary, replace beans defined in your configuration before the container completes the startup process. Configured `org.springframework.beans.factory.config.BeanPostProcessor` implementations are executed before a bean is injected in other beans that depend on it. For example:

- The `AutowiredAnnotationBeanPostProcessor` is a framework bean created automatically when you configure Spring. It's responsible for looking for `@Autowired` and `@Injected` properties and injecting their values.
- The `InitDestroyAnnotationBeanPostProcessor` looks for `InitializingBean` implementations (or `@PostConstruct` methods) and `DisposableBean` implementations (or `@PreDestroy` methods) and executes those methods at the appropriate stages in the life cycle.
- Some post-processors are actually capable of *replacing* the bean. The `AsyncAnnotationBeanPostProcessor` looks for beans with `@Async` methods and replaces those beans with proxies so that the `@Async` methods can be called asynchronously.

Most bean post-processors that you require, like the ones mentioned previously, are created for you automatically. However, to support validation of method arguments and return values, you need to create an `org.springframework.validation.beanvalidation.MethodValidationPostProcessor` to proxy the execution of validated methods. This isn't as simple as just instantiating a `MethodValidationPostProcessor` bean because by default it uses the validation provider on the classpath (without your `MessageSource`). Instead, you want to configure it to use the `LocalValidatorFactoryBean` you created earlier.

```
...

@Bean
public LocalValidatorFactoryBean localValidatorFactoryBean() { ... }


@Bean
public MethodValidationPostProcessor methodValidationPostProcessor()
{
    MethodValidationPostProcessor processor =
            new MethodValidationPostProcessor();
    processor.setValidator(this.localValidatorFactoryBean());
    return processor;
}

@Bean
public ObjectMapper objectMapper() { ... }

...
```

This MethodValidationPostProcessor looks for classes annotated with @org.springframework.validation.annotation.Validated or @javax.validation.executable.ValidateOnExecution and proxies them so that argument validation occurs on annotated parameters before method execution and return value validation occurs on annotated methods after method execution. Two sections from now you learn how to annotate class methods to activate this process.

### Making Spring MVC Use the Same Validation Beans

Unlike the MethodValidationPostProcessor you just created, which uses a Validator instance, Spring MVC controller form object and argument validation uses a Spring Validator instance. This supports providing Errors arguments to methods that expect @Valid parameters because the Errors interface is simpler to use than a set of ConstraintViolations. Fortunately, the LocalValidatorFactoryBean implements both validator interfaces, but by default Spring MVC creates a separate Spring Validator instance that masks the one created in the root application context.

To alter this default configuration, you just need to change the ServletContextConfiguration class you created in previous chapters to override WebMvcConfigurerAdapter's getValidator method and return the validator created in the root application context.

```
@Inject SpringValidatorAdapter validator;

...

@Override
public Validator getValidator()
{
    return this.validator;
}

...
```

With this change, Spring MVC uses your configured validator to validate appropriate controller handler method arguments, and your Spring Bean Validation is now complete.

## ADDING CONSTRAINT VALIDATION ANNOTATIONS TO YOUR BEANS

For Bean Validation, your Spring applications mainly deal with two types of beans:

- POJOs or JavaBeans-like entities and form objects that are typically method parameters or return types
- Spring Beans like @Controllers and @Services that use those POJOs as method parameters and return types

Both these types of beans use Bean Validation constraint annotations, but in different ways. In this section you experiment with applying constraint annotations to POJOs, and in the next section you learn how to complete this process by applying annotations to your Spring Beans.

## Understanding the Built-in Constraint Annotations

Although you can create your own constraint annotations any time you like, the Bean Validation API comes with several built-in annotations that satisfy the most common validation requirements. These are all very simple constraints, but in many cases they are all you need to use. All these constraints are in the package `javax.validation.constraints`.

- `@Null` — You can apply this to any type, and it ensures that the annotated target is `null`.
- `@NotNull` — You can also apply this to any type. It ensures that the target is *not* `null`.
- `@AssertTrue` and `@AssertFalse` — These ensure that their annotated targets are `true` and `false`, respectively. As such, the field, parameter, or method (return value) that they annotate must be of the type `boolean` or `Boolean`. A `null Boolean` is considered valid for either constraint, so combine these with `@NotNull` if you do not accept `null` values.
- `@DecimalMax` — This defines an upper limit for a numeric type, specified with the `value` attribute. It may annotate fields, parameters, and methods (return values) of type `BigDecimal`, `BigInteger`, `CharSequence` (`String`), `byte`, `Byte`, `short`, `Short`, `int`, `Int`, `long`, and `Long`. The primitives `double`, `Double`, `float`, and `Float` are not supported due to precision concerns. `CharSequence`s are converted to a decimal before validation, and `null` values are considered valid. The optional `inclusive` attribute specifies whether the test should be inclusive (less than or equal to) or exclusive (less than), and defaults to inclusive (`true`).
- `@DecimalMin` — This is the counterpart to `@DecimalMax`. It applies to all the same types with the same rules. It also contains an `inclusive` attribute.
- `@Digits` — You can use this to ensure that the annotated target is a parseable number (if it's a `CharSequence`) and then tests the limits of that number's parts (whether it's a `CharSequence`, `BigDecimal`, `BigInteger`, `byte`, `Byte`, `short`, `Short`, `int`, `Int`, `long`, or `Long`). The mandatory `integer` attribute specifies the maximum number of integral digits (before the decimal point) allowed, whereas the required `fraction` attribute specifies the maximum number of fractional digits (after the decimal point) allowed. As always, `null` values are considered valid.
- `@Future` — Ensures that the `Date` or `Calendar` field, parameter, or method (return value) is at some point in the future, however near or distant. As of Bean Validation 1.1, there is no support for Java 8 Date and Time API types. `null` values are considered valid.
- `@Past` — Ensures that `Date` and `Calendar` targets are at some point in the past.
- `@Max` and `@Min` — These are similar to `@DecimalMax` and `@DecimalMin`, but they do not support `CharSequence` targets, and they do not host an `inclusive` attribute — they are always inclusive. Targets that are `null` are considered valid.
- `@Pattern` — This defines a regular expression `regexp` that the target `CharSequence` (`String`) must match, and it considers `null` values to be valid. It hosts an optional `flags` attribute that supports an array of any of `Pattern.Flag` enum values. Supported flags are:

    - `CANON_EQ` — Enables canonical equivalence
    - `CASE_INSENSITIVE` — Enables case-insensitive matching
    - `COMMENTS` — Enables white space and comments in the pattern
    - `DOTALL` — Turns dotall mode on
    - `MULTILINE` — Turns multiline mode on
    - `UNICODE_CASE` — Enables Unicode case folding
    - `UNIX_LINES` — Turns Unix lines mode on
- `@Size` — This defines inclusive `max` and `min` limits for the length of a `CharSequence` (`String`), the number of values in a `Collection`, the number of entries in a `Map`, or the number of elements in an array of any type.

## Understanding Common Constraint Attributes

As you can see, you have a wide array of constraints to choose from. In addition to the constraint-specific annotation attributes already mentioned, *all* constraint annotations also have the following optional attributes. These attributes must also be present in any custom constraints you create.

- `message` — This `String` attribute defines what message should be displayed to the user. If the message is enclosed in curly braces (for example, `message="{employee.firstName.notBlank}"`) it represents a message code that must be localized prior to display. Otherwise, it is simply a hard-coded message. This defaults to a message code that is different for each constraint type.
- `groups` — This is an array of `Class`es that defines what validation group or groups this constraint belongs to. By default the array is empty, meaning the constraint belongs only to the default group. Validation groups will be covered in more detail later in this section.
- `payload` — This is another array of `Class`es, and the classes must extend `javax.validation.Payload`. Payloads provide some type of meta-information to the validation provider or `ConstraintValidator` evaluating the constraint. This makes payloads nonportable between validation providers for built-in constraint types (the API defines no payload types), but it can be useful for custom constraints. You can use payloads for just about anything you put your mind to on custom constraints, so their theoretical use is outside the scope of this book.

Finally, all these constraint annotations define inner annotations called `@List` that permit the application of multiple constraints of that type to a target. For example, you can annotate a target with multiple `@Max` constraints using the `@Max.List` annotation. The segment on validation groups later in this section demonstrates one possible use for these lists.

## Putting Constraints to Use

To gain an understanding of the basic use of these built-in constraints, take a look at the Employee POJO from the HR-Portal project. It is based on the hypothetical employee validation business logic you saw at the beginning of the chapter.

```
public class Employee
{
    private long id;

    @NotNull(message = "{validate.employee.firstName}")
    private String firstName;

    @NotNull(message = "{validate.employee.lastName}")
    private String lastName;

    private String middleName;

    @NotNull(message = "{validate.employee.governmentId}")
    private String governmentId;

    @NotNull(message = "{validate.employee.birthDate}")
    @Past(message = "{validate.employee.birthDate}")
    private Date birthDate;

    @NotNull(message = "{validate.employee.gender}")
    private Gender gender;

    @NotNull(message = "{validate.employee.badgeNumber}")
    private String badgeNumber;

    @NotNull(message = "{validate.employee.address}")
    private String address;

    @NotNull(message = "{validate.employee.city}")
    private String city;

    @NotNull(message = "{validate.employee.state}")
    private String state;

    @NotNull(message = "{validate.employee.phoneNumber}")
    private String phoneNumber;

    @NotNull(message = "{validate.employee.email}")
    @Pattern(
            regexp = "^[a-z0-9`!#$%^&*'{}?/+=|_~-]+(\\.[a-z0-9`!#$%^&*'{}?/+=" +
                    "|_~-]+)*@([a-z0-9]([a-z0-9-]*[a-z0-9])?)+(\\.[a-z0-9]" +
                    "([a-z0-9-]*[a-z0-9])?)*$",
            flags = {Pattern.Flag.CASE_INSENSITIVE},
            message = "{validate.employee.email}"
    )
    private String email;

    @NotNull(message = "{validate.employee.department}")
    private String department;

    @NotNull(message = "{validate.employee.location}")
    private String location;

    @NotNull(message = "{validate.employee.position}")
```

```
        private String position;

        // mutators and accessors
    }
```

You should notice some things right away:

- Most of the fields are annotated `@NotNull` except for `manager` and `middleName`.
- There is no replacement for the `trim().length() > 0` check performed on so many of the fields earlier, which could become a problem quickly.
- The e-mail regular expression could become cumbersome if used in many places.
- `birthDate` is checked only to ensure it's in the past, not to ensure the employee is at least 18 years old. For that matter, `birthDate` must be a legacy date type to use the built-in constraints, but you'd probably prefer to use the Java 8 date types.
- The employee department, location, and position are not checked to make sure that they exist.

You can address many of the issues with custom constraints. However, not every check is appropriate for Bean Validation tools. Checking that the department, location, and position exist requires other business logic and, likely, database queries, so tasks like these are best left up to manual validation.

> **NOTE** *Near the end of this chapter, you learn how to write your own custom validation constraints and meet needs like string length, date boundary, and e-mail validation. However, there are also options other than creating custom constraints. Hibernate Validator has proprietary constraints you can use, but doing so ties you to always using Hibernate Validator as your provider.*
>
> *Another option is the Bean Validation Constraint Extensions project (Maven artifact* `net.nicholaswilliams.java.validation:validation-api-constraint-extensions`*), which provides* `null`*-intolerant versions of all the built-in constraints, as well as constraints for e-mail, credit card number, IP address, Java 8 Date and Time, Joda Time, and other targets. Because this library contains only constraints and is not a Bean Validation provider, it is safe to use with any provider.*

## Using @Valid for Recursive Validation

So far you have been annotating simple field types like `String`s and primitives with validation constraints. But what if your bean contains a complex field that itself is annotated with validation constraints? For example, consider the following beans:

```
public class Train
{
    @NotNull
    private String name;

    @NotNull
```

```
        private Station origin;

        @NotNull
        private Station destination;

        @NotNull
        private Person engineer;

        @NotNull
        private Person conductor;

        // mutators and accessors
    }
```

The `Station` and `Person` fields in this case are POJOs with their own fields, and those fields are also annotated with validation constraints. These nested objects are not automatically validated. To ensure that they are validated, you annotate the fields of these types with `@Valid`, which indicates that a field, parameter, or method (return value) should result in cascading validation.

```
public class Train
{
    @NotNull
    private String name;

    @NotNull
    @Valid
    private Station origin;

    @NotNull
    @Valid
    private Station destination;

    @NotNull
    @Valid
    private Person engineer;

    @NotNull
    @Valid
    private Person conductor;

    // mutators and accessors
}
```

If `Station` or `Person` contains fields that are also marked with `@Valid`, validation continues recursively as deep as it needs to. However, validators detect infinite loops caused by cyclical references and terminate validation of a field without error after it circles back on itself.

## Using Validation Groups

Validation groups provide a way to enable and disable certain constraints based on the groups to which they belong as well as which groups are currently active. This is extremely similar to Spring Framework's Bean Definition Profiles. A group is represented by any arbitrary marker interface. The interface need not have any constants or methods because they are not used. Instead, the interface's

`Class` object identifies the group when declaring the constraint. Then, at validation time, the `Validator` applies only constraints whose group `Classes` are specified in the call to the `validate`, `validateProperty`, or `validateValue` methods.

For example, consider a multistep data entry UI, where fields are successively filled out on each page. You would want to validate that the appropriate field values are provided for each step, but you might want to store all this in the same form object. Using groups, this is easy:

```
public interface UiScreen1 { }

public interface UiScreen2 { }

public interface UiScreen3 { }

public class Form
{
    @NotNull(groups = UiScreen1.class)
    private String field1;

    @NotNull(groups = UiScreen2.class)
    private String field2;

    @NotNull(groups = UiScreen2.class)
    private String field3;

    @NotNull(groups = UiScreen3.class)
    private String field4;

    // mutators and accessors
}
```

Then, when you're ready to validate, you just pass in the appropriate group class or classes on each call to the `Validator`, and it applies constraints matching those groups. Use the `javax.validation.groups.Default` group if you also want to evaluate constraints without defined groups.

```
// in method for step 1
Set<ConstraintViolation<Form>> violations =
    validator.validate(form, Default.class, UiScreen1.class)

// in method for step 2
Set<ConstraintViolation<Form>> violations =
    validator.validate(form, Default.class, UiScreen1.class, UiScreen2.class)

// in method for step 3
Set<ConstraintViolation<Form>> violations =
    validator.validate(form, Default.class, UiScreen1.class, UiScreen2.class,
            UiScreen3.class)
```

If a constraint declares no groups, it is assumed to be in the `Default` group. Likewise, if a call to `validate`, `validateProperty`, or `validateValue` specifies no groups, it is assumed to apply to the `Default` group.

Validation groups are also useful for applying the same constraint different ways depending on the group. Using `@Size.List` and `@Size`, for example, you can specify that a `String` field must be one length if validated in one group and another length if validated in another group (or groups).

```
public class BusinessObject
{
    @Size.List({
            @Size(min = 5, max = 100, groups = {Default.class, Group1.class}),
            @Size(min = 20, max = 75, groups = Group2.class)
    })
    private String value;

    // mutators and accessors
}
```

As usual, Spring also makes it easier to utilize validation groups. Instead of having to access the validator directly, you can specify in an annotation which groups should be active when validating an object. You learn more about that in the next section.

## Checking Constraint Legality at Compile-Time

The Java language has rules about which annotations you can use where, specified with the `java.lang.annotation.ElementType` values provided in the `@java.lang.annotation.Target` annotation on a particular annotation definition. However, the rules about where you can apply validation constraints are much more complex than supported natively.

For example, constraint annotations are allowed for `ElementyType.METHOD` (and others) at compile time, but this ignores the fact that constraints are allowed only on instance methods and not static methods (a distinction that `ElementType` does not make). Likewise, constraints are allowed only on instance fields and not static fields, but the compiler cannot enforce that, either. Even more important, different constraints are limited to different types (you cannot use `@Future` on `String`s, for example), and you need a way to ensure that you use these constraints correctly.

Hibernate Validator comes with a compile-time annotation processor that hooks into the compiler and causes the code to not compile if the stricter constraint application rules are not followed. This makes applying validation constraints much easier because you know when you compile whether you've used them correctly. Otherwise, you won't find out until validation of an object fails with a `javax.annotation.ConstraintDeclarationException`. Using the annotation processor is easy: simply add the following Maven dependency to your project.

```
<dependency>
    <groupId>org.hibernate</groupId>
    <artifactId>hibernate-validator-annotation-processor</artifactId>
    <version>5.1.0.Final</version>
    <scope>compile</scope>
    <optional>true</optional>
</dependency>
```

The reason this dependency is marked as optional is that the library isn't actually needed at run time. It's needed only at compile time so that the compiler can detect and use the annotation processor it contains. The upside of doing it this way is that the processor gets applied automatically in both your Maven build and your IDE compilation. The downside is that the classes in the artifact are technically available to your classes at compile time, meaning your IDE will suggest them. (Though you don't have to use them.)

You have other ways to apply annotation processors in Maven and your IDE. For example, you can add the dependency to the compiler plug-in's dependencies instead of the project dependencies, and this then removes the classes from your classpath but forces you to separately set up the processor in your IDE. Examination of this technique and others is outside the scope of this book. You should consult the documentation for the Java compiler, Maven, and your IDE for more information.

## CONFIGURING SPRING BEANS FOR METHOD VALIDATION

So far, you've created a bean capable of validation (`Employee`), but you haven't written any code to validate it yet. By now, you have likely discovered that you can use the `Validator`'s `validate`, `validateProperty`, or `validateValue` methods to validate this bean, but what you really want is for the validation to happen automatically without using the `Validator` directly. As usual, Spring makes this easy. You've already done half the work by setting up the `MethodValidationPostProcessor`, which proxies Spring beans that should have their method parameters and return values validated. Now you just need to mark your Spring bean methods to indicate which return values or parameter should be validated.

### Annotating Interfaces, Not Implementations

Using the programming by contract paradigm, developers rely on the contract of a bit of code to fulfill certain requirements or perform certain actions without concerning themselves with how those requirements are met. In Java, interfaces are considered the primary approach to programming by contract. You already explored this significantly in Chapter 14. You create an interface with methods defined indicating what implementations are supposed to do. Often you use Javadoc documentation to elaborate on the contract that the interface guarantees. Then consumers of the interface use it blindly without needing to know or even caring how the implementation works.

Constraint annotations are an extension of a programming contract. In addition to telling the `Validator` how to validate an object, they also tell the consumer of an API what to expect of a class's behavior. For example, a method annotated `@NotNull` is guaranteed to never return `null`, so you don't have to check for `null` before using its return value. Naturally, you might wonder what good these constraints would do on an implementation class, and the answer is: none. In fact, they could do harm.

Consider this scenario: You are calling a method on an interface and none of its parameters have constraint annotations. However, the underlying implementation indicates that one of the integer parameters is `@Max(12L)`. When you call the interface method, you might supply a value of 15 thinking it's okay, but the implementation throws an exception because you violated a constraint that you didn't know applied. For this reason, you are forbidden from constraint annotating the implementation of a method specified in an interface. If you annotate such a method, the `Validator` throws a `ConstraintDeclarationException` at run time. This is another area in which the Hibernate Validator Annotation Processor comes in handy because it detects errors like this during compilation.

When using constraint annotations for method validation, you must always annotate the interface, not the implementation. This ensures that the annotations expand on the contract that the programmer relies on. If developers use an intelligent IDE with code completion, it informs them of these additional contract requirements as they use each method.

## Using Constraints and Recursive Validation on Method Parameters

Now that you have an `Employee` entity to work with, you need a service for saving and retrieving `Employees`. The following interface defines such a service as simply as possible.

```
public interface EmployeeService
{
    public void saveEmployee(Employee employee);

    public Employee getEmployee(long id);

    public List<Employee> getAllEmployees();
}
```

Think about the business rules that need to be applied to the arguments to `getEmployee` and `saveEmployee`. When retrieving a single `Employee`, you know that the ID is always positive. So to indicate this contract, annotate the *`id`* parameter with `@Min`.

```
    public Employee getEmployee(
            @Min(value = 1L,
                    message = "{validate.employeeService.getEmployee.id}") long id
    );
```

This is simple enough; the `Validator` ensures that the ID is greater than or equal to 1 and returns a validation error with the given message code otherwise. Saving an `Employee` is slightly more complex. You want to ensure that the *`employee`* parameter is not `null`, but you also want the `Employee` to be validated so that its constraints are met. To do this, you simply need the `@NotNull` constraint and the `@Valid` annotation to indicate recursive validation.

```
    public void saveEmployee(
            @NotNull(message = "{validate.employeeService.saveEmployee}")
            @Valid Employee employee
    );
```

Now the `Validator` first checks that the `Employee` isn't `null` and returns a validation error with the given message code if it is. If it's not `null`, the `Validator` applies all the constraints you previously declared on the `Employee`'s properties and returns the appropriate validation error or errors if the `Employee` isn't valid.

## Validating Method Return Values

In addition to ensuring that consumers of your interfaces follow the proper rules when supplying values to methods, you also want to guarantee that implementations follow the rules regarding return values. The `getAllEmployee` method from the `EmployeeService` interface should never return `null`. If there are no `Employees` to retrieve, it should return an empty list instead. Enforcing this contract is as simple as annotating the method `@NotNull`.

```
@NotNull
public List<Employee> getAllEmployees();
```

Notice that no message code is provided for this constraint. Unlike a method parameter constraint, whose status is typically driven by user input, a return value constraint indicates an implementation problem, which is an unexpected problem that should be addressed in code, not by the user. This is similar to the conceptual difference between checked and unchecked exceptions. Checked exceptions should be expected and handled gracefully, whereas unchecked exceptions usually indicate a programming error. You certainly may provide a message code for return value constraints, but it is unnecessary. This constraint never fails if the application is programmed correctly, so creating localized messages is a waste of time.

Also notice that the `getEmployee` method is not annotated `@NotNull`. This is intentional; if the employee doesn't exist, the consumer wants to get a `null` value back. To make it clearer that a `null` return value is permitted, you could create a `@Nullable` annotation and decorate such methods with that. An annotation such as this would not be enforced in the `Validator` (it indicates only that the return value *may* be `null`, not that it *must* be `null`), but it would improve the contract of your interface.

> **NOTE** *You can, of course, enforce these restrictions at compile time using a static code analyzer. Various tools are available (such as FindBugs and IntelliJ Contract Annotations) that provide annotations such as* `@NonNull` *and* `@Nullable`*, as well as annotation processors that check for these annotations and make sure the byte code isn't capable of violating the restriction (or checks* `@Nullable` *values before using them). Such tools can ensure during compilation that you don't violate the contract, and they can cut down on the number of possible bugs and runtime* `NullPointerException`*s and* `UnsupportedOperationException`*s. There were discussions of creating a standard set of static code analysis-eligible annotations (*`@NonNull`*,* `@Nullable`*, and* `@Readonly`*) in Java 8, but that did not happen.*

## Indicating That a Class Is Eligible for Method Validation

So now that you have defined your interface's method validation contract, you need to tell Spring's `MethodValidationPostProcessor` to actually apply validation to executions of the method. You have a couple of options here. You can either use the standard `@ValidateOnExecution` annotation or Spring's `@Validated` annotation. Each has its advantages and disadvantages. `@ValidateOnExecution` is more granular because you can annotate individual methods as well as an interface (to apply to all its methods), whereas you can use `@Validated` only on a class or interface. On the other hand, you can use `@Validated` on method parameters, but you cannot use `@ValidateOnExecution` on method parameters.

If you want to specify the validation groups that should be applied during method execution, you can use `@javax.validation.GroupSequence` with `@ValidateOnExecution` on the class. `@Validated`, on the other hand, enables you to specify validation groups directly within it without an extra annotation and also enables you to specify different groups for different MVC controller method parameters in the same controller class. (You cannot do this with `@ValidateOnExecution` and `@GroupSequence`, because `@GroupSequence` can only be used on a class.) Unfortunately, neither the standard annotations nor `@Validated` enables specification of different groups for method parameters in the same non-controller class. In nearly all cases, `@Validated` is simpler to use.

```
@Validated
public interface EmployeeService
{
    ...
}
```

If you wanted the validation to use only those constraints in a certain group or groups, you could specify those groups in the `@Validated` annotation.

```
@Validated({Default.class, Group1.class})
public interface EmployeeService
{
    ...
}
```

Your application needs an implementation of the `EmployeeService`. The default implementation that follows is full of no-operation methods because you don't need to actually save any data to demonstrate that validation works properly. Notice that the implementation lacks any validation-related annotations. This is the way it should be because the interface contains that contract. The `getAllEmployees` method returns `null`, which is in violation of the contract. You demonstrate that as well later in the section.

```
@Service
public class DefaultEmployeeService implements EmployeeService
{
    @Override
    public void saveEmployee(Employee employee)
    {
        // no-op
    }

    @Override
    public Employee getEmployee(long id)
    {
        return null;
    }

    @Override
    public List<Employee> getAllEmployees()
    {
        return null;
    }
}
```

## Using Parameter Validation in Spring MVC Controllers

In addition to validating the method execution of your services, repositories, and other beans, Spring can also validate specified parameters in MVC controller handler methods. To demonstrate this you need an `EmployeeController` and `EmployeeForm`. The `EmployeeForm` lacks many of the fields in `Employee`, but that's okay. You're not trying to actually create `Employees`; you're trying to demonstrate Bean Validation. The `EmployeeForm` uses both `@NotNull` and `@Size` because some browsers send blank strings and other browsers send `null` values for form fields.

```
public class EmployeeForm
{
    @NotNull(message = "{validate.employee.firstName}")
    @Size(min = 1, message = "{validate.employee.firstName}")
    private String firstName;

    @NotNull(message = "{validate.employee.lastName}")
    @Size(min = 1, message = "{validate.employee.lastName}")
    private String lastName;

    private String middleName;

    // mutators and accessors
}
```

The controller contains a `listEmployee` handler method that responds to the index request and lists employees. As you might expect, this request fails with a `ConstraintViolationException` because the default `getAllEmployees` method returns `null` in violation of the contract. It also contains a simple handler method for getting the employee creation form. All this is standard fare that you have seen and done before.

```
@Controller
public class EmployeeController
{
    @Inject EmployeeService employeeService;

    @RequestMapping(value = "/", method = RequestMethod.GET)
    public String listEmployees(Map<String, Object> model)
    {
        model.put("employees", this.employeeService.getAllEmployees());
        return "employee/list";
    }

    @RequestMapping(value = "/create", method = RequestMethod.GET)
    public String createEmployee(Map<String, Object> model)
    {
        model.put("employeeForm", new EmployeeForm());
        return "employee/create";
    }

    ...
}
```

The last method that the controller contains is responsible for handling submission of the employee creation form. It does some new things that probably aren't familiar to you. First, the form parameter is annotated `@Valid`, which tells Spring to validate the `EmployeeForm` before executing the method. Normally, constraint violations would result in an exception, but the presence of the `Errors` parameter means Spring passes the validation errors in to the method instead of throwing an exception, allowing you to handle them gracefully. (This only works for controller methods.) The method first checks for the presence of form errors and returns the user to the form view if errors exist. It then copies the form contents into an `Employee` object and attempts to save the employee, which fails because the employee is not complete. If constraint violations are detected, it sets those to the model and returns the user to the form view.

```
@RequestMapping(value = "/create", method = RequestMethod.POST)
public ModelAndView createEmployee(Map<String, Object> model,
                                   @Valid EmployeeForm form, Errors errors)
{
    if(errors.hasErrors())
    {
        model.put("employeeForm", form);
        return new ModelAndView("employee/create");
    }

    Employee employee = new Employee();
    employee.setFirstName(form.getFirstName());
    employee.setLastName(form.getLastName());
    employee.setMiddleName(form.getMiddleName());

    try
    {
        this.employeeService.saveEmployee(employee);
    }
    catch(ConstraintViolationException e)
    {
        model.put("validationErrors", e.getConstraintViolations());
        return new ModelAndView("employee/create");
    }

    return new ModelAndView(new RedirectView("/", true, false));
}
```

## Displaying Validation Errors to the User

This process has likely raised some questions about why you validate the submitted data twice. Remember that the `EmployeeService` encapsulates your core business logic. The controller is just a user interface that sits in front of it. You could have other user interfaces — such as web services or desktop applications — that sit in front of it. The same business rules should apply evenly across all user interfaces; thus, the constraints should be applied in the service.

Why validate the form at all, then? Well, as you can see in the following JSP code, Spring can associate form validation errors with form fields on the screen. This enables you to display an error related to the *`firstName`* property, for example, next to the First Name field — a much better user experience. However, this works only if it's the form object that was validated, so you must validate the form object. To catch validation errors that were omitted from the form validation or that can be applied only in the business logic (such as testing that the department exists), you must also validate the object in the business layer and have a way of displaying non-form validation errors to users gracefully. The `/WEB-INF/jsp/view/employee/create.jsp` file, part of which is shown in the following code snippet, displays both types of errors.

```
<h2><spring:message code="title.create.employee" /></h2>
<c:if test="${validationErrors != null}"><div class="errors">
    <ul>
        <c:forEach items="${validationErrors}" var="error">
            <li><c:out value="${error.message}" /></li>
        </c:forEach>
    </ul>
</div></c:if>
<form:form method="post" modelAttribute="employeeForm">
    <form:label path="firstName"><spring:message code="form.first.name" />
    </form:label><br />
    <form:input path="firstName" /><br />
    <form:errors path="firstName" cssClass="errors" /><br />

    <form:label path="middleName">
        <spring:message code="form.middle.name" />
    </form:label><br />
    <form:input path="middleName" /><br />
    <form:errors path="middleName" cssClass="errors" /><br />

    <form:label path="lastName"><spring:message code="form.last.name" />
    </form:label><br />
    <form:input path="lastName" /><br />
    <form:errors path="lastName" cssClass="errors" /><br />

    <input type="submit" value="Submit" />
</form:form>
```

Now that you have a user interface, it's time to take Bean Validation for a test drive:

1. Compile the application and start Tomcat in your IDE.
2. Go to `http://localhost:8080/portal/` and you should immediately see an HTTP 500 error with a `ConstraintViolationException` in your browser window. This is expected and means Bean Validation is working properly because the `DefaultEmployeeService` illegally returned `null` from the `getAllEmployees` method.
3. Now go to `http://localhost:8080/portal/create` and you should see the employee creation form.
4. Without filling in any of the fields, submit the form. You should see a screen like that in Figure 16-1, where the First Name and Last Name fields have errors below them. This means that your form object failed to validate because you didn't supply these values.
5. Fill in these fields and submit the form again. Now you should see a different set of errors, as shown in Figure 16-2. These errors are the result of Bean Validation intercepting the `saveEmployee` method on the `EmployeeService` and ensuring that your `Employee` met all the business rules.

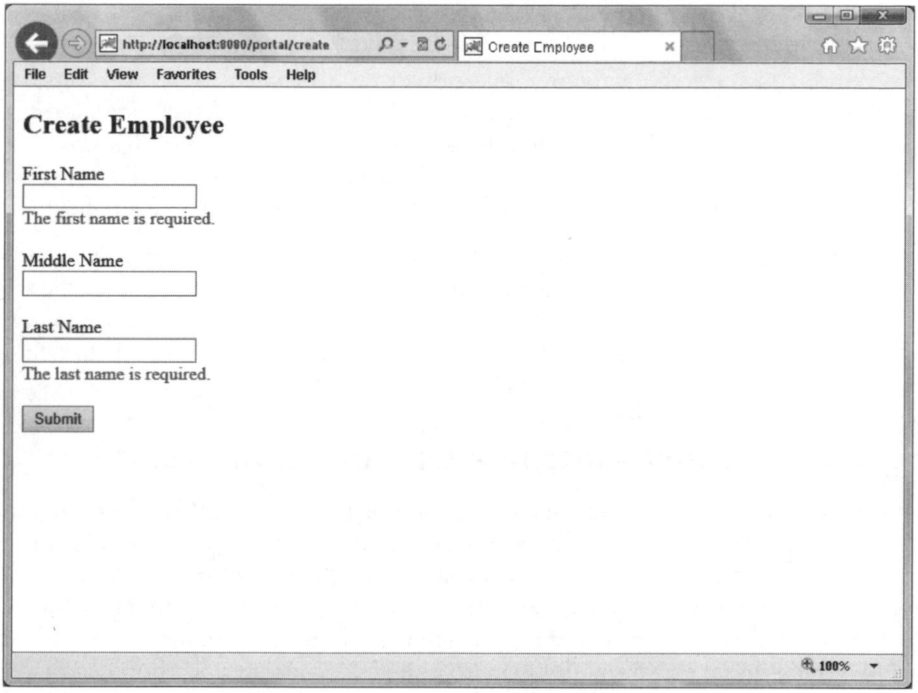

http://localhost:8080/portal/create
Create Employee
File Edit View Favorites Tools Help
Create Employee
First Name
The first name is required.
Middle Name
Last Name
The last name is required.
Submit
100%

FIGURE 16-1

http://localhost:8080/portal/create
Create Employee
File Edit View Favorites Tools Help
Create Employee
The birth date is required.
The position is required.
The location is required.
The e-mail must be a valid e-mail address.
The state is required.
The government ID is required.
The phone number is required.
The address is required.
The department is required.
The gender is required.
The badge number is required.
The city is required.
First Name
Jane
Middle Name
Last Name
Smith
Submit
100%

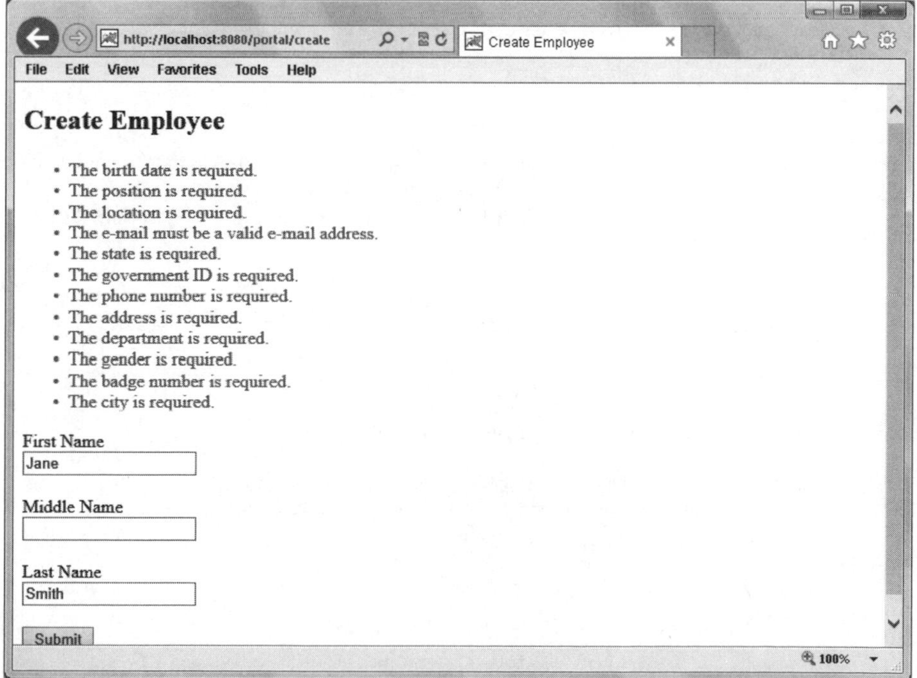

FIGURE 16-2

# WRITING YOUR OWN VALIDATION CONSTRAINTS

By now, you've probably noticed that your application can use a few custom constraints. For example, the use of `@NotNull` throughout `Employee` is not sufficient to detect blank strings. `EmployeeForm` uses `@NotNull` *and* `@Size`, but this still does not detect strings that are only spaces. What you really need is a `@NotBlank` constraint. Furthermore, that e-mail regular expression is aggravating if you need to use it many times, and an `@Email` constraint would sure help with that.

Fortunately, writing custom constraints in Bean Validation is exceptionally easy. The Custom-Constraints project available on the `wrox.com` code download site is an extension of the HR-Portal project that adds the custom constraints `@com.wrox.site.validation.NotBlank` and `@com.wrox.site.validation.Email`. Now start with the `@Email` constraint first because, believe it or not, it's easier.

## Inheriting Other Constraints in a Custom Constraint

In Bean Validation, constraints can inherit from one another. Of course, this is not the same thing as one class inheriting from another because you cannot extend annotations. However, per convention, constraint annotations usually include a target of `ElementType.ANNOTATION_TYPE`. When a constraint annotation is located, the `Validator` determines if the annotation definition is annotated with any other constraints. If so, it combines all the additional constraints with the logic defined by the original constraint (if any) into a single, composite constraint. In this sense, the constraint inherits all the constraints with which it is annotated. If for some reason you need to create a constraint that cannot be inherited, you simply omit `ElementType.ANNOTATION_TYPE` from the definition. With all this in mind, take a look at the `@Email` definition.

```
@Target({ElementType.METHOD, ElementType.FIELD, ElementType.ANNOTATION_TYPE,
        ElementType.CONSTRUCTOR, ElementType.PARAMETER})
@Retention(RetentionPolicy.RUNTIME)
@Documented
@Constraint(validatedBy = {})
@Pattern(regexp = "^[a-z0-9`!#$%^&*'{}?/+=|_~-]+(\\.[a-z0-9`!#$%^&*'{}?/+=|" +
        "_~-]+)*@([a-z0-9]([a-z0-9-]*[a-z0-9])?)+(\\.[a-z0-9]" +
        "([a-z0-9-]*[a-z0-9])?)*$", flags = {Pattern.Flag.CASE_INSENSITIVE})
@ReportAsSingleViolation
public @interface Email
{
    String message() default "{com.wrox.site.validation.Email.message}";

    Class<?>[] groups() default {};

    Class<? extends Payload>[] payload() default {};

    @Target({ElementType.METHOD, ElementType.FIELD, ElementType.ANNOTATION_TYPE,
            ElementType.CONSTRUCTOR, ElementType.PARAMETER})
    @Retention(RetentionPolicy.RUNTIME)
    @Documented
    static @interface List {
        Email[] value();
    }
}
```

There's a lot going on here, so take a look at it line by line, starting with the annotations:

- `@Target` — This annotation indicates which language features this annotation can be placed on. The values listed are pretty standard and should be used for most constraints.
- `@Retention` — Indicates that the annotation must be retained at run time. If not, Bean Validation will not detect it.
- `@Documented` — This means that the Javadoc of targets marked with this annotation should indicate the annotation's presence. This is especially useful when programming in an IDE because it makes the contract more visible.
- `@Constraint` — This is a must: It's what indicates that this annotation represents a Bean Validation constraint, so all constraint definitions have to be annotated with this. Without this, your constraint is ignored. `@Constraint` also indicates which `ConstraintValidator` implementation or implementations are responsible for validating your constraint. However, in this case no `ConstraintValidator` is necessary.
- `@Pattern` — This is another constraint, indicating that this constraint inherits the constraint declared with `@Pattern`. This is the same regular expression seen earlier, but now you won't have to duplicate the regular expression every time you use it. You can just use the `@Email` annotation, instead.
- `@ReportAsSingleViolation` — Indicates that the composite constraint should be considered one constraint and use `@Email`'s message instead of `@Pattern`'s message. It is very rare that you should ever create a constraint that inherits other constraints without using `@ReportAsSingleViolation`.

Within the annotation are three attributes: `message`, `groups`, and `payload`. These are the standard attributes that must be present in all constraints. Without one or more of these, use of `@Email` would result in a `ConstraintDefinitionException`. The `@Email.List` inner annotation, like all the Bean Validation list annotations, defines a way to specify multiple `@Email` constraints on a target.

## Creating a Constraint Validator

The `@NotBlank` constraint looks nearly identical to `@Email`. For the most part, it has the same annotations, attributes, and features. Instead of being annotated with `@Pattern`, it's annotated with `@NotNull`. In this case `@NotBlank` should imply non-`null`, so you inherit the `@NotNull` constraint to accomplish this. (If you anticipate needing to define targets that can be `null` but cannot be blank strings, you would simply remove `@NotNull` from this annotation.)

```
@Target({ElementType.METHOD, ElementType.FIELD, ElementType.ANNOTATION_TYPE,
        ElementType.CONSTRUCTOR, ElementType.PARAMETER})
@Retention(RetentionPolicy.RUNTIME)
@Documented
@Constraint(validatedBy = {NotBlankValidator.class})
@NotNull
@ReportAsSingleViolation
public @interface NotBlank
{
```

```
    String message() default "{com.wrox.site.validation.NotBlank.message}";

    Class<?>[] groups() default {};

    Class<? extends Payload>[] payload() default {};

    @Target({ElementType.METHOD, ElementType.FIELD, ElementType.ANNOTATION_TYPE,
            ElementType.CONSTRUCTOR, ElementType.PARAMETER})
    @Retention(RetentionPolicy.RUNTIME)
    @Documented
    static @interface List {
        NotBlank[] value();
    }
}
```

However, unlike `@Email`, it can't inherit all its functionality. It needs a `ConstraintValidator` to test whether the value is blank. The following `NotBlankValidator` class, declared in the `@Constraint` annotation on the `@NotBlank` annotation, accomplishes this.

```
public class NotBlankValidator
        implements ConstraintValidator<NotBlank, CharSequence>
{
    @Override
    public void initialize(NotBlank annotation)
    {

    }

    @Override
    public boolean isValid(CharSequence value, ConstraintValidatorContext context)
    {
        if(value instanceof String)
            return ((String) value).trim().length() > 0;
        return value.toString().trim().length() > 0;
    }
}
```

With both new constraints in place, take a look at the Employee and `EmployeeForm` POJOs. Both have had most of their `@NotNull` constraints replaced with `@NotBlank`, and `EmployeeForm` no longer uses `@Size`. The *`email`* field in Employee is changed to use `@Email`, and a similar *`email`* field is added to `EmployeeForm` so that you can see e-mail validation in action.

```
    @NotNull(message = "{validate.employee.email}")
    @Email(message = "{validate.employee.email}")
    private String email;
```

Also, an e-mail form field is added to the `employee/create` view JSP. To finish up:

1. Compile and start the application and go to `http://localhost:8080/portal/create`.
2. Submit the form with no values in any fields, and you see that the `@NotBlank` constraint works.
3. Now enter data in all the fields, but in the Email Address field enter an invalid e-mail address, such as one without the `@` character.

4. When you submit the form again, the Email Address field is still marked in error because the value is not a valid e-mail address.
5. Enter a valid e-mail address and submit the form again and form validation passes, showing instead the business layer validation errors.

## Understanding the Constraint Validator Life Cycle

`@NotBlank` and its `NotBlankValidator` are, of course, very simple. You could perform many advanced tasks within this validator depending on the constraint type, value type, and constraint attributes available. To understand the things you can do, you first need to understand the life cycle of a `ConstraintValidator`.

When the `Validator` comes across a constraint annotation on a field, parameter, other constraint, and so on, it first checks whether the constraint is annotated with other constraints. If it is, it handles those constraints first. Next, it checks whether the constraint has any defined `ConstraintValidators`. If it does not, the value is considered valid as long as it also passes all the inherited constraints. If it does, it finds the `ConstraintValidator` that is the closest compatible match with the target type. For example, you may create a constraint that supports `CharSequences`, `ints`, and `Integers`. For such a constraint, you likely need two different `ConstraintValidators`:

```
public class IntValidator
        implements ConstraintValidator<MyConstraint, Integer> { ... }

public class StringValidator
        implements ConstraintValidator<MyConstraint, CharSequence> { ... }

@Constraint(validatedBy = {IntValidator.class, StringValidator.class})
...
```

After it finds a matching `ConstraintValidator`, the `Validator` instantiates and calls the `initialize` method on the `ConstraintValidator`. This method is called once *per use* of the constraint. If you have a class with 10 fields and 5 of them use your constraint, 5 instances of the `ConstraintValidator` are constructed and initialized. Those instances are cached and reused, the same instance each time for a given field. The `initialize` method enables your code to obtain values from the specific annotation instance for a particular use (such as the `min` and `max` attributes of the `@Size` annotation). This way, you can make decisions about how your constraint validates the target value just once, making execution of the `isValid` method more efficient. Only after `initialize` returns does the `Validator` call `isValid`, and it then calls `isValid` each subsequent time the field, parameter, or other target is validated.

With this knowledge, you can do some pretty complex things with custom constraints. For example, you can create a constraint that applies only to types instead of fields or parameters and use it to apply some business rule that considers the values of multiple fields of the annotated type. The possibilities are quite numerous and largely outside the scope of this book. The Hibernate Validator reference documentation and JSR 349 specification both have plenty of information about the ways you can create custom validators. You can also look through the source code of the Bean Validation Constraint Extensions project mentioned in a note earlier in the chapter.

## INTEGRATING VALIDATION IN THE CUSTOMER SUPPORT APPLICATION

The Customer-Support-v13 project, available for download from the wrox.com code download site, demonstrates a more thorough integration of Bean Validation 1.1. It doesn't really use anything new that you haven't seen yet in this chapter, but it is a more stable application with validation business logic applied to forms, POJOs, and beans. The TicketController.TicketForm and AuthenticationController.LoginForm objects now use constraint annotations to ensure that form fields aren't left blank, and the corresponding submit methods in the controller use the Errors object and the ConstraintViolationException to detect and report errors back to the user.

```
@RequestMapping(value = "create", method = RequestMethod.POST)
public ModelAndView create(Principal principal, @Valid TicketForm form,
                           Errors errors, Map<String, Object> model)
        throws IOException
{
    if(errors.hasErrors())
        return new ModelAndView("ticket/add");
    ...
    try
    {
        this.ticketService.save(ticket);
    }
    catch(ConstraintViolationException e)
    {
        model.put("validationErrors", e.getConstraintViolations());
        return new ModelAndView("ticket/add");
    }
    ...
}

@RequestMapping(value = "login", method = RequestMethod.POST)
public ModelAndView login(Map<String, Object> model, HttpSession session,
                          HttpServletRequest request, @Valid LoginForm form,
                          Errors errors)
{
    if(UserPrincipal.getPrincipal(session) != null)
        return this.getTicketRedirect();

    if(errors.hasErrors())
    {
        form.setPassword(null);
        return new ModelAndView("login");
    }

    Principal principal;
    try
    {
        principal = this.authenticationService.authenticate(
                form.getUsername(), form.getPassword()
        );
    }
```

```
        catch(ConstraintViolationException e)
        {
            form.setPassword(null);
            model.put("validationErrors", e.getConstraintViolations());
            return new ModelAndView("login");
        }
        ...
    }
```

One interesting thing to note is that the `Attachment` has constraints to ensure that name and content type are not blank and that the attachment contents contain at least 1 byte. Then the list of attachments in the `Ticket` uses the `@Valid` annotation to ensure recursive validation of all the attachments for the ticket.

```
public class Attachment
{
    @NotBlank(message = "{validate.attachment.name}")
    private String name;

    @NotBlank(message = "{validate.attachment.mimeContentType}")
    private String mimeContentType;

    @Size(min = 1, message = "{validate.attachment.contents}")
    private byte[] contents;

    // mutators and accessors
}

public class Ticket
{
    // other fields

    @Valid
    private Map<String, Attachment> attachments = new LinkedHashMap<>();

    // mutators and accessors
}
```

To ensure that `Tickets` are valid before they are saved, the `TicketService` is `@Validated` and contains constraints on all its methods to enforce the contract of the interface.

```
@Validated
public interface TicketService
{
    @NotNull
    List<Ticket> getAllTickets();
    Ticket getTicket(
            @Min(value = 1L, message = "{validate.ticketService.getTicket.id}")
                long id
    );
    void save(@NotNull(message = "{validate.ticketService.save.ticket}")
            @Valid Ticket ticket);
}
```

Likewise, the `AuthenticationService` is also `@Validated` with constraints to ensure that the username and password aren't blank.

```
@Validated
public interface AuthenticationService
{
    Principal authenticate(
            @NotBlank(message = "{validate.authenticate.username}")
                String username,
            @NotBlank(message = "{validate.authenticate.password}")
                String password
    );
}
```

With these notes made, compile the project, start Tomcat from your IDE, and go to `http://localhost:8080/support/`. You should notice that validation now works on the login screen and the ticket creation screen, and you can still log in and create tickets.

## SUMMARY

In this chapter you learned about Bean Validation 1.1 (JSR 349, which replaced JSR 303), Hibernate Validator 5.1, and using Bean Validation and Hibernate Validator with Spring Framework. You explored the various aspects of configuring Bean Validation in the Spring container, as well as adding constraint annotations to POJOs and form objects that you want validated. You also learned how to qualify your Spring beans for automatic method validation and trigger form validation in your Spring MVC controller handler methods. Finally, you experimented with creating custom constraints and got a glimpse of some of the many things you can do with custom Bean Validation constraints.

In the next chapter, you explore using Spring MVC controllers as RESTful web services and learn about many of the intricacies involved with that, including error handling and HTTP response status codes.

# 17

# Creating RESTful and SOAP Web Services

## IN THIS CHAPTER

- What are web services?
- How do you use Spring MVC to configure RESTful web services?
- How to test your web service endpoints
- How best to utilize Spring Web Services for SOAP

## WROX.COM CODE DOWNLOADS FOR THIS CHAPTER

You can find the `wrox.com` code downloads for this chapter at `http://www.wrox.com/go/projavaforwebapps` on the Download Code tab. The code for this chapter is divided into the following major examples:

- Web-Service Project
- Customer-Support-v14 Project

## NEW MAVEN DEPENDENCIES FOR THIS CHAPTER

In addition to the Maven dependencies introduced in previous chapters, you also need the following Maven dependencies:

```
<dependency>
    <groupId>org.springframework</groupId>
    <artifactId>spring-aop</artifactId>
    <version>4.0.2.RELEASE</version>
    <scope>compile</scope>
</dependency>
```

## UNDERSTANDING WEB SERVICES

Creating *web services* for your applications is a task that you will inevitably face in the future, if you haven't already. This is because web services provide a way for non-human clients to interact with your web application. Usually there is still a human interacting with a web service client, but at this stage that doesn't matter. You aren't creating clients that use web services in this chapter — just web services. (In the section "Creating an OAuth Client Application" of Chapter 28, you use Spring Framework tools to create a web service client.)

Typically to create a web service, you need a way to allow non-human clients to programmatically use and even discover your web application's resources. This is becoming increasingly important as mobile applications become more prevalent and the traditional desktop browser experience approaches retirement. Mobile applications tend to rely on a web application to perform their main tasks, serving only as user interfaces on the mobile device. This enables someone who has many devices (mobile or otherwise) to share an experience across devices.

Today, many application developers are opting to exclusively create web services and write single-page JavaScript applications that interact directly with those web services. This model will eventually become the rule rather than the exception because it means demanding less development time from application developers while giving user interface developers greater power to create elegant applications across platforms.

Traditional web service developers — the pioneers who thought up the concepts and invented the technologies that empower web services — will tell you that you have only one kind of web service: SOAP. Anything else (RESTful, for example) is perhaps good on its own merits, but not technically a web service. Indeed, the World Wide Web Consortium (W3C) states at `http://www.w3.org/TR/2004/NOTE-ws-gloss-20040211/#webservice`:

> *A Web service is a software system designed to support interoperable machine-to-machine interaction over a network. It has an interface described in a machine-processable format (specifically WSDL). Other systems interact with the Web service in a manner prescribed by its description using SOAP-messages, typically conveyed using HTTP with an XML serialization in conjunction with other Web-related standards.*

This book does not debate the merits of calling or not calling certain technologies web services. Instead, it abides by the spirit of the first sentence in the quote from the W3C. For the purposes of this book, a web service is *any* software system that supports machine-to-machine interaction over a computer network using an interoperable, machine-processable protocol and format. This includes SOAP and RESTful web services, and other web service technologies created in their own right. In this chapter, you explore SOAP and RESTful web service creation in Spring Framework. You get only an introduction into the concepts of these two web service technologies because entire books have been written about each.

## In the Beginning There Was SOAP

No, we're not talking about the substances you use to wash your hands and take a shower. In fact, some developers claim to feel dirtier after using SOAP, not cleaner. But I digress. *SOAP*, which originally stood for *Simple Object Access Protocol*, is a protocol for machine-to-machine interaction using structured data in the form of XML messages. In version 1.2 of the protocol (the first adopted by the W3C) the acronym was dropped and the word SOAP stood on its own. Of course, SOAP wasn't really the beginning of web services in the general sense because other technologies such as XML-RPC existed long before SOAP did. However, the adoption of SOAP is generally thought of as the turning point when web services started to become more prevalent among enterprises.

SOAP sports three main characteristics that drive its popularity:

- It's extensible because it's easy to add other features, such as security, on top of the base protocol.
- It's neutral because it doesn't matter what transport mechanism you use — HTTP, JMS, AMQP, SMTP, TCP, and others are all options.
- It's independent because SOAP doesn't rely on or endorse any particular programming model.

SOAP does, however, encourage the development concept of *contract-first* design. The *Web Services Descriptive Language* (*WSDL*) technology defines a way to establish a contract that users should observe and the web service promises to abide by. It defines the location of the web services available at a particular location and the data format for requests to and responses from those web services. Generally written using *XSD* (sometimes referred to as *XML Schema Definition*), the contract is usually created before any code for the web service is written, and the web service is created to follow the contract. This is similar to the concept of *test-driven development* — in which unit and application tests are written before the application, and then the application is written to make the tests pass — and stands in stark contrast to *contract-last design*, where the web service is created first and then the contract is written to match it.

Contract-first design has its merits, and of course it's always best to clearly define your users' needs and write an application that meets them instead of writing an application and then figuring out how it meets your users' needs. But clearly defining users' needs and writing a WSDL are two different things, and often it is much easier to explicitly define the contract in plain human language, write web service code that meets the requirements, and then automatically generate the very complex WSDL document using XML tools. In this book, you take this approach and avoid having to deal with writing a WSDL file manually.

SOAP is not a simple protocol. Each SOAP message (request or response) starts with a root element called the *SOAP Envelope*. All the information about the message is contained within this envelope. The envelope has an optional *SOAP Header* element (not to be confused with HTTP headers) that contains application-specific information such as authentication details. Also within the envelope is the mandatory *SOAP Body* element, which contains the instructions and data of the request or response. Finally, the envelope of a response can also have an optional *SOAP Fault* element describing any errors that occur while processing a request.

The details of each of these elements are many and largely defined by the WSDL. Writing and dealing with WSDL documents can be a complicated and convoluted task at times, and the more automation you can cleanly integrate into the process, the better. To make matters worse, XML is one of the most verbose and bandwidth- and processor-hungry data formats known. Although SOAP can be very useful and very powerful, it is, thankfully, not the only option.

## RESTful Web Services Provide a Simpler Approach

*Representational State Transfer* (*REST*) is a web service concept that, in a lot of ways, is very similar to SOAP. The REST architecture consists of servers and clients. Clients make state transitions through actions (requests to servers to obtain or change the state of resources) and servers process the requests and return appropriate resources. A resource may be any logical concept that is understood by both the client and the server, and it is transmitted in an agreed-upon representation. REST does not depend on or specify the resource type or representation. Resources may be absolutely any type of data imaginable. Their representations may be plain text, HTML, XML, YAML, JSON, binary data, or any other format understood by both the client and the server. REST systems operate using URLs that indicate the resource type, *verbs* that indicate the action to be performed on the resource, and *media types* (MIME types) that indicate the representation of the resource in the request and in the response. It would be quite natural if this reminded you of HTTP and the World Wide Web, and this is not by coincidence. Roy Fielding is one of the authors of HTTP 1.0 and 1.1 and defined representational state transfer as part of his doctoral dissertation in 2000. The World Wide Web is, by its nature, the largest REST system in existence.

A major principle behind RESTful web services is that there aren't a lot of major operations that need to be performed on a resource. These procedures are generally referred to as *CRUD* operations: Create, Read, Update, and Delete. The methods designated in the HTTP specification easily map to these verbs: `POST`, `GET`, `PUT`, and `DELETE`, respectively. SOAP uses the envelope element to describe the action to perform (method to execute), whereas REST relies on the HTTP protocol to provide the envelope. SOAP also uses the envelope to identify the resource being acted upon, whereas REST relies on the HTTP URL.

In a RESTful web service, the `Content-Type` request header informs the server of the representation of the request body, the `Accept` header or file extension requests a particular response representation, and the `Content-Type` response header informs the client of the representation of the response body.

With this information you should start to see some advantages and disadvantages forming for each protocol. RESTful web services are tied to HTTP, whereas SOAP is protocol-independent, a win for SOAP to be sure. Although it would not be impossible to create a RESTful web service without using HTTP, remember that a RESTful web service is a web service built on top of a REST protocol; it is not REST itself. So creating a non-HTTP RESTful web service would involve creating a REST protocol with URLs, verbs, and media types similar to HTTP that could serve as an envelope for the request and response. At that point you might as well use HTTP. RESTful web services are completely independent of data format, however, which is not something SOAP can boast; it requires XML. SOAP also has redundancies when used with HTTP because it is essentially an envelope within an envelope. The envelope element duplicates functionality that could be provided with the URL and HTTP methods. (It must do this to remain protocol-neutral.)

One of the key selling points for RESTful web services is the lack of a WSDL. To be clear, this does not mean that RESTful web services are contract-last. They can be contract-first just as easily as SOAP can be, but the contract is defined using plain-language documentation and freely available, public APIs as opposed to a complex XSD.

Some RESTful web services providers do still go so far as to publish XML Schema (XSD) or JSON Schema documents for their XML- or JSON-based RESTful web services, respectively, and that can also help define the contract. For this reason and many others, REST has become the predominant web service architecture, overtaking and surpassing SOAP in both adoption and first-class support in software frameworks. Spring Framework, for example, supports REST directly within the MVC framework, but for SOAP web services, you must use the separate Spring Web Services project. In this chapter you primarily explore the creation of RESTful web services using Spring, but near the end of the chapter you get a glimpse of using Spring Web Services to create SOAP web services.

## Understanding Discoverability

Another important feature of RESTful web services is their discoverability. Using a combination of URLs and, at times, the `OPTIONS` HTTP method, clients can discover the resources available at a web service without access to a contract, and then at each resource, clients can then discover the actions available for the resource. Although many RESTful web service providers do not support discovery today, it is a central tenet of the REST architecture. The World Wide Web is discoverable automatically. As a user, you can open a web browser and go to any home page. From that home page, you can discover other pages within the website using hyperlinks. Clicking a hyperlink takes you to a new page that could have its own hyperlinks. In this way, without any prior knowledge of the contents of the site, you can find resources on it and interact with those resources in some fashion.

This same constraint is placed on the official REST application architecture. REST clients should be able to use a RESTful web service without any prior knowledge of the resources available on this web service. This concept, known as *Hypermedia as the Engine of Application State* (*HATEOAS*), uses hypertext (XML, YAML, JSON, or whatever format you choose) combined with hyperlinks to inform the client of the structure of the web service. For example, a request and response to a web service's base URL using `GET` might look something like this:

```
> GET /services/Rest/ HTTP/1.1
> Accept: application/json

< 200 OK
< Content-Type: application/hal+json
<
< {
<     "_links": {
<         "self": { "href": "http://example.net/services/Rest" },
<         "account": { "href": "http://example.net/services/Rest/account" },
<         "order": { "href": "http://example.net/services/Rest/order" }
<     }
< }
```

With this data, the client now knows the resources available at the web service. If it wants to explore accounts further, it has a couple of choices. First, it can simply make a `GET` request to the resource. This is called a *collection request*, or a request to a *collection URI*, and returns every resource of that type available.

```
> GET /services/Rest/account HTTP/1.1
> Accept: application/json

< 200 OK
< Content-Type: application/json
<
< {
<    "value": [
<        {
<            "id": 1075,
<            "name": "John Smith",
<            ...
<        }, {
<            "id": 1076,
<            "name": "Adam Green",
<            ...
<        }
<    ]
< }
```

This has a couple of disadvantages. First, this collection could be very large — enormous, even. Imagine asking Amazon.com's web service to return every product, and you can quickly understand the problem. The obvious solution is paging resources, and in most cases requiring pagination to avoid nightmare response scenarios. (In the next section you explore pagination in more detail when implementing a Spring REST controller.) Another problem is that this list contains the resource data but not links to the resources. One option is to return a list of links, but that makes using the collection request useless for displaying lists of resources to an end user. For this reason, many web services use a combination of properties and a link within a collection response.

Another action a client can take to explore the accounts resource further is to make an `OPTIONS` request to the resource.

```
> OPTIONS /services/Rest/account HTTP/1.1
> Accept: application/json

< 200 OK
< Allow: OPTIONS,HEAD,GET,POST,PUT,PATCH,DELETE
<
< {
<    "GET": {
<        "description": "Get a resource or resources",
<        "resourceTemplate": "http://example.net/services/Rest/account/{id}",
<        "parameters": {
<            "$select": {
<                "type": "array/string",
<                "description": "The properties to be returned for each resource.",
<            },
<            "$filter" ...
<        }
<    },
<    "POST" ...
< }
```

The `OPTIONS` response can be especially powerful. Not only can it tell a client what actions are available for a resource type, but also it can be filtered according to the client's privileges. For example, if a client has permission to view but not create, update, or delete, the `Allow` response header value would be `OPTIONS,HEAD,GET`. In addition, different actions might be available for different individual resources based on any number of factors (including privileges), as demonstrated in the following two requests and their responses:

```
> OPTIONS /services/Rest/account/1075 HTTP/1.1
> Accept: application/json

< 200 OK
< Allow: OPTIONS,HEAD,GET,PUT,PATCH,DELETE
< ...

> OPTIONS /services/Rest/account/1076 HTTP/1.1
> Accept: application/json

< 200 OK
< Allow: OPTIONS,HEAD,GET
< ...
```

The primary problem with discoverability in RESTful web services is that there is no single agreed-upon standard for the content of discovery responses. The links response in the first example is the JSON representation of *Hypertext Application Language* (*HAL*), one of several emerging standards but by no means the only one. The collection request for accounts was just a standard JSON collection, nothing more. And the `Allow` header in the `OPTIONS` response is standard and universal, but the response body is completely made up, which is what many vendors do.

The lack of a universal standard has likely led to so few vendors implementing discoverability. You need to evaluate your needs and the technology at the time to determine the best discoverability standard to use. You may even decide not to support discoverability and to tell clients to read the manual, and that's okay. The good news is that implementing RESTful web services in Spring Framework doesn't depend on the resources or representations you decide on, so adopting one standard over another won't change the Spring techniques you learn about in this chapter.

## Using URLs, HTTP Methods, and HTTP Status Codes

As you read earlier, RESTful web services use request URLs to identify the requested resource and HTTP methods to ascertain the action wanted. They also use HTTP status codes to reveal the result of a request. Different status codes apply to different types of requests. However, there are a few status codes that are universal and apply to all types of requests:

- `400 Bad Request` indicates that the request made by the client was unsupported or unrecognized. This is usually because the proper request syntax was not followed. For example, if a required field of a resource were left blank on a `POST` or `PUT`, that would result in a `400 Bad Request` response. The response body should include information about why the request was bad in the representation format agreed upon or in the default representation in absence of agreement.

- `401 Unauthorized` signals that authentication and authorization are required before accessing the resource or performing the requested state transition. The content of the response varies based on the authentication protocol in use (such as OAuth).
- `403 Forbidden` indicates that the client, though authenticated, does not have permission to access the resource or perform the requested state transition. Depending on the authentication protocol in use, it's possible that re-authenticating with more requested privileges could resolve this condition.
- `404 Not Found`, quite simply, tells the client that the requested resource does not exist. It should never be used to indicate that a resource exists but the state transition is simply not supported or allowed. That is what `405 Method Not Allowed` and `403 Forbidden` are for.
- `405 Method Not Allowed` means that the state transition (HTTP method) requested is not supported. This should never be used to indicate that the client does not have permission to perform the state transition; `403 Forbidden` is reserved for that.
- `406 Not Acceptable` indicates that the representation format requested in the `Accept` header is not supported by the server. For example, the client may have requested `application/xml`, but the server can generate only `application/json`. In these cases, the server may simply return the default supported representation instead of `406 Not Acceptable`, and that is what most vendors do.
- `415 Unsupported Media Type` is very similar to `406 Not Acceptable`. It indicates that the `Content-Type` header in the request (the representation of the request entity) is a type that is not supported by the server. The server may also include an `Accept` response header indicating which media types the server supports. It's possible that both the `Accept` request header value and the `Content-Type` request header value can be unsupported media types. In such a case, the `415 Unsupported Media Type` response takes precedence because `406 Not Acceptable` is an optional response.
- `500 Internal Server Error` signals that an error occurred while processing the request. The response content should include as much information about the error as is safe and possible in the representation format agreed upon or in the default representation in absence of agreement.

The rest of this section covers the syntax and semantics of each HTTP method supported by RESTful web services, including other HTTP status codes meaningful to these methods.

## OPTIONS

As demonstrated previously, `OPTIONS` is one of the few standardized discovery mechanisms available. When a request is made to a resource URL with the `OPTIONS` method, the server must return a `200 OK` response containing an `Allow` header whose contents is a comma-separated list of the HTTP methods supported for the resource. If the client is authenticated, the `Allow` header may instead contain the HTTP methods that the client is authorized to invoke for the resource. Optionally, the server may also return a response body describing how to use each HTTP method for that resource. The response body should be in the representation form agreed upon or in the default representation in the absence of any agreement. If the `PATCH` method is one of the supported methods, the response should also contain the `Allow-Patch` header, which specifies a comma-separated list of the representations (media types) permitted for `PATCH` requests, which may differ for other types of requests.

There are some exceptions to these requirements:

- If the resource does not exist, the server should return `404 Not Found` instead of `200 OK` with the `Allow` header.
- If no methods are permitted on a resource without authentication, the server should return `401 Unauthorized`.
- If the client is authenticated but does not have permission to invoke any actions on the resource, the server should return `403 Forbidden`.

`OPTIONS` requests are considered *nullipotent* (safe); that is, they should never, under any circumstances, result in modification of any resources.

> **NOTE** *Some web services enable* Cross-Origin Resource Sharing (CORS). *This special, relatively new protocol enables authorized browser applications to bypass the AJAX* same-origin policy *using a set of specialized headers. If you want your web services to be directly accessible from JavaScript applications, you need to enable CORS support. The full details of this are outside the scope of this book. However, CORS-enabled web services* must *support* `OPTIONS` *requests for* all *resources and, when responding to* `OPTIONS` *requests,* must *include the* `Access-Control-Allow-Methods` *response header, whose contents are identical to the* `Allow` *header.*

## HEAD and GET

Whenever `GET` is supported and allowed on a resource, `HEAD` must also be supported and allowed. The only difference between `GET` and `HEAD` is that a `HEAD` response must have no response body. The `HEAD` response must have headers identical to what would be in a `GET` response. `GET` requests are used to obtain a resource or resources. A URL such as `/services/Rest/account` indicates that the client wants to obtain all accounts or a filtered list of accounts. Typically, filter, order, and pagination instructions are included in query string parameters.

A request URL such as `/services/Rest/account/1075` indicates that the client wants to obtain a single account with the unique identifier `1075`. Some vendors also support relational URLs such as `/services/Rest/account/1075/order` and `/services/Rest/account/1075/order/1522`, signaling requests for a (possibly filtered) list of orders for account `1075` and for order `1522` belonging to account `1075`, respectively. This recursion can, theoretically, continue as far as the limits on URL length will permit. `/services/Rest/account/1075/order/1522/item/12` could return a particular line item from an order for an account.

> **NOTE** *In the URLs demonstrated here, the* `account` *and* `order` *path segments are singular. This is not required — it's just a choice. The URLs could instead contain* `accounts` *and* `orders` *path segments. Which you use is up to you, but you should pick one and remain consistent across your resources. Generally speaking, using singular path segments does result in shorter URLs, which permit more contents in the query string when needed.*

The server should respond `200 OK` for successful `GET` and `HEAD` requests and include the resource or resources requested in the agreed-upon (or default) representation in the response body for `GET` requests.

`GET` and `HEAD` requests are also nullipotent and should not have any side effects for resources on the server.

## POST

`POST` requests are used to create new resources on the server. A `POST` request should always be directed at a collection URI (`/services/Rest/account`), but it can also be directed at a subordinate collection URI (`/services/Rest/account/1075/order`). A `POST` request to an individual *element URI* (`/services/Rest/account/1075`) should result in a `405 Method Not Allowed` response. In a successful `POST` request, the server creates the requested resource and returns `201 Created`. The response should include a `Location` header with the URL for the newly created resource.

For example, a `POST` request to `/services/Rest/account` to create a new account might return `http://www.example.com/services/Rest/account/9156` in the `Location` header. The response body should be the created resource because it would be returned with a `GET` request to the URL in the `Location` header.

A `POST` request is non-nullipotent (non-safe — the request does result in modification of one or more resources) and non-*idempotent* (making multiple identical `POST` requests results in multiple created resources).

## PUT

A `PUT` request results in the replacement of a resource on the server. For this reason, `PUT` requests are used to update existing resources. `PUT` requests, unlike `POST` requests, are never made to collection URIs. Instead, they are made to individual element URIs and subordinate element URIs (`/services/Rest/account/1075`, `/services/Rest/account/1075/order/5122`). A `PUT` request to a collection URI or subordinate collection URI should result in a `405 Method Not Allowed` response. The response to a successful `PUT` request should be `204 No Content` and its body should be empty.

`PUT` requests are, obviously, non-nullipotent. They should, however, be idempotent. Two or more successive, identical `PUT` requests should have no side effects other than those in the first `PUT` request.

One area that this can be a challenge is if the resource being updated includes a "last modified" timestamp or a version number. To abide by the restriction of idempotence, the service should update the resource timestamp and/or version number for `PUT` requests only if the underlying entity truly changed. Such a requirement can actually be quite challenging to implement, so many vendors implement `PUT` in a partially idempotent manner, documenting that the timestamp and version number will still be updated in identical `PUT` requests.

## PATCH

PATCH requests are very similar to PUT requests in both purpose and semantics. PATCH is a relatively new HTTP method, added only in the last several years. It is not part of the original HTTP/1.1 specification. PATCH requests, like PUT requests, are also intended to update resources at individual element URIs. However, a PATCH request indicates only a partial update of a resource, not a complete replacement of the resource.

For example, if a PATCH request to /service/Rest/account/1075/order/5122 contains only the shippingAddress property, then only the shippingAddress on the order will be updated. Other properties will remain unchanged (except, possibly, timestamps and version numbers). This is an extremely powerful request method, but it is also quite challenging to implement. To support PATCH, your application must accept a very flexible set of properties in the request entity, and then update *only* those resource properties that are present in the request. You cannot merely use a check for null because the PATCH may be intentionally setting a property value to null.

The response to a successful PATCH request should be either 200 OK or 204 No Content. It's your choice whether to return the full, updated entity or no content in the response body. If PATCH is supported, the requested media type is supported, and the PATCH request content is understood and parsed successfully, but the server still cannot apply the patch (for example, because the patch would make the entity invalid), the server should respond with 422 Unprocessable Entity. If the client uses the If-Match request header or If-Unmodified-Since request header to define a precondition for the patch and that precondition fails, the server should return 412 Precondition Failed. If multiple requests attempt to patch a resource simultaneously and that is not permitted, the server should return 409 Conflict.

PATCH requests, like PUT requests, are non-nullipotent and should be idempotent.

## DELETE

A DELETE request, naturally, is used to delete a resource. A DELETE request may be made against an individual element URI — in which case that single resource is deleted — or it may be made against a (possibly filtered) collection URI — in which case all the matching resources are deleted. Allowing the deletion of multiple resources is often not desirable, so this capability is usually not supported. Upon successful deletion of a resource, the server should respond 200 OK with the deleted resource in the response body or 204 No Content with no content in the response body. If for some reason the server accepts the delete command but cannot execute it immediately (perhaps the resource is in use), it may return 202 Accepted. In this case, the response body should contain a resource URL that the client can use to follow up on the request and check on its status at a later time.

DELETE requests are obviously non-nullipotent, but their idempotence is an interesting topic. Deleting a resource may result in setting a flag on that resource but retaining its data (a *soft delete*), or it may result in actually permanently and irrevocably eliminating the resource's data (a *hard delete*). When employing soft deletes, multiple identical DELETE requests always return the same response and have no additional side effects, making DELETE idempotent. However, when using hard deletes a second identical DELETE request always results in 404 Not Found because the resource no longer exists. Technically this is considered non-idempotent because the response differs, but it doesn't actually have different side effects and is still the best practice when accepting DELETE requests for hard deletes.

## CONFIGURING RESTFUL WEB SERVICES WITH SPRING MVC

One of the great things about RESTful web services is how neatly they work within an existing HTTP infrastructure, and this is demonstrated plainly in Spring Framework. Technically speaking, you don't have to do anything special to create RESTful web services. You can simply create a `@Controller`, add some `@RequestMapping` methods to it, and begin operating a RESTful web service. Practically speaking, however, it is unlikely that you will want to reuse your existing `DispatcherServlet` application context for your web services. Think about some of the beans you have previously configured in this application context: There are various message converters for handling all sorts of request and response formats; there's the `SessionLocaleResolver` that certainly doesn't apply to stateless REST requests; and there are the `ViewResolver` and `RequestToViewNameResolver` that are completely unnecessary for responding to web service requests. It's only logical, then, to create a separate `DispatcherServlet` and application context configured appropriately to form your RESTful web services.

In this section you explore configuring this separate `DispatcherServlet` and creating REST controllers. You start by looking at how to segregate your web and REST controllers so that they don't cross contexts, and then you create and bootstrap another application context configuration. You also look at how to properly handle error conditions in your services. Finally, you create a REST controller and use `@RequestMapping` for discovery and representational state transfer for both XML and JSON clients. You can follow along in the Web-Service project available for download from the `wrox.com` code download site.

### Segregating Controllers with Stereotype Annotations

Recall from Chapters 12 and 13 that the `@Controller` annotation serves two purposes. As an `@Component`, it is responsible for marking your controllers as Spring-managed beans eligible for instantiation and dependency injection. However, in the context of Spring MVC, it is also responsible for marking beans to be scanned for `@RequestMapping`. A bean marking with `@RequestMapping` cannot respond to requests if it is not annotated with `@Controller`. Thus, your REST controllers must, like your web controllers, be marked with `@Controller`.

Of course, this presents some challenges. You don't want your REST controllers to be picked up by component scanning for your web `DispatcherServlet`, and you don't want your web controllers to be picked up by component scanning for your REST `DispatcherServlet`, either. The obvious solution is to place your web controllers in a separate package from your REST controllers and component scan only the appropriate package in each application context. This is certainly an easy approach as well, and in most cases it can satisfy any use cases you might have. However, there is another way to tackle this problem: meta-annotations.

Spring Framework's `@Component` stereotype annotations are, for lack of a better word, inherited. `@Controller`, `@Service`, and `@Repository` are all annotated with `@Component`. This means you can create your own stereotype annotations, too, by meta-annotating them with an existing `@Component`. It isn't just `@Component` that is inherited, either. You can meta-annotate a custom annotation with `@Controller`, for example, giving your annotation the same force as `@Controller`. This is especially important because it means that your custom annotations can mark controllers for request mapping, which solves the controller segregation problem quite nicely. With this in mind, take a look at the `@com.wrox.config.annotation.WebController` and `@com.wrox.config.annotation.RestEndpoint` annotations in the Web-Service project.

```
@Target({ ElementType.TYPE })
@Retention(RetentionPolicy.RUNTIME)
@Documented
@Controller
public @interface WebController
{
    String value() default "";
}

@Target({ ElementType.TYPE })
@Retention(RetentionPolicy.RUNTIME)
@Documented
@Controller
public @interface RestEndpoint
{
    String value() default "";
}
```

These annotations are practically identical, but their semantic meanings have important differences. Both indicate that the target bean is a controller eligible for request mapping. However, `@WebController` marks controllers for traditional web requests, whereas `@RestEndpoint` denotes RESTful *web service endpoints*. The lone `value` attribute serves the same purpose here as it does in other stereotype annotations: It provides a way to specify the bean name that overrides the default bean name pattern.

## Creating Separate Web and REST Application Contexts

On their own, these custom annotations don't do you any good. You can place them on your controllers and endpoints, but the `ServletContextConfiguration` class you have used in previous chapters picks them all up in its component scan for `@Controller`. As such, you need to update this configuration to scan only for your `@WebController` annotation. To remove any ambiguity about its purpose, it's also a good idea to rename this class to `WebServletContextConfiguration`.

```
@Configuration
@EnableWebMvc
@ComponentScan(
        basePackages = "com.wrox.site",
        useDefaultFilters = false,
        includeFilters = @ComponentScan.Filter(WebController.class)
)
public class WebServletContextConfiguration extends WebMvcConfigurerAdapter
{
    ...
}
```

None of the code within this class has changed from previous chapters. All you have done here is change the types of stereotype annotations that mark beans belonging to this application context. Now you need to create a new application context — one that looks for `@RestEndpoint` and that is more suited to RESTful web services. The `RestServletContextConfiguration` in Listing 17-1 does just that.

**LISTING 17-1: RestServletContextConfiguration.java**

```
@Configuration
@EnableWebMvc
@ComponentScan(
        basePackages = "com.wrox.site",
        useDefaultFilters = false,
        includeFilters = @ComponentScan.Filter(RestEndpoint.class)
)
public class RestServletContextConfiguration extends WebMvcConfigurerAdapter
{
    @Inject ObjectMapper objectMapper;
    @Inject Marshaller marshaller;
    @Inject Unmarshaller unmarshaller;
    @Inject SpringValidatorAdapter validator;

    @Override
    public void configureMessageConverters(
            List<HttpMessageConverter<?>> converters
    ) {
        converters.add(new SourceHttpMessageConverter<>());

        MarshallingHttpMessageConverter xmlConverter =
                new MarshallingHttpMessageConverter();
        xmlConverter.setSupportedMediaTypes(Arrays.asList(
                new MediaType("application", "xml"),
                new MediaType("text", "xml")
        ));
        xmlConverter.setMarshaller(this.marshaller);
        xmlConverter.setUnmarshaller(this.unmarshaller);
        converters.add(xmlConverter);

        MappingJackson2HttpMessageConverter jsonConverter =
                new MappingJackson2HttpMessageConverter();
        jsonConverter.setSupportedMediaTypes(Arrays.asList(
                new MediaType("application", "json"),
                new MediaType("text", "json")
        ));
        jsonConverter.setObjectMapper(this.objectMapper);
        converters.add(jsonConverter);
    }

    @Override
    public void configureContentNegotiation(
            ContentNegotiationConfigurer configurer)
    {
        configurer.favorPathExtension(false).favorParameter(false)
                .ignoreAcceptHeader(false)
                .defaultContentType(MediaType.APPLICATION_JSON);
    }

    @Override
    public Validator getValidator()
    {
```

```
        return this.validator;
    }

    @Bean
    public LocaleResolver localeResolver()
    {
        return new AcceptHeaderLocaleResolver();
    }
}
```

This class is similar to `WebServletContextConfiguration` in several ways, but it also has many important differences. It lacks any view resolution or multipart support because those features are simply not needed. It has fewer message converters, focusing only on the tasks of marshalling and unmarshalling JSON and XML and forgetting about `String`s, forms, and `byte` arrays. The `configureContentNegotiation` method takes a slightly different approach, supporting only the `Accept` header for content negotiation (that is, after all, the RESTful standard). You still need a Spring `Validator`, of course. Bean validation has its uses in RESTful web services, too: You can mark `@RequestBody` entity parameters with `@Valid`.

A `LocaleResolver` can also come in handy: Language does not affect request and response representation, but it can be used to localize error messages at the client's request. In this case you'd use the `AcceptHeaderLocaleResolver` instead of the `SessionLocaleResolver` (as a general rule, there are no sessions in REST), and you no longer need the `LocaleChangeInterceptor` because the client specifies the wanted locale (if any) on every request.

With a new REST application context read to go, you need to bootstrap it properly. This is done in the `Bootstrap` class as usual. The existing `DispatcherServlet` declaration has been renamed so that it is less ambiguous, and a new `DispatcherServlet` declaration has been added.

```
AnnotationConfigWebApplicationContext webContext =
        new AnnotationConfigWebApplicationContext();
webContext.register(WebServletContextConfiguration.class);
ServletRegistration.Dynamic dispatcher = container.addServlet(
        "springWebDispatcher", new DispatcherServlet(webContext)
);
dispatcher.setLoadOnStartup(1);
dispatcher.setMultipartConfig(new MultipartConfigElement(
        null, 20_971_520L, 41_943_040L, 512_000
));
dispatcher.addMapping("/");

AnnotationConfigWebApplicationContext restContext =
        new AnnotationConfigWebApplicationContext();
restContext.register(RestServletContextConfiguration.class);
DispatcherServlet servlet = new DispatcherServlet(restContext);
servlet.setDispatchOptionsRequest(true);
dispatcher = container.addServlet(
        "springRestDispatcher", servlet
);
dispatcher.setLoadOnStartup(2);
dispatcher.addMapping("/services/Rest/*");
```

You'll notice that the new Servlet lacks a multipart configuration, which is to be expected. You can use multipart requests with RESTful web services, but that is rare and the topic is beyond the scope of this book. The code also sets the `DispatcherServlet`'s `dispatchOptionsRequest` property to `true`. Normally `DispatcherServlet` ignores `OPTIONS` requests and defers to the default `HttpServlet` behavior in these cases. To support discovery, you must tell the `DispatcherServlet` to dispatch `OPTIONS` requests to your RESTful endpoints just like any other request.

## Handling Error Conditions in RESTful Web Services

How you handle and respond to erroneous requests and error conditions in your RESTful web services is almost as important as how you handle and respond to successful requests. Consumers of your RESTful APIs expect meaningful status codes and error messages when something goes wrong, and they certainly don't want to get back the standard container HTML-formatted error pages.

Spring Framework's support for graceful error handling has evolved a lot in the last 3 or 4 years. You can easily find a half-dozen approaches or more in a quick search of the web, and most of them still use old, outdated, and even deprecated tactics. This chapter does not address these old ways of handling errors but instead focuses on the features added in Spring 3.0 and 3.2.

### Changing HTTP Response Codes

One of the things you need to handle in your web services is requests to resources that don't exist. Sure, Spring can return `404 Not Found` when requests are made to URLs without method mappings, but what if a request is made to `/services/Rest/account/10` and the account with identifier `10` doesn't exist. According to the RESTful standards, you're also suppose to return `404 Not Found`. In the earliest days you simply had to use the `HttpServletRequest` everywhere to set the response status. Now it is much simpler. From a coding standpoint, the easiest way to report such an issue is to throw an exception. So, create an exception.

```
@ResponseStatus(HttpStatus.NOT_FOUND)
public class ResourceNotFoundException extends RuntimeException
{
    ...
}
```

The only thing special about this exception is the `@org.springframework.web.bind.annotation.ResponseStatus` annotation, added in Spring 3.0. When placed on an exception declaration, this tells Spring Framework to return a `404 Not Found` status code. Without this, throwing such an exception from a controller method would normally result in a `500 Internal Server Error`. There are other uses for `@ResponseStatus` as well, but you'll see those later in this section.

### Declaring Exception Handlers

Another thing to consider is the problem of bean validation. In your web controllers in Chapter 16, you caught `ConstraintViolationExceptions` and then added the individual violations to your model to display to the user. It would be great if there was an easy way to do something similar in your endpoint controllers, and indeed there is. The `@org.springframework.web.bind.annotation.ExceptionHandler` annotation, also added in Spring 3.0, enables you to mark a method as an exception handler. It has nearly the same semantics as `@RequestMapping`, enabling you to return most of the same return types and accept most of the same method arguments.

```
@ExceptionHandler({ ConstraintViolationException.class })
@ResponseStatus(HttpStatus.BAD_REQUEST)
@ResponseBody
public ErrorResponse handleBeanValidationError(ConstraintViolationException e)
{
    ...
}
```

The problem with this pattern is that it requires you to have the necessary `@ExceptionHandler` methods on *all* your controllers. You could inherit from a base controller with these methods defined, but that then prevents you from extending other classes when needed.

## Using the Controller Advice Pattern

Spring 3.2 introduced the concept of the *controller advice* pattern with the `@org.springframework.web.bind.annotation.ControllerAdvice` annotation. Classes marked with `@ControllerAdvice`, which is a `@Component`, are Spring-managed beans that advise controllers. At this time you can add `@ExceptionHandler`, `@InitBinder`, and `@ModelAttribute` methods to a controller advice class, and the advice those methods supply apply to all controllers. Being a `@Component`, `@ControllerAdvice` classes would normally get automatically instantiated in your root application context. You don't want this because you don't want such advice to apply to web controllers and endpoint controllers alike, so you need to exclude this annotation from your root component scanning.

```
...
@ComponentScan(
        basePackages = "com.wrox.site",
        excludeFilters =
        @ComponentScan.Filter({Controller.class, ControllerAdvice.class})
)
public class RootContextConfiguration
...
```

Before you can create controller advice for your endpoint controllers, consider that you might want to also create advice for your web controllers at some point. So, instead of using `@ControllerAdvice` directly, it would be best to create your own stereotype annotation specific to RESTful endpoint controllers.

```
@Target({ ElementType.TYPE })
@Retention(RetentionPolicy.RUNTIME)
@Documented
@ControllerAdvice
public @interface RestEndpointAdvice
{
    String value() default "";
}
```

The last thing you need to do is configure the component scanning for the REST application context to make it pick up `@RestEndpointAdvice` classes.

```
...
@ComponentScan(
        basePackages = "com.wrox.site",
        useDefaultFilters = false,
        includeFilters =
        @ComponentScan.Filter({RestEndpoint.class, RestEndpointAdvice.class})
)
public class RestServletContextConfiguration extends WebMvcConfigurerAdapter
...
```

Now you can create a controller advice to handle errors. The `com.wrox.site.exception.RestExceptionHandler` in Listing 17-2 does just that. It has two inner classes, `ErrorItem` and `ErrorResponse`, which help it achieve the goal of cleanly reporting errors back to the user. The lone `handle` method, annotated with `@ExceptionHandler`, converts all the constraint violations into `ErrorItem`s, places them in an `ErrorResponse`, and returns the `ErrorResponse` wrapped in a `ResponseEntity` with the status code set to `400 Bad Request`.

Notice how the `@ExceptionHandler` annotation indicates which exceptions the method is capable of handling. You could put multiple exceptions in this annotation to have a single method handle multiple errors. Because Spring always calls the most specific match, you could also create a catchall handle method that took any instance of `Exception`. Spring would call the method that most closely matched the thrown exception and then only call your catchall method as a last resort.

**LISTING 17-2: RestExceptionHandler.java**

```
@RestEndpointAdvice
public class RestExceptionHandler
{
    @ExceptionHandler(ConstraintViolationException.class)
    public ResponseEntity<ErrorResponse> handle(ConstraintViolationException e)
    {
        ErrorResponse errors = new ErrorResponse();
        for(ConstraintViolation violation : e.getConstraintViolations())
        {
            ErrorItem error = new ErrorItem();
            error.setCode(violation.getMessageTemplate());
            error.setMessage(violation.getMessage());
            errors.addError(error);
        }

        return new ResponseEntity<>(errors, HttpStatus.BAD_REQUEST);
    }

    public static class ErrorItem
    {
        private String code;
        private String message;

        @XmlAttribute
        public String getCode() { ... }
        public void setCode(String code) { ... }
        @XmlValue
```

```
        public String getMessage() { ... }
        public void setMessage(String message) { ... }
    }

    @XmlRootElement(name = "errors")
    public static class ErrorResponse
    {
        private List<ErrorItem> errors = new ArrayList<>();

        @XmlElement(name = "error")
        public List<ErrorItem> getErrors() { ... }
        public void setErrors(List<ErrorItem> errors) { ... }
        public void addError(ErrorItem error) { ... }
    }
}
```

You may have realized this by now, but the `@ResponseStatus` annotation you placed on your `ResourceNotFoundException` isn't all that helpful in a REST context. For exceptions thrown within web controllers, it would be helpful, and you could leave the annotation there to make the exception remain useful in a web context, but because it results in the container HTML error page being returned, it's not ideal for REST responses. A better idea would be to add a second `handle` method to the `RestExceptionHandler` to handle that exception *and* Spring's `NoSuchRequestHandlingMethodException` (thrown when the incoming request matches no controller methods). That exercise and the exercise of creating a catchall method are left up to you.

## Mapping RESTful Requests to Controller Methods

To create a web service, you first need a business layer to expose with it. The `AccountService` interface continues with the account example URLs used so far in this chapter. It specifies methods for listing, getting, saving, and deleting accounts. The details of the `DefaultAccountService` implementation are unimportant; it's a standard in-memory store of accounts. You can look at it in the Web-Service project.

```
@Validated
public interface AccountService
{
    @NotNull
    public List<Account> getAllAccounts();
    public Account getAccount(long id);
    public Account saveAccount(
            @NotNull(message = "{validate.accountService.saveAccount.account}")
            @Valid Account account
    );
    public void deleteAccount(long id);
}
```

The implementation of this service, which is managed in the root application context, is accessible to both the web and REST `DispatcherServlet` application contexts, as demonstrated at the top of the `AccountController` and `AccountRestEndpoint`. The details of the `AccountController` are also unimportant. It is the standard web controller that you are used to creating.

```
@WebController
public class AccountController
{
    @Inject AccountService accountService;
    ...
}

@RestEndpoint
public class AccountRestEndpoint
{
    @Inject AccountService accountService;
    ...
}
```

Using `@RequestMapping` in a RESTful endpoint is very much like using it in a web controller. Technically speaking, you can write request handler methods with all the same parameter rules and return types; although in reality this is usually not the case. It doesn't make sense to return a `ModelAndView`, `View`, `String` view name, `Model`, `Map`, model attribute, `Callable`, or `DeferredResult` from a RESTful web service handler method. Typically you want to return a `@ResponseBody` response entity object or an explicit `ResponseEntity<?>` that can be written back to the client, or `void` or `ResponseEntity<Void>` if no content should be returned to the client. Method parameters usually consist of `@PathVariable` and `@RequestParam` parameters and, for `POST` and `PUT` requests, `@RequestBody` request entities. As with web controllers, request entities should be form or command objects lacking the fields that you don't want your clients to set (usually at least the resource identifier). Response entities returned from your methods can be the same business objects you normally operate on (not form objects), but you should refrain from returning any type of `Collection` or `Map`. Although these can easily be converted to a JSON representation, they cannot be converted into an XML representation.

The first methods you'll notice in the `AccountRestEndpoint` are the discovery methods, which respond to `OPTIONS` requests. There are two methods: one for collection requests and one for individual resource requests. These methods are fairly simple and always return the same allowed options, but you could implement security checks here and return only those options that the authenticated client has access to.

```
@RequestMapping(value = "account", method = RequestMethod.OPTIONS)
public ResponseEntity<Void> discover()
{
    HttpHeaders headers = new HttpHeaders();
    headers.add("Allow", "OPTIONS,HEAD,GET,POST");
    return new ResponseEntity<>(null, headers, HttpStatus.NO_CONTENT);
}

@RequestMapping(value = "account/{id}", method = RequestMethod.OPTIONS)
public ResponseEntity<Void> discover(@PathVariable("id") long id)
{
    if(this.accountService.getAccount(id) == null)
        throw new ResourceNotFoundException();

    HttpHeaders headers = new HttpHeaders();
    headers.add("Allow", "OPTIONS,HEAD,GET,PUT,DELETE");
    return new ResponseEntity<>(null, headers, HttpStatus.NO_CONTENT);
}
```

As indicated in the OPTIONS response, clients may GET either the collection or individual resources. This is implemented in the read methods. The collection read is dangerous because it doesn't page the results. If the database contained 1,000,000 accounts, this method would return all 1,000,000 of them. Normally you would use request parameters or headers to filter and limit the results returned from this method. It's also best to automatically limit the number of results returned if the client fails to specify any filters or limits. These methods demonstrate the use of @ResponseBody for returning response entities and @ResponseStatus to indicate which HTTP status Spring should respond to the request with.

```
@RequestMapping(value = "account", method = RequestMethod.GET)
@ResponseBody @ResponseStatus(HttpStatus.OK)
public AccountList read()
{
    AccountList list = new AccountList();
    list.setValue(this.accountService.getAllAccounts());
    return list;
}

@RequestMapping(value = "account/{id}", method = RequestMethod.GET)
@ResponseBody @ResponseStatus(HttpStatus.OK)
public Account read(@PathVariable("id") long id)
{
    Account account = this.accountService.getAccount(id);
    if(account == null)
        throw new ResourceNotFoundException();
    return account;
}
```

Notice that the individual read returns a single Account and throws a ResourceNotFoundException (which results it a 404 Not Found) if the Account requested isn't found. The @ResponseStatus for the method is ignored in this case, and the @ResponseStatus for the exception (or the exception handler) is given higher precedence. Meanwhile, the collection read returns an AccountList (instead of a List<Account>). If your web service were supporting JSON only, you would just need a List<Account> and not the specialized AccountList object. AccountList enables the response to be represented with XML as well. This is something you must pay particular attention to when writing RESTful web service endpoints. Representing request and response entities is much simpler with JSON than it is with XML, and so special considerations must be made when supporting both. Some service providers opt to support only JSON requests and responses to avoid these complexities, and you may decide to take that route as well. You could also create separate handler methods for XML and JSON responses; although, that can sometimes make your job even more complicated.

```
@XmlRootElement(name = "accounts")
public static class AccountList
{
    private List<Account> value;

    @XmlElement(name = "account")
    public List<Account> getValue()
    {
        return value;
```

```
        }

        public void setValue(List<Account> accounts)
        {
            this.value = accounts;
        }
    }
```

The create and update methods (POST and PUT, respectively) shown in the following code snippet are responsible for adding new accounts and saving changes to existing accounts. Notice that update throws a ResourceNotFoundException, just like the individual read method, if the resource being updated doesn't exist. It also returns void and responds 204 No Content when the resource is successfully updated, whereas create responds 201 Created, returns the created entity, and includes a Location header in the response with the URL for the created resource. It uses Spring's org.springframework.web.servlet.support.ServletUriComponentsBuilder to create the URL so that it contains your application's domain name and context path.

```
    @RequestMapping(value = "account", method = RequestMethod.POST)
    public ResponseEntity<Account> create(@RequestBody AccountForm form)
    {
        Account account = new Account();
        account.setName(form.getName());
        account.setBillingAddress(form.getBillingAddress());
        account.setShippingAddress(form.getShippingAddress());
        account.setPhoneNumber(form.getPhoneNumber());
        account = this.accountService.saveAccount(account);

        String uri = ServletUriComponentsBuilder.fromCurrentServletMapping()
                .path("/account/{id}").buildAndExpand(account.getId()).toString();
        HttpHeaders headers = new HttpHeaders();
        headers.add("Location", uri);

        return new ResponseEntity<>(account, headers, HttpStatus.CREATED);
    }

    @RequestMapping(value = "account/{id}", method = RequestMethod.PUT)
    @ResponseStatus(HttpStatus.NO_CONTENT)
    public void update(@PathVariable("id") long id, @RequestBody AccountForm form)
    {
        Account account = this.accountService.getAccount(id);
        if(account == null)
            throw new ResourceNotFoundException();
        account.setName(form.getName());
        account.setBillingAddress(form.getBillingAddress());
        account.setShippingAddress(form.getShippingAddress());
        account.setPhoneNumber(form.getPhoneNumber());
        this.accountService.saveAccount(account);
    }
```

Though simple, the final method of interest in the AccountRestEnpdoint is delete. Like read and update it throws a ResourceNotFoundException if the resource doesn't exist. It then deletes the resource if it does exist and responds 204 No Content.

```
    @RequestMapping(value = "account/{id}", method = RequestMethod.DELETE)
    @ResponseStatus(HttpStatus.NO_CONTENT)
```

```
    public void delete(@PathVariable("id") long id)
    {
        if(this.accountService.getAccount(id) == null)
            throw new ResourceNotFoundException();
        this.accountService.deleteAccount(id);
    }
```

## Improving Discovery with an Index Endpoint

The discovery methods in the `AccountRestEndpoint` help clients learn about the account resource and what they can do with it, but it doesn't complete the RESTful discovery mechanism. Typically you would create an index endpoint that lists your web service's available resources. In the simplest sense, this is just a static list of links in your code, created with your application's domain name and context path in front. The `IndexRestEndpoint` in Listing 17-3 does just this. It returns resource links using the HAL standard, and because this standard has very different XML and JSON representations, it uses some helper POJOs and two different discovery methods to return the appropriate response. `@RequestMapping`'s `produces` attribute helps identify which method should be called based on the request's `Accept` header.

**LISTING 17-3: IndexRestEndpoint.java**

```
@RestEndpoint
public class IndexRestEndpoint
{
    @RequestMapping(value = {"", "/"}, method = RequestMethod.GET,
            produces = {"application/json", "text/json"})
    @ResponseBody @ResponseStatus(HttpStatus.OK)
    public Map<String, Object> discoverJson()
    {
        ServletUriComponentsBuilder builder =
                ServletUriComponentsBuilder.fromCurrentServletMapping();

        Map<String, JsonLink> links = new Hashtable<>(2);
        links.put("self", new JsonLink(builder.path("").build().toString()));
        links.put("account",
                new JsonLink(builder.path("/account").build().toString()));

        Map<String, Object> response = new Hashtable<>(1);
        response.put("_links", links);
        return response;
    }

    @RequestMapping(value = {"", "/"}, method = RequestMethod.GET,
            produces = {"application/xml", "text/xml"})
    @ResponseBody @ResponseStatus(HttpStatus.OK)
    public Resource discoverXml()
    {
        ServletUriComponentsBuilder builder =
                ServletUriComponentsBuilder.fromCurrentServletMapping();

        Resource resource = new Resource();
        resource.addLink(new Link("self", builder.path("").build().toString()));
```

*continues*

**LISTING 17-3** *(continued)*

```
            resource.addLink(new Link("account",
                    builder.path("/account").build().toString()));
            return resource;
        }

        public static class JsonLink
        {
            private String href;

            public JsonLink(String href) { ... }
            @XmlAttribute
            public String getHref() { ... }
            public void setHref(String href) { ... }
        }

        public static class Link extends JsonLink
        {
            private String rel;

            public Link(String rel, String href) { ... }
            @XmlAttribute
            public String getRel() { ... }
            public void setRel(String rel) { ... }
        }

        @XmlRootElement
        public static class Resource
        {
            private List<Link> links = new ArrayList<>();

            @XmlElement(name = "link")
            public List<Link> getLinks() { ... }
            public void setLinks(List<Link> links) { ... }
            public void addLink(Link link) { ... }
        }
    }
```

# TESTING YOUR WEB SERVICE ENDPOINTS

Testing web services, whether RESTful or SOAP, is an interesting challenge. Unlike standard web pages, you can't just open up your browser and go to your application's URL. This might work for `GET` requests, but that's about it. You could create a user interface for the service, and indeed that's how many people test their web services. But this has the disadvantage of adding another variable to the equation: What if your user interface has bugs? Sometimes you need to test your web services absent all other variables, and for that you need some kind of web service testing tool.

## Choosing a Testing Tool

There are a lot of tools available, and which one you choose depends on what type of testing you want to perform. Of course, you can (and should) unit test your web services, just like you unit test your business logic and repositories, for which you would use an automated unit-testing tool such as JUnit or TestNG. There's also integration testing, which involves testing many components of your system interacting as they would in the real world. Among other tools used by quality assurance teams around the world, JUnit and TestNG can also lend a hand in this arena. Another common testing requirement is load testing, which helps determine the performance characteristics, bottlenecks, and breaking points of a system. There are many tools available for this, including free tools such as JMeter and The Grinder, and expensive, enterprise tools such as NeoLoad and LoadRunner.

However, another common testing approach (one you have used throughout this book) is functional testing. Sometimes the easiest and quickest way to tell if a system works is to open it up and try it out. With a mobile app, that involves using the app on your phone or tablet. Functional testing a desktop application, likewise, involves opening and using the application on your desktop or notebook computer. Testing a web application is as simple as opening your browser and entering the application's URL.

But how do you functionally test a web service? You need a tool that enables you to easily create and manipulate HTTP requests and view the responses. The command-line tool cURL is a contender, but it involves a lot of overhead and manual typing for each request, and any authentication more complicated than HTTP basic authentication is difficult. It would be helpful if the tool could remember authentication and preset header values and format the JSON and XML responses to make it more readable. Fiddler is one option that can be very useful for functional testing web services, and it supports these features. Fiddler has many other uses, though, and can be a little cumbersome to use for just that purpose. There are several REST client web browser plug-ins for Chrome and Firefox that are handy specifically for testing RESTful web services. In this section you use the RESTClient Firefox add-on, but there are a lot of tools to choose from, and you can and should choose the one that works best for you. You can download the RESTClient Firefox add-on here at `http://restclient.net/`.

## Making Requests to Your Web Service

After installing the RESTClient extension in Firefox, follow these steps:

1. Open up RESTClient by clicking the square red button with the orange circle — shown here in the margin — to the right of the address and search bars.
2. Click the Headers menu and click Custom Header.
3. Enter **`Content-Type`** in the Name and **`application/json`** in the Value, check the favorites box, and click Okay.
4. Repeat step 3 for **`Content-Type`** and **`application/xml`**, **`Accept`** and **`application/json`**, and **`Accept`** and **`application/xml`**. This saves quick-access headers that you can easily grab whenever needed. Make sure you clear the Headers bar in RESTClient when you are done. To do this, click the Remove All button.
5. Compile and start the Web-Service application from your IDE.

6. Add the `application/json` `Content-Type` and `Accept` headers to the Headers bar in RESTClient, select **`GET`** from the method, enter **`http://localhost:8080/financials/services/Rest/`** in the URL, and press Send. The response body will be a list of links returned by the `RestIndexEndpoint` controller.
7. Try changing the method to **`OPTIONS`** and the URL to **`http://localhost:8080/financials/services/Rest/account`**. The `AccountRestController` will respond with `204 No Content` and an `Allow` header of all the actions you are allowed to perform on the collection resource.
8. Change the method back to **`GET`**, enter **`http://localhost:8080/financials/services/Rest/account`** in the URL, and press Send. The response body should have an empty list in it. Try the URL **`http://localhost:8080/financials/services/Rest/account/1`**, and your web service should respond with a `404 Not Found`. This is because you don't have any accounts yet.
9. To fix this, change the URL back to **`http://localhost:8080/financials/services/Rest/account`**, change the method to **`POST`**, and enter the value shown in Figure 17-1 in the Body field. After you send this request your web service will respond `400 Bad Request`.

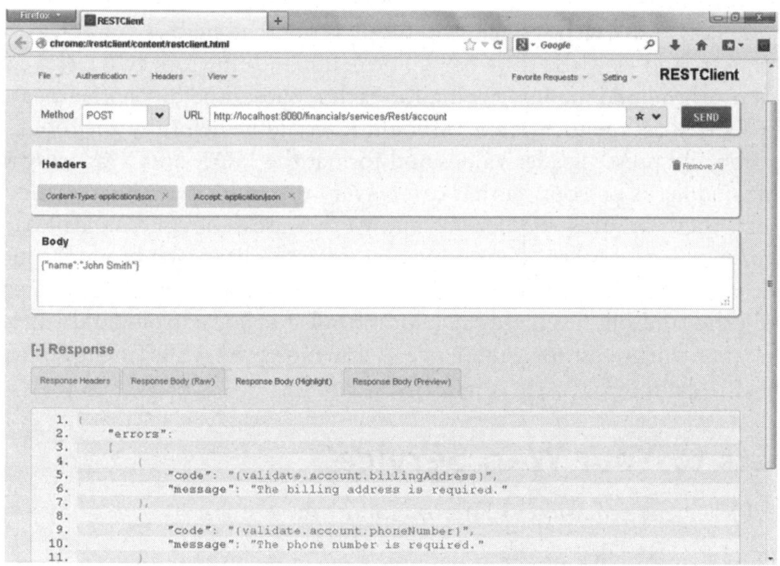


FIGURE 17-1

10. Check the response body, and it should look like Figure 17-1. This means that bean validation threw a `ConstraintViolationException` and your `RestExceptionHandler` converted the exception into a JSON REST response.
11. Now repeat this process with XML: Change the `Content-Type` and `Accept` headers to `application/xml` and the Body field to the value shown in Figure 17-2. You'll get the same response back, only formatted XML instead of JSON.
12. Figure 17-3 shows a successful `POST` with the complete JSON request body to successfully create an account. Perform this `POST` and take a look at the response headers, where you'll see a `Location` URL for the resource that was just created.

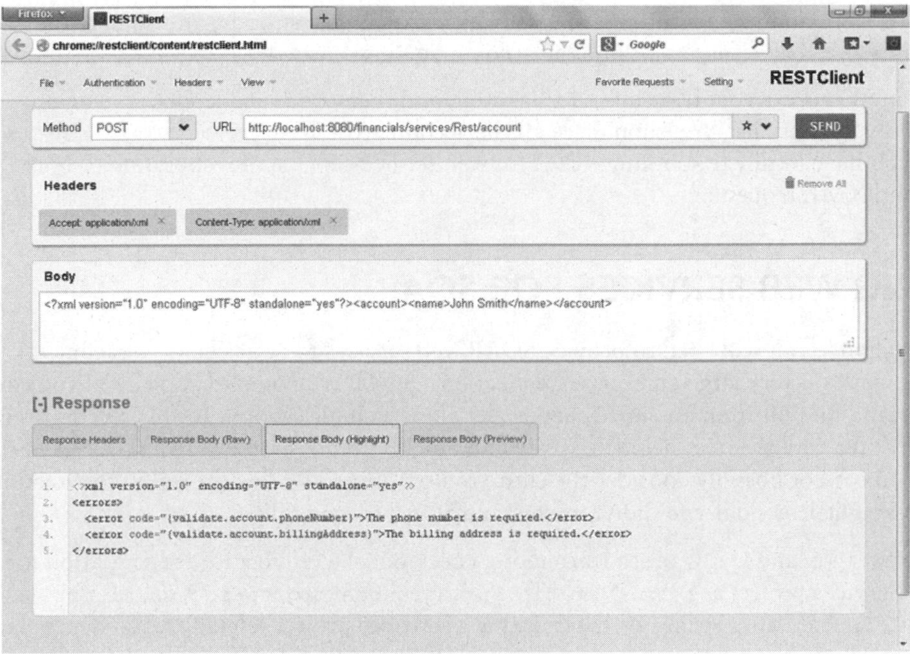


FIGURE 17-2

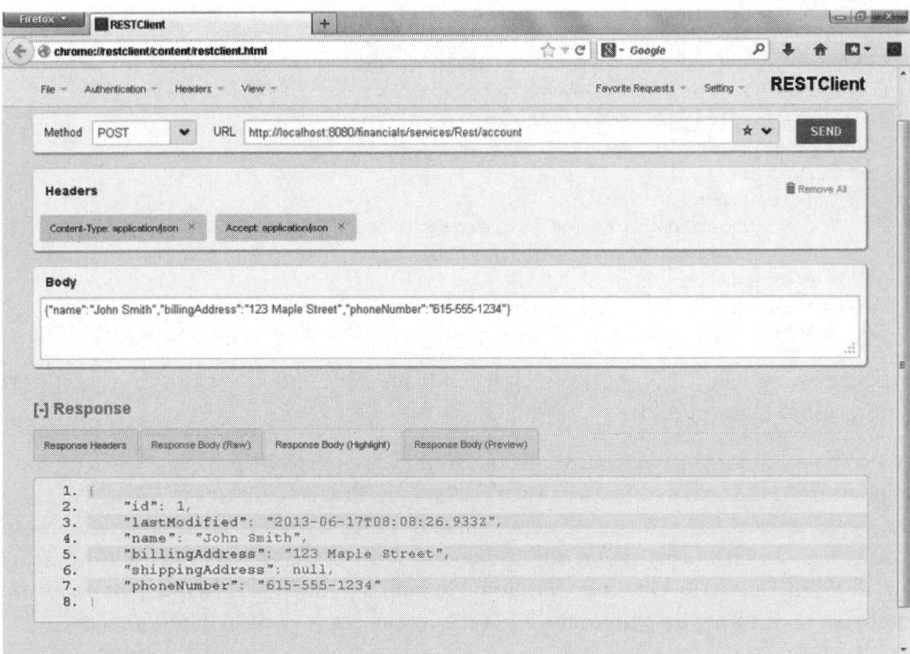


FIGURE 17-3

13. Copy this URL and paste it into the URL field, clear the request body, and change the method to `GET`. The response will be the account you just created.

14. Create a few more accounts, using XML as well, and then try the collection `GET` again. Instead of an empty list, you should see all the accounts you have created so far. This testing means you have a fully functioning RESTful web service capable of responding to both JSON and XML requests.

## USING SPRING WEB SERVICES FOR SOAP

There's a decent chance you will need to provide SOAP web services to your clients someday, especially if you work on very large enterprise applications. SOAP is a complex topic, and you can't get a full understanding of it from an entire chapter, let alone a single section. In this section you are briefly introduced to a tool that can help you easily and quickly create simple SOAP services: Spring Web Services. You cannot possibly consider the entire toolset offered by this project in this section, and it would do you little good if you didn't understand SOAP thoroughly.

If this topic interests you and you want to learn more, check out the reference documentation for the Spring Web Services project at `http://static.springsource.org/spring-ws/sites/2.0/reference/html/index.html`. Spring Web Services is a separate project related to and dependent on Spring Framework. It is meant to work side-by-side with existing Spring-based code, such as web controllers and RESTful endpoints.

To use Spring Web Services, you need an additional Maven dependency not mentioned at the beginning of this chapter:

```
<dependency>
    <groupId>org.springframework.ws</groupId>
    <artifactId>spring-ws-core</artifactId>
    <version>2.1.4.RELEASE</version>
    <scope>compile</scope>
    <exclusions>
        <exclusion>
            <groupId>javax.xml.stream</groupId>
            <artifactId>stax-api</artifactId>
        </exclusion>
    </exclusions>
</dependency>
```

The transient Java Streaming API for XML (StAX) dependency is excluded because it is part of the Java 6 and higher Standard Edition API.

To follow along with the work for this section, see the Customer-Support-v14 project available for download from the wrox.com code download site. It already contains a `RestServletContextConfiguration`, a `RestExceptionHandler`, and an `IndexRestEndpoint` — all similar to what you've seen so far in this chapter. It also contains a `TicketRestEndpoint` for managing tickets via a RESTful JSON or XML API, and you should examine it and test it as much as you want. In this section you focus on creating an endpoint for managing tickets via a SOAP web service.

> **NOTE** *You'll probably notice that the* `TicketRestEndpoint` *has no security protecting it from unauthorized access. For that matter, the SOAP endpoint has no security, either. The simple form authentication this application uses is not appropriate for web services. In Part IV of this book you learn how to secure web services using OAuth. Until then, your web services remain unprotected.*

## Writing Your Contract-First XSD and WSDL

Spring Web Services enforces contract-first development strictly. You must define your XML contract before you can do anything else. The good news is that there are some tools that can help you do this. Consider what you might want a `Ticket` to look like in XML format.

```
<ticket xmlns="http://example.com/xmlns/support">
    <id>12</id>
    <customerName>John Doe</customerName>
    <dateCreated>2014-01-17T12:36:00Z</dateCreated>
    <subject>Foo</subject>
    <body>Bar</body>
    <attachment>
        <name>spacer.gif</name>
        <mimeContentType>image/gif</mimeContentType>
        <contents>R0lGODlhAQABAAAAACH5BAEKAAEALAAAAAABAAEAAAICTAEAOw==</contents>
    </attachment>
</ticket>
```

You also know that you want to create new tickets, so you need a `<ticketForm>` element.

```
<ticketForm xmlns="http://example.com/xmlns/support">
    <subject>Foo</subject>
    <body>Bar</body>
    <attachment>
        <name>spacer.png</name>
        <mimeContentType>image/png</mimeContentType>
        <contents>iVBORw0KGgoAAAANSUhEUgAAAAEAAAABAQMAAAAl21bKAAAAA1BMVEUAAACne
j3aAAAAAXRSTlMAQObYZgAAAApJREFUCB1jYAAAAAIAAc/INeUAAAAASUVORK5CYII=</contents>
    </attachment>
</ticketForm>
```

You need to read and delete an individual ticket, so you need a `<ticketRequest>` element and an identical `<deleteTicket>` element. Finally, you need a way to select all tickets, so an empty `<ticketsRequest>` element should do the trick.

```
<ticketRequest xmlns="http://example.com/xmlns/support">
    <id>12</id>
</ticketRequest>
```

Given these examples, your IDE can help generate XSD schema code. In IntelliJ IDEA, for example, you can create temporary XML files with each element by following these steps:

1. Right-click anywhere within XML contents, and click Generate XSD Schema from XML File.
2. In the dialog that appears, make sure that the Design Type field is set to local elements/global complex types, and then click OK.
3. The generated XSD schema file is quite close to what you want and requires only a few minor changes to indicate expected element types, specify how often types can appear, and so on. The XSD files need to be merged into one XSD file for all actions on your web service.

Listing 17-4 shows the resulting XSD schema file `/WEB-INF/xsd/soap/support.xsd`.

**LISTING 17-4: support.xsd**

```
<?xml version="1.0" encoding="UTF-8"?>
<xs:schema attributeFormDefault="unqualified" elementFormDefault="qualified"
           targetNamespace="http://example.com/xmlns/support"
           xmlns:xs="http://www.w3.org/2001/XMLSchema"
           xmlns:support="http://example.com/xmlns/support">
    <xs:element name="ticketsRequest" type="support:ticketsRequestType" />
    <xs:element name="ticketRequest" type="support:selectTicketType" />
    <xs:element name="createTicket" type="support:createTicketType"/>
    <xs:element name="deleteTicket" type="support:selectTicketType"/>
    <xs:element name="ticket" type="support:ticketType" />
    <xs:element name="tickets" type="support:ticketsType" />
    <xs:complexType name="ticketType">
        <xs:sequence>
            <xs:element type="xs:long" name="id" minOccurs="0"/>
            <xs:element type="xs:string" name="customerName" minOccurs="0"/>
            <xs:element type="xs:dateTime" name="dateCreated" minOccurs="0"/>
            <xs:element type="xs:string" name="subject"/>
            <xs:element type="xs:string" name="body"/>
            <xs:element type="support:attachmentType" name="attachment"
                        minOccurs="0" maxOccurs="unbounded"/>
        </xs:sequence>
    </xs:complexType>
    <xs:complexType name="ticketsRequestType">
        <xs:sequence />
    </xs:complexType>
    <xs:complexType name="selectTicketType">
        <xs:sequence>
            <xs:element type="xs:long" name="id"/>
        </xs:sequence>
    </xs:complexType>
    <xs:complexType name="createTicketType">
        <xs:sequence>
            <xs:element type="support:ticketType" name="ticket"/>
        </xs:sequence>
    </xs:complexType>
    <xs:complexType name="ticketsType">
        <xs:sequence>
            <xs:element type="support:ticketType" name="ticket" minOccurs="0"
```

```
                                    maxOccurs="unbounded"/>
            </xs:sequence>
        </xs:complexType>
        <xs:complexType name="attachmentType">
            <xs:sequence>
                <xs:element type="xs:string" name="name"/>
                <xs:element type="xs:string" name="mimeContentType"/>
                <xs:element type="xs:base64Binary" name="contents"/>
            </xs:sequence>
        </xs:complexType>
    </xs:schema>
```

The XSD is all you need in this case: Spring Web Services considers this enough contract and creates the WSDL for you automatically. To effect this WSDL creation, you have to first configure Spring Web Services.

## Adding the SOAP Dispatcher Servlet Configuration

Unlike Spring Framework, Spring Web Services does not support Java-based programmatic configuration. However, you need component scanning for your SOAP application context, so it's easiest to create a hybrid configuration. The `SoapServletContextConfiguration` scans for `@org.springframework.ws.server.endpoint.annotation.Endpoint` components and imports the `soapServletContext.xml` XML configuration.

```
@Configuration
@ComponentScan(
        basePackages = "com.wrox.site",
        useDefaultFilters = false,
        includeFilters = @ComponentScan.Filter(Endpoint.class)
)
@ImportResource("classpath:com/wrox/config/soapServletContext.xml")
public class SoapServletContextConfiguration
{
    @Bean
    public WebServiceMessageFactory messageFactory()
    {
        SaajSoapMessageFactory factory = new SaajSoapMessageFactory();
        factory.setSoapVersion(SoapVersion.SOAP_12);
        return factory;
    }
}
```

The explicit `messageFactory` bean (the name is important) overrides the default message factory so that the supported SOAP version is 1.2 instead of the default 1.1. There are several enhancements in SOAP 1.2 regarding protocol binding, extensibility, and XML formats that are beyond the scope of this book. The `soapServletContext.xml` file tells Spring Web Services to configure endpoints based on annotations and to use the XSD schema file you created earlier to generate the WSDL.

```
<?xml version="1.0" encoding="UTF-8"?>
<beans xmlns="http://www.springframework.org/schema/beans"
       xmlns:sws="http://www.springframework.org/schema/web-services"
       xmlns:xsi="http://www.w3.org/2001/XMLSchema-instance"
       xsi:schemaLocation="http://www.springframework.org/schema/beans
```

```
            http://www.springframework.org/schema/beans/spring-beans-4.0.xsd
            http://www.springframework.org/schema/web-services
            http://www.springframework.org/schema/web-services/web-services-2.0.
xsd">

    <sws:annotation-driven marshaller="jaxb2Marshaller"
                           unmarshaller="jaxb2Marshaller" />
    <sws:dynamic-wsdl id="support" portTypeName="Support"
                      locationUri="/services/Soap/" createSoap11Binding="false"
                      createSoap12Binding="true"
                      targetNamespace="http://example.com/xmlns/support">
        <sws:xsd location="/WEB-INF/xsd/soap/support.xsd" />
    </sws:dynamic-wsdl>

</beans>
```

Because `@Endpoint` is also a `@Component`, you need to change the `RootContextConfiguration` to ensure that only the SOAP dispatcher Servlet context instantiates and manages SOAP endpoint classes.

```
...
@ComponentScan(
        basePackages = "com.wrox.site",
        excludeFilters = @ComponentScan.Filter({
                Controller.class, ControllerAdvice.class, Endpoint.class
        })
)
public class RootContextConfiguration
...
```

You'll need to bootstrap the SOAP dispatcher Servlet so that it uses the `SoapServletContextConfiguration`. Spring Web Services has a special `DispatcherServlet` implementation `org.springframework.ws.transport.http.MessageDispatcherServlet` that handles SOAP requests. The following code from the `Bootstrap` class creates this Servlet, sets its application context, and instructs it to transform WSDL locations to requests.

```
        ...
        AnnotationConfigWebApplicationContext soapContext =
                new AnnotationConfigWebApplicationContext();
        soapContext.register(SoapServletContextConfiguration.class);
        MessageDispatcherServlet soapServlet =
                new MessageDispatcherServlet(soapContext);
        soapServlet.setTransformWsdlLocations(true);
        dispatcher = container.addServlet("springSoapDispatcher", soapServlet);
        dispatcher.setLoadOnStartup(3);
        dispatcher.addMapping("/services/Soap/*");
        ...
```

Having configured Spring Web Services, you are now ready to create a SOAP endpoint.

## Creating a SOAP Endpoint

Endpoints are the key concept of Spring Web Service's server support. Unlike controllers, whose handler methods are directly tied to HTTP requests and responses, Spring Web Service SOAP endpoints can serve SOAP requests made via HTTP, XMPP, SMTP, JMS, and more. Just like `@Controller` marks a controller whose `@RequestMapping` methods should be scanned and mapped to requests, `@Endpoint` marks an endpoint whose `@org.springframework.ws.server.endpoint.annotation.PayloadRoot` methods, `@org.springframework.ws.soap.server.endpoint.annotation.SoapAction` methods, and/or `@org.springframework.ws.soap.addressing.server.annotation.Action` methods are handlers for incoming SOAP requests on any protocol. Endpoint methods' parameters correspond to elements of the request, whereas return types indicate response contents.

As far as method parameters are concerned, you have a great deal of flexibility as to which content types you want to accept depending on how you prefer to access the XML content in requests. For example, a method parameter of type `SoapMessage`, `SoapBody`, `SoapEnvelope`, or `SoapHeader` (all in package `org.springframework.ws.soap`) is passed the corresponding content from the SOAP request. Similar to `@RequestBody`, if a method parameter is annotated `@org.springframework.ws.server.endpoint.annotation.RequestPayload`, Spring Web Services converts the request payload to the designated type. Supported request payload types are:

- `javax.xml.transform.Source` or its subinterfaces
- `org.w3c.dom.Element`
- `org.dom4j.Element` if dom4j is on the classpath
- `org.jdom.Element` if JDOM is on the classpath
- `nu.xom.Element` if XOM is on the classpath
- `javax.xml.stream.XMLStreamReader` or `javax.xml.stream.XMLEventReader` in Java SE 6 or higher, or if StAX is on the classpath
- Any type annotated with `@javax.xml.bind.annotation.XmlRootElement` in Java 6 or higher, or if JAXB is on the classpath
- Any type supported by the Spring OXM Unmarshaller if `<sws:annotation-driven>` is configured with the `unmarshaller` attribute.

Similarly, methods annotated `@org.springframework.ws.server.endpoint.annotation.ResponsePayload` can have return types `Source` or its subinterfaces, `org.w3c.dom.Element`, `org.dom4j.Element`, `org.jdom.Element`, `nu.xom.Element`, any type annotated `@XmlRootElement`, and any type supported by the Spring OXM Marshaller (if `<sws:annotation-driven>` is configured with the `marshaller` attribute). A method that returns `void` has no response content (an empty SOAP envelope).

Because of this method parameter and return type support, you can reuse several of the parameter and return types created for the `TicketRestEndpoint` in the `TicketSoapEndpoint` in Listing 17-5. As you can see, this endpoint has many similarities with the REST endpoint, but it also has several differences. This endpoint uses the payload root element names to match to endpoint action methods using the `@PayloadRoot` annotation, but you could instead use the `SOAPAction` header with the `@SoapAction` annotation or the Web Services Addressing standard (`http://www.w3.org/2005/08/addressing`) with the `@Action` annotation.

### 17-5: TicketSoapEndpoint.java

```
@Endpoint
public class TicketSoapEndpoint
{
    private static final String NAMESPACE = "http://example.com/xmlns/support";

    @Inject TicketService ticketService;

    @PayloadRoot(namespace = NAMESPACE, localPart = "ticketsRequest")
    @ResponsePayload
    public TicketWebServiceList read()
    {
        TicketWebServiceList list = new TicketWebServiceList();
        list.setValue(this.ticketService.getAllTickets());
        return list;
    }

    @PayloadRoot(namespace = NAMESPACE, localPart = "ticketRequest")
    @Namespace(uri = NAMESPACE, prefix = "s")
    @ResponsePayload
    public Ticket read(@XPathParam("/s:ticketRequest/id") long id)
    {
        return this.ticketService.getTicket(id);
    }

    @PayloadRoot(namespace = NAMESPACE, localPart = "createTicket")
    @ResponsePayload
    public Ticket create(@RequestPayload CreateTicket form)
    {
        Ticket ticket = new Ticket();
        ticket.setCustomerName("WebServiceAnonymous");
        ticket.setSubject(form.getSubject());
        ticket.setBody(form.getBody());
        if(form.getAttachments() != null)
            ticket.setAttachments(form.getAttachments());

        this.ticketService.save(ticket);

        return ticket;
    }

    @PayloadRoot(namespace = NAMESPACE, localPart = "deleteTicket")
    @Namespace(uri = NAMESPACE, prefix = "s")
    public void delete(@XPathParam("/s:deleteTicket/id") long id)
    {
        this.ticketService.deleteTicket(id);
    }

    @XmlRootElement(namespace = NAMESPACE, name = "createTicket")
    public static class CreateTicket
    {
        private String subject;
        private String body;
```

```
        private List<Attachment> attachments;

        public String getSubject() { ... }
        public void setSubject(String subject) { ... }
        public String getBody() { ... }
        public void setBody(String body) { ... }
        @XmlElement(name = "attachment")
        public List<Attachment> getAttachments() { ... }
        public void setAttachments(List<Attachment> attachments) { ... }
    }
}
```

Compile and start the Customer Support application and test it out. Go to `http://localhost:8080/support/services/Soap/support.wsdl` in any normal browser window to view your auto-generated WSDL. Create some tickets with the graphical user interface, and then try out the RESTful web service interface with the RESTClient browser plug-in. You can also use RESTClient to test the SOAP web service interface. You need to use `Accept` and `Content-Type` request headers with the value `application/soap+xml`. Because SOAP envelope requests can be so complex to create by hand, included are the four following requests that you can use to test your service. Requests should be made to `http://localhost:8080/support/services/Soap/` with method `POST` regardless of action.

```
<soap:Envelope xmlns:soap="http://www.w3.org/2003/05/soap-envelope">
  <soap:Header/>
  <soap:Body>
    <support:ticketsRequest xmlns:support="http://example.com/xmlns/support"/>
  </soap:Body>
</soap:Envelope>

<soap:Envelope xmlns:soap="http://www.w3.org/2003/05/soap-envelope">
  <soap:Header/>
  <soap:Body>
    <support:ticketRequest xmlns:support="http://example.com/xmlns/support">
      <id>1</id>
    </support:ticketRequest>
  </soap:Body>
</soap:Envelope>

<soap:Envelope xmlns:soap="http://www.w3.org/2003/05/soap-envelope">
  <soap:Header/>
  <soap:Body>
    <support:deleteTicket xmlns:support="http://example.com/xmlns/support">
      <id>1</id>
    </support:deleteTicket>
  </soap:Body>
</soap:Envelope>

<soap:Envelope xmlns:soap="http://www.w3.org/2003/05/soap-envelope">
  <soap:Header/>
  <soap:Body>
    <support:createTicket xmlns:support="http://example.com/xmlns/support">
      <subject>Foo</subject>
      <body>Bar</body>
```

```
        <attachment>
          <name>spacer.gif</name>
          <mimeContentType>image/gif</mimeContentType>
          <contents>R0lGODlhAQABAAAAACH5BAEKAAEALAAAAAABAAEAAAICTAEAOw==</contents>
        </attachment>
      </support:createTicket>
    </soap:Body>
  </soap:Envelope>
```

## SUMMARY

You have covered a lot of content in this chapter. First, you were introduced to the concept of web services and learned about SOAP, the beginning of modern web services. You explored the RESTful web service standard and learned how to provide RESTful web services to your clients. You investigated how to create RESTful web services using standard Spring MVC controllers and created your own stereotype annotations to differentiate web controllers and RESTful web service endpoints. You also very briefly learned about the Spring Web Services project and how it can be used to create SOAP web service endpoints for your application.

In the next and final chapter of Part II, you explore how Spring Framework messages and web application clustering can make your application more flexible, scalable, and reliable.

# 18

# Using Messaging and Clustering for Flexibility and Reliability

## IN THIS CHAPTER

- Deciding when to use messaging and clustering
- How to add messaging support to your application
- Distributing your messages across a cluster
- Using Advanced Message Queuing Protocol to distribute events

## WROX.COM CODE DOWNLOADS FOR THIS CHAPTER

You can find the `wrox.com` code downloads for this chapter at `http://www.wrox.com/go/projavaforwebapps` on the Download Code tab. The code for this chapter is divided into the following major examples:

- Publish-Subscribe Project
- WebSocket-Messaging Project
- AMQP-Messaging Project

## NEW MAVEN DEPENDENCIES FOR THIS CHAPTER

This chapter has no new Maven dependencies that you will use in future chapters. You'll continue to use the Maven dependencies introduced in all previous chapters. You'll use the following dependency only in the last section of this chapter and not in any other chapters.

```
<dependency>
    <groupId>com.rabbitmq</groupId>
    <artifactId>amqp-client</artifactId>
    <version>3.2.3</version>
    <scope>compile</scope>
</dependency>
```

# RECOGNIZING WHEN YOU NEED MESSAGING AND CLUSTERING

*Messaging* and *clustering* are two critical features of enterprise applications. Interestingly, messaging and clustering capabilities can stand on their own and enhance your applications independently, but they can also work hand-in-hand to improve the flexibility, reliability, scalability, and availability of your applications. In this chapter you learn about what each topic brings to the table individually and how to use them together with Spring Framework in a Java EE web application environment.

## What Is Application Messaging?

The term *messaging* can have a lot of meanings. When you communicate with your friends and colleagues using e-mails and text messages, you participate in messaging. If you use an instant messaging service such as Jabber, AIM, Skype, or Lync, that's messaging, too. Even signaling someone with Morse code is a form of messaging.

Application messaging, however, doesn't apply to any of these behaviors. *Application messaging* is the exchanging of information, usually regarding events, between disparate units of an application. Though some type of human interaction usually triggers the exchange of application messages, it rarely happens at the instruction of or to the knowledge of the application users. Application messaging is a crucial component of any large application. It enables parts of an application to notify other parts of the application about activities taking place, data changing, caches becoming stale, and any number of other events. Application messaging can potentially take many forms, but the most common are *Remote Procedure Call* (*RPC*) and the *publish-subscribe pattern* (*pub/sub*).

### Understanding Publish-Subscribe

In RPC, messages are exchanged by way of the *client-server paradigm*. A client connects to a server (perhaps with a persistent connection, or possibly once per procedure call) and executes a specified procedure (or method). In Java, this is more commonly known as *Remote Method Invocation* (*RMI*), which is really just the Java-specific native RPC protocol that uses interfaces and Java serialization.

In general, the problem with RPC and the client-server paradigm is that the caller (or client) must know something about the message recipient (or server). In a local sense (within the same running application) RPC doesn't even apply. A simple method invocation is the analog to RPC within a single running application. To understand how this can be problematic, consider a human resources management system that, at first, contains a simple database of employee data. A new component of the system needs to send a tax record to the local government when a new employee is hired, so the employee service is updated to call the tax record service. Now a payroll system needs to create a payroll entry for the employee, so the employee service is updated to call the payroll service. Also, the system needs an insurance component for managing employees on the group policy, so the employee service is updated once again to call the insurance service.

Before you know it, 10 or 20 system components all have hooks hard-wired into the employee service. Not only must the employee service have knowledge of these systems and how they work to call them, but also the tests for the employee service must provide mock implementations for all these components to test that they are properly called. As each of these systems interlocks with the rest, you discover you have created an inordinately complex system not unlike a ball of yarn, and pulling on the wrong thread to change a feature can unravel the whole thing. Yes, RPC has its purposes but not for application messaging in this nature.

Such a system is *tightly coupled*. To better understand the drawbacks of this pattern, apply it to your social networking activities. When you sign up for a social networking platform, you add "friends" to your account, and those friends in return add you to theirs. If you were to follow the same client-server paradigm, each time you update your status or post a link, you must send a message to each of your friends about it so that they see it. This can get out of hand quickly.

Actually, social networking is a perfect example of the publish-subscribe pattern. On Twitter, for example, users subscribe to other users. When a user publishes content, his subscribers are notified of that content automatically — he doesn't have to manually send the content to each of his subscribers. This system is *loosely coupled*. The publisher of the content doesn't care who is subscribed and doesn't need to know anything about its subscribers for them to receive his published content. The subscriber, likewise, doesn't need to know who is publishing a particular type of content. (It could be multiple sources.) A publisher may have zero subscribers or it may have hundreds of subscribers. This decouples the systems and makes them less complex (and easier to test).

A pub/sub system contains three roles: *publisher*, *subscriber*, and *broker*. The broker is responsible for maintaining a list of who is subscribed to which *topics* and dispatching messages to the appropriate subscribers when a publisher broadcasts content to a relevant topic, as shown in Figure 18-1. In the Twitter example, Twitter is the broker and you are both publisher and subscriber. When you subscribe to another Twitter user, you notify Twitter (by clicking the Follow button) that you want to subscribe to his content. When that user publishes a tweet, Twitter makes sure that it appears on the Tweets list on your Twitter homepage. By now you may realize that a pub/sub publisher may also be a subscriber (and often is). For that matter, there is no technical reason why a broker cannot also be a publisher and/or a subscriber (though that is less common). You can never have more than one broker, however, except when two or more brokers work together in a load-sharing or failover configuration that mimics one logical broker (a *broker cluster*).

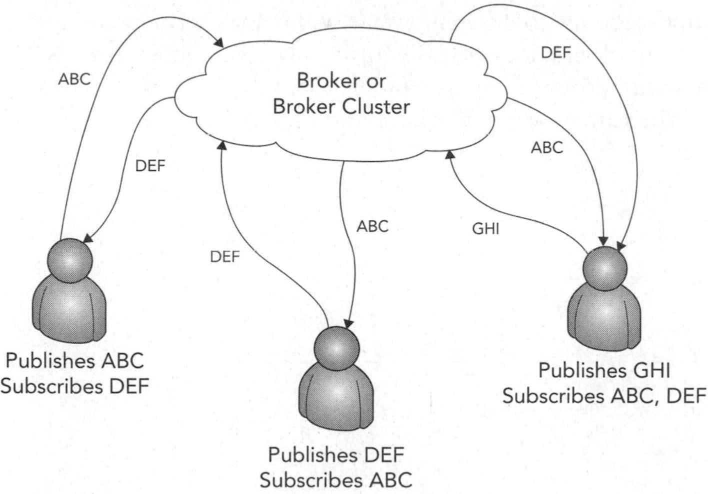


**FIGURE 18-1**

## Using Spring Framework's Application Events and Listeners

Without any special configuration, Spring Framework automatically acts as a message broker in a pub/sub environment. To publish messages, you call the `publishEvent` method on an instance of `org.springframework.context.ApplicationEventPublisher` and pass it an instance of `org.springframework.context.ApplicationEvent`. You can obtain an `ApplicationEventPublisher` in a Spring-managed bean either through dependency injection or by implementing `org.springframework.context.ApplicationEventPublisherAware`. With an `ApplicationEventPublisher` instance, you can publish as many events as you want as often as you need to.

Subscribing to events is equally easy. Given an event `FooEvent extends ApplicationEvent`, a Spring bean needs only to implement `org.springframework.context.ApplicationListener<FooEvent>` to subscribe to `FooEvent` messages. To subscribe to `BarEvent`, implement `ApplicationListener<BarEvent>`. You can create and subscribe to a hierarchy of events, too. For example, consider the following event definitions:

```
public class TopEvent extends ApplicationEvent { }
public class MiddleEvent extends TopEvent { }
public class CenterEvent extends TopEvent { }
public class BottomEvent extends MiddleEvent { }
```

Given this, a bean that implements:

- `ApplicationListener<ApplicationEvent>` subscribes to all events
- `ApplicationListener<TopEvent>` subscribes to `TopEvent`, `MiddleEvent`, `CenterEvent`, and `BottomEvent`
- `ApplicationListener<MiddleEvent>` subscribes to `MiddleEvent` and `BottomEvent`
- `ApplicationListener<CenterEvent>` subscribes only to `CenterEvent`
- `ApplicationListener<BottomEvent>` subscribes only to `BottomEvent`

Because Java does not permit you to implement the same interface more than once, even with different type arguments, you cannot subscribe to different events without subscribing to their common ancestor. This isn't always desirable, especially if the only common ancestor is `ApplicationEvent` — Spring comes with dozens of built-in events that are published for many different reasons at any given time. You can, however, work around this with the clever use of `@Bean` and anonymous inner classes:

```
@Service
public class FooService
{
    public void doSomething() { }

    @Bean
    public ApplicationListener<BarEvent> fooService$barEventListener()
    {
        return new ApplicationListener<BarEvent>()
        {
            @Override
```

```
                public void onApplicationEvent(BarEvent e)
                {
                    FooService.this.doSomething();
                }
            }
        }

        @Bean
        public ApplicationListener<BazEvent> fooService$bazEventListener()
        {
            return new ApplicationListener<BazEvent>()
            {
                @Override
                public void onApplicationEvent(BazEvent e)
                {
                    FooService.this.doSomething();
                }
            }
        }
    }
```

Of course, as powerful as this pub/sub support built in to Spring Framework is, it's local. It works only within a given Spring container or, more important, within a single JVM. In many cases, you need pub/sub to work across servers in a cluster, which begs the question, "What is clustering, exactly?"

## What Is Clustering?

Clustering has many meanings. Speaking strictly in terms of a definition, a cluster is a group of something. Use of the word cluster can refer to geology, biology, chemistry, astronomy, food, technology, and a number of other things. Houses can be built in a cluster, cities can be formed in a cluster, and people can gather in clusters.

In computer terminology, however, an *application cluster* is a group of two or more applications working together toward the same goal so that you can use them as a single system. Typically, this involves two or more physical or virtual servers running the same services and performing the same tasks, sharing a load evenly distributed among the servers. It can also involve two or more identical services running on the same physical or virtual machine in the same manner. For example, two or more Apache Tomcat installations can form a cluster whether they run all on the same server, all on different servers, or in some combination. What matters most isn't where these services live, but whether they are configured to work cooperatively on the same tasks.

### Understanding Distributable Java EE Applications

Strictly speaking, a Java EE web application is considered distributable as long as the `<distributable/>` tag is present in its deployment descriptor *and* in all `/META-INF/web-fragment.xml` descriptors in any JAR files packaged in its `/WEB-INF/lib` directory. If a JAR file does not contain a `web-fragment.xml` file, it is not considered a web fragment, so it doesn't count. If a single JAR with a `web-fragment.xml` lacking `<distributable/>` is present in an application, or if the deployment descriptor is lacking `<distributable/>`, the application is considered non-distributable.

This doesn't mean anything without understanding what, precisely, a distributable Java EE application is. The `<distributable/>` element indicates that the web application was written to deploy to multiple JVMs running on the same host or on different hosts. In almost all cases, this means that all attributes written to `HttpSessions` are `Serializable`. Containers are allowed to support non-`Serializable` session attributes in distributable applications, but they are not required to, and most simple Servlet containers do not. Tomcat, for example, throws an `IllegalArgumentException` if a `<distributable/>` application adds a non-`Serializable` attribute to a session. The point of using `Serializable` session attributes is that it permits `HttpSessions` to be shared among servers in a cluster, which is perhaps the most important reason for using `<distributable/>`. If two or more containers are configured to work in a cluster, they may share `HttpSession` data across the cluster only for distributable applications.

## Understanding HTTP Sessions, Stickiness, and Serialization

Why would you want to have `HttpSession` data shared across servers in a cluster? The answer to that is quite simple and boils down to the reasons you use a cluster to begin with: scalability and availability. A single server cannot service an infinitely increasing number of users. When a server fails, you want your users transparently shuffled to other servers. Because the majority of applications interact with users using sessions, it's important for that session data to be shareable across a cluster. This can serve two purposes:

- If a server fails, a user can be sent to a different server and that server will have all the same session data for the user that the failed server had.
- In an ideal world, consecutive user requests can be handled independently of which server receives the request, so a user's requests can conceivably be handled on different servers every time without losing session information.

For either of these scenarios to work properly, you must make your session attributes `Serializable`. Because Java objects cannot live beyond the confines of a single Java Virtual Machine, `HttpSessions` must be serialized before being sent to other servers in the cluster — whether over shared memory, a file system, or a network connection. This pattern presents two interesting challenges with solutions for both.

First, sometimes session attributes simply cannot be 100 percent `Serializable`. This is especially true for legacy applications that are upgraded and refactored. For example, a session attribute may (for whatever reason, however bad) hold on to a database connection or open file handle. These attributes obviously cannot be serialized and shared across the cluster — or can they? The `javax.servlet.http.HttpSessionActivationListener` interface specifies a special type of attribute that knows when it is about to be serialized and sent to other servers in a cluster or has just been deserialized on a server. Any session attribute that implements this interface is notified when it is about to be sent to other servers (via the `sessionWillPassivate` method) and when it has just been received from another server (via the `sessionDidActivate` method). In the aforementioned examples, a session attribute could re-open a database connection marked `transient` in `sessionDidActivate`.

A more common problem with clustered sessions is performance. For complete server independence to be possible, the server must serialize and share an `HttpSession` every time you update a session attribute *as well as* on every request (so that the `lastAccessTime` property stays up-to-date). This can present a real performance issue in some cases. (Although it still has a net benefit over using only one server.)

For this reason and others, the concept of session stickiness is an important consideration whenever you deploy a distributable application. How session stickiness is configured varies from one container and load balancer to the next, but the concept is the same: Within a single session, all that session's requests are handled in the same JVM. Sessions are serialized and shared across the cluster only periodically, as often as is practical by the performance standards set by the deployment team.

Sharing sessions less often can cause problems: Imagine having added several items to your shopping cart, and on the next request, the items are no longer in your shopping cart. With sticky sessions, you are always sent to the same server unless your session ends or the server fails, and the problem of session state inconsistency is mitigated. This is not without its downside. Server failures are not predictable, and sessions are rarely left in a consistent state when a failure occurs. When possible, it is always best to maintain session state across the cluster every time a session is updated.

## Configuring Your Container to Support Clustered Applications

The process of configuring application clustering varies wildly across Java EE application servers and Servlet containers. For example, if you install GlassFish Domain Administration Server (DAS), you can use the web applications on that server to automatically create and configure GlassFish clusters and nodes. Then all you have to do is deploy a `<distributable/>` application to a cluster, and GlassFish distributes the application to the cluster nodes with session migration activated automatically.

Conversely, Tomcat and most standalone Servlet containers are a little more complicated to configure. Out-of-the-box, Tomcat does not perform any application distribution. Two Tomcat servers running the same application are just that — two different Tomcat servers running the same application. They have no knowledge of each other and no way to share session data. You must first configure all the Tomcat servers in a cluster to recognize each other and coordinate session migration. You must then tell them *how* to share session data with each other — via TCP sockets, a database, or some other means.

You also have to set up load balancing across your Tomcat cluster nodes. You can achieve this in many different ways, but you usually approach it using one of the techniques shown in Figures 18-2 and 18-3.

In the first, more common scenario, a standard network traffic load balancer accepts requests inbound to your website's IP address and round-robins requests between two or more Apache HTTPD or Microsoft IIS web servers (refer to Figure 18-2). These web servers run a variation of the Apache Tomcat Connector — mod_jk for Apache or isapi_redirect for IIS. The Apache Tomcat Connector knows about the performance metrics of the Tomcat servers it is connected to and can route the request to the Tomcat server with the smallest load. This is a very valuable intelligent load balancing that is used in many enterprises across the world. It has some drawbacks, however — namely that it doesn't support WebSocket traffic (yet).

An alternative and equally viable solution is using the network load balancer to intelligently balance traffic between the Tomcat instances directly (refer to Figure 18-3). Although this load balancer cannot measure the performance metrics that the Apache Tomcat Connector can, good network load balancers can make very accurate performance measurements by issuing simple, periodic health-check requests and then measuring the relative time it takes each server to respond.

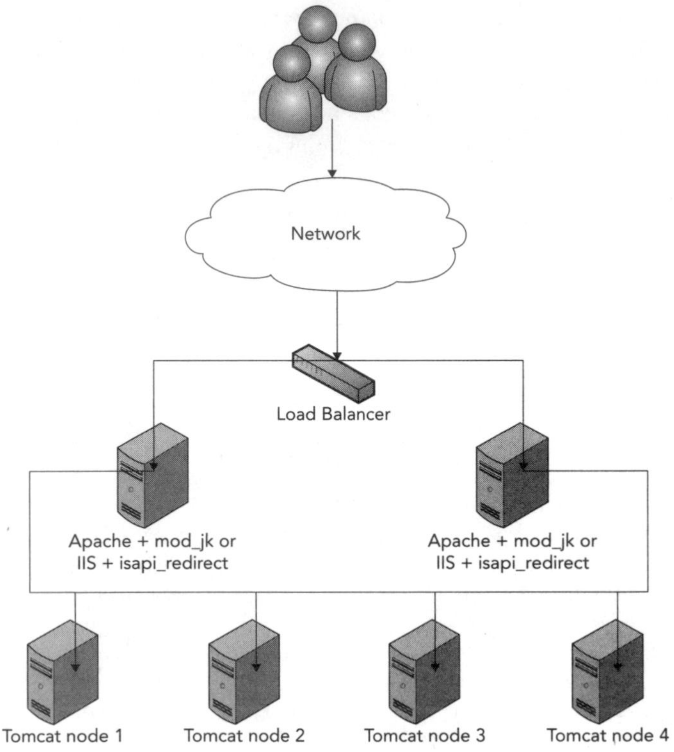


**FIGURE 18-2**

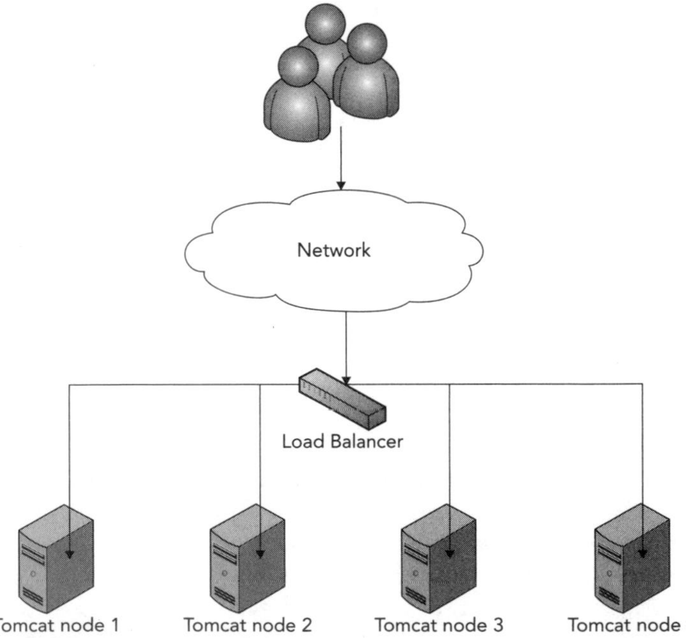


**FIGURE 18-3**

When you have your cluster nodes in place and your load balancing configured, you must configure Tomcat cluster communications and session migration. The simplest way to do this is to add the following element inside the `<Engine>` or `<Host>` elements in Tomcat's `conf/server.xml`:

```
<Cluster className="org.apache.catalina.ha.tcp.SimpleTcpCluster"/>
```

This activates the default session migration configuration. Nodes are assumed to always reside on different hosts (and can use the same ports) and announce themselves over the subnet multicast address. Sessions are transmitted over TCP connections established to all the nodes in the cluster. However, this is just the default, and you can customize many things about the cluster configuration. You can set it up to use a database or shared file system, and you can change the ports the clustering operates on. You can also adjust the algorithm that Tomcat uses to determine when to share sessions and with which nodes to share sessions. The process of configuring a cluster of two or more Tomcat servers is quite complex, and this book is not about Tomcat server administration. As such, this chapter does not walk you through setting up and testing a clustered Tomcat environment.

> **NOTE** *The load balancing techniques described here are also applicable to GlassFish clusters. In addition to supporting standard load balancing, GlassFish supports the mod_jk and isapi_redirect Apache Tomcat Connectors. Configuring cluster communications and session migration, however, is completely different.*

# How Do Messaging and Clustering Work Together?

As you may already realize, `HttpSession` migration across a cluster is useful but does not meet all the needs you may have when building a web application. Similarly, Spring's support for local messaging is powerful, but it lacks the capability to send messages to other nodes in a cluster. Some form of distributed messaging can meet the needs that are not met with `HttpSession` migration in `<distributable/>` applications.

## Identifying Uses for Distributed Messaging

To understand how a distributed messaging system should operate, you must first understand the possible uses for sending messages across a cluster. Why would you need such a system, and how could it benefit you? Here are just a few scenarios that can benefit from the addition of a clustered messaging system. With a little effort, you can probably think of others specific to your business needs.

- **Large applications often store settings for controlling application behavior in a database of some type.** Because the settings are usually numerous and frequently accessed, reloading the settings from the database on every request (or more often, if tasks run in the background) can introduce performance problems. On the other hand, caching the settings and refreshing them periodically can result in incorrect behavior on servers operating with a stale cache. With a distributed message system, the server that handles the request to update the settings can send a message to other servers in the cluster instructing them to clear their settings cache. Furthermore, you can tailor specialized messages to groups of settings so that a smaller number of cached settings are reloaded. You can apply this pattern to caches of all sorts, not just settings.

- **Different services may run on different servers in a cluster.** In cases in which this is desirable, services that want to subscribe to a particular topic must receive messages from across the cluster, not just locally.
- **Some tasks cannot start and complete within the confines of a single HTTP request.** You may start these tasks, such as data imports and exports, on a schedule or in reaction to a request, but usually they must be completed in the background. In these cases, it's often necessary to provide a way to check on the status of a background task. Distributed messaging enables all the servers in your application cluster to know the task's status so that a status-check request to any server can return a useful response.

## Recognizing Problems with Distributed Messaging

Distributed messages across a cluster may seem like the magic bullet at this point, but it's important to understand that it comes with its own set of problems. None of these problems are critical, and you can deal with them all so long as you understand them properly.

One common issue is the asynchronicity of messaging in a cluster. Of course, this is a drawback of the pub/sub pattern in general: Messages are published and then execution continues. There is no "reply" process in pub/sub. If you have a particular need for the send-and-reply model, RPC is better suited for this task — for that matter, any type of web service can meet this requirement as well as, sometimes better than, RPC. However, the asynchronicity issue is more exaggerated in a clustered environment. The same application usually receives and reacts to a message within milliseconds, but other applications in a cluster may not receive a message for whole seconds. This latency is something you should be aware of and plan for. Do not write your applications in such a way that they depend on these messages being delivered and handled quickly.

Another issue is deliverability. Messages sent within the same application are essentially guaranteed to be delivered to subscribers. Because of the short timeframes between message transmission and message delivery, it takes an extremely unusual situation (such as a JVM crash) to prevent message delivery. For that matter, in Spring Framework, the `ApplicationEventPublisher`'s `publishEvent` method does not return until all subscribers receive the message, so any code executed after this method can count on subscribers receiving the message.

Messages published to a cluster are a different story, however. Because of the latency involved in the publishing of cluster messages, this almost always happens in a separate thread. After you publish a message intended for the cluster from your code, you have no guarantee that any subscribers will receive it. Some systems do provide delivery receipts, but that's a different subject. Generally speaking, when using clustered messaging you should make your application robust enough that delivery failures are not critical.

## Understanding How WebSockets Can Help

In Chapter 10, you explored WebSockets and even experimented with using them to send simple messages between Servlets in a "cluster." In reality, these Servlets were in the same web application, but the implication was clear. WebSockets are a game-changing technology that can drastically simplify communication between applications in a cluster. Indeed, a WebSocket channel can serve as a channel for the delivery of application messages. You have two primary ways to use WebSockets in application messaging:

- **Your application can open WebSocket connections to every other application in your cluster and send messages over that connection.** The target code (Spring Framework) acts as the message broker and delivers the messages to the appropriate subscribers. This works well but depends on some kind of discovery mechanism — a common method is to use subnet multicast packets. When an application completes its startup process, it sends a packet to the multicast address and all applications listening for this packet receive it. Using the information in the packet, other applications in the cluster open WebSocket connections to the application that sent it. In this way applications can automatically recover from a failure simply by rebroadcasting the multicast packet.
- **You can use WebSockets to communicate with a message broker.** Such a pattern is specified in the *WebSocket Application Messaging Protocol* (*WAMP*, not to be confused with Windows-Apache-MySQL-PHP), which you can read about at `http://wamp.ws/spec`. In WAMP, the message broker resides within a different service (or on a different server). The logical broker may be a cluster of broker servers behind a load balancer. Applications open persistent WebSocket connections to the broker and send subscription requests and messages and receive messages over the connection. Spring Framework, in this case, is no longer the primary broker. Combined with Spring Framework you can implement this one of many ways. For example, you can use the broker to simply rebroadcast all `ApplicationEvent` messages and Spring's pub/sub support to deliver the messages to the right subscribers. Or you can use Spring's pub/sub support only for local messages and WAMP only for cluster messages, independently of each other. You could also forego Spring Framework's pub/sub support altogether and use WAMP exclusively. Which approach you take is solely up to you and largely depends on the needs of your application.

## Introducing Java Message Service 2.0 (JSR 343)

One older but industry-tested and reliable distributed messaging technology is *Java Message Service* (*JMS*). JMS was first specified in 2001 and updated with version 1.1 in 2002. It gained widespread adoption across the Java world and remained largely unchanged until JSR 343, which formalized JMS 2.0 in 2013. JMS 2.0 didn't introduce any significant conceptual changes; instead, it cleared up ambiguities in the specification, simplified the API while leaving the existing API for backward compatibility, added support for Java 7 `AutoCloseable` resources, and integrated more completely with the entire Java EE suite.

JMS supports several different messaging patterns but has first-class support for pub/sub with the concept of topics, publishers, and subscribers. JMS, then, acts as a message broker. One advantage of using JMS is the optional ability to place a message in a queue. The message then sits there until an interested consumer processes the message. When processed, the message is removed from the queue and no other interested consumers can process it. This process can be transactional, too, guaranteeing that a message is *never* marked processed until a consumer *successfully* processes it and that *exactly one* consumer successfully consumes the message.

It's important to understand that JMS is an API, not a protocol. JMS's standard API makes it simple to swap out the JMS provider with little or no changes to your code. However, the JMS standard specifies only a set of interfaces for the provider to implement, and the provider implements the underlying protocol however it likes. In fact, it's possible and even likely that different implementations cannot interoperate and share messages between them. This can have a lot of drawbacks, and for that reason, JMS is generally not the best choice if you anticipate your application ever having to communicate with other applications that are written against different providers or on different platforms.

You can integrate JMS with Spring Framework in many of the same ways that you can integrate WAMP, including making it operate exclusive to, independently of, and in cooperation with Spring's pub/sub support. Spring also has first-class support for JMS features, abstracting away some of the headaches associated with the 1.1 API. Unfortunately, JMS is difficult to use outside of a full Java EE application server (including Tomcat and standalone applications). For this reason, this book does not cover JMS in more detail.

### Introducing Advanced Message Queuing Protocol

The *Advanced Message Queuing Protocol* (*AMQP*) standard was formalized to solve the interoperability problems with JMS and other JMS-like specifications. Unlike JMS, which specifies a Java API, AMQP specifies a wire protocol for transmitting messages and enables providers to specify their own language-dependent APIs for using the protocol. This permits a multitude of applications written by different vendors on different platforms to use a common messaging protocol and communicate and collaborate with each other effectively.

The project began in 2003 with the goal of improving monetary transaction communications between financial institutions. AMQP 1.0 was released in 2011 and adopted as a standard exactly one year later. Though it originated in the financial services industry, it has gained widespread adoption across industries.

AMQP, like other standards, supports pub/sub as well as transactional message queuing and point-to-point (targeted) messaging. You can integrate it with Spring Framework using the same techniques as WAMP and JMS. Spring Framework does not have built-in AMQP support, but the Spring AMQP project provides the capability to seamlessly integrate AMQP messaging solutions into your Spring Framework application. You don't have to use Spring AMQP to work with AMQP messaging, however. This chapter covers using an AMQP broker and an AMQP Java client library for messaging in the "Distributing Events with AMQP" section.

## ADDING MESSAGING SUPPORT TO YOUR APPLICATION

Adding publish-subscribe messaging to an application is really easy with Spring Framework. One common use-case for this is to notify subscribers when users log in to or out of the application. The Publish-Subscribe project on the `wrox.com` code download site does just this. It contains the same Spring configuration you have progressively built over the last several chapters along with several events and listeners and a controller to publish events.

### Creating Application Events

If your application is going to publish and subscribe to events when users log in or out, it probably makes sense for those events to inherit from a common, authentication-related ancestor. An `AuthenticationEvent` forms a good basis for this.

```
public abstract class AuthenticationEvent extends ApplicationEvent
{
    public AuthenticationEvent(Object source)
    {
        super(source);
    }
}
```

The `LoginEvent` and `LogoutEvent`, then, extend `AuthenticationEvent` to form a hierarchy of authentication events.

```
public class LoginEvent extends AuthenticationEvent
{
    public LoginEvent(Object source)
    {
        super(source);
    }
}

public class LogoutEvent extends AuthenticationEvent
{
    public LogoutEvent(Object source)
    {
        super(source);
    }
}
```

The mysterious event source, mandatory when constructing the event, is anything you want or need it to be. The point of the event source is to identify the cause of the event, and that cause only has meaning in the context of the event's meaning. For example, an event published when an employee is added to a human resources system might have the employee entity or identifier as the source. Likewise, authentication-related events should probably contain the `Principal`, username, user credentials, or some other user identifier as the source of the event. With this in mind, the `LoginEvent` and `LogoutEvent` make more sense with a `String` username source.

```
public class LoginEvent extends AuthenticationEvent
{
    public LoginEvent(String username)
    {
        super(username);
    }
}

public class LogoutEvent extends AuthenticationEvent
{
    public LogoutEvent(String username)
    {
        super(username);
    }
}
```

## Subscribing to Application Events

Of course, the whole purpose of creating application events is so that interested parties can subscribe to and receive the messages. In fact, it's entirely likely that you will create events only on an as- and when-needed basis. After all, publishing thousands of different messages wastes effort and computer resources if nobody is listening for them. In this case, three different parties (pieces of program logic) are all interested in varying authentication messages. Why they're interested in these messages is unimportant; the publisher doesn't care — it just knows that it must publish them. The `AuthenticationInterestedParty`, for one reason or another, subscribes to all types of authentication messages.

```
@Service
public class AuthenticationInterestedParty
        implements ApplicationListener<AuthenticationEvent>
{
    private static final Logger log = LogManager.getLogger();

    @Override
    public void onApplicationEvent(AuthenticationEvent event)
    {
        log.info("Authentication event for IP address {}.", event.getSource());
    }
}
```

The `onApplicationEvent` method of this bean is called for any login *or* logout messages. The `LoginInterestedParty` and `LogoutInterestedParty` beans, however, subscribe only to login and logout messages, respectively.

```
@Service
public class LoginInterestedParty implements ApplicationListener<LoginEvent>
{
    private static final Logger log = LogManager.getLogger();

    @Override
    public void onApplicationEvent(LoginEvent event)
    {
        log.info("Login event for IP address {}.", event.getSource());
    }
}

@Service
public class LogoutInterestedParty implements ApplicationListener<LogoutEvent>
{
    private static final Logger log = LogManager.getLogger();

    @Override
    public void onApplicationEvent(LogoutEvent event)
    {
        log.info("Logout event for IP address {}.", event.getSource());
    }
}
```

All these beans perform the same simple action: When they receive events to which they are subscribed, they write messages to the log. Of course, you can do so much more with this action than log it. You could send notifications like e-mails or text messages or create or delete a record in the database, just to name a few.

Keep in mind that message delivery is performed synchronously with the publication method execution, so an action that takes a long time to complete can slow down message delivery to other subscribers and delay return of control to the method that originally published the message. If you have a message-handling action that you know, or reasonably suspect, may take a long time to complete, you should run it asynchronously in a separate thread. Thankfully, this is somewhere that Spring's asynchronous method execution can come in handy. An `@Async` `onApplicationEvent` method, like any other `@Async` method, hands off to Spring's task executor. The revised `LogoutInterestedParty` takes advantage of this feature.

```
@Service
public class LogoutInterestedParty implements ApplicationListener<LogoutEvent>
{
    private static final Logger log = LogManager.getLogger();

    @Override
    @Async
    public void onApplicationEvent(LogoutEvent event)
    {
        log.info("Logout event for IP address {}.", event.getSource());

        try
        {
            Thread.sleep(5000L);
        }
        catch(InterruptedException e)
        {
            log.error(e);
        }
    }
}
```

## Publishing Application Events

Now that you have created several events and beans that subscribe to those event messages, you need a way to publish events so that you can test this publish-subscribe support. The simplest approach is to just create a standard web controller that enables you to alternate between publishing the `LoginEvent` and `LogoutEvent`.

```
@WebController
public class HomeController
{
    @Inject ApplicationEventPublisher publisher;

    @RequestMapping("")
    public String login(HttpServletRequest request)
    {
        this.publisher.publishEvent(new LoginEvent(request.getRemoteAddr()));
```

```
            return "login";
        }

        @RequestMapping("/logout")
        public String logout(HttpServletRequest request)
        {
            this.publisher.publishEvent(new LogoutEvent(request.getRemoteAddr()));
            return "logout";
        }
    }
```

The `login` method publishes a `LoginEvent` and returns the login view name. Because this simple application lacks an actual authentication system, the controller uses the IP address of the request origin so that the event source can be properly demonstrated. The `/WEB-INF/view/login.jsp` view is quite simple, providing only a link to the logout action.

```
<!DOCTYPE html>
<html>
    <head>
        <title>Login</title>
    </head>
    <body>
        <a href="<c:url value="/logout" />">Logout</a>
    </body>
</html>
```

The `logout` method is nearly identical to `login`, publishing a `LogoutEvent` and returning the logout view name. `/WEB-INF/view/logout.jsp` links back to the login page. This way, you can pull up either page and quickly alternate between "logging in" and "logging out."

```
<!DOCTYPE html>
<html>
    <head>
        <title>Login</title>
    </head>
    <body>
        <a href="<c:url value="/" />">Login</a>
    </body>
</html>
```

Testing this pub/sub setup is easy.

1. Compile and start the application from your IDE and open your favorite browser.
2. Go to `http://localhost:8080/messaging/` and then look at the `application.log` file in Tomcat's `logs` directory. You should see log entries from the `AuthenticationInterestedParty` and `LoginInterestedParty` beans at the end of the log file.
3. Click the logout link in the browser, and log entries from `AuthenticationInterestedParty` and `LogoutInterestedParty` appear in the log tail. Notice that the log entry written in `LogoutInterestedParty` came from a different thread than the other entries. This is because of Spring's asynchronous method execution, which invokes the `@Async` method in a background thread so that message publication can continue quickly.

You can continue to click the logout and login links, and the code keeps on writing entries to the log file.

> **NOTE** *You may wonder about the terms* event *and* message *and how they are related. You can think about this many different ways, but put simply there's not really a difference, and this book uses the terms interchangeably. Spring Framework uses the word "event" largely because the system is based off Java's* `java.util.EventObject` *and* `EventListener` *concepts (which are used heavily throughout Java Swing). But the notion of triggering events and the notification of event listeners really isn't different from pub/sub messaging. It's all about how you use the tools, not what they're named. For that matter, application messages are, in all cases, published as a result of some type of event occurring, so the word "event" is a fair name for an object representing a message.*

# MAKING YOUR MESSAGING DISTRIBUTABLE ACROSS A CLUSTER

You're probably pleasantly surprised by how easy it was to add local pub/sub messaging to your Spring Framework application. Distributing this messaging across all application nodes in your cluster is a more complicated task. First you must pick a protocol that you want to use for sending messages. Next you must create a custom *event multicaster* to correctly distribute events using the chosen protocol. In Spring Framework, the multicaster (an implementation of `org.springframework.context.event.ApplicationEventMulticaster`) is the bean responsible for taking all published events and delivering them to the appropriate subscribers. Finally, testing is an interesting challenge because you can test distributed messages only by running two or more instances of the application.

In this section, you explore some of the basic event changes necessary to support distribution, and then you implement a WebSocket multicaster. This multicaster uses direct communication instead of a WAMP broker. As a result, the connections between nodes form a *complete undirected simple graph* — in a cluster with *n* nodes, each node has a degree of *n*–1 (meaning it has *n*–1 WebSocket connections because it connects to every other node in the cluster). This is demonstrated in Figure 18-4, which shows a four-node cluster.

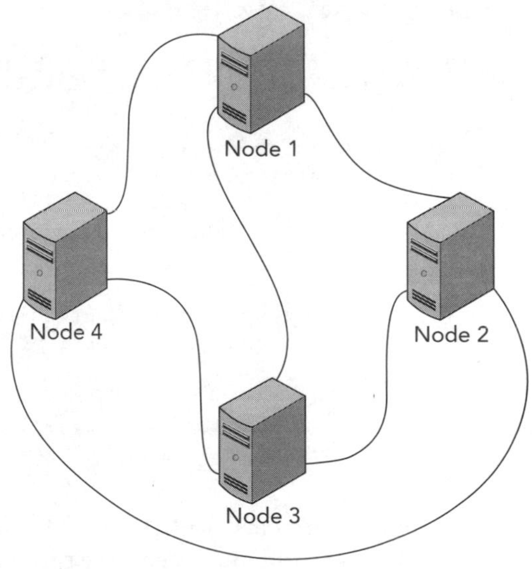


FIGURE 18-4

Of course, this pattern assumes you want to integrate Spring Framework's pub/sub messaging with your distributed messaging protocol of choice. This chapter does not cover how to use these tools independently. You can follow along using the WebSocket-Messaging project available for download from the `wrox.com` code download site. It is an extension of the Publish-Subscribe project you saw earlier.

## Updating Your Events to Support Distribution

Before you can start publishing events, you need to prepare them for distribution. But you must address a couple of problems with the standard `ApplicationEvent`.

First, `EventObject` (which `ApplicationEvent` extends) defines its source to be `transient`. This means that the source is excluded when the event is serialized. To eliminate this problem, you must ensure that the source is `Serializable` and then add some support to the event to properly deserialize the otherwise-transient value. The source can never be `null`; you will get `NullPointerExceptions` throughout Spring if an event has a `null` source.

Also, you need to put measures in place to stop events from repeatedly rebroadcasting. Because the multicaster ultimately re-multicasts events it receives from other nodes, it must know not to then rebroadcast those events back to the other nodes. Otherwise, the events will circle infinitely. A base `ClusterEvent` class can take care of these problems fairly easily.

```
public class ClusterEvent extends ApplicationEvent implements Serializable
{
    private final Serializable serializableSource;
    private boolean rebroadcasted;

    public ClusterEvent(Serializable source)
    {
        super(source);
        this.serializableSource = source;
    }

    final boolean isRebroadcasted()
    {
        return this.rebroadcasted;
    }

    final void setRebroadcasted()
    {
        this.rebroadcasted = true;
    }

    @Override
    public Serializable getSource()
    {
        return this.serializableSource;
    }

    private void readObject(ObjectInputStream in)
            throws IOException, ClassNotFoundException
    {
        in.defaultReadObject();
        this.source = this.serializableSource;
    }
}
```

The event implements `Serializable` so that it can be serialized. It defines a copy of `source` that is not `transient` and implements the special-purpose `readObject` deserialization method to copy the non-transient source to the original source after deserialization. It also overrides `getSource` so that users of the class know that the source is always `Serializable`. Finally, it adds a `rebroadcasted` flag to identify events that were already distributed across the cluster. The `AuthenticationEvent` in the WebSocket-Messaging project is different (from the event in the Publish-Subscribe project) in that it extends `ClusterEvent` (instead of `ApplicationEvent`) and takes a `Serializable` object as its source.

## Creating and Configuring a Custom Event Multicaster

The standard event multicaster, `org.springframework.context.event.SimpleApplicationEventMulticaster`, doesn't have any built-in support for message clustering. The `ClusterEventMulticaster` in Listing 18-1 extends `SimpleApplicationEventMulticaster` to implement special clustering behavior. The `multicastEvent` method executes the default behavior in the superclass and then, if the event is of type `ClusterEvent`, publishes the event to the cluster. This behavior is important because it means you can control whether a particular message type is local-only or cluster-wide by extending or not extending `ClusterEvent`. The `publishClusteredEvent` method sends the event to every endpoint registered in the multicaster.

You haven't seen `ClusterMessagingEndpoint` yet, but you take a look at that next. `registerEndpoint` and `deregisterEndpoint` deal with the registration of endpoints — added when a connection is opened and removed when a connection is closed. The `registerNode` method connects to another node via WebSockets (you'll see where this gets invoked soon), and `handleReceivedClusteredEvent` sets the `rebroadcasted` flag on an event before multicasting it. Finally, `shutdown` closes all WebSocket endpoints.

**LISTING 18-1:** ClusterEventMulticaster.java

```
public class ClusterEventMulticaster extends SimpleApplicationEventMulticaster {
    private static final Logger log = LogManager.getLogger();
    private final Set<ClusterMessagingEndpoint> endpoints = new HashSet<>();
    @Inject ApplicationContext context;

    @Override
    public final void multicastEvent(ApplicationEvent event) {
        try {
            super.multicastEvent(event);
        } finally {
            try {
                if(event instanceof ClusterEvent &&
                        !((ClusterEvent)event).isRebroadcasted())
                    this.publishClusteredEvent((ClusterEvent)event);
            } catch(Exception e) {
                log.error("Failed to broadcast distributable event to cluster.",
                        e);
            }
        }
    }

    protected void publishClusteredEvent(ClusterEvent event) {
```

*continues*

**LISTING 18-1** *(continued)*

```
            synchronized(this.endpoints) {
                for(ClusterMessagingEndpoint endpoint : this.endpoints)
                    endpoint.send(event);
            }
        }

        protected void registerEndpoint(ClusterMessagingEndpoint endpoint) {
            if(!this.endpoints.contains(endpoint)) {
                synchronized(this.endpoints) {
                    this.endpoints.add(endpoint);
                }
            }
        }

        protected void deregisterEndpoint(ClusterMessagingEndpoint endpoint) {
            synchronized(this.endpoints) {
                this.endpoints.remove(endpoint);
            }
        }

        protected void registerNode(String endpoint) {
            log.info("Connecting to cluster node {}.", endpoint);
            WebSocketContainer container = ContainerProvider.getWebSocketContainer();
            try {
                ClusterMessagingEndpoint bean =
                        this.context.getAutowireCapableBeanFactory()
                                .createBean(ClusterMessagingEndpoint.class);
                container.connectToServer(bean, new URI(endpoint));
                log.info("Connected to cluster node {}.", endpoint);
            } catch (DeploymentException | IOException | URISyntaxException e) {
                log.error("Failed to connect to cluster node {}.", endpoint, e);
            }
        }

        protected final void handleReceivedClusteredEvent(ClusterEvent event) {
            event.setRebroadcasted();
            this.multicastEvent(event);
        }

        @PreDestroy
        public void shutdown() {
            synchronized(this.endpoints) {
                for(ClusterMessagingEndpoint endpoint : this.endpoints)
                    endpoint.close();
            }
        }
    }
```

Configuring Spring to use your multicaster is simple: The `RootContextConfiguration` class defines an `applicationEventMulticaster` bean as follows. It's important that the bean name match the name used here for Spring to recognize it.

```
@Bean
public ClusterEventMulticaster applicationEventMulticaster()
{
    return new ClusterEventMulticaster();
}
```

## Using WebSockets to Send and Receive Events

`ClusterMessagingEndpoint` in Listing 18-2 is actually one of the simplest WebSocket endpoints you have seen so far in this book, but it's also unique in that it's annotated `@ServerEndpoint` *and* `@ClientEndpoint`. This is perfectly legal: After a connection is established, WebSocket clients and servers are identical in capabilities and responsibilities, so it's possible to write an endpoint that can serve as both ends of the endpoint.

The way this endpoint is written, each node has exactly one connection to every other node and messages pass in both directions across the connection. On open the endpoint registers itself with the multicaster, and on close it deregisters itself. When it receives an event message, it sends the event to the multicaster, and its `send` method is called from the multicaster to send events to the cluster. Its `Codec` uses standard Java serialization to send event messages over the wire.

**LISTING 18-2: ClusterMessagingEndpoint.java**

```
@ServerEndpoint(
        value = "/services/Messaging/{securityCode}",
        encoders = { ClusterMessagingEndpoint.Codec.class },
        decoders = { ClusterMessagingEndpoint.Codec.class },
        configurator = SpringConfigurator.class
)
@ClientEndpoint(
        encoders = { ClusterMessagingEndpoint.Codec.class },
        decoders = { ClusterMessagingEndpoint.Codec.class }
)
public class ClusterMessagingEndpoint
{
    private static final Logger log = LogManager.getLogger();
    private Session session;
    @Inject ClusterEventMulticaster multicaster;

    @OnOpen
    public void open(Session session) {
        Map<String, String> parameters = session.getPathParameters();
        if(parameters.containsKey("securityCode") &&
                !"a83teo83hou9883hha9".equals(parameters.get("securityCode"))) {
            try {
                log.error("Received connection with illegal code {}.",
                        parameters.get("securityCode"));
                session.close(new CloseReason(
                        CloseReason.CloseCodes.VIOLATED_POLICY, "Illegal Code"
```

*continues*

**LISTING 18-2** *(continued)*

```
                ));
            } catch (IOException e) {
                log.warn("Failed to close illegal connection.", e);
            }
        }

        log.info("Successful connection onOpen.");
        this.session = session;
        this.multicaster.registerEndpoint(this);
    }

    @OnMessage
    public void receive(ClusterEvent message) {
        this.multicaster.handleReceivedClusteredEvent(message);
    }

    public void send(ClusterEvent message) {
        try {
            this.session.getBasicRemote().sendObject(message);
        } catch (IOException | EncodeException e) {
            log.error("Failed to send message to adjacent node.", e);
        }
    }

    @OnClose
    public void close() {
        log.info("Cluster node connection closed.");
        this.multicaster.deregisterEndpoint(this);
        if(this.session.isOpen()) {
            try {
                this.session.close();
            } catch (IOException e) {
                log.warn("Error while closing cluster node connection.", e);
            }
        }
    }

    public static class Codec implements Encoder.BinaryStream<ClusterEvent>,
            Decoder.BinaryStream<ClusterEvent> {
        @Override
        public ClusterEvent decode(InputStream stream)
                throws DecodeException, IOException { ... }
        @Override
        public void encode(ClusterEvent event, OutputStream stream)
                throws IOException { ... }
        @Override public void init(EndpointConfig endpointConfig) { }
        @Override public void destroy() { }
    }
}
```

## Discovering Nodes with Multicast Packets

You now have a multicaster and WebSocket endpoint that work together to coordinate event broadcasting and multicasting. However, neither of these can initiate communications with other nodes without knowing where those other nodes are. This can happen one of two ways: configuration or discovery. Configuration is a simple concept: You place a properties or XML file in each application node that provides instructions that node uses to connect to all other nodes. You should be able to figure out this approach on your own.

Discovery is the more challenging and interesting technique, so it's covered here. The `ClusterManager` class in Listing 18-3 first starts listening on a multicast address for packets coming from other nodes. After the root application context starts, it begins periodically checking if the application's URL is publicly accessible. This is important: If it sends a broadcast packet before the application completely starts, other nodes might fail trying to connect to it. When it can access the application's URL, it sends a discovery packet to the multicast group announcing itself as joining the cluster. Nodes that are already running receive the packet and connect to the WebSocket URL in it. If other nodes start after this node, this node connects to the WebSocket URL in the packets it receives. This way, each node connects to all other nodes exactly once.

**LISTING 18-3: ClusterManager.java**

```
@Service
public class ClusterManager implements ApplicationListener<ContextRefreshedEvent>
{
    private static final Logger log = LogManager.getLogger();
    private static final String HOST= InetAddress.getLocalHost().getHostAddress();
    private static final int PORT = 6789;
    private static final InetAddress GROUP = InetAddress.getByName("224.0.0.3");

    private final Object mutex = new Object();
    private boolean initialized, destroyed = false;
    private String pingUrl, messagingUrl;
    private MulticastSocket socket;
    private Thread listener;
    @Inject ServletContext servletContext;
    @Inject ClusterEventMulticaster multicaster;

    @PostConstruct
    public void listenForMulticastAnnouncements() throws Exception {
        this.pingUrl = "http://" + HOST + ":8080" +
                this.servletContext.getContextPath() + "/ping";
        this.messagingUrl = "ws://" + HOST + ":8080" +
                this.servletContext.getContextPath() +
                "/services/Messaging/a83teo83hou9883hha9";

        synchronized(this.mutex) {
            this.socket = new MulticastSocket(PORT);
            this.socket.joinGroup(GROUP);
            this.listener = new Thread(this::listen, "cluster-listener");
```

*continues*

**LISTING 18-3** *(continued)*

```
            this.listener.start();
        }
    }

    private void listen() {
        byte[] buffer = new byte[2048];
        DatagramPacket packet = new DatagramPacket(buffer, buffer.length);
        while(true) {
            try {
                this.socket.receive(packet);
                String url = new String(buffer, 0, packet.getLength());
                if(url.length() == 0)
                    log.warn("Received blank multicast packet.");
                else if(url.equals(this.messagingUrl))
                    log.info("Ignoring our own multicast packet.");
                else
                    this.multicaster.registerNode(url);
            } catch (IOException e) {
                if(!this.destroyed)
                    log.error(e);
                return;
            }
        }
    }

    @PreDestroy
    public void shutDownMulticastConnection() throws IOException {
        this.destroyed = true;
        try {
            this.listener.interrupt();
            this.socket.leaveGroup(GROUP);
        } finally {
            this.socket.close();
        }
    }

    @Async
    @Override
    public void onApplicationEvent(ContextRefreshedEvent event) {
        if(this.initialized)
            return;
        this.initialized = true;

        try {
            URL url = new URL(this.pingUrl);
            log.info("Attempting to connect to self at {}.", url);
            int tries = 0;
            while(true) {
                tries++;
                URLConnection connection = url.openConnection();
                connection.setConnectTimeout(100);
                try(InputStream stream = connection.getInputStream()) {
```

```
                    String response = StreamUtils.copyToString(stream,
                            StandardCharsets.UTF_8);
                    if(response != null && response.equals("ok")) {
                        log.info("Broadcasting multicast announcement packet.");
                        DatagramPacket packet =
                                new DatagramPacket(this.messagingUrl.getBytes(),
                                        this.messagingUrl.length(), GROUP, PORT);
                        synchronized(this.mutex) {
                            this.socket.send(packet);
                        }
                        return;
                    } else
                        log.warn("Incorrect response: {}", response);
                } catch(Exception e) {
                    if(tries > 120) {
                        log.fatal("Could not connect to self within 60 seconds.",
                                e);
                        return;
                    }
                    Thread.sleep(400L);
                }
            }
        } catch(Exception e) {
            log.fatal("Could not connect to self.", e);
        }
    }
}
```

## Simulating a Cluster with Multiple Deployments

In a cluster, you normally have a single application deployed on two or more different Servlet container installations at the exact same context path (for example, `http://node1.example.org:8080/messaging` and `http://node2.example.org:8080/messaging`). In fact, if you want to share `HttpSession` data across session nodes you *must* do this; you cannot share session data between applications deployed at different contexts (for security reasons).

There are no shortcuts for testing session clustering. There is, however, a shortcut for testing clustered messaging: You can deploy the same application to the same server at multiple context paths. This is easy to do, but you must change a few logging statements so that it's obvious looking at the log file what's going on.

First, the `LoginEvent` and `LogoutEvent` publish in the `HomeController` using the context path as the event source instead of the IP address. This enables you to know which node an event originated from.

```
...
        this.publisher.publishEvent(new LoginEvent(request.getContextPath()));
...
        this.publisher.publishEvent(new LogoutEvent(request.getContextPath()));
...
```

Also, the `AuthenticationInterestedParty`, `LoginInterestedParty`, and `LogoutInterestedParty` use `@Injected ServletContexts` to log the context path for the application that receives the event as well as the context path for the application that sends the event (via the event source).

```
...
    @Inject ServletContext servletContext;

    @Override
    public void onApplicationEvent(AuthenticationEvent event)
    {
        log.info("Authentication event from context {} received in context {}.",
                event.getSource(), this.servletContext.getContextPath());
    }
...
```

You are now ready to test the distributed messaging. To start:

1. Make sure that the application is configured in your IDE to deploy to `/messaging1` on your Tomcat server.
2. Build the WAR file artifact, and copy the artifact from the project output directory to Tomcat's `webapps` directory, renaming the copied WAR file to **`messaging2.war`** in the process.
3. Start Tomcat from your IDE, and pay close attention to the log output. `/messaging2` probably starts first (depending on which IDE you use), and when it sends its multicast packet it is the only node in the cluster. No other nodes connect to it. `/messaging1` starts next and logs to the same file. When it sends its multicast packet, `/messaging2` receives the packet and connects to `/messaging1` using the WebSocket URL in the packet.
4. Open your browser and go to `http://localhost:8080/messaging1`; then look at the log file. You see a log entry with the message "Authentication event from context /messaging1 received in context /messaging1" followed shortly by another log entry "Authentication event from context /messaging1 received in context /messaging2." You also see the log entries "Login event for context /messaging1 received in context /messaging1" and "Login event for context /messaging1 received in context /messaging2." Click the logout link in the browser, and you see four similar log entries appear again notifying you about the logout.
5. Go to `http://localhost:8080/messaging2` and look at the log file again. This time the log entries are reversed: "Authentication event from context /messaging2 received in context /messaging2," "Authentication event from context /messaging2 received in context /messaging1," and so on. This means you are successfully using Spring Framework's pub/sub events and WebSockets to distribute messages throughout an application cluster.
6. If you feel really brave, shut down Tomcat and make another copy of the WAR file, naming it **`messaging3.war`**. Start Tomcat again and repeat the testing process, trying out the third URL as well.
7. When you finish testing, make sure you delete the `messaging`*`n`*`.war` files and corresponding `/messaging`*`n`* directories from Tomcat's `webapps` directory.

# DISTRIBUTING EVENTS WITH AMQP

Because you have lots of ways to implement distributed messaging in your applications, this book can cover only a limited number of them. In the previous section you explored using direct WebSocket connections, which formed a complete basic graph. The problem with this configuration is that it is not very scalable. It works well in small clusters, but the number of connections increases nonlinearly as the cluster size increases. If you took graph theory classes in school, you'll remember that the number of edges in a connected graph $K_n$ with $n$ vertices is $\frac{n(n-1)}{2}$. Although a four-node cluster may have only six total connections, an 8-node cluster has 28 total connections and a 16-node cluster has 120 connections. If you're running a cluster with hundreds of nodes, you're looking at tens of thousands of connections (hundreds per node). You should understand the scalability issue at this point.

Other messaging protocols such as WAMP, JMS, and AMQP are much more scalable because all messages in the cluster flow through a central broker. As a result, the configuration forms a *connected simple graph* that is 1-regular (each node has one connection) with the exception of the broker (which has $n$–1 connections), and the total number of connections equals the number of nodes minus the broker. This is demonstrated in Figure 18-5, which shows a six-node cluster with a broker. For high-availability and scalability, you can arrange multiple brokers in a cluster to form a single logical broker. This increases the total number of connections only slightly, if at all.

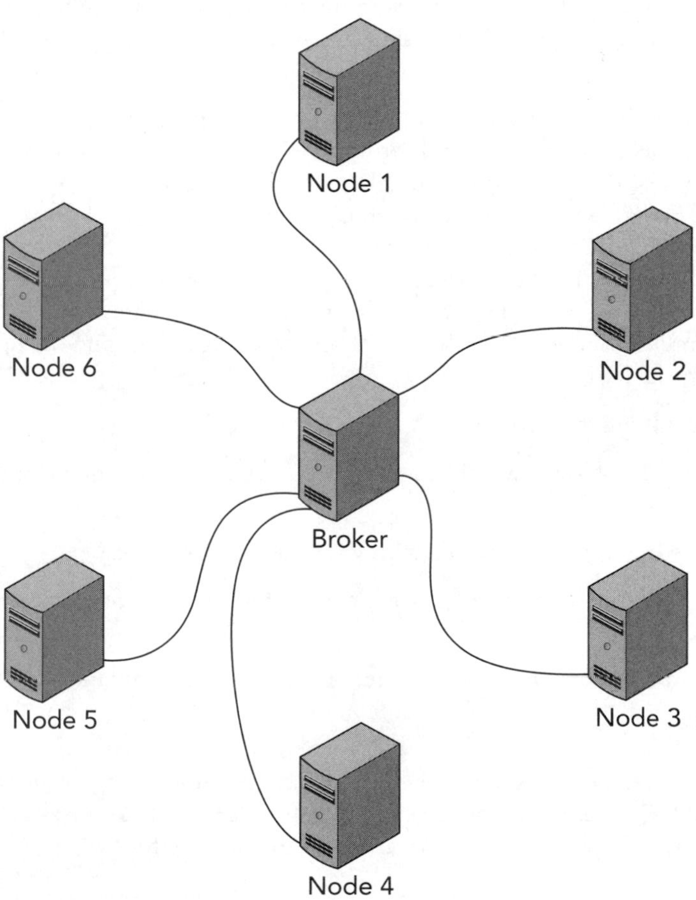


FIGURE 18-5

JMS is a natural selection for such a task in a Java EE environment. However, JMS is quite difficult to configure in a standalone application or in a Servlet-only container like Tomcat because it requires adding libraries to the Tomcat installation and changing the Tomcat configuration extensively to support them. Therefore, this section covers one way to use Advanced Message Queuing Protocol (AMQP) for distributed messaging in your application.

In this configuration, the broker does not manage multiple pub/sub topics. Instead, it simply delivers all messages to all nodes, and Spring Framework (acting as a local broker) delivers the correct messages to subscribers. You can alternatively use AMQP directly and independently of `ApplicationListeners` to manage pub/sub for multiple topics on the broker. Although this section does not cover the second option, it should be clear from the simple code samples how you can accomplish this.

## Configuring an AMQP Broker

Several different AMQP provider implementations are available to give you options when choosing an AMQP broker to use in your environment. By far the most popular and powerful implementation is RabbitMQ, a free and open source AMQP server that also provides paid, enterprise support when necessary. This section does not serve as a configuration and administration guide for RabbitMQ, but it does walk you through downloading, installing, and using it in its default configuration in less than 10 minutes.

RabbitMQ is written with and runs on Erlang, a concurrent programming language with garbage collection and a virtual runtime environment, similar to Java. (Though the syntax is vastly different.) Before you can install RabbitMQ you must download `http://www.erlang.org/download.html` and install Erlang. On most Linux distributions you can use the package management system, but on Red Hat/Fedora/CentOS systems you need to download it from the website. If you install on Windows, you also need to download `http://technet.microsoft.com/en-us/sysinternals/bb896655.aspx` and install `handle.exe` from Windows Sysinternals. (Place `handle.exe` somewhere in Program Files, such as `C:\Program Files\Sysinternals`, and then put that directory on the `PATH` system variable.)

After you install these prerequisites, follow these steps:

1. Download the server from the RabbitMQ website `http://www.rabbitmq.com/download.html`.
2. Click the Installation Guides link that corresponds with your operating system.
3. Install the server as directed. (For Windows, just run the executable and be sure to tell it to install the Windows service.)
4. If you installed RabbitMQ in a Unix environment, execute the following command:

   ```
   rabbitmq-plugins enable rabbitmq_management
   ```

   If you installed RabbitMQ in Windows instead, open a command prompt, change your current directory to the RabbitMQ `sbin` directory (for example, `C:\Program Files (x86)\RabbitMQ Server\rabbitmq_server-3.1.3\sbin`), and then execute the following command:

   ```
   .\rabbitmq-plugins.bat enable rabbitmq_management
   ```

This command enables the web management console, which is disabled by default.

5. If you installed RabbitMQ in Windows, open up Service Manager and restart the RabbitMQ service. On other operating systems, start or restart the service or binary as applicable.
6. At this point you should now be able to access RabbitMQ in your favorite browser at `http://localhost:15672/`. Log in with the username guest and the password guest, which are the defaults upon installation. If you cannot access the management console, check your installation steps again and consult the documentation to see where you went wrong.

That's all you need to do to get a basic RabbitMQ server up and running. In a production environment, of course, you would lock down security and fine-tune the configuration for performance.

## Creating an AMQP Multicaster

Creating an `ApplicationEventMulticaster` that uses AMQP to distribute events is simple. You can follow along in the AMQP-Messaging project available for download on the `wrox.com` code download site. This project is very similar to the WebSocket-Messaging project you looked at earlier, and it contains the exact same `ClusterEvent`. There is no `ClusterManager` or `ClusterMessagingEndpoint`. All the logic is contained within the `ClusterEventMulticaster` in Listing 18-4, which has a `multicastEvent` method identical to the one in WebSocket-Messaging.

**LISTING 18-4: ClusterEventMulticaster.java**

```
public class ClusterEventMulticaster extends SimpleApplicationEventMulticaster {
    private static final Logger log = LogManager.getLogger();
    private static final String EXCHANGE_NAME = "AMQPMessagingTest";
    private static final String HEADER = "X-Wrox-Cluster-Node";

    private final AMQP.BasicProperties.Builder builder =
            new AMQP.BasicProperties.Builder();
    private Connection amqpConnection;
    private Channel amqpChannel;
    private String queueName;
    private Thread listener;
    private boolean destroyed = false;

    @Override
    public final void multicastEvent(ApplicationEvent event) { ... }

    protected void publishClusteredEvent(ClusterEvent event) throws IOException {
        this.amqpChannel.basicPublish(EXCHANGE_NAME, "", this.builder.build(),
                SerializationUtils.serialize(event));
    }

    @PostConstruct
    public void setupRabbitConnection() throws IOException {
        ConnectionFactory factory = new ConnectionFactory();
```

*continues*

**LISTING 18-4** *(continued)*

```
            factory.setHost("localhost");
            this.amqpConnection = factory.newConnection();
            this.amqpChannel = this.amqpConnection.createChannel();

            this.amqpChannel.exchangeDeclare(EXCHANGE_NAME, "fanout");
            this.queueName = this.amqpChannel.queueDeclare().getQueue();
            this.amqpChannel.queueBind(this.queueName, EXCHANGE_NAME, "");

            Map<String, Object> headers = new Hashtable<>();
            headers.put(HEADER, this.queueName);
            this.builder.headers(headers);

            this.listener = new Thread(this::listen, "RabbitMQ-1");
            this.listener.start();
        }

        @PreDestroy
        public void shutdownRabbitConnection() throws IOException {
            this.destroyed = true;
            this.listener.interrupt();
            this.amqpChannel.close();
            this.amqpConnection.close();
        }

        private void listen() {
            try {
                QueueingConsumer consumer = new QueueingConsumer(this.amqpChannel);
                this.amqpChannel.basicConsume(this.queueName, true, consumer);

                while(!this.destroyed) {
                    QueueingConsumer.Delivery delivery = consumer.nextDelivery();
                    Object header = delivery.getProperties().getHeaders().get(HEADER);
                    if(header == null || !header.toString().equals(this.queueName)) {
                        ClusterEvent event = (ClusterEvent)SerializationUtils
                                .deserialize(delivery.getBody());
                        event.setRebroadcasted();
                        this.multicastEvent(event);
                    }
                }
            } catch(Exception e) {
                if(!this.destroyed)
                    log.error("Error while listening for message deliveries.", e);
            }
        }
    }
```

Most of the interesting work happens in the `setupRabbitConnection` and `listen` methods. `publishClusteredEvent` is one line of code, and the `shutdownRabbitConnection` method simply closes resources. `setupRabbitConnection` first establishes a connection to the `localhost` RabbitMQ server and then opens a channel. It then sets up an exchange called `AMQPMessagingTest` and sets the exchange to fanout mode.

> **NOTE** *An exchange is a mechanism for defining how messages are delivered to queues. Fanout mode means that all published messages get delivered to all queues. You can learn more about these topics, and channels, in the RabbitMQ documentation. Exploring them further is outside the scope of this book.*

Next, this method asks RabbitMQ to create a random queue (which is unique to this node) and bind the queue to the channel and exchange. The properties builder to which it creates and assigns the custom `X-Wrox-Cluster-Node` header is used when sending each message. That way, when the message is received, the node can ignore messages that it sent. Finally, it starts a listener thread to listen for incoming messages.

The `listen` method is responsible for receiving and multicasting messages delivered from RabbitMQ. It creates a consumer and binds the consumer to the channel and queue. The consumer then blocks on each call to `nextDelivery` until the next message arrives. The listener checks all received messages to ensure they came from different nodes (not from itself) and then deserializes and multicasts the event to the local application. Notice that the sample code uses Java serialization to deliver messages, which ironically means only Java applications can use messages in this environment. For your purposes here, this is okay. If you want to communicate with applications on other platforms, you could simply use a more portable format, such as JSON.

## Running the AMQP-Enabled Application

You can test the AMQP-Messaging application in the exact same manner that you tested WebSocket-Messaging:

1. Ensure that RabbitMQ is running.
2. Make sure that the application is configured in your IDE to deploy to `/messaging1` on your Tomcat server.
3. Build the WAR file artifact, rename it to **`messaging2.war`**, and copy it into Tomcat's `webapps` directory.
4. Start Tomcat for your IDE and the `/messaging1` and `/messaging2` applications should start up.
5. Navigate to `http://localhost:8080/messaging1` and `http://localhost:8080/messaging2` and alternate clicking the logout and login links. You should see identical log entries as when you tested the WebSocket-Messaging application. Again, you can also create and deploy a third WAR file named **`messaging3.war`** to try out a simulated cluster of three nodes.
6. With Tomcat running, go to the RabbitMQ web management console and click the Queues menu item at the top. You should see a screen like Figure 18-6, showing the random queues that RabbitMQ created for your application instances.
7. When you finish testing, make sure you delete the `messaging`*`n`*`.war` files and corresponding `/messaging`*`n`* directories from Tomcat's `webapps` directory.

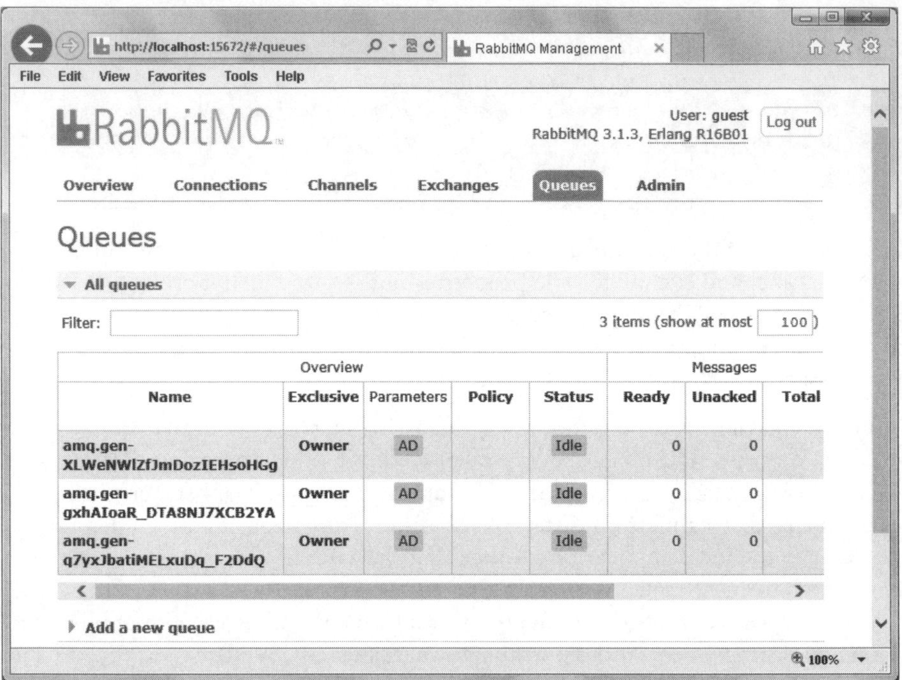


FIGURE 18-6

# SUMMARY

You have covered a lot in this chapter. You were introduced to the concepts and challenges of clustering Java EE web applications, and you learned about technologies and approaches that empower this important feature of any enterprise application. You explored the publish-subscribe messaging pattern and learned about how you can use Spring Framework's `ApplicationEvent` and `ApplicationListener` to implement publish-subscribe locally. You also learned about WebSockets, WAMP, JMS, and AMQP and how these technologies can all help you send application messages across a cluster. You experimented integrating Spring's application messaging and WebSockets to directly send messages between applications. You then explored some reasons that this configuration isn't very scalable. Finally, you learned how to install a RabbitMQ server and used it to broker AMQP messages using Spring's application messaging.

This concludes Part II of the book, which introduced you to Spring Framework and its most powerful features. In Part III, you learn about persisting application data to a database using the Java Persistence API and Hibernate ORM within a Spring application.

# PART III
# Persisting Data with JPA and Hibernate ORM

# 19

# Introducing Java Persistence API and Hibernate ORM

**IN THIS CHAPTER**

- Understanding data persistence
- What is an Object-Relational Mapper?
- Understanding Hibernate ORM
- How to prepare a relational database
- How to use the Maven dependencies in this Part

**WROX.COM CODE DOWNLOADS FOR THIS CHAPTER**

There are no code downloads for this chapter.

**NEW MAVEN DEPENDENCIES FOR THIS CHAPTER**

There are no new Maven dependencies for this chapter. Continue to use the Maven dependencies introduced in all previous chapters.

## WHAT IS DATA PERSISTENCE?

With few exceptions, every application needs persistence in some form or another. But what exactly is persistence? Put simply, *persistence* is making some form of data last across multiple executions of an application. In that sense, logging is a form of persistence because it persists diagnostic information about program execution so that you can analyze it while or after the application executes. Indeed, you can persist logging information to a flat file, an XML file, a JSON file, a database, or any number of other media, as is the case with all other forms of persistence.

Generally, however, persistence does not refer to logging. Instead, it refers to the saving of *entities* within the application to some storage media. Entities can be anything — people, users, tickets, forum posts, shopping carts, store orders, products, news articles, and more. The list goes on, and this entire book is not long enough to enumerate them all. In software development, an entity contains data but usually no logic of significance. Entities are passed between units of a program and encapsulate properties that the program uses.

In the Spring Framework applications you built in Part II of this book, your controllers created entities and handed them off to services to apply business rules, and then those services handed the entities off to repositories that stored the entities in memory using maps. Likewise, when your controllers received requests for one or more entities, they passed those requests on to the services that retrieved the stored entities from the repositories. In Java entities are POJOs; in C# entities are POCOs. Other languages have equivalent jargon for these data types.

An in-memory persistence map, however, is not sufficient in the real world. The data does not exist on every node in the cluster, and it disappears when the application shuts down. When considering how to persist data, you have many options and no one option is the "magic bullet." Every option is right for certain use cases. Nevertheless, there are some storage media that are more common or popular than others, for better or worse.

## Flat-File Entity Storage

A natural approach to entity persistence is to use the native file systems that the operating system provides. A likely scenario involves directories for each entity type, with each file in a directory representing a distinct entity named for that entity's *surrogate key* (*SK*). An SK is a unique identifier for an entity that enables you to individually locate it within the storage medium. As a filename, the SK acts as a sort of index so that the entity can be located quickly.

Data stored within a flat file can take many formats. It can be persisted as a Java serialized object (or serialized object of some other language) or represented using key-value pairs, XML, or JSON. The Java serialized form enables extremely efficient storage and retrieval but eliminates portability entirely. Only other Java applications can access the entity.

Either way, in general, flat file storage is extremely slow and difficult to manage compared to its alternatives. Each entity CRUD operation results in the opening of a file handle, immediate writing of data to the filesystem, and then closing of the file handle. The overhead from this is enormous and especially hinders entity location operations that involve more than just the surrogate key, such as searching on the properties of an entity. For this reason, flat-file entity storage is useful only for the smallest and most basic cases, such as application settings.

## Structured File Storage

Structured file storage is similar to flat-file storage in many ways. It uses the operating system's file system to store application data in files, and CRUD operations often result in the repeated opening and closing of file handles. However, instead of relying on directories and individual files to store entities, structured file storage systems often create large files that store many entities in one file using a predetermined structure that the program can understand. Instead of one directory per entity type, you often have one file per entity type. This has the advantage that search operations are much more efficient; they can be performed against a single file instead of many hundreds or thousands of files. However, individual lookups by surrogate key can suffer from such an arrangement. Often it is necessary to create a smaller index file of some type that makes it easier to identify the location of records within the larger data file.

If this sounds a lot like a relational database to you, you are correct. Many relational databases work in a very similar manner. Btrieve, one of the earliest databases of the sort, stored entities in files like this using the Indexed Sequential Access Method (ISAM) format. There are many differences between relational databases and structured file storage systems, however, namely that structured file storage tends to be proprietary and happen directly within the application code, whereas relational databases are based on a somewhat-portable standard and usually run within another application. More important, structured file storage is usually ignorant of the relationships between entities. The capability to relate different entities is a hallmark of relational databases. In this sense, Btrieve was a structured file storage system and not a relational database; however, it did have a concept of transactions common in today's relational databases.

## Relational Database Systems

If you're reading this book, you probably already know about *relational database management systems* (*RDBMSs*). In fact, you're going to have to know about them to read this and the next five chapters. Relational databases store entities as *records* in *tables*, and each table stores exactly one type of entity (though a complex entity may include data from multiple tables). These tables consist of a strict *schema* that defines the names, types, and sizes of the various fields or *columns*. You cannot store records in a table with columns that don't already exist, and you can also not store records in a table with `null` values for columns that are `NOT NULL`. Typically, a table contains a single *primary key* column (or, sometimes, several columns forming a composite primary key) that acts as the entity's surrogate key. You interact with relational databases using the ANSI standard *Structured Query Language* (*SQL*), a language designed to manipulate table schema and data content in a universal way.

Unfortunately, there are no relational databases that abide by the ANSI standard fully, and most also define their own proprietary extensions that aren't supported by other databases. For example, Oracle calls its SQL implementation PL/SQL, whereas Microsoft SQL Server uses Transact-SQL or T-SQL. This makes it difficult to create all but the most basic SQL statements that work across all databases, and nearly impossible to form `CREATE TABLE` or `ALTER TABLE` statements that work on more than one database.

> **NOTE** *It is a matter of great contention whether SQL is pronounced "sequel" or "es-kyu-el." This author prefers the pronunciation "sequel" for two important reasons. First, it's historically correct. When it was first developed in the 1970s, SQL was originally called Structured English Query Language (SEQUEL for short). However, SEQUEL was already trademarked, so it was shortened to SQL. Second, "sequel" is simply easier to say. Because you're reading this book and not listening to it, you can pronounce it however you like.*

In Java, you interact with relational databases using *Java Database Connectivity* (*JDBC*). You obtain a `java.sql.Connection` to a relational database, either using the `java.sql.DriverManager` or from some kind of `java.sql.DataSource` like a connection pool, and then you execute statements against that `Connection`. For simple statements that contain no parameters, you use the `java.sql.Statement`, and for complex statements that contain one or more parameters, you use `java.sql.PreparedStatement`. There is even a `java.sql.CallableStatement` for executing stored procedures and functions. These interfaces provide the capability to execute SQL statements against a database to query or manipulate data. Saving entities to and retrieving entities from a database involves mapping column names to POJO properties. This is the challenge that you tackle in this part of the book.

## Object-Oriented Databases

*Object-oriented database management systems* (*OODBMSs*), often just called object databases, are an attempt to solve the natural disconnect between object-oriented entities and relational databases. They use the same model of representing data that object-oriented programming languages do.

One principal of object databases is to store this data in such a manner that SQL can still be used to manipulate and retrieve objects. Unfortunately, this causes a number of problems due to object inheritance. Another approach involves storing JSON or XML within text columns in a database and using proprietary SQL extensions to query within that data, but the capability of indexing this data for efficient retrieval is minimal. The key problem with object databases is the attempt to maintain a strict schema. It is primarily for this reason that object databases have never really caught on, despite their having been around since the 1980s.

## Schema-less Database Systems

A schema-less database is, naturally, a database that lacks a strict schema. The term *NoSQL*, coined in 1998, is typically used to describe such databases. NoSQL databases are a relatively new phenomenon, having become popular only in the last 5 to 10 years. NoSQL databases solve a lot of problems not easily solved in relational databases, such as flexible fields and object inheritance. There are a number of different types of NoSQL databases, the most common of which are *document-oriented databases*.

Even though it lacks a strict structure, a document database encodes data in a consistent and well-known format, such as XML or JSON (or BSON, the compact, binary version of JSON). A *document* is roughly synonymous with a record in a relational database, and a *collection* is roughly synonymous with a table. Documents in a collection, though they must not adhere to a particular schema, are generally similar to each other. When two documents in a collection contain a property with the same name, best practices dictate that those properties are the same type and have the same semantic meaning.

Most document databases tend to have extremely fast insertion times, sometimes orders of magnitude better than relational databases. They are sometimes not quite as fast for indexed lookups as relational databases, but they can store data on much larger scales than can relational databases. Some document databases can store many hundreds of gigabytes or even terabytes of data without sacrificing insertion performance. This makes document databases ideal for storing logging- and auditing-related data. Some of the more popular document databases include MongoDB, Apache CouchDB, and Couchbase Server.

Another popular type of NoSQL database is a *key-value store*. It is much like it sounds, storing key-value pairs in a very flat manner. This can be likened to a Java `Map<String, String>`, though some key-value stores are multivalue and can store data more like a `Map<String, List<String>>`. Some popular key-value stores include Apache Cassandra, Freebase, Amazon DynamoDB, memcache, Redis, Apache River, Couchbase, and MongoDB. (Yes, some document databases double as key-value stores.)

*Graph databases* are NoSQL databases that focus on object relationships. In a graph database objects have attributes (properties), objects have relationships to other objects, and those relationships have attributes. Data is stored and represented as a graph, with relationships between entities existing naturally, not in the contrived manner created with foreign keys. This makes it easy, for example, to solve the degrees of separation problem, finding relationships between entities that might not have been realized at insertion time. Perhaps the most popular graph database is Neo4j. Though Neo4j is written in Java and despite its name, it can work on any platform. It is, however, very well suited for Java applications.

NoSQL databases do not operate on any type of standard like ANSI SQL. As such, there is no common way (like JDBC) to access any two NoSQL databases. This, of course, is a natural downside to using NoSQL databases, but there is an upside as well. Each NoSQL database comes with its own client library, and most of these client libraries can take Java objects and store them directly in the database in whatever format the database requires. This eliminates the task of mapping POJOs to "tables" and properties to "columns," and thus makes NoSQL an attractive alternative to relational databases for entity storage. Because the approach to every NoSQL database is different, and because NoSQL client libraries obviate the need for object-relational mappers, this book does not cover them further.

## WHAT IS AN OBJECT-RELATIONAL MAPPER?

To date, relational databases are the most common databases in use. You can find them backing nearly all major enterprise software, storing everything from entities to application settings to auditing records. However, storing object-oriented entities in a relational database is often not a simple feat and requires a great deal of repetitive code and conversion between data types. *Object-relational mappers*, or *O/RMs*, were created to solve this problem. An O/RM persists entities in and retrieves entities from relational databases without the programmer having to write SQL statements and translate entity properties to statement parameters and result set columns to entity properties.

This chapter and the next five cover object-relational mappers and how to use them to persist entities in your application. Before you can truly recognize how an O/RM can help, you need to understand the problem.

### Understanding the Problem of Persisting Entities

To understand the scale of the code necessary to persist and retrieve persisted entities, consider the following repository method, which retrieves a product record from the database and copies its data to a hypothetical `Product` object.

```
public Product getProduct(long id) throws SQLException
{
    try(Connection connection = this.getConnection();
        PreparedStatement s = connection.prepareStatement(
                "SELECT * FROM dbo.Product WHERE productId = ?"
        ))
    {
        s.setLong(1, id);
        try(ResultSet r = s.executeQuery())
        {
            if(!r.next())
                return null;

            Product product = new Product(id);
            product.setName(r.getNString("Name"));
            product.setDescription(r.getNString("Description"));
            product.setDatePosted(r.getObject("DatePosted", Instant.class));
            product.setPurchases(r.getLong("Purchases"));
            product.setPrice(r.getDouble("Price"));
            product.setBulkPrice(r.getDouble("BulkPrice"));
            product.setMinimumUnits(r.getInt("MinimumUnits"));
            product.setSku(r.getNString("Sku"));
            product.setEditorsReview(r.getNString("EditorsReview"));

            return product;
        }
    }
}
```

As you well know, there are some things missing from this picture. For one, this method has no error handling, which in reality is needed. Also, store products generally have many more properties than this — the code here is very conservative. This method could easily be many times the length that it is. Then there's creating a new `Product`:

```
public void addProduct(Product product) throws SQLException
{
    try(Connection connection = this.getConnection();
        PreparedStatement s = connection.prepareStatement(
                "INSERT INTO dbo.PRODUCT (Name, Description, DatePosted," +
                        "Purchases, Price, BulkPrice, MinimumUnits, Sku," +
                        "EditorsReview) VALUES (?, ?, ?, ?, ?, ?, ?, ?, ?)",
                new String[] { "ProductId" }
        ))
    {
        s.setNString(1, product.getName());
        s.setNString(2, product.getDescription());
        s.setObject(3, product.getDatePosted(), JDBCType.TIMESTAMP);
        s.setLong(4, product.getPurchases());
        s.setDouble(5, product.getPrice());
        s.setDouble(6, product.getBulkPrice());
        s.setInt(7, product.getMinimumUnits());
        s.setNString(8, product.getSku());
        s.setNString(9, product.getEditorsReview());

        if(s.executeUpdate() != 1)
```

```
                throw new SaveException("Failed to insert record.");

            try(ResultSet r = s.getGeneratedKeys())
            {
                if(!r.next())
                    throw new SaveException("Failed to retrieve product ID.");
                product.setProductId(r.getLong("ProductId"));
            }
        }
    }
```

And, of course, you must also provide methods for updating and deleting products. (Though, arguably, the delete method is vastly easier to implement.)

These methods may not seem awful on their own, but consider a more complex product entity, and then start thinking about product reviews, shopping carts, orders, shipping, searching, users, store administration, discounts and coupons, merchants (if you allow your users to sell their own products), payments, refunds, and more. An online store could easily have many dozens or even hundreds of different entities, each with code very similar to this, each requiring a lot of SQL and use of `Statements` and `ResultSets`.

No doubt, before you were done with it you would likely begin to write your own set of utilities to make this task easier. Likely this utility would involve some form of reflection so that it could handle any entity type. So if this tool were already written for you, and already tested extensively by a community of users, wouldn't that be easier?

## O/RMs Make Entity Persistence Easier

A good O/RM can greatly simplify this long, tedious code that's vulnerable to typos and hard to unit test effectively. O/RMs use reflection to analyze entities and line up their properties to the columns of the relational database tables they are stored in. Using an O/RM, the previous code becomes something more like this:

```
public Product getProduct(long id)
{
    return this.getCurrentTransaction().get(Product.class, id);
}

public void addProduct(Product product)
{
    this.getCurrentTransaction().persist(product);
}
```

Even better, adding methods to update and delete products is just as easy, and far easier than using straight JDBC:

```
public void updateProduct(Product product)
{
    this.getCurrentTransaction().update(product);
}

public void deleteProduct(Product product)
{
    this.getCurrentTransaction().delete(product);
}
```

As you can see, this code is much more palatable. In fact, if you're clever you could even make it generic to an extent so that you could write this code in an abstract class and use it for any class. Of course, that's not all there is to it. An O/RM can't just "know" what tables and columns to map an entity or entities to, nor can it always know how the data types should line up. (Although, often it can figure out a great deal of this information on its own.) When using an O/RM, you must create formal mapping instructions telling the O/RM how to map your entities. This can take many different forms depending on which O/RM you use, which is kind of a problem. After you create dozens or hundreds of entity mappings using the proprietary format of a particular O/RM, it becomes extremely difficult to switch to another O/RM at any given point in the future. There could be all kinds of reasons to switch to another O/RM: Perhaps you need a feature that a different O/RM offers, or you discovered that the O/RM you use doesn't perform well and you want one that performs better. Either way, significant work would be required to switch to a different O/RM.

There are some other consequences of using O/RMs that some consider problematic. For one, the high level of abstraction that comes with using an O/RM can make it hard to understand what happens behind the scenes. What happens when you call the `persist` method to persist an entity to the database? You know that the entity gets inserted into the table, but is that enough? Should you know more?

Many argue yes, and to an extent they are right. It's important to understand how an O/RM works to some degree because, if it's generating poor SQL statements, it could result in bad application performance. But there's certainly no reason to understand the exact inner workings of an O/RM. You can always perform load testing against an O/RM to ensure its performance is adequate, and you can set up statement logging on your database server to analyze the statements it generates for acceptable quality.

In addition, O/RMs are often cited as a reason for poor database design decisions, and perhaps that's correct. But does it matter? Well, that depends. First, if you use your database for some means other than merely as persistence storage (for example, as a data warehouse), of course design matters. However, if your database's only purpose is storing the data for your application, it is a means to an end, nothing more. As long as it works and works well, it's not necessarily bad that the database tables aren't pretty. Of course, both of these statements ignore a simple fact: You create the database. It's true that many O/RMs can generate table schema automatically based on your mapping instructions, but this should never be used in a production environment. You should always create the tables and columns yourself. If your database is poorly designed, it is your doing, not the fault of the O/RM.

In the end, only you can make the decision about whether an O/RM is applicable to your use cases, but in most cases the benefits far outweigh the drawbacks.

## JPA Provides a Standard O/RM API

One of the earliest O/RMs was TopLink, developed for Smalltalk in the early 1990s. Its developers, The Object People (hence the "Top" in TopLink), released TopLink for Java in 1998, and in 2002 Oracle Corporation purchased TopLink for Oracle Fusion Middleware. Over the course of many years and code donations to Sun Microsystems and eventually Eclipse Foundation, TopLink became

EclipseLink. (However, TopLink still exists today as an Oracle product.) In addition to mapping objects to relational databases, TopLink and EclipseLink can also map objects to XML documents.

Another O/RM, iBATIS, started in 2002 and continued as an Apache Software Foundation project until 2010, when it was retired and replaced with MyBatis at Google Code. iBATIS was written for Java, .NET, and Ruby, and MyBatis for Java and .NET. Hibernate ORM, perhaps one of the most popular Java O/RMs, started in 2001 and has evolved significantly. Its *Hibernate Query Language* (*HQL*) closely resembles SQL but is used for querying entities instead of tables. NHibernate is a .NET port of Hibernate ORM, bringing similar features to the .NET platform.

The problem with having so many different O/RMs is flexibility. An application written to use Hibernate, for example, cannot easily be changed to use EclipseLink or MyBatis without significant refactoring of the domain layer. The Java Persistence API was created to solve this problem and provide a standard API for Java object persistence in relational databases using O/RM technology. Programming solely against the Java Persistence API allows you to switch out O/RM implementations with minimal effort when the need arises.

JPA 1.0 was standardized in 2006 under JSR 220 as part of the Java EE 5 umbrella. It unified the Java Data Objects (JDO) API and the EJB 2.0 Container Managed Persistence (CMP) API and included many features inspired by or based on TopLink and Hibernate ORM. It also defined the *Java Persistence Query Language* (*JPQL*), a query language nearly identical to HQL. It had some drawbacks, however:

- It lacked a standard way to lookup objects based on complex criteria without using JPQL. Because many developers preferred a pure Java approach without a query language, they often used provider-specific features such as Hibernate's `Criteria`.
- One of the core principles of JPA is the ability to transform the limited set of SQL data types to Java data types such as the primitives and their wrappers, `Strings`, `Enums`, `Dates`, `Calendars`, and more. JPA specified a limited set of data type transformations that all implementations must support but unfortunately provided no way to define custom converters to handle other data types. Some implementations support additional data types (for example, Hibernate ORM supports all the Joda Time types), but relying on that ties you to a particular implementation. Implementations also often provided a way to specify your own custom data types, but that still ties you to a particular implementation.
- JPA 1.0 lacked support for collections of entities within other entities, multiple levels of nested entities, and ordered lists.

JSR 317 standardized JPA 2.0 in 2009 as part of Java EE 6 and added better support for collections of entities, nested entities, and ordered lists. It also added support for automatically generating database schema based on the defined entities and integrating with the Bean Validation API. Perhaps most important, it added a standard criteria API that enables pure Java entity lookup without the use of JPQL. Unfortunately, it still lacked support for custom data type conversion, causing many developers to continue relying on proprietary implementation features such as Hibernate's `UserType`. JPA 2.1 finally satisfied this need for custom data types. Part of Java EE 7, JPA 2.1 was standardized with JSR 338 in 2013. In addition to custom data types, it included enhancements to JPQL, support for stored procedures, and improvements to the JPA 2.0 criteria API to support bulk update and delete operations.

Sun's GlassFish application server contained the reference implementation of JPA 1.0, based on the code donated from Oracle's TopLink. After JPA 1.0 Sun donated the code to Eclipse, and TopLink became EclipseLink. Despite Hibernate's overwhelming popularity, EclipseLink was chosen as the reference implementation for JPA 2.0 and 2.1. BatooJPA, DataNucleus, EclipseLink, Hibernate ORM, ObjectDB, Apache OpenJPA, IBM WebSphere, and Versant JPA are just some of the JPA 2.0 providers. As of this writing, only EclipseLink, DataNucleus, and Hibernate have released JPA 2.1 implementations.

> **NOTE** *JPA implementations use JDBC for executing SQL statements, but you will never have to deal with this detail. You will always use the Java Persistence API, never the JDBC API directly.*

## Why Hibernate ORM?

In this book you use Hibernate ORM as the JPA implementation for your sample projects. This may seem curious, as Hibernate is neither the original Java O/RM nor the JPA reference implementation — both of those titles belong to EclipseLink. However, Hibernate is a very mature and stable project with a large support community and thousands of how-to articles online. You can easily get help with Hibernate when you need to, but the global knowledge base for EclipseLink is simply not as extensive. (Hibernate is also what this author knows best.)

Hibernate ORM also supports lazy loading of collections without having to manipulate the bytecode of your entities. EclipseLink, on the other hand, must weave bytecode decorations into your entities to achieve this, and that can be tricky to configure. The good news is that you do not have to use Hibernate just because this book does. You will be working with the Java Persistence API, so you can easily switch to a different JPA implementation whenever you like.

# A BRIEF LOOK AT HIBERNATE ORM

The next several chapters focus on using the Java Persistence API for persisting entities in your applications. You will not use the implementation provider (Hibernate ORM) API directly. In fact, the provider libraries you use in this book have a runtime scope in the Maven file, preventing you from using them directly. However, there are times when using the provider API is necessary, as discussed in the previous section. Though continued improvements to the JPA standard make this less and less likely, you need to understand the libraries you use. As such, this section introduces you to Hibernate ORM and how it works outside of the scope of JPA.

## Using Hibernate Mapping Files

Recall from the previous section that, before you can persist an entity using an O/RM, you must first define a mapping of that entity's fields to the corresponding relational database columns. When you use JPA for this, you always use annotations to map an entity. Between Hibernate ORM 3.0 and 3.5 you could use proprietary Hibernate annotations modeled after the JPA annotations to map an entity through the separate Hibernate Annotations project. Since Hibernate ORM 3.5, the proprietary annotations have been bundled with the Hibernate core library, and Hibernate has also supported the JPA annotations. Prior to Hibernate 3.0, however, you were required to use XML mapping files using the Hibernate Mapping XML schema. These files have the extension `.hbm.xml` and contain instructions that tell Hibernate how to save entities to and retrieve entities from a relational database. You can still use XML mappings today if you prefer, but only if you use Hibernate ORM directly, without JPA.

Hibernate XML mapping files always contain the `<hibernate-mapping>` root element. Within that, one or more `<class>` elements indicate mappings given class names and the tables they map to. Though it is possible to include multiple mappings within a single mapping file by using multiple `<class>` elements, the best practice is to use one file per entity, with the file named after the class. For example, the mapping file for the `Product` class would be `Product.hbm.xml`. It is also best practice to include the mapping files alongside your entity classes in the package structure (in the resources directory), so the mapping file for `com.wrox.entities.Product` would be `com/wrox/entities/Product.hbm.xml`.

Within a `<class>` element, the `<id>` element specifies a single-column, single-field surrogate key, whereas the mutually exclusive `<composite-id>` element specifies a multi-column, multi-field surrogate key. One or more `<property>` elements map class fields to database columns. For most use cases the mapping can be completely represented using attributes of `<property>`, but for more complex use cases, you may need to use the nested `<column>` element.

> **NOTE** *You may have noticed this section referring to mapping entity "fields" to database columns. In this case the word "field" refers to a JavaBean property (an instance field with an accessor and a mutator). In both JPA and Hibernate ORM, all mapped fields must be JavaBean properties by default. (However, you can specify different behavior.) The field name is determined by removing the "get" or "is" prefix from the getter and converting the first character to lowercase. (The field name is* not *determined by examining the backing instance field.) Contrary to what it may sound like when called "field," JPA and Hibernate entity fields do not need backing instance fields. A matching getter and setter are sufficient to qualify as an entity field.*

If you continue with the product example, creating a mapping for the `Product` class is pretty simple:

```
<?xml version="1.0" encoding="UTF-8" ?>
<!DOCTYPE hibernate-mapping PUBLIC "-//Hibernate/Hibernate Mapping DTD 3.0//EN"
                "http://www.hibernate.org/dtd/hibernate-mapping-3.0.dtd">
<hibernate-mapping>
    <class name="com.wrox.entities.Product" table="Product" schema="dbo">
        <id name="productId" column="ProductId" type="long" unsaved-value="0">
            <generator class="identity" />
        </id>
        <property name="name" column="Name" type="string" length="60" />
        <property name="description" column="Description" type="string"
                  length="255" />
        <property name="datePosted" column="DatePosted"
                  type="java.time.Instant" />
```

```
            <property name="purchases" column="Purchases" type="long" />
            <property name="price" column="Price" type="double" />
            <property name="bulkPrice" column="BulkPrice" type="double" />
            <property name="minimumUnits" column="MinimumUnits" type="int" />
            <property name="sku" column="Sku" type="string" length="12" />
            <property name="editorsReview" column="EditorsReview" type="string"
                    length="2000" />
        </class>
    </hibernate-mapping>
```

Most of this should be fairly self-explanatory. The `productId` field is mapped to the `ProductId` column and uses identity generation (`IDENTITY` columns in Microsoft SQL Server, `AUTO_INCREMENT` columns in MySQL, and so on). The other properties are all simple fields mapped to simple columns. You could also create `<map>`, `<list>`, and `<set>` properties, and use elements like `<one-to-many>` and `<many-to-one>` to associate entities with each other. There are dozens of pages' worth of mapping examples and instructions in the Hibernate ORM 4.3 user manual `http://docs.jboss.org/hibernate/orm/4.3/manual/en-US/html/`. Because you use only JPA mappings in this book, no further examples are covered here.

## Understanding the Session API

The primary unit for performing work within Hibernate ORM is the `org.hibernate.Session` interface. A Hibernate `Session` is nothing like an `HttpSession` or a WebSocket `Session`. Hibernate `Session`s represent the life of a transaction from start to finish. Depending on how your application is architected, that might be less than a second or several minutes; and in a web application, it could be one of several transactions in a request, a transaction lasting an entire request, or a transaction spanning multiple requests. A `Session`, which is *not* thread-safe and must be used only in one thread at a time, is responsible for managing the state of entities.

When an entity is retrieved from the database, it is attached to the `Session` and remains part of the `Session` until the `Session` (and its transaction) ends. This way, certain properties of an entity can be loaded in a lazy manner, as long as they are accessed during the life of the `Session`. Likewise, when an entity is added or updated, those changes are also attached to the `Session`, and when an entity is deleted from the database, it is removed from the `Session`. As you'll learn later, this is very similar to how JPA's `EntityManager` works.

Finding an entity by its surrogate key is simple using the `get` method on a `Session` instance:

```
return (Product)session.get(Product.class, id);
```

If the specified product does not exist, `get` simply returns `null`. To add a new entity, pass it to the `save` method.

```
session.save(product);
```

This method returns the generated ID of the entity being added; though you don't usually need to use the returned value. After calling this method, the ID property of the entity you passed in to the method will have been updated with the generated ID. An alternative to `save` is `persist`, which also adds a new entity. The key difference is that `persist` is safer: It will never result in an `INSERT` if the transaction has already closed, whereas `save` *will* result in an extra-transaction insert. As such, persist is usually the preferred method. However, the INSERT triggered by persist isn't guaranteed to execute until flush time, so persist does not return the generated ID, and the entity's ID property may or may not have been set when persist completes. If you need the ID right away, you should flush the Session after saving the entity:

```
session.persist(product);
session.flush();
```

Flushing a Session simply causes any pending statements to execute immediately; it does not end the transaction. As such, you may call flush as many times as you need during the life of a Session. Closing a Session or committing its transaction automatically flushes the Session. The reasoning behind flushing Sessions lies in how Hibernate queues statements. In a transaction involving more than one action, the actions might not actually execute in the order you specify. At flush time, all actions since the last flush are executed in the following order:

- All entity insertions in the order you added them
- All entity updates in the order you updated them
- All collection deletions in the order you deleted them
- All collection element insertions, updates, and deletions in the order you executed them
- All collection insertions in the order you added them
- All entity deletions in the order you deleted them

As such, if you need to guarantee that an action or actions execute before some other action or actions, you must call flush between them. The only exception is save, which always executes an INSERT immediately regardless of flushing. (But remember, persist is subject to flushing.)

> **WARNING** *Flushing affects only the writing of* Session *changes to the database. The changes you make to a* Session *are reflected immediately in memory. Be careful with this behavior because it can be the source of many mix-ups.*

Updating an entity is a little tricky to understand. You could use the update method, as in the following snippet:

```
session.update(product);
```

However, this works only if the entity has not already been attached to the Session (if you did not use get, save, or persist for this entity during the transaction). If the entity has already been attached, update throws an exception. Because of this it's almost always best to use the merge method, which works whether the entity has or hasn't already been attached to the Session:

```
session.merge(product);
```

Deleting an entity is quite straightforward:

```
session.delete(product);
```

Entity eviction is an interesting concept in Hibernate. Calling the `evict` method causes the entity to be detached from the `Session`, but it does not result in any changes to the database like deleting the entity.

```
session.evict(product);
```

If you want to evict all the entities attached to a session, you can call the `clear` method. Note that `evict` cancels any pending changes for the evicted entity that have not already been flushed. Likewise, `clear` cancels all pending changes on all entities in the `Session` (including insertions and deletions) that have not already been flushed.

Getting a single entity using its surrogate key is certainly not the only type of query you will ever need to perform. You will want to look up single entities and collections of entities using multiple criteria. You can use either the `org.hibernate.Criteria` API or the `org.hibernate.Query` API to perform both of these tasks. The following two `return` statements result in the exact same single entity:

```
return (Product)session.createCriteria(Product.class)
        .add(Restrictions.eq("sku", sku))
        .uniqueResult();

return (Product)session.createQuery("FROM Product p WHERE p.sku = :sku")
        .setString("sku", sku)
        .uniqueResult();
```

Note that `Product` in the HQL query refers to the entity name, not the table name, and in both places `sku` refers to the `sku` property of the entity, not the `Sku` field in the database table. Likewise, both of the following `return` statements result in a `List` of `Products` posted less than a year ago whose names start with "java":

```
return (List<Product>)session.createCriteria(Product.class)
        .add(Restrictions.gt("datePosted",
                Instant.now().minus(365L, ChronoUnit.DAYS)))
        .add(Restrictions.ilike("name", "java", MatchMode.START))
        .addOrder()
        .list();

return (List<Product>)session.createQuery("FROM Product p WHERE
datePosted > :oneYearAgo AND name ILIKE :nameLike ORDER BY name")
        .setParameter("oneYearAgo",
                Instant.now().minus(365L, ChronoUnit.DAYS))
        .setString("nameLike", "java%")
        .list();
```

There are many other things that you can do with the `Session` API, but these basic tasks should meet many of your needs.

## Getting a Session from the SessionFactory

`Sessions` don't just appear out of nowhere. A `Session` is associated with a JDBC database connection, and something must create the connection or retrieve it from a `DataSource`, instantiate the `Session` implementation, and attach the `Session` to the connection, all before it can be used. It's also necessary to "look up" an existing `Session` if one is already in progress for the current context instead of creating a new Session every time you need to perform an action. The org.hibernate.SessionFactory interface exists for just this purpose. It contains several methods for building Sessions, opening Sessions, and retrieving the "current" Session. For example, to open a new Session, you can call the openSession method:

```
Session session = sessionFactory.openSession();
```

This opens a Session with all the default settings (DataSource, interceptors, and so on) configured for the SessionFactory. Sometimes, however, it's necessary to override those settings. You might need to use a connection to a different database for some special purpose:

```
Session session = sessionFactory.withOptions()
        .connection(connection).openSession();
```

Or perhaps you need to intercept all SQL statements to modify them in some way. For example, your mappings may specify something like schema="@SCHEMA@", and at run time you replace that with a value from a setting, parameter, or other variable:

```
Session session = sessionFactory.withOptions()
        .interceptor(new EmptyInterceptor() {
            @Override
            public String onPrepareStatement(String sql)
            {
                return sql.replace("@SCHEMA@", schema);
            }
        })
        .openSession();
```

Hibernate ORM also has a concept of stateless sessions, represented by org.hibernate.StatelessSession. Particularly well-suited for bulk data operations, a StatelessSession can do many of the same things that a Session can, but it does not hold on to attached entities like a Session does. You can open a default StatelessSession with openStatelessSession and a custom StatelessSession using withStatelessOptions.

Perhaps one of the most important features of a SessionFactory is its capability to hold and retrieve the "current" Session. (No such ability exists for StatelessSessions due to their stateless nature.) But what exactly is the "current" Session? Unlike Sessions, SessionFactorys are thread-safe, so the "current" Session is not simply the last one opened with openSession. Rather, the meaning of "current" is defined by the supplied implementation of org.hibernate.context.spi.CurrentSessionContext. The most common implementation is org.hibernate.context.internal.ThreadLocalSessionContext, which stores the current session in a java.lang.ThreadLocal. Any calls to getCurrentSession retrieve the session previously opened within the current thread, if any.

```
        Session session = sessionFactory.openSession();
    ...
        Session session = sessionFactory.getCurrentSession();
```

## Creating a SessionFactory with Spring Framework

SessionFactorys can be tricky to configure, and in a web application it is extremely important that resources are properly cleaned up at the end of each request. Failing to do so could result in memory leaks or (worse) data leaks across applications. As with so many other things, Spring Framework makes creating a `SessionFactory` easier and manages the creation and closure of `Sessions` and transactions on your behalf so that you don't have to worry about that repetitive code everywhere in your application. When configuring Hibernate ORM in Spring, you use one of two Spring classes to create a `SessionFactory`.

If you configure Spring using XML, it's easiest to define an `org.springframework.orm.hibernate4.LocalSessionFactoryBean` bean, a special type of Spring bean that creates and returns a `SessionFactory`. `LocalSessionFactoryBean` also implements `org.springframework.dao.support.PersistenceExceptionTranslator`, so it can serve as a translator that converts Hibernate ORM exceptions to Spring Framework generic persistence exceptions.

When using Java configuration, however, the `org.springframework.orm.hibernate4.LocalSessionFactoryBuilder` is a simpler approach. It extends `org.hibernate.cfg.Configuration` to provide some shortcuts for configuring a `SessionFactory` in your Spring Framework application. This approach is shown in the following Java configuration snippet:

```
...
@EnableTransactionManagement
public class RootContextConfiguration
        implements AsyncConfigurer, SchedulingConfigurer
{
    ...
    @Bean
    public PersistenceExceptionTranslator persistenceExceptionTranslator()
    {
        return new HibernateExceptionTranslator();
    }

    @Bean
    public HibernateTransactionManager transactionManager()
    {
        HibernateTransactionManager manager = new HibernateTransactionManager();
        manager.setSessionFactory(this.sessionFactory());
        return manager;
    }

    @Bean
    public SessionFactory sessionFactory()
    {
        LocalSessionFactoryBuilder builder = new
                LocalSessionFactoryBuilder(this.dataSource());

        builder.scanPackages("com.wrox.entities");
        builder.setProperty("hibernate.default_schema", "dbo");
        builder.setProperty("hibernate.dialect",
                MySQL5InnoDBDialect.class.getCanonicalName());

        return builder.buildSessionFactory();
    }
    ...
}
```

With this configuration, Spring Framework can automatically create a `Session` prior to an `@org.springframework.transaction.annotation.Transactional` service or a repository method being invoked and close the `Session` after that method returns. If a `@Transactional` method calls other `@Transactional` methods, the current `Session` and transaction remain in effect. Then, you need to have only an `@Injected` `SessionFactory` in your repositories and call `getCurrentSession` whenever you need to use the `Session`. You learn more about `@EnableTransactionManagement` and `@Transactional` in Chapter 21.

## PREPARING A RELATIONAL DATABASE

To complete and use the examples and sample projects in the rest of this book, you need to have access to a relational database for storing persisted entities. You could use a 100 percent Java embedded database like HyperSQL `http://hsqldb.org/` , but that would defeat the purpose of replacing the in-memory repositories you have been using so far in this book. Instead, the examples will be more effective if you use a separate, standalone relational database like MySQL, PostgreSQL, or Microsoft SQL Server.

The examples in this book assume you have access to a relational database; if you do not, you need to install one. In addition, the examples are written for and tested against a MySQL server because it is the most popular, free database system available. However, there is no reason why you shouldn't be able to use any relational database to complete the examples. Most of the code works completely independently of any particular database (that is, after all, part of the point of an ORM), but you need to do a bit of independent thinking when using the configuration code show throughout the examples. For example, whenever you see something database-specific like the `MySQL5InnoDBDialect` class used in the previous section, you need to figure out the appropriate replacement for your database of choice. You also need to translate the MySQL database, table, and index creation statements to the appropriate statements for your database of choice.

In addition to showing you how to install a JDBC driver and create connection resources in Tomcat, this section also helps you install a local MySQL server in case you do not already have access to a database you would like to use. If you plan on using some other database *you should still read this section!* It contains important information that also applies to your database vendor.

### Installing MySQL and MySQL Workbench

To install MySQL Database, follow these steps:

1. Go to the MySQL download website (`http://dev.mysql.com/downloads/`) and download the MySQL Community Server and MySQL Workbench products.
2. For MySQL Community Server, select the appropriate platform (Mac OS X, Windows, SuSE, and so on) and download the correct installer or archive for your platform version.
3. Follow the installation instructions for your operating system to install MySQL Community Server on your computer. The installer should guide you through the process.

4. If presented with a Setup Type screen, you can usually just choose Developer Default, as shown in Figure 19-1. This installs everything you need to develop with MySQL, including extensions for Microsoft Excel if you're on a Windows system. If you want to install only certain features, choose the Custom setup type, and select the features you want to install on the screen, as shown in Figure 19-2.

> **NOTE** *Many Linux distributions offer MySQL in their package management systems, and it may be easier for you to install MySQL using that approach. However you install it,* you must use MySQL 5.6.12 or newer — *earlier versions do not support some of the features used in the following chapters. When downloading from the MySQL site, you do not have to create an account or log in. You can click the "No thanks, just start my download" link to skip this process.*

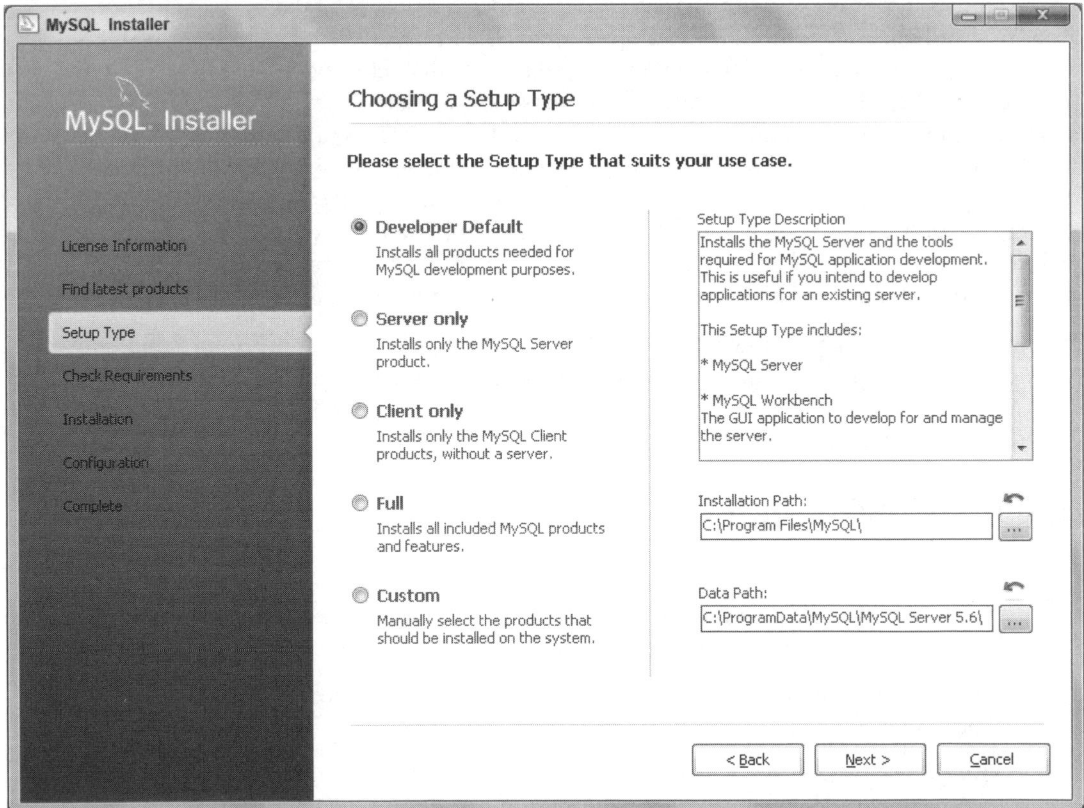


FIGURE 19-1

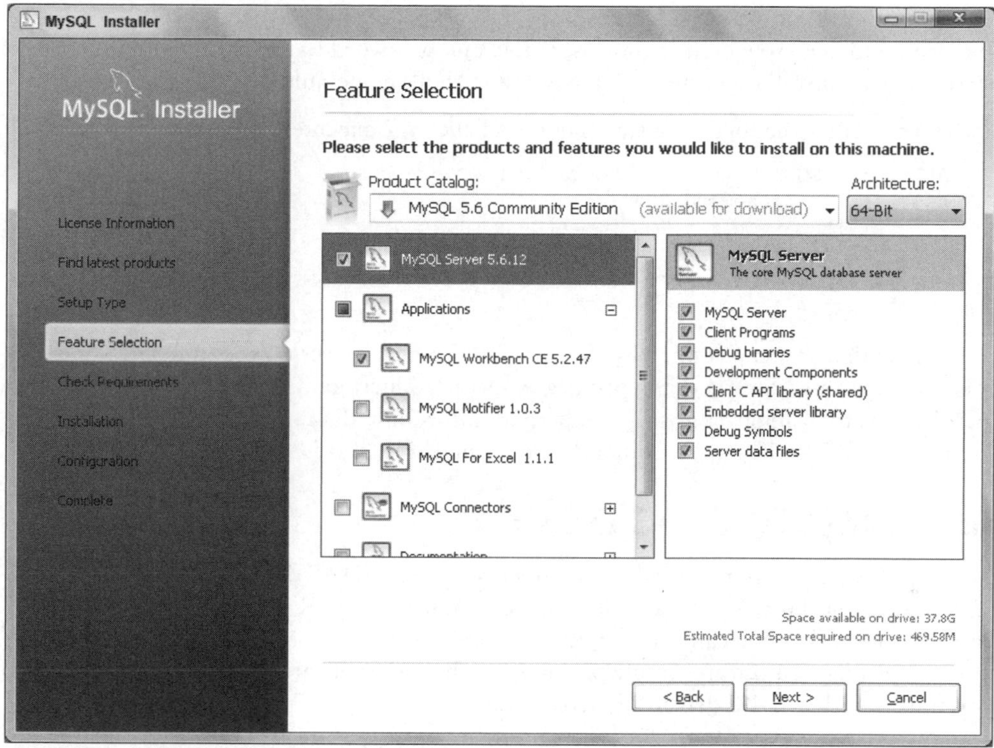


FIGURE 19-2

MySQL Workbench is a database browser and management tool similar to Microsoft SQL Server Management Studio and Oracle SQL Developer. Some of the examples and screen shots in this book tell you to execute queries against your MySQL database and show you what the results should look like in Workbench. You can, of course, use whatever tool you prefer to perform these tasks. If you ran an installer for the MySQL server and that installer included Workbench, you do not need to do anything further to install Workbench. Otherwise, to download and install Workbench, you should select the appropriate platform and download the correct installer or binary for your platform version. Installing Workbench is a simpler process than installing MySQL Community Server, and Workbench is typically not found in standard package management repositories.

For the most part, your MySQL Community Server should be ready to go after installation. It requires no extra configuration to get started for development purposes; however, in its default configuration it is not optimized for performance and it is not secure. The default configuration should be sufficient to use the examples and perform the tasks detailed in this book. You will, however, need to create a username and password that your applications can use to access databases through JDBC.

> **NOTE** *The details of managing a MySQL Community Server are outside the scope of this book, but the MySQL website has plenty of resources that help you configure it to meet your needs.*

To create this username and password, open MySQL Workbench and connect to your local MySQL installation. You will need to enter the root username and password to log in; if you did not set up a root password during installation, the root password is blank by default.

In the query editor, enter the following statements and click the execute icon to execute them:

```
GRANT ALL PRIVILEGES ON *.* TO 'tomcatUser'@'localhost'
    IDENTIFIED BY 'password1234';
GRANT ALL PRIVILEGES ON *.* TO 'tomcatUser'@'127.0.0.1'
    IDENTIFIED BY 'password1234';
GRANT ALL PRIVILEGES ON *.* TO 'tomcatUser'@'::1' IDENTIFIED BY 'password1234';
FLUSH PRIVILEGES;
```

This creates a user that you can connect with from your Tomcat server on the same machine. Of course, this user is granted far too many privileges. On a production machine, you would want to limit its permissions to a single database, and perhaps allow only data manipulation and prohibit schema manipulation. For the purposes of a developer machine, this is sufficient.

## Installing the MySQL JDBC Driver

MySQL, like most other relational database vendors, supplies a JDBC driver for connecting to MySQL databases from Java. You need to download this driver (a JAR file) and place it in your Tomcat installation so that you can use it from your applications. This may strike you as odd because other JAR files you use are simply packaged with your applications in `/WEB-INF/lib`. You must *never* do this with a JDBC driver for two reasons:

- Most important, doing so can cause a memory leak. JDBC drivers automatically register themselves with the `java.sql.DriverManager`, which is part of the Java SE core libraries. If your application includes a JDBC driver in `/WEB-INF/lib`, the `DriverManager` holds on to the driver classes forever, even if your application is undeployed. The application server then cannot fully undeploy your application, resulting in a memory leak.
- It's a best practice to have the application server manage your JDBC `DataSources`. Application servers have built-in systems for managing connection pools, improving the performance of database connections in your applications. For the application server to be able to manage these connections, you must load the JDBC driver in the application server class loader instead of the web application class loader.

Installing the MySQL JDBC driver in Tomcat is extremely easy. On the MySQL download website mentioned previously, locate the Connector/J product. This is the JDBC driver. It is platform-independent, so all you need to do is download the ZIP or TAR archive (whichever is easiest for you to use on your computer). Extract the JAR file from the archive, and copy it to `C:\Program Files\Apache Software Foundation\Tomcat 8.0\lib` (or the equivalent directory for your Tomcat installation).

That's all there is to it. The next time Tomcat starts, the MySQL JDBC driver becomes available to all web applications.

> **WARNING** *As of the time of this writing, the MySQL JDBC driver is* mostly *compatible with JDBC 4.1, which was part of Java 7. Java 8 includes JDBC 4.2. The only significant changes in JDBC 4.2 are the addition of the Java 8 Date and Time types for SQL* `DATE`*,* `TIME`*, and* `DATETIME` *types. Because the MySQL Driver is not yet compatible with JDBC 4.2, you cannot use the Java 8 Date and Time types directly with JDBC statements and result sets — yet. JDBC vendors usually release new versions of their drivers 6 months to several years after a new Java/JDBC version is released, or it may not. By the time you read this, the MySQL driver may already be JDBC 4.2-compliant. Make sure you download the latest version and consult the Connector/J documentation to see if it is JDBC 4.2-compliant. This cautionary note also applies to any other JDBC drivers you may use.*

## Creating a Connection Resource in Tomcat

Creating a pooled connection `DataSource` in Tomcat is quite straightforward and takes only a few minutes. Any time you use a new database for an example or sample project, this book instructs you to create a Tomcat connection resource. You will likely want to refer back to this section from time to time to remember how to do that. Instead of creating a brand new resource every time and having dozens of resources by the end of the book, it is also acceptable to simply create one resource and change it every time you need to.

1. To create a connection resource, open `C:\Program Files\Apache Software Foundation\Tomcat 8.0\conf\context.xml` (or the equivalent in your Tomcat installation) in your favorite text editor.
2. Add the following `<Resource>` element between the beginning and end `<Context>` elements:

```
<Resource name="jdbc/DataSourceName" type="javax.sql.DataSource"
          maxActive="20" maxIdle="5" maxWait="10000"
          username="mysqluser" password="mysqlpassword"
          driverClassName="com.mysql.jdbc.Driver"
          url="jdbc:mysql://localhost:3306/databaseName" />
```

3. For each example you must replace *`jdbc/DataSourceName`* with the appropriate data source name (which should always start with `jdbc/`) and *`databaseName`* with the correct database name. *`mysqluser`* and *`mysqlpassword`* should be replaced with the user (`tomcatUser`) and password (`password1234`) that you previously created for Tomcat to access MySQL. You can reuse this username and password for all the examples in this book.

This `<Resource>` definition causes Tomcat to expose the connection pool `DataSource` as a JNDI resource so that it can be looked up via JNDI by any application.

# A NOTE ABOUT MAVEN DEPENDENCIES

The Maven dependencies you use in this part of the book aren't quite as straightforward as you may be used to. Most of the Java EE dependencies you have used up to this point are the actual Java EE specification libraries from the Maven Central Repository, such as `javax.servlet:javax.servlet-api:3.1.0` and `javax.websocket:javax.websocket-api:1.0`. However, other Java EE components have different licenses that prohibit binary distribution in Maven Central.

The legal absurdities that result in this are beyond the scope of this book, but suffice it to say that there is no "official" `javax.persistence` (Java Persistence API) artifact in Maven Central for JPA 2.0 or 2.1. You may also come across similar situations for other Java EE components in the future. However, the implementation providers for these APIs publish identical, unofficial API artifacts in Maven Central and it is safe to use those. The best practice is to use the API published by the reference implementation in these cases because it is the most likely to be 100 percent correct. When you see the following Maven dependency in the next chapter, know that this is the Java Persistence API 2.1 artifact provided by the reference implementation EclipseLink. It is compatible with any JPA implementation, including Hibernate ORM.

```
<dependency>
    <groupId>org.eclipse.persistence</groupId>
    <artifactId>javax.persistence</artifactId>
    <version>2.1.0</version>
    <scope>compile</scope>
</dependency>
```

Hibernate ORM also publishes an `org.hibernate.javax.persistence:hibernate-jpa-2.1-api:1.0.0` artifact for JPA 2.1, and you can use it if you prefer. The only alternative to using provider-published artifacts is to manually download the official JARs from the Java website, but that does not work well with Maven projects and is really not necessary. Fortunately, this is the exception and not the norm for Java EE components.

# SUMMARY

This brief preparatory chapter introduced you to Object-Relational Mappers (O/RMs) and the Java Persistence API (JPA). It explained the history and evolution of both and explained the advantages of using JPA instead of a proprietary O/RM API. You also got a brief introduction to using Hibernate ORM outside of JPA. However, in the rest of this book, you use only the JPA classes and interfaces. You learned that you must have access to a relational database for the rest of the book and were given instructions for installing and setting up MySQL for this purpose. Finally, you learned how to install a JDBC driver in Tomcat and configure a Tomcat connection pool `DataSource`.

In upcoming chapters, you use JPA to persist all sorts of entities to relational databases. You also learn about the different techniques that you can employ to map entities to database tables and explore adding, updating, deleting, reading, and searching entities in various manners.

# 20

# Mapping Entities to Tables with JPA Annotations

## IN THIS CHAPTER

- Understanding and working with simple entities
- Designing and utilizing a persistence unit
- How to map complex data types

### WROX.COM CODE DOWNLOADS FOR THIS CHAPTER

You can find the wrox.com code downloads for this chapter at http://www.wrox.com/go/projavaforwebapps on the Download Code tab. All the code for this chapter is contained within the following examples:

- Entity-Mappings Project
- Enums-Dates-Lobs Project

### NEW MAVEN DEPENDENCIES FOR THIS CHAPTER

In addition to the Maven dependencies introduced in previous chapters, you also need the following Maven dependencies. The Hibernate persistence API and JBoss transaction API transient dependencies are excluded because they conflict with the standard dependencies already declared. The XML API dependency is excluded because it is already part of Java SE 7 and newer. Finally, JBoss Logging is excluded not out of necessity, but out of clarity, because a dependency on a newer version was declared in an earlier chapter.

```
<dependency>
    <groupId>org.eclipse.persistence</groupId>
    <artifactId>javax.persistence</artifactId>
    <version>2.1.0</version>
    <scope>compile</scope>
</dependency>

<dependency>
```

```
        <groupId>javax.transaction</groupId>
        <artifactId>javax.transaction-api</artifactId>
        <version>1.2</version>
        <scope>compile</scope>
    </dependency>

    <dependency>
        <groupId>org.hibernate</groupId>
        <artifactId>hibernate-entitymanager</artifactId>
        <version>4.3.1.Final</version>
        <scope>runtime</scope>
        <exclusions>
            <exclusion>
                <groupId>org.hibernate.javax.persistence</groupId>
                <artifactId>hibernate-jpa-2.1-api</artifactId>
            </exclusion>
            <exclusion>
                <groupId>org.jboss.spec.javax.transaction</groupId>
                <artifactId>jboss-transaction-api_1.2_spec</artifactId>
            </exclusion>
            <exclusion>
                <groupId>xml-apis</groupId>
                <artifactId>xml-apis</artifactId>
            </exclusion>
            <exclusion>
                <groupId>org.jboss.logging</groupId>
                <artifactId>jboss-logging</artifactId>
            </exclusion>
        </exclusions>
    </dependency>
```

# GETTING STARTED WITH SIMPLE ENTITIES

In this chapter, you learn how to map entities to relational database tables using JPA annotations. A vast number of both simple and complex mapping options are available to you, and this chapter attempts to cover most of them. To make understanding this process simpler, you do not use Spring Framework in this chapter. Instead, you use simple Servlets to execute JPA code and persist and list the entities you create. All the examples are contained within the Entity-Mappings project, available for download from the `wrox.com` code download site.

## ANNOTATION-BASED OR XML-BASED MAPPINGS?

You do not have to use annotations to map entities in your application. Instead, you can use the `/META-INF/orm.xml` file to create XML-based mappings similar to Hibernate ORM mappings. Showing you how to create both annotation-based and XML mappings would take twice as many pages and is simply not practical. Annotations are the easiest and preferred method for mapping JPA entities, so this book covers only that technique. If you are also interested in learning about XML mappings, the XML mapping elements and their attributes are essentially identical to the mapping annotations and their attributes. A good IDE, such as IntelliJ IDEA, can provide code hints based on the `orm.xml` XSD. To help you start with this, an empty `orm.xml` file looks like this:

```
<?xml version="1.0" encoding="UTF-8"?>
<entity-mappings xmlns="http://xmlns.jcp.org/xml/ns/persistence/orm"
  xmlns:xsi="http://www.w3.org/2001/XMLSchema-instance"
  xsi:schemaLocation="http://xmlns.jcp.org/xml/ns/persistence/orm
        http://xmlns.jcp.org/xml/ns/persistence/orm_2_1.xsd"
  version="2.1">

</entity-mappings>
```

## Marking an Entity and Mapping It to a Table

The first two and most basic JPA mapping annotations are `@javax.persistence.Entity` and `@javax.persistence.Table`. `@Entity` marks a class to indicate that it is an entity. Every entity must have this annotation. By default, an entity name is equal to the unqualified entity class name, so the following `com.wrox.site.entities.Author` class has an entity name of `Author`.

```
@Entity
public class Author implements Serializable
{
    ...
}
```

You can customize the entity name by specifying the `name` attribute on the `@Entity` annotation as on the `com.wrox.site.entities.Publisher` class.

```
@Entity(name = "PublisherEntity")
public class Publisher implements Serializable
{
    ...
}
```

The table name to which an entity maps defaults is the entity name. So the default table name for `Author` is `Author` and the default table name for `Publisher` is `PublisherEntity`. You can change the table name using the `name` attribute of `@Table`.

```
@Entity
@Table(name = "Authors")
public class Author implements Serializable
{
    ...
}

@Entity(name = "PublisherEntity")
@Table(name = "Publishers")
public class Publisher implements Serializable
{
    ...
}
```

Now these two classes map to the tables `Authors` and `Publishers`, respectively. You have several other things you can do with this annotation as well. For example, you can use the `schema` attribute to override database connection's user's default schema (assuming the database you use supports schemas). You can also use the `catalog` attribute to indicate that the table exists in a *catalog* other than the catalog selected in the database connection. In JDBC and JPA, "catalog" is a generic term for a collection of database tables. Most relational database systems use the term "database" instead.

The `com.wrox.site.entities.Book` entity demonstrates the use of the `uniqueConstraints` attribute.

```
@Entity
@Table(name = "Books", uniqueConstraints = {
        @UniqueConstraint(name = "Books_ISBN", columnNames = { "isbn" })
})
public class Book implements Serializable
{
    ...
}
```

`uniqueConstraints` is a special attribute used exclusively for schema generation. JPA providers can automatically generate database schema based off of your entities, and this attribute enables you to indicate that a particular column or columns should form a unique constraint. As of JPA 2.1, you can also use the `indexes` attribute to specify indexes that JPA should create when using schema generation.

```
@Entity
@Table(name = "Books", uniqueConstraints = {
        @UniqueConstraint(name = "Books_ISBNs", columnNames = { "isbn" })
},
indexes = {
        @Index(name = "Books_Titles", columnList = "title")
})
public class Book implements Serializable
{
    ...
}

@Entity
@Table(name = "Authors", indexes = {
        @Index(name = "Authors_Names", columnList = "AuthorName")
})
public class Author implements Serializable
{
    ...
}

@Entity(name = "PublisherEntity")
@Table(name = "Publishers", indexes = {
        @Index(name = "Publishers_Names", columnList = "PublisherName")
})
public class Publisher implements Serializable
{
    ...
}
```

Of course, because you use `uniqueConstraints` and `indexes` only when schema generation is enabled, you have no need to specify them if schema generation is disabled (the default).

> **WARNING** *Schema generation is a dangerous feature. Although it's helpful for development purposes, it should* never *be used in a production environment. The schema generated by this process is not always pretty and is not guaranteed to be correct. As a best practice, this author* never *uses schema generation. The development process should also include development of the schema you use in production so that it is tested thoroughly through all stages of product maturity.*

## Indicating How JPA Uses Entity Fields

By default, JPA providers access the values of entity fields and map those fields to database columns using the entity's JavaBean property accessor (getter) and mutator (setter) methods. As such, the names and types of the private fields in an entity do not matter to JPA. Instead, JPA looks at only the names and return types of the JavaBean property accessors. You can alter this using the `@javax.persistence.Access` annotation, which enables you to explicitly specify the access methodology that the JPA provider should employ.

```
@Entity
@Access(AccessType.FIELD)
public class SomeEntity implements Serializable
{
    ...
}
```

The available options for the `AccessType` enum are `PROPERTY` (the default) and `FIELD`. With `PROPERTY`, the provider gets and sets field values using the JavaBean property methods. `FIELD` makes the provider get and set field values using the instance fields. As a best practice, you should just stick to the default and use JavaBean properties unless you have a compelling reason to do otherwise.

The rest of the JPA annotations are mostly property annotations. You explore many of these, such as `@Id`, `@Basic`, `@Temporal`, and more, in the rest of this chapter. Technically speaking, you can put these property annotations on either the private fields or the public accessor methods. If you use `AccessType.PROPERTY` (default) and annotate the private fields instead of the JavaBean accessors, the field names must match the JavaBean property names. However, the names do not have to match if you annotate the JavaBean accessors. Likewise, if you use `AccessType.FIELD` and annotate the JavaBean accessors instead of the fields, the field names must also match the JavaBean property names. In this case, they do not have to match if you annotate the fields. It's best to just be consistent and annotate the JavaBean accessors for `AccessType.PROPERTY` and the fields for `AccessType.FIELD` — this eliminates any source of confusion.

> **WARNING** *You should* never *mix JPA property annotations and JPA field annotations in the same entity. Doing so results in unspecified behavior and is very likely to cause errors.*

# Mapping Surrogate Keys

One of the first things you must do when mapping JPA entities is create surrogate keys, also called primary keys or IDs, for those entities. Every entity should have an ID, which can be one field (and thus a single column) or multiple fields (and thus multiple columns). As a result, you have many different approaches for mapping an ID.

## Creating Simple IDs

First, you can mark any JavaBean property with `@javax.persistence.Id`. This annotation can go on the private field or the public accessor method and indicates that the property is the entity's surrogate key. The property may be any Java primitive, primitive wrapper, `String`, `java.util.Date`, `java.sql.Date`, `java.math.BigInteger`, or `java.math.BigDecimal`. Some providers may also eventually support Java 8 Date and Time types for this field; however, at this time none do. (Even so, such use would not be portable.) JPA 2.2 will likely require support for these types.

If your entity class does not have an `@Id` property, the JPA provider looks for a property named `id` (with accessor `getId` and mutator `setId`) and uses it automatically. This property must also be a primitive, primitive wrapper, `String`, `java.util.Date`, `java.sql.Date`, `BigInteger`, or `BigDecimal`.

As a best practice, entity IDs (primary keys) should usually be `int`s, `long`s, `Integer`s, `Long`s, or `BigInteger`s. Generally speaking, however, using an `int` or `Integer` limits the number of entities your table can hold to 2,147,483,647. `BigInteger`s are tricky to deal with and don't automatically cast to primitives like wrappers do, and `String`s are harder to index and look up than numbers. There are few cases in which a `long` or `Long` isn't appropriate for an entity ID, so this book exclusively uses `long`s except when demonstrating other types of entity IDs. However you do it, if you have schema generation enabled, the JPA provider automatically creates a primary key constraint for ID columns. You do not need to specify a unique constraint in `@Table`.

You can, whenever you want, create an entity with an ID that is manually generated and assigned. However, this is rarely desired because it requires extra, repetitive, unnecessary work. Typically, you want your entity IDs to be automatically generated in some manner. You can accomplish this using the `@javax.persistence.GeneratedValue` annotation. `@GeneratedValue` enables you to specify a generation strategy and, if necessary, a generator name. For example, the `Book` and `Author` entity IDs use `javax.persistence.GenerationType.IDENTITY` to indicate that the database column the ID is stored in can generate its own value automatically.

```
@Entity
...
public class Book implements Serializable
{
    ...
    @Id
    @GeneratedValue(strategy = GenerationType.IDENTITY)
    public long getId()
    {
        return this.id;
    }
    ...
```

```
}

@Entity
...
public class Author implements Serializable
{
    ...
    @Id
    @GeneratedValue(strategy = GenerationType.IDENTITY)
    public long getId()
    {
        return this.id;
    }
    ...
}
```

This is compatible with MySQL `AUTO_INCREMENT` columns, Microsoft SQL Server and Sybase `IDENTITY` columns, PostgreSQL `SERIAL` and `DEFAULT NEXTVAL()` columns, Oracle `DEFAULT SYS_GUID()` columns, and more. You cannot use `GenerationType.IDENTITY` with databases that do not support the auto-generation of column values, but all the most common relational databases support this.

At the very least, in any database that supports before-insert triggers you can use a trigger to generate a value for a column (a very common technique for Oracle databases using sequences), and that column becomes compatible with `GenerationType.IDENTITY`. However, you can use other generators so that you don't have to employee triggers and trickery to accomplish this. Because many databases such as Oracle and PostgreSQL support sequences, you can use `@GeneratedValue` combined with `@javax.persistence.SequenceGenerator` to tell the JPA provider to generate the value using a sequence.

```
@Entity
public class SomeEntity implements Serializable
{
    ...
    @Id
    @GeneratedValue(strategy = GenerationType.SEQUENCE,
            generator = "SomeEntityGenerator")
    @SequenceGenerator(name = "SomeEntityGenerator",
            sequenceName = "SomeEntitySequence")
    public long getId()
    {
        return this.id;
    }
    ...
}
```

The `generator` attribute of `@GeneratedValue` corresponds with the `name` attribute of `@SequenceGenerator`, and generator names are global. This means that you can create a single `@SequenceGenerator` on one entity and reuse it for multiple entities. (However, you may also use a separate sequence for each entity.)

```
@Entity
public class SomeEntity implements Serializable
{
    ...
```

```
        @Id
        @GeneratedValue(strategy = GenerationType.SEQUENCE,
                generator = "GlobalGenerator")
        @SequenceGenerator(name = "GlobalGenerator", sequenceName = "GlobalSequence",
                allocationSize = 1)
        public long getId()
        {
            return this.id;
        }
        ...
    }

    @Entity
    public class AnotherEntity implements Serializable
    {
        ...
        @Id
        @GeneratedValue(strategy = GenerationType.SEQUENCE,
                generator = "GlobalGenerator")
    public long getId()
        {
            return this.id;
        }
        ...
    }
```

Alternatively, you can create a generator that multiple entities share using the `<sequence-generator>` element in `orm.xml`.

```
<?xml version="1.0" encoding="UTF-8"?>
<entity-mappings xmlns="http://xmlns.jcp.org/xml/ns/persistence/orm"
                 xmlns:xsi="http://www.w3.org/2001/XMLSchema-instance"
                 xsi:schemaLocation="http://xmlns.jcp.org/xml/ns/persistence/orm
        http://xmlns.jcp.org/xml/ns/persistence/orm_2_1.xsd"
                 version="2.1">
    <sequence-generator name="GlobalGenerator" sequence-name="GlobalSequence"
                        allocation-size="1" />
</entity-mappings>

@Entity
public class SomeEntity implements Serializable
{
    ...
    @Id
    @GeneratedValue(strategy = GenerationType.SEQUENCE,
            generator = "GlobalGenerator")
    public long getId()
    {
        return this.id;
    }
    ...
}

@Entity
public class AnotherEntity implements Serializable
```

```
{
    ...
    @Id
    @GeneratedValue(strategy = GenerationType.SEQUENCE,
            generator = "GlobalGenerator")
public long getId()
    {
        return this.id;
    }
    ...
}
```

Using `@SequenceGenerator` (or `<sequence-generator>`), you can specify the `schema` and `catalog` attributes to specify which schema and database the sequence belongs to. If you enable JPA schema generation, you can also use `initialValue` (`initial-value`) and `allocationSize` (`allocation-size`) to indicate the sequence's initial value and to specify how much it increases with each insert operation. `initialValue` defaults to 0, and `allocationSize` defaults to 50.

You can also use a `@javax.persistence.TableGenerator`, as demonstrated in `Publisher`, to use a separate table that acts as a database sequence. Like `@SequenceGenerator`, you can also create a `@TableGenerator` (or `<table-generator>`) that multiple entities share. `@TableGenerator` has the same `name`, `schema`, `catalog`, `initialValue`, and `allocationSize` attributes that `@SequenceGenerator` provides, with the same purposes and defaults. Its other attributes are as follows:

- `table` indicates the name of the generator database table.
- `pkColumnName` indicates the name of the primary key column for the generator table.
- `pkColumnValue` indicates the value of the primary key column for this generator.
- `valueColumnName` indicates the name of the value column.

Before inserting a record, the provider selects the value for the given `pkColumnValue` from the sequence table, increments the value for that record, and then uses the value as the primary key for the record being inserted.

```
...
public class Publisher implements Serializable
{
    ...
    @Id
    @GeneratedValue(strategy = GenerationType.TABLE,
            generator = "PublisherGenerator")
    @TableGenerator(name = "PublisherGenerator", table = "SurrogateKeys",
            pkColumnName = "TableName", pkColumnValue = "Publishers",
            valueColumnName = "KeyValue", initialValue = 11923,
            allocationSize = 1)
    public long getId()
    {
        return this.id;
    }
    ...
}
```

The default values for `table`, `pkColumnName`, `pkColumnValue`, and `valueColumnName` are not mandated in the specification and may vary from one provider to the next. For example, if you omit `pkColumnValue`, Hibernate ORM uses the entity table name as the value, whereas EclipseLink uses the generator name. Relying on these default values is not portable. If you care about the name of the table, the name of its columns, and the values of its primary key column, you should specify a different `@TableGenerator` on every entity. If you don't care, you can omit the `@TableGenerator` annotation completely and use `@GeneratedValue(strategy = GenerationType.TABLE)` only. This results in the provider creating a single table for all your `GenerationType.TABLE` entities and a separate row in the table for each entity.

The common use case for `@TableGenerator` is using JPA with an existing, legacy database. Usually, identity and sequence IDs are sufficient for all purposes. If you prefer, you may place `@SequenceGenerator` or `@TableGenerator` on an entity class as opposed to the property or field. However, you must always place `@GeneratedValue` on the property or field.

## Creating Composite IDs

Composite IDs consisting of multiple fields and columns are more challenging to map than standard surrogate keys. You can take one of two different approaches to define composite IDs. The first technique involves using multiple `@Id` properties combined with `@javax.persistence.IdClass`. The separate class specified in the `@IdClass` annotation must contain properties that match all the `@Id` properties on the entity class.

```
public class JoinTableCompositeId implements Serializable
{
    private long fooParentTableSk;
    private long barParentTableSk;

    public long getFooParentTableSk() { ... }
    public void setFooParentTableSk(long fooParentTableSk) { ... }

    public long getBarParentTableSk() { ... }
    public void setBarParentTableSk(long barParentTableSk) { ... }
}

@Entity
@Table(name = "SomeJoinTable")
@IdClass(JoinTableCompositeId.class)
public class JoinTableEntity implements Serializable
{
    private long fooParentTableSk;
    private long barParentTableSk;
    ...
    @Id
    public long getFooParentTableSk() { ... }
    public void setFooParentTableSk(long fooParentTableSk) { ... }

    @Id
    public long getBarParentTableSk() { ... }
    public void setBarParentTableSk(long barParentTableSk) { ... }
    ...
}
```

Looking at this, you may immediately wonder what the point of the `JoinTableCompositeId` class is. After all, can't the JPA provider just use the two `@Id` columns to persist entities without a class with redundant properties? Well, yes, but then how would you look up an entity by its ID? When looking up an entity by its ID, you use the `find` method on the `javax.persistence.EntityManager`:

```
JoinTableEntity entity = entityManager.find(JoinTableEntity.class, id);
```

The find method doesn't accept multiple ID arguments. It accepts only one ID argument, so you must create a `JoinTableCompositeId` instance with which to locate the entity:

```
JoinTableCompositeId compositeId = new JoinTableCompositeId();
compositeId.setFooParentTableSk(id1);
compositeId.setBarParentTableSk(id2);

JoinTableEntity entity = entityManager.find(JoinTableEntity.class, compositeId);
```

The `@IdClass` solution might seem a bit clunky to you because of the duplicate properties on the classes, and indeed that's a legitimate concern. The alternative to `@Id` and `@IdClass` is using `@javax.persistence.EmbeddedId` with `@javax.persistence.Embedded` to embed the composite ID class as the ID property.

```
@Embeddable
public class JoinTableCompositeId implements Serializable
{
    private long fooParentTableSk;
    private long barParentTableSk;

    public long getFooParentTableSk() { ... }
    public void setFooParentTableSk(long fooParentTableSk) { ... }

    public long getBarParentTableSk() { ... }
    public void setBarParentTableSk(long barParentTableSk) { ... }
}

@Entity
@Table(name = "SomeJoinTable")
public class JoinTableEntity implements Serializable
{
    private JoinTableCompositeId id;

    @EmbeddedId
    public JoinTableCompositeId getId() { ... }
    public void setId(JoinTableCompositeId id) { ... }
}
```

This solution may be a lot more palatable to you, and as such it is a much more common approach to composite IDs. Whichever technique you use, you should map the `fooParentTableSk` and `barParentTableSk` properties to the appropriate database columns using the mapping annotations you learn about throughout this chapter — such as `@Column`, `@Basic`, `@Enumerated`, `@Temporal`, and `@Convert`. You should place the mapping annotations on the composite ID class properties for the `@Embeddable` solution and on the entity class properties for the `@IdClass` solution. You learn more about `@Embeddable` and its other uses in Chapter 24.

## Using Basic Data Types

To make your life easier, JPA automatically maps certain data types without any further instruction from you. If any properties are found on an entity (or fields if using `AccessType.FIELD`) with the following types, they are automatically mapped as basic properties to standard SQL data types. Some providers coerce these basic data types to other SQL data types as well.

- Properties of type `short` and `Short` are mapped to `SMALLINT`, `INTEGER`, `BIGINT`, or equivalent fields.
- `int` and `Integer` properties are mapped to `INTEGER`, `BIGINT`, or equivalent SQL data types.
- `long`, `Long`, and `BigInteger` properties are mapped to `BIGINT` or equivalent fields.
- Properties of type `float`, `Float`, `double`, `Double`, and `BigDecimal` are mapped to `DECIMAL` or equivalent SQL data types.
- `byte` and `Byte` properties are mapped to `BINARY`, `SMALLINT`, `INTEGER`, `BIGINT`, or equivalent fields.
- Properties of type `char` and `Char` are mapped to `CHAR`, `VARCHAR`, `BINARY`, `SMALLINT`, `INTEGER`, `BIGINT`, or equivalent fields.
- Properties of type `boolean` and `Boolean` are mapped to `BOOLEAN`, `BIT`, `SMALLINT`, `INTEGER`, `BIGINT`, `CHAR`, `VARCHAR`, or equivalent fields.
- `byte[]` and `Byte[]` properties are mapped to `BINARY`, `VARBINARY`, or equivalent SQL data types.
- `char[]`, `Character[]`, and `String` properties are mapped to `CHAR`, `VARCHAR`, `BINARY`, `VARBINARY`, or equivalent SQL data types.
- Properties of type `java.util.Date` and `Calendar` are mapped to `DATE`, `DATETIME`, or `TIME` fields, but you *must* supply additional instructions using `@Temporal`. In the "Mapping Complex Data Types" section, you learn about this and how to better control how these values are stored.
- Properties of type `java.sql.Timestamp` are always mapped to `DATETIME` fields.
- Properties of type `java.sql.Date` are always mapped to `DATE` fields.
- Properties of type `java.sql.Time` are always mapped to `TIME` fields.
- Enum properties are mapped to `SMALLINT`, `INTEGER`, `BIGINT`, `CHAR`, `VARCHAR`, or equivalent fields. By default enums are stored in their ordinal form, but you can alter this behavior using `@Enumerated`. You explore that more in the section "Mapping Complex Data Types."
- Any other properties implementing `Serializable` are mapped to `VARBINARY` or equivalent SQL data types and converted using standard Java serialization and deserialization.

If you want to more explicitly indicate that a field is mapped, you can annotate it with `@Basic`. All the same data type restrictions and rules apply for `@Basic` properties and fields. You can also use the annotation's `fetch` attribute to indicate whether a property's value is retrieved from the database eagerly (`javax.persistence.FetchType.EAGER`, the default if not specified) or only when accessed (`FetchType.LAZY`).

Eager fetching means the field value is retrieved from the database at the same time the entity is retrieved from the database. This may or may not involve additional SQL statements, depending on whether the field value resides in a different table. Lazy fetching causes the provider to retrieve the value only when the field is accessed — it is not retrieved when the entity is initially retrieved. Not specifying the `fetch` attribute (or explicitly specifying `FetchType.EAGER`) is a *requirement* that the provider fetch the value eagerly. However, specifying `FetchType.LAZY` is only a *hint* to fetch the value lazily. The provider may not support lazy access and may fetch the value eagerly anyway. As such, you should consult your provider's documentation before relying on this feature. You learn more about lazy fetching in Chapter 24.

Finally, you can use `@Basic`'s `optional` attribute to indicate that the property may be `null`. (This is only a hint and is useful for schema generation.) This is ignored for primitives, which may never be `null`. The completed `Book` entity in Listing 20-1 demonstrates the usage of `@Basic`.

**LISTING 20-1: Book.java**

```
@Entity
@Table(name = "Books", uniqueConstraints = {
        @UniqueConstraint(name = "Books_ISBNs", columnNames = { "isbn" })
},
indexes = {
        @Index(name = "Books_Titles", columnList = "title")
})
public class Book implements Serializable
{
    private long id;
    private String isbn;
    private String title;
    private String author;
    private double price;
    private String publisher;

    @Id
    @GeneratedValue(strategy = GenerationType.IDENTITY)
    public long getId()
    {
        return this.id;
    }

    public void setId(long id)
    {
        this.id = id;
    }

    @Basic(optional = false)
    public String getIsbn()
    {
        return this.isbn;
    }

    public void setIsbn(String isbn)
```

*continues*

**LISTING 20-1** *(continued)*

```
        {
            this.isbn = isbn;
        }

        @Basic(optional = false)
        public String getTitle()
        {
            return this.title;
        }

        public void setTitle(String title)
        {
            this.title = title;
        }

        @Basic(optional = false)
        public String getAuthor()
        {
            return this.author;
        }

        public void setAuthor(String author)
        {
            this.author = author;
        }

        @Basic
        public double getPrice()
        {
            return this.price;
        }

        public void setPrice(double price)
        {
            this.price = price;
        }

        @Basic(optional = false)
        public String getPublisher()
        {
            return this.publisher;
        }

        public void setPublisher(String publisher)
        {
            this.publisher = publisher;
        }
    }
```

## Specifying Column Names and Other Details

By default, JPA maps entity properties to columns with the same name. Referring to the `Book` entity in Listing 20-1, the `id`, `isbn`, `title`, `author`, `price`, and `publisher` properties are automatically mapped to database columns named `Id`, `Isbn`, `Title`, `Author`, `Price`, and `Publisher`, respectively. However, this is not always wanted and sometimes the column names must be different for any number of reasons. Using the `@javax.persistence.Column` annotation you can customize the column name and more to fine-tune how the JPA provider persists values to that property's column. `@Column` has many attributes that serve a variety of purposes, several of them related to JPA schema generation.

The `name` attribute indicates to which database column the property is mapped. It is closely related to the `table` attribute, which specifies the table that the column exists in, and defaults to the primary table for the entity. You use this when an entity is stored in multiple tables (something you explore more in Chapter 24). The `boolean` attributes `insertable` and `updatable` indicate whether the property value is persisted on insert and update, respectively. Both default to `true`. The rest of `@Column`'s attributes are for schema generation. `nullable` specifies whether the column should be `NULL` or `NOT NULL` and defaults to `true` (`NULL`). `unique` is a shortcut for the `@UniqueConstraint` annotation, useful when the unique constraint contains only one column and you don't care what the constraint's name is. It is `false` (non-unique) by default.

The `length` attribute, used only for `VARBINARY` and `VARCHAR` columns, indicates how long the column should be and defaults to 255. The `scale` and `precision` attributes both default to 0 and indicate the scale (number of digits before the decimal point) and precision (number of digits after the decimal point) for decimal columns. You must provide a nonzero value for `precision` for decimal columns if you use schema generation. Finally, `columnDefinition` provides a way to specify the actual SQL used to generate the column. If you use this, it will likely not be portable across different database systems.

The completed entity `Author` in Listing 20-2 demonstrates `@Column` for changing the default column name for its properties. `Publisher` in Listing 20-3 also demonstrates the schema generation attribute `nullable`, which is ignored unless schema generation is enabled.

**LISTING 20-2: Author.java**

```
@Entity
@Table(name = "Authors", indexes = {
        @Index(name = "Authors_Names", columnList = "AuthorName")
})
public class Author implements Serializable
{
    private long id;
    private String name;
    private String emailAddress;

    @Id
    @GeneratedValue(strategy = GenerationType.IDENTITY)
    @Column(name = "AuthorId")
    public long getId()
```

*continues*

**LISTING 20-2** *(continued)*

```
    {
        return this.id;
    }

    public void setId(long id)
    {
        this.id = id;
    }

    @Basic
    @Column(name = "AuthorName")
    public String getName()
    {
        return this.name;
    }

    public void setName(String name)
    {
        this.name = name;
    }

    @Basic
    public String getEmailAddress()
    {
        return this.emailAddress;
    }

    public void setEmailAddress(String emailAddress)
    {
        this.emailAddress = emailAddress;
    }
}
```

**LISTING 20-3: Publisher.java**

```
@Entity(name = "PublisherEntity")
@Table(name = "Publishers", indexes = {
        @Index(name = "Publishers_Names", columnList = "PublisherName")
})
public class Publisher implements Serializable
{
    private long id;
    private String name;
    private String address;

    @Id
    @GeneratedValue(strategy = GenerationType.TABLE,
            generator = "PublisherGenerator")
    @TableGenerator(name = "PublisherGenerator", table = "SurrogateKeys",
            pkColumnName = "TableName", pkColumnValue = "Publishers",
            valueColumnName = "KeyValue", initialValue = 11923,
```

```
                allocationSize = 1)
        @Column(name = "PublisherId")
        public long getId()
        {
            return this.id;
        }

        public void setId(long id)
        {
            this.id = id;
        }

        @Basic
        @Column(name = "PublisherName", nullable = false)
        public String getName()
        {
            return this.name;
        }

        public void setName(String name)
        {
            this.name = name;
        }

        @Basic
        @Column(nullable = false)
        public String getAddress()
        {
            return this.address;
        }

        public void setAddress(String address)
        {
            this.address = address;
        }
    }
```

# CREATING AND USING A PERSISTENCE UNIT

Now that you have created and mapped some entities, you are almost ready to use those entities. You still need to create the database tables and configure the JPA provider, and then you can write code that uses the persistence API to persist and retrieve your entities.

## Designing the Database Tables

For this exercise you need to use MySQL Workbench or your SQL data tool of choice to create a database and several tables. You can find the schema definition statements in this section in the `create.sql` file of the Entity-Mappings project you downloaded from the `wrox.com` code download site. Open Workbench and log in to your local server using the root user.

Create a database named `EntityMappings` by entering the following SQL statement in the query editor and clicking the execute icon.

```
CREATE DATABASE EntityMappings DEFAULT CHARACTER SET 'utf8'
  DEFAULT COLLATE 'utf8_unicode_ci';
```

This database uses the character set `utf8` and the collation `utf8_unicode_ci`. You should use this in almost all circumstances. These values are the optimum values for correctly storing and retrieving character data from any language. If you need to override these values, you can set character sets and collations individually on tables and columns, but you'll rarely need to use something other than these two. After you create the database, you then need to create the three tables for the `Book`, `Author`, and `Publisher` entities. Remember that you pluralized the table names using the `@Table` annotation.

```
USE EntityMappings;

CREATE TABLE Publishers (
  PublisherId BIGINT UNSIGNED NOT NULL PRIMARY KEY,
  PublisherName VARCHAR(100) NOT NULL,
  Address VARCHAR(1024) NOT NULL,
  INDEX Publishers_Names (PublisherName)
) ENGINE = InnoDB;

CREATE TABLE Authors (
  AuthorId BIGINT UNSIGNED NOT NULL PRIMARY KEY AUTO_INCREMENT,
  AuthorName VARCHAR(100) NOT NULL,
  EmailAddress VARCHAR(255) NOT NULL,
  INDEX Publishers_Names (AuthorName)
) ENGINE = InnoDB;

CREATE TABLE Books (
  Id BIGINT UNSIGNED NOT NULL PRIMARY KEY AUTO_INCREMENT,
  Isbn VARCHAR(13) NOT NULL,
  Title VARCHAR(255) NOT NULL,
  Author VARCHAR(100) NOT NULL,
  Price DECIMAL(6,2) NOT NULL,
  Publisher VARCHAR(100) NOT NULL,
  UNIQUE KEY Books_ISBNs (Isbn),
  INDEX Books_Titles (Title)
) ENGINE = InnoDB;
```

There is nothing special about these tables. They contain very simple columns that cleanly correlate to the entity property names and data types. The key here is that you write your code first and design a database that supports your code. This is the preferred approach when designing most types of applications because creating your database first can result in forcing your code to adhere to the database. What matters the most is that the application does what the user needs, and that happens in code. JPA makes it really simple to create entities and then create a database that merely supports those entities.

Finally, recall that you told JPA to use a table generator for the `Publisher` surrogate key, so you need to create the appropriate generator table to support this requirement.

```
USE EntityMappings;

CREATE TABLE SurrogateKeys (
  TableName VARCHAR(64) NOT NULL PRIMARY KEY,
  KeyValue BIGINT UNSIGNED NOT NULL,
  INDEX SurrogateKeys_Table_Values (TableName, KeyValue)
) ENGINE = InnoDB;
```

That's all there is to it. The database is created and ready to use for persisting your entities. You need only create a `<Resource>` in Tomcat's `conf/context.xml` file (as a child element of the root `<Context>` element) to give you a way to access the database from a web application.

```
<Resource name="jdbc/EntityMappings" type="javax.sql.DataSource"
          maxActive="20" maxIdle="5" maxWait="10000"
          username="tomcatUser" password="password1234"
          driverClassName="com.mysql.jdbc.Driver"
          url="jdbc:mysql://localhost/EntityMappings" />
```

## Understanding Persistence Unit Scope

A *persistence unit* is a configuration and a set of entity classes logically grouped together. This configuration controls the `javax.persistence.EntityManager` instances attached to the persistence unit, and an `EntityManager` in a particular persistence unit can manage *only* the entities defined in that persistence unit. For example, given two persistence units `Foo` and `Bar`, an `EntityManager` instantiated for persistence unit `Foo` can manage only the entities defined in persistence unit `Foo`. It cannot manage the entities defined only in `Bar`. However, it's possible to define an entity in multiple persistence units. If an entity is defined in both `Foo` and `Bar`, an `EntityManager` instantiated for persistence unit `Foo` or `Bar` can access the entity.

You can define one or more persistence units within a file named `persistence.xml`. You must place this file (and `orm.xml` if you choose to map your entities with XML) in a `META-INF` directory. But in which `META-INF` directory should you place them? As you likely know, a web application can have many different `META-INF` directories, for example:

```
mappings.war!/META-INF
mappings.war!/WEB-INF/classes/META-INF
mappings.war!/WEB-INF/lib/something.jar!/META-INF
```

The first example is the web application `META-INF` directory. Unlike other `META-INF` directories, this directory is not on the classpath. You cannot access its contents using classpath resource location. This directory is exclusively for files that the Servlet container uses. For example, you can place a `context.xml` file in this directory and put Tomcat `<Resource>` definitions within it. (However, this works only for Tomcat, not for other containers.) You cannot, however, put `orm.xml` or `persistence.xml` in this directory because the JPA provider cannot find them there.

The JPA provider *can* find persistence files in the `/WEB-INF/classes/META-INF` directory and in the `META-INF` directories of any JAR files on the classpath. Where you place your `persistence.xml` file determines the *persistence unit scope*. The most important thing to understand about the persistence unit scope is that `persistence.xml` and `orm.xml` share the same scope, so you should always place them in the same `META-INF` directory if you use `orm.xml`.

The scope defines what code can access the persistence unit. A persistence unit is visible to the defining component and the components it defines. Generally speaking (though some providers are more lax), if you define a persistence unit in `/WEB-INF/classes/META-INF/persistence.xml`, it is visible to the application classes and to any components (JAR file classes) included in `/WEB-INF/lib`. If you define a persistence unit in `META-INF/persistence.xml` within a JAR file in `/WEB-INF/lib`, it is visible only to the code in that JAR file. Likewise, a persistence unit defined at the top level of an EAR file is visible to all components (WAR files, application JAR files, or EJB-JAR files) of that EAR, but persistence units defined within the components of that EAR are not visible to other components or to the EAR itself.

When defining a persistence unit in a WAR file, you typically want to place that persistence unit in `/WEB-INF/classes/META-INF/persistence.xml`. It is especially important to do this in a container that does not provide a JPA implementation, such as Tomcat (which is just a Servlet container and not a full Java EE application server). In these cases you have to provide your own JPA implementation (in this book you use Hibernate ORM, remember) and that implementation, embedded within a JAR of your application, acts more like a standalone application than a web application within a persistence container.

## Creating the Persistence Configuration

To use the entities you create, you must define a persistence unit. Doing so is simple. Create a `persistence.xml` file not dissimilar from a deployment descriptor, but with far fewer options to worry about. The root element of a persistence configuration file is `<persistence>`. This element may contain one or more `<persistence-unit>` elements. No other elements are within `<persistence>`. `<persistence-unit>` has two attributes: `name` specifies the name of the persistence unit and `transaction-type` indicates whether this persistence unit uses *Java Transaction API (JTA)* transactions or standard local transactions.

You must specify a `name`, which is how you locate the persistence unit in code. If not specified, `transaction-type` defaults to `JTA` in a Java EE application server and `RESOURCE_LOCAL` in a Java SE environment or simple Servlet container. However, to prevent unexpected behavior it's best to always set this value explicitly instead of relying on a default value.

> **NOTE** *The Java Transaction API, like JPA, is part of the Java EE stack. JTA is a* transaction-processing monitor *that coordinates transactions across multiple resources, such as a database and an application messaging system (JMS, AMQP, and so on). JTA is mentioned further in Chapters 21 and 22.*

`<persistence-unit>` contains the following inner elements. None of them are required (so `<persistence-unit>` may be empty); however, you must specify whichever elements you use in the following order:

- `<description>` contains a useful description for this persistence unit. Although it makes reading the persistence file easier, it has no semantic value.
- `<provider>` specifies the fully qualified class name of the `javax.persistence.spi.PersistenceProvider` implementation used for this persistence unit. By default, when you look up the persistence unit, the API will use the first JPA provider on the classpath. You can include this element to mandate a specific JPA provider.
- You can use either `<jta-data-source>` or `<non-jta-data-source>` (but not both) to use a JNDI `DataSource` resource. You may use `<jta-data-source>` only if `transaction-type` is `JTA`; likewise you may use `<non-jta-data-source>` only if `transaction-type` is `RESOURCE_LOCAL`. Specifying a `DataSource` causes the persistence unit to use that `DataSource` for all entity operations.

- <mapping-file> specifies the classpath-relative path to an XML mapping file. If you don't specify any <mapping-file>, the provider looks for orm.xml. You may specify multiple <mapping-file> elements to use multiple mapping files.
- You can use one or more <jar-file> elements to specify a JAR file or JAR files that the JPA provider should scan for mapping-annotated entities. Any @Entity, @Embeddable, @javax.persistence.MappedSuperclass, or @javax.persistence.Converter classes found are added to the persistence unit.
- You can use one or more <class> elements to indicate specific @Entity, @Embeddable, @MappedSuperclass, or @Converter classes that should be added to the persistence unit. You must annotate the class or classes with JPA annotations.
- Using <exclude-unlisted-classes /> or <exclude-unlisted-classes>true</exclude-unlisted-classes> indicates that the provider should ignore classes not specified with <jar-file> or <class>. Omitting <exclude-unlisted-classes> or using <exclude-unlisted-classes>false</exclude-unlisted-classes> causes the JPA provider to scan the classpath location of the persistence file for JPA-annotated classes. If persistence.xml is located in a JAR file, that JAR file (and only that JAR file) is scanned for classes. If persistence.xml is located in a directory-based classpath location (such as /WEB-INF/classes), that directory (and only that directory) is scanned for classes. Prior to Hibernate 4.3.0 and Spring Framework 3.2.5, specifying this element with the value false was incorrectly interpreted as true.
- <shared-cache-mode> indicates how entities are cached in the persistence unit (if the JPA provider supports caching, which is optional). NONE disables caching, whereas ALL enables caching for all entities. ENABLE_SELECTIVE means that only entities annotated @javax.persistence.Cacheable or @Cacheable(true) (or marked as cacheable in orm.xml) are cached. DISABLE_SELECTIVE results in caching of all entities except those annotated @Cacheable(false) (or marked as non-cacheable in orm.xml). The default value, UNSPECIFIED, means that the JPA provider decides what the effective default is. Hibernate ORM defaults to ENABLE_SELECTIVE, but relying on this is not portable.
- <validation-mode> indicates if and how Bean Validation should be applied to entities. NONE means that Bean Validation is not enabled, whereas CALLBACK makes the provider validate all entities on insert, update, and delete. AUTO has an effective value of CALLBACK if a Bean Validation provider exists on the classpath and an effective value of NONE if no Bean Validation provider exists on the classpath. If you enable validation, the JPA provider configures a new Validator to validate your entities. If you have configured a special Spring Framework Validator with your custom localized error codes, the JPA provider ignores it. As such, it's best to set the validation mode to NONE and use Bean Validation before your persistence layer is invoked.
- <properties> provides a way to specify other JPA properties, including standard JPA properties (such as JDBC connection string, username, and password, or schema generation settings) as well as provider-specific properties (such as Hibernate settings). You specify one or more properties using nested <property> elements, each with a name and value attribute.

The `persistence.xml` file in the Entity-Mappings project, shown next, mandates Hibernate ORM as the JPA provider, uses the `DataSource` resource you created in the Tomcat `context.xml` file, explicitly enables scanning of all classes in `/WEB-INF/classes` for entity annotations, enables caching only for annotated entities, and disables Bean Validation. It also contains a property to ensure that schema generation is disabled (just in case).

```
<?xml version="1.0" encoding="UTF-8"?>
<persistence xmlns="http://xmlns.jcp.org/xml/ns/persistence"
             xmlns:xsi="http://www.w3.org/2001/XMLSchema-instance"
             xsi:schemaLocation="http://xmlns.jcp.org/xml/ns/persistence
        http://xmlns.jcp.org/xml/ns/persistence/persistence_2_1.xsd"
             version="2.1">

    <persistence-unit name="EntityMappings" transaction-type="RESOURCE_LOCAL">
        <provider>org.hibernate.jpa.HibernatePersistenceProvider</provider>
        <non-jta-data-source>
            java:/comp/env/jdbc/EntityMappings
        </non-jta-data-source>
        <exclude-unlisted-classes>false</exclude-unlisted-classes>
        <shared-cache-mode>ENABLE_SELECTIVE</shared-cache-mode>
        <validation-mode>NONE</validation-mode>
        <properties>
            <property name="javax.persistence.schema-generation.database.action"
                      value="none" />
        </properties>
    </persistence-unit>

</persistence>
```

## Using the Persistence API

Using the persistence API is quite easy. Most of the code is spent handling transactions and resources. Saving and retrieving entities is simple. The `EntityServlet` adds and displays entities using the persistence API. The first things you should look at are the `init` and `destroy` methods, which, respectively, create a `javax.persistence.EntityManagerFactory` on startup and close it on shutdown.

```
@WebServlet(
        name = "entityServlet",
        urlPatterns = "/entities",
        loadOnStartup = 1
)
public class EntityServlet extends HttpServlet
{
    private final Random random;
    private EntityManagerFactory factory;

    public EntityServlet()
    {
        try
        {
            this.random = SecureRandom.getInstanceStrong();
        }
        catch(NoSuchAlgorithmException e)
```

```
        {
            throw new IllegalStateException(e);
        }
    }

    @Override
    public void init() throws ServletException
    {
        super.init();
        this.factory = Persistence.createEntityManagerFactory("EntityMappings");
    }

    @Override
    public void destroy()
    {
        super.destroy();
        this.factory.close();
    }

    ...
}
```

The `createEntityManagerFactory` method obtains the persistence unit named `EntityMappings` from the configuration in `persistence.xml` and creates a new `EntityManagerFactory` for that persistence unit. In a full Java EE application server, you wouldn't have to perform these extra steps. Instead, you could do something like this:

```
public class EntityServlet extends HttpServlet
{
    private final Random random;

    @PersistenceContext("EntityMappings")
    EntityManagerFactory factory;

    ...
}
```

This tells the container to create and inject the `EntityManagerFactory` for you. However, this won't work unless the container provides JPA and dependency injection, which Tomcat does not. In the next chapter you learn how to simplify this using Spring Framework tools.

The `EntityServlet` responds to `GET` and `POST` requests. For `GET` requests, it queries entities and displays them using `/WEB-INF/jsp/view/entities.jsp`. First, it creates an `EntityManager` and starts a transaction through that manager. It then uses the `javax.persistence.criteria.CriteriaBuilder`, `javax.persistence.criteria.CriteriaQuery`, and `javax.persistence.TypedQuery` to list all the `Publishers`, `Authors`, and `Books`, taking care to commit the transaction and close the manager when it's through, and roll back the transaction if an error occurs.

```
    @Override
    public void doGet(HttpServletRequest request, HttpServletResponse response)
            throws ServletException, IOException
    {
        EntityManager manager = null;
        EntityTransaction transaction = null;
```

```
        try
        {
            manager = this.factory.createEntityManager();
            transaction = manager.getTransaction();
            transaction.begin();

            CriteriaBuilder builder = manager.getCriteriaBuilder();

            CriteriaQuery<Publisher> q1 = builder.createQuery(Publisher.class);
            request.setAttribute("publishers", manager.createQuery(
                    q1.select(q1.from(Publisher.class))
            ).getResultList());

            CriteriaQuery<Author> q2 = builder.createQuery(Author.class);
            request.setAttribute("authors", manager.createQuery(
                    q2.select(q2.from(Author.class))
            ).getResultList());

            CriteriaQuery<Book> q3 = builder.createQuery(Book.class);
            request.setAttribute("books", manager.createQuery(
                    q3.select(q3.from(Book.class))
            ).getResultList());

            transaction.commit();

            request.getRequestDispatcher("/WEB-INF/jsp/view/entities.jsp")
                    .forward(request, response);
        }
        catch(Exception e)
        {
            if(transaction != null && transaction.isActive())
                transaction.rollback();
            e.printStackTrace(response.getWriter());
        }
        finally
        {
            if(manager != null && manager.isOpen())
                manager.close();
        }
    }
```

For POST requests, EntityServlet persists a new Publisher, a new Author, and a new Book. Of course, the values are all very mundane and repetitive because they aren't based on user input, but the demonstration is clear: Using JPA is easy. As with doGet, doPost also starts, commits, and rolls back a transaction as necessary.

```
    @Override
    public void doPost(HttpServletRequest request, HttpServletResponse response)
            throws ServletException, IOException
    {
        EntityManager manager = null;
        EntityTransaction transaction = null;
        try
        {
            manager = this.factory.createEntityManager();
            transaction = manager.getTransaction();
```

```
            transaction.begin();

            Publisher publisher = new Publisher();
            publisher.setName("John Wiley & Sons");
            publisher.setAddress("1234 Baker Street");
            manager.persist(publisher);

            Author author = new Author();
            author.setName("Nicholas S. Williams");
            author.setEmailAddress("nick@example.com");
            manager.persist(author);

            Book book = new Book();
            book.setIsbn("" + this.random.nextInt(Integer.MAX_VALUE));
            book.setTitle("Professional Java for Web Applications");
            book.setAuthor("Nicholas S. Williams");
            book.setPublisher("John Wiley & Sons");
            book.setPrice(59.99D);
            manager.persist(book);

            transaction.commit();

            response.sendRedirect(request.getContextPath() + "/entities");
        }
        catch(Exception e)
        {
            if(transaction != null && transaction.isActive())
                transaction.rollback();
            e.printStackTrace(response.getWriter());
        }
        finally
        {
            if(manager != null && manager.isOpen())
                manager.close();
        }
    }
```

To test the project, follow these steps:

1. Compile it and start Tomcat from your IDE. Go to `http://localhost:8080/mappings/entities` in your browser of choice, and click the Add More Entities button a few times.
2. Shut down Tomcat and start it back up.
3. Go back to `http://localhost:8080/mappings/entities` and the entities should still be there, persisted between instances of the virtual machine.

4. Now open MySQL Workbench and execute the following statements, as shown in Figure 20-1. Take a look at each result tab, and you can see the values that Hibernate ORM inserted into your database tables.

```
USE EntityMappings;
SELECT * FROM Publishers;
SELECT * FROM Authors;
SELECT * FROM Books;
SELECT * FROM SurrogateKeys;
```

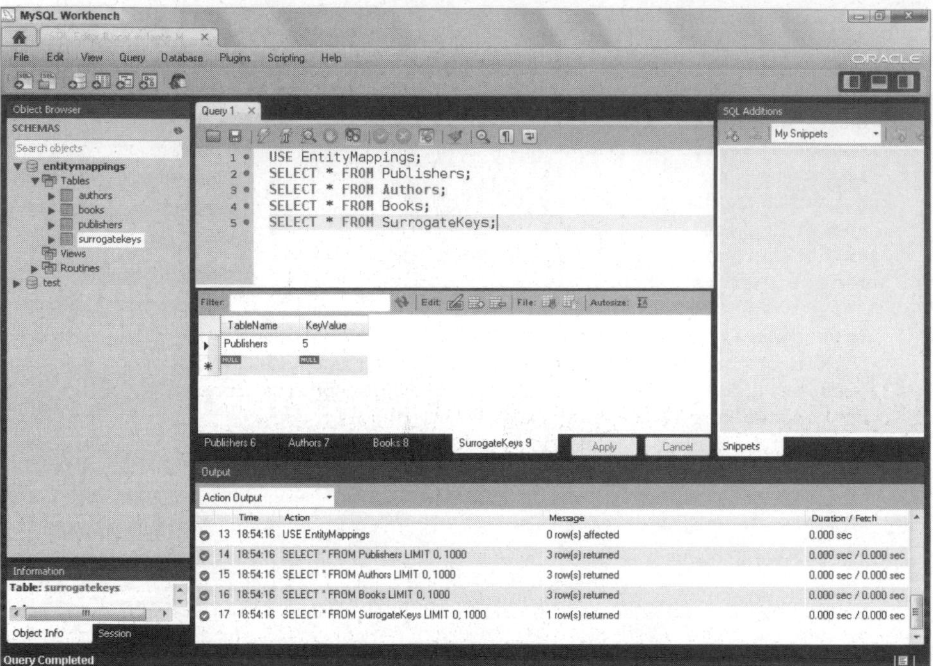


**FIGURE 20-1**

# MAPPING COMPLEX DATA TYPES

You should have a reasonable grasp on the basics of mapping entities by this point, but you still have some missing pieces. In this section, you learn how to properly map complex data types, such as enums, dates, times, and large objects. You explore even more advanced mapping tasks (such as inheritance, nested entities, and custom data types) in Chapter 24. For this section you use the Enums-Dates-Lobs project available for download from the `wrox.com` code download site. This project extends the Entity-Mappings project you worked on earlier in the chapter, and the code in this section represents additions to that project.

## Using Enums as Entity Properties

As discussed earlier, a JPA provider can automatically persist entity properties that are enums without any special configuration. However, the standard way that enums are persisted may not be what you want. Consider the following `Gender` enum:

```
public enum Gender
{
    MALE,
    FEMALE,
    UNSPECIFIED
}
```

The `Author` entity has a `gender` property of type `Gender` that indicates the author's gender.

```
...
public class Author implements Serializable
```

```
{
    ...
    private Gender gender;

    ...

    public Gender getGender()
    {
        return this.gender;
    }

    public void setGender(Gender gender)
    {
        this.gender = gender;
    }
}
```

Used like this, the JPA provider persists the enum using the integer ordinal value. So an `Author` with the gender `MALE` has a value 0 in the gender column in the database. Likewise, the persisted values for `FEMALE` and `UNSPECIFIED` are 1 and 2, respectively. This presents a couple of challenges.

- You can't look at the database tables directly (such as through MySQL Workbench) and recognize the data automatically. You will see only 0s, 1s, and 2s in the gender column, not useful descriptions.
- If someone alters the enum and reorders the constants (for example, to alphabetize them), all previously persisted data is now corrupt — obviously a big problem.

This default behavior remains the same whether the database column is a numeric column (such as `INT`) or a string column (such as `NVARCHAR`). Fortunately, JPA provides the `@javax.persistence.Enumerated` annotation that enables you to change how this value is persisted. `@Enumerated`'s sole attribute is (ironically) an enum, `javax.persistence.EnumType`. The default behavior corresponds to `EnumType.ORDINAL`. Your other option is `EnumType.STRING`, which tells the JPA provider to persist the enum in its `String` format (the name of the constant). This is both refactor-safe (unless, of course, someone changes the constant names, but that's a bigger problem) and easy to view directly in the database.

```
    @Enumerated(EnumType.STRING)
    public Gender getGender()
    {
        return this.gender;
    }
```

When using `EnumType.STRING`, not only must your column be a string-type column (which is probably obvious), but it must also be a *Unicode* column (such as `NVARCHAR`, or `VARCHAR` with a UTF-8 or UTF-16 character set). (The exception to this rule is when the database vendor has support for native `ENUM` column types.) The reason for this is that Java enum constants may contain characters that won't properly store in non-Unicode columns. Of course, you can always simply avoid using such characters; however, because `Strings` in Java are always Unicode, it's usually best to make all your text columns Unicode so that character set translation doesn't have to take place.

The new definition for the `Authors` table follows and uses the special MySQL `ENUM` data type to provide an additional layer of metadata and validation in the database and to consume less space when storing the data.

```
CREATE TABLE Authors (
  AuthorId BIGINT UNSIGNED NOT NULL PRIMARY KEY AUTO_INCREMENT,
  AuthorName VARCHAR(100) NOT NULL,
  EmailAddress VARCHAR(255) NOT NULL,
  Gender ENUM('MALE', 'FEMALE', 'UNSPECIFIED') NULL,
  INDEX Publishers_Names (AuthorName)
) ENGINE = InnoDB;
```

## Understanding How JPA Handles Dates and Times

Dates and times have been perhaps the biggest challenge to software developers since the beginning of software. Dealing with JDBC is no exception to that challenge. JPA makes it somewhat easier, but you still have challenges to consider. JDBC 4.2 (Java SE 8) contains significant improvements that make dealing with database dates and times simpler (due to the Java 8 Date and Time API), but JPA will likely not adapt to those changes until version 2.2 or 2.3. Most relational databases have three primary date-related data types: `DATE`, `TIME`, and `DATETIME`. Some databases also have `TIMESTAMP` data types, but these are largely the same as `DATETIME`, and you can consider them equivalent when you use JDBC (and, thus, JPA). You should always be cognizant of the purpose, features, and limitations of the different date-related data types that your database vendor supplies, and choose the one that best meets your needs for a given property.

In previous versions of JDBC, your only options for inserting a date, time, or date-time were the `setDate`, `setTime`, and `setTimestamp` methods of `PreparedStatement`. These methods require a `java.sql.Date`, a `java.sql.Time`, and a `java.sql.Timestamp`, respectively. Likewise, `ResultSet`'s `getDate`, `getTime`, and `getTimestamp` methods return a `Date`, a `Time`, and a `Timestamp`, and its `updateDate`, `updateTime`, and `updateTimestamp` methods function the same as the three `PreparedStatement` methods. These types are stored in the database as follows:

- A `Date` is stored as just the date (year, month, and day only).
- A `Time` is stored as just the time (hour, minute, and second only).
- A `Timestamp` is a combination of the two, always being stored as the year, month, day, hour, minute, and second.

JDBC 4.2 added the capability of inserting or retrieving any `Object` as a date, time, time-with-time-zone, date-time, or date-time-with-time-zone using the `setObject(int, Object, java.sql.SQLType)` method on `PreparedStatement` and the `updateObject(int, Object, SQLType)`, `updateObject(String, Object, SQLType)`, `getObject(int, Class)`, and `getObject(String, Class)` methods on `ResultSet`. Of course, you can use these methods only with types the driver vendor supports, but all JDBC 4.2 vendors are expected to support the appropriate Java 8 Date and Time types in addition to `java.util.Date`, `Calendar`, `java.sql.Date`, `Time`, and `Timestamp`. The `SQLType`s that correlate to date and time types follow:

- `java.sql.JDBCType.DATE` (stores date only)
- `JDBCType.TIME` (stores time only)
- `JDBCType.TIME_WITH_TIMEZONE` (stores time and time zone only)
- `JDBCType.TIMESTAMP` (stores date and time only)
- `JDBCType.TIMESTAMP_WITH_TIMEZONE` (stores date, time, and time zone)

Some database systems, such as Microsoft SQL Server, support time and date-time columns that store a time zone as well, in addition to the standard time and date-time columns that always match the server time zone. Other databases, such as MySQL, support time and date-time columns only in the server time zone. The `TIME_WITH_TIMEZONE` and `TIMESTAMP_WITH_TIMEZONE` constants are only valid for those vendors that support the combination time zone columns. You should use them sparingly, and only when supported. For the vast majority of cases, you should store times and date-times in the server time zone and convert them to other time zones only when necessary.

> **WARNING** *You should exercise caution whenever using the latest JDBC 4.1 and JDBC 4.2 features. Many drivers, such as those for MySQL and Microsoft SQL Server, have not even caught up to the JDBC 4.1 features added to Java 7 in July 2011. In fact, as of the time of this writing, PostgreSQL's JDBC driver supports only the JDBC 3.0 features introduced in Java 4 in February 2002. PostgreSQL claims to have a partially complaint JDBC 4.0 driver that includes the Java 6 features released in December 2006, but that driver is far from complete and throws* `AbstractMethodErrors` *in many places. Oracle is the only major vendor that currently supports JDBC 4.1. You can expect this trend to continue, so it may be many years before you can use the new JDBC 4.2 features in MySQL, Microsoft SQL Server, and PostgreSQL.*

Using JPA, properties of type `java.sql.Date` are stored only as dates (using `PreparedStatement.setDate`). Even if the database column is a `DATETIME`, the time of the column is given all zeroes. Likewise, `Time` properties are stored only as times (using `PreparedStatement.setTime`), and the database columns must be `TIME` (or equivalent) columns only. `Timestamp` properties are automatically stored with both the date and time parts, and the corresponding database columns must be `DATETIME` (or equivalent). Where things can get tricky is if your entities contain `java.util.Date` or `Calendar` properties. For these you must use the `@javax.persistence.Temporal` annotation to tell the provider how to persist the type. The `value` attribute expects a `javax.persistence.TemporalType`, and its options follow:

- `TemporalType.DATE` (converts the `Date` or `Calendar` property to and from a `java.sql.Date`)
- `TemporalType.TIME` (converts the property to and from a `Time`)
- `TemporalType.TIMESTAMP` (converts the property to and from a `Timestamp`)

You may not use `@Temporal` on properties that are already `java.sql.Date`, `Time`, or `Timestamp` types. The `Publisher` entity's `dateFounded` property uses a `Calendar` to store the date the `Publisher` was founded and stores the value in a `DATE` column.

```
...
public class Publisher implements Serializable
{
    ...
    private Calendar dateFounded;

    ...

    @Temporal(TemporalType.DATE)
```

```
        public Calendar getDateFounded()
        {
            return dateFounded;
        }

        public void setDateFounded(Calendar dateFounded)
        {
            this.dateFounded = dateFounded;
        }
    }

    CREATE TABLE Publishers (
      PublisherId BIGINT UNSIGNED NOT NULL PRIMARY KEY,
      PublisherName VARCHAR(100) NOT NULL,
      Address VARCHAR(1024) NOT NULL,
      DateFounded DATE NOT NULL,
      INDEX Publishers_Names (PublisherName)
    ) ENGINE = InnoDB;
```

Of course, this isn't really ideal. You don't want to use a `java.util.Date` or `Calendar` to hold just a date, and the `java.sql.Date` is as much of a pain to work with as `java.util.Date`. (It even extends `java.util.Date`, which is just plain weird.) What you really want to do here is use the new `java.time.LocalDate` as the entity property, but the JPA provider won't know what to do with that type. In Chapter 24 you learn how to write converters so that you can use the Java 8 Date and Time types.

## Mapping Large Properties to CLOBs and BLOBs

Sometimes a `CHAR`, `VARCHAR`, `NCHAR`, or `NVARCHAR` column, usually restricted to a few thousand characters, just isn't big enough. This is also the case for storing binary data in a `BINARY` or `VARBINARY` column. Most database systems provide a way to store *Large Objects (LOBs)* that can hold many millions or even billions of bytes. The text form of a LOB is a *Character Large Object (CLOB)*, whereas the binary form is a *Binary Large Object (BLOB)*.

JDBC provides different, optimized mechanisms for storing and retrieving LOBs that aren't compatible with the standard `setString` and `setBytes` methods, so you have to tell JPA to store values you anticipate could be very large as LOBs instead of standard columns. You do this with the `@javax.persistence.Lob` annotation. `String` and `char[]` properties annotated with `@Lob` are persisted as CLOBs. All other types, such as `byte[]` and `Serializable` properties, are persisted as BLOBs. The `Book` entity uses a `@Lob` property to store a preview of the first few pages of the book in PDF form.

```
    public class Book implements Serializable
    {
        ...
        private byte[] previewPdf;

        ...
        @Lob
        public byte[] getPreviewPdf()
        {
```

```
        return previewPdf;
    }

    public void setPreviewPdf(byte[] previewPdf)
    {
        this.previewPdf = previewPdf;
    }
}

CREATE TABLE Books (
  Id BIGINT UNSIGNED NOT NULL PRIMARY KEY AUTO_INCREMENT,
  Isbn VARCHAR(13) NOT NULL,
  Title VARCHAR(255) NOT NULL,
  Author VARCHAR(100) NOT NULL,
  Price DECIMAL(6,2) NOT NULL,
  Publisher VARCHAR(100) NOT NULL,
  PreviewPdf MEDIUMBLOB NULL,
  UNIQUE KEY Books_ISBNs (Isbn),
  INDEX Books_Titles (Title)
) ENGINE = InnoDB;
```

> **NOTE** *You may combine* `@Enumerated`, `@Temporal`, *and* `@Lob` *with* `@Basic` *to enable lazy loading or mark the property as optional. However, as with other basic types, you do not* have to use `@Basic` *if you do not want or need to.*

Testing the Enums-Lobs-Dates project is essentially the same as testing the Entity-Mappings project:

1. Run the `create.sql` in MySQL Workbench to create the `EnumsLobsDates` database and its tables.
2. Update Tomcat's JNDI resources to point to the new database.

```
<Resource name="jdbc/EnumsDatesLobs" type="javax.sql.DataSource"
          maxActive="20" maxIdle="5" maxWait="10000"
          username="tomcatUser" password="password1234"
          driverClassName="com.mysql.jdbc.Driver"
          url="jdbc:mysql://localhost/EnumsDatesLobs" />
```

3. Go to `http://localhost:8080/mappings/entities` in your browser of choice, and click the Add More Entities button a few times. It should behave exactly as it did before, but with the addition of the author's gender and the publisher's foundation date (which is just today's date for the example).
4. You can also query the tables using MySQL Workbench to see the data you inserted. You need to convert the `PreviewPdf` column to a hexadecimal string for display using MySQL's `hex` function:

```
USE EnumsDatesLobs;
SELECT * FROM Publishers;
SELECT * FROM Authors;
SELECT Id, Isbn, Title, Author, Price, Publisher, hex(PreviewPdf) FROM Books;
SELECT * FROM SurrogateKeys;
```

## SUMMARY

In this chapter, you explored the basics of mapping entities using JPA annotations and saw a brief example of XML mappings using `orm.xml`. You learned about `persistence.xml`, what purpose it serves, what a persistence unit is, and how persistence unit scope works. You created several tables in MySQL and experimented with using the persistence API to store data in and retrieve data from those tables. You also learned about some important steps and considerations involved when dealing with enums, dates, times, date-times, and LOBs.

You haven't yet put the persistence API to full use, and there are many parts about finding, inserting, updating, and deleting entities that you still need to learn. In the next chapter you explore the persistence API more thoroughly, using Spring Framework to take care of the mundane work of injecting the persistence unit and managing transactions.

# 21

# Using JPA in Spring Framework Repositories

## IN THIS CHAPTER

- Understanding Spring repositories and taking advantage of transactions
- Setting up persistence in Spring Framework
- Implementing and using JPA repositories
- Converting data with DTOs and entities

## WROX.COM CODE DOWNLOADS FOR THIS CHAPTER

You can find the wrox.com code downloads for this chapter at http://www.wrox.com/go/projavaforwebapps on the Download Code tab. The code for this chapter is divided into the following major examples:

- Spring-JPA Project
- Customer-Support-v15 Project

## NEW MAVEN DEPENDENCIES FOR THIS CHAPTER

In addition to the Maven dependencies introduced in previous chapters, you also need the following Maven dependency:

```
<dependency>
    <groupId>org.springframework</groupId>
    <artifactId>spring-orm</artifactId>
    <version>4.0.0</version>
    <scope>compile</scope>
```

```
        </dependency>

        <dependency>
            <groupId>org.javassist</groupId>
            <artifactId>javassist</artifactId>
            <version>3.18.1-GA</version>
            <scope>runtime</scope>
        </dependency>
```

# USING SPRING REPOSITORIES AND TRANSACTIONS

Before Object-Relational Mappers became so common and the JPA Persistence API was first released, Spring Framework's `org.springframework.jdbc.core.JdbcTemplate` provided a standard, simplified way to persist and retrieve entities using JDBC in Spring Framework applications. In addition to making table-to-entity translation easier, the `JdbcTemplate` also recognized the various vendor-specific `SQLExceptions` and error codes that a JDBC driver could throw and translated them to members of the hierarchy of `org.springframework.dao.DataAccessExceptions`. For example, failure to insert a record due to a unique key conflict in Oracle, Microsoft SQL Server, MySQL, or any other supported database would result in the unambiguous `org.springframework.dao.DuplicateKeyException`. Today the `JdbcTemplate` still exists, but its power is far outmatched next to JPA or a standalone O/RM tool.

Nevertheless, there are some tasks that are still difficult or verbose to perform using JPA. For example, creating an `EntityManager` and managing transactions manually in every method consumed the vast majority of the persistence code you wrote in the previous chapter. More important, transactions often include selecting and manipulating multiple types of entities. You need a way to create an `EntityManager`, start a transaction, and share it across multiple repositories during the scope of a single unit of work.

Thankfully, Spring Framework provides tools for just such a need and more. In previous Spring versions, the `org.springframework.orm.jpa.JpaTemplate` provided a mechanism similar to `JdbcTemplate` for using the persistence API within Spring Framework applications. However, `JpaTemplate` was deprecated in Spring 3.1 and removed in Spring 4.0 in favor of new support for using the persistence unit `EntityManager` directly. In this chapter, you explore how to configure and use Spring Framework transactions, shared `EntityManagers`, and JPA exception translation.

## Understanding Transaction Scope

In Spring Framework, you control transactions using the `org.springframework.transaction.PlatformTransactionManager`. You define a `PlatformTransactionManager` appropriate to your environment and chosen persistence technology within the root application context. The methods in this interface are not important — you'll never use it directly and you'll only configure an implementation. Spring manages starting, committing, and rolling back transactions automatically on your behalf. This is accomplished using the `@org.springframework.transaction.annotation.Transactional` or `@javax.transaction.Transactional` annotations. You can annotate interfaces, classes, interface methods, and class methods with these annotations. Annotating an interface or class has the effect of annotating all the methods in that interface or class. Annotating a method in an interface or class that is also annotated has the effect of overriding the annotation on the interface or class.

Spring begins a transaction when it encounters an annotated method. The transaction's scope covers the execution of that method, the execution of any methods that method invokes, and so on, until the method returns. Any managed resources that are covered by the configured `PlatformTransactionManager` and that you use during the transaction scope participate in the transaction. For example, if you use the `org.springframework.jdbc.datasource.DataSourceTransactionManager`, a `Connection` retrieved from the linked `DataSource` participates in the transaction automatically. Likewise, Java Message Service actions performed during a transaction managed by the `org.springframework.jms.connection.JmsTransactonManager` participate in that transaction.

The transaction terminates one of two ways: Either the method completes execution directly and the transaction manager commits the transaction, or the method throws an exception and the transaction manager rolls the transaction back. By default, any `java.lang.RuntimeException` results in a rolled back transaction. Using either of the `@Transactional` annotations you can expand or restrict this filter to refine what triggers a transaction rollback.

There is, of course, a bit of magic involved in all this, and you must use these resources in a specific way for the transaction scope to apply. How this works varies from one `PlatformTransactionManager` implementation to another and from one resource type to another.

## Using Threads for Transactions and Entity Managers

The transaction scope discussed previously is limited to the thread the transaction begins in. The transaction manager then links the transaction to managed resources used in the same thread during the life of the transaction. When using the Java Persistence API, the resource you work with is the `EntityManager`. It is the functional equivalent of Hibernate ORM's `Session` and JDBC's `Connection`. Normally, you would obtain an `EntityManager` from the `EntityManagerFactory` before beginning a transaction and performing JPA actions. However, this does not work with the Spring Framework model of managing transactions on your behalf.

The solution to this problem is the `org.springframework.orm.jpa.support.SharedEntityManagerBean`. When you configure JPA in Spring Framework, it creates a `SharedEntityManagerBean` that proxies the `EntityManager` interface. This proxy is then injected into your JPA repositories. When an `EntityManager` method is invoked on this proxy instance, the following happens in the background:

- If the current thread already has a real `EntityManager` with an active transaction, it delegates the call to the method on that `EntityManager`.
- Otherwise, Spring Framework obtains a new `EntityManager` from the `EntityManagerFactory`, starts a transaction, and binds both to the current thread. It then delegates the call to the method on that `EntityManager`.

When the transaction is either committed or rolled back, Spring unbinds the transaction and the `EntityManager` from the thread and then closes the `EntityManager`. Future `@Transactional` actions on the same thread (even within the same request) start the process over again, obtaining a new `EntityManager` from the factory and beginning a new transaction. This way, no two threads use an `EntityManager` at the same time, and a given thread has only one transaction and one `EntityManager` active at any given time.

Instead of marking `EntityManager` fields in your repositories as `@Inject` or `@Autowired`, you use the `@javax.persistence.PersistenceContext` annotation to indicate that Spring should inject a proxy for the `EntityManager`.

```
@PersistenceContext
EntityManager entityManager;
```

Normal `EntityManagers` are not thread-safe, and they always require you to start a transaction before using them. However, obtaining a `@PersistenceContext EntityManager` *from Spring Framework* means that your repository can use this instance in multiple threads, and behind the scenes each thread has its own `EntityManager` instance with a transaction managed on your behalf.

Another advantage to using `@PersistenceContext` is that you can specify a persistence unit name for a given `EntityManager` instance. This way, you can define multiple persistence context configurations in your Spring application context and discriminate which `EntityManager` instance you intend to use in a repository by specifying its name.

```
public class FooRepository
{
    @PersistenceContext(unitName = "fooUnit")
    EntityManager entityManager;
    ...
}

public class BarRepository
{
    @PersistenceContext(unitName = "barUnit")
    EntityManager entityManager;
    ...
}
```

When using JPA in Spring Framework, you can use one of two `PlatformTransactionManager` implementations.

- The most standard and common is `org.springframework.orm.jpa.JpaTransactionManager`, and it is what you use throughout this book. This implementation can manage the transactions only for `EntityManager` actions and only for a single persistence unit, but in many cases that is all you need.
- If you want to use multiple persistence units in your application (as in the previous example), or manage transactions across multiple types of resources (such as `EntityManagers` and Java Message Service resources), you need the `org.springframework.transaction.jta.JtaTransactionManager` or one of its subclasses (`WebLogicJtaTransactionManager` on WebLogic servers; `WebSphereUowTransactionManager` on WebSphere servers). This implementation requires a Java Transaction API provider, so to use it you need a full Java EE application server or a complex standalone JTA configuration (as is the case with Tomcat).

JTA is an extensive topic and difficult to configure outside a full Java EE application server, so it is not covered further in this book. There are many JTA tutorials online, and your application server documentation should be a useful resource.

## Taking Advantage of Exception Translation

In the days of direct JDBC usage, dealing with exceptions could be a nightmare. Every JDBC driver vendor had its own set of exceptions that extended `java.sql.SQLException`, and the error codes associated with those exceptions also varied based on the vendor. If you wanted to know in code precisely why an error occurred, you either restricted your code to a single vendor and figured out that vendor's exception pattern or you tested for every vendor's exceptions in your catch blocks. This process was tedious at best and often led to writing more code than you actually spent performing the work in the first place.

As O/RMs became more popular, some defined a useful exception hierarchy and some did not. The Java Persistence API defines a modest exception hierarchy starting at `javax.persistence.PersistenceException`, but even it is missing some key features (like an exception to indicate that a unique key violation occurred). Then in the realm of NoSQL tools, each client library defines its own set of checked or unchecked exceptions, and none of them inherit from a common persistence exception, making the problem even more daunting.

Spring Framework and its associated data tools (such as Spring Data NoSQL) solve this problem by defining a thorough hierarchy of persistence exceptions inheriting from `org.springframework.dao.DataAccessException`. This group contains a lot of exceptions and this book does not cover them all. Suffice it to say whether you use JDBC, Hibernate or another O/RM directly, JPA, Java Data Objects, or NoSQL, you can look for exceptions in this hierarchy instead of the technology-specific exceptions.

There are two key concepts to achieving this *exception translation* in your applications. First, you must configure one or more `org.springframework.dao.support.PersistenceExceptionTranslator` implementations in your root application context. There are different `PersistenceExceptionTranslator` implementations for different technologies. If you use multiple persistence technologies in your application — such as JPA and NoSQL — you need to configure an implementation that handles them all or configure multiple implementations. (Spring automatically chains them using the `org.springframework.dao.support.ChainedPersistenceExceptionTranslator`.)

Spring Framework has a variety of `PersistenceExceptionTranslators` to handle different persistence technologies. The `org.springframework.orm.jpa.LocalContainerEntityManagerFactoryBean` that you configure in the next section is also a `PersistenceExceptionTranslator` capable of translating JPA exceptions and the underlying JDBC error codes into `DataAccessExceptions`. By merely defining this bean, you have configured exception translation for JPA. If you use multiple persistence technologies, you can configure an implementation for each technology.

After you configure exception translation, you must next annotate your repositories with `@Repository`. This tells Spring that the annotated bean is eligible for exception translation using the configured `PersistenceExceptionTranslators`. If the repository methods throw any persistence exceptions, the `PersistenceExceptionTranslators` translate those exceptions as appropriate. Note that this means that you cannot catch translated `DataAccessExceptions` from the repository itself, because translation has not taken place yet. You can catch `DataAccessExceptions` only in code that calls repository methods.

> **NOTE** *If you look at all the* `PersistenceUnitTranslator` *implementations that Spring Framework and its tools provide, you notice that there is no plain JDBC exception translator. When you use JDBC in Spring repositories, it is expected that you'll use the* `JdbcTemplate`*. Because the* `JdbcTemplate` *is a Spring Framework tool and not a third-party class, it has persistence translation built in to it.*

## CONFIGURING PERSISTENCE IN SPRING FRAMEWORK

Configuring JPA in Spring is actually very straightforward, but you need to understand several options and this section explains them to you. Generally speaking, the Spring JPA configuration process has three parts:

- Create or look up a `DataSource`.
- Create or look up a persistence unit and configure Spring to inject it in your repositories.
- Set up transaction management so that `@Transactional` methods are properly handled.

You can follow along in the Spring-JPA project available for download from the `wrox.com` code download site. This project starts with the standard Spring bootstrap and configuration that you used at the end of Part II.

### Looking Up a Data Source

The first thing you need to do is make a `DataSource` available to your application. You have a few different ways to do this. For example, if you need to simply test something quickly, use Spring's `org.springframework.jdbc.datasource.DriverManagerDataSource` to create a `DataSource` on demand:

```
@Bean
public DataSource springJpaDataSource()
{
    DriverManagerDataSource dataSource = new DriverManagerDataSource();
    dataSource.setUrl("jdbc:mysql://localhost/SpringJpa");
    dataSource.setUsername("tomcatUser");
    dataSource.setPassword("password1234");
    return dataSource;
}
```

However, this creates a simple `DataSource` that returns single-use `Connections`. Because it does not provide connection pooling, it really should never be used in a production environment of any type. In a standalone application, you could use Apache Commons DBCP and Apache Commons Pool to create and return a pooled `DataSource`. Usually, you would read a properties file with the URL, username, and password information so that changing the connection details won't require a recompilation of code. On an application server or Servlet container, however, the easiest thing to do is to define a `DataSource` on the server (as you did in the previous chapter) and look that `DataSource` up from your `RootApplicationContext`. This is what the Spring-JPA project does.

```
@Bean
public DataSource springJpaDataSource()
{
    JndiDataSourceLookup lookup = new JndiDataSourceLookup();
    return lookup.getDataSource("jdbc/SpringJpa");
}
```

> **NOTE** *Connection pooling is similar to the thread pooling concept you learned about in Part II. A connection pool contains multiple, idle connections waiting to be used. These connections are borrowed from the pool and then returned and reset when they are no longer needed. This way, the overhead of constantly opening and closing connections is avoided. A* `DataSource` *configured in your application server or Servlet container uses connection pooling.*

While you're working on this, don't forget to define the `DataSource` resource in Tomcat's `context.xml` configuration file. (You'll learn about the `defaultTransactionIsolation` attribute in the next section.)

```
<Resource name="jdbc/SpringJpa" type="javax.sql.DataSource"
          maxActive="20" maxIdle="5" maxWait="10000"
          username="tomcatUser" password="password1234"
          driverClassName="com.mysql.jdbc.Driver"
          defaultTransactionIsolation="READ_COMMITTED"
          url="jdbc:mysql://localhost/SpringJpa" />
```

In this sample application, you use a standard `DataSource` that cannot participate in JTA transactions. This is sufficient for the examples in this book, but if you want a transaction to span multiple `DataSources` or multiple technologies (such as JMS), you must define and lookup a JTA-capable `DataSource`. This is possible, though very difficult, in Tomcat. Your best bet is to use a full Java EE application server for this purpose.

## Creating a Persistence Unit in Code

Perhaps the most important thing you must do when configuring Spring Framework's JPA support is setting up your persistence unit. You already explored creating a persistence unit in the `/WEB-INF/classes/META-INF/persistence.xml` file in Chapter 20, but you are not restricted to this technique when using Spring Framework.

To properly set up JPA, you need to configure a bean that implements `org.springframework.orm.jpa.AbstractEntityManagerFactoryBean`. Beans of this type can create `SharedEntityManagerBeans` that manage the thread-bound, transaction-linked `EntityManagers` in your repositories.

The simplest approach is to configure an `org.springframework.orm.jpa.LocalEntityManagerFactoryBean`. This bean requires that `/META-INF/persistence.xml` exists and reads the persistence unit configuration settings from that file. When you configure the `LocalEntityManagerFactoryBean`, you specify the name of the persistence unit that it should use.

```
@Bean
public LocalEntityManagerFactoryBean entityManagerFactoryBean()
{
    LocalEntityManagerFactoryBean factory =
            new LocalEntityManagerFactoryBean();
    factory.setPersistenceUnitName("SpringJpa");
    factory.setJpaVendorAdapter(new HibernateJpaVendorAdapter());
    factory.setDataSource(this.springJpaDataSource());
    return factory;
}
```

This is perfectly sufficient, but it is quite inflexible as far as solutions go. A more useful implementation is `org.springframework.orm.jpa.LocalContainerEntityManagerFactoryBean`, which does not require `/META-INF/persistence.xml` to exist. You could, for example, place your persistence file in a package instead of `META-INF` and then tell `LocalContainerEntityManagerFactoryBean` where the persistence file lives.

```
@Bean
public LocalContainerEntityManagerFactoryBean entityManagerFactoryBean()
{
    LocalContainerEntityManagerFactoryBean factory =
            new LocalContainerEntityManagerFactoryBean();
    factory.setPersistenceXmlLocation(
            "classpath:com/wrox/config/persistence.xml"
    );
    factory.setPersistenceUnitName("SpringJpa");
    factory.setJpaVendorAdapter(new HibernateJpaVendorAdapter());
    factory.setDataSource(this.springJpaDataSource());
    return factory;
}
```

Perhaps most important, you don't even *need* a persistence file with `LocalContainerEntityManagerFactoryBean`. You can omit the persistence XML location and persistence unit name entirely and create the persistence unit configuration using pure Java code. This is how the `RootContextConfiguration` in the Spring-JPA project configures its persistence unit.

```
@Bean
public LocalContainerEntityManagerFactoryBean entityManagerFactoryBean()
{
    Map<String, Object> properties = new Hashtable<>();
    properties.put("javax.persistence.schema-generation.database.action",
            "none");

    HibernateJpaVendorAdapter adapter = new HibernateJpaVendorAdapter();
    adapter.setDatabasePlatform("org.hibernate.dialect.MySQL5InnoDBDialect");

    LocalContainerEntityManagerFactoryBean factory =
            new LocalContainerEntityManagerFactoryBean();
    factory.setJpaVendorAdapter(adapter);
    factory.setDataSource(this.springJpaDataSource());
    factory.setPackagesToScan("com.wrox.site.entities");
    factory.setSharedCacheMode(SharedCacheMode.ENABLE_SELECTIVE);
    factory.setValidationMode(ValidationMode.NONE);
```

```
        factory.setJpaPropertyMap(properties);
        return factory;
    }
```

Examine this code carefully, because a lot of things are happening. First, it creates a map to hold JPA configuration properties — in this case, the schema generation property. Next, it creates an `org.springframework.orm.jpa.vendor.HibernateJpaVendorAdapter` and sets it as the adapter for the factory. This is a special Spring pattern that does a few things:

- It tells the `LocalContainerEntityManagerFactoryBean` which `PersistenceProvider` to use (`org.hibernate.jpa.HibernatePersistenceProvider`). This replaces `<provider>` from `persistence.xml`.
- It tells the `SharedEntityManagerBean` which extended `EntityManagerFactory` interface it will proxy (`org.hibernate.jpa.HibernateEntityManagerFactory`) and which extended `EntityManager` interface it will proxy (`org.hibernate.jpa.HibernateEntityManager`).
- It tells Spring how to properly translate the Hibernate ORM-specific JPA exceptions to `DataAccessExceptions`.
- It informs transaction management about any extra steps that should be used when beginning and ending transactions to deal with any special issues that might arise.
- It configures Hibernate ORM to use the correct dialect for the database you use. Hibernate attempts to detect the proper dialect to use, but for MySQL it always selects `org.hibernate.dialect.MySQLDialect`. This legacy dialect is only for MySQL 4.x and should not be used with MySQL 5.x. It's safest to always manually specify this value.

There are more than 50 different Hibernate ORM dialects. Table 21-1 lists the most common Hibernate ORM dialects and which database versions they support.

**TABLE 21-1:** Common Hibernate Dialects

| DATABASE NAME & VERSION(S) | DIALECT CLASS |
|---|---|
| H2 Database Engine | `org.hibernate.dialect.H2Dialect` |
| HyperSQL 1.8+, 2.x+ | `org.hibernate.dialect.HSQLDialect` |
| MySQL 4.x Generic | `org.hibernate.dialect.MySQLDialect` |
| MySQL 4.x MyISAM Engine | `org.hibernate.dialect.MySQLMyISAMDialect` |
| MySQL 4.x InnoDB Engine | `org.hibernate.dialect.MySQLInnoDBDialect` |
| MySQL 5.x+ Generic + MyISAM | `org.hibernate.dialect.MySQL5Dialect` |
| MySQL 5.x+ InnoDB Engine | `org.hibernate.dialect.MySQL5InnoDBDialect` |
| Oracle Database 8i | `org.hibernate.dialect.Oracle8iDialect` |
| Oracle Database 9i | `org.hibernate.dialect.Oracle9iDialect` |

*continues*

**TABLE 21-1** *(continued)*

| DATABASE NAME & VERSION(S) | DIALECT CLASS |
|---|---|
| Oracle Database 10g, 11g+ | `org.hibernate.dialect.Oracle10gDialect` |
| PostgreSQL 8.1 | `org.hibernate.dialect.PostgreSQL81Dialect` |
| PostgreSQL 8.2+ | `org.hibernate.dialect.PostgreSQL82Dialect` |
| Microsoft SQL Server 2000 | `org.hibernate.dialect.SQLServerDialect` |
| Microsoft SQL Server 2005 | `org.hibernate.dialect.SQLServer2005Dialect` |
| Microsoft SQL Server 2008, 2012+ | `org.hibernate.dialect.SQLServer2008Dialect` |
| Sybase 10 | `org.hibernate.dialect.SybaseDialect` |
| Sybase 11.9.2+ | `org.hibernate.dialect.Sybase11Dialect` |
| Sybase ASE 15+ | `org.hibernate.dialect.SybaseASE15Dialect` |
| Sybase Anywhere 8+ | `org.hibernate.dialect.SybaseAnywhereDialect` |

`HibernateJpaVendorAdapter` is just one implementation of `org.springframework.orm.jpa.JpaVendorAdapter`. Spring also has adapters for EclipseLink and OpenJPA that help configure Spring correctly for those JPA vendors, and you can easily create your own implementation to support another vendor if necessary. Note that the `LocalEntityManagerFactoryBean` and `LocalContainerEntityManagerFactoryBean` can function without a `JpaVendorAdapter` implementation, but they may not function as well as they could. It's best to always supply this.

> **NOTE** *Instead of calling* `setDatabasePlatform` *on the adapter, you could call* `setDatabase` *and pass it one of the* `org.springframework.orm.jpa.vendor.Database` *enum constants. Then the* `HibernateJpaVendorAdapter` *would select the Hibernate dialect class for you. However, it also selects only* `MySQLDialect` *for MySQL databases, selects the SQL Server 2000 dialect for SQL Server databases, and so on. Although this is a convenient tool, you're better off telling Hibernate exactly which dialect to use so that it works the best it possibly can. Otherwise, you might not get the correct dialect for your database.*

After configuring the vendor adapter, the code sets the `DataSource` to the one you configured earlier. This replaces the `<non-jta-data-source>` element in `persistence.xml` and also sets the `transaction-type` for the persistence unit to `RESOURCE_LOCAL`. (Calling `setJtaDataSource` is the equivalent of `<jta-data-source>` and setting `transaction-type` to `JTA`.)

It then tells the `LocalContainerEntityManagerFactoryBean` to scan the package `com.wrox.site.entities` for entity beans. This is equivalent to `<exclude-unlisted-classes>true</exclude-unlisted-classes>` and listing out each entity class with `<class>`, except that Spring detects and registers the entity classes for you. This starts up significantly faster than

`<exclude-unlisted-classes>false</exclude-unlisted-classes>` because Spring limits its scanning to the package or packages you specify, whereas the JPA provider would have to scan many more packages and classes. The configuration then sets the shared cache mode (equivalent to `<shared-cache-mode>`), the validation mode (equivalent to `<validation-mode>`), and the JPA properties.

> **NOTE** *In general, you really shouldn't need to understand much about coding with Hibernate ORM as long as you use JPA. However, you do need to know about some things, such as dialects. For your reference, you can view the Hibernate ORM 4.3 API documentation at* `http://docs.jboss.org/hibernate/orm/4.3/javadocs/`*. Before selecting a dialect for your particular database, you should view the API documentation for* `org.hibernate.dialect.Dialect` *and its subclasses.*

## Setting Up Transaction Management

Configuring transaction management is the last step to setting up JPA in Spring Framework. Though it is not especially tricky, there are some things to watch out for. You initially activate transaction management and `@Transactional` method interception by annotating the `RootContextConfiguration` with `@org.springframework.transaction.annotation.EnableTransactionManagement`. Like the `@EnableAsync` annotation that you are already using, `@EnableTransactionManagement` results in Spring dynamically advising your `@Transactional` bean methods. However, you must do this with care.

First, you must configure `@EnableAsync` and `@EnableTransactionManagement` with the same `AdviceMode` (`PROXY` or `ASPECTJ`) and the same `proxyTargetClass` value. As discussed in Chapter 14, the easiest approach is to use `AdviceMode.PROXY` with `proxyTargetClass` set to `false`.

### A NOTE ABOUT SPRING FRAMEWORK METHOD ADVICE

Spring Framework can advise your methods using AspectJ pointcuts or proxies. Using `AdviceMode.PROXY` enables proxies, meaning proxy classes wrap around advised methods to execute advice code before and after the methods as necessary. You can create these proxy methods using dynamic proxies (`proxyTargetClass = false`), which are part of the standard Java SE API. This is the preferred, best-practice proxy technique. However, dynamic proxies can advise only methods that are specified in an interface, and they apply only if the consuming code uses the interface instead of the actual class. If you need to advise public methods that are only part of the class and not part of an interface, you must use CGLIB proxies (`proxyTargetClass = true`). The important downside to remember about using CGLIB proxies is that your bean constructors execute twice, not once, so plan accordingly.

*continues*

*continued*

When you use dynamic proxies, the method advice they provide applies only when another class executes methods on the Spring-managed bean instance. If a method invoked on an instance of `FooBean` executes another method on the same instance of `FooBean` (with or without using `this`), the method advice does not execute. (See `org.springframework.aop.framework.AopContext` for an ugly way to do this, which you should avoid whenever possible.) CGLIB proxies override every non-final method on a class, so method advice *is* applied when `FooBean` calls another `FooBean` method (with or without using `this`). However, Spring cannot create CGLIB proxies for final classes.

If these two options still do not meet your needs, you can use AspectJ pointcuts with load-time weaving enabled. Load-time weaving actually modifies the compiled bytecode of your classes as they are loaded, adding the method advice directly to the bytecode. This works on final and non-final classes and methods, and on methods called from within the same object. An object doesn't even have to be a Spring-managed bean for method advice to apply! (This is very useful for legacy applications.) You enable this by setting the advice mode to `AdviceMode.ASPECTJ`, decorating your root context configuration class with `@EnableLoadTimeWeaving(aspectjWeaving=EnableLoadTimeWeaving.AspectJWeaving.ENABLED)`, and adding the following Maven dependency to your project:

```
<dependency>
    <groupId>org.springframework</groupId>
    <artifactId>spring-aspects</artifactId>
    <version>4.0.2.RELEASE</version>
    <scope>runtime</scope>
</dependency>
```

You explore using AspectJ load-time weaving more in Chapter 24. However you choose to configure method advice in your application, you must configure it the same way for every feature that uses it. For example, you must configure it the same way for `@EnableAsync` as for `@EnableTransactionManagement`. If you configure them differently, Spring picks one configuration and uses it for both, which may cause unexpected results.

Also, it's important to consider the order of execution of these two proxies. If the transaction management proxy executes before the asynchronous proxy, then actions associated with setting up an asynchronous method are included in transaction management, and thread-binding the transaction may not work properly. The `RootContextConfiguration` class uses the `order` attribute of these two annotations to ensure that the proxies execute in the correct order (asynchronous operations proxy before the transaction management proxy).

```
@Configuration
@EnableScheduling
@EnableAsync(
        mode = AdviceMode.PROXY, proxyTargetClass = false,
        order = Ordered.HIGHEST_PRECEDENCE
```

```
)
@EnableTransactionManagement(
        mode = AdviceMode.PROXY, proxyTargetClass = false,
        order = Ordered.LOWEST_PRECEDENCE
)
@ComponentScan(
        basePackages = "com.wrox.site",
        excludeFilters =
        @ComponentScan.Filter({Controller.class, ControllerAdvice.class})
)
public class RootContextConfiguration implements
...
```

Any time you use `@EnableTransactionManagement` you must supply a default implementation of the `PlatformTransactionManager`. For JPA resources you should use the `org.springframework.orm.jpa.JpaTransactionManager`. Its constructor binds to an `EntityManagerFactory`, so you should use the `LocalContainerEntityManagerFactoryBean` you created earlier to construct the `JpaTransactionManager`.

```
    @Bean
    public PlatformTransactionManager jpaTransactionManager()
    {
        return new JpaTransactionManager(
                this.entityManagerFactoryBean().getObject()
        );
    }
```

By default, transaction management looks for a bean named `txManager` and then falls back to the first bean it can find that implements `PlatformTransactionManager`. However, it's possible to have multiple `PlatformTransactionManagers` in an application context. In this case, Spring may choose the wrong default transaction manager to handle `@Transactional` methods. To protect against this, your configuration class can implement `TransactionManagementConfigurer` and Spring always uses the manager returned from `annotationDrivenTransactionManager` as the default manager for `@Transactional` methods.

```
@Configuration
@EnableScheduling
@EnableAsync(
        mode = AdviceMode.PROXY, proxyTargetClass = false,
        order = Ordered.HIGHEST_PRECEDENCE
)
@EnableTransactionManagement(
        mode = AdviceMode.PROXY, proxyTargetClass = false,
        order = Ordered.LOWEST_PRECEDENCE
)
@ComponentScan(
        basePackages = "com.wrox.site",
        excludeFilters =
        @ComponentScan.Filter({Controller.class, ControllerAdvice.class})
)
public class RootContextConfiguration implements
        AsyncConfigurer, SchedulingConfigurer, TransactionManagementConfigurer
{
    ...
    @Bean
```

```
        public PlatformTransactionManager jpaTransactionManager()
        {
            return new JpaTransactionManager(
                    this.entityManagerFactoryBean().getObject()
            );
        }
        ...
        @Override
        public PlatformTransactionManager annotationDrivenTransactionManager()
        {
            return this.jpaTransactionManager();
        }
        ...
    }
```

Notice that this method simply calls the `@Bean` `jpaTransactionManager` method so that the chosen bean name (`jpaTransactionManager`) is preserved.

# CREATING AND USING JPA REPOSITORIES

Using JPA in Spring repositories is easier than using JPA on its own because you don't have to deal with transactions and the `EntityManagerFactory`. This section shows you the simple steps involved in doing this as well as how to demarcate transaction boundaries in your services. You also create a generic repository for handling many different types of entities using common code. The Spring-JPA project uses the `Book`, `Author`, and `Publisher` entities you created in the previous chapter, minus the `previewPdf` property of the `Book`, and uses the same database creation script except for the database name `SpringJpa`.

## Injecting the Persistence Unit

You're going to have three repositories — one for each entity. This is a common and useful pattern, but by no means required. You could create a repository for several related entities, for example. But using one repository per entity enables you to create generic repository code, something you learn about later in the section. The repositories each implement an interface, which you explore in more detail later in the section.

```
public interface AuthorRepository { ... }
public interface BookRepository { ... }
public interface PublisherRepository { ... }
```

To perform JPA operations in the repository implementations, you need an `EntityManager` instance. As discussed earlier, all you need to do is declare an `EntityManager` field and mark it with the `@PersistenceContext` JPA annotation. You don't need to annotate the field `@Inject` or `@Autowired`; `@PersistenceContext` serves this purpose as well. Because `@PersistenceContext` came before Spring Framework's support for JPA, there is no Spring-equivalent for `@PersistenceContext`, so this annotation is all you need to worry about.

```
@Repository
public class DefaultAuthorRepository implements AuthorRepository
{
```

```
    @PersistenceContext EntityManager entityManager;

    ...
}

@Repository
public class DefaultBookRepository implements BookRepository
{
    @PersistenceContext EntityManager entityManager;

    ...
}

@Repository
public class DefaultPublisherRepository implements PublisherRepository
{
    @PersistenceContext EntityManager entityManager;

    ...
}
```

You'll recall from earlier in the chapter that the `EntityManager` injected here isn't the one provided by the JPA vendor (Hibernate ORM). Instead, it's a proxy instance for the real thing and automatically delegates to the transaction-linked, thread-bound `EntityManager` created for a previous method invocation in the same transaction and thread (or creates a new `EntityManager` and transaction if one has not been created yet).

## Implementing Standard CRUD Operations

For now your repositories need to perform only the simplest operations — returning single entities and lists of entities, adding entities, updating entities, and deleting entities. This is easily represented in the `AuthorRepository` interface.

```
public interface AuthorRepository
{
    Iterable<Author> getAll();

    Author get(long id);

    void add(Author author);

    void update(Author author);

    void delete(Author author);

    void delete(long id);
}
```

The implementation for these methods in Listing 21-1 takes a slightly different approach than you used in the `EntityServlet` in the previous chapter. Instead of the newer criteria API, it uses the Java Persistence Query Language (JPQL) to look up entities. As you can tell, JPQL is very similar to ANSI SQL; however, there are of course some differences. For example, the identifiers in the `SELECT` clause identify which entities are returned, not which columns are returned as in a SQL query. A JPQL query can use multiple entities in a `WHERE` clause but return only one of them in the `SELECT` clause. Also, the identifiers in the FROM clause identify the entity names, not the table names as in a SQL query.

**LISTING 21-1: DefaultAuthorRepository.java**

```
@Repository
public class DefaultAuthorRepository implements AuthorRepository
{
    @PersistenceContext EntityManager entityManager;

    @Override
    public Iterable<Author> getAll()
    {
        return this.entityManager.createQuery(
                "SELECT a FROM Author a ORDER BY a.name", Author.class
        ).getResultList();
    }

    @Override
    public Author get(long id)
    {
        return this.entityManager.createQuery(
                "SELECT a FROM Author a WHERE a.id = :id", Author.class
        ).setParameter("id", id).getSingleResult();
    }

    @Override
    public void add(Author author)
    {
        this.entityManager.persist(author);
    }

    @Override
    public void update(Author author)
    {
        this.entityManager.merge(author);
    }

    @Override
    public void delete(Author author)
    {
        this.entityManager.remove(author);
    }

    @Override
    public void delete(long id)
    {
        this.entityManager.createQuery(
                "DELETE FROM Author a WHERE a.id = :id"
        ).setParameter("id", id).executeUpdate();
    }
}
```

## Creating a Base Repository for All Your Entities

Think for a minute about the `AuthorRepository` and the methods it specified, and then think about the methods that the `BookRepository` and `PublisherRepository` should specify. You should immediately notice a similarity:

```
public interface BookRepository
{
    Iterable<Book> getAll();
    Book get(long id);
    void add(Book book);
    void update(Book book);
    void delete(Book book);
    void delete(long id);
}

public interface PublisherRepository
{
    Iterable<Publisher> getAll();
    Publisher get(long id);
    void add(Publisher publisher);
    void update(Publisher publisher);
    void delete(Publisher publisher);
    void delete(long id);
}
```

If you consider the implementations for these methods, you should quickly realize that they are nearly identical to the `DefaultAuthorRepository` class. You'd be right to wonder whether there's a way to write code that can take care of all your entities. To be most useful, such a repository needs to use generics. Following best practices and starting with an interface, consider what it might look like.

```
@Validated
public interface GenericRepository<I extends Serializable, E extends Serializable>
{
    @NotNull
    Iterable<E> getAll();

    E get(@NotNull I id);

    void add(@NotNull E entity);

    void update(@NotNull E entity);

    void delete(@NotNull E entity);

    void deleteById(@NotNull I id);
}
```

The generic type variable *`I`* represents the type of the surrogate key for your entities — usually a `long`, but not always, which is why this is a variable. *`E`* represents the entity type. Using the Bean Validation `@NotNull` constraint is a great way to tell repository users and implementers that `null` parameters and `null` returned lists are not tolerated. Due to the ambiguity of *`I`* and *`E`* here (they could, in theory, be the same types), the compiler cannot distinguish between a method parameter of type `I` and a method parameter of type `E`. Therefore, the `delete` and `deleteById` methods must have different names.

> **NOTE** *JPA does not strictly require entities or their surrogate keys to be* `Serializable`*, but this is a best-practice restriction to enforce.*

Now your repository interfaces need only to extend this parent interface and specify the type variables applicable to the entities they provide access to.

```
public interface AuthorRepository extends GenericRepository<Long, Author>
{

}

public interface BookRepository extends GenericRepository<Long, Book>
{
    Book getByIsbn(String isbn);
}

public interface PublisherRepository extends GenericRepository<Long, Publisher>
{

}
```

The `AuthorRepository` and `PublisherRepository` interfaces don't define any methods because they don't need to. The methods are all defined in the `GenericRepository` interface, and the type variable values make the method argument types and return types concrete. The `BookRepository` defines an additional method to look books up by ISBN — a common need.

The next logical step is to define common implementations for all the `GenericRepository` methods. As of Java 8, you *could* take the unique approach of using default methods:

```
@Validated
public interface GenericRepository<I extends Serializable, E extends Serializable>
{
    @NotNull
    default Iterable<E> getAll()
    {
        ...
    }

    ...
}
```

However, this is a bad choice for several reasons:

- Default methods are not designed for the purpose of replacing abstract classes. They were created so that you can make improvements to interfaces without breaking existing implementations. For example, Java 8 collections were improved using default methods without breaking thousands of existing `Collection`, `List`, `Set`, `Map`, `Iterable`, and `Iterator` implementations. Default methods have a different semantic meaning than concrete methods in abstract classes and should not be used for this purpose.

- You need an injected `EntityManager` to execute code in these methods, and you cannot obtain that in an interface.
- You need access to the type (`Class`) of *`I`* and *`E`* to perform safe JPA query operations. The best way to obtain this (and the only way if you want to make these values `final`) is in a constructor, which an interface cannot have.

A more appropriate approach is to use a generic base class, and this can satisfy all your needs. You have a few things to consider when deciding how to approach this. The first is how to determine the `Class` instance for the type variables. The simplest approach is to require them in the constructor:

```
public abstract class
        GenericBaseRepository<I extends Serializable, E extends Serializable>
    implements GenericRepository<I, E>
{
    protected final Class<I> idClass;
    protected final Class<E> entityClass;

    public GenericBaseRepository(Class<I> idClass, Class<E> entityClass)
    {
        this.idClass = idClass;
        this.entityClass = entityClass;
    }

    ...
}
```

This would work, but it seems silly to require these constructor arguments when the information is already there in the implementation's type variable arguments. Fortunately, you can access the arguments to these type variables, though not without some effort.

```
public abstract class
        GenericBaseRepository<I extends Serializable, E extends Serializable>
    implements GenericRepository<I, E>
{
    protected final Class<I> idClass;
    protected final Class<E> entityClass;

    @SuppressWarnings("unchecked")
    public GenericBaseRepository()
    {
        Type genericSuperclass = this.getClass().getGenericSuperclass();
        while(!(genericSuperclass instanceof ParameterizedType))
        {
            if(!(genericSuperclass instanceof Class))
                throw new IllegalStateException("Unable to determine type " +
                        "arguments because generic superclass neither " +
                        "parameterized type nor class.");
            if(genericSuperclass == GenericBaseRepository.class)
                throw new IllegalStateException("Unable to determine type " +
                        "arguments because no parameterized generic superclass " +
                        "found.");

            genericSuperclass = ((Class)genericSuperclass).getGenericSuperclass();
```

```
            }

            ParameterizedType type = (ParameterizedType)genericSuperclass;
            Type[] arguments = type.getActualTypeArguments();
            this.idClass = (Class<I>)arguments[0];
            this.entityClass = (Class<E>)arguments[1];
        }
    }
```

This constructor may confuse you some, so take a look at it piece by piece. When a class extends `GenericBaseRepository`, that class's superclass is `GenericBaseRepository`. More important, `GenericBaseRepository` is its *generic superclass* and thus should be a `ParameterizedType` with type arguments. Now you could just call `((ParameterizedType) this.getClass().getGenericSuperclass()).getActualTypeArguments()`, but that works only if every repository inherits directly from `GenericBaseRepository` and is `final`. Not only is this restriction not ideal, but it also won't work with Spring Framework's transaction proxying and exception translation. So the loop walks up the inheritance tree, inspecting each type it encounters until it finds a `ParameterizedType`. If it encounters a type that isn't a `Class`, it can't walk the tree further. If it encounters its own type, it has walked the tree too far. Both conditions are arguably impossible, but worth testing for nonetheless. When it finds a `ParameterizedType`, it has found the superclass where the type variable arguments are specified. It then retrieves those arguments from the type and assigns them to the fields.

This constructor is the only value the `GenericBaseRepository` provides. It does not provide an `EntityManager` or method implementations because you may want to have a mixture of JPA and non-JPA repositories in your application. Determining the type arguments has nothing to do with JPA, so it's best to put this behavior in its own superclass. The `GenericJpaRepository` in Listing 21-2 does all the interesting JPA work.

**LISTING 21-2: GenericJpaRepository.java**

```
public abstract class
        GenericJpaRepository<I extends Serializable, E extends Serializable>
    extends GenericBaseRepository<I, E>
{
    @PersistenceContext protected EntityManager entityManager;

    @Override
    public Iterable<E> getAll()
    {
        CriteriaBuilder builder = this.entityManager.getCriteriaBuilder();
        CriteriaQuery<E> query = builder.createQuery(this.entityClass);

        return this.entityManager.createQuery(
                query.select(query.from(this.entityClass))
        ).getResultList();
    }

    @Override
    public E get(I id)
    {
        return this.entityManager.find(this.entityClass, id);
```

```
    }

    @Override
    public void add(E entity)
    {
        this.entityManager.persist(entity);
    }

    @Override
    public void update(E entity)
    {
        this.entityManager.merge(entity);
    }

    @Override
    public void delete(E entity)
    {
        this.entityManager.remove(entity);
    }

    @Override
    public void deleteById(I id)
    {
        CriteriaBuilder builder = this.entityManager.getCriteriaBuilder();
        CriteriaDelete<E> query = builder.createCriteriaDelete(this.entityClass);

        this.entityManager.createQuery(query.where(
                builder.equal(query.from(this.entityClass).get("id"), id)
        )).executeUpdate();
    }
}
```

Some notes about the previous code:

- The original `DefaultAuthorRepository` demonstrated the Java Persistence Query Language, but this is not easy to use when you don't know the actual entity name (which you can't in a generic repository). The `GenericJpaRepository` uses the criteria API, instead, to return the list of all entities and delete by ID.
- The `deleteById` method works only if all your entities have a property named `id`, which is the case here. If the surrogate key property names differ, you have to get the entity by the ID and then call the `remove` method.
- The `DefaultAuthorRepository` and `DefaultPublisherRepository` no longer need any methods because their methods are already defined in the `GenericJpaRepository`.
- Only the `DefaultBookRepository` needs a method, which implements the additional `getByIsbn` method specified in the `BookRepository` interface.

```
@Repository
public class DefaultAuthorRepository extends GenericJpaRepository<Long, Author>
    implements AuthorRepository
{

}

@Repository
```

```
public class DefaultBookRepository extends GenericJpaRepository<Long, Book>
        implements BookRepository
{
    @Override
    public Book getByIsbn(String isbn)
    {
        CriteriaBuilder builder = this.entityManager.getCriteriaBuilder();
        CriteriaQuery<Book> query = builder.createQuery(this.entityClass);
        Root<Book> root = query.from(this.entityClass);

        return this.entityManager.createQuery(
                query.select(root).where(builder.equal(root.get("isbn"), isbn))
        ).getSingleResult();
    }
}

@Repository
public class DefaultPublisherRepository
        extends GenericJpaRepository<Long, Publisher>
        implements PublisherRepository
{

}
```

The JPA criteria API is not the most intuitive API and is certainly more difficult to use than Hibernate ORM's criteria API. Unlike Hibernate's API, which is designed solely to make it easy to add expressions and restrictions to an entity lookup, this API is designed to mimic the query language itself. The `getAll` criteria in `GenericJpaRepository` can literally be read, "Select from entity," which is identical to the JPQL query you created earlier for this purpose, minus ordering instructions. If order is important, you have a few options. You could override the method as needed, or you could specify a constructor argument that subclasses use to specify default order instructions. Ordering is not difficult with the criteria API.

```
...
Root<Book> root = query.from(Book.class);

return this.entityManager.createQuery(
        query.select(root).orderBy(builder.asc(root.get("name")))
).getResultList();
```

The new query can be read, "Select from `Book` ordered by `Book.name` ascending." Notice that the code created the root query type first because it needed to use `Book` in both the `FROM` and `ORDER BY` clauses. This may seem redundant because the `CriteriaQuery` instance is already typed, but remember that the `CriteriaQuery` is typed to the object that will be returned. The query may use types other than the return type. Although you may often find JPQL easier to use, you can perform any of the same options using the criteria API. Which you use is up to your use case and personal preference.

## Demarking Transaction Boundaries in Your Services

As mentioned earlier, you tell Spring Framework when and how to start and end a transaction using Spring's `@Transactional` annotation or JTA's `@Transactional` annotation. Spring's annotation is a little more powerful and flexible than JTA's annotation.

Using @javax.transaction.Transactional, you can define a blacklist of exceptions that should not trigger a rollback using the dontRollbackOn attribute, a whitelist of exceptions to override the default rollback rule of all RuntimeExceptions using rollbackOn, and the rule for when and how a transaction is created using the Transactional.TxType enum value attribute. Transactional.TxType has the following enum constants:

- MANDATORY indicates a transaction must already exist, a new transaction may not be created, and an exception must be thrown if a transaction does not already exist.
- NEVER indicates that a transaction must not already exist, a transaction must not be used, and an exception must be thrown if a transaction already exists.
- NOT_SUPPORTED means that a transaction must not be used, and if one already exists, it must be suspended so that the code can execute outside of a transaction. When the code finishes executing, any suspended transaction must be resumed.
- REQUIRED means that a transaction must be used. If no transaction exists, it should be started before the method executes and completed after the method returns. If a transaction already exists, it should be used and allowed to continue after the method returns.
- REQUIRES_NEW is exactly what it sounds. Like REQUIRED, it indicates that if no transaction exists, it should be started before the method executes and completed after the method returns. However, if a transaction already exists, it should be suspended and a new transaction started before the method executes, and the new transaction should be completed and the original transaction resumed after the method returns.
- SUPPORTS is perhaps the most flexible instruction. It means that an existing transaction must be used, but if no transaction already exists, the method must execute without a transaction.

@org.springframework.transaction.annotation.Transactional has attributes noRollbackFor, rollbackFor, and propagation with the same semantic meaning as dontRollbackOn, rollbackOn, and value, respectively, in JTA's annotation. It also has noRollbackForClassName and rollbackForClassName attributes that accept String class names instead of Classes. The org.springframework.transaction.annotation.Propagation enum has the same constants with the same meanings as Transactional.TxType.

In addition, Propagation has a NESTED constant that creates a nested transaction if one already exists or a new transaction if none already exists. NESTED is not supported when using the JpaTransactionManager. It *may* be supported when using the JtaTransactionManager with some JTA providers, but using it is not portable. The default rule is REQUIRED for both @Transactional annotations, and in almost all cases, this is sufficient for your purposes.

Spring's annotation also contains several other useful attributes. isolation enables you to specify the transaction isolation level using the org.springframework.transaction.annotation.Isolation enum. This attribute is not supported and is ignored for the JpaTransactionManager and the JtaTransactionManager. The transaction isolation level for these managers is always the isolation level specified in the JPA or JTA DataSource configuration or the default isolation level for the JDBC driver, if none is specified in the DataSource. Because the default varies from one JDBC driver to the next, it's best to always specify the isolation level when defining the

DataSource resource. The available isolation levels are NONE, READ_COMMITTED, READ_UNCOMMITTED, REPEATABLE_READ, and SERIALIZABLE. For more information about what these mean you should consult the documentation for your database server. In this book, you always use READ_COMMITTED.

readOnly is another attribute available in Spring's @Transactional annotation that is not supported for the JpaTransactionManager and JtaTransactionManager. It instructs the underlying transaction system that writes should be forbidden in the transaction and defaults to false. The timeout attribute is supported when you use the JtaTransactionManager but not when you use the JpaTransactionManager. It restricts the amount of time that a transaction may consume before ending in an exception and rollback.

When using the JTA @Transactional annotation, Spring always uses the default PlatformTransactionManager. Remember, this is the one returned by the TransactionManagementConfigurer method, or the one named txManager in the absence of TransactionManagementConfigurer if there are multiple transaction managers, or the only transaction manager if there is just one. However, you can use Spring's @Transactional annotation with multiple PlatformTransactionManager beans. If you omit the value attribute, it uses the default transaction manager, but you can specify a bean name in the value attribute and the PlatformTransactionManager with that bean name used.

```
@Configuration
@EnableTransactionManagement(
        mode = AdviceMode.PROXY, proxyTargetClass = false,
        order = Ordered.LOWEST_PRECEDENCE
)
public class RootContextConfiguration implements TransactionManagementConfigurer
{
    ...
    @Bean
    public PlatformTransactionManager jpaTransactionManager()
    {
        return new JpaTransactionManager(
                this.entityManagerFactoryBean().getObject()
        );
    }

    @Bean
    public PlatformTransactionManager dataSourceTransactionManager()
    {
        return new DataSourceTransactionManager(this.springJpaDataSource());
    }

    @Override
    public PlatformTransactionManager annotationDrivenTransactionManager()
    {
        return this.jpaTransactionManager();
    }
    ...
}
```

The previous configuration creates two PlatformTransactionManager beans, one for JPA and one for simple DataSource actions. The JpaTransactionManager acts as the default transaction manager. Using this configuration, the actionOne method in the following service executes under the control of the default (JPA) transaction manager. Likewise, `actionTwo` executes explicitly using the `JpaTransactionManager` while `actionThree` executes explicitly using the `DataSourceTransactionManager`.

```
public SomeService
{
    @Transactional
    public void actionOne();

    @Transactional("jpaTransactionManager")
    public void actionTwo();

    @Transactional("dataSourceTransactionManager")
    public void actionThree();
}
```

When using either of the `@Transactional` annotations, you may annotate an interface, individual interface methods, a class, or class methods. If you annotate an interface, it is equivalent to annotating the methods of that interface. Likewise, annotating a class is equivalent to annotating the methods of that class. When demarking transaction boundaries in code in your application, the best practice is to annotate the concrete class or class methods, not the interface or interface methods. Annotating an interface or its methods, `@Transactional` works only when dynamic proxies (`proxyTargetClass = false`) are in use. If you ever need to enable CGLIB proxies (`proxyTargetClass = true`), the interface annotations will stop working. Unlike Bean Validation annotations, which establish a contract on the interface, `@Transactional` is an implementation detail and doesn't belong in the contract. Annotating service methods is demonstrated with the `DefaultBookManager` implementation in Listing 21-3. Although `DefaultBookManager` does not show it, a `@Transactional` method can access and manipulate multiple entities using multiple repositories, all within the same transaction context.

**LISTING 21-3: DefaultBookManager.java**

```
@Service
public class DefaultBookManager implements BookManager
{
    @Inject AuthorRepository authorRepository;
    @Inject BookRepository bookRepository;
    @Inject PublisherRepository publisherRepository;

    @Override
    public List<Author> getAuthors()
    {
        return this.toList(this.authorRepository.getAll());
    }

    @Override
    public List<Book> getBooks()
    {
        return this.toList(this.bookRepository.getAll());
```

*continues*

**LISTING 21-3** *(continued)*

```
    }

    @Override
    public List<Publisher> getPublishers()
    {
        return this.toList(this.publisherRepository.getAll());
    }

    private <E> List<E> toList(Iterable<E> i)
    {
        List<E> list = new ArrayList<>();
        i.forEach(list::add);
        return list;
    }

    @Override
    public void saveAuthor(Author author)
    {
        if(author.getId() < 1)
            this.authorRepository.add(author);
        else
            this.authorRepository.update(author);
    }

    @Override
    public void saveBook(Book book)
    {
        if(book.getId() < 1)
            this.bookRepository.add(book);
        else
            this.bookRepository.update(book);
    }

    @Override
    public void savePublisher(Publisher publisher)
    {
        if(publisher.getId() < 1)
            this.publisherRepository.add(publisher);
        else
            this.publisherRepository.update(publisher);
    }
}
```

## Using the Transactional Service Methods

You needn't do anything different when using `@Transactional` service methods. From the consumer's perspective, the transaction happens transparently. The `BookController` works similarly to the `EntityServlet` in Chapter 20: It lists the `Authors`, `Books`, and `Publishers` for `GET` requests and creates them for `POST` requests.

```
@WebController
public class BookController
{
    private final Random random;

    @Inject BookManager bookManager;

    public BookController()
    {
        try
        {
            this.random = SecureRandom.getInstanceStrong();
        }
        catch(NoSuchAlgorithmException e)
        {
            throw new IllegalStateException(e);
        }
    }

    @RequestMapping(value = "/", method = RequestMethod.GET)
    public String list(Map<String, Object> model)
    {
        model.put("publishers", this.bookManager.getPublishers());
        model.put("authors", this.bookManager.getAuthors());
        model.put("books", this.bookManager.getBooks());

        return "entities";
    }

    @RequestMapping(value = "/", method = RequestMethod.POST)
    public View add()
    {
        Publisher publisher = new Publisher();
        publisher.setName("John Wiley & Sons");
        publisher.setAddress("1234 Baker Street");
        publisher.setDateFounded(Calendar.getInstance());
        this.bookManager.savePublisher(publisher);

        Author author = new Author();
        author.setName("Nicholas S. Williams");
        author.setEmailAddress("nick@example.com");
        author.setGender(Gender.MALE);
        this.bookManager.saveAuthor(author);

        Book book = new Book();
        book.setIsbn("" + this.random.nextInt(Integer.MAX_VALUE));
        book.setTitle("Professional Java for Web Applications");
        book.setAuthor("Nicholas S. Williams");
        book.setPublisher("John Wiley & Sons");
        book.setPrice(59.99D);
        this.bookManager.saveBook(book);

        return new RedirectView("/", true, false);
    }
}
```

To test it, follow these steps:

1. Make sure you add the `DataSource` resource definition to Tomcat's `context.xml` file and run the `create.sql` database creation script in MySQL Workbench to create the necessary database tables.

```
<Resource name="jdbc/SpringJpa" type="javax.sql.DataSource"
          maxActive="20" maxIdle="5" maxWait="10000"
          username="tomcatUser" password="password1234"
          driverClassName="com.mysql.jdbc.Driver"
          defaultTransactionIsolation="READ_COMMITTED"
          url="jdbc:mysql://localhost/SpringJpa" />
```

2. Compile the application and start Tomcat from your IDE.
3. Go to `http://localhost:8080/repositories/` and click the Add More Entities button a few times, just like you did in the previous chapter.

You should see entities appearing in both the browser and the database tables. Looking up individual entities by ID (and ISBN) is an exercise left up to you.

# CONVERTING DATA WITH DTOS AND ENTITIES

The Customer-Support-v15 application, available for download from the `wrox.com` code download site, uses the `LocalContainerEntityManagerFactoryBean` and transaction management you configured in Spring-JPA. It also has the same `GenericRepository` interface and `GenericBaseRepository` and `GenericJpaRepository` abstract classes. However, changing the Customer Support application to use JPA repositories and a MySQL database is not as simple as that. The `Ticket` class has properties that you can't yet convert using the JPA mechanisms you have learned about so far — the `Instant` date created and the `Map` of attachments. The easiest way to account for this is to treat the `Ticket` as a *Data Transfer Object (DTO)* and create a separate `TicketEntity` for persisting to the database.

## Creating Entities for the Customer Support Application

You need a few different entities in your application, and you can reuse some existing objects. `Attachment`, for example, just needs to be moved to `com.wrox.site.entities`, annotated, and given an ID property and a foreign key reference to the ticket.

```
@XmlRootElement(name = "attachment")
@Entity
public class Attachment implements Serializable
{
    private static final long serialVersionUID = 1L;

    private long id;
    private long ticketId;
    @NotBlank(message = "{validate.attachment.name}")
    private String name;
    @NotBlank(message = "{validate.attachment.mimeContentType}")
    private String mimeContentType;
    @Size(min = 1, message = "{validate.attachment.contents}")
```

```
        private byte[] contents;

        @Id
        @Column(name = "AttachmentId")
        @GeneratedValue(strategy = GenerationType.IDENTITY)
        public long getId() { ... }
        public void setId(long id) { ... }

        @Basic
        public long getTicketId() { ... }
        public void setTicketId(long ticketId) { ... }

        @Basic
        @Column(name = "AttachmentName")
        public String getName() { ... }
        public void setName(String name) { ... }

        @Basic
        public String getMimeContentType() { ... }
        public void setMimeContentType(String mimeContentType) { ... }

        @XmlSchemaType(name = "base64Binary")
        @Lob
        public byte[] getContents() { ... }
        public void setContents(byte[] contents) { ... }
    }
```

The `UserRepository` and `UserPrincipal` change significantly because users are stored in the database now. `UserPrincipal` also moves to the `com.wrox.site.entities` package and now has an ID, username, and password. You should never store a password plain text or even weakly hashed in the database, therefore the password is persisted strongly hashed with a salt.

```
    @Entity
    @Table(uniqueConstraints = {
            @UniqueConstraint(name="UserPrincipal_Username", columnNames="Username")
    })
    public class UserPrincipal implements Principal, Cloneable, Serializable
    {
        private static final long serialVersionUID = 1L;
        private static final String SESSION_ATTRIBUTE_KEY = "com.wrox.user.principal";

        private long id;
        private String username;
        private byte[] password;

        @Id
        @Column(name = "UserId")
        @GeneratedValue(strategy = GenerationType.IDENTITY)
        public long getId() { ... }
        public void setId(long id) { ... }

        @Override
        @Transient
        public String getName() { ... }

        @Basic
        public String getUsername() { ... }
```

```
        public void setUsername(String username) { ... }

        @Basic
        @Column(name = "HashedPassword")
        public byte[] getPassword() { ... }
        public void setPassword(byte[] password) { ... }

        ...
    }
```

Because `Ticket` contains an `Instant` and a `Map`, you need to create a `TicketEntity` to transfer data to and from the DTO `Ticket`. It looks a lot like `Ticket` but uses a `Timestamp` for the date created and has a foreign key reference to the customer's `UserPrincipal` ID instead of the customer name.

```
    @Entity
    @Table(name = "Ticket")
    public class TicketEntity implements Serializable
    {
        private static final long serialVersionUID = 1L;

        private long id;
        private long userId;
        private String subject;
        private String body;
        private Timestamp dateCreated;

        @Id
        @Column(name = "TicketId")
        @GeneratedValue(strategy = GenerationType.IDENTITY)
        public long getId() { ...}
        public void setId(long id) { ... }

        @Basic
        public long getUserId() { ... }
        public void setUserId(long userId) { ... }

        @Basic
        public String getSubject() { ... }
        public void setSubject(String subject) { ... }

        @Basic
        public String getBody() { ... }
        public void setBody(String body) { ... }

        @Basic
        public Timestamp getDateCreated() { ... }
        public void setDateCreated(Timestamp dateCreated) { ... }
    }
```

These are all the entities you need for now. You also need a database schema that you can store these entities in, and the initial four users that were hard-wired in Java code in previous chapters.

```
    CREATE DATABASE CustomerSupport DEFAULT CHARACTER SET 'utf8'
      DEFAULT COLLATE 'utf8_unicode_ci';

    USE CustomerSupport;

    CREATE TABLE UserPrincipal (
```

```
  UserId BIGINT UNSIGNED NOT NULL AUTO_INCREMENT PRIMARY KEY,
  Username VARCHAR(30) NOT NULL,
  HashedPassword BINARY(60) NOT NULL,
  UNIQUE KEY UserPrincipal_Username (Username)
) ENGINE = InnoDB;

CREATE TABLE Ticket (
  TicketId BIGINT UNSIGNED NOT NULL AUTO_INCREMENT PRIMARY KEY,
  UserId BIGINT UNSIGNED NOT NULL,
  Subject VARCHAR(255) NOT NULL,
  Body TEXT,
  DateCreated DATETIME NOT NULL,
  CONSTRAINT Ticket_UserId FOREIGN KEY (UserId)
    REFERENCES UserPrincipal (UserId) ON DELETE CASCADE
) ENGINE = InnoDB;

CREATE TABLE Attachment (
  AttachmentId BIGINT UNSIGNED NOT NULL AUTO_INCREMENT PRIMARY KEY,
  TicketId BIGINT UNSIGNED NOT NULL,
  AttachmentName VARCHAR(255) NULL,
  MimeContentType VARCHAR(255) NOT NULL,
  Contents BLOB NOT NULL,
  CONSTRAINT Attachment_TicketId FOREIGN KEY (TicketId)
    REFERENCES Ticket (TicketId) ON DELETE CASCADE
) ENGINE = InnoDB;

INSERT INTO UserPrincipal (Username, HashedPassword) VALUES ( -- password
  'Nicholas', '$2a$10$x0k/yA5qN8SP8JD5CEN.6elEBFxVVHeKZTdyv.RPra4jzRR5SlKSC'
);
INSERT INTO UserPrincipal (Username, HashedPassword) VALUES ( -- drowssap
  'Sarah', '$2a$10$JSxmYO.JOb4TT42/4RFzguaTuYkZLCfeND1bB0rzoy7wH0RQFEq8y'
);
INSERT INTO UserPrincipal (Username, HashedPassword) VALUES ( -- wordpass
  'Mike', '$2a$10$Lc0W6stzND.9YnFRcfbOt.EaCVO9aJ/QpbWnfjJLcMovdTx5s4i3G'
);
INSERT INTO UserPrincipal (Username, HashedPassword) VALUES ( -- green
  'John', '$2a$10$vacuqbDw9I7rr6RRH8sByuktOzqTheQMfnK3XCT2WlaL7vt/3AMby'
);
```

The repositories for the entities are simple. The interfaces all extend `GenericRepository` and the implementations all extend `GenericJpaRepository`. `UserRepository` requires a custom method implementation so that users can be looked up by username, and `AttachmentRepository` needs a method to look up attachments for a particular ticket.

```
public interface UserRepository extends GenericRepository<Long, UserPrincipal>
{
    UserPrincipal getByUsername(String username);
}

@Repository
public class DefaultUserRepository
        extends GenericJpaRepository<Long, UserPrincipal>
        implements UserRepository
{
    @Override
    public UserPrincipal getByUsername(String username)
```

```
    {
        return this.entityManager.createQuery(
                "SELECT u FROM UserPrincipal u WHERE u.username = :username",
                UserPrincipal.class
        ).setParameter("username", username).getSingleResult();
    }
}

public interface TicketRepository extends GenericRepository<Long, TicketEntity>
{ }

@Repository
public class DefaultTicketRepository
        extends GenericJpaRepository<Long, TicketEntity>
        implements TicketRepository { }

public interface AttachmentRepository extends GenericRepository<Long, Attachment>
{
    Iterable<Attachment> getByTicketId(long ticketId);
}

@Repository
public class DefaultAttachmentRepository
        extends GenericJpaRepository<Long, Attachment>
        implements AttachmentRepository
{
    @Override
    public Iterable<Attachment> getByTicketId(long ticketId)
    {
        return this.entityManager.createQuery(
                "SELECT a FROM Attachment a WHERE a.ticketId = :id ORDER BY a.id",
                Attachment.class
        ).setParameter("id", ticketId).getResultList();
    }
}
```

## Securing User Passwords with BCrypt

You need to update the services in the Customer Support application to use the new repositories. The `TemporaryAuthenticationService`, renamed to `DefaultAuthenticationService`, is significantly more secure now. It uses the industry-standard jBCrypt Java implementation of the BCrypt hash algorithm, provided by the following Maven dependency.

```
<dependency>
    <groupId>org.mindrot</groupId>
    <artifactId>jbcrypt</artifactId>
    <version>0.3m</version>
</dependency>
```

When used correctly, BCrypt is extremely strong. It is designed to be extremely slow. This may seem counterintuitive, but in reality it doesn't add a significant amount of time to login or saving a user. Where the performance impact is felt is when generating billions of sample passwords in a dictionary attack — using a different salt for each password, it is extremely expensive and impractical to attack a compromised password database.

You should never use a quick-hash algorithm like MD5 or any of the SHA algorithms, because modern password-hacking systems can generate billions of dictionary comparisons per second. BCrypt is the most powerful and well-tested password-hashing algorithm to date, and you should stick to it when securing user passwords. It uses an iteration count, represented as a power of 2, to determine the number of rounds of hashing to apply. For example, with an input iteration count of 10, hashing is applied 1,024 times. Each round uses a small, constant amount of memory that makes it difficult to implement with hardware only, so modern password-hacking systems can generate only small numbers of dictionary comparisons per second. The `DefaultAuthenticationService` in Listing 21-4 uses the new `UserRepository` and BCrypt to save and authenticate users.

**LISTING 21-4: DefaultAuthenticationService.java**

```
@Service
public class DefaultAuthenticationService implements AuthenticationService
{
    private static final Logger log = LogManager.getLogger();
    private static final SecureRandom RANDOM;
    private static final int HASHING_ROUNDS = 10;
    static
    {
        try
        {
            RANDOM = SecureRandom.getInstanceStrong();
        }
        catch(NoSuchAlgorithmException e)
        {
            throw new IllegalStateException(e);
        }
    }

    @Inject UserRepository userRepository;

    @Override
    @Transactional
    public UserPrincipal authenticate(String username, String password)
    {
        UserPrincipal principal = this.userRepository.getByUsername(username);
        if(principal == null)
        {
            log.warn("Authentication failed for non-existent user {}.", username);
            return null;
        }

        if(!BCrypt.checkpw(
                password,
                new String(principal.getPassword(), StandardCharsets.UTF_8)
        ))
        {
            log.warn("Authentication failed for user {}.", username);
            return null;
```

*continues*

**LISTING 21-4** *(continued)*

```
        }

        log.debug("User {} successfully authenticated.", username);

        return principal;
    }

    @Override
    @Transactional
    public void saveUser(UserPrincipal principal, String newPassword)
    {
        if(newPassword != null && newPassword.length() > 0)
        {
            String salt = BCrypt.gensalt(HASHING_ROUNDS, RANDOM);
            principal.setPassword(BCrypt.hashpw(newPassword, salt).getBytes());
        }

        if(principal.getId() < 1)
            this.userRepository.add(principal);
        else
            this.userRepository.update(principal);
    }
}
```

## Transferring Data to Entities in Your Services

The `DefaultTicketService` in Listing 21-5 uses the new `TicketRepository`, `AttachmentRepository`, and `UserRepository` to get and save `Tickets` and `TicketEntitys`. Because the application uses `Tickets` but the database persists `TicketEntitys`, the data must be transferred between the two different POJOs throughout the `DefaultTicketService`. The code makes significant use of lambdas, method references, and the Java 8 Collections Stream API to reduce the code necessary to achieve this.

**LISTING 21-5: DefaultTicketService.java**

```
@Service
public class DefaultTicketService implements TicketService
{
    @Inject TicketRepository ticketRepository;
    @Inject AttachmentRepository attachmentRepository;
    @Inject UserRepository userRepository;

    @Override
    @Transactional
    public List<Ticket> getAllTickets()
    {
        List<Ticket> list = new ArrayList<>();
        this.ticketRepository.getAll().forEach(e -> list.add(this.convert(e)));
        return list;
    }

    @Override
```

```
@Transactional
public Ticket getTicket(long id)
{
    TicketEntity entity = this.ticketRepository.get(id);
    return entity == null ? null : this.convert(entity);
}

private Ticket convert(TicketEntity entity)
{
    Ticket ticket = new Ticket();
    ticket.setId(entity.getId());
    ticket.setCustomerName(
            this.userRepository.get(entity.getUserId()).getUsername()
    );
    ticket.setSubject(entity.getSubject());
    ticket.setBody(entity.getBody());
    ticket.setDateCreated(Instant.ofEpochMilli(
            entity.getDateCreated().getTime()
    ));
    this.attachmentRepository.getByTicketId(entity.getId())
            .forEach(ticket::addAttachment);
    return ticket;
}

@Override
@Transactional
public void save(Ticket ticket)
{
    TicketEntity entity = new TicketEntity();
    entity.setId(ticket.getId());
    entity.setUserId(this.userRepository.getByUsername(
            ticket.getCustomerName()
    ).getId());
    entity.setSubject(ticket.getSubject());
    entity.setBody(ticket.getBody());

    if(ticket.getId() < 1)
    {
        ticket.setDateCreated(Instant.now());
        entity.setDateCreated(new Timestamp(
                ticket.getDateCreated().toEpochMilli()
        ));
        this.ticketRepository.add(entity);
        ticket.setId(entity.getId());
        for(Attachment attachment : ticket.getAttachments())
        {
            attachment.setTicketId(entity.getId());
            this.attachmentRepository.add(attachment);
        }
    }
    else
        this.ticketRepository.update(entity);
}

@Override
```

*continues*

**LISTING 21-5** *(continued)*

```
        @Transactional
        public void deleteTicket(long id)
        {
            this.ticketRepository.deleteById(id);
        }
    }
```

You should be used to testing the Customer Support application now, but this time your tickets will persist in the database:

1. Create the following `DataSource` resource in your Tomcat's `context.xml` file, and make sure you run the `create.sql` script to create the database and tables.

```
<Resource name="jdbc/CustomerSupport" type="javax.sql.DataSource"
          maxActive="20" maxIdle="5" maxWait="10000"
          username="tomcatUser" password="password1234"
          driverClassName="com.mysql.jdbc.Driver"
          defaultTransactionIsolation="READ_COMMITTED"
          url="jdbc:mysql://localhost/CustomerSupport" />
```

2. Compile the application, and start Tomcat from your IDE.
3. Go to `http://localhost:8080/support/` and log in as one of the pre-existing users in the database.
4. Create a ticket or two, attach some files, and restart Tomcat. The tickets should still be there, persisted in the database.

You can and should query the database tables in MySQL Workbench to see the persisted entities.

## SUMMARY

In this chapter, you have learned a lot about using JPA and Hibernate ORM in Spring Framework. You experimented with creating a `LocalContainerEntityManagerFactoryBean`, learned about the different ways that Spring Framework advises methods, explored transaction management using `@Transactional` and the `JpaTransactionManager`, and created a generic repository that can handle most standard CRUD operations for all your entities. You learned how Spring can completely replace the `persistence.xml` file and create a persistence unit in memory, reducing the amount of XML you have to write. You also compared the criteria API to JPQL and saw the advantages and disadvantages of both. Finally, you explored protecting user passwords using the secure BCrypt password slow-hashing algorithm before persisting the passwords in the database.

However, you may think that there's still an awful lot of code to write, especially when looking up persisted entities. What if you need to look up an entity many different ways using many different fields? What about ordering and paging results, which can complicate the matter further? In the next chapter you learn how Spring Data JPA can make writing your JPA repositories even easier — by making it unnecessary to write them at all.

# 22

# Eliminating Boilerplate Repositories with Spring Data JPA

## IN THIS CHAPTER

- Understanding Spring Data's unified data access
- Creating Spring Data JPA repositories
- How to refactor the Customer Support application

## WROX.COM CODE DOWNLOADS FOR THIS CHAPTER

You can find the `wrox.com` code downloads for this chapter at `http://www.wrox.com/go/projavaforwebapps` on the Download Code tab. The code for this chapter is divided into the following major examples:

- Spring-Data-JPA Project
- Customer-Support-v16 Project

## NEW MAVEN DEPENDENCIES FOR THIS CHAPTER

In addition to the Maven dependencies introduced in previous chapters, you also need the following Maven dependency. The SLF4J JCL bridge is excluded because your use of Log4j 2 makes this bridge unnecessary.

```
<dependency>
    <groupId>org.springframework.data</groupId>
    <artifactId>spring-data-jpa</artifactId>
    <version>1.5.0.RELEASE</version>
```

```
        <scope>compile</scope>
        <exclusions>
            <exclusion>
                <groupId>org.slf4j</groupId>
                <artifactId>jcl-over-slf4j</artifactId>
            </exclusion>
        </exclusions>
    </dependency>

    <dependency>
        <groupId>org.slf4j</groupId>
        <artifactId>slf4j-api</artifactId>
        <version>1.7.5</version>
        <scope>runtime</scope>
    </dependency>
```

# UNDERSTANDING SPRING DATA'S UNIFIED DATA ACCESS

In Chapter 20, you learned how powerful the Java Persistence API can be, and in Chapter 21 you learned how Spring Framework can make using JPA even easier. Spring takes care of all your transaction management and `EntityManager` creation and closing so that you don't have to. It even eliminates the need to include a `persistence.xml` file in your application! Perhaps most helpful of all, you created a generic, base repository that all your repositories can extend, providing the basic CRUD operations without having to write them for every repository.

But let's face it: *Most* of your repositories need more than the standard CRUD operations. For starters, you often need to perform basic lookups with uniquely constrained columns other than the primary key. In the last chapter's Spring-JPA project, you added a method to look up books by their ISBN, whereas in the Customer-Support-v15 project, your `UserRepository` included a method for looking up users by their usernames.

Then sometimes you need to filter entities with multiple fields. For example, as a system administrator you may need to find people by their first and last name or their phone number, which may return multiple results. Then there's searching, such as looking for products with certain keywords or finding support tickets with content matching a search phrase. Finally, there is perhaps the most difficult task to tackle: You cannot simply return a `List` of all entities or even all entities matching a filter. This neither performs well nor is easy to utilize in your user interfaces. (Imagine returning 10,000,000 records from the database just to display 50 of them on the screen.) So you must implement paging of results somehow, and while doing this you must keep result ordering in mind at all times.

## Avoiding Duplication of Code

Ordering and paging results is possible using both the Java Persistence Query Language and the criteria API. However, there are no shortcuts. Both operations require you to construct and execute two separate queries: one to return a count of results and another to return a subset of results. The following code demonstrates performing this using JPQL. You have already learned how to filter results, so the code focuses solely on pagination and applies no filtering.

```
TypedQuery<Long> countQuery = this.entityManager.createQuery(
        "SELECT count(b) FROM Book b WHERE predicates...", Long.class
);
long totalRows = countQuery.getSingleResult();

TypedQuery<Book> pagedQuery = this.entityManager.createQuery(
        "SELECT b FROM Book b WHERE predicates... " +
            "ORDER BY b.title ASC, b.isbn DESC", Book.class
);
pagedQuery.setFirstResult(startRecordNumber);
pagedQuery.setMaxResults(maxPerPage);
List<Book> singlePage = pagedQuery.getResultList();
```

Performing the same task with the criteria API is more verbose but works better for generic queries of unknown entity types.

```
CriteriaBuilder builder = this.entityManager.getCriteriaBuilder();

CriteriaQuery<Long> pageCriteria = builder.createQuery(Long.class);
Root<Book> root = pageCriteria.from(Book.class);
TypedQuery<Long> countQuery = this.entityManager.createQuery(
        pageCriteria.select(builder.count(root))
                .where(predicates...)
);
long totalRows = countQuery.getSingleResult();

CriteriaQuery<Book> criteria = builder.createQuery(Book.class);
root = criteria.from(Book.class);
TypedQuery<Book> pagedQuery = this.entityManager.createQuery(
        criteria.select(root)
                .where(predicates...)
                .orderBy(builder.asc(root.get("title")),
                         builder.desc(root.get("isbn")))
);
pagedQuery.setFirstResult(startRecordNumber);
pagedQuery.setMaxResults(maxPerPage);
List<Book> singlePage = pagedQuery.getResultList();
```

In both of these examples, *`startRecordNumber`* and *`maxPerPage`* are input variables indicating, respectively, the zero-based index of the first entity on the page and the maximum number of entities to return. *`totalRows`* is the number of matching rows that you would return, whereas *`singlePage`* is the list of entities that you would return. (Obviously, you would need to return some kind of holder object that contained both of these values.) Although both of these examples are still easier than writing database-specific SQL and using raw JDBC, they're not exactly friendly. Where you see `predicates...` in both examples is where you would put `WHERE` statements to filter results, meaning you have to create these predicates and set parameters *twice*, identically. The Hibernate ORM-specific API is slightly easier, enabling you to construct criteria once and reuse them to generate the record count *and* the limited list of entities.

But even if you were to use the easier, Hibernate-proprietary API, you still have to do this anywhere you need to page results — and that's most places that you return a list of entities. That's a lot of code to write (and test). Eventually, you would try to create a generic way to specify filters, ordering information, and paging instructions for any generic lookup of any entity in your base repository class. But is that really necessary?

Thankfully, it's not. Spring Data, a Spring project separate from but dependent on Spring Framework, can write your repositories for you. All you have to do is create an interface and Spring Data dynamically generates the necessary code to implement that interface at run time. Figure 22-1 shows the normal program execution path that you have become accustomed to in Spring Framework. Your controllers are written against your service interfaces. Spring intercepts calls to those interfaces and performs any necessary tasks, such as Bean Validation, starting a transaction, or invoking the method asynchronously. When the service method returns, Spring may also perform further Bean Validation and commit or rollback a transaction.

Likewise the service code is written against the repository interfaces. When you invoke a repository method, Spring again performs any necessary tasks like starting a transaction. When the method returns, Spring converts any thrown exception to a `DataAccessException`. It's that repository code that you really don't need. It contains no business logic (that should be in the service) or user

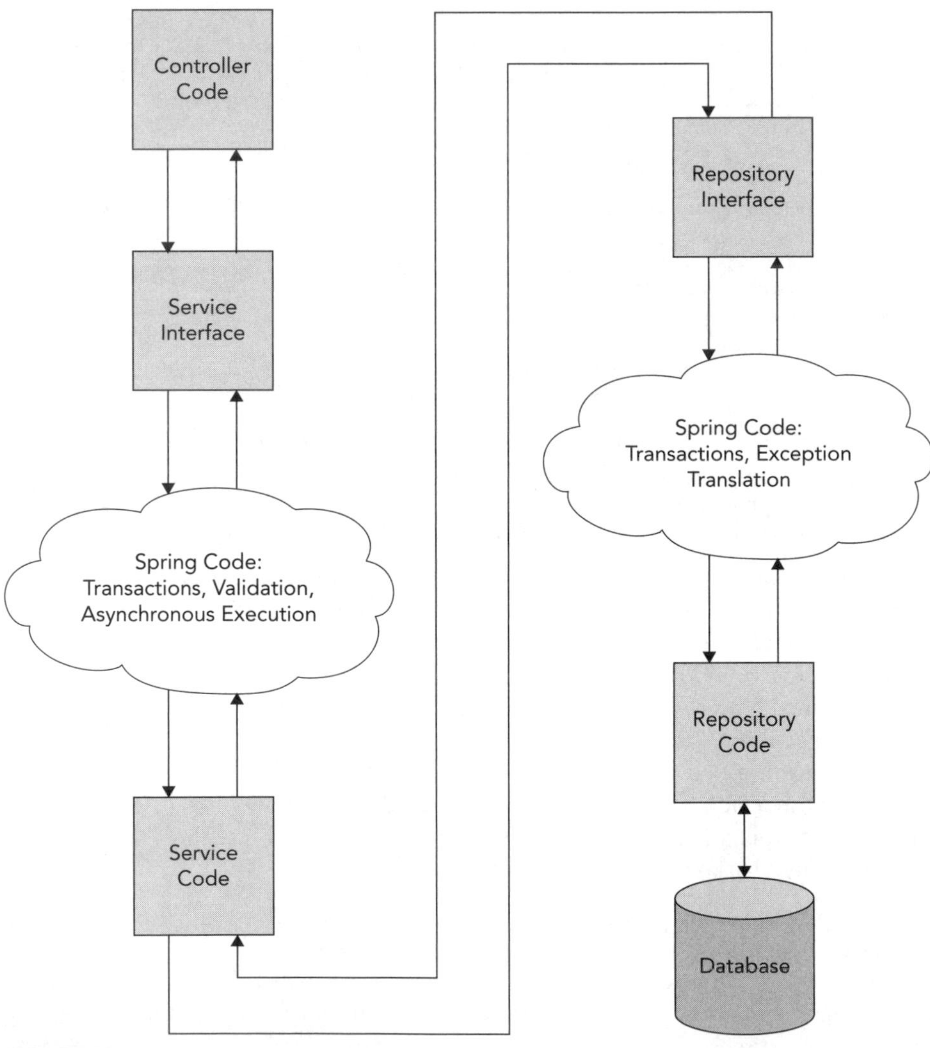


FIGURE 22-1

interface logic (that should be in the controller), so there's nothing special that your application should need to do in the repository. It's boilerplate code for persisting and retrieving entities.

When you use Spring Data, that repository code gets written for you. There are very few cases when you would ever need to write repository code that Spring Data couldn't handle automatically, and facilities exist to handle those rare occasions. Figure 22-2 shows this new program execution path. Much of it remains the same because controllers and services contain logic proprietary to your application. But after you execute a method on your repository interface, that's the end of code written by you. Spring Framework and Spring Data handle everything that happens beyond that point.

Spring Data supports a variety of data access methodologies, including JPA, `JdbcTemplate`, NoSQL, and more. Its primary subproject, Spring Data Commons, provides a core toolset that all other subprojects use to create repositories. The Spring Data JPA subproject provides support for repositories implemented against the Java Persistence API.

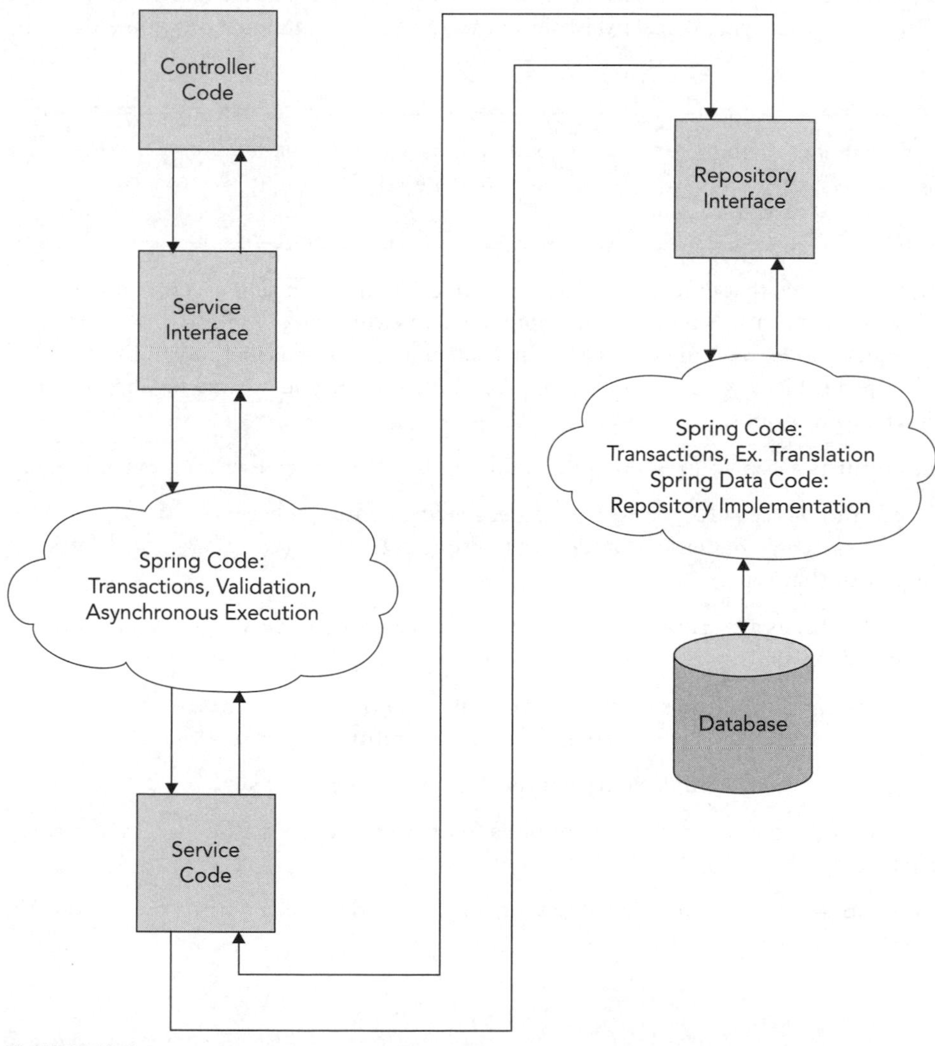


**FIGURE 22-2**

> **NOTE** *You use many different classes from Spring Data Commons and Spring Data JPA, and this book cannot tell you every detail about all of them. You should review and bookmark the Spring Data Commons API Documentation* `http://docs.spring.io/spring-data/commons/docs/1.7.x/api/` *and the Spring Data JPA API Documentation* `http://docs.spring.io/spring-data/jpa/docs/1.5.x/api/` *for future reference.*

## Using the Stock Repository Interfaces

One of the tools supplied by Spring Data Commons is the `org.springframework.data.repository.Repository<T, ID extends Serializable>` interface. All Spring Data repository interfaces must extend this marker interface, which specifies no methods. Only interfaces extending `Repository` are eligible for dynamic implementation. The generic type parameters `T` and `ID` capture the entity type and identifier type, respectively, similar to the `GenericRepository` you created in Chapter 21.

> **NOTE** *The type parameters are reversed in Spring Data from what you created in* `GenericRepository`. *Also, the* `ID` *parameter must implement* `Serializable`, *but no such restriction is enforced for* `T`.

You may create an interface that extends `Repository` directly, but because it specifies no methods, you will probably never do this. A more useful approach is to extend `org.springframework.data.repository.CrudRepository<T, ID>`, which specifies numerous methods for basic CRUD operations. This interface is very similar to the `GenericRepository` you created in Chapter 21, but uses a few different conventions.

- `count()` returns a `long` representing the total number of unfiltered entities extending `T`.
- `delete(T)` and `delete(ID)` delete the single, specified entity, whereas `delete(Iterable<? extends T>)` deletes multiple entities and `deleteAll()` deletes every entity of that type.
- `exists(ID)` returns a `boolean` indicating whether the entity of this type with the given surrogate key exists.
- `findAll()` returns all entities of type `T`, whereas `findAll(Iterable<ID>)` returns the entities of type `T` with the given surrogate keys. Both return `Iterable<T>`.
- `findOne(ID)` retrieves a single entity of type `T` given its surrogate key.
- `save(S)` saves the given entity (insert or update) of type `S` where `S` extends `T`, and returns `S`, the saved entity.
- `save(Iterable<S>)` saves all the entities (again, `S` extends `T`) and returns the saved entities as a new `Iterable<S>`.

All Spring Data projects already know how to implement all these methods for a given type. You'll notice, however, that this repository still doesn't specify methods that support paging and sorting. This is so that these methods don't clutter any repositories that you don't want to support paging and sorting. If you want a repository to provide paging and sorting methods, its interface can extend `org.springframework.data.repository.PagingAndSortingRepository<T, ID extends Serializable>`.

- `findAll(Sort)` returns all `T` entities as an `Iterable<T>` sorted with the provided `Sort` instructions.
- `findAll(Pageable)` returns a single `org.springframework.data.domain.Page<T>` of entities sorted and bounded with the provided `Pageable` instructions.

An `org.springframework.data.domain.Sort` object encapsulates information about the properties that should be used to sort a result set and in what direction they should be sorted. An `org.springframework.data.domain.Pageable` encapsulates a `Sort` as well as the number of entities per page and which page to return (both `int`s). In a web application, you don't usually have to worry about creating `Pageable` objects on your own. Spring Data provides two `org.springframework.web.method.support.HandlerMethodArgumentResolver` implementations that can turn HTTP request parameters into `Pageable` and `Sort` objects, respectively: `org.springframework.data.web.PageableHandlerMethodArgumentResolver` and `org.springframework.data.web.SortHandlerMethodArgumentResolver`.

All these predefined methods are helpful, and the standardized `Sort` and `Pageable` objects definitely come in handy, but you still have no way to find specific entities or lists of entities using anything other than surrogate keys — at least, not without creating your own method implementations. This is where Spring Data's *query methods* come in to play.

## Creating Query Methods for Finding Entities

Query methods are specially defined methods that tell Spring Data how to find entities. The name of a query method starts with `find...By`, `get...By`, or `read...By` and is followed by the names of properties that should be matched on. The method parameters provide the values that should match the properties specified in the method name (in the same order the properties are listed in the method name if the values are of the same type). The method return type tells Spring Data whether to expect a single result (`T`) or multiple results (`Iterable<T>`, `List<T>`, `Collection<T>`, `Page<T>`, and so on). So, for example, in a `BookRepository` you might need to locate a book by its ISBN, author, or publisher:

```
public interface BookRepository extends PagingAndSortingRepository<Book, Long>
{
    Book findByIsbn(String isbn);
    List<Book> findByAuthor(String author);
    List<Book> findByPublisher(String publisher);
}
```

The algorithm that analyzes these methods knows that `findByIsbn` should match the `Book`'s `isbn` property to the method parameter and that the result should be unique. Likewise, it knows that `findByAuthor` and `findByPublisher` should match multiple records using the `author` and publisher Book properties, respectively. Notice that the property names referenced in the repository method names match the JPA property names of the Book entity — this is the convention that you must follow. In most cases, this is also the JavaBean property names. Of course, an author can write many books and a publisher most certainly publishes many, so you probably need your query methods to support pagination.

```
public interface BookRepository extends PagingAndSortingRepository<Book, Long>
{
    Book findByIsbn(String isbn);
    Page<Book> findByAuthor(String author, Pageable instructions);
    Page<Book> findByPublisher(String publisher, Pageable instructions);
}
```

You can put multiple properties in your query method name and separate those properties with logical operators as well:

```
List<Person> findByFirstNameAndLastName(String firstName, String lastName);
List<Person> findByFirstNameOrLastName (String firstName, String lastName);
```

Many databases ignore case when matching string-based fields (either by default or as an optional configuration), but you can explicitly indicate that case should be ignored using IgnoreCase:

```
Page<Person> findByFirstNameOrLastNameIgnoreCase(String firstName,
                                                 String lastName,
                                                 Pageable instructions);
```

In the preceding example, only the last name ignores case. You can also ignore case on the first name using the method name findByFirstNameIgnoreCaseOrLastNameIgnoreCase, but that is very verbose. Instead, you can tell Spring Data to ignore the case for all String properties using findByFirstNameOrLastNameAllIgnoreCase.

Sometimes properties are not simple types. For example, a Person might have an address property of type Address. Spring Data can also match against this property if the parameter type is Address, but often you don't want to match on the whole address. You may want to return a list of people in a certain postal code, for example. This is easily accomplished using Spring Data *property expressions*.

```
List<Person> findByAddressPostalCode(PostalCode code);
```

Assuming Person has an address property and that property's type has a postalCode property of type PostalCode, Spring Data can find the people in the database with the given postal code. However, property expressions can create ambiguity in the matching algorithm. Spring Data greedily matches the property name before looking for a property expression, not unlike a regular expression might greedily match an "or more" control character. The algorithm could match on a different property name than you intended, and then fail to find a property within that property's type matching the property expression. For this reason, it's best to always separate property expressions using an underscore:

```
Page<Person> findByAddress_PostalCode(PostalCode code, Pageable instructions);
```

This removes the ambiguity so that Spring Data matches on the correct property.

You undoubtedly remember that method names begin with find...By, get...By, or read...By. These are *introducing clauses*, and By is a delimiter separating the introducing clause and the criteria to match on. To a large extent, you can place whatever you want to between `find`, `get`, or `read` and `By`. For example, to be more "plain language," you could name a method `findBookByIsbn` or `findPeopleByFirstNameAndLastName`. `Book` and `People` are ignored in this case. However, if the word `Distinct` (matching that case) is in the introducing clause (such as `findDistinctBooksByAuthor`), this triggers the special behavior of enabling the distinct flag on the underlying query. This may or may not apply to the storage medium in use, but for JPA or `JdbcTemplate` repositories, it's the equivalent of using the `DISTINCT` keyword in the JPQL or SQL query.

In addition to the `Or` and `And` keywords that separate multiple criteria, the criteria in a query method name can contain many other keywords to refine the way the criteria match:

- `Is` and `Equals` are implied in the absence of other keywords, but you may explicitly use them. For example, `findByIsbn` is equivalent to `findByIsbnIs` and `findByIsbnEquals`.
- `Not` and `IsNot` negate any other keyword except for `Or` and `And`. `Is` and `Equals` are still implied in the absence of other keywords, so `findByIsbnIsNot` is equivalent to `findByIsbnIsNotEqual`.
- `After` and `IsAfter` indicate that the property is a date and/or time that should come after the given value, whereas `Before` and `IsBefore` indicate that the property should come before the given value. Example: `findByDateFoundedIsAfter(Date date)`.
- `Containing`, `IsContaining`, and `Contains` indicate that the property's value may start and end with anything but should contain the given value. This is similar to `StartingWith`, `IsStartingWith`, and `StartsWith`, which indicate that the property should start with the specified value. Likewise, `EndingWith`, `IsEndingWith`, and `EndsWith` indicate that the property should end with the specified value. Example: `findByTitleContains(String value)` is equivalent to the SQL criteria `WHERE title = '%value%'`.
- `Like` is similar to `Contains`, `StartsWith`, and `EndsWith`, except that value you provide should already contain the appropriate wildcards (instead of Spring Data adding them for you). This gives you the flexibility to specify more advanced patterns. `NotLike` simply negates `Like`. Example: `findByTitleLike(String value)` could be called with value `"%Catcher%Rye%"` and would match "The Catcher in the Rye" and "Catcher Brings Home Rye Bread."
- `Between` and `IsBetween` indicate that the property should be between the *two* specified values. This means that you must provide two parameters for this property criterion. You can use `Between` on any type that may be compared mathematically in this manner, such as numeric and date types. Example: `findByDateFoundedBetween(Date start, Date end)`.
- `Exists` indicates that something should exist. Its meaning may vary wildly between storage mediums. It is roughly equivalent to the `EXISTS` keyword in JPQL and SQL.
- `True` and `IsTrue` indicate that the named property should be `true`, whereas `False` and `IsFalse` indicate that the named property should be `false`. These keywords do not require method parameters because the value is implied by the keywords themselves. Example: `findByApprovedIsFalse()`.

- `GreaterThan` and `IsGreaterThan` indicate that the property is greater than the parameter value. You can include the parameter value in the bounds with `GreaterThanEqual` or `IsGreaterThanEqual`. The inverse of these keywords are `LessThan`, `IsLessThan`, `LessThanEqual`, and `IsLessThanEqual`.
- `In` indicates that the property value must be equal to at least one of the values specified. The parameter matching this criterion should be an `Iterable` of the same type of the property. Example: `findByAuthorIn(Iterable<String> authors)`.
- `Null` and `IsNull` indicate that the value should be `null`. These keywords also do not require method parameters because the value is implied.
- `Near`, `IsNear`, `Within`, and `IsWithin` are keywords useful for certain NoSQL database types but have no useful meaning in JPA.
- `Regex`, `MatchesRegex`, and `Matches` indicate that the property value should match the `String` regular expression (do not use `Pattern`) specified in the corresponding method parameter.

# Providing Custom Method Implementations

As you can tell, the query method language is really quite powerful. There's not a whole lot you can't do with Spring Data interface methods. In almost all cases, you can simply create an interface, sit back, and let Spring Data do the work for you. Every once in a while, however, you'll come across a situation that Spring Data can't handle. One example of this is performing full-text searching, something you'll explore more in Chapter 23.

Another example is user-generated dynamic queries. Usually you want to strictly structure the queries a user can perform on persisted data. Allowing a user to filter on virtually any property can have disastrous performance implications. But where you understand the risks and plan accordingly, such a tool can be extremely powerful and useful for your users. It is also not possible to achieve this using standard Spring Data query methods.

> **NOTE** *Although Spring Data does not provide a standard mechanism for performing dynamic queries, Spring Data JPA does provide two proprietary mechanisms for doing so using the JPA criteria API or Querydsl* (`http://www.querydsl.com/`) *predicates. If you use JPA repositories, you can use one of these mechanisms. If you use some other Spring Data repository type, you may still have to create your own mechanism for dynamic queries.*

Whatever feature you decide that Spring Data cannot achieve on its own, adding custom behavior to a Spring Data repository is generally very easy. You can take one of two approaches or both at once as the need arises: customizing an individual repository or customizing all repositories.

## Customizing an Individual Repository

The first step in customizing an individual repository is to create an interface *for that customization*. This interface should be separate from the actual repository interface and should specify all methods (at least one) that have custom implementations for your repository. The repository interface should then extend the customization interface.

```
public interface BookRepositoryCustomization
{
    public Page<Book> findBooksWithQuery(DynamicQuery query, Pageable p);
    public Page<Book> searchBooks(String searchQuery, Pageable p);
}

public interface BookRepository
    extends PagingAndSortingRepository<Book, Long>, BookRepositoryCustomization
{
}
```

You can name the repository and customization interfaces whatever you want; these names are just examples. When Spring Data finds `BookRepository`, it first looks for a class in the same package named `BookRepositoryImpl` (or whatever you named the interface plus `Impl`) and instantiates and wires that class as any ordinary Spring bean. This class should implement the `BookRepositoryCustomization` interface and provide the behavior for its methods. Spring Data delegates to this implementation when the customized methods are invoked on the `BookRepository`. For all other methods, Spring Data provides the standard Spring Data implementations. The following snippet demonstrates this implementation. The actual code that makes up the methods is unimportant, and the `DynamicQuery` class is just a hypothetical holder for dynamic query criteria.

> **NOTE** *You can change the class name suffix that Spring Data looks for from* `Impl` *to something else — more on that in the next section.*

```
public class BookRepositoryImpl
    implements BookRepositoryCustomization
{
    @PersistenceContext EntityManager entityManager;

    @Override
    public Page<Book> findBooksWithQuery(DynamicQuery query, Pageable p)
    {
        // code to implement finding books
    }

    @Override
    public Page<Book> searchBooks(String searchQuery, Pageable p)
    {
        // code to implement searching books
    }
}
```

Customizing an individual repository may be a fairly common occurrence if you make heavy use of full-text searching or dynamic querying. You won't see a working example in this chapter, but in Chapter 23 you use this customization technique to implement searching methods.

## Customizing All Repositories

As you can see, customizing an individual repository is really easy. In nearly all customization scenarios, you'll either customize only a few of your repositories or the customizations will be different for all repositories. In these cases, individual customization is the route you want to take. However, in the rarest circumstances you might want to provide the same customized method to *all* your repositories of a particular type (such as all your JPA repositories). This is a significantly more complicated process. First, you must create a new interface that extends the project-specific interface and specifies the custom method or methods.

```
@NoRepositoryBean
public interface CustomRepository<T, ID extends Serializable>
        extends JpaRepository<T, ID>
{
    public void customOperation(T entity);
}
```

Notice that the interface extends `org.springframework.data.jpa.repository.JpaRepository` (which in turn extends `CrudRepository` and `PagingAndSortingRepository`). Each Spring Data subproject provides one or more repository interfaces that extend the base Spring Data Commons repository interfaces. Using Spring Data JPA as an example here, the `CustomRepository` must extend `JpaRepository`, the interface that Spring Data JPA scans for.

You must also annotate `CustomRepository` with `@org.springframework.data.repository.NoRepositoryBean`. Because `CustomRepository` itself extends `Repository` (by way of `JpaRepository extends PagingAndSortingRepository extends CrudRepository`), Spring Data JPA would normally detect it and create an implementation of it. You don't want this — `CustomRepository` is supposed to merely be a base interface for your repositories. `@NoRepositoryBean` tells Spring Data to not create an implementation for this interface. (If you look at the API documentation for `CrudRepository`, `PagingAndSortingRepository`, and `JpaRepository`, they are all annotated `@NoRepositoryBean` as well.)

After specifying your new interface, you must extend the base repository class provided by the Spring Data JPA project.

```
public class CustomRepositoryImpl<T, ID extends Serializable>
        extends SimpleJpaRepository<T, ID>
        implements CustomRepository<T, ID>
{
    private Class<T> domainClass;
    private EntityManager entityManager;

    public CustomRepositoryImpl(Class<T> domainClass, EntityManager entityManager)
    {
        super(domainClass, entityManager);
        this.domainClass = domainClass;
        this.entityManager = entityManager;
    }

    public CustomRepositoryImpl(JpaEntityInformation<T, ?> information,
                                EntityManager entityManager)
    {
        super(information, entityManager);
        this.domainClass = information.getJavaType();
```

```
        this.entityManager = entityManager;
    }

    public void customOperation(T)
    {
        // code to implement custom operation
    }
}
```

The `org.springframework.data.jpa.repository.support.SimpleJpaRepository` is the class that provides base support for predefined interface methods, such as `findOne(ID)` and `save(T)`. If you want to also provide Querydsl support, you should extend `org.springframework.data.jpa.repository.support.QueryDslJpaRepository` instead of `SimpleJpaRepository`.

Now comes the challenging bit of providing custom behavior for all your repositories. Spring Data JPA does not use your `CustomRepositoryImpl` as its base repository class automatically. You must create a factory bean to perform this task and replace the default factory bean with your factory bean.

```
public class CustomRepositoryFactoryBean<R extends JpaRepository<T, ID>, T,
                                         ID extends Serializable>
        extends JpaRepositoryFactoryBean<R, T, ID>
{
    @Override
    protected RepositoryFactorySupport createRepositoryFactory(EntityManager e)
    {
        return new CustomRepositoryFactory<T, ID>(e);
    }

    private static class CustomRepositoryFactory<T, ID extends Serializable>
            extends JpaRepositoryFactory
    {
        private EntityManager entityManager;

        public CustomRepositoryFactory(EntityManager entityManager)
        {
            super(entityManager);
            this.entityManager = entityManager;
        }

        @Override
        @SuppressWarnings("unchecked")
        protected Object getTargetRepository(RepositoryMetadata metadata)
        {
            return new CustomRepositoryImpl<T, ID>(
                    (Class<T>) metadata.getDomainType(), this.entityManager
            );
        }

        @Override
        protected Class<?> getRepositoryBaseClass(RepositoryMetadata metadata)
        {
            return CustomRepositoryImpl.class;
        }
    }
}
```

Just like the `LocalContainerEntityManagerFactoryBean` acts as a factory for creating `EntityManagerFactorys`, `CustomRepositoryFactoryBean` acts as a factory for creating `CustomRepositoryFactorys`. The `CustomRepositoryFactory` stores the `EntityManager` and responds to calls for new `CustomRepository` instances. Because `CustomRepositoryImpl` (in its own code and by way of extending `SimpleJpaRepository`) already implements all the base methods specified in `CrudRepository`, `PagingAndSortingRepository`, `JpaRepository`, and `CustomRepository`, Spring Data JPA needs only to take the created `CustomRepositoryImpl` instance and dynamically add implementations for the methods specified in any extending interfaces (such as `BookRepository` or `PersonRepository`).

The final step of adding this custom behavior to all your JPA entities is to configure Spring Data JPA to use the `CustomRepositoryFactoryBean` instead of the default `JpaRepositoryFactoryBean`. You learn how to do that in the next section. Because you'll probably never have to add the same custom method to all the repositories for a given database type, this book does not provide an actual working example; however, you can create one from the sample code shown here. In some cases, it may simply be easier to create a customization interface and implementation as if you were customizing an individual repository and then apply that interface to all your repositories.

# CONFIGURING AND CREATING SPRING DATA JPA REPOSITORIES

In the previous section you explored using Spring Data to write repository interfaces and learned how it can completely replace your hand-written interfaces. Although the text occasionally mentioned Spring Data JPA (such as when adding custom method implementations), everything you read about applies to Spring Data in general, and you can apply the techniques you learned to not just Spring Data JPA, but also a host of other Spring Data projects that support different database types. Now you'll switch gears and learn about Spring Data JPA specifically, how to use it, and how to configure it. In Chapter 21, you learned how to configure JPA in Spring Framework. If you did not read Chapter 21, you need to go back and catch up now. The configuration introduced in that chapter is heavily used in this section for setting up Spring Data JPA.

Configuring Spring Data JPA and creating repositories for it to implement are both very simple tasks. The beauty of using any Spring Data project is that there really isn't a lot for you to do unless you need to implement custom behavior. In this section, you explore getting Spring Data JPA set up and running using the Spring-Data-JPA project available for download from the `wrox.com` code download site. It is based on the Spring-JPA project you worked on in Chapter 21. Its entities are identical and use the existing database, database table schema, and Tomcat `DataSource` resource.

## Enabling Repository Auto-Generation

Configuring Spring Data JPA doesn't involve very much effort. You have only a handful of options to consider. As with Spring Framework, you can take two different configuration approaches: XML or Java. This section tells you about both, but only Java configuration is demonstrated in the Spring-Data-JPA project. Be sure to read about the XML namespace configuration even if you don't intend to use it because it introduces some concepts important to the Java configuration.

## Using the XML Namespace Configuration

You use two XML namespaces when you configure Spring Data JPA. The first, `http://www.springframework.org/schema/data/repository`, is the core namespace for Spring Data Commons. (In this book, the namespace prefix is `data`.) All Spring Data projects use this namespace in some fashion to configure repository generation. In some cases, a Spring Data project, like Spring Data JPA, may extend some of the types defined in the Spring Data Commons namespace to create additional elements. That is, indeed, the case with the Spring Data JPA namespace, `http://www.springframework.org/schema/data/jpa` (with a `data-jpa` namespace prefix in this book).

Spring Data has the capability of populating your database with data using the repositories it generates. It does this using either XML or JSON files. This book does not go into details about this feature because you should only use it in a development environment, and it can be very dangerous in production systems. However, should you need to configure this feature you would use one of the following XML namespace elements, all from the Spring Data Commons namespace.

- `<data:jackson-populator>` defines a bean that populates entities using a JSON file by way of the Jackson Data Processor 1.x `ObjectMapper`. You must specify the name or names of your JSON files using the `locations` attribute. You can customize the name of this bean using the `id` attribute. If you have already created and configured an `ObjectMapper` 1.x bean, you should put the name of that bean in the `object-mapper-ref` attribute so that Spring Data uses that mapper.
- `<data:jackson2-populator>` also defines a bean that populates entities using a JSON file but makes use of the Jackson Data Processor 2.x `ObjectMapper`. It also has a required `locations` attribute, the optional `id` bean name attribute, and an `object-mapper-ref` attribute for referencing the `ObjectMapper` 2.x bean.
- `<data:unmarshaller-populator>` defines a bean that populates entities using an XML file. Its `locations` attribute must point to one or more XML files containing entity definitions. Because a Spring `Unmarshaller` requires some configuration (which you learned about in Chapter 17), you must specify the `Unmarshaller` bean name using the required `unmarshaller-ref` attribute. You can also customize the bean name with the `id` attribute.

In the current version of Spring Data Commons, these are the only elements the namespace contains. You'll never need them unless you decide to enable entity auto-population. The Spring Data Commons namespace does define some core types that serve as the foundation for the two Spring Data JPA namespace elements.

The `<data-jpa:repositories>` element is the central element for configuring repository generation using Spring Data and Spring Data JPA. Most of its attributes and sub-elements come from the Commons namespace and are available to other project namespace elements, such as `<data-mongo:repositories>` and `<data-neo4j:repositories>`. The common attributes include:

- `base-package` — This is the only required attribute. Spring Data JPA looks in this package, and any subpackages for interfaces that extend `Repository` and aren't annotated `@NoRepositoryBean`. Then it generates implementations for these interfaces.

- `named-queries-location` — If you use named queries with your Spring Data project of choice, you can use this attribute to define the location of a `.properties` file containing these named queries. This does not apply to Spring Data JPA, which instead uses the JPA standard `<named-query>` elements in `orm.xml` and `@javax.persistence.NamedQuery` and `@javax.persistence.NamedQueries` annotations on entity classes to define named queries.
- `repository-impl-postfix` — This defines the suffix that Spring Data appends to a repository interface to locate the custom method implementations. It defaults to `Impl`, which is why the `BookRepository`'s custom method implementation class in the previous section was named `BookRepositoryImpl`. You can use this attribute in most Spring Data projects including Spring Data JPA, but it does not apply to them all. If you use a good IDE, it tells you whether you can use this element.
- `query-lookup-strategy` — This attribute specifies how Spring Data creates queries for your query methods. The default, `create-if-not-found`, is usually sufficient. It means that Spring Data should look for a named query that matches the method name, and if it doesn't exist, create a method automatically using the algorithm described in the previous section (remember: `find...By`). The value `create` disables looking up named queries and uses only the query method algorithm. The final value, `use-declared-query`, disables the query method algorithm, uses only named queries, and fails if a match is not found.
- `factory-class` — This enables you to specify a different default repository factory bean and is where you configure the `CustomRepositoryFactoryBean` you saw in the previous section. This attribute applies only to some Spring Data projects, including Spring Data JPA.
- `transaction-manager-ref` — Spring Data JPA and some other Spring Data projects support transactional repositories. If this is the case, you can specify the name of the `PlatformTransactionManager` bean that the repositories should use. If you do not specify this, Spring Data JPA determines the default `PlatformTransactionManager` using the same algorithm that Spring Framework uses. It's safest to always specify this attribute when applicable.

The common sub-elements that you use within `<data-jpa:repositories>` and any other Spring Data project namespace `repositories` elements are:

- `<data:include-filter>` — Use one or more of these to define additional criteria that must be met before an interface is eligible for auto-generation. These criteria replace the standard `Repository` interface requirement. This element is identical to the `<context:include-filter>` element you learned about for `<context:component-scan>` in Chapter 12.
- `<data:exclude-filter>` — Use one or more of these to exclude certain repository interfaces from being eligible for auto-generation. This element is the analog of `<context:exclude-filter>` for `<context:component-scan>`.

As an example of using these sub-elements, consider the following code. Normally enabling Spring Data JPA repositories would scan for all interfaces extending `Repository`. However, if you were using both Spring Data JPA and Spring Data MongoDB, they would both scan for `Repository`, which would result in duplicate repositories and serious problems. Using the elements that follow eliminates the default scanning (for `Repository`) and activates more specific scanning — for interfaces that extend `JpaRepository` for Spring Data JPA and `MongoRepository` for Spring Data MongoDB. (Alternatively, you could simply place these repositories in separate packages.)

```
        <data-jpa:repositories base-package="com.sample">
            <data:include-filter type="assignable"
                                 expression="org.springframework.data.jpa.
    repository.JpaRepository" />
        </data-jpa:repositories>

        <data-mongo:repositories base-package="com.sample">
            <data:include-filter type="assignable"
                                 expression="org.springframework.data.mongodb.
    repository.MongoRepository" />
        </data-mongo:repositories>
```

Spring Data JPA defines an additional `entity-manager-factory-ref` attribute so that you can specify the `EntityManagerFactory` that Spring Data JPA should use for its JPA operations. Because you typically have a `LocalContainerEntityManagerFactoryBean` configured, you should reference that bean directly.

When using Spring Data JPA, you can configure entity auditing using the `<data-jpa:auditing>` element. With auditing enabled, Spring Data can set certain entity properties for you whenever an entity is saved, such as the user who saved it or the date and time saved. Some other Spring Data projects also have this element (but with a different namespace prefix). All projects that offer this element support the following attributes:

- `auditor-aware-ref` — This is the bean name of an `org.springframework.data.domain.AuditorAware<U>` implementation that determines the currently authenticated user or `Principal`. Without this reference, auditing does not record the user who modified a record.
- `set-dates` — This is a `boolean` attribute that indicates whether creation and modification dates should be set whenever an entity is created or saved. It defaults to `true`.
- `date-time-provider-ref` — Use this attribute to specify the bean name of an `org.springframework.data.auditing.DateTimeProvider` implementation for determining the date and time to use for auditing purposes. The default is `org.springframework.data.auditing.CurrentDateTimeProvider`. Prior to Spring Data Commons 1.7, using a provider required you to have Joda Time on your classpath. As of version 1.7, the `DateTimeProvider` is now based on a `Calendar`, and Joda Time is no longer required.
- `modify-on-creation` — This attribute, which defaults to `true`, indicates whether you want to set the modification date on creation, too. If `false`, the modification date is saved only on update.

This may seem like a lot, but in reality the typical Spring Data JPA configuration is likely to look very much like this:

```
<?xml version="1.0" encoding="UTF-8"?>
<beans xmlns="http://www.springframework.org/schema/beans"
       xmlns:xsi="http://www.w3.org/2001/XMLSchema-instance"
       xmlns:data-jpa="http://www.springframework.org/schema/data/jpa"
```

```
       xsi:schemaLocation="http://www.springframework.org/schema/beans
            http://www.springframework.org/schema/beans/spring-beans-4.0.xsd
            http://www.springframework.org/schema/data/jpa
            http://www.springframework.org/schema/data/jpa/spring-jpa-1.3.xsd">

    <data-jpa:repositories base-package="com.sample"
                           transaction-manager-ref="jpaTransactionManager"
                           entity-manager-factory-ref="entityManagerFactoryBean"/>

</beans>
```

If you're configuring auditing, custom scanning filters, auto-population, and a different query method strategy, your configuration might look more like this:

```
<?xml version="1.0" encoding="UTF-8"?>
<beans xmlns="http://www.springframework.org/schema/beans"
       xmlns:xsi="http://www.w3.org/2001/XMLSchema-instance"
       xmlns:data="http://www.springframework.org/schema/data/repository"
       xmlns:data-jpa="http://www.springframework.org/schema/data/jpa"
       xsi:schemaLocation="http://www.springframework.org/schema/beans
            http://www.springframework.org/schema/beans/spring-beans-4.0.xsd
            http://www.springframework.org/schema/data/repository
            http://www.springframework.org/schema/data/repository/spring-
repository-1.6.xsd
            http://www.springframework.org/schema/data/jpa
            http://www.springframework.org/schema/data/jpa/spring-jpa-1.3.xsd">

    <data:jackson2-populator locations="classpath:com/sample/config/inserts.json"
                             object-mapper-ref="objectMapper" />

    <data-jpa:repositories base-package="com.sample"
                           transaction-manager-ref="jpaTransactionManager"
                           entity-manager-factory-ref="entityManagerFactoryBean"
                           query-lookup-strategy="create">
        <data:include-filter type="annotation"
                             expression="com.sample.MyRepository" />
    </data-jpa:repositories>

    <data-jpa:auditing auditor-aware-ref="auditorAwareImpl" />

</beans>
```

## Using the Java Configuration

The `@org.springframework.data.jpa.repository.config.EnableJpaRepositories` annotation replaces the `<data-jpa:repositories>` namespace element. It registers the same necessary beans and contains the same configuration options as the XML namespace element. These include:

- `basePackages` and `basePackageClasses` replace the attribute `base-package`.
- `namedQueriesLocation` replaces the attribute `named-queries-location`.
- `repositoryImplementationPostfix` replaces `repository-impl-postfix`.

- `queryLookupStrategy` replaces `query-lookup-strategy` and uses the `org.springframework.data.repository.query.QueryLookupStrategy.Key` enum.
- `repositoryFactoryBeanClass` replaces `factory-class`.
- `transactionManagerRef` replaces the `transaction-manager-ref` attribute.
- `entityManagerFactoryRef` replaces the `entity-manager-factory-ref` attribute.
- `includeFilters` and `excludeFilters` replace the `<data:include-filter>` and `<data:exclude-filter>` elements and use the `@ComponentScan.Filter` annotation that you are already familiar with.

The `RootContextConfiguration` class in the Spring-Data-JPA project uses `@EnableJpaRepositories` to set up Spring Data JPA. It requires no other special beans to be configured.

```
@Configuration
...
@EnableJpaRepositories(
        basePackages = "com.wrox.site.repositories",
        entityManagerFactoryRef = "entityManagerFactoryBean",
        transactionManagerRef = "jpaTransactionManager"
)
...
public class RootContextConfiguration implements
        AsyncConfigurer, SchedulingConfigurer
{
    ...
}
```

If you are happy with the default values of Spring Data's `set-dates` and `modify-on-creation` auditing settings, you can configure auditing with pure Java. Just define a bean that implements `AuditorAware` and Spring Data can find it. However, if you need to change one or both of these values to `false`, you must use the XML namespace and `@ImportResource` to include the XML configuration in your Java configuration.

For the most part, however, you configure auditing on an entity-by-entity basis. In previous versions of Spring Data Commons, auditable entities had to implement `org.springframework.data.domain.Auditable<U, ID extends Serializable>` where `U` is the user or `Principal` type. This interface defined very rigid property names, and timestamps had to use Joda Time. All auditable entities had to have `createdBy`, `createdDate`, `lastModifiedBy`, and `lastModifiedDate` properties. As of Spring Data Commons 1.5, you can use annotations to flag entity properties as auditable properties. An entity class may have at most one of each of the following property annotations (including in properties inherited from superclasses). You may choose to have one auditable property or all four.

- `@org.springframework.data.annotation.CreatedBy` properties are set to the logged-in user when the entity is created. The Java type must match the type returned by the `AuditorAware` implementation.

- `@org.springframework.data.annotation.CreatedDate` properties are set to the current date and time when the entity is created. Prior to Spring Data Commons 1.7, the only supported Java types were `long`, `Long`, `java.util.Date`, and `org.joda.time.DateTime`. As of Spring Data Commons 1.7, you can also use `Calendar` and the Java 8 Date and Time types `Instant`, `LocalDateTime`, `OffsetDateTime`, and `ZonedDateTime`. You cannot, however, use Timestamp. Whatever type or types you choose, the persistence technology you are using (JPA, MongoDB, and so on) must also support those types.
- `@org.springframework.data.annotation.LastModifiedBy` properties are set to the logged-in user when the entity is updated. The Java type must match the type returned by the `AuditorAware` implementation.
- `@org.springframework.data.annotation.LastModifiedDate` properties are set to the current time when the entity is updated. It supports the same types as `@CreatedDate`.

## Configuring Spring MVC Support

As mentioned in the previous section, Spring Data can automatically convert request parameters into Spring Web MVC handler method arguments for `Pageable` and `Sort`. In addition, using your repositories, it can automatically convert request parameters and path variables to your entity types as Spring Web MVC handler method arguments. For example, you could create a handler method like this:

```
@RequestMapping("/person/{id}")
public String viewPerson(@PathVariable("id") Person person)
{
    // method implementation
}
```

Spring Data can take the ID from the URL, retrieve the `Person` object from the `Person` repository implementation it created using `findOne(ID)`, and automatically provide that `Person` to your controller method. This eliminates the step of manually retrieving the `Person` from the repository using a `long` ID method parameter.

Configuring this support, which is new in Spring Data Commons 1.6, is really quite easy. Just annotate your `DispatcherServlet` configuration class (or classes, if you have multiple `DispatcherServlets`) with `@org.springframework.data.web.config.EnableSpringDataWebSupport`. This automatically registers an `org.springframework.data.repository.support.DomainClassConverter`, which converts request parameters and path variables into your entities. It also registers the `PageableHandlerMethodArgumentResolver` and `SortHandlerMethodArgumentResolver` beans, enabling conversion of `Pageables` and `Sorts` from request parameters. This is demonstrated in the `WebServletContextConfiguration`.

```
@Configuration
@EnableWebMvc
@EnableSpringDataWebSupport
@ComponentScan(
        basePackages = "com.wrox.site",
        useDefaultFilters = false,
        includeFilters = @ComponentScan.Filter(WebController.class)
```

```
)
public class WebServletContextConfiguration extends WebMvcConfigurerAdapter
{
    ...
}
```

The beans registered by using `@EnableSpringDataWebSupport` contain many settings that are initialized to default values. These settings include things like parameter names, maximum page sizes, and default `Pageable` and `Sort` values when request parameters are missing. These defaults might be acceptable for you, but if they are not, you need to omit the `@EnableSpringDataWebSupport` annotation and register these beans manually. This is demonstrated in `RestServletContextConfiguration`.

```
@Configuration
@EnableWebMvc
@ComponentScan(
        basePackages = "com.wrox.site",
        useDefaultFilters = false,
        includeFilters =
        @ComponentScan.Filter({RestEndpoint.class, RestEndpointAdvice.class})
)
public class RestServletContextConfiguration extends WebMvcConfigurerAdapter
{
    private static final Logger log = LogManager.getLogger();

    @Inject ApplicationContext applicationContext;
    ...
    @Override
    public void addArgumentResolvers(List<HandlerMethodArgumentResolver>
                                             resolvers)
    {
        Sort defaultSort = new Sort(new Sort.Order(Sort.Direction.ASC, "id"));
        Pageable defaultPageable = new PageRequest(0, 20, defaultSort);

        SortHandlerMethodArgumentResolver sortResolver =
                new SortHandlerMethodArgumentResolver();
        // sortParameter defaults to "sort"
        sortResolver.setSortParameter("$paging.sort");
        sortResolver.setFallbackSort(defaultSort);

        PageableHandlerMethodArgumentResolver pageableResolver =
                new PageableHandlerMethodArgumentResolver(sortResolver);
        pageableResolver.setMaxPageSize(200);
        pageableResolver.setOneIndexedParameters(true); // page starts at 1, not 0
        // pagePropery defaults to "page" and sizeProperty to "size"
        //   The following is equal to .setPageProperty("$paging.page") and
        //   .setSizeProperty("$paging.size");
        pageableResolver.setPrefix("$paging.");
        pageableResolver.setFallbackPageable(defaultPageable);

        resolvers.add(sortResolver);
        resolvers.add(pageableResolver);
    }
```

```
    @Override
    public void addFormatters(FormatterRegistry registry)
    {
        if(!(registry instanceof FormattingConversionService))
        {
            log.warn("Unable to register Spring Data JPA converter.");
            return;
        }

        // DomainClassConverter adds itself to the registry
        DomainClassConverter<FormattingConversionService> converter =
                new DomainClassConverter<>((FormattingConversionService)registry);
        converter.setApplicationContext(this.applicationContext);
    }
    ...
}
```

## Writing and Using Spring Data JPA Interfaces

Unless you have dozens or hundreds of repositories, you'll likely spend more code configuring Spring Data JPA than creating repositories. The new `AuthorRepository`, `BookRepository`, and `PublisherRepository` interfaces in the Spring-Data-JPA project are practically empty. The `GenericRepository`, `GenericBaseRepository`, `GenericJpaRepository`, `DefaultAuthorRepository`, `DefaultBookRepository`, and `DefaultPublisherRepository` from the previous chapter's Spring-JPA project are gone because they are no longer needed. Just think of all the code you've eliminated!

```
public interface AuthorRepository extends CrudRepository<Author, Long>
{

}

public interface BookRepository extends CrudRepository<Book, Long>
{
    Book getOneByIsbn(String isbn);
}

public interface PublisherRepository extends CrudRepository<Publisher, Long>
{

}
```

Using these new interfaces requires only minor changes to the `DefaultBookManager` service. `saveAuthor()`, `saveBook()`, and `savePublisher()`, which previously called `add()` if the ID was less than one and `update()` otherwise, now simply call the `save()` method on the appropriate repository. The `getAuthors()`, `getBooks()` and `getPublishers()` methods previously used the `getAll()` repository methods and now use the `findAll()` repository methods.

```
    ...
    @Override
    @Transactional
    public List<Author> getAuthors()
    {
        return this.toList(this.authorRepository.findAll());
```

```
    }
    ...
    @Override
    @Transactional
    public void saveAuthor(Author author)
    {
        this.authorRepository.save(author);
    }
    ...
```

You may wonder why the repositories return an `Iterable<T>` instead of a `List<T>`, and why you have to take the extra step of iterating over the `Iterable<T>` to convert it to a `List<T>`. O/RMs usually back the `Lists` of entities they return directly with the JDBC `ResultSet`. This improves performance and allows the calling code to begin executing immediately while the database is still returning data to the application. However, returning from the `@Transactional` method commits the transaction and closing the JDBC `Connection`, thus closing the `ResultSet`. When an O/RM returns a `List` or other `Iterable`, it is best to iterate over the entire portion of the list that you require and copy the contents of the `Iterable` into another collection before exiting the transaction context. This ensures that all the entity data has been successfully read from the database before the transaction ends.

> **NOTE** *You probably noticed that the JPA repository interfaces you created extended* `CrudRepository` *from Spring Data Commons instead of* `JpaRepository` *from Spring Data JPA. You should only extend the interface whose methods you want to expose to your services. In most cases you shouldn't need to expose the fact that your repositories use JPA, and so you shouldn't extend* `JpaRepository`. *If you want to expose pagination capabilities, extend* `PagingAndSortingRepository`. *Only if you need to expose JPA-specific behavior, such as batch deletions or* `EntityManager` *flushing, should you extend* `JpaRepository`.

Testing the application is just like testing the Spring-JPA project in Chapter 21:

1. If you never tested the Spring-JPA project from Chapter 21, be sure that you run the `create.sql` script in MySQL Workbench to create the necessary database tables, and that you create the `DataSource` resource in Tomcat's `context.xml` file.

    ```
    <Resource name="jdbc/SpringJpa" type="javax.sql.DataSource"
              maxActive="20" maxIdle="5" maxWait="10000"
              username="tomcatUser" password="password1234"
              driverClassName="com.mysql.jdbc.Driver"
              defaultTransactionIsolation="READ_COMMITTED"
              url="jdbc:mysql://localhost/SpringJpa" />
    ```

2. Compile the code and start Tomcat from your IDE. Go to `http://localhost:8080/repositories/` and you should see the entities that you created when you tested Spring-JPA in Chapter 21.

3. Click Add More Entities a few more times and more entities should appear on the screen and in the database tables.

You are using JPA and Hibernate ORM without having written any persistence code!

# REFACTORING THE CUSTOMER SUPPORT APPLICATION

Of course, the Customer Support application that you have been building throughout the book can make thorough use of Spring Data and Spring Data JPA. In fact, you can significantly reduce the amount of code you need in the application and make improving the application even easier.

In this section, you can follow along in the Customer-Support-v16 project available for download on the `wrox.com` code download site. It uses the same `@EnableJpaRepositories` configuration that you created in the previous section in `RootContextConfiguration`. However, it does not use `@EnableSpringDataWebSupport` in `WebServletContextConfiguration`. Instead, it manually creates the `SortHandlerMethodArgumentResolver` and `PageableHandlerMethodArgumentResolver` so that sensible defaults are applied, just like in `RestServletContextConfiguration`.

## Converting the Existing Repositories

Like in the Spring-Data-JPA project, you'll notice that:

- The `GenericRepository`, `GenericBaseRepository`, and `GenericJpaRepository` no longer exist in the Customer-Support-v16 project.
- The `DefaultAttachmentRepository`, `DefaultTicketRepository`, and `DefaultUserRepository` are also gone.
- The `AttachmentRepository`, `TicketRepository`, and `UserRepository` interfaces now extend `CrudRepository` and moved to the `com.wrox.site.repositories` package.

You don't even need to change the additional methods that `AttachmentRepository` and `UserRepository` define; they are already compatible with the Spring Data query method algorithm.

```
public interface AttachmentRepository extends CrudRepository<Attachment, Long>
{
    Iterable<Attachment> getByTicketId(long ticketId);
}

public interface TicketRepository extends CrudRepository<TicketEntity, Long>
{

}

public interface UserRepository extends CrudRepository<UserPrincipal, Long>
{
    UserPrincipal getByUsername(String username);
}
```

The changes to these repositories require a few tweaks to the services that use them. For example, the `saveUser` method in the `DefaultAuthenticationService` needs to use the repository's new `save` method instead of `add` and `update`.

```
    @Override
    @Transactional
    public void saveUser(UserPrincipal principal, String newPassword)
    {
```

```
        if(newPassword != null && newPassword.length() > 0)
        {
            String salt = BCrypt.gensalt(HASHING_ROUNDS, RANDOM);
            principal.setPassword(BCrypt.hashpw(newPassword, salt).getBytes());
        }

        this.userRepository.save(principal);
    }
```

In the `DefaultTicketService`, uses of:

- `getAll` become `findAll`.
- `get` become `findOne`.
- `add` and `update` become `save`.
- `deleteById` become `delete`.

The changes are minor but extend throughout the class, so the code is not included here. You'll notice that the changes in the Customer-Support-v16 project do not include taking advantage of the pagination provided by Spring Data. Updating existing code for pagination is an exercise left up to you. Later in this section you'll use pagination for ticket comments as an example.

> **NOTE** *In the former* `GenericRepository` *interface, both type parameters extended* `Serializable`*, so having* `delete(E)` *and* `delete(I)` *methods was ambiguous and wouldn't compile. This is why* `GenericRepository` *defined* `delete(E)` *and* `deleteById(I)` *methods. In* `CrudRepository`*, only the* `ID` *type parameter extends* `Serializable`*, so it is possible to overload the* `delete` *method in this fashion. Thus,* `CrudRepository`*'s methods are* `delete(T)` *and* `delete(ID)`.

## Adding Comments to Support Tickets

One of the major features missing from the Customer Support system right now is ticket commenting. What good is reporting a ticket if nobody can comment on it? With JPA, Spring Data, and Spring Data JPA, adding commenting to the Customer Support application is really easy. You'll still have to change business logic and the user interface, but the persistence layer is taken care of for you. First you create the comment entity and repository and then update the services to manipulate comments. When done with this, you need to add comments to the user interface.

### Creating the Entity and Repository

You want to start by creating a `TicketComment` POJO, of course. It looks remarkably similar to a ticket but lacks a subject.

```
public class TicketComment
{
    private long id;

    @NotBlank(message = "{validate.ticket.comment.customerName}")
```

```
    private String customerName;

    @NotBlank(message = "{validate.ticket.comment.body}")
    private String body;

    private Instant dateCreated;

    // mutators and accessors omitted
}
```

Because you still can't persist entities with `Instant` properties, you need to create a separate `TicketCommentEntity`. `TicketComment` then serves as a DTO.

```
@Entity
@Table(name = "TicketComment")
public class TicketCommentEntity implements Serializable
{
    private static final long serialVersionUID = 1L;

    private long id;
    private long ticketId;
    private long userId;
    private String body;
    private Timestamp dateCreated;

    @Id
    @Column(name = "CommentId")
    @GeneratedValue(strategy = GenerationType.IDENTITY)
    public long getId() { ... }
    public void setId(long id) { ... }

    @Basic
    public long getTicketId() { ... }
    public void setTicketId(long ticketId) { ... }

    @Basic
    public long getUserId() { ... }
    public void setUserId(long userId) { ... }

    @Basic
    public String getBody() { ... }
    public void setBody(String body) { ... }

    @Basic
    public Timestamp getDateCreated() { ... }
    public void setDateCreated(Timestamp dateCreated) { ... }
}
```

You also need a new MySQL table to persist comments to. Be sure to run the following creation statement, which you can also find in `create.sql`, on your Customer Support database.

```
CREATE TABLE TicketComment (
  CommentId BIGINT UNSIGNED NOT NULL AUTO_INCREMENT PRIMARY KEY,
  TicketId BIGINT UNSIGNED NOT NULL,
  UserId BIGINT UNSIGNED NOT NULL,
```

```
    Body TEXT,
    DateCreated TIMESTAMP(6) NULL,
    CONSTRAINT TicketComment_UserId FOREIGN KEY (UserId)
      REFERENCES UserPrincipal (UserId) ON DELETE CASCADE ,
    CONSTRAINT TicketComment_TicketId FOREIGN KEY (TicketId)
      REFERENCES Ticket (TicketId) ON DELETE CASCADE
) ENGINE = InnoDB;
```

Finally, creating the `TicketCommentRepository` is the simplest step of all because all you have to do is define an interface and let Spring Data take care of the rest.

```
public interface TicketCommentRepository
        extends CrudRepository<TicketCommentEntity, Long>
{
    Page<TicketCommentEntity> getByTicketId(long ticketId, Pageable p);
}
```

## Updating the Services

The service layer should also be fairly easy to update. You need methods for getting the comments for a ticket, saving a comment, and deleting a comment. You won't really need to do anything more than that with comments. The following three methods added to the `TicketService` interface take care of that well. The `TicketService` makes sense as a home for these because comments are inextricably linked to tickets.

```
@NotNull
Page<TicketComment> getComments(
        @Min(value = 1L, message = "{validate.ticketService.getComments.id}")
            long ticketId,
        @NotNull(message = "{validate.ticketService.getComments.page}")
            Pageable page
);
void save(
        @NotNull(message = "{validate.ticketService.save.comment}")
        @Valid TicketComment comment,
        @Min(value = 1L, message = "{validate.ticketService.saveComment.id}")
            long ticketId
);
void deleteComment(long id);
```

The implementations for `save` and `deleteComment` in `DefaultTicketService` are fairly standard and mimic the counterpart methods for tickets. `getComments` is interesting, however, because it must convert the `Page<TicketCommentEntity>` returned by the repository into a `Page<TicketComment>`. In Chapter 24, you'll learn how to use `Instants` in entities so that you can get rid of this extra work.

```
@Override
@Transactional
public Page<TicketComment> getComments(long ticketId, Pageable page)
{
    List<TicketComment> comments = new ArrayList<>();
    Page<TicketCommentEntity> entities =
            this.commentRepository.getByTicketId(ticketId, page);
    entities.forEach(e -> comments.add(this.convert(e)));
```

```
        return new PageImpl<>(comments, page, entities.getTotalElements());
    }

    private TicketComment convert(TicketCommentEntity entity)
    {
        TicketComment comment = new TicketComment();
        comment.setId(entity.getId());
        comment.setCustomerName(
                this.userRepository.findOne(entity.getUserId()).getUsername()
        );
        comment.setBody(entity.getBody());
        comment.setDateCreated(Instant.ofEpochMilli(
                entity.getDateCreated().getTime()
        ));

        return comment;
    }
```

## Commenting from the User Interface

Updating the user interface is the last step to adding comments to the customer support application. The changes to the `TicketController` are small. First, the `view` method needs a `Pageable` argument (which Spring Data automatically resolves for you) and two simple lines of added code.

```
        model.put("comments", this.ticketService.getComments(ticketId, page));
        model.put("commentForm", new CommentForm());
```

The controller also needs a method for adding new comments. The comment form exists on the ticket-viewing page so that the user can view the ticket and other comments while commenting. Therefore, this method defers to the `view` method if validation errors occur.

```
    @RequestMapping(value = "comment/{ticketId}", method = RequestMethod.POST)
    public ModelAndView comment(Principal principal, @Valid CommentForm form,
                                Errors errors, Map<String, Object> model,
                                Pageable page,
                                @PathVariable("ticketId") long ticketId)
    {
        Ticket ticket = this.ticketService.getTicket(ticketId);
        if(ticket == null)
            return this.getListRedirectModelAndView();

        if(errors.hasErrors())
            return this.view(model, page, ticketId);

        TicketComment comment = new TicketComment();
        comment.setCustomerName(principal.getName());
        comment.setBody(form.getBody());

        try
        {
            this.ticketService.save(comment, ticketId);
        }
        catch(ConstraintViolationException e)
        {
```

```
            model.put("validationErrors", e.getConstraintViolations());
            return this.view(model, page, ticketId);
        }

        return new ModelAndView(new RedirectView(
                "/ticket/view/" + ticketId, true, false
        ));
    }
```

The JSP code for displaying and adding comments is long, and a large chunk of it is dedicated to pagination. You can view the code in `/WEB-INF/jsp/view/ticket/view.jsp`. Everything after line 21 displays and adds comments. As you read the code, you will probably determine that you could do even more with the page links (such as adding first and last page links, and not displaying links to every single page if there are many pages). You should quickly realize that duplicating that code everywhere you need paging is not desirable. A custom JSP tag is just the thing to solve this problem, and creating this tag is an exercise left up to you.

You are now ready to test the updated Customer Support application using these steps:

1. If you did not test the application in Chapter 21, make sure you run the `create.sql` script and add the `DataSource` resource to Tomcat's `context.xml` file. If you did, make sure you add the `TicketComment` table to the database.
2. Compile the project and start Tomcat from your IDE.
3. Go to `http://localhost:8080/support/` in your favorite browser, log in, and comment on some of the tickets you created in Chapter 21.
4. Create more tickets if you like, and try creating different comments signed in as different users.
5. Add more than 10 comments to a ticket so that you can test pagination. Using Spring Data JPA, you have easily refactored and added comments to the support system.

You may have noticed that the SOAP and RESTful web services are not updated to address creating and returning comments. This, also, is an exercise that is left to you.

## SUMMARY

In this chapter, you explored how Spring Data and Spring Data JPA can eliminate the tedious, repetitive task of writing repository code. You learned about creating Spring Data repository interfaces and writing Spring Data query methods, and also how Spring Data creates the implementations for these interfaces on-the-fly. You were briefly introduced to adding custom behavior to Spring Data repositories, which you explore further in the next chapter. Finally, you added comments to support tickets in the Customer Support application with minimal effort thanks to Spring Data and demonstrated how easy it is to paginate data because of Spring Data's `Pageable`, `Page`, and `Sort` objects.

In the next chapter you learn about various approaches to data searching and explore how to integrate native MySQL full-text searching and universal Apache Lucene full-text searching into your JPA repositories.

# 23

# Searching for Data with JPA and Hibernate Search

## IN THIS CHAPTER

- Searching basics
- How to locate objects with advanced criteria
- Using full-text indexes with JPA
- Using Apache Lucene and Hibernate Search to index your data

## WROX.COM CODE DOWNLOADS FOR THIS CHAPTER

You can find the `wrox.com` code downloads for this chapter at `http://www.wrox.com/go/projavaforwebapps` on the Download Code tab. The code for this chapter is divided into the following major examples:

- Advanced-Criteria
- Customer-Support-v17 Project
- Search-Engine Project

## NEW MAVEN DEPENDENCY FOR THIS CHAPTER

In addition to the Maven dependencies introduced in previous chapters, you also need the following Maven dependency only for the section that covers Apache Lucene, Hibernate Search, and the Search-Engine project.

```
<dependency>
    <groupId>org.hibernate</groupId>
    <artifactId>hibernate-search-orm</artifactId>
    <version>4.5.0.Final</version>
    <scope>compile</scope>
</dependency>
```

# AN INTRODUCTION TO SEARCHING

Searching through data takes many different forms. You might use a tool like grep, find, Agent Ransack, Spotlight, or Windows Search to locate a file on your hard drive. You could look for matching filenames or matching file contents. Perhaps most familiar to you, searching might involve opening your web browser and using a popular search tool such as Google to find content on the Internet. Or maybe you have a Gmail account and you use the search bar at the top of a Gmail page to find e-mails and create filters from search patterns.

If you like to shop online, you probably have a favorite store, and it's likely you have used its search tool to find products that interest you. As a developer, undoubtedly you have used a search tool in your IDE to find specific files or classes, keywords in a project, or code in a code file. You might have used the GitHub search to find code in an Open Source repository and then used your browser's search tool to locate specific keywords on a page. Perhaps you have a social networking profile and use its search tool to locate people you know or find topics you are interested in. And, of course, who could forget the tried-and-true (and least accurate) method of searching: manually looking through paper documents in your filing cabinet or microfiche in a library to find the data you are looking for.

In all these different approaches to searching, two undeniable truths emerge: Indexed searching is faster than non-indexed searching, and creating indexes makes creating content take longer.

### WAIT — INDEXES OR INDICES?

The intersection of language and computer jargon often results in some interesting disputes. For example, do you use computer mice or computer mouses? (This author uses computer mouses.) The word "index" in plural form has traditionally been "indices," but this has changed somewhat in recent years. Some people learn the phrase, "Books have indexes; math has indices." Because mathematical indices also have important meanings in computer science, many people prefer the word "indexes" when referring to a technological but non-mathematical index in the plural form. This book uses the word "indexes" as well.

## Understanding the Importance of Indexes

Take the filing cabinet as an example. You could throw all your documents in the first available spot in the filing cabinet as soon as you get them. This would be very fast and with the drawers closed would take on the appearance of being very organized. But finding that one bill six months after you got it *will* prove to be a time-consuming task.

Alternatively, you could create folders in your filing cabinet to organize all the bills together — all your insurance paperwork together, all your research on a particular topic together, and so on. Suddenly, finding that bill is much easier. Instead of looking through the entire filing cabinet (or, worse, cabinets) until you find the bill, you can open the drawer you know it's in, reach into the Bills folder, and sift through the handful of similar documents until you find the right one. The downside is that inserting the bill into the filing cabinet takes longer. You can't just open a drawer, throw it in, and walk away. You have to find the right drawer for the document type, locate the appropriate folder, create a new folder if the appropriate one doesn't exist, and then insert the document.

Indexing your documents also involves a certain amount of occasional reorganization. If a certain drawer or folder gets too full, you might make smaller, less narrow categories and reclassify some or all of your documents. The point that should be abundantly clear by now is that keeping your documents organized isn't free. It's not even cheap and can consume considerable time. The same is true of indexes containing digital information. The question that you must always ask yourself is, "Is the price worth the benefit?"

Compare searching for a document using grep versus using Mac OS X's Spotlight feature. If you grep a small folder's contents, it will likely return results fairly quickly. So will Spotlight. But what about an entire hard disk containing hundreds of thousands of files? Grep could take several minutes or even hours to return results, whereas Spotlight still takes mere seconds. The difference is in the approach. Grep must open and read every document every time it searches whereas Spotlight keeps an index of file contents and uses that index instead. The cost is in disk performance: Every time you save a file, Spotlight must update the index. Every few days or hours (depending on how active your computer is) Spotlight cranks up the CPU to reorganize its indexes. Much of the time you never notice it, but sometimes your machine briefly slows down. Is this expense worth the immeasurable increase in searching speed? For most users, it absolutely is.

An index is any kind of structure that makes finding data easier. Indexes take many forms depending on what's doing the indexing. Many relational databases make heavy use of *B-tree indexes*, which store ordered data very well. Text-heavy data stores that need to search based on how closely the content matches a search query often use *full-text indexes*. Google's search uses a closely guarded indexing algorithm that most people know little about. All these indexes, for their purposes, have a benefit (faster searching) and a cost. For most indexes that cost is slower saving of data. For search engines like Google that cover content created by third parties, the cost is the expense of operating "crawlers" that index the data after it is updated.

So how do you know whether an index is worth the cost? That's a complicated question whose answer could fill many, many chapters. Generally speaking, the cost of an index is directly related to the ratio of writes to reads. A system that performs significantly more reads than writes can afford more indexes and more complicated indexes than a system that performs more writes than reads. Sometimes this ratio varies for different parts of a system. For example, a database table holding news articles is updated far less often than a database table holding comments on those news articles. Therefore, the news article table can have more indexes and more complicated indexes than the comments table for approximately the same cost. The value of that index is then related to the cost versus the ratio of reads that use the index to reads that don't use the index.

Determining how and where to create indexes is a learned art and often involves painstaking analysis of query types and ratios, bottlenecks, and the output of profiling tools. But generally speaking, if you want to search any large amount of data in a reasonable amount of time, you *will* need one or more indexes. Without any indexes your search will be unbearably slow and probably affect the performance of other areas of your application. What kind of indexing technology you use largely depends on your storage medium, computer language, and programming methodologies.

## Taking Three Different Approaches

This chapter explores three different approaches to searching and indexing:

- Simple indexes with complex queries
- Full-text searching using database vendor indexes
- Full-text searching using Apache Lucene and Hibernate Search

This is by no means an exhaustive analysis, but it does cover some of the most common techniques adopted by other Java, JPA, and relational database programmers. All these approaches integrate with the Java Persistence API in some way or another, but you can use them all outside of a JPA environment as well. After you have learned about these three different techniques, you should be at a good jumping-off point for integrating any other searching and indexing technologies you may want to use into your applications.

# USING ADVANCED CRITERIA TO LOCATE OBJECTS

Perhaps the most obvious solution initially, is that you can use the criteria API to find objects in many different ways. Like all the solutions presented in this chapter, it is the best choice for some situations and a bad choice for other situations. One place in which it excels is in building dynamic queries. In a dynamic query, a user provides expected values for one or more fields, possibly indicates whether all or any of the criteria should be met, and submits the search. This isn't something as simple as the user typing in a person's first and last names to find a Person object in the application. You don't need the criteria API for that; you can simply create a Spring Data query method named `findByFirstNameAndLastName` to satisfy this requirement.

In a dynamic query, you don't know at compile time what fields the user wants to search on, so you can't write even the most complex query method to power the search. From the user side, a dynamic query might look something like Figure 23-1. There's no official name for this; it's just another type of search. You may call it something different. This book, consistently calls it a dynamic query.

In this search screen, you can include as few or as many of the fields in your query as you want. The query currently entered should find all white females with the last name of Sanders living in Hawaii, United States. The criteria are implicitly grouped with the `AND` logical operator, but fields without the check box checked are not included in the query. You cannot perform this search with a static query known at compile time. This is a dynamic query, and the best way to approach it is with the criteria API.

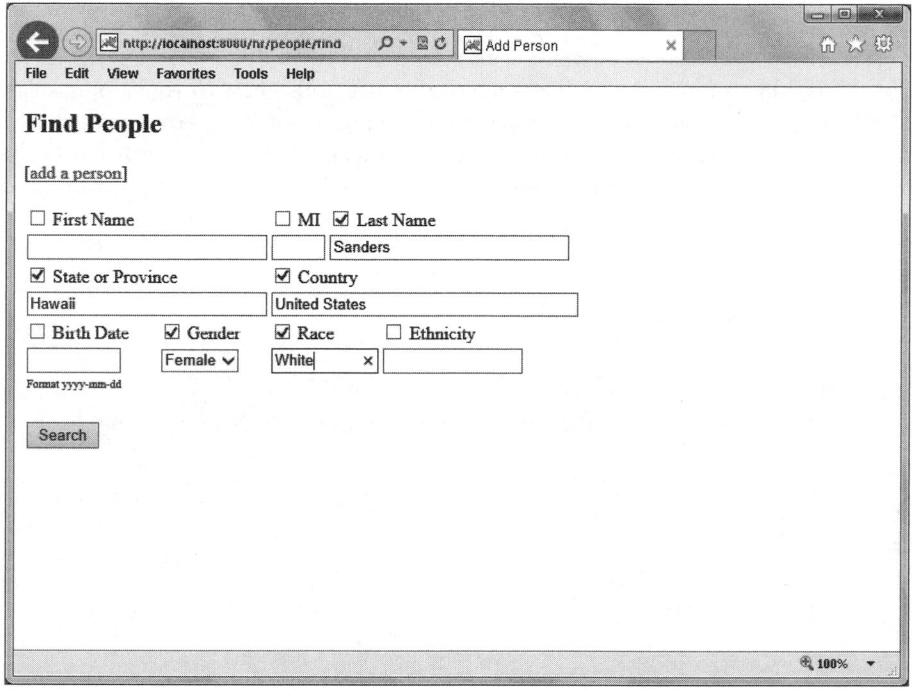


FIGURE 23-1

# Creating Complex Criteria Queries

Continuing with the example search screen in Figure 23-1, assume your application has the following `Person` entity with appropriate mutator and accessor methods. You can follow along with this section in the Advanced-Criteria project available for download on the `wrox.com` code download site.

```
@Entity
@Table(name = "Person")
public class Person
{
    private long id;
    private String firstName;
    private String middleInitial;
    private String lastName;
    private String state;
    private String country;
    private Date birthDate;
    private Gender gender;
    private String race;
    private String ethnicity;

    // mutators and accessors
}
```

## Representing Search Criteria in an API

You can't use the JPA criteria API to create search criteria and pass them down through the layers of your application. This API requires an `EntityManager` instance and access to your domain layer, which shouldn't be accessible from your user interface layer. You need some way to convey the search query from the user interface to the repository. Because this is likely not the only entity that you want to search in this manner, you need to reuse this mechanism across your application, so it can't be `Person`-specific.

```
public class Criterion
{
    private final String propertyName;
    private final Operator operator;
    private final Object compareTo;

    public Criterion(String propertyName, Operator operator, Object compareTo)
    { ... }

    // accessors

    public static enum Operator
    {
        EQ, NEQ, LT, LTE, GT, GTE, LIKE, NOT_LIKE, IN, NOT_IN, NULL, NOT_NULL
    }
}

public interface SearchCriteria extends List<Criterion>
{
}
```

The API is simple: A search involves a list of one or more `Criterion` instances. Each `Criterion` represents a comparison between a property on an entity and a value, using the `Operator` enum to determine how to perform that comparison. For now, it permits only the AND-ing of criteria because that's all you need for this search and it's easier to implement. If you want to add an AND/OR toggle or add AND/OR groupings, you can create extra features in the `SearchCriteria` interface to do that. (This is a task you can do on your own.)

## Adding a Custom Search Method

Your repository needs a custom search method that can accept a `SearchCriteria` argument. It should also accept a `Pageable` and return a `Page<Person>` so that search results can be retrieved in pages. However, you don't want to rewrite this method for every repository, so you need to make it generic. This requires some of the clever trickery you used in Chapter 21 to get the type arguments for a generic class.

First, create an interface to reflect what you want the searchable repository to do. Your `Person` repository interface should extend this interface to indicate that people are searchable.

```
public interface SearchableRepository<T>
{
    Page<T> search(SearchCriteria criteria, Pageable pageable);
}

public interface PersonRepository extends JpaRepository<Person, Long>,
        SearchableRepository<Person>
{
}
```

All searchable repositories can share a common implementation of the `search` method you create, so it makes sense to implement a common base class for your custom repository implementations. The code in `search` needs to know the `Class` for `T`, but you could also have other common base classes that need this information. So create a base class for abstracting the type argument and a base class for searching.

```
abstract class AbstractDomainClassAwareRepository<T>
{
    protected final Class<T> domainClass;

    @SuppressWarnings("unchecked")
    protected AbstractDomainClassAwareRepository()
    {
        Type genericSuperclass = this.getClass().getGenericSuperclass();
        while(!(genericSuperclass instanceof ParameterizedType))
        {
            if(!(genericSuperclass instanceof Class))
                throw new IllegalStateException("Unable to determine type " +
                        "arguments because generic superclass neither " +
                        "parameterized type nor class.");
            if(genericSuperclass == AbstractDomainClassAwareRepository.class)
                throw new IllegalStateException("Unable to determine type " +
                        "arguments because no parameterized generic superclass " +
                        "found.");

            genericSuperclass = ((Class)genericSuperclass).getGenericSuperclass();
        }

        ParameterizedType type = (ParameterizedType)genericSuperclass;
        Type[] arguments = type.getActualTypeArguments();
        this.domainClass = (Class<T>)arguments[0];
    }
}

abstract class AbstractSearchableJpaRepository<T>
        extends AbstractDomainClassAwareRepository<T>
        implements SearchableRepository<T>
{
```

```
    @PersistenceContext protected EntityManager entityManager;

    @Override
    public Page<T> search(SearchCriteria criteria, Pageable pageable)
    {
        return null;
    }
}
```

Right now the search method is stubbed out, but you'll fill it in in a minute. You added `SearchableRepository<Person>` to the `PersonRepository` interface, but Spring Data still doesn't know how to find the search method implementation. To solve this, you need a `PersonRepositoryImpl` class. Notice that this class implements *only* `SearchableRepository<Person>` (by way of extending `AbstractSearchableJpaRepository<Person>`). It does not implement `PersonRepository` because Spring Data JPA does that for you.

```
public class PersonRepositoryImpl extends
AbstractSearchableJpaRepository<Person>
{
}
```

## Creating Queries from Search Input

Now you still need to complete the `search` method implementation. It needs to do several things:

- Convert the `SearchCriteria` into a JPA `CriteriaQuery<Long>` to count the number of matching records.
- Convert the `SearchCriteria` into a JPA `CriteriaQuery<T>` to retrieve actual entities.
- Order the records properly using the `Sort` information in the `Pageable` parameter.
- Apply the `Pageable` limits to the query to retrieve the correct page.
- Convert the query results to a `Page<T>` with a fully initialized list of entities.

As you start to think about all the options in the `Criterion.Operator` enum, you should quickly realize how much code this consumes. Because you have to convert the `SearchCriteria` twice, that conversion should be in a separate method. However, even this method would contain 12 `if` statements or 12 `case` statements (one for each `Operator`) — not the most object-oriented approach. Why perform such onerous logic when the `Operator` enum is naturally polymorphic?

As it turns out, you can represent each `Criterion` with a `javax.persistence.criteria.Predicate` (not to be confused with Java 8's `java.unit.function.Predicate`). In a general sense (and in the case of both `Predicate` interfaces), a predicate is just a `boolean` expression. In the sense of the JPA and Java 8 interfaces, a `Predicate` is a `boolean` expression that you can evaluate at some later point. Each `Operator` constant can precisely evaluate to a `Predicate` using the `Criterion`, `Root`, and `CriteriaBuiler` as input. The `Operator` enum in Listing 23-1 defines an abstract `toPredicate` method, implemented in each constant.

**LISTING 23-1: Criterion.java**

```
public class Criterion
{
    // previously printed code

    public static enum Operator
    {
        EQ {
            @Override
            public Predicate toPredicate(Criterion c, Root<?>r, CriteriaBuilder b)
            {
                return b.equal(r.get(c.getPropertyName()), c.getCompareTo());
            }
        }, NEQ {
            @Override
            public Predicate toPredicate(Criterion c, Root<?>r, CriteriaBuilder b)
            {
                return b.notEqual(r.get(c.getPropertyName()), c.getCompareTo());
            }
        }, LT {
            @Override @SuppressWarnings("unchecked")
            public Predicate toPredicate(Criterion c, Root<?>r, CriteriaBuilder b)
            {
                return b.lessThan(
                        r.<Comparable>get(c.getPropertyName()), getComparable(c)
                );
            }
        }, LTE {
            @Override @SuppressWarnings("unchecked")
            public Predicate toPredicate(Criterion c, Root<?>r, CriteriaBuilder b)
            {
                return b.lessThanOrEqualTo(
                        r.<Comparable>get(c.getPropertyName()), getComparable(c)
                );
            }
        }, GT {
            @Override @SuppressWarnings("unchecked")
            public Predicate toPredicate(Criterion c, Root<?>r, CriteriaBuilder b)
            {
                return b.greaterThan(
                        r.<Comparable>get(c.getPropertyName()), getComparable(c)
                );
            }
        }, GTE {
            @Override @SuppressWarnings("unchecked")
            public Predicate toPredicate(Criterion c, Root<?>r, CriteriaBuilder b)
            {
                return b.greaterThanOrEqualTo(
                        r.<Comparable>get(c.getPropertyName()), getComparable(c)
                );
            }
        }, LIKE {
```

*continues*

**LISTING 23-1** *(continued)*

```
        @Override
        public Predicate toPredicate(Criterion c, Root<?>r, CriteriaBuilder b)
        {
            return b.like(
                    r.get(c.getPropertyName()), getString(c)
            );
        }
    }, NOT_LIKE {
        @Override
        public Predicate toPredicate(Criterion c, Root<?>r, CriteriaBuilder b)
        {
            return b.notLike(
                    r.get(c.getPropertyName()), getString(c)
            );
        }
    }, IN {
        @Override
        public Predicate toPredicate(Criterion c, Root<?>r, CriteriaBuilder b)
        {
            Object o = c.getCompareTo();
            if(o == null)
                return r.get(c.getPropertyName()).in();
            if(o instanceof Collection)
                return r.get(c.getPropertyName()).in((Collection) o);
            throw new IllegalArgumentException(c.getPropertyName());
        }
    }, NOT_IN {
        @Override
        public Predicate toPredicate(Criterion c, Root<?>r, CriteriaBuilder b)
        {
            Object o = c.getCompareTo();
            if(o == null)
                return b.not(r.get(c.getPropertyName()).in());
            if(o instanceof Collection)
                return b.not(r.get(c.getPropertyName()).in((Collection) o));
            throw new IllegalArgumentException(c.getPropertyName());
        }
    }, NULL {
        @Override
        public Predicate toPredicate(Criterion c, Root<?>r, CriteriaBuilder b)
        {
            return r.get(c.getPropertyName()).isNull();
        }
    }, NOT_NULL {
        @Override
        public Predicate toPredicate(Criterion c, Root<?>r, CriteriaBuilder b)
        {
            return r.get(c.getPropertyName()).isNotNull();
        }
    };

    public abstract Predicate toPredicate(Criterion c, Root<?> r,
```

```
                                                    CriteriaBuilder b);

        @SuppressWarnings("unchecked")
        private static Comparable<?> getComparable(Criterion c) {
            Object o = c.getCompareTo();
            if(o != null && !(o instanceof Comparable))
                throw new IllegalArgumentException(c.getPropertyName());
            return (Comparable<?>)o;
        }

        private static String getString(Criterion c) {
            if(!(c.getCompareTo() instanceof String))
                throw new IllegalArgumentException(c.getPropertyName());
            return (String)c.getCompareTo();
        }
    }
}
```

Using the `toPredicate` method, the code to convert the `SearchCriteria` into a `CriteriaQuery` is much simpler:

```
    ...
    public Page<T> search(SearchCriteria criteria, Pageable pageable)
    {
        CriteriaBuilder builder = this.entityManager.getCriteriaBuilder();

        CriteriaQuery<Long> countCriteria = builder.createQuery(Long.class);
        Root<T> countRoot = countCriteria.from(this.domainClass);
        long total = this.entityManager.createQuery(
                countCriteria.select(builder.count(countRoot))
                        .where(toPredicates(criteria, countRoot, builder))
        ).getSingleResult();

        CriteriaQuery<T> pageCriteria = builder.createQuery(this.domainClass);
        Root<T> pageRoot = pageCriteria.from(this.domainClass);
        List<T> list = this.entityManager.createQuery(
                pageCriteria.select(pageRoot)
                        .where(toPredicates(criteria, pageRoot, builder))
                        .orderBy(toOrders(pageable.getSort(), pageRoot, builder))
        ).setFirstResult(pageable.getOffset())
                .setMaxResults(pageable.getPageSize())
                .getResultList();

        return new PageImpl<>(new ArrayList<>(list), pageable, total);
    }

    private static Predicate[] toPredicates(SearchCriteria criteria, Root<?> root,
                                            CriteriaBuilder builder)
    {
        Predicate[] predicates = new Predicate[criteria.size()];
        int i = 0;
        for(Criterion c : criteria)
            predicates[i++] = c.getOperator().toPredicate(c, root, builder);
        return predicates;
    }
    ...
```

This code executes the five steps previously enumerated. The `toOrders` method invocation (in bold) is a static import from `org.springframework.data.jpa.repository.query.QueryUtils` that turns a Spring Data `Sort` into JPA ordering instructions. The `search` method returns a new `org.springframework.data.domain.PageImpl` with the `Pageable` information, total record count, and list of results. Remember that the list returned by the JPA provider may be lazy-loaded and thus won't populate until iterated. This is why the code wraps the list in a new `ArrayList`.

> **NOTE** *The unfortunate part about the* `search` *method is the need to convert the* `SearchCriteria` *to a* `CriteriaQuery` *twice. Some JPA implementations let you reuse the* `Root` *object for multiple queries, in which case you could avoid this additional step. However, the JPA specification is unclear on this; therefore, such use is not portable.*

The Advanced-Criteria project contains a `MainController`, a `/WEB-INF/jsp/view/people/add.jsp`, and a `/WEB-INF/jsp/view/people/find.jsp` that comprise the user interface for creating and searching people. `MainController` uses `PersonService`, and `DefaultPersonService` uses `PersonRepository`. The details are unimportant because they don't contain anything you haven't seen already in this book. However, you should know that the current user interface is limited — it only supports `AND`-ing all criteria together, and it only supports the `EQ` operator. Feel free to extend the user interface yourself further to support other operators, such as `LT`, `GT`, `LIKE`, and so on. In doing so, you will quickly realize that creating useful dynamic querying is an enormous task.

To test the existing, limited user interface:

1. Be sure to run `create.sql` in MySQL Workbench and create the following `DataSource` resource in Tomcat's `context.xml` configuration file.

    ```
    <Resource name="jdbc/AdvancedCriteria" type="javax.sql.DataSource"
              maxActive="20" maxIdle="5" maxWait="10000"
              username="tomcatUser" password="password1234"
              driverClassName="com.mysql.jdbc.Driver"
              defaultTransactionIsolation="READ_COMMITTED"
              url="jdbc:mysql://localhost/AdvancedCriteria" />
    ```

2. Compile the project and start Tomcat from your IDE, then go to `http://localhost:8080/hr/people/add` in your favorite browser. Add several people with different names, genders, birth dates, races, and locations to your database using this screen.
3. Once you have added enough people to perform a useful test of searching, go to `http://localhost:8080/hr/people/find`. You should see a screen like the previous Figure 23-1. Try different search queries to see how they change the results you see. To test paging, you will need to perform a search that matches more than 10 people.

## Using OR in Your Queries

By now you should recognize that the criteria API is exceptionally powerful. So powerful, in fact, that it can even be dangerous — giving your users unfettered access to create queries on any columns can have disastrous performance consequences. But so far all you have done is specified a lot of simple-expression `Predicates` in the `where` method. All these `Predicates` are `AND`-ed together, which of course isn't enough for all situations. Suppose you know a person's birthdate and the name "Cooper," but you don't know whether that's the first or last name. You would need to `OR` the first and last name `Predicates`, and then `AND` the result of that and the birthdate `Predicate`. So how do you accomplish this with the criteria API?

As you should know from everyday programming experience, when you `AND` or `OR` two or more `boolean` expressions, the result itself is a `boolean` expression. Likewise, using the criteria API you can `AND` or `OR` two or more `Predicates` to create another `Predicate`. The `where` method is an implicit `AND` if you supply multiple `Predicates`, but you can explicitly `AND` or `OR` `Predicates` together, as well. Returning to the person named "Cooper," you could accomplish this with the following code where *n* is the name "Cooper" and *b* is the birthdate:

```
criteria.select(root)
        .where(
                builder.or(
                        builder.equal(root.get("lastName"), n),
                        builder.equal(root.get("firstName"), n)
                ),
                builder.equal(root.get("birthDate"), b)
        );
```

The `or` method here accepts multiple `Predicates` and returns a `Predicate` with those `Predicates` `OR`-ed. The `where` method, again, acts as an implicit `AND` of the `OR`-ed predicates and the birth date predicates. If you prefer to explicitly `AND` criteria, you could rewrite the same query like this:

```
criteria.select(root)
        .where(
                builder.and(
                        builder.or(
                                builder.equal(root.get("lastName"), n),
                                builder.equal(root.get("firstName"), n)
                        ),
                        builder.equal(root.get("birthDate"), b)
                )
        );
```

Using the `or` and `and` methods, which you can nest as deeply as you need to mimic levels of parenthesis in code or SQL, you can execute some fairly complex queries. Most of the time you don't need queries like this for standard searching situations, but this level of complexity will likely come in handy in batch situations and background jobs.

```
pageCriteria.select(pageRoot)
        .where(
                builder.or(
                        builder.and(
                                builder.equal(expr),
                                builder.equal(expr),
                                pageRoot.get("property").in(expr)
                        ),
                        builder.or(
                                builder.lessThan(expr),
                                builder.greaterThanOrEqualTo(expr)
                        )
                ),
```

```
                builder.and(
                        builder.equal(expr),
                        builder.greaterThan(expr)
                )
        );
```

## Creating Useful Indexes to Improve Performance

As you read earlier, any time you search through data you're going to need one or more indexes. But it's important to understand up front that you can't index for every scenario. The more you index a database table, the more it slows down for inserts, updates, and deletes. Your exact goal will vary between every application, and a detailed discussion on the intricacies of database indexing is an entire book on its own. Every database system is different, and no guidelines work for everything. Generally speaking, however, you should aim for having 95 percent of queries contain at least the first column in at least one index, and a majority of queries contain two or more columns in at least one index. ("Contain" here means in the `WHERE` clause.) You should prioritize your most heavily run queries over the less common ones. This might mean running a trace program against your database to capture statistics on which queries run how often. Depending on which database server you use, you likely have tools available to analyze queries and get a glimpse of which indexes are needed, if any.

Remember that a `LIKE` comparison can use an index unless it *starts* with a wildcard — when this happens, it will trigger a scan. Scanning is bad (very slow), so when you know you'll be performing a `LIKE` comparison starting with a wildcard, try to include at least one other criterion that can *always* use an index. For example, you could require the user to specify a date range or automatically limit the results to those created or updated within the last year.

`OR`-ed criteria can utilize indexes but not as efficiently as `AND`-ed criteria in most cases. So if you have to `OR` something, try to include an indexed `AND` as well, if possible.

Keep in mind that a query must contain the first column in an index before it can use any other columns in that index. So if you have an expensive query with one column in the `WHERE` clause and no indexes start with that column, you're going to have a problem. It does you no good for an index to have that column as the second or third column in the index.

Finally, unique constraints are your friend. They are the fastest indexes other than the primary key. (In some databases like Oracle, you must explicitly create the index to match the constraint.) If you're creating a `User` table and you think, "I'll enforce username uniqueness in the code," take a step back. The unique constraint doesn't just enforce uniqueness — it also gives you a very efficient means for locating records that you are very likely to look up using that one column (otherwise, why would you care about uniqueness?). Enforce uniqueness in the code, for sure — that's a best practice. *But add the unique constraint, too.*

# TAKING ADVANTAGE OF FULL-TEXT INDEXES WITH JPA

Though different trends exist in different industries and types of applications, these days most users prefer entering a search query into a single text box for searching data. You have several ways to approach this use case, but *full-text searches* are a very common solution. In a full-text search, a search engine analyzes every single word in every single document in the database and comes up with matches that contain relevance scores. Different search engines calculate relevance in different ways, but generally speaking it involves measuring how closely a result matches a search query and how close the search terms are to each other in a particular result. A result that contains an exact phrase matching the search will have a higher relevance score than a result that merely contains all the words but not together.

Such a search can be far more expensive than simple `LIKE` comparisons, but specialized *full-text indexes* can make the task much more efficient. These indexes store every word that exists in the indexed data along with how many times each word appears (the most common words are weighted less important than the least common words) and which records it appears in, among other statistics and analysis. When a full-text search is performed, the database can quickly find matches using the index and then calculate the relevance of the results. This technique is so much more efficient than a brute-force full-text search that most databases *require* you to have a full-text index before you are allowed to perform a full-text search.

In this section you explore how to create full-text indexes in MySQL, how to use those indexes in a JPA repository, and how to make full-text searching more portable with other relational databases. You add full-text searching to the Customer Support project that you have been working on throughout the book, enabling your users and employees to easily search through your support tickets. You can follow along with the text in the Customer-Support-v17 project, available for download from the `wrox.com` code download site.

## Creating Full-Text Indexes in MySQL Tables

MySQL, like most databases, requires a full-text index if you want to perform full-text searches. It has supported full-text indexes for more than 10 years as part of the MyISAM database engine, but during most of that time *only* MyISAM tables could house full-text indexes. This meant that you could create a transactional table (InnoDB), or a full-text-capable table (MyISAM), but you couldn't create a table that was both transactional and full-text-capable. However, as of MySQL 5.6.4 you can now create full-text indexes in InnoDB tables, a feature thousands of users have been awaiting for years. This, finally, enables you to have fully ACID-compliant tables that also support full-text searching. This change in MySQL is not without its caveats, so you should keep these things in mind:

- MyISAM and InnoDB are different engines within the MySQL umbrella, so naturally their full-text implementations and algorithms are not identical. This is not to say that one is better than the other, but keep this in mind when switching from MyISAM to InnoDB. However, using full-text searching and indexing in MyISAM and InnoDB is *syntactically* identical.
- The InnoDB full-text engine is still very young. (Only 12 patch versions, 5.6.5 through 5.6.16, have been released since full-text support was added.) As such, it is bound to have bugs that have not yet been identified and fixed. Don't let this stop you from using it, though! The community needs your help finding and reporting issues.
- Although MyISAM has 543 default *stopwords* (words that are filtered out from the index due to their commonness), InnoDB has only 36 default stopwords. Some people have complained for some time that MyISAM has too many stopwords, and this was addressed in InnoDB (without breaking backward compatibility for MyISAM users). The MySQL

documentation (`http://dev.mysql.com/doc/refman/5.6/en/`) provides instructions for adding to and removing from the stopword list for both engines.

- The relevance scores calculated by the InnoDB engine are completely different from those calculated by the MyISAM engine, so you cannot compare scores from a query run against a MyISAM table with scores from a query run against an InnoDB table. That wouldn't be a good practice, anyway.
- The MyISAM `ft_min_word_length` configuration setting and the InnoDB `innodb_ft_min_token_size` configuration setting serve essentially the same purpose but default to different values. If you previously used MyISAM full-text search, you may want to alter the `innodb_ft_min_token_size` setting to one that works well for you.
- Several critical InnoDB full-text bugs have been fixed lately. Make sure you are running at least MySQL 5.6.16, 5.7.3, or better!

If you are familiar with creating full-text indexes on MyISAM tables, the task is no different on InnoDB, except that you can add only one full-text index at a time. A table *can* have multiple full-text indexes, but for some reason they must be added in separate statements. For purposes of the Customer Support application, which you have been working on since Part I, you want ticket subjects, ticket bodies, and comment bodies to be indexed. Open MySQL Workbench and run the following statements, which create the necessary full-text indexes.

```
USE CustomerSupport;
ALTER TABLE Ticket ADD FULLTEXT INDEX Ticket_Search (Subject, Body);
ALTER TABLE TicketComment ADD FULLTEXT INDEX TicketComment_Search (Body);
```

If you have not used the Customer Support application in previous chapters, you should run the entire `create.sql` script provided with the downloaded project and create the appropriate `DataSource` resource in Tomcat's `context.xml` configuration file.

> **NOTE** *When you create these full-text indexes, MySQL will issue a warning with the message, "124 InnoDB rebuilding table to add column FTS_DOC_ID." Do not let this concern you; it is normal. MySQL adds a hidden column to full-text indexed InnoDB tables to uniquely identify each indexed record. You will never see this column, and it will not interfere with normal use of the table. If a table has multiple full-text indexes, MySQL adds only this one hidden column, and all indexes for that table share it.*

## Creating and Using a Searchable Repository

As before, you need to customize your repositories to make them searchable. This starts with a slightly different `SearchableRepository` than you used in the previous section. You also need a way to return not just the `Ticket`, but also its relevance to the result. This requires the use of a custom JPA result set mapping, something you have not done yet but will do in this section. For the purposes of returning the entity and the relevance, the new `SearchResult` class serves as a wrapper for both.

```
public class SearchResult<T>
{
    private final T entity;
    private final double relevance;

    public SearchResult(T entity, double relevance)
    {
        this.entity = entity;
        this.relevance = relevance;
    }

    // accessors
}

public interface SearchableRepository<T>
{
    Page<SearchResult<T>> search(String query, boolean useBooleanMode,
                                 Pageable pageable);
}

public interface TicketRepository extends JpaRepository<TicketEntity, Long>,
        SearchableRepository<TicketEntity>
{
}
```

## Searching with Native Queries and Custom Mappings

JPA doesn't support full-text searching natively. There is no provision in the criteria API or JPQL for performing full-text searches. However, JPA does enable you to perform native queries. Native queries are executed directly in the database instead of being interpreted by the JPA provider like JPQL queries. As such, you must write native queries in the SQL syntax supported by your database vendor, not in JPQL syntax. You can use a native query to execute a full-text search on a database. Unfortunately, native queries are not `TypedQuery`s, but you can still provide the domain `Class` when creating them, so the provider still knows how to translate the result set into the correct entities.

In addition to this, you need to retrieve both the `TicketEntity` and a custom column, search relevance, from the database using just one query. This means that you can't use a standard query with just the domain `Class`. Instead, you need to define a custom result set mapping that tells JPA what to do with the extra columns. This is achieved by marking the `TicketEntity` class with the `@javax.persistence.SqlResultSetMapping` annotation.

```
@Entity
@Table(name = "Ticket")
@SqlResultSetMapping(
        name = "searchResultMapping.ticket",
        entities = { @EntityResult(entityClass = TicketEntity.class) },
        columns = { @ColumnResult(name = "_ft_scoreColumn", type = Double.class) }
)
public class TicketEntity implements Serializable
{
    ...
}
```

A custom result set mapping is named, and you reference that name when creating a query that should use the mapping. You can then use one or more of the `entities`, `columns`, and `classes` attributes to specify how the result set should map. Using `entities`, you can specify one or more managed JPA entities that should be mapped from the result. (So you could, for example, return multiple different entities using one query.) The `columns` attribute enables you to map individual columns to scalar values. In this case, `_ft_scoreColumn` maps to a `Double`. Finally, the `classes` attribute is an array of `@javax.persistence.ConstructorResult` annotations. Using this, you can map multiple scalar columns to the constructor of any class, and that class is constructed and returned using those columns.

`@SqlResultSetMapping` does not replace the mapping instructions for the entity it appears on. In fact, it doesn't even have to appear on an entity that it maps — it just has to appear on some entity somewhere so that the JPA provider can discover the custom result set mapping. If you don't want to use the annotation for this purpose, you can use XML mappings instead. The following XML is identical to the previous use of `@SqlResultSetMapping`:

```
<?xml version="1.0" encoding="UTF-8"?>
<entity-mappings xmlns="http://xmlns.jcp.org/xml/ns/persistence/orm"
                 xmlns:xsi="http://www.w3.org/2001/XMLSchema-instance"
                 xsi:schemaLocation="http://xmlns.jcp.org/xml/ns/persistence/orm
        http://xmlns.jcp.org/xml/ns/persistence/orm_2_1.xsd"
                 version="2.1">

    <sql-result-set-mapping name="searchResultMapping.ticket">
        <entity-result entity-class="com.wrox.site.entities.TicketEntity" />
        <column-result name="_ft_scoreColumn" class="java.lang.Double" />
    </sql-result-set-mapping>

</entity-mappings>
```

Normally you would place this XML in `/META-INF/orm.xml`. However, you can specify a different classpath location for this file using `<mapping-file>` in `persistence.xml`. You can also use Spring Framework's `LocalContainerEntityManagerFactoryBean` to specify a different classpath location:

```
@Bean
public LocalContainerEntityManagerFactoryBean entityManagerFactoryBean()
{
    ...
    factory.setJpaPropertyMap(properties);
    factory.setMappingResources("com/wrox/config/mappings.xml");
    return factory;
}
```

The `TicketRepositoryImpl` implements the custom search method for searching tickets in the database. Notice that there is no `AbstractSearchableJpaRepository` as in the Advanced-Criteria project. Although you could make full-text searching a generic affair, it involves a lot of code and is extremely complicated. A generic repository needs to be aware of the table and schema for each entity, as well as the columns indexed in the full-text index. In addition, the query for searching the tickets isn't your ordinary full-text search query. If it were, it would look something like this:

```
SELECT *, MATCH(Subject, Body) AGAINST('search phrase') AS _ft_scoreColumn
  FROM Ticket
  WHERE MATCH(Subject, Body) AGAINST('search phrase')
  ORDER BY _ft_scoreColumn DESC, TicketId DESC;
```

In this case, however, the user wants to find matching tickets *and* tickets with matching comments, which requires a much more complicated query.

```
public class TicketRepositoryImpl implements SearchableRepository<TicketEntity>
{
    @PersistenceContext EntityManager entityManager;

    @Override
    public Page<SearchResult<TicketEntity>> search(String query,
                                                    boolean useBooleanMode,
                                                    Pageable pageable)
    {
        String mode = useBooleanMode ?
                "IN BOOLEAN MODE" : "IN NATURAL LANGUAGE MODE";
        String matchTicket = "MATCH(t.Subject, t.Body) AGAINST(?1 " + mode + ")";
        String matchComment = "MATCH(c.Body) AGAINST(?1 " + mode + ")";

        long total = ((Number)this.entityManager.createNativeQuery(
                "SELECT COUNT(DISTINCT t.TicketId) FROM Ticket t " +
                        "LEFT OUTER JOIN TicketComment c ON c.TicketId = " +
                        "t.TicketId WHERE " + matchTicket + " OR " + matchComment
        ).setParameter(1, query).getSingleResult()).longValue();

        @SuppressWarnings("unchecked")
        List<Object[]> results = this.entityManager.createNativeQuery(
                "SELECT DISTINCT t.*, (" + matchTicket + " + " + matchComment +
                        ") AS _ft_scoreColumn " +
                        "FROM Ticket t LEFT OUTER JOIN TicketComment c " +
                        "ON c.TicketId = t.TicketId " +
                        "WHERE " + matchTicket + " OR " + matchComment + " " +
                        "ORDER BY _ft_scoreColumn DESC, TicketId DESC",
                "searchResultMapping.ticket"
        ).setParameter(1, query)
                .setFirstResult(pageable.getOffset())
                .setMaxResults(pageable.getPageSize())
                .getResultList();

        List<SearchResult<TicketEntity>> list = new ArrayList<>();
        results.forEach(o -> list.add(
                new SearchResult<>((TicketEntity)o[0], (Double)o[1])
        ));

        return new PageImpl<>(list, pageable, total);
    }
}
```

As you can see, the `TicketRepositoryImpl` handles not only searching, but also paging the results properly. The first query counts the matching tickets and tickets with matching comments, whereas the second query returns the appropriate tickets. The second query adds the relevance score of the ticket and the comments together so that tickets that match and also have comments that match have an increased score; then it sorts by that score descending. This also ensures that tickets that don't match, but which have comments that match, are included at the appropriate location in the sort. For pagination to work properly, the order of results must be deterministic. Because it is possible for two records to share the same relevance, you should always add a backup sort. Sorting by the primary key descending is a great option, as newer results are typically more relevant to most users.

> **NOTE** *Don't worry that the same* `MATCH` *criteria appear in both the* `SELECT` *and the* `WHERE` *clauses in the query. The MySQL query optimizer recognizes this and knows to evaluate them only once.*

The list of results must be cast and unchecked warnings suppressed due to the lack of a `TypedQuery`. Because you use a custom result set mapping (notice how the second query references the `searchResultMapping.ticket` named result set mapping), the query returns a list of `Object` arrays. The `Object` arrays are the length of the number of mappings specified in the `@SqlResultSetMapping` annotation. Because you have two mappings (one for the `TicketEntity` entity and one for the `Double` scalar value), the `Object` arrays in the result `List` each contain two elements. The lambda expression in bold populates the result list with `SearchResults` created from those `Object` arrays.

## Adding Search to the User Interface

You need to add a search method to the `TicketService`, which is a straightforward task. The bulk of the work is not significantly different from the `getAllTickets` and `getComments` methods.

```
public interface TicketService
{
    ...
    Page<SearchResult<Ticket>> search(
            @NotBlank(message = "{validate.ticketService.search.query}")
                String query,
            boolean useBooleanMode,
            @NotNull(message = "{validate.ticketService.search.page}")
                Pageable pageable
    );
    ...
}

public class DefaultTicketService implements TicketService
{
    ...
    @Override
    @Transactional
    public Page<SearchResult<Ticket>> search(String query, boolean useBooleanMode,
                                             Pageable pageable)
    {
        List<SearchResult<Ticket>> list = new ArrayList<>();
        Page<SearchResult<TicketEntity>> entities =
                this.ticketRepository.search(query, useBooleanMode, pageable);
        entities.forEach(r -> list.add(
                new SearchResult<>(this.convert(r.getEntity()), r.getRelevance())
        ));

        return new PageImpl<>(list, pageable, entities.getTotalElements());
    }
    ...
}
```

> **NOTE** *The search method implementation must create a new set of* `SearchResult` *objects, which is unfortunate and reinforces the need to get rid of the DTO process and figure out how to persist the* `Ticket` *directly, mapping the* `Instant` *field and the attachments automatically. Don't give up. You learn about this in the next chapter!*

Adding search to the controller is equally easy. You just need a simple method for displaying the empty search form and another simple method for processing it. You also need the new `SearchForm` command object, which is just a POJO.

```
public class TicketController
{
    ...
    @RequestMapping(value = "search")
    public String search(Map<String, Object> model)
    {
        model.put("searchPerformed", false);
        model.put("searchForm", new SearchForm());

        return "ticket/search";
    }

    @RequestMapping(value = "search", params = "query")
    public String search(Map<String, Object> model, @Valid SearchForm form,
                         Errors errors, Pageable pageable)
    {
        if(errors.hasErrors())
            model.put("searchPerformed", false);
        else
        {
            model.put("searchPerformed", true);
            model.put("results", this.ticketService.search(
                    form.getQuery(), form.isUseBooleanMode(), pageable
            ));
        }

        return "ticket/search";
    }
    ...
}
```

The view, `/WEB-INF/jsp/view/ticket/search.jsp`, is long but straightforward, so it isn't printed here. It has a trivial form for providing a query and enabling Boolean search operators, paging just like you saw in the previous chapter, and listing just like in `/WEB-INF/jsp/view/ticket/list.jsp`. There's also a new link to the search page in `/WEB-INF/tags/template/basic.tag`. The view displays each result's relevance in its raw form, which isn't very meaningful to most users. Making this value meaningful is an exercise left up to you.

Now you can give it a try! Compile the project and start Tomcat from your IDE. Log in to the support application at `http://localhost:8080/support/` and make sure you have several tickets with different content so that your search doesn't return everything. Then click the search link, enter a search phrase, and submit the form. Be sure to try searching for things that you know will return no results, too. You're now searching records!

## Making Full-Text Searching Portable

As written now, the `search` method in `TicketRepositoryImpl` is strictly MySQL-specific. It won't work in any other relational database. So how do you make this method portable? Well, quite simply, you can't — at least not completely. Not every relational database supports full-text searching, so you can never make this feature completely portable. Such is the case with many JPA features, however, like identity-generated IDs (which Oracle doesn't support, for example). It *is* possible to have general portability, supporting all databases that support full-text searching.

Achieving this is no simple task. General things — such as executing the queries and handling pagination — could happen in a generic sense. But you would need a different implementation for generating the native SQL queries for each supported relational database. You would then have to either detect the underlying database somehow or require configuration of some type. (Not unreasonable — you almost always have to configure the Hibernate ORM dialect.) So before you go to this trouble, you have to ask yourself whether you actually need it. Realistically, you will usually work only with a single relational database in a particular application. If you switch or add another database, you can add support for its full-text searching as needed.

Alternatively, you could use the open source project JPA Native Full-Text Search (Maven artifact `net.nicholaswilliams.java.jpa.search:fulltext-core`). Its goal is to provide a generic, self-configuring JPA full-text integration that works across multiple databases and can support all your entities without you having to write any queries. However, it is still a very young project and needs contributors to support all the different SQL dialects and test all its features.

# INDEXING ANY DATA WITH APACHE LUCENE AND HIBERNATE SEARCH

As you have seen so far, full-text search is an extremely powerful tool that can be indispensable to you and your users. However, it's not always an option available to you. Perhaps you use a relational database that doesn't support full-text searching, such as HyperSQL. Or maybe you use a combination of databases and want the search to be consistent across all of them. Perhaps you even use other storage options, such as XML or JSON files, or a NoSQL database that doesn't support full-text search. It could even be that you simply don't like the way the full-text search works in your database but don't have the option of switching. Thankfully, there is no rule that you must use the full-text search tools provided by your database vendor. There are plenty of other options that can meet your searching needs. One of those is Apache Lucene.

Apache Lucene is an umbrella project, encompassing several open source search software projects. One of those is Lucene Core. Lucene Core is a Java-based search engine that also provides advanced tools, such as spell checking, hit highlighting, and advanced search analysis. It is arguably much more advanced and feature-rich than full-text search provided by most databases, and powers the search on sites such as Twitter, Apple, and Wikipedia.

Apache Solr is a search server powered by Lucene Core. It provides high-performance HTTP, XML, JSON, Ruby, and Python APIs, caching, replication, and a graphical server administration interface. You can use Lucene Core with or without Solr using its client Java API. Even better, using the Hibernate project Hibernate Search, you can integrate Lucene Core and JPA/Hibernate so that searches against the Lucene Core search engine return your JPA entities from wherever they are stored. You can use Hibernate Search with the Hibernate ORM API directly or with JPA, but only if Hibernate is your JPA provider. If you use some other JPA provider (such as OpenJPA or EclipseLink), you need to use the Lucene API directly.

For the rest of this chapter, you can follow along in the Search-Engine project, available for download from the `wrox.com` code download site. Wherever you see the term Lucene, you can assume it refers to Apache Lucene Core. Likewise, anywhere you see Solr refers to Apache Solr.

> **WARNING** *This book is presenting Apache Lucene only as an alternative to the other searching approaches detailed in this chapter. Lucene is a huge project with many facets, and it is outside the scope of this book to serve as a definitive guide on Lucene's features or configuration. You get only a cursory look at the search engine and using it with Hibernate Search, and you should not use it in a production environment without considerably more research and understanding of how it works.*

## Understanding Lucene Full-Text Indexing

Lucene works in a simple CRUD fashion, much like the Java Persistence API and Hibernate ORM. Although you persist entities in JPA, you persist *Lucene documents* using Lucene's API. These documents are not the same as the documents you persist in NoSQL document databases. A Lucene document contains only a document identifier and the data you want to be indexed. This document ID must somehow tie to the full entity from which it comes so that you can relate these pieces of data on retrieval. The common practice is to simply use the primary key of the entity as the document ID for the Lucene document.

In this sense, Lucene is very much an advanced full-text index to supplement your database's capabilities. More important, its indexing and matching analysis capabilities are far beyond what most full-text indexes offer. It can identify words that sound alike, such as "through" and "thru" or "cat" and "kat," and causes searches for one to match the other. It can also recognize related words and words with the same roots. For example, a search for "run" could also match "ran" and "running," whereas a search for "there" might also match "their" and "they're."

Synonyms are another one of its strengths, where a search for "hop" can match results with "hop," "jump," and "leap" in the index. One of Lucene's extremely useful features is its capability to spell-check queries and indexed data (when enabled), enabling it to suggest matches for misspelled queries and find results that might have misspelled matches in them. It does all this while sporting impressive performance statistics, which you can read about on its website at `http://lucene.apache.org/core/`.

Another great feature of Lucene is that you can configure its indexing to happen asynchronously. This means that your create, update, and delete actions are not slowed down by the full-text indexing process. This is a very useful capability that modern relational databases simply cannot offer with their full-text indexing.

When you use Apache Lucene on its own, you index data (and remove deleted data from the index) by calling the Lucene Java API. This applies whether you use Lucene within the same Java process (similar to an in-memory database) or use Solr as a Lucene search server. This book does not cover the Lucene API. Instead, you use Hibernate Search, which provides a simpler interface for indexing and searching JPA and Hibernate ORM entities. Hibernate ORM and Hibernate Search automatically index your entities in Lucene when you add and update them through JPA, and retrieve your persisted entities through JPA when you search for them in Lucene.

## Annotating Entities with Indexing Metadata

Instead of manually configuring Lucene for indexing all your entities and managing the Lucene API each time you add or update an entity, you can annotate the entities you want indexed with Hibernate Search annotations so that Hibernate Search does all this for you. Just think of Lucene as the JDBC API and Hibernate Search as the O/RM for Lucene. The Search-Engine project represents an extremely primitive forum where users can post messages. It doesn't have any reply capabilities. The `User` entity is obviously a simple entity. It contains only an ID and a username.

```
@Entity
@Table(name = "UserPrincipal")
public class User
{
    private long id;
    private String username;

    @Id
    @Column(name = "UserId")
    @GeneratedValue(strategy = GenerationType.IDENTITY)
    public long getId() { ... }
    public void setId(long id) { ... }

    @Basic
    @Field
    public String getUsername() { ... }
    public void setUsername(String username) { ... }
}
```

This entity is just a standard JPA entity. In this case, you don't actually need to perform full-text searches on the user entity, but you do need the ability to search for forum postings by the usernames of the users who created them. So how does that work? Take a look at the `ForumPost` entity.

```
@Entity
@Table(name = "Post")
@Indexed
public class ForumPost
{
    private long id;
    private User user;
```

```
        private String title;
        private String body;
        private String keywords;

        @Id
        @DocumentId
        @Column(name = "PostId")
        @GeneratedValue(strategy = GenerationType.IDENTITY)
        public long getId() { ... }
        public void setId(long id) { ... }

        @ManyToOne(fetch = FetchType.EAGER, optional = false)
        @JoinColumn(name = "UserId")
        @IndexedEmbedded
        public User getUser() { ... }
        public void setUser(User user) { ... }

        @Basic
        @Field
        public String getTitle() { ... }
        public void setTitle(String title) { ... }

        @Lob
        @Field
        public String getBody() { ... }
        public void setBody(String body) { ... }

        @Basic
        @Field(boost = @Boost(2.0F))
        public String getKeywords() { ... }
        public void setKeywords(String keywords) { ... }
    }
```

`ForumPost` uses two JPA annotations that you haven't learned about yet: `@ManyToOne` and `@JoinColumn`. You explore them more in the next chapter, but for now they are necessary to demonstrate Hibernate Search's capabilities. This entity is also an `@org.hibernate.search.annotations.Indexed` entity. The `@Indexed` annotation indicates that this entity is eligible for full-text indexing. Hibernate Search automatically creates or updates the document for this entity whenever you add or save it. The `@org.hibernate.search.annotations.DocumentId` annotation tells Hibernate Search which property is the document ID. It is placed on the `id` property solely for demonstration purposes; if you leave it off, Hibernate Search automatically falls back to the property annotated `@Id`.

`@org.hibernate.search.annotations.IndexedEmbedded` is an annotation of interest. It tells Hibernate Search that the property is itself an entity with indexed fields that should be indexed as part of this document. This way, you can include the `user` property in your searches and find postings based on the users that made them.

The `@org.hibernate.search.annotations.Field` annotation is used on both the `User` and `ForumPost` entities. It marks a property as one that should be full-text indexed and eligible for searching, and it has many different attributes that can affect the way the property is indexed and stored. Understanding how to use these attributes requires the in-depth understanding of Lucene that this book does not include. In many cases the default values are very safe to go with. In the

ForumPost entity, the keywords property is literally given an extra boost with the @org.hibernate.search.annotations.Boost annotation and the boost attribute. This specifies a factor by which the relevance score derived from the keywords property should be increased. In this case, the property contains user-specified keywords that the author feels best indicate the content of the posting. Therefore, it makes sense that keywords should have greater weight in the scores.

The create.sql file in the Search-Engine project creates the SearchEngine database and the necessary tables for these entities. It also populates the User table with several users. You should open MySQL Workbench and execute this script to create the database, and then create the following DataSource resource in Tomcat's context.xml configuration file:

```
<Resource name="jdbc/SearchEngine" type="javax.sql.DataSource"
          maxActive="20" maxIdle="5" maxWait="10000"
          username="tomcatUser" password="password1234"
          driverClassName="com.mysql.jdbc.Driver"
          defaultTransactionIsolation="READ_COMMITTED"
          url="jdbc:mysql://localhost/SearchEngine" />
```

# Using Hibernate Search with JPA

When you have entities that are index-ready, you must configure Hibernate Search for indexing and use the Hibernate Search and Apache Lucene APIs to perform searches. Then it's just a matter of creating another searchable repository using the Spring Data customization you should be very familiar with by now.

## Configuring Hibernate Search

Configuring Hibernate Search is simple. You just need to add the following two properties (in bold) to the EntityManagerFactory you configure in the RootContextConfiguration class.

```
@Bean
public LocalContainerEntityManagerFactoryBean entityManagerFactoryBean()
{
    Map<String, Object> properties = new Hashtable<>();
properties.put("javax.persistence.schema-generation.database.action",
            "none");
    properties.put("hibernate.search.default.directory_provider",
            "filesystem");
    properties.put("hibernate.search.default.indexBase", "../searchIndexes");

    HibernateJpaVendorAdapter adapter = new HibernateJpaVendorAdapter();
    adapter.setDatabasePlatform("org.hibernate.dialect.MySQL5InnoDBDialect");

    LocalContainerEntityManagerFactoryBean factory =
            new LocalContainerEntityManagerFactoryBean();
    factory.setJpaVendorAdapter(adapter);
    factory.setDataSource(this.searchEngineDataSource());
    factory.setPackagesToScan("com.wrox.site.entities");
    factory.setSharedCacheMode(SharedCacheMode.ENABLE_SELECTIVE);
    factory.setValidationMode(ValidationMode.NONE);
    factory.setJpaPropertyMap(properties);
    return factory;
}
```

Adding these two properties did several things.

- It enabled Hibernate ORM's use of Hibernate Search.
- It specified that the full-text indexing should use Lucene standalone (no Solr) and save indexes to the local filesystem.
- It specified `../searchIndexes` (relative to the current directory) as the location for saving the full-text indexes.

Of course, this isn't safe if you use a cluster of Tomcats or access these indexes from more than one JVM at a time. You can also use these and similar properties with different values to configure Hibernate Search to use a Solr server, thus making this safe for a clustered environment. For the purposes of testing locally, this configuration is sufficient.

## Creating a Lucene Searchable Repository

Creating a Lucene search-enabled repository is certainly different but not really more difficult than the native full-text repository you created in the previous section. As is typical, you start off with some basic interfaces like `SearchableRepository` and `ForumPostRepository`.

```
public interface SearchableRepository<T>
{
    Page<SearchResult<T>> search(String query, Pageable pageable);
}

public interface ForumPostRepository extends JpaRepository<ForumPost, Long>,
        SearchableRepository<ForumPost>
{
}
```

As usual, the hard work happens in `ForumPostRepositoryImpl`, as shown in Listing 23-2. One of the key things that makes this different is the use of the `org.hibernate.search.jpa.FullTextEntityManager`, the pivotal interface in the Hibernate Search JPA integration. It extends `EntityManager` to add full-text capabilities to it. Unlike the `EntityManager` that Spring Framework injects, which is really a thread-bound, transaction-linked `EntityManager` proxy that delegates to a new `EntityManager` for each new transaction, the `FullTextEntityManager` is the real thing. This means that you have to create a new instance each time the `search` method is called (which is really all that is happening behind the scenes when you use Spring's injected `EntityManager` proxy). Furthermore, Hibernate Search can create a `FullTextEntityManager` only if it has access to the actual Hibernate ORM `EntityManager` implementation (as opposed to a wrapper or the proxy).

**LISTING 23-2: ForumPostRepositoryImpl.java**

```
public class ForumPostRepositoryImpl implements SearchableRepository<ForumPost>
{
    @PersistenceContext EntityManager entityManager;

    EntityManagerProxy entityManagerProxy;

    @Override
```

*continues*

**LISTING 23-2** *(continued)*

```
    public Page<SearchResult<ForumPost>> search(String query,
                                                Pageable pageable)
    {
        FullTextEntityManager manager = this.getFullTextEntityManager();

        QueryBuilder builder = manager.getSearchFactory().buildQueryBuilder()
                .forEntity(ForumPost.class).get();

        Query lucene = builder.keyword()
                .onFields("title", "body", "keywords", "user.username")
                .matching(query)
                .createQuery();

        FullTextQuery q = manager.createFullTextQuery(lucene, ForumPost.class);
        q.setProjection(FullTextQuery.THIS, FullTextQuery.SCORE);

        long total = q.getResultSize();

        q.setFirstResult(pageable.getOffset())
                .setMaxResults(pageable.getPageSize());

        @SuppressWarnings("unchecked") List<Object[]> results = q.getResultList();
        List<SearchResult<ForumPost>> list = new ArrayList<>();
        results.forEach(o -> list.add(
                new SearchResult<>((ForumPost)o[0], (Float)o[1])
        ));

        return new PageImpl<>(list, pageable, total);
    }

    private FullTextEntityManager getFullTextEntityManager()
    {
        return Search.getFullTextEntityManager(
                this.entityManagerProxy.getTargetEntityManager()
        );
    }

    @PostConstruct
    public void initialize()
    {
        if(!(this.entityManager instanceof EntityManagerProxy))
            throw new FatalBeanException("Entity manager " + this.entityManager +
                    " was not a proxy");

        this.entityManagerProxy = (EntityManagerProxy)this.entityManager;
    }
}
```

> **NOTE** *If you were using the Hibernate API directly (and not JPA), you would use the* `org.hibernate.search.FullTextSession` *interface, which adds full-text features to* `org.hibernate.Session`*, instead of* `FullTextEntityManager`*.*

To solve this problem, the `initialize` method first casts the `EntityManager` to an `org.springframework.orm.jpa.EntityManagerProxy`, an interface that the Spring-injected `EntityManager` implements. This method is called only once, but `getFullTextEntityManager` is called every time a `FullTextEntityManager` is needed, and only within a transaction. It calls `getTargetEntityManager` on the `EntityManagerProxy` to retrieve the actual Hibernate ORM `EntityManager` implementation. It then uses the `org.hibernate.search.jpa.Search` static method `getFullTextEntityManager` to get the `FullTextEntityManager` from the underlying `EnityManager` instance.

When the `search` method has a `FullTextEntityManager`, it creates an `org.hibernate.search.query.dsl.QueryBuilder` for the `ForumPost` entity. It then uses this builder to create an `org.apache.lucene.search.Query` for the query string supplied and the `ForumPost` fields you want to search. Notice the use of dot notation (the bold in Listing 23-2) to trigger searching the `username` field of the `User` entity in the `user` field. You can use the dot notation to nest as many levels deep as you need to into indexed embedded entities. Also note that you could use the Lucene API directly to create this query, instead of the `QueryBuilder`, if you wanted.

Next, the code retrieves an `org.hibernate.search.jpa.FullTextQuery` for the Lucene `Query` and the `ForumPost` entity. The `FullTextQuery` is a `javax.persistence.Query` capable of executing all the necessary Lucene and JPA queries. It sets the projections for the query, telling Hibernate Search to return the entity as the first element in an `Object` array (`FullTextQuery.THIS`) and the relevance score as the second element (`FullTextQuery.SCORE`) for each result in the result list. This is practically identical to the technique you used in the previous section to retrieve the entity and the score together.

Finally, the code gets the expected total result size, sets the pagination boundaries, gets the result list, and converts it to a `Page` of `SearchResult<ForumPost>s`. The only caveat to keep in mind is that Lucene does not participate in the JPA transaction, so it's possible that the number of results can change between the call to `getResultSize` and `getResultList`.

## Testing the Search Engine

The last step that you need to take before testing your Apache Lucene repository is to create a transactional service, controller, and user interface. The `MainService` and `DefaultMainService` are extremely simple, and really serve only as a `@Transactional`-marked pass-through between the controller and the repository. The `MainController` is equally simple. It forgoes many of the validation and checking routines that you are used to because this is just a test of Lucene's searching capabilities. It responds to requests for the homepage with a simple form for creating new forum postings in the view `/WEB-INF/jsp/view/add.jsp`. The controller methods that handle searching should look very familiar to you because they are nearly identical to those in the `TicketController` from the Customer Support application. Finally, the `/WEB-INF/jsp/view/search.jsp` view handles displaying the search form, search results, and paging, also in a fashion very similar to the Customer Support application.

Now that you have reviewed the rest of this code, take the following steps to test it out:

1. Compile the application and start Tomcat from your IDE. You should see the Lucene index files directory appear in the Tomcat home directory (likely `C:\Program Files\Apache Software Foundation\Tomcat 8.0` if you use Windows).
2. Go to `http://localhost:8080/forums/` in your favorite browser and create several forum postings first. Alternate the usernames you supply for each posting between Nicholas, Sarah, Mike, and John. These are the users prepopulated in the database you created earlier.
3. After you create several postings with varying content, click the search link and try some different search queries. Make sure you also search for one or two usernames to find postings by those users.

## SUMMARY

You covered a great deal of material in this chapter. You learned about some basic concepts of searching and indexing data, and explored how you can create extremely complex queries using the JPA criteria API. You were introduced to the concept of full-text searching, and learned how to create full-text indexes in MySQL and execute full-text searches using JPA. You also explored Apache Lucene and Hibernate Search, and created indexed entities and a repository capable of searching for those entities using a Lucene full-text index. It's important to note that you really only scratched the surface with Apache Lucene and Hibernate Search. Many hundreds of pages could be written about their use and capabilities, and hopefully this chapter has spurred your interest to research those topics further.

The next chapter wraps up the Java Persistence API topics. You learn how to create some complex mappings and finally include those Java 8 Date and Time types in your entities using JPA converters. You also learn about those `@ManyToOne` and `@JoinTable` annotations you saw in the last section of this chapter.

# 24

# Creating Advanced Mappings and Custom Data Types

## IN THIS CHAPTER

- Why convert nonstandard data types?
- How to embed POJOs inside entities
- How to define relationships between entities
- Using revisions and timestamps to version entities
- How to define common entity ancestors
- How to map `Collection`s and `Map`s of basic and embedded values
- Using multiple tables to store entities
- Constructing programmatic triggers
- Using load time weaving to lazy load simple properties

## WROX.COM CODE DOWNLOADS FOR THIS CHAPTER

You can find the `wrox.com` code downloads for this chapter at `http://www.wrox.com/go/projavaforwebapps` on the Download Code tab. The code for this chapter is divided into the following major examples:

- Advanced-Mappings Project
- Customer-Support-v18 Project

## NEW MAVEN DEPENDENCIES FOR THIS CHAPTER

There are no new Maven dependencies for this chapter. Continue to use the Maven dependencies introduced in all previous chapters.

# WHAT'S LEFT?

So far you've done some cool things with JPA. From simple lookups to complex queries to advanced searching, you've thoroughly explored the Java Persistence API and its CRUD capabilities.

So what's left? Well, you've only touched the surface on the ways you can map objects to database tables. So far your entities have been very straightforward, containing only basic types that the JPA provider can directly and unambiguously convert to and from relational database field types. In reality, your entities will not be so trivial. You have already seen this problem with the `TicketEntity` and `TicketCommentEntity` in the Customer Support application. For example, it would be a lot easier to simply persist the `Instant` creation date, but instead you have to use a `Timestamp` in your entities. Hopefully, JPA 2.2 (or whatever comes next, which may be JPA 3.0) will support the Java 8 Date and Time types natively, but right now you need a different solution.

> **NOTE** *To help ensure the inclusion of Java 8 Date and Time support in the next version of JPA, go to* `https://java.net/jira/browse/JPA_SPEC-63` *and vote on the feature request. You need to create a Java.net account or log in using your existing Java.net account to vote.*

So as a starting point, take a look at some of the things you still need to learn to make the most out of your JPA entities:

- Convert simple types that aren't natively supported, such as `Instants`, `LocalDateTimes`, `java.net.InetAddresses`, and more.
- Map POJO property types with entities in addition to basic properties. For example, you might have a `PhoneNumber` object that contains components of a phone number stored in multiple columns but that isn't an entity on its own.
- Define one-to-many, many-to-one, and many-to-many relationships. A great example is retrieving the `Attachments` on a `Ticket` at the same time that you retrieve the `Ticket`. Of course, this relationship should be lazy so that you don't unnecessarily load a bunch of `Attachments` while simply listing `Tickets`. Another example is retrieving a `Ticket` and the `UserPrincipal` that created the `Ticket` at the same time.
- Version entities, keeping track of how many times they are updated.
- Define properties common to many entities in a base class that those entities inherit from. This way, you don't have to duplicate code for things such as IDs, auditing, and versioning.
- Store key-value pairs as a `Map` within entities. The values may even need to be other entities.
- Retrofit existing databases and applications. Not every application can start with a domain model and then create a suitable database. In these situations, it sometimes helps to split the data for an entity across several tables, and you need a way to get all this data into one entity.
- Define custom behavior that takes place before or after a CRUD operation on an entity.

As you can see, you're just getting started. In this chapter, you cover all these topics, and when you're done, you'll have virtually unlimited ways to use JPA entities. For most of the chapter, you can follow along in the Advanced-Mappings project, available for download on the `wrox.com` code download site. This chapter covers the mappings in that project but does *not* mention the Spring Data JPA repositories, services, controllers, or (simple) user interfaces with which you are already so familiar. At any time during the chapter, you can compile and start the project from your IDE, go to `http://localhost:8080/mappings`, and use the links on the homepage to test out the entity mappings.

At the end of the chapter, you employ the topics you have mastered to make the task of persisting entities in the Customer Support application easier.

## CONVERTING NONSTANDARD DATA TYPES

In Chapter 20, you learned about the `@Basic`, `@Lob`, `@Enumerated`, and `@Temporal` types that JPA vendors are required to support. This list is extensive, but by no means does it fulfill your every need. You have already seen that it does not include the new Java 8 Date and Time types. (But keep your eyes peeled for support for this in the next version of JPA.) Some providers do support additional types — for example, Hibernate ORM automatically supports Joda Time data types. Hibernate ORM 5.0 might even support the Java 8 Date and Time types at some point. However, relying on this support is non-portable because it's nonstandard. If you switch providers someday, your entities may stop working.

So what can you do about this? In previous versions of JPA, you couldn't do anything that was portable. Before JPA 2.1, there was no standard way to persist and retrieve simple types (types that aren't themselves POJOs) that weren't natively supported. This greatly limited your options. As a result, most of the major providers supply proprietary APIs that let you define custom data types. Using Hibernate ORM, you can implement `org.hibernate.usertype.UserType` or `org.hibernate.usertype.CompositeUserType` and then annotate a property with `@org.hibernate.annotations.Type` to specify the `UserType` or `CompositeUserType` implementation class responsible for that property. However, this is no more portable than relying on nonstandard basic types supported by a particular provider, and it breaks as soon as you switch providers.

This problem was finally resolved in JPA 2.1 with *attribute converters*, though they are not without their drawbacks.

### Understanding Attribute Converters

An *attribute converter* is any class that implements `javax.persistence.AttributeConverter`. The purpose of an attribute converter is to convert entity properties between non-supported simple types and supported basic types. This works in nearly all circumstances. Using JDBC, you must eventually convert pretty much any simple type you can imagine into one of the supported basic types before you can save the value to your database. For example, if you create a custom `UnsignedLong` class capable of holding unsigned long integers, the only way you can get such a value into and out of the database is by calling `PreparedStatement`'s `setBigDecimal` method and `ResultSet`'s `getBigDecimal` method. This means that you can easily fulfill this need in JPA by implementing an `AttributeConverter` that converts between `UnsignedLongs` and `BigDecimals`.

The special case, ironically, is converting types that involve dates and times. The `setDate`, `setTime`, `setTimestamp`, `getDate`, `getTime`, and `getTimestamp` methods in JDBC deal with `java.sql.Dates`, `Times`, and `Timestamps`. As of JDBC 4.1, you must use these types for setting and retrieving dates and times in a database. JDBC 4.2, you'll recall, adds methods that support more types than this. Having direct access to the JDBC API and a JDBC 4.2 driver, the following code is the correct way to persist `Instant`, `LocalDateTime`, `LocalDate`, `LocalTime`, `OffsetDateTime`, `OffsetTime`, and `ZonedDateTime` properties.

```
statement.setObject(1, instant, JDBCType.TIMESTAMP);
statement.setObject(2, localDateTime, JDBCType.TIMESTAMP);
statement.setObject(3, localDate, JDBCType.DATE);
statement.setObject(4, localTime, JDBCType.TIME);
statement.setObject(5, offsetDateTime, JDBCType.TIMESTAMP_WITH_TIMEZONE);
statement.setObject(6, offsetTime, JDBCType.TIME_WITH_TIMEZONE);
statement.setObject(7, zonedDateTime, JDBCType.TIMESTAMP_WITH_TIMEZONE);
```

Likewise, you would retrieve these value types with code similar to the following:

```
instant = resultSet.getObject("instant", Instant.class);
localDateTime = resultSet.getObject("localDateTime", LocalDateTime.class);
localDate = resultSet.getObject("localDate", LocalDate.class);
localTime = resultSet.getObject("localTime", LocalTime.class);
offsetDateTime = resultSet.getObject("offsetDateTime", OffsetDateTime.class);
offsetTime = resultSet.getObject("offsetTime", OffsetTime.class);
zonedDateTime = resultSet.getObject("zonedDateTime", ZonedDateTime.class);
```

However, an `AttributeConverter` does not have access to the `PreparedStatement` and `ResultSet` objects. It can convert only between the custom type and a target type supported by JPA. Therefore, you must either write `AttributeConverters` that convert between these types and `java.sql.Date`, `Time`, and `Timestamp`, or you must still use proprietary vendor APIs such as Hibernate's `UserType`. You should recall from Chapter 20 that it could be years before all the major relational database vendors provide JDBC 4.2 drivers. Without support for these new methods, resorting to `UserType` is futile. So your best bet is to stick with `AttributeConverters`.

## Understanding the Conversion Annotations

Implementing an `AttributeConverter` is just the first step to creating and using the attribute converter. There are also several easily confused annotations that you must utilize to make your converter work. The first of these is `@javax.persistence.Converter`. A concrete class implementing `AttributeConverter` *must* either be annotated with `@Converter` or specified in a `<converter>` element in a JPA mapping file (such as `orm.xml`). Furthermore, if a converter you want to use is not in the root of your persistence unit, or you have `<exclude-unlisted-classes>` enabled, you must indicate that the converter is a managed class using `<class>` or `<jar-file>` in `persistence.xml`. `@Converter`'s `autoApply` attribute (which defaults to `false`) indicates whether the JPA provider should automatically apply the converter to matching properties. The definition of an attribute converter would therefore normally look like this:

```
@Converter
public class InstantConverter implements AttributeConverter<Instant, Timestamp>
{
    ...
}
```

If `autoApply` is `false` or omitted (it defaults to `false`), you must use the similarly named `@javax.persistence.Convert` annotation on JPA properties to indicate which properties the converter applies to. You use `@Convert`'s `converter` attribute to specify the `Class` of the applicable converter. You can annotate a field (if you use field property access), accessor method (if you use method property access), or entity with `@Convert`. If you annotate the entity, you must also specify the `attributeName` attribute. The following three uses of `@Convert` are all equivalent.

```
public class MyEntity
{
    @Convert(converter = InstantConverter.class)
    private Instant dateCreated;

    ...

    public Instant getDateCreated() { ... }
    public void setDateCreated(Instant instant) { ... }

    ...
}

public class MyEntity
{
    private Instant dateCreated;

    ...

    @Convert(converter = InstantConverter.class)
    public Instant getDateCreated() { ... }
    public void setDateCreated(Instant instant) { ... }

    ...
}

@Convert(attributeName = "dateCreated", converter = InstantConverter.class)
public class MyEntity
{
    private Instant dateCreated;

    ...

    public Instant getDateCreated() { ... }
    public void setDateCreated(Instant instant) { ... }

    ...
}
```

If you use the latter approach, you may have multiple attributes that need converting. Though it would likely be easier just to annotate the individual properties, you can use the `@javax.persistence.Converts` annotation to group multiple `@Convert` annotations at the entity level.

```
@Converts({
    @Convert(attributeName = "dateCreated", converter = InstantConverter.class),
    @Convert(attributeName = "dateModified", converter = InstantConverter.class)
})
```

```
public class MyEntity
{
    private Instant dateCreated;
    private Instant dateModified;

    ...

    public Instant getDateCreated() { ... }
    public void setDateCreated(Instant instant) { ... }

    public Instant getDateModified() { ... }
    public void setDateModified(Instant instant) { ... }

    ...
}
```

## Creating and Using Attribute Converters

In many cases your attribute converters will be very simple. The `InstantConverter` in the Advanced-Mappings project has only one line of code in each method.

```
@Converter
public class InstantConverter implements AttributeConverter<Instant, Timestamp>
{
    @Override
    public Timestamp convertToDatabaseColumn(Instant instant)
    {
        return instant == null ? null:new Timestamp(instant.toEpochMilli());
    }

    @Override
    public Instant convertToEntityAttribute(Timestamp timestamp)
    {
        return timestamp == null ? null:Instant.ofEpochMilli(timestamp.getTime());
    }
}
```

The `User` entity demonstrates use of the custom attribute converter to persist the `dateJoined` property without having to use a DTO and service to convert the value.

```
@Entity
@Table(name = "UserPrincipal")
public class User
{
    private long id;
    private Instant dateJoined;
    private String username;

    @Id
    @Column(name = "UserId")
    @GeneratedValue(strategy = GenerationType.IDENTITY)
    public long getId() { ... }
    public void setId(long id) { ... }

    @Convert(converter = InstantConverter.class)
```

```
    public Instant getDateJoined() { ... }
    public void setDateJoined(Instant dateJoined) { ... }

    @Basic
    public String getUsername() { ... }
    public void setUsername(String username) { ... }
}
```

Finally, in `RootContextConfiguration` the `com.wrox.site.converters` package is added to the `LocalContainerEntityManagerFactoryBean`'s `packagesToScan` property. This ensures that the converter is added to the persistence unit so that it can be used within the application.

```
    @Bean
    public LocalContainerEntityManagerFactoryBean entityManagerFactoryBean()
    {
        ...
        factory.setDataSource(this.advancedMappingsDataSource());
        factory.setPackagesToScan("com.wrox.site.entities",
                "com.wrox.site.converters");
        factory.setSharedCacheMode(SharedCacheMode.ENABLE_SELECTIVE);
        ...
    }
```

# EMBEDDING POJOS WITHIN ENTITIES

Sometimes it's inconvenient for your entity properties to be mere simple types. Consider the classic telephone number conundrum: A `Person` has a phone number, but you want to store the country code and phone number in separate columns. You could create properties `phoneNumberCountryCode` and `phoneNumberNumber`, but that's awkward. A more desirable solution would be to have a `phoneNumber` property of type `PhoneNumber`, which in turn has properties `countryCode` and `number`. Such an approach is possible using JPA *embeddable types*. Embeddable types are intrinsically part of their enclosing entity. They are always stored in the same table as the entity and share the same ID as the entity. They are not and cannot be actual entities.

## Indicating That a Type Is Embeddable

In a lot of ways, an embeddable type looks very much like an entity. It can contain any number of properties with annotations such as `@Basic`, `@Column`, `@Lob`, `@Temporal`, `@Enumerated`, `@Convert`, and more. However, it cannot be annotated `@Entity` or `@Table`, and it cannot contain any properties annotated `@Id` or `@EmbeddedId`. It can contain properties of other embeddable types.

To mark a class as embeddable, all you have to do is annotate it with `@javax.persistence.Embeddable`. Demonstrated in the following `PhoneNumber` class, this annotation indicates that it may be embedded as a property within any entity in your application. Like `@Entity` classes, `@Embeddable` classes must be registered as managed classes in your persistence unit. This means you must either specify them in `<class>` or `<jar-file>` elements in your persistence unit configuration, leave `<exclude-unlisted-classes>` disabled in your persistence unit configuration, or include them in the scanned classes discovered by Spring's `LocalContainerEntityManagerFactoryBean`. By placing `PhoneNumber` in the `com.wrox.site.entities` package, it is automatically discovered and added to the persistence unit.

```
@Embeddable
public class PhoneNumber
{
    private String countryCode;
    private String number;

    @Basic
    @Column(name = "PhoneNumber_CountryCode")
    public String getCountryCode() { ... }
    public void setCountryCode(String countryCode) { ... }

    @Basic
    @Column(name = "PhoneNumber_Number")
    public String getNumber() { ... }
    public void setNumber(String number) { ... }
}
```

Notice that `PhoneNumber` contains two properties, each mapped to its own column. Any entity may include a `PhoneNumber` property provided that entity's table has two columns named `PhoneNumber_CountryCode` and `PhoneNumber_Number`.

## Marking a Property as Embedded

Actually embedding an embeddable type is equally easy. Simply mark a property of that type with the `@javax.persistence.Embedded` annotation. You must not mark the property with any other annotations, such as `@Basic`, `@Temporal`, or `@Column`. This is demonstrated in the `Person` entity.

```
@Entity
public class Person
{
    private long id;
    private String firstName;
    private String lastName;
    private PhoneNumber phoneNumber;

    @Id
    @Column(name = "PersonId")
    @GeneratedValue(strategy = GenerationType.IDENTITY)
    public long getId() { ... }
    public void setId(long id) { ... }

    @Basic
    public String getFirstName() { ... }
    public void setFirstName(String firstName) { ... }

    @Basic
    public String getLastName() { ... }
    public void setLastName(String lastName) { ... }

    @Embedded
    public PhoneNumber getPhoneNumber() { ... }
    public void setPhoneNumber(PhoneNumber phoneNumber) { ... }
}
```

> **NOTE** *Use of* `@Embedded` *is only for non-ID properties in your entities. You can use embeddable types as composite entity IDs, but you must annotate the ID property with* `@javax.persistence.EmbeddedId` *instead of* `@Embedded`*. You explored creating composite IDs like this in Chapter 20.*

As mentioned earlier, embeddable types can themselves contain embedded properties. A great example of this is the following `Address` and `PostalCode` POJOs.

```
@Embeddable
public class PostalCode
{
    private String code;
    private String suffix;

    @Basic
    @Column(name = "PostalCode_Code")
    public String getCode() { ... }
    public void setCode(String code) { ... }

    @Basic
    @Column(name = "PostalCode_Suffix")
    public String getSuffix() { ... }
    public void setSuffix(String suffix) { ... }
}

@Embeddable
public class Address
{
    private String street;
    private String city;
    private String state;
    private String country;
    private PostalCode postalCode;

    @Basic
    @Column(name = "Address_Street")
    public String getStreet() { ... }
    public void setStreet(String street) { ... }

    @Basic
    @Column(name = "Address_City")
    public String getCity() { ... }
    public void setCity(String city) { ... }

    @Basic
    @Column(name = "Address_State")
    public String getState() { ... }
    public void setState(String state) { ... }

    @Basic
    @Column(name = "Address_Country")
    public String getCountry() { ... }
```

```
    public void setCountry(String country) { ... }

    @Embedded
    public PostalCode getPostalCode() { ... }
    public void setPostalCode(PostalCode postalCode) { ... }
}
```

## Overriding Embeddable Column Names

The PostalCode is designed so that it can be used on its own *or* as part of an Address. The problem is the column names. As written, the Person table will have columns Address_Street, Address_City, Address_State, Address_Country, PostalCode_Code, and PostalCode_Suffix. It's not obvious by these names that the postal code columns are part of the address. You can easily fix this in the Person entity using the @javax.persistence.AttributeOverride annotation, which allows you to alter these column names in the entity in which they are used. You can also use the @javax.persistence.AttributeOverrides annotation, which enables you to group multiple @AttributeOverride annotations.

```
@Entity
public class Person
{
    ...
    private Address address;

    ...

    @Embedded
    @AttributeOverrides({
            @AttributeOverride(name = "postalCode.code",
                    column = @Column(name = "Address_PostalCode_Code")),
            @AttributeOverride(name = "postalCode.suffix",
                    column = @Column(name = "Address_PostalCode_Suffix"))
    })
    public Address getAddress() { ... }
    public void setAddress(Address address) { ... }
}
```

The name attribute uses dot notation to indicate the property whose column details are being overridden. Because the Address entity contains a property named postalCode, the first part of both names is postalCode. This name is based off the property name, not the property type, so if Address's PostalCode property were named zip, the first part of the override names would be zip. The second parts of the names are the properties within PostalCode being overridden.

With this dot notation, you can keep specifying overrides deeper and deeper and deeper. Attribute overrides also make it possible to use the same embeddable type multiple times in any given entity (or other embeddable type). You simply need to override all the column names in all but one of the uses. (Although more commonly you would simple override them all.) With these changes, the following statement creates the appropriate table and columns for the Person entity.

```
CREATE TABLE Person (
  PersonId BIGINT UNSIGNED NOT NULL AUTO_INCREMENT PRIMARY KEY,
  FirstName VARCHAR(60) NOT NULL,
  LastName VARCHAR(60) NOT NULL,
```

```
    PhoneNumber_CountryCode VARCHAR(5) NOT NULL,
    PhoneNumber_Number VARCHAR(15) NOT NULL,
    Address_Street VARCHAR(100) NOT NULL,
    Address_City VARCHAR(100) NOT NULL,
    Address_State VARCHAR(100) NULL,
    Address_Country VARCHAR(100) NOT NULL,
    Address_PostalCode_Code VARCHAR(10) NOT NULL,
    Address_PostalCode_Suffix VARCHAR(5)
) ENGINE = InnoDB;
```

# DEFINING RELATIONSHIPS BETWEEN ENTITIES

As you have already seen, it is very common for entities to be related to other entities. `Tickets` in the Customer Support application have `Attachments`, for example, and so far you have had to manage that relationship within the service layer. However, this extra step is unnecessary. You may still want to use it in certain situations, especially if a particular entity has *many* relationships to other entities. But those special circumstances aside, you can define entity relationships directly within those entities, and the JPA provider can retrieve the entities you need at the time you need them.

## Understanding One-to-One Relationships

One-to-one relationships might just be the ones you are least likely to define. A one-to-one relationship means that entity A is related to at most one entity B, and entity B is related to at most one entity A. Generally speaking, such a relationship violates the rules of normal form and accepted object-oriented design practices. However, in some situations it's a more practical approach to solve a peculiar problem. For example, if an entity contains hundreds of properties, you might want to group those properties into sub-entities where all the related properties belong to their own entity. The following mythical `Employee` entity demonstrates such a use case.

```
@Entity
public class Employee
{
    private long id;
    ...
    private EmployeeInfo info;

    @Id
    @Column(name = "EmployeeId")
    @GeneratedValue(strategy = GenerationType.IDENTITY)
    public long getId() { ... }
    public void setId(long id) { ... }

    ...

    @OneToOne(mappedBy = "employee", fetch = FetchType.LAZY,
            cascade = CascadeType.ALL, orphanRemoval = true)
    public EmployeeInfo getInfo() { ... }
    public void setInfo(EmployeeInfo employeeInfo) { ... }
}

@Entity
```

```
public class EmployeeInfo
{
    private long id;
    private Employee employee;
    ...

    @Id
    public long getId() { ... }
    public void setId(long id) { ... }

    @OneToOne(mappedBy = "info")
    @Column(name = "EmployeeId")
    public Employee getEmployee() { ... }
    public void setEmployee(Employee employee) { ... }

    ...
}
```

If wanted, you may define the relationship on only one side or the other. For example, you could have the `info` property in `Employee` but omit the `employee` property in `EmployeeInfo` (or vice versa). In this case, the relationship is bidirectional, so you must annotate the `info` property on `Employee` and the `employee` property on `EmployeeInfo` with `@javax.persistence.OneToOne`, and both must specify the `mappedBy` attribute.

This attribute tells the JPA provider which property on the other end of the relationship maps back to "this" entity. The `fetch` attribute indicates when the related entities should be retrieved from the database using the `javax.persistence.FetchType` enum. `FetchType.EAGER` means that the JPA provider *must* retrieve the values when the entity is retrieved. On the other hand, `FetchType.LAZY` serves as a *hint* to the JPA provider that it can wait and fetch the values only when the property is first accessed (which may be never, thus saving a trip to the database). However, JPA providers are not required to support lazy loading, so these values may be loaded eagerly anyway. Here, the fetch attribute defaults to `FetchType.EAGER`, and that's usually okay for one-to-one relationships. Hibernate ORM and EclipseLink both support lazy loading, but for one-to-one relationships you must enable class weaving. You learn more about how to do this in the "Refining the Customer Support Application" section.

The `cascade` attribute of `@OneToOne` indicates what should happen to the related entity when operations are performed on the entity specifying cascade instructions. Using the `java.persistence.CascadeType` enum you can specify one or more of the values `DETACH`, `MERGE`, `PERSIST`, `REFRESH`, and `REMOVE`. Each one indicates an `EntityManager` operation that should cascade to the related entity. You can also use `ALL` as a shortcut for specifying all 5 values. For one-to-one relationships, you generally do not want to specify cascade instructions within the owned entity. However, you may want to specify cascade instructions within the owning entity. The related `orphanRemoval` attribute indicates whether orphaned entities should be deleted from the database. The default (`false`) means that if you set the `Employee`'s `info` property to `null`, the `EmployeeInfo` record in the database *will not be deleted*. This is almost always not what you want to happen, so you should specify `true`, as indicated in the example.

Finally, the `optional` attribute indicates whether the relationship is optional. If set to `false` it indicates there must *always* be a value on both sides of the relationship. It defaults to `true`, which means that one side of the relationship may be `null`.

## Using One-to-Many and Many-to-One Relationships

One-to-many and many-to-one relationships are a much more common scenario that you will face in your applications. They are very closely related. In fact, whenever you specify a one-to-many relationship on an entity, you often specify a corresponding many-to-one relationship on the other entity. In a one-to-many relationship, *one* entity A has a relationship to *many* entities B. This is usually represented by a collection of some sort in A that stores instances of B. A many-to-one relationship is simply the opposite. So in this specific case, entity B already has a many-to-one relationship with entity A.

Entities are related in such a manner by design, not by annotation. If an entity has a one-to-many relationship with another entity, that other entity *will* necessarily have a many-to-one relationship with the first entity. However, what you can control is whether you *advertise* that relationship to JPA. In the Customer Support application you've worked on previously, `Ticket` has a one-to-many relationship to `Attachment`, and `Attachment` a many-to-one relationship to `Ticket`, but the JPA provider knew nothing about this. You need only advertise one or more sides of this relationship if you want to navigate from an entity to its relations. You do this by creating *navigational properties*, as demonstrated in the `Applicant` and `Resume` entities in the Advanced-Mappings project.

```
@Entity
public class Applicant
{
    private long id;
    private String firstName;
    private String lastName;
    private boolean citizen;
    private Set<Resume> résumés = new HashSet<>();

    @Id
    @Column(name = "ApplicantId")
    @GeneratedValue(strategy = GenerationType.IDENTITY)
    public long getId() { ... }
    public void setId(long id) { ... }

    @Basic
    public String getFirstName() { ... }
    public void setFirstName(String firstName) { ... }

    @Basic
    public String getLastName() { ... }
    public void setLastName(String lastName) { ... }

    @Basic
    public boolean isCitizen() { ... }
    public void setCitizen(boolean citizen) { ... }

    @OneToMany(fetch = FetchType.LAZY, cascade = CascadeType.ALL,
            orphanRemoval = true)
    @JoinColumn(name = "ApplicantId")
    public Set<Resume> getRésumés() { ... }
    public void setRésumés(Set<Resume> résumés) { ... }
```

```
}

@Entity
@Table(name = "Applicant_Resume")
public class Resume
{
    private long id;
    private String title;
    private String content;

    @Id
    @Column(name = "ResumeId")
    @GeneratedValue(strategy = GenerationType.IDENTITY)
    public long getId() { ... }
    public void setId(long id) { ... }

    @Basic
    public String getTitle() { ... }
    public void setTitle(String title) { ... }

    @Lob
    public String getContent() { ... }
    public void setContent(String content) { ... }
}
```

> **NOTE** *Wait, what's that? Are those character accents in variable and method names? This is legal? Yes! In Java, there is no rule against accented alphabetic characters in type names, method names, and identifiers. Because the word "resume" without accents is a completely different word meaning to restart or un-pause, you wouldn't want to use that, would you? Unfortunately, the ZIP format is less cooperative than Java. If the entity class were also named* `Résumé`, *the* `Résumé.java` *filename would get corrupted in the ZIP file that you downloaded. Because of this, the example code had to leave the accents off the* `Resume` *and* `ResumeRepository` *class names. However, the* `RésuméForm` *class uses accents because it is an inner class of* `MainController`, *and so doesn't affect the filename. Databases are likewise less tolerant of accented characters in object names, so the* `Applicant_Resume` *table lacks the accents.*

In this example, an applicant (presumably a job applicant) can have multiple résumés. The `Applicant` entity defines a navigational property named `résumés` containing a `Set` of `Resumes`. This property allows a piece of code holding an `Applicant` to *navigate* to that applicant's `Resumes` directly without having to go back to the service or repository. In this case the *advertised* relationship is unidirectional because the `Resume` class does not contain a navigational property back to `Applicant`. But on further thought, you probably want code that obtains a `Resume` to navigate back to the `Applicant` who created it. Making the advertised relationship bidirectional is as simple as adding the navigational property to `Resume` and tweaking the navigational property on `Applicant`.

```
@Entity
public class Applicant
{
    ...

    @OneToMany(mappedBy = "applicant", fetch = FetchType.LAZY,
            cascade = CascadeType.ALL, orphanRemoval = true)
    public Set<Resume> getRésumés() { ... }
    public void setRésumés(Set<Resume> résumés) { ... }
}

@Entity
@Table(name = "Applicant_Resume")
public class Resume
{
    private long id;
    private Applicant applicant;
    ...

    @ManyToOne(fetch = FetchType.EAGER, optional = false)
    @JoinColumn(name = "ApplicantId")
    public Applicant getApplicant() { ... }
    public void setApplicant(Applicant applicant) { ... }

    ...
}
```

The `@javax.persistence.OneToMany` and `@javax.persistence.ManyToOne` annotations contain many of the same attributes as `@OneToOne`. `@OneToMany` lacks an `optional` attribute because such a concept doesn't apply to a collection of values. (A collection can always be empty.) Only `@OneToMany` contains a `mappedBy` attribute because in a bidirectional one-to-many-to-one relationship, only the one-to-many side needs this information. `@OneToMany` is also the only one of the two annotations with an `orphanRemoval` attribute because such an action makes sense only from that side of the relationship.

You may have noticed that the `@javax.persistence.JoinColumn` annotation moved from original `Applicant` to the new property in `Resume`. This annotation, largely similar to the `@Column` annotation, specifies the column details for the column that joins these two tables. (If the foreign key is composite, you can use `@javax.persistence.JoinColumns` to group multiple annotations.) In a unidirectional one-to-many relationship, it goes on the only side of the relationship it can: the `@OneToMany` side (`Applicant`). For these relationships, it indicates which column in the *other* entity's table contains "this" entity's primary key. However, in a unidirectional many-to-one relationship or a bidirectional one-to-many-to-one relationship, it belongs on the `@ManyToOne` side of the relationship (`Resume`). For these relationships `@JoinColumn` indicates which column in "this" entity's table contains the *other* entity's primary key. It also replaces the `@Column` annotation for that property.

Instead of a `Set` of `Resumes`, you could use a `List` of `Resumes` and maintain their order in some fashion. To do this, you annotate the `List` property (the `@OneToMany` side) with `@javax.persistence.OrderColumn` and specify the `name` of the column in the `Applicant_Resume` table that the Resumes should be ordered by. You can also specify a Map of Resumes. In this case, you need to pick some column from the Applicant_Resume table to serve as the key of the Map. You could annotate the Map property with @javax.persistence.MapKey, which means that the Map keys are the @Id properties of the Resumes. Alternatively, you could use @javax.persistence.MapKeyColumn to specify the name of an Applicant_Resume column, such as Title, to serve as the Map keys.

One final note: With Map properties, you can still use @OrderColumn to get a Map whose entries (as returned by entrySet()) and values (as returned by values()) are ordered according to that column.

The final versions of the Applicant and Resume entities map to the following MySQL schema:

```
CREATE TABLE Applicant (
  ApplicantId BIGINT UNSIGNED NOT NULL AUTO_INCREMENT PRIMARY KEY,
  FirstName VARCHAR(60) NOT NULL,
  LastName VARCHAR(60) NOT NULL,
  Citizen BOOLEAN NOT NULL
) ENGINE = InnoDB;

CREATE TABLE Applicant_Resume (
  ResumeId BIGINT UNSIGNED NOT NULL AUTO_INCREMENT PRIMARY KEY,
  ApplicantId BIGINT UNSIGNED NOT NULL,
  Title VARCHAR(100) NOT NULL,
  Content TEXT NOT NULL,
  CONSTRAINT Applicant_Resume_Applicant FOREIGN KEY (ApplicantId)
    REFERENCES Applicant(ApplicantId) ON DELETE CASCADE
) ENGINE = InnoDB;
```

## Creating Many-to-Many Relationships

Many-to-many relationships are simply a natural extension of one-to-many and many-to-one relationships. In a many-to-many relationship, each side of the relationship can relate to multiple entities on the other side of the relationship. A common example of this is the relationship between a school and a student. A school can have many students, and a student can have multiple schools. Thus, a School entity would have a Set, List, or Map of Students, and the Student entity would in turn have a Set, List, or Map of Schools.

You can advertise one or both sides of a many-to-many relationship using @javax.persistence.ManyToMany. It has the cascade, fetch, and mappedBy attributes that you are well used to. You must specify mappedBy if, and only if, the advertised relationship is bidirectional, and as usual its value should point to the property on the opposite end of the relationship. You specify mappedBy only on one side of the relationship (the non-owner side, in whatever way you define ownership).

When advertising a many-to-many relationship (unidirectional or bidirectional), the JPA vendor attempts to guess the name of the join table and its columns. For your sanity, it's best to remove the guessing variable and specify the @javax.persistence.JoinTable annotation. You place this annotation only on the owner side of the relationship (the opposite side that you specify mappedBy). In addition to the table name and other details, this annotation contains joinColumns and inverseJoinColumns attributes. You use joinColumns to specify one or more @JoinColumns that indicate which column or columns "this" (the owning) entity's primary key maps to. Likewise, you use inverseJoinColumns to specify one or more @JoinColumns that indicate which column or columns the other (owned) entity's primary key maps to. In the School and Student example described earlier, the mapping would look like this on the School entity:

```
@ManyToMany(fetch = FetchType.LAZY)
@JoinTable(name = "School_Student",
        joinColumns = { @JoinColumn(name = "SchoolId") },
        inverseJoinColumns = { @JoinColumn(name = "StudentId") })
public List<Student> getStudents() { ... }
public void setStudents(List<Student> students) { ... }
```

# ADDRESSING OTHER COMMON SITUATIONS

Several other common situations exist that are simple to address and don't require entire sections by themselves. Do not construe this to mean they aren't useful; some of them may be the most useful of all for your needs. This includes topics such as versioning entities, defining common entity ancestors, and adding Collections and Maps to your entities, all of which are addressed in this section.

## Versioning Entities with Revisions and Timestamps

At the simplest, you may take any approach to versioning entities that you like. The JPA provider treats a version property as it would any other property, and persists and retrieves it normally. However, you can define a special kind of version property that helps the JPA provider ensure integrity and avoid concurrent modifications when performing merge operations. To create such a property, you annotate it with @javax.persistence.Version.

@Version properties can be ints, Integers, longs, Longs, shorts, Shorts, or Timestamps (and perhaps, in a future version, Instants). You must *never* set the value of a @Version property manually; the JPA provider does this for you. When writing changes for an entity to the database, the provider increments the version in the UPDATE statement and includes a WHERE clause that fails to evaluate to true if the version has already changed. For example, if the table for a versioned entity is MyEntity, the @Id property column is EntityId, and the integer @Version property column is VersionNumber, the UPDATE statement would look something like this:

```
UPDATE MyEntity SET [other values[,...]], VersionNumber = VersionNumber + 1
  WHERE EntityId = ? AND VersionNumber = ?;
```

If this statement fails to update any records, some other thread or process has deleted or updated the entity already. The JPA provider throws a javax.persistence.OptimisticLockException if this happens.

Because manually setting the @Version property is bad and can cause serious problems in your application, the best practice is to make the mutator method protected or package-private, thus reducing the likelihood that some code will accidentally set it.

### UNDERSTANDING OPTIMISTIC LOCKING VERSUS PESSIMISTIC LOCKING

Optimistic locking allows two or more threads to read the same entity simultaneously but allows only one of those threads to update the entity. This can and will prevent concurrent modification of an entity. However, if you prefer to lock the row at the database so that only one thread may read the entity at the any given time, you can do so by specifying the `javax.persistence.LockModeType` enum constant `PESSIMISTIC_READ` in any of the `EntityManager` methods that support it (that is, any methods that affect only one entity at a time). When using Spring Data JPA, you can achieve the same thing by annotating a repository interface method with `@org.springframework.data.jpa.repository.Lock` and specifying `LockModeType.PESSIMISTIC_READ` as its `value` attribute. If you need to add `@Lock` to a method in a superinterface, just override it in your interface.

When using pessimistic locking, two types of failures can occur. The first is a failure to obtain a lock that results in the database rolling back the transaction. Such an error is fatal to the transaction and results in a `javax.persistence.PessimisticLockException` (also rolling back the JTA transaction if one exists). However, the database locking failure may result in only the rollback of a single statement. In this case, the failure is transient and results in a `javax.persistence.LockTimeoutException`. It is up to you to handle the `LockTimeoutException` by either retrying the statement or rolling back the transaction. In almost all cases, optimistic locking is sufficient, and you shouldn't need to enable pessimistic locking.

## Defining Abstract Entities with Common Properties

After you create several entities, you'll probably notice that they contain at least a few of the same properties over and over again. For example, you might realize that all your entities have IDs, creation dates, last modification dates, and `@Version` properties. Instead of redefining these properties every time you create an entity, you can create a *mapped superclass* that defines the entities once.

A mapped superclass is very much like an entity. It contains no `@Table` annotation, and the `@javax.persistence.MappedSuperclass` annotation replaces the `@Entity` annotation, but otherwise you can map any properties within it just like you would in a normal entity. The properties in a mapped superclass always map to the same table as the eventual `@Entity` class that extends it. You are not limited to a single mapped superclass in the hierarchy, either. You can define any number of mapped superclasses and an entity inherits the properties of all the mapped superclasses that are its ancestors.

A mapped superclass or entity can override the column mappings of properties it inherits by overriding the accessor method and redefining the `@Column` annotation. However, this doesn't work if you use field access instead of method access, so in those cases, you have to annotate the class with `@AttributeOverride`, specify the property name in the `name` attribute, and provide the new `@Column` definition. You cannot override annotations such as `@Basic`, `@Lob`, `@Temporal`, `@Enumerated`, `@Convert`, and other JPA type annotations. If a mapped superclass defines a `@Transient` property, its subclasses cannot override that property to make it non-`@Transient`.

Likewise, a mapped superclass or entity cannot override a non-`@Transient` method from one of its ancestors and make it `@Transient`.

The `BaseEntity` mapped superclass in the Advanced-Mappings project defines the simple `id` property that all extending entities will have. `VersionedEntity`, another mapped superclass, extends `BaseEntity` to specify a `@Version` property for optimistic locking. Finally, the `AuditedEntity` mapped superclass extends `VersionedEntity` and specifies creation and modification date properties.

```
@MappedSuperclass
public abstract class BaseEntity
{
    private long id;

    @Id
    @GeneratedValue(strategy = GenerationType.IDENTITY)
    public long getId() { ... }
    public void setId(long id) { ... }
}

@MappedSuperclass
public abstract class VersionedEntity extends BaseEntity
{
    private long version;

    @Version
    @Column(name = "Revision")
    public long getVersion() { ... }
    void setVersion(long version) { ... }
}

@MappedSuperclass
public abstract class AuditedEntity extends VersionedEntity
{
    private Instant dateCreated;
    private Instant dateModified;

    @Convert(converter = InstantConverter.class)
    public Instant getDateCreated() { ... }
    public void setDateCreated(Instant dateCreated) { ... }

    @Convert(converter = InstantConverter.class)
    public Instant getDateModified() { ... }
    public void setDateModified(Instant dateModified) { ... }
}
```

You can now create as many entities as you want that extend any of these mapped superclasses. The `NewsArticle` entity that follows extends `AuditedEntity` and inherits all its superclasses' properties. Its SQL schema reflects the overridden `id` property column name.

```
@Entity
@AttributeOverride(name = "id", column = @Column(name = "ArticleId"))
public class NewsArticle extends AuditedEntity
{
    private String title;
```

```
        private String content;

        @Basic
        public String getTitle() { ... }
        public void setTitle(String title) { ... }

        @Basic
        public String getContent() { ... }
        public void setContent(String content) { ... }
    }

    CREATE TABLE NewsArticle (
      ArticleId BIGINT UNSIGNED NOT NULL AUTO_INCREMENT PRIMARY KEY,
      Revision BIGINT UNSIGNED NOT NULL,
      DateCreated TIMESTAMP(6) NULL,
      DateModified TIMESTAMP(6) NULL,
      Title VARCHAR(100) NOT NULL,
      Content TEXT NOT NULL
    ) ENGINE = InnoDB;
```

Like `@Entity` classes, `@MappedSuperclasses` must be registered as managed classes in your persistence unit. This means you must either specify them in `<class>` or `<jar-file>` elements in your persistence unit configuration, leave `<exclude-unlisted-classes>` disabled in your persistence unit configuration, or include them in the scanned classes discovered by Spring's `LocalContainerEntityManagerFactoryBean`. By placing `BaseEntity`, `VersionedEntity`, and `AuditedEntity` in the `com.wrox.site.entities` package, they are automatically discovered and added to the persistence unit.

## Mapping Basic and Embedded Collections

Up to this point, you have created entities with basic- and embedded-type properties and properties that are collections of other entities. However, sometimes you just need a simple collection of a basic or embedded type. For example, an employee usually has multiple phone numbers and addresses. You could add two or three phone number properties and two or three address properties, but why restrain it this way? It not only violates database normal form, but it violates good object-oriented design practices as well. It makes more sense to have either a `List` or `Set` of phone numbers and addresses, depending on whether order is important to you. In JPA you mark a field that is a collection of basic or embedded types with the `@javax.persistence.ElementCollection` annotation.

`@ElementCollection` has a `targetClass` attribute that may or may not be required in certain situations. It specifies the type of the elements stored in the `Collection`. If you use an untyped `Collection` (which you should really never, ever do because it is unsafe), you *must* specify the `targetClass` attribute. However, as long as you use generics (such as `List<String>` or `Set<Address>`) the JPA provider can discover the element type (`String`, `Address`) automatically and you *must not* specify the `targetClass` attribute. The `fetch` attribute indicates whether the `Collection` values should be retrieved from the database eagerly or lazily, and defaults to `FetchType.LAZY`.

You are now probably wondering about the restriction described earlier on embedded types: They must exist within the same table as the entity that contains them. Well, this is only part of the story.

They may exist in a separate table if they are part of a collection property. In this case, the collection defaults to storing in a table whose name is equal to the containing entity's table name followed by an underscore followed by the property name. Certain assumptions are also made about the column names based on the types and property names. Consider the `Employee` entity as an example.

```
@Entity
public class Employee
{
    private long id;
    private String firstName;
    private String lastName;
    private List<String> phoneNumbers = new ArrayList<>();
    private Set<Address> addresses = new HashSet<>();

    @Id
    @Column(name = "EmployeeId")
    @GeneratedValue(strategy = GenerationType.IDENTITY)
    public long getId() { ... }
    public void setId(long id) { ... }

    @Basic
    public String getFirstName() { ... }
    public void setFirstName(String firstName) { ... }

    @Basic
    public String getLastName() { ... }
    public void setLastName(String lastName) { ... }

    @ElementCollection(fetch = FetchType.EAGER)
    public List<String> getPhoneNumbers() { ... }
    public void setPhoneNumbers(List<String> phoneNumbers) { ... }

    @ElementCollection(fetch = FetchType.LAZY)
    public Set<Address> getAddresses() { ... }
    public void setAddresses(Set<Address> addresses) { ... }
}
```

With these default mappings, an `Employee`'s phone numbers are assumed to reside in the database table `Employee_PhoneNumbers` with a foreign key column named `EmployeeId` and a `PhoneNumber` column containing the phone number. The `Employee`'s addresses are assumed to reside in `Employee_Addresses`, also with an `EmployeeId` foreign key column. However, because the `Address` class you created earlier in the chapter is an embeddable type with its own mappings, the JPA provider doesn't have to make assumptions and knows the columns for it are `Address_Street`, `Address_City`, `Address_State`, `Address_Country`, `PostalCode_Code`, and `PostalCode_Suffix`. These may not be the names you want, so you can customize them:

```
@Entity
public class Employee
{
    ...
    @ElementCollection(fetch = FetchType.EAGER)
    @CollectionTable(name = "Employee_Phone", joinColumns = {
            @JoinColumn(name = "Employee", referencedColumnName = "EmployeeId")
```

```
    })
    @OrderColumn(name = "Priority")
    public List<String> getPhoneNumbers() { ... }
    public void setPhoneNumbers(List<String> phoneNumbers) { ... }

    @ElementCollection(fetch = FetchType.LAZY)
    @CollectionTable(name = "Employee_Address", joinColumns = {
            @JoinColumn(name = "Employee", referencedColumnName = "EmployeeId")
    })
    @AttributeOverrides({
            @AttributeOverride(name = "street", column =@Column(name = "Street")),
            @AttributeOverride(name = "city", column = @Column(name = "City")),
            @AttributeOverride(name = "state", column = @Column(name = "State")),
            @AttributeOverride(name = "country", column=@Column(name = "Country"))
    })
    public Set<Address> getAddresses() { ... }
    public void setAddresses(Set<Address> addresses) { ... }
}
```

The `@javax.persistence.CollectionTable` annotation allows you to customize the table name and the columns that it joins on. `@javax.persistence.OrderColumn` enables you to specify the column that orders the elements in the `Collection` (which applies only if the collection is a `List` instead of a `Set`). In a `Collection` holding a basic type, you can use `@Column` to specify the name of the column in which the values are stored inside the collection table. However, if the `Collection` holds embedded types, you must use `@AttributeOverride` and `@AttributeOverrides`. As mapped here, the `Employee` entity resides in the following MySQL schema:

```
CREATE TABLE Employee (
  EmployeeId BIGINT UNSIGNED NOT NULL AUTO_INCREMENT PRIMARY KEY,
  FirstName VARCHAR(50) NOT NULL,
  LastName VARCHAR(50) NOT NULL
) ENGINE = InnoDB;

CREATE TABLE Employee_Phone (
  Employee BIGINT UNSIGNED NOT NULL,
  Priority SMALLINT UNSIGNED NOT NULL,
  Number VARCHAR(20) NOT NULL,
  CONSTRAINT Employee_Phone_Employee FOREIGN KEY (Employee)
    REFERENCES Employee (EmployeeId) ON DELETE CASCADE
) ENGINE = InnoDB;

CREATE TABLE Employee_Address (
  Employee BIGINT UNSIGNED NOT NULL,
  Street VARCHAR(100) NOT NULL,
  City VARCHAR(100) NOT NULL,
  State VARCHAR(100) NULL,
  Country VARCHAR(100) NOT NULL,
  PostalCode_Code VARCHAR(10) NOT NULL,
  PostalCode_Suffix VARCHAR(5),
  CONSTRAINT Employee_Address_Employee FOREIGN KEY (Employee)
    REFERENCES Employee(EmployeeId) ON DELETE CASCADE
) ENGINE = InnoDB;
```

> **NOTE** *In addition to embeddable types and the standard basic types, you can also store types that require conversion within* `Collection` *properties. Just annotate the* `Collection` *property with* `@Convert` *as if it were any other basic property.*

## Persisting a Map of Key-Value Pairs

Although its name suggests it applies only to `Collection` properties, `@ElementCollection` can also mark a `Map` property for persistence. `Map` properties are always stored with the key and value in the same table, which has the same default name as `Collection` properties and which you can also customize using `@CollectionTable`. You use `@Column` to specify the name of the column that stores the `Map` *value*, and `@javax.persistence.MapKeyColumn` to specify the name of the column that stores the map *key*. `Map` properties should also always use generics, but if for some reason they cannot, use the `targetClass` attribute of `@ElementCollection` to specify the *value* class and `@javax.persistence.MapKeyClass` to specify the *key* class.

Both the key and the value may be any of the basic types, including enum and temporal types, any types that require an attribute converter, and any embeddable types. As with `Collection` properties, you do not have to specify the `@Embedded` annotation on `Map` properties whose keys or values are embeddable types. Enumerated types follow the same semantics as for basic properties, and you can override these semantics with the usual `@Enumerated` annotation for the `Map` *value* and the `@javax.persistence.MapKeyEnumerated` annotation for the *key*. Likewise, you can customize the semantics for temporal types with the usual `@Temporal` for the `value` and `@javax.persistence.MapKeyTemporal` for the `key`.

Using `Map` properties is a great way to store supplemental entity properties that you don't know about at compile time, such as custom fields. This is demonstrated with the following new `Employee` property and the table to which it's mapped.

```
@Entity
public class Employee
{
    ...
    private Map<String, String> extraProperties = new HashMap<>();

    ...

    @ElementCollection(fetch = FetchType.EAGER)
    @CollectionTable(name = "Employee_Property", joinColumns = {
            @JoinColumn(name = "Employee", referencedColumnName = "EmployeeId")
    })
    @Column(name = "Value")
    @MapKeyColumn(name = "KeyName")
    public Map<String, String> getExtraProperties() { ... }
    public void setExtraProperties(Map<String, String> extraProperties) { ... }
}

CREATE TABLE Employee_Property (
  Employee BIGINT UNSIGNED NOT NULL,
```

```
    KeyName VARCHAR(100) NOT NULL,
    Value VARCHAR(255) NOT NULL,
    CONSTRAINT Employee_Property_Employee FOREIGN KEY (Employee)
      REFERENCES Employee(EmployeeId) ON DELETE CASCADE
  ) ENGINE = InnoDB;
```

## Storing an Entity in Multiple Tables

Although an unlikely and unusual scenario, you can persist an entity in multiple tables. Don't confuse this with the concept of `Collection` or `Map` properties residing in separate tables — that's an expected practice mandated by good normal form. Instead, this particular scenario actually breaks normal form by storing basic properties of an entity in separate tables. In an absurd example, an `Employee`'s first name might be stored in table `Employee1`, whereas his last name is stored in table `Employee2`. This is usually a symptom of legacy databases, poorly designed databases retrofitted for object-relational mapping, or entities that exceed the number of columns permitted in a single table by the underlying database vendor.

By default, all the non-`Collection`, non-`Map` properties of an entity are assumed to reside in the primary table. This is the table specified in `@Table` or, in the absence of `@Table`, the table with the same name as the entity. If some of an entity's properties reside in a secondary table, you should annotate it with `@javax.persistence.SecondaryTable` to specify the name and (optionally) other details of the table. If an entity has multiple secondary tables, you can use `@javax.persistence.SecondaryTables` to group multiple `@SecondaryTable` annotations. Then, throughout the entity, each property should be annotated with `@Column` to indicate which table it belongs to. The `@Id` property must *always* reside in the primary table.

A secondary table is assumed to have a column of the same name and type as the primary key column of the primary table, and that column should be the primary key for the secondary table. You can customize the details of this column in the `@SecondaryTable` annotation.

Though mapping an entity to multiple tables is not demonstrated in the Advanced-Mappings project, the `Employee` entity might look something like this in such a scenario:

```
@Entity
@Table(name = "Employee")
@SecondaryTables({
        @SecondaryTable(name = "Employee2", pkJoinColumns = {
                @PrimaryKeyJoinColumn(name = "Employee",
                        referencedColumnName = "EmployeeId")
        })
})
public class Employee
{
    ...

    @Id
    @Column(name = "EmployeeId")
    @GeneratedValue(strategy = GenerationType.IDENTITY)
    public long getId() { ... }
    public void setId(long id) { ... }

    @Basic
```

```
        @Column(name = "FirstName", table = "Employee")
        public String getFirstName() { ... }
        public void setFirstName(String firstName) { ... }

        @Basic
        @Column(name = "LastName", table = "Employee2")
        public String getLastName() { ... }
        public void setLastName(String lastName) { ... }

        ...
    }
```

# CREATING PROGRAMMATIC TRIGGERS

To a large extent, the relational database triggers that you may have used in the past should exist as business logic in your services. This removal of all business logic from the database is the last step to completely abstracting your application from its storage mechanism and allowing you to easily switch out the storage mechanism as the need arises. Equally important, it reinforces the view of the application as the goal and the database as simply a means to that goal. However, there may be times where your entity needs a little bit of persistence logic of its own. The classic example is when updating versioning- and auditing-related fields. (Although you may simply want to let Spring Data take care of that for you.) Though not strictly related to mapping, JPA allows you to add special annotations to your entities that define programmatic triggers in Java code instead of relying on database triggers.

## Acting before and after CRUD Operations

You can define a trigger on any entity by creating a method that executes the logic you want and annotating it with one of the trigger annotations. These methods, officially called *lifecycle event handlers* or *lifecycle event callback methods*, are instance methods and have access to all the properties of the entity. This means that the methods can use and modify those properties however you want. In addition to annotating methods in a concrete entity, you can also annotate methods on a mapped superclass to create triggers that apply to all entities that inherit from that mapped superclass. Of course, such triggers could safely use and modify only the properties of the mapped superclass and its ancestors.

The `@javax.persistence.PostLoad` annotation defines a read trigger, executing after the entity is constructed and populated from the `ResultSet`. It is the only trigger annotation that does not have a counterpart that executes before the operation because that would not be possible for reads. The other annotations, all in the same package, are as follows:

- `@PrePersist` methods are executed before the entity is persisted: immediately after the `persist` method is called on the `EntityManager` and immediately before the entity is actually attached to the `EntityManager`. Note that in a long-running transaction, it could be a long time after this method executes before the entity is actually written to the database.
- `@PostPersist` methods are invoked immediately after the entity is actually written to the database (either during flush or commit, whichever comes first). The transaction could still roll back after this method is called.

- `@PreUpdate` methods are invoked as soon as the `EntityManager` detects that the entity has changed. It's important to understand that, when using JPA, you don't actually have to call `merge` to update an entity unless the instance is modified after a transaction is committed. Calling any of the mutator methods on an entity changes the entity, and those changes are written to the database when the transaction is committed even if you do not call `merge`. As soon as the entity has been changed by a mutator invocation, the `@PreUpdate` trigger fires. In a long-running transaction, it could be a long time after this method executes before the entity is actually written to the database.
- `@PostUpdate` methods are executed immediately after the changes to the entity are written to the database. The transaction could still roll back after this method is called.
- `@PreRemove` methods are invoked when the entity is marked for removal (deletion) from the `EntityManager`. In a long-running transaction, it could be a long time after this method executes before the entity is actually written to the database.
- `@PostRemove` methods are invoked immediately after the entity is actually deleted from the database. The transaction could still roll back after this method is called.

A trigger method may serve as a trigger for multiple events (for example, it could be annotated with both `@PrePersist` and `@PreUpdate`), but an entity may have no more than one method annotated for a particular event. This includes inherited trigger methods, meaning for example that a `@PostRemove` method in an entity will disable any `@PostRemove` methods that it inherits from mapped superclasses. However, it won't disable that same method from being called for other events it may be annotated for, such as `@PostUpdate`.

Trigger methods must return void and have no arguments. They can be named anything and be public, protected, package-private, or private, but they must not be static. To prevent unusual behavior, they should never call `EntityManager` or `Query` methods or access any other entities. If a trigger method throws an exception, the transaction is rolled back. (So you could, for example, use trigger methods to prevent illegal modifications.)

The `Person` entity you created earlier demonstrates use of all the different trigger methods to log the life cycle of an entity.

```
@Entity
public class Person
{
    ...

    private static final Logger log = LogManager.getLogger();

    @PostLoad void readTrigger()
    {
        log.debug("Person entity read.");
    }

    @PrePersist void beforeInsertTrigger()
    {
        log.debug("Person entity about to be inserted.");
```

```
        }

        @PostPersist void afterInsertTrigger()
        {
            log.debug("Person entity inserted into database.");
        }

        @PreUpdate void beforeUpdateTrigger()
        {
            log.debug("Person entity just updated by call to mutator method.");
        }

        @PostUpdate void afterUpdateTrigger()
        {
            log.debug("Person entity just updated in the database.");
        }

        @PreRemove void beforeDeleteTrigger()
        {
            log.debug("Person entity about to be deleted.");
        }

        @PostRemove void afterDeleteTrigger()
        {
            log.debug("Person entity about deleted from database.");
        }
    }
```

## Using Entity Listeners

*Entity listeners* are closely related to the trigger methods you just read about. An entity listener is a construct for defining trigger methods outside of an entity class. These methods are called external trigger methods or *external lifecycle event handlers*, in contrast to internal trigger methods you just learned about that exist as part of the entity class or its superclasses. External trigger methods enable you to keep this logic truly separate from your entity classes. Entity listeners must have public, no-argument constructors and may define any or all the trigger methods previously described. However, there are a few minor differences:

- **The external trigger methods defined in an entity listener must have a single argument: the entity that caused the lifecycle event.** You can make the type of the argument as vague (a mapped superclass or even just `Object`) or as specific (the exact entity type) as you want.
- **Entity listeners are inherited from mapped superclasses just like internal trigger methods are, except they do not override inherited entity listeners.** This means that you *can* have multiple trigger methods execute for a particular lifecycle event on the same entity.

When executing trigger methods, the provider first invokes all external trigger methods and then invokes all internal trigger methods. External trigger methods in entity listeners execute starting at the highest point in the mapped superclass ancestry and complete with the actual entity class. You can also define default entity listeners that execute before all others. These entity listeners apply to all entities anywhere in your application, but you can define a default entity listener only in a mapping file (such as `orm.xml`).

Writing an entity listener class is as simple as creating a class and adding trigger methods to it. The class does not have to implement any interfaces or extend any superclasses. (However, it certainly can implement or extend other types if that helps you in some way.) After you create an entity listener, you have to attach it to an entity using the `@javax.persistence.EntityListeners` annotation. You can place this annotation on an entity class or mapped superclass to attach the listener or listeners to that entity class or mapped superclass, for example:

```
@EntityListeners(Listener1.class)
@MappedSuperclass
public abstract class AbstractEntity
{
    ...
}

@EntityListeners({ Listener2.class, Listener3.class })
@Entity
public class ConcreteEntity extends AbstractEntity
{
    ...
}
```

If you create an entity that extends a mapped superclass but you do not want to inherit the mapped superclass's entity listeners, you can annotate the entity with `@javax.persistence.ExcludeSuperclassListeners`. You can also annotate a mapped superclass with `@ExcludeSuperclassListeners` to stop inheritance of its superclass listeners for it and for its subclasses. Likewise, you can annotate an entity or mapped superclass `@javax.persistence.ExcludeDefaultListeners` to exclude all default listeners for it and for its subclasses.

## REFINING THE CUSTOMER SUPPORT APPLICATION

With the tools that you have learned about in this chapter, you can make many improvements to the Customer Support application you have been working on throughout this book. To start with, you can stop using `Ticket` as a DTO for `TicketEntity`, get rid of `TicketEntity` altogether, and start using `Ticket` as an entity directly. This is made possible using the `InstantConverter` you created earlier in the chapter.

You can also define a relationship between `Tickets` and `Attachments` so that you can automatically retrieve a ticket's attachments when you retrieve the `Ticket` entity. Speaking of attachments, you can now add attachments to `TicketComments`, using a join table and a relationship with `Attachment` similar to that in `Ticket`. You can also directly associate the `UserPrincipal` to a `Ticket` or `TicketComment`. Finally, you can ensure that an `Attachment`'s content is loaded lazily so that you don't load potentially hundreds of megabytes of data when listing the attachments on a ticket and its comments. The Customer-Support-v18 project, available for download from the `wrox.com` code download site, accomplishes all these things.

## Mapping a Collection of Attachments

Because you'll now use Attachments for both Tickets and TicketComments, the Attachment entity no longer needs a ticketId property, and the corresponding table no longer needs a TicketId column. Instead, use the following join tables, found in create.sql, to relate Attachments to both Tickets and TicketComments.

```
USE CustomerSupport;

CREATE TABLE Ticket_Attachment (
  SortKey SMALLINT NOT NULL,
  TicketId BIGINT UNSIGNED NOT NULL,
  AttachmentId BIGINT UNSIGNED NOT NULL,
  CONSTRAINT Ticket_Attachment_Ticket FOREIGN KEY (TicketId)
    REFERENCES Ticket (TicketId) ON DELETE CASCADE,
  CONSTRAINT Ticket_Attachment_Attachment FOREIGN KEY (AttachmentId)
    REFERENCES Attachment (AttachmentId) ON DELETE CASCADE,
  INDEX Ticket_OrderedAttachments (TicketId, SortKey, AttachmentId)
) ENGINE = InnoDB;

CREATE TABLE TicketComment_Attachment (
  SortKey SMALLINT NOT NULL,
  CommentId BIGINT UNSIGNED NOT NULL,
  AttachmentId BIGINT UNSIGNED NOT NULL,
  CONSTRAINT TicketComment_Attachment_Comment FOREIGN KEY (CommentId)
    REFERENCES TicketComment (CommentId) ON DELETE CASCADE,
  CONSTRAINT TicketComment_Attachment_Attachment FOREIGN KEY (AttachmentId)
    REFERENCES Attachment (AttachmentId) ON DELETE CASCADE,
  INDEX TicketComment_OrderedAttachments (CommentId, SortKey, AttachmentId)
) ENGINE = InnoDB;
```

If you have been running previous versions of the Customer Support application in earlier chapters, you need to migrate the data in the TicketId column to the Ticket_Attachment table and then drop the TicketId column. The following statements, commented out in create.sql, take care of this for you.

```
USE CustomerSupport;

INSERT INTO Ticket_Attachment (SortKey, TicketId, AttachmentId)
    SELECT @rn := @rn + 1, TicketId, AttachmentId
        FROM Attachment, (SELECT @rn:=0) x
        ORDER BY TicketId, AttachmentName;
CREATE TEMPORARY TABLE $minSortKeys ENGINE = Memory (
  SELECT min(SortKey) as SortKey,TicketId FROM Ticket_Attachment GROUP BY TicketId
);
UPDATE Ticket_Attachment a SET a.SortKey = a.SortKey - (
  SELECT x.SortKey FROM $minSortKeys x WHERE x.TicketId = a.TicketId
) WHERE TicketId > 0;
DROP TABLE $minSortKeys;
ALTER TABLE Attachment DROP FOREIGN KEY Attachment_TicketId;
ALTER TABLE Attachment DROP COLUMN TicketId;
```

Mapping the Ticket-Attachment and TicketComment-Attachment relationships is easy. First, the Ticket no longer has a getAttachment method to retrieve an Attachment by name. Attachments are not strictly related to `Tickets` anymore, so individual retrieval must use the ID instead of the name. The following mapping joins the `Ticket` and `Attachment` entities:

```
@OneToMany(fetch = FetchType.LAZY, cascade = CascadeType.ALL,
        orphanRemoval = true)
@JoinTable(name = "Ticket_Attachment",
        joinColumns = { @JoinColumn(name = "TicketId") },
        inverseJoinColumns = { @JoinColumn(name = "AttachmentId") })
@OrderColumn(name = "SortKey")
@XmlElement(name = "attachment")
@JsonProperty
public List<Attachment> getAttachments()
{
    return this.attachments;
}
```

Whereas the following joins `TicketComment` with its `Attachments`:

```
@OneToMany(fetch = FetchType.EAGER, cascade = CascadeType.ALL,
        orphanRemoval = true)
@JoinTable(name = "TicketComment_Attachment",
        joinColumns = { @JoinColumn(name = "CommentId") },
        inverseJoinColumns = { @JoinColumn(name = "AttachmentId") })
@OrderColumn(name = "SortKey")
@XmlElement(name = "attachment")
@JsonProperty
public List<Attachment> getAttachments()
{
    return this.attachments;
}
```

Notice that a ticket's attachments are loaded lazily, whereas a comment's attachments are loaded eagerly. Why? When listing tickets, you don't list their attachments. Therefore, you have no reason to load the information that you don't need. Instead, in the `DefaultTicketService` you can tell Hibernate to load the attachments for an individually retrieved ticket by calling a method on the attachment list during the transaction. (Remember that `getNumberOfAttachments` calls the `size` method of the `List<Attachment>`.)

```
@Override
@Transactional
public Ticket getTicket(long id)
{
    Ticket ticket = this.ticketRepository.findOne(id);
    ticket.getNumberOfAttachments();
    return ticket;
}
```

However, this is different for comments. When listing the comments while viewing a ticket, you also want to list their attachments. Thus, you load comments' attachment lists eagerly. Because `Attachment` is shared between both these entities, the relationship is unidirectional. (`Attachment` does not have `@ManyToOne Ticket` or `Comment` properties.) `Attachment` does not have any navigational properties back to `Ticket` or `TicketComment`.

One of the upsides to this change is the improved simplicity of the `DefaultTicketService`. You no longer have to translate between DTOs and entities, eliminating a lot of code. You can view the refactored service, in addition to the updated controller and views, in the downloaded project.

## Lazy Loading Simple Properties with Load Time Weaving

Now that both tickets and their comments can have attachments, you needlessly load a significant amount of data just by viewing a ticket. If a ticket has several 10-megabyte attachments, and each comment has several 10-megabyte attachments, viewing a ticket could load hundreds of megabytes of data that isn't being used. This would be an enormous performance problem. What you really need to do is lazy load the `Attachment`'s `contents` property:

```
@Lob
@Basic(fetch = FetchType.LAZY)
@XmlElement
@XmlSchemaType(name = "base64Binary")
@JsonProperty
public byte[] getContents()
{
    return this.contents;
}
```

Then in the `DefaultTicketService` you would load this content only when getting an individual ticket (for download):

```
@Override
@Transactional
public Attachment getAttachment(long id)
{
    Attachment attachment = this.attachmentRepository.findOne(id);
    if(attachment != null)
        attachment.getContents();
    return attachment;
}
```

However, it isn't that simple. Lazy loading works automatically for properties that are `Map`s and `Collection`s (`List`s and `Set`s) because those are interfaces, and Hibernate ORM comes with proxy implementations of those interfaces that run the necessary queries to load the data only when the `Map` or `Collection` property is used in some way (its size is calculated, it is iterated over, and so on). For you to lazy load simple properties of types like `byte[]` or `String`, or `@OneToOne` or `@ManyToOne` properties, Hibernate must instrument the bytecode of the entities so that it can intercept the method calls to retrieve those properties. It cannot do this out-the-door without some configuration.

First, you have to set up an environment capable of bytecode instrumentation. You have three different ways to do this:

- **Attach a Java agent to the JVM (see the `java` command's `-agent` argument), which uses a class file transformer to inspect and, if necessary, transform all classes loaded by the class loaders in that JVM.** This is a bit heavy-handed for an application server or Servlet container environment, though. You need something that applies to a single application.
- **Use Hibernate's `org.hibernate.tool.instrument.InstrumentTask` Ant task (either in your Ant script or through the Ant plug-in in your Maven POM).** This task modifies the bytecode of your entities at build time, right after you compile them and before you deploy your application. Other O/RMs provide similar mechanisms for decorating bytecode at build time.
- **Use load-time bytecode weaving.** You see this final approach in the Customer-Support-v18 project.

With Spring Framework's load time weaving feature, you can transform classes when they are loaded from their class files using one of several pluggable `org.springframework.instrument.classloading.LoadTimeWeaver` implementations. The fallback implementation is one that uses a Java agent as previously mentioned, but this is not necessary here. A better option is to use a weaver that takes advantage of the instrumentable `ClassLoader` provided by the container.

GlassFish, JBoss, WebLogic, and WebSphere all provide instrumentable `ClassLoaders` that Spring can take advantage of. Prior to Tomcat 8.0 you had to tell Tomcat to use a special `ClassLoader` (provided by Spring) that extended the default Tomcat `ClassLoader`. However, Tomcat 8.0 now provides an instrumentable `ClassLoader` that Spring can use automatically.

Configuring Spring Framework's load time weaving is as simple as adding `@org.springframework.context.annotation.EnableLoadTimeWeaving` to the `RootContextConfiguration`. It automatically detects and uses Tomcat's instrumentable `ClassLoader`. Telling Hibernate ORM to use this load time weaver requires one additional Hibernate property.

```
...
@EnableLoadTimeWeaving
...
public class RootContextConfiguration implements
        AsyncConfigurer, SchedulingConfigurer, TransactionManagementConfigurer
{
    ...
    @Bean
    public LocalContainerEntityManagerFactoryBean entityManagerFactoryBean()
    {
        ...
        properties.put("hibernate.ejb.use_class_enhancer", "true");
        ...
    }
    ...
}
```

The final thing you must consider is XML and JSON serialization of these entities. However you instrument these classes (statically at build time, with an agent, or dynamically with load time weaving), Hibernate can add any number of unspecified fields and methods to your entities. This is okay because they won't interfere with your normal use of these entities, but JAXB (which you use for XML serialization) and Jackson Data Processor (which you use for JSON serialization) do not know what to do with these fields and methods. The solution to this is telling JAXB and Jackson to ignore the properties of your entities *by default* using `@XmlAccessorType` and `@JsonAutoDetect`, adding `@XmlElement` and `@JsonProperty` to the properties that you *do* want serialized, and removing `@XmlTransient` and `@JsonIgnore` from the properties that you *do not* want serialized.

```
...
@XmlAccessorType(XmlAccessType.NONE)
@JsonAutoDetect(creatorVisibility = JsonAutoDetect.Visibility.NONE,
        fieldVisibility = JsonAutoDetect.Visibility.NONE,
        getterVisibility = JsonAutoDetect.Visibility.NONE,
        isGetterVisibility = JsonAutoDetect.Visibility.NONE,
        setterVisibility = JsonAutoDetect.Visibility.NONE)
public class Ticket implements Serializable
```

```
{
    ...
    @XmlElement
    @JsonProperty
    public long getId() { ... }
    ...
}

...
@XmlAccessorType(XmlAccessType.NONE)
@JsonAutoDetect(...)
public class TicketComment implements Serializable
{
    ...
    @XmlElement
    @JsonProperty
    public long getId() { ... }
    ...
}

...
@XmlAccessorType(XmlAccessType.NONE)
@JsonAutoDetect(...)
public class Attachment implements Serializable
{
    ...
    @XmlElement
    @JsonProperty
    public long getId() { ... }
    ...
}
```

After you review all the changes to the Customer Support application, compile the project, start Tomcat from your IDE, and go to `http://localhost:8080/support` in your browser. Log in, create a ticket or two, and add comments with attachments to see how it all works. If you place a breakpoint in the `TicketController`'s `view/{ticketId}` method, you'll see that any attachments on the ticket or ticket comments have `null contents` fields. The contents are loaded only when downloaded through the `attachment/{attachmentId}` method.

> **NOTE** *You may notice that the RESTful and SOAP web services don't work fully anymore. This is because a* `Ticket` *requires a* `UserPrincipal` *and won't save without it. You fix this in Chapter 28 when you learn about securing your web services.*

## SUMMARY

In this chapter you learned just about everything else you need to know about mapping entities in JPA. You explored creating attribute converters to handle nonstandard types and embedding POJOs within your entities using `@Embeddable` and `@Embedded`, and creating relationships between entities that are automatically or lazily loaded. You also saw how to version entities and create common entity ancestors, add `Collections` and `Maps` of basic and embedded values to your entities, store entities in multiple tables, and finally create triggers in Java code that activate before or after various CRUD operations. You also further refined the Customer Support application to get rid of its DTOs, simplify its service layer, and enhance ticket comments with attachments.

This concludes Part III of this book. It did not cover every minute detail of JPA and its APIs, and it omitted much of the XML mapping syntax that provides an alternative to using annotations. Instead, it focused on the critical tools that you need every day in your applications and showed you how to use these tools smarter with libraries like Spring Framework, Spring Data JPA, and Hibernate Search. The few tidbits you may still want to know about JPA, such as its XML mapping syntax, you can now read about and easily understand simply by downloading the specification document at `http://download.oracle.com/otndocs/jcp/persistence-2_1-fr-eval-spec/index.html`.

In Part IV, the final part of this book, you'll explore keeping your application secure from unauthorized access using Spring Security and related tools.

# PART IV
# Securing Your Application with Spring Security

# 25

# Introducing Spring Security

### IN THIS CHAPTER

- Understanding authentication and authorization
- Integrating Spring Security

### WROX.COM CODE DOWNLOADS FOR THIS CHAPTER

There are no code downloads for this chapter.

### NEW MAVEN DEPENDENCIES FOR THIS CHAPTER

There are no new Maven dependencies for this chapter. Continue to use the Maven dependencies introduced in all previous chapters.

## WHAT IS AUTHENTICATION?

When many people think of *authentication*, they think of a mechanism that determines whether someone has access to a system. Although this process is related to authentication, it is actually *authorization*. When you check whether someone has access to some system, building, file, or other object, you are checking whether they are *authorized* to use the target resource in the requested manner. The first step to authorization is authentication. The president of a company may be authorized to view some confidential file, but until you authenticate his identity, you can't be sure he is really the president or someone posing as the president. If he is someone posing as the president, you should not authenticate him and therefore not authorize him.

You encounter authentication and authorization on a daily basis. When you log in to your computer network at work in the morning, this authenticates you and establishes your identity. Your permissions on the network then determine which systems you are authorized to access based on your identity. If you go to pick up your niece from school one afternoon because her parents are stuck in traffic, the school first checks your ID to make sure you are who you say you are. This is authentication. They will then check the girl's file to see if your name is among those authorized to pick her up. Assuming it is, then and only then, they let you leave with her. If you enter a military installation, they immediately check your ID to, again, make sure you are who you say you are. Sometimes, they'll perform further checks, such as a fingerprint or retina scan, to more securely authenticate you. They may ask you for the "color of the day," or the "password of the day." When they are convinced that your authentication is valid, they check that you are authorized to access the area you are attempting to access.

Although it is true that authentication and authorization are necessarily and inextricably related, they are not the same concept. Going forward, you must remember the difference. In this chapter you explore the nuances and techniques involved in both authentication and authorization. You then take a look at Spring Security, a framework that you use in this fourth and final part of the book, so you can add security to your web applications.

# Integrating Authentication

Though it does not necessarily have to be the first security component that you integrate into your application, authentication is the first step that your users must take to participate in protected activities or access protected resources in your application. Whether they authenticate through a trusted third party or directly through mechanisms your application provides, your users must establish their identity before you can authorize them. How this happens is a topic of great interest. You can take dozens of different approaches to create authentication mechanisms. Some are better than others, but most are roughly equivalent. Which you use is largely up to your particular business and security needs, and often the desires and technological savvy of your users drive it.

## Anonymous Authentication

Anonymous authentication is certainly the simplest form of authentication that exists. You may be thinking, "How is anonymous authentication actually authentication? I thought authentication was about verifying someone's identity?" This statement may be true, but it's entirely relative to your definition of identity. For example, you may need to assert only that the browser visiting a page is the same browser that visited the previous page just a few moments ago. HTTP sessions achieve this by way of session ID tokens. Because a browser sends the same session ID token back to your server every time it visits a page on your site, you can tie these requests together as belonging to the same identity. You may simply not care *who* that visitor is. Instead, you just want to know whether it's the same person. This is a form of anonymous authentication.

More broadly, you can think of anonymous authentication as merely the absence of any other form of authentication. Most web applications support anonymous authentication up to a point. Twitter, for example, enables you to view users' feeds, trending topics, and more without "logging in." This is anonymous authentication. However, if you want to tweet something or follow other users, you must authenticate in some way that establishes your Twitter ID.

Many sites permit you to perform some basic tasks and access some resources with anonymous authentication, requiring a higher level of authentication only if you want to perform protected activities or access protected resources. This is particularly true of many forums on sites throughout the Internet, where you usually can read any post anonymously but can create new posts only after authenticating. Still other sites require no authentication—you can do anything with anonymous authentication. Some sites, though rare, do not permit you to view or do anything anonymously. The Customer Support application you have worked on throughout this book is one example of disallowing anonymous authentication.

## Password Authentication

Undoubtedly, when you were a kid you had some kind of fort, clubhouse, or tree house that you invited your friends over to. Before they could enter, you might have asked them for "the password." Without the secret word or phrase that granted them access, they couldn't come in. You didn't ask them for their username and password. That was too complex. You just wanted to know if they knew "the password." The earliest recorded use of *passwords* came from ancient Rome, where the Roman military used passwords, called watchwords, to authenticate members of the military whom they met. This was important because the military was so large that most of its members did not know every other member. The only way to tell friend from foe was to ask for the password. If the person knew the password, they were friend. If not, they were the enemy.

One of the problems with this system may already be immediately obvious to you. Roman enemies eventually caught on, and when confronting a Roman soldier they would ask for the password before the Roman soldier got the chance. The Roman soldier would then immediately state the password, not realizing he was handing it over to the enemy, who could then use the password maliciously. To counter this problem, the use of passwords eventually evolved into the use of passwords and counter-passwords. In World War II, the United States 101st Airborne Division used passwords and counter-passwords during the Battle of Normandy in Normandy, France. Paratroopers would yell out the password "flash" as a challenge, and ground forces would respond with "thunder." In this way both the paratroopers and the ground forces mutually established their identities as U.S. forces.

This password/counter-password approach is very similar to modern approaches involving web applications, where users expect an HTTPS certificate confirming the identity of the site before they provide their authentication credentials. If a user were to give his credentials to a malicious site posing as the intended site, that site could then use those credentials to do harm. Mutual authentication helps prevent such attacks, known as *man-in-the-middle attacks*.

One of the earliest recorded uses of computerized *password authentication* occurred at MIT in 1961. Its Compatible Time-Sharing System had a LOGIN command that required a user password to access the time-shared resources. Since that time, protecting passwords on computers and websites has been a never-ending battle. In the 1970s Robert Morris, while working on a UNIX system, came up with the idea of storing one-way hashes of passwords instead of the passwords themselves. In theory, because these hashes were irreversible, hackers could not determine the actual passwords and use them to access protected resources. The technique of storing one-way hashes has continued to this day, and remains the most secure way of protecting user passwords in case a password data store is breached.

Of course, as you likely know, hash-cracking hardware and software has become continually more advanced, and the algorithms that calculate the hashes have had to become more advanced to stay ahead of the hackers. Modern password-hacking computers contain as many as 30 *Graphics Processing Units* (*GPUs*). A GPU, usually used for the intense number-crunching necessary for rendering graphics on a display, is better-suited for quickly computing hashes of passwords than is a standard CPU. Furthermore, it is much easier to create a system with dozens of GPUs than with dozens of CPUs. Using special software capable of taking advantage of this power, hackers can generate billions of password hashes *per second*. This enables hackers to quickly mount a *dictionary attack* on a password database by calculating hashes for billions of possible password combinations and comparing those hashes to the hashes in the password database. Today's advanced hash-calculating algorithms, such as BCrypt, are designed to be very slow and utilize memory resources, making it difficult or impossible for GPU-based attacks.

## Usernames and Passwords

It's unlikely you will protect your applications with just a password. A single password means anyone who authenticates to your site has the same identity. It also makes changing the password more difficult—you must notify everyone who knows it—and makes the password less secure. Undoubtedly, you're already familiar with the alternative approach of assigning usernames and passwords. Each user has a unique username that no other user shares and a password associated solely with that username.

To authenticate and establish his or her identity, the user must enter the username and password when prompted. Sometimes the username is a user-chosen value, such as a name, nickname, or a "handle" by which the user prefers to be known. Other times the username might be the user's e-mail address, simplifying a system that would otherwise have to store both the username and e-mail address. And then sometimes the username is a system-assigned value over which the user has no control. This is common in employee portals to HR systems such as e-payroll sites. The username is often the employee's assigned employee ID number. Banks sometimes use customers' account numbers as their usernames.

The origin and meaning of the username is really unimportant to the purpose of *username-password authentication*. With this type of authentication, you establish a unique identity for each user. The username serves as that identity, while the password authenticates the identity as genuine. Username-password authentication is the basis for many different methods of authentication, such as form authentication, operating system authentication, and more. You likely use some form of username-password authentication most, if not all, of the times you authenticate for websites, applications, and systems.

## Basic and Digest Authentication

Basic access authentication is an HTTP authentication protocol that enables both proactive authentication requests and authentication challenge responses. When a resource protected by basic authentication receives a request lacking credentials, it responds with HTTP status code `401 Not Authorized` and the `WWW-Authenticate` header, as in the following sample response header:

```
HTTP/1.1 401 Not Authorized
Date: Sun, 25 Aug 2013 21:46:47 GMT
WWW-Authenticate: Basic realm="Multinational Widget Corp. Customer Support"
```

When the browser receives this response, it prompts the user for a username and password in a modal window containing the text from the *realm* header parameter. If the user cancels, the browser cancels the request. If the user enters a username and password, the browser re-sends the exact same request with an `Authorization` header containing the word `Basic` followed by a space and the Base64-encoded username and password separated by a colon. So if the username is "John" and the password is "green," the browser encodes "John:green" and re-sends the request as follows:

```
GET /support HTTP/1.1
Host: www.example.org
Authorization: Basic Sm9objpncmVlbg==
```

The server decodes the header and compares the username and password to the credential database stored server-side. Although the credentials are incorrect, the server keeps responding with `401 Not Authorized` and the `WWW-Authenticate` header. Assuming the credentials check out, the user is authenticated and a normal response is returned. The browser then caches the authentication and re-sends it automatically on every subsequent request to that resource or its children. Typically, this cache expires after some time of inactivity.

One of the upsides of basic authentication is that it doesn't require login pages, cookies, or HTTP session ID tokens. It can also function without a server `401` challenge response and without the user having to manipulate the `Authorization` header. Users can embed credentials directly in the request URL, and their browser or command-line client, such as Wget or cURL, converts those credentials to the Authorization header automatically. Such a URL might look like `http://John:green@www.example.org/support`.

Of course, this protocol is extremely vulnerable in many ways. First and foremost, the username and password are sent in plain text. (Base64 is only an encoding algorithm; it does not employ any hashing or encryption.) Any malicious party sniffing packets on the network can observe and capture the credentials in transit. The party can then use those credentials for nefarious purposes. Even if the party is not interested in the credentials themselves, it can simply replay the request and access the protected resources. Both these problems are serious, but become nonexistent if the requests and responses take place over HTTPS. HTTPS protects the credentials from snooping (man-in-the-middle) and prevents *replay attacks*. However, a third problem remains; the password is often stored plaintext on the server side, which is an additional vulnerability. Most modern web servers, however, provide mechanisms for storing the passwords using one-way hashes, instead.

Where HTTPS is either not an option or not wanted, server and client can still achieve some level of security using a similar protocol known as *digest access authentication*. This protocol uses the MD5 checksum algorithm to calculate a series of one-way hashes so that the password is never transmitted over the wire. In addition, two different *nonces* (a *server nonce* and a *client nonce* or *cnonce*) and a serial request number prevent replay attacks so hackers cannot simply replay the requests and view the protected resources. In response to a request without credentials, a server responds with `401 Not Authorized` and the header `WWW-Authenticate: Digest`, including the *realm* parameter and several other header parameters:

- *algorithm* indicates which technique the client should use to create the *first hash*. If unspecified, the default value is `"MD5"`, and means that the first hash is calculated as `MD5(`*username*`:`*realm*`:`*password*`)`. The other valid value is `"MD5-sess"`, meaning the first hash is calculated as `MD5(MD5(`*username*`:`*realm*`:`*password*`):`*nonce*`:`*cnonce*`)`.

- *qop* indicates the *quality of protection* and may either be `"auth"` (the default) or `"auth-int"`, or it may be `"auth,auth-int"` (in which case the client chooses which to use). If the client chooses `"auth"`, the *second hash* is calculated as `MD5(requestMethod:requestUri)`. If the client chooses `"auth-int"`, the second hash is calculated as `MD5(requestMethod:requestUri:MD5(requestBody))`. The `"auth-int"` option applies only to requests that include a request body (`POST`, `PUT`, and so on), so servers usually ask for `"auth,auth-int"` and clients respond with `"auth-int"` for requests with bodies and `"auth"` for requests without.
- *opaque* is a required parameter of random string data. It must be hexadecimal or Base64-encoded. The client must return the *opaque* parameter value untouched. It has no special meaning and it provides no instructions; it's just a sanity check.
- *nonce* contains the server nonce. It must be random and guaranteed to never repeat for any two `401 Not Authorized` responses. The client must return the *nonce* parameter value untouched. Because the server sends a `401 Not Authorized` response only until the client authenticates, the client sends the same server nonce for every request—the most recent server nonce.

> **NOTE** *A nonce is a special token used to prevent replay attacks. Every time a client makes a request to a server it generates a random token and includes that token in the request. The server stores nonce tokens to ensure that no two requests use the same nonce. Often, nonces are paired with timestamps so that the server doesn't have to store nonces forever—nonces with timestamps older than a certain amount of time are always rejected. This requires the nonce and timestamp to be involved in the hash calculation so that an attacker can't simply change the nonce or timestamp to replay the request.*

After the client has calculated the first and second hashes, it then calculates the *final hash* or *response hash*. (Response here means response to the authentication challenge, not server response.) If *qop* is unspecified, the final hash is calculated as `MD5(firstHash:nonce:secondHash)`. If *qop* is specified, the final hash is `MD5(firstHash:nonce:nc:cnonce:qop:secondHash)` where *nc* is the client nonce counter, also called the serial request number.

The second approach is more secure, so modern servers almost always specify *qop*. When the client sends a follow-up request with credentials in response to the challenge response, it calculates all the hashes and puts the final hash in the *response* parameter of the `Authorization` header. It also includes the *qop* parameter with the chosen quality of protection, unless the server omitted that parameter.

Finally, it includes *username*, *realm*, *nonce*, *uri*, *nc*, *cnonce*, and *opaque* parameters with the expected values. (*cnonce* must be regenerated at every request, and it and *nc* must never repeat.) When the server receives the request, it recalculates all the hashes the same way the client should have, basing them on the provided parameters. (Passwords are stored hashed as `MD5(username:realm:password)`, so that hash is already calculated.) If the final hash matches the value in the *response* parameter, the client successfully authenticated.

This exchange is demonstrated in the following sample requests and responses, assuming the same username, realm, and password as before:

***REQUEST 1***

```
GET /support HTTP/1.1
Host: www.example.org
```

***RESPONSE 1***

```
HTTP/1.1 401 Not Authorized
Date: Sun, 25 Aug 2013 21:46:47 GMT
WWW-Authenticate: Digest realm="Multinational Widget Corp. Customer Support",
                         algorithm="MD5-sess", qop="auth,auth-int",
                         nonce="d41d8cd98f00b204e9800998ecf8427e",
                         opaque="66ffcd4fb3f0ceb07195b60fa7991592"
```

***REQUEST 2***

```
GET /support HTTP/1.1
Host: www.example.org
Authorization: Digest realm="Multinational Widget Corp. Customer Support",
                      username="John", qop="auth", uri="/support",
                      nc="000001"
                      nonce="d41d8cd98f00b204e9800998ecf8427e",
                      opaque="66ffcd4fb3f0ceb07195b60fa7991592",
                      cnonce="9dba9637e8635a4d912075cd6ea55530",
                      response="4b4a3883cc8d220fc105e81a9592331c"
```

***RESPONSE 2***

```
HTTP/1.1 200 OK
Date: Sun, 25 Aug 2013 21:47:10 GMT
Content-Type: text/html;charset=UTF-8
Content-Length: 11485
...
```

***REQUEST 3***

```
GET /support/ticket/list HTTP/1.1
Host: www.example.org
Authorization: Digest realm="Multinational Widget Corp. Customer Support",
                      username="John", qop="auth", uri="/support/ticket/list",
                      nc="000002"
                      nonce="d41d8cd98f00b204e9800998ecf8427e",
                      opaque="66ffcd4fb3f0ceb07195b60fa7991592",
                      cnonce="361a1ce4535219d9208b61a3f5aa9706",
                      response="456fd32109400477064cafce92090662"
```

***RESPONSE 3***

```
HTTP/1.1 200 OK
Date: Sun, 25 Aug 2013 21:49:31 GMT
Content-Type: text/html;charset=UTF-8
Content-Length: 15817
...
```

Because the *cnonce* and *nc* change every request and the server remembers their values for some time, replay attacks are prevented. Because the password is never sent across the wire and is stored in hashed format, it is kept secure. Fortunately, the server handles this process for you, so as a programmer you don't have to worry about the details. Depending on the server environment, you need only to declare that a particular resource is protected by basic or digest authentication. However, due to the most recent attacks on MD5, which rendered it largely obsolete, digest authentication is generally not something you should rely on anymore, outside of the security of HTTPS. Even over HTTPS, you should still use digest over basic when possible. Note that although all modern browsers support digest authentication, none of the most popular browsers support `auth-int` quality of protection.

## Form Authentication

HTTP form authentication is the protocol with which you are likely most familiar. Its implementation is simple: When the client attempts to access a protected resource, the server redirects the client with `302 Found`, `303 See Other`, or `307 Temporary Redirect` to a different page with a login form containing username and password fields. The user enters the username and password in the form, just as he would in a modal window with basic or digest authentication. If the credentials are incorrect, the server continues to redirect the user back to the login form, informing him that the login attempt failed. If the credentials are correct, the server sends the user back to his original destination or (if the server is not well behaved) to the application homepage. There is nothing special or important to highlight about this authentication mechanism. You probably use it every day. Like basic authentication, the credentials are sent in plaintext form across the web, so you should utilize HTTPS to protect these credentials whenever possible.

## Microsoft Windows Authentication

Like basic, digest, and form authentication, Windows authentication requires the user to provide a username and password. In fact, these credentials may be presented using basic or form authentication. In these cases, the primary difference is that the credentials are checked against a Windows domain controller instead of an internal credential database. However, these situations are still primarily basic or form authentication. *Integrated Windows Authentication* (*IWA*) uses SPNEGO, Kerberos, or NTLMSSP to capture the Windows credentials of clients on their machine and securely pass those to the server automatically without including the password in the request. When this works, the process is transparent to users. They are never prompted with a modal window or login form to provide credentials because the protocol detects the Windows credentials automatically.

However, this is only possible in certain situations. Typically, users must use Microsoft Internet Explorer. Mozilla Firefox can support NTLMSSP, but only if users go to `about:config` and configure the site address in the `network.automatic-ntlm-auth.trusted-uris` property (which contains a comma-separated list of trusted sites that may request IWA). Most Internet users are simply not technologically savvy enough to make this change, so often Firefox is not an option. Google Chrome supports IWA, but with stricter security settings that Internet Explorer defines. A site must be qualified in the Local Intranet security zone before Chrome permits IWA to proceed.

Of course, all this assumes that users connect from a Microsoft Windows machine, which today is much less likely than it was 10 years ago. Many users today are on Mac OS X or Linux machines, incapable of providing Windows domain credentials. For this reason, Integrated Windows Authentication is often deployed only for internal resources in corporate environments in which users work in uniform environments. Public sites rarely use IWA for user authentication. Also, when you cannot guarantee that all user environments are Windows machines running supported browsers, you must provide backup options such as basic or form authentication backed by the Windows domain controller.

> **NOTE** Simple and Protected GSSAPI Negotiation Mechanism (SPNEGO), Kerberos, *and* NT LAN Manager Security Support Provider (NTLMSSP) *are different and related protocols concerning protocol negotiation and challenge-response authentication. You do not use them in this book, so it is out of scope to define them further.*

## Client Certificates

*Client certificate authentication* is a different approach to certifying a user's identify. In involves no usernames or passwords, making it significantly more secure. In fact, client certificate authentication is one of the most secure authentication protocols available. As a part of the SSL protocol, client certificate authentication requires HTTPS. When you connect to a server via HTTPS, that server identifies itself with a server SSL certificate. It presents its public key, signed by a trusted certificate authority, and signs its communications with your browser using its private key. Client certificates are essentially the reverse of this.

During "registration" (the process during which users would normally create a username and password), the server tells a user's browser to generate a public/private key pair. The browser stores the private key securely on the user's machine and transmits the public key to the server. From then on, the browser presents the public key to the server for identity purposes and signs the communications to the server with the private key. The disadvantage to using this protocol is that users can't easily use a new or different computer to authenticate with your site. They must back up their public/private key pair and restore it on the other computers they want to use. However, the advantage to this is the added security: Users' credentials cannot easily be compromised. A hacker must take control of a user's computer to use his credentials.

Many highly sensitive applications requiring strong security utilize client certificate authentication. Its benefits are attractive, but it requires a higher level of technological know-how than most Internet users possess today, which also makes it one of the most rarely used web authentication protocols.

## Smart Cards and Biometrics

Two other alternatives to username-password authentication variants are *smart cards* and *biometrics*. A smart card is a special integrated circuit that a user can carry around in his pocket and plug in to his computer when he needs to authenticate. Like a government-issued ID card or magnetic employee security passcard, the smart card contains information asserting the user's identity. Presentation of this smart card serves to authenticate the holder as that user. Microsoft Internet Explorer, Mozilla Firefox, and Google Chrome all support smart cards, although with varying levels of configuration complexity.

Biometrics involves capturing the fingerprints, voiceprint, iris scan, DNA, or other biological identity from the user and requires re-presentation of this identity each time the user authenticates. Most browsers support biometrics in some fashion or another using vendor-supplied plug-ins that integrate with the biometrics hardware being used. Biometrics is an extremely complex topic that is far outside the scope of this book.

Although smart cards and biometrics are both possible solutions for web application authentication, they are more typically used for authenticating people entering buildings or signing on to corporate or government computer systems.

## Claims-Based Authentication

So far you have learned about various authentication mechanisms that you can implement directly in your application. *Claims-based authentication* is the mechanism that you get to *not* implement. With claims-based authentication, your application trusts a third-party application to authenticate users on your behalf. You neither care nor need to know how this third-party application performs the authentication process. If you have ever used Facebook to authenticate for another site, you have used claims-based authentication. Typically in claims-based authentication, when users attempt to access a protected resource in your application, you simply redirect them to the third-party application. After successful authentication, they return to your site with one or more claims asserting their identity. These claims, issued by the third-party application, are easily validated using a callback request to the application to retrieve this validation, as shown in Figure 25-1. Many different protocols, such as OAuth and SAML, implement or enable claims-based authentication mechanisms. You can also use claims for authorization purposes, something you explore more later in this section.

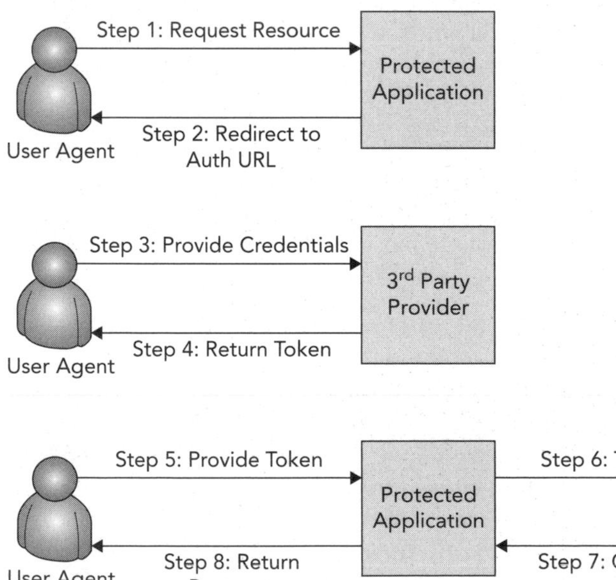


**FIGURE 25-1**

In some cases, your system communicates directly with the third-party system to exchange credentials for claims. Two common examples are Microsoft Windows's *Active Directory* domain authentication and the *Lightweight Directory Access Protocol* (*LDAP*). The direct claims-based authentication process is shown in Figure 25-2.

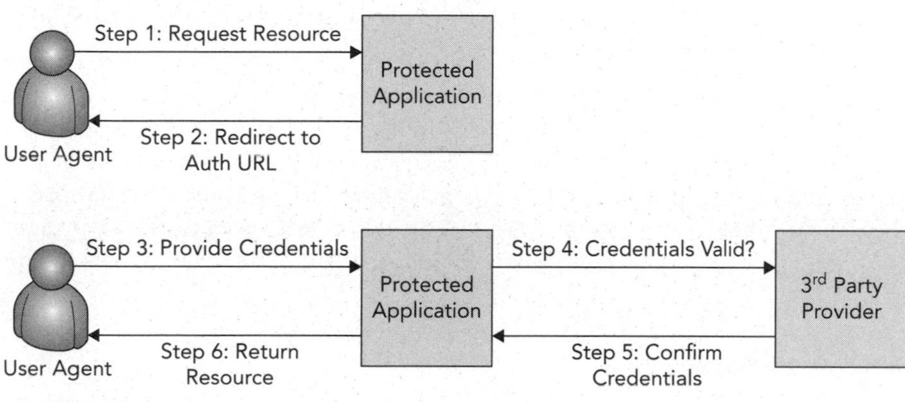


**FIGURE 25-2**

This may seem like a simpler, and therefore more desirable, approach to take, but it's not always the best option (or even an available option). Users appreciate the feeling of security that comes from accessing the same login page whenever they use their credentials for a given security service. Consider this: If a site asked you to authenticate using your Google account, would you prefer to be redirected to Google's website to log in, or would you prefer to give the potentially untrusted site your Google credentials? Your answer to this question should make it clear why the first approach is often the desired approach. Direct authentication is typically reserved for highly trusted applications, and usually only within the same organization or company that controls the authentication service.

## Multi-Factor Authentication

All the mechanisms described so far have involved only one authentication factor. With username-password authentication and its many derivatives, providing a username and password is all the user must do. For client certificate authentication, the user must simply present the correct client certificate. The same is true for biometrics, smart cards, and claims-based authentication. In all these mechanisms, only the single step is required to successfully authenticate a user. Today, many web applications require or can require *multi-factor authentication* (*MFA*). Gmail, Twitter, Facebook, Amazon.com, WordPress, and many others all provide options for users to enable multi-factor authentication.

Multi-factor authentication requires a user to perform two or more steps to assert his identity. This may include, for example, presenting a client certificate *and* a username and password. More commonly, after submitting a username and password, many sites send a text message to the user's known phone number containing a special code that the user must enter into the web application before proceeding.

More secure solutions include devices such as keychain dongles with simple LCD screens or smartphone apps that display a secure six- to nine-digit code, which rotates using a secure random generator every 30 to 60 seconds. These dongles contain a highly accurate clock and a factory-installed random seed, enabling the server that knows the random seed to predict the number being displayed at any given moment. The smartphone apps communicate securely with a token server to coordinate the display of the correct token. When users enter their normal credentials (username and password, certificate, and so on), they are challenged to enter the number displayed on their dongle or in their smartphone app.

Although the concept of multi-factor authentication is simple, its security advantages are significant and should be fairly obvious by this point. It is extremely unlikely that an attacker could both provide credentials and receive a text message sent to a user or view the numbers on a user's dongle or smartphone app simultaneously. All these examples have included only two factors of authentication. Add in a third or fourth and the level of security increases even further. For these reasons, multi-factor authentication is becoming more popular every day, and you can expect this trend to continue.

# Understanding Authorization

After users have been authenticated—by one of these methods or some other method—you can check their authorization to perform certain actions in the system. Even the simplest systems usually have at least two different types of users: low-privilege users and administrators. These two levels of access are different types of authorization. Users who are authorized to administer the application see additional menu items and can perform more tasks than users who aren't authorized to administer the application. However, an authorization system does not require that access levels create a hierarchy of some type, where each level is more powerful than the next. More typical applications require many different authorizations, and some of them may have equal "power" but for different tasks.

A great example of this is a forum system. Consider a website with two different forums: a product forum and an art forum. User A may be authorized to moderate the topics in the product forum, whereas User B is authorized to moderate the topics in the art forum. Both users have equal "power" as moderators, but they are authorized to moderate different forums.

Similarly, in a very large application, you may have different administrator-like authorizations. For example, some employees can administer users, whereas others manage product listings and still others oversee news articles. All these employees have the same "power" over their respective areas, but the authorizations differ so that they cannot manage each other's systems.

## Using Principals and Identities

The first step to establishing a user's authorization is to represent that user in some standard form. Although you may create this in whatever form you like, in Java the convention is to implement `java.security.Principal`. At a minimum, a `Principal` should hold the identity of a user. Remember, the identity is what you authenticate. You confirm the user is who she claims to be, so that identity should be stored in the `Principal`. An identity could simply be a username, or it could be lots of other information, such as legal name, birth date, address, and phone number. Any code in your system can then know by the presence of the `Principal` in the security context that the identity it contains has been authenticated. So what else is the `Principal` useful for?

In addition to storing the identity, a `Principal` can also store information about which actions the user is authorized to take. With this information, any code in the application can access the security context, obtain the current `Principal`, and determine whether the user is authorized to do what he is attempting. You have many ways to represent this information; you learn about some standard techniques next. More important, you should make the representations immutable, constant objects, such as enum constants or interned `Strings`. Otherwise, a `Principal` with many authorizations can have a significant memory footprint, which is not good for performance.

## Roles, Groups, Activities, and Permissions

Choosing a method for representing authorization privileges is largely a matter of personal preference, but there are advantages and disadvantages of most techniques. No matter how you handle authorization, your goal essentially boils down to this: You need to establish whether a user has permission to do what he's asking to do. On the surface, it sounds rather simple. But it's a task that should be well thought-out and well planned because when you go down a particular road in a large application, it is very difficult to back out.

One of the most common and well-known approaches is to assign all your users to roles. For example, in a forum system you can create Poster, Moderator, and Administrator roles. Posters can post messages and replies; moderators can do these things and delete messages and replies; and administrators can do everything moderators can in addition to deleting and banning users and managing moderators. The advantages to this approach should be fairly obvious: With a simple radio button, you can indicate whether a user is a poster, moderator, or administrator, making the management of permissions straightforward. However, with this approach you end up with code that looks like this:

```
public void deleteMessage(long id)
{
    if(security.userInRole("moderator"))
    {
        ...
    }
}

public void deleteReply(long id)
{
    if(security.userInRole("moderator"))
    {
        ...
    }
}
```

What happens when you decide you want to have different moderators for messages and replies? You have to alter, recompile, retest, and redeploy your application. Planning for such a change is really as simple as making permissions as granular as possible. The best way to approach this is to think of which activities your users will undertake. In the forum example, these are the activities you might expect to see:

- Creating a post
- Creating a reply
- Editing your post
- Editing your reply
- Deleting your post
- Deleting your reply
- Deleting someone else's post
- Deleting someone else's reply
- Temporarily banning a user
- Permanently banning a user
- Deleting users
- Assigning user permissions

With this set of activities, checking a user's authorization isn't much different from the previous example:

```
public void deleteMessage(long id)
{
    if(security.userHasActivity("DELETE_OTHER_MESSAGE") ||
        isOwnMessage() && security.userHasActivity("DELETE_OWN_MESSAGE"))
    {
        ...
    }
}

public void deleteReply(long id)
{
    if(security.userHasActivity("DELETE_OTHER_REPLY") ||
        isOwnReply() && security.userHasActivity("DELETE_OWN_REPLY"))
    {
        ...
    }
}
```

Perhaps the easiest way to determine which activities you need is to simply look at the methods in your services. Odds are you need one activity per method. The method name is usually an indicator as to what the activity is. Some methods, such as those in the previous code, may need two activities. In this case, deleting one's own message is a different activity from deleting another user's message.

Although this granularity reduces the chances of your application requiring recompilation, it also increases the effort required to manage user permissions. When editing a user you must choose one or more permissions from a list of many permissions. In a very large system with hundreds of activities, this list quickly becomes hard to manage for every user. It is not strictly necessary, but you could employ the concept of user groups, where the users in a group inherit the ability to perform all the activities that the group can perform. You can easily change the activities that many users can perform by simply changing the group to which they belong. If you find that a particular user or users need different permissions, you just move them to a different group. This is nearly identical to the concept of roles, except that groups can be dynamically created and changed at run time instead of requiring a code change.

> **NOTE** *Okay. Roles? Permissions? Groups? What's the difference, really? Who decides what these are called? In this book these terms simply differentiate several conventions. You can call them whatever you want internally. It doesn't matter whether you name them roles or groups; it only matters how you use them.*

One way to define groups is to make them `Principals`. With an abstract `Principal` implementation designed so that it holds activity permissions, you can then extend that `Principal` to form your user and group `Principals`. The user `Principal` can then have a group `Principal` as an object property (or perhaps a list of group `Principals`, depending on your needs). This is just one example, and there are many different ways to approach it.

### Claims-Based Authorization

Earlier in this section, you explored the concept of claims-based authentication. Claims-based authorization is the complement to this concept. In claims-based authorization, the user's identity claim includes the activities for which the user has permission. One example of such a system is Microsoft's Active Directory. When you authenticate on a machine using your Windows domain credentials, the domain controller gives that machine your identity claim (username, real name, e-mail address, and other information attached to your domain user) and your authorization claims (the domain permissions assigned to you). The domain groups you belong to are part of your identity claim, and thus you inherit the permissions assigned to those groups as well. This is a combination claims-based authentication and authorization system.

If you choose claims-based authentication, you may, but do not have to, use claims-based authorization. Often the third-party system with which you authenticate your users has no knowledge of your application, so any claimed authorizations it could present are useless to your application. In these cases, you have an extra step to take after a user's identity claim is returned from the authentication system: You must locate the permissions within your own system that are assigned to the identity from the authentication system.

## WHY SPRING SECURITY?

For the rest of this book, you learn how to integrate security into your applications using Spring Security. Although many Java security frameworks are available, Spring Security is perhaps the most popular for web applications and, being a Spring project, integrates seamlessly with Spring Framework. Note that just as a full Java EE application server can provide IoC, dependency injection, and persistence provider services, it can also provide a full security framework. However, as with Part II and III, this part focuses on an alternative to container security for those applications unable or unwilling to use container security.

## Understanding the Spring Security Foundation

Spring Security provides authentication and authorization services. You can configure it to completely handle these services for you automatically, or you can provide code to perform key operations to customize its behavior. In addition to using JDBC or one of your services or repositories to authenticate users, Spring Security comes with built-in systems to authenticate and (if wanted) authorize using Microsoft's Active Directory, Jasig's Central Authentication Service (CAS), *Java Authentication and Authorization Service* or *JAAS* (a *Pluggable Authentication Module*, or *PAM*, implementation), LDAP, and *OpenID*, all of which are claims-based services. With Spring Security, you can secure web-based and client-side applications; however, it is certainly designed for web applications and requires additional effort to use in client-side applications.

The central interface around which Spring Security revolves is `org.springframework.security.core.Authentication`. It extends `Principal` to provide some additional information about an identity. For example, the `getIdentity` method returns an `Object` that represents the identity of the `Principal`. This object is commonly a username (a `String`, and therefore often the same value returned by `getName`) but can also be some other object, such as an `X509` identity representation or e-mail address object. `getCredentials` returns the credentials that supposedly prove the identity is genuine. This property is generally used only during the authentication process and then erased when authentication is complete. In the common case, the `Object` it holds is a password (also a `String`). `isAuthenticated` indicates whether the principal is authenticated (and, thus, its identity has been proven sufficiently), whereas `setAuthenticated` is the mechanism for changing this indicator. This is also typically used only during the authentication process.

`Authentication` also provides the user's `org.springframework.security.core.GrantedAuthority`s by way of the `getAuthorities` method. A `GrantedAuthority` could be a role, if you use role-based authorization, or an activity permission, if you use activity-based authorization. Because it's not the name that matters, only how you use it, `GrantedAuthority` can serve both purposes.

When you authenticate against a service like LDAP or Active Directory, Spring Security automatically fills the `Authentication`'s authorities with the directory groups to which the user belongs. In this case, the groups are actually acting like roles in role-based authentication. You can customize this behavior by writing a little more code to replace these groups with your local permission sets or with the permissions assigned to those groups, thereby turning it into activity-based authorization.

The final core interface that you will always use is `org.springframework.security.authentication.AuthenticationProvider`. As the name implies, this is the provider of authentication services in your application. Its `authenticate` method accepts an unauthenticated `Authentication` containing the credentials to prove the identity, and then it can either mark the `Authentication` as authenticated and return the same object, return a completely different `Authentication` instance representing the authenticated principal, or throw an `org.springframework.security.core.AuthenticationException` if authentication fails. Spring

Security comes with `AuthenticationProvider` implementations for Active Directory, CAS, JAAS, LDAP, OpenID, JDBC (using a table schema that you configure), and more. You can also provide your own implementation for more customized authentication behavior.

## Using Spring Security's Authorization Services

You have a few different ways to use authorization in Spring Security, and they are not mutually exclusive. One approach is to use global method security annotations. This is perhaps one of the best approaches because it can enforce security within your services instead of within your UI—particularly important if you have multiple user interfaces that utilize the same services. You simply annotate your service methods with one of several different security-related annotations, and Spring Security ensures the current `Authentication` has the proper `GrantedAuthority`(s) to execute the method. You learn more about which annotations you can use and how to use them in the upcoming chapters.

Another option is to define method interception rules within the Spring Security configuration. These rules are similar to Aspect Oriented Programming join points. As with the security annotations, you can define rules that intercept your service methods, making this another attractive option for protecting your code with authorization rules. Depending on the complexity of your application, you might find it easier to set up method interception rules than annotations. In addition, if you use XML configuration, you can change method interception rules without recompiling (which may or may not be something you want). You cannot achieve this using annotations.

Your final option is to define URL interception rules. This is sometimes the simplest approach, but it has several disadvantages. First, you can apply it only to web applications and not to other types of applications. Also, if you have multiple web user interfaces (for example, web, REST, and SOAP), you must define the interception rules for every user interface. It's easy to define these rules inconsistently, which can lead to authorization vulnerabilities. In almost all cases, you want to secure your services using either annotations or configured rules, binding all existing and future user interfaces to these security requirements. Even if you use method security, you usually want to define a handful of URL security rules surrounding your login and logout screens. In the following chapters you explore all these options.

# Configuring Spring Security

To be clear, you must use Spring Framework to utilize Spring Security. Spring Security's configuration is closely tied to Spring Framework's configuration, and it makes heavy use of the `ApplicationContexts` to manage its security contexts.

When setting up Spring Security, you can use an XML, Java, or hybrid configuration. Java configuration is new to Spring Security 3.2. In some ways, it is similar to Spring Framework's Java configuration, but it also has many key differences. One important difference is you don't have many configuration-related annotations (there are only two). Instead, your `@Configuration` classes implement configuration interfaces with methods that are called to set up your security context programmatically. This is because although Spring Framework has only one configuration per application context, Spring Security can have multiple configurations per application context.

For example, in a Web MVC context you can have one, two, or a dozen different security contexts based on URLs within that context. Each context requires a separate configuration, so you define methods within your `@Configuration` classes that use Spring Security configuration classes to add each security context you need to define. You explore this in more detail in the following chapters. More important, because the Java configuration is considerably more verbose than the Spring Framework Java configuration, you see each configuration using both XML and Java.

## SUMMARY

In this short introductory chapter, you learned about the differences between authentication and authorization and came to understand why you need both for effective security. You explored the many different approaches you can take for authentication and authorization, such as username and password authentication, basic and digest authentication, form authentication, role-based authorization, and activity-based authorization. Finally, you were introduced to Spring Security, the authentication and authorization framework you use for the remainder of this book. You learned about its `Authentication`, `GrantedAuthority`, and `AuthenticationProvider` interfaces and how they form the foundation for Spring Security's operation. You also took a quick look at the different ways you can use Spring Security's authorization services and configure Spring Security within your Spring Framework applications.

In the next chapter you create your first Spring Security-enabled application and learn how to authenticate your users to meet your various needs.

# 26

# Authenticating Users with Spring Security

## IN THIS CHAPTER

- Adding Spring Security Authentication to your application
- Using Form Login, JDBC, LDAP, and OpenID
- Protecting against session fixation and limiting user sessions
- Remembering users between sessions
- Creating a custom authentication provider
- Mitigating cross-site request forgery attacks

## WROX.COM CODE DOWNLOADS FOR THIS CHAPTER

You can find the `wrox.com` code downloads for this chapter at `http://www.wrox.com/go/projavaforwebapps` on the Download Code tab. The code for this chapter is divided into the following major examples:

- Authentication-App Project
- Customer-Support-v19 Project

## NEW MAVEN DEPENDENCIES FOR THIS CHAPTER

In addition to the Maven dependencies introduced in previous chapters, you also need the following Maven dependencies:

```
<dependency>
    <groupId>org.springframework.security</groupId>
    <artifactId>spring-security-web</artifactId>
    <version>3.2.0.RELEASE</version>
```

```
        <scope>compile</scope>
    </dependency>

    <dependency>
        <groupId>org.springframework.security</groupId>
        <artifactId>spring-security-config</artifactId>
        <version>3.2.0.RELEASE</version>
        <scope>compile</scope>
    </dependency>

    <dependency>
        <groupId>org.springframework.security</groupId>
        <artifactId>spring-security-crypto</artifactId>
        <version>3.2.0.RELEASE</version>
        <scope>compile</scope>
    </dependency>
```

You no longer need the following dependency because Spring Security includes a BCrypt implementation in its distribution.

```
    <dependency>
        <groupId>org.mindrot</groupId>
        <artifactId>jbcrypt</artifactId>
        <version>0.3m</version>
    </dependency>
```

# CHOOSING AND CONFIGURING AN AUTHENTICATION PROVIDER

One of the first things you must do is choose which mechanism to use to authenticate your users. As you saw in the previous chapter, Spring Security has many built-in `AuthenticationProvider` implementations that support several different mechanisms. You can also create your own implementation, making the possibilities limitless. After you choose a mechanism, you simply need to configure it and set up your security context. In this section, you explore the various built-in providers and configuration of Spring Security authentication. In the next section, you create your own `AuthenticationProvider` implementation to perform more customized authentication steps.

> **NOTE** *If you have not read Chapter 5 and you are unfamiliar with the concepts of* `HttpSessions`*, session identifiers, or session fixation attacks and other session vulnerabilities, it is strongly recommended that you go back and read Chapter 5 before continuing. There are concepts mentioned in this chapter that you may not understand otherwise.*

## Configuring a User Details Provider

One of the simplest `AuthenticationProvider` implementations you can use is the `org.springframework.security.authentication.dao.DaoAuthenticationProvider`. The core concept of this provider is that it uses a *Data Access Object*, in the form of an `org.springframework.security.core.userdetails.UserDetailsService` implementation, to retrieve `org.springframework.security.core.userdetails.UserDetails` objects by username.

The `UserDetails` object contains information about a user, such as the username and password, the `GrantedAuthoritys`, and whether the user is enabled, expired, and locked out. These objects working together form a generic authentication provider. Instead of worrying about the details of authenticating a user, you simply provide a mechanism for retrieving details about your users, allowing Spring Security to manage the authentication process. Of course, you can also choose from various default `UserDetailsService` implementations.

The easiest way to get started with the `DaoAuthenticationProvider` is to employ the `org.springframework.security.provisioning.InMemoryUserDetailsManager`. This simple implementation is not intended for production use, but it's perfect for simple test applications and demonstrations—such as the Authentication-App project available for download from the `wrox.com` code download site.

There's a key difference in how you configure Spring Security versus how you configure Spring Framework. Spring Security operates through a series of `Filter` implementations that handle the various implementation details behind the scenes. This is necessary to ensure that all requests to your application are properly intercepted and secured as appropriate. Because of this, you do not configure Spring Security in your separate `DispatcherServlet` application contexts. Instead, you always configure it in your root application context, even if you intend to secure your different `DispatcherServlet` application contexts with different security principles. Configuring Spring Security consists of two key steps: registering the filters and setting up the security rules.

## Setting Up the Spring Security Filters

For registering the filters using a Java configuration, Spring Security comes with an abstract `WebApplicationInitializer` implementation that takes care of this for you. Remember, `WebApplicationInitializer` is the Spring Framework interface that it uses to initialize Servlet 3.0 and newer applications. Spring's `ServletContainerInitializer` implementation discovers all `WebApplicationInitializer` implementations and initializes them. In previous chapters, you created a `Bootstrap` class that implemented `WebApplicationInitializer` to register all your Spring Framework listeners and Servlets.

When using Spring Security's Java configuration, all you have to do is extend `org.springframework.security.web.context.AbstractSecurityWebApplicationInitializer`. It takes care of registering all the proper security-related filters. However, you must be careful to order all the filters in your application appropriately. The filters in your application must execute in the following order:

- Filters that handle logging of nearly any type, such as logging requests or adding fish tags to the Log4j 2 `ThreadContext`
- All Spring Security filters
- Filters that handle security-sensitive logging, such as adding the current user to the Log4j 2 `ThreadContext`
- Filters that handle multitenancy decisions (In a multitenant application, you need to determine which tenant a request belongs to as early as possible.)
- All other filters in their appropriate orders

In the simple Authentication-App project, you aren't using any filters, so you don't have to worry about ordering just yet. You look at that in the next section. For now, just create a `SecurityBootstrap` class that extends `AbstractSecurityWebApplicationInitializer`.

```
public class SecurityBootstrap extends AbstractSecurityWebApplicationInitializer
{
}
```

Notice that the class doesn't have any fields or methods; that's because it doesn't need any. This is enough to register Spring Security's filters. It also sets the session tracking mode to cookies only. If you choose a different way of tracking sessions (URLs or SSL session IDs), you need to override the `getSessionTrackingModes` method to indicate this:

```
public class SecurityBootstrap extends AbstractSecurityWebApplicationInitializer
{
    @Override
    protected Set<SessionTrackingMode> getSessionTrackingModes()
    {
        return EnumSet.of(SessionTrackingMode.SSL);
    }
}
```

However, using session cookies is the simplest solution and works fine for this purpose, so accepting the default is all you need to do. If you aren't using Java configuration, simply add Spring Security's `DelegatingFilterProxy` to your deployment descriptor. This class is a filter proxy that wraps around all Spring Security's filters and orders them internally.

```
<filter>
    <filter-name>springSecurityFilterChain</filter-name>
    <filter-class>
        org.springframework.web.filter.DelegatingFilterProxy
    </filter-class>
</filter>

<filter-mapping>
    <filter-name>springSecurityFilterChain</filter-name>
    <url-pattern>/*</url-pattern>
    <dispatcher>ERROR</dispatcher>
    <dispatcher>REQUEST</dispatcher>
</filter-mapping>
```

Remember, if you choose to go this route, the `DelegatingFilterProxy` must still appear in the order previously mentioned, where the Spring Security filters belong. If you are programmatically registering filters anywhere else, you probably need to stick to extending `AbstractSecurityWebApplicationInitializer`.

## Configuring the Login Mechanism and Protected URLs

Now that the Spring Security filters have been registered, you can proceed with configuring Spring Security for your application. Placing this in the root application context would normally involve adding more code to the `RootContextConfiguration` you created and have used since Part II. However, that class is getting a little crowded, and the security configuration could eventually get quite large, so an alternative and attractive approach is to create a new configuration class and import it from the `RootContextConfiguration`.

```
...
@ComponentScan(
        basePackages = "com.wrox.site",
        excludeFilters =
        @ComponentScan.Filter({Controller.class, ControllerAdvice.class})
)
@Import({ SecurityConfiguration.class })
public class RootContextConfiguration implements
        AsyncConfigurer, SchedulingConfigurer, TransactionManagementConfigurer
{
    ...
}

@Configuration
@EnableWebMvcSecurity
public class SecurityConfiguration extends WebSecurityConfigurerAdapter
{
    @Override
    protected void configure(AuthenticationManagerBuilder builder)
            throws Exception
    {
        builder
                .inMemoryAuthentication()
                        .withUser("John")
                        .password("password")
                        .authorities("USER")
                    .and()
                        .withUser("Margaret")
                        .password("green")
                        .authorities("USER", "ADMIN");
    }

    @Override
    public void configure(WebSecurity security)
    {
        security.ignoring().antMatchers("/resource/**");
    }

    @Override
    protected void configure(HttpSecurity security) throws Exception
    {
        security
                .authorizeRequests()
                    .antMatchers("/signup", "/about", "/policies").permitAll()
                    .antMatchers("/secure/**").hasAuthority("USER")
                    .antMatchers("/admin/**").hasAuthority("ADMIN")
                    .anyRequest().authenticated()
                .and().formLogin()
                    .loginPage("/login").failureUrl("/login?error")
                    .defaultSuccessUrl("/secure/")
                    .usernameParameter("username")
                    .passwordParameter("password")
```

```
                    .permitAll()
                .and().logout()
                    .logoutUrl("/logout").logoutSuccessUrl("/login?loggedOut")
                    .invalidateHttpSession(true).deleteCookies("JSESSIONID")
                    .permitAll()
                .and().csrf().disable();
    }
}
```

A lot is going on in this code, so let's take it apart and examine it piece by piece.

There are two annotations that you should know about here that are very similar: `@org.springframework.security.config.annotation.web.configuration.EnableWebSecurity` and `@org.springframework.security.config.annotation.web.servlet.configuration.EnableWebMvcSecurity`. The first annotation enables Spring Security web authentication and authorization features. The second annotation additionally enables integration with Spring Web MVC controllers. Unless you aren't using Spring Web MVC, you should always use `@EnableWebMvcSecurity`. Any time you annotate a `@Configuration` class with `@EnableWebSecurity` or `@EnableWebMvcSecurity`, that class must either implement `org.springframework.security.config.annotation.web.WebSecurityConfigurer` or extend `org.springframework.security.config.annotation.web.configuration.WebSecurityConfigurerAdapter`. Extending `WebSecurityConfigurerAdapter` is a much simpler approach, and there's no reason you should ever need to do otherwise.

The `configure(AuthenticationManagerBuilder)` method sets up the `AuthenticationProvider` that you should use for authenticating users. You don't have to actually use the `InMemoryUserDetailsManager` directly to use an in-memory user database. Both the Java and XML configuration options provide shortcuts for configuring the `InMemoryUserDetailsManager`. In this method, you create two default users in memory and assign the appropriate `GrantedAuthority`s. Yes, this is an authorization detail, but sometimes it's hard to keep these details from spilling over.

> **NOTE** *You probably noticed that the* `configure(AuthenticationManagerBuilder)` *method refers to an authentication* manager, *whereas the book has been referring to an authentication* provider. *Technically, Spring Security's authentication power resides within an* `org.springframework.security.authentication.AuthenticationManager` *implementation. Although you* could *technically implement this interface, you never should. The default and only implementation,* `org.springframework.security.authentication.ProviderManager`, *delegates to one or more* `AuthenticationProvider` *implementations. This enables you to have multiple ways to authenticate users. Later in this section, you look at an example of this: "remember me" authentication.*

The `configure(WebSecurity)` method is fairly simple. In this case, all it does is keep Spring Security from evaluating access to resources (JavaScript, style sheets, images, and so on) for security concerns. `configure(HttpSecurity)` does most of the hard work. First, it defines several URL patterns and how they are protected. Again, this is an authorization detail, but it's necessary to set up some minimal level of authorization to make Spring Security require users to log in.

The `permitAll` invocation instructs Spring Security to allow all access to the `/signup`, `/about`, and `/policies` URLs. Everything under the `/secure/` URL requires the user to have the `USER` permissions, whereas access to `/admin/` and everything under it requires the `ADMIN` permission. Any other request simply requires authentication, regardless of permissions.

Next, calling `formLogin` begins the process of configuring username and password authentication by way of a login form. It sets up the URL where the login form should reside; the URL where users go when authentication fails; and the name of the request parameters for the username and password in the submitted login form. Finally, calling `logout` configures the URL that should trigger a logout and the URL to send the user to after they have logged out. The `permitAll` invocations in these two places ensure that users can access the login and logout URLs without first authenticating (for obvious reasons). *Cross-Site Request Forgery* (*CSRF*) protection is enabled in Java configuration by default. (It is disabled in XML configuration by default.) CSRF protection is a complex topic covered in the next section, so it's disabled for now using the call to `csrf` followed by the call to `disable`.

> **NOTE** *You probably wondered about the difference between ignoring URLs in* `configure(WebSecurity)` *and permitting all access to URLs in* `configure(HttpSecurity)`. *Ignoring URLs makes those URLs skip most of Spring Security's internal filters. This is important because you want access to static resources to be as fast as possible, and skipping the Spring Security internal filters ensures this speed. Permitting all access to URLs still sends requests to those URLs through the Spring Security internal filters, which adds necessary overhead for secured URLs.*

The available options when configuring these settings are too numerous to list them all. The API documentation at `http://docs.spring.io/spring-security/site/docs/3.2.x/apidocs/` is your friend, and you should reference it often. The process that Spring Security follows here is fairly simple. If Spring Security detects users attempting to access a secured URL, it redirects them to the configured login URL.

You must supply the view that implements the login form and ensure that it submits using `POST` to the same URL. However, you do not have to implement the code that handles the submitted form. When Spring Security detects a `POST` to the configured URL, it extracts the username and password using the configured parameters, finds a configured `AuthenticationProvider` that supports authentication using an `org.springframework.security.authentication.UsernamePasswordAuthenticationToken` (in this case, that provider is the `DaoAuthenticationProvider` with the `InMemoryUserDetailsManager`), and authenticates the user with that provider. If authentication fails, Spring Security redirects the user to the failure URL. If authentication succeeds, it sends the user to the original intended URL (or the default URL if users came straight to the login screen).

Finally, if Spring Security detects a request to the configured logout URL, it clears the authentication, invalidates the `HttpSession`, deletes the session cookie, and redirects the user to the configured success URL.

As you can see here, the Spring Security Java configuration uses a fluent API, which is in stark contrast to the Spring Framework Java configuration. This is by necessity, not just by design. It makes configuring the various (and sometimes duplicate) components of security fairly simple, and your IDE's code hinting can help you figure out what your options are for each component. However, not everyone likes fluent APIs, and some developers prefer to take a different approach. The following XML configuration is identical to the Java configuration in the Authentication-App. You could import it from your `RootContextConfiguration` using `@ImportResource` instead of `@Import`.

```
<?xml version="1.0" encoding="UTF-8"?>
<beans:beans xmlns="http://www.springframework.org/schema/security"
             xmlns:beans="http://www.springframework.org/schema/beans"
             xmlns:xsi="http://www.w3.org/2001/XMLSchema-instance"
             xsi:schemaLocation="http://www.springframework.org/schema/security
         http://www.springframework.org/schema/security/spring-security-3.2.xsd
         http://www.springframework.org/schema/beans
         http://www.springframework.org/schema/beans/spring-beans-4.0.xsd">

    <authentication-manager>
        <authentication-provider>
            <user-service>
                <user name="John" authorities="USER" password="password" />
                <user name="Margaret" authorities="USER,ADMIN" password="green" />
            </user-service>
        </authentication-provider>
    </authentication-manager>

    <http security="none" pattern="/resource/**" />

    <http use-expressions="true">
        <intercept-url pattern="/signup" access="permitAll" />
        <intercept-url pattern="/about" access="permitAll" />
        <intercept-url pattern="/policies" access="permitAll" />
        <intercept-url pattern="/login" access="permitAll" />
        <intercept-url pattern="/logout" access="permitAll" />
        <intercept-url pattern="/secure/**" access="hasAuthority('USER')" />
        <intercept-url pattern="/admin/**" access="hasAuthority('ADMIN')" />
        <form-login login-page="/login"
                    login-processing-url="/login"
                    authentication-failure-url="/login?error"
                    default-target-url="/secure/"
                    username-parameter="username"
                    password-parameter="password" />
        <logout logout-url="/logout"
                logout-success-url="/login?loggedOut"
                invalidate-session="true"
                delete-cookies="JSESSIONID" />
    </http>

</beans:beans>
```

## Setting Up Session Fixation Protection

You should be familiar with the problem with HTTP session fixation attacks and how they can leave your users vulnerable to having their accounts on your site compromised. In Chapter 5 you explored ways to mitigate these attacks. Thankfully, Spring Security comes with built-in utilities to mitigate these attacks as well. Prior to Servlet 3.1, developers had to resort to creating new sessions, copying the data from one session to the next, and then invalidating the old session. Spring Security made this task very easy—just a simple configuration switch controlled the behavior. By default, session fixation protection is enabled in Spring Security because session fixation attacks are a major problem in web applications. Servlet 3.1 added the `changeSessionId` method to `HttpServletRequest` to make session fixation protection vastly simpler, and Spring Security 3.2 includes support for this method. You can fine-tune this process in your configuration.

```
@Configuration
@EnableWebMvcSecurity
public class SecurityConfiguration extends WebSecurityConfigurerAdapter
{
    ...
    @Override
    protected void configure(HttpSecurity security) throws Exception
    {
        ...
                .invalidateHttpSession(true).deleteCookies("JSESSIONID")
                .permitAll()
            .and().sessionManagement()
                .sessionFixation().changeSessionId()
            .and().csrf().disable();
    }
    ...
}
```

The previous code retrieves the session management configuration and instructs Spring Security to use the Servlet 3.1 `changeSessionId` method for protecting against session fixation attacks. To be clear, this isn't actually necessary. By default, Spring Security uses the `changeSessionId` mechanism for applications running on Servlet 3.1 containers and newer. You can also select

- `newSession`, which creates a new session without copying existing session attributes.
- `migrateSession`, which creates a new session and copies all existing attributes.
- `none`, which disables session fixation protection.

`migrateSession` is the default when your application runs in a Servlet 3.0 or older container. Configuring session fixation protection in XML is just as easy:

```
<http use-expressions="true">
    ...
    <session-management session-fixation-protection="migrateSession" />
</http>
```

## Limiting the Number of User Sessions

Sometimes it's desirable to limit the number of sessions a single user can hold at once. This prevents them from using your site from multiple computers, browsers, or locations at once, and is typically used as a security feature to ensure that only one person uses a given set of credentials. Using the session management configuration, you can restrict the number of simultaneous sessions. The following Java and XML configurations enable this feature.

```
@Configuration
@EnableWebMvcSecurity
public class SecurityConfiguration extends WebSecurityConfigurerAdapter
{
    ...
    @Override
    protected void configure(HttpSecurity security) throws Exception
    {
        ...
                    .invalidateHttpSession(true).deleteCookies("JSESSIONID")
                    .permitAll()
                .and().sessionManagement()
                    .sessionFixation().changeSessionId()
                    .maximumSessions(1).expiredUrl("/login?maxSessions")
                .and().and().csrf().disable();
    }
    ...
}

    <http use-expressions="true">
        ...
        <session-management session-fixation-protection="changeSessionId">
            <concurrency-control max-sessions="1"
                                 expired-url="/login?maxSessions" />
        </session-management>
    </http>
```

When configured with a maximum number of sessions, the default behavior is to expire an existing session if a user logs in again. In this case, when the holder of the original session attempts to access that session again, they will be redirected to `/login?maxSessions`. This isn't always the desired behavior. Instead, you can instruct Spring Security to prevent the second login and return an unauthorized response, allowing the original session to continue unabated.

```
@Configuration
@EnableWebMvcSecurity
public class SecurityConfiguration extends WebSecurityConfigurerAdapter
{
    ...
    @Override
    protected void configure(HttpSecurity security) throws Exception
    {
        ...
                    .invalidateHttpSession(true).deleteCookies("JSESSIONID")
                    .permitAll()
                .and().sessionManagement()
                    .sessionFixation().changeSessionId()
                    .maximumSessions(1).maxSessionsPreventsLogin(true)
                .and().and().csrf().disable();
    }
    ...
}

    <http use-expressions="true">
        ...
```

```
        <session-management session-fixation-protection="changeSessionId">
            <concurrency-control max-sessions="1"
                                 error-if-maximum-exceeded="true" />
        </session-management>
    </http>
```

Note that the configuration option for this behavior has a different name in the new Java configuration than it has in the XML configuration. Of course, you can enable session concurrency control without changing the default session fixation protection. Just leave off the `sessionFixation().option()` code or the `session-fixation-protection` XML attribute.

To enable concurrency control, you must also configure a special Spring Security listener that publishes `HttpSession`-related events. This allows Spring Security to build a session registry that it can use to detect concurrent sessions. The simplest way to enable this listener is to override the `enableHttpSessionEventPublisher` method in your `SecurityBootstrap` class.

```
public class SecurityBootstrap extends AbstractSecurityWebApplicationInitializer
{
    @Override
    protected boolean enableHttpSessionEventPublisher()
    {
        return true;
    }
}
```

If you use an XML configuration instead, you can just manually add the listener to your deployment descriptor.

```
    <listener>
        <listener-class>
            org.springframework.security.web.session.HttpSessionEventPublisher
        </listener-class>
    </listener>
```

Whichever approach you take to configure this listener, if you deploy your application in a clustered environment, you must take care to properly synchronize sessions among all the nodes in your cluster. Otherwise, the listener will not be aware of all the sessions and it will not properly limit the number of sessions a user can hold.

The Authentication-App contains a basic controller that responds to the simple URLs that Spring Security is protecting. The details of this controller are unimportant and contain nothing that you aren't already used to. To test it out, simply follow these steps:

1. Compile the project and start Tomcat from your IDE.
2. Go to `http://localhost:8080/authentication/about`, `http://localhost:8080/authentication/signup`, and `http://localhost:8080/authentication/policies`. You can access these pages without logging in.
3. Now go to `http://localhost:8080/authentication/secure/` or any URL under it, and Spring Security asks you to log in. Enter in bad credentials and Spring Security returns you to the login screen and tells you the login failed.
4. Enter in correct credentials and you should be granted access.

5. Click the Log Out link to log out and then log in with a different set of credentials. Logged in as **John**, try to go to `http://localhost:8080/authentication/admin/`, and Spring Security prevents access.
6. Log out and log back in as **Margaret** and Spring Security should let you access the admin pages.

## Using the JDBC User Details Service

As mentioned earlier, the `InMemoryUserDetailsManager` is just a test implementation that you should never use in a production application. It was useful for this demonstration, but what other options are available? If you store your users in a database (typical for most applications), the `org.springframework.security.provisioning.JdbcUserDetailsManager` provides a simple mechanism for obtaining `UserDetails` objects from your database. You simply give it a `DataSource` and configure SQL queries for obtaining users and their permissions from the database.

```
@Configuration
@EnableWebMvcSecurity
public class SecurityConfiguration extends WebSecurityConfigurerAdapter
{
    ...
    @Inject DataSource dataSource;

    @Override
    protected void configure(AuthenticationManagerBuilder builder)
            throws Exception
    {
        builder
                .jdbcAuthentication()
                    .dataSource(this.dataSource)
                    .usersByUsernameQuery("SELECT Username, Password, Enabled " +
                            "FROM User WHERE Username = ?")
                    .authoritiesByUsernameQuery("SELECT Username, Permission " +
                            "FROM UserPermission WHERE Username = ?")
                    .passwordEncoder(new BCryptPasswordEncoder());
    }
    ...
}
```

Most of this configuration should be self-explanatory. The "users by username" SQL query must return a result set with the columns containing the username, password, and enabled/disabled flag, in that order. The "authorities by username" SQL query must return a result set with the columns containing the username and authority name, in that order. Both queries must require exactly one parameter, the username of the user to locate.

Of course, you should never store users' passwords in the database in plain text, and Spring Security's `org.springframework.security.crypto.password.PasswordEncoder` interface provides a mechanism for comparing passwords to hashed passwords. All you have to do is return the hashed password column in your configured "users by username" query and provide the appropriate `PasswordEncoder` implementation to handle the hashed password format. The `org.springframework.security.crypto.bcrypt.BCryptPasswordEncoder` provides a standard implementation for using the BCrypt hashing algorithm to compare user passwords.

The following XML configuration is identical to the Java configuration for the JDBC user details service.

```
<authentication-manager>
    <authentication-provider>
        <jdbc-user-service data-source-ref="dataSource"
                           users-by-username-query=
"SELECT Username, Password, Enabled FROM User WHERE Username = ?"
                           authorities-by-username-query=
"SELECT Username, Permission FROM UserPermission WHERE Username = ?" />
        <password-encoder hash="bcrypt" />
    </authentication-provider>
</authentication-manager>
```

### Using Other User Details Services

In addition to the `JdbcUserDetailsManager`, there is also an `org.springframework.security.ldap.userdetails.LdapUserDetailsManager` and an `LdapUserDetailsService`, but these classes are purely for information retrieval. You cannot use them for the actual authentication process because they cannot obtain a password from an LDAP provider. You learn more about these next. There are no other bundled `UserDetailsService` implementations, but you may define your own fairly simply. Just create a `UserDetailsService` implementation, obtain an instance of it in your `SecurityConfiguration` class (either by creating it manually or injecting it), and add it to the security configuration.

```
@Configuration
@EnableWebMvcSecurity
public class SecurityConfiguration extends WebSecurityConfigurerAdapter
{
    ...
    @Inject MyUserDetailsService myUserDetailsService;

    @Override
    protected void configure(AuthenticationManagerBuilder builder)
            throws Exception
    {
        builder.userDetailsService(this.myUserDetailsService)
                .passwordEncoder(new BCryptPasswordEncoder());
    }
    ...
}
```

Configuring your custom `UserDetailsService` using XML is essentially the same.

```
<authentication-manager>
    <authentication-provider user-service-ref="myUserDetailsService">
        <password-encoder hash="bcrypt" />
    </authentication-provider>
</authentication-manager>
```

## Working with LDAP and Active Directory Providers

To be sure, the `DaoAuthenticationProvider` class and corresponding `UserDetailsService` interface are very handy for quickly getting Spring Security up and running in simple situations. But real life is rarely that simple, and often much more complex authentication mechanisms are called for. Claims authentication using the Lightweight Directory Access Protocol is one example. For this, Spring Security comes with an `org.springframework.security.ldap.authentication.LdapAuthenticationProvider`.

This provider is necessary because you can't always obtain a password (hashed or otherwise) from an LDAP server. For example, the most common authentication strategy is called Bind, where users essentially "log in" to the LDAP server, thereby establishing their identity. The `LdapAuthenticationProvider` authenticates directly with the LDAP server rather than redirecting users to an authentication server. It has several options, but you should never need to configure it directly. Instead, you can use the Java configuration shortcuts or XML namespace.

```
@Configuration
@EnableWebMvcSecurity
public class SecurityConfiguration extends WebSecurityConfigurerAdapter
{
    ...
    @Override
    protected void configure(AuthenticationManagerBuilder builder)
            throws Exception
    {
        builder
                .ldapAuthentication()
                    .contextSource()
                        .url("ldap://ldap1.example.org:389/dc=example,dc=org
ldap://ldap2.example.org:389/dc=example,dc=org")
                        .managerDn("uid=admin,ou=system")
                        .managerPassword("bindPassword")
                        .and()
                    .userSearchFilter("(uid={0})")
                    .userSearchBase("ou=people")
                    .groupSearchBase("ou=groups");
    }
    ...
}

    <ldap-server manager-dn="uid=admin,ou=system" manager-password="bindPassword"
                 url="ldap://ldap1.example.org:389/dc=example,dc=org
ldap://ldap2.example.org:389/dc=example,dc=org" />

    <authentication-manager>
        <ldap-authentication-provider user-search-filter="(uid={0})"
                                      user-search-base="ou=people"
                                      group-search-base="ou=groups" />
    </authentication-manager>
```

These configurations assume that anonymous access is not enabled on the server, and thus provides a manager distinguished name and password with which to bind other users. If your server allows anonymous access, you could omit these values. Multiple servers for redundancy and high availability are specified by separating the URLs with a space, as is the LDAP convention. These configurations also assume that the users could be located in multiple nodes in the directory (a typical scenario), and specify a user search base and filter for locating users anywhere within the base node. If your users are always located on the same node, you could omit the search filter and base properties and instead use the `userDnPatterns`/`user-dn-pattern` properties. The group search base properties instruct Spring Security how to locate the LDAP groups to which your users belong. This is necessary if you also want to take advantage of the directory for claims-based authorization, but you can omit it otherwise. To further restrict the groups returned, you can specify a `groupSearchFilter`/`group-search-filter`.

> **WARNING** *LDAP is a complex topic that is outside the scope of this book. It is very easy to misconfigure an LDAP client of any type, and doing so can make your application insecure or inaccessible, depending on the mistakes made. You should* always *consult your LDAP server administrator before attempting to integrate LDAP authentication into your application.*

Earlier you read about the `LdapUserDetailsManager` and `LdapUserDetailsService` classes. These can obtain `UserDetails` from the LDAP server, but they cannot obtain password information for authenticating users. So what are they for? Well, you don't strictly need them. The previous configuration works for authenticating users against an LDAP server. However, if you want to provide a "remember me" checkbox on your login screen in an LDAP-enabled application and use the XML configuration, you must also configure an `LdapUserDetailsManager` or `LdapUserDetailsService`. (There is a slight difference in how these classes resolve users that is outside the scope of this book.)

When a "remembered" user returns and is authenticated automatically, this service obtains the user's details from the LDAP server (and ensures the user is not deleted, disabled, or locked out). You should configure the service with the same search and filter details as the `LdapAuthenticationProvider`. The Java configuration takes care of this for you automatically. You learn more about "remember me" authentication later in this section.

Spring Security also has built-in support for Windows Domain Active Directory authentication. This support uses LDAP and, thus, requires that you enable LDAP on your domain controllers. (It is enabled by default, but some domain administrators disable it to simplify security measures). It also means that the `org.springframework.security.ldap.authentication.ad.ActiveDirectoryLdapAuthenticationProvider` is closely related to the `LdapAuthenticationProvider`—both extend `org.springframework.security.ldap.authentication.AbstractLdapAuthenticationProvider`.

Configuring the `LdapAuthenticationProvider` to properly connect to a Windows domain controller is a very complex task. Because the LDAP structure is always the same across all Windows domain controllers, Spring Security provides the `ActiveDirectoryLdapAuthenticationProvider` to greatly simplify this task. It also translates the Microsoft-proprietary error codes returned by domain controllers into more useful error messages than the generic `LdapAuthenticationProvider` can provide. All you need to do is provide the default Windows domain name (used when the username does not contain an explicit domain) and the URL or URLs for the domain controller's LDAP server(s), as demonstrated in the following Java and XML configurations.

```
@Configuration
@EnableWebMvcSecurity
public class SecurityConfiguration extends WebSecurityConfigurerAdapter
{
```

```
    ...
    @Override
    protected void configure(AuthenticationManagerBuilder builder)
            throws Exception
    {
        builder.authenticationProvider(
                new ActiveDirectoryLdapAuthenticationProvider(
                        "example.com",
                        "ldap://dc1.example.com:389/ ldap://dc2.example.com:389/"
                )
        );
    }
    ...
}
```

```
    <beans:bean id="activeDirectoryProvider"
                class="org.springframework.security.ldap.authentication.ad.
ActiveDirectoryLdapAuthenticationProvider">
        <beans:constructor-arg value="example.com" />
        <beans:constructor-arg value="ldap://dc1.example.com:389/
ldap://dc2.example.org:com/"/>
    </beans:bean>

    <authentication-manager>
        <authentication-provider ref="activeDirectoryProvider" />
    </authentication-manager>
```

**NOTE** *To use Spring Security's LDAP support, you need to add the following Maven dependency to your project, which also pulls in an external dependency on the Spring LDAP project.*

```
<dependency>
    <groupId>org.springframework.security</groupId>
    <artifactId>spring-security-ldap</artifactId>
    <version>3.2.0.RELEASE</version>
    <scope>compile</scope>
</dependency>
```

## Authenticating with OpenID

Spring Security also provides built-in support for OpenID authentication. If you aren't interested in OpenID authentication, you can skip to the section "Remembering Users." This part of the section assumes that you have some knowledge of how OpenID authentication works and refers to several OpenID concepts without elaborating on what they are. Because OpenID is a claims-based authentication system that requires users to be redirected to the provider, you don't need an `AuthenticationProvider` implementation, and you won't configure a form login mechanism. Instead, you configure an OpenID login mechanism that redirects the user to the OpenID provider's login form when necessary.

You also need a page to handle the first stage of OpenID login—presenting your users with the list of OpenID providers you support and a field for them to enter their OpenID identifier. When your users submit this form, Spring Security takes over, redirecting them to the proper provider URL and completing the callback authentication process when they return from the provider.

```
@Configuration
@EnableWebMvcSecurity
public class SecurityConfiguration extends WebSecurityConfigurerAdapter
{
    @Override
    public void configure(WebSecurity security)
    {
        security.ignoring().antMatchers("/resource/**");
    }

    @Override
    protected void configure(HttpSecurity security) throws Exception
    {
        security
                .authorizeRequests()
                    .antMatchers("/signup", "/about", "/policies").permitAll()
                    .antMatchers("/secure/**").hasAuthority("USER")
                    .antMatchers("/admin/**").hasAuthority("ADMIN")
                    .anyRequest().authenticated()
                .and().openidLogin()
                    .loginPage("/login")
                    .failureUrl("/login?error")
                    .defaultSuccessUrl("/secure/")
                    .authenticationUserDetailsService(new MyUserDetailsService())
                    .attributeExchange("https://www.google.com/.*")
                        .attribute("firstname").required(true)
                        .type("http://axschema.org/namePerson/first")
                        .and()
                        .attribute("lastname").required(true)
                        .type("http://axschema.org/namePerson/last")
                        .and()
                        .attribute("email").required(true)
                        .type("http://axschema.org/contact/email")
                        .and()
                    .and()
                    .attributeExchange(".*yahoo.com.*")
                        .attribute("fullname").required(true)
                        .type("http://axschema.org/namePerson")
                        .and()
                        .attribute("email").required(true)
                        .type("http://axschema.org/contact/email")
                        .and()
                    .and()
                .and().logout()
                    .logoutUrl("/logout").logoutSuccessUrl("/login?loggedOut")
                    .invalidateHttpSession(true).deleteCookies("JSESSIONID")
                    .permitAll()
                .and().sessionManagement()
                    .sessionFixation().changeSessionId()
                    .maximumSessions(1).maxSessionsPreventsLogin(true)
                .and().and().csrf().disable();
    }
}
```

This configuration sets up the OpenID login mechanism and configures attribute exchanges with two common providers. If you need to configure attribute exchanges with many providers, it probably makes more sense to create private methods to handle the setup for each. The configuration also sets up the familiar login page, failure URL, and default success URL, which you previously configured for the form login mechanism.

The `loginPage` is the view you provide containing the OpenID identifier field (the field name must be `openid_identifier`) and buttons for all of the providers you support. The `MyUserDetailsService` is a theoretical `org.springframework.security.core.userdetails.AuthenticationUserDetailsService` implementation of your design capable of accepting an `org.springframework.security.openid.OpenIDAuthenticationToken` and returning a corresponding `UserDetails` object. You must provide a `UserDetailsService` implementation if you decide to also enable "remember me" authentication. You can use the same `UserDetailsService` for both of these purposes.

As you can tell, the details involved in configuring OpenID in Spring Security are numerous and could fill an entire chapter. If you want to see more examples, the sample code in the Spring Security GitHub repository (`https://github.com/spring-projects/spring-security`) is a great resource.

**NOTE** *To use Spring Security's OpenID support, you need to add the following Maven dependencies to your project (the first as a direct dependency, the others to force usage of more recent transient dependencies with many bug fixes and security improvements). This dependency pulls in many transient dependencies.*

```
<dependency>
     <groupId>org.springframework.security</groupId>
     <artifactId>spring-security-openid</artifactId>
     <version>3.2.0.RELEASE</version>
     <scope>compile</scope>
</dependency>

<dependency>
     <groupId>commons-codec</groupId>
     <artifactId>commons-codec</artifactId>
     <version>1.9</version>
     <scope>runtime</scope>
</dependency>

<dependency>
     <groupId>org.apache.httpcomponents</groupId>
     <artifactId>httpclient</artifactId>
     <version>4.3.1</version>
     <scope>runtime</scope>
</dependency>
```

## Remembering Users

Many sites offer remember-me authentication. The concept typically involves a check box on the login screen where users can indicate that the site should remember their browser and log them in automatically next time. This works by saving a cookie in the users' browser to identify them on their next visit.

To be clear, this is a security vulnerability waiting to happen. All an attacker must do is obtain access to the user's cookies and he can then access your application on behalf of the user. You can somewhat lessen the security concerns by having remember-me tokens that expire quickly or can be used only once, but in reality the vulnerability still exists. You should never use remember-me authentication when protecting any kind of sensitive information, such as healthcare data, financial or tax records, or employment information. However, for low-security situations (such as user forums and news sites with comment capability) this compromise is sometimes acceptable in the name of user convenience.

Spring Security offers remember-me authentication by way of a special `org.springframework.security.authentication.RememberMeAuthenticationProvider`. If you decide you want to enable remember-me services, add a check box to your login screen with the field name `remember-me` (or `_spring_security_remember_me` when using XML configuration), and then simply switch on remember-me services in your configuration:

```
@Configuration
@EnableWebMvcSecurity
public class SecurityConfiguration extends WebSecurityConfigurerAdapter
{
    ...
    @Override
    protected void configure(HttpSecurity security) throws Exception
    {
        ...
                    .maximumSessions(1).maxSessionsPreventsLogin(true)
                .and().and().csrf().disable()
                .rememberMe().key("myApplicationName");
    }
    ...
}

    <http use-expressions="true">
        ...
        <remember-me key="myApplicationName"/>
    </http>
```

If your login process takes place over SSL (as it should), set `useSecureCookie` (or `use-secure-cookie`) to `true` in order to increase security. This eliminates one avenue with which attackers can obtain your users' remember-me cookies. You can also use `tokenValiditySeconds` (or `token-validity-seconds`) to control how long remember-me tokens are valid before they expire, further limiting a stolen token's usefulness. As discussed previously, remember-me services require a `UserDetailsService` implementation in order to work properly. Without this, remember-me services cannot function. If you have multiple `UserDetailsServices`, you must pick the one that you want to support remember-me services for and specify it with `userDetailsService` (or `user-service-ref`).

There is also a slightly more secure version of the remember-me services that requires a `DataSource` and a table with a specific schema. Use of this feature is detailed in the Spring Security documentation, but in general this author recommends that you never use remember-me services.

## Exploring Other Authentication Providers

Several other built-in `AuthenticationProviders` come with Spring Security. `org.springframework.security.cas.authentication.CasAuthenticationProvider` manages authentication using Jasig Central Authentication Service. Both `org.springframework.security.authentication.jaas.DefaultJaasAuthenticationProvider` and `org.springframework.security.authentication.jaas.JaasAuthenticationProvider` use a Java Authentication and Authorization Service provider; however, `JaasAuthenticationProvider` relies on a particular JAAS implementation that might not be available on all Java Virtual Machines, whereas the `DefaultJaasAuthenticationProvider` can work with any JAAS implementation.

`org.springframework.security.web.authentication.preauth.PreAuthenticatedAuthenticationProvider` is an interesting implementation. It operates on the basis that you'll encounter some situations in which you cannot or do not want to use Spring Security for authentication purposes, but you do want to take advantage of its authorization capabilities. Such scenarios could include client certificate authentication (which only the Servlet container can handle), SiteMinder authentication, and other authentication handled directly within the Servlet container. When configuring pre-authentication, you must carefully tell Spring Security how to properly and securely recognize pre-authenticated requests.

`org.springframework.security.authentication.rcp.RemoteAuthenticationProvider` is a very similar provider that applies to slightly different situations in which authentication is also handled externally and Spring Security is still responsible for authorization.

The final built-in provider is `org.springframework.security.access.intercept.RunAsImplAuthenticationProvider`. You can use this to temporarily replace the current `Authentication` with an `Authentication` for a different `Principal` with (potentially) different `GrantedAuthoritys`. One example use case for this is to run certain code in privileged mode while running the majority of your code with a user holding fewer permissions.

The configuration details for these providers are numerous, and trying to print them all in this book would not make sense. You will find that the Spring Security API documentation and GitHub repository samples mentioned earlier are very useful for learning about these providers.
You should also consult the Spring Security reference documentation (`http://docs.spring.io/spring-security/site/docs/3.2.x/reference/html/`) for more information.

# WRITING YOUR OWN AUTHENTICATION PROVIDER

As useful as all these built-in authentication mechanisms are, sometimes they're not enough. Thankfully, writing your own `AuthenticationProvider` is fairly simple, and in this section you do just that. You can follow along in the Customer-Support-v19 project, available for download from the `wrox.com` code download site. This is the project you have been progressively improving and refactoring since Chapter 3, and the only tasks that remain to complete it are adding authentication and authorization. If you have not been working on this project since the beginning, don't worry!

The project is self-contained and you can run it as soon as you download it. This section covers only the changes made to the project to add authentication to the Customer Support application.

Early on, you added a rudimentary system for username and password form authentication to the application. This was necessary to complete some of the more basic features required in the project. Now, you can replace this home-baked authentication with the enterprise features of Spring Security. This section shows you how to do this and also introduces you to Cross-Site Request Forgery attacks and the mitigation features that Spring Security 3.2 introduces.

# Bootstrapping in the Correct Order

As you may recall, the Spring Framework, Servlet, and filter configuration in the Customer Support application is much more complex than what you created in the sample Authentication-App. One important problem is that the `LoggingFilter` performs two tasks: adding a fish tag (in the form of a UUID) and the logged-in username to the Log4j 2 `ThreadContext`. The problem with this is that the username does not become available until after the Spring Security filter chain executes, meaning that filter code must run last. However, running the fish tagging code last would exclude Spring Security logging from including the fish tag, which is not desirable. Because of this, you must split the logging filter into two filters and bootstrap everything in the proper order.

## Splitting the Logging Filter

Splitting the logging filter is not a complicated task. Replace the `LoggingFilter` with a `PreSecurityLoggingFilter` and a `PostSecurityLoggingFilter`. The `PreSecurityLoggingFilter` is responsible for setting up the fish tag and clearing both the fish tag and the username when the request is complete.

```
public class PreSecurityLoggingFilter implements Filter
{
    @Override
    public void doFilter(ServletRequest request, ServletResponse response,
                         FilterChain chain) throws IOException, ServletException
    {
        String id = UUID.randomUUID().toString();
        ThreadContext.put("id", id);
        try
        {
            ((HttpServletResponse)response).setHeader("X-Wrox-Request-Id", id);
            chain.doFilter(request, response);
        }
        finally
        {
            ThreadContext.remove("id");
            ThreadContext.remove("username");
        }
    }
    ...
}
```

The `PostSecurityLoggingFilter` is even simpler. It uses a static method on Spring Security's `org.springframework.security.core.context.SecurityContextHolder` class to obtain the current `org.springframework.security.core.context.SecurityContext`. This context is request-local,and holds the `Authentication` that belongs to the current request and HTTP session. The `PostSecurityLoggingFilter` delegates removal of the username from the `ThreadContext` to the `PreSecurityLoggingFilter` so that the username can exist on the `ThreadContext` for as long as possible.

```
public class PostSecurityLoggingFilter implements Filter
{
    @Override
    public void doFilter(ServletRequest request, ServletResponse response,
                         FilterChain chain) throws IOException, ServletException
    {
        SecurityContext context = SecurityContextHolder.getContext();
        if(context != null && context.getAuthentication() != null)
            ThreadContext.put("username", context.getAuthentication().getName());

        chain.doFilter(request, response);
    }
    ...
}
```

## Ordering Multiple Bootstrap Classes

Now that you have split up the logging filter, it's important that all your application components are initialized in the proper order. The `PreSecurityLoggingFilter` must be registered first, followed by the Spring Security filter chain and finally the `PostSecurityLoggingFilter`. Because Spring Framework registers only a `ServletContextListener` and several Servlets, it doesn't really matter where in that process you initialize Spring Framework. It won't interfere with the filter execution order.

Ordering multiple Spring Framework `WebApplicationInitializers` is really easy. All you have to do is annotate the classes with `@org.springframework.core.annotation.Order`, providing a value corresponding to the precedence of the initializer. The lowest value corresponds to the highest precedence, so `-2,147,483,648` is the highest precedence possible. The highest value corresponds to the lowest precedence, so the lowest precedence possible is `2,147,483,647`. For your purposes, it's easiest just to number the three bootstrap classes you need as `1`, `2` and `3`. The classes are grouped in the `com.wrox.config.bootstrap` package, and `FrameworkBootstrap` replaces the old `Bootstrap` class from previous versions. The ellipsis represents the Spring Framework bootstrap code that hasn't changed. The only major differences are that the previous `AuthenticationFilter` is gone and the `PreSecurityLoggingFilter`, not the previous `LoggingFilter`, is registered here.

```
@Order(1)
public class FrameworkBootstrap implements WebApplicationInitializer
{
    private static final Logger log = LogManager.getLogger();

    @Override
    public void onStartup(ServletContext container) throws ServletException
    {
        log.info("Executing framework bootstrap.");

        ...

        FilterRegistration.Dynamic registration = container.addFilter(
```

```
                "preSecurityLoggingFilter", new PreSecurityLoggingFilter()
        );
        registration.addMappingForUrlPatterns(null, false, "/*");
    }
}
```

Next, you need to bootstrap Spring Security's filter chain. Other than the addition of the `@Order` annotation and a logging statement (to demonstrate that ordering is correct), this is identical to the `SecurityBootstrap` you created for the Authentication-App project.

```
@Order(2)
public class SecurityBootstrap extends AbstractSecurityWebApplicationInitializer
{
    private static final Logger log = LogManager.getLogger();

    @Override
    protected boolean enableHttpSessionEventPublisher()
    {
        log.info("Executing security bootstrap.");

        return true;
    }
}
```

The final step in the bootstrapping process is to register the `PostSecurityLoggingFilter` in the new `LoggingBootstrap` class. Now when Spring Framework starts up, it executes these bootstrap classes in the order they appear here.

```
@Order(3)
public class LoggingBootstrap implements WebApplicationInitializer
{
    private static final Logger log = LogManager.getLogger();

    @Override
    public void onStartup(ServletContext container) throws ServletException
    {
        log.info("Executing logging bootstrap.");

        FilterRegistration.Dynamic registration = container.addFilter(
                "postSecurityLoggingFilter", new PostSecurityLoggingFilter()
        );
        registration.addMappingForUrlPatterns(null, false, "/*");
    }
}
```

## Creating and Configuring a Provider

Now that logging and Spring Security are set up to bootstrap in the correct order, it's time to create your own `AuthenticationProvider` implementation. Because you use the `UserPrincipal` entity as an identity throughout the application, the easiest thing to do is simply update `UserPrincipal` to implement `Authentication`. Then you can return it from your `AuthenticationProvider` implementation.

> **NOTE** *Making* `UserPrincipal` *extend* `Authentication` *is just one approach. In the next chapter you explore another approach—extending* `UserDetails`.

## Converting the User Principal and Authentication Service

For the most part, the `UserPrincipal` remains largely unchanged. Its mapping is the same, and it still implements `Principal` and `Serializable`, but indirectly by way of implementing `Authentication`. The only major change is the addition of the `getAuthorities`, `getPrincipal`, `getDetails`, `getCredentials`, `isAuthenticated`, and `setAuthenticated` methods specified in `Authentication`. Their implementation is boilerplate. In the next chapter you map user authorities to a new database table that stores user permissions.

The most important changes are to the `AuthenticationService` interface, and its `DefaultAuthenticationService` implementation. `AuthenticationService` now extends `AuthenticationProvider`, overriding its `authenticate` method to clarify that this provider returns only `UserPrincipals`.

```
@Validated
public interface AuthenticationService extends AuthenticationProvider
{
    @Override
    UserPrincipal authenticate(Authentication authentication);

    void saveUser(
            @NotNull(message = "{validate.authenticate.saveUser}") @Valid
                UserPrincipal principal,
            String newPassword
    );
}
```

The implementation of the `saveUser` method hasn't changed any. `authenticate` has obviously changed a great deal, and the `supports` method indicates that this `AuthenticationProvider` can authenticate using only `UsernamePasswordAuthenticationTokens`. After casting the `Authentication` to a `UsernamePasswordAuthenticationToken` and retrieving the username and password, `authenticate` erases the plain-text password stored in the token so that it can't accidentally leak anywhere. It then retrieves the `UserPrincipal` and runs through the standard checks it previously ran through. After the user identity has been confirmed, it sets the `authenticated` flag to `true` (in bold) to confirm the authentication succeeded.

```
@Service
public class DefaultAuthenticationService implements AuthenticationService
{
    ...

    @Override
    @Transactional
    public UserPrincipal authenticate(Authentication authentication)
    {
        UsernamePasswordAuthenticationToken credentials =
                (UsernamePasswordAuthenticationToken)authentication;
        String username = credentials.getPrincipal().toString();
        String password = credentials.getCredentials().toString();
```

```
            credentials.eraseCredentials();

            UserPrincipal principal = this.userRepository.getByUsername(username);
            if(principal == null)
            {
                log.warn("Authentication failed for non-existent user {}.", username);
                return null;
            }

            if(!BCrypt.checkpw(
                    password,
                    new String(principal.getPassword(), StandardCharsets.UTF_8)
            ))
            {
                log.warn("Authentication failed for user {}.", username);
                return null;
            }

            principal.setAuthenticated(true);
            log.debug("User {} successfully authenticated.", username);

            return principal;
        }

        @Override
        public boolean supports(Class<?> c)
        {
            return c == UsernamePasswordAuthenticationToken.class;
        }

        ...
    }
```

Now you just need to configure Spring Security to use the `AuthenticationService` implementation as the `AuthenticationProvider`. This is demonstrated in the `SecurityConfiguration` class in Listing 26-1, which is `@Imported` from the `RootContextConfiguration` class. Notice that it lets Spring Framework inject the `AuthenticationService` bean automatically and then simply wires it in from the `configure(AuthenticationManagerBuilder)` method. The `configure(WebSecurity)` method excludes static resources and a possible favicon from Spring Security's filter chain, whereas `configure(HttpSecurity)` requires authentication for all requests and sets up the form login and logout mechanisms, similar to the code in the Authentication-App. It does a few other things, too, which you'll look at soon.

**LISTING 26-1: SecurityConfiguration.java**

```
@Configuration
@EnableWebMvcSecurity
public class SecurityConfiguration extends WebSecurityConfigurerAdapter
{
    @Inject AuthenticationService authenticationService;

    @Bean
```

*continues*

**LISTING 26-1** *(continued)*

```
        protected SessionRegistry sessionRegistryImpl()
        {
            return new SessionRegistryImpl();
        }

        @Override
        protected void configure(AuthenticationManagerBuilder builder)
                throws Exception
        {
            builder.authenticationProvider(this.authenticationService);
        }

        @Override
        public void configure(WebSecurity security)
        {
            security.ignoring().antMatchers("/resource/**", "/favicon.ico");
        }

        @Override
        protected void configure(HttpSecurity security) throws Exception
        {
            security
                    .authorizeRequests()
                        .anyRequest().authenticated()
                    .and().formLogin()
                        .loginPage("/login").failureUrl("/login?loginFailed")
                        .defaultSuccessUrl("/ticket/list")
                        .usernameParameter("username")
                        .passwordParameter("password")
                        .permitAll()
                    .and().logout()
                        .logoutUrl("/logout").logoutSuccessUrl("/login?loggedOut")
                        .invalidateHttpSession(true).deleteCookies("JSESSIONID")
                        .permitAll()
                    .and().sessionManagement()
                        .sessionFixation().changeSessionId()
                        .maximumSessions(1).maxSessionsPreventsLogin(true)
                        .sessionRegistry(this.sessionRegistryImpl())
                    .and().and().csrf()
                        .requireCsrfProtectionMatcher((r) -> {
                            String m = r.getMethod();
                            return !r.getServletPath().startsWith("/services/") &&
                                    ("POST".equals(m) || "PUT".equals(m) ||
                                            "DELETE".equals(m) || "PATCH".equals(m));
                        });
        }
    }
```

## Replacing the Session Registry

You probably wondered why the `SecurityConfiguration` class in Listing 26-1 manually creates the Spring Security `SessionRegistryImpl` bean and then (in bold) injects it into the session management configuration. Won't Spring Security create this bean automatically? Yes, Spring Security will do that, but in doing so the `SessionRegistry` won't be exposed to the entire application as a bean. Early in the book you created your own `com.wrox.site.SessionRegistry` using `SessionListener` (an implementation of `HttpSessionListener` and `HttpSessionIdListener`). Spring Security's `SessionRegistry` can replace this functionality completely. By manually creating the `SessionRegistryImpl` bean, you expose the bean to your application so that you can use it in other application beans outside of Spring Security classes. The `SessionListController` now uses Spring Security's `SessionRegistry` instead of the legacy `com.wrox.site.SessionRegistry`.

```
@WebController
@RequestMapping("session")
public class SessionListController
{
    @Inject SessionRegistry sessionRegistry;

    @RequestMapping(value = "list", method = RequestMethod.GET)
    public String list(Map<String, Object> model)
    {
        List<SessionInformation> sessions = new ArrayList<>();
        for(Object principal : this.sessionRegistry.getAllPrincipals())
            sessions.addAll(this.sessionRegistry.getAllSessions(principal, true));

        model.put("timestamp", System.currentTimeMillis());
        model.put("numberOfSessions", sessions.size());
        model.put("sessionList", sessions);

        return "session/list";
    }
}
```

Using Spring Framework's publish-subscribe messaging, Spring Security publishes a variety of messages when certain authentication events occur. These different events are all detailed in the API documentation, but the ones that are of the most use to you include the following:

- `org.springframework.security.authentication.event.AbstractAuthenticationFailureEvent`, published when authentication fails for some reason. Its subclasses indicate more detailed reasons for the failure.
- `org.springframework.security.authentication.event.AuthenticationSuccessEvent`, published when authentication succeeds. However, this might also include automatic authentication events, such as remember-me authentication. If you want to know only about interactive authentication, use `org.springframework.security.authentication.event.InteractiveAuthenticationSuccessEvent`.
- `org.springframework.security.web.authentication.session.SessionFixationProtectionEvent`, published when session fixation protection causes the session to change (for example, session migration or `changeSessionId`).
- `org.springframework.security.core.session.SessionDestroyedEvent`, published when a session is destroyed (either on log out or session timeout).

Previously, the ChatEndpoint used the legacy com.wrox.site.SessionRegistry to subscribe to events regarding the destruction of sessions. You can learn about these events now simply by implementing ApplicationListener<SessionDestroyedEvent>. However, only singleton beans can implement ApplicationListener<?>. Because ChatEndpoint is not a singleton bean (instead, a new instance is created for every new WebSocket connection), it cannot implement this method. (Spring Framework logs a warning and ignores it.) To solve this problem, the com.wrox.site .chat.SessionDestroyedListener class acts as a proxy, listening for destroyed sessions and forwarding the events on to all active WebSocket connections.

Speaking of ChatEndpoint, it now uses the SecurityContextHolder to obtain the UserPrincipal in the EndpointConfigurator.

```
public static class EndpointConfigurator extends SpringConfigurator
{
    ...
    @Override
    public void modifyHandshake(ServerEndpointConfig config,
                                HandshakeRequest request,
                                HandshakeResponse response)
    {
        ...
        config.getUserProperties().put(
                PRINCIPAL_KEY,
                SecurityContextHolder.getContext().getAuthentication()
        );
        ...
    }
    ...
}
```

## Modifying the Authentication Controller

The AuthenticationController is vastly simplified now. It doesn't have to handle login or logout commands, so those methods have been removed. Spring Security takes care of all that for you. The only thing AuthenticationController must still do is render the login view (and only after checking the SecurityContextHolder to make sure the user isn't already logged in). Although it never actually uses the LoginForm (because it doesn't process a submitted login anymore), it still adds the LoginForm to the model so that you can use the Spring Framework <form:form> tag in the login view. You cannot use <form:form> without a command object.

```
@WebController
public class AuthenticationController
{
    @RequestMapping(value = "login", method = RequestMethod.GET)
    public ModelAndView login(Map<String, Object> model)
    {
        if(SecurityContextHolder.getContext().getAuthentication() instanceof
                UserPrincipal)
            return new ModelAndView(new RedirectView("/ticket/list", true, false));

        model.put("loginForm", new LoginForm());
        return new ModelAndView("login");
```

```
        }

        public static class LoginForm { ... }
    }
```

# Mitigating Cross-Site Request Forgery Attacks

Cross-Site Request Forgery (CSRF) is one of the worst known web vulnerabilities. In a CSRF attack, the attacker takes advantage of a user's existing login on a site the attacker wants access to. The attack typically takes one of two forms. In a login attack, the malicious site is often disguised as the site the user wants to log in to. (Many times this is combined with a phishing attack.) Users enter their credentials and attempt to log in. The malicious site first captures the credentials and then forwards the credentials on to the real site. Because users successfully log in to the real site, they never notice that they have given their credentials to an attacker. These attacks are tough to pull off on sites that use HTTPS to secure their login forms, assuming users are conditioned to look for a valid certificate.

To understand the other type of attack, consider a scenario in which the user logs into his online banking software. Still logged in, he opens another browser tab where he sees an alert saying he won $1,000. Unfortunately, when he clicks that button, it doesn't give him $1,000. Instead, an invisible form submits to his banking software behind the scenes and, in a cruel twist of irony, transfers $1,000 out of his account and into the attacker's account.

You can mitigate both kinds of attacks using the *synchronizer token pattern*. In this pattern, a securely random token string is generated for each request to the application. That token is persisted as an attribute within the `HttpSession` and added as a hidden form field to any forms on the screen. If one of those forms is submitted, the application checks to make sure the submitted token matches the token in the session and permits form processing to continue only if the token matches. The attacker cannot know this token in advance, so he cannot include it in the submitted form used to trick the user.

For login attacks, the synchronizer token pattern cannot prevent the attack completely. All it can do is let users know that the attack occurred and that the attacker has their credentials. In this case, users must change their password immediately. As a best practice, the application should require this. For all other CSRF attacks, this pattern can prevent the attacks. Because the form is never processed, the damage is never done. Of course, if the submitted form contains sensitive data, some risk still exists, and the user should be notified.

## Configuring CSRF Protection

Spring Security can protect your users from CSRF attacks automatically. By default, this protection is enabled when you use Java configuration, but it's disabled by default for XML configuration (to maintain existing behavior from previous versions). In its standard configuration, it requires the CSRF token (either as a request parameter or request header) for all `POST`, `PUT`, `DELETE`, and `PATCH` requests (that is, those requests that can have side effects) that Spring Security's filter chain processes (even those that are `permitAll`). Only requests ignored and excluded from the chain (for example, in `configure(WebSecurity)`) are unprotected. However, this is not always desirable for all secured URLs. In the Customer Support application, for example, you should not include CSRF protection on the RESTful and SOAP web services because they don't use web forms. The requireCsrfProtectionMatcher call in Listing 26-1 overrides the default request matcher for CSRF protection, excluding the web services from CSRF protection.

> **NOTE** *Although the lambda expression certainly helps, the CSRF configuration in Listing 26-1 is awkward at best because you have to define a new matcher. In Chapter 28 you learn a better way to configure this when you add authentication and authorization to your web services.*

## Securing Web Forms

After you configure CSRF protection to your needs, how do you protect your forms? Well, to a certain extent you don't have to do anything. As long as you configured Spring Security with @EnableWebMvcSecurity instead of @EnableWebSecurity, anywhere you use the <form:form> tag with verb POST, PUT, PATCH, or DELETE, Spring Security automatically adds a hidden CSRF token field. This is why you still want to use <form:form> for the login view—so CSRF protection happens automatically. (If you configured Spring Security with only @EnableWebSecurity, you must create a bean of type org.springframework.security.web.servlet.support.csrf .CsrfRequestDataValueProcessor to enable this feature.) Spring Security automatically looks for the CSRF token for any requests that match the configured request matcher.

The only time you must take extra steps to add CSRF protection is when you use standard HTML <form>s without Spring's <form:form>, when you submit hidden forms generated by JavaScript, and when you submit Ajax calls to the server. In these cases, it is your responsibility to add the CSRF field or header to the form or request. Spring Security also makes this easy by registering an EL variable *_csrf* of type org.springframework.security.web.csrf.CsrfToken in all your JSP views. All you have to do is use the token properties to manually add the proper values to your form or JavaScript. The postInvisibleForm JavaScript function in the Customer Support application starts and joins chat sessions and logs out of the application. A simple tweak to this function protects any code that submits forms in that manner.

```
var postInvisibleForm = function(url, fields) {
    var form = $('<form id="mapForm" method="post"></form>')
            .attr({ action: url, style: 'display: none;' });
    for(var key in fields) {
        if(fields.hasOwnProperty(key))
            form.append($('<input type="hidden">').attr({
                name: key, value: fields[key]
            }));
    }
    form.append($('<input type="hidden">').attr({
        name: '${_csrf.parameterName}', value: '${_csrf.token}'
    }));
    $('body').append(form);
    form.submit();
};
```

While you're securing forms, you should know that the "best practice" today is to disable autocomplete for login forms. This protects users who share computers with other people, such as in a public library. Making this change is as simple as adding autocomplete="off" to the

`<form:form>`, `<form:input>`, and `<form:password>` tags in `login.jsp`. With CSRF protection enabled, Spring Security requires the logout to happen over `POST`. It does not respond to logout requests over `GET`. This is why the login link in the Customer Support application now submits an invisible form.

After reviewing all these changes, compile the project and start Tomcat from your IDE. Log in to the application at `http://localhost:8080/support/` and you shouldn't really notice a difference creating, listing, and searching tickets and chatting with support. From the user's perspective the application performs essentially the same; however, it is much more secure and robust now. You still need to handle users with different permissions—something that is coming up in the next chapter.

## HTTP SECURITY HEADERS IN SPRING SECURITY 3.2

Over the past few years, industry experts and working groups have proposed and adopted several security-related HTTP headers meant to instruct browsers to enable certain security mechanisms. These headers were formulated to combat different web vulnerabilities, such as Cross-Site Scripting (XSS) and Clickjacking (User Interface Redress) attacks.

Spring Security 3.2 adds support to automatically set these headers to "best practices" values, making your application as secure as possible. As with CSRF protection, these headers are added to the responses only for any URLs that Spring Security's filter chain processes. If you use XML configuration, these headers are disabled by default to maintain the same behavior from previous versions. However, if you use Java configuration, these headers are enabled by default, meaning you should understand how they work and what they do to determine whether you need to disable any of them.

- `Cache-Control` is set to `no-cache, no-store, max-age=0, must-revalidate` and `Pragma` is set to `no-cache`. This tells client browsers and proxies to never cache the data your site returns, protecting confidential information that may be contained therein.
- `X-Content-Type-Options` is set to `nosniff`, instructing browsers to never guess the MIME content type of pages and resources. Instead, browsers must rely solely on the `Content-Type` header. This is much more secure than guessing and helps prevent XSS attacks, but it means you must ensure your server always returns a valid `Content-Type` header for all requests.
- `Strict-Transport-Security` is set to `max-age=31536000 ; includeSubDomains`, which helps protect users from man-in-the-middle attacks during future redirects from HTTP to HTTPS. This header is set only on responses delivered over HTTPS and tells browsers to always use HTTPS to access the site and its subdomains for the next year.

*continues*

*continued*

- `X-Frame-Options` is set to `DENY`, preventing the responses from displaying within a frame. This helps prevent Clickjacking attacks.
- `X-XSS-Protection` is set to `1; mode=block`. As a result, if a browser detects a suspicious script that could contain XSS, it disables the script entirely instead of trying to disable only the suspect parts.

To enable these security headers in XML configuration, simply add `<headers />` to the `<http>` configuration to which you want it to apply. To disable these headers in Java configuration, do something like the following:

```
@Override
protected void configure(HttpSecurity security) throws Exception
{
    security
            ...
            .and().headers().disable();
}
```

You can also control each header type individually. The following is the equivalent to enabling them all (or not disabling them):

```
@Override
protected void configure(HttpSecurity security) throws Exception
{
    security
            ...
            .and().headers().cacheControl().contentTypeOptions()
                .frameOptions().httpStrictTransportSecurity()
                .xssProtection();
}
```

# SUMMARY

In this chapter, you explored authentication with Spring Security. You also learned about some ways that Spring Security is a total security solution, such as through CSRF mitigation and the new HTTP security headers added in Spring Security 3.2. You experimented with various authentication mechanisms and created your own authentication provider for the Customer Support application. Finally, you learned about the XML and Java configuration options and how Spring Security Java configuration differs significantly from Spring Framework Java configuration.

In the next chapter you complete the authentication-authorization story, learning about the various ways to check user permissions and ensure only authorized users perform secured actions.

# Using Authorization Tags and Annotations

## IN THIS CHAPTER

- Checking authorization rules in code
- Declaring URL and method security
- Using common and Spring Security annotations
- Understanding authorization decisions
- Creating access control lists for object security
- Using Spring Security's tag library

## WROX.COM CODE DOWNLOADS FOR THIS CHAPTER

You can find the `wrox.com` code downloads for this chapter at `http://www.wrox.com/go/projavaforwebapps` on the Download Code tab. The code for this chapter is included in the following example:

- Customer-Support-v20 Project

## NEW MAVEN DEPENDENCIES FOR THIS CHAPTER

In addition to the Maven dependencies introduced in previous chapters, you also need the following Maven dependency:

```
<dependency>
    <groupId>org.springframework.security</groupId>
    <artifactId>spring-security-taglibs</artifactId>
    <version>3.2.0.RELEASE</version>
    <scope>runtime</scope>
</dependency>
```

# AUTHORIZING BY DECLARATION

In Chapter 25, you explored some of the different approaches you can take to authorization. There are a lot of techniques and technologies you can use, and it would not be correct to say that any one approach is better than the others. A lot depends on your individual needs, the architecture of your application, and the approach you take to authentication. The instinctual approach might be to simply place authorization code within your code. A very common technique, and one often considered a best practice, is to authorize by declaration. In this technique, your code or its configuration declares rules that determine who can do what, and a security mechanism intercepts access to your code to enforce those rules on your behalf. This pattern is similar to the transactional pattern you explored in Part III of this book. In this section, you explore various ways to implement both approaches, and learn about the conventions and tools available in Spring Framework.

## Checking Permissions in Method Code

Normally, your code would need to check that the user is authorized to perform an action using code like this:

```
public void doSomeAction(...)
{
    if(security.userCanPerformAction("ACTION_1"))
    {
        // code that performs the action
    }
    else
        throw new AccessDeniedException("Not authorized to perform action.");
}
```

However, this can quickly litter your services with duplicate code. Consider a service that manages forum postings and replies:

```
public Post getPost(long id)
{
    if(security.userCanPerformAction("READ_POST")) {
        // code that returns post
    } else
        throw new AccessDeniedException("Not authorized to perform action.");
}

public Page<Post> listPosts(long forumId, Pageable pageable)
{
    if(security.userCanPerformAction("LIST_POSTS")) {
        // code that lists posts
    } else
        throw new AccessDeniedException("Not authorized to perform action.");
}

public void savePost(Post post)
{
    if(security.userCanPerformAction("SAVE_POST")) {
        // code that saves post
    } else
        throw new AccessDeniedException("Not authorized to perform action.");
```

```
    }

    public void deletePost(Post post)
    {
        if(security.userCanPerformAction("DELETE_POST")) {
            // code that deletes post
        } else
            throw new AccessDeniedException("Not authorized to perform action.");
    }

    public Reply getReply(long id)
    {
        if(security.userCanPerformAction("READ_REPLY")) {
            // code that returns reply
        } else
            throw new AccessDeniedException("Not authorized to perform action.");
    }

    public Page<Reply> listReplies(long postId, Pageable pageable)
    {
        if(security.userCanPerformAction("READ_REPLIES")) {
            // code that lists replies
        } else
            throw new AccessDeniedException("Not authorized to perform action.");
    }

    public void saveReply(Reply reply)
    {
        if(security.userCanPerformAction("SAVE_REPLY")) {
            // code that saves reply
        } else
            throw new AccessDeniedException("Not authorized to perform action.");
    }

    public void deleteReply(Reply reply)
    {
        if(security.userCanPerformAction("DELETE_REPLY")) {
            // code that deletes reply
        } else
            throw new AccessDeniedException("Not authorized to perform action.");
    }
```

Of course, this code is simplistic. It ignores the fact that users might be permitted to view only certain posts and replies, and it doesn't account for the difference between moderators deleting other users' posts and users deleting their own posts. Even so, at least 24 lines of code are dedicated just to checking authorization rules in this one service, and the code is quite repetitive. You could remove some duplication using callbacks and lambda expressions, like so:

```
    public Post getPost(long id)
    {
        return security.doSecured("READ_POST", () -> {
            // code that returns post
        });
    }

    ...
```

Although this is certainly an improvement, you still end up duplicating some code. It also isn't the cleanest approach because all your service code ends up being placed within callback lambdas. In addition, think about how you would unit test any of the previous code examples. It wouldn't be easy! Each test would have to set up an `Authentication` with the correct `GrantedAuthority`s to check both the positive case (code executes because the user is authorized) and the negative case (code does not execute because the user is not authorized). You would have to do this for *all* your code, re-testing authorization checks wherever you go. Should you really be coupling this code?

Generally speaking, you don't want to take any of these approaches. In fact, Spring Security has only limited support for this first technique and no support for the second. (However, you can implement your own service to support the second approach.) Spring Security's filter chain wraps all `HttpServletRequest` objects and implements the `getUserPrincipal`, `getRemoteUser`, and `isUserInRole` methods, which return the `Authentication` object, authenticated username, and authorization check results, respectively. Within a Spring Web MVC controller, you can ask for a `Principal` as a handler method parameter, cast it to an `Authentication`, and check its `GrantedAuthority`s to determine access. However, this is a bit clunky. You can improve this technique slightly by implementing a `HandlerMethodArgumentResolver` that provides `Authentication` or `List<GrantedAuthority>` handler method parameters, but this still has its problems.

As of Spring Security 3.2, another approach involves annotating a controller method parameter with `@org.springframework.security.web.bind.annotation.AuthenticationPrincipal`. As long as you use the `@EnableWebMvcSecurity` configuration annotation, Spring Security registers a `HandlerMethodArgumentResolver` that can provide values for `@AuthenticationPrincipal` arguments. An `@AuthenticationPrincipal` argument can be of any type — the key is that its type must match the type returned by the `getPrincipal` method of the `Authentication` your application uses. In most cases this will be a `UserDetails` implementation, as in the following example:

```
@RequestMapping(value = "addMessage", method = RequestMethod.POST)
public View addMessage(MessageForm form,
                       @AuthenticationPrincipal MyUserDetails user)
{
    ...
}
```

All these techniques work for controllers; however, if you intend to enforce authorization in your services (as you should), you have to pass this information as arguments to your services, which is not ideal. Another option is to use the `SecurityContextHolder` to obtain the current `Authentication` and check its `GrantedAuthority`s. This is better suited for enforcing authorization in your services, but it still involves a lot of code in each method and makes unit testing difficult. If you want to take this approach, you should create some helper classes that do most of the repetitive work.

So what should you do? Why does Spring Security not provide better tools for this? Spring Security emphasizes a declarative approach to authorization, so much so that it provides no helpers for programmatic checking. Declarative authorization decouples your business logic from your authorization logic, which in the end is going to save you a lot of trouble. You can implement declarative authorization a few different ways. The rest of this section provides an overview of these methods and how they work in Spring Security.

## Employing URL Security

You already explored one approach to declarative security in Chapter 26: URL security. This involves declaring URL patterns and defining rules for who can access those URL patterns. You have already seen the `permitAll`, `authenticated`, and `hasAuthority` rules. Although you can avoid using URL security, it does make some things very simple. In the Customer Support application, for example, you used URL security to declare that all URLs require a user to be logged in, but excluded the login and logout URLs from this rule. `permitAll`, `authenticated`, and `hasAuthority` are *authorization expression functions* that largely mean exactly what they say. There are several expression functions that you can choose from:

- `denyAll` prevents everyone from accessing the given resource. (It always evaluates to `false`.) This is handy if you need to temporarily block access to a particular URL, but it has little long-term value.
- `permitAll` is the opposite of `denyAll`. It enables anyone to access the resource, whether they have been authenticated. (It always evaluates to `true`.)
- `hasAuthority(String)` evaluates to `true` if the user has the specified `GrantedAuthority` passed as an argument to the function.
- `hasAnyAuthority(String...)` enables you to specify multiple `GrantedAuthoritys` and evaluates to `true` if the user has *at least one* of these authorities.
- `hasRole(String)` is a synonym for `hasAuthority` and does the same thing. Which you use is just a matter of preference. If you want to avoid the appearance of role-based authorization, you'll probably choose `hasAuthority`.
- `hasAnyRole(String...)` is a synonym for `hasAnyAuthority`.
- `hasPermission` is a special expression function that checks a user's permission to access a particular resource based on more than just that user's roles or authorities. For example, it can check that a user can access a specific forum, which may differ from one forum to the next. Using `hasPermission` is a complex subject that's detailed in the section on access control lists.
- `isAnonymous` evaluates to `true` if the user is anonymously authenticated (in other words, they are *not* "logged in").
- `isRememberMe` evaluates to `true` if the user is authenticated using remember-me authentication.
- `isAuthenticated` is the opposite of `isAnonymous` — it evaluates to `true` if the user is not anonymous (in other words, they are "logged in").
- `isFullyAuthenticated` evaluates to `true` if `isAuthenticated` is `true` and `isRememberMe` is `false`. You can use this to mitigate some of the dangers of remember-me authentication. You can permit limited access to nonsensitive resources whenever `isAuthenticated` but protect more sensitive resources by allowing access only if `isFullyAuthenticated`.

- `hasIpAddress(String)` evaluates to `true` if the user's request originates from the given IP address. You can also specify a *Classless Inter-Domain Routing* (*CIDR*) block (such as 65.128.76.0/24), and `hasIpAddress` evaluates to `true` if the user's IP address belongs to that block of IP addresses.
- `getAuthentication` returns the `Authentication` object, which you can use to perform more complex or specialized comparisons that evaluate to a Boolean value.

Spring Framework Expression Language (Spring EL or SpEL) is the force that powers use of these authorization functions. This book has not covered SpEL, but it's really quite simple. It's very similar to the Java Unified Expression Language, and you can learn much of what you need to learn about it using Spring Security expressions. If you want more information, however, you can find it in the Spring Framework Reference Documentation (`http://docs.spring.io/spring/docs/4.0.x/spring-framework-reference/html/expressions.html`).

When using XML configuration, you define URL access rules within the `<intercept-url>` inner element of `<http>`. By default, the `access` attribute acts like a `hasAnyRole` or `hasAnyAuthorities`. It simply accepts a comma-separated list of `GrantedAuthority`s, and the user must have one of them to access matching URLs. Note that the order these `<intercept-url>` tags appear is important. Spring Security evaluates the first rule that a URL matches, so if you reverse the order of these two rules, anyone could access the `/admin/` URLs.

```
<http>
    <intercept-url pattern="/admin/**" access="ADMINISTRATOR" />
    <intercept-url pattern="/**" access="USER" />
    <form-login ...>
    <logout ...>
</http>
```

To use the authorization expression functions within the `access` attribute, you must enable expressions within the `<http>` element. Enabling expressions is as simple as setting the `use-expressions` attribute to `true`. After you do this, you can no longer provide a simple comma-separated list of `GrantedAuthority`s to the access attribute. You must use expressions. You use one or more of the security functions combined with the Boolean operators `or` and `and`, and parentheses if necessary, to form an entire security expression. With this syntax you can define very simple and very complex rules for protecting your application's web resources. For example, to specify that accessing the administration panel requires being fully authenticated (not remember-me), having administrator privileges, and connecting from a range of internal IP addresses, you could configure it like this:

```
<http use-expressions="true">
    <intercept-url pattern="/admin/**" access="isFullyAuthenticated
and hasAuthority('ADMINISTRATOR') and hasIpAddress('192.168.0.0/24')" />
    <intercept-url pattern="/**" access="hasAuthority('USER')" />
    <form-login ...>
    <logout ...>
</http>
```

In this case, if the user is authenticated using remember-me authentication, he is asked to fully authenticate ("log in") before accessing the administration panel. If the user does not have the `ADMINISTRATOR` `GrantedAuthority` or is connecting from a prohibited IP address, he receives a

403 Forbidden HTTP error. Of course, you could use or instead of and, but that wouldn't make sense. Then only one of the three conditions would have to be met to permit access to the administration panel.

Java configuration is a little different in that it supports only security expressions. This is natural considering how different Java configuration is from XML configuration already, and how the defaults of many settings differ between these types. When you select a URL pattern in Java configuration (either with anyRequest, antMatchers, or regexMatchers), the object returned is an org.springframework.security.config.annotation.web.configurers .ExpressionUrlAuthorizationConfigurer.AuthorizedUrl. With this object you can either call the access method to create a complex SpEL expression identical to what you'd create in an XML configuration, or you can use one of the convenience methods named after the security functions to create simple expressions. The following Java configuration is identical to the previous XML configuration. (Note, again, that the order of the URL matchers is important.)

```
@Override
protected void configure(HttpSecurity security) throws Exception
{
    security
            .authorizeRequests()
                .antMatchers("/admin/**").access("isFullyAuthenticated and " +
                        "hasAuthority('ADMINISTRATOR') and " +
                        "hasIpAddress('192.168.0.0/24')")
                .antMatchers("/**").hasAuthority("USER")
            .and().formLogin()
    ...
}
```

**WARNING** *Although the* hasRole *and* hasAnyRole *security functions are identical to the* hasAuthority *and* hasAnyAuthority *security functions, this is not the case for the Java configuration convenience methods. The* hasRole *and* hasAnyRole *convenience methods prepend the authorities passed in to them with* ROLE_. *This is fine if the authorities you use start with* ROLE_. *In this case, just leave off* ROLE_ *and it is added for you. However, if your authorities do not start with* ROLE_, *you need to stick with* hasAuthority *and* hasAnyAuthority.

Using declarative URL security certainly has its advantages. It's easy to configure and apply to broad sets of URLs, the expressions are very flexible, and if you use an XML configuration, you can alter the authorization rules without recompiling the application. It's definitely an improvement over evaluating security restrictions in all your application methods. However, two glaring disadvantages often discourage use of this feature:

- **It ties authorization to the web tier** — If another user interface is created that performs the same task, forgetting to define duplicate security rules for that user interface compromises the security of that feature.
- **It makes refactoring more risky** — If your user interface changes and your authorization rules don't, your security could again be compromised.

And, of course, this completely ignores the possibility that you might not even have a web tier to begin with! The previous code that evaluated authorization rules within your methods had one thing going for it — the rules were applied within your services. This meant that the rules were always applied uniformly across all user interfaces. You'll find that it makes the most sense to apply a few simple rules at the UI for convenience while applying more precise and complex rules within the services themselves.

# Using Annotations to Declare Permissions

So how do you evaluate authorization rules within your services without actually writing authorization code in your services? You approached a similar need for database transactions in Part III using annotations — by annotating your service methods with `@Transactional`, the Spring Framework transaction proxy ensured that a transaction started before your methods executed and that it committed or rolled back after your methods completed. You can apply the same pattern to add security to your service methods — annotate them with one or more security-related annotations to declare the `GrantedAuthority`s the user must have or permission expressions that must evaluate successfully before the user is permitted to invoke the requested action.

## Common Annotations for Authorization

The Common Annotations API, part of Java EE, specifies several authorization annotations that you can use for just this purpose. They are all found in the `javax.annotation.security` package.

- `@DeclareRoles`, which isn't any use in a Spring Security environment, provides a way to list all of the roles (or permissions, or actions, and so on) your application uses.
- `@DenyAll` prohibits access to everyone. Of course, this annotation has limited use as well. Annotating a method with this means that external actors (another class) can never execute it. An object can normally execute its own `@DenyAll` methods because proxies aren't applied in this situation. However, if you use bytecode weaving instead of interface or CGLIB proxies (which you learned about in Chapter 24), even that won't work. As such, few situations require you to use this annotation. If you mark an entire class or interface with this annotation, it prevents execution of all that class's methods.
- `@PermitAll` is, naturally, the opposite of `@DenyAll`. It declares that everyone may execute this method. Although this may seem equally useless, it can actually be quite useful. To understand why, you must first understand the next annotation.
- `@RolesAllowed` can be deceiving because its name suggests it works only for role-based authorization. Remember what you learned in Chapter 25: It's not what you call it; it's how you use it. `@RolesAllowed` specifies one or more roles (or permissions or `GrantedAuthority`s) that a user must have to execute the method. The user is not required to have all these roles, just one of them. If specified on a class or interface, this annotation applies to all the methods in that class. If specified on both a class and a method, the restrictions for the method typically add to the restrictions for the class. However, if the method annotation specifies roles also specified in the class annotation, the method restrictions completely override the class restrictions. Furthermore, if a class is marked with `@RolesAllowed` and one of its methods is marked `@PermitAll`, anyone may execute that method.

- `@RunAs` instructs the container to run the method as a different user. However, this annotation is only useful in a full Java EE container when you use container-supplied authorization. Spring Security does not provide support for this annotation.

Using the `@RolesAllowed` annotation is straightforward. Just add it to any method or class (of a Spring-managed bean) and specify one or more permissions in the annotation value.

```
@RolesAllowed("ADMINISTRATOR")
public interface SettingsMutatorService
{
    @RolesAllowed({"ADD_GENERAL_SETTING", "ALTER_GENERAL_SETTING"})
    void saveGeneralSettings(Map<String, Object> settings);

    @RolesAllowed({"ALTER_MEMBERSHIP_SETTING"})
    void saveMembershipSettings(Map<String, Object> settings);

    ...
}
```

If a user attempts to invoke a method without sufficient permissions, an `org.springframework.security.access.AccessDeniedException` is thrown. You don't normally need to worry about catching this exception. As a `RuntimeException`, it causes any related transaction to roll back and propagate without any efforts on your part. Spring Security's filter chain then catches the exception and returns a `403 Forbidden` error to the user. In a few scenarios, you might need to catch this exception, but usually you need to do so only for non-web applications.

As you can see, the `@RolesAllowed` and `@PermitAll` annotations can be useful, but that's about it. There's little point in using the other three annotations when you use Spring Security. So is that all there is? These annotations are useful, but they are completely ignorant of what the user is requesting a method to do. You can't use `@RolesAllowed` to restrict access to some forum posts but not all forum posts if they all come through the same method. Fortunately, Spring Security provides a more robust set of annotations to meet your needs.

## The Secured Annotation

The `@org.springframework.security.access.annotation.Secured` annotation was Spring Security's first pass at declarative security annotations. It came before Java EE 5 was released and thus before the Common Annotations API was available. Practically speaking, `@Secured` is identical to `@RolesAllowed`. It accepts one or more `GrantedAuthoritys`, and a user may execute an annotated method only if that user has at least one of those `GrantedAuthoritys`.

There is one minor difference, however. `@RolesAllowed` works with any values, but `@Secured` requires the values you specify to start with `ROLE_`. Any `GrantedAuthoritys` you specify that do not start with `ROLE_` are ignored. This is due to the varying members in the access decision voter pattern, which you learn more about in the next section. If you do not want all your permission names to start with `ROLE_`, you should avoid `@Secured` and use `@RolesAllowed` instead. As with `@RolesAllowed`, you can specify `@Secured` on a class or interface to affect all the methods in that class or interface, or you can specify it on individual methods, or both. The same precedence and overriding rules apply in the third case.

```
@Secured("ADMINISTRATOR")
public interface SettingsMutatorService
{
    @Secured({"ADD_GENERAL_SETTING", "ALTER_GENERAL_SETTING"})
    void saveGeneralSettings(Map<String, Object> settings);

    @Secured({"ALTER_MEMBERSHIP_SETTING"})
    void saveMembershipSettings(Map<String, Object> settings);

    ...
}
```

## Pre- and Post- Annotations for Authorization

Spring Security's pre- and post-execution authorization annotations are the core of Spring Security's modern declarative authorization power. This group of four annotations, all in the `org.springframework.security.access.prepost` package, enables you to use the expressions you read about previously either before or after (or before and after) a method executes. As with `@RolesAllowed` and `@Secured`, you can specify these annotations on the class or interface, on individual methods, or both. If you specify the same pre- or post- annotation on a method *and* its class, the method annotation completely overrides the class annotation.

`@PreAuthorize` is the annotation you'll likely use the most of any annotations Spring Security supports. A security expression you specify in `@PreAuthorize` is evaluated before the method executes. The expression may reference any of the method arguments using the parameter name preceded by a `#`. For example, if the method has a parameter named *`employee`*, you could access the value of this argument using *`#employee`* in the expression. The exposed SpEL variables have the same types as the parameters they correspond to, and you can call methods on and access properties of the arguments.

```
@PreAuthorize("isFullyAuthenticated and hasAuthority('USER')")
public interface UserService
{
    @PreAuthorize("#userId == authentication.principal.userId or " +
                  "hasAuthority('CHANGE_OTHER_USER_PASSWORD')")
    void changePassword(long userId, String oldPassword, String newPassword);

    @PreAuthorize("#user.userId == authentication.principal.userId or " +
                  "hasAuthority('CHANGE_OTHER_USER_DETAILS')");
    void updateDetails(User user);

    @PreAuthorize("#user.userId == 0 and ( isAnonymous or " +
                  "hasAuthority('CREATE_NEW_USER') )")
    void addUser(User user);

    ...
}
```

If the expression evaluates to `true`, method execution continues. If the expression evaluates to `false`, the method is not invoked and an `AccessDeniedException` is thrown. Here, you have to be careful with the resolution of parameter names. Prior to Java 8, SpEL could not discover parameter names *unless your classes were compiled with debug information*. This meant putting classes compiled with debug symbols into production, which some developers prefer to avoid. In addition to this, interfaces don't contain debug information, so Spring Security cannot discover the parameter names of interface methods using debug symbols.

With Java 8's new parameter name reflection feature and as of Spring Security 3.2, parameter name discovery is more reliable and is also available for interfaces. You must compile your code with the `-parameters` compiler option to enable parameter name reflection. However, there are still circumstances under which it cannot work, such as if bean proxies interfere with the process. You can use parameter names if you carefully control your environment, but a better option (also new to Spring Security 3.2) is to annotate your method parameters to specify their names within Spring Security expressions. You can do this using `@org.springframework.security.access.method.P` or Spring Data's `@Param` (if you are using Spring Data).

```
@PreAuthorize("#u.userId == 0 and ( isAnonymous or " +
              "hasAuthority('CREATE_NEW_USER') )")
void addUser(@P("u") User user);
```

Spring Security 3.2's default configuration determines expression parameter variable names using the following checks, in order of precedence. You learn how to customize this later in the section.

1. If the parameter is annotated with `@P`, the name specified in that annotation is used. This is true even if `@Param` is also present.
2. If `@Param` is on the classpath and the parameter is annotated with `@Param` but not `@P`, the name specified in `@Param` is used.
3. If Java 8 parameter name reflection information is available, the name of the method parameter is used.
4. If debug symbols are available, the name of the method parameter is used.

> **WARNING** *When you enable pre- and post- annotations for authorization, Spring Security applies an implicit* `@PreAuthorize("permitAll")` *restriction to all applicable methods that do not explicitly specify* `@PreAuthorize`*. This means that any user can invoke methods not annotated with* `@PreAuthorize`*. To be clear, this isn't really any different from the behavior of* `@Secured` *and* `@RolesAllowed` *— in the absence of these annotations, access to a method is unrestricted. (Of course, URL security is still applied regardless of the status of your authorization annotations.)*

`@PostAuthorize` is essentially the same as `@PreAuthorize`, except that it evaluates after a method completes execution. The expression in this annotation cannot access the method arguments, but it can access the value the method returned using the EL variable *`returnObject`*, which has the same type as the method return type.

```
@PostAuthorize("returnObject.userId == authentication.principal.userId");
User getUser(long id);
```

Very few scenarios require you to use this annotation (you can replace this simple example with `@PreAuthorize`) because the method executes even if the user doesn't have permission. It *can* result in a rolled back transaction (assuming you order your proxies correctly), and it *can* prevent the user from obtaining the return value of the method execution, but if it's important to you that the method invocation has no side effects without permission, you should use `@PreAuthorize` instead.

`@PostFilter` is a particularly powerful annotation that allows you to filter the value returned from the method. You can use this annotation only on methods that return a `Collection` or array type. An EL variable named *`filterObject`* is available to the SpEL expression specified in `@PostFilter`. This variable has the type of the elements stored in the `Collection`. The expression is evaluated once for every value in the `Collection` or array, and values for which the expression evaluates to `false` are removed from the `Collection` or array before continuing. If the returned value is not a `Collection` or array, it results in an `IllegalArgumentException`. You can use this annotation for checks as simple as ensuring that the logged in user sees only objects that they "own" or "manage" (for example, the objects' theoretical `userId` property values match the principal's `userId` property). Or you can perform more advanced filtering using access control lists, which you learn about in the "Creating Access Control Lists for Object Security" section.

```
@PostAuthorize("returnObject.userId == authentication.principal.userId or " +
              "hasPermission(returnObject, 'read') or " +
              "hasPermission(returnObject, 'admin')")
User getUser(long id);

@PostFilter("hasPermission(filterObject, 'read') or " +
            "hasPermission(filterObject, 'admin')")
List<User> getManagedUsers();
```

`@PreFilter` is similar to `@PostFilter`, except that it acts on a method argument instead of a method's return value. The method parameter must be a `Collection` of elements (arrays are not supported for this annotation), and a *`filterObject`* variable will be exposed to the SpEL expression with the same type as the elements in the `Collection`, just like with `@PostFilter`. If the method has only one parameter that is a `Collection`, Spring Security can detect it automatically. If you have multiple `Collection` parameters, you must specify the name of the parameter you want to filter using the annotation's `filterTarget` attribute. That parameter name is matched to the method parameter using the process previously described for `@PreAuthorize`. There are very few uses for this annotation, and you will likely find that you never use it.

> **WARNING** *Although filtering method arguments and return values is useful, it cannot completely replace in-method security checks. More important, this technique is incompatible with pagination; it works only for methods that normally return an unpaged collection of a particular object. If you try to combine it with pagination, pages would possibly not have the correct number of results, and also may not have the same number of results from page to page. Also, filtering after the fact can often be a detriment to performance. To restrain lists based on user permissions, you still usually want to alter the logic that retrieves the data (for example, changes the SQL query to exclude results the user can't see). As such, you can never completely eliminate authorization code within your services. You can, however, almost completely replace it with declarative authorization.*

As you can see, Spring Security's pre- and post-execution authorization annotations are significantly more powerful than the Common Annotations API or `@Secured`. There is very little you can't do with these annotations given SpEL as the expression engine. However, you may have been confused by the sample use of the `hasPermission` function that you still haven't learned about. `hasPermission` makes use of Spring Security's access control list, which you learn about in the "Creating Access Control Lists for Object Security" section.

> **NOTE** *If you don't want to use SpEL expressions and prefer* `@Secured` *or* `@RolesAllowed`*, but you still want the advantage of the* `isAnonymous`*,* `isRememberMe`*, and* `isFullyAuthenticated` *security functions, just use the special-case permissions/roles* `IS_AUTHENTICATED_ANONYMOUSLY`*,* `IS_AUTHENTICATED_REMEMBERED`*, and* `IS_AUTHENTICATED_FULLY`*. They have the same effect as these functions.*

## Understanding the Benefits of Using Annotations

After seeing how you can essentially write code within some of these annotations, you might wonder how this is an improvement over writing the code in the service method. Didn't you read earlier that separating the authorization logic from the business logic was a key goal? Doesn't this just relocate the problem? Remember what you read earlier about unit testing your services: It becomes much harder to do this when you must create a `SecurityContext` and test positive and negative cases for every unit test. Using annotations in this matter eliminates this problem. Because the authorization check is merely *declared* in the annotation, it is never evaluated during your unit tests. This allows your tests to focus on testing the actual business logic that your code implements.

Another important point is that authorization rules are really a contract. When you create a `UserService` interface, you do so to establish a contract about what all `UserService` implementations must do, regardless of how they do it. Now imagine swapping out implementations of this `UserService`. Would those implementations suddenly have different authorization rules, too? No. The authorization rules are not an implementation detail. They are part of the contract, and as such they don't belong in the implementation — they belong in the interface. Spring Security's annotation support lets you (but does not require you to) declare these authorization rules in your interfaces so that they are part of the contract and apply to any implementation. This is a vast improvement over embedding the authorization checks in your application code.

## Configuring Annotation Support

Annotation support is disabled in Spring Security by default. You must enable annotation support to use any of the annotations covered in this section; otherwise, they are ignored. To enable annotation support you first need to expose the `AuthenticationManager` as a bean. Because you can have multiple web security configurations (which you learn about in the next chapter), the `WebSecurityConfigurerAdapter` does not expose the `AuthenticationManager` bean by default. (Otherwise, you could have duplicate beans.) Overriding the configuration adapter's `authenticationManagerBean` method allows the exposure of this bean.

Next, you need to add `@org.springframework.security.config.annotation.method.configuration.EnableGlobalMethodSecurity` to your configuration class and configure its attributes. Three of these attributes allow you to specify which annotations you want to support. `jsr250Enabled` controls support for the Common Annotations API, whereas `securedEnabled` controls support for `@Secured` and `prePostEnabled` for the pre- and post-execution annotations. By default, support for all three types is disabled because the attributes default to `false`. The following configuration enables support for all three groups using the `SecurityConfiguration` class you created in Chapter 26:

```
@Configuration
@EnableWebMvcSecurity
@EnableGlobalMethodSecurity(
        jsr250Enabled = true, securedEnabled = true, prePostEnabled = true
)
public class SecurityConfiguration extends WebSecurityConfigurerAdapter
{
    ...
    @Bean
    @Override
    public AuthenticationManager authenticationManagerBean() throws Exception
    {
        return super.authenticationManagerBean();
    }
    ...
}
```

In most cases, however, you won't want to enable all three groups of annotations. In fact, intermixing these groups can result in unspecified outcomes that might not be what you expect. You should usually pick one of the three annotation groups and stick with it throughout your application. In these last two chapters of the book, you work with the pre- and post- annotations exclusively.

You also need to pay attention to proxy ordering. You should recall from Part III (when you added `@EnableTransactionManagement` to your `RootContextConfiguration`) that all Spring Framework features that wrap beans with proxies must be configured the same way and should be ordered appropriately. If you use `AdviceMode.PROXY` on one, you should use it on all of them. If you set `proxyTargetClass` to `false` on one, you should do the same on all of them. Like `@EnableAsync` and `@EnableTransactionManagement`, `@EnableGlobalMethodSecurity` provides `mode`, `proxyTargetClass`, and `order` attributes to control these features because it configures a proxy that wraps your beans. You should use the same `mode` and `proxyTargetClass` values that you use for `@EnableAsync` and `@EnableTransactionManagement`. As for order, generally speaking the Spring Security proxy should execute before any other proxies on the same method. More important, it should always execute before the asynchronous execution and transaction management proxies.

```
@Configuration
@EnableWebMvcSecurity
@EnableGlobalMethodSecurity(
        prePostEnabled = true, order = 0,
        mode = AdviceMode.PROXY, proxyTargetClass = false
)
```

```
public class SecurityConfiguration extends WebSecurityConfigurerAdapter
{
    ...
}
```

The previous code is comparable to the following XML configuration:

```
<?xml version="1.0" encoding="UTF-8"?>
<beans:beans xmlns="http://www.springframework.org/schema/security"
             xmlns:beans="http://www.springframework.org/schema/beans"
             xmlns:xsi="http://www.w3.org/2001/XMLSchema-instance"
             xsi:schemaLocation="http://www.springframework.org/schema/security
         http://www.springframework.org/schema/security/spring-security-3.2.xsd
         http://www.springframework.org/schema/beans
         http://www.springframework.org/schema/beans/spring-beans-4.0.xsd">

    <global-method-security pre-post-annotations="enabled"
                            proxy-target-class="false" order="0" />

    ...

</beans:beans>
```

You have many ways to further customize global method security. You can create custom decision managers, expression handlers, invocation managers, metadata sources, and method advices. In an XML configuration you do this using other `<global-method-security>` attributes or sub-elements. Using Java configuration you must extend `org.springframework.security.config.annotation.method.configuration.GlobalMethodSecurityConfiguration` and override one or more of its methods to customize the configuration defaults further.

For example, the `hasPermission` security function is handled using an implementation of `org.springframework.security.access.PermissionEvaluator`. Normally you would configure an `org.springframework.security.acls.AclPermissionEvaluator` (which uses Spring Security's access control list features to evaluate object permissions) for this purpose. If you want to use a custom implementation, you just need to override the `createExpressionHandler` method and customize the `PermissionEvaluator` it uses. You could also call the handler's `setParameterNameDiscoverer` method to configure an alternative parameter name discovery protocol.

```
@Configuration
@EnableWebMvcSecurity
public class SecurityConfiguration extends WebSecurityConfigurerAdapter
{
    ...

    @Configuration
    @EnableGlobalMethodSecurity(
            prePostEnabled = true, order = 0,
            mode = AdviceMode.PROXY, proxyTargetClass = false
    )
    public static class AuthorizationConfiguration
            extends GlobalMethodSecurityConfiguration
    {
        @Override
        public MethodSecurityExpressionHandler createExpressionHandler()
```

```
        {
            DefaultMethodSecurityExpressionHandler handler =
                    new DefaultMethodSecurityExpressionHandler();
            handler.setPermissionEvaluator(new CustomPermissionEvaluator());
            return handler;
        }
    }
}
```

This code uses a new configuration syntax you haven't seen before. `SecurityConfiguration` already extends `WebSecurityConfigurerAdapter`, so it can't extend another class. To get around this, you just need to define a separate configuration class that extends `GlobalMethodSecurityConfiguration`. Using an inner class allows you to still group the entire security configuration in this file and also eliminates the need to `@Import` the `AuthorizationConfiguration`. (Spring Framework automatically imports static inner `@Configuration` classes of other `@Configuration` classes.) If you create a configuration class that extends `GlobalMethodSecurityConfiguration`, you must annotate it with `@EnableGlobalMethodSecurity`. You may have only one configuration class marked with this annotation, and only one configuration class may extend `GlobalMethodSecurityConfiguration`.

## Defining Method Pointcut Rules

As you might understand, some development teams prefer not to decorate their interfaces and classes with more and more annotations. There are arguably some down sides to using security annotations. For example, changing your authorization rules means recompiling your interfaces or their implementations. It may be easier to recompile your configuration classes or, more important, you might keep your configuration in XML files so that you can change the configuration without any recompilation. Within the `<global-method-security>` XML tag, you can define one or more AspectJ pointcut expressions and corresponding permissions or roles (comma-separated for `or`-ing multiple permissions for a single pointcut). Spring Security applies those restrictions to any bean methods matching the AspectJ pointcut, for example:

```
<global-method-security>
    <protect-pointcut expression="execution(* com.wrox.site.admin.*(*))"
                      access="ADMIN" />
</global-method-security>
```

Unfortunately, this feature does not support SpEL security expressions, which limits its usefulness. (Spring Security JIRA issue SEC-1663 documents a feature request to add expression support if you are truly interested.) It also requires you to learn about the very complex AspectJ pointcut expression syntax, which is beyond the scope of this discussion. Although method pointcut rules are useful for applying very simple restrictions to large numbers of methods with minimal code, this book recommends you stick to using the pre- and post-execution annotations for method security. Method security pointcuts are not explored further in this book.

# UNDERSTANDING AUTHORIZATION DECISIONS

To a large extent, you can configure Spring Security to handle most authorization scenarios without customizing its implementation. However, you may occasionally need to customize something, and understanding how Spring Security determines authorization decisions makes this process much simpler. Understanding this decision-making process also helps you troubleshoot behavior that doesn't match your intentions or desires. Finally, grasping Spring Security's access decision making is critical if you decide to switch from Spring Security's default decision-making settings to alternative settings that Spring Security provides. This section covers the decision-making process and the interfaces and implementations that power it.

## Using Access Decision Voters

*Access Decision Voters* are the key actors in the decision-making process. A typical Spring Security configuration contains multiple voters, which are implementations of `org.springframework.security.access.AccessDecisionVoter`. Just like members of a governmental body vote on whether to pass legislation, `AccessDecisionVoters` vote on whether to permit access to some part of the application. When a voter is polled for its opinion on whether access should be granted, it casts its vote based on the specific knowledge that voter is given. If it isn't given enough information to make an informed vote (for example, some other feature it doesn't know about is the only feature protecting a resource), it returns `AccessDecisionVoter.ACCESS_ABSTAIN` from its `vote` method to abstain from voting. If it does have enough information and believes access should be granted, it returns `AccessDecisionVoter.ACCESS_GRANTED`. Likewise, it returns `AccessDecisionVoter.ACCESS_DENIED` if it believes access should not be granted.

Several `AccessDecisionVoter` implementations are available, and Spring Security configures the appropriate one for you based on the security features you enable and disable. Your application may use just one or it may use many `AccessDecisionVoters`. The existing implementations are detailed in the following list.

- `org.springframework.security.acls.AclEntryVoter` casts its vote based on Spring Security's access control lists. If the resource accessed is not protected with the `hasPermission` expression function, `AclEntryVoter` abstains from voting. This voter isn't automatically configured, and in fact you will probably never use it. You have better ways to configure access control lists, which you explore in the next section.
- `org.springframework.security.access.vote.AuthenticatedVoter` acts on the special-case roles `IS_AUTHENTICATED_ANONYMOUSLY`, `IS_AUTHENTICATED_REMEMBERED`, and `IS_AUTHENTICATED_FULLY`. If the resource is not protected with one of these roles, `AuthenticatedVoter` abstains.
- The `org.springframework.security.access.annotation.Jsr250Voter` votes for any methods protected using the Common Annotations API (JSR 250). For example, if a method is annotated with `@RolesAllowed`, the `Jsr250Voter` votes based on the permissions specified in that annotation. This voter is enabled only if you enable support for JSR 250 annotations. When enabled, it votes only if a JSR 250 annotation is present for the method (or its class or interface). If one is not present or the access decision is for a non-method resource (such as a URL), this voter abstains.
- `org.springframework.security.access.prepost.PreInvocationAuthorizationAdviceVoter` casts a vote based on the `@PreAuthorize` and `@PreFilter` annotations. It is enabled only if pre- and post-execution annotation support is enabled. It abstains for non-method resources or when the annotations aren't

present for a method (or its class or interface). There is no voter for `@PostFilter` and `@PostAuthorize` — Spring Security handles these annotations as a special case because voters are used only before resource access.

- The `org.springframework.security.access.vote.RoleHierarchyVoter` uses Spring Security's role hierarchy system to make access decisions. You must create it manually if you enable the role hierarchy system, and it abstains if role hierarchy restrictions are not present on the protected resource being accessed. This book does not detail the role hierarchy system because use of role-based authorization is generally discouraged (see Chapter 25).
- `org.springframework.security.access.vote.RoleVoter` votes for resources protected with non-expression URL restrictions, method pointcut restrictions, or the `@Secured` annotation, and abstains for all other cases. It votes only if one or more listed "roles" start with the `ROLE_` prefix (which is why you can use only `ROLE_`-prefixed permissions with `@Secured`). This voter is enabled if you have `@Secured` annotations enabled, if you have `use-expressions` set to `false` in an XML `<http>` configuration element, or if you use method pointcut restrictions.
- The `org.springframework.security.web.access.expression.WebExpressionVoter` makes its decisions based on expressions protecting URL resources. It abstains for method protection decisions and in the absence of an expression protecting a particular URL. It is enabled if you use Java configuration or have `use-expressions` set to `true` in an XML `<http>` configuration element.

This pattern of voting "yes," "no," or "abstain" is very common in technologies that control access. For example, nearly all firewall systems have rules that evaluate to "accept," "deny," or "neutral." If you recall Log4j 2 filters from Chapter 11, you know that they, too, use a similar pattern. It's an extremely flexible architecture that essentially supports every possible rule.

## Using Access Decision Managers

As you can see, there are several built-in voters, and it's possible that multiple voters could be enabled simultaneously. In fact, multiple voters could have a non-abstaining opinion on a particular access decision. So how does Spring Security reconcile these differences? It uses *Access Decision Managers* to coordinate the votes of one or more voters and turn them into a final decision on the fate of an access request.

To continue the analogy of a governing body, a decision manager, which implements `org.springframework.security.access.AccessDecisionManager`, acts like a prime minister or speaker of the governing body. It tallies up the votes and determines whether the appropriate rules are met to grant access. Ultimately, the decision managers are the components that decide whether to throw an `AccessDeniedException`.

Your application could have multiple decision managers configured simultaneously. If you enable global method security, this creates a decision manager to manage access to protected methods. This decision manager can use most of the aforementioned voters. Likewise, configuring URL restrictions in your HTTP configuration creates another decision manager for controlling access to your application URLs. The `WebExpressionVoter` exists solely to service this manager because it has no purpose elsewhere in your application.

Spring Security ships with three standard `AccessDecisionManager` implementations; however, you can easily create your own. You can use these implementations for method security, URL security, or anything else that calls for a decision manager. By default, access is denied when all voters abstain, but each standard implementation provides a setting to determine whether to grant access in this scenario.

## Deciding by Affirmation

The `org.springframework.security.access.vote.AffirmativeBased` is the default and perhaps the simplest decision manager. This decision manager grants access if *at least one* non-abstaining voter approves. Even if other voters reject access, this decision manager still grants access if at least one voter returns `ACCESS_GRANTED`. You can probably see why this pattern is problematic in some cases, but in most cases it is perfectly sufficient. You typically won't have two URL restrictions match a request, but if you do, it's usually fine to allow access if at least one rule permits it. The same applies to method restrictions. Rarely do you use both `@Secured` and `@PreAuthorize` on the same method, for example, but if you did, it's logical to conclude those conditions should be `or`-ed together, not `and`-ed.

## Deciding by Consensus

Consensus decisions are probably the kind you are most familiar with. All republican and democratic forms of government operate on some principal of decisions made by consensus, whether it's a simple majority or two-thirds of a governing body agreeing. The `org.springframework.security.access.vote.ConsensusBased` decision manager operates on the simple majority principle. If 50-percent-plus-1 non-abstaining voters approve, access is granted.

For example, if you have all 7 voters enabled, 4 voters abstain, 2 voters vote to grant access, and 1 votes to deny access, access is granted. However, if 1 votes to grant and 2 vote to deny, access is denied. Of course, you have the problem of ties, in which the same number of grant and deny votes are cast. For this case, the `ConsensusBased` decision manager provides a setting for determining the tiebreaker policy. By default, access is granted in the event of a tie.

## Deciding by Unanimity

The natural conclusion to the set of standard decision managers is the one that requires all non-abstaining voters to vote yes — `org.springframework.security.access.vote.UnanimousBased`. All non-abstaining voters must vote to grant access; otherwise, this decision manager denies access. This is a very strict policy but, nevertheless, is appropriate in some cases.

Configuring a different `AccessDecisionManager` for global method security is really straightforward. If your `@Configuration` class doesn't extend `GlobalMethodSecurityConfiguration`, make that change. Then simply override the `accessDecisionManager` method to return a `ConsesusBased`, a `UnanimousBased`, or some custom implementation. Don't forget to include the voters in whatever manager you decide to return. Configuring a different decision manager for web security is equally easy: just add it to the `configure(HttpSecurity)` method.

```
    @Override
    protected void configure(HttpSecurity security) throws Exception
    {
        security
                .authorizeRequests()
                    .accessDecisionManager(new CustomDecisionManager())
        ...
    }
```

# CREATING ACCESS CONTROL LISTS FOR OBJECT SECURITY

So far this chapter has presented a relatively naïve approach to authorization, in which only a user's permissions or whether he "owns" a resource or object determine his access to that resource. Sometimes this approach is perfectly sufficient. Simple applications, especially applications with minimal user input, usually operate with very few authorization rules. Even applications like user forums, which seem fairly complicated, are actually simple in terms of authorization. However, sometimes you need much more complicated solutions.

An *access control list* (or *ACL*) is a more complex approach to object security, which defines per-user, per-object permissions. For a given object type `Foo`, a user `Bar` might have completely different permissions for different instances of that object. This goes beyond the idea of user ownership: A user might administer some instances, write others, delete others, read others, and finally not access others at all. Operating system file permissions, such as those in Microsoft Windows and Apple Mac OS X, are based on ACL principles. Linux operating systems also support ACL permissions; however, by default, they are not enabled and many Linux users are unfamiliar with using them.

## Understanding Spring Security ACLs

If you have ever managed file permissions in Windows or Mac OS X, or in Linux with ACL permissions enabled, you are very familiar with how ACLs work. Every file on your filesystem has a set of permissions, and for any given file, you can define different permissions for each user with access to that file system.

As you can imagine, a system that supports this is not trivial. In addition to containing complex permission management mechanisms, a system requires a significant set of backing data to hold these permissions. If you imagine an application with one million records of a given type in a system with one million users, you could potentially have one trillion pieces of data just to record those users' permissions for that one object type! No matter how efficiently you store that data, you're still looking at several terabytes of data. Understand that this is an extreme scenario (most users would have permissions to access only a small percentage of each data type), but undoubtedly you can see how important it is for you to design such a system well.

Spring Security comes with a mature, industry-tested ACL system that provides fine-grained control over your users' permissions. The central player in this system is the `org.springframework.security.acls.model.Acl` interface. It represents the access control list for a single domain object, and every domain object has exactly one `Acl`. It generically encapsulates the ID of the domain object in the form of an `org.springframework.security.acls.model.ObjectIdentity`, the ID of the owner of the domain object (the user that created it) in the form of an `org.springframework.security.acls.model.Sid`, and a list of all the permissions assigned to every user allowed to use that object in some way in the form of a `List` of `org.springframework.security.acls.model.AccessControlEntrys`.

Each `AccessControlEntry` encapsulates the ID of the user that holds that entry and the `org.springframework.security.acls.model.Permission` assigned to the entry. Permissions are represented with bitmasks — a highly efficient storage mechanism where each bit of a number represents a single permission. For example, bit 1 might control permission to read, whereas bit 2 controls permission to write. An `Acl` can also contain a parent `Acl`, in which case it inherits the `AccessControlEntrys` of that parent.

> **NOTE** *Bit masking can be a scary term to even seasoned developers. This same technique is used for standard Unix filesystem permissions and many other application and operating system activities. Rest assured, Spring Security abstracts away all the bit masking horror; you should never have to deal with it directly. The standard* `Permission` *implementation,* `org.springframework.security.acls.domain.BasePermission`*, understands the permissions* `read`, `write`, `create`, `delete`, *and* `admin`, *which are sufficient for most use cases. If you need to support other permissions, you must implement your own* `Permission` *class and tell it how to convert the bitmasks for your implementation.*

There are two standard implementations for `Sid`: `org.springframework.security.acls.domain.PrincipalSid` corresponds to an `Authentication`, whereas `org.springframework.security.acls.domain.GrantedAuthoritySid` corresponds to a `GrantedAuthority`. The latter is useful if you use `GrantedAuthoritys` to represent roles or groups and you want to grant permission to everyone in a particular role or group. With both these implementations, the `Sid` is ultimately represented with the `String` form of the `Authentication` or `GrantedAuthority` (the username or authority name). If you want to represent these with, say, a `long` user ID, you can easily implement your own `Sid`.

The ACL system is powered by an implementation of `org.springframework.security.acls.model.AclService`. This service can load ACLs by object identifier for use in permission evaluation. It is what enables you to use the `hasPermission` expression function to control access to your methods — calling this function loads the ACL for the given domain object using the `AclService` implementation.

If you want to, you can implement your own `AclService`, but this is not recommended. Spring Security's `org.springframework.security.acls.jdbc.JdbcAclService` is designed to very efficiently store ACLs in a relational database and retrieve them in a high-performance manner. The JAR artifact for `spring-security-acl` contains SQL scripts that create the necessary tables for MySQL/MariaDB (`createAclSchemaMySql.sql`), PostgreSQL (`createAclSchemaPostgresql.sql`), and HSQLDB (`createAclSchema.sql`). If you decide to use a different database, you can easily translate one of these scripts. Because `JdbcAclService` uses standard ANSI SQL features for data manipulation, it should be compatible with nearly any popular relational database.

Four ACL tables serve the following functions:

- `acl_sid` uniquely defines each `Sid` in the system for referential integrity with other tables. Typically, you have one row in this table for every user in your system, assuming you use only `PrincipalSid` or similar.
- `acl_class` uniquely defines each domain object class in the application. Like `acl_sid`, this table is used for referential integrity.
- `acl_object_identity` corresponds to the `Acl` class and holds the `ObjectIdentity`, owner `Sid`, and other `Acl` properties. You'll have one row in this table for every ACL-protected domain object in your system.
- `acl_entry` maps to the `List` of `AccessControlEntrys` in each `Acl`.

> **WARNING** *The* `acl_entry` *table has the potential to grow to many billions or even trillions of records, depending on the number of domain objects in your application, the number of persisted instances of those domain objects, and the number of users in your system. You should always monitor this table for performance problems and adjust indexing, system properties, or hardware as appropriate.*

## Configuring Access Control Lists

If you're going to implement your own ACL system, how you configure it is largely determined by how you design it. You either need to implement `AclService` and modify the `DefaultMethodSecurityExpressionHandler` to provide it with an `AclPermissionEvaluator` that uses this service, or just define your own `PermissionEvaluator` implementation.

Configuring Spring Security's ACL implementation is significantly more involved, but when set up correctly, it does most of the work for you. You would start by creating the Spring Security ACL methods in your application and defining an inner `@Configuration` class for global method security.

```
@Configuration
@EnableGlobalMethodSecurity(
        prePostEnabled = true, order = 0,
        mode = AdviceMode.PROXY, proxyTargetClass = false
)
public static class MethodAuthorizationConfiguration
        extends GlobalMethodSecurityConfiguration
{
    private static final Logger log = LogManager.getLogger();

    ...
}
```

> **NOTE** *The* `spring-security-acl` *Maven artifact is already a run-time dependency of other Spring Security artifacts you have included in your application. However, if you are going to use ACL you need to make this dependency a compile-time dependency.*
>
> ```
> <dependency>
>     <groupId>org.springframework.security</groupId>
>     <artifactId>spring-security-acl</artifactId>
>     <version>3.2.0.RELEASE</version>
>     <scope>compile</scope>
> </dependency>
> ```

You need to configure an implementation of `org.springframework.security.acls.domain.AclAuthorizationStrategy`. The ACL system uses this to determine whether the current principal has permissions to actually access administrative functions of the ACL service (such as changing the ACL for a particular object). The standard implementation permits use of these administrative methods if the principal is the owner of the object, has the administrative permission for the object, or has any of the granted authorities listed in the strategy constructor.

```
@Bean
public AclAuthorizationStrategy aclAuthorizationStrategy()
{
    return new AclAuthorizationStrategyImpl(
            new SimpleGrantedAuthority("ADMINISTRATOR")
    );
}
```

Next, you need to configure an `org.springframework.security.acls.model.PermissionGrantingStrategy`. This interface allows you to customize how permissions are evaluated, but the standard implementation is usually sufficient. It needs an `org.springframework.security.acls.domain.AuditLogger` for logging ACL authorization events. Configured as shown in the following code, it uses a lambda expression to provide logging behavior. You could take many different approaches, such as using the default `org.springframework.security.acls.domain.ConsoleAuditLogger` that logs to standard output.

```
@Bean
public PermissionGrantingStrategy permissionGrantingStrategy()
{
    return new DefaultPermissionGrantingStrategy((granted, entry) -> {
        if (!granted)
            log.info("Access denied for [{}].", entry);
    });
}
```

Now, you need to set up an `org.springframework.security.acls.model.AclCache` implementation. For optimized performance, the ACL system needs to cache entries until the next time they are changed. Spring Security comes with `AclCache` implementations capable of using either Ehcache (a popular open source distributed cache system for Java) or Spring Framework's cache system. For demonstration purposes, Spring Framework's cache based on `java.util.concurrent.ConcurrentMap` is sufficient. If you have a clustered application, you must provide an appropriate distributed cache implementation.

```
@Bean
public AclCache aclCache()
{
    return new SpringCacheBasedAclCache(
            new ConcurrentMapCache("Security-Acl"),
            this.permissionGrantingStrategy(),
            this.aclAuthorizationStrategy()
    );
}
```

After configuring these base systems, you need to set up the JDBC ACL implementation and add the `PermissionEvaluator`. The `JdbcAclService` and `org.springframework.security.acls.jdbc.BasicLookupStrategy` work together to efficiently retrieve ACL entries using your application `DataSource` and cache them when appropriate. The `AclPermissionEvaluator` and `org.springframework.security.acls.AclPermissionCacheOptimizer` work together to evaluate `hasPermission` expressions.

```
@Inject DataSource dataSource;

@Bean
public LookupStrategy lookupStrategy()
{
    return new BasicLookupStrategy(
            this.dataSource,
            this.aclCache(),
            this.aclAuthorizationStrategy(),
            this.permissionGrantingStrategy()
    );
}

@Bean
public AclService aclService()
{
    return new JdbcAclService(this.dataSource, this.lookupStrategy());
}

@Override
public MethodSecurityExpressionHandler createExpressionHandler()
{
    DefaultMethodSecurityExpressionHandler handler =
            new DefaultMethodSecurityExpressionHandler();
    handler.setPermissionEvaluator(new AclPermissionEvaluator(
            this.aclService()
    ));
    handler.setPermissionCacheOptimizer(new AclPermissionCacheOptimizer(
            this.aclService()
    ));
    return handler;
}
```

Finally, you can add `hasPermission` expressions to your methods to restrict access based on ACL permissions. For the most part, this entire configuration consists of simple Spring beans, and you should be very familiar with how to configure these components using XML. If you use an XML configuration, you need to configure the `DefaultMethodSecurityExpressionHandler` with its evaluator and optimizer as a standard bean and then use the Spring Security namespace to assign it to global method security:

```
<?xml version="1.0" encoding="UTF-8"?>
<beans:beans xmlns="http://www.springframework.org/schema/security"
             xmlns:beans="http://www.springframework.org/schema/beans"
             xmlns:xsi="http://www.w3.org/2001/XMLSchema-instance"
             xsi:schemaLocation="http://www.springframework.org/schema/security
         http://www.springframework.org/schema/security/spring-security-3.2.xsd
         http://www.springframework.org/schema/beans
         http://www.springframework.org/schema/beans/spring-beans-4.0.xsd">

    <global-method-security pre-post-annotations="enabled" order="0"
                            proxy-target-class="false">
        <expression-handler ref="expressionHandler" />
    </global-method-security>

</beans:beans>
```

## Populating ACLs for Your Entities

So far you have seen how to use ACLs, but you still need to populate ACLs for your entities. Spring Security does not do this for you automatically. Any time you create an entity, you must populate its owner, administrator, and other user permissions for that entity. Likewise, you may need service methods specifically for modifying the permissions for an entity, where user interfaces are provided for this purpose. You can manually populate the ACL database tables if you want, but Spring Security does provide a simpler approach to this task. You can create `ObjectIdentity`, `Sid`, `Permission`, and `Acl` instances and persist them to the database using an `org.springframework.security.acls.model.MutableAclService`, similar to the way you would use an Object-Relational Mapper.

To make this possible, you must first replace your `JdbcAclService` with a mutable version of it, `org.springframework.security.acls.jdbc.JdbcMutableAclService`. It also requires a reference to the caching bean because it must update the cache whenever an ACL changes.

```
@Bean
public MutableAclService aclService()
{
    return new JdbcMutableAclService(
            this.dataSource, this.lookupStrategy(), this.aclCache()
    );
}
```

Using the mutable service is easy. In any of your services, you can obtain an `@Injected MutableAclService` and then use it to insert or update the ACL, where appropriate. The following code updates an existing ACL or inserts a new ACL if one does not already exist. The `ObjectIdentityImpl` constructor used expects the entity to have a `getId` method. Alternatively, you can use the constructor that accepts a `Class<?>` object type and a `Serializable` ID value. If the mutable ACL service has to create a new ACL, it assigns the current principal as the owner of the object. You can change this by calling the `setOwner` method on the `MutableAcl`. This code gives another user read and write permissions on the forum post.

```
ObjectIdentityImpl identity = new ObjectIdentityImpl(forumPost);

MutableAcl acl;
try
{
    acl = (MutableAcl)this.mutableAclService.readAclById(identity);
}
catch(NotFoundException e)
{
    acl = this.mutableAclService.createAcl(identity);
}

Authentication otherUser = this.userService.getUser("OtherUserName");
PrincipalSid sid = new PrincipalSid(otherUser);
acl.insertAce(acl.getEntries().length, BasePermission.READ, sid, true);
acl.insertAce(acl.getEntries().length, BasePermission.WRITE, sid, true);
this.mutableAclService.updateAcl(acl);
```

Although Spring Security's ACL system is very powerful, it can be overkill. You don't need ACLs in every application, and if you can create a useful, secure application without ACLs, you're usually better off. More important, using ACLs unnecessarily can make performance suffer. Integrating Spring Security's ACL system into your application is an exercise left up to the reader.

# ADDING AUTHORIZATION TO CUSTOMER SUPPORT

In the last chapter, you created a simple application to demonstrate Spring Security authentication and then integrated authentication into the Customer Support application. In this chapter, you improve the security of the Customer Support application using Spring Security authorization. You can obtain the Customer-Support-v20 project from the `wrox.com` code download site. If you have not been following along with the Customer Support application from previous chapters, don't worry. The downloaded project is ready to compile and start, so you don't need to be familiar with previous work completed in the application. You should, however, take a look at the authentication added in Chapter 26.

Before you start, there's one thing you should know: Spring Security's error messages are already localized in several languages for your convenience. Just add the resource bundles to your `RootContextConfiguration`'s `messageSource` bean:

```
...
messageSource.setBasenames(
        "/WEB-INF/i18n/titles", "/WEB-INF/i18n/messages",
        "/WEB-INF/i18n/errors", "/WEB-INF/i18n/validation",
        "classpath:org/springframework/security/messages"
);
...
```

## Switching to Custom User Details

When you added authentication to the Customer Support application in Chapter 26, you created a custom `Authentication` object and `AuthenticationProvider` implementation. This demonstrated that you could do this, if you need to, but it really wasn't necessary. In fact, it's not the best practice, either, so you should avoid it if you can. Instead, the convention is to provide a `UserDetailsService` implementation and, if necessary, a custom `UserDetails`.

## Deciding on a User Details Implementation

When you design your system, ultimately you need to decide whether you want to couple the user object for persistence purposes with the user object for authentication and authorization purposes. The advantage to separating them is that you really don't need (or even want) a mutable user object carried around in the security context, and keeping them separate enforces this mantra. However, the advantage to making them the same object is that you don't have to do as much work to embed the user entity in other entities. Ultimately, only you can decide the approach that works best for you.

For simplicity, the Customer Support application combines the `UserDetails` implementation and the entity in the same object. The changes to `UserPrincipal` are pretty simple. It now implements `UserDetails` instead of `Authentication` and also implements `org.springframework.security.core.CredentialsContainer` so that Spring Security clears the password when the authentication process is complete.

```
...
public class UserPrincipal implements UserDetails, CredentialsContainer, Cloneable
{
    private static final long serialVersionUID = 1L;

    private long id;
    private String username;
    private byte[] hashedPassword;
    private Set<UserAuthority> authorities = new HashSet<>();
    private boolean accountNonExpired;
    private boolean accountNonLocked;
    private boolean credentialsNonExpired;
    private boolean enabled;

    // userId and username properties

    @Basic(fetch = FetchType.LAZY)
    @Column(name = "HashedPassword")
    public byte[] getHashedPassword() { ... }
    public void setHashedPassword(byte[] password) { ... }

    @Transient
    @Override
    public String getPassword()
    {
        return this.getHashedPassword() == null ? null :
                new String(this.getHashedPassword(), StandardCharsets.UTF_8);
    }

    @Override
    public void eraseCredentials()
    {
        this.hashedPassword = null;
    }

    @Override
    @ElementCollection(fetch = FetchType.LAZY)
```

```
    @CollectionTable(name = "UserPrincipal_Authority", joinColumns = {
            @JoinColumn(name = "UserId", referencedColumnName = "UserId")
    })
    public Set<UserAuthority> getAuthorities() { ... }
    public void setAuthorities(Set<UserAuthority> authorities) { ... }

    @Override
    @XmlElement @JsonProperty
    public boolean isAccountNonExpired() { ... }
    public void setAccountNonExpired(boolean accountNonExpired) { ... }

    @Override
    @XmlElement @JsonProperty
    public boolean isAccountNonLocked() { ... }
    public void setAccountNonLocked(boolean accountNonLocked) { ... }

    @Override
    public boolean isCredentialsNonExpired() { ... }
    public void setCredentialsNonExpired(boolean credentialsNonExpired) { ... }

    @Override
    @XmlElement @JsonProperty
    public boolean isEnabled() { ... }
    public void setEnabled(boolean enabled) { ... }

    ...
}
```

This, of course, requires some additional columns in the `UserPrincipal` table. If this is the first time you've run the Customer Support application, just run the SQL script in `create.sql` in the application to create all the tables and indexes you need. Otherwise, use the following code to add the necessary columns.

```
USE CustomerSupport;
ALTER TABLE UserPrincipal
  ADD COLUMN AccountNonExpired BOOLEAN NOT NULL DEFAULT TRUE,
  ADD COLUMN AccountNonLocked BOOLEAN NOT NULL DEFAULT TRUE,
  ADD COLUMN CredentialsNonExpired BOOLEAN NOT NULL DEFAULT TRUE,
  ADD COLUMN Enabled BOOLEAN NOT NULL DEFAULT TRUE;
ALTER TABLE UserPrincipal
  MODIFY COLUMN AccountNonExpired BOOLEAN NOT NULL,
  MODIFY COLUMN AccountNonLocked BOOLEAN NOT NULL,
  MODIFY COLUMN CredentialsNonExpired BOOLEAN NOT NULL,
  MODIFY COLUMN Enabled BOOLEAN NOT NULL;
```

The `UserAuthority` class is simple: It's just an embeddable POJO that implements `GrantedAuthority`. `@CollectionTable` in `UserPrincipal` maps `UserAuthority` to the `UserPrincipal_Authority` table.

```
@Embeddable
public class UserAuthority implements GrantedAuthority
{
    private String authority;

    public UserAuthority() { }

    public UserAuthority(String authority)
```

```
    {
        this.authority = authority;
    }

    @Override
    public String getAuthority() { ... }

    public void setAuthority(String authority) { ... }
}

CREATE TABLE UserPrincipal_Authority (
  UserId BIGINT UNSIGNED NOT NULL,
  Authority VARCHAR(100) NOT NULL,
  UNIQUE KEY UserPrincipal_Authority_User_Authority (UserId, Authority),
  CONSTRAINT UserPrincipal_Authority_UserId FOREIGN KEY (UserId)
    REFERENCES UserPrincipal (UserId) ON DELETE CASCADE
) ENGINE = InnoDB;
```

## Using the New User Details Entity

The old `AuthenticationService` no longer needs to handle authentication. Instead, it extends `UserDetailsService`, so it makes sense to rename it to `UserService` (and its implementation to `DefaultUserService`).

```
@Validated
public interface UserService extends UserDetailsService
{
    @Override
    UserPrincipal loadUserByUsername(String username);

    ...
}

@Service
public class DefaultUserService implements UserService
{
    ...

    @Override
    @Transactional
    public UserPrincipal loadUserByUsername(String username)
    {
        UserPrincipal principal = userRepository.getByUsername(username);
        // make sure the authorities and password are loaded
        principal.getAuthorities().size();
        principal.getPassword();
        return principal;
    }

    ...
}
```

The configuration needs just a slight tweak to use the `DaoConfigurationProvider` backed by the `UserService` and tell Spring Security to erase credentials after authentication.

```
@Configuration
@EnableWebMvcSecurity
public class SecurityConfiguration extends WebSecurityConfigurerAdapter
{
    @Inject UserService userService;

    ...

    @Override
    protected void configure(AuthenticationManagerBuilder builder)
            throws Exception
    {
        builder
                .userDetailsService(this.userService)
                        .passwordEncoder(new BCryptPasswordEncoder())
                .and()
                .eraseCredentials(true);
    }

    ...
}
```

When your users authenticate, the `UserPrincipal` object is stored in the resulting `Authentication` object. You can call the `Authentication`'s `getPrincipal` method to retrieve the corresponding `UserPrincipal`. In previous versions of Spring Security this would be quite cumbersome in your controllers because you would have to cast the `Principal` to an `Authentication` and then call `getPrincipal` and cast that to a `UserPrincipal`. Because of Spring Security 3.2's new `@AuthenticationPrincipal` annotation you learned about earlier, you can simply add annotated `UserPrincipal` parameters to your controller methods. Note that this wouldn't be possible if `UserPrincipal` still implemented `Authentication` as in Chapter 26.

```
@WebController
@RequestMapping("ticket")
public class TicketController
{
    ...
    @RequestMapping(value = "create", method = RequestMethod.POST)
    public ModelAndView create(@AuthenticationPrincipal UserPrincipal principal,
                               @Valid TicketForm form, Errors errors,
                               Map<String, Object> model)
            throws IOException
    {
        ...
    }
    ...
}
```

## Securing Your Service Methods

In Chapter 26, you added a single, simple authorization rule that protects all URLs by requiring authentication. Now you need to secure your service methods so that only certain users can perform certain tasks. First, you have to enable global method security. This is as simple as adding `@EnableGlobalMethodSecurity` to the `SecurityConfiguration` class — enabling pre- and post-execution annotations in the process — and exposing the `AuthenticationManager` as a bean. There is no need to create an inner class extending `GlobalMethodSecurityConfiguration` in this case, because nothing in the method security configuration needs to be customized.

```
@Configuration
@EnableWebMvcSecurity
@EnableGlobalMethodSecurity(
        prePostEnabled = true, order = 0, mode = AdviceMode.PROXY,
        proxyTargetClass = false
)
public class SecurityConfiguration extends WebSecurityConfigurerAdapter
{
    ...
    @Bean
    @Override
    public AuthenticationManager authenticationManagerBean() throws Exception
    {
        return super.authenticationManagerBean();
    }
    ...
}
```

> **NOTE** *The order for the global method security proxy is set to 0 here. In addition, the proxy order for asynchronous method execution is 1, whereas the proxy order for transactional support is 2. This ensures that security always runs first, followed by asynchronous method execution, and finally transaction operations.*

Protecting the `TicketService` is straightforward. You can protect all the methods using `@PreAuthorize` and fairly simple expressions. However, because you want users to edit only their own tickets and comments (unless they have an administrator-level privilege to edit anyone's comment), you must split up the `save` methods for `Tickets` and `TicketComments` into `create` and `update` methods. The `TicketController`, `TicketRestEndpoint`, and `TicketSoapEndpoint` must then be updated with the changed method names (not shown here). Notice the use of `@P` to indicate the parameter names for Spring Security expressions.

```
...
public interface TicketService
{
    @NotNull
    @PreAuthorize("hasAuthority('VIEW_TICKETS')")
    List<Ticket> getAllTickets();
    @NotNull
    @PreAuthorize("hasAuthority('VIEW_TICKETS')")
    Page<SearchResult<Ticket>> search(...);
    @PreAuthorize("hasAuthority('VIEW_TICKET')")
    Ticket getTicket(...);
    @PreAuthorize("#ticket.id == 0 and hasAuthority('CREATE_TICKET')")
    void create(@NotNull(message = "{validate.ticketService.save.ticket}")
                @Valid @P("ticket") Ticket ticket);
    @PreAuthorize("(authentication.principal.equals(#ticket.customer) and " +
            "hasAuthority('EDIT_OWN_TICKET')) or hasAuthority('EDIT_ANY_TICKET')")
    void update(@NotNull(message = "{validate.ticketService.save.ticket}")
                @Valid @P("ticket") Ticket ticket);
    @PreAuthorize("hasAuthority('DELETE_TICKET')")
```

```
    void deleteTicket(long id);

    @NotNull
    @PreAuthorize("hasAuthority('VIEW_COMMENTS')")
    Page<TicketComment> getComments(...);
    @PreAuthorize("#comment.id == 0 and hasAuthority('CREATE_COMMENT')")
    void create(
            @NotNull(message = "{validate.ticketService.save.comment}")
            @Valid @P("comment") TicketComment comment,
            @Min(value = 1L, message = "{validate.ticketService.saveComment.id}")
                long ticketId
    );
    @PreAuthorize("(authentication.principal.equals(#comment.customer) and " +
            "hasAuthority('EDIT_OWN_COMMENT')) or " +
            "hasAuthority('EDIT_ANY_COMMENT')")
    void update(@NotNull(message = "{validate.ticketService.save.comment}")
                @Valid @P("comment") TicketComment comment);
    @PreAuthorize("hasAuthority('DELETE_COMMENT')")
    void deleteComment(long id);

    @PreAuthorize("hasAuthority('VIEW_ATTACHMENT')")
    Attachment getAttachment(long id);
}
```

You also need to secure chat requests, which introduces a few more complications. Here, you must not only check that users are authorized to perform the task, but also that they are actually members of the chat session when they send a message or leave the session.

```
public interface ChatService
{
    @PreAuthorize("authentication.principal.username.equals(#user) and " +
            "hasAuthority('CREATE_CHAT_REQUEST')")
    CreateResult createSession(@P("user") String user);
    @PreAuthorize("authentication.principal.username.equals(#user) and " +
            "hasAuthority('START_CHAT')")
    JoinResult joinSession(long id, @P("user") String user);
    @PreAuthorize("authentication.principal.username.equals(#user) and " +
            "(#user.equals(#session.customerUsername) or " +
            "#user.equals(#session.representativeUsername)) and " +
            "hasAuthority('CHAT')")
    ChatMessage leaveSession(@P("session") ChatSession session,
                             @P("user") String user, ReasonForLeaving reason);
    @PreAuthorize("authentication.principal.username.equals(#message.user) and " +
            "(#message.user.equals(#session.customerUsername) or " +
            "#message.user.equals(#session.representativeUsername)) and " +
            "hasAuthority('CHAT')")
    void logMessage(@P("session") ChatSession session,
                    @P("message") ChatMessage message);
    @PreAuthorize("hasAuthority('VIEW_CHAT_REQUESTS')")
    List<ChatSession> getPendingSessions();

    ...
}
```

You must also consider something else, however. Currently, Spring Security has no support for handling WebSocket sessions. This is a planned feature for Spring Security 4.0, which will hopefully release by the middle of 2014. That version should take care of many things for you, such as overriding the `Principal` in the `Session` and closing WebSocket sessions when `HttpSessions` are logged out. Indeed, it could get rid of a great deal of code in your application. For now, however, you must take some special steps on your own. When a WebSocket session is handed off and asynchronous communications begin, the Security Context is cleared. To compensate, you must create a method to handle secured operations.

```
private void doSecured(SecuredAction secureAction)
{
    SecurityContextHolder.setContext(this.securityContext);
    try
    {
        secureAction.execute();
    }
    finally
    {
        SecurityContextHolder.clearContext();
    }
}

@FunctionalInterface
private static interface SecuredAction
{
    void execute();
}

public static class EndpointConfigurator extends SpringConfigurator
{
    ...
    @Override
    public void modifyHandshake(ServerEndpointConfig config,
                                HandshakeRequest request,
                                HandshakeResponse response)
    {
        ...
        config.getUserProperties().put(SECURITY_CONTEXT_KEY,
                SecurityContextHolder.getContext());
        ...
    }
    ...
}
```

You then have to make sure that all `@OnOpen`, `@OnClose`, `@OnMessage`, and `@OnError` methods (and any other methods that the WebSocket container could invoke) execute within a secured action. For example, here is the new `@OnError` method:

```
@OnError
public void onError(Throwable e)
{
    this.doSecured(() -> {
        log.warn("Error received in WebSocket session.", e);

        synchronized(this)
        {
            if(this.closed)
```

```
                    return;
                this.close(ChatService.ReasonForLeaving.ERROR,
                        "error.chat.closed.exception");
            }
        });
    }
```

The last thing you need to think about is the session list. This is an administrative function, but the service (Spring Security's `SessionRegistry`) is not in your control, so you cannot add security annotations to the service. For this, you will need to fall back to standard URL security rules in your `SecurityConfiguration`.

```
    @Override
    protected void configure(HttpSecurity security) throws Exception
    {
        security
                .authorizeRequests()
                    .antMatchers("/session/list")
                        .hasAuthority("VIEW_USER_SESSIONS")
                    .anyRequest().authenticated()
        ...
    }
```

Now that you know what all the secured actions in your application are, you need to assign permissions to your users. If you just ran the `create.sql` script earlier in the section, this was already done for you. Otherwise, you must find the following four inserts in the script and run them to grant the authorities. The inserts assume you still have the pre-populated users (Nicholas, Sarah, Mike, and John) in your database, and they grant standard "customer" permissions to Nicholas, Sarah, and Mike, and "representative" permissions to John.

```
USE CustomerSupport;
INSERT INTO UserPrincipal_Authority (UserId, Authority)
  VALUES (1, 'VIEW_TICKETS'), (1, 'VIEW_TICKET'), (1, 'CREATE_TICKET'),
    (1, 'EDIT_OWN_TICKET'), (1, 'VIEW_COMMENTS'), (1, 'CREATE_COMMENT'),
    (1, 'EDIT_OWN_COMMENT'), (1, 'VIEW_ATTACHMENT'), (1, 'CREATE_CHAT_REQUEST'),
    (1, 'CHAT');

INSERT INTO UserPrincipal_Authority (UserId, Authority)
  VALUES (2, 'VIEW_TICKETS'), (2, 'VIEW_TICKET'), (2, 'CREATE_TICKET'),
    (2, 'EDIT_OWN_TICKET'), (2, 'VIEW_COMMENTS'), (2, 'CREATE_COMMENT'),
    (2, 'EDIT_OWN_COMMENT'), (2, 'VIEW_ATTACHMENT'), (2, 'CREATE_CHAT_REQUEST'),
    (2, 'CHAT');

INSERT INTO UserPrincipal_Authority (UserId, Authority)
  VALUES (3, 'VIEW_TICKETS'), (3, 'VIEW_TICKET'), (3, 'CREATE_TICKET'),
    (3, 'EDIT_OWN_TICKET'), (3, 'VIEW_COMMENTS'), (3, 'CREATE_COMMENT'),
    (3, 'EDIT_OWN_COMMENT'), (3, 'VIEW_ATTACHMENT'), (3, 'CREATE_CHAT_REQUEST'),
    (3, 'CHAT');

INSERT INTO UserPrincipal_Authority (UserId, Authority)
  VALUES (4, 'VIEW_TICKETS'), (4, 'VIEW_TICKET'), (4, 'CREATE_TICKET'),
    (4, 'EDIT_OWN_TICKET'), (4, 'VIEW_COMMENTS'), (4, 'CREATE_COMMENT'),
    (4, 'EDIT_OWN_COMMENT'), (4, 'VIEW_ATTACHMENT'), (4, 'CREATE_CHAT_REQUEST'),
    (4, 'CHAT'), (4, 'EDIT_ANY_TICKET'), (4, 'DELETE_TICKET'),
    (4, 'EDIT_ANY_COMMENT'), (4, 'DELETE_COMMENT'), (4, 'VIEW_USER_SESSIONS'),
    (4, 'VIEW_CHAT_REQUESTS'), (4, 'START_CHAT');
```

## Using Spring Security's Tag Library

Now that you've configured method security, your services are secured against unauthorized access. However, is it really a good user experience to click a link only to be greeted with an "Access Denied" message? You need to improve your views so that users can't see actions they can't perform. The creators of Spring Security thought about pretty much everything, so you have a tag library at your disposal to make this task easy.

```
<%@ taglib prefix="security" uri="http://www.springframework.org/security/tags" %>
```

The `<security:accesscontrollist>` tag, which you won't use here, allows you to perform checks against the access control list for an object. In the `domainObject` attribute, you use an EL expression (not a SpEL expression) to provide a domain object exposed as an EL variable. In the `hasPermission` attribute, you specify one or more (comma-separated) object permissions that the user must have on that domain object. The code nested within the tag is not evaluated unless the user has those permissions for the given domain object. Spring Security 4.0 will include `<security:csrfField>` and `<security:csrfMetaTags>` tags that output, respectively, a CSRF form field and CSRF HTML `<meta>` elements. JavaScript code can use these HTML `<meta>` elements to reference the CSRF field and header name and CSRF token value.

The `<security:authentication>` tag is very useful. It allows you to output properties of the current `Authentication`. The `WEB-INF/tags/template/basic.tag` file demonstrates this by printing out the username for the current principal.

```
<br />Welcome, <security:authentication property="principal.username" />!
```

The tag you'll use most often is `<security:authorize>`. Its nested contents are evaluated only if the authorization rule defined with its attributes evaluates to `true`. If you specify the `access` attribute, it evaluates the value as a security expression (so you can use `hasAuthority` and the other functions). The `url` attribute allows you to specify an application-relative URL, and Spring Security finds and evaluates the matching URL security rule, if any. If you use `url`, you can also specify `method` to restrict the permitted HTTP methods. You cannot specify `access` and `url` at the same time. `basic.tag` demonstrates using `<security:authorize>` to hide links that the user isn't authorized to access.

```
<security:authorize access="hasAuthority('VIEW_TICKETS')">
    <a href="<c:url value="/ticket/list" />">...</a><br />
    <a href="<c:url value="/ticket/search" />">...</a><br />
</security:authorize>
<security:authorize access="hasAuthority('CREATE_TICKET')">
    <a href="<c:url value="/ticket/create" />">...</a><br />
</security:authorize>
<security:authorize access="hasAuthority('CREATE_CHAT_REQUEST')">
    <a href="javascript:void 0;" onclick="newChat();">...</a><br />
</security:authorize>
<security:authorize access="hasAuthority('VIEW_CHAT_REQUESTS')">
    <a href="<c:url value="/chat/list" />">...</a><br />
</security:authorize>
<security:authorize access="hasAuthority('VIEW_USER_SESSIONS')">
    <a href="<c:url value="/session/list" />">...</a><br />
</security:authorize>
```

All the Spring Security tags provide `var` attributes like so many other tags you have used. For the `<security:authorize>` and `<security:accesscontrollist>` tags, the specified variable contains the `boolean` result of evaluating the rule. The tag cannot have nested content if you use this attribute. For the other tags, the tag output is stored in the specified variable. `WEB-INF/jsp/view/chat/list.jsp` demonstrates using the `var` attribute with `<security:authorize>` to omit links from the list if the user doesn't have the `START_CHAT` authority.

```
<security:authorize access="hasAuthority('START_CHAT')"
                    var="canJoin" />
<spring:message code="message.chatList.instruction" />:<br /><br />
<c:forEach items="${sessions}" var="s">
    <c:choose>
        <c:when test="${canJoin}">
            <a...>${s.customerUsername}</a><br />
        </c:when>
        <c:otherwise>${s.customerUsername}</c:otherwise>
    </c:choose>
    ...
```

With these changes to the views, the Customer Support application is ready to go. Go ahead and compile it, start Tomcat from your IDE, and go to `http://localhost:8080/support`. Log in as different users and test out that the authorization system works properly by listing and creating tickets, listing sessions, and taking part in a chat session. If you want, you can set the system property `spring.security.disableUISecurity`, which disables the `<security:authorize>` tags so that their contents are always rendered, making it easier to attempt unauthorized access to resources and ensure that method security is working properly.

> **NOTE** *If you have never run the Customer Support application before, or you do not remember the usernames and passwords for it, consult the* `create.sql` *script. Each user's* `INSERT` *statement includes a SQL comment with the plain-text password for that user.*

## SUMMARY

You have learned a lot about authorizing users in Spring Security in this chapter. You explored URL security and global method security, and compared a number of different method security annotations and how to use them. You learned about how Spring Security makes access decisions and how voters can contribute to those decisions, and also learned about Spring Security's powerful access control list (ACL) system. Finally, you added authorization to Multinational Widget Corporation's Customer Support application. You converted the `UserPrincipal` from an `Authentication` to a `UserDetails`, configured method security, added user interface security with the security tag library, and took special steps to maintain the `SecurityContext` in a WebSocket endpoint.

Only one thing remains to finish off the Customer Support application: you still have web service endpoints that aren't secured and aren't fully functional. In the next and final chapter of the book, you learn about web service security and OAuth, and you integrate Spring Security OAuth into the Customer Support application.

# 28

# Securing RESTful Web Services with OAuth

## IN THIS CHAPTER

- ➤ Understanding web service security
- ➤ An introduction to OAuth
- ➤ A comparison of OAuth 1.0a and 2.0
- ➤ Using OAuth with Spring Security
- ➤ Finishing the Customer Support application
- ➤ Writing an OAuth Client application

## WROX.COM CODE DOWNLOADS FOR THIS CHAPTER

You can find the `wrox.com` code downloads for this chapter at `http://www.wrox.com/go/projavaforwebapps` on the Download Code tab. The code for this chapter is divided into the following major examples:

- ➤ Customer-Support-v21 Project
- ➤ OAuth-Client Project

## NEW MAVEN DEPENDENCIES FOR THIS CHAPTER

In addition to the Maven dependencies introduced in previous chapters, you also need the following Maven dependencies:

```
<dependency>
    <groupId>org.springframework.security.oauth</groupId>
    <artifactId>spring-security-oauth2</artifactId>
    <version>1.0.5.RELEASE</version>
```

```
        <scope>compile</scope>
    </dependency>

    <dependency>
        <groupId>commons-codec</groupId>
        <artifactId>commons-codec</artifactId>
        <version>1.9</version>
        <scope>runtime</scope>
    </dependency>

    <dependency>
        <groupId>org.apache.httpcomponents</groupId>
        <artifactId>httpclient</artifactId>
        <version>4.3.1</version>
        <scope>runtime</scope>
    </dependency>
```

# UNDERSTANDING WEB SERVICE SECURITY

So far in Part IV, you have explored the concepts and technologies associated with authentication and authorization and applied your newfound knowledge to securing web-based graphical user interfaces. In Chapter 17 you learned about SOAP and RESTful web services, but up until now, you have left those web services unprotected. In this chapter you learn about web service security and various approaches to securing your web service resources. You explore the OAuth standard and integrate it into the Customer Support application. Finally, you create a very simple web service client for testing the Customer Support RESTful web service.

## Comparing Web GUI and Web Service Security

Securing your web services is a very different task from securing your web GUI. You no longer need to worry about certain vulnerabilities. Because you have no graphical forms that your users must fill out, you don't have to worry about cross-site request forgeries. Because of a lack of JavaScript, you don't have to worry about cross-site scripting. And because you aren't using HTTP sessions and cookies, you aren't affected by session fixation attacks; however, you may face new and similar vulnerabilities.

Now, don't be mistaken. This isn't to say that the developers of client web applications that use your web services don't have to worry about these vulnerabilities — they do. Also, if you use your web services to back your web user interfaces, you still have to keep these vulnerabilities in mind. But if you're serving up a web service only for other applications to consume, these issues aren't your concern.

A host of security concerns still apply to your web services. You have to worry about man-in-the-middle attacks, which as usual you can address by using strong SSL mechanisms. You have to worry about stolen authentication tokens, something you learn about in the next section. Presumably you'll want to authenticate your web service users and ensure they are authorized to perform certain tasks, but it's possible your web services provide different features than your web GUI and you don't need authentication. (It's equally possible the other way around, too.) You also have to remember all kinds of HTTP protocol vulnerabilities, just like you would with a web GUI.

Assuming you want to authenticate users of your web services (which is typical), how do you do it? Forget about authentication *mechanisms* (basic, form, LDAP, and so on) momentarily. Do you even want the same users? For a lot of organizations, the answer to this question is "Yes." For others, it's "No." As with so many other things, it completely depends on your business needs. There is no requirement, technical or otherwise, that you secure your web GUI and web services with the same set of users. Of course, understand that if you expose the same data through your web GUI and web services, your users will fully expect that the services require the same users because other users shouldn't see their private data. This chapter emphasizes the approach of using the same set of users.

After you answer these questions, the next step is to determine which authentication mechanism (or mechanisms) to use for your web services. You have plenty of choices along with some standard conventions, which you explore in this chapter.

## Choosing an Authentication Mechanism

You explored several authentication mechanisms in Chapter 26, and most of these are applicable to web services in some form or another. For example, you could enforce basic or digest authentication for your web services, which would actually fit really well with the stateless nature of REST. SOAP can be either stateful or stateless, but in either case, basic and digest still work really well for these types of web services. However, both mechanisms have one major problem: The client application must know and retain the credentials for the entire duration that the web services are in use. This may be fine if the client application is the user, but if your users want to use a third-party application that connects to your web services, they will likely be uncomfortable or unwilling to provide that application with their credentials.

Another option is to have your users authenticate directly with your application and then give the client application a token of some type to assert that authentication. This is actually the basic concept behind form authentication and HTTP sessions: Your users authenticate using a form on your site, and in turn your application gives the user's browser (the client application) a token (a session ID cookie) to assert that authentication on future requests. The advantage of using this approach is that your users never have to give the client application their credentials, which improves both actual and perceived security. This highlights one important concept of security: understanding the difference between actual and perceived security.

If you take some action that makes your users perceive a higher level of security, they are happier, and thus that makes your business more successful. However, the action might not actually make them safer. Sometimes this is okay: If your users are genuinely safe using your site and making them actually safer isn't achievable, but you can make them feel safer, it can help your business. But if your site is susceptible to one or more attacks and you make your users feel safer, this creates a false sense of security, which is dangerous and can hurt you and your users. Essentially, every security-related change you make to your site can have one of the following consequences, presented in the order you should prefer those consequences to occur:

1. **You make a change that actually makes your users safer and also makes them feel safer.** This is a win-win and should always be your goal.
2. **You make a change that actually makes your users safer but has no impact on how they perceive their safety.** This is still a good thing, and you should not altogether avoid it. Your users are still better off regardless of whether they know it.

3. **You make a change that actually makes your users safer but makes them feel less safe.** This is a bad thing. The increased safety does no good if users stop using your site because they feel unsafe. You can almost always avoid this dilemma by approaching the change with a better public relations approach.
4. **You make a change that actually makes your users less safe and also makes them feel less safe.** Obviously, this is a very bad thing. Don't make your users less safe. However, if your users decide they feel *unreasonably* less safe they'll stop using your site, and only you suffer the consequences.
5. **You make a change that actually makes your users less safe but makes them feel the same or, worse, safer.** Yes, this is actually worse than consequence number 4. You may benefit in the short term, and in fact it's possible you never get caught. But chances are your users will eventually suffer the consequences, and when they figure out they were duped, they will probably come after you for compensation.

Obviously, you want to design an authentication and authorization system such that every feature achieves consequence number 1. Because this is only possible in a perfect world, your realistic goal is to stick to consequences 1 and 2, with as many features resulting in consequence number 1 as possible. If your security features include ones that result in consequences 3, 4, or 5, you must take a step back and re-evaluate your approach.

Returning to the idea of your users authenticating directly with your application and returning an assertion token back to the client application, this approach is not without its downsides.

- **You run the risk of the token being stolen.** This risk is not substantially different from the risk of the credentials being stolen. In fact, if you change tokens very frequently (at least once per day) you can actually make things more secure because users are typically unwilling to change their passwords that often.
- **You have the problem of token forgery.** You can mitigate this fairly simply (and you learn about this in the next section).

Regardless of these downsides, tokens are a very safe and effective approach and one used across the industry to protect web services. As usual, it makes little sense to try to reinvent the wheel, and there are already tools available to integrate strong security in web service applications. One of those, which you use in this chapter, is OAuth.

## INTRODUCING OAUTH

OAuth is an open standard for authorization founded by Blaine Cook of Twitter, Larry Halff of Ma.gnolia, Chris Messina, an open source advocate who has worked for Google and several other companies, and David Recordon, an open standards advocate from Facebook. You may already wonder about the use of the word authorization to describe OAuth. Aren't you supposed to be finding a solution to authentication? No, you already have a solution! In fact, you have many solutions! Basic, digest, form, Windows, certificates, smart cards — the list goes on.

You don't need a new way to establish your users' identities; you're already an expert on that. What you really need is a way to continue to use that authentication on future requests to establish that the user is *authorized* to access the web service. This, of course, emphasizes the blurry line that draws the boundary between authentication and authorization. The two are closely related and very much depend on one another. To an extent, you can even consider authentication as a form of authorization. At the very least, authentication is always the first step in authorization. To be clear, OAuth is an authorization standard, but it is closely tied to authentication.

> **WARNING** *This book is not an authoritative guide to any version of OAuth. The many details and nuances of OAuth simply cannot be covered in a single chapter. This chapter helps you start with a simple OAuth system, but you should not deploy OAuth into your production environment without reading the specifications and supporting documents. You can find the IETF standards documents for OAuth 1.0a, OAuth 2.0, and OAuth 2.0 Bearer Tokens* at `http://tools.ietf.org/html/rfc5849`, `http://tools.ietf.org/html/rfc6749`, and `http://tools.ietf.org/html/rfc6750`, *respectively.*

## Understanding the Key Players

All versions of OAuth have official terms that identify the key players in the authentication and authorization process. It's important to know these terms and understand the role each player makes during an OAuth session. These terms are used often and without further clarification throughout the text, so make sure you understand them clearly before proceeding.

- The *client* is any HTTP application capable of making requests to a web service API using OAuth. It can be a JavaScript application, a web browser plug-in, a desktop application, a mobile application, or anything else you can think of. More important, the client is not the user or person authenticating with your application.
- A *protected resource* is, quite simply, a resource in your application that is protected from unauthorized access. It can be accessed only in an OAuth-authenticated request.
- A *resource owner* is some entity authorized to access these protected resources. The resource owner might be an organization, a person, or even another application—generally speaking, it is what you think of as the user. The resource owner uses the client to connect to your application and retrieve or manipulate protected resources.

## The Beginning: OAuth 1.0

OAuth began when several of its founders were implementing OpenID for their respective organizations. Larry Halff, for example, was trying to come up with a way for his OpenID users to connect their Mac OS X Dashboard Widgets to Ma.gnolia's web services. After a brief consultation, the founders determined that there was no current open authorization standard for web service APIs, and OAuth was born.

The founders formed an open standards discussion group in April 2007, and started working on the OAuth standard. It went through several revisions, during which Eran Hammer joined the discussion group. In October 2007, the group released the OAuth Core 1.0 final draft. In 2009, it was discovered that OAuth 1.0 was vulnerable to a form of session fixation attack. The details of this attack are outside the scope of this book, but you can read about them on Eran Hammer's blog at `http://hueniverse.com/2009/04/explaining-the-oauth-session-fixation-attack/`. For this reason, you should consider the OAuth 1.0 draft unsafe, and you should not use it.

## The Standard: OAuth 1.0a

The *Internet Engineering Task Force* (*IETF*) met in 2008, and discussed taking on the OAuth 1.0 draft as an Internet working standard. OAuth enjoyed wide community support, and an IETF group worked on it for nearly 2 years. It was publicly approved and published as Internet standard RFC 5849 in April 2010. Officially, it is OAuth Core 1.0 Revision A and incorporates a fix for the session fixation attack identified in OAuth 1.0 in 2009. It is normally referred to simply as OAuth 1.0a and is considered an authorization *protocol*. (For the purposes of this book, that means it describes how implementations *must* behave.) This part of the section gives a brief overview of how OAuth 1.0a functions, including identifying the changes made to mitigate the session fixation vulnerability.

### Understanding OAuth 1.0a Terminology

The standard defines several terms that are specific to OAuth 1.0a. The *server* is you, or rather your application. The client makes requests to the server and, assuming it is authorized, the server returns responses to the client. The generic concept of the server is responsible for authentication and authorization services and for hosting your protected resources. *Credentials* are a pair of values capable of establishing an identity. The pair consists of an identifier (such as a username or public key) and a secret (such as a password or private key). In OAuth 1.0a, there are three types of credentials.

- *Client credentials* authenticate the client (remember: not the user) making the request. Client credentials are important because they allow you to restrict which applications can access your web services on behalf of your users.
- *Temporary credentials* are, as the name implies, temporary, and are used during the authentication process to link all the steps together securely.
- *Token credentials* are credentials returned by the authentication service to the client that the client uses to authorize all future requests for the resource owner. A *token*, like a username, is a unique identifier (sometimes a completely random string, sometimes more meaningful). After a resource owner properly authenticates, the server issues a token to the client. Combined with a shared secret to form the token credentials, the token associates requests with the authenticated resource owner.

### Using OAuth 1.0a to Authenticate and Authorize

The flow of OAuth-authenticated requests is straightforward, even if the concept seems confusing. Diagrams make it easier to understand, so this section has several. When a resource owner wants to access a protected resource on the server using a client, exactly one of three things is true:

> **NOTE** *Figures 28-1 through 21-3 are discussed later in this chapter and appear surrounded by more discussion about what's shown in the figures. Please refer forward to these figures as you work through this list.*

- The client has no token credentials for that resource owner and cannot access the protected resource (the upcoming Figure 28-1).
- The client has valid token credentials for that resource owner and can access the protected resource (Figure 28-2).
- The client has expired or revoked token credentials for that resource owner and cannot access the protected resource (Figure 28-3).

Each of these situations results in a different set of actions that occur to ultimately grant access to the protected resource (assuming such access is permitted). In the case that the client has no token credentials for the resource owner, it first (transparent to the resource owner) makes an empty HTTP `POST` request to the *temporary credentials request endpoint* (for which the client already knows the URL). This request uses the `Authorization: OAuth` header and several authorization header *protocol parameters* to authenticate the client with the server.

- *`realm`* names the application or resource ultimately being accessed, just like with standard basic or digest authentication.
- *`oauth_consumer_key`* contains the identifier from the client credentials (which the client obtained from the server ahead of time).
- *`oauth_signature_method`* is the signature mechanism being employed.
- *`oauth_timestamp`* is the timestamp of when the request was made, specified in seconds since the Unix epoch.
- *`oauth_nonce`* is a unique identifier for the request that is never repeated (to prevent replay attacks).
- *`oauth_callback`* is the URI that the server should return the client to after the client has authenticated and granted access to the client.
- *`oauth_signature`* is a signature calculated using all these parameters, various parts of the request, and the secret from the client credentials.

> **NOTE** *To be clear, the* `Authorization` *header is only one approach that the client may use to transmit protocol parameters. It may also use request entity parameters when the request is* `x-www-form-urlencoded` *(less preferred) and request URL parameters (least preferred). Use of the* `Authorization` *header is the preferred mechanism because Internet proxies tend to be better behaved and not cache these types of requests.*

The secret is never transmitted in the request — it doesn't need to be because the client uses the secret to generate the signature. The signature is always either HMAC-SHA1 (symmetric, using the secret or secrets as a salt) or RSA-SHA1 (asymmetric, using a private key to generate the signature). Because the server also knows the symmetric secret, it can calculate what the signature *should be* if the client uses the right secret and ensures that the signature matches the expected value. For asymmetric signatures, the server can verify the private key-generated signature using the matching public key.

Either way, if the signature is valid, permission is granted and the server permits the client to proceed with the authorization. The server returns `400 Bad Request` if the request contains any unsupported parameters or protocol versions and `401 Unauthorized` if the signature fails verification, the credentials are invalid, the token is expired, or the nonce is invalid or has already been used. At this point the server returns an `x-www-form-urlencoded` format `200 OK` response to the client, containing the temporary credentials in the response body. The *`oauth_token`* response parameter contains the temporary identifier, whereas *`oauth_token_secret`* contains the temporary secret. Because the secret is included in plain text in the response, the standard requires that this request and response happen over TLS (for example, HTTPS). *`oauth_callback_confirmed`* is the third required response parameter and differentiates from older versions of the protocol. It must always have the value `true`. This is all shown as Steps 1 through 2 in Figure 28-1.

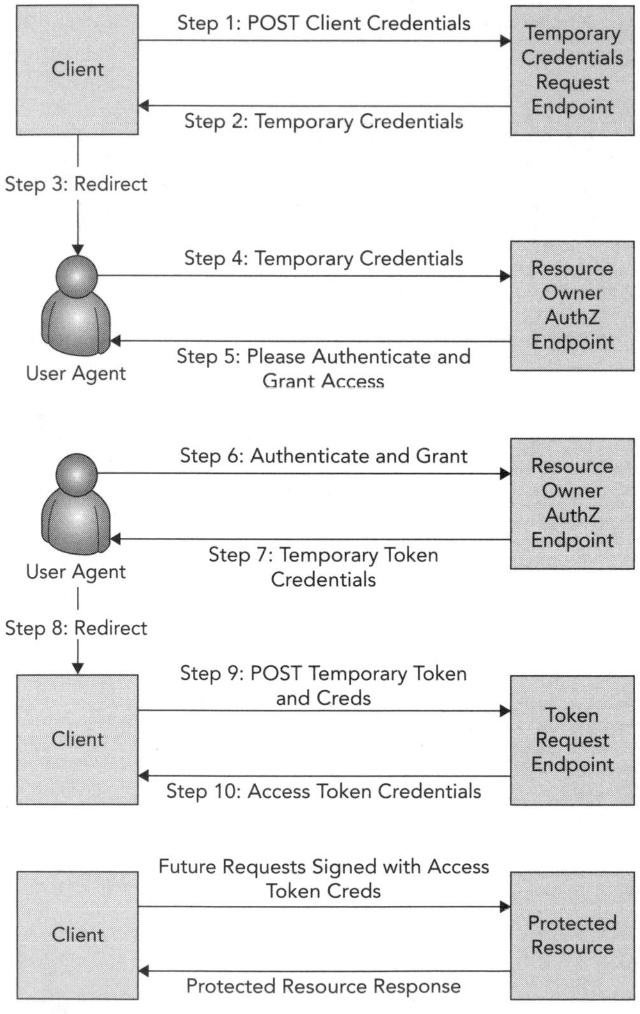


**FIGURE 28-1**

Now that the client has temporary credentials, it can redirect the resource owner to the server's *resource owner authorization endpoint* with the temporary `oauth_token` in a request parameter (Steps 3 and 4). This is where the server takes over the authentication process. If the resource owner is already authenticated (for example, has a current HTTP session on the server), the server proceeds directly to the grant screen. (Although, for enhanced security the server may ask the resource owner to authenticate again.) Otherwise, it asks the resource owner to authenticate by the normal means (Step 5, which may be form authentication, basic, digest, Windows — you get the idea).

After the resource owner has successfully authenticated, the server proceeds to the grant screen (also Step 5). On the grant screen, the server tells the resource owner which protected resources the client wants to access and asks for permission to grant that access. If the resource owner approves (Step 6), the server redirects the resource owner to the client's callback URI. The redirect request contains the temporary `oauth_token` and a one-use-only `oauth_verifier` parameter with a random string value (Steps 7 and 8). The `oauth_verifier` parameter mitigates the aforementioned session fixation attack.

> **NOTE** *You may wonder why the callback URI and not the callback URL is referred to. The callback URI might not be a standard web URL. A web URL wouldn't work if the client application were a desktop or mobile application instead of a web application. The callback URI could be an application-proprietary protocol URI that the browser or operating system understands. When the browser sees this URI, it can then open the target application and pass the request parameters to it in a previously agreed-upon manner.*
>
> *For example,* `mailto:nicholas@example.org` *opens up a mail client to send a message to* `nicholas@example.org`*. More realistically,* `fb://notifications` *opens the Facebook app to the notifications list, while* `twitter://timeline` *opens the Twitter app to the timeline. Generally speaking, an application developer must register his URI with some recognized authority, such as Apple or Google, in order to use the URI effectively.*

When the client receives the callback redirect, it makes a new behind-the-scenes empty `POST` request to the *token request endpoint* (Step 9). This request again contains the `Authorization: OAuth` header with largely the same value. (Obviously, the timestamp and nonce differ.) It also includes the `oauth_token` and `oauth_verifier` header parameters contained in the callback redirect and omits the `oauth_callback` parameter that is no longer needed. This time, the request is signed with the temporary secret. The server authenticates the request, verifies that the token and verifier parameters match the grant approved by the resource owner, and returns token credentials to the client using the `oauth_token` and `oauth_token_secret` response parameters. At this point the server expires the temporary credentials so that they can no longer be used (Step 10).

This may seem like a complicated and lengthy process, but it all transpires in a matter of just a few seconds. More important, although the standard strongly recommends using TLS for all communications, the temporary credentials and token retrieval steps are the only steps that the standard requires to use TLS because a secret is included in plain text in each response.

When the client has the token credentials, it can access protected resources (with or without the resource owner's immediate presence). Each future request to a protected resource again contains the `Authorization: OAuth` header with the `oauth_token` from the token credentials and no `oauth_verifier` or `oauth_callback` header parameters. These requests are all signed using both the client credentials secret and the token credentials secret. The server verifies that the token and signature are valid before permitting access to protected resources, as shown in Figure 28-2.

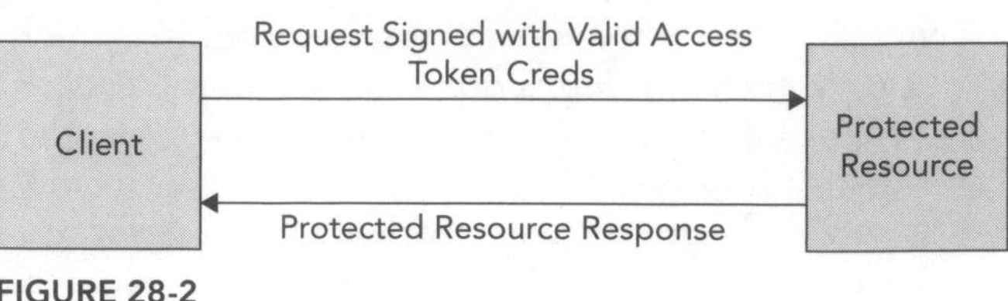


**FIGURE 28-2**

Token credentials may be but do not have to be perpetual. Servers may expire token credentials periodically, or a resource owner may request that token credentials be revoked (for example, the resource owner decides he does not want the client to have access to his data anymore). When this happens, the server responds to the next protected resource request with a `401 Unauthorized` response. The client can then start the process of obtaining temporary credentials, authorizing the resource owner, and exchanging temporary credentials for token credentials again. This is demonstrated in Figure 28-3.

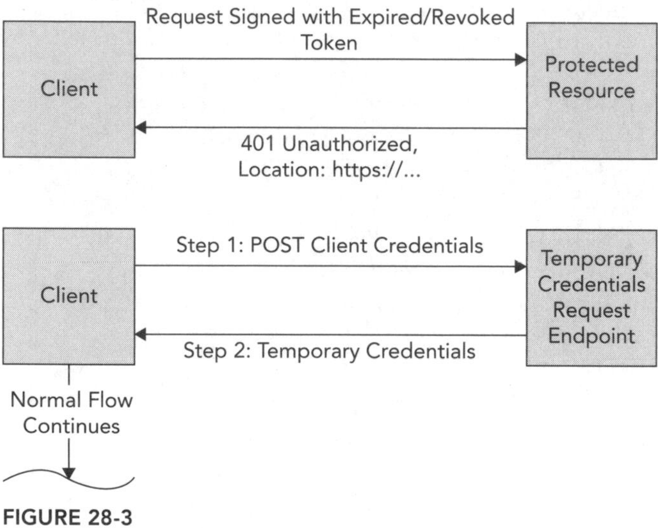


**FIGURE 28-3**

> **WARNING** *The OAuth 1.0a standard includes no specifications for the structure, content, or length of any of the various tokens included in this process (the client credential identifier, temporary credential identifier, and token credential identifier). This can take whatever form and length the provider wants. The tokens can consist of random data, or they can contain a predictable structure that the provider understands. As such, clients should make no assumptions and place no limits on these tokens.*

## Facing Some Challenges with OAuth 1.0a

OAuth 1.0a is a very secure protocol, but it is not without its weaknesses. First, OAuth initially experienced some ambiguities concerning the order in which various parts of requests would appear in the signature. For example, when listing out the URL, method, headers, and parameters that required signatures, it was not initially clear in what order the request parameters should be placed. This led to different implementations using different orderings and, thus incompatibility between implementations. Since then, the spec was clarified in favor of a determinist order for request parameters appearing in the signature, but some legacy implementations still remain.

OAuth 1.0a took some heavy criticism for its signature requirements in general. Some in the industry felt nothing was gained by signing virtually every part of the request. Although this technique ensures that requests and responses aren't tampered with, the security it provides could be more easily and effectively achieved using TLS. Instead, many argued, the signature should include only the parameters of the `Authorization` header. This would be sufficient to achieve the ultimate goal of establishing that the client held the correct secret without sending the secret over the wire or introducing unnecessary complexity.

Another common complaint is that OAuth 1.0a, as written, essentially assumes that the resource owner is a person and that the client is always untrusted. The strict flow of OAuth 1.0a omits two important use cases:

- The client application is also the resource owner and thus can authenticate solely with its client credentials.
- The client application is created by the same organization as the server. This means the resource owner trusts the client application and is willing to enter authentication credentials directly in the client, thus creating a better user experience.

For this reason, many implementations have created extensions to the OAuth 1.0a protocol that better support these two use cases. For example, you can optionally use Spring Security OAuth without a resource owner that authenticates separately (and instead treats the client as the resource owner). In this approach, every request always includes the client credentials identifier and is signed with the client credentials secret. This technique is called *Two-Legged OAuth* (in contrast to the unofficial name for the standard, *Three-Legged OAuth*) and is widely supported among implementations. This makes these implementations somewhat at odds with the specification, but only if you configure them in this manner. By default, they should still be standards compliant (that is, Three-Legged).

> **NOTE** *After reading about OAuth 1.0a, it may have occurred to you that it is a very stateful protocol. In fact, token credentials are very much like HTTP session ID cookies (although there are some important security differences). But isn't the point of RESTful web services to provide a stateless architecture? It's true that OAuth's statefulness stands in stark contrast to REST's statelessness. But, really, you simply can't avoid this (at least, not securely). To achieve true statelessness, the client must send the resource owner's credentials on every request (similar to the basic and digest approaches discussed earlier). This is simply not as secure with untrusted, third-party clients, and resource owners will not tolerate that lack of trust. A secure authentication and authorization system demands a stateful protocol.*

# The Evolution: OAuth 2.0

The ink had barely dried on the OAuth 1.0a publication when the IETF OAuth working group began developing OAuth 2.0. Its final draft was published in October 2012 as the Proposed Standard RFC 6749. In the Internet Standards Track, Proposed Standard is the entry-level maturity for standards. After sufficient feedback and revisions, standards eventually move from Proposed Standard to Draft Standard. When in Draft Standard, few changes are made, but some revisions are still possible to resolve problems with the standard. The third and final maturity is Internet Standard, meaning the standard is adopted and is ready for widespread use.

As of October 2013, OAuth 2.0 was still a Proposed Standard. RFC 2026 says this means it is unsuitable for use in "disruption-sensitive environments" (meaning don't use it in production). Nevertheless, and despite this warning, it has already been widely adopted across the industry, and many providers, such as Facebook and Twitter, require the use of OAuth 2.0.

OAuth 2.0 is the successor to and replacement for OAuth 1.0a, and it is not backward compatible. OAuth 1.0a clients cannot use OAuth 2.0 servers (and OAuth 2.0 clients cannot use OAuth 1.0a servers), but implementations are permitted to support both standards simultaneously. Most important, OAuth 2.0 is not a protocol; instead, it is a framework that describes how a protocol might (but is not required to) be implemented. This has been the source of much controversy, which is covered later in this section.

## Using OAuth 2.0 Terminology

Like OAuth 1.0a, OAuth 2.0 defines some of its own terminology. OAuth 2.0 acknowledged that protected resources and the authentication/authorization system do not always reside on the same server, so the server in OAuth 1.0a has been divided into the *resource server* and *authorization server* in OAuth 2.0.

Credentials are a different story altogether. In general you still have client credentials in some form, but temporary and token credentials are not directly addressed. Similar concepts may be present based on the authorization grant type chosen, or you can add extensions to OAuth 2.0 that incorporate different credential types.

## Understanding Authorization Grants

One of the key features in OAuth 2.0, and certainly one of its strengths, is that it takes into account the various use cases for web service API authorization. The assumption is no longer made that all resource owners are separate from clients and that all clients are untrusted. The standard defines four built-in *authorization grant* types as well as the process for authenticating and authorizing with each of those types, and it allows you to add additional grant types through extensions. All grant types follow the basic flow demonstrated in Figure 28-4, although each differs in exactly how the authorization grant is obtained.

As with OAuth 1.0a, the client authenticates with the authorization server (but not the resource server) using the client credentials any time the client makes a direct (behind-the-scenes) request to the authorization server. This always happens regardless of which grant type is chosen. All clients have public client identifiers. Clients may also have secrets that complete the client credentials. Authorization servers must be aware of the difference between *confidential clients* (clients that can reasonably be expected to keep their secret secret) and *public clients* (clients who may be unable to hold secrets, such as open source applications whose secrets ship with the applications).

Authorization servers must not rely on client credentials authorization alone to establish the identity of a public client. Generally, clients authenticate with the authorization server using HTTP basic authentication. This is the only mechanism providers are required to support for client authentication, although they may support other mechanisms.

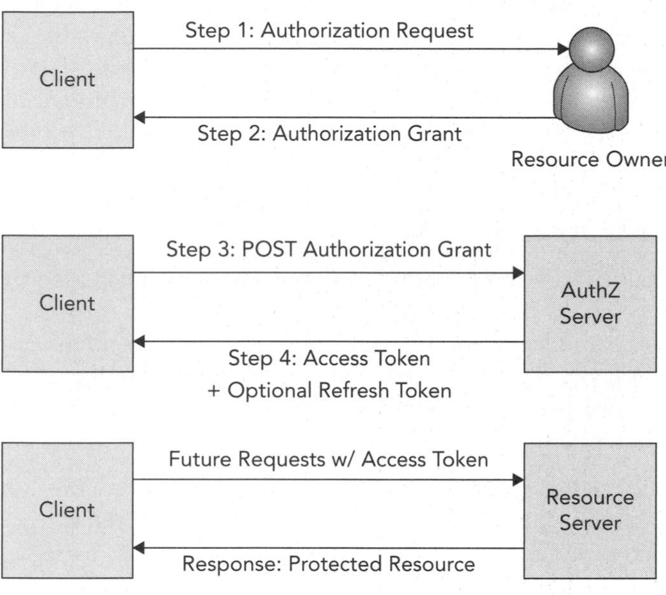


**FIGURE 28-4**

The *Authorization Code Grant* is the functional equivalent of Three-Legged OAuth 1.0a. The client redirects the resource owner to the authorization server's *authorization endpoint* when it needs to obtain an access token and includes the request parameters `response_type` (set to "code" for this grant type), `client_id` (from the client credentials), `redirect_uri` (the URI to send the resource owner to after authorization is approved), `scope` (the optional token scope, to restrict its access), and `state` (an optional but recommended parameter that prevents CSRF attacks).

When the resource owner completes the authentication and grant stage on the authorization server, the server redirects the resource owner to the *redirection endpoint* as in OAuth 1.0a, including an *authorization code* in the `code` response parameter and a `state` parameter containing the same value from the request `state` parameter, if it was provided. This authorization code is the authorization grant from Figure 28-4. The client then makes a behind-the-scenes `POST` back to the authorization server's *token endpoint* and exchanges the authorization code for an *access token*. The request for an access token includes the request parameters `grant_type` (set to "authorization_code" for this grant type), `code` (the authorization code just received), `redirect_uri` (the original `redirect_uri` parameter value sent to the authorization endpoint), and `client_id`. The response is in JSON format, containing root-level values `access_token`, `token_type` (for example, `bearer`), `expires_in` (a value in seconds), `refresh_token` (optional, if refresh tokens are enabled), and echoes of any other request parameters sent.

The nature of this token is not actually defined in the framework. Instead, application developers can choose one of several extensions (or create their own) to determine what the access token looks like, where it lives, how it's derived, and when and if it expires. However it's implemented, the access token is then used to access protected resources on the resource server. How the access token is used (for example, request parameters or the `Authorization` header) is also undefined and left up to the access token type chosen.

*Implicit Grants* are extremely similar to Authorization Code Grants and are still the functional equivalent of Three-Legged OAuth 1.0a, although demonstrably less secure. In an Implicit Grant, the resource owner still goes to the authorization server to authenticate and grant access to the client. This request is nearly identical to the Authorization Code Grant except that the *`response_type`* parameter is set to "token." However, the callback redirect does not include an authorization code to be exchanged for an access token. Instead, the callback contains the access token directly (thus removing the middle step from the basic flow in Figure 28-4). The parameters are *`access_token`*, *`token_type`*, *`expires_in`*, *`scope`*, and *`state`*. (Refresh tokens are prohibited for this grant type.) Because the client now has the access token, it does not make a request to the token endpoint for it.

You can probably point out some obvious security holes in this grant type, and for this reason the standard indicates you should use it only in very limited circumstances. For example, a browser application *might* not be susceptible to the problems typically exposed by this grant type. Because most browser applications are written in JavaScript, the Authorization Code Grant can introduce performance hits that the Implicit Grant easily remedies, without seriously impacting security. With that said, it is not recommended that you use Implicit Grants.

A *Client Credentials Grant*, demonstrated in Figure 28-5, is the functional equivalent of Two-Legged OAuth 1.0a, finally codified within the standard. In this grant type, the client contacts the token endpoint and exchanges its client credentials for an access token. The request contains a *`grant_type`* parameter set to "client_credentials" and an optional *`scope`* parameter. The client authenticates via the usual process—basic authentication. The response includes the usual `access_token`, `token_type`, and `expires_in` JSON values. (Refresh tokens are also prohibited for this grant type.) In this way, the client acts as its own resource owner, and the client credentials serve as the authorization grant referred to in Figure 28-4. The client can then use the access token to access protected resources on the resource server on its own behalf, instead of on behalf of some other resource owner.

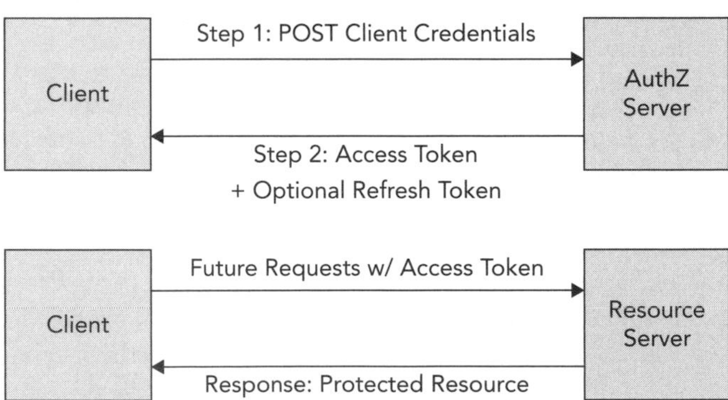


**FIGURE 28-5**

The *Resource Owner Password Credentials Grant*, as shown in Figure 28-6, is both the most user-friendly and *potentially* the most insecure grant type. Using this grant type, the resource owner provides her credentials (username and password, public and private key, and so on) directly to the client and never has to redirect to the authorization endpoint. These resource owner credentials are the authorization grant referred to in Figure 28-4. The client then forwards these credentials on to the token endpoint on the resource owner's behalf, and exchanges them for an access token.

The request's `grant_type` parameter is set to "password" this time, and the request also contains `username`, `password`, and `scope` parameters. The `username` and `password` parameters are generic parameters for the resource owner's credentials and might not actually contain a username and password. The JSON response is the same as for the Authorization Code Grant type. Again, the returned access token can then be used to access protected resources on the resource server.

When dealing with desktop and mobile applications, this grant type undoubtedly provides the best user experience. Instead of swapping between an application and a browser (sometimes frequently) just to authenticate, the resource owner can stay within a single application. Of course, this presents the obvious security implication that the resource owner must give his credentials, unencrypted and unsecured, to the client application. Because of this, the best practice is to use this grant type *only when the organization that created the application is also the organization that hosts the authorization server*. This is the one circumstance in which the client can be fully trusted with the resource owner's credentials. You should never allow third-party clients to use Resource Owner Password Credentials Grant.

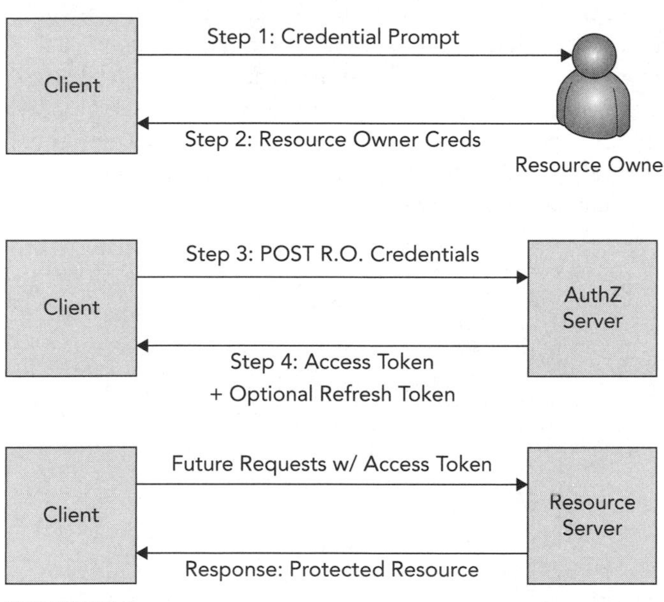


**FIGURE 28-6**

> **NOTE** *You may have noticed that there is no replacement in OAuth 2.0 for the temporary credentials request endpoint. This is because OAuth 2.0 makes no use of temporary credentials and does not make an initial request to get temporary credentials before redirecting the client to the authorization server. Although this does simplify the process somewhat, it can also be seen as a vulnerability. Because of this, you should* always *employ the* `state` *parameter to help defend against some of the problems this might pose.*

## Using Bearer Tokens

You probably noticed that you haven't read anything about the format of the `Authorization` header and the parameters passed to and from the resource server. That's because it's not specified! To be more precise, the OAuth 2.0 standard doesn't mandate these. Instead, these formats and parameters depend entirely on which type of access token you choose. The standard and recommended access token implementation, however, is *bearer tokens*. Specified in RFC 6750 (also a Proposed Standard), bearer tokens are exactly what they sound like: Whoever bears the token holds the grant. This is identical to HTTP session ID tokens, and at first it might sound identical to OAuth 1.0a token credentials, but in reality it is very, very different (and potentially very insecure).

Recall that OAuth 1.0a token credentials contain two parts: the identity (the token) and the secret. The token is sent with every request, but the secret is not. Instead, the client uses the secret to generate a signature that the server can duplicate or validate. The presence of the correct token and a valid signature establishes authorization. Bearer tokens do not use signatures. In fact, there is no signature process at all.

While the community argued for easier-to-implement signatures that used only the `Authorization` header contents, the working group decided to get rid of signatures completely. This means that the bearer token is the only thing necessary to access protected resources on behalf of the resource owner. If the bearer token is compromised, there is no specified process for revoking it. Instead, the specification prefers short-lived bearer tokens that expire quickly to mitigate stolen tokens. However, to keep the resource owner from having to constantly authenticate, the standard also specifies a concept of *refresh tokens*. When issuing a bearer token, the authorization server *may also* (but is not required to) issue a refresh token. When the bearer token expires, the client may contact the authorization server and exchange the refresh token for new bearer and refresh tokens, all without the resource owner having to authenticate again. This is visualized in Figure 28-7.

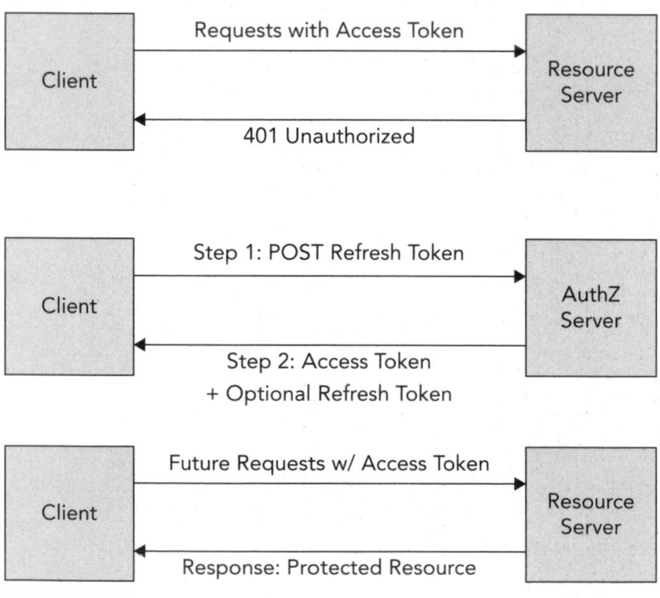


**FIGURE 28-7**

There are obvious problems with this approach, most notably the ability to steal bearer tokens. The working group also did away with nonces and timestamps while they were at it, making the framework susceptible to replay attacks. (But again, it's just a framework, and you can build a protocol more secure than the framework specifies.) To mitigate concern about all these issues, the working group made two arguments.

- They asserted that there was no reason to make OAuth more secure than HTTP session IDs because session IDs were already the weakest link in web security.
- The standard states that using TLS should avoid all these problems because the encrypted traffic cannot be intercepted and decrypted. (Use of TLS is an optional part of the standard for most communications, just as it is in OAuth 1.0a. It is required only where secrets are sent in the clear.)

However, there are two powerful counterarguments to these statements:

- Using the weakest link argument results in web security never improving; when the next working group attempts to improve HTTP session ID security, it can point to OAuth 2.0 as the weakest link and claim, again, that there's no point in improving security.
- SSL is only as strong as the weakest implementation involved in a conversation. Sometimes clients are misconfigured and don't properly validate the server certificate chain. If this happens, a man-in-the-middle can easily step in and pose as the resource server, stealing the bearer token and using it until it expires. (This particularly impacts RESTful web services, where this vulnerability can make the intended discovery process a more dangerous affair.) For this reason, there has been widespread disagreement with the bearer tokens proposed standard in the open standards community.

## Overcoming the Controversy of OAuth 2.0

Bearer tokens are not the only controversy OAuth 2.0 has encountered. A point of contention for many open standards community members is the lack of any real "teeth" in the standard. Nearly every feature is optional or has exceptions in which the implementation is allowed to omit it. In fact, the standard specifically says in Section 1.8 (emphasis added in this book):

> *OAuth 2.0 provides a rich authorization framework with well-defined security properties. However, as a rich and highly extensible framework with many optional components, on its own,* ***this specification is likely to produce a wide range of non-interoperable implementations.***

By 2012, many community members, and even some working group members, decided they had enough. Eran Hammer, who had been with OAuth since almost the beginning, removed his name from the standard, resigned as chief editor, and withdrew from the working group. He wrote a series of blog posts and hosted a series of talks that harshly criticized the process of the working group and the results of the OAuth 2.0 standard. Of particular interest, he claims the standard was intentionally designed with enterprises in mind, making it so vague that the enterprises involved could sell their consulting services for implementing the standard. David Recordon also withdrew from the working group and removed his name from the standard, although he has not spoken publicly about his decision. Even with these departures, the OAuth 2.0 proposed standard was published in October 2012 and is likely to advance to Internet Standard without these major issues resolved.

## Using MAC As a Bearer Token Alternative

Several members of the OAuth working group, as well as other community members, have proposed an alternative to the bearer tokens extension that would add a good deal of security to OAuth 2.0 and eliminate many of the current complaints (except for the interoperability problems). The Message Authentication Code (MAC) Tokens extension specifies a different type of token that uses message signatures to establish that the client holds the secret without ever transmitting the secret on the wire. Although this is a significant improvement over the recommended bearer tokens extension — and, arguably, the fact that such an extension can be created is a huge testament to OAuth 2.0's design — the proposal is not without its drawbacks.

Although the intended track for this proposal is Standards Track, currently it is only an Internet Draft. It has not become a Proposed Standard yet, and it does not have an assigned RFC number. As of this writing, the current draft is version 4, which expires January 16, 2014. At that point, the draft could move to Proposed Standard, be renewed as another draft version, or be abandoned. Even if it isn't abandoned, it could take several years before it is an Internet Standard, making it an unappealing solution for many organizations.

## Which Version of OAuth Should You Use?

So which should you use? Well, that's up to you. Reasons exist for using and not using each version. OAuth 1.0a is more stable, more mature, and more industry tested. It has no known current vulnerabilities, and most developers familiar with OAuth are at least familiar with OAuth 1.0a. However, OAuth 2.0 is more extensible, does support the useful additional grant types, and is inevitably the future of OAuth. Because the major players (such as Twitter, Facebook, and Google, to name a few) have already adopted OAuth 2.0, it is unlikely that OAuth 1.0a will remain in common use for long. If you don't like the future of OAuth, you can always explore other solutions. If you do decide to use OAuth 2.0, you should not use bearer tokens. Instead, use a more secure token type (such as MAC tokens) or create your own token system that uses message signatures to establish authorization.

The rest of this chapter explores the create-your-own-token approach. Using Spring Security, you implement OAuth 2.0 with your own token system and create a very simple client capable of consuming your services.

> **NOTE** *It is important to point out an irony: One of the goals of the OAuth 2.0 project was to reduce non-interoperability between implementations. Often, OAuth 1.0a clients had to use provider-supplied libraries to work properly with the provider's authorization/resource servers. However, the non-interoperability built into OAuth 2.0 almost guarantees that this problem will get worse, not better. Creating your own token system—which is essentially required to use OAuth 2.0 securely—ensures that you will have to provide your clients with client libraries that interface with your proprietary OAuth 2.0 implementation.*

# USING SPRING SECURITY OAUTH

Spring Security provides ample support for OAuth 1.0a and 2.0 through its Spring Security OAuth subproject. In addition to securing your protected resources in a provider application, Spring Security OAuth can also help you securely access OAuth-protected resources in a client application. Spring Security OAuth support is divided into two Maven artifacts:

- `spring-security-oauth` provides OAuth 1.0 and 1.0a support.
- `spring-security-oauth2` provides OAuth 2.0 support.

The classes in these artifacts are organized into different packages, so you can use them simultaneously — but only with some caveats. Although you can protect different sets of URLs with different OAuth versions, you cannot protect the same URLs with OAuth 1.0(a) and OAuth 2.0 simultaneously. You can write a client application that uses Spring Security OAuth to access both OAuth 1.0(a) and OAuth 2.0 services.

This book cannot cover all four Spring Security OAuth scenarios: OAuth 1.0(a) provider, OAuth 1.0(a) client, OAuth 2.0 provider, and OAuth 2.0 client. It must, however, cover provider and client scenarios; otherwise, you won't have a way to test your application. Because OAuth 2.0 will eventually replace OAuth 1.0a, you learn about Spring Security OAuth 2.0 support in this chapter. Due to the insecurity of Bearer Tokens, this chapter also covers implementing your own token system. Support for OAuth 1.0 has some similarities and also some significant differences. You can learn more about OAuth 1.0 support in the reference documentation (`https://github.com/spring-projects/spring-security-oauth/wiki/oauth1`).

## Creating on OAuth 2.0 Provider

The Spring Security OAuth 2.0 Provider implementation is divided into two components:

- Authorization server implementation
- Resource server implementation

This corresponds to the OAuth 2.0 specification, which accounts for the authorization services and resource services residing on different servers.

If you want, you can use Spring Security OAuth just for the authorization server or just for the resource server. However, more than likely you will use it for both the authorization server and the resource server, on either the same or different servers. For the sake of simplicity, the examples in this chapter assume both the authorization server and the resource server exist on the same server and on all servers in a cluster. This last part is important because you can persist tokens in memory only for simple, non-clustered applications. Any application that is clustered must persist tokens using a more persistent means.

### Managing Client Details

In Chapters 26 and 27, you learned about Spring Security's `UserDetails` and `UserDetailsService` interfaces. Spring Security OAuth includes similar interfaces: `org.springframework.security`

.oauth2.provider.ClientDetails and org.springframework.security.oauth2.provider .ClientDetailsService.

ClientDetails specifies information about an OAuth client that is permitted to access the application. Because clients can access resources on their own behalf (such as for the Client Credentials Grant), ClientDetails includes a Collection of GrantedAuthoritys that the client holds. It provides the client ID and the client secret, which authenticate clients for authorization requests and for Client Credentials Grant access token requests. ClientDetails also indicates the set of grants the client is permitted to request, the resources that the client can access (null if unrestricted), and the OAuth scope or scopes the client is restricted to (null if unrestricted).

Likewise, the ClientDetailsService enables you to load a ClientDetails instance by client ID. Whenever a client authenticates, Spring Security OAuth loads the client using the ClientDetailsService and compares the client secret to the one in the HTTP basic Authorization header. The authorization server component of Spring Security OAuth requires a UserDetailsService to function properly. The two default implementations of this service are in the same package.

- InMemoryClientDetailsService is configured on its startup with all the clients your application supports.
- JdbcClientDetailsService uses a hard-coded table definition for storing and retrieving client details.

Because clients authenticate using HTTP basic authentication, which Spring Security already supports, you configure a standard authentication manager with a DaoAuthenticationProvider and an org.springframework.security.oauth2.provider.client .ClientDetailsUserDetailsService.

## Understanding the Authorization Server

When a client needs to access one of your protected resources but does not have an access token, it redirects the resource owner to your authorization endpoint. Spring Security OAuth's authorization server hosts this authorization endpoint. It presents an approval screen, processes its submission, generates the authorization code, and redirects the resource owner back to the client application. It also responds to token endpoint requests to exchange authorization codes for access tokens, as well as to exchange client credentials and resource owner credentials for access tokens. When configuring the authorization server, you must also configure Spring Security to protect the authorization endpoint. This way, Spring Security requires the user to authenticate and have the necessary authority for accessing the authorization endpoint. (Spring Security OAuth already protects the token endpoint with HTTP basic authentication using the client credentials.)

Configuring the authorization server is very complex and varies significantly depending on your application. This book cannot possibly go over all the possible combinations, but this section does provide some general information. The next section shows you an example of one possible configuration.

## Configuring Code and Token Services

To configure the authorization server, you must first configure services capable of storing and retrieving authorization codes and access tokens. org.springframework.security.oauth2

.provider.code.AuthorizationCodeServices specifies an interface for creating, storing, and consuming authorization codes. The authorization server uses this service to create an authorization code when a resource owner approves authorization for a client. When the client contacts the authorization server to exchange the authorization code for an access token, it uses the AuthorizationCodeServices to "consume" the authorization code. When consumed, the authorization code cannot be used again. The authorization server then uses an implementation of org.springframework.security.oauth2.provider.token.AuthorizationServerTokenServices to create access and refresh tokens and return those tokens to the client. The implementation must persist the tokens somehow so that the resource server can retrieve them later.

On future requests to the resource server, the org.springframework.security.oauth2.provider.token.ResourceServerTokenServices provides a mechanism for obtaining the Authentication object associated with an access token. The Authentication is originally created when the resource owner authenticates, and it is attached to the authorization code when the resource owner authorizes the client. When the authorization code is later exchanged for an access token, the Authentication is attached to the access token so that it can be referenced each time the client accesses a protected resource. This allows Spring Security's authorization services to access the resource owner's user details and authorities during requests to protected resources.

The two standard AuthorizationCodeServices implementations are in the same package as the interface.

- InMemoryAuthorizationCodeServices creates authorization codes made of random letters and numbers and persists them in memory. This implementation is fantastic and optimized to perform well, but it is only useful if your application is not running in a cluster. Even load balancer sticky sessions may not work properly with authorization endpoints and token endpoints. There's a good chance the client's next request will hit a different server, and the InMemoryAuthorizationCodeServices bean will have no record of the authorization code generated on another server. So if you plan on clustering your application (which you most likely do), you need to plan on persisting authorization codes in a central location, such as a database.
- JdbcAuthorizationCodeServices also creates random authorization codes and provides a simple mechanism for storing them in a relational database between creation and exchange. You can customize the INSERT, SELECT, and DELETE statements to manage the codes. Of course, you can also create your own implementation if you want.

org.springframework.security.oauth2.provider.token.DefaultTokenServices is the only standard implementation of AuthorizationServerTokenServices. It is also the only standard ResourceServerTokenServices implementation. It handles the creation, storage, and retrieval of bearer tokens and uses an org.springframework.security.oauth2.provider.token.TokenStore to manage the actual persistence of the tokens. You can choose from the InMemoryTokenStore (which suffers from the same drawbacks in a clustered environment) or the JdbcTokenStore, or you can implement these interfaces on your own.

You configure these services as simple Spring beans. If you choose to use in-memory implementations, Spring Security OAuth provides XML namespace elements to simplify creating these beans. In most cases, the in-memory implementations are chosen by default when you configure Spring Security OAuth without specifying otherwise. Because the in-memory implementations are not suitable for clustered environments, you need to change these defaults.

The Spring Security OAuth 2.0 XML schema URI is `http://www.springframework.org/schema/security/oauth2`. You can add this schema to any Spring Beans XML file (use the recommended `oauth2` namespace prefix) to configure OAuth 2.0 support. If you want to configure OAuth 1.0 using XML, use the `http://www.springframework.org/schema/security/oauth` XML schema URI (and the recommended `oauth1` namespace prefix). Because these schemas are separate, you can configure both OAuth 1.0 and OAuth 2.0 components simultaneously. The `<oauth2:authorization-server>` element configures the authorization server. Its `client-details-service-ref` attribute allows you to specify a reference to a `ClientDetailsService` bean, whereas `token-services-ref` indicates an instance of `AuthorizationServerTokenServices`. You can also customize the endpoint URLs using the *`authorization-endpoint-url`* and *`token-endpoint-url`* attributes (which default to *`/oauth/authorize`* and *`/oauth/token`*, respectively).

Within this element you can specify several other elements that control which grant types are supported. By default, all grant types are supported. The `<authorization-code>`, `<implicit>`, `<client-credentials>`, and `<password>` elements control the Authorization Code Grant, Implicit Grant, Client Credentials Grant, and Resource Owner Credentials Grant, respectively. There is also the special `<refresh-token>` grant element because refresh tokens work very much like a special type of grant.

Each of these grant-control elements has a `disabled` attribute that you can set to `true` to disable the grant type. The `<authorization-code>` element also contains an `authorization-code-services-ref` attribute that enables you to customize the `AuthorizationCodeServices` to use. Likewise, `<password>` includes an `authentication-manager-ref` attribute that lets you specify an alternative `AuthenticationManager` instance.

> **NOTE** *You probably wondered about the lack of details for Java configuration. Although Java configuration should be present in Spring Security OAuth 1 and 2 version 2.0.x, this version does not come out until after this book is printed, so the Java configuration isn't covered in this book. At the time of writing, Spring Security OAuth Java configuration is incomplete and lacks many of the features that the XML namespace offers. Be sure to check the next edition of this book for a revised, Java-only configuration of Spring Security OAuth 2.*

## Using the Resource Server

As you have read, the resource server is responsible for controlling access to protected resources. It ensures that requests are accompanied with access tokens, checks those access tokens for validity, and redirects unauthorized requests to the authorization endpoint. The word "server" can be a confusing term for this feature because it's not a server at all. The resource server is simply a `Filter` implementation and some supporting classes. It doesn't actually serve requests; instead, it intercepts requests to resources that your application serves. The resource server uses the `ResourceServerTokenServices` bean you read about earlier to look up and verify the access tokens included in resource requests.

The resource server has fewer moving parts and is easier to configure using the `<oauth2:resource-server>` XML configuration element. In most cases, you need to specify the `token-services-ref` attribute, which should be a reference to a `ResourceServerTokenServices` bean. Also, if you use OAuth resource IDs, you should specify the resource ID that this server is protecting using the `resource-id` attribute; otherwise all resource IDs are allowed. This is the last piece to put into place to set up Spring Security OAuth in your applications. The next section demonstrates a real-life example.

## Using OAuth Security Expressions

In Chapter 27 you learned about Spring Security's authorization expressions, which you can use for both URL and method security, such as when using the `@PreAuthorize` annotation. Spring Security OAuth extends this expression support to provide an *`oauth2`* SpEL variable available to all expressions. This variable is essentially a namespace for several authorization functions, and it is never `null` (even if the method is not executed as part of an OAuth-protected resource). These additional authorization functions are as follows:

- `#oauth2.denyOAuthClient()` returns `true` if the current authentication is *not* an OAuth authentication. This is useful for prohibiting remote (OAuth) end users from accessing certain features in your application, even if they normally have sufficient authority.
- `#oauth2.clientHasRole(String)` returns `true` if the *client* has the specified granted authority. To check whether the *resource owner* has the granted authority, use the standard `hasAuthority` or `hasRole` functions instead.
- `#oauth2.clientHasAnyRole(String...)` returns `true` if the *client* has at least one of the specified granted authorities. To check whether the *resource owner* has at least one of the granted authorities, use the standard `hasAnyAuthority` or `hasAnyRole` functions instead.
- `#oauth2.hasScope(String)` returns `true` if the OAuth authentication has the specified OAuth scope.
- `#oauth2.hasAnyScope(String...)` returns `true` if the OAuth authentication has at least one of the specified OAuth scopes.
- `#oauth2.isClient()` returns `true` if the current authentication belongs to an OAuth *client* (for example, using Client Credentials Grant).
- `#oauth2.isUser()` returns `true` if the current authentication belongs to an OAuth resource owner (for example, using Authorization Code Grant, Implicit Grant, or Resource Owner Password Credentials Grant).

To use these new expressions, you need to configure the extended expression support and replace the existing expression support. If you use XML configuration, you can use the `<oauth2:expression-handler>` and `<oauth2:web-expression-handler>` elements to configure the method security and web security expression handlers, specify bean IDs for them, and inject references to those beans into any other configuration components that need them. Java configuration is equally easy. Just extend `GlobalMethodSecurityConfiguration` and override `createExpressionHandler` to create an `OAuth2MethodSecurityExpressionHandler` instead of the default (`DefaultMethodSecurityExpressionHandler`). Likewise, when defining your URL expressions, replace the default expression handler (`DefaultWebSecurityExpressionHandler`) with an `OAuth2WebSecurityExpressionHandler`.

## Creating an OAuth 2.0 Client

The flip side to protecting your services with OAuth is accessing OAuth-protected resources from a client application. As mentioned earlier, Spring Security OAuth can take care of this for you, too.

To understand how the Spring Security OAuth client component works, you must first know about Spring Framework's `org.springframework.web.client.RestOperations`. This interface specifies a basic set of RESTful web service operations. Using an implementation of this interface, you can `GET` an entity or collection of entities from a web service, `DELETE` an entity, `POST` a new entity, `PUT` an update to an entity, retrieve the `HEAD` for a resource, determine the `OPTIONS` for a resource, and more. The default implementation of this interface, `org.springframework.web.client.RestTemplate`, is the only class you should ever need to access RESTful web services. The toolset is very complete and very well tested, and also provides mechanisms for intercepting requests and responses and manipulating them (for example, to add or change request headers).

However, `RestTemplate` does not provide built-in support for any type of security. Although you could manually implement OAuth authorization using an interceptor, this is unnecessary because Spring Security OAuth supplies an implementation that does this already. `org.springframework.security.oauth2.client.OAuth2RestOperations` extends the `RestOperations` interface to specify OAuth-related methods. Likewise, `org.springframework.security.oauth2.client.OAuth2RestTemplate` extends `RestTemplate` to implement `OAuth2RestOperations` and provide OAuth 2.0 client support.

### Configuring the OAuth REST Template

You should keep one important thing in mind when using `OAuth2RestTemplate`. With the standard `RestTemplate`, you can reuse a single `RestTemplate` bean anywhere in your application for accessing any web service endpoint anywhere on the web. This is because the `RestTemplate` is completely stateless and stores no identifying information between requests. This is not the case for the `OAuth2RestTemplate`, however — and it may not be the case for any `RestTemplate` that you configure with an interceptor, depending on what that interceptor does.

When you configure an `OAuth2RestTemplate`, you provide it with an `org.springframework.security.oauth2.client.resource.OAuth2ProtectedResourceDetails`. This specifies the client ID, client secret, and other information that the template should use when authorizing with the resource server. It represents either a single remote resource or a group of resources that all accept the same client credentials and access tokens. As such, if you are going to access multiple web services protected with different resource servers, you need to define multiple `OAuth2RestTemplate` beans and qualify them on injection using Spring's `@Qualifer` or Java EE's `@javax.inject.Qualifier` (as covered in Chapter 12).

In a standalone application (one that is not hosted on the web), using the `OAuth2RestTemplate` is fairly simple. You use it just like any other `RestTemplate` instance, except that you create an instance per client credentials instead of one, global instance. You need to provide each `OAuth2RestTemplate` with an `org.springframework.security.oauth2.client.OAuth2ClientContext` implementation capable of determining the correct client context and access code (if any) for a particular request. Typically, you store this information on either a per-thread basis or globally for the entire JVM.

If an access token is invalid or the OAuth-protected request was otherwise rejected, the `OAuth2RestTemplate` methods throw the appropriate exceptions. If, however, the resource owner is not authorized yet and needs to be redirected to the authorization endpoint (because you are using Authorization Code Grant or Implicit Grant), the methods throw an `org.springframework.security.oauth2.client.resource.UserRedirectRequiredException`.

Upon catching this exception your code can launch a browser window, redirect the request, or do whatever else is necessary to send the end user to the authorization endpoint to authorize the client. Remember that even your standalone applications must receive the redirect from the authorization endpoint to receive the authorization code (or access token for Implicit Grants). In a standalone application, this means that your application must register a proprietary application-launcher URI scheme with the operating system and installed browsers, or it must include an embedded browser within the application. If this is not an option, you need to use Client Credentials Grant or Resource Owner Password Credentials Grant.

## Using the REST Template in a Web Application

Using the `OAuth2RestTemplate` in a web application is even simpler than in a standalone application because Spring Security's filter chain can take care of much of the hard work for you. The `<oauth2:resource>` element creates an `OAuth2ProtectedResourceDetails` bean with the given configuration options. You can configure the client ID and secret, authorization endpoint URL, access token endpoint URL, and more with this element. You can use it as many times as necessary to define multiple resources that your application will use. (Alternatively, you could just manually create `<bean>`s or `@Beans` instead of using the shortcut element.)

After you define the protected resources your application will use, you can use one or many `<oauth2:rest-template>` elements to define `OAuth2RestTemplate` beans that use those protected resource details. You can then use these templates in your other beans to access protected resources. The templates are configured with special session-scoped client contexts, which means that multiple users can execute template code simultaneously and that code will use the access token bound to each user's session in a thread-safe manner.

For these features to work, you must enable the OAuth client filter in the filter chain. This is easy using the namespace configuration. Just add the `<oauth2:client>` element to your XML configuration, and add the defined filter to your `<http>` element or elements:

```
<oauth2:client id="oauth2ClientFilter" />

<http ...>
    ...

    <custom-filter ref="oauth2ClientFilter"
                   after="EXCEPTION_TRANSLATION_FILTER" />
</http>
```

You may find this obvious, but you should note that these special session-scoped templates work only in the course of or in response to HTTP requests to your application. You can use these templates "in the background" as long as the background thread is spawned by an HTTP request handling thread (so that the `Authentication` and session information is inherited). However, in such a case, you must be careful to ensure the access token is obtained before the thread is handed off. You cannot use these templates for purely scheduled tasks for two obvious reasons:

- A scheduled task cannot be redirected to an authorization endpoint.
- Because the filter is never invoked, the template code running in a scheduled task cannot select the correct access token for an authenticated end user.

If you want to use an `OAuth2RestTemplate` in a purely scheduled task, you need to use the Client Credentials Grant for those tasks. You must configure the `OAuth2RestTemplate` manually in these cases.

> **NOTE** *Although this may go without saying, you can't use the Spring Security OAuth Client features without also using Spring Security authentication. The client features require the presence of the Spring Security context and other components.*

# FINISHING THE CUSTOMER SUPPORT APPLICATION

Customer-Support-v21, available for download on the `wrox.com` code download site, is the final version of the Customer Support application. You have worked on this project since Chapter 3, and it looks very different from the first version. For the most part, it is very much the same as the project you worked on in the previous chapter. The last and only remaining puzzle piece is in place — securing the web services from unauthorized access. Though OAuth is typically employed for RESTful web services, you do not need to exclude it from consideration for SOAP web services, and for simplicity's sake the Customer Support application secures both types of web services using OAuth.

The key to making OAuth 2 tokens secure is avoiding transmission of access tokens for protected resource requests. You can easily achieve this by taking a page out of the OAuth 1 playbook — use the token to generate a signature for each request instead of transmitting the actual token. You need to avoid some of the unnecessary complexities of OAuth 1 signatures, so there's really no need to sign the URL, request parameters, request body, headers, and other request properties.

However, you do need to sign a different piece of data for every request; otherwise, the signature will always be the same and an attacker can easily replay it. This presents an opportunity to tackle two problems at once — you also need to prevent replay attacks in general. The simplest way to do this is to include nonces in your requests, and the nonces can serve as a signature item for ensuring a different signature value on every request. This section covers designing this nonce and token system and implementing it provider-side using Spring Security OAuth. The next section demonstrates creating an OAuth client capable of consuming these protected resources.

## Generating Request Nonces and Signatures

Generating secure nonces and signature tokens is actually really simple. Keep in mind that a nonce doesn't establish the authenticity of a request or the authentication of the user initiating it. It merely serves as a salt for the signature that prevents the token from being stolen and an identifier for the request that prevents it from being replayed. Nonces should be random so that they cannot be predicted. However, because true randomness does not preclude repetition, nonces should be paired with timestamps. The provider should ensure that any given nonce-timestamp combination is unique. Therefore, to prevent an attacker from merely changing the timestamp and reusing the nonce to replay a request, the signature token should include the timestamp in addition to the nonce.

At this point, you already know that your signature token should at least include the access token (but only as a salt for the signature), nonce, and timestamp. What else should it include? Well, for the provider to find the correct access token for verifying the signature, the request needs to include some type of identifier that the provider can use to look up the access token from the token store. Because the request will include this identifier, it makes sense to include the identifier in the signature as well.

OAuth 1.0a includes the client ID in every protected resource request to ensure that only the client to whom the access token was issued can use the access token, but OAuth 2.0 lacks this security feature. Including the client ID in protected resource requests is trivial, and including the client ID in the signature ensures it has not been tampered with. As a final sanity check, including some component of the request in the signature wouldn't hurt. It doesn't have to be as complicated as OAuth 1.0a and include request parameters, post variables, and several headers — something as simple as the request method or URL will do. Syntactically, a signature might look something like this:

```
SHA1( clientId "," tokenId "," nonce "," timestamp "," method "," tokenValue )
```

With a client ID of `TestClient`, a token ID of `y8FglFPKzW`, a nonce of `i74K5E4y4B`, a timestamp of `1381292470`, the request method `POST`, and a token value of `Y4KPI2432489ey50i3hK`, the signature can be described as follows:

```
SHA1( TestClient,y8FglFPKzW,i74K5E4y4B,1381292470,POST,Y4KPI2432489ey50i3hK )
```

The calculated value of the signature is then as follows:

```
ead5cea9b0d6474f597467bb13dba9d78ca5923b
```

The client ID, token ID, and token value are the same for every protected resource request from the same client and resource owner. Only the nonce and timestamp values change every single request. The request method, of course, always reflects the method for the given request.

You need a way to transmit all this data with each request. The standard mechanism for authorizing protected resource requests is to include the `Authorization` header in each request. When the header value starts with the word "Bearer" followed by a space, the rest of the value represents the bearer token. For this scheme, you can use the word "Signing" instead of "Bearer" and then use comma-separated key-value pairs in the value for the token information. Using the previously described values and signature, the `Authorization` header in a request would look like this (new lines added for clarity are omitted from the actual header value):

```
Authorization: Signing client_id=TestClient, token_id=y8FglFPKzW,
                       nonce=i74K5E4y4B, timestamp=1381292470,
                       signature=ead5cea9b0d6474f597467bb13dba9d78ca5923b
```

Notice that the token value does not appear in the header because the goal is to not have to transmit the token to prove the client holds it. The request method does not appear in the header, either, because it's simply part of the request. Although the order the values appear in the signature is very important, the order they appear in the header is not. When the provider receives the request, all it has to do is use the token ID to look up the token value, ensure the specified client is the holder of the token, check that the nonce has never been used before, and then recalculate the signature with the given information. If the signature matches the one provided, the authenticity of the access token is established. If the signature does not match, the request must be rejected.

> **WARNING** *A theoretical alternative to the standard bearer token system specified in the OAuth 2.0 documentation was just described. This alternative has not been reviewed by the OAuth community or by security experts. Although this proposal provides significantly greater security than bearer tokens, you should evaluate it carefully and thoroughly and consult with your organization's security officer before using it in your production applications. You should use the same due diligence before using OAuth in general.*

> **NOTE** *If you wanted to increase the level of security even further, you could use asymmetric public-private key pairs to generate and verify signatures instead of using a shared secret token as a signature salt. The added benefit is that the authorization server never stores the secret (private key) — only the client has this information. Even if the entire OAuth credentials database were stolen, attackers would not be able to use the public keys therein to compromise your system. Furthermore, as long as the client generated the key pair instead of the server, the private key would never need to travel over the wire — that is extremely secure. This technique would require significantly more effort and is left up to the reader to explore further.*

# Implementing Client Services

You need a way to define the clients that are permitted to access your web services. For a simple system with a very static and stable set of internally developed clients, you could just use Spring Security OAuth's `InMemoryClientDetailsService`, but this is not sufficient in most circumstances. You could use the `JdbcClientDetailsService`, but if you're already using JPA, Spring Data, and Spring Framework transactions, it might be easier to simply create your own implementation.

## Creating a Client Entity

The client entity is fairly straightforward. It needs to implement `ClientDetails` and map to several database tables. Because you're customizing this, you'll encounter some `ClientDetails` properties that you can safely hardwire for your situation. For example, you might want to require the client to always present a secret and a scope, not be allowed to use refresh tokens, not have any additional information, and always have the same authority or authorities. This is demonstrated in the abbreviated `WebServiceClient` entity that follows (which uses some of the advanced mapping techniques you learned about in Chapter 24).

```
@Entity
public class WebServiceClient implements ClientDetails, Serializable
{
    // fields

    @Id @Column(name = "WebServiceClientId")
    @GeneratedValue(strategy = GenerationType.IDENTITY)
    public long getId() { ... }
    public void setId(long id) { ... }

    @Override
    public String getClientId() { ... }
    public void setClientId(String clientId) { ... }

    @Override
    public String getClientSecret() { ... }
    public void setClientSecret(String clientSecret) { ... }

    @Override @Column(name = "Scope")
    @ElementCollection(fetch = FetchType.EAGER)
    @CollectionTable(name = "WebServiceClient_Scope", joinColumns = {
            @JoinColumn(name = "WebServiceClientId",
                    referencedColumnName = "WebServiceClientId")
    })
    public Set<String> getScope() { ... }
    public void setScope(Set<String> scope) { ... }

    @Override @Column(name = "GrantName")
    @ElementCollection(fetch = FetchType.EAGER)
    @CollectionTable(name = "WebServiceClient_Grant", joinColumns = {
            @JoinColumn(name = "WebServiceClientId",
                    referencedColumnName = "WebServiceClientId")
    })
    public Set<String> getAuthorizedGrantTypes() { ... }
    public void setAuthorizedGrantTypes(Set<String> authorizedGrantTypes) { ... }

    @Override @Column(name = "Uri")
    @ElementCollection(fetch = FetchType.EAGER)
    @CollectionTable(name = "WebServiceClient_RedirectUri", joinColumns = {
            @JoinColumn(name = "WebServiceClientId",
                    referencedColumnName = "WebServiceClientId")
    })
    public Set<String> getRegisteredRedirectUri() { ... }
    public void setRegisteredRedirectUri(Set<String> uri) { ... }

    private static final Set<String> RESOURCE_IDS = new HashSet<>();
    private static final Set<GrantedAuthority> AUTHORITIES = new HashSet<>();
    static {
        RESOURCE_IDS.add("SUPPORT");
        AUTHORITIES.add(new SimpleGrantedAuthority("OAUTH_CLIENT"));
    }

    @Override @Transient
    public Set<String> getResourceIds() { return RESOURCE_IDS; }

    @Override @Transient
```

```
        public Collection<GrantedAuthority> getAuthorities() { return AUTHORITIES; }

        @Override @Transient
        public Integer getAccessTokenValiditySeconds() { return 3600; }

        @Override @Transient
        public Integer getRefreshTokenValiditySeconds() { return -1; }

        @Override @Transient
        public Map<String, Object> getAdditionalInformation() { return null; }

        @Override @Transient
        public boolean isSecretRequired() { return true; }

        @Override @Transient
        public boolean isScoped() { return true; }
    }
```

## Providing Client Details

The Spring Data repository interface that supports this entity is simple and eliminates any hard work on your part.

```
public interface WebServiceClientRepository
        extends CrudRepository<WebServiceClient, Long>
{
    WebServiceClient getByClientId(String clientId);
}
```

The `WebServiceClientService` interface extends `ClientDetailsService` to clarify that the service always returns `WebServiceClient` entities, and the implementation is straightforward. Notice that `loadClientByClientId` never returns `null`. If a client cannot be found, it throws Spring Security OAuth's `ClientRegistrationException` to indicate that the client is not valid. Also notice that the service does not provide any mechanism for registering new clients. (Likewise, there is no UI for doing so.) How this happens varies greatly from one business case to another and is an exercise left up to you.

```
public interface WebServiceClientService extends ClientDetailsService
{
    @Override
    WebServiceClient loadClientByClientId(String clientId);
}

public class DefaultWebServiceClientService implements WebServiceClientService
{
    @Inject WebServiceClientRepository clientRepository;

    @Override
    @Transactional
    public WebServiceClient loadClientByClientId(String clientId)
    {
        WebServiceClient client = this.clientRepository.getByClientId(clientId);
        if(client == null)
            throw new ClientRegistrationException("Client not found");
        return client;
    }
}
```

The project's `create.sql` file adds four new tables to the Customer Support database and inserts a test client into those tables. If you have not worked with the customer support application in previous chapters, you need to run the entire `create.sql` script and create the appropriate Tomcat `DataSource` resource (named `jdbc/CustomerSupport`). If you have an existing database to upgrade, be sure to run the create statements for these four tables. The data inserted into the new tables for the test client follows. (The client password is the BCrypt-hashed value of "y471l12D2y55U5558rd2.")

```
INSERT INTO WebServiceClient (ClientId, ClientSecret) VALUES (
    'TestClient', '$2a$10$elDBcfb/ZKyuNgOPK5.70Oi4gN2EuhU2yONPsoF3avx9.Hd/b8BTa'
);

INSERT INTO WebServiceClient_Scope (WebServiceClientId, Scope)
  VALUES (1, 'READ'), (1, 'WRITE'), (1, 'TRUST');

INSERT INTO WebServiceClient_Grant (WebServiceClientId, GrantName)
  VALUES (1, 'authorization_code');

INSERT INTO WebServiceClient_RedirectUri (WebServiceClientId, Uri)
  VALUES (1, 'http://localhost:8080/client/support');
```

Also if you are upgrading an existing database, you need to grant permissions for accessing the web services. The following statement from the `create.sql` script adds this permission to the users Nicholas and John (assuming you have kept the default users in your database).

```
INSERT INTO UserPrincipal_Authority (UserId, Authority)
  VALUES (1, 'USE_WEB_SERVICES'), (4, 'USE_WEB_SERVICES');
```

## Implementing Nonce Services

Spring Security OAuth 2 doesn't specify any type of nonce-related interfaces because nonces aren't a standard part of OAuth 2.0. However, fabricating a system of your own is really quite trivial. There's very little to the nonce entity, repository, and service. Be sure to run the SQL create statement if you have an existing database to upgrade.

```
@Entity
@Table(name = "OAuthNonce")
public class Nonce implements Serializable
{
    private static final long serialVersionUID = 1L;

    private long id;
    private String value;
    private long timestamp;

    public Nonce() { }
    public Nonce(String value, long timestamp) { ... }

    @Id @Column(name = "OAuthNonceId")
    @GeneratedValue(strategy = GenerationType.IDENTITY)
    public long getId() { ... }
    public void setId(long id) { ... }

    public String getValue() { ... }
```

```
    public void setValue(String value) { ... }

    @Column(name = "NonceTimestamp")
    public long getTimestamp() { ... }
    public void setTimestamp(long timestamp) { ... }
}

CREATE TABLE OAuthNonce (
  OAuthNonceId BIGINT UNSIGNED NOT NULL AUTO_INCREMENT PRIMARY KEY,
  Value VARCHAR(50),
  NonceTimestamp BIGINT NOT NULL,
  UNIQUE KEY OAuthNonce_Value_Timestamp (Value, NonceTimestamp)
) ENGINE = InnoDB;
```

The `NonceRepository` uses a technique you learned about in Chapter 22 but didn't experiment with — using `@org.springframework.data.jpa.repository.Query` to define a query for a method that doesn't match a standard Spring Data repository method pattern. The `@org.springframework.data.jpa.repository.Modifying` annotation tells Spring Data that this method modifies data (as opposed to reading data) and should be executed as such.

```
public interface NonceRepository extends CrudRepository<Nonce, Long>
{
    Nonce getByValueAndTimestamp(String value, long timestamp);

    @Modifying
    @Query("DELETE FROM Nonce n WHERE n.timestamp < :timestamp")
    void deleteWhereTimestampLessThan(long timestamp);
}
```

The purpose of the delete method is fairly simple. Because nonces must be stored to check for duplication, the nonce table will fill up rather quickly if your server load is heavy. A simple solution to this problem is to periodically delete nonces with timestamps older than a few minutes and simply reject requests with older timestamps. This requires system clocks on client applications to be fairly accurate, which is not an unreasonable requirement for a secure system.

The `deleteOldNonces` method in `DefaultOAuthNonceServices` uses Spring Framework scheduling to delete nonces older than 2 minutes each minute. Remember that for a scheduled method to also be transactional, either the method must be specified in the interface or, if you don't want to expose it, Spring Framework must use CGLIB proxies instead of JDK proxies (`proxyTargetClass` must be set to `true` throughout your application). Also note that the `OAuthNonceService` doesn't even expose the `Nonce` entity because it's simply not necessary for such a simple service.

```
public interface OAuthNonceServices
{
    void recordNonceOrFailIfDuplicate(String nonce, long timestamp);
}

public class DefaultOAuthNonceServices implements OAuthNonceServices
{
    @Inject NonceRepository nonceRepository;

    @Override @Transactional
    public void recordNonceOrFailIfDuplicate(String nonce, long timestamp)
    {
```

```
        if(this.nonceRepository.getByValueAndTimestamp(nonce, timestamp) != null)
            throw new InvalidTokenException("Duplicate nonce value [" + nonce +
                    "," + timestamp + "]");

        this.nonceRepository.save(new Nonce(nonce, timestamp));
    }

    @Transactional @Scheduled(fixedDelay = 60_000L)
    public void deleteOldNonces()
    {
        this.nonceRepository.deleteWhereTimestampLessThan(
                (System.currentTimeMillis() - 120_000L) / 1_000L
        );
    }
}
```

## Implementing Token Services

As you learned earlier, Spring Security OAuth has both an `InMemoryTokenStore` and a `JdbcTokenStore` that you can use with the `DefaultTokenServices`. `DefaultTokenServices` and the `JdbcTokenStore` are perfectly sufficient for bearer tokens, but you need something a little more custom for your signature-based tokens.

First, you have to implement `OAuth2AccessToken`, which you can easily make into an entity and create a repository for. Then you need to implement `AuthorizationServerTokenServices` and `ResourceServerTokenServices`.

### Designing a Token Entity

When storing access tokens, you must have a way to associate access tokens with the `Authentication` (user) that authorized access for the client. This `Authentication` is an `OAuth2Authentication` to provide additional information for Spring Security OAuth 2 internals.

For the built-in bearer token support, Spring Security OAuth simply serializes the `OAuth2Authentication` and stores it in a column in the access token table. There's no reason you can't do the same in this case. The `SigningAccessToken` entity implements `OAuth2AccessToken` and provides the `OAuth2Authentication` as an entity property. It also provides a `key` property for looking up an access token by the token ID included in protected resource requests. The `additionalInformation` property enables you to add custom key-value pairs that are sent back to the client in the response to the access token request. This is how you tell the client about the token identifier that it must send along with its signed requests.

The `SigningAccessToken` is lengthy and not printed here, but you can review it in the Customer-Support-v21 project. It's important to know that the entity maps to two new tables: `OAuthAccessToken` and `OAuthAccessToken_Scope`. If you upgrade an existing database, be sure to run the create statements for these tables found in `create.sql`.

### Creating and Retrieving Tokens

The repository for the access token entity is another simple Spring Data repository with two additional lookup methods. Notice that this repository interface is different in that it extends `JpaRepository` instead of `CrudRepository`. Though unfortunate, it is necessary to leak the JPA details because the service that uses this repository needs to call the `flush` method.

```
public interface SigningAccessTokenRepository
        extends JpaRepository<SigningAccessToken, Long>
{
    SigningAccessToken getByKey(String key);
    SigningAccessToken getByValue(String value);
}
```

The service that creates and retrieves access tokens is significantly more involved. Not only does it implement both `AuthorizationServerTokenServices` and `ResourceServerTokenServices` for simplicity, it also provides an additional method for looking access tokens up by the token identifier (the `key` property). This method is specified in the `SigningAccessTokenServices` interface.

```
public interface SigningAccessTokenServices
        extends AuthorizationServerTokenServices, ResourceServerTokenServices
{
    SigningAccessToken getAccessToken(String key);
}
```

`DefaultAccessTokenServices` in Listing 28-1 implements this interface and supplies all the logic necessary to create and retrieve signature-based access tokens. The `refreshAccessToken` method throws an `UnsupportedOperationException` because refresh tokens aren't necessary for signature-based tokens, and in this particular case you want to require your users to re-authorize clients whenever an access token expires.

The `DefaultAuthenticationKeyGenerator` can generate a deterministic key (which you use for the token identifier) based on a given `OAuth2Authentication`. The authorization server calls the `createAccessToken` method when the client connects to exchange an authorization code for an access token. It might also call `getAccessToken(OAuth2Authentication)` in some situations, and the deterministic key generator makes it possible to look up the access token. The authorization server also calls `refreshAccessToken`, except in this project where refresh tokens are disabled.

The `getAccessToken(String)` method specified in `SigningAccessTokenServices` is what you use in the resource server to look up the access token using the key provided by the client. The resource server would normally use the other two methods to retrieve tokens and authentications by the token value, but in the custom resource server implementation you create later in this section, these methods are unnecessary. You have to use `getAccessToken(String)` instead because client connections include the token identifier and not the token value.

**LISTING 28-1: DefaultAccessTokenServices.java**

```
public class DefaultAccessTokenServices implements SigningAccessTokenServices
{
    AuthenticationKeyGenerator authenticationKeyGenerator =
            new DefaultAuthenticationKeyGenerator();

    @Inject SigningAccessTokenRepository repository;

    @Override @Transactional
    public OAuth2AccessToken createAccessToken(OAuth2Authentication auth)
            throws AuthenticationException
    {
```

```
        String key = this.authenticationKeyGenerator.extractKey(auth);
        SigningAccessToken token = this.repository.getByKey(key);
        if(token != null)
        {
            if(token.isExpired())
            {
                this.repository.delete(token);
                this.repository.flush();
            }
            else
            {
                token.setAuthentication(auth); // in case authorities changed
                this.repository.save(token);
                return token;
            }
        }

        token = new SigningAccessToken(
                key,
                UUID.randomUUID().toString(),
                new Date(System.currentTimeMillis() + 86_400_000L), // one day
                auth.getAuthorizationRequest().getScope(),
                auth
        );

        this.repository.save(token);

        return token;
    }

    @Override @Transactional
    public OAuth2AccessToken getAccessToken(OAuth2Authentication auth)
    {
        return this.repository.getByKey(
                this.authenticationKeyGenerator.extractKey(auth)
        );
    }

    @Override @Transactional
    public SigningAccessToken getAccessToken(String key)
    {
        return this.repository.getByKey(key);
    }

    @Override @Transactional
    public OAuth2AccessToken readAccessToken(String tokenValue)
    {
        return this.repository.getByValue(tokenValue);
    }

    @Override @Transactional
    public OAuth2Authentication loadAuthentication(String tokenValue)
            throws AuthenticationException
    {
        SigningAccessToken token = this.repository.getByValue(tokenValue);
```

```
        if(token == null)
            throw new InvalidTokenException("Invalid token " + tokenValue + ".");

        if(token.isExpired())
        {
            this.repository.delete(token);
            throw new InvalidTokenException("Expired token " + tokenValue + ".");
        }

        return token.getAuthentication();
    }

    @Override
    public OAuth2AccessToken refreshAccessToken(String refreshToken,
                                                AuthorizationRequest request)
            throws AuthenticationException
    {
        throw new UnsupportedOperationException();
    }
}
```

## Customizing the Resource Server Filter

Normally you would configure the Spring Security OAuth 2 resource server using the XML namespace element `<oauth2:resource-server>`. This creates an `org.springframework.security.oauth2.provider.authentication.OAuth2AuthenticationProcessingFilter` that intercepts protected resource requests and then extracts and validates the access token. This filter is written specifically for bearer tokens and is not easily extended, so you must implement your own filter in this case.

The `OAuthSigningTokenAuthenticationFilter` handles all this for you. This class is also lengthy and most of it isn't printed here. The `parseHeader` method parses the `Authorization` header, ensures that it is a `Signing` value, and returns a `Map<String, String>` of the parameters in the header. `doFilter` calls `parseHeader` to determine if the header is present and then passes the map of header parameter values on to the `authenticate` method. This method, which follows, does the hard work of calculating the signature, checking it against the provided signature, validating the token, and ensuring the request doesn't contain an old or duplicate nonce.

```
    private void authenticate(Map<String, String> header,
                              HttpServletRequest request)
    {
        String tokenId = header.get("token_id");
        if(tokenId == null)
            throw new InvalidTokenException("Header [" + header +
                    "] missing token_id.");

        SigningAccessToken token = this.tokenServices.getAccessToken(tokenId);
        if(token == null)
            throw new InvalidTokenException("Token [" + tokenId + "] not found.");

        OAuth2Authentication authentication = token.getAuthentication();
        AuthorizationRequest authorizationRequest =
                authentication.getAuthorizationRequest();

        String clientId = header.get("client_id");
```

```
        if(!authorizationRequest.getClientId().equals(clientId))
            throw new InvalidTokenException("Client ID does not match token.");

        Collection<String> resourceIds = authorizationRequest.getResourceIds();
        if(this.resourceId != null && resourceIds != null &&
                !resourceIds.isEmpty() && !resourceIds.contains(this.resourceId))
            throw new InvalidTokenException("Resource ID not permitted.");

        String timestamp = header.get("timestamp");
        String nonce = header.get("nonce");
        if(timestamp == null || nonce == null)
            throw new InvalidTokenException("Header missing timestamp or nonce.");

        String toSign = clientId + "," + tokenId + "," + nonce + "," +
                timestamp + "," + request.getMethod().toUpperCase() + "," +
                token.getValue();
        String signature = new String(Base64.getEncoder().encode(
                DIGEST.digest(toSign.getBytes(StandardCharsets.UTF_8))
        ), StandardCharsets.UTF_8);
        String presentedSignature = header.get("signature");
        if(!signature.equals(presentedSignature))
            throw new InvalidTokenException("Missing or invalid signature.");

        long timestampValue = Long.parseLong(timestamp);
        long now = System.currentTimeMillis() / 1_000L;
        if(timestampValue < now - 60L || timestampValue > now + 60L)
            throw new InvalidTokenException("Header timestamp out of range.");

        this.nonceServices.recordNonceOrFailIfDuplicate(nonce, timestampValue);

        request.setAttribute(OAuth2AuthenticationDetails.ACCESS_TOKEN_VALUE,
                token.getValue());
        authentication.setDetails(this.authenticationDetailsSource.buildDetails(
                request
        ));
        SecurityContextHolder.getContext().setAuthentication(authentication);
    }
```

One of the key points of this method is that it accepts only requests with timestamps that are within 1 minute of the current time. Because the nonce service you created earlier deletes nonces after they are 2 minutes old, you should allow only nonces created within a 2-minute window (1 minute before and after the current timestamp). This means clients accessing your web services need to have clocks up to date within 1 minute of your servers' clocks. Today, Network Time Protocol is standard and enabled by default on all operating systems for all different types of devices, so this shouldn't be a serious challenge for your users.

> **NOTE** *Replacing the standard Spring Security OAuth 2 authentication-processing filter is only necessary because Spring Security OAuth 2 does not provide a mechanism for plugging in additional token types. Hopefully, Spring Security OAuth 2 version 2.0 will provide a plug-in mechanism for supplying alternative token types to avoid this problem, but that won't be known until after this book is published.*

## Reconfiguring Spring Security

The last step to completing your OAuth 2 provider is to configure it in Spring Security. Though you configured Spring Security using pure Java in previous chapters, Spring Security OAuth does not yet support Java configuration. Although you could theoretically create a hybrid Spring Security configuration that combines the XML namespace and Java configuration features, this is more trouble than it's worth. You're better off using the XML namespace configuration exclusively.

You'll notice the `SecurityConfiguration` class no longer exists. It has been replaced with a `securityConfiguration.xml` file in the resources directory, and the `RootContextConfiguration` has been changed to import the XML file:

```
...
@ImportResource({ "classpath:com/wrox/config/securityConfiguration.xml" })
public class RootContextConfiguration implements
        AsyncConfigurer, SchedulingConfigurer, TransactionManagementConfigurer
{
    ...
}
```

The XML configuration starts with the namespace imports and definition of some basic beans.

```
<?xml version="1.0" encoding="UTF-8"?>
<beans:beans xmlns="http://www.springframework.org/schema/security"
             xmlns:beans="http://www.springframework.org/schema/beans"
             xmlns:oauth2="http://www.springframework.org/schema/security/oauth2"
             xmlns:xsi="http://www.w3.org/2001/XMLSchema-instance"
             xsi:schemaLocation="...">

    <beans:bean id="userService" class="com.wrox.site.DefaultUserService" />
    <beans:bean id="webServiceClientService"
                class="com.wrox.site.DefaultWebServiceClientService" />
    <beans:bean id="clientDetailsUserService"
                class="org.springframework.security.oauth2.provider.client.
ClientDetailsUserDetailsService">
        <beans:constructor-arg ref="webServiceClientService" />
    </beans:bean>

    <beans:bean id="sessionRegistry"
                class="org.springframework.security.core.session.
SessionRegistryImpl" />

    <beans:bean id="webSecurityExpressionHandler"
                class="org.springframework.security.oauth2.provider.expression.
OAuth2WebSecurityExpressionHandler" />
    <beans:bean id="methodSecurityExpressionHandler"
                class="org.springframework.security.oauth2.provider.expression.
OAuth2MethodSecurityExpressionHandler" />

    <beans:bean id="passwordEncoder"
                class="org.springframework.security.crypto.bcrypt.
BCryptPasswordEncoder" />

    ...

</beans:beans>
```

Notice the configuration of the password encoder, session registry, and `DefaultUserService` that you configured with Java in previous chapters. It also configures the Spring Security OAuth 2 expression handlers to replace the stock expression handlers and the `DefaultWebServiceClientService` you created for looking up your OAuth clients. The `ClientDetailsUserDetailsService` is a special bridge between the `ClientDetailsService` and `UserDetailsService` interfaces, and is necessary for the authentication manager to function properly for the access token endpoint. For bearer tokens you would normally define the `DefaultTokenServices` and a `TokenStore`. For example, you could configure this:

```
    <beans:bean id="tokenStore"
                class="org.springframework.security.oauth2.provider.token.
InMemoryTokenStore" />

    <beans:bean id="tokenServices"
                class="org.springframework.security.oauth2.provider.token.
DefaultTokenServices">
        <beans:property name="tokenStore" ref="tokenStore" />
        <beans:property name="supportRefreshToken" value="true" />
        <beans:property name="clientDetailsService"
                        ref="webServiceClientService" />
    </beans:bean>
```

Instead, you just need to configure your `DefaultAccessTokenServices`.

```
    <beans:bean id="tokenServices"
                class="com.wrox.site.DefaultAccessTokenServices" />
```

Next you need to configure several other OAuth and authentication management components. The `UserApprovalHandler` handles the resource owner response to the request to authorize a client. The `OAuth2AccessDeniedHandler` handles access denied errors and returning responses with the client-requested content type. The `OAuth2AuthenticationEntryPoint` does the same thing, except for authentication errors instead of access denied errors. The first `<authentication-manager>` creates the authentication manager for the authentication you configured in Chapter 26, whereas the second one creates a special authentication manager just for handling client requests to the access token endpoint.

```
    <beans:bean id="userApprovalHandler"
                class="org.springframework.security.oauth2.provider.approval.
TokenServicesUserApprovalHandler">
        <beans:property name="tokenServices" ref="tokenServices" />
    </beans:bean>

    <beans:bean id="oauthAccessDeniedHandler"
                class="org.springframework.security.oauth2.provider.error.
OAuth2AccessDeniedHandler" />

    <beans:bean id="oauthAuthenticationEntryPoint"
                class="org.springframework.security.oauth2.provider.error.
OAuth2AuthenticationEntryPoint" />

    <authentication-manager>
        <authentication-provider user-service-ref="userService">
            <password-encoder ref="passwordEncoder" />
```

```
        </authentication-provider>
    </authentication-manager>

    <authentication-manager id="oauthClientAuthenticationManager">
        <authentication-provider user-service-ref="clientDetailsUserService">
            <password-encoder ref="passwordEncoder" />
        </authentication-provider>
    </authentication-manager>

    <oauth2:authorization-server token-services-ref="tokenServices"
                client-details-service-ref="webServiceClientService"
                user-approval-page="oauth/authorize" error-page="oauth/error">
        <oauth2:authorization-code />
    </oauth2:authorization-server>
```

The `<oauth2:authorization-server>` element is an important part of the OAuth configuration. It sets up the authorization endpoint (`/oauth/authorize` relative to your application root) and access token endpoint (`/oauth/token`) and handles requests to those URLs. The configured authorization server even handles responding to these requests automatically with an HTML authorization form. However, this form is very generic and obviously won't be styled to match your site. In most cases, therefore, you'll want to replace it. The `user-approval-page` attribute enables you to specify a Spring MVC view name for the form that displays the authorization request, whereas the `error-page` attribute enables you to specify a view name for the error page displayed when an authorization error occurs.

The view names in this case match the `/WEB-INF/jsp/view/oauth/authorize.jsp` and `/WEB-INF/jsp/view/oauth/error.jsp` files. The EL variables and form field names in these JSPs are standard to Spring Security OAuth and should not vary.

The next thing you need to configure is the resource server filter. Normally, you would configure it with something like this:

```
    <oauth2:resource-server id="resourceServerFilter" resource-id="SUPPORT"
                            entry-point-ref="oauthAuthenticationEntryPoint"
                            token-services-ref="tokenServices" />
```

This handles bearer tokens out-of-the-box, but because you're using custom tokens, you need to configure your nonce services and custom resource server filter manually:

```
    <beans:bean id="nonceServices"
                class="com.wrox.site.DefaultOAuthNonceServices" />
    <beans:bean id="resourceServerFilter"
                class="com.wrox.site.OAuthSigningTokenAuthenticationFilter">
        <beans:property name="authenticationEntryPoint"
                        ref="oauthAuthenticationEntryPoint" />
        <beans:property name="nonceServices" ref="nonceServices" />
        <beans:property name="tokenServices" ref="tokenServices" />
        <beans:property name="resourceId" value="SUPPORT" />
    </beans:bean>
```

After you have all this configured, the final step is to configure global method security and HTTP security. Global method security is straightforward, and the first two `<http>` elements configure URL patterns that are excluded from all security filters.

```
<global-method-security pre-post-annotations="enabled" order="0"
                        proxy-target-class="true">
    <expression-handler ref="methodSecurityExpressionHandler" />
</global-method-security>

<http security="none" pattern="/resource/**" />
<http security="none" pattern="/favicon.ico" />
```

The next <http> element configures the security for the access token endpoint. This ensures that clients authenticate with their client ID and secret using HTTP basic authentication before they can exchange authorization codes for access tokens. Note that the order in which these <http> elements appear is very important because each request uses the first configuration that it matches. Also note that this configuration is stateless, meaning HTTP sessions are not created for requests to the access token endpoint.

```
<http use-expressions="true" create-session="stateless"
      authentication-manager-ref="oauthClientAuthenticationManager"
      entry-point-ref="oauthAuthenticationEntryPoint" pattern="/oauth/token">
    <intercept-url pattern="/oauth/token"
                   access="hasAuthority('OAUTH_CLIENT')" />
    <http-basic />
    <access-denied-handler ref="oauthAccessDeniedHandler" />
    <expression-handler ref="webSecurityExpressionHandler" />
</http>
```

The following <http> element is also stateless and uses the custom resource server filter you created earlier to protect your web services with your signature-based access tokens. It also ensures that resource owners are granted the `USE_WEB_SERVICES` authority before they are allowed to use your web services. This doesn't replace the `@PreAuthorize` checks you added to all of your services—those still apply as well.

```
<http use-expressions="true" create-session="stateless"
      entry-point-ref="oauthAuthenticationEntryPoint" pattern="/services/**">
    <intercept-url pattern="/services/**"
                   access="hasAuthority('USE_WEB_SERVICES')" />
    <custom-filter ref="resourceServerFilter" before="PRE_AUTH_FILTER" />
    <access-denied-handler ref="oauthAccessDeniedHandler" />
    <expression-handler ref="webSecurityExpressionHandler" />
</http>
```

The final <http> element is essentially identical to the `HttpSecurity` configuration you created with Java in Chapters 26 and 27 but with two minor tweaks.

- Although Java configuration permits the login form to submit to the same URL at which the form displays, XML configuration does not, so the login form now posts to `/login/submit`.
- This configuration protects the OAuth authorization endpoint with standard web security so that users must log in and have the `USE_WEB_SERVICES` granted authority before they can grant access to a client.

Note the use of the <csrf> element to enable CSRF protection, which is disabled by default for XML configuration.

```
<http use-expressions="true">
    <intercept-url pattern="/session/list"
                   access="hasAuthority('VIEW_USER_SESSIONS')" />
    <intercept-url pattern="/oauth/**"
                   access="hasAuthority('USE_WEB_SERVICES')" />
    <intercept-url pattern="/login/**" access="permitAll()" />
    <intercept-url pattern="/login" access="permitAll()" />
    <intercept-url pattern="/logout" access="permitAll()" />
    <intercept-url pattern="/**" access="isFullyAuthenticated()" />
    <form-login default-target-url="/ticket/list" login-page="/login"
                login-processing-url="/login/submit"
                authentication-failure-url="/login?loginFailed"
                username-parameter="username" password-parameter="password" />
    <logout logout-url="/logout" logout-success-url="/login?loggedOut"
            delete-cookies="JSESSIONID" invalidate-session="true" />
    <session-management invalid-session-url="/login"
                        session-fixation-protection="changeSessionId">
        <concurrency-control error-if-maximum-exceeded="true" max-sessions="1"
                             session-registry-ref="sessionRegistry" />
    </session-management>
    <csrf />
    <expression-handler ref="webSecurityExpressionHandler" />
</http>
```

At this point you have successfully created and configured an OAuth 2.0 provider using Spring Security OAuth. You'll notice that the web service endpoints also take advantage of `@AuthenticationPrincipal` to obtain the `UserPrincipal` in their handler methods.

The other thing you'll want to look at before moving on is the `TicketService` interface and `DefaultTicketService` implementation. These were updated so that your code can optionally specify lambda expressions that fetch properties within the transaction that are normally lazy-loaded, ensuring that the values can be properly serialized. The `TicketRestEndpoint` and `TicketSoapEndpoint` controllers then take advantage of this expansion capability. Of course, this is just one approach to solve this problem and is far from the best-performing solution. Ultimately, you need a way to tell Jackson Data Processor and other utilities when to ignore lazy-loaded properties that haven't been fully loaded. This is a difficult task that is left up to you because it is outside the scope of this book.

The changes you've made here don't do you a lot of good just yet because you have no way to test them. The next and final section of this chapter helps you create a simple OAuth 2 client for testing the provider and Customer Support application.

## CREATING AN OAUTH CLIENT APPLICATION

Fortunately, Spring Security OAuth doesn't just include provider implementations. It also has client implementations, making the consumption of OAuth protected resources much simpler. Currently, the Spring Security OAuth 2 client supports accessing only RESTful web services because it is strictly tied to the `OAuth2RestTemplate` class you read about earlier. Efforts are under way to make this support more generic in the next version so that other clients, such as SOAP clients, can take advantage of the OAuth client features.

The OAuth-Client project, available for download from the `wrox.com` code download site, demonstrates using Spring Security OAuth and the `OAuth2RestTemplate` to access the Customer Support application's RESTful web service.

When you open it up, the first thing you'll notice is that it has the `Ticket`, `Attachment`, and `UserPrincipal` classes (minus JPA annotations) and `TicketWebServiceList` class from the Customer-Support-v21 application. This makes it easy for the client to deserialize responses from the Customer Support web service. In fact, it is very common for providers to distribute artifacts containing the published data types like `Ticket` and `Attachment` so that clients can more reliably use the related web services.

The OAuth-Client project also provides a very simple `AuthenticationController` and login screen for handling logins to the application through Spring Security.

## Customizing the REST Template

Normally, the out-of-the-box client configuration would be straightforward and work fine for your needs, but you're using custom signature-based tokens, so you need to perform some customization. This customization is not nearly as extensive as was necessary for your OAuth provider implementation. All you need to do is extend `OAuth2RestTemplate` to override the `createRequest` method and use your custom access token protocol instead of the default bearer tokens. The `OAuth2SigningRestTemplate` in Listing 28-2 implements the client token signature generation. It generates a random nonce using a UUID, creates the signature string, generates the signature, and then adds the header with necessary parameters to the request.

**LISTING 28-2: OAuth2SigningRestTemplate.java**

```
public class OAuth2SigningRestTemplate extends OAuth2RestTemplate
{
    private static final Logger log = LogManager.getLogger();
    private static final MessageDigest DIGEST;
    static {
        try {
            DIGEST = MessageDigest.getInstance("SHA-1");
        } catch (NoSuchAlgorithmException e) { // not possible
            throw new IllegalStateException(e);
        }
    }

    private final OAuth2ProtectedResourceDetails resource;

    public OAuth2SigningRestTemplate(OAuth2ProtectedResourceDetails resource)
    { ... }
    public OAuth2SigningRestTemplate(OAuth2ProtectedResourceDetails resource,
                                     OAuth2ClientContext context) { ... }

    @Override
    protected ClientHttpRequest createRequest(URI uri, HttpMethod method)
            throws IOException
    {
```

*continues*

**LISTING 28-2** *(continued)*

```
            OAuth2AccessToken token = this.getAccessToken();

            String tokenType = token.getTokenType();
            if(!StringUtils.hasText(tokenType))
                tokenType = OAuth2AccessToken.BEARER_TYPE;

            if("Signing".equalsIgnoreCase(tokenType))
            {
                String clientId = this.resource.getClientId();
                String tokenId = token.getAdditionalInformation()
                        .get("token_id").toString();
                String nonce = UUID.randomUUID().toString();
                long timestamp = System.currentTimeMillis() / 1_000L;

                String toSign = clientId + "," + tokenId + "," + nonce + "," +
                        timestamp + "," + method + "," + token.getValue();
                String signature = new String(Base64.getEncoder().encode(
                        DIGEST.digest(toSign.getBytes(StandardCharsets.UTF_8))
                ), StandardCharsets.UTF_8);

                String header = "Signing client_id=" + clientId + ", token_id=" +
                        tokenId + ", timestamp=" + timestamp + ", nonce=" + nonce +
                        ", signature=" + signature;

                ClientHttpRequest request =
                        this.getRequestFactory().createRequest(uri, method);
                log.debug("Created [{}] request for [{}].", method, uri);
                log.debug("toSign = [{}], signature = [{}]", toSign, signature);
                request.getHeaders().add("Authorization", header);
                return request;
            }
            else
                throw new OAuth2AccessDeniedException(
                        "Unsupported access token type [" + tokenType + "].");
        }
    }
```

## Configuring the Spring Security OAuth Client

Much of the Spring Security configuration for the OAuth-Client project is very boilerplate. It contains many things you've already seen and is imported from the `RootContextConfiguration` just like in the Customer Support application.

The `<authentication-manager>` element declares a simple in-memory user service with two hard-coded users, whereas the `<http>` element defines straightforward authentication and authorization rules. `<oauth2:resource>` and `<oauth2:client>` are new features that you have not used before. The first defines a third-party protected resource that this client consumes, including its authorization and access token endpoints, the client ID, the client secret, and more. If your client accessed protected resources from multiple providers, you would define multiple resource elements. The client element, however, is always used exactly once — it defines a filter that catches `UserRedirectRequiredExceptions` and redirects the user to the proper authorization endpoint when one of these occurs.

```
<?xml version="1.0" encoding="UTF-8"?>
<beans:beans xmlns="http://www.springframework.org/schema/security"
             xmlns:beans="http://www.springframework.org/schema/beans"
             xmlns:aop="http://www.springframework.org/schema/aop"
             xmlns:oauth2="http://www.springframework.org/schema/security/oauth2"
             xmlns:xsi="...">

    <oauth2:resource id="oAuth2ClientBean" client-authentication-scheme="header"
                     client-id="TestClient" client-secret="y471l12D2y55U5558rd2"
                     authentication-scheme="header" type="authorization_code"
                     scope="READ,WRITE,TRUST"
        user-authorization-uri="http://localhost:8080/support/oauth/authorize"
        access-token-uri="http://localhost:8080/support/oauth/token" />

    ...

    <authentication-manager>
        <authentication-provider>
            <user-service>
                <user name="Steve" password="apple" authorities="USER" />
                <user name="Bill" password="orange" authorities="USER" />
            </user-service>
        </authentication-provider>
    </authentication-manager>

    <oauth2:client id="oAuth2ClientFilter" />

    <http use-expressions="true">
        <intercept-url pattern="/login/**" access="permitAll()" />
        <intercept-url pattern="/login" access="permitAll()" />
        <intercept-url pattern="/logout" access="permitAll()" />
        <intercept-url pattern="/**" access="hasAuthority('USER')" />
        <session-management invalid-session-url="/login"
                            session-fixation-protection="changeSessionId" />
        <csrf />
        <form-login authentication-failure-url="/login?loginFailed"
                    login-page="/login" login-processing-url="/login/submit"
                    username-parameter="username" password-parameter="password"
                    default-target-url="/" />
        <logout logout-url="/logout" logout-success-url="/login?loggedOut"
                delete-cookies="JSESSIONID" invalidate-session="true" />
        <custom-filter ref="oAuth2ClientFilter"
                       after="EXCEPTION_TRANSLATION_FILTER" />
    </http>

</beans:beans>
```

The last thing you have to configure is the `RestTemplate` implementation. If you were using the default bearer token type, this configuration would be as simple as follows:

```
    <oauth2:rest-template id="customerSupportRestTemplate"
                          resource="oAuth2ClientBean" />
```

However, because you have created a custom `RestTemplate`, you must configure it by hand. This is complex and involves creating a request-scoped access token request and wrapping it in a proxy, creating a session-scoped client context and wrapping it in a proxy, and finally creating the custom `RestTemplate` that consumes these other beans. These are all things that the `<oauth2:rest-template>` element normally does for you automatically. Like `<oauth2:resource>`, you configure one `RestTemplate` for every protected resource your application accesses.

```
    <beans:bean name="accessTokenRequestProxy" scope="request"
                class="org.springframework.security.oauth2.client.token.
DefaultAccessTokenRequest">
        <aop:scoped-proxy />
        <beans:constructor-arg index="0" value="#{request.parameterMap}" />
        <beans:property name="currentUri"
                        value="#{request.getAttribute('currentUri')}" />
    </beans:bean>
    <beans:bean name="clientContextProxy" scope="session"
                class="org.springframework.security.oauth2.client.
DefaultOAuth2ClientContext">
        <aop:scoped-proxy />
        <beans:constructor-arg index="0" ref="accessTokenRequestProxy" />
    </beans:bean>
    <beans:bean id="customerSupportRestTemplate"
                class="com.wrox.site.OAuth2SigningRestTemplate">
        <beans:constructor-arg index="0" ref="oAuth2ClientBean" />
        <beans:constructor-arg index="1">
            <beans:bean class="org.springframework.security.oauth2.config.
OAuth2ClientContextFactoryBean">
                <beans:property name="resource" ref="oAuth2ClientBean" />
                <beans:property name="bareContext">
                    <beans:bean class="org.springframework.security.oauth2.client.
DefaultOAuth2ClientContext" />
                </beans:property>
                <beans:property name="scopedContext" ref="clientContextProxy" />
            </beans:bean>
        </beans:constructor-arg>
        <beans:property name="messageConverters">
            <beans:list value-type="org.springframework.http.converter.
HttpMessageConverter">
                <beans:bean class="org.springframework.http.converter.json.
MappingJackson2HttpMessageConverter">
                    <beans:property name="objectMapper" ref="objectMapper" />
                </beans:bean>
            </beans:list>
        </beans:property>
    </beans:bean>
```

> **NOTE** *This complex configuration is required because Spring Security OAuth 2 support provides no mechanism for plugging in additional token types, which means you must extend the* `OAuth2RestTemplate` *and configure the extended class instead. Hopefully Spring Security OAuth 2 version 2.0 will provide a plug-in mechanism for supplying alternative token types to avoid this problem, but that won't be known until after this book is published.*

## Using the REST Template

Using the custom `OAuth2RestTemplate` is perhaps the simplest part of the OAuth-Client project. The `SupportController` retrieves a list of all `Tickets` from the Customer Support web service and forwards the request to a view that displays all the titles. If the user currently logged in to the client application doesn't have an access token for the web service, a `UserRedirectRequiredException` will result and the user will be redirected to the authorization endpoint.

After returning to this controller with an authorization code, Spring Security OAuth 2 contacts the access token endpoint and exchanges the code for an access token. It can then use the access token to securely access the Customer Support web services.

```
@WebController
public class SupportController
{
    private static final Logger log = LogManager.getLogger();

    @Inject @Qualifier("customerSupportRestTemplate")
    RestTemplate webService;

    @RequestMapping("support")
    public String getTickets(Map<String, Object> model)
    {
        TicketWebServiceList list = this.webService.getForObject(
                "http://localhost:8080/support/services/Rest/ticket",
                TicketWebServiceList.class
        );
        model.put("tickets", list);

        return "support";
    }
}
```

> **WARNING** *You probably noticed by now that you aren't using HTTPS anywhere in these applications. If you use bearer tokens, you* must *use HTTPS for* all *requests to the authorization server and the resource server (even though the standard mandates it only for the redirect endpoint and access token endpoint). If you use signature-based tokens like those here, you still* must *use HTTPS for the redirect endpoint and access token endpoint. However, using it for all resource server communications becomes much less necessary and depends on the sensitivity of the data with which your system works. Either way, setting up HTTPS is overkill for the sample applications in this book and is outside the scope of this chapter. Be sure to follow best security practices in your real applications.*

## Testing the Provider and Client Together

Testing the provider and client together requires a little more effort but isn't too difficult.

1. Open up the OAuth-Client project in your IDE, and build the exploded web application artifact.

2. Find this artifact directory (likely named `oauth-client-1.0.0-SNAPSHOT`) in the Maven `target` directory, and copy it to your Tomcat `webapps` directory (probably `C:\Program Files\Apache Software Foundation\Tomcat 8.0\webapps` on Windows machines).
3. Rename the copied directory to `client`.
4. Open the Customer-Support-v21 project in your IDE and compile it.
5. Start the Customer Support application in Tomcat from your IDE just like you have throughout the rest of the book. As Tomcat starts up it first deploys the client application because it already exists in the `webapps` directory, and then it deploys the Customer Support application. (To be clear, the order is not actually important.).
6. After Tomcat has fully started, go to `http://localhost:8080/client` and log in with one of the users hard-coded into the client application. The landing page gives you instructions for authorizing the application.
7. Simply click the link and you are redirected to the Customer Support application to log in.
8. Log in with one of the Customer Support application users and you land on the authorization page.
9. Grant access to the client application, and you are finally redirected back to `http://localhost:8080/client/support` with the authorization code. Spring Security OAuth 2 obtains an access token behind the scenes and then accesses the protected resource.

You should now see the list of `Ticket` subjects in the client application, which means that both your OAuth provider and client work.

## SUMMARY

This chapter covered a lot of concepts and technologies involved in securing your web services against unauthorized access. You learned about OAuth and compared the OAuth 1.0a and OAuth 2.0 standards. You did not do a deep dive into the OAuth standards, and you should read the specifications before putting an implementation for either OAuth version into a production environment. You explored how OAuth 2.0 works in Spring Security OAuth, including how Spring Security OAuth can help you create resource provider applications *and* client applications. Finally, you completed the Customer Support application by securing its web services using OAuth, and you created a sample client application to prove that the OAuth implementation works.

This book started with a simple introduction into the structure of a basic Java EE web application. You learned about Servlets, JSPs, custom JSP tags, HTTP sessions, filters, WebSockets, and application logging with Log4j 2. Next, you explored Spring Framework and its powerful features to help you create world-class applications. After that you experimented with the Java Persistence API and learned how Spring Data makes entity persistence as simple as a few lines of code. Finally, in the last part you learned how to make your application secure using Spring Security, form authentication, and OAuth.

You will never finish learning all there is to learn about Java EE, Spring Framework, and Java persistence (continuous learning is part of the fun!), but this book has handed you the tools you need and put you on the road to creating advanced, enterprise applications that can serve you and your customers well.

Every day new versions of the tools you used in this book are released, and each new version brings with it features that can improve your applications. Look for these new versions and for future editions of this book to stay up to date on the latest technologies and approaches for professional Java web application development.

# INDEX

## Numbers and Symbols

## A

## B

## C

## D

## F

## G



## H

## J

## M

## N



## O

## P

## Q



## R

## S

## T

## U



## V

## W

## X

# Apache License, Version 2.0

Some of the source code demonstrated in this book or available for download from wrox.com is subject to the terms of the Apache License, Version 2.0. This license is included here in its entirety.

Source `http://www.apache.org/licenses/LICENSE-2.0`

Version 2.0, January 2004

## Terms and Conditions for Use, Reproduction, and Distribution

1. **Definitions.** "License" shall mean the terms and conditions for use, reproduction, and distribution as defined by Sections 1 through 9 of this document.

"Licensor" shall mean the copyright owner or entity authorized by the copyright owner that is granting the License.

"Legal Entity" shall mean the union of the acting entity and all other entities that control, are controlled by, or are under common control with that entity. For the purposes of this definition, "control" means (i) the power, direct or indirect, to cause the direction or management of such entity, whether by contract or otherwise, or (ii) ownership of fifty percent (50%) or more of the outstanding shares, or (iii) beneficial ownership of such entity.

"You" (or "Your") shall mean an individual or Legal Entity exercising permissions granted by this License.

"Source" form shall mean the preferred form for making modifications, including but not limited to software source code, documentation source, and configuration files.

"Object" form shall mean any form resulting from mechanical transformation or translation of a Source form, including but not limited to compiled object code, generated documentation, and conversions to other media types.

"Work" shall mean the work of authorship, whether in Source or Object form, made available under the License, as indicated by a copyright notice that is included in or attached to the work (an example is provided at the end of this page).

"Derivative Works" shall mean any work, whether in Source or Object form, that is based on (or derived from) the Work and for which the editorial revisions, annotations, elaborations, or other modifications represent, as a whole, an original work of authorship. For the purposes of this License, Derivative Works shall not include works that remain separable from, or merely link (or bind by name) to the interfaces of, the Work and Derivative Works thereof.

"Contribution" shall mean any work of authorship, including the original version of the Work and any modifications or additions to that Work or Derivative Works thereof, that is intentionally submitted to Licensor for inclusion in the Work by the copyright owner or by an individual or Legal Entity authorized to submit on behalf of the copyright owner. For the purposes of this definition, "submitted" means any form of electronic, verbal, or written communication sent to the Licensor or its representatives, including but not limited to communication on electronic mailing lists, source code control systems, and issue tracking systems that are managed by, or on behalf of, the Licensor for the purpose of discussing and improving the Work, but excluding communication that is conspicuously marked or otherwise designated in writing by the copyright owner as "Not a Contribution."

"Contributor" shall mean Licensor and any individual or Legal Entity on behalf of whom a Contribution has been received by Licensor and subsequently incorporated within the Work.

2. **Grant of Copyright License.** Subject to the terms and conditions of this License, each Contributor hereby grants to You a perpetual, worldwide, non-exclusive, no-charge, royalty-free, irrevocable copyright license to reproduce, prepare Derivative Works of, publicly display, publicly perform, sublicense, and distribute the Work and such Derivative Works in Source or Object form.

3. **Grant of Patent License.** Subject to the terms and conditions of this License, each Contributor hereby grants to You a perpetual, worldwide, non-exclusive, no-charge, royalty-free, irrevocable (except as stated in this section) patent license to make, have made, use, offer to sell, sell, import, and otherwise transfer the Work, where such license applies only to those patent claims licensable by such Contributor that are necessarily infringed by their Contribution(s) alone or by combination of their Contribution(s) with the Work to which such Contribution(s) was submitted. If You institute patent litigation against any entity (including a cross-claim or counterclaim in a lawsuit) alleging that the Work or a Contribution incorporated within the Work constitutes direct or contributory patent infringement, then any patent licenses granted to You under this License for that Work shall terminate as of the date such litigation is filed.

4. **Redistribution.** You may reproduce and distribute copies of the Work or Derivative Works thereof in any medium, with or without modifications, and in Source or Object form, provided that You meet the following conditions:

1. You must give any other recipients of the Work or Derivative Works a copy of this License; and
2. You must cause any modified files to carry prominent notices stating that You changed the files; and
3. You must retain, in the Source form of any Derivative Works that You distribute, all copyright, patent, trademark, and attribution notices from the Source form of the Work, excluding those notices that do not pertain to any part of the Derivative Works; and
4. If the Work includes a "NOTICE" text file as part of its distribution, then any Derivative Works that You distribute must include a readable copy of the attribution notices contained within such NOTICE file, excluding those notices that do not pertain to any part of the Derivative Works, in at least one of the following places: within a NOTICE text file distributed as part of the Derivative Works; within the Source form or documentation, if provided along with the Derivative Works; or, within a display generated by the Derivative Works, if and wherever such third-party notices normally appear. The contents of the NOTICE file are for informational purposes only and do not modify the License. You may add Your own attribution notices within Derivative Works that You distribute, alongside or as an addendum to the NOTICE text from the Work, provided that such additional attribution notices cannot be construed as modifying the License. You may add Your own copyright statement to Your modifications and may provide additional or different license terms and conditions for use, reproduction, or distribution of Your modifications, or for any such Derivative Works as a whole, provided Your use, reproduction, and distribution of the Work otherwise complies with the conditions stated in this License.

5. **Submission of Contributions.** Unless You explicitly state otherwise, any Contribution intentionally submitted for inclusion in the Work by You to the Licensor shall be under the terms and conditions of this License, without any additional terms or conditions. Notwithstanding the above, nothing herein shall supersede or modify the terms of any separate license agreement you may have executed with Licensor regarding such Contributions.

6. **Trademarks.** This License does not grant permission to use the trade names, trademarks, service marks, or product names of the Licensor, except as required for reasonable and customary use in describing the origin of the Work and reproducing the content of the NOTICE file.

7. **Disclaimer of Warranty.** Unless required by applicable law or agreed to in writing, Licensor provides the Work (and each Contributor provides its Contributions) on an "AS IS" BASIS, WITHOUT WARRANTIES OR CONDITIONS OF ANY KIND, either express or implied, including, without limitation, any warranties or conditions of TITLE, NON-INFRINGEMENT, MERCHANTABILITY, or FITNESS FOR A PARTICULAR PURPOSE. You are solely responsible for determining the appropriateness of using or redistributing the Work and assume any risks associated with Your exercise of permissions under this License.

8. **Limitation of Liability.** In no event and under no legal theory, whether in tort (including negligence), contract, or otherwise, unless required by applicable law (such as deliberate and grossly negligent acts) or agreed to in writing, shall any Contributor be liable to You for damages, including any direct, indirect, special, incidental, or consequential damages of any character arising as a result of this License or out of the use or inability to use the Work (including but not limited to damages for loss of goodwill, work stoppage, computer failure or malfunction, or any and all other commercial damages or losses), even if such Contributor has been advised of the possibility of such damages.

9. **Accepting Warranty or Additional Liability.** While redistributing the Work or Derivative Works thereof, You may choose to offer, and charge a fee for, acceptance of support, warranty, indemnity, or other liability obligations and/or rights consistent with this License. However, in accepting such obligations, You may act only on Your own behalf and on Your sole responsibility, not on behalf of any other Contributor, and only if You agree to indemnify, defend, and hold each Contributor harmless for any liability incurred by, or claims asserted against, such Contributor by reason of your accepting any such warranty or additional liability.

## How to Apply the Apache License to Your Work

To apply the Apache License to your work, attach the following boilerplate notice, with the fields enclosed by brackets "[]" replaced with your own identifying information. (Don't include the brackets!) The text should be enclosed in the appropriate comment syntax for the file format. We also recommend that a file or class name and description of purpose be included on the same "printed page" as the copyright notice for easier identification within third-party archives.

```
:::text
Copyright [yyyy] [name of copyright owner]
Licensed under the Apache License, Version 2.0 (the "License"); you
may not use this file except in compliance with the License. You may
obtain a copy of the License at

http://www.apache.org/licenses/LICENSE-2.0

Unless required by applicable law or agreed to in writing, software
distributed under the License is distributed on an "AS IS" BASIS,
WITHOUT WARRANTIES OR CONDITIONS OF ANY KIND, either express or
implied. See the License for the specific language governing permis-
sions and limitations under the License.
```